ISRAEL:

THE CHALLENGE
OF THE
FOURTH DECADE

ISRAEL:

THE CHALLENGE
OF THE
FOURTH DECADE

By ALON BEN-MEIR

Cyrco Press, Inc., Publishers • New York and London

International Standard Book Number: 0–915326–19–1

Library of Congress Catalog Card Number: 77–90077

Cyrco Press, Inc., Publishers, New York

Printed in the United States of America

To Prime Minister Begin

Whose inspiring leadership and vision
have given rise to renewed hope,
to spiritual rejuvenation and idealism.

ACKNOWLEDGMENT

IN the preparation of this work I have been fortunate in receiving generous assistance and good advice from many individuals to whom I owe special thanks and with-' out whom this work would have been incomplete.

First, I shall express my profound gratitude to my very good friend, Dr. Roger Nye, for his encouragement, his advice, and above all, for his editorial efforts. Special expressions of gratitude should also go to my research assistant, Leslie Flum, who worked tirelessly to provide me with the necessary materials, and to my secretary, Miriam Mehler, for her devotion and cheerful patience in typing and retyping the manuscript.

I am especially grateful to many of my friends in Israel and in the United States who contributed significantly to the quality of this work. I would like particularly to mention Professor Ira Sharkansky, Ambassador Ira Hirsch-mann, Professor Victor LeVine, Rabbi Robert Jacobs, publisher Philip Hochstein, Alfred Fleishman, Joan Fredricks, research analyst, Rabbi Arnold Asher, David Konoson, and my two assistants, Shirley Langfeld and Selma Silverstein, for their technical help and care.

Finally, I also extend my thanks to many individuals for their encouragement and spiritual support. To name only a few: publisher Milton Firestone, editor Ann Shapiro, Dr. Mayer Mehler, Dr. Amitai Etzioni, editor Llewllyn Howland, III, Executive Director of the Canadian Jewish Congress Alan Rose, Dr. Alan Eberstein, Terri Eberstein, and my publisher Benjamin Rosenzweig who deserves my special gratitude.

Although I have been influenced by many writers, I take full responsibility for my analysis and interpretation. Needless to say, all the shortcomings of this book are mine as well.

CONTENTS

9

FOREWORD

IN past debates concerning the Arab-Israeli crisis, very little, if any, attention has been paid to the Israeli social, economic, and political conditions that could have a direct or indirect bearing on the process of peace between Israel and the Arab states. The purpose of this book is to argue that unless drastic measures are taken to begin correcting some of these conditions, peace with the Arab states would be most fragile, if attainable at all.

For example, one of the most important factors that has a direct effect on the process of peace negotiations is the political makeup of the Israeli government. Political fragmentation in Israel in the past has undoubtedly inhibited the government from taking any major initiative that might have provoked serious opposition from within and outside the coalition government. For this reason, it becomes clear that unless some sort of political reform takes place in Israel, or a national government (in which most parties participate) is formed, the chances for an overall settlement with the Arab states will not improve.

In addition to the political situation in Israel, there are other internal problems that have added further restraints against the process of peace. The Israeli social and ethnic class struggle is a case in point. Very few Jewish and/or Israeli leaders, if any, admit that Israel's social and ethnic struggle is bad enough to warrant serious debate. Yet most of those leaders, including former Prime Minister Yitzhak Rabin, know very well that there exists an explosive situation between the various class strata in Israel and that what might have contained that explosion was and still is the common outside danger. Would the intense relationship that exists between the Sephardic and Ashkenazi communities, for example, remain dormant once the danger from the border is removed?

Israel's demographic posture is another factor that is of the utmost importance in the minds of many Israeli officials when they consider the extent of territorial concessions to be granted to the Arab states or when they plan new settlements and the movement of people from one locality to another. It is also obvious that the greater the Jewish population in Israel, the safer and more confident Israelis feel because population growth relates directly to Israel's military posture and to a greater inventory of human resources. How and from what sources can Israel draw sufficient manpower in order to sustain a Jewish majority, particularly in the wake of not only the decline in the birth rate and in Jewish immigration to Israel but the increase in emigration?

A difficult issue is the Palestinian question. Although I am advocating that some sort of Palestinian entity would have to be eventually established on part or all of the West Bank and the Gaza Strip, it would be presumptuous to be specific as to the exact dimensions of such a newly developed entity in terms of borders and social, economic, and political relationships with Israel and/or Jordan. Yet the Palestinian problem is an enduring feature of the Arab-Israel crisis and without its satisfactory solution, peace between Israel and the Arab states may not be durable. To what extent will the Arab Palestinians and Israel moderate their positions so that the fulfillment of the national aspirations of each will not necessarily be attained at the expense of the other?

No survey of Israel's challenges for the next decade can be complete until one examines one other factor that directly influences Israel's political, military, and economic posture, i.e., Israel's relationship with the United States. In the past three decades the unequivocal overall support of the United States has contributed appreciably to what Israel is today. The future relations between Israel and the United States will undoubtedly markedly affect Israel's stance toward the Arab states. What is the course that Israel must choose to maintain maximum independence despite the fact that close relations remain crucial to its very survival?

Another extremely critical aspect of the situation that is analyzed in this book is the relationship between Israel and diaspora Jewry and the extent to which the Jewish communities around the world, especially in the United States, influence Israel's political conduct as well as its social and economic postures. In answering the criticism that I have received for not writing this book in Hebrew and for not living in Israel, I submit, first, that I do not share the view that one must live in Israel in order to be qualified to address Israeli problems. And, second, that the problems Israel is facing have never been exclusive to Israel. The Jewish communities throughout the diaspora have contributed immensely toward shaping Israel's socio-economic and political characteristics. The time has come for both sides to reexamine the requisites of their relationship and to overcome the misperceptions of the past that have resulted in serious disservice to both sides. The purpose of this book therefore is to awaken the American Jewish reader who has either ignored the problem or has been unwilling to be exposed to it.

The task of criticizing some of Israel's major problems, which may have serious implications for Israel and world Jewry, is not an easy one. Although critics can easily attack almost any issue, such criticism remains empty rhetoric unless it is followed by constructive suggestions. Although I have attempted persistently to provide some practical alternatives and new choices, at times it has been extremely difficult to spell out proposals on matters that are of a volatile nature and on which the element of time impacts, such as the political development of the Palestinian dilemma and Israel's demographic posture.

One other aspect of this book that must be clarified at the outset is that Israel's present social, economic and political problems are *not* the products of the Begin regime but have been inherited from its predecessor, the Labor government. While the Begin government should be exempted from that responsibility, it is challenged to face up to these critical problems and provide some equitable solutions for them. Prime Minister Begin and his team undoubtedly possess the leadership and the ingenuity to deal with these problems effectively. Begin, who for decades has been voicing much of the same criticism from the opposition benches, has now the his-. toric opportunity to make Israel not only the true haven for the Jews but also a light by which all humanity can seek a better tomorrow.

Finally, one thing that I would like the reader to bear in mind: Although my criticism may be harsh at times, and although I may resort to extreme positions to explain my viewpoint, only the following sentiments have guided me along an uneasy path—my love for and everlasting commitment to the state of Israel and its security.

ALON BEN-MEIR

St. Louis, Mo.

INTRODUCTION

How difficult and at times extremely unpopular
to state one's views on matters concerning Israel!
"Be agreeable," (and even complacent) I've often been told,
"for we have had our share of criticism.
Our foes criticize us for what we are,
and our friends rebuke us for what we are not."
But silence has never been the habit of the Jew,
and complacency finds no room in his heart.

Throughout this work
I attempt to analyze and criticize
some of Israel's policies, both foreign and domestic.
At times my criticism may seem severe,
but its severity emanates from deep and personal concern,
concern that has not been widely voiced

in a concentrated form such as this.
The time has come to stop indulging in self-praise;
the time is now to reevaluate our goals and our priorities;
now is the time when we must research our souls.
If Israel is at the center of our hearts,
we are obligated to state what is on our minds.
For only through an honest dialogue,
a sincere exchange,
an ongoing constructive debate,
can we reach the depth, the fullness of our true selves.
Thus I tackle some of Israel's dilemmas.
I criticize, I warn, I alert, and I cry,
for I am a concerned Jew,
and I refuse to be a silent one.
I hope my criticism will be taken in good faith,
for faith is all one needs
to pursue an uneasy avenue
and a course that pleases but a few.

Whenever I think about the concept of Judaism,
of Jews and Israel,
I feel as though I am taken back and forth
through generations and centuries;
when I relive the past,
I see glory: yet it is mingled with pain.
When I reflect upon the present time,
I feel proud, yet uncertain;
and when I try to envision the future,
I see great fulfillment lying ahead—
yet it is mixed with anxiety.
Yes,
glory and pain,

pride and uncertainty,
great fulfillment and anxiety
constitute the makeup of a Jew.

Soon Jews in Israel and Jews around the world
will celebrate the thirtieth birthday of the state of Israel.
Indeed, there will be great reason to rejoice
and great memories to cherish.
Lucky are we who witnessed the fulfillment of a dream;
lucky are we who witnessed history as it wrote itself
       in time.
Yet this glorious chapter in our history
was not written without pain.
Our pride was not renewed without bloodshed.
Our achievements and successes in many walks of life
were not reached without anxiety.
Pogroms, mass slaughter,
persecutions, and misery
have for generations been the lot of the Jew.
Yet even now,
after realizing the greatest dream of all,
a Jewish state, a haven, a refuge, a home,
and the realization of the prayer—"next year in Jeru-
       salem"—
we still cannot claim total victory.
For Israel is facing multiple crises,
crises with deadly implications
that may jeopardize its very existence.

The time for complacency has passed.
No longer can Israeli officials
ignore, misconceive, neglect, or defer

what must be tackled now.
Israel must win a new set of victories.
Victories over its own internal weaknesses,
over the social, economic, and political crises
that may explode at any time:
Victory over the ethnic and class struggle in Israel—
a struggle that may jeopardize the unity of the country,
a struggle that at best has been ignored,
a struggle that lay dormant because of outside danger—
that will unleash its destructive potential
once the danger is removed.
Victory over misguided immigration policies,
policies of inequality in absorption
and waste in manpower and resources.
Victory over emigration from Israel
that has reached epidemic proportions
and may endanger Israel's viability
as a Jewish state created for the Jews.
Victory over red tape and an inflated bureaucracy.
Victory over the misperceived public relations campaign
that clouds Israel's image
and renders disservice to Israel's stature
in the world community;
victory over an awkward political system
that has fragmented Israeli society and
weakened its national security.
And, finally
those victories that will give us
peace with our enemy.
To these crises we must direct our attention.
To these problems the new Israeli government
must address itself.

There is no room for indecisiveness and irresolution.
There is no time for ambivalence and equivocation.
There is no place for a stalemated government and vacil-
   lating leaders.

Let us not be misled
by Israel's military power,
the victories of the War of Independence,
the Sinai Campaign,
the Six Day War,
and the Yom Kippur War.
All have not yet guaranteed the peace,
for diplomacy did not follow
where force left off.
Military power is nothing but a tool,
but in Israel it has often been mistaken for an end.
We moved from one military victory to another,
believing in the invincibility of our own creation,
thinking that the Arabs would soon acquiesce.
Let us therefore not assume that the job is done
nor that the future is settled.
Let us not confuse the building of a nation, a home,
with its preservation.
We can draw strength from the past three decades
but not guarantees for the future.
We can draw on our past experiences,
but we must not abandon the search.
We can rely on our perseverance,
but we cannot lose touch with reality:
the reality of American strategic interest in the region,
the reality of the Israelis' new set of priorities,
the reality of the Arab Palestinians,

the reality of oil and petrodollars,
and the reality of the West's vulnerability to Arab black-
    mail.

In its almost thirty years of independence Israel
has surpassed in many fields even its own goals;
goals that were considered
unattainable by any stretch of the imagination.
Yet its achievements and successes
in medicine, technology, science, agriculture
education, aviation, and the martial arts
would have been drastically reduced
without the direct and indirect support of world Jewry
and the United States of America.
The continuation of Israel's steadfastness,
better yet, its very existence,
hinges on the preservation of this unique relationship
with world Jewry, on the one hand,
and with the United States, on the other.

But
in this context, too,
no partnership can endure
unless its members demonstrate the capacity to be tolerant,
the ability to withstand criticism, and
the fortitude to perform under adverse conditions.
The partnership of Israel and world Jewry
embodies a unique emotional affinity
that can be fortified steadily
only through self-appraisal and
open debate,
not senseless recrimination;

through uninhibited exchange
and open communication.
Israel and world Jewry must remain coequal,
united in their dreams,
in their aspirations,
and in their hopes.
For these are the prerequisites of their survival.

Those who question the need
for a continuous exchange between Israel and world Jewry
must be aware that
the affinity between Israel and world Jewry
is not a luxury,
nor a quality added for good measure.
It is the very crux of their separate and mutual well-being;
it is the ultimate guarantor of their existence,
for only through the demonstration of this affinity
will a Jew cease to be considered a stranger,
a beggar, an outsider, a foreigner.
No longer will a Jew be treated as a bastard of humanity,
for now he has a place of his own.
Here he can reciprocate and offer hospitality,
for he has his own nation, his own refuge, his own home,
a home that must be guarded
with everything that we may ever have,
for it is the only home in which
whatever we have has any meaning at all.

I

THE NEED FOR POLITICAL REFORM OR A "NATIONAL GOVERNMENT"

G OVERNMENT policies in a democracy are often reflections of the country's internal social, economic, and political divisions, leaving the government little margin for formulating its foreign policy independent of the pressures of various constituencies. In a democracy a consistent long-range foreign policy cannot easily be achieved unless the government and the political system enjoy popular support. By contrast, in a dictatorial or totalitarian regime, such as China, Cuba, and Russia, foreign policy is largely formulated by an individual or a group that does not overly concern itself with the interests of the various political or economic factions that may be allowed to exist. Authoritarian leaders are able to formulate foreign policy from the overall perspective of national interest and thereby retain an advantage over democracies in decisiveness and flexibility. In a democracy, on the other hand, the necessary relationship between the government and various political factions and economic sectors may at times result in the creation of policies that reflect private, short-term interests and lack of decisiveness and far-sightedness. The problem is further exacerbated when the democratic government is a coalition government, such as in Israel, in which one has to rely on a narrow margin of support in the parliament for its continued existence.

The Concept of National Government

Because of political complexities and profound disagreements, it has been extremely difficult to form a "national government" in Israel, that is, a governing coalition of all political parties, excluding the Communists. In fact, only on one occasion during Israel's existence has agreement been reached to form such a government for the sake of demonstrating national unity. That was in 1967, when the number of seats represented in the cabinet was 106, which represented 89 percent of the membership in the Knesset or parliament. The formation of such a "wall-to-wall cabinet," in the words of Golda Meir, was undoubtedly prompted by the 1967 war. A major attempt was made to portray the government as one of unity. Because of the differences over policies, the National Religious party pulled out in 1969, to be followed by Gahal in 1971, leaving the government with a total of 72 seats. (See Appendix I)

Since the Yom Kippur War of October 1973, the discontent of the Israeli general public with the performance of its Labor government has been intensifying—economic austerity, on the one hand, and political uncertainty, on the other, have added to the sense of insecurity. The government's failure to administer Israel's affairs competently has further weakened general public confidence in its ability to handle more complicated issues, particularly in foreign affairs and in relations with the Arab states. However, before discussing further the desire for a stronger government with capable and competent leadership, it is necessary to review the political process in Israel and its particular makeup. Such a review will provide the basis for our contention that *Israel is clearly moving toward political dislocation* unless political reforms are instituted in the near future.

Israel's Internal Politics

Unlike the United States or Great Britain, where a dominant two-party system exists, Israel contains various interest groups and ideologies that have been represented by as many as twenty-five political parties. The Israelis prefer that their government represent a consensus of several party ideologies rather than one particular political philosophy. The government's desire to secure maximum participation, heightened by jealousies among the various parties, also contributes to the country's political fragmentation. One other element that may have contributed to the abundance of political parties in Israel is the fact that most parties existed before the foundation of the state. In fact, every single Jewish party that was elected to the second Knesset had been in existence before the establishment of Israel.

In the last ten years many smaller parties have been absorbed by the larger ones, but they have maintained their individual ideologies as separate sects within the larger parties. In the December 1973 election there were still more than ten parties campaigning for the 120 seats in the Knesset. And in the May 1977 election some six new parties emerged. However, only two—the Democratic Movement for Change, headed by Yigal Yadin, and Shlom Zion, headed by General Eric Sharon—have been able to make a serious impression on the Israeli voters.

Since Israel's independence in 1948, the Labor party has ruled Israel with the cooperation of other smaller parties. The Labor party has never had a sufficient number of seats (a minimum of 61) to form a majority government of its own but has retained power through the formation of a coalition government consisting of several (mostly religious) parties. One reason behind the inclusion of the religious parties in the coalition government was to prevent them from stirring up trouble on religious matters that are under their jurisdiction. A second reason was that their demands are generally related to internal religious issues that the leading party, the Labor Alignment, or the Mapai before it, could live with. Also, a smaller party is often invited to participate, even though its support in the Knesset is not required, so that if one party drops out of the coalition, there would still be enough seats represented in the cabinet to maintain a government. A vote of "lack of confidence" in the government by 61 or more members forces the prime minister to tender his or her resignation, which in effect brings down the whole government. In such a case, the president of Israel has the obligation to call on another party— usually the second largest—to form a government. Failure to do so results in a new election.

A case in point that illustrates the fragility of this political system is the recent government crisis in Israel that was precipitated by the dismissal of the National Religious party by former Premier Yitzhak Rabin. Consequently, the support of ten members of the National Religious party in the Knesset was lost, leaving the government with only 57 votes out of 120. A minority government thus faced a motion of "no confidence" by the opposition that would have compelled the government to fall. To prevent such an occurrence, Rabin tendered his own resignation to the president, in effect dissolving the government. The failure of the second largest party, the Likud, headed by Menahem Begin, to form a new government has forced the president to exercise his second option—to ask Rabin to serve as head of a caretaker government until the new election, which was advanced from November to May 1977.

This political system has several weaknesses that are relevant to our discussion:

1) The Israeli voter chooses among parties, not among individual representatives. Israel is not divided into constituencies, such as in Great Britain where each constituency has its own representative in parliament. In effect, the individual member of parliament in Israel is not accountable to the people per se but to the party leaders. Thus, representation in parliament does not necessarily reflect the social and economic makeup of society. By not being able to elect their own representatives, a majority of Israelis are not represented in the Knesset in proportion to their numbers.

Unfortunately, this situation is self-perpetuating. Under the existing system each party puts up one single list of candidates in the entire country. The veterans of the party machine usually have a dominant say on the appointments committee that puts together the list of candidates. The veterans make sure their names are placed in a safe spot so that their reelection is guaranteed. Acting as a group, the veteran politicians also maintain a high degree of cohesion, which minimizes the occurrence of unexpected changes. Furthermore, in analyzing coalition formation and the party system, it should be noted that Israel's political parties play a significant role in the social and economic life of the country. The various parties open and operate medical clinics, publish newspapers, and organize many social activities that have a direct influence on individual Israelis.

2) Party discipline in parliament is strong; that is, a member of parliament must vote on behalf of the government's policies when his party is part of the government coalition. Hence, very few members of a governing coalition have the audacity to argue against the government, fearing expulsion in the next election.

3) Because of the fact that no single party is often able to form a government, coalition government has become a way of life. Compromise and give-and-take become essential exercises for the sake of political stability. Coalition partners may find themselves at odds over some proposal that may result in the resignation of the smaller party. Such an incident could force the government as a whole to resign if the number of parliamentary members is not large enough to support it.

4) The principle of proportional representation in Israel allows a seat to any party that can win one percent of the total vote. This factor has enabled many **splinter**

groups to register as independent parties, further encouraging political division, on the one hand, and weakening the main parties, on the other. Even the main parties in Israel, namely, the Likud and the Labor Alignment, are themselves combinations of four smaller parties. This situation makes the ideological lines of the major parties blurry and ambiguous to a large extent. Thus the voters in the December 1973 and May 1977 elections were not able to determine precisely what the policies of the parties were and how they would perform in the face of growing dissatisfaction among the voters in general.

5) Another weakness of the Israeli political system is the fact that the party's prestige rests on the individual who heads the party. By clinging to the existing leadership, however, party members have created a generation gap within the party so that no qualified young successors have been groomed to take over. Thus, the parties have found themselves compelled to turn to the army for leadership, which has further increased the army's influence over civilian matters. Furthermore, the idea of national security has always been profoundly important in Israeli politics, and this factor greatly affects the size and makeup of the coalition government—particularly in times of tension and war.

The leadership situation has affected the opposition parties even more than the Labor party from which all of Israel's prime ministers except Menahem Begin have been chosen since 1948. The victory of the Likud party in May 1977 made it possible for Begin to head the first Israeli non-Labor government in 29 years. In their book, *Who Rules Israel?*, Yuval Elizur and Eliahu Salpeter elucidate this political pattern. Permanent coalition versus the opposition status of the respective parties helps to mold both the mentality displayed and the patterns of recruitment used by both sides. The opposition parties, having never experienced full political power, find it difficult to recruit able young men into their ranks. In the ruling parties, however, status and advancement depend largely on the individual's power in his administrative job, and so the recruitment of young talent is easier.

A government that does not enjoy a winning coalition of at least four or five Knesset members beyond the 61-member majority is often weak. It will be unable to take steps of national magnitude because of fear that one or two members might defect. A vote on returning the West Bank to Jordan, for example, might well bring down the government regardless of the political makeup of the coalition, unless, of course, a consensus had been reached in advance. Such being the case, the Begin government experienced difficulty reaching a consensus on these issues. In fact, any Israeli government could fall because of issues of far less magnitude than that of surrendering the West Bank to any Arab state. For example, the forceful evacuation of a group of Jewish settlers (Gush Emunim) from Kadum in the Samaria region of the West Bank could have caused a coalition crisis because of the lack of consensus about this sensitive issue even between ministers of the Knesset and members of their own party. For this reason the three settlements in that region were legalized by the Begin government.

The Israel political system therefore lends itself to political fragmentation, often resulting in a lack of cohesive policies even on matters of national magnitude. And, as such, compromise between the opposing points of view has been difficult to achieve and the development of deep-rooted political and economic cleavages is given even more impetus because of personality clashes and personal rivalries for power.

Political and Economic Crises

In the aftermath of the Yom Kippur War Israel suffered severe psychological, economic, and, to a lesser extent, military setbacks. Although Israel, on the surface, recuperated psychologically and militarily, especially in the wake of the Entebbe operation of July 4, 1976, it has been unable to cope with the mounting economic and political difficulties resulting from the war. The reasons behind these developments are varied and complicated. The following reasons are only the most pertinent:

1) *The Leadership Vacuum:*

In the wake of the disastrous Yom Kippur War, Israel found itself searching for a new leader to play the role of savior. Prime Minister Golda Meir and Defense Minister Moshe Dayan were forced to leave their government posts under public pressure. With the removal of Dayan as a political successor to Golda Meir, the late Pinhas Sapir (who was another contender for the premiership) was also pressured to take a back seat, for he too symbolized the failure of the old generation.

Once the main contenders were removed as viable candidates, Yigal Allon was also cast aside mainly because of his controversial and "dovish" views. Above all, however, the political machine of the Labor Alignment was not ready to consider anyone who might incur the slightest disapproval of the various factions of the party. In other words, the new candidate was supposed to have the aura of a leader, moderate views, the fewest political enemies, and the acceptance of Golda Meir herself. It was clear that the party was more concerned with maintaining some harmony among the opposing groups, even at the expense of electing a leader who lacked some of the fundamental qualifications required to lead a besieged nation. Thus Yitzhak Rabin was selected by the Labor party machine.

Despite his brilliant military record, Rabin failed to assert himself as a leader (his reelection to head the list of the Labor Alignment notwithstanding). His military experiences and his diplomatic tenure in Washington did not guarantee automatic success in political life, especially when the prevailing conditions were so highly volatile and uncertain. Rabin lacks vision, decisiveness, and political adaptability, all of which are essential qualities in a leader. General Ariel Sharon, the Yom Kippur War hero, who resigned as military adviser to Rabin in early April 1976, claimed in a TV interview in Israel that the Israeli government is incapable of standing up to American pressure. General Sharon added that he felt compelled to resign because he wanted to alert the Israeli public to the dangers inherent in the continuation of the Rabin government.

In a similar view, expressed at the same time, Rabbi Alexander Schindler, chairman of the Conference of Presidents of Major Jewish Organizations, told an audience in Israel that Israel's world image was that of a nation without strong leadership. Rabbi Schindler added that the world view of Israel was that its leadership could not stand up to the challenges of the region. Whether this allegation is true or not, Rabbi Schindler emphasized, makes no difference as long as the world perceives Israel in that light.

In a report published by the Jewish Telegraphic Association, Uzi Benjamin discussed the disenchantment of many professors who joined the Rabin government but decided to quit because of political pressure and personality clashes with the various ministries. For example, Professor Yuval Neeman, until late 1976 adviser to the defense minister on cabinet policy, and Professor Michael Bruno, adviser to the finance minister on government economic policy, are among those who departed. According to Professor Bruno, there are many more who have decided to quit their jobs because of differences of opinion. Professors who joined the civil service learned of the huge political price that Israeli society pays for the survival of the Rabin government; they realized that in order to maintain the existence of the cabinet, former Premier Yitzhak Rabin had to water down his plans to cut the budget of the defense ministry. They saw how the cabinet had acceded to pressure applied by different economic interest groups (banks, trade unions, industrialists), thus gnawing away at its economic policy. Some of these professors were stunned by what they described as the incompetence to carry out cabinet resolutions; they became disillusioned with the weakness of the cabinet as a governing and consensual body. They were further disillusioned by the inner struggle among cabinet ministers and by the haphazard way in which policies were laid down.

With discontent growing not only among the ranking

members of the Labor Alignment but also throughout Israel's populace, the need for a Ben-Gurion style of leadership is expressed by the vast majority of the Israeli public. Restoration of public confidence in the government has become a prerequisite of the government's execution of its foreign and domestic policies.

These were the conditions that, to a large extent, contributed to the creation of the Democratic Movement for Change, headed by Professor Yigal Yadin. It was the disenchantment of thousands of Israelis with the Labor Alignment that gave impetus to the Yadin movement. And indeed, the election of May 1977 has shown that the Israeli populace is ready for some degree of political change.

What has further aggravated the situation are those chronic problems that have subjected the government to daily criticism.

2) *Economic Dislocation:*

Another aspect of the pre-May 17, 1977 crisis is Israel's chronically weak economic condition. One of the main repercussions of the Yom Kippur War was economic dislocation that stemmed from several interrelated factors:

(a) The general mobilization of Israel's armed forces during and after the Yom Kippur War resulted in severe damage to Israel's industry and consequently caused a serious drop in Israel's GNP growth rate.

(b) Heavy military losses, especially in equipment and general materiel, were sustained during Israel's initial military setback. It was estimated that the total economic loss to Israel as a result of the war was in excess of eight billion dollars (for the United States this would be equivalent to 640 billion dollars). These heavy losses have set back Israel's economy by at least ten years.

(c) The cost of the Yom Kippur War added a burden to the already overburdened economy. The need for greater military preparedness, notwithstanding the disengagement accords with Syria and Egypt, has compelled the government to budget a far greater sum for defense, estimated at almost 50 percent of Israel's GNP. Such unparalleled military expenditures caused a direct decline in civilian industry. General economic uncertainties have given impetus to an inflationary spiral (rising to 32 percent during 1975) that, coupled with increased unemployment and the devaluation of the lira (Israeli pound), has become a steady feature of the economy. The deterioration of the Israeli economy has reached a dangerous stage; no easy cure is readily available. Government attempts to alleviate the situation have not as yet shown many positive results, particularly when the Israeli political situation has itself been a disruptive factor.

3) *Lack of Political Cohesiveness:*

Essentially, the Israeli political crisis of December 1976 originated within the Labor Alignment party that consists of four different factions: Mapai, Ahdoet Avoda, Mapam, and Rafi. The disagreements among the various factions are ideological and political in nature; yet they also reflect personal disagreements and even animosities among the leaders of the different factions, most of whom covet the premiership.

Former Defense Minister Shimon Peres, who lost his bid to head the list of the Labor Alignment, is hawkish in his attitude toward the Arab-Israeli crisis. He also favors a comprehensive new economic program. Former Foreign Minister Yigal Allon is essentially dovish; he is ready to make major concessions and negotiate with any Palestinian representative who recognizes Israel's right to exist. Rabin, representing the third side of the triangular debate, has taken the middle road, fearing drastic measures in either direction. There are many other areas of disagreement. The settlement of Israeli Jews in the Samaria region of the West Bank, the policies best suited for economic recovery, the future of the Gaza Strip and the West Bank, the course that should be adopted for future negotiations with the Arab states—these and other major issues deepened the schisms among Rabin, Peres, and Allon and brought the government to a critical showdown.

As proof of the weakness of the Rabin government, former Prime Minister Golda Meir was enlisted by Rabin and other Labor party leaders to restore party unity by taking an active part in the Labor party's new leadership forum. It was hoped that the inclusion of Mrs. Meir would save the Labor party from the ideological and financial ills that threaten to rend it asunder. And indeed, the active participation of Golda Meir helped to secure the very thin margin recorded in favor of Rabin during the Labor convention in February 1977, a margin without which Peres might have been able to defeat Rabin for the leadership of the party. (In the wake of Rabin's bank account scandal, Peres was subsequently elected to head the Labor party.)

Despite the change in leadership, the Rabin episode contributed to the loss inflicted on the Labor party in the May 1977 election. Yet it would be unfair if we were to attribute all that was lost by the Labor party to Rabin himself. The Labor party has long been a target, blamed for whatever ills the country was facing. In addition, the corruption within the party, as revealed by the guilty plea of Asher Yadlin (former head of the Kupat Holim), who admitted that he accepted bribes on behalf of the Labor party treasury, and other such revelations, badly affected Labor's strength on the eve of the election. The Yadlin case was widely viewed as a representative sample of what was happening within the governing party hierarchy, against whom charges of bribery, fraud, and tax evasion were frequently leveled.

Despite these developments, the Labor party was not hurt as much as its antagonists—the Likud and the Democratic Movement for Change—expected. The political processes in Israel often work contrary to those of other democratic countries.

As indicated earlier, political factionalism in Israel is actually desired. Although Israelis encourage a multiparty system, they remain, by and large, loyal to their party affiliations regardless of the discontent caused throughout the years.

To illustrate this paradox of Israeli politics, let us examine the Israeli election of December 1973.

After the Yom Kippur War in October 1973, the dissatisfaction of the Israelis with their government reached its peak. The mishandling of the war and the fact that the country was on the verge of bankruptcy had agitated every voter. Yet, when all the votes were counted, the Labor Alignment lost only 6 seats over the previous election, and in fact it maintained a proportionate majority within the Knesset. The second parliamentary bloc, the Likud, gained 8 seats. The overall picture shows that the voting behavior of the Israeli population has remained consistent in every election. In addition, "Prior to 1973, a good deal of the change of vote was within factional groupings. The parties of the left lost voters to one another . . . the individual party may be exposed to a substantial swing in its vote from election to election. Yet, when examined in terms of factional groupings, a much more stable picture was provided. . . . Parties of the left never won fewer than sixty-four nor more than sixty-nine seats in the Knesset in the seven elections which took place through 1969. In 1973, however, they won fifty-nine seats, the center parties ranked between twenty-seven and thirty-four seats (forty-three in 1973), the religious parties between fifteen and eighteen seats (fifteen in 1973). . . . The Labor party retained many of the characteristics of a dominant party. The 1973 elections, viewed in the perspective of the Labor party's declining claim to dominance, must be viewed as part of a process, and not as a break with the past." (Alan Arian, *Comparative Politics*, vol. 8, No. 1, pp. 152–53, p. 163) For this reason one may ask—if the disaster of the Yom Kippur War did not cause a drastic change in the Israeli parliamentary picture (see Appendix 2), what would it take to ensure meaningful social and political change? As a matter of fact, even those citizen-soldiers mobilized by the war did not vote much differently in the election of 1973 than they did previously. The army vote gave the Likud 41.28 percent as opposed to 39.54 percent for the Alignment. In the general population the division was 28.6 percent and 39.8 percent. respectively. Although it is true that the Likud outpaced the Alignment in the army returns, even before the war it was well known that the Likud was strong among younger voters. The Alignment won from army voters almost exactly the same share as it did from the general population. (Alan Arian, *Comparative Politics*, October 1975, p. 160)

There is a variety of reasons that explains Israeli political orientation and behavior. Some of them are socioeconomic, and others are inherent in the Israeli character.

(a) The strong and well-organized labor unions within the Histadrut (the Labor Federation) are very loyal to the political core of the Labor Alignment. As Elizur and Salpeter have shown in their book, *Who Rules Israel?*, the economic enterprises of the Histadrut, including banks, factories, corporations, and even luxury hotels, can be counted on to supply the funds for election campaigns and to provide jobs for minor functionaries, while the unions, today comprising more than half a million members, help to bring in the votes. This is the reason why, despite the continuous friction between the Histadrut and the government over the latter's economic policy, social legislation, and educational system, government leaders are careful to preserve the unique place of the Histadrut within the framework of Israeli democracy. The powerful labor organizations can muster at will all the necessary support for the Labor government. Only a few workers dare to defect from the party line; by and large, the votes of the workers are locked in.

(b) There is a special incentive for the big corporations, such as Solel Bonei, Bank Hapoalim, Eged, Dan, and many others, to maintain an amicable relationship with the Labor party—not only because it has been in power since the creation of the state but also because the bureaucrats on both sides are not willing to rock the boat, particularly when most of these corporations have become essential factors in the Labor party's power base.

(c) Average Israelis associate themselves with the leaders of their political parties rather than with the parties' political philosophy. This may explain, at least in part, the return of Golda Meir to an active role in the Labor party hierarchy in the face of the government's singular lack of inspiring leadership.

(d) Most parties have been making the same political pronouncements for years with very little change in leadership. What would compel an Israeli to vote for another party, especially in the absence of a new, viable movement that can provide, first, an alternative to the existing political system, and, second, can engender wide support from both the extreme and the moderate right?

A partial answer to this question was given in the election of May 1977. For the first time since 1948, a credible movement was developing—headed by a man who commanded a great deal of respect from Israeli voters. However, the fact that the Democratic Movement for Change was not able to generate an absolute, or even a relative, majority was indicative of the political orientation explained earlier. Although the Yadin movement ranked third after Likud and the Labor Alignment, it signals the beginning of a new political era that may eventually lead toward a more equitable political system— a system subject more and more to the scrutiny of the people and in which the checks and balances among government branches are enforced.

4) *Military Domination:*

Unlike most democratic countries, the military establishment in Israel wields enormous influence over security matters, and, to a great extent, over the conduct of foreign policy. By and large the civilian authority has formulated its policies based on assessments, domestic and foreign, received from the military establishment. The military in Israel still is the principal source from which the civilian authority draws its information, seeks analyses and evaluations, and asks for recommendations for action.

In their book, *Who Rules Israel?*, Yuval Elizur and Eliahu Salpeter have stressed the fact that the intelligence branch of the defense establishment exerts enormous influence over the civilian authority. The evaluations and reports of military intelligence carry much weight in determining the size of the armed forces and the level of weaponry. The defense concepts developed by the military elite are also translated directly into government policy and thereby have a direct impact on Israel's foreign policy and international political position.

There are several reasons that account for the creation of this unique relationship between the Israeli military and the civilian authorities. In examining these reasons I will argue that changes need to be made in the relationship. In a word, the Israeli government should begin to adopt policies of reconciliation with the Arab states, policies that conflict with the philosophy of the defense establishment. This does not mean that the civilian authorities should seek to weaken the Israeli forces but it does mean that they should develop independent political thinking to which army intelligence may contribute but not dominate.

(a) *The Garrison State:* Since its formation Israel has depended on the military for its survival. With Arab violence steadily increasing since 1936, and with Israel's back to the sea, the strength of the Israeli army constituted the difference between survival and probable annihilation. Having performed so successfully, the military became the focal point of Israeli life. Military men ranked the highest in popular esteem and prestige.

The successive victories of the Israeli army in the War of Independence in 1948, the Sinai Campaign of 1956, and the Six Day War of 1967 created a euphoria and a feeling of absolute superiority over the Arab states. This overconfidence backfired in the Yom Kippur War of 1973, when the Israeli army was caught by surprise. Overreliance on the military, then, did not prove at all justified.

The Agranatt Commission, appointed by the Israeli government to investigate the war, was explicit in its critical findings: 1) There was a general lack of preparedness on the part of the military forces. 2) The mobilization of the reserves was delayed—possibly for political reasons. 3) No contingency plans were available in case of a surprise attack. 4) There was a miscalculation of enemy intent as well as serious misinterpretations of general data. 5) The enemy's capability to wage an all-out war was underestimated. 6) Military forces in the south were strategically misplaced. 7) There was unwarranted, total reliance on the Israeli army regulars to contain the enemy and to initiate a counterattack. 8) Inexperienced young generals were in charge of highly sensitive and important areas such as the Southern Command. 9) Excessive self-confidence on the part of the military leadership prevailed. 10) The civilian political leadership placed total reliance on the military's evaluations.

The toll of the war was exceedingly high and the blunders of some of the military officers and of the defense establishment in general were well inscribed in the minds of the average Israelis. Given the volatile situation in the Middle East, the reliance of Israel on its military has been virtually unavoidable, but total reliance has proved dangerous.

One point that should be clarified is that there is no contradiction between overreliance by the civilian authorities on the military establishment and the failure to use military forces when needed. Before the Yom Kippur War the only means by which the Arab army could have been discouraged from launching a surprise attack would have been Israeli military preparedness. Yet the government failed to make use of the instrument that was designed to perform that very task. The irony was that even the decision by the government not to mobilize the reserve forces soon enough was partly attributable to military intelligence.

Although the Israeli military is constitutionally subordinate to the civilian authority, this does not by itself guarantee a nonmilitary approach to civilian problems. The military ethic in Israel is predominant and often leaves very little room for independent thinking.

(b) *Administrative Inefficiency in the Private Sector:* In addition to the fact that the military establishment in Israel exerts tremendous influence over security and foreign affairs, retired generals and other high-ranking officers, it seems automatically, have assumed positions of authority in the private sector as well. The general policy of both

the civilian and the military authorities has been to promote the integration of army officers into civilian life both
during their service tenure and after retirement. The
private business sector, for its part, has often been eager
to bring ex-army officers into its enterprises, for civilian
employers believe that ex-army officers will bring efficiency
and smoothness of operation to their companies. As a
result, large numbers of army officers have transferred
to leadership roles in civilian establishments. The result
is that generals and other officers out of uniform have
been able to exert considerable influence on the Israeli
civilian sector.

Far from being at the instigation of the military, the
circumstances of hostile neighbors and the vacuum of
leadership in the nonmilitary sectors have created a situation that only retired army personnel can fill. Army
personnel has been diffused among the industrial techno-
crats and the bureaucratic elite in Israel. In the words
of Amos Perlmutter, author of *The Military and Politics
in Israel*, "A tacit but highly institutionalized pattern has
been established between the army and society for the
benefit of a vigorous and mobile army, officer turnover
in the military is rapid; the society then absorbs the
much-needed retired young officers. The military in Israel, as a pressure group similar to those in other non-
praetorian states where the civilian is formally and
informally supreme, will nevertheless continue to challenge the civilian."

The military in Israel has become a part of the social,
psychological, and emotional fabric without which most
Israelis would feel insecure. Although the Israeli social
and mental balance may depend to a large extent on the

continuation of "militarism" as a way of life, it should be stated clearly that undue militarism of the Israeli society is often translated into public policies and attitudes that are not consistent with Israel's long-range plans of reconciliation with the Arab states. Although no one who is concerned with Israel's security and future would dream of advocating the weakening of Israel's military posture for the sake of appearing conciliatory, one can nevertheless promote an intellectual and spiritual atmosphere less dependent on military achievements. Operations such as the Entebbe rescue of the airline hostages from Uganda in July 1976 are important factors in maintaining Israeli morale. But such military achievements must not be the prime, or only, source that sustains high morale—an important ingredient for the normal functioning of Israeli society. Lacking other sources, the misconception about the "invincibility" of the Israeli soldier may arise again under conditions that might be both misleading and dangerous.

The Need for Political Reform

Considering the political peculiarities of the Israeli system, the most ideal solution would be a major political reform that would provide more direct representation, on the one hand, and the reduction of the various political factions to a two- or three-party system, on the other. For the last three decades many Israeli politicians, including David Ben-Gurion (Israel's first prime minister), attempted to introduce some changes into the electoral system but failed because of the consistent opposition that was mounted in various degrees of intensity by most of the political parties, including the Labor Alliance.

The opposition to political change was primarily motivated by the desire of the various parties for self-
perpetuation. With the emergence of the Democratic
Movement for Change the chances for some political
reforms are better now than ever before. For the first
time in Israel's history, a party has run on a platform
committed to political change. The response of the voters
is indicative of a new political awareness among an
appreciable number of Israelis who have been frustrated
by and indignant about the existing system and were
waiting for an opportunity to demonstrate their feelings.
Yet the success or failure of Yigal Yadin in implementing
his program will largely depend on: 1) whether or not
the Yadin movement will be joined by other small political
parties such as Flato-Sharon, the independent Liberals,
and Citizens Rights, whose independent survival will
remain ineffective and rather precarious; and 2) to what
extent the Yadin movement will broaden its popular base
among Labor's social strata. The new party, according
to one of its founders, Mordechai Abir, "will move toward
implementing its political reform in two stages—knowing
that under the present political makeup the new movement cannot bring about all the changes it needs or
wants." If the Democratic Movement for Change can
demonstrate a capacity to lead and enlarge its grassroots
support, the chances are that the new movement may
indeed succeed in bringing a new dimension to the Israeli
political system. The two stages, according to Mordechai
Abir, include, first: "the adoption of electoral reform,
dissolution of the Ninth Knesset after 12 to 18 months
needed for requisite legislation, and the holding of new
elections; and second, the beginning of administrative

reform of the government through the creation of a small inner cabinet which should point an end to the present paralysis at the top." (*Jerusalem Post*, Feb. 8, 1977, p. 10)

Although political reforms are still ideals, pioneered by by the new Democratic Movement for Change, short of achieving those ideals, the formation of a national government may prove to be a viable alternative and a means by which political reforms may become attainable.

The pros and cons of a national government (in which most parties would form a coalition government) are numerous. In the past the idea was rejected by both Golda Meir and Yitzhak Rabin. Their opposition to including the Likud party was primarily based on the supposition that the two prime partners, namely, the Likud and Labor, would not reconcile their political differences regarding issues of national magnitude. The future of the occupied territories, for example, was often cited as the main stumbling block; yet, as indicated earlier, lacking a two- or three-party system, the Israeli government by and large has been inhibited from taking any action that could have provoked serious opposition not only from the opposition parties but from within the government itself. A national government could not have hindered efforts to solve some of the major problems that were, and still are, facing the nation. Furthermore, a national government would have been able to accelerate the process of bringing forth new faces, badly needed for positions of leadership.

Rabin and Golda Meir have not solved the leadership vacuum. Rabin is inept and incapable of giving Israel the leadership that it desperately needs; Golda Meir is too old and rigid—she could be a liability rather than an asset.

A national government would succeed in bringing together the best available minds in the economic, social, military, and political fields. Contrary to what the Rabin government has maintained, it would also provide a coherent and cohesive approach to Israel's problems. Although the diversity of views and opinions within such a national government would be great, such a government must still be formed on the premise of national needs and requirements.

The question of reconciling the "hawkish" views of Menahem Begin and the unequivocally dovish views of Professor Yadin was addressed by the veteran Mapam leader Ya'acov Hazan, who said: "Anyone who is not an out-and-out Land of Israel movement annexationist is necessarily a dove." If one accepts this definition, then individuals such as Sharon, Yadin, Dayan, Eban, Peres, Bar-Lev, and Rabin can and must work together for the sake of the country without necessarily compromising their principles and beliefs.

Issues of national magnitude, such as the surrender of major territories, should be resolved by referendum—let the people decide which way the nation should go. The task of the politicians is to make their cases to the people. The Arab-Israeli crisis is not a political issue that can be misrepresented to the Israeli voter. Israelis in general have lived most of their lives, and in many cases all of their lives, amid crisis. The time has come for Israeli leaders to begin to give some credit to the Israeli people.

As to the question of why a national government would be any more united than the previous one if it has even more diverse views within it, let me repeat that a diversity of political viewpoints is inherent in the Israeli political system. The purpose of national unity in government is not to force a unity of political view but rather to reach a consensus and allow an open discussion that will shed some light on the many issues that have been dealt with exclusively in the past by the Labor Alignment that has been prejudiced as well as committed to old dogmas.

A national government should relieve Israel of much internal and external political pressure. A national government should be formed on the premise of a national emergency, and partisan politics should be set aside. Any other government, short of a government formed by a single party with an absolute majority, would only portray an intransigence or weakness that would lead to increased demands by the Arab states and the Arab Palestinians. Finally, a government of national unity would prevent, or at least forestall, a new political crisis that could bring Israel to the brink of economic and political disaster. The leaders of the various political parties sooner or later will have to come to grips with the real problems. If they do not support such a move in the national interest, they will have to face the Israeli electorate that, against its will, may take positions that could lead to anarchy or revolution. In either case, Israel's national character, its political allegiance, and its social and economic structure will be in jeopardy.

Conclusion

Israel is facing not only a danger to its physical security but also attacks of an economic, political, and psychological (propaganda) nature. No country can afford to be complacent about its shortcomings when it is besieged and partially surrounded by enemies sworn to its liquidation. No country in such circumstances can afford the luxury of internal strife, haggling, distrust, and vicious rivalries for power.

The May election has so far provided some encouraging signs; whether the Democratic Movement for Change will finally succeed in bringing the desired political changes remains to be seen. Its success or failure, however will signal the course that Israel will follow for the next decade. If political fragmentation persists and if the lack of consensus to create a national government continues to prevail, then indeed Israel will continue to suffer social and economic ills, and recovery may not be in sight until a severe shakeup of the entire system occurs.

Prime Minister Begin has so far demonstrated an ability to lead. His desire to form a national government should indeed be welcomed. It is now up to the Labor Alignment to follow the lead of the Democratic Movement for Change and join forces with Begin to meet today's challenges. One such grave challenge is Israel's ethnic and class struggle to which we now turn our attention.

II

ISRAEL'S
ETHNIC AND
CLASS STRUGGLE

THE class and ethnic struggle in Israel between Jews of different backgrounds constitutes one of Israel's internal dilemmas that require special attention. This problem is unique in many ways. First, it has manifested itself daily in social contacts between the two groups even though it has been a subdued conflict, without much overt friction. Second, it is potentially dangerous, but very little if anything has been done by the Labor government to avert a major confrontation in the future. And, finally, although this social and ethnic struggle will determine Israel's future character, the problem is being relegated to the "natural" processes of social evolution rather than directed toward some desirable outcome.

What kind of outcome can be anticipated when the relationship between the various Jewish ethnic groups is steadily deteriorating and when alarming symptoms of a deep social fissure are apparent? How many more years can any Israeli government hope to minimize the importance of this explosive situation?

The concern that has been voiced by some observers, including this writer, is not by any means directed toward only those ethnic groups that have suffered the most. Rather it is concern for the well-being of the state of Israel as a whole. In fact, it is my judgment that the danger to Israel's security that emanates from within— the class and ethnic struggle—is as severe as that emanating from the extremist Arab states.

If Israel's social and ethnic schism has not yet posed an imminent threat to the state, it is merely because an outside enemy that poses a danger to the entire population has been a source of unity. Throughout modern Israel's history the level of social tensions has been inversely related to the extent of the threat on its borders, that is, the lower the external threat, the higher the social discontent within; the higher the border tension, the greater the social harmony.

After almost thirty years of statehood, Israel still has not developed the social and political mechanisms, such as equitable political representation, that serve to promote social equilibrium and harmony. Democratic elections by secret ballot, freedom of speech and of the press, welfare reforms, and land distribution have not been sufficient in themselves to bring about a narrowing of the social and economic disparities among various classes in Israel.

Although Israel contains more than seventy different linguistic groups, the population may be divided into two major classes: 1) the "Western Jews" (Ashkenazim) who immigrated to Israel from the Western hemisphere, including East European Jews; and 2) the "Oriental Jews" (Sephardim) who came mainly from Middle Eastern countries, North Africa, and South America and who are distinguishable by their relatively darker skin. In 1970, 27.5 percent of the 2,562,000 Jews in Israel had been born in Europe-America, 26.3 percent in Asia-Africa, and 46.2 percent in Israel. (C.B.S., *Statistical Abstract of Israel*, 22:45) In their article, "The Dynamics of Social Inequalities"(*Social Dynamics* 1 (1) pp. 63–79, 1975, p. 66), Sammy Smooha and Yochanan Peres point out that if all foreign-born Israelis from Asia and Africa (excluding South Africa) and their descendants are included in the Oriental group, the total contribution of that group would be raised to 52 percent in 1970. "In spite of their numerical preponderance," Smooha and Peres continue, "Orientals are a subordinate group. They suffer from the disadvantages of late arrival in the state, poor skills, and inexperience in living in an industrial, democratic society."

According to another scholar, Eva Etzioni-Halevy, the disadvantages of the Oriental Jew are deep-rooted and widespread in effect: "Originating from a more traditional culture, the Orientals encountered serious difficulties in becoming integrated into Israel's relatively modernized economic, occupational and educational structures. Thus, they tended to gravitate into lower-ranking occupations, and their children evidenced disproportionately high rates of school attrition. On the political scene, Orientals were successfully absorbed into existing organizations. But they were not accorded any major power positions in them. In addition, they came to be regarded by many as somewhat lower in social status than Westerners. . . . What counts is that contrary to prevailing expectations the socioeconomic gaps were not narrowed as time went on." ("Protest Politics in the Israeli Democracy," *Political Science Quarterly*, vol. 90, No. 3, Fall 1975, p. 501)

There are several reasons why class and ethnic disparities between the Sephardic Jew and the Ashkenazi Jew have been perpetuated. Some are circumstantial, some cultural, and still others are the result of the short-sightedness and, at times, the deliberate policies of the government dating from the early days of Israel's independence.

1) *The Privilege of Circumstance:* The vast majority of the early settlers were Jews from Eastern Europe, especially from Poland and Russia. Being the first pioneers, from the turn of the century through the late forties, they laid the foundations of the Jewish political entity in Palestine. It was only natural, therefore, that they would hold the highest positions, particularly since the number of Sephardic Jews was insignificant at the time. The situation could not be condemned if it were not for the fact that those who were in power from the inception of the state clung to their positions as if each of them was totally indispensable.

In his book, *The Israelis, Founders and Sons,* Amos Elon, a noted Israeli journalist, observed that in the Israeli system a forty-five or fifty-year-old man aspiring for public office is still regarded as an ambitious young man. To illustrate the tenacious hold of the Ashkenazi Jews in power, Elon gave a brief survey of Israel's Knesset (parliament). In the first Israeli parliament (1949) the average age of the members was forty-three. The average age in the sixth parliament (1969) was sixty-three. During the intervening 20 years, the average age of the members had risen exactly 20 years! Furthermore, Elon stressed that between 1949 and 1970 of the 277 members of parliament, 74 percent were born in Eastern Europe of Eastern European parents. "Despite the vast changes in the ethnic composition of the Jewish-Israeli population, the predominance of Eastern Europeans in the sixth and seventh Knessets of 1965 and 1969 was almost as marked as it had been in the Knessets elected in 1961, 1959, 1955, and 1949." The danger in the stubborn staying power of the older, Ashkenazi Jews is, of course, that without adequate provisions for a periodic turnover in political personnel, governments tend to produce stale leaders and sterile policies.

The number of Sephardic Jews in positions of high authority is quite small. In fact, power disparities vary from an extreme differentiation on positions such as mayors of large towns to a near equality in minor positions such as secretaries-general of workers' councils in smaller towns. "The wide range is not random, but falls into a significant pattern of increasing power disparity with higher levels. This generalization (the more powerful the position, the smaller the Oriental representation) is confirmed by examination of differentials in power disparities. . . . When positions are classified into three ranks . . . Oriental representation tends to be smaller at the middle and higher ranks compared with the lower ranks." (*Social Dynamics* 1 (1), 1975, pp. 73–74)

Eva Etzioni-Halevy points out that although the representation of Sephardim in high-ranking posts of authority has somewhat increased—Sephardim have been appointed to posts of speaker of the Knesset and chairman of the Foreign Affairs and Security Committee, and the number of Sephardic government ministers has increased from one (minister of police) to two (the addition being the minister of agriculture)—there has been no meaningful change. Some cabinets contained two Sephardic ministers, but the key positions of authority were still retained by Westerners. Twenty-one ministers, including the prime minister, are Ashkenazim; the ministry of defense, the ministry of foreign affairs, the treasury, and the ministry of education and culture are retained in Ashkenazi hands. (*Political Science Quarterly*, vol. 90, No. 3, p. 510) Although Sephardic Jews voted heavily for the Likud party, Prime Minister Begin has maintained the same ratio of Sephardic representation in his new government.

An economic element that has also served to perpetuate social class differences relates to the fact that the majority of Sephardic Jews came to Israel with limited financial resources. In contrast, by 1950 most of the Ashkenazim in Israel had been able to establish themselves economically, a factor that had a direct bearing not only on their standards of living but also on their ability to enhance their own education and that of their children. With the limited resources of the Israeli government, very few Sephardic Jews have been able to obtain scholarships to pursue higher studies beyond the free elementary level. (See Appendix 3)

Economic differences between the two classes are real and critical. Studies of relative inequalities indicate that a Sephardic family income ranges between 57 percent to 74 percent of income received by an Ashkenazi family. More fundamentally, there has been an increase in the absolute gap in purchasing power; the gap between the two groups increased from IL 168 in 1956–57 to IL 307 in 1971. (*Social Dynamics* 1 (1), p. 66)

More indicators of the economic gap may be cited. In 1968–69, 30 percent of the Sephardim were in the lowest fifth based on income distribution, compared to only 12 percent of the Ashkenazi population. (Public Inquiry Commission, 1971:24) Twice as many Sephardim as Ashkenazim receive assistance from welfare bureaus, and 3.7 times as many are "hard-core" welfare recipients. (C.B.S., *Statistical Abstract of Israel*, 22:593)

In his book, *The Kingdom of Oil*, Ray Vickers confirmed that the Sephardic Jews of Israel are at the low end of the social and economic scale, often living as an inferior minority despite their numerical majority. The children of Sephardic parentage total 70 percent of the school classes at the elementary level, approximately 16 percent finish high school, and only 3 percent complete university education. In some respects, Vickers notes, "the Oriental Jew is the 'black' of Israel."

Educational inequality is further explored by Smooha and Peres, who are concerned with the same pyramidal situation that Vickers analyzed. In 1969–70, Sephardim constituted 61.2 percent of all primary school students, 42.6 percent of all students in post-primary education, and 13.2 percent of students in higher education. (C.B.S., *Statistical Abstract of Israel*, 22:557, 561, 568) In the judgment of Peres and Smooha, "This low representation among college students will restrict the entry of Orientals, who constitute over 50 percent of the Jewish population, into Israeli elites. Higher education has increasingly become a prerequisite for entry to such positions." For this reason, it has become imperative to begin the process of narrowing the ethnic gap by making educational facilities far more accessible to the children of Sephardic origin; free high school and university education may be one of the main prerequisites.

An attempt by the ministry of education to integrate schools by busing some of the students of Sephardic background to better schools has failed, according to Havir Shimoni, a Knesset member of the Labor Alignment. The ministry of education programs were neither encompassing nor serious. What is needed to improve the deteriorating condition of the underprivileged is far more than busing. Smaller classrooms, better qualified teachers, and, most important, the creation of conditions at home that will be more conducive to studying are all needed in preparation for higher education.

However, in this regard too, the prospects are far from encouraging. It appears likely that the incidence of extremely low Sephardic attendance at universities may be aggravated in the future by the steady increase of tuition fees from an average of 3,000 Israeli lira to approximately 10,000 Israeli lira. Many academicians and social observers warn that increased fees for higher education will widen the gap between the affluent and the underprivileged classes of Israeli society because only those in the higher income categories will be able to send their children to the universities. The most alarming aspect of this situation, however, relates to the fact that the bulk of the universities' budgets is underwritten by the government. In effect, the government is subsidizing the education of the rich, often at the expense of the poor.

2. *Political Inhibition:* The Sephardic Jews by and large

did not participate in the governing of their countries of origin, nor did they experience Western-style democracy. Thus, a lack of political awareness and a lack of a sense of political efficacy have undoubtedly inhibited their active participation in Israeli politics. The politically unsophisticated image that the Sephardic Jewish immigrants projected masked their capacity to adjust and contribute effectively to the shaping of the multiethnic society. The error of the Western political elite was not in creating a class of politically disoriented citizens but in accepting the situation, an acquiescence that reflected fear of future competition from the Oriental Jews who exceeded fifty percent of the total Israeli population by 1955. There are at least two results of this policy of inaction:

a) It has made Israel appear a totally Western country, in effect strengthening the Arab claims that Israel is a Western entity planted in the heart of the Middle East and that there is nothing Oriental about it. Many Arab politicians and intellectuals have repeatedly pointed to the fact that there has not been a single Sephardic Jew in an important post. Arab students have ridiculed the fact that the Israeli government for more than two decades has managed to appoint a Sephardic Jew to the post of police minister. This is not even lip service, they argued; it is an insult to the integrity of the Sephardic Jew.

b) Many thousands of educated Sephardic Jews have been "forced into exile" by virtue of their inability to combat the inertia and social inequality of the political bureaucracy. Many of these men and women are intellectuals who grew weary and disheartened and emigrated to Europe, Canada, and the United States in search of a better future. The Israeli loss in terms of human resources has been indeed formidable. Many of these "exiled" Jews succeeded in becoming highly respected citizens of their new countries where they have made contributions to science, medicine, and business.

3) *Sephardic Disunity:* Political inhibition was a Sephardic characteristic, and most of the Sephardic professionals and intellectuals submitted almost without opposition to the new Israeli environment that did not encourage them to take a more active part in the political process. In this regard, the Sephardic community must itself be blamed for its ineptitude and inability to organize politically. The Sephardic community continues to cling to its own social and cultural habits. Deeply involved with day-to-day problems, it leaves the country in the hands of the politically sophisticated parties controlled predominantly by Ashkenazi Jews.

What has further contributed to the Sephardic lack of participation in the political life of the country, for which they must assume full responsibility, may be summarized as follows:

a) Disunity among the various Sephardic communities who came to Israel from more than twenty-five different countries with different cultural backgrounds and social habits. For example, the difference in cultural background between a Jew from Iraq and his counterpart from Yemen is far greater than the difference between a Jew from Iraq and a Jew from Britain or France.

b) The Sephardic community has been unable to produce leaders who could (1) represent the whole mix of the Sephardic community; and (2) remain independent and not allow themselves to be coopted into existing parties that were seeking the so-called Sephardic leaders in order to change their own image.

c) Lack of political maturity forced many emerging Sephardic leaders into serious infighting among themselves as well as with their constituents. Distrust and at times animosity between two contending leaders were fairly common phenomena.

d) Most of the Sephardic leaders have spread themselves too thin instead of forming one political movement or even joining, in a bloc, an existing party that could lead to positions of authority. They elected to join various political parties, carrying very little weight in their respective capacities, if they carried any weight at all.

Finally, many of these leaders grew weary of the political and social squabbling and reluctantly gave up their hopes for effective political participation. Some left the country altogether; the majority, however, remains in Israel biding time.

4) *Shortsightedness:* There are several spheres in which the Labor government could have taken a more active, ameliorative role but elected instead to ignore the "race problem" by denying its existence. It is the policy of not acknowledging the severe Sephardic-Ashkenazi schism that has been the main factor in perpetuating and even enlarging that schism.

The Israeli army, for example, which is supposed to be recruited on the basis of social equality, has not become a melting pot. Ironically, it maintains the same ratio of Sephardic to Ashkenazi Jews as that in the political sphere. There has not been a single officer of Sephardic origin who reached the top two ranks of general. This lack of opportunity has been especially disheartening to so many young and vigorous Sephardic Jews not because many of them aspire to be generals but because their achievement of very high rank is most unlikely. Another source of disheartenment is the knowledge that even those few Sephardic Jews who reached high political positions were not necessarily chosen because of their personal capabilities; rather, they were coopted into office by an establishment anxious to alter its image of Eastern European ethnocentricity without really changing the makeup of the establishment itself.

5) *Political and Social Expediency:* One other development that has further aggravated the prospects for an integrated Israeli society is the way in which Israel's social and economic institutions have evolved. With the expansion of the economy in the late 1940s and early 1950s, a great demand arose for skilled workers. There were two options open to the authorities at the time—either to initiate a massive program to educate the incoming Sephardic Jews in technical and professional fields, or to attempt to import skilled Jews from the diaspora in order to meet emerging needs. The decision to adopt the second option was made and rationalized on two different but interrelated grounds:

First, the concept of *Avoda Ivrit* (Jewish labor) was one of the main principles of the Zionist movement. The retention of labor in the hands of Jews was, and still is to a great extent, considered a fundamental manifestation of Zionist ideology. After all, it was justifiably maintained, the state was created for the Jews who had been persecuted for centuries and it is they who should receive first priority. Therefore, if the Israeli authorities were to recruit thousands of unskilled workers from the Sephardic community and train them for skilled jobs, they would create a vacuum in the unskilled sector of the economy and would have to turn to Arab laborers who could eventually dominate the Israeli working class. Although the Israeli government and private sector opened their doors to Arabs with Israeli citizenship, the problem of absorbing thousands of Arab laborers from the occupied territories became rather acute. The government was compelled to provide jobs for the new labor forces without being able to improve the qualifications of the unskilled Sephardic laborers to any appreciable degree. And at the same time the concept of Jewish labor yielded to the new conditions.

Second, importing skilled Ashkenazi labor from North America and Europe, it was thought, had many advantages. It would bring more Jews to the state of Israel—another nationalist fulfillment—and it would be economically beneficial, for the cost of bringing skilled workers motivated by ideological fervor would be far less than that of educating unskilled and unmotivated laborers. The high expectation of massive Jewish emigration from North America and Western Europe has not as yet been fulfilled, but the efforts to keep Israel Westernized continue.

And, finally, it was considered politically and socially farsighted to seek skilled men and women from abroad in order to maintain a kind of social and numerical equilibrium between the Ashkenazi and Sephardic communities, especially when the latter was clearly moving toward a majority. Western Jewry, and particularly the Jewish community in the United States, further encouraged Israel's efforts to remain predominantly Western not only in political and technological fields but in social and cultural development as well. Therefore, in considering the future makeup of the Israeli society, one must consider the important role played by the diaspora Jewry that is, of course, predominantly Western. According to Philip Hochstein, the editor of *The Jewish Week* in New York, "Israel is enormously dependent upon and influenced by Western and especially American opinion. We in America are not prepared emotionally, even if intellectually, for an Israel that would be a merging of the Western and Oriental. American Jews are well disposed toward supporting the rights of American minorities to an equal share of American society. That is because we are predisposed both to social justice and to a Western culture. We naturally would give lip service to the ideal of social justice in Israel for Moroccans and other Orientals, but our dream of Israel is of a rescued European Jewry. American Jewry will be a drawback, not a spur, to the realization of a cultural integration in Israel that appreciatively embraces Oriental culture. We will, of course, favor legislation to ensure equality for the Orientals, but we are not at all prepared or even willing to feel that Israel should be substantially Orientalized."

6) *Protectzia* (*Favoritism*): Favoritism by the government of one ethnic group over the other is not an unusual phenomenon in Israel. In mid-June 1976, for example, Havir Shimoni, a long-time champion of the rights of the Sephardic community, charged the Israeli government with intentional acts of inequality. In discussing a bill that would have allowed underqualified Jewish dental practitioners from the U.S.S.R. to practice dentistry in Israel, Shimoni maintained that it smelled of "racism."

He further explained that licensing immigrant dentists by administrative means rather than by requiring them to complete a professional course of study could lead to the "Levantinization of the dental profession in Israel." For years we have been told how important it was to maintain the country's high academic standards, a campaign that actually prevented the successful absorption of Asian and African immigrants into society. Now, he concluded, "When the interests of Russian immigrants are at stake, everybody is ready to look aside and forget."

In government occupations there is a similar inequality. With the shift of power from the legislative to the administrative branch of government, caused by the bureaucratization of society as a whole, Sephardim in Israel have been channeled into the former branch. In the late 1960s the index of Sephardic representation in the Knesset was 18 percent, compared with only 4 percent in top state administration, 13 percent in other key state posts (such as appointed supreme court justices), and 0 percent for major-generals. Administrative posts in Zionist organizations also appear to be closed to Sephardim: In 1969–70 none of the directors and only 4 of the 53 members of the legislative body of the Jewish Agency were Sephardim. In comparing these figures with those of the fifties, we find only a relative and not an absolute improvement in the late sixties. In Histadrut headquarters Sephardic representation among top-ranking officials is only 19 percent, and among top managers of the Histadrut industrial complex it is a mere 4 percent. Yet Sephardic representation is 26 percent among members of the legislative body. (Smooha and Peres, cited above)

As we have already indicated, despite the existing

schism between the two communities, only occasional waves of bitterness have swept the Oriental community. The first incident was a protest in Haifa that took place immediately before the 1956 war. No governmental policy changes resulted from that outbreak. In 1967 a movement for unified action started to mobilize in one Sephardic sector. It abated for a while and was then revived in 1971 with the creation of the Israeli "black panthers" group. The name was derived from the American group that advocated violence to overcome racial discrimination. This group has remained active in Israel, although it is less belligerent than it was previously. In the Histadrut election of 1973, the black panthers were able to marshal 4 percent of the vote. But despite this marginal success the Sephardic community has by and large remained dormant, although it contains a steadily growing momentum for action.

By 1970 the Israeli class struggle had become the number one social dilemma, often seeming to threaten the nation's unity. What stopped the situation from developing into an open clash undoubtedly was the continual external tension applied by the Arab states. Arab hostility has been a unifying factor in Israel. Without it social disintegration might have occurred long ago. Social and political differences have been set aside in the wake of a common danger; the eventual removal of the threat from the borders might stir and release the centrifugal forces that have so far remained dormant for the sake of national security. A dangerous situation of political and social confrontation could result.

A warning is evident in the following conclusion by Smooha and Peres: ". . . By the early seventies a new,

Israeli-born generation of Orientals had come of age. This generation widely resembles and interacts intensively with its Ashkenazi counterpart, and is thus becoming more and more impatient with its comparatively inferior socio-economic and power achievements." ("The Dynamics of Ethnic Inequalities," *Social Dynamics* 1 (1), 1975)

The stability of any peace agreement with the Arab states will depend on the degree to which Israel becomes a Middle Eastern country rather than a European one. Israel will not be able to reach a peace of reconciliation with the Arab states as long as more than 50 percent of its population is a "neglected minority." Any Israeli government that does not recognize the necessity of involving the Sephardic Jews fully in the higher echelons of government, the military, and business will only bring Israel closer to social and economic disruption. Furthermore, Israel's claim of being the haven of the oppressed Jews would be put to the test if the disenchantment of the Sephardic Jews persists. The Arab states could, and undoubtedly would, capitalize on this disenchantment by simply opening up their borders and countries to Sephardic Jews desirous of returning to their countries of origin or of immigrating to another Arab state. Although the response might not be in the thousands, the hundreds who might heed such an invitation would inflict a severe blow to Israel's position and prestige in the eyes of the world community.

The increase in emigration from Israel during the past few years is indicative of the general disenchantment of many Israelis with existing conditions. Although the vast majority of yordim are *not* of Sephardic ethnicity, the situation will continue to be serious unless it is effectively tackled by the government.

Prospects: In recent years the Israeli government seems to have taken more notice of the growing and alarming situation caused by the Sephardic-Ashkenazi schism. An attempt has been made by public and private Israeli agencies to reduce educational, social, and economic gaps between Ashkenazi and Sephardic Jews. The Labor government also adopted a progressive tax system that gave more tax relief to large families with smaller incomes. And in the educational field, many scholarships were granted to students of Sephardic ethnicity.

Yet despite these programs, the general condition of the Sephardic community has not improved much. There are still misconceptions on the part of officials in government as well as in the private sector who continue to view Israel's class struggle as a natural phenomenon, citing other countries that may have encountered the same experience. It must be noted that Israel's dilemmas are its own—the danger that may result from the perpetuation of social inequality cannot be taken lightly because other countries have not done better. There is one Israel and one Jewish people both jointly and independently facing increasing danger from within and without. The state of Israel cannot afford the "luxury" of intensive class struggle regardless of how many countries may have suffered or continue to suffer the same ills.

To understand official Israeli thinking, the old cliché used by Aharon Yedlin, Israel's former education and culture minister, during his visit to the United States in March 1976, is quite revealing. In his statement to the press at the office of the National Council of Jewish

Women, Yedlin rejected the concept of the "melting pot" as an appropriate goal for the integration of Jews coming from more than one hundred countries to settle in Israel. "Israel does not have a racial problem," Yedlin asserted. "Israel's problem is fundamentally one of bringing up to modern standards of knowledge and competence the children from the Oriental countries, whose families are far behind those from Western countries."

What is absurd in the Yedlin attitude is that most, if not all, of the culturally deprived children have been born in Israel to Sephardic parents and that these children have inherited the very same deprivation as that of their parents, namely, the lack of educational opportunity. After all, there has been no mass Sephardic immigration to Israel during the last twenty years or so. What has happened to all the Sephardic children that were born after 1955? Have they been able to advance within the new Israeli society without being subjected to unfavorable social and economic conditions that create a *de facto* situation of racial and ethnic inequality?

Whether there has been a deliberate policy of ethnic inequality in Israel is hardly relevant; that which helps to create and perpetuate a social schism does not necessarily require an overt or covert policy by either the government or any particular influential faction. Social cleavages based on ethnic affiliation may gain in intensity and momentum by any one or a combination of the following: 1) if there is a refusal to acknowledge the existence of the crisis in the first place; 2) if there exists an attitude of complacency, a lack of a strong desire to effect a positive change on the part of Israeli officials as well as diaspora Jewry; 3) if the authorities use the pretext of limited financial resources in order not to improve the situation; and 4) if no action or very little action is taken to bridge the gap.

Thus one might state that while the Labor government has not adopted a policy of *deliberate* segregation of the Sephardic and Ashkenazi Jews, it has either ignored the problem for many years or has refused to acknowledge its serious and alarming existence. Western Jewry maintains its silence, for it is consistent with its social and cultural beliefs that Israel should remain Westernized because the nation was created for European Jewry in the first place.

How does any Israeli government hope to integrate its people—by hope alone? For how long can Israel's national security vis-à-vis the Arabs be used as a pretext for inaction toward the economically and culturally deprived children of the community? If Jewish children, who are supposedly one of the most fundamental components on which Israel's future security depends, are not given top or at least equal priority for access to the military defense structure, who will stand fast in defending Israel in ten, fifteen, or twenty years? How can any government hope to instill feelings of nationalism, love, and affection for the country itself, when these children—70 percent of all children in Israel—feel deprived at an early age? Are they deprived because of circumstances or only by virtue of being who they are?

The importance of dealing with this unfortunate situation is reiterated by Smooha and Peres: "Ethnic gaps between Orientals and Ashkenazim are appreciably discrepant and persistent; therefore, should external tensions recede, serious ethnic conflicts are expected to erupt. . . . The expansion of social services or opportunities has not sufficiently levelled off the socioeconomic differences and power disparities. At the same time, the absolute improvement in living conditions tends to revolutionize expectations, and the growing absolute inequality becomes more and more salient. Consequently, the sense of relative deprivation is heightened and unrest is stirred among subordinate groups." They conclude that, "more radical means beyond the existing institutional arrangements and policies of the Western welfare societies appear necessary if elimination of ethnic or racial inequalities at a rapid pace is desired. It does not suffice to 'raise the floor' by subsidizing the underprivileged while the ceiling is determined by free competition. Ethnic equality can be approached only if the deprived progress *faster* and *at the expense of* the privileged."

This writer is well aware that many Israelis and diaspora Jews may vehemently disagree with some of the statements made above. However, despite the sensitivity of the subject and regardless of taste and feeling, regardless of pain and agony, it is worthy of Israel, the only haven for the oppressed and persecuted Jews, and it is worthy of the Jewish people, both Sephardic and Ashkenazi, who have paid a dear price for making Israel a reality, to state the case without frills, without ambiguity, and without compromise. *Israel's ultimate survival depends largely on its ability to create an integrated and harmonious society*—a society of Israelis, not of Ashkenazi and Sephardic Jews; a Middle Eastern society that thinks and conceives and behaves in Middle Eastern terms; a society that has all the benefits and the advantages of the Western world but with Eastern application, conduct, and flavor; a society that rejects the misconceptions and misperceptions of Eastern Jewish and Arab inferiority; a society that is dedicated to sharing power equally with all segments of the population regardless of their ethnic affiliations.

In this respect the American Jewish community *must* support Israel. In fact, it must pioneer programs geared toward such an end, for Israel's ultimate social and ethnic harmony or disruption will have serious repercussions not only on Israel's social structure but on the entire diaspora Jewry, particularly that of the United States who helped Israel become what it is today. Furthermore, the Sephardic Jewish community in Israel and throughout the diaspora must consolidate its forces, use its resources, and struggle for changes—*now*, not for some future day. Only by being united in their dreams and aspirations for the good of the country and only through hard work and perseverance can Jews of the Sephardic community make Israel a home not only for themselves but for all Jews regardless of ethnic background.

This cannot come about easily; few remedial recommendations, vital as they may be, can be carried out by a single decision made by individuals or the government. It is a hard and a long process—a process that may take many years; a process that will require great financial and human resources; a process that demands sacrifices in many other fields that are equally important. And, finally, it is a process that requires ingenuity, patience, and perseverance. Above all, it requires *good will* and a *beginning* to be made by all who have a stake in Israel's well-being and future. We now turn to Israel's demographic challenge for the next decade.

III

DEMOGRAPHIC
CONDITIONS
IN ISRAEL:
A DANGEROUS
PROSPECT

M ANY observers of the political and social scene in
Israel agree that demographic conditions have an
immediate and direct bearing on its future. Israel's population growth affects not only the prospects for peace
with the Arab states but also the very existence of Israel
as a sovereign Jewish state. In fact, these observers, including this writer, believe that if the prospects for peace
between the Arab states and Israel have improved, it is
partly because of the fact that the Israeli Jewish population
has more than tripled since the creation of Israel in 1948.

However, demographers have also observed that Israel's
sovereignty as a Jewish state might very well be threatened if certain present population trends continue, namely:
unchecked Israeli emigration; limited immigration to Is-

rael; a reduced birth rate among Jews in general; greater intermarriage and conversion; and, finally, misconceived governmental policies toward the occupied territories. Several Jewish leaders have expressed alarm at the prospect of the continuation of these demographic developments in Israel. What further aggravates the situation is that many Israeli officials seem to adopt an attitude of complacency toward the deterioration of Israel's demographic position.

From the psychological, military, and sociopolitical points of view, a solid and sustainable Jewish majority in Israel, say, 75 percent of the total population, will in itself be a considerable deterrent to any Arab extremist states or groups who plan to bring about the elimination of Israel or its absorption by force or subversion. Based on the pre-1967 borders, the Jewish/Arab population ratio in Israel stood at 87 percent/13 percent. In order to maintain more or less the same proportion, it would seem imperative for Israel to aim at doubling its Jewish population from roughly three million now to six million by the year 2000.

There are political, territorial, economic, and demographic measures that must be adopted by the Israeli authorities if a Jewish majority is to be maintained. Although some of these measures have already been undertaken, other policies should be enacted by the government if only to improve coordination among the various governmental departments and agencies that are directly and indirectly involved with questions of population growth, planning, and absorption.

1) *Territorial Measures: Annexation:* One factor that will contribute to the retention of a solid Jewish majority

through the next three decades is the size and the demographic makeup of the territory that Israel might annex. It seems clear that if Israel were to annex any part of the occupied territories, which would result in the absorption of more than three hundred thousand Arabs, the Jewish-Arab ration of 87/13 percent would shift drastically in favor of the Arabs. If, for example, Israel retains all of the occupied territories, the Jewish population in Israel would move toward a clear minority by the year 2000 if Jewish immigration continues to decline. On the other hand, the return of all the occupied territories, with the exception of the Golan Heights and East Jerusalem (with a total Arab population of approximately 75,000), would enable the Jewish population to retain its clear majority through the year 2000.

There are several political factions and parties in Israel, such as the Likud, the National Religious party, and some leaders of the Labor Alignment, who believe that Israel should not return either the Gaza Strip or the West Bank to the Arab states or to any new Arab entity formed in these regions. However, the acceptance of the Arab Palestinians presently residing in the West Bank and the Gaza Strip as Israeli citizens with equal rights would most likely create a social crisis leading to the disintegration of Israel's identity as a Jewish state.

Even Arab spokesmen recognize that Israeli assimilation of the refugees would dilute the Jewish identity of the state. For example, Cecil Hourani, speaking of the Arab Palestinians, observed, "If Israel accepts the Arabs within the territories she controls as full Israeli citizens with equal civil and political rights, the concept of Israel as a Jewish state will have to be changed. Israel will no

longer be a Jewish state; it will become a Jewish-Arab
state, in other words, a secular state in which nationality
will be a function of residence or citizenship." More
subtly, in March 1976 the PLO declared that "the
liquidation of Israel by force might not be necessary;
Israel will disappear through a demographic change that
the Arabs can and should bring about."

Many Israelis are also alarmed about the future social
makeup of the country. Yehoshua Arieli, an Israeli writer,
questions seriously the wisdom of those who advocate
annexation of the territories without serious consideration
of the likely repercussions that such an act may produce.
"The state of Israel's uniqueness," Arieli contends, "lies
first and foremost in the simple fact that it was formed
and exists in order to solve the problem of the Jewish
people as a whole." Arieli further observes, "In practice,
we can assume that the Arab Palestinians would never
be ready to accept citizenship, and if they accept it, with
their 40 percent minority, it would undoubtedly form an
irredentist movement destroying the democratic structure
of the country and compelling us, against our will, to move
from a situation of equality to increasing repression."

To be sure, any contemplated mass absorption of Palestinian Arabs into the Israeli social structure through an
act of annexation or otherwise will be potentially dangerous. The emergence of a new social and racial balance
could easily threaten the very existence of the state. For
these compelling reasons, the Israeli government must
act with extreme caution, especially in the densely populated West Bank and the Gaza Strip (estimated at over
one million persons).

2) *Jewish Birth Rate:* There has been a dramatic drop

in the Jewish birth rate worldwide over the last five decades. Many Jewish demographic experts and leaders in and outside the state of Israel view this decrease with much alarm. The birth rate is one aspect of the Jewish population dilemma that must be examined rather thoroughly.

The world Jewish population is estimated at about 14,145,000, according to the *American Jewish Year Book* whose 1977 edition has recently been published. This figure represents a drop of 86,000 from the population cited in last year's issue. Although not all of this drop was related to the decrease in birth rate, there is sufficient evidence to indicate that the world Jewish community is reaching zero population growth.

The impact of this decreasing birth rate on the Jewish family, on Jewish education, and on the synagogue is discussed in *Analysis*, the scholarly publication of the Institute for Jewish Policy Planning and Research of the Synagogue Council of America by its acting director, George E. Johnson (*The Impact of Family Formation Patterns on Jewish Communal Involvement*), Dr. Harold S. Himmelfarb, assistant professor of sociology at Ohio State University (*Fertility Trends and Their Effects on Jewish Education*), and Rabbi Mordecai Waxman, former president of the Rabbinical Assembly and the International Association of Conservative Rabbis and rabbi of Temple Israel in Great Neck (*Surviving the Infertility Years: The Synagogue and the Community*).

A study has shown that if current patterns of Jewish fertility persist, the average Jewish family within a few years will have between 1.7 and 1.9 children—well below the 2.1 level necessary for replacement. The great growth of the American Jewish community between the 1880s and the 1920s resulted not from reproduction but from immigration, and this growth subsided as restrictive immigration laws went into effect.

The current population profile reveals that a wide gap has already opened at the lower ages. The children of the "baby boom," between 1946 and 1960, the period following the end of the war, who are now between 17 and 29, constitute 28 percent of the population, whereas the children born since 1960 make up not much more than 17 percent of the total. (*The Jewish Week-Examiner*, February 27, 1977)

Because of their increased concentration in urban areas, historically, by and large, Jews have been ahead of even the Christian community in reducing their birth rate. Their death rate, which had long declined, began to level off because of the relatively larger number of old people in the Jewish population, itself the result of the previous decline in Jewish mortality. In Lodz, Poland, for example, in the period 1919–29, when Jewish infant mortality of 134–154 per 1,000 contrasted favorably with the corresponding non-Jewish mortality of 171–203 per 1,000, *the ratios were reversed* in the case of persons over 70. At the beginning of the twentieth century, this trend was so clear that, in 1908, Felix A. Theilhaber (in *Der Untergang der Deutschen Juden*) warned his German coreligionists that if these demographic weaknesses were to continue unabated, German Jewry without the aid of immigration from the outside would decline rapidly and ultimately die out. (*Encyclopaedia Judaica*, Book 13, p. 888)

These tendencies became more pronounced during and

after World War I. In the years 1911–26 the Prussian population registered an excess of births over deaths of 3,019,100. But the Jewish population, conversely, showed the reverse: an "excess mortality" of 18,252. In 1925–28 the Prussian general population gained 1,182,056 persons, while the Prussian Jews lost 5,090 through natural causes. (H. Silbergleit, *Bevoelkerungs* . . . p. 39) Furthermore, a Jewish census taken in Buffalo, New York in 1938 testified to a marked decline in the Jewish birth rate.

In 1926 Soviet Jews had a birth rate of only 24.6 per 1,000 (as against 35.9 per 1,000 thirty years before and 43.3 per 1,000 for the Soviet population as a whole), the lowest of all major nationalities in the Soviet Union. Such large cities as Vienna and Budapest actually had an excess of Jewish mortality over natality (2,709 deaths versus 1,343 births in Vienna, and a still larger excess of 1,588 deaths over births in Budapest in 1932). Even in Warsaw in 1925–29 the Jewish ratio of 15.5 births versus 11.1 deaths per 1,000 contrasted with that of 22.4 versus 15.4 among the city's Christians. On a world scale, these decreases in the births of European and Soviet Jews were partially compensated for by an increase in North America and in Asia and North Africa.

Although the downturn in the Jewish birth rate is not exclusive to Israel, its effect on Israel is serious. Apart from the immediate loss of a certain number of Jews that could have been born and were not, Israel is also losing potential Jewish immigrants because of the general global decline in the Jewish birth rate, especially in the United States and Russia.

There are many factors that have a direct bearing on the Jewish birth rate in general. The differences between the Jewish birth rate in Israel and that in the United States (with the largest Jewish concentration) or Russia (third largest concentration—Israel is second) are directly related to the social, educational, and economic conditions of these communities.

1) *Social Factors:* The integration of Jews into modern societies has been characterized by the mass movement to cities or suburbs, the obtaining of higher education, and an ascent in social status. Although these developments contributed to a lower fertility rate in both Jewish and non-Jewish communities, they had far more effect on the Jewish fertility rate. Urbanized and educated Jews were faced with a personal conflict: whether to pursue individual goals and hopes or community goals. The choice was between the desire to lead the "good life" in a materialistic way and the desire to aid the larger Jewish "nation."

a) Conversion: The social pressures that were often imposed on Jewish communities, such as in Russia, coupled with a forcible draft for long-term military service, substantially increased the number of Jews who converted to Christianity, especially in the nineteenth century. Although there are not enough accurate data to verify the number of Jews who left their community and converted, the cumulative information available indicates that these numbers have increased alarmingly.

b) Intermarriage: Intermarriage interferes with the growth of the Jewish population in two ways. 1) Religiously divided couples, as a rule, raise their children as Christians rather than as Jews, and 2) in many cases, in order to avoid further complications, they refrain from having children altogether or have one child only.

At a symposium sponsored by the University of Haifa during the first week of July 1976, a group of Jewish scholars and leaders from Israel and other countries voiced concern about the problem of Jewish assimilation and its most serious consequence, intermarriage. In the view of this distinguished group, intermarriage poses a far greater threat to the Jewish people—particularly to the state of Israel. This major problem was cited throughout the symposium as one for which no easy cure is available. The ramifications of assimilation are complex, and the progress being made to rectify the situation is extremely slow. Furthermore, the causes of assimilation are numerous and not subject to one decisive remedial action.

According to Professor Joseph Nedava of Haifa University, the Jewish population today could have reached 200 million worldwide if it were not for assimilation. Professor Shmuel Ettinger from the Hebrew University in Jerusalem spoke of the contemporary paradox of a renewed feeling of solidarity accompanying increasing cultural, social, and political assimilation, and here even Israel is affected. In Great Britain the assimilation of Jews is not so severe as in the case of American Jewry. Still, according to Professor S. A. McCartney of Oxford University, the anticolored feeling that is spreading in Britain may also have an anti-Semetic content that encourages assimilation. Otherwise British Jewry has felt no need for assimilation.

In the Soviet Union, which has the third largest Jewish concentration, recent studies show, according to Dr. A. Altschulter of Hebrew University, that intermarriage has reached 50 percent. Conversely, Professor Yaacob Poyi of Tel Aviv University maintains that because the Soviet Union does not recognize the Jews in Russia as a minority, a Jew cannot easily assimilate. His card is stamped "Jew," and he is not accepted by the surrounding population. This factor causes many of them to consider emigration. Unfortunately, however, the vast majority is not allowed to emigrate.

According to a World Zionist report published recently, the intermarriage rate is soaring in Latin America, reaching 60 percent in some places. Haim Finkelstein, head of W.Z.O.'s education department, after returning from a visit to Latin America (June 1976), said, "There is a great deal of apathy among many local Jews to this situation of intermarriage." It would seem, he continued, that "the situation will not improve unless greater efforts are being undertaken in the field of education." He cited a variety of educational projects, including Jewish teacher training colleges, to help alleviate the situation.

c) The Holocaust: One other important factor within the framework of social causes affecting the Jewish birth rate was the holocaust. It has been estimated that on the eve of World War II Jews numbered close to 17 million. By 1945 this number was reduced to 11 million. Not all of the 6 million Jews were killed by the Nazi extermination squads; considerable losses were sustained among Jewish soldiers in the Russian army, the American army, and others.

Demographers believe that the Jewish losses should have been easily made up by the natural growth of the Jewish population during the six years of war. Other nations, such as Germany, Italy, Japan, and Russia, recovered their biological strength, and in two decades

(1940–60) increased their population by 25–33 percent. The Jewish people, if allowed to continue their natural population growth, would have reached 19–20 million by 1960. But when a census was taken in 1960, the count showed only 12,800,000. Thus, these experts concluded, a serious imbalance in the progress of natural increase had occurred as a result of the holocaust. An onslaught of postwar anti-Semetic feeling with its inhibitive repercussions further aggravated this imbalance.

Although an intensified religious education may help alleviate the deteriorating situation, a substantial increase in Jewish fertility faces serious obstacles. One obstacle that must be underlined is an ideological one of which Jews have been the main advocates. The population explosion and the international cry for imposing some limitations on population growth (in one state in India it is already mandatory) make the Jewish case self-defeating. Many young Jews (especially in the diaspora) find it extremely difficult to justify their advocacy of birth control, knowing that what they are advocating may be detrimental to the Jewish people.

Forecasts of an increased fertility rate among the Jews in the diaspora seem very discouraging. Concerted efforts will have to be directed toward the Jewish population in Israel that seems to hold the real key to Israel's future demographic stability. (See Appendix 4)

2) *Educational and Religious Factors:* One other environmental element affecting the Jewish birth rate, especially in the diaspora, is religious practice. Such scholars as Steven M. Cohen of Owens College and Paul Ritterband of City College of New York have observed that religious education in general and religious involvement appear

to have a positive effect on the birth rate. Because, by and large, fewer young Jewish couples these days are getting involved in religious practice, their concern with large families and self-perpetuation is lessening. The population deficit now being experienced by diaspora Jewry might be partially relieved by a greater focus on religious values and a deeper personal involvement in religion as a stimulant to higher fertility.

Dr. Harold S. Himmelfarb, in his study *Fertility Trends and Their Effect on Jewish Education,* pointed out that in 1961–62 total Jewish school enrollment was estimated at 588,995 students. He stated that there were approximately 1.370,000 Jewish youngsters between the ages of 3 and 17 in 1961–62, an enrollment of 43 percent of all youngsters in a Jewish school. For the 1974–75 year, it was fewer than 400,000, a decline of one-third in fourteen years. "Was this due to a decline of children or lack of interest?" he asked. (*The Jewish Week-Examiner,* February 27, 1977)

The declining enrollment in Sunday Hebrew schools and Hebrew day schools, where Jewish education is emphasized indirectly, affects Jewish fertility, particularly in the diaspora. Lack of funds for the support of these schools to further Jewish education, on the one hand, and lack of ideological motivation among younger adults, on the other, have reduced the involvement of increased numbers of Jews in Jewish community life. Rabbi Bertram W. Korn observed at the National Jewish Welfare Board in New Orleans in March 1976 that "We are the best educated Jewry that has ever lived. We read more than any Jews who have ever lived. We are more sophisticated in music, art, literature, political science, social work, science, law, and medicine than any Jews who have ever lived. We are aware of the depth of everything *but* Judaism. We know less about our heritage and tradition than the average eight year old Jewish child 150 years ago. *Our Judaism is catastrophically superficial, irrelevant, peripheral, and remote.*"

In a similar vein, Rabbi Arthur Hertzberg, president of the American Jewish Congress, stated in April 1976 that the American Jewish community had stopped regarding anti-Semitism as a problem because it was "no longer forced into a physical or psychological ghetto." He continued, "Young American Jews have a weakening sense of Jewish identity and see their task as fighting for the rights of others—the disadvantaged at home and the beleaguered Jewish communities abroad." Religious education is considered by many scholars to be one of the most important factors having a direct relation to fertility rates. As such, it can be argued that the general tendency toward Reformed Judaism and away from religious orthodoxy has probably contributed to the general decline in Jewish fertility. On the east coast of the United States, for example, there is a definite swing toward orthodoxy, especially Chassidic groups that seems to have affected the birth rate in these areas by an increase of at least 8 per 1,000.

3) *Economic Factors:* Curiously, economic factors seem to work both ways. Young Jewish couples in the United States, for example, who are in the higher income brackets seem to favor a lower birth rate. Jews of the same age in Israel favor a lower fertility rate although their economic status is far lower proportionately. By the same token, young couples with higher incomes in Israel tend to have 3–4 children versus 2–3 children among lower

income parents. Although generally poor families in Asia and Africa tend to have a greater number of children, Jews worldwide tend to be more influenced by their general social status and level of education than by their economic position. Although some of the social and economic conditions that lead to an increase or decrease in the Jewish fertility rate in Israel and the diaspora may be similar, the methods prescribed for increasing the fertility rates in the two spheres are different.

In the diaspora, according to Rabbi Irving Greenberg, chairman of the Institute for the Study of Modern Jewish Life at City College in New York, the emphasis should be on living a rich Jewish life style, for the more a Jew is imbued with Jewish culture and religious experience, the greater are his desire and awareness in preserving Judaism, of which fertility is an integral part. These will be the decisive elements in the Jewish continuity from which Israel can draw. As suggested by George Johnson of the Institute of Jewish Policy Planning and Research in Washington, D.C., synagogues will have to shift their focus more toward meeting adult needs and interests. In addition, Johnson recognizes a need for upgrading the quality and content of Jewish home life.

In Israel, although the government encourages large families, most newly-wed Israelis find themselves in a predicament when the size of their families is being planned. Eva Etzioni-Halevy, in her "Protest Politics in the Israeli Democracy," dwells on the difficulties young couples face in their attempts to acquire even modest apartments. Most of these young people have just been released from the army and find the financial problems of housekeeping simply insurmountable. To gather the initial sum required for a down payment would necessitate years of strenuous savings, while prices, in all probability, would continue to soar, in the end making the accumulated savings inadequate. Even if successful in gathering such a sum, the couple would then have to repay various loans and mortgages that would weigh heavily on their budget precisely when they were starting a family.

By 1970 there were 70,000 Jewish couples in Israel who had been married within the previous three years. Of these, 10 percent were found to be still living with their parents, and 48 percent were dissatisfied with their housing conditions. By and large, the financial condition of young people is not conducive to raising large families. Government austerity programs announced in July 1975 included a levy on imports and higher taxes on property, travel, capital gains, and luxuries. Combined with the recent rise in the cost of arms and fuel imports (from $700 million in 1972 to $2,350 million in 1974 and double this amount by 1977), the effect has been to reduce further the desirability of having large families. The public's~ general lack of confidence in better prospects for the immediate future also contributes to the slow-down in the birth rate.

The Israeli government will have to provide new and far-reaching economic and social incentives to young couples in order to encourage them to have larger families. To reach the six million target by the year 2000 would require a minimum of three to four children per family. The government may also be able to modify the newly adopted abortion law to reduce to a minimum the number of abortions (estimated at one million in the last twenty-five years) and to ensure that abortions will be performed only when the mother's health is in danger or in such cases as rape, incest, or probable birth defects. In fact, abortions in Israel are so widespread as to be a *de facto* birth control method for a relatively large segment of the Israeli population. The section of the abortion law that aroused the ire of its opponents states that a woman may demand an abortion—and get it—if giving birth "is liable to cause her or her children serious harm by virtue of the difficult situation prevailing in the woman's family, social milieu, or surroundings." Opponents branded this section legal recognition of abortion as an instrument of family planning and thus abhorrent. (*Jerusalem Post*, February 8, 1977)

Although the pros and cons on abortion may continue for many years to come, it is obvious that both the opponents of the bill and its supporters have erred by taking rather extreme positions. Abortion should and must be legal when it applies to some of the cases mentioned above, but that it should be used as a birth-control method because of social and/or economic difficulties stands in total contradiction to Israel's future welfare.

An increased birth rate as the principal means of population growth in Israel is most crucial, for unless all Israeli social and psychological behavior is geared toward self-multiplication, merely the immigration of Jews to Israel will not be sufficient to sustain a Jewish majority over the Arab Palestinians in the long run (regardless of the Palestinians' eventual place of residence). The present net birth rate of Jews in Israel stands at 21.5 per 1,000 versus 45.6 per 1,000 among Arabs in Israel. If these rates are maintained, absorption of additional hundreds of thousands of Arabs without an equivalent influx of

Jewish immigrants will cause a demographic setback in Israel that might seriously weaken the Jewish identity of the country. The disastrous civil war in Lebanon between Christians and Moslems illustrates the danger of such a demographic imbalance. Therefore, greater emphasis should be put on the expansion of the Jewish fertility rate. Although internal Israeli population growth is bound to be a slow process, it is a process within the reach of the Israelis and not subject to external forces. In contrast, mass Jewish immigration to Israel is often subject to outside social, economic, and political conditions beyond Israeli control.

Although there may be more than one solution to the problem of the decreasing birth rate in Israel, especially in the wake of the newly adopted liberalized abortion law, combined efforts by world Jewry and the Israeli government should produce more positive results. Such efforts should be directed toward improving the conditions under which an increased birth rate can become not only possible but desirable as well. (See the proposal, Appendix 5.)

4) *Discouraging Emigration:* One other significant factor affecting Israeli population growth is the number of Jews who leave Israel after a stay of a few years. There are many circumstances that oblige these Israelis to leave. Among them are: 1) economic difficulties; 2) social or political disenchantment; 3) personal fear or apprehension about Israel's future; 4) a search for better job opportunities and earning power; and 5) lack of compelling ideological motivations. In considering these causes, it becomes obvious that the burden of changing the

situation falls heavily on the Israeli government and the Jewish Agency.

In attempting to understand the causes behind the steady increase, in both absolute and relative figures, in emigration from Israel, one immediately finds himself at odds with anyone in Israel who is connected with the department of absorption. In this office there is a general attitude of superficiality, recrimination, and at times, indifference. Many officials elect to dismiss the whole issue by telling half-truths or by treating it as a fact of life that should be accepted. Instead, I would contend that the crisis of emigration from Israel is a problem of no less importance than are the Arab threats. Why is a crisis such as this, one that will surely affect the future well-being of the state, being neglected? Whatever happened to the ideology of the Zionist movement that has rested primarily on immigration to Israel?

Sufficient data have not been collected regarding the number of Jews who have left Israel permanently and those who have left but intend to go back. But the general limited statistics that were obtained from various sources (the United States Census Bureau, United States Immigration and Nationalization authorities, and the *Statistical Abstract of Israel*) show conclusively that in the United States alone, for example, there are close to 275,000 Israelis and that by all indications these numbers will climb to 300,000 or more before 1980.

Recently a special edition of the armed forces weekly magazine was sent to 11,000 Israeli reservists living in the United States, highlighting the degree to which emigration is causing a manpower crisis in the Israeli army.

According to Richard Mathews, emigration is considered by those who stay almost as treachery. People deciding to leave encounter social isolation from their friends and neighbors. (*The Middle East*, December 1976)

a) *Government Apathy:* In mid-June 1976, the Knesset was asked by the Likud alignment to open an official investigation of emigration from Israel. The proposal was stricken from the agenda by the Labor minister, Moshe Baram, who contended that there was no reason for such an investigation and that the situation did not warrant a parliamentary act. The position of Mr. Baram was only too consistent with that of the former premier Yitzhak Rabin who had chosen to dismiss the whole issue of emigration by labeling those who left Israel as "dregs" and "deserters." The Rabin position illustrates how shortsighted an Israeli official can be. The Jewish Agency, in an effort to combat the emigration phenomenon, established a special department in February 1976 for the prevention of emigration. In spite of this, the wave of emigants from Israel continues to swell. Because the former Israeli government could not be proud of this exodus, it deliberately chose to ignore the problem.

One of the most alarming developments, however, is related to Jews of Sephardic origin. A sensation was caused recently by a report that ten families from Morocco, who had raised a generation of children in Israel, had decided to return to their native country. This was followed by a public call from King Hassan of Morocco, inviting all of his former Jewish citizens to return to their "home." No Israeli official likes to talk about this, but the fact remains that Jews such as those from Morocco were never able to integrate into Israeli society.

b) *Government Measures:* This alarming phenomenon

of Israeli emigration must not be treated with complacency and half-measures. There are specific reasons that compel Jews, young and old, to leave Israel for better havens. Some of these causes may be beyond the authority of Israeli officials, such as business ambitions, personal fear, cases that could be linked to marriage, education, and so forth. But when the causes are purely indigenous, where the government can exercise an indispensable role, and where practical measures ought to yield real results, then it is incumbent upon the Begin government to rethink the policies of absorption and family planning, rearrange some of the priorities, and "wage war" against the trend that has been diluting Israel's human and, consequently, scientific and economic resources. However, no persuasion on the part of any government to encourage permanent residence will suffice unless it is accompanied by specific measures to eliminate the causes that encourage emigration from Israel in the first place. It is undoubtedly a formidable task; yet it is one that is absolutely crucial to Israel's future demographic position.

Far greater resources, human as well as financial, will have to be allocated by the Israeli government to "combat" emigration and to reduce it to the absolute minimum. More opportunities in the scientific and the technological fields, larger government subsidies for education, some tax relief for younger couples, a revitalization of ideological and spiritual motivation, increasing the enrollment capacity of the universities—these and other measures should contribute to the stabilization, if not the reduction, of the exodus. Although it is undoubtedly impossible to eliminate emigration short of imposing a ban on all travel abroad, the rate at which Israelis are leaving must be slowed or the effect on Israel could be critical.

In a recent survey that was presented by the chairman of the Zionist Council, Arye Zimuki, it was shown that the majority of Israel's youth regards emigration from Israel (yerida) as a phenomenon highly damaging to the state. According to the survey, this position is more widely shared by religious youth (85 percent), although 75 percent of secular youth adopted the same position.

The problem of emigration is especially significant not only because of the estimated three hundred and fifty thousand emigrants who have left Israel since the early fifties (over 10 percent of the Israeli population), but also because of the psychological repercussions that such departures have on other Jews, both in Israel and in the diaspora. Thus, it would seem that an appreciable reduction in the number of emigrants would almost certainly result in an increase in the number of new immigrants who would feel more secure in following the footsteps of those who immigrated to Israel and have stayed.

5) *Encouraging Immigration:* The final important aspect of the Israeli demographic condition involves the immigration of Jews to Israel from other parts of the world. Because Jewish birth rates in Israel are now substantially lower than those of the Arabs, Jewish immigration to Israel is considered by the Israelis their most important source of population. It represents an almost "instant" growth. While, of course, massive Jewish immigration to Israel can provide the desired result, it is very unlikely that millions of Jews from North America and Russia would either have the desire to settle in Israel or be allowed to do so. The difficulties imposed on the Soviet

Jews wanting to leave Russia and the lack of a strong ideological motivation on the part of the North American and West European Jews make the prospect of Jewish immigration *en masse* rather doubtful.

According to Richard Mathews, between 1971 and 1975, over 100,000 Soviet Jews were allowed to leave the Soviet Union. Even today they represent about half of Israel's annual rate of immigration, but the economic advantage that they provide is almost outweighed by the political disadvantage of the spectacle of so many disavowing the Jewish state in Vienna.

Even if all those who left Russia this year went on to Israel, the numbers would still show a fall from previous years. In 1973 about 35,000 Soviet Jews arrived (with an 8 percent dropout rate); in 1976 about 12,000 were due (after a dropout averaging about 50 percent).

In his article "Let My People Go—But Where?" Paul Jacobs reiterated more or less the same findings that indicate conclusively that the prospects for massive immigration to Israel do not seem very promising. "In 1973, when the Soviet government first allowed Jews to emigrate in sizable numbers, theoretically to join their families in Israel, 34,741 Russian Jews left the country. Ninety-six percent actually went to Israel—although some emigrated again later on.

"In 1974, 20,634 Jews were allowed out and 81 percent made the journey from Vienna, their first stop, to Tel Aviv. Some of them didn't remain in Israel either.

"By 1975, when 13,229 Jews departed, the percentage of those who opted to settle in Israel dropped again, this time to 63 percent. And again the real percentage was lower because of those who departed from Israel after they arrived there. During 1976, at least 50 percent of the Jewish emigrants had become dropouts." (*Present Tense*, Winter 1977)

These figures were also confirmed by Uzi Narkis, director general of the Jewish Agency immigration department, who noted a continuing rise of dropouts among Soviet Jewish emigrants after they reach Vienna.

In addition, the fact that so many Israelis have left Israel (an estimated 17,500 in 1975 alone) has undoubtedly further discouraged those Russian Jews allowed to leave Russia who desire to immigrate to Israel. It was estimated in mid-1976 that there were at least 2,000 Russian Jews at transit centers in Austria destined to arrive in the United States instead of Israel. The Israeli authorities fear that the estimated 60 percent "dropout" of Russian Jews who leave Russia but choose not to immigrate to Israel may harm Soviet emigration as a whole because it tends to discredit the claim of a Jewish impulse to go to the homeland.

There has been intensive argument in the Jewish press, among Jewish organizations, and within the Labor government concerning whether Israel or the Jewish Agency should help those Russian Jews who exit Russia with an Israeli visa but decide to immigrate elsewhere. In an editorial that appeared in *Ha'aretz*, Israel's most prestigious daily newspaper, on September 22, 1976, the problem was vividly and eloquently stated: "The controversy around the giving of aid to Jews leaving the Soviet Union but dropping out in Vienna arouses a basic question: to what limits is Israel—Nation and People—responsible for each other. . . . It is true that the dropouts are a propaganda asset in the hands of the Soviets. It is also true that they arouse doubts in the world as to the nature of the Jewish national revival, on the basis of which we were able to recruit non-Jewish opinion in favor of eased emigration from the Soviet Union. . . . But it must be remembered that the people of Israel have an ancient tradition of redeeming prisoners. The question of who are to be redeemed and what they will do afterwards has nothing to do with the matter: the redemption itself is the supreme value. For this reason, Israel cannot oppose assistance to the dropouts; she must also continue granting her patronage to any Jew who wants to leave the Soviet Union. Israel is entitled to hope that all will immigrate and to use her influence toward that objective. But she must not cross the border line and deny aid to those who leave, for that would be a denial of one of the fundamental values of the People of Israel."

To be sure, Jews who are allowed to leave Russia should be free to go to the country of their choice. To get out of Russia is an end in itself, and it should remain the prime motivation behind Israel's policy. What Russian Jews decide to do once they have left Russia depends to a great extent on the social and economic quality of life in Israel and the psychological and emotional environment that they encounter once they are there. No amount of pressure will force a Russian emigrant to go to or stay in Israel if he continues to feel deprived either on ideological or professional grounds.

Herbert Bernstein, the former director of the New York Association of New Americans (NYANA) has recently indicated, based on studies conducted by the Jewish Agency and HIAS, the worldwide Jewish migration agency, that "the departure of Russian Jews from Israel is also linked to their places of origin in the U.S.S.R. and consequently their Jewish identification. Jews from central Russian republics where more assimilated, professional Jews reside, have the highest 'dropout' rate (leave Israel after a short stay, or do not immigrate to Israel in the first place) as do newcomers from Odessa. On the other hand, Jews from the Baltic states and Moldavia, especially non-Ashkenazi Jews who tend to have a greater sense of Jewish identification and less opportunity outside Israel, remain there."

According to Richard Mathews, emigration from the West as a whole is characterized by a high dropout rate as well. After the first five years, up to 40 percent of Western emigrants have returned home.

The sharp drop in immigration to Israel from both East and West—notwithstanding the increase in Jewish emigration from France, South Africa, and South America—was in fact the focus of the Jewish Agency, which met in mid-July 1976. According to Moshe Rivlin, the former director general of the Jewish Agency, the drop in immigration to Israel is highly significant. As a result, a reexamination of all the methods and procedures in the area of immigration to and absorption in Israel has become necessary. Two committees were established to examine thoroughly all matters concerning immigration. One is the Horev Committee, appointed jointly by the Rabin government and the Jewish Agency under the chairmanship of Haifa University President Amos Horev. The second was established by the Jewish Agency alone under Harvard University Professor Richard Rosenblum. Regardless of what the ultimate recommendation by these committees may be, the belief is that there will be a call for massive changes in the entire immigration procedure.

Stanley Sloane of New Jersey, one of the U.J.A.'s fifteen national chairmen and a shrewd observer of Jewish life, stated in a recent (July 1976) interview with David Landau, Jewish Telegraphic Association writer, that the time has come when we must stop talking about immigration to Israel and start doing something about it. "Awareness and conviction of the diaspora leadership are prerequisite to increased immigration of American Jews to Israel. We Americans come away with the conclusion that it is up to us to get involved in Aliyah (immigration) . . . to exhort our fellow citizens, and to act in a practical way to turn exhortation into realization. The Zionist proponents of Aliyah, urging others to go but not showing the example themselves, have been positively detrimental to Aliyah."

The aliyah potentials are among the estimated two million urban American Jews, Sloane observed. Approximately half of these are elderly, but the others constitute an obvious reservoir for an initial mass movement of American olim (immigrants) to Israel. These Jews, usually in the middle or the lower-middle income brackets, are struggling continually to make a living and, at the same time, face worsening problems concerning ecology and the quality of life. Eventually, and for most of them within the next decade, the need to relocate will become pressing. Their options, as they see them, are to move to a nearby neighborhood, moving piecemeal away from negative social influences, or to make the more difficult transition to suburbia where life is more expensive. Our task is to convince and persuade these young urban Jewish families, many of them only loosely affiliated with organized Jewry, that they have a third option: Israel. Part of this persuasion must be in the form of material arrangements for their settlement and absorption in Israel. Mr. Sloane would consider it a moderate success if, say, 2 percent finally agree to go to Israel, which would mean 20,000 American Jews immigrating to Israel each year. Finally, Mr. Sloane observed that although throughout history migration movements are begun by the economically weak, the more affluent quickly catch on and follow suit. This was the case when mass Eastern European Jewish immigration hit America. First, it was the poor, but the more affluent quickly followed. In addition, Richard Mathews emphasizes that the volume of emigration of Jews from the United States has a diffierent significance but is also a test of faith of almost crisis proportions. The United States has one of the largest Jewish communities in the world, but they have always seemed more willing to support Israel with their check books and to use the country as a holiday resort than to live there. This is in spite of the fact that Zionist organizations have emissaries in many American cities specifically to encourage immigration to Israel. Ehud Avriel, Israel's former consul general in Chicago, believes that Israel should tell American Jews simply and directly that the Jewish state needs aliyah now more than anything else and that the tasks and challenges facing Israel are too many to be fulfilled by the people of Israel alone.

Avriel contends that any Jew who considers himself a Zionist "must understand that his personal involvement in the building of Israel is a must. The State of Israel is not yet standing on solid ground. The tasks are numerous

and I believe that if we make this clear the response of
the American Jewish community will be one of understanding." Israeli representatives in the United States and
elsewhere, Avriel asserted, must be identified completely
with the "Zionist solution" that, he said, means aliyah
to Israel. According to Avriel, Israel can be a special
answer for American Jewish youth who seek new meaning
and new challenges in their lives. "Israeli society can give
young American Jews the feeling that with their activity
they can shape the society they live in," he stated. "Israeli
society, unlike American society, is in a process of development and formation, and American youngsters can take
part in its molding and future."

The aliyah of, say, half a million from America to
Israel, it is believed, far from weakening United States
Jewry would actually strengthen it.

a) *The Russian Dilemma:* Israel's recent handling of
the whole issue of Jewish emigration from Russia was
not in conformity with either the concept of quiet diplomacy, which is imperative in dealing with Russia, or with
realistic conditions in Israel itself.

The Soviet Union's repudiation of the 1972 trade agreement with the United States is only one example from
which a lesson should be learned. Whether the Soviet
repudiation was truly related to the Jackson Amendment
(tying United States-Soviet trade to the right of Russian
citizens to emigrate) is irrelevant. The Soviets used the
Jackson Amendment as an excuse to disavow the agreement. Since 1975, the number of Jews emigrating from
Russia has been far lower than in previous periods. Thus
it would appear that excessive publicity regarding the
"Russian understanding"—which apparently was never

made clear—as to how many Jews would be allowed to leave Russia once the trade agreement became law did not serve the Jewish cause in Russia.

It is usual to castigate the Russians for this behavior. Yet several considerations remain: 1) The Russians could not submit to public pressure from abroad and thereby admit weakness; 2) Arab pressure on Russia must have had some effect; after all, while Russia was in effect supplying Israel with manpower, the United States was supplying Israel with military hardware. What else would Israel need to maintain its "expansionist" posture, as the Arabs claim? 3) Soviet authorities considered Jewish emigration as a purely Russian internal problem and thus viewed foreign interference in the matter as inadmissible; 4) Knowing the dire need for manpower in Israel, the Russians recognized that Jewish immigration could be used as an effective political tool to extract a variety of concessions from both Israel and its supporters in the United States.

b) *Brussels II* is another case in point. There were two conferences on Soviet Jewry that took place in Brussels during February 1971 and February 1976. Brussels I directly and indirectly helped the Jewish cause in Russia, for some 110,000 Russian Jews left Russia between the two conferences. Brussels II, on the other hand, was ill-conceived from the point of view of timing and reasonable expectations.

If the idea behind Brussels II was to generate further pressure on Russia, then the opportunity was lost because of premature publicity and the impracticality of increased emigration from Russia at that particular time. First, the Jewish press attributed the 110,000 exit visas that were granted by the Russians after Brussels I to the success of the first conference. By then publicizing this inaccurate information, the Jewish press in effect challenged the Russians to bow to new resolutions. Anyone who understood the Russian mind could have no difficulty predicting that Russia's reaction would be exactly the opposite.

The timing and planning of Brussels II for the year 1976 was also unfortunate. The main source of pressure on Russia comes from the United States, but the Russians did not expect any intensified American pressure during an election year. In addition, since mid-1973, Israel has undergone severe economic and political strains as one critical development after another in the Middle East has brought to bear the focus of the United States and the Soviet Union. These conditions undoubtedly rendered a disservice to Brussels II. The honorary chairman of the conference, former Prime Minister Golda Meir, stated in a conciliatory fashion that the conference "is not directed against the Soviet Union or anyone else; it is directed toward and for the benefit of Jews." Still the Russian authorities remain intransigent on the immigration issue.

c)*Internal Conditions in Israel:* Economic, social, and political problems in Israel have further aggravated the demographic situation. For many Russian Jews, the social structure in Israel is a real deterrent to immigration. The Labor government and the officials of the Jewish Agency have not been able to revitalize the ideological motivation that was the major cause of Jewish immigration in earlier years. Many Russian Jews were appalled to find how much apathy and indifference exist in Israel. Moreover, many of these Russian Jews, who are highly educated professionals, do not consider themselves refugees escaping the danger of physical annihilation. To them, ideological motives play an important part, and they are unwilling to change countries for obscure political reasons.

Furthermore, many immigrants find integration difficult. "When it comes to employment, for example, the immigrant sometimes finds his new home is not in a part of the country to his liking—opportunities for jobs may be limited or it may be necessary to travel long distances to work. He may have to be retrained in a new skill, or he may find his professional qualification is not recognized." (Richard Mathews, "Immigration and Emigration: The Crisis Facing Israel," *The Middle East*, December 1976)

For all these reasons, there are certain measures that must be adopted by the Begin government in order to make immigration more of a challenge than an adventure. These measures include:

1) liberalizing Israeli trade and industrial laws in order to encourage greater foreign investments and/or transfers of businesses;

2) aiming for a realistic number of emigrants from North America and Russia corresponding to Israel's absorption ability, without any unnecessary hardship to newcomers that could result in a proportionately higher number of emigrants leaving Israel later on;

3) negotiating with Russia by means of quiet diplomacy to increase Jewish immigration; refraining from making public any information regarding numbers of Russian Jews in order not to subject Russia to pressure from either the Arab states or fanatical groups within Russia who oppose the immigration of Jews to Israel;

4) applying the same treatment to all immigrants ir-

respective of their countries of origin. Not applying the same measures in the past has helped, for example, to create a social schism between the Sephardic and the Ashkenazi communities; and

5) addressing itself to its own inflated bureaucracy and reorganizing the various departments that are directly or indirectly connected with foreign investments, immigration, and absorption, and weeding out all superfluous personnel.

Former Defense Minister Shimon Peres, in his recent bid for the premiership, suggested that every immigrant family should receive a monetary allocation to facilitate its absorption and to relieve it of the need to grapple with red tape involved in the absorption institutions. The allocation should vary according to the family's size and financial needs. Peres told the Labor party's diaspora study circle that he would recommend appointing a minister without portfolio to coordinate the treatment of new immigrants by the different ministries in place of the present ministry of absorption. The minister without portfolio would also bear responsibility for maintaining contact with the Jews in the diaspora, he said.

Peres also proposed that communities abroad should surround Jerusalem with housing projects for members who want to immigrate. (*Jerusalem Post*, February 8, 1977)

Some of Peres's recommendations may indeed improve the situation; yet Israel's demographic position is one that requires intensive study; goals will have to be reexamined and priorities will have to be rearranged. There must be a better correlation between demographic policies and the realities of demographic problems. Questions of absorption, immigration to and emigration from Israel, an increased birth rate, and a cautious policy in the occupied territories (see the chapter on Israel and the Palestinians) are all interrelated and require cohesive planning with one goal in mind: the multiplication of Israel's population by the year 2000. This goal is an attainable one, but one that demands far greater resources and a concentrated effort by Israel and world Jewry.

IV

THE ARAB
PALESTINIANS:
A NEW PROSPECT

FOR an understanding of the complex Palestinian issue it is necessary to distinguish between the Palestinians as a people and the Palestinian Liberation Organization (PLO) as a political organization whose means (including the use of terror) and objectives have not always coincided with the human needs of the Palestinian people. The fact that the Arab states and the international community have sought to bundle both groups together and treat them as one entity has not served the Arab Palestinian cause nor has it brought their problem any closer to solution. Therefore one must not accept the notion that the PLO and the Arab Palestinians are one and the same, only because the U.N. has given the PLO its "seal of approval."

It is the position of this writer that while Israel under the Labor Alignment was consistent in its search for peace it was at the same time misguided in its attempts to bring together the necessary elements in order to reach a reconciliation with the Arab states. Israel's initiation of peaceful contacts has either been directed to the wrong party or offered at the wrong time. Although Israel has considered the four Arab states that surround it—namely Syria, Lebanon, Jordan, and Egypt, as the main antagonists, it has systematically ignored the main party to the crisis—the Arab Palestinians. Israel's lack of a definitive policy toward the Arab Palestinians after 1967 has in effect helped to nourish various Palestinian liberation movements and has given impetus to their reemergence as important elements in the Arab-Israeli crisis. As Dr. Nahum Goldmann, president of the World Jewish Congress, has said, "Let the Israelis for once—and they have not done that as yet—produce a plan of their own for a peace proposal and recognition of the Arabs. Let us see what would be the reaction of the Arabs to the Israeli plan. If they reject it, the whole world would see that the Arabs are bluffing."

For example, after the civil war in Jordan in September of 1970, when the Palestinian Liberation Organization (PLO) ceased to be, by all responsible accounts, a viable element in the anti-Israel struggle, Israel's consistent refusal to consider the Arab Palestinians a separate factor deserving special attention brought Arab Palestinian nationalism once again to the fore. (History has repeated itself in Lebanon, in 1976.) Many Israelis, Arabs, and Western observers believe that if Israel had been prepared to deal with the Palestinian Arab problem, particularly when it became logistically capable of doing so after 1967, then the whole international upsurge during 1974–76 in favor of the Palestinians and the widespread and increasing recognition of the PLO might have been avoided. Israel's position toward the Palestinians, however, has been ill-conceived, impractical, and, to a large extent, inconsistent from the viewpoint of Israel's preservation.

The following should help explain some of the causes that have contributed to Israel's misperception of the entire Arab Palestinian situation:

Political Fragmentation: Israel's sociopolitical makeup is one that has never been conducive to a unified approach toward issues of national importance and security. In the Israeli democracy, the coalition form of government depends on a minority faction for support, the government is often open to group pressures exerted by these smaller parties, and more often than not, the latter succeed in imposing their will on the majority.

In the case of the Arab Palestinians, for example, we find that most of the religious parties in Israel are strenuously opposed to the return of the West Bank or the Gaza Strip to any Arab state or to the Arab Palestinians. Because these political parties are part of the coalition government, they hold the key to whether or not the government survives a vote of confidence in the parliament over this issue. Yet before 1967, when there was no occupied territory involved, the Labor government contended that the Palestinian refugee situation was an Arab problem. Apart from occasional cosmetic moves, such as the reunion of families, very little action was taken to resolve the problem of the Arab Palestinians.

One other aspect that must be noted in considering the Israeli position toward the Arab Palestinians is the emergence of the PLO as the "sole representative" of the Arab Palestinians and its acceptance as such by the

Arab states and the UN. In this regard, Israel tacitly accepted the new role bestowed on the PLO; for only by considering the PLO and the Arab Palestinians one entity could Israel justify its refusal to negotiate with the Arab Palestinians. After all, Israel is not expected to negotiate with any party that has sworn to liquidate it. On the other hand, Israel has maintained its policies of social and economic reconciliation with the Arab Palestinians throughout the occupied territories because in effect it seeks to separate the interests of the PLO from those of the Arab Palestinians. Here again is evidence of a contradictory policy, perhaps unavoidable by the very nature of the problem.

The Arab states, for their part, have chosen to perpetuate the Arab Palestinian issue for political reasons and have indeed succeeded in keeping it before the international community for almost three decades. While Israel may not have been in a position to do much about it before the Six Day War of 1967, it could indeed have taken the initiative afterward. Yet the governments of Golda Meir and Rabin failed to produce an alternative solution, partly because of shortsightedness on the part of its political leaders, and partly because of the weakness inherent in a coalition government that has not commanded wide support since 1967. Thus, no Israeli government has been able to formulate any far-reaching solution to the Arab Palestinian problem without facing virtual collapse.

Social and Economic Objections: Because an increase in the number of Arabs in Israel would threaten the majority rule of the Jews, as we saw in the previous chapter, Israel has objected in principle to the concept of "repatriation" endorsed unanimously by the Arab states. Israel has rejected that concept on the grounds that resettlement of all the Palestinians in Israel would not be repatriation but rather their alienation from the rest of Arab society. In any case, Israeli leaders have contended, differences of language, culture, heritage, national identity, and loyalty would not permit easy assimilation of the Palestinian refugees with the Jews. Furthermore, repatriation of the Arab Palestinians would create a racial crisis that might lead to the disintegration of Israel's identity as a Jewish state. The Israeli population would eventually be dominated numerically by a majority of Arabs, if not by other means, by the natural birth rate. In addition to the potential danger that acceptance of the Arab refugees *en masse* would pose to the very nature of Israel, Israel could not assume the new economic burdens that hundreds of thousands of refugees would entail. Israel's fragile economy, it was maintained, was in no position to create economic conditions conducive to social harmony and brotherhood.

These contentions appear reasonable and acceptable, particularly if related to the pre-1967 situation. But after 1967, with the military occupation of the West Bank and other territories, the situation changed drastically. The question of repatriation was no longer a viable one. Nor were the socioeconomic conditions present to support a continuation of the policy of "no action" by the Israeli authorities. The "Dayan Doctrine" that was followed in the West Bank and the Gaza Strip both provided for the social and economic integration of the Palestinians and their political and national separation from Israel. How did the Labor government expect to maintain thereafter a working relationship with the Arab Palestinians who could not help but view the Israeli presence as a foreign occupation? It would seem that Israel's leaders were indeed naive to suppose that the Arab Palestinians would eventually repress their national aspirations in favor of a higher standard of living in Israel.

While Israel was making impressive social and economic progress in the West Bank and the Gaza Strip after 1967, the Labor government had many options open for creating an amicable solution on its own, not in conjunction with any other Arab state or the PLO. It could thereby have defused the Arab states' claim of "sponsorship" of the Palestinian refugee cause. But the opportunity was lost.

Military Influence: For obviously justifiable reasons, Israel is extremely sensitive about all matters that fall within its concept of "national security." It is only natural that the question of the Arab Palestinians falls within the jurisdiction of the army. Being entrusted with the task of security, and to a large extent, the survival of the state, the army has been able to extend its authority and influence beyond what by democratic norms is considered its legitimate sphere of authority. Before 1967 the Israeli army had the responsibility of safeguarding the security of Israel from its neighbors while at the same time overseeing the Arab Israelis (estimated in 1967 at 350,000). After the Six Day War the role of the army became greater; it was charged not only with keeping order throughout the occupied territories but also with the full responsibility for administrative duties in those territories.

Although the army in Israel has always been fully

involved in all policy planning, it is the *determining factor* in planning policies that relate directly or indirectly to the occupied territories. Being sensitive to all security matters, the army tends to treat the occupied territories as a source of trouble and as a menace to Israel's security. In addition, the new territories provide easier terrain to protect, and from a strictly military point of view, continued occupation or control over the territories is therefore advisable.

In addition to pure logistics and the security point of view, there is the psychological and emotional aspect that further strengthens the army's hand. The military sacrifices and hardships that accompanied the four Arab-Israeli wars have created in the army an emotional barrier that tends to block the consideration of nonmilitary alternatives. This barrier to detached analysis cannot be easily removed. Army officers continue to advocate to the Israeli government that the present borders constitute the safest frontiers, and short of a total peace, they say, Israel would be advised to maintain indefinitely its control over most of the occupied territories.

The Israeli Arabs: One final factor that may have indirectly contributed to Israel's reluctance to find an acceptable formula for the Arab Palestinians before and after 1967 is the Arab minority in Israel. Many Israeli leaders, although sympathetic to the Israeli Arabs, feel that regardless of circumstances and conditions, in the final analysis the loyalties of Israeli Arabs lie with their brethren in the other Arab states and with the Palestinians. That is not to say that the Israeli Arabs are completely disloyal; however, if and when it comes to a choice between supporting the Israeli cause or the Arab cause, they will not hesitate to support the latter.

Other Israelis have been more radical in their views regarding the Israeli Arabs' loyalty. Many of them believe that the Arab minority is nothing less than a fifth column and that when the time comes, they will be eager to join other Arab forces in bringing about the destruction of the state of Israel. The disturbances of April 1976, caused by Israeli Arabs in northern Israel in support of the Arab Palestinians in the West Bank, are pointed to as true manifestations of the Arab Israelis' loyalty.

Regardless of the accuracy of these views, ethnic and class differences between Arabs and Jews do exist in Israel. They have manifested themselves on a variety of levels, particularly in social status, standard of living, and education. The outbreak of rioting in the Galilee in the summer of 1976, although ostensibly meant to express opposition to government plans to expropriate land in the area, in fact reflected the Arab frustration over not enjoying the same economic and political advantages in Israel as did the Jews. In the words of Atallah Mansaur, an Israeli Arab who is a member of the editorial staff of the independent and well-regarded newspaper *Haaretz*, "This gap (between Jews and Arab Israelis) is a time bomb that may explode and cause more damage to peace in Israel and to its international reputation." It is no secret that the majority of the Israeli Arabs feel deprived in one way or another.

Because of the lack of a consensus regarding an overall solution to the Arab Palestinian situation, Israeli authorities have elected since 1967 to let time take its own course and to hope for the best. Israel failed to take any creative initiative after the 1967 war, choosing instead to work toward creating harmonious relations between the Arab Palestinians and the Israelis in the hope of eventually reconciling their differences. This accommodating attitude, it was thought, would defuse the national aspirations of the Arab Palestinians. Although Israel was successful in ameliorating the Israeli-Arab situation on social and economic levels, this success was insufficient to subdue or eliminate the deeper Palestinian nationalism. For this reason the Likud government is challenged to find a new resolution regarding the Palestinian problem.

Yet if current conditions are carefully examined and the available options are studied, it is possible that the overwhelming support that the PLO gained in the 1976 municipal elections in the West Bank can be turned around to benefit Israel as well as the Arab Palestinians. Although the result of the election may seem grim to some Israeli officials, still the fact that Israel was able to hold a democratic election in these territories reflects the Israeli commitment to freedom and good will. The utter lack of free elections in almost every other part of the Arab world stands in total contrast.

The outcome of the election surely must have been anticipated and now cannot be ignored. A dialogue between the two sides should be commenced even though it may prove difficult in the beginning. In the words of Israel's former Defense Minister Shimon Peres, the results of the election constitute a national challenge. Israel must open up a dialogue with the new representatives in the West Bank and regain the good will built up in the early years of the occupation. All other options, as we shall see, have no realistic basis and are inherently dangerous to the welfare of all concerned. To these options we shall now turn our attention.

There are, in fact, five different options available to Israel. None of the first four options, if considered seriously, can provide all that the Israelis or the Arab Palestinians expect. They will have to be ruled out because they are implausible or impractical under present conditions. The fifth option, however, offers a realistic solution that if carefully carried out, may provide the basis for an Israeli-Palestinian agreement.

1) *Annexing the Occupied Territories:* Annexation as an option has been steadily losing ground. Recent developments in the West Bank, such as the general elections, have strengthened appreciably the position of those Israelis who feel that annexation must be ruled out. The antiannexation group argues that territorial annexation as such would mean having to absorb more than one million Arabs into the social fabric—a situation that would eventually create severe economic, political, and national security problems in Israel. Furthermore, the fact that the natural increase of the Arab population is almost twice the rate of the Israeli population growth (41 per 1,000, not allowing for any influx of Jewish immigrants into Israel) indicates that the Arab minority of today will move to a clear majority by the year 2000 at the latest. In such a situation, the state of Israel would lose its Jewish identity and its purpose as a home for all Jews who are seeking a sanctuary and a life style of their own.

Furthermore, it is estimated that after annexation the number of Arab Palestinians in Israel would reach at least 1,500,000. This "minority" with the potential of becoming a majority would surely not accept a subordinate position or second-class citizenship. Israel would have to choose between (a) granting complete and equal opportunity to all its citizens, thereby increasing the possibility that the Jewish state would lose its character and become a secular state (such an outcome might be welcomed by the Arab states and even by the PLO that has been advocating this solution for some time); or (b) granting a lesser or a second-class citizenship to the Palestinians that in the long run would force Israelis to become repressive against their own will. Because neither of these results is desirable, the option of annexation must be ruled out as a viable solution.

In a comprehensive essay published in the *Jerusalem Post* on June 29, 1976, former Foreign Minister Abba Eban emphasized the lack of any common ground—cultural, historical, or psychological—between Arabs and Jews that might promote unity and sociopolitical harmony if, for example, the West Bank and the Gaza Strip were annexed by Israel. "No unity without consent, that is the crux. The military victory has failed to have any marked effect on the sharp duality of experience between the river and the area. To pass from the area of Israeli law into the realm of the military administration is to undertake a voyage of drastic transition. . . . Every taste and sound and smell, every dream and hope in Nablus and Ramallah is foreign to every taste and sound and smell and dream and hope in Tel Aviv, Dagania, Holon and Dimona." After recounting a historical survey showing why unity cannot work without consent, Abba Eban stated the key dilemma: "Let us face the hard truth: *If the West Bank and the Gaza Arabs were annexed, our principles would not allow us to withhold citizenship, and our vital*

interest would not allow us to grant it" [Italics added].
He concluded with a recommendation: "Israel's sovereignty as a Jewish state came to birth through partition.
It would dwindle with partition's death. We must tell
the nation frankly that an agreed new partition is a
'concession' not only to Arab demands, but also to Israeli
interests and conceptual truth. Faced by the fallacious
but earnest élan of Gush Emunim, it is time for Israeli
leaders to enter the intellectual arena and undertake their
educative role."

2) *Returning the West Bank to Jordan:* The official
Israeli position regarding the future of the Gaza Strip
and the West Bank has never been entirely clear, but in
the past Israel has expressed the desire to see the problem
of the Arab Palestinians solved as an integral part of the
Jordanian territorial problem. Israel contends that the Arab
Palestinians are part of Jordan and that Jordan is naturally
the only place that should constitute their homeland.
Furthermore, any solution of the status of the West Bank
should be incorporated into the overall peace settlement
with Jordan. This should prevent, Israel argues, the
creation of a new Arab-Palestinian state that, in the words
of former premiers Rabin and Golda Meir, "would be
an ideal place to be pointed directly at Israel, a launching
pad, as it were, to continue their Holy War."

In an interview with Thomas W. Lippman of *The
Washington Post* (December 30, 1976), Egyptian President Sadat said that "any Palestinian state that is created
on the West Bank must be formally linked with Jordan."
Then he added: "We (Egypt and Jordan) issued a
declaration and I was attacked vehemently by the Palestinians at that time. My idea was and still is that a certain

relationship between the Palestinians and Jordan should be declared to take place whenever the Palestinian state is created." Sadat added further that this could take the form of a confederation or "whatever model they agree on between them." He also insisted that Israeli withdrawal from the occupied territories must be swift, total, and completed in a single phase and that Lebanon must be a full participant in the Geneva peace conference. Shlomo Avineri, director general of the Foreign Ministry, said in a radio interview (January 2) that Sadat's support for a Palestinian-Jordanian linkage might pave the way for resuming the Geneva conference, "but it is certainly not enough" by itself. He said that Arab insistence on PLO participation at Geneva remained a major obstacle and is unacceptable to Israel. On the other hand, Avineri thought that Sadat's remarks could signify the beginning of a serious erosion of Arab support for the PLO and, if continued, could provide the basis for a dialogue between Israel and its neighbors. (*JTA Daily News Bulletin*, January 3, 1977)

Here again the point is being missed, for regardless of what arrangement can be made between a Palestinian entity and Jordan and however Sadat may phrase such an agreement, Israel and the Arab states will have to recognize that an independent Palestinian entity is the prerequisite of any kind of Palestinian-Jordanian collaboration. Israel may feel that Sadat's newly adopted position has helped to make its own goals more attainable; yet the reality of the situation does not suggest that such a development will change the basic need of the Palestinians for self-expression.

Furthermore, recent developments are making the option of returning the West Bank to Jordan less and less attractive. First, there is no guarantee that King Hussein will take any permanent position short of securing (a) peace with Israel and (b) total control over affairs in his country. In fact, in his address to the Los Angeles World Affairs Council on April 6, 1976, King Hussein asserted: "The Palestinian people should be enabled to exercise their inalienable right of self-determination, including the right to establish an independent state in Palestine if they so desire."

Second, thus far very few Palestinian leaders have indicated any desire to reunite the West Bank with Jordan while the civil war of 1970 is still fresh in the minds of most Palestinians. The April 1976 elections in the West Bank drew the line between the Arab Palestinian and the Israeli perceptions of a future settlement. Arab leaders contend that the vote demonstrated the preference of the residents of the area for an independent Palestinian state on the West Bank and the Gaza Strip. Khamil Khalef, the militant mayor of Ramallah, stated this case: "Could the message be more clear?" he asked. "The vote shows the whole world that the Palestinians want to establish their own national entity, and not be linked to either Jordan or Israel."

Third, past experience in northern Iraq with the Kurds and the more recent civil war in Lebanon have shown that the Arabs, despite many common characteristics, have not sufficient political maturity to tolerate different religious sects, let alone share political power with them on an equal footing.

It has become increasingly clear since the Israeli take-over of the West Bank and the Gaza Strip that the Arab

Palestinians have very little love for the Jordanian monarchical government and little in common with it in
terms of national aspirations. No Palestinian leader has
expressed a desire to go back to the old situation, namely,
that of Jordanian control. Why, then, has the Labor
government continued to insist that the fate of the Arab
Palestinians is tied to that of their "brothers," the Jordanians? Why has it always been assumed that a new
third country, say, in the West Bank, would be a greater
menace to Israel than the one *combined* state under
Jordanian rule? Who is to guarantee that the new "unified"
country would not by chance or by choice turn against
Israel, with or without King Hussein? Arab politics today,
as we have stated on many occasions before, is based less
on considerations of immediate gains and losses than on
considerations of long-term advantages, that is, Arab
leaders know very well that time is working in their favor.

3) *Marking Time:* The option of waiting for a more
favorable time before deciding on the fate of the Arab
Palestinians was advocated primarily by former Premier
Rabin. Rabin maintained, at least since 1975, that Israel
should take advantage of the American presidential elections in 1976 and continue to bide its time because the
Ford Administration would probably not take any drastic
action in an election year. And if a Democratic president
were elected, he would most likely consider the Israeli
dilemma in a more favorable light than would a Republican.

Although Rabin may have been correct in his estimate
of the greater responsiveness to Israel's needs on the
part of a Democratic president, President Carter, however, made it clear (February 1977) that although Israel's

survival and security remain unequivocal American commitments, an Arab Palestinian entity is not inconsistent with those commitments. From its first days in office, the new American administration has been under mounting Arab pressure for new initiatives in the Middle East. Although Saudi Arabia's linkage of oil prices to progress toward an Arab-Israeli settlement may or may not be effective pressure on the Carter Administration, President Carter still seems to think that the element of time is critical and that a continued stalemate will reverse the existing trend for a peaceful resolution of the Arab-Israeli crisis.

High-ranking Israelis, such as former Foreign Minister Abba Eban, maintain that time is not on Israel's side. For example, Eban stated in an interview with the *New York Times* on April 19, 1976 that "Time is of the essence and unhappily for us, time is running out. We ought to grasp the central issues now and involve the U.S. in solving them. I don't see how it will be better for us later on; economically, I don't think we'll be less dependent on the U.S. Also the Arab monetary power is only beginning to make itself felt." Eban contended that the debut speech made by former United States Ambassador William Scranton at the United Nations should be understood as a signal to Israel that the United States also believes that time is not working in Israel's favor. "Even in the American-Israeli relationship gaps are beginning to show." The Rabin strategy of postponing the issue seems not to have stood on firm ground.

Marking time may have a certain validity if Israel has a definite basis for economic recovery or if one were able to separate the Middle East situation from American interests in that region. But they are inextricably linked. For example, a Republican administration would have undoubtedly remained committed to Israel's survival but would not have hesitated to use any pressure against Israel that it deemed necessary in order to further the "normalization" process with the Arab nations. In effect, this would have meant that if further territorial concessions by Israel—even short of total peace—were considered essential to promote American interests, then Israel would have been pressured to make such concessions.

This situation has not changed to any appreciable degree under the new Democratic administration. President Jimmy Carter will undoubtedly continue to act prudently when it comes to the question of Israel's future. But, as indicated above, President Carter has expressed his views on the Palestinian issue. He recognizes the fact that an equitable solution to the problem in the West Bank and the Gaza Strip must be found. Although not ruling out the possibility of a separate entity for the Arab Palestinians, he gave his unequivocal commitment to the state of Israel. Furthermore, Carter has advocated recognition by the PLO of the state of Israel as a first step in any solution. Essentially, therefore, very little if any change in policy may be expected from the Democratic administration. President Carter may, however, be a little more flexible regarding grants and loans for military aid or other economic assistance, but none of these factors will have a direct bearing on the Palestinian issue.

When it comes to fundamentals, the president of the United States, regardless of his political party affiliation, will act solely in America's national interest. Although all American administrations since Israel's creation have recognized the important political role that Israel plays in the Middle East, no administration in the future can afford to overlook any opportunities that the Arab world may offer. It can be argued convincingly that the present strategic interests of the United States lie more in the Arab world than in Israel principally because of America's dependence on the vast quantities of oil there. It would seem, however, that the moral commitment of the United States to Israel as well as its strategic perceptions of the Middle East have swayed the pendulum of American policy in Israel's favor.

Before we turn to the last two options, some serious consideration should be given to the positions of other nations, particularly that of the Soviet Union, on the Palestinian issue.

Throughout this argument a great deal of emphasis has been placed on the important role that the United States will continue to play in achieving an Arab-Israeli peace agreement. The fact that the Soviet Union's role was underplayed should not necessarily be taken to mean that the Soviet Union does not have much to say about a future agreement among the contending parties. The Soviet Union's attitude toward the Arab-Israeli conflict remains critical notwithstanding Soviet reverses in Egypt and more recently in Syria. According to Professor Victor LeVine (Washington University, St. Louis), "Should the U.S.S.R. continue to suffer reverses and blows to its prestige because it cannot rely on its clients to remain constant, then it may very well see itself cutting its losses by helping the United States push to a settlement. Its championing of the PLO, Iraq and South Yemen is beginning to rebound unpleasantly." It would seem therefore that any new major peace offensive in the Middle East will have to receive at least the tacit agreement of the Soviet Union. The Soviet Union may at the present time, for reasons of its own, be more amicable to an Arab-Israeli accord than at any time before. To be sure, the Soviet Union does not want to see Israel destroyed, for that would also put an end to Russian influence in the Middle East. On the other hand, the Soviet Union will not be willing to support any peace agreement that might substantially reduce or completely eliminate its influence in the region. After all, it is argued, most of the Arab states would not have wanted to be dependent militarily and politically on the Soviet Union had it not been for the conflict with Israel. In sum, then, the Soviet Union will continue to weigh its overall losses and gains to determine its course of action. The Russian position, although it may appear at times ambivalent, has been supportive of both UN Resolutions 242 and 338 that confirm and reconfirm the right of both the Israelis and the Arab Palestinians to a secure haven of their own.

Israel also cannot overlook the position of many of its friends such as Great Britain, France, West Germany, and others who have gone on record recognizing the Arab Palestinian need for a homeland. After the debate on the Palestinian problem in the United Nations Security Council on January 2, 1976, all the nations represented, including the United States, supported the motion that recognized the right of the Arab Palestinians to self-determination. The United States vetoed the final resolution, however, on the grounds that there was a need to preserve the framework for negotiations established in previous resolutions, specifically Resolutions 242 and 338 that recognized Israel's right to exist with secure boundaries. In the course of the debate, the United States affirmed: 'There can be no durable solution unless every effort is made to promote a solution of the key issues of a just and lasting peace, based on Resolutions 242 and 338, taking into account *the legitimate interests of all the people in the area, including the Palestinian people,* and respect for the right to independent existence of all states in the area." (See Resolutions 242 and 338, Appendixes 6 and 7)

For these reasons, the option of waiting for an opportune moment does not seem to offer good prospects. The Arab position is improving with time. Why wait? Why not act now, when Israel stands to gain much more than it can gain at a later date? An Israeli initiative between 1967 and 1973 would have yielded far greater results, for after the Yom Kippur War, Israel became increasingly more vulnerable politically and even militarily. Prospects suggest that the picture will not improve.

4) *Maintaining the Status Quo:* This option calls for perpetuating Israeli control over the West Bank and the Gaza Strip, an option that no one in a responsible position from either camp, Israeli or Arab, believes viable because of its inherent explosiveness. There are, however, small militant groups in Israel who believe that indefinite military control will allow Israel to exercise its policies at will and decide unilaterally the future of the West Bank and the Gaza Strip. After all, these groups maintain, Israeli sacrifices in terms of money and manpower have been formidable; why should all that be thrown away?

This particular position has been losing momentum, for

those who are familiar with the volatile situation in the whole region know of the danger of renewed war. Military strength by itself may stall undesirable developments, but it cannot indefinitely stop adverse occurrences from taking place. Maintaining the status quo, thus, is a thing of the past. In the words of Fahad Kawasme, the newly elected Arab mayor of Hebron, the recent change in leadership in the West Bank is nothing less than a revolution. "Without any doubt, the change is the end of one era and the beginning of a period of intensified national consciousness among the peoples of the occupied area."

5) *Creating and Safeguarding a Palestinian Entity:* If the four options discussed above are impractical and unrealistic, what is left for Israel is an option that can satisfy to a great extent the Palestinians' demand for nationhood with a minimum risk to Israel's security. It is hardly relevant whether the Palestinians constitute a "people." The fact remains that the Arab Palestinians have lived for almost three decades where they are now living. Short of driving them out of these territories or dispersing them, which is unthinkable, the only solution left is self-rule. *With self-rule they can find fulfillment* and satisfy their national needs without serious risk or damage to Israel. This writer thinks that such a solution would be the most beneficial one, for *it is an answer that gives Israel the greatest degree of security by allowing Israel to retain some control over the evolution of affairs.*

To be sure, the establishment of a Palestinian entity can be considered only as an integral part of an overall peaceful settlement between Israel and the Arab states. No responsible observer would advocate that Israel should unilaterally withdraw from the West Bank and the Gaza

Strip for the purpose of testing the Arabs' intentions. No surrender of territory can be conceived of without simultaneous reciprocity by the Arab states. However, what must be clarified publicly is Israel's own position regarding its willingness to support the establishment of a Palestinian entity *within the framework of total peace.* Such a declaration of willingness will serve notice to the Arab Palestinians, the Arab states, and the international community that Israel's intentions are meritorious. In sum, Israel will have to make it clear that it too considers the 1967 borders, with some minor changes, the basis for negotiations toward a peace settlement. By stating its intent, Israel will be able 1) to discredit the Arabs' claim of Israel's expansionism, and 2) to challenge the Arab Palestinians to accept an offer that they will find very difficult to refuse.

What gave further impetus to this proposition are the most recent developments in the Middle East which were precipitated by the historic visit of President Anwar El-Sadat of Egypt to Israel. Egypt's determination to continue the process of face-to-face negotiation with Israel for the purpose of achieving a lasting peace in the Middle East has caused a serious political turmoil among the Arab states. The PLO, which ostensibly champions the cause of the Arab Palestinians, has decided to join Algeria, Iraq, Libya and Syria in their opposition to the Sadat initiative. By adopting this extreme position of no negotiation with Israel, the PLO may have lost a historic opportunity to become a true political force in any future Arab-Israeli peace conference. The PLO refusal to attend the Cairo preliminary peace conference has further demonstrated the extremism of the PLO and its true intentions regarding

Israel. This particular development should indeed be capitalized upon by the Likud government. For the first time in a decade Israel can move toward a de facto political separation between the interests of the PLO and those of the Arab Palestinians. For the first time Israel can show to the international community that the PLO does not seek peace and that Israel is prepared to find an amicable solution to the Arab Palestinian problem under the framework of a peace agreement with Egypt and Jordan. Such an approach will undoubtedly be supported by Western Europe, the United States and the rest of the Western hemisphere, including some nations in Africa and Asia. Contrary to the Labor government, the Likud government will not lose sight of these new opportunities as they unfold. A dialogue between Israel and the legitimate representative of the Arab Palestinians should begin. The Palestinian representative should be democratically elected from among the Arab Palestinians in the Gaza Strip and the West Bank. And for the first time a de facto situation may be created demonstrating that the PLO is not the sole representative of the Arab Palestinians, that the PLO *does not* represent the real aspirations of the Arab Palestinians for peace, and that the PLO defiance of President Sadat further proves its intransigence and ill designs against the sovereignty of Israel.

Some of the principles that must guide the Likud government initiative toward the creation of Palestinian self-rule are: 1) All the Israeli settlements in the West Bank and Gaza Strip must remain intact. These settlements do not have to be necessarily linked to the eventual boundaries that may be established through negotiation. The durability of any peace agreement with the Palestinians will depend to a large extent on the degree of economic, cultural and social intercourse between them and the Israelis. The existence of these settlements will help sustain those changes and thereby transform the Arab-Israeli relationship into permanent good neighborly relations.

2) Israeli military presence will be retained for a period of perhaps 10–15 years, until such time when a reversal in the relationship between Israel and the newly established Palestinian entity becomes extremely undesirable to the latter.

3) All territories from which Israel is to eventually withdraw will have to remain demilitarized. Israel, with the support of Jordan and perhaps Egypt, should assume the military protection of the Palestinian entity. Such an arrangement will not only help to maintain the status quo but will also relieve the new entity from the burden of military expenditure.

It should be clear that the objectives of both sides must be met—namely, self-rule for the Arab Palestinians and security for Israel. If one is not to be achieved at the expense of the other, flexibility must be employed to meet the realities of the situation. In addition, if Israel's armed forces would commit themselves to preserving the territorial integrity of the new entity during the early stages of its development, this would undoubtedly discourage outside radical factions or states from taking irresponsible measures against it—actions that could affect its political status.

In the context of such an Israeli initiative that would be *only declaratory*, it would have to be reaffirmed by Israel that the future of the Old City of Jerusalem is not subject to negotiation; on this unique issue Israel must take an irrevocable stance. Jerusalem will have to remain united, while the Arabs and the Christians should have *total and complete control over their holy shrines and absolute freedom of worship.* The Arab residents in a united Jerusalem will enjoy equal citizenship and will be eligible to vote and to be elected to any post in the municipality. (For a more comprehensive analysis of this issue, see *The Middle East: Imperatives and Choices*, by Alon Ben-Meir, Decalogue Books, 1975, pp. 185–217.)

There is also the possibility that the Jordanian government may join Israel in these efforts, for regardless of the political boundaries eventually agreed upon, *social and economic cooperation among Israel, Jordan, and the newly established entity will be the prerequisite of the creation of a workable and lasting settlement.* Consensus in the region indicates clearly that the Palestinian Arabs, including some moderate members of the PLO, favor such cooperation with Israel.

The Advantages to Israel: The advantages to Israel that would result from the establishment of a Palestinian entity are numerous. The most important ones should be mentioned:

1) By taking the initiative Israel will be able to defuse the Arabs' persistent claims on behalf of the Palestinians regarding their right to self-determination. Once Israel makes its support of a Palestinian entity clear, it will "throw the ball back to the Arab states," including the Palestinians, and thus test their true intentions.

2) The political pressure exerted against Israel by the international community, and particularly the United States, would be drastically curtailed. Moreover, it would

encourage the United States to define its commitment to Israel and what the American role in future peace efforts would be.

3) In the wake of Israel's readiness to help establish a Palestinian entity, Arab economic pressure on the United States will lessen because the Arab claims of Israeli "stalling" will have little validity.

4) Finally, Israel will be able to turn its efforts toward a more constructive role in the West Bank and the Gaza Strip, replacing the posture of foreign occupation that must inevitably increase tension.

The current situation in the West Bank is extremely volatile and politically dangerous. Israel will sooner or later have to choose between acts of severe repression against the Arab Palestinians or coming to terms with them. Regardless of the course that Israel chooses, the West Bank and the Gaza Strip are ideologically and politically in the process of transformation. Neither the process itself nor the goal of transformation is consistent with Israel's stated intentions or desires. Unless Israel comes up with a new approach and imaginative policy toward the region, political uncertainties and extremism, which are inherently dangerous, will continue to prevail.

V

ISRAELI-JEWISH
PUBLIC RELATIONS
FAILURE

ELI Wiesel, one of our most celebrated writers, in an interview with Morton A. Reichbeck, an associate editor of *Business Week*, recently summed up the inefficiency of Jewish-Israeli public relations in the following terms: "Israel has always been poor in explaining itself. And often I wonder why? After all, we who are the masters of public relations, experts on Madison Avenue; I think Jews can explain everything but themselves. They explain potato chips, they can explain cars, they can explain any cause you give them but themselves." To emphasize his point, Mr. Wiesel looked to history: "Moses is an example. He should have been the speaker, the PR expert, but he stuttered. You can't explain it, and this is still going on. It's a mystery." (*Present Tense Magazine of World Jewish Affairs*, Spring 1976, pp. 44–45)

Mr. Wiesel's statement summarizes the dilemma that Israel faces in its public relations efforts. Israel's intensified efforts to explain its policies and position, especially since the October war of 1973, have not been making much headway. For example, the onslaught against Israel in the United Nations, led by the Soviet Union and enthusiastic Arab states, began with the attempt to expel Israel and ended with the passage of the resolution equating Zionism with racism. The Communist bloc, the third world nations, and the Arab states have consistently attempted to discredit Israel and thereby delegitimize its sovereign existence. The acceptance of the PLO as an equal party to the Arab-Israel crisis and the unrelenting "attacks" by the Security Council in its effort to portray Israel as an outlaw country are further examples of the hostile climate of opinion that Israel finds itself in.

These systematic attacks, accusations, and allegations have indeed put Israel on the defensive. While Israel was (and still is) trying to coordinate its forces in order to explain its position vis-à-vis the Arab states, the latter, supported by the Soviet bloc, have been able to wage such a propaganda campaign as to render Israel a very serious setback in its own explanatory and persuasive efforts.

The Jewish-Israeli public relations effort thus needs a thorough reexamination. Apart from the lack of well-coordinated campaigns, the Israeli public relations effort has failed to recognize that times have changed and that the tools employed before to counter the Arab-Communist "attacks" are no longer suitable. New efforts, better tools, a more imaginative approach, better coordination, and preventive measures, more funds, and more qualified personnel—all are required urgently in order to combat one of the most vicious propaganda onslaughts in modern times.

During the fifties and sixties, Jews in the diaspora and in Israel grew accustomed to the availability of ample intellectual and financial resources for conducting public relations campaigns against assaults by the Arab and Communist propagandists. In fact, the Israeli and the Jewish organizations' public relations campaigns were so successful during that period that they prompted some United States officials, among them the chairman of the Joint Chiefs of Staff, General George S. Brown, to assert (with no foundation) that "the Jews in the United States own or control most of the banks and the press." The influence that American Jewish leaders and Israeli lobbyists have been able to exercise is not generated at all through "Jewish ownership" of either the press or the banking system in the United States. Rather, that influence arose out of the ingenuity of some Jewish-Israeli lobbyists, on the one hand, and also, and more important, the lack or the inadequacy of the Arab propaganda counter-campaign, on the other.

Since the Yom Kippur War of October 1973, we have been witnessing a dramatic change in the effectiveness of Jewish public relations and Arab propaganda. Israeli and American public relations officials can no longer attain early success in influencing public opinion. Since October 1973, the propaganda war between the Arab states and Israel has become the focal point of the cold war that has prevailed between them. The "battle" for American and West European public opinion is being waged with a far greater degree of sophistication, manpower, and finance on both sides. In addition, the changing moods and priorities of the American public and the international community at large have compelled both sides to re-assess their wars of propaganda and to adopt suitable measures to ensure greater success.

To appreciate the disparity between the Arab and Israeli approaches to propaganda and their successes in terms of American and West European public responsive-ness, we can outline six major differences: limited audi-ences versus mass appeal, moral and legal versus emotional and expedient, uncoordinated versus coordinated effort, defensive versus offensive, politics versus policies, and, finally, underfinanced and understaffed versus a profusion of funds and an abundance of competent manpower. These differences indicate why the Israeli-Jewish public relations campaign has been lagging behind its Arab counterpart and what must be done to rectify the situa-tion. The differences also illustrate why the Arab propa-gandists have been generating greater sympathy for and receptivity to their cause.

1. *Limited Audience versus Mass Appeal*

The Israeli public relations campaign, supported, for example, by the National Jewish Community Relations Advisory Councils in the United States, has been directed mainly toward intellectuals and more sophisticated audi-ences, many of them Jewish. To be sure, the Jewish organizations as well as Israeli officials keep explaining themselves to one another; each is flattered with the other's achievements, and when a non-Jewish personality is involved, he or she is often paid to say what Jewish audiences like to hear. Furthermore, even when Israeli officials visit the United States they come essentially to address Jewish audiences and primarily to encourage further and greater support for Israel. Yet very seldom would the same speaker take the time to address himself to a non-Jewish group for the simple purpose of better public relations.

Contrary to this approach, Arab propagandists have been directing their attention to the general public—average persons—in the United States who often lack the desire or the capacity to search for deep and involved explanations in matters of foreign affairs. Hence the broader impact and success of the Arab propaganda initiative.

Economic, racial, and political difficulties that have engulfed the United States and other Western democracies in recent years have undoubtedly further contributed to the apathy of the average Westerner who has become less and less concerned with abstract ideologies abroad and more and more attuned to inflation, unemployment, and bread-and-butter issues at home. Arab propagandists have never failed to remind Western Europeans and Americans how important the continuation of the flow of oil is to their industries, how critical oil prices are to economic recovery and a balanced budget, and how many more jobs are created for every billion dollars' worth of trade with the Arab states. Israeli public relations officials took very little note of this economic anxiety permeating the general American and West European public and thus left the field almost exclusively to the Arab propagandists who spared no effort to exploit the opportunity of appealing to a broader audience.

Philip Hochstein, the editor and publisher of *The Jewish*

Week and American Examiner in New York, shed further light on this important issue. "What is really hurting Israel's cause in American public opinion," Hochstein asserts, "is oil. In the absense of a national energy program having a credible claim to pointing to energy independence, it will be extremely difficult to preserve American preference for Israel in the Middle East. If the Jews in America were to take militant leadership in fighting for an independent energy program, it would become possible to keep a connection in the American mind between American pride and Israel's survival."

Hochstein admits that this is a big order that would require a transformation in the quality of American leadership, for, he maintains, "It is not as easy to raise funds for backing an energy program as it is for defending ourselves against moribund anti-Semitism or self-defeating Arab propaganda. . . . Therefore, count on our defense agencies perpetuating themselves with scare counterpropaganda instead of doing a constructive job."

2. *Moral and Legal versus Emotional and Expedient*

Israeli and Jewish public relations people have always viewed the moral and legal aspects of the Middle East crisis as the main components that argue in Israel's favor. Yet recent experiences in the UN (e.g., the invitation to Yassir Arafat to address that body and his greeting with a standing ovation, the granting of permanent status to the PLO in the General Assembly, the UN resolution equating Zionism with racism, the persistent attempts of the UN majority members to delegitimize Israel) have shown that morality is an expendable and relative commodity and that legality can be disposed of, even by such "democratic" and free nations as France and Japan. One is dismayed to find that some Western democracies are falling prey to Arab petro-blackmail. The former United States Ambassador to the UN, Daniel Patrick Moynihan, stated that "Nothing is farther apart than Zionism and racism. Israel can be anything else but racist, unless it ceases to be Zionist."

While the Israelis were demanding legal or historical rights with an emphasis on morality, the Arab propagandists were concentrating on the human aspect of the Arab Palestinian situation. They played on issues charged with emotion, with an eye to the general public, portraying the Arab "minority" as the underdog, "suffering" from severe injustices resulting from dislocation, mistreatment, and abuse. These exaggerated protestations psychologically prepared the general public and then prompted sympathy for the Arab cause. This indoctrination of the general public was instrumental in helping to prepare the groundwork for the passage of yet another unfortunate resolution. The Human Rights Commission, meeting in Geneva, overwhelmingly approved a resolution in February 1976 that accused Israel of committing "war crimes" in the territories that it captured in 1967. The only country that voted against it was the United States, while Britain, France, Italy, West Germany, Austria, Canada, and others abstained. Here again, oil and the petrodollar have only begun to make their impact felt.

To illustrate the potency of the Arabs' propaganda, consider this: For nearly thirty years the Arab states have managed to bring the plight of the Palestinian refugees to the attention of the UN General Assembly, using the humane and tragic aspects of the situation to undermine Israel's position. At no time have the sacrifice and the hardship of over 600,000 Sephardic Jews, refugees from Arab countries, living now in Israel, been brought to the attention of the international community. Most of these Jews left their fortunes behind in Arab countries, and yet no one of international stature made an issue out of their misfortune. It is no surprise, then, to find a growing public responsiveness among the American and West European people toward the Arab Palestinians.

One point that must be clarified: Although Western Europe and Japan may or may not be concerned with the morality of the Arab-Israeli crisis, they are concerned with oil and oil prices. The fact that the Arab states were able to present the Palestinian case in a credible fashion and on a humanitarian basis provided Western Europe and Japan with a perfect pretense for supporting the Palestinian cause.

In the face of all this, one might well ask: What can stop the Arab propagandists from spreading their false protestations of "inhumane" treatment of the Arab Palestinians at the hands of the Israelis when a counteroffensive campaign to put matters into proper perspective continues to be lacking! It is no wonder, therefore, that one finds that the Arab states, supported by the Soviets, continue their onslaught against Israel, taking advantage of every opportunity to discredit Israel in the eyes of the international community.

3. *Uncoordinated versus Coordinated Effort*

The third important aspect of the Israeli public relations crisis is the political and the organizational fragmentation that results in inconsistent and disunified public relations policies. Often conflicting or unclear statements emanate from several Israeli ministers or their subordinates. Often differing statements are made by the Israeli mission to the United States and by the Israeli embassy in Washington and in other important capitals. Finally, the heads of Jewish organizations have added to the overall confusion by filling the pages of scores of newspapers with their often contradictory statements and declarations.

The Israeli settlements in the West Bank, for example, constitute an issue on which there was no agreement among Yitzhak Rabin, Yigal Allon, and Shimon Peres. Each of the three key position holders in the former Israeli government made his views clear: Rabin was ambivalent regarding the settlement of Gush Emonim, the army base in the Samaria region of the West Bank, Allon wanted the settlers to leave, and Peres insisted that they should stay. Not only has Israel been losing credibility, but, worse, Israel has become more vulnerable to the Arab propagandists' assault because of its lack of a unified position among key officials in government regarding important issues. That is not to say, of course, that the Arab states are completely unified in their public relations efforts. However, the one fundamental thing that they all share is their basic position toward Israel. Although there is a vast disparity among Arabs on most other political issues, they have been able to demonstrate a unity when it comes to Israel and matters of national magnitude. The degree of unity among the Arab members of OPEC is an example, Saudi Arabia's disagreement on oil prices notwithstanding.

In addition to the absence of one voice coming from Israeli officials, there are in the United States scores of

Jewish organizations that deal with public relations, directly or indirectly. To mention only a few: the American Jewish Congress, the Conference of Presidents of Major Jewish Organizations, Coordinating Board of Jewish Organizations, National Jewish Community Relations Advisory Council, World Jewish Congress, National Jewish Informational Service for the Propagation of Judaism, B'nai B'rith, American Zionist Federation, and the America Israel Public Affairs Committee.

Although the National Jewish Community Relations Advisory Council has been acting as a center with the prime function of coordinating the public relations effort, the various organizations still, by and large, maintain their traditional independence in this field, a factor that produces a diversity of opinions and approaches. For example, Rabbi Arthur Hertzberg, the president of the American Jewish Congress, explained in 1976 that there are at least three organizations dealing with the Arab boycott problem: the American Jewish Congress, the American Jewish Committee, and the Anti-Defamation League of B'nai B'rith. "A great deal of money is spent; each has legal counsel, research staff, office and clerical help. The polite thing to say would be that the situation is not so bad; but I'll say it outright, that it stinks. Organizations have to show constantly that they are doing something, that they are saving the Jewish people. There is a tendency to jump into a popular problem."

Philip Hochstein, an astute observer of Jewish life, put more of the blame on Jewish organizations. "The problem," he said, "is more in America than Israel. While it is true that the Israelis have been smug and inept about their public relations, the greater part of the problem lies in the defect of the American Jewish community. . . . We have a number of bureaucratized defense organizations that may have rendered important service, in the past, in combating anti-Semitism, especially in combating Nazi propaganda during the early war period before America entered the war. These establishments have been prolonging their existence by championing Israel, but I fear that they have been more successful in perpetuating themselves than in helping Israel."

The PLO situation is another case in point. It is a well-known fact that the official position of the Israeli government is one of never negotiating with the PLO. Yet in the past some members of the Israeli cabinet, among them former Foreign Minister Allon and his Director General Uri Avneri, have more than once announced that Israel should negotiate with any party that recognizes its right to exist as a sovereign state with secure borders. Many other Jewish leaders throughout the world have taken ambivalent positions, supporting Israel's official position, on the one hand, and advocating some sort of dialogue with the PLO, on the other. In fact, numerous high-ranking Jewish and Israeli individuals have met with PLO representatives despite Israel's objections.

This lack of coordinated policy on one of the main problems of the Middle East crisis has been fully exploited by the PLO spokesmen and other Arab propagandists. Although the PLO does not agree on many issues, their representatives have never failed to inform important American and other Western European visitors to the Arab states of their—the PLO's—"moderate" approach versus Israel's intransigence. Simultaneously, PLO officials have capitalized on the disagreement within

Israel and between Israeli and American Jewish leaders. If the official position of the Labor government was against negotiation with the PLO under any circumstances, then that position should have been supported by all the members of the Israeli cabinet. By not adopting a unified approach toward the PLO the Labor government under Rabin could easily be accused of intransigence, particularly since some of its members were prepared to deal with the PLO under certain conditions. Had Israel, however, separated the interests of the Arab Palestinians from those of the PLO it could have readily dismissed the need to negotiate with the PLO—after all, Israel could not be expected to negotiate its own demise.

4. *Defensive versus Offensive*

American public affairs officials have perceived their work as largely defensive in nature, designed to create and promote a credible relationship with the public. Such a relationship, they argue, must be based on the truth, the whole truth. Although one cannot conceive of advocating the willful and demagogic spreading of lies in order to improve one's position, telling the whole truth may hardly be appropriate at times, particularly when one's opponents have already established a consensus among themselves to the contrary. If one waits to be accused of or smeared by unfounded accusations and lies, merely replying with the truth as the main tool for one's defense makes one lose effectiveness, credibility, and momentum. Instead, the truth should be accompanied by an *offensive* counterattack in order to force the opponents to answer charges as well.

To demonstrate the tendency of the public to accept

propagated lies, one should only recall the fact that seventy-four nations accepted the slander that Zionism and racism stand on an equal footing. Before the passage of this resolution in the United Nations, one could say without exaggeration that hundreds of thousands of Jews around the world refused to be directly associated with Zionism. To these Jews, Zionism was simply an unattractive term with which they disliked being identified. In the eyes of these Jews, Zionism as a movement should have ceased to exist immediately upon the establishment of the state of Israel. To these Jews, for the Zionist movement to focus on anything beyond the establishment of Israel, such as mass immigration of Jews to Israel and the plight of Russian Jewry, only places uncalled for burdens on the Jewish communities living in the diaspora.

When the resolution equating Zionism with racism was adopted by the General Assembly, however, many Jews suddenly awoke to a new reality. Because Zionism has always been connected with Judaism they could not escape the repercussions of such a degrading pronouncement and thereby mobilized some of their strength for a limited campaign to tell the *truth* about Zionism—the very truth that they were ashamed to be connected with before.

But for the non-Jews who have committed themselves to the "equation," for whatever reason or consideration, no amount of *post facto* truth could completely reverse their newly found "convictions." (The Mexican government did reverse its position after it became clear that its tourist trade was suffering from the Jewish American ban on travel to Mexico.) Although it is too early to assess the damage that may result from such a resolution, it is certain that the position of many Jewish communities around the world will erode further, particularly the positions of those who are living under totalitarian regimes in Asia, South America, and in the Communist bloc.

Yet if Zionism had been portrayed realistically—as an ideology and a philosophy that promotes social justice, human welfare, and dignity, while seeking a refuge for the Jewish people in their historical and rightful land for which they have paid in blood; and if Jews, especially the ultra-reformed Jewish communities, had truly associated themselves with this concept of Zionism—certainly the Arab onslaught against Zionism would not have taken the course that it did. The successful campaign by well-trained Arab propagandists hit a weak spot in Jewish life and left millions of Jews in shock.

5. *Politics versus Policies*

Because of internal fragmentation and diversity of opinion, Israel so far has not been able to produce a comprehensive plan for resolving the Middle East crisis. In fact, no diplomatic stance adopted by the Labor government has been free from politicking. The government and the parliamentary opposition often fall prey to their eagerness to upstage each other, resulting in the premature disclosure of their diplomatic tactics. In contrast, the Arab states, despite their political, social, and economic instabilities and factional orientations, have been able to demonstrate a capacity for agreement in their disputes with Israel, and a unified approach to their propaganda campaign against Israel. Thus, political gestures proffered by Israel toward the Arab states to demonstrate its good will for the sake of peace and

stability have been turned around by the Arab propagandists and labeled superficial and ill-intended.

To illustrate the lack of diplomatic sophistication on the
part of the former Israeli leadership, one should cite the
offer made by Prime Minister Yitzhak Rabin to Egypt in
February 1975 to surrender the Mitla and Gidi passes,
including the oil fields at Abu Rudais, in exchange for a
nonbelligerency agreement. As Rabin had set the pre-
conditions, Egypt immediately seized the opportunity,
determining not to make any political concessions to
Israel. As a result, Israel was pressured into surrendering
the passes and the oil fields during the final stages of
Kissinger's "shuttle diplomacy" (September 1975). This
agreement became known as the second "interim peace
agreement" with Egypt; yet it was signed without a nonbelligerency clause and without any major political concession on the part of Egypt.

All this is not to say that the interim peace agreement
between Israel and Egypt is a disadvantage to Israel
from the public relations point of view. Rather, the point
is that Israel had lost its bargaining position even before
the start of the bargaining. Having known the extent to
which Israel might concede, Egypt's President Anwar
Sadat was shrewd enough to hold to his position and,
through an intensive propaganda campaign, was able to
portray Israel as *intransigent*, thereby subjecting it to
diplomatic pressure from the international community.
One might add that even United States officialdom accepted the "validity" of Sadat's argument and declared
publicly Israel's intransigence.

One other example that demonstrates the serious weakness in the Israeli perception of policy making and its

conveyance to the public is Israel's announcement in March 1976 of its readiness to surrender vast areas of the Sinai and the West Bank in return for a state of nonbelligerency with all the Arab states. Here again, what should have been a secret, and thereby possibly used as a bargaining tool, was given away by making it public. The former Secretary of State Kissinger's expressed dismay over the matter was not without cause. In negotiating with the Arab states, "convincing" Israel to accept nonbelligerency in return for the surrender of most of the occupied territories is completely different from an agreement announced in advance by Israel.

It is only natural for the Arab states to take advantage once again of this diplomatic weakness by aiming for much higher goals and probably achieving them. After all, that is the essence of bargaining. Arab propagandists have already gone to work and no doubt will further prepare public opinion to pressure Israel for substantial concessions. Untimely disclosure of political flexibility by Israel, *short of a total peace, cannot but be interpreted as weakness by the Arabs and their propagandists.*

Yet some of the Arab states' political maneuvering and propaganda onslaught may have backfired. Representatives of the Arab states seem to have the ability to learn fast. A top Israeli diplomat at the UN explained that the Arabs soon realized that their extreme demands caused revulsion. This was the reason for their low-key approach during 1976–77. In a way, their behavior became more sophisticated, and this is a cause for alarm to Israel. The anti-Israel forces at the UN concluded that Israel could be more effectively isolated by introducing "moderate" resolutions that Israel's traditional allies, namely, the United States and Western Europe, could support.

This new tactic was effectively used by the Egyptians in the debate on the Middle East. The Assembly overwhelmingly adopted a carefully worded Egyptian resolution calling for the reconvening of the Geneva Mideast peace conference. It was approved by a vote of 122–2, with 8 abstentions. Only the United States and Israel voted against it. Israel's isolation, along with the United States, was underscored by the fact that not one European country opposed the resolution and, in fact, most of them supported it. As a result of the vote, Israel and the United States appeared to be against reconvening the Geneva talks, although in reality they supported the resumption of the talks but without the participation of the PLO.

Although the resolution cannot be implemented without the approval of the Security Council, its adoption gave the Arabs and the PLO, which is to head the new state, according to the resolution, a propaganda victory. The status of the PLO, which had been in eclipse because of the civil war in Lebanon, was strengthened as a result of the resolution.

The recent pattern of voting among the nine European countries that in previous years voted in unison on Mideast issues is a cause for concern to Israel. Although in the past all nine voted against anti-Israel resolutions or some of them abstained, there was an erosion in their support for Israel in last year's Assembly session. Only Britain, West Germany, and the Netherlands continued to demonstrate their traditional support for Israel. In June 1977 the West European countries adopted for the first time a united position calling for the establishment of a Palestinian entity as a part of an overall Arab-Israeli peace agreement.

A few months earlier, during the first quarter of 1977, the Arab states began a new peace offensive, portraying themselves as peace seekers and Israel as an opponent of peace. President Sadat, who led the Egyptian peace parade, gained once again.

6. *Availability of Funds and Manpower*

The better financed and the better staffed an organization is, the better chance it has to succeed in performing its task. In this regard, Jewish-Israeli public relations organizations have been unable to match their Arab counterparts in terms of finance and competent manpower. While the Jewish-Israeli side has been relying primarily on limited contributions and volunteer work, the Arab propagandists have demanded and received from their governments an annual budget in excess of $50 million, enabling them to recruit West Europeans, including West Germans, as professional propagandists in an advisory capacity and as field directors. As stated in *The Jerusalem Post*, February 8, 1977, "Thus, the American public can expect to be hearing more and more from the combined and strengthened Arab lobby in Washington. With virtually unlimited petrodollars at their disposal, the Arab states will try to win new friends in America. Israel's supporters know that they must redouble their efforts to get their message across. As diplomatic efforts to resolve the dispute continue this year, the Arab-Israeli propaganda battle in Washington is sure to escalate."

The availability of funds has also afforded the Arab propagandists the opportunity to penetrate financially troubled institutions and consequently exert influence. For example, the Arab League has established a five-year propaganda plan "to sell the American people on the idea that the Palestinian and Jerusalem issues—and not the Arabs' rejection of Israel's right to exist—are the crux of the Middle East conflict," the Anti-Defamation League of B'nai B'rith disclosed. And details of a $45 million a year Arab "master plan" designed to indoctrinate the American people have also been disclosed.

The Arabs and their supporters in the United States have divided their campaign into six separate but loosely coordinated components:

1) The various organizations representing Arab Americans;

2) The official representatives of the Arab governments and the Arab League;

3) The oil companies, especially the *Aramco* members, that have actively supported the Arab cause;

4) The pro-Arab research groups;

5) The humanitarian groups that raise funds for Palestinian refugees;

6) The well-paid lawyers and public relations consultants hired by Arab governments to represent Arab interests. (*Jerusalem Post*, February 8, 1977)

Says Dr. Ghada Talhami, the director of the Arab Information Center (AIC) in Chicago: "After decades of silence and inactivity, Arab Americans are beginning to organize to change United States attitudes toward Arabs and to tell their story. . . . No longer does the Arab in America strive to maintain a low ethnic profile."

While the expenditure of funds cannot as yet be pinpointed, the Anti-Defamation League disclosed that there is evidence of an increasing flow of funds to American campuses where there are more than 25,000 Moslem students, half of them from the Arab world.

Observing that educational institutions, their students, and faculties are priority targets of the Arab propaganda campaign, Arnold Forster, ADL's general counsel and associate director, pointed out: "The Organization of Arab Students, which appeared to be moribund, has been revived, its units in various parts of the country reactivated and a new O.A.S. periodical—'The Arab Student Bulletin'—published and distributed from its new headquarters in East Lansing, Michigan." (*Near East Report,* June 9, 1976)

Against this background of "money power," Jewish-Israeli public relations people have been unable to generate enough financial support from either the various Jewish organizations or from the state of Israel, resulting in the limited recruitment of qualified personnel. Although hundreds of millions of dollars are being spent by Jews on local Jewish and Israeli needs, the public relations campaign has been neglected by both Israel and the Jewish leadership in various countries, especially in the United States. It is this financial deficiency that accounts to a great extent for the Jewish-Israeli public relations setback.

A Suggested Solution

What is to be done? *Public relations and propaganda are among the most formidable tools used during war or peace.* Winning the public support of the international community is of foremost importance; no party to any crisis, whether right or wrong, can afford to ignore this reality. Israel has been lagging behind; it has lost important ground and stands to lose a great deal more, especially in the wake of the insurmountable amount of petrodollars that the Arabs have put to use in promoting their interests.

Suitable measures, severe as they may be, must be adopted, including the transformation of an existing organization to perform this task. The America Israel Public Affairs Committee (AIPAC) may be the most suitable. Such an organization should include representatives of Jewish leadership worldwide. It should be empowered to conduct a public relations campaign while receiving *proper* and *timely* guidelines from Israel and feedback from numerous and widespread Jewish organizations. This reconstructed entity should be financed primarily by the state of Israel and to a lesser extent by Jewish and non-Jewish philanthropies. For the following reasons it should not be engaged directly or indirectly in any fund-raising activities of its own: 1) There is already an abundance of Jewish organizations that are geared to the task of fund raising. 2) The financing of the new organization by others will discourage it from going out on its own and spending additional sums for public relations purposes, such as is the case now, and, finally, 3) The new organization should concentrate all of its efforts on public relations work and not be troubled with financing.

Among other things, this agency should be responsible for: (1) the recruitment of qualified public relations men and women from all ethnic backgrounds; (2) the coordination of policies and decisions on tactics and strategies; (3) the creation and upgrading of a national speakers' bureau geared to non-Jewish audiences; (4) the dissemination of information and reports to the news media; and (5) the publication of a weekly bulletin, reflecting a unified approach, to be mailed to all major institutions and prominent individuals, especially non-Jews.

Adequate budget funds must be allocated. Budgeting and finances will have to be determined on the basis of need and of circumstance.

The reconstructed AIPAC will not replace local Jewish organizations such as JCRC, ADL, American Jewish Committee, and so forth but will constitute an overall supervisory agency, serving as a clearinghouse when a consensus is needed, providing uniformity, finances, competent manpower, and general guidance.

These suggestions are not by any means complete, but they do offer some guidelines for today's new requirements. Unless some new approaches are immediately adopted, Israel and the Jewish community will soon find themselves isolated and on the defensive, answering false charges rather than attacking injustices.

Israeli and Jewish leaders throughout the diaspora must therefore take a fresh look at the overall situation, reexamine the rules of this new cold war, and begin to work harmoniously. Whatever these efforts may entail, they must be undertaken. Leaders who underestimate the crucial importance of timely and effective public relations will be the first to fall victim to their shortsightedness.

Finally, in the words of Philip Hochstein: "The relationship between Israel and the Jewish community has been one of the blind leading the blind. We in America want the Israelis to be our surrogates in leading a Jewish life, and the Israelis want us to be their magic rubber stamps. Neither is likely to survive without the other; yet their intercommunication could hardly be more misleading."

VI

ISRAELI-U.S. RELATIONS: MISPERCEPTIONS AND PROSPECTS

FOR the most part, the relationship between the United States and Israel has been stable over the years. Such stability has been possible primarily because both countries share the same ideological and political philosophies and have a mutuality of interest in the economic and strategic spheres. Although American-Israeli friendship remains basically sound, recent developments in the Middle East have pressured each side into reassessing its policies and taking a clearer stance vis-à-vis the other.

On the one hand, the political fragmentation and the diversity of political views that exist in Israel are raising serious questions about the country's ability to produce a coherent policy that can form the basis for a permanent settlement in the Middle East. In addition, Israel has become more dependent on the United States politically, economically, and militarily. On the other hand, the strategic needs of the United States are changing in the post-Vietnam era. American officials view the volatile situation in the Middle East with growing concern and are questioning the Israelis' wisdom in handling their affairs.

In view of these changes, several questions are raised that warrant some thoughtful answers: 1) What is the basis of the American commitment to Israel, and how is this commitment perceived by United States officials in relation to America's political needs? 2) How does one reconcile Israel's growing economic and military dependence on the United States with Israel's own political interests that diverge from those of the United States? 3) Is the United States government's moral commitment to the survival of Israel consistent with its moral obligations to the American people? How does this commitment conform with America's perception of peace in the Middle East? 4) Are the new political and economic realities in the Middle East consistent with Israel's continued dependence? 5) What are the prospects for future American-Israeli relations? 6) And, finally, what are the imperatives of the United States-Israeli relationship? What are the policy choices that will not only ensure the continuation of a special relationship between the two countries but will secure a just and lasting peace in the Middle East?

As I shall attempt to argue, a deep and lasting United States-Israeli friendship is the absolute prerequisite of a final peace. In turn, the prospects for friendship will depend ultimately on the United States and Israel's ability *to coordinate their efforts*. Both countries *must reach a complete understanding on all critical issues* concerning national security, national borders, and the Arab Palestinians.

The Basis of the American Commitment to Israel

Since Israel was established in 1948, the United States has been a most enthusiastic supporter and a permanent friend. The American-Israeli special relationship was at first predicated on the American sense of duty toward the dispersed and persecuted Jews, particularly after the horror of the Second World War. The Truman Administration felt morally committed to the Jewish nationalist aspirations for statehood. This moral obligation, with its historical basis in the period 1942–52, remained the cornerstone of the United States commitment to the preservation of the state of Israel.

A new dimension was added to the United States support of Israel when it became clear to the American government between 1952 and 1955 that Israel could play an important role on behalf of the United States in the Middle East. New developments were rapidly evolving in this period: the rise of Nasser in Egypt, the arms deal between Egypt and Czechoslovakia, the nationalization of the Suez Canal, and the Russian commitment to build the Aswan Dam. (It should be added parenthetically that the democratic nature of the Israeli political system was an extra factor in Israel's favor that accelerated the process of improved relations with the United States. The relationship was essentially predicated on the American moral commitment and strategic interests.) Over the years the United States has maintained close ties with many authoritarian and nondemocratic countries, such as Saudi Arabia, Jordan, South Korea, Iran, Vietnam, and various Latin American nations, as long as there existed mutual economic or strategic interests. The truth of the matter is that since World War II the United States as a global power has used its political influence and military power for the purpose of maintaining stability and continuity around the world regardless of the nature of the political systems with which it allied.

Very few Israeli leaders grasped the full implications of their relationship with the United States. As early as 1953, when it became clear that the Soviet Union was moving toward supporting the Arab states at the expense of Israel, Israel was unable to translate this political setback with the Soviets into new gains in its relationship with the United States.

Israel was faced with both a dilemma and an opportunity. The dilemma was how to reconcile its loss of Soviet support in the face of intensified Arab radicalism, and the opportunity was how to use its new role as a promoter and protector of American interests in the entire region. There was no specific time in which Israel was confronted with this dilemma and opportunity. The situation evolved as early as 1950 and was completed in 1955 with the arms deal between Egypt and Czechoslovakia. Israel failed to realize that there was an opportunity that could allow it *to play a dominant role in the Middle East as an ally and a protector of United States interests* and to be recognized as such by the American people.

Since 1955 Israel's growing dependency on American political, economic, and military support has been explained to the American people on the basis of America's commitment to Israel's survival and not on the basis of the important role that Israel has played (and continues to play) on behalf of American strategic and economic interests. These interests, accepted by American leaders regardless of their party affiliations, include: 1) continuing Israeli adherence to United States dictates; 2) maintaining the balance of power in the Middle East; 3) containing Soviet influence in the region, and most recently, 4) gaining leverage with the Arab states through the substantial United States influence over Israel.

Israel's Dependence on the United States

The growing dependence of Israel on the United States has become a source of alarm to many Israelis as well as to American officials. On the one hand, the United States feels compelled to continue its traditional support of Israel, although there are naturally some divergent interests between the two countries. On the other hand, Israel, faced with growing Arab military and economic power, has become significantly dependent on the United States for its survival. Despite the negative repercussions that dependency leads to, the United States actively pursued, and Israel could not prevent, policies that resulted in Israel's rising dependence.

A brief historical survey will show that United States actions and initiatives clearly encouraged such dependence. The debacle of the Sinai Campaign in 1956, for example, illustrates the extent of Israeli subordination to the United States. The Eisenhower Administration's threat to impose economic sanctions against Israel unless it agreed to surrender to Egypt all of the then-occupied territory proved effective. It reminded Israel's leaders that their country was vulnerable and dependent on United States economic aid. The Sinai episode made

Israel a protectorate of the United States, and from that time on, Israel has been unable to exercise political freedom on any major issue that also substantially affects American interests in the region.

American arms deliveries and financial support (1956–67) were the main factors that contributed to Israel's "lightning victory" of 1967. Israeli retention of the occupied territories between 1967 and 1973 was possible primarily because the United States did not demand their return. Arms deliveries to Israel during 1973 were managed in such a way as to heighten Israeli independence on the United States. As Israel turned the tide of the war in 1973, it was again the United States that denied the Israeli forces total victory over the Egyptians. And in the recovery period since the October war of 1973, Israel has become even more dependent on United States financial and military assistance.

All American presidents since 1948 have affirmed the United States commitment to Israel. In 1967 and 1973 Presidents Johnson and Nixon challenged the Soviet Union to halt actual moves against Israel. Even during the last two months of the Ford Administration, as political analysts wrote about the "eroding U.S.-Israel relationship," President Ford went on record to reconfirm the United States commitment. During a dinner with the American Jewish Committee in May 1976, he stated that "while America must and will preserve friendship with all nations, this will never be done at the expense of America's commitment to Israel." He assured the audience that "our commitment to Israel will meet the test of American steadfastness and resolve." Significantly, former President Ford made the strongest statement ever made by any

United States president when he said, "America will remain the ultimate guarantor of Israel's freedom."

The American Congress has been even more supportive of Israel than have the last five presidents. A majority of senators and congressmen have promised their unrelenting support for Israel. For example, Congressman Morris Udall of Arizona, in his 1976 bid for the Democratic presidential nomination, explained his support for Israel in the following way: "The U.S. has a deep commitment to the security and integrity of Israel. That commitment is soundly based, I believe, on an objective assessment of our own national interests. Israel is the only functioning democracy and fully dependable ally of the U.S. in one of the most crucial and unstable regions of the globe. Above and beyond that, we have a moral tie with Israel that extends all the way back to our role in her establishment in 1948. It is in our own political and ethical interest to strengthen that tie in the years ahead."

Senator Frank Church told a Jewish audience on March 3, 1975 that "Our support of Israel is not a sentimental matter; it is a matter of our own national interest." President Jimmy Carter vowed, "My prime commitment as president would be to the preservation of the state of Israel. I would provide whatever economic and military aid is necessary to permit Israel to defend itself against any foreseeable attack. America's commitment to Israel should be unshakeable."

In conclusion, the problems of Israel's increased dependence are not necessarily based on fears of a change of mood or attitude on the part of the United States. Rather a heightened dependence and an absolute commitment by the United States to the preservation of the state of Israel raise questions as to whether Israel has become a United States satellite and, for all practical purposes, has lost its political independence.

Moral Obligation and National Interest

It is not easy to prove whether erosion has taken place in the relationship between Israel and the United States because of either minor misunderstandings or major policy divergences. Regardless of denials emanating from Washington and Jerusalem, there are serious differences as to what the next step should be in untangling the deadlock in Arab-Israeli affairs. In addition, many American officials, despite their pronouncements of total moral commitment to Israel, believe that times have changed and that the present interests of the United States in the Middle East are being adversely affected by Israel's stance. The American government, regardless of political party, faces vexing questions of morality and national interest. Political theorist Sidney Hook captured the essence of the difficulty of dealing with these issues. "It should be clear that every troubled situation of moral choices is one in which the choice is not between good or bad, right or wrong, but between good and good, right and right. . . . One good may be overridden by a greater good, one obligation by a more pressing one." ("Intelligence, Morality and Foreign Policy," *New York Times*, May 1, 1976)

Many American and Israeli observers are sounding some concern about the long-term strength of moral commitments. They cite recent examples of moral deterioration that has swept a majority of nations: the equating of Zionism with racism, the granting of observer status to the PLO at the UN, the indifference of the international community toward the civil war in Lebanon. The United States was not involved in any of these acts. But whenever morality is cast aside for the sake of political and economic expediency, the past promises and future intentions of any nation are in doubt. The questioning of commitments is particularly serious when one's very survival is at stake.

In an attempt to dispel the doubts of those concerned with the durability of the United States commitment to Israel, Dr. Kissinger, in his address before the American Jewish Congress in April 1976, explained the concept of moral commitment: "Tension is unavoidable between moral values, which are invariably cast in absolute terms, and efforts to achieve them, which of necessity involve compromise." He went on to say that "Morality without pragmatic action is empty, just as pragmatism without moral direction is like a rudderless ship. For Americans foreign policy has always been more than a search for stability. Americans have a vision of a world of justice that drives all our efforts. . . . Our responsibility to conduct a moral, farsighted and realistic policy has grown in recent years." In this context the former secretary of state reaffirmed that "the survival and the security of Israel are unequivocal and permanent moral commitments of the United States. Israel is a loyal friend and a fellow democracy, whose very existence represents the commitment of all free people." Kissinger concluded his remarks by stating, "We will never abandon Israel, either by failing to provide crucial assistance or by misconceived or separate negotiations or by irresolution when challenged to meet our own responsibility to maintain the global balance of power."

Philosopher and theologian Michael Novack characterized the moral side of Israeli-United States relations in a
more decisive fashion in the March 1975 issue of *Com-
monweal*: "Our self-interest in Israel is pre-eminently
moral . . . a betrayal of Israel would be worse than
Munich in 1938; it would leave life in the United States
without moral savor."

However, the Israelis are generally unwilling to gamble
their future on those arguments. After all, it can be easily
maintained that America's greater moral obligation is to
itself, and if, for example, selling advanced weapons to
the Arab states serves American interests, then that practice should continue. Senator Henry Jackson (D–Washington) opposes this reasoning: "For practical considerations
of the military balance and for moral reasons as well, I
believe that we cannot continue the present policy of
profligate military support to those countries whose pledge
to continue the war with Israel makes them candidates
for a new round of aggression." Senator James Abourezk
(D–South Dakota) warns that "We cannot continue to
support both sides militarily; with the United States and
the Soviet Union sending arms to Middle East countries,
it can only lead to an enormous and dangerous buildup."

While this debate over the basis for and the extent of
the United States commitment to Israel continues, the
political realities in the Middle East are rapidly changing,
almost daily. For example: 1) the United States has a
growing interest in the Arab investment or "recycling" of
petrodollars; 2) United States-Arab trade is accelerating;
3) the Arab states are stockpiling modern armaments with
all the implications for leverage and warfare that this entails; 4) the United States is gaining a deeper foothold in

Egypt and is working to influence other Arab states in the region. In this evolving setting American and Israeli policymakers are called on to reassess and redefine their interests and policies for the future. The years ahead may require changes in national priorities based on these new developments and alignments among the participants.

New Realities and Dependency

In order to understand what factors might motivate the United States to reassess its policies in the Middle East, some mention should be made of the basis for American interest in that region, given the new realities in the region and Israeli dependency.

First, the American people would like to see a permanent peace settlement in the Middle East. The general consensus is that a solution of the Arab-Israeli crisis is necessary, even at the expense of returning all of the occupied territories to the Arabs. On the particular issue of territory, there is a fundamental difference between the position of Israel and that of the United States. The United States believes that a return of most of the occupied territory will open an avenue leading to a peaceful settlement, whereas Israel believes that the Arab-Israeli crisis essentially is a matter of the Arabs' accepting Israel in principle as a sovereign state and that the Palestinian problem and all territorial questions are of secondary importance. What further aggravates United States-Israeli relations is the establishment of more Israeli settlements in some of the occupied territories. The United States views these activities as a serious obstacle to peace.

One American intellectual (Noam Chomsky, professor of linguistics at M.I.T.) has gone so far as to say: "If the situation continues as it is with a permanent military confrontation and with Israel continuing to settle the occupied region, then in effect Israel is signing its death warrant."

Second, Israel perceives its very survival as being in danger, maintaining that total dependence on the United States for military, economic, and political aid leaves very little political flexibility with which to approach the Arab states. More specifically, Israel does not believe that its relationship with the United States is being reciprocated and believes that the Arabs sense not only a certain weakness in Israeli-United States relations that is inherent in dependency but are taking full advantage of it.

The United States believes that its particular interests in the Middle East dictate the pursuit of several interrelated objectives: (a) preventing a new round of Arab-Israeli warfare that could involve a confrontation with the Soviet Union; (b) preventing renewed instability in the Middle East that would give Russia a new opportunity to exploit; (c) preventing new oil embargoes that would disrupt economic relations with Western Europe and Japan as well as damage American industry; (d) preventing an increased burden on the American economy that renewed hostilities would aggravate; (e) encouraging trade with the oil-rich Arab states that in 1975 exceeded $10 billion; (f) encouraging the normalization of relations between Egypt and the United States that is considered of high priority; and (g) maintaining relative stability in the price of oil that has a direct effect on the economic recovery of the Western Hemisphere, Europe, and Japan. The United States is striving to maintain momentum and ensure stabilization in the Middle East in the hope that the radical Arab states (Syria, Libya, Algeria, Iraq) will find it in their interests to prefer ties with the West to confrontation.

The United States believes that pursuing these seven objectives will not only not be detrimental to Israel's survival but will be in the interest of all parties concerned. In the words of former UN Ambassador Charles W. Yost, "We must continue to support both sides. Our primary interest is to prevent the outbreak of new hostilities. We must help both sides in order to maintain our credibility and our friendship with both sides."

Third, Israel sees itself involved in a situation of permanent war—a war for survival. Israel does not perceive its disagreement with the Arab states as peripheral in nature but as the central confrontation in which there can be only one victim—Israel. Despite heavy losses that Israel might be able to inflict on the Arab states in the case of a major war, the Arab armies and economies cannot be totally destroyed. But one cannot say the same for Israel. It is for this reason that Israel cannot treat the question of survival in a sanguine way. The uncomfortable question must be raised: To what extremes will America go to ensure the national survival of any other country, including Israel? If the existence of Israel is deemed desirable, what measures will the United States take in its defense in an age when nuclear attack makes the sudden death of entire cultures possible?

Many American officials maintain that the United States commitment to Israel does not contradict the new realities of the Middle East. The United States needs a strong and viable friend such as Israel, a fellow democracy to depend on. These officials, among them President

Carter and his Secretary of State Cyrus Vance, believe that United States policy in the Middle East is consistent with its commitment to Israel and that mutual trust and confidence will undoubtedly prevail despite differences in national interests.

The new realities of the Middle East are not similarly perceived by other knowledgeable individuals such as former Secretary of Defense James K. Schlesinger. In a speech before the seventeenth annual policy conference of the America Israel Public Affairs Committee on May 4, 1976, Mr. Schlesinger, speaking of the Ford Administration, stated: "The part that most concerns me is the *undermining of the moral basis of our support for the state of Israel.* And that, of course, is reflected in parallel tactics that were employed in earlier times by us in our negotiations in Southeast Asia. There has been a tendency to place the blame for nonprogress, slow progress of negotiations on Israel, to assert that stagnation is bad, that momentum and progress are good, and that failure to achieve momentum is a direct consequence of Israeli intransigence. The finger of blame has been pointed at Israel."

Mr. Schlesinger, who has since become energy chief in the Carter Administration, continues to believe that the United States interest in the Middle East has actually been strengthened, not weakened, by Israel's political and military posture. Today, more than ever before, the United States needs Israel. "So I turn to the strategic significance of Israel, of growing importance in terms of worldwide balance, in large degree an importance that is symbolic, a barometer of United States intentions. And that symbolic importance has increased as the posture of the United

States has decayed and the question of American stead-fastness has increasingly arisen in the wake of our diffi-culties in Southeast Asia, Africa, and our domestic cohesion. Because of that significance of Israel has his-torically grown, and today Israel and American sup-port of Israel is taken as an indicator of American steadfastness."

In summary, several conclusions can be drawn. These conclusions will also form the basis for examining future Israel-United States relations.

First: It would seem that as the power of the Arab countries grows, America's interests in the Middle East are defined increasingly in economic terms. Therefore, moral commitments (such as that to Israel) may have to be reexamined in order to adjust America's commitments to its interests.

Second: Israel's increasing political, economic, and military dependence on the United States has reached a dangerous point—a situation that has not yet been recon-ciled with America's interests in the Arab world. With normal and friendly relations lacking between the Arab states and Israel, any improved relations between the Arab states and the United States will have to be, at least to a certain extent, at the expense of the relationship between Israel and the United States. Israel's dependence on the United States affords the latter the opportunity to move closer to the Arab states at the expense of Israel, without risking Israel's friendship in the process.

Third: The United States has never accepted the idea that Israel should retain any sizable part of the occupied territory, except for "cosmetic" changes. The United States views Israel's policy of settling even larger areas of the occupied territory as a serious obstacle to peace, endangering the momentum toward peace that was generated after the second interim settlement with Egypt in September 1975. The United States considers this territorial aspect of the Arab-Israeli crisis the most important; consequently, the Carter Administration resolved not to allow this obstacle to hinder future peace negotiations regardless of Israel's sensitivity.

Fourth: The element of time is not working in Israel's favor. Israel's chances for economic recovery in the next three to four years do not seem very good. If numbers, whether in terms of dollars, military equipment, or manpower, have any meaning in the Middle East crisis, then the odds are against Israel. As time goes on, the cards in the hands of the Arabs (as President Sadat of Egypt has said) are improving. There is no reason to believe that Israeli economic or military power will reach such proportions in the near future as to render Israel totally independent of the United States. The international political trends and the present balance of power between East and West further indicate that Israel will be further locked into United States defenses and on American terms.

Fifth: Domestic politics in Israel and the United States are not conducive to the continuation of the present ambiguous situation. Israel, on the one hand, is politically fragmented and continues to depend on a coalition government in which no consensus has been reached regarding the occupied territories. The American people and the Congress are still haunted by the tragedy of United States intervention in Vietnam. The American public generally does not take the time to differentiate between the role

that Israel is playing in support of United States interests in the Middle East and the role that South
Vietnam was supposed to have played in Southeast Asia.
American officials generally do not speak of the vital
importance of Israel to American economic, political, and
strategic interests. Israel has usually been portrayed as
a United States protectorate, not as a full-fledged ally
deserving American support. Economic and military aid
to Israel is often begrudged as a heavy burden on the
American economy instead of viewed as an integral part
of America's defense budget.

Sixth, and finally: Dr. Kissinger's impact on United
States foreign policy will undoubtedly continue to be
felt for many years after his retirement. He set the tone
for United States long-range policies. Regardless of the
political affiliation of the administration, it is unlikely
that any considerable change will take place in American
foreign policy in general or toward Israel in particular.
Israel will continue to be perceived as an "expensive
friend" but, unfortunately, few public statements will
explain the advantages of such a friendship. This is not
to say that the administration is preparing the American
public for the renunciation of Israel, for Carter's commitment to the survival of Israel is unshakeable and irrevocable. By the same token, however, the Carter Administration is preparing Israel to settle for much less. The
danger of United States involvement in another Middle
East war is almost always mentioned in the same breath
as the danger of a possible confrontation with the Soviet
Union with all its perilous implications. In other words,
the United States has resolved not to allow Israel to
be the instigator of a possible thermonuclear war. Whether

such a contention is made for effect alone or because it is believed that there is some validity to it is hardly relevant. The American people will continue to view renewed hostilities in the Middle East with apprehension.

Relationship in Prospect

The critical question of where the United States-Israeli relationship is heading occupies concerned quarters on both sides. To answer this question, we must examine the basic misperceptions that exist between the two countries and suggest what must be done to rectify the situation.

It is the contention of this writer that if there is a slowdown in the movement toward a peaceful settlement between Israel and the Arab states, it is at least in part attributable to the lack of agreement between the United States and Israel concerning what constitutes the basic principles of an Arab-Israeli peace.

The Arab states and Israel agree that the United States is the major, if not the only, power that can influence both sides to make necessary concessions. Both sides also agree that the United States, through the efforts of former Secretary of State Kissinger, has been able to gain the confidence of each and has created momentum for the continuation of negotiations. In addition, the United States itself feels compelled (because of vital interests in the region) to continue its efforts to achieve peace between the contending parties while there is still some momentum left.

The United States has felt frustrated in its recent efforts to move the parties to a closer position. This failure, as indicated before, has been largely attributed, according to one State Department specialist, to "Israeli intransigence." Israel's policies in the occupied areas are deemed to contradict the United States vision of a peaceful settlement. William Scranton, former United States Ambassador to the UN, opened his debut speech by asserting that the United States considered Israel's policy of settling the occupied territories a serious obstacle to peace. The State Department, when subsequently questioned about the matter, replied that there was nothing new in Ambassador Scranton's speech. This, after all, was United States policy since the Israeli occupation of these territories in 1967, and there is no reason to assume that the Carter Administration has a different view on the subject. Yet the United States has done very little if anything since 1967 to pressure Israel into returning these territories. Between 1967 and 1972 the United States was preoccupied with the war in Vietnam. The Middle East was then going through a period of relative tranquillity. After the stunning victory in 1967, Israel was beginning to feel almost independent of any American and Arab pressure to change the status quo. The Arab states were busy rebuilding their defeated armies and just beginning to grasp the economic and, consequently, the political power that their "black gold" was to confer on them.

As the war in Vietnam wound down at the end of 1972, and the (U.S. Secretary of State William P.) Rogers Plan to implement an interim agreement between Israel and Egypt failed to achieve a breakthrough, developments began to accelerate in the Middle East, culminating in the Yom Kippur War of October 1973. It was only then that the United States took a new, hard look at the whole situation in the Middle East, a festering conflict that had brought the country twice, in 1967 and 1973, to the brink of a direct confrontation with the Soviet Union. The year 1973, therefore, was a turning point; the United States determined then to bring the Arab-Israeli war to an end—a peaceful end that would require great sacrifices from both the Arab states and Israel.

Israel, on the one hand, faced the dilemma of surrendering tangible territory considered vital to its security and hence its survival—in exchange for intangible Arab concessions, mostly political in nature, that might be revoked at any time.

The Arab states, on the other hand, could not offer anything more than their acceptance of Israel's right to exist, in effect renouncing the long-held idea of ejecting the Jewish state from their midst. Their acceptance of coexistence with Israel was and still is conditional on Israel's total surrender of all territories and Israel's recognition of the right of the Arab Palestinians to have a home of their own.

In sum, although both sides have indeed come closer than ever before in terms of their professed peaceful intentions, what has been lacking is a decisive role by the mediator—the United States—to bring both sides one step closer and compel them to define their vague intentions.

What should have followed after the second interim peace with Egypt in September 1975 was the formulation by Israel and the United States of a cohesive peace plan with mutually shared objectives. *Israel-United States understanding and agreement have become fundamental* to any new peace initiative in the Middle East. The United

States and Israel must develop a comprehensive plan according to which all problems of territory, security, and economics would be settled. The Arabs fully understand and appreciate Israel's dependence on the United States. They are also aware of the fact that the United States has never overtly or tacitly expressed a sentiment that would support Israel's retention of substantial parts of the occupied territories.

The United States government has reaffirmed time and again that an ultimate solution of the Arab-Israeli crisis must be based on UN Resolutions 242 and 338, adopted after the wars of 1967 and 1973. Both resolutions call on Israel to withdraw from the occupied territories to secure borders and declare that all nations in the area must respect one another's sovereignty. Israel and the Arab states accepted the resolutions at the time, but difficulties arose from the clause that urged Israel to withdraw to secure borders, for the Arab states maintain that "secure borders" mean essentially the 1967 lines. (See the full text of Resolutions 242 and 338, Appendixes 6 and 7.)

Because the United States government views Resolutions 242 and 338 as the basis for any future Middle East peace negotiation, the first order of the day should be the removal of all ambiguities from these two resolutions, and the exact interpretation of each clause should be resolved. Such an agreement between the United States and Israel will constitute one of the main requisites for peace in the Middle East. It would therefore be imperative that the United States and Israel reach a clear understanding on these critical issues and thereby avoid any possible misperceptions in the future.

It should be clear to Israeli as well as to American

officials that *insofar as the Arab states perceive any schism between the United States and Israel, they will find it to their advantage to maintain their hard line.* After all, time is working in their favor; they stand to gain in economic and political strength as time goes on, slowly compelling the United States once again to reassess its policies toward the Middle East. There is no doubt that the reassessment of United States policies in the Middle East, which the Ford Administration undertook between April and July 1975, rendered a serious blow to Israeli prestige and policy independence. By July 1975, the United States was ready to exert further pressures on Israel and compel it to accept the second Sinai accord with Egypt two months later. The United States position was not necessarily adopted out of friendship for Egypt nor out of dislike for Israel; Washington believed that an agreement would be in the best interests of all parties concerned, and indeed it proved to be so. Yet the way in which the whole process of negotiation evolved at the time cast heavy shadows on Israel and made it appear intransigent and, in the end, wholly dependent on United States good will.

Dependency and Choices

Israel's dependence on the United States cannot be viewed as temporary and transitional. United States policies in the Middle East have generally been directed toward subjecting the Arab states and Israel to greater United States influence, the aim being to achieve greater stability and thereby reduce Soviet influence while protecting other American interests. Israel's increased dependency on the United States, therefore, has been encouraged by United States officials. Israel, misguided by some of its own leaders, was forced to fight the Yom Kippur War that resulted in a formidable number of losses—an outcome that made it even more dependent than before on United States supplies and good will. The seven good years that followed the 1967 Six Day War, during which Israel was able to exercise some political independence, ended, and partial dependence on the United States became absolute. The future does not seem to hold much better prospects for Israel's political independence. What choices does Israel have, given the reality of dependence?

Marking Time

Some Israeli circles believe that once the present economic hardship passes, Israel will be in a much better position to say "no" to the United States. This notion, advocated by Yitzhak Rabin, does not seem to rest on solid ground. As former Israeli Foreign Minister Abba Eban put it: "I don't see how it will be better for us later on. Economically I don't think we will be less dependent on the United States. Even the most optimistic view about our economic recovery doesn't create a picture of improvement within that period. Also the Arab monetary power is only beginning to make itself felt. We ought to grasp the central issues now and involve the U.S. in resolving them. Before the 1973 war there were really three options: one could move forward to peace, backward to war, or mark time. Since 1973 the third option is out."

Other than moving forward to peace under the auspices of the United States, the ultimate guarantor of Israel's security (according to former President Ford), other options will not produce a permanent solution, and some may even produce a far more perilous situation.

Nuclear Weapons as a Deterrent

One such perilous choice includes nuclear weapons. This option is being advocated by Robert W. Tucker, professor of international relations at Johns Hopkins University. Professor Tucker maintains that Israel's precarious situation between dependence on the United States and Arab intransigence leaves very little room to exercise the flexibility needed to ensure its survival.

The acquisition of nuclear weapons by Israel would have deterrent value only if it became a *known* factor, that is, if the Arabs were aware of their existence. However, arms races escalate, and it would seem only logical and imperative for the Arab states to follow suit and obtain similar weapons in order to maintain the balance of power. No nation since the end of World War II has resorted to nuclear weapons when the option of employing conventional weapons was available. The possession of nuclear weapons by the United States, France, the Soviet Union, and others did not prevent wars in Vietnam, Korea, and the Middle East where the United States was involved directly or indirectly. Neither Israel nor the Arab states is likely to use nuclear weapons except as a last resort. Therefore, how would the acquisition of nuclear weapons reduce Israel's dependence on the United States for economic aid and conventional military hardware? It would not. And what would prevent the various terrorist movements from intensifying their activities in Israel?

To be sure, the employment of nuclear weapons in the Middle East as a means of preventing war would be inconsistent with Israel's strategic needs. The acquisition of nuclear weapons by Israel would not prevent a renewed conventional war with the Arab states—a continuous war that would drain Israel of its economic and military resources. Such a war of attrition could be maintained almost indefinitely until such time as the Arab states acquire nuclear weapons of their own. In such an eventuality, neither side would have a decisive advantage. Therefore, as Winston Churchill put it, there must be options other than being subjected to the horror of "a balance of terror." The Arab states surely do not want to annihilate Israel if that act would foreclose the possibility that a new Palestinian society could function normally in its place. By the same token, Israel would not be able to destroy the entire Arab world or the greater part of it without facing repercussions that would far outweigh its "gain." In short, neither the Arab states nor Israel will be able to inflict serious damage on the other without the fear of being subjected to a counterattack and, consequently, to unacceptable damage. For these reasons, a far more perilous situation would emerge if both the Arab states and Israel were to start to build stockpiles of nuclear weapons.

Conclusion

The intricacies of the Arab-Israeli crisis and its volatility make it extremely difficult to deal separately with its various components. The Arab states, the Soviet Union, Israel, the United States, the PLO, and the Arab Palestinians all have very high stakes in the Middle East. It is important to remember that seldom has there been such a steady, harmonious, friendly relationship between two states as has existed between the United States and Israel. Regardless of all the reasons that help to sustain United States-Israeli friendship, the most formidable force holding the two countries together is a genuine commitment to the preservation of dignity and the freedom of man. Ultimately only American consistency in the pursuit of these values can ensure Israel's freedom. Only through a conscious awareness of their mutual needs, interests, and values can the United States and Israel bring about a lasting and just peace in the Middle East. Regardless of how much influence the Soviet Union may have in the Middle East, regardless of how disruptive Arab radical forces may be, *full agreement between the United States and Israel on all pending issues is the absolute prerequisite of a negotiated settlement among Israel, the Arab states, and the Palestinians.*

Many political observers of the Middle East scene believe that the visit of President Sadat of Egypt to Israel (November 1977) and the subsequent face-to-face meeting between Israel and Egypt have made the United States' role as mediator only a marginal one. While this political assessment may appear to be correct, in reality, however, it is not. The United States role will remain extremely important, especially when the Arabs and the Israelis begin to negotiate the real problems that separate them, namely those of the Arab Palestinians and the surrender of important parts of the territories presently under Israeli control. The U.S. relationship with Israel will undoubtedly be put once again to the test of time.

VII

WORLD JEWRY
AND ISRAEL

A^S Israel approaches the thirtieth anniversary of its establishment in 1948, a review of Israel's relationship with its most loyal and ardent supporters, world Jewry, is appropriate and, in fact, essential. Such a review is necessary because after almost thirty years of statehood, misperceptions involving the two have developed. Clear and open dissent has been surfacing on both sides, raising important questions regarding the very nature and the ultimate prospects of the Israeli-world Jewry relationship.

Although Jewish scholars and Jewish leaders from both sides do not question the importance of a spirited and close relationship, they do argue against the means usually employed in the process of maintaining that partnership. The argument goes more or less in the following fashion:

1) Because the interdependence of the two sides is so

deeply rooted, it is important to put into proper perspective all the tenets that constitute the foundations of Israeli-world Jewry relations, for only through the manifestation of these basic tenets can both sides look forward to an even greater collaboration in the future and, therefore, to a more successful partnership.

2) Because conditions in the Middle East are of such great concern to the four nations in which the bulk of world Jewry resides (United States, Britain, Russia, France) and from which Israel expects the greater part of support in terms of money and manpower, it behooves the Israeli government to pursue policies that will not unduly subject the Jewish communities in those countries to uncomfortable situations in which they are forced to defend their loyalty to their respective countries.

3) Because American Jewry has by far the greatest leverage on Israel of all the Jewish communities throughout the diaspora and because American influence over Israel and other countries in the Middle East is far greater than the influence of all the other powers combined, it follows that Israel and American Jewry must maintain a relationship that will continue to encourage the United States government to act favorably on behalf of Israel. For the American Jewish leadership to rubberstamp Israeli policies is not consistent with Israel's goals or with American Jewish interests. Indeed, constructive criticism of Israel's policies by Jewish activists may even give the American Jewish community the appearance of being independent, thereby becoming more credible and effective when it is necessary for it to support Israel's policies.

The purpose of this analysis is to show that the existing

relationship between world Jewry and Israel should be reexamined in view of the changing political and economic environment of world Jewry, on the one hand, and of Israel's independent existence, on the other. First, we must examine the basic tenets of the Israel-world Jewry relationship—the foundations of their emotional and cultural affinity.

Emotional Affinity: Origins

Unlike the relationship between other minorities and their native lands, the emotional affinity between the Jewish minorities that are scattered in more than 100 countries and the state of Israel is unique. Its uniqueness is characterized by several interrelated factors that constitute the very makeup of a typical Jew—regardless of his place of residence.

Although ethnic minorities in the United States (e.g., Italians, Mexicans, and Puerto Ricans) may maintain strong emotional ties with the countries of their origin, their ties are based primarily on religious, cultural, and psychological factors that together establish a subtle emotional bond. This bond is not subject to any immediate threat or rupture and is not cemented by the sharing of a common historical experience that is the basis for permanent anxiety and fear. The Italian and Mexican minorities in the United States, for example, do not fear the dismantling of Italy or Mexico and therefore feel less apprehension and concern about their former countries in comparison with the Jewish minority in the United States. But what makes the world Jewry-Israeli emotional affinity so much more deeply ingrained is the interdependency of a whole set of political, economic, cultural, and psychological factors, without which neither side would feel safe or fulfilled.

The viability of the Israeli-world Jewry relationship hinges primarily on a continual exchange between the two. Ever since the idea of creating a Jewish state was conceived in the early 1900s, Jewish nationalism (Zionism) has incorporated in its ideology not only a political platform to which any individual can subscribe but also a platform designed to meet Jewish needs alone. All the components that characterized the movement as being exclusively Jewish were included. Therefore, religion, with its spiritual, psychological, and moral implications, was incorporated in the Zionist movement and became an integral part of the political basis of the state. In other words, the emotional affinity between world Jewry and Israel exists by virtue of the common religious, cultural, and historical heritage that both sides share and is reinforced by continual interaction.

A factor that is fundamental in understanding the emotional affinity between world Jewry and Israel that other ethnic minorities have never experienced is the historical connection between the Jews and Israel. Here again, the very existence of Israel is viewed as the fulfillment of a dream—a dream that many Jewish generations shared but were unable to realize. Once the state of Israel became a reality, the generations of persecutions and pogroms to which Jews were subjected began to be perceived in a different light. None of that would have happened, many scholars assert, if Israel had been in existence and Jews could have had a refuge of their own. Therefore, although Jews may now feel safe in their countries of origin, say, for example, in the United

States, France, Britain, and other countries, their fears or uncertainties have not completely been removed. In this sense Israel represents a hope, a future alternative, a last resort, a refuge—in short, a home to which they can go if and when the need arises. However, even if they cannot go and occupy that home by choice (Russian Jewry is a case in point), the fact remains that such a home does exist and does proclaim the Jewish right of self-determination. It has brought self-confidence, self-esteem, and respect. Now Jews can think of themselves as free; they have a home of their own; they are no longer wanderers, no longer alone. Israel will stand and will fight for them. (The July 1976 raid on Uganda's Entebbe airport and the release of the Israeli airline hostages is a vivid example of this commitment.)

This is the very essence of the emotional affinity and the very basic component of the world Jewry-Israel relationship, a relationship that was cast in common terror, has existed in danger, and will continue to exist because the emotional and the intellectual survival of one side has become the prerequisite of the survival of the other.

Emotional Affinity: Possible Deterioration?

For the last two decades many Jews have tended to believe that the unique relationship between world Jewry and Israel contains built-in safeguards sufficient to prevent, first, any emotional erosion between the two sides and, second, any deterioration of Jewish values among world Jewry itself. Recent developments, however, indicate that both assumptions are false. Neither the Israeli-world Jewry relationship nor the Jewish identity of many hundreds of thousands of Jews in the diaspora has been immune to outside pressure. It would seem that too much has been taken for granted on the part of Israel and world Jewry and too little has been done to stop or at least inhibit some undesirable trends that are emerging.

Among the causes that have contributed to the degradation of values among Israeli-world Jewry, the following are the most pertinent:

1) *The Devaluation of the Holocaust*: Initially the holocaust served as a shield against anti-Semitism. As the memories of the holocaust began to fade away, especially among those who were born a few years before or after the Second World War, two simultaneous phenomena began to surface. First, because the past has inevitably been distorted over time and the experience of the holocaust has been downgraded, many non-Jews no longer feel guilty. Thus non-Jews, and even some Jews, do not find it difficult to take a position against Israel. The existence of Israel is no longer considered a direct consequence of the holocaust, and thereby Israel has become more and more subjected to criticism, without any guilt feelings on the part of the critics. According to Eli Wiesel, a noted Jewish writer, what has contributed to this "devaluation" is the fact that "the holocaust has been commercialized for purposes of fund raising, etc." In addition, the holocaust has been "over-exposed to institutionalization and frequently superficial studies" by what he regards as "intellectual dilettantes." In short, it has become a commonplace, "exploited for cheap ventures."

2) *Lack of Pioneering Spirit*: The early days of the establishment of Israel were strongly characterized as

the pioneering period. This perspective helped appreciably to engender an enthusiasm and a sense of strong affiliation among Jews in the diaspora and especially among young people. Since the late 1960s, however, Israel has failed to generate the same enthusiasm, first, because the Israelis themselves began to lose the pioneering spirit and the fervor that accompanied the very idea of living in Israel, and, second, because Israel took too much for granted and reduced its contact with the diaspora Jewry through the various Jewish organizations (to which more than 70 percent of the Jews do not subscribe). Third, Jewish organizations that often act as liaisons between Israel and the Jewish community have multiplied: Because many of these organizations were neither equipped nor designed to play such a role, they failed to portray Israel in the way that it should have been portrayed, and they even inadvertently excluded scores of Jews from Israel and Jewish causes in general. Finally, one other very important factor that has affected both Israel and world Jewry is the absence of ideological revival. Many Jewish organizations, including the Zionist organization that spearheaded the creation of the state of Israel, continued to exist after the establishment of Israel. That existence was based on emotional and sentimental motivations that are neither adequate for nor consistent with the special needs of the Jews in the diaspora today. These Jewish organizations have existed in a void since 1948 because they have refused to cease operating upon the completion of their missions and have been unable or unwilling to rejuvenate themselves ideologically by assuming new roles on behalf of the Jewish people. In the words of Philip Hochstein, an astute observer of Jewish life,

"American Jewry needs to escape from the bureaucracies that may have served well enough as rescuers during the Hitler period but are now even more defunct than the Israeli political establishment." The results of this bureaucratic perpetuation unaccompanied by ideological revival have been damaging both to Israel and world Jewry, for instead of regenerating new interest on the part of young adults, a growing sense of alienation and disenchantment has been developing. Those who disagree with this observation often cite the enrollment of young leadership in organizations such as the Jewish Federation and the United Jewish Appeal. Analysis of this assumption will clearly indicate that erosion among the young leadership has surfaced and dismay is often expressed by individuals who leave the organizations. There is no doubt that an organization such as the U.J.A. fulfills a fundamental function in Jewish life, but how can this and many other organizations hope to continue to generate interest and mass participation without even paying lip service to ideological revival? It is misleading and most damaging to continue to portray Israel as the ultimate beneficiary of organizational efforts as well as using Israel as both the cause and the objective of major activities. The danger in which Israel has existed for the last three decades is no longer sufficient in itself to create that necessary "push" that stimulates many Jews, especially young adults. These young men and women are looking for fulfillment that the U.J.A., Israel Bonds, B'nai B'rith, or the Z.O.A. cannot provide in their ideological and social settings. Newcomers to the Jewish scene are searching for a new horizon in which great ideals go hand in hand with tangible and practical achievements. Together Israel and the major Jewish organizations can begin a process in which Israel's needs in terms of money and manpower remain consistent with an ideological revival. Yet such a revival would be impossible when, for example, the Zionist organization continues to advocate the importance of Aliyah (immigration) to Israel, while Israel has failed in its efforts to keep those who are already there.

3) *Insufficient Jewish Education*: Not enough has been done on the part of Israel and on the part of Jews throughout the diaspora to further Jewish education. The creation of the state of Israel, the development of Hebrew, and the revival of Jewish consciousness are not sufficient to strengthen Jewish religious values and engender spiritual enrichment that is lacking in Israel itself as well as among Jews outside Israel. The religious education of a Jewish boy or girl usually ends at the early age of sixteen. The majority of Jews do not even send their children to Sunday school, let alone to higher Jewish education. According to Mordechai Bar On, who for almost nine years was the head of the World Zionist Organization's youth and Hechalutz department, "American Jewry is worried about its creative survival. It is quite obvious that Jewish education in the United States does not answer the educational needs. Integral Jewish education and Sunday schools show very little achievement." The percentage of Jewish boys and girls who attend Hebrew academy or a yeshiva is very small. However, what must be emphasized is that yeshiva students and the Orthodox Jewish population in reality have proportionately far greater impact than their numbers would suggest. It could be said that the Orthodox Jewish com-

munity is the remnant that keeps the Jewish existence in the diaspora alive. Without this minority group, the Jewish cultural and religious commitment would have eroded to a far more alarming degree.

Economic Support

After the deep emotional bond, the second basic component of Israeli-world Jewry relations is the economic support that is given to Israel in progressively greater amounts year after year. Although grateful for economic aid, Israel has also made it known that it is the duty of world Jewry to continue its financial support. The Jewish communities have been willing to accept this obligation. Yet in this sphere, too, there are some serious problems developing that neither side is willing to admit.

Motivation: For many Jews, Israel's need constitutes sufficient reason to give and give generously. There are those, of course, who give because to them donations are a way to cleanse their consciences. There are those who give because they feel that they must—their status in the community compels them to be generous in order not to fall out of grace as far as the rest of the community is concerned. Some give because of the honor involved; they seek recognition and like to be in the spotlight. And, finally, there are those who give because they were asked by a friend or a relative whom they cannot turn down either because they expect reciprocity or because it is their turn to reciprocate.

Although there are other kinds of donors, what is significant about the categories mentioned above is, first, that they represent the main givers, and, second, only a small percentage of them contributes because Israel is thought to be in need. These are the facts to which all professional fund raisers will attest. Their relevance to our discussion is as follows: 1) The growing economic needs of Israel are forcing the major fund-raising Jewish organization—the United Jewish Appeal (U.J.A.) in conjunction with the Jewish Federation—to exert far greater pressure on a small percentage of the Jewish community for greater contributions; 2) The multiplicity of Jewish organizations that raise funds for other local or overseas causes is unnecessary and at best redundant. Ironically, most of these organizations seem to be attracted to the same relatively small group of individuals who are known as philanthropists and who are perceived to be staunch supporters of Israel and other Jewish causes; 3) Because the motivation to give is usually the prerequisite of giving, appeals on behalf of Israel's security, which is a sensitive issue in Jewish life, have often been improperly used. Leon Dulzin, treasurer of the Jewish Agency, discerns a pattern in donations to the United Jewish Appeal. They follow a curve that rises sharply at times of military crisis, declines sharply as conditions return to normal, but then rises again in a gradual but steady slope. (Gil Sedan, *JTA News Bulletin*, January 19, 1977); 4) Although the United Jewish Appeal and the Jewish Federation are well entrenched in most Jewish communities, other fund-raising organizations vigorously compete for funds, further disenchanting the donors and alienating many potential ones; 5) Although most of the funds are raised in the name of Israel—at least, Israel has always been portrayed as the focal point in fund-raising efforts—a large percentage of these funds is spent on local American Jewish needs, not always justifiable or acceptable to the giver. For example, why should a Jewish community center be viewed as more important than Hebrew day schools that are continually struggling for funds? For this reason, growing numbers of donors bypass the various organizations and make their contributions directly or contribute to a cause not necessarily related to Israel; 6) Finally, the fact that contributions to charitable organizations, including the U.J.A., are tax deductible encourages many donors to give more or even to give in the first place.

Continued financial support of Israel by world Jewry—based on current fund-raising methods and ideologies—does not, it appears, have good prospects. Israel's financial needs will steadily increase while many Jews, for a variety of reasons, will tend either to reduce their financial support or will advocate some drastic changes in the method of fund raising and the way that funds are allocated. According to Leon Dulzin, what prompts a significant number of philanthropists to make annual contributions is tension on Israel's borders, if not the renewed outbreak of hostilities between Israel and the Arab states. It is very sad indeed that only a direct danger to Israel's security can create the necessary motivation.

"The economic arena is one way in which more concrete involvement can come to expression," Abba Eban once observed. "What is lacking is a commensurate pace of effort and sacrifice between the two sides of the Jewish people." In a similar vein but with more boldness, Stanley Sloan, a sophisticated observer of Jewish history and past national chairman of the U.J.A., stated in an interview that "The time has come, in terms of Jewish need, for American Jewry to step up the giving. We have come up in a relatively short time from fifty million to five hundred million dollars a year. Now we must state our aim: one billion dollars a year, and having stated it, we must strive to attain it. We have to reach more people while at the same time maintaining the level of intensity of our operation." According to Mr. Sloan's estimate, the U.J.A. now reaches only 50 percent of American Jews, but only half of them, namely, 25 percent, gives "responsibly" (according to their means). "We must get up to 50 percent responsible giving among all American Jews."

Whether the present relationship between the giver (world Jewry) and the recipient (Israel) is a healthy one, the fact remains indisputable that this exchange must continue for the mutual benefit of both. For its part Israel must play a far greater role in developing Jewish consciousness throughout the diaspora, a role necessitated by growing apathy among members of the younger generation. It is incumbent upon world Jewry, on the one hand, to give a far greater measure of its human and financial resources, for the safer that Israel is, the greater will Israel become the bastion of Judaism and a force for worldwide Jewish identity. To be sure, for world Jewry Israel is the single, most important source of spiritual and moral strength. It is for this reason that Israel's strength or weakness in the economic, political, and military spheres relates directly to the *morale* of Jews outside Israel. Therefore, monetary support of Israel, which has a direct bearing on its military prowess, has become a moral responsibility and becomes a burden on the consciences of those who do not respond to Israel's financial needs.

Political Support

World Jewry renders crucial support to Israel in the political sphere as well. Jewish lobbying in the countries where there is a concentration of Jews, such as Great Britain, France, South Africa, and, particularly the United States, is significant and at times plays a critical role in determining the political and financial decisions made concerning Israel.

Recently this lobbying by Jewish groups has been criticized. Such criticism is coming from quarters not necessarily hostile to Israel—often they are very strong supporters of Israel—but from those who believe that the Jewish community, for example in the United States, might lose an appreciable degree of its political influence if it fails to distinguish between what is really important to Israel and what is not. To be sure, a clear distinction must be made between issues that are important to Israel, concerning which the support of world Jewry is imperative, and those that are neither detrimental to Israel's security nor crucial to its well-being. Indiscriminate support of Israel's positions by world Jewry tends to raise questions about the credibility of Jewish leadership. Discriminating between what warrants total support by world Jewry and what should be left to the Israeli government to handle with another government would place world Jewry in a position of credibility, thereby avoiding charges of "undue influence" on Congress, such as that made by the chairman of the Joint Chiefs of Staff, General George Brown, in his 1976 confirmation hearings.

The whole problem of political support can be illustrated by the following examples:

1) In March 1975, when former United States Secretary of State Henry Kissinger failed to achieve a second interim agreement between Israel and Egypt, Israel was portrayed by the American press as "intransigent." At the same time, Prime Minister Rabin was hailed as a courageous man by American Jewry because he was able to say "no" to the United States despite the importance of continued American good will toward Israel. The support by American Jews of the Rabin position was spontaneous. They gave little consideration to the official stance of the United States government or to how desperate the United States was for a political success, particularly after the disastrous setback in Vietnam. In August of the same year, when the second interim peace agreement was finally accepted, Rabin was hailed again by American Jewry for his courage in taking the necessary "risks for peace." A reserved response in both instances by American Jewry would undoubtedly have put its leaders in a better light and, consequently, in a better position of influence.

2) The sale of military hardware to Israel's Arab neighbors is undoubtedly a sensitive issue that concerns not only the Jews in the United States but also many other Americans who believe that the United States should supply the world, including the Arab states, with everything but weapons. But, here again, one has to distinguish between the sale of certain equipment and its political implications—its importance to the United States. When the United States government announced the sale of six C-130 planes to Egypt, the Israeli government immediately voiced its opposition. American Jewry followed suit without consulting United States officials. Although this

writer does not advocate the sale of military hardware to the Arab states as a tool of political influence, a distinction must be made between massive sales of offensive weapons (such as jet fighters or air-to-air missiles to Saudi Arabia), on the one hand, and a limited sale of six C-130 transport planes, on the other.

If the sale of six planes to Egypt—which does not constitute a military threat to Israel—can bring the United States one step closer to Egypt and increase American influence there, that alone should constitute sufficient reason for American Jewry to support it. Opposition to the sale of arms must be based on the merit of each deal. It is not wise for American Jewry to oppose a relatively small sale because the sale might create a precedent. They must remember that the very survival of Israel depends on the good will of the United States and that the United States obligation is to reconcile its commitment to the survival of the state of Israel with American national interests.

3) Finally, Israel asked for, and American Jewry was very active in supporting, the attachment of the Jackson amendment (promoting the free emigration of Russian Jews) to the United States-Soviet trade bill of 1972. Russia immediately repudiated the agreement, and the number of Jews consequently allowed to leave Russia totaled less than half that of previous years. There are many political, moral, and economic arguments for the Jackson amendment. But what is related to our argument is whether American Jewry should have openly supported the amendment or whether quiet diplomacy should have been employed for the purpose of securing the freedom of oppressed Soviet Jews. Would not the result

have been far more positive with quiet diplomacy? The only way that one can judge is by the results. Unfortunately, the results of the Jackson amendment have been very poor so far. Israel's losses in potential manpower are incredibly high. The number of Jews who immigrated to Israel from Russia in 1973 was 33,458; in 1974 the number dropped to 16,808, followed by an additional decrease in 1975 and 1976. (Israel Immigration and Absorption Office, Table V-3. See Appendix 8)

The overzealousness of some Jewish leaders was described in an article by Ira Silverman. In a 1974 memorandum on the role played by American Jewish leaders in supporting the Jackson-Vanik amendment on Soviet Jewish emigration, Elihu Bergman, a Harvard professor (then acting as a consultant to the National Conference on Soviet Jewry), blamed several leaders involved for problems encountered in that struggle. "The record of Jackson-Mills-Vanik through its enactment by the House demonstrates how the decision-making structure can be preempted and manipulated by one or two individuals who occupy, however temporarily, key positions. However distinguished their service or noble their motivations, individuals so inclined to assert themselves can do mischief and damage. . . ." Bergman cites the fact that "economic affluence, rather than the unique qualifications for the job at stake, is too frequently the principal determinant of recruitment to a leadership role.' . . . Then too there is a tendency for an 'old boy' network to develop among those in leadership positions, as a result of which something other than the merits of an issue influence decision-making." (Ira Silverman, *Present Tense*, Winter 1977, vol. 4, No. 2)

The Right of Dissent

The analysis of spontaneous and uncritical support by world Jewry of Israel's political position brings us to one of the most sensitive problems facing Israel and the Jewish communities in the diaspora. The question is whether Jews should be allowed to criticize Israel publicly and to whom such criticism should be directed.

Living in the United States, Britain, or France, for example, gives one the constitutional right to say what he or she wants, when he or she wants, provided that he or she does not incite others to commit illegal acts. Thus, an activist Jew or any advocate may say what he or she chooses when he or she chooses without necessarily being subject to harassment by the government. However, this right may not be freely exercised by an activist Jew in the diaspora if he chooses to express views publicly—especially to the non-Jewish media—that do not conform with Israel's official policy. Israeli officials claim to understand and interpret events in Israel better than can any Jew who is not living there. Jewish communities in the diaspora are told in effect: "Because you are not physically involved with our day-to-day problems, you have no right to tell us how to handle our affairs and how to react to situations that are indigenous to the Middle East in general and to Israel in particular."

At least two basic assumptions are wrong here. One is that living in the Middle East or in Israel is supposed to qualify one as a critic. That is to say, one becomes completely inept in his perception of the realities of the Middle East solely because he does not live there. The Labor government gives no credit whatsoever to diaspora Jewry for their ability to make their own intelligent evaluations of the Israeli situation and to recommend, even if only for the sake of argument, new policies or approaches to some of the Middle East problems. The Israeli government also fails to understand that living in the midst of the problems may not be conducive to objective judgment, for one easily becomes enveloped in problems and often loses perspective on the real issues!

What further exacerbates this situation is the fact that ironically a majority of the Jewish communities not only accept the Israeli viewpoint *but they themselves have become ardent advocates of the Israeli position and demand absolute adherence to it in the name of solidarity.* "It is necessary, in fact imperative, for us to demonstrate our sympathy with and support of the Israeli position," they maintain, "so that our own governments will be encouraged to take measures favorable to Israel."

One striking example that portrays this situation is the question of the Arab Palestinians and the PLO. Israel's position has always been clear, namely, no recognition and no negotiation with the Palestinians. The problem involves identifying the Arab Palestinians with the PLO, as if they exist as one entity. Although no one who is well informed about the Middle East situation can advocate to the Israeli government that it negotiate with the PLO as a political organization before that organization recognizes Israel's right to exist, one *can* ask why negotiations with the Arab Palestinians in the West Bank and the Gaza Strip have not been attempted. After all, the argument goes, if the Arab Palestinians in the West Bank were able to elect in the spring of 1976 their own mayors and councilmen, who are clearly pro-PLO, why not organize them into constituencies, let them elect their own political representatives, and then let them open negotiations with Israel? Even such a moderate approach, when voiced by Jews outside Israel, is considered interference with Israel's internal problems. Those of us who live on the other side of the globe are not allowed to say what is in our hearts.

It is hoped that the blunder of the October war is still so fresh in our minds that we can learn a lesson. After the "lightning victory" of 1967, Israel found no reason to move toward solving the Palestinian problem. The years between 1967 and 1973 were marked by tranquillity and significant social and economic progress in the West Bank and the Gaza Strip. Because Israel wanted to maintain that status quo world Jewry acquiesced, supporting Israel's position of doing nothing. It is possible that Israel's blunders during the 1973 Yom Kippur War were *related to the complacency of world Jewry*, complacency that gave Israel a feeling of confidence and a message of "do nothing; we're with you." Future historians may develop more insight into the relationship that prevailed at that particular time. But it is interesting to speculate: Had the leadership of world Jewry questioned Israel's position during those "seven fat years" (1967–73), perhaps the Yom Kippur War could have been deferred or prevented, or perhaps Israel might have been better prepared. My contention is that complacency cannot and will not serve Israel's interests, and if Israel is too sensitive to take any advice or criticism, then Israel is either too weak to withstand outside pressure or too arrogant to accept it.

As to the argument that dissent negatively affects the policies or positions of the home governments of Jewish critics, this writer does not recall any incident in which overt criticism of Israel's activities had that effect. Indeed, it stands to reason that when Jewish leaders decide to take a position that is not in conformity with the official Israeli position, such independent leadership proves itself more credible. Thus, when they are supportive of Israel's position, the critics' views may be taken more seriously. With credibility there would be less chance of their becoming subject to criticism by local groups or open to accusations of being disloyal. Trude Weiss-Rosmarin, the articulate editor of *The Jewish Spectator* and a keen observer of American Jewish life, repeatedly tells her readers that major Jewish organizations will not tolerate dissent, especially if criticism of policies of the Israeli government is involved. In her editorial in the Summer 1976 issue of *The Jewish Spectator*, she wrote: "In the context of the obligation to *defend* and also *to do battle* for this freedom (of expression), I do not wish to consider whether the criticism that irks so many in the American Jewish establishment is valid and justified. What concerns and troubles me is that in this Bicentennial year American Jewish leaders are so un-American and so un-Jewish as to denounce persons who, in consonance with American and Jewish tradition, speak freely in keeping with the dictates of their conscience. The *principle* involved in the attempt of American-Jewish organizations to silence *Jewish* criticism of Israel is an *ethical* issue. Under attack and at stake is the cornerstone of democracy: freedom of expression and the freedom to dissent and to criticize." (Ira Silverman, *Present Tense*, Winter 1977, vol. 4, No. 2)

In a comprehensive essay in the January-February issue

of the *Women's American ORT Reporter*, Rabbi Eugene B. Borowitz, professor of education and Jewish religious thought at HUC-JIR in New York City, sharply denounced the attitudes generally adopted by Jewish leaders regarding the inadmissibility of dissent on matters concerning Israel. "We have," Rabbi Borowitz maintained, "over a period of decades come to the point where we practice the value called democratic pluralism—but with one exception: affairs concerning the State of Israel. It is obviously something of a communal anomaly to call for openness in discussion on everything but not to do so with regard to the State of Israel. Moreover, it is an interesting irony that for many years it was the Zionists and the intensely Jewish members of our community who led the fight for democracy, but who now insist that with regard to the State of Israel it has serious limits. . . . this (dissent) being a matter of the survival of the State of Israel or the Jewish people, indeed I'd agree, in the face of clear and present danger, survival would be a reason for keeping quiet. But the word 'survival' cannot be taken at face value. It should not be made a code word for 'shut up.' For 20-some years now 'survival' has been used to silence all criticism about the State of Israel within the American Jewish community.

"One last comment, particularly for religious leaders. Should not something be done to set limits to the co-optation of religious life to serve the national needs of the State of Israel? We gave Yom Kippur away for bonds, which perhaps we can justify though it is an investment not a charity and we take interest from fellow Jews. Then we are told that *Shavuot* Sunday ought to be used for Federation mobilization day. And the U.J.A. suggests working through its Rabbinical Council that we get congregations to agree to 100% pledging with the congregation taking the responsibility of collecting the pledges people do not pay. . . .

"The real problem is what shall be done with the feeling of dissent which now truly exists? . . . It would be far better for leadership to sponsor dissent."

To be sure, Jews in the diaspora are not and should not be in positions to decide for the Israeli government. But this need not exclude their active intellectual contributions. In the words of Rabbi Arthur Hertzberg, president of the American Jewish Congress, speaking at the opening session of the annual congress sponsored by the American-Israeli dialogue in July 1976: "I do not mean to deny either the sovereignty or the preeminence of Israeli political leadership, but the leaders of the rest of the Jewish world must be brought into the ongoing process of thinking and planning to deal with our interrelated problems. I am a Zionist because I am a citizen of the Jewish nation, not because I may carry an Israeli passport. It is wrong to say that the battle of American Jewry for support of Israel must be commanded from Jerusalem."

In summing up, world Jewry and Israel must learn to tolerate Jewish dissent. Such dissent may force Israel from time to time to explain itself. It may at times render temporarily a direct or indirect disservice to Israel's cause, but the advantages of criticism far outweigh the disadvantages of mindless acquiescence. For Israel to maintain a viable partnership with world Jewry, it must accept that restrictive element in any partnership that allows either partner to investigate or to question the actions of the other. Israel cannot expect to maintain a one-sided partnership in which it can always dictate the rules and then change them when suitable. The majority of Jews live outside Israel, and they have a tremendous stake in its survival. Because the dividend that they receive from Israel is important to their intellectual and spiritual as well as their emotional well-beings, their advice should be sought without automatic consent being required for the continuation of a healthy partnership.

The pros and cons of dissent will undoubtedly continue to be debated for many years to come. The representatives of major Jewish organizations will continue their campaign against dissidents, for to tolerate dissent would essentially mean to give away an appreciable portion of their power base. The dissidents, on the other hand, will continue to press for the right to air their views and speak out on issues regardless of whether they are in conformity with the official Israeli position. So far both sides have erred, for they have resorted to extreme methods. While continuing to use terms such as freedom and democratic procedure, many dissidents fail to join Jewish organizations and fail to attempt to change things from within. On the other hand, Jewish leadership, which, after all, is self-appointed, has allowed threats, smearing, and harassment to be used to subdue dissent. Both fail to draw the line where Israel may be hurt and where Israel's security of survival is used as a pretense for selfish and narrow interests. One thing, however, must be stated unequivocally: Jewish survival would have been impossible without free debate, open dialogue, and two-way communication. Nothing will stifle the Jewish community more than coercion and undue pressure by individuals who enjoy the exercise of power at the expense of a silent majority. Some of these self-appointed "prosecutors," unfortunately, will go to any length to protect their precarious positions in the eyes of the Jewish community. Yet attacks on individuals or on policies advocated by Israeli officials and/or American Jewish leaders cannot be responsible and constructive unless the critics demonstrate: 1) first-hand knowledge of the issue in question; and 2) the ability to produce some credible alternatives, untainted by empty rhetoric. Only then will a dissident be taken seriously and only then will his or her opponents (the establishment) assume a defensive posture—answering constructive criticism rather than degrading dissident friends and responding in a shallow and damaging way to those who care about the great cause of Israel's survival.

The Jewish Press

The Jewish press has also been under attack by various factions of the Jewish-Israeli community. The charges and countercharges against the American press and the Israeli press have been numerous and may be summarized as follows:

1) *The American Jewish Press*: The American Jewish press is deficient, for it does not live up to the standard of unbiased reporting. A great deal of this deficiency may be attributed to financial difficulties. Murray Zuckoff, New York editor of the J.T.A., sharply criticized the Jewish press in America for its tendency to give in to the pressure of local "machers." In his address at the World Conference of Jewish Journalists, which met at

Beit Agzom in Israel in January 1977, Zuckoff stated that the tendency was to try to divert legitimate news gathering by the Jewish press. In "trying to enforce and limit the kind of news that the Jewish press should deal with, one realizes that the Jewish press is working according to certain commandments given by Jewish organizations. Such commandments might say—thou shall print everything we say, or, thou shall hallow and glorify our name."

2) *Lack of Communication between the Israeli and American Press*: Although the Israelis may have a ragged and sometimes irresponsible press, they are utterly contemptuous of the American Jewish press. The Israeli press is highly effective, for example, in the investigation of corruption in government, yet it is inconsistent in dealing with the quality of life in Israel. Many Israeli editors and journalists have elected to ignore the problems of Israel's social and ethnic struggle and the problems of immigration to and emigration from Israel. The Israeli press must assume full responsibility for contributing to the perpetuation of some of Israel's chronic sociopolitical problems. A more responsive press in Israel would have been able to awaken both the Israeli society and the American Jewish community to some of the unpleasant realities that have so far been ignored or covered up. The American Jewish press, however, has continued to accept the official Israeli dogmas, especially because nothing to the contrary has been communicated by the Israeli press.

3) *Military Censorship in Israel*, complicated by stiff organizational guidelines in the Jewish press: Although Israeli law requires that all material pertaining to national security be submitted to censorship, before publication

the government freely uses military censorship in order to suppress embarrassing information or any kind of criticism that the government deems too critical of itself. One vivid example of this indiscriminate censorship was the fact that for three weeks before the Yom Kippur War of October 1973, the Israeli media were aware of troop concentrations by both Syria and Egypt. Yet the Israeli government chose to suppress this information for reasons of national security. One wonders what would have happened if the Israeli press had reported this concentration of Arab forces. Would the Egyptians and the Syrians still have carried out the attack? Better yet, would the Israeli government have acted the way it did had the Arab concentration of forces become common knowledge? Furthermore, how would the American Jewish community have reacted had the alarm been sounded in every Jewish paper in the United States?

4) *Dissent and Free Press*: Dissent is another alarming problem that must be faced by the members of the Jewish-Israeli press—not only to maintain their integrity as free people but also to live up to the code of ethics, duty, and responsibility of their profession. Responsible dissent is the essence of a free society and is the basis for its well-being; it is the core of its responsible functioning. The Jewish-Israeli press has so far paid nothing but lip service to dissenting views. One of the messages that was clearly conveyed to the Jewish press during the World Conference of Jewish Journalists was that the Jewish press around the world must not shy away from dissent and dispute. Most journalists stated that dissent is in the best tradition of Jewish life and that the right to dissent is an important element in ensuring a viable and

progressive Jewish press. It is high time for the Jewish and the Israeli press to open their pages to responsible dissent: Past blunders and coverups might have been avoided had dissident voices been given fair play.

If the Jewish press continues to subordinate its professional integrity and responsibility to the whims of an unenlightened bureaucracy, then indeed the Jewish press will lose not only its value as an educational instrument but also its moral responsibility and commitment to the Jewish community.

The Relationship in Prospect

The continuation of a progressive and viable relationship between world Jewry and Israel is of vital importance to both sides. Some of the misperceptions on both sides were not taken seriously enough in the past, and little has been done to correct these misperceptions. In recent years, however, more and more prominent individuals from both sides have been raising questions about the measures needed not only to prevent an erosion in world Jewry-Israel relations but also to bring about a better and more satisfactory and rewarding relationship for both parties. Before we attempt to enumerate the various fields in which a great deal of improvement must take place, it should be noted that a clear definition of responsibilities must be achieved, first, in order to ensure a sense of partnership, efficiency, and economy. This division of responsibility will become clearer as we detail the fields in which improvement is urgently needed.

1) *Education.* Jewish education and the development of a Jewish identity among Jewish youth throughout the diaspora have been recognized as the very foundations

of Jewish continuity and longevity. However, in this critical sphere not too much has been accomplished. The various Jewish organizations, and particularly the synagogues, have been satisfied with providing elementary Jewish education, including the Hebrew language, to their boys and girls up to the age of thirteen, and at times to the age of sixteen. In this context, Sunday schools have played the prime role. Yet after the age of sixteen, very little, if anything, has been done to further the Jewish education of young adults or to develop in any other way their sense of Jewishness, for apart from some Hebrew day schools, which a very small percentage of Jewish boys and girls attend, there are no major Jewish institutions capable of or equipped to undertake this formidable task of providing a Jewish orientation for the greater part of Jewish youth. The most important segment of the Jewish population on which the future of world Jewry and, to a great extent, the future of Israel depends— the Jewish high school and university student—has been virtually neglected. These young men and women, who embody the very future of Jewish existence, have been left entirely to themselves, and the only Jewish influence that they receive, if any, is from their parents, and this, of course, only when the parents are eager to convey their own identity to their children.

Recent informal studies indicate that Jewish parents throughout the diaspora, apart from the Orthodox community, are by and large preoccupied with their own affairs and attach very little importance to the development of a Jewish identity in their children. The repercussions of this situation are most alarming and in many ways extremely dangerous. Without proper and adequate

Jewish orientation and without a developing Jewish identity and affinity among youth not only will the Jewish people in general face a severe demography that may threaten their very existence and independence as an organic entity but also will subject Israel to the possibility of losing its Jewish identity altogether because of receiving insufficient numbers of Jewish immigrants to offset the losses in natural birth rate. (See *Demographic Conditions in Israel: A Dangerous Prospect,* pp. 75–107)

Thus, furthering Jewish education among high school and university students is a prerequisite of the future spiritual and physical strength of world Jewry and Israel. *No effort can be spared and no resources can be too dear to pay in reaching these young men and women and confronting them with all that Jews and Israel stand for.* Only through an intensive, continuous, and unrelenting campaign among this group can Israel and world Jewry expect Jewish continuity. Jewish education and the orientation of Jewish youth is the key to aliyah to Israel, future financial support, strong political lobbying for Israel, the steady influx of Western technology for Israel's industry, and, above all, it is the key to Israel's future security and world Jewry's future existence.

Achieving this mass indoctrination would require a substantial amount of money and a small army of qualified personnel to design and conduct a special campaign geared toward this vulnerable aspect of Jewish life. Millions of dollars will have to be spent annually on literature, lecturers, scholarships to Israel, seminars, symposia, and other educational programs. Indeed, even if millions of dollars have to be taken from other important fields, it would still be justified, for the importance of Jewish education ranks even higher in the long run than the military itself.

The duty of Jewish education falls first and foremost on the Jewish organizations throughout the diaspora—especially the U.J.A., which raises the bulk of funds from the Jewish community. The U.J.A. must allocate a substantial sum for the purpose of reaching young adults. The U.J.A. should completely eliminate or reduce its support to a variety of Jewish institutions, such as community centers that can either be self-supporting or settle for much less, as well as increase its financial support to Hebrew day schools that are the cornerstones of Jewish education in any community. In the final analysis, a reexamination of the list of priorities is a must. *The development of Jewish education beyond the Bar Mitzvah age must receive top priority.*

Israel's role is no less important. Israel should provide not only funds but also the national identity, the pioneering spirit, and the psychological and intellectual motivation. *In this regard world Jewry and Israel face a crisis of identity; assimilation and intermarriage have reached epidemic proportions; apathy and ignorance have engulfed the mass of Jews; Jewish tradition and cultural heritage have given way to secular pursuits; and the end result could be a Jewish calamity no less severe than the holocaust itself.*

It is not enough to build magnificent and beautiful synagogues and temples. It is not enough to attend services for social purposes or for putting on appearances. *It is what is done with the children throughout their childhood and adulthood that will determine the fate of the Jews and Israel.* The job is a formidable one, and time is not in our favor. We must "begin yesterday."

2) *Public Relations.* Israel's prestige directly affects Jewish communities throughout the diaspora in their relations with the rest of the citizens of their respective countries. For this reason, Israel must take all steps necessary to avoid situations that will compel any Jewish community anywhere to go on the defensive. Raymond Aron, a Sorbonne University philosophy professor and a noted journalist, observed that although Jews in a certain community may be clumsy in handling themselves and thereby cause anti-Semitism in that particular community, Israeli clumsiness is far more dangerous because the Jews of all countries are implicated. For this reason, Israel must be extremely careful in the conduct of its political affairs and in formulating its political stance on any issue. Israel must ensure that the way that it is portrayed to the outside world is such that Jews around the world will find it easy to explain as well as take pride in explaining its positions.

Jewish leaders throughout the diaspora should embark upon a real assessment of the role that they have been playing and the role that they should play. In recent years disagreements and a lack of coordination between Israel's and world Jewry's positions gave the appearance of a serious policy cleavage. To be sure, the way that Israel is perceived by world Jewry determines to a large extent the way world Jewry responds to Israel's needs and requirements. Although Israel, on the one hand, has failed to convey honestly to world Jewry any problem that might prove embarrassing, such as Israel's ethnic inequality, world Jewry, on the other hand, has failed to probe below the surface; it simply swallows the official dosage.

3) *Immigration, "Aliyah."* Jewish immigration to Israel from Eastern and Western Europe and from North America must also be rated as an issue of top priority. In this regard, North American Jewry has not responded in great numbers, and over 50 percent of Soviet Jewry who are allowed to leave Russia choose to settle in the United States or in other Western democracies rather than in Israel. (For an analysis of immigration—aliyah to Israel and Israel's general demographic problems—see *Demographic Conditions in Israel: A Dangerous Prospect*, pp. 75–107.) These two problems, lack of massive immigration to Israel from North America and the settling of Russian Jews outside Israel, were the subject of a U.J.A. study mission in Jerusalem in July 1976. Many leaders attending the conference voiced serious alarm at the lack of prospects of aliyah in large numbers to Israel. Among the well-known speakers, former Foreign Minister Abba Eban voiced serious criticism of world Jewry leaders who, in his words, "have done very little to encourage immigration to Israel. Our greatest danger is that the Jewish people lose the conviction of our eternity. . . . Israel's continued survival lies in the nature of the depth of Jewish solidarity, because Israel alone in the Middle East does not possess the rationale for stability. . . . We are an island in an ocean of hate. Israel's 'demographic drought' is the single source of our vulnerability. Three million pairs of shoulders are not enough to sustain the burden of Jewish identity. There is no involvement on the part of world Jewry with Israel's demographic predicament."

Although Eban rejected the idea that Israel's social class inequalities discourage large-scale Jewish immigration to Israel, he noted that these imperfections exist because not enough Jews are coming to Israel. "You cannot create weaknesses by your calculated absence and then invoke those weaknesses as a reason for not coming to correct them."

Abba Eban's position does not, however, reflect the views of many others, including this writer, who believe that Israel itself has fallen far short in its efforts to make the country a haven for many potential immigrants, including Soviet Jews.

Conclusion

World Jewry and Israel must show a far greater capacity to work closely together. Israel must be willing to enter into this renewed spiritual and physical partnership and cease to view world Jewry as a commodity or as a source from which it can draw money and manpower. Although Israel reciprocates by supplying world Jewry with continual dosages of dignity, pride, spiritual fulfillment, and religious and cultural enrichment, still world Jewry must become far more involved in Israel's immediate, internal problems. World Jewry, especially the young, must be exposed to the other side of Israel. Most of the Jews in the diaspora hear and see only the bright side. Israeli officials tend to portray only the positive and the glamorous side of Israel. It is one way of saying, "Look what we can do with your support. Imagine how much more we could achieve with greater support." In addition, Israel's military might has always been used as an example of its remarkable achievements, and who can deny the stunning victories of Israel's armed forces in 1948, 1956, 1967, and even in 1973. And if the victory in 1973 was not complete and left some unfulfilled expectations, the Entebbe operation in Uganda in July 1976, with its spectacular rescue of the airplane hostages, restored Israel's and world Jewry's pride in the Israeli military.

Although Israel has made great strides in many fields, especially in agriculture and industry, there are many other sides to Israel that require attention in the next decade. A look at the "other Israel" reveals a serious domestic class and ethnic struggle, an unwieldy bureaucratic machine that often consumes more than it can produce, a terrible need for better housing, rearrangement of immigration and absorption priorities, and, finally, an educational blight depriving tens of thousands of young Oriental Jews of the elementary right to attend high school, not to mention the university, because of their inferior economic and social status.

These are the sides that world Jewry should see and help to correct. It is in this other side where the real Jewish need lies, and it is there where *the challenge of the fourth decade must begin.* The Israeli army can be only as strong as the strength of the Israeli spirit, and the source of this spirit and high morale must be generated from within. Israel must fight its adversaries and must win if it has no other course. But military victories over the Arab states and their supporters in the Middle East or in Africa cannot and must not be the only source of pride and satisfaction. Peace with the Arab states must first be won *inside* Israel. When Israel can conquer its own weaknesses, and when world Jewry ceases to fantasize about Israel's infallibility, a real victory will become possible.

An open dialogue, a continuous exchange, and a permanent, mutual inquiry are fundamental elements in any partnership. Neither Israel nor world Jewry can afford to be complacent about the role of the other. Both sides must march together to meet the uncertainties of the future, for Jewish destiny is for all Jews to share.

EPILOGUE

W ITH the upset victory of the opposition right-wing Likud party in the Israeli election of May 1977, Israel has entered a new political era. The implications may prove to be far more serious for Israel's socioeconomic, political, and military postures than most Western political observers have contemplated. This writer believes that Begin's election left a profound impression on the Arab world. There is absolutely no doubt that the historic visit of Sadat to Israel would have been unthinkable had Rabin, for example, been the Prime Minister of Israel. What the Egyptian President saw in Begin was a leader with decisiveness, insight and conviction; to President Sadat of Egypt, Begin was his true counterpart with whom he could deal effectively.

Contrary to his predecessor, Yitzhak Rabin, Prime Minister Begin was able immediately upon assuming the

Premiership to generate respect and popularity throughout Israel and the world Jewry. World leaders from the East and West have also been extremely impressed with Begin's vitality, sincerity and straightforwardness—all of which are important elements for mutual respectability and confidence.

Premier Menachem Begin has become the prime minister of Israel in a critical period in its history. His success or failure will leave a deep and profound impression on Israel and the Middle East. No Israeli prime minister since David Ben-Gurion declared Israel's independence in 1948 has carried a heavier burden of responsibility for Israel and for world Jewry as Menachem Begin carries now. The fate of Israel, and, to a large extent, that of the Jewish community throughout the diaspora, depends on how well Begin uses his authority to achieve peace with the Arabs and prosperity and social justice at home.

Because of my conviction that Premier Begin is best equipped to lead Israel toward the noble goals of peace, prosperity and social justice, I am proud to dedicate this work in his honor.

Appendix 1

*TABLE 1: Parties Represented in Cabinets

Party / Cabinet #	1	2	3	4	5	6	7	8	9	10	11	12	13	14	15	16	17	18
Mapam							9	9	9				8	8	8			
Ahdut Ha'avodah							10	10	7	8	8	8						
Mapai	46	46	45	45	45	45	40	40	47	42	42	42	45**	45	45	56	56	51
Rafi														10†	10			
N. R. P.	16	16	8	8	8	8	11	11	12	12	12	12	12	12	12	12	12	10
Agudat Yisrael			3															
Sephardim	4	4																
Progressives	5	5		4	4	4	5	5	6				5§	5	5	4	4	4
General Zionist				20	20													
Gahal														26	26	26		
Independent		1							1									
Total seats represented	71	72	56	77	77	57	75	75	82	62	62	62	70	106	106	98	72	65
Ministries	12	13	13	16	16	16	16	16	16	16	16	16	16	21	21	22	18	23

Cabinet # 1 1949-50; 2 1950-51; 3 1951-52; 4 1952-54; 5 1954-55; 6 1955; 7 1955-58; 8 1958-59; 9 1959-61; 10 1961-63; 11 1963-64; 12 1964-65; 13 1965-67; 14 1967-69; 15 1969; 16 1969-71; 17 1971-74; 18 1974.

*Adapted from *Comparative Political Studies*, vol. 8, No. 2, July 1975.

**1965 A.A. and Mapai ran as Alignment.

§Name change to Independent Liberals.

†Rafi was dissident wing Mapai party; enlarged Alignment changed name to Labor party.

Appendix 2

*Table 2: Vote Change Caused by War, 1969 Vote, 1973 Vote, and Future Vote

1969 Vote	1973 Vote	Future Vote	Vote Change Caused by War		
			N	Yes %	No %
Same	Alignment	Same	127	4	96
		Uncertain	175	8	92
	Likud	Same	93	11	89
		Uncertain	62	13	87
	Religious	Same	45	4	96
		Uncertain	17	24	76
Different	Alignment	Same	6	33	67
		Uncertain	33	73	27
	Likud	Same	22	77	23
		Uncertain	71	85	15
	Religious	Same	1	100	—
		Uncertain	7	57	43
		Total	659	23	77

Variable distributions:

1969 Vote	1973 Vote	Future Vote
Same 79%	Alignment 52%	Same 45%
Different 21%	Likud 38%	Uncertain 55%
	Religious 10%	

*From Alan Arian, *Comparative Politics*, vol. 8, No. 1, October 1975.

Appendix 3

MONTHLY FAMILY INCOME (IN CURRENT ISRAELI POUNDS) 1956/57–1971

	1956/ 57[a]	1957/ 58[b]	1963/ 64[b]	1963/ 64[c]	1965[d]	1966[d]	1967[d]	1968[d]	1969[d]	1970[d]	1971[d]
Asia–Africa	219	172	402	477	517	567	558	642	692	808	893
Europe–America	300	304	640	671	717	825	925	908	1000	1100	1200
Index of Equality											
Relative	73	57	63	71	72	69	60	71	69	73	74
Absolute	–81	–132	–238	–194	–200	–258	–367	–266	–308	–292	–307

Sources: [a] C.B.S. Family Expenditure Surveys, 1956/57 and 1959/60, Special Series 148, pp. CXXIV–CXXV.

[b] C.B.S. Saving Survey, 1963/64, Special Series 217, Table 5, p. XXIX.

[c] C.B.S. Family Expenditure Survey, 1963/64, Special Series 200.

[d] C.B.S. Statistical Abstract of Israel, 23:271.

Appendix 4

Live Births and Total Fertility, By Live Birth Order During Life of Mother

Not known	6+	5	4	3	2	1	Total	
								Jews
								Absolute Numbers
1,389	963	495	882	2,290	4,707	6,952	17,678	1948
2,048	2,717	1,390	2,395	5,527	10,924	11,358	36,359	1950
924	5,361	2,415	3,942	6,715	11,878	11,104	42,339	1955
20	7,736	2,998	3,935	6,793	11,304	12,195	44,981	1960
91	8,093	2,831	4,291	8,234	12,900	14,871	51,311	1965
194	6,000	2,812	5,673	11,572	15,655	19,303	61,209	1970
225	5,791	2,929	6,081	12,081	16,943	21,488	65,463	1971
147	5,244	2,914	5,744	11,321	17,286	21,834	64,490	1972
123	4,842	2,800	5,456	11,579	18,506	23,480	66,786	1973
107	4,750	2,866	5,931	12,572	20,896	23,423	70,545	1974
								Total Fertility Per Thousand Women
x	177	97	163	422	889	1,330	3,078	1948
x	318	159	273	629	1,238	1,284	3,901	1950
x	491	212	347	591	1,037	966	3,644	1955
x	616	237	314	538	877	913	3,495	1960
x	575	201	302	577	879	933	3,467	1965
x	413	186	366	717	837	888	3,407	1970
x	391	187	375	706	840	937	3,436	1971
x	344	177	337	621	797	907	3,183	1972
x	306	162	306	596	807	935	3,121	1973
x	295	163	321	619	869	912	3,179	1974

Live Birth Order

Non-Jews

Absolute Numbers

204	3,516	1,218	1,338	1,406	1,368	1,434	10,484	1958
–	4,264	1,378	1,412	1,422	1,544	1,791	11,811	1960
41	5,681	1,483	1,563	1,797	2,119	2,151	14,835	1965
287	7,219	1,854	2,111	2,290	2,702	3,171	19,634	1970
190	7,442	1,937	2,181	2,361	3,066	3,259	20,436	1971
117	7,419	1,972	2,190	2,686	3,190	3,480	21,054	1972
73	7,346	2,103	2,321	2,940	3,394	3,582	21,754	1973
91	7,276	2,104	2,595	3,104	3,456	3,995	22,621	1974

Total Fertility Per Thousand Women

x	3,212	866	862	853	793	726	7,312	1958
x	3,563	924	893	832	842	938	7,992	1960
x	4,001	822	797	863	964	973	8,420	1965
x	3,445	719	788	813	902	981	7,650	1970
x	3,316	705	758	783	942	930	7,433	1971
x	3,175	694	724	837	924	944	7,298	1972
x	3,025	708	735	866	925	924	7,212	1973
x	2,919	695	790	869	901	970	7,143	1974

Statistical Abstract of Israel, 1975, no. 26
Central Bureau of Statistics

Appendix 5
Direct Financial Support to Young Israeli Families

One positive measure, recently evolved by Joan Fredricks, is the creation of an instrumentality through which an American family can foster the birth of a child in Israel by "adoption," provided the young Israeli family already has two or more children.

The meaning of the term "foster" is the partial financial sponsorship of the birth of a child to an *Israeli* couple who might want to have a third or fourth child but is unable to carry the additional financial burden.

The usefulness of this particular approach is multiple:

1) It will create a unique relationship between the sponsoring family and the recipient.

2) It will further strengthen and deepen the link to Israel by the American family.

3) It will ease the financial burden on the Israeli government, which cannot shoulder a heavier load beyond its present financial subsidies to large families.

4) Finally, it will bring about a new generation of Israelis who will have a special bond with their "godparents"—better yet—a living relationship conducive to harmony and greater affinity.

To implement such a program, many technical problems will have to be solved. Among the most important are: whether monetary gifts by an American family would be tax deductible and whether such a gift would be tax exempt in Israel. We have reason to believe that these two obstacles could be overcome.

Pioneer Women: The one agency or organization that could execute such a program may be the Pioneer Women of America. The Pioneer Women's organization has performed a magnificent role on behalf of the Jewish people and Israel. Pioneer Women would fill this role perfectly not only because of the implication of their name (Pioneer Women for an increased birth rate in Israel) but because of their day-to-day functions.

The Pioneer Women's organization is probably the only Jewish organization that is fully equipped to handle such an undertaking. It has all the human resources necessary to reach a very large segment of the American Jewish community and establish the first contact between an American family and a young Israeli family.

The Financial Assistance in Practical Terms: The financial assistance in real terms should range between $25 and $50 per month. Such financial help could go a long way toward the rearing of a child and his or her education and well-being. The funds would be sent on a monthly basis directly to the recipient (with the Pioneer Women as the conveyor to insure tax deductibility), with the organization maintaining a liaison position in case of a disruption in the relationship between the donor and the recipient, or if and when either the donor or the recipient decides to end the relationship. Naturally, the Pioneer Women would maintain and keep all records and would be accountable only to their own board of directors.

Appendix 6

United Nations Security Council Resolution 242 November 22, 1967

The Security Council
Expressing its continuing concern with the grave situation in the Middle East,

Emphasizing the inadmissibility of the acquisition of territory by war and the need to work for a just and lasting peace in which every state in the area can live in security,

Emphasizing further that all Member States in their acceptance of the Charter of the United Nations have undertaken a commitment to act in accordance with Article 2 of the Charter,

1. *Affirms* that the fulfillment of Charter principles requires the establishment of a just and lasting peace in the Middle East which should include the application of both the following principles:

  (i) Withdrawal of Israeli armed forces from territories occupied in the recent conflict;

(ii) Termination of all claims or states of belligerency and respect for and acknowledgment of the sovereignty, territorial integrity and political independence of every State in the area and their right to live in peace within secure and recognized boundaries free from threats or acts of force;

2. *Affirms further* the necessity

(a) For guaranteeing freedom of navigation through international waterways in the area;

(b) For achieving a just settlement of the refugee problem;

(c) For guaranteeing the territorial inviolability and political independence of every State in the area, through measures including the establishment of demilitarized zones;

3. *Requests* the Secretary-General to designate a Special Representative to proceed to the Middle East to establish and maintain contacts with the States concerned in order to promote agreement and assist efforts to achieve a peaceful and accepted settlement in accordance with the provisions and principles in this resolution;

4. *Requests* the Secretary-General to report to the Security Council on the progress of the efforts of the Special Representative as soon as possible.

Appendix 7
United Nations Security Council Resolution 338

After Dr. Kissinger's return to the United States, the Security Council was immediately convened as a matter of urgency by both the Soviet Union and the United States in a night session on October 21, and in the early hours of October 22, the Council adopted a resolution, presented jointly by the United States and the Soviet Union, calling for a cease-fire in the Middle East. Adopted by 14 votes to zero, with China abstaining, the resolution (338 of 1973) was worded as follows:

"The Security Council

"(1) Calls upon all parties to the present fighting to cease all firing and terminate all military activity immediately, no later than 12 hours after the moment of the adoption of this decision, in the positions they now occupy;

"(2) Calls upon the parties concerned to start immediately after the cease-fire the implementation of Security Council 242 in all of its parts [i.e., the resolution of November 22, 1967—for text, see page 25029];

"(3) Decides that, immediately and concurrently with the cease-fire, negotiations start between the parties concerned under the appropriate auspices aimed at establishing a just and durable peace in the Middle East."

Appendix 8

Immigrants and Tourists Settling, By Period of Immigration and Continent of Birth (Jews)

Period of Immigration	Percentages			Absolute Numbers			
	Europe–America	Asia–Africa	Total	Not Known	Europe–America	Asia–Africa	Total
1914–19 V 1948	89.6	10.4	100.0	22,283	385,066	44,809	452,158
1948–1974	51.0	49.0	100.0	20,768	780,284	748,795	1,549,847
1948–1968	45.5	54.5	100.0	19,807	578,837	691,966	1,290,610
1948–1951	51.4	49.6	100.0	19,130	336,623	330,986	686,739
1952–1954	24.0	76.0	100.0	32	12,982	41,051	54,065
1955–1957	31.7	68.3	100.0	613	52,138	112,185	164,936
1958–1960	63.7	36.3	100.0	12	48,106	27,369	75,487
1961–1964	40.1	59.9	100.0	14	91,462	136,570	228,046
1965–1968	46.1	53.9	100.0	6	37,526	43,805	81,337
1969–1974	78.0	22.0	100.0	1,068	201,447	56,722	259,237
1948	85.6	14.4	100.0	11,856	77,032	12,931	101,819
1949	52.7	47.3	100.0	5,325	123,384	110,867	239,576
1950	50.5	49.5	100.0	1,692	85,112	83,411	170,215
1951	29.2	70.8	100.0	257	51,095	123,777	175,129
1952	29.7	70.3	100.0	2	7,242	17,124	24,369
1953	28.3	71.7	100.0	13	3,202	8,111	11,326
1954	13.8	86.2	100.0	16	2,538	15,816	18,370

							Year
8.7	91.3	100.0	6	3,243	34,229	37,478	1955
14.0	86.0	100.0	3	7,911	48,320	56,234	1956
58.0	42.0	100.0	604	40,984	29,636	71,224	1957
55.3	44.7	100.0	2	14,977	12,103	27,082	1958
66.3	33.7	100.0	4	15,855	8,036	23,895	1959
70.5	29.5	100.0	6	17,274	7,230	24,510	1960
52.9	47.1	100.0	7	25,215	22,416	47,638	1961
22.6	77.4	100.0	3	13,874	47,451	61,328	1962
31.8	68.2	100.0	4	20,453	43,907	64,364	1963
58.4	41.6	100.0	–	31,920	22,796	54,716	1964
53.6	46.4	100.0	–	16,470	14,266	30,736	1965
57.7	42.3	100.0	–	9,080	6,650	15,730	1966
38.2	61.8	100.0	–	5,480	8,847	14,327	1967
31.6	68.4	100.0	6	6,496	14,042	20,544	1968
56.0	44.0	100.0	361	21,063	16,380	37,804	1969
62.8	37.2	100.0	254	22,952	13,544	36,750	1970
75.4	24.6	100.0	190	31,471	10,269	41,930	1971
86.4	13.6	100.0	146	48,170	7,572	55,888	1972
89.5	10.5	100.0	116	48,998	5,772	54,886	1973
90.0	10.0	100.0	2	28,792	3,185	31,979	1974

Statistical Abstract of Israel, 1975
Central Bureau of Statistics,
Statistical Abstract of Israel, 1975.

TWENTIETH
CENTURY EUROPE

TWENTIETH CENTURY EUROPE

A HISTORY

C. E. Black
Princeton University

E. C. Helmreich
Bowdoin College

FOURTH EDITION

Alfred · A · Knopf   New York

THIS IS A BORZOI BOOK
PUBLISHED BY ALFRED A. KNOPF, INC.

Copyright, 1950, ©, 1959, 1966, 1972 by Alfred A. Knopf, Inc. All rights reserved under International and Pan-American Copyright Conventions. Published in the United States by Alfred A. Knopf, Inc., New York, and simultaneously in Canada by Random House of Canada Limited, Toronto. Distributed by Random House, Inc., New York.

PUBLISHED, 1950. *Reprinted four times.*
SECOND EDITION, *Revised, Reset, and Printed from New Plates,* 1959.
Reprinted three times.
THIRD EDITION, 1966. *Reprinted seven times.*
FOURTH EDITION, 1972.

Trade Edition: ISBN: 0-394-47274-8
Text Edition: ISBN: 0-394-31638-x
Library of Congress Catalog Card Number: 73-152714
Manufactured in the United States of America
987654321

T O

Louise Roberts Helmreich

A N D

Corinne Manning Black

PREFACE

TO THE FOURTH EDITION

THE rapid development of events in contemporary Europe calls for periodic revisions of this text. As in earlier editions, we have kept the idea in mind that a useful text should be adaptable to the varying emphases of individual instructors on areas or events. The material on the period since World War II has been thoroughly revised and to some extent rearranged. It has seemed appropriate, in view of changing world conditions, to gather the material on former colonies into a chapter on decolonization. This chapter, however, has been so organized that instructors who wish to do so can still assign the relevant sections along with the postwar history of the former imperial states. The material on the United Nations in this edition is presented in two chapters—on the founding and framework of that organization and on its activity over the past twenty-five years. Here too the material may be read together as a single topic. Considerations of time or interest may lead some instructors to omit the history of some of the smaller states, but we have continued to provide accounts for those who wish to include these countries in their view of Europe. The bibliography has been continued and brought up to date, as have the appendices, maps, and illustrations.

C. E. BLACK

E. C. HELMREICH

PREFACE

TO THE THIRD EDITION

IT is with a sense of gratitude to the users of this text that we send forth this third edition. The material has been brought up to date, and a new map and appendix giving essential data on present day Africa have been added. The extensive bibliography has been so well received in the past that we have been encouraged to enlarge it by adding more titles than we have dropped.

C. E. BLACK
E. C. HELMREICH

PREFACE

TO THE SECOND EDITION

IN revising this text and bringing it up to date, we have taken advantage of the experience gained from its extensive use in the classroom. The organization of the material has been simplified somewhat, and a sharper distinction has been drawn between the great powers and the smaller countries.

Many useful suggestions have been received from teachers and students. We are particularly grateful to Harold C. Deutsch, Dwight C. Lee, Louis L. Snyder, and Henry R. Winkler, whose detailed comments proved to be most valuable.

Special acknowledgements for assistance in the final preparation of the revised text are also due to Leroy D. Cross, for typing important sections of the manuscript; to Frank G. Denig, for work on the bibliography; and to Louise Roberts Helmreich, for indispensable help in innumerable ways.

C. E. BLACK
E. C. HELMREICH

PREFACE

EACH generation must interpret history anew, and the profound political and ideological problems which face the world in the aftermath of World War II make it all the more necessary to reappraise the first half of the twentieth century. The authors have centered their study on the European continent, for it is here that the problems of the age have developed in their most acute form. At the start of the century Europe was at the height of its prestige and influence, and even at the present low ebb of its fortunes it commands a position, by virtue of its relationship to the great issues of this era, which is matched by no other comparable region.

A real effort has been made in this volume to give a thorough-going exposition of the problems of the states of eastern Europe, in view of the greatly increased significance of their role during the past fifty years. The authors have also given consideration to the world-wide character of Europe's problems. This applies both to the extensive overseas possessions of the European states, and to the independent non-European states which have had a decisive influence on the events of the twentieth century. Particularly significant among the latter is of course the United States, which had just begun to assume its role as a world power at the start of the century but which now shares the center of the stage. Due consideration has therefore been given to the participation of the United States in the two World Wars which had Europe as their center, and to its role in the great economic depression which was in many ways the most important turning point of the period. Special attention has also been given to the countries of the Near East, which occupy an important position on the periphery of the European continent and continue as in the past to serve as a sensitive barometer of European relationships. The independent states of Africa and Asia have also been given consideration, in so far as their policies have affected the main drama on the European stage.

In presenting their materials the authors have sought a compromise between organization by period and by country. The two main periods in which the domestic political developments of the various countries are narrated in chronological order are those from the first peace settlement to the world depression, and from the depression to World War II. In adopting this form of organization, the authors believe that the advantages of stressing the significance of the depression as a turning point will outweigh the disadvantages of interrupting the narrative in the early 1930's. Such a division makes it possible to keep the picture of Europe as a whole and the simultaneous developments in its various states constantly before the eyes of the reader. The book is nevertheless planned to provide considerable elasticity of treatment, and those desiring to obtain an uninterrupted account of the political development of a given country for the entire period between the two World Wars may do so by reading the appropriate chapters or sections out of sequence. During the two world crises, and the periods immediately preceding and following them, the developments in the individual countries are subordinated to the larger framework of events.

The writing of contemporary history presents many problems of selection and interpretation, to which there is no solution that can hope to gain general acceptance today. The authors are well aware, as individuals who are in general agreement with the objectives being pursued by the Western democracies, that they cannot lay claim to any definitive interpretation of the turbulent period to which this volume is devoted. At the same time they recognize that all of the dominant political trends of this age—including both communism and fascism—represent genuine efforts to solve its problems, and they have therefore attempted to present these diverse views with respect if not with conviction. In attempting to offer a sympathetic exposition of the problems of contemporary Europe and of efforts at their solution, the authors trust that they have taken full advantage of the relative detachment afforded by their American background.

The maps and charts, which have been specially drawn for this volume by Mr. Theodore R. Miller, offer a number of new features. It is hoped that these, as well as the appendices, will prove useful aids to the understanding of the complex problems of contemporary Europe. In preparing this volume the authors have received advice and assistance which they are happy to acknowledge from the following friends and colleagues: Professor Gordon A. Craig, Professor Arthur C. Cressy, Professor Athern P. Daggett, Professor Jean L. Darbelnet, Lieutenant Colonel Andrew J. Goodpaster, Jr., Professor Jeter A. Isely, Professor Robert R. Palmer, and Professor Robert B. Warren. We are grateful to Professor Howard M. Ehrmann, Dr. Harry N. Howard, and Professor Lawrence D. Steefel for their readings of parts of the manuscript. The authors also wish to acknowledge the assistance of Mr. Leroy D. Cross in the typing of the tables, bibliography, and appendices. Finally, a very particular debt of gratitude is owed to Louise Roberts Helmreich, who devoted much time and skill to the editing of the manuscript.

C. E. BLACK

E. C. HELMREICH

CONTENTS

PART I. THE FIRST WORLD CRISIS

PART II. THE GREAT POWERS AND THE SEARCH FOR AN EQUILIBRIUM

PART III.   THE SMALLER POWERS
IN THE INTERWAR PERIOD

PART IV.   THE SECOND WORLD CRISIS

ILLUSTRATIONS

MAPS

BY THEODORE R. MILLER

CHARTS

TABLES

I

THE
FIRST WORLD
CRISIS

CHAPTER

1

The Heritage of the Twentieth Century

The Dynamic Age: *Industrialism; Expansion of Production; Economic Institutions; Social Change.*
The Ideologies of Progress: *Materialism; Nationalism; Liberalism; Socialism.*
The European State System, 1900–14: *The Western Democratic States; Decline of the Eastern Empires.*
Europe and the World: *Sovereignty and Interdependence; Imperialism; Security Through Alliances; Militarism.*

The Dynamic Age

INDUSTRIALISM. Through two world wars and a great economic crisis, Europe has been struggling in the twentieth century to find a political system that will permit its diverse and gifted peoples to live at peace without too great sacrifice of independence on the part of the individual, the national group, the economic class, or the sovereign state. History knows of numerous past ages in which a degree of political stability and social harmony have been achieved, but the solution worked out by one age is never suited to another, and the problems of Europe in the twentieth

century are of a magnitude and intensity never known before. While all
human history has been dynamic, the development of science and the consequent growth of the industrial system since the middle of the eighteenth
century have resulted in social and political adjustments so extensive that
the last two hundred years may safely be labeled "The Dynamic Age."

A survey of the history of Europe during the first half of the twentieth
century reveals a wide variety of controversial problems. It is nevertheless
a sound generalization to say that the central source of unrest has lain in
the contest between the traditional political ideals and institutions centered in sovereign national states, and the economic and social realities
that have to an increasing degree come into conflict with the European
state system. The expanding economy created problems more rapidly than
they could be solved in an orderly fashion by the political institutions that
Europe inherited from the nineteenth century, and as a consequence the
continent became involved in an unprecedented series of wars and economic crises. A glance at Europe as it looked during the first decade of the
twentieth century will provide a panorama of the dilemmas which confronted it.

It is generally agreed that the principal element of change which dis-
tinguishes the Dynamic Age from earlier periods has been the rapid
growth of science and technology. The application of this new knowledge
to economic and social activity, which resulted in the increasing use of
machines in place of manual labor, may for the sake of convenience be
characterized by the general term of "industrialism." Behind this phenomenon lay many centuries of investigation, yet the final flowering of this
achievement occurred in so brief a time as compared with the long sweep
of human history that it may properly be called revolutionary. The application of science to technology in the eighteenth century led to the introduction of a wide variety of machines and processes which facilitated the
expansion of production, and by the end of the nineteenth century industrialism had established itself all over the continent and in many other parts
of the world. While many believed in 1900 that the end of technological
progress was in sight, at least in its current phase, Europe was in fact only
on the threshold of new technological achievements which were destined
further to increase the possibilities of industrial production and to place
new resources of power in the hands of its inhabitants.

What interests us here is less, however, the scientific principles underlying the new inventions or the processes permitting the ever-expanding
conversion of coal and water-power into steam and electricity, than the
impact of these technological developments on the social and economic
life of the inhabitants of the European continent. Had it been possible for
them to enjoy the benefits of their new wealth and power while remaining
within the framework of ideas and institutions which they had known in
the past, there is little reason to believe that the history of the twentieth
century would have been any more dramatic than that of the nineteenth.
This was unfortunately not within the realm of possibility. The organiza-

tion of Europe had in fact been closely related to the livelihood and folk-ways of its inhabitants, and when they changed, it soon became malad-justed. It is therefore important to see what was the measure of the expansion of production, the nature of the resulting social changes and their impact on ideas and ideals, in order to understand the problems that European statesmen faced at the outset of the twentieth century.

EXPANSION OF PRODUCTION. The most characteristic result of indus-trialism was the rapid expansion of production in all the aspects of the economy which it influenced. This is reflected clearly in the figures for the production of such fundamental components of the industrial system as coal, pig iron, and steel:

TABLE 1

EXPANSION OF PRODUCTION *

		UNITED KINGDOM	FRANCE	GERMANY
Steel	1865:	225	41	97
(*thousands of*	1900:	5,130	1,565	6,645
metric tons)	1910:	6,374	3,506	13,698
Pig Iron	1865:	4,892	989	882
(*thousands of*	1900:	9,003	2,714	7,549
metric tons)	1910:	10,380	4,032	14,793
Coal	1860:	80.0	8.1	12.3
(*thousands of*	1900:	225.2	32.7	109.3
metric tons)	1913:	292.0	40.9	277.3

* Adapted from S. B. Clough and C. W. Cole: *Economic History of Europe* (New York, 1941), pp. 538, 545.

These figures on three basic elements of the economy could be matched by many others to illustrate the expansion of material wealth which Europe was witnessing at the start of the twentieth century.

A parallel expansion took place in agricultural production. The use of fertilizers and machinery made larger crops possible, and their rotation and variation permitted better use of soil and climate. At the same time the quantity and quality of livestock was raised through improved breed-ing and care. In contrast to industry, however, the agriculture of the more highly industrialized states found it difficult both to meet the demands of an increasing population and to compete successfully with Eastern Europe and the Americas. As a result, European agriculture went through a diffi-cult period of readjustment from which it was only emerging at the start of the twentieth century.

The expansion of industrial production and the need for larger imports of agricultural goods led to a vast growth in commerce and trade. The rail-road mileage of Europe had grown from 1,818 miles in 1840 to 176,179 miles in 1900, while merchant shipping grew from 186,000 net tons of steamships in 1850 to 19,045,000 in 1910. World commerce, in which Eu-rope had the major share, grew from 2.8 billion dollars in value in 1840 to 20 billion dollars in 1900. By 1910 this figure had been doubled to 40 billion dollars. A similar development took place in domestic commerce.

While the twentieth century thus opened in an atmosphere of continuous expansion in almost every aspect of the European economy, it did not expand steadily but rather in fits and starts. So spontaneous and unregulated an expansion was bound to create as many problems as it solved, and dislocations took the form of business crises that were the result of the fluctuations of prices. These, in turn, reflected the demand and production of all the various products on the market, the supply of gold on which the currencies were based, and other variables characteristic of the economic system. By the first decade of the twentieth century it had been noted that business activity tended to develop in cycles of prosperity and depression. Thus the depression of 1846–48 was followed by a period of prosperity which ended in 1857. A new period of expansion lasted until 1873, and was followed by a twenty-year period of generally falling prices. A general rise in prices took place in the early 1900's, but the upward trend was interrupted in 1900–01 and 1907–09. At the start of the new century, business leaders were nevertheless hardly as conscious of the uncertainties of the industrial system as they were of its potential resources.

ECONOMIC INSTITUTIONS. The growth of industrialism was accompanied by a rapid transformation and development of the institutions devoted to the organization of business and trade. The economic system at the opening of the twentieth century is known by the general term "capitalism." It is a term which has been variously defined, but its essential characteristics are the private ownership of the raw materials and tools of production and exchange, the accumulation of profits in the form of capital, and the investment of capital in the development of new businesses or the maintenance and expansion of old. Arising with the expansion of commerce at the end of the middle ages, the techniques of capitalism gradually developed until by the end of the nineteenth century they constituted the backbone of the industrial system.

The principal task of capitalist institutions was the administration of profits and investments, and this was done by a variety of banks, corporations, and insurance companies. Central banks were established by the principal governments, dealing either directly with large or small businesses or indirectly through private banks. The latter had tended originally to specialize in the financing either of commercial transactions or of business enterprises, but by the beginning of the twentieth century these institutions were being consolidated into larger banks doing a wide variety of business. The credit made available by these banks was generally invested in joint stock companies, or corporations, which in a wide variety of forms administered the production and exchange of goods. The functions of banks and corporations were distinct, but as the capitalist system grew more complex they tended to become inextricably intermingled. By the early 1900's, manufacturing companies and commercial enterprises were forming cartels and mergers on a regional or functional basis, for the purpose of increasing efficiency and reducing competition. These in turn maintained close personal and organizational affiliations with the larger banking firms, with the result that control over large amounts of capital and hence over the livelihood of many thousands of persons frequently lay in the hands of a few individuals.

Parallel to the development of these dominant capitalist institutions, which tended to centralize the administration of capital in relatively few hands, were two other institutions which represented a somewhat different trend while retaining the central capitalist principle of private enterprise. These were the co-operative societies and the insurance companies. The initial purpose of the co-operatives, which were founded in the 1840's, was to reduce the cost of consumption goods to low-income groups by forming joint stock companies in which anyone could buy shares, and then distributing the profits in proportion to the amount of goods purchased by members at the co-operative stores. The co-operatives later went into the production of foodstuffs and household supplies, and by the early 1900's exercised an important influence all over Europe and were welded into an international organization. While the co-operatives served to safeguard the interests of the low-income groups, a far wider variety of interests were protected against the uncertainties of the capitalist system by insurance companies. The various forms of industrial and marine insurance had had a long history. This principle was now extended by certain governments in the form of social insurance for personal hazards such as death, accident, and unemployment. The insurance business was handled in part by private organizations and increasingly in certain countries of Central Europe by the state.

By the turn of the century, the system of private enterprise had also been extended to agriculture. In England and Ireland, as well as in Spain and parts of the Habsburg empire, feudal ownership had been supplanted by large estates worked by tenant farmers who often earned only a precarious living. In most other parts of Western Europe, on the other hand, small holdings were the rule. Here the farmers operated in many respects like small capitalists, borrowing money to make improvements and investing their profits in new equipment. In Russia the peasants were not freed until the 1860's, and the government found it difficult to negotiate a settlement which would provide the peasants enough land to live on and at the same time give adequate compensation to the landlords. After 1905, the government finally made a deliberate effort to settle peasants on the land as independent small holders with the assistance of state banks. This practice of extending state loans was in wide use in Europe by the early 1900's as a means of facilitating the adaptation of the small landowners to the capitalist system.

The capitalist system prided itself on the extent to which private enterprise was able to assume responsibility for industry and commerce, but important functions nevertheless remained to the state. The crucial function of issuing and administering the currency was the responsibility of the state, although the general adoption of the gold standard raised the regulation of money above the level of purely national policy. In addition, the state had accumulated by the end of the nineteenth century a variety of responsibilities in the fields of public works, education, social services, and defense. In accomplishing these tasks, the state dispensed sums equal by 1913 to some 20 per cent of the national income in Great Britain, 14 per cent in France, and 8 per cent in Germany. These sums were raised by a variety of indirect levies, and by direct taxes on income, inheritance, business, and property. Except in the case of Great Britain, even the increasingly heavy taxes did not produce sufficient income to cover budgetary expenditures, and national governments resorted increasingly to borrowing. In all the major European countries with the exception of Great Britain, the national debt was growing rapidly in the opening years of the twentieth century.

SOCIAL CHANGE. The significance of the impact of industrialism was its effect on the life and habits of the peoples of Europe. One of the most immediate and obvious results of the great economic expansion that took place in the nineteenth century was the rapid increase in the population. The population of Europe as a whole grew from 188 million in 1800 to 400 million in 1900, and increased again to 462 million by 1914. Some idea of the growth of population in the principal countries is given by the following table:

TABLE 2

GROWTH OF POPULATION (*in 000's*) *

	ENGLAND AND WALES	RUSSIA (*European*)	GERMANY (*1871 boundaries*)	FRANCE	ITALY
1850:	17,928	57,234	35,310	35,784	24,348
1900:	32,528	103,464	56,367	38,962	32,475
1910:	36,075	142,500	64,926	39,602	34,671

* Adapted from Clough and Cole: *Economic History of Europe*, p. 667; and W. Bowden, M. Karpovich, and A. P. Usher: *An Economic History of Europe Since 1750* (Boston, 1937), p. 21. See also Appendix I of this text.

This phenomenon may be explained both by the improvement in medical care, and by the greatly expanded resources of food and employment which Europe offered by the start of the new century. By the early 1900's the rate of increase was beginning to decline in Western Europe, but the rapid increase was due to continue in the Eastern European countries for several generations.

Of equal importance to the increase in population was its movement from rural areas to industrial cities. While no more than one quarter of the population of France lived in towns over 2,000 in the eighteenth century, about 45 per cent was urban at the start of the twentieth. In England, the proportion of urban population rose from about one half in the middle of the century, to three quarters by 1900. The urban population of Germany rose, even more rapidly, from 36 per cent in 1871 to 60 per cent in 1910. Even in agricultural Russia, the agrarian population declined in proportion from 95 per cent to about 80 per cent during the nineteenth century.

For an area with such a wide variety of conditions as those possessed by the European continent in 1900, it is difficult to make sound generalizations. It nevertheless appears that the great wealth produced by industrialism was relatively slow in making its benefits felt to the great majority of the population. The initial effects of industrialization were in most cases to bring great hardships to the workers in terms of living conditions, and to concentrate economic wealth and control in relatively few hands. By 1900 the most severe phase of the adjustment had nevertheless been passed in Western Europe, and the material benefits of industrialism were more widely felt. Compulsory elementary education, for instance, was enforced in the more advanced countries, and literacy among adults had reached a high level by the turn of the century. As one moved into Eastern Europe conditions became much worse, however, and in Russia the literacy of persons over ten years of age stood at only 45 per cent in 1914, although it was considerably higher in the cities.

The Ideologies of Progress

MATERIALISM. The scientific thought that had contributed so much to the technological advances of industrialism also had an important impact on the thinking of Europe's leaders regarding the relations of man and the universe. The humility of man in the face of the mysteries of the world around him had already begun to give way to a greater self-confidence in the seventeenth and eighteenth centuries, but this could not match the supreme assurance with which most leaders of European thought faced the world in 1900. In the physical sciences, improvements and refinements were constantly being made in the mechanistic system associated with the names of Galileo and Newton. Developments in thermodynamics and electricity, and the rapid discovery of new chemical elements, appeared to confirm more definitely than ever the accepted view that the world was like a great machine whose broad principles were already understood and whose intimate workings would soon be discovered. A similar development had taken place in the biological sciences, which had constructed a world of germs, cells, and heredity giving every evidence of explaining the essential nature of life. Moreover, when Darwin's simple and understandable theory of natural selection was adapted to social science, new reasons for optimism were soon apparent.

The scientific approach, which at the opening of the twentieth century was so self-assured, was bound to diffuse a spirit of optimism in the field of social thought. Economists, political scientists, and sociologists drew easy analogies from the recent discoveries of science, and adopted a positivist attitude which concerned itself primarily with factual analysis. Like a plant or an animal, the evolution of human society and institutions from the earliest times was described, and every hope was entertained that the progress which the past had recorded would be extended into the indefinite future.

The widespread belief in the scientific soundness of rational analysis and in the inevitability of material progress had by the early 1900's become a direct challenge to the established religious beliefs that had ruled men's minds for so many centuries. What had once been regarded as the revealed truths of the Bible had already, in the minds of many persons, been undermined by the work of scholars who had demonstrated the extent to which Christianity had drawn on the Oriental, Classical, and Hebrew traditions. The traditional faith was now further weakened by the general acceptance of a scientific scheme which greatly reduced, if it did not eliminate, the workings of a divine will in the affairs of men and nature. While the state was taking over many of the social functions formerly performed by the church, the spiritual authority that the latter had inspired was being denied by many influential groups. The religious leaders met this threat to the church's authority in various ways, some seeking to show that the spiritual realm was not affected by the claims of science, and others attempting to establish their doctrines on new foundations that would attract the loyalty of the disciples of materialism. These controversies were at their height when the twentieth century opened, and they contributed powerfully to the spirit of the age.

NATIONALISM. There were many reasons why loyalty to the groups that spoke a common language and had common historical traditions—the sentiment known as nationalism—should have had such a powerful emotional hold on the peoples of Europe at the opening of the twentieth century. The great changes in the nineteenth century had taken place primarily within the framework of the national states, and their success had been predicated upon the acceptance of common language and loyalties. The legal structure of the economy and the broad popular education that had been stimulated and demanded by industrialism had both been based on the state system, while the sacrifices and hardships that these required were generally made in the name of national interest. Moreover, the popular scientific beliefs current at the start of the century tended to strengthen the idea that a common language and tradition were as natural a basis for social and political organization as was a common shape of leaf and bark for the classification of trees.

At the same time, nationalism filled many of the spiritual needs of the age. The peasants of Europe had for centuries been guided in their habits and beliefs by local custom and tradition, generally adapted and administered by the church. In the latter half of the nineteenth century millions of peasants left the villages that had been their homes for many generations and went to live in urban environments under entirely new conditions. While they took with them some of their traditional habits, they left many more behind. When urbanization was accompanied by the spread of popular education, as was frequently the case, the loss of traditional beliefs was generally followed by a decline of faith in the authority of the church. By this means a large sector of the population before long had no authority to which it could turn for all the psychological and social services that had traditionally been administered by the local community and the church.

It was only natural that the national state should fill this void. National feeling had the quality of being able to satisfy man's desire for friendship and membership in a group, and to give the satisfaction and security that come from belonging to an organized society. The national state had also by 1900 become almost the sole organization bringing together within a unified system the laws that governed man's public and private affairs, the education that taught him everything from the alphabet as a child to his professional knowledge as a mature person, and, in an increasing number of countries, the social security that guaranteed him medical assistance, unemployment insurance, and a retirement pension. Few institutions in the past had claimed to meet so many of the needs of man in society as did the modern national state, and fewer yet had ever held the loyalty of its members by a stronger emotion than nationalism. That dynasties, religion, and ideological loyalties still had a powerful hold over the peoples of Europe in the early 1900's can be amply demonstrated, but they were everywhere in full retreat before the powerful thrust of nationalism.

If national feeling did not develop its full emotional and social drive until the end of the nineteenth century, it had become a powerful political weapon much earlier. Without tracing its history back to Shakespeare, or to Chaucer as some would have it, one may cite the Reformation as an example of the hold which national feeling was able to exercise even when confronted with the powerful attraction of a religion with universal claims. The propagandists of the French Revolution found nationalism a powerful weapon against the dynastic loyalties which were predominant in Europe at the end of the eighteenth century, and until the middle of the nineteenth national feeling was a sentiment which bound the new industrial forces with the more radical republicans as opposed to the interests of the landed gentry. Only in the latter part of the nineteenth century, when the economic groups that dominated the industrial system had achieved political power, did nationalism become a doctrine of conservatism rather than of revolt. At the start of the twentieth century, nationalism was the dominant emotional bond that provided Europeans with a community, a tradition, a set of moral standards, a legal framework for business transactions, and a motivation for political activity.

LIBERALISM. The landed gentry, which had governed Europe since the Middle Ages through dynastic states, relinquished its predominant political position only gradually. The French Revolution is generally regarded as the classic case of the transfer of political power from the landed interests to those that derived their strength from commerce and industry, although this process had been started earlier and more gradually in England and did not take place until the twentieth century in some parts of Eastern Europe. The middle class, or the bourgeoisie, as those who derive their income from the management of commerce and industry are generally known, did not achieve stable political power even in Western Europe until the middle of the nineteenth century. Allied during the first part of the century with the working-class movements, the efforts of the middle class to displace the gentry had culminated in the widespread revolutions of 1848. In the course of these disturbances both the middle class and the landed gentry had been impressed by the violence and excesses of the working class, and the middle class ended by assimilating the gentry rather than displacing it. This alliance of the middle class with the gentry was most fully achieved in England, but it was also characteristic of the entire continent. The interests of the working class and of the peasantry were protected to a greater or lesser degree by the ruling groups, but in no country did their political organizations achieve sufficient strength to give them political office of cabinet rank.

The middle class thus held effective political power at the opening of the twentieth century, and the philosophy and principles that characterized its outlook and guided its policies are known under the general term of "liberalism." Developed in an age in which the middle class was asserting the interests of commerce and industry against those of a dominant gentry, liberalism laid special emphasis on the freedom of the individual from all controls by the state. The ideology of progress and change taught that in a vigorous and free competition the best man would survive, and it was the task of liberalism to develop the legal framework of political and economic institutions best suited to the needs of progress. The typical liberalism of the early 1900's thus stressed the extension of suffrage and education, the enforcement of civil liberties, and the adoption of parliamentary government. In the economic field, liberalism favored letting the law of supply and demand run its free course in determining the price of goods and the cost of labor. In its more abstract form, liberalism set the greater freedom of the individual as the goal towards which society should be directed, and believed that the path of freedom would lead man to happiness.

At the same time, the early 1900's were years of intense nationalism, and many who marched behind the banner of liberalism were inclined to believe that the individual could achieve his fullest expression only within the boundaries of a well-organized and secure national state. As competition became sharper among the industrialized states, many who felt their business interests to be threatened turned to the state for protection. They tended to place national interest above individual liberty, and modified their liberalism by transferring to the state many of the attributes of authority and independence with which they had formerly endowed the individual. By the turn of the century, conservative parliamentary parties in a number of countries had begun to call themselves "national liberals."

SOCIALISM. As the ideology of material progress, liberalism in the broadest sense predominated throughout Europe. In countries where agrarian interests still played an important part, as was the case with Austria-Hungary, the tenets of liberalism possessed wide appeal. Even in peasant Russia the emperor found it necessary in 1905 to permit the establishment of a semi-parliamentary regime, although he did not have the wisdom nor did the middle class have the skill or strength to make the full transition to parliamentary government. While the agrarian interests were finding a satisfactory place for themselves in the liberal structure, the workers were not satisfied with their position and were gradually organizing in an effort to secure a greater share in the determination of policy. The working-class ideologies which were juxtaposed to the tenets of liberalism are generally grouped under the broad term of "socialism."

Most workers were not convinced that they had a great deal to gain if the laws of supply and demand were allowed to operate unhindered. Without any personal resources to fall back on, and without any systematic assistance from society, they felt that they were largely at the mercy of the employers when bargaining for better wages and working conditions. The policies of the liberal parties which predominated in the parliaments of Europe tended to favor employers over employees, and so the latter turned to organizing in order to obtain greater political influence. The utopian societies which socialist thinkers had set as their goal in the early part of the nineteenth century were soon abandoned in favor of trade unions, mutual assistance organizations, and co-operative societies. While these programs helped to solve the economic problems of the workers, political power could only be obtained through the organization of political parties, and it was to these that they turned by the end of the nineteenth century.

A wide variety of socialist teachings inspired the labor parties at the turn of the century, and of these the most influential were those of Marx and Engels [see below, pp. 191–94]. Marx's views gained a predominant influence by virtue of their simplicity and appeal, although there was no full agreement on the details of the Marxian program. The principal tenet of the political program of Marxism and related social doctrines was that the socialist parties should win political power and exert their influence to enlist the power of the state in the interests of the workers. They favored steeply graduated income taxes, social security programs, public education and housing, and ultimately the ownership by the state of all the means of production. Unlike the liberals, the socialists believed in principle that the interests of the individual could be achieved better through international co-operation than by national rivalry. Like the liberals, however, the socialists tended to appeal to national loyalties when it served their party organizations to do so. In no European country had the socialists won political leadership by the first decade of the twentieth century, but they were gaining steadily in electoral strength and the time was in sight when in the normal course of events they would be participating in the formation of cabinets.

The European State System, 1900–14

The expansion of commerce in the Western Mediterranean and North Atlantic sea lanes in the sixteenth and seventeenth centuries, which prepared the way for the subsequent development of industrialism, had given an important head start to the peoples of Western Europe. Located in the center of the new sphere of business activity, and relatively secure from foreign invasion, England early took the lead in developing modern parliamentary institutions and during the nineteenth century possessed the most stable traditions of democratic freedom. France and its neighbors on the Atlantic seaboard had by the early 1900's caught up with England and in certain respects passed it, and the recently unified states of Germany and Italy had been functioning for some two generations as constitutional states. Farther east, the peoples of Europe lived in the multinational and predominantly agrarian empires of Austria-Hungary, Russia, and Turkey, or had only recently achieved independence. In the great empires important remnants of the dynastic autocracies of the past still persisted, and in the Balkan countries that had been liberated in the nineteenth century, the development of parliamentary institutions had been delayed by the demands of national unification.

THE WESTERN DEMOCRATIC STATES. In their most advanced form, parliamentary institutions were solidly based on full civil liberties, public education in the primary grades, and more or less universal manhood suffrage. No country met the highest standards set by the liberals in all of these fields, but all were working towards them as best they could. The broad agreement as to the desirability of the parliamentary system did not, of course, imply any general consensus as to the specific policies which should be adopted. Wide divergencies existed among the political parties on such questions as taxation, tariff rates, and the allotment of appropriations to the various branches of government. The question of the intervention of the government in the economic life of the country, either to rescue private enterprise in distress or to protect public welfare, was likewise a burning issue everywhere. For the democratic theorists of the early 1900's the important thing was the maintenance of free discussion and decision by majority vote within the parliamentary framework; as long as democratic procedures were followed, mistakes could be rectified and injustices eventually compensated for.

By the opening decade of the twentieth century, the major countries that had advanced farthest along the road surveyed by liberal democrats were France and Great Britain. While the British had a sounder tradition of parliamentary government and a more stable cabinet system, the French had established public education on a more democratic basis and in the face of many obstacles had contributed more to the diffusion of liberal ideas on the continent. In France the more advanced liberals established themselves in power after 1902 under the leadership of Combes, Rouvier, Clemenceau, and Briand. In an atmosphere of considerable political agitation, a law was passed in 1905 disestablishing the Roman Catholic church. This act deprived the church of the fiscal support of the state, while the latter voluntarily gave up the right which it had enjoyed of passing on the appointment of the higher clergy. During this period the income tax was raised, social legislation was passed, and measures were taken to restrict the use of strikes on the part of the trade unions. The socialists cooperated with the radicals on some of these measures, but on the whole pursued an independent policy and were not strong enough to play a determining role. Far weaker was the royalist minority, which was reorganized in 1898 as the *Action Française*. As foreign affairs began to take precedence over social problems in the years after 1910, the balance of political power swung to the more nationalistic moderates led by Barthou and Poincaré.

The Conservatives, headed by Salisbury, were in power in England at the time of Queen Victoria's death in 1901, and continued to govern for several more years under Balfour (1902–05). The era that came to an end with the death of the Queen had been a brilliant one for the empire, but signs of international strife had already appeared in the Far East, in North Africa, and most embarrassingly of all in the South African Boer War. An extensive program of domestic reform was undertaken by the Liberal cabinets of Campbell-Bannerman (1905–08) and Asquith (1908–16). This program included an extension of the educational system, regulation of the liquor business, accident compensation, and health and unemployment insurance for workingmen. Even more important was Lloyd George's budget of 1909 which provided for increased income and inheritance taxes, and levies on various forms of unearned income. The whole Liberal program was opposed by the Conservatives, and this opposition culminated in the rejection of the budget of 1909 by the House of Lords. This stand by the upper house led to a great constitutional crisis, involving the question whether a hereditary House of Lords could be permitted in a modern democracy to stop legislation desired by a House of Commons which was based on universal suffrage.

In true democratic fashion, general elections were held in January and December, 1910, and in each case the country returned a Liberal majority, although somewhat reduced in strength. The House of Lords finally capitulated, and accepted the Parliament Bill of 1911, in which its right to veto a money bill was taken away. The Lords retained the power only to delay for two years, but not to veto permanently, other measures. The Liberals now passed two further pieces of reform legislation: the National Insurance Act of 1911, and the Minimum Wage Law of 1912. The perennial question of home rule for Ireland was also injected into the constitutional struggle, and the Liberals sponsored a Home Rule Bill providing for parliamentary government for the whole of Ireland. This controversial measure was finally adopted in September, 1914. Its implementation was, however, suspended because of the war, and the door was left open for a reconsideration of the status of the Protestants of northern Ireland, who feared that in

a unitary state their interests would be discriminated against by the Catholic majority.

Similar to France and Great Britain in the general temper of their political regimes were the Lowland kingdoms of Belgium and the Netherlands, and the Scandinavian kingdoms of Denmark, Norway, and Sweden.
The Lowland countries leaned towards a more conservative form of democracy, and in both monarchies the election laws fell considerably short of
providing equal and universal suffrage. In Belgium the conservative Clericals were continuously in power, while in the Netherlands the Clericals
alternated in power with a weak Liberal party. Important social legislation
was nevertheless passed in the Netherlands, and both countries developed
a spirit of toleration in the face of deep religious and ethnic cleavages. The
spirit of cautious reform was symbolized by the ruling monarchs. In 1890
Queen Wilhelmina started her long reign of fifty-eight years, and in 1909
Albert I succeeded his uncle, Leopold II, in Belgium.

Developing in relative peace after the Napoleonic wars, the three Scandinavian kingdoms reached full maturity as democratic and parliamentary
states during the early years of the twentieth century. Denmark established
a parliamentary system based on broad suffrage in 1914–15, having already
gone a long way in providing social legislation and in establishing its agriculture and dairy farming on a sound basis. Norway and Sweden had been
united under a single crown since 1815, but their political traditions and
economic interests were divergent, and in 1905 the separation of the two
states was negotiated peacefully. Norway had already introduced universal
manhood suffrage, and in 1907 this privilege was extended to women. All
three Scandinavian states were destined to benefit greatly from their relative isolation from the wars and turmoils of the twentieth century. During
the long reigns of their modern monarchs, Haakon VII (1905–57) in Norway, Gustavus V (1907–50) in Sweden, and Christian X (1912–47) in
Denmark, they developed a level of political stability and social welfare
which was the envy of the whole world.

Similar in its achievements as a small and peaceful democracy, although quite different in its social and political structure, was the republic
of Switzerland. Organized as a federal state, Switzerland had a bicameral
legislature in which the twenty-two cantons were represented in the upper
house, while the lower was elected on the basis of universal suffrage. The
executive authority was exercised by a Federal Council of seven, one of
whom was elected by the legislature each year to serve as president of the
republic. Under this system of government Switzerland had a unique record of civic freedom, and it was frequently chosen as the headquarters for
international organizations and conferences. This stability was achieved in
spite of wide differences of language among the inhabitants of Switzerland.

The western states bordering on the Mediterranean Sea were not so
well adapted to the conditions of industrialism as were their northern
neighbors, and on the whole made slower progress towards the goal set by
the ideology of liberalism. Upon its establishment in 1861, the kingdom of

Italy had inherited the liberal Piedmontese Constitution of 1848. This provided for a parliamentary system with a bicameral legislature, elected under a suffrage system that was made almost universal in 1912. The economic poverty of the country, however, aggravated by a rapidly growing population, prevented the establishment of a fully stable political regime. The governments under Giolitti (1903–05, 1906–09, 1911–14) struggled incessantly with social unrest, and to these troubles was added a disastrous earthquake in Sicily in 1908 which took some 150,000 lives. In the latter part of the nineteenth century Italy had suffered humiliating defeats in its African ventures, and these were to some extent redressed in 1911–12 by the victory over Turkey in Tripoli. On the whole, however, the early years of the long reign of Victor Emmanuel III (1900–44) were not much happier than the later.

Spain and Portugal presented a picture which was even less in harmony with the times. The prestige of the Spanish monarchy suffered greatly as a consequence of defeat at the hands of the United States in 1898. The conservative regime met political opposition from the liberals, the republicans, and a vigorous socialist party. There was also a strong movement in the province of Catalonia, which desired an autonomous government. Alfonso XIII (1902–31) did not succeed in fulfilling his monarchical function of providing a rallying point for patriotic leaders, and the political parties wrestled ineffectually with their social and economic problems. In Portugal the decline in monarchical competence went even further, and the assassination of Carlos I in 1908 was followed by the deposition two years later of Manuel II. The republic that was established in 1910 under the leadership of Braga and Arriaga adopted an advanced liberal program, but attempts at reform were soon stifled by the social unrest accompanying World War I.

Of all the countries that had adopted constitutional government, Germany presented the most puzzling contrasts. In both a geographical and a political sense the German Empire represented a transition between the parliamentary systems of the West and the dynastic traditions of the East. The rapid industrialization of Germany at the end of the nineteenth century had produced a strong middle class, and both employers and workers had built up powerful political organizations in the National Liberal and Social Democratic parties. At the same time the Progressive People's party stood for a more moderate form of parliamentary liberalism. The strongly authoritarian and dynastic Conservative party, by contrast, relied heavily on the support of the Prussian landed gentry and wielded important influence. Between these two trends, and frequently holding the balance of political power, was the Center party, which represented the Catholic interests in Germany.

In the fields of science, scholarship, and popular education Germany was a leader in Europe, and its society contained many of the elements which make for a highly developed political life. German political culture was nevertheless characterized also by a widespread acceptance of militarism and authoritarianism. Centuries of disunity and strife had apparently bred in the German people a feeling of deep political insecurity, and they were inclined to entrust their nation's welfare to the military leadership of the landed gentry that had successfully engineered Germany's unification in the decade before 1870. This tendency was well illustrated by the fatuous emperor William II, who retained constitutional powers in the realm of military and foreign affairs throughout his long reign (1888–1918) thus placing himself beyond the reach of the parliament. The government was headed by Chancellors Bülow (1900–09) and Bethmann-Hollweg (1909–17), who lacked the firmness of character to stem the impulsiveness of their emperor. Germany achieved a remarkable record in the fields of social legislation, public administration, and municipal government, and within certain limits it enjoyed vigorous and democratic political activity. The crucial decisions of foreign affairs, which in the European system formed the keystone of national politics, nevertheless remained in the hands of the dynasty and were made in large measure without the participation of the German people.

DECLINE OF THE EASTERN EMPIRES. The political outlook in Eastern Europe at the opening of the twentieth century presented a vastly different picture from that in the more fully industrialized states of the West. The Austrian, Russian, and Turkish empires had consolidated their rule over Eastern Europe in the eighteenth century. Despite the widely different traditions they represented, they had many traits in common. All three were dynastic empires in which the landed gentry, and other privileged military and bureaucratic groups around the throne, wielded political power out of all proportion to the numbers or interests they represented. Moreover, industrialization had made relatively slow headway in these strongholds of agriculture, and a middle class that could challenge the dynastic system was only beginning to make its strength felt. The governments of all three empires still retained vigorous authoritarian traits, although in the case of Austria these were softened by the urbanity and inefficiency of the central administrative organs. Any tendency towards a liberalization of the rigid bureaucratic system was held back by the presence of large minority populations in each of the three empires. These minorities were eager to win a degree of autonomy, and were quick to take advantage of any concession of political rights to set in motion important changes of frontier and government.

Closest to the Western tradition was the Habsburg empire of Austria-Hungary. The complex constitutional structure evolved by this empire is described elsewhere [see below, pp. 36–40], but attention may be drawn here to the many forces that were tending to tear the empire apart. The greatest source of division was the mixture of nationalities. While the two political units comprising the state were dominated by the Germans and the Magyars, respectively, the Slavic minorities actually comprised 46 per cent of the population of the empire in 1910. The German-speaking Austrians (23 per cent) and the Magyars (20 per cent) together accounted for only 43 per cent of the population, while a variety of minority groups made up the remaining 11 per cent. Yet there were many loyalties holding the empire together, despite the diversity of the population. Such institutions as the Roman Catholic church, the privileged aristocracy, and the army drew their support from numerous national groups and found a common symbol in the aging emperor, Francis Joseph I, who was coming to the end of his long reign (1848–1916). Similarly the large bureaucracy, drawn from the middle class, and the important business interests living on the extensive commerce that formed the lifeblood of the empire, found it to their advantage to support the large political structure whose collapse would have meant their ruin. With such a complex balance of loyalties the conduct of parliamentary government was difficult, and even the introduction of universal suffrage in the Austrian part of the empire in 1907 failed to contribute greatly to its political stability.

In Russia minority questions played a secondary role, and the major problem faced by Nicholas II during his stormy reign (1894–1917) was that of retaining his autocratic powers in face of demands for constitutional reform on the part of a liberal middle class and gentry, and a growing socialist movement. For many generations the social and political conditions in Russia had favored the centralized and autocratic system of government established in the eighteenth century. This regime had the support of a large army, bureaucracy, and police force. It also had as a powerful source of support the Orthodox church, which was administered as a branch of the government. Important agrarian and civic reforms were put through in the latter half of the nineteenth century, but these had been accomplished without sacrifice of the absolute power of the emperor. To this absolute power Nicholas II clung with a tenacity born of his early education as heir to the throne of the Romanovs, and nurtured by his own short-sightedness and the tenacious will of his German-born wife, the Empress Alexandra. There was nevertheless an important body of educated Russian opinion which, while recognizing that conditions in Russia differed from those in Western Europe, held that the important step from autocracy to parliamentary government was long overdue. This view was held by informed persons of all classes, although there were many opinions as to the precise direction reform should take. While many favored a gradual transition from limited suffrage to full parliamentary democracy, following the evolutionary process through which most Western states had passed, there was also a revolutionary strain in Russian thought which had arisen in reaction to the limitations placed on political activity in Russia.

All of these tendencies came to the fore in the winter of 1904–05, when a disastrous war with Japan in the Far East revealed the inefficiency of the old regime and made the government particularly vulnerable to attack. Discontent found expression in civic unrest culminating in a general strike in October, 1905, which brought transportation and business to a standstill. Nicholas II thereupon issued his October Manifesto, which promised a constitution and a parliamentary assembly, and as proof of his good intentions he appointed the able Witte as prime minister. The terms of the new constitution were published in the following spring, and it turned out that Nicholas had no intention of relinquishing his autocratic powers. When the Parliament, or Duma, met, only the conservative Octobrists were satisfied with its limited consultative powers. The liberal Constitutional Democratic party, or Cadets, which had won the largest number of seats, refused to co-operate with the government and forced a dissolution of the first Duma. The extremist Social Revolutionary and Social Democratic parties were even more violent in their opposition. Despite this opposition, the government found it possible through a liberal use of force and with the aid of foreign loans to restrict further the powers of the Duma and even to withdraw some of the meager concessions which the emperor had made during the crisis of 1905–06. This policy was executed by the vigorous prime minister Stolypin (1906–11), and the assassination that terminated his career was symbolic of the antagonism aroused by the policies of Nicholas II during his later years.

The Turkish Empire was passing through a somewhat parallel period of change. The bulk of the empire was in Asia, but in 1900 European Turkey, including the capital city of Constantinople, had a population of some 6,000,000. Moreover, this region played an important role in European affairs, on account of the restless nationalism of its inhabitants and the constant interference of the great powers. Turkey had known several centuries of greatness in which it had built a powerful empire through a combination of military strength and administrative ability. The empire had experienced a period of decline since the seventeenth century, however, and it had already lost a large proportion of its possessions in Europe. This decline had given rise to a strong reform movement within the government, and many attempts had been made in the course of the nineteenth century to reorganize the empire along more modern lines. Abdul Hamid II had even experimented with a constitution during the first year of his reign (1876–1909), but had soon returned to the more traditional methods of oppression. When the twentieth century opened, the westernized elements of the ruling class, known as the Young Turks, were preparing to take action. An opportunity was offered during an international crisis in 1908, and the Sultan was forced to restore the constitution of 1876, which provided for an elected parliament. When the Sultan tried to regain his authority a year later, he was replaced by his brother, Mohammed V (1909–15). Turkey was still far from being a modern parliamentary state, but an important step had been taken and henceforth policies were to be determined by vigorous, Western-minded leaders.

The minority peoples of Eastern Europe were destined to play a crucial role in the history of that continent in the twentieth century, and by 1900 the process of national liberation had already made substantial achievements in the Balkan peninsula. Since the Turkish Empire was the furthest advanced in the process of disintegration, it was the countries of Southeastern Europe which first gained their independence. The first steps towards independence were taken by Montenegro in 1799, by Serbia in 1804, by Greece in 1821, by Rumania in 1856, and by Bulgaria in 1878. In each of these countries the nationalist movements had adopted the Liberal ideology of Western Europe, and constitutional systems were established giving the peoples of this region an apprenticeship in the techniques of self-government. In every case, however, only partial independence had been gained during the nineteenth century, and in 1900 each country had fellow-nationals in adjacent territory still under foreign sovereignty. The desire to liberate the remaining minorities inevitably took precedence over the trend towards parliamentary government, and democratic processes were regularly sacrificed in the interest of national unity and military preparedness. This tendency towards authoritarian methods was generally favored by the monarchs, in most cases foreign-born, who used the unfulfilled nationalist aims as an excuse for retaining royal prerogatives. The alliance of Balkan states which successfully defeated Turkey in 1912–13, and the subsequent strife that broke out among the allies, was a characteristic incident in the nationalist activity that absorbed public attention at the expense of political maturity. Only in Greece was distinct progress made towards democratic parliamentary government, when constitutional reforms were adopted in 1911 under the leadership of Venizelos.

The minorities living in Austria-Hungary and Russia became increasingly restless, but the increase of their civil rights within the traditional structure was their goal rather than independence. In Austria-Hungary, the Croats and the Slovenes were particularly sensitive to the success of nationalism in the Balkans. Closely akin to the Serbs in language and aspirations, these two Slavic national minorities joined with the kindred peoples in Bosnia and Herzegovina to form an area of continual resistance against the restraints imposed by the Austrian and Hungarian regimes. The Rumanian minority in the Hungarian province of Transylvania was similarly aroused by the success of their compatriots in neighboring Rumania, as were the Italians in the region around Trieste by the strident nationalism of independent Italy. The Czechs and Slovaks, living in the Austrian provinces of Bohemia and Moravia and in northern Hungary, lacked the stimulation of a neighboring national state and expressed their discontent by constant agitation for autonomous rights. Less fortunate were the Poles, who, divided among Germany, Austria, and Russia, had to contend with all three empires. While Germany and Austria granted them substantial civil rights, the largest number of Poles lived in Russia, where they were able to engage in formal political activity only after 1905. The Finns were more fortunate in being organized as a separate Grand Duchy, and despite constant Russian encroachments were able to preserve certain autonomous rights. The large Jewish minority in Russia, on the other hand, found itself largely without rights or sympathy and the object of systematic discrimination by the government. Large numbers of Russian Jews emigrated to the United States, while others found solace in the Zionist movement which aspired to the establishment of a Jewish state in Palestine.

Europe and the World

SOVEREIGNTY AND INTERDEPENDENCE. Few problems were more characteristic of Europe at the beginning of the twentieth century than the conflict between the desire of each state to strengthen its control over all
phases of national life, and the increasing interdependence of the European peoples in their social, economic, and cultural activity. The weakening of traditional local institutions through urbanization and the powerful
emotional ties that now bound people into national groups had served to
thrust ever-increasing power into the hands of national states. At the same
time, this tendency had been intensified by the great expansion of legal machinery necessary for the smooth working of the industrial system. As the
only source of authority, it was again to the national state that the new
powers of incorporation and regulation accrued. The national state thus
commanded both the emotional loyalty of its citizens, who looked to it for
security, and the power to control the corporate social and economic activity of its inhabitants. The strength and welfare of a person's national state
was, at least for the average Western European at the opening of the
twentieth century, the value which took precedence over all others.

Yet in fact the social and economic activities of the European peoples
were by no means restricted by their national frontiers. Raw materials and
markets knew no boundaries, and many European businessmen recognized
that they had more to gain on an international than on a national basis. At
about the turn of the century, in the field of textiles, steel rails, dyes, and
numerous raw materials, international trusts were organized in which producers drew up agreements regarding prices, volume of production, and
the division of markets. Similarly, in the field of finance, national boundaries were easily broken down when banks could increase their profits by
pooling their resources with respect to specific geographical spheres of investment. The governments themselves were not entirely consistent in
dealing with the problem of economic interdependence. On the whole,
tariffs were being raised at the turn of the century and each country was
seeking to protect domestic industries from foreign competition. Among
the great powers only Great Britain felt secure enough to maintain a free
trade policy during a period when competition was becoming increasingly
sharp. In certain fields, however, European governments recognized the
advantages of co-operation. Full international co-operation obtained in the
fields of telegraph and postal services, rail and water transportation, patents
and copyrights, and the like. Likewise, most of the currencies were regulated under the conventions of the Latin Monetary Union.

Like the European-wide, and frequently world-wide, economic institutions that grew out of the industrial era, in spite of the strong attractions of
national sovereignty, social and political activity was not confined within
national frontiers. Religion was by its very nature a system of beliefs for
which national frontiers had little intrinsic meaning, and of the organized
churches the Roman Catholic had the most impressive record of interna-

tional activity. Following on the long and eventful pontificate of Leo XIII (1878–1903), Pius X during his briefer tenure of office (1903–14) continued the work of his predecessor in reorganizing the administration of the church and in combating attempts to revise its dogmas. By providing an alternative source of authority to the state in matters of faith for the 160,-000,000 Roman Catholics in Europe, the Catholic church tended to temper somewhat the more extreme nationalist movements. The Protestant and Eastern Orthodox churches were organized on a national basis, but they likewise served to some degree as a counterforce to the predominant nationalist trend. Of the political parties, the Socialists were the most vigorous to press the point that the interests of the European peoples could best be served by internationalism. The Second International, founded in 1889, was an active force in stimulating the co-operation of the various socialist parties despite the strong pull that each party felt towards purely national policies. The various national trade union organizations and co-operative movements were similarly joined to form international bodies at the turn of the century. Liberal leaders interested in promoting world peace generally placed emphasis on the development of international law. The various conventions drawn up by the Second International Peace Conference at The Hague, in 1907, were typical of the efforts made in this direction.

IMPERIALISM. The claim of the European states to full sovereignty over their respective inhabitants was further weakened by the fact that in most cases they could not provide a satisfactory livelihood for their rapidly growing populations. As a result, no less than 50,000,000 persons emigrated from Europe in the century after 1820. The largest number went to the United States to seek a better living, but many others also settled in Latin America, Africa, Asia, and Australia. Investments likewise overflowed national frontiers, in search of larger returns than could be obtained at home. In 1914 British foreign investments amounted to four billion pounds, of which over one half was invested outside of the empire. French and German investments in 1914, amounting to some forty-five billion francs and twenty-seven billion marks respectively, were invested primarily outside of their empires. The emigrations of peoples and of capital are only the most striking examples of the limited and almost fictional character of the authority claimed by the national states of Europe. The legal structure and the dominant political institutions of Europe were organized on a national basis, and to a very considerable degree the chief emotional loyalty of the European peoples was to their national state. At the same time many of the activities of the European peoples, particularly in the economic field, bore little relation to national frontiers. The result of this situation was that national leaders throughout Europe developed a deep-seated feeling of insecurity.

This sense of insecurity on the part of the European national states was reflected in the eagerness with which they competed to extend their sovereignty over the unoccupied portions of the world. This imperialism, which was a continuation of the colonial expansion of earlier centuries, was greatly intensified after 1870 and reached its climax at the turn of the century. By 1914 the European states had extended their rule over some twenty million square miles of non-European territory, with a total population estimated at almost 500,000,000. The following table provides a general picture of the extent and distribution of these possessions:

TABLE 3

OVERSEAS POSSESSIONS OF EUROPEAN STATES, 1914 *
(*Population in 000's*)

	AFRICA	ASIA	AUSTRALIA AND PACIFIC	AMERICA AND N. ATLANTIC	TOTALS
Belgium	15,000.0	....	....	....	15,000.0
Denmark	....	....	....	125.8	125.8
France	26,681.2	14,773.0	81.1	450.9	40,986.2
Germany	11,428.4	168.9	636.5	....	12,041.6
Great Britain	37,990.2	323,865.9	6,551.5	10,096.8	378,504.4
Italy	1,373.2	....	....	....	1,373.2
Netherlands	....	38,000.0	....	140.6	38,140.6
Portugal	8,243.6	895.8	....	....	9,139.4
Spain	235.8	....	....	....	235.8
				Grand Total	495,547.0

* Adapted from *Statesman's Year-Book*, 1914.

The significance of European imperialism is that by the turn of the century it had very largely failed of its principal aims. It did serve temporarily and in a limited degree to relieve the pressure of population and to provide new opportunities for investment, new markets, and new sources of raw material. European imperialism failed in its major implicit objective, however, which was to provide economic and political security for the national states of Europe. By 1900 substantially all territory available for imperial occupation had been taken, and the process had contributed little or nothing towards a solution of the political problems of the European states. As they extended their sovereignty over distant regions, the European states found that their responsibilities and difficulties increased with their possessions. While some countries were more successful than others in their imperial ventures, and Germany was comparatively unsuccessful because of its late arrival on the scene, no European state was strong enough to feed its inhabitants or nourish its industries without extensive reliance on commercial interchange with rival states.

SECURITY THROUGH ALLIANCES. Unable to achieve security through imperialism, the European states after the turn of the century turned increasingly to alliances in an effort to attain the security that they were unable to achieve singlehanded. Certain elements of the alliance system had existed for a generation before 1900, and now the European states re-examined their traditional ties and formed new ones. As a result, the European great powers found themselves divided on the eve of World War I into two groups: the Triple Alliance, comprising Germany, Austria-Hungary, and Italy; and the Triple Entente, including France, Russia, and Great Britain.

The basic agreement of the Triple Alliance was the alliance formed between Germany and Austria-Hungary in 1879 and renewed periodically. It provided that if either country were attacked by Russia, the other would come to its aid. In 1882 Italy joined this group. Germany and Italy were to aid each other in case of aggression by France, and if any of the three allies were attacked by two or more great powers, the others were pledged to come to its aid. As the years passed, relations between France and Italy improved, and in 1902 they exchanged letters promising each other to remain neutral in case either was attacked by one or more powers. Technically this promise was not contrary to Italy's obligations under the Triple Alliance, since this too was a defensive agreement and Italy was pledged to aid Germany only in case of a French attack. In reality, however, Italy had a foot in each camp and made the best use it could of this advantageous position. For a time Rumania also was associated with the Triple Alliance, having made an agreement with Germany and Austria-Hungary in 1883 which was aimed at mutual protection against a Russian attack. The events of the Balkan wars of 1912–13 resulted in a change in Rumania's outlook, and by the outbreak of the war it leaned more towards Russia than towards Germany.

The Triple Entente was of more recent date than the Triple Alliance, its rival, having originated in a series of agreements between France and Russia negotiated in 1891–94. These agreements provided for mutual military assistance in case either of the two countries were attacked by Germany, alone or in alliance with Italy or Austria-Hungary. They provided also that both France and Russia would mobilize immediately in case one or more of the members of the Triple Alliance mobilized. Within a few years Great Britain moved towards closer relations with France and Russia. Long an advocate of "splendid isolation," Great Britain had become impressed with the dangers of isolation by the rise of German naval power, and the costly competition with France in North Africa and with Russia in Central Asia. Britain's exposed position had been clearly revealed during the war against the Boers in South Africa (1899–1902), and an indication of a change in policy had been given in 1902 with the conclusion of an alliance with Japan. Having failed on several occasions to reach an understanding with Germany, Great Britain now turned to France and negotiated an agreement in 1904 providing for a friendly settlement of their differences in Egypt and Morocco. A similar agreement was reached between Great Britain and Russia in 1907, which provided for a division of spheres of influence in Persia, the recognition of British interests in Afghanistan, and a joint promise to respect the territorial integrity of the Chinese province of Tibet. In contrast to an "alliance," an "entente" is less specific in its terms and less binding in its obligations. The Triple Entente nevertheless represented a clear-cut rival to the Triple Alliance, and was so regarded. The

Entente was considerably strengthened by secret general staff conversations between Great Britain and France which, without making definite commitments, provided for a mutually convenient disposition of the military and naval forces of the two countries in case of a war with Germany.

MILITARISM. This diplomatic activity was accompanied by vigorous military and naval preparations on the part of all the great powers. Differences in the relative importance of land and sea defense, in the size and location of overseas possessions, and in the population of the home country,

TABLE 4

MILITARY EXPENDITURES OF THE GREAT POWERS *

	STANDING ARMY (000)	ARMY APPROPRIA- TION ($000,000)	NAVAL TONNAGE (000)	NAVAL APPROPRIA- TION ($000,000)	TOTAL DEFENSE EXPENDI- TURE ($000,000)	COST PER CAPITA HOME POPULA- TION ($)
Triple Alliance						
Germany						
1870	403	48	42	6	54	1.33
1890	487	121	190	23	144	2.95
1914	812	442	1305	112	554	8.52
Austria-Hungary						
1870	247	37	73	4	41	1.16
1890	337	58	66	6	64	1.56
1914	424	143	372	38	182	3.48
Italy						
1870	334	32	70	7	39	1.44
1890	262	56	242	23	79	2.63
1914	305	92	498	49	141	3.81
Triple Entente						
British Empire						
1870	302	67	633	49	116	3.74
1890	355	88	679	69	157	4.03
1914	381	147	2714	237	384	8.53
France						
1870	380	75	457	35	110	3.03
1890	502	142	319	44	186	4.87
1914	846	197	900	90	287	7.33
Russia						
1870	700	98	363	12	110	1.34
1890	647	123	180	22	145	1.32
1914	1300	324	679	118	441	2.58

	STANDING ARMY (000)	ARMY APPROPRIA-TION ($000,000)	NAVAL TONNAGE (000)	NAVAL APPROPRIA-TION ($000,000)	TOTAL DEFENSE EXPENDI-TURE ($000,000)	COST PER CAPITA HOME POPULA-TION ($)
Non-European Powers						
Japan						
1870	70	. . .	. . .	. . .	. . .	. . .
1890	74	18	41	6	24	.60
1914	250	48	700	48	96	1.75
United States						
1870	37	58	175	22	80	1.98
1890	27	45	40	22	67	1.06
1914	98	174	895	140	314	3.20
Total Great Powers						
1870	2473	416	1813	135	551	1.70
1890	2691	653	1757	216	869	2.12
1914	4416	1568	8065	832	2400	4.27

* Adapted from Quincy Wright: A *Study of War* (2 vols.; Chicago, 1942), Vol. 1, pp. 670–1.

make it difficult to compare the expenditures on armaments of the great powers. The accompanying table nevertheless makes possible several generalizations which help to clarify the situation. In terms of total expenditures for defense in 1914, Germany and Russia had the largest budgets, and were followed in order by Great Britain, France, Austria-Hungary, and Italy. In terms of defense expenditures per capita of home population, on the other hand, a somewhat different picture emerges. On this basis, Great Britain and Germany are in the lead and France follows closely, while Italy, Austria-Hungary, and Russia are far behind. Judged by European standards, the military expenditures of Japan in 1914 were very modest, while those of the United States approximated the per capita rate of the secondary European powers.

In addition to the armaments race, the growing acerbity of the relations between the two rival groups was reflected in a bitter duel for influence over public opinion. The traditional hatreds of Europe were revived and taught to schoolchildren in the textbooks that the various governments prepared for their public school systems. Persons beyond the reach of the schools were subjected to the irresponsible daily fulminations of the many journalists, politicians, and professors who made their living as press agents for the various national causes. The recently founded popular daily newspapers had already discovered that the more sensational their news, the more copies of their paper would be sold. A vicious circle was thus started, in which the youth of Europe was taught a narrow nationalist doctrine in place of a broader political understanding, and this prepared them to accept as a matter of course the unrestrained hatred with which the press was increasingly filled.

The antagonisms that were so soon to lead to open warfare were concentrated in two main centers of rivalry: that between Germany, and France and England; and that between Russia and Austria-Hungary. The former had its immediate origin in the French defeat in 1871 and the German annexation of the province of Alsace-Lorraine. The French had never forgotten this defeat, and the Germans had lived in constant apprehension lest the French find some way to take revenge. Germany and England, on the other hand, had enjoyed friendly relations until the turn of the century, for German land power and British sea power appeared to complement each other. A shortsighted German policy of pressing colonial expansion at the expense of friends in Europe had left the country increasingly isolated, while its rapidly expanding industrial plant had given its statesmen a false sense of power. It was the navy constructed during this surge of self-confidence which finally convinced the British that no compromise with Germany was possible. More important for the immediate origins of the war, however, was the conflict in the Balkans between Russia and Austria-Hungary. Involving as it did, in the last analysis, the honor and domestic security of the two great empires, their attitude on Balkan issues steadily stiffened until finally war seemed preferable to compromise.

CHAPTER

2

The Coming of the Crisis

Testing the Alliance Systems: *The Russo-Japanese War, 1904–05; The First Morocco Crisis, 1905–06; The Annexation Crisis; The Second Morocco Crisis, 1911; The Haldane Mission, 1912.*

Tensions in Southeastern Europe: *The Habsburg Empire; The South Slav Problem; The First Balkan War, 1912–13; The Second Balkan War, 1913.*

The Alliance Systems, 1912–14.

The Outbreak of Hostilities: *The Assassination of Francis Ferdinand; Repercussions in Europe; The Ultimatum to Serbia; Involvement of the Powers.*

T HE FAILURE of Germany and Britain to achieve a broad understanding in their negotiations at the turn of the century had led to the conclusion of the Anglo-French Entente on April 8, 1904, but the division of Europe into two camps was not yet definite. Britain's relations with France's ally, Russia, remained uncertain; the war which broke out between Russia and England's ally, Japan, in 1904, made any close accord between England and Russia seem remote indeed. There was always an inclination to strike up friendships outside the general alliance pattern in order to settle particular issues, and certain powers in each alliance grouping found it convenient to work at times with members of the opposite group to check the sometimes inconvenient demands of their own special friends. This was relatively easy to do, since the powers in theory, and often in fact, still acted together as the Concert of Europe.

Testing the Alliance Systems

THE RUSSO-JAPANESE WAR, 1904–05. The statesmen of both Russia and Germany had for years stressed for more than they were worth the historic ties of friendship which existed between the Hohenzollern and Romanov dynasties, whose common interest in upholding the monarchical principle always provided a common meeting ground. Regularly the Kaiser and the Tsar had written each other in English, and with the outbreak of war in the Far East the number of Willy-Nicky letters (so called from the signatures used) increased. The Kaiser assured the Tsar of his friendship and hailed him as the champion of the white race against the Yellow Peril. Germany even agreed to provide coal for the Russian Baltic fleet on its long voyage to Far Eastern waters. The British warned Germany that this might be considered by Japan as a breach of neutrality and intimated that if Japan were drawn into war with Germany for such a reason, Britain would be bound by the Anglo-Japanese Alliance of 1902 to join in the war. The tension was not lessened by the Dogger Bank Incident, in which a jittery Russian admiral took some British fishing vessels in the murky North Sea for Japanese torpedo boats and sank them forthwith. Feeling ran high, although this particular incident was settled peacefully enough by an international commission. The Kaiser took advantage of this situation to press for a more definite understanding with Russia. In July, 1905, the Tsar and the Kaiser personally negotiated an alliance at Björkö, which never went into effect, due chiefly to the objections of the Russian foreign minister, who considered that it conflicted with the French-Russian alliance. This stillborn treaty marked the failure of Germany to set up a new pattern of alliances based on Russian-German friendship.

THE FIRST MOROCCO CRISIS, 1905–06. For some time the German foreign office had been aware that the French government was preparing to extend its influence over Morocco, where, by the International Convention of Madrid of 1880, all powers had been awarded equal rights. Indeed, by a series of agreements—with Italy (December, 1900), with Britain (April, 1904), and with Spain (October, 1904)—France had acquired practically a free hand in Morocco in return for concessions on her part in other areas. The Germans did not know exactly the content of these agreements and they could not be sure that the information which they had received from "secret sources" was complete. One thing was certain: the French government had not made a deal with Germany, and any change in status in Morocco as contemplated by France would curtail the general international rights of the other powers. Since the United States in general advocated the open-door policy, the Germans believed they could count on American support in any protests they might make.

In the spring of 1905 the Kaiser, while on his way to Corfu, stopped off at Tangier for a ceremonial visit to the Sultan of Morocco and made speeches calling for freedom of trade and equality in Moroccan affairs. The German foreign office now suggested a conference of all the powers signatory to the Madrid Convention of 1880 to arrange for reform and to protect the interests of all countries in Morocco. Delcassé, the French foreign minister, who had slowly been preparing the way for French ascendency there, saw his whole policy thwarted by this German plan and hence opposed such a conference. Fortunately for the peace of the world at that time, the French cabinet as a whole was not in full agreement with Delcassé. Premier Rouvier, unwilling to run the risk of war, forced Delcassé to resign, and it was finally agreed to hold an international conference at Algeciras in January, 1906. At this conference the Germans won a nominal victory, inasmuch as the independence and integrity of Morocco with equal economic rights for all powers was affirmed. Actually France and Spain won material advantages, since they were given special control over Moroccan reform.

The Germans had not achieved their objective of disrupting the Entente between France and England. In fact, the German embassy in London reported that the British press "was more French than the French" in the Morocco question. During the crisis the French had repeatedly pressed the English for definite commitments in regard to aid, should war break out, and this pressure led to important Anglo-French military and naval conversations. These developed in the following years in such a fashion that by 1911 the French chief of staff told the Russian generals "that the French army would concentrate as quickly as the German army, and that from the twelfth day it would be in a position to take the offensive against Germany, *with the aid of the English army on its left wing.*" [1]

These German efforts to detach France from her allies were a factor in influencing England and Russia to find ways to settle their differences. At Algeçiras Britain and Russia were drawn closer together by their common support of France, and in 1907 the Entente Cordiale was converted into the Triple Entente.

THE ANNEXATION CRISIS. In 1908 another crisis occurred when Austria-Hungary decided to annex outright the small Slav-inhabited territories of Bosnia-Herzegovina, which she had administered since 1878. This decision was reached as a result of the Young Turk Revolution of 1908, which threatened to strengthen Turkey's control over its European territories, and it was sanctioned by a meeting between the Russian and Austrian foreign ministers in September, 1908, at Buchlau in Bohemia. Just what was agreed upon at this conference is in much dispute. It seems clear that the Russian minister agreed to the Austrian annexation of Bosnia-Herzegovina, and that the Austrian in turn accepted the opening of the Straits to Russian warships. The Russian minister then left on a leisurely visit to

[1] Quoted in Sidney B. Fay: *The Origins of the World War* (2 vols.; New York, 1928), Vol. I, p. 213.

the other Western capitals, only to be confronted on his arrival in Paris with the news of the Austrian occupation of the provinces. Thus he had not been given the opportunity to approach the French and British foreign offices, and when he did raise the question of the Straits, his inquiries were deftly turned aside. The result was that Austria had secured her part of the bargain, but Russia was left empty-handed.

Since the Austrian action was clearly a violation of the Treaty of Berlin, the Russian foreign minister now proposed that an international conference be called to confirm the changes, but Austria refused to submit the annexation to the arbitration of a conference. Serbia had a special grievance, in view of the fact that these provinces were inhabited by her fellow-nationals, and brought pressure to bear on Russia for assistance. A flood of anti-Austrian propaganda came out of Belgrade, and soon the Austrians had mobilized a large part of their forces. The lines were not yet clearly drawn, however, and when in February, 1909, the Turks were persuaded to accept an Austrian offer of a monetary payment for the "loss of crown property," the Russians agreed to a German proposal to recognize the annexation by an exchange of notes among the powers. This satisfied the Russian demand that any change in the Treaty of Berlin required the consent of the signatory powers, but it avoided the ticklish question of a conference. On March 31, 1909, Serbia was persuaded to make a declaration in Vienna recognizing the annexation of the two provinces, and within a few weeks both the Austrian and Serbian armies were demobilized. The crisis was ended, but it had done much to make the European statesmen aware of the claims of Serbian nationalists and to aggravate the differences between Russia and Austria in the Balkans.

So far as the alliance system as such was concerned, this crisis served mainly to deepen the pattern already drawn. Although Britain and France were not as yet prepared to grant Russia all her desires—chiefly the Straits—they went far at this time in accepting and supporting Russia's Serbian policy. On the other hand, the blunders of the Russian foreign office had only drawn Germany and Austria-Hungary closer. Before the crisis ended, the Kaiser declared that, if the need arose, Germany would take its place "in shining armor" beside Austria-Hungary. Italy, vexed by Austrian policy, was the exception to the rule, and her future defection from the Triple Alliance was foreshadowed by the Racconigi Agreement negotiated secretly with Russia in 1909. This agreement provided for co-operation between Italy and Russia against Austria-Hungary in the Near East. Further, Italy promised to work for Russia's interests in the question of the Straits, while Russia agreed to support Italy's claims to Tripoli and Cyrenaica. The Annexation Crisis and the developments growing out of it thus mark another step in Italy's shift from the Triple Alliance to the Triple Entente.

THE SECOND MOROCCO CRISIS, 1911. The special rights awarded to Spain and France at the Conference of Algeçiras to supervise reforms in Morocco gave these powers a welcome opportunity. France developed an extensive police organization for which there was great need, since the Sultan was both unable and disinclined to maintain order. A new German-French agreement on Morocco (February 9, 1909), resulting from a dispute over consular immunity in connection with deserters from the French foreign legion, reaffirmed the independence and integrity of the country, although Germany recognized France's special political interests. In return Germany again was promised equality in economic matters.

Within the next two years political unrest in Morocco increased, and with it the extension of French influence. New loans brought the Sultan completely under French dominance, but even the Germans realized that conditions in Morocco were so chaotic that expansion of French control was inevitable, and they were willing to make concessions at a price. When the French occupied the city of Fez in the spring of 1911, the Germans expected compensations that were not forthcoming. The gunboat *Panther* was sent to Agadir, ostensibly to protect German interests, whereupon the Second Morocco Crisis rapidly gathered momentum. The Germans wanted to bring pressure on the French for concessions in the Congo, in return for German recognition that Morocco constituted a French bailiwick. The French, naturally, would not agree and received warm support from the British chancellor of the exchequer, Lloyd George, who backed France in the famous Mansion House speech. On the other hand, the Russians, having just achieved a working accord with Germany on railway building in the Near East (Potsdam Agreement of November 4–5, 1910), had no desire to become involved in a war with Germany over French colonial questions. The Russian foreign office urged the French to make concessions, saying that the Russian army was unprepared. France finally agreed on November 4, 1911, to cede to Germany some 100,000 square miles of the French Congo, which gave the German Cameroons much-needed river outlets, in return for the right to establish a protectorate over Morocco.

The Second Morocco Crisis did much to strengthen the ties between England and France. At its height, important military conversations took place between the French and British military staffs. The most striking thing about the Second Morocco Crisis was its revelation of the sharp antagonism between Germany and England over German colonial expansion in Africa. Statesmen in both countries were profoundly disturbed and made valiant efforts to remedy the situation.

THE HALDANE MISSION, 1912. Back of the German-English antagonism, which had increased steadily in the first decade of this century, lay naval rivalry. The German navy had only come into being as a result of the naval laws of 1898 and 1900, which provided for a seventeen-year building program. The British admiralty was not slow to react and as early as 1904 reorganized its fleet so as to retain an overwhelmingly strong force in the North Sea. The next year the British laid the keel for the first dreadnought. These ships gave the British navy superiority over anything else afloat. Unfortunately they not only doubled the cost of building capital ships, but they also created a situation in which the building of a few German dread-

ROYAL COUSINS   *Emperor William II of Germany and King George V of England on parade in London, 1911.*

noughts would make a good portion of the British fleet obsolete. In 1906 and 1908 Germany enacted additional navy bills, not with the intention of building a fleet equal to Britain's, but rather of providing for one that Germany claimed was necessary to protect its commerce and colonies against France as much as England. It was often termed a "risk navy," one strong enough to make the British hesitate to attack and one to lend weight to Germany's colonial demands. The British, however, were determined to maintain a two-power standard, which meant a navy as large as the combined navies of any two other powers. The British were convinced that their navy was a necessity, while, as Churchill phrased it, the German navy was a luxury.

The British were interested in slowing down the German building program in order to lighten the British military budget. In Germany, particularly after Bethmann-Hollweg became chancellor in 1909, there was a real desire to improve relations with Britain. The result was that there were repeated attempts after 1908 to come to some sort of understanding on naval matters. These negotiations proceeded at a snail's pace and became involved in other discussions on a variety of subjects — the Baghdad Railway, Persia, African colonies, and a political formula of friendship. At the conclusion of the Second Morocco Crisis, the need to discuss a naval agreement seemed more pressing than ever. Bethmann-Hollweg reminded the British ambassador that he was still awaiting the British reply as to an exchange of naval information. It took some time to arrange matters, but finally in February, 1912, Viscount Haldane, as the representative of the British cabinet, headed a small mission to Berlin.

The conversations at Berlin were conducted in a friendly atmosphere. The British wanted to prevent, or at least slow down materially, the building program of the new German naval law of 1912. The Germans in exchange wanted the British to agree to a mutual declaration of neutrality in case either became involved in a war. This a certain section of the British cabinet and the permanent officials of the foreign office were unwilling to do, since any such statement would jeopardize their relations with Russia and France. Without some sort of political agreement the Germans were unwilling to reduce their naval building program, and so the Haldane Mission, like other such attempts, ended in failure. Nevertheless, relations between Germany and Britain did not deteriorate as might have been expected. As one authority has stated, the Haldane Mission "was successful in its larger object of restoring a considerable measure of confidence between the two governments." [2] In fact, relations between the two powers were considerably improved by the upright and loyal co-operation between the German and English governments in the localization of the Balkan Wars in 1912–13.

On the other hand, the Triple Entente remained intact, and France took the occasion of the German-English naval negotiations to press for a

[2] G. P. Gooch: "Lord Haldane," *Contemporary Review* (1928), 134:429.

more explicit statement of Entente relationships. The result was the Anglo-French naval understanding of July, 1912, according to which the British withdrew battleships from the Mediterranean, concentrating them in the North Sea. In return the French shifted their battleships from Brest to the Mediterranean. Also, an exchange of letters between Grey, the British foreign secretary, and Paul Cambon, the French ambassador at London, in November, 1912, formulated the obligations of each power in case war should arise. England technically still held a free hand, but such agreements tended definitely to restrict her freedom of choice.

Tensions in Southeastern Europe

In Southeastern Europe the rivalries of the great powers had long been manifest, and it was here that the incident took place which led to the opening of hostilities in World War I. The war of 1914 must be considered in general as the natural outcome of the cleavage between the alliance systems of Europe, but the immediate issue over which they clashed might be termed the question of Yugoslav unification. That this turned into a World War, because of the international tensions of the time, lends especial significance to the nationality problems of Austria-Hungary and the peculiar nature of that state in relation to the development of Serbian nationalism.

THE HABSBURG EMPIRE. The rise of nationalism and of democratic ideas in the early nineteenth century led to serious revolutions in the Austrian Empire in 1848. These were put down, and for a time an effort was made to govern the whole Empire as a centralized state from Vienna. This, however, proved to be impossible, and in 1867 a unique governmental structure was devised under which the Habsburg lands were divided into an Empire of Austria, with its capital at Vienna, and a Kingdom of Hungary, with its capital at Budapest. A long history of feudal succession, marriages, and conquests had determined which of the many Habsburg lands were placed within each state, and a glance at the map will show how peculiar these boundaries were [see map, p. 37]. After 1878, when Austria-Hungary obtained the right to occupy Bosnia-Herzegovina, these provinces were administered jointly as *Reichsland* (Imperial Province) by the common minister of finance. They were inhabited mainly by Catholic Croatians and Orthodox Serbians, although a strong Mohammedan minority was present. In the Austrian Empire were included many Slavic nationalities, as well as Italians and Germans, the latter constituting the most powerful group. Hungary was inhabited predominantly by Magyars, although there were heavy minority settlements in some provinces. Hungary also included the ancient autonomous Kingdom of Croatia-Slavonia, inhabited by Croatians and Serbians.

The government of the Dual Monarchy was a complicated business. A brief description of it indicates the difficulty of securing governmental reforms which might have lessened, if not completely solved, the nationality problems of the Habsburg state. Francis Joseph ruled over both states,

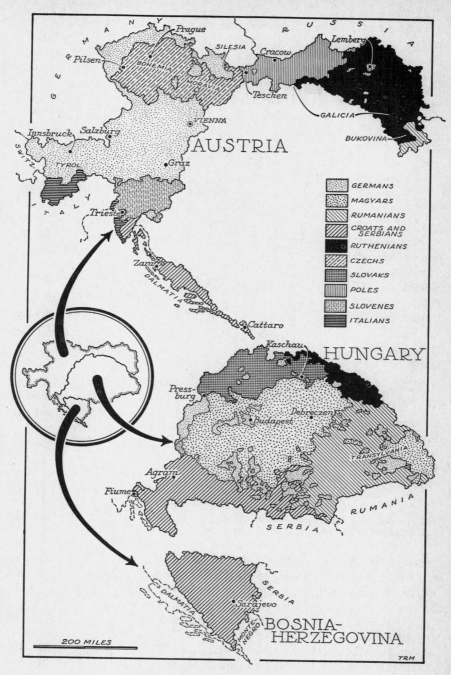

MAP 1   *Austria and Hungary, 1914*

as Emperor of Austria and as King of Hungary. Each state had its own ministry and its own bicameral Parliament that controlled internal affairs. The chambers of these Parliaments named delegations from their membership to serve as a sort of Parliament for the whole realm. These delegations met separately and enacted the limited amount of legislation which was in their competence. If they failed to agree, a joint session was held, where, without discussion or debate, a vote was taken. There were three

TABLE 5

THE NATIONALITIES OF AUSTRIA-HUNGARY *

(*Census of 1910*)

NATIONALITY	AUSTRIA	HUNGARY (*including Croatia-Slavonia*)	BOSNIA-HERZEGOVINA	AUSTRIA-HUNGARY *as a whole*
Czechs, Moravians, and Slovaks	6,435,983			⎱ 8,403,953
Slovaks		1,967,970		⎰
Poles	4,967,984			4,967,984
Ruthenians	3,518,854	472,587		3,991,441
Slovenes	1,252,940			1,252,940
Serbs and Croats	788,334		1,823,000	⎱
Serbs		1,106,471		⎬ 5,545,967
Croats		1,833,162		⎰
Total Slavs	16,959,095	5,380,190	1,823,000	24,162,285
Germans	9,950,266	2,037,435		11,987,701
Magyars	10,974	10,050,575		10,061,549
Rumanians	275,115	2,949,032		3,224,147
Italians	768,422			768,422
Others	583,126	469,255	109,000	1,161,381
Totals	28,546,998	20,886,487	1,932,000	51,365,485

* Compiled from *Statesman's Year-Book* 1914, pp. 649, 664, and from Oscar Jaszi: *The Dissolution of the Habsburg Monarchy* (Chicago, 1929), pp. 271–82.

common ministries: those of foreign affairs, finance, and war, appointed by the Emperor and responsible to him. Economic questions, railroad arrangements, and customs rates, as well as the quotas of the common financial budget, were settled by treaty every ten years.

The Common War Ministry administered the common army, while the state armies were each in charge of a separate Defense Ministry. It was only on the adamant insistence of Emperor Francis Joseph, in the face of Magyar demands for change, that German was maintained as the language of command in the common army. Recruits from the different national groups, of course, had to be instructed in their native languages.

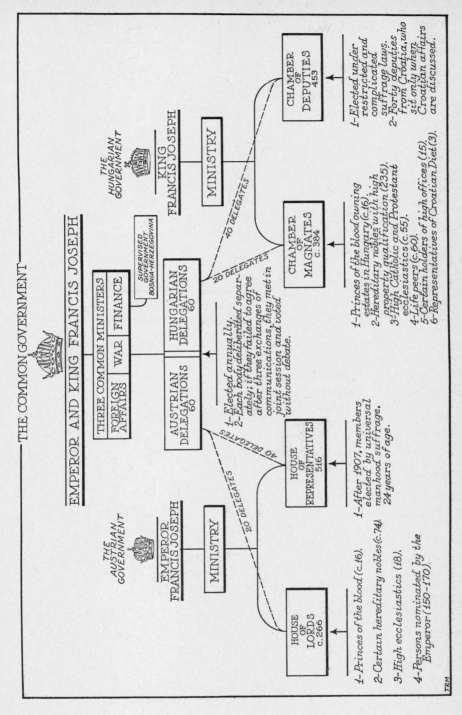

CHART I   The Government of Austria-Hungary

The members of the Austro-Hungarian officer corps had to be good linguists, if nothing else. In fact they were able enough, and their loyalty to the Emperor-King was one of the main cohesive forces within the Empire. There was only one common Austro-Hungarian navy, which was designed primarily for use in the Adriatic Sea.

To conduct the affairs of the realm, particularly foreign policy, was a difficult task. When any major decisions were to be made, Crown Councils — consisting of the common ministers, various departmental advisers, and also members of each of the state governments — were held. Approval of the Emperor-King had then to be obtained. For example, Berchtold, as foreign minister, had to consult the premiers of Austria and Hungary and obtain their approval before undertaking any measures against Serbia in 1914. Also, the consent of the sovereign was no mere formality, as it was in England. Francis Joseph still directed foreign policy to a remarkable degree.

Judged by liberal standards, Austria was more advanced than Hungary. Austria, for example, granted universal manhood secret suffrage to all its peoples in 1907, while in Hungary suffrage was oral and remained on a restricted basis. In Austria the various nationalities had a share in governmental positions, in schools, and in various aspects of cultural life. In Hungary there was more domination on the part of the Magyars, who not only monopolized governmental offices but also controlled the industrial and cultural life of the state.

The Austro-Hungarian Monarchy was truly a dual state under German and Magyar hegemony. Some leaders had hopes of establishing "Trialism" by creating a South Slav state within the Empire, thus establishing a Triple rather than a Dual Monarchy. The Magyars were particularly hostile to this innovation, since it would mean the breakup of their historic Hungarian state. Then, too, the establishment of a self-governing South Slav state within the Monarchy would almost certainly have also involved making fundamental changes on behalf of the Czechs, Slovaks, Poles, and Rumanians. Some leaders eagerly looked forward to a genuine federal state. But no one knew what the end would be if reformers began tinkering with the structure of the state; Francis Joseph preferred not to venture on new paths.

THE SOUTH SLAV PROBLEM. In the early Middle Ages various Slavic tribes, which we today refer to as South Slavs, spread over Southeastern Europe. The Slovenes, who came under Austria, and the Croatians, under Hungary, were both subject as Roman Catholics to Western influence. The Serbians, who settled farther south, became members of the Eastern Orthodox church under the influence of Constantinople. The Bulgarians in the heart of the peninsula were descendants of Mongol conquerors who had been gradually absorbed by the local Slavic population.

In the late Middle Ages most of these Slavs were incorporated into the vast Ottoman Empire, which at the height of its power controlled all the Balkans and the central Danubian basin almost to the gates of Vienna.

It was the Habsburg emperors who took the lead in pushing the Turks back from Central Europe in the seventeenth and eighteenth centuries, but most of the Slavs remained under Turkish rule.

In 1817, as a result of several insurrections, the Sultan recognized a Hereditary Prince of Serbia, and Belgrade became the capital of a small autonomous Serbian state. At Cetinje, in the mountains north of Lake Scutari, Prince-Bishops headed a rival Serbian state known as Montenegro. At the Congress of Berlin in 1878, when the powers worked out new political alignments in the Balkans, both Serbia and Montenegro were recognized as independent states with addition of territory. Rivalry developed between the two states—or rather between their two dynasties—although it was clear that Serbia was destined to assume the leadership of the mounting Serbian national movement, and it was Serbia that led the opposition to the annexation of Bosnia-Herzegovina by Austria.

Russian interest in the Balkan states had grown tremendously in the nineteenth century. In this century it was Russia rather than Austria that waged war against Turkey. Four times in the nineteenth century—1806–12, 1828–29, 1854–56, and 1877–78—and once again in 1914, Russian armies clashed with the Turks. Russia of course had her own territorial and imperialistic interests in mind. On the other hand, her growing determination to see that the interests of the Slavic peoples and of the Orthodox church were safeguarded was not without altruistic aspects. Pan-Slavism, while synonymous with imperialism, also meant, at least for some Slavic peoples, independence and liberty. The great role which Russia played in the liberation of the Balkan peoples is not to be forgotten. Russia had fought to liberate Rumanians, Greeks, Serbs, and Bulgars from the Turks; she was not disposed to see them dominated by Austria-Hungary.

With the achievement of independence in 1878, Serbian leaders began to talk of Serbia as the Piedmont of a large South Slav state. Just as Italy had been unified by the addition of Italian-inhabited territory to the Kingdom of Piedmont, so these Serbian leaders too would create a large unified Serbian state. This meant liberating the Serbs who still remained under Turkish rule and also taking away certain lands from Austria-Hungary. And just as the Carbonari and Mazzini's "Young Italy" played a great role in Italian unification, so in Serbia ardent patriots formed societies to work for a large united South Slav state.

Serbia had been plagued in the nineteenth century by dynastic rivalry between the Obrenovich and Karageorgevich families. In 1903 a band of conspirators assassinated the Obrenovich rulers, King Alexander and Queen Draga, and placed their rival, Peter Karageorgevich, on the throne. The inner circle of these conspirators continued to exercise a dominating influence on Serbian politics. One of the first results of the change in rulers was a Serbian foreign policy oriented towards St. Petersburg.

THE FIRST BALKAN WAR, 1912–13. The Annexation Crisis left Serbia in an intransigent mood. A "National Defense Society," better known under its Serbian name *Narodna Odbrana,* had been founded for the purpose of resisting the annexation. This organization established centers throughout Serbia and even on Austrian and Turkish territory. Although it was allegedly a cultural and propaganda organization, it did train some men in bomb throwing, the art of blowing up bridges, and other activities which might be useful in case of emergency. For some more zealous individuals the National Defense Society did not proceed with sufficient speed. In 1911 a number of its members founded another very secret organization, commonly known as the Black Hand. This organization, in the words of its constitution, preferred terroristic action to intellectual propaganda. The membership was so secretly guarded that individuals were designated only by number, and outside of the leaders at the central bureau no one knew who was a member. Many *emigrés* from Bosnia-Herzegovina or Macedonia wandering about Belgrade became members of the organization, but it also included some of the leading functionaries of Serbia.

Turkish misrule in Macedonia and Albania had caused numerous revolts there. Ardent patriots and members of the Black Hand urged the Serbian government to alleviate the plight of their fellow nationals in Macedonia. The Bulgarian government was pressed by the Macedonian Revolutionary Organization to do likewise. Urged on by these groups, and with the guidance and aid of the Russian government, the Serbian and Bulgarian governments revised their alliance of 1904. The new agreement, signed on March 13, 1912, laid the foundation for what is known as the Balkan League. It should be pointed out that this agreement was directed against both Turkey and Austria-Hungary. Subsequent military conventions laid down the obligations of each country in case of war with either power. Definite division of spoils was arranged in case of a successful war against Turkey. Later this basic agreement was supplemented by a treaty of alliance between Greece and Bulgaria, an oral agreement between Bulgaria and Montenegro, and a treaty of alliance between Serbia and Montenegro. Negotiations between Serbia and Greece were under way when war broke out between the Balkan allies and Turkey in October, 1912.

In 1911–12, Italy had taken advantage of the Moroccan Crisis to attack Turkey, seizing Tripolitania in North Africa. This provided a favorable moment for the Balkan states. With unexpected speed they overwhelmed the Turkish armies. An armistice was arranged in December, 1912, but when terms of peace could not be agreed upon, hostilities were resumed. Finally on May 30, 1913, under the guidance of the great powers, the Balkan states and Turkey signed preliminary peace terms. Turkey ceded to the allies all territory beyond a line drawn from Enos on the Aegean Sea to Media on the Black Sea [see map, p. 43]. After four centuries of conflict Turkey had finally been driven almost completely from Europe, but, thanks to rivalry among the great powers, retained possession of Constantinople.

THE SECOND BALKAN WAR, 1913. The Balkan states now faced the task of dividing their spoils. This was not easy to do amicably, in part be-

MAP 2 *Partition of European Turkey, 1878–1914*

cause of the interference of the great powers. First, the powers had forced
Bulgaria to cede some territory in the Dobruja to Rumania, on the theory
that Rumania had a right to compensations because the other Balkan
states were about to receive large additions of territory. Rumania had furnished no aid in the war, and Bulgaria naturally felt aggrieved. Second,
the powers insisted upon the formation of an independent Albanian state
to satisfy Austria-Hungary, which was strongly opposed to Serbian expansion to the Adriatic coast. Thus Serbia also had a grievance. As compensation Serbia demanded territory which had not been assigned to her in the
Serbian-Bulgarian treaty. Immediately after the signing of the Preliminary
Peace of London with Turkey, Serbia entered into a secret alliance with
Greece to hold out for a common Serbian-Greek boundary at the expense
of Bulgaria.

In the Serbian-Bulgarian treaty of 1912 appeared a clause that dated
back to an earlier treaty of 1904 to the effect that the Tsar was to arbitrate
in case of a territorial dispute between Serbia and Bulgaria. The Bulgarian
leaders, pressed on by the Macedonian Revolutionary Organization, whose
members were opposed to dividing Macedonia with anyone, now launched
a sudden attack on the Serbian and Greek armies in Macedonia. It seems
clear that this was done in the belief that it would hurry the Tsar into
making an arbitral award. The Bulgarians believed that Russia would do
her best to prevent the breakup of the Balkan League. Instead, Russia
withdrew, giving her blessing to what is known as the Second Balkan War
(June 29 to August 10, 1913). It has often been charged that Austria encouraged Bulgaria to attack Serbia and Greece and promised her aid, but
examination of the Austrian and Bulgarian documents (only published in
the twenties) does not support this thesis.

In spite of the immediate efforts of certain Bulgarian leaders to call off
the attack, the Serbs and Greeks were only too eager to put a forcible end
to what they considered Bulgarian arrogance. Montenegro and Rumania
joined in the fray and even Turkey seized the opportunity to retake Adri-
anople from the Bulgarians. The Second Balkan War thus found Greece,
Serbia, Montenegro, Rumania, and Turkey fighting Bulgaria. The outcome, of course, was obvious and the Bulgarians hastened to seek an armistice. The final peace terms were signed at Bucharest on August 10, 1913.
Greece and Serbia received a common frontier, while Bulgaria, although
it obtained some former Turkish territory in Macedonia and Thrace and
an outlet on the Aegean Sea, was given far less than either ethnography
or her efforts in the common war against Turkey would justify. The necessity of ceding a further strip of the Dobruja to Rumania was especially
galling to the Bulgarians.

After the Peace of Bucharest each of the former enemies of Turkey
had to negotiate separate peace treaties with the Sultan. These were easily
arranged except in the case of Greece, and in spite of many mediatory
efforts of the great powers, Greece and Turkey had not settled their differences when the Great War broke out. Serbia was reluctant to with-

draw her troops from certain sections which the great powers had awarded to the newly created Albanian state. Austria-Hungary, with the tacit, if not enthusiastic, consent of the great powers, undertook to see that Serbia did not mock the will of the Concert of Europe. In October, 1913, an ultimatum was dispatched to Belgrade demanding that Serbia withdraw her troops from Albania. This time Serbia complied, an action which met with the full approval of the Russian foreign office. The presentation of this ultimatum was a precedent for the famous ultimatum of July, 1914.

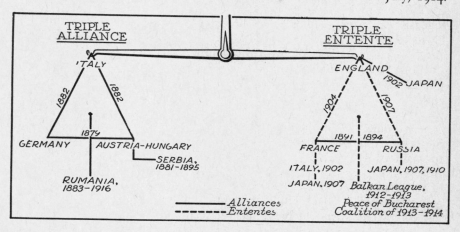

CHART II   *The European Alliance Systems Before 1914*

The Alliance Systems, 1912–14

It was common knowledge that the Bulgarians resented the Peace of Bucharest and would do their best to overthrow it. This fact tended to unite Serbia, Greece, Rumania, and Montenegro into an informal coalition with a common interest in upholding the peace settlement. The original Balkan League had been broken up, for this new coalition took its place, with Rumania included instead of Bulgaria. From August, 1913, to July, 1914, and even beyond, the powers made great efforts to line up this coalition, or certain members of it, with their alliance systems.

Austria-Hungary felt the new situation most acutely, for she considered the enlarged Serbia a danger to her own domestic stability. Having liberated the Serbs living in Turkey, ardent Serbian nationalists turned their eyes towards the Slavs living under "Habsburg oppression." Moreover, Rumanian national spirit was awakened, and the Rumanians began to cast greedy glances towards the Habsburg lands inhabited by many fellow nationals. Rumanian-Serbian friendship made the leaders at Vienna skeptical of the loyalty of Rumania as an ally. It was also obvious that French and Russian influence at Bucharest was in the ascendency. The Balkan Wars had important repercussions within the Dual Monarchy, where the mixture of nationalities became constantly more dangerous to the state. Some diplomats began to say that Austria-Hungary had replaced Turkey as the "sick man of Europe." This analogy was well known to the statesmen at Vienna, and they were determined to show that the old Monarchy still had vitality.

In spite of the early renewal of the Triple Alliance in December, 1912, and the formal co-operation of Italy on various questions during the Balkan Wars, Italy's relations with Austria-Hungary were not good. Austria's Balkan policy was suspect at Rome, and there was an increase in irredentist agitation aiming at the annexation of the Italians within the Dual Monarchy. On the other hand, Rome and Bucharest began to draw closer together as their ties with the Triple Alliance weakened.

The relations between the Triple Alliance and Triple Entente had at times been very strained during the Balkan Wars. Both Austria-Hungary and Russia mobilized parts of their armies, and on several occasions hostilities threatened. Germany and England co-operated in exercising a moderating influence and did much to keep the Concert of Europe functioning. The improved relations between Germany and England slowly began to manifest themselves in colonial negotiations. In the spring of 1914 Britain and Germany came to a settlement, not only on the vexed question of the Baghdad Railway but also in regard to their interests in the Portuguese colonies, another problem of long standing. The treaties were all but completed when war broke out in 1914.

The years 1912–14 brought a good example of the Concert of Europe in action at the Ambassadorial Conference in London, and one can cite numerous differences within each of the two major alliance groups. Yet the over-all picture is nevertheless one of Europe divided into two opposing camps. England did not permit her co-operation with Germany or Austria-Hungary to jeopardize her Entente agreements with France and Russia. Poincaré, who came to dominate the French political scene at this time, worked incessantly at strengthening Entente ties. By mutual support in diplomatic negotiations and by conversations between the military and naval staffs of the three countries, the Entente had become much more firmly knit together. The events of the Balkan Wars also gave these countries a decided advantage in this troubled area and shifted the balance of power to the side of the Entente. When the Young Turks sought to reorganize their army by calling in a German expert, Liman von Sanders, such vigorous Entente protests followed that an international crisis threatened (November–December, 1913). A compromise was finally reached, but the Entente had served notice that its members would not countenance German domination of Turkish affairs.

The Outbreak of Hostilities

The heir apparent to the throne of Austria-Hungary, Francis Ferdinand, was a man of ability and intelligence. He was particularly critical of the methods of the Budapest government, which had imposed a Magyar domination over the other nationalities within the Hungarian kingdom. Reputedly he was favorable to the idea of a Triple Monarchy (Trialism). Who could tell if a self-governing, economically prosperous Slav state with a Habsburg king might not prove more attractive to the Slavs along the Adriatic than a small, poverty-stricken Serbia or Montenegro? Optimists even held that such a state might have an attraction for the Slavs of other states, a possibility which was deeply dreaded by the Serbian leaders, who for years had been carrying on agitation within the Monarchy. To these agitators it seemed that the removal of Francis Ferdinand might not only end the possibility of Trialism, but would almost surely lead to a firmer Austro-Hungarian policy in Bosnia-Herzegovina. More police measures, more oppression could only lead to an increase in Serbian national restlessness and a longing to join with the Serbian state which had but recently achieved great glory in the Balkan Wars.

THE ASSASSINATION OF FRANCIS FERDINAND. In September, 1913, shortly after the close of the Second Balkan War, Francis Ferdinand, as Inspector in Chief of the Austro-Hungarian army, began to lay plans for an inspection of the two army corps which were regularly stationed in Bosnia. It was decided that he should attend the regular spring maneuvers accompanied by his wife. It was to be an official visit such as royalty for centuries have paid to parts of their territories in order to tighten the bonds of loyalty between sovereign and subjects. The maneuvers were held as planned; the Archduke and his wife, amid popular acclaim, made a shopping trip through the bazaars of Sarajevo, and the couple were scheduled to return to Vienna at 5 a.m. on Monday, June 29, 1914. Truly the life of royalty is not all a bed of roses. Only one thing remained and that was the official trip to the city of Sarajevo, which was to be made on Sunday morning, June 28. Meanwhile the Archduke and his wife were staying at the pleasant summer watering place of Ilidze, a short distance from the city.

On Sunday morning the official party—the Archduke, his wife, and Potiorek, the Governor of Bosnia—left Ilidze riding in an open touring car. The plan was to proceed along the main boulevard to the City Hall, where official greetings were to be exchanged. Suddenly a man stepped forward and threw a bomb, which landed on the folded-down top of the car and bounded into the street. The occupants of the next car were seriously injured. After the Archduke had seen that all the wounded were taken to a hospital, the cavalcade proceeded to the City Hall and went through the scheduled program. Plans were then changed. Instead of driving through the old parts of the city on his return journey, the Archduke decided to visit the hospital. The chauffeur of the Archduke's car, however, made the turn towards the old parts of the city as first planned. He was ordered to stop and take the route to the hospital. At this moment an assassin, Gavrilo Princip, who had stationed himself at that corner, pulled out a revolver and shot both the Archduke and his wife. Visitors to Sarajevo today can view the plaque attached to the building at this corner honoring the

SARAJEVO *Archduke Francis Ferdinand, heir to the Habsburg throne, and his wife, at Sarajevo shortly before their fateful assassination, June 28, 1914.*

deed that was indirectly to lead to the formation of a large Serbian state. In the annals of history, all sorts of deeds and events make heroes.

REPERCUSSIONS IN EUROPE. The assassins and several accomplices, who were immediately arrested, proved to be Serbians native to Bosnia (therefore Austrian nationals) who had just returned to Sarajevo from Belgrade. It was soon evident that they were members of some secret organization, which one was not too clear, and that they had obtained the weapons they used in Serbia. The Austrian government had recently made the mistake of using documents, which turned out to be forged, for the prosecution of certain treason trials involving South Slavs. The Austrians were now all the more careful in using material that came to hand. They dispatched to Sarajevo a special investigator, Baron von Wiesner, to make an on-the-spot investigation. His telegraphic report stated that although it was clear that the Pan-Serbian propaganda was being carried on with the knowledge and support of the Serbian government, there was no direct evidence to implicate the Serbian government in the assassination plot. Potiorek, who, as Governor of Bosnia, saw the telegram, did not agree with it and reported that without doubt the Serbian government knew of the plot. Wiesner on his return to Vienna stated that it was indeed unlikely that the Serbian government did not have wind of the assassination plot, but at Sarajevo he could find no document to prove this.

In Vienna, the Austrian leaders felt certain that some Serbian governmental officials were involved in the assassination plot. Much painstaking research has subsequently proved that they were correct. But the Austrians made their charges against Serbian officers and functionaries belonging to the old, officially recognized propaganda organization, the National Defense Society. The plot actually had been planned and put into execution by members of the Serbian Black Hand Society, founded in 1911. Many members of the Black Hand held high positions in the Serbian army and in other governmental services. It is also clear that members of the Serbian cabinet had received word of the plot and that they did not take adequate steps to warn the Austrian government. They could, of course, make the excuse that they did not know for certain that the plan would be carried through. The Serbian government at times had its own difficulties with this same group of conspirators, and to say that the government had knowledge of some of their plans is not to say that it approved them. That the Serbian government backed nationalistic agitation and anti-Austro-Hungarian propaganda, however, no one could deny. Serbia was following a policy directed towards the breakup of the Dual Monarchy.

The news of the assassination aroused heartfelt sympathy at the capitals of Europe. There was feeling similar to that which King Edward expressed in connection with the assassination of King Alexander of Serbia in 1903. In 1905 he said:

> *My particular business is that of being king. King Alexander was also by his trade a king. As you see, we belonged to the same guild, as labourers or professional men. I cannot be indifferent to the assassination of a member of my guild. We should be obliged to shut up our businesses if we, the kings, were to consider the assassination of kings as of no consequence at all.*[3]

The Austrian officials definitely counted on fraternal monarchical feeling and horror of assassination to help keep the armies of Europe quiet while they undertook to put Serbia in order. All through the Balkan Wars the Viennese officials had tended to deal with the Serbian menace by peaceful means. Serbia had been kept from the Adriatic Sea; she had been forced by an ultimatum in October, 1913, to withdraw from Albania. In

---

[3] Quoted in Sidney Lee: *King Edward: A Biography* (2 vols.; New York, 1925, 1927), Vol. II, p. 273, from Edward Legge: *King Edward in His True Colors*, pp. 81–2.

spite of these diplomatic victories, or perhaps because of them, Pan-Serb agitation had increased. The Serbians were openly demanding the disintegration of the Austro-Hungarian realm. As one reads the documents for 1913–14 in the great Austrian collection, one realizes that the Austrian leaders had come to the conclusion that this cancer in the side of the Monarchy could be cured only by a radical operation. Only through war could the Pan-Serb agitation be stilled. A defeated Serbia, from which ample bits of territory could be ceded to Bulgaria, Albania, and perhaps even Rumania, would then no longer act as a Pied Piper to the Slavs of the Monarchy. Great powers in the past had often resorted to war with less provocation. In July, 1914, with a few notable exceptions, the Austrian leaders were resolved to undertake a punitive war with Serbia.

With this end in view, the Austrians sent Count Hoyos as a special emissary to Berlin to inform William II officially of the assassination. He carried with him a long document that had been drawn up before the assassination, discussing at great length the reasons why Austria and Germany should make an alliance with Bulgaria. The German statesmen not only agreed to this, but added that Austria was the one to decide what steps it was necessary to take against Serbia. This was the famous "blank check" that caused the Austrians to feel that they had unconditional German backing. The German statesmen also suggested that it was best to undertake any punitive measures that were contemplated against Serbia as soon as possible, while European feeling was still stirred with revulsion against the assassination.

THE ULTIMATUM TO SERBIA. At Vienna things moved slowly. The authorities wanted to present as airtight a case against Belgrade as possible and undertook elaborate investigations. Events ran more swiftly, and in the end the Austrians made small use of their material and presented their case badly and tardily at the European capitals. It is true that they had to win over Count Tisza, Premier of Hungary, who in the beginning was absolutely opposed to a war with Serbia. He feared a general war and for political reasons was also opposed to acquisition of Slavic territory. Then, too, the Viennese statesmen thought they would have a better chance of avoiding a general war if they waited until the French President, who was on a visit to Russia, had embarked on his homeward journey. They were afraid that Poincaré, a fiery Lorrainer, might inflame the Russians if he were in their midst when news of the Austrian demands broke. With great care they proceeded to draw up the terms of the ultimatum, which were designedly couched so that Serbia would reject them. If by any chance she did accept them, then Austria's position would be so preponderant in Serbia that it would be equal to a military victory.

In the opening paragraphs the ultimatum mentioned the hostile propaganda which for years had been going on in Serbia with the blessing of the government. Certain Serbian frontier officials and other functionaries were charged with complicity in the plot that led to the assassination of Francis Ferdinand. The Serbian government was asked to print a prescribed disavowal of Pan-Serb agitation in its official journal and make the disavowal an order of the day to the army. In addition the Serbian government was asked to accede to ten specific demands. These had to do with the suppression of agitation against Austria-Hungary, the dissolution of secret societies, the dismissal and arrest of certain officials who were to be named by Austria-Hungary, and the right of the Austro-Hungarian gov-

STRENGTHENING THE ENTENTE *Grand Duke Nicholas, Emperor Nicholas II, President Poincaré of France, and Empress Alexandra Fedorovna at a garden party in honor of the French statesman, St. Petersburg, July, 1914.*

ernment to share in Serbian investigations to be undertaken within Serbia. A time limit of forty-eight hours was set for the Serbian reply. At 6 P.M. on July 23, 1914, Baron Giesl, the Austrian minister, handed the ultimatum to the Serbian foreign office. That same evening Poincaré embarked from St. Petersburg and was on the high seas when he heard of the ultimatum.

The Serbian government immediately asked for more time to study the note, but this was refused. At a little before 6 P.M. on July 25 the Serbian reply was handed to Baron Giesl. By that time Serbia had already ordered the mobilization of her army. Giesl compared the reply with the instructions he had received, declared the answer unsatisfactory, and broke off relations. Along with his whole staff, he caught the 6:30 train out of Belgrade. Events had truly begun to march. That same day Francis Joseph was persuaded to designate July 28 as the beginning of mobilization against Serbia and Montenegro. This involved only a partial mobilization of the forces of the Monarchy.

The Serbian reply was conciliatory in form, but it clearly did not entirely meet the Austrian demands. The Serbian government immediately circularized this reply to the capitals of Europe, where it made a favorable impression. Even the German Emperor was astonished at how far the Serbs had gone toward accepting the Austrian demands, and made this marginal note on the morning of July 28:

> A *brilliant performance for a time-limit of only 48 hours. This is more than one could have expected! A great moral success for Vienna; but with it every reason for war drops away, and Giesl ought to have remained quietly in Belgrade! After such a thing, I should never have ordered mobilization!—W*.[4]

In Vienna the reaction was different, for the Serbian reply was considered evasive, and the Austrians were determined to see the thing through. On the morning of July 28 war was declared on Serbia. When the Austrian diplomatic representatives informed the various governments of the sending of an ultimatum, they promised to submit a dossier providing evidence to support the charges made against Serbia. This voluminous document— some forty large pages in length—was sent by post from Vienna on July 25. By the time it was presented to the European foreign offices the news of Austria's declaration of war had spread over the world. Now no one took time to read or to be influenced by Austrian explanations.

INVOLVEMENT OF THE POWERS. From the time the ultimatum had been issued, statesmen of all the great powers had taken steps to bring about delay or compromise. The Austrian declaration of war brought renewed mediatory proposals, particularly on the part of England and Germany. At first Germany held to the plan of localizing the conflict, which led her to refuse English proposals for a general European conference. It was doubtless with a similar idea that Austria moved so rapidly into war with Serbia. The wires of Europe were hot with telegrams from Berlin and London, suggesting this or that way out, and the Kaiser sent a personal appeal to the Tsar. However, no statesman was now able to stop the course of events which had actually been laid down during the past decades.

The statesmen in Vienna always hoped that their war with Serbia would remain localized. They knew there was danger of Russian intervention, but they took the fatalistic attitude that if Russia should take this occasion to march it meant that Russia would sooner or later attack the Monarchy anyway. In case of a general war they felt certain of Germany's support. On the other side, Russia had given diplomatic support to Serbia

---

[4] Translated from the German documents by Fay: *Origins of the World War*, Vol. II, p. 348.

in both the crises of 1908 and 1912–13, and on more than one occasion had told Serbian leaders that she would not leave them in the lurch. Russia always claimed to be the protector of the small Slav Orthodox states. Another humiliation of Serbia, with its reflection on Russia, would dangerously threaten Russian prestige and honor in the Balkans, as Pan-Slav writers were constantly pointing out. Russia had the persistent ambition to acquire the Straits, an ambition recognized as unlikely to be fulfilled without a general European war, and hoped also to obtain the Polish and Ruthenian territories of the Dual Monarchy. Underlying the acceptance of the challenge of war lay hopes like these, to which should be added France's desire to recover Alsace-Lorraine, Britain's desire to curb German naval and colonial ambitions, Italy's desire for Trentino, and Germany's desire for a "place in the sun." Russia's determination to stand by Serbia and the resulting train of events made a general European war out of what seemed like a local Balkan squabble, for Germany was just as certainly bound to stand by Austria-Hungary. The alignment of the powers meant that France would stand with Russia, once Germany was involved. When the British Empire was drawn in, the European War became a world conflict.

It would be difficult to determine the exact moment when a general war became inevitable. When military circles in both Russia and Germany gained the upper hand, as they did in those hectic days, war could be the only outcome. General mobilization of the armies was very important, for once this took place it was generally accepted that war would follow. On July 25 Russia took the first steps towards mobilization. Soldiers on leave were recalled, garrisons were put on a war footing, grain and horses were purchased, and a variety of other measures were set in motion, devised for what was designated as a "period preparatory to war." On the 29th the Tsar agreed to general mobilization, which was later changed to partial mobilization upon the receipt of a telegram from the German Emperor. The next day, however, general Russian mobilization was again ordered. On July 31 Germany proclaimed a "state of threatening danger of war" and sent an ultimatum to St. Petersburg asking for assurance within twelve hours that Russia would stop her military preparations. That same day Austria, which had only been mobilized against Serbia, decreed general mobilization. French mobilization preceded German by a few minutes on August 1. Having received no reply from St. Petersburg, Germany, on the evening of August 1, declared war against Russia. The die was cast. Under the terms of the French-Russian alliance, France was now bound to enter the conflict. The Germans did not wait for the French to act, but on August 3, having failed to obtain assurances of neutrality from Paris, declared war on France. Britain, on the morning of August 2 had, as previously agreed, assured France that Britain would protect the French northern coasts in case of an attack. A request made to Belgium on August 2 that the German army be permitted to march through Belgium was refused. The Germans, pleading military necessity, violated Belgian neutrality. That this was a direct violation of the international treaty of 1839, which established Belgium as a neutralized state, the German chancellor admitted in a speech in the Reichstag. He promised to make good the wrong done to Belgium, but later to the British ambassador made an unfortunate reference to the Treaty of 1839 as a "scrap of paper." His words were picked up immediately by his enemies and the sanctity of treaties and international law became one of the heralded war aims of the Allies. On August 4 England declared war on Germany, ostensibly because of the attack on Belgium. While Britain would in any case have found it difficult to remain aloof with honor, the invasion of Belgium created a justification for war which was rooted deep in Britain's past: that no great power should control the Low Countries has always been a cardinal principle of British policy.

Montenegro declared war on Germany on August 10, and on August 23 Japan entered the conflict. Only Italy and Rumania among the original members of the alliance blocs ventured to stand aside. On the grounds that Austria-Hungary's attack on Serbia was an offensive war, these countries maintained that they were under no alliance obligations to enter the conflict. From the beginning, however, they hardly planned on a permanent policy of neutrality. On September 23, 1914, Italy and Rumania signed a secret treaty under which these two former members of the Triple Alliance agreed to concert their policies in regard to the war.

Many attempts have been made to place the responsibility of causing the war on this or that statesman, country, or chain of events. It is easy to get involved in endless "ifs," particularly in regard to the immediate origins of the war. "If Francis Ferdinand had not attended the maneuvers in Sarajevo?" "If Germany had not promised Austria her support?" "If Russia had not backed Serbia?" "If Britain had made it absolutely clear to Germany that she would enter the War?" "If Austria had undertaken a thorough reorganization of her Empire?" Such speculation is, of course, futile. The War of 1914 cannot be accounted for by any one error of statesmanship. In its immediate origins and perhaps also in historical perspective it is comparable to the Italian-Austrian War of 1859 and the Prussian-Austrian War of 1866. All three were anti-Habsburg national wars of liberation. In other aspects it was but a continuation of the Balkan Wars of 1912–13. Because of the rivalry of the great powers and their military commitments, it developed into a conflict of unprecedented scope, involving the organization of the continent of Europe and the balance of power in the world.

CHAPTER

---— 3 ——---

World War I

The First Year: *Military Power and Strategy; The Initiative of the Central Powers; The Search for Allies.*

The War of Attrition: *Military Deadlock; The War Beyond Europe; The Impact of the War; War Aims and Secret Treaties.*

The Turn of the Tide: *Unrestricted Submarine Warfare; Intervention of the United States; The Critical Months; Collapse of the Eastern Front.*

Victory of the Allies: *Victory in the West; Armistice.*

---◆---

The First Year

MILITARY POWER AND STRATEGY. In the course of the past century, and in particular during the generation or two preceding World War I, the major European countries built up armies and navies and drew up plans of attack in preparation for what many regarded as an almost inevitable war. The Central Powers—Germany and Austria-Hungary —were as active as any in this regard. Although the population of these two countries, a total of about 120,000,000 in 1914, was no more than half that of the six countries united against them at the outset of the war, the Central Powers had the advantage of superior organization and a central strategic position. At the head of their military machine was the redoubtable

German General Staff, which had exhibited great skill and vigor in the German wars against Austria and France a generation earlier. Well aware of Germany's difficult position between France in the west and Russia in the east, Schlieffen, Chief of Staff from 1891 to 1906, had developed a plan calling for a rapid and decisive blow against France before the Russians were fully mobilized. In the east, Germany would have the assistance of the Austro-Hungarian army against Russia and Serbia. The army of Germany's ally likewise had behind it a long military tradition. Its apparent strength was to a considerable degree counterbalanced, however, by the fact that a large proportion of the soldiers were recruited from among the minorities of the empire and were, therefore, of doubtful loyalty. The important Czech, Slovak, and southern Slav minorities in particular felt no loyalty to the empire and were in fact eager to see it defeated by the Russians and Serbs.

Against the Central Powers at the start of the war were arrayed France, the British Empire, Belgium, Russia, Serbia, and Montenegro. Shortly before the war French military thinking had fixed on the plan known as No. 17, which had in view a direct attack with full force against the center of the German front, hoping thus to stop the expected German attack before it got very far into France. In dealing with the Germans, France could expect very little assistance on land from her Western allies. England could send only a few divisions across the channel initially, while the Belgian army was trained primarily to man the Belgian fortifications. In the east was the large and unwieldy Russian army. While the Russian army could not be counted on for any rapid movements or complicated maneuvers, the Western allies depended heavily on it to keep a sizable number of German and Austrian troops occupied in the eastern theater of the war. At Russia's side, at the start of the war on the eastern front, was the small but valiant Serbian army.

Counting only the men already available or readily mobilized for the first battles of the war, the Central Powers had about 150 infantry divisions as against 170 for the Allies. In addition, the Central Powers were faced with the problem of fighting a war on two fronts. It was in an effort to overcome these handicaps that Germany and Austria, taking advantage of their superior communications and more complete military preparedness, struck the initial blows of the war. Once the Allies mobilized and organized their superior resources, the task of the Central Powers would become far more difficult, if not impossible.

THE INITIATIVE OF THE CENTRAL POWERS. On August 3, 1914, Germany declared war on France and on the following day on Belgium as well, as her troops crossed the frontier into that country. England replied immediately to the violation of Belgian soil with a declaration of war on Germany. After making certain modifications of the Schlieffen Plan—which had the effect of weakening the force of the initial German blow—Moltke, the German Chief of Staff, sent five strong armies towards France through Belgium and Luxembourg, while a weak left wing comprising two armies attacked France from the east. Belgium was rapidly reduced, and in the latter part of August the main body of German troops crossed over into France. The small British expeditionary force that landed at the channel ports was at first of little assistance, but under the able leadership of Joffre, the French put up a vigorous resistance. Fighting at times no more than twenty miles from Paris, they threw back the Germans in a decisive battle on the Marne River. By the end of September, 1914, the two great armies were facing each other along a line which extended across northern France and a corner of Belgium. The Germans had been stopped and, despite their most vigorous efforts, were never again able to recover all the ground they had lost in September. The Allies, on the other hand, were able to hold the Germans, but were not strong enough to throw them back out of France and Belgium [see map, p. 62–3].

In the east the Russian armies, led by Grand Duke Nicholas, uncle of Emperor Nicholas II, attacked on a wide front from the Baltic Sea to the Carpathian Mountains. In the north they almost reached the German city of Königsberg in East Prussia, but they were resoundingly defeated in the battle of Tannenberg by the Germans under the expert leadership of Hindenburg and Ludendorff. In the south the Russians fared better against the armies of Austria-Hungary, occupying the greater part of the province of Galicia. While the west remained for the Germans the more important of the two fronts, the constant threat of the Russians prevented them from concentrating sufficient troops against France and England to force a decision. Farther south the armies of Austria-Hungary twice tried to overrun Serbia in the first months of the war, and both times they were thrown back.

The Central Powers could take the initiative on land, but at sea the Allies had the advantage. The British fleet, under the command of Jellicoe, was able from the start to maintain a decisive superiority over the German naval forces in the North Sea in addition to fulfilling its many other responsibilities all over the world. The British nevertheless fought a cautious war at sea, for the navy held the key to their security. As Churchill phrased it, the navy "could lose the war in an afternoon" by a mistaken move. Beyond the waters of the British Isles the Germans had a few small successes. At the start of the war they had several warships stationed at various points in the Pacific, Atlantic, and Mediterranean, and they sank almost fifty British freighters before they were put out of action. Three times as many German merchantmen were seized and destroyed by the British, however, and at the end of 1914 the Allies were almost complete masters of the seas.

In the Mediterranean two important German naval units, the battle cruiser *Goeben* and the light cruiser *Breslau*, managed to evade the enemy forces and startled the world on August 10 by entering the strategically important Turkish Straits connecting the Mediterranean with the Black Sea. There they were to play an important role in helping bring Turkey into the war on the side of the Central Powers. The Russian navy, bottled up as it was in the Baltic and Black seas and still suffering from its defeat at the hands of the Japanese in 1905, could play no more than a defensive role on a very limited scale. In addition to containing the Russian fleet in the Baltic, the German navy served to keep open the increasingly important trade routes to the Scandinavian states.

THE SEARCH FOR ALLIES. Even before the results of the first battles on the eastern and western fronts were known, both the Allies and the Central Powers began making plans for winning over the other countries that could contribute men, supplies, and strategic positions to their respective causes. In the sharp rivalry that thus developed, bribes in money and territory were freely offered, and the statesmen of the countries not yet involved in the war saw in this international bargain counter a chance to achieve the national aims which in peacetime had filled their patriotic speeches.

Of the neutrals at the start of the war, Turkey was one of the most important. Both as political sovereign of the Ottoman Empire and as nominal religious leader of all Moslems, the Turkish Sultan was an ally well worth having. Moreover, Turkey was the master of the vital Straits— the Bosphorus, the Sea of Marmora, and the Dardanelles—which connect the Black Sea and the Mediterranean. By gaining control of this waterway, the Central Powers could cut off the main line of communications between Russia and her Western allies. A secret treaty of alliance between Germany and Turkey had already been concluded on August 1, but it was not until the end of October that Turkey, by bombarding Russian Black Sea ports, provoked the Allies into declaring war on her. The presence in the port of Constantinople of the two German cruisers the *Goeben* and the *Breslau*, which were nominally incorporated into the Turkish navy, was an important factor in strengthening the hand of those Turkish groups that favored the German alliance. It was these German-built cruisers, along with other Turkish warships, that took the initiative in the sudden bombardment of the Russian ports which brought Turkey into the war on the side of the Central Powers.

When the war in Europe started, Japan had a treaty of alliance with England and agreements with both France and Russia, under which the special interests of Japan in the Far East were recognized. To Japan, the European war provided an opportunity to expand and consolidate her empire in the Far East while the major Western powers with interests in that region were elsewhere engaged. Japan's initial objective was the seizure of Germany's Asian possessions, and shortly after the start of the war she opened hostilities against Germany. After a brief campaign, she occupied the German treaty zone of Kiaochow, including the port of Tsingtao, on the Shantung peninsula. Japan also occupied the German islands north of the equator, including the Marshalls, the Marianas, the Carolines, and Palau. The German colonial islands south of the equator were occupied by Australian and New Zealand forces [see maps, pp. 489 and 568].

An effort was now made to obtain the participation of Japanese troops in the European war itself, but the Japanese government held that all of its troops were needed to defend its interests in the Far East, although Japan did contribute to the eastern front by shipping supplies to Russia. In January, 1915, in a secret note to the Chinese government, Japan presented its famous twenty-one demands, which included transfer to Japan of the German possessions in Shantung, commercial rights in southern Manchuria, and various other economic and political restrictions on China. After delaying for several months, China was finally forced to concede the greater part of these demands. Russia's agreement to Japan's new position of influence in China was obtained in July, 1916, in return for the recognition of Russian influence in the Chinese province of Outer Mongolia. With these and other moves, Japan rapidly increased her position of influence in the Far East during the course of the war.

Although associated primarily with the Central Powers in the diplomacy of the prewar generation, Italy maintained that she was not in fact committed to join them in the conflict that broke out in the summer of 1914, since it was not a defensive war as specified in the alliance treaty. For practical purposes, Italy faced the choice of remaining neutral in return for territorial concessions in Austria and Southeastern Europe from the Central Powers, or of joining the Allies and receiving additional compensation in the Eastern Mediterranean region and in North Africa. In reaching its decision the Italian government, headed by Salandra and his foreign minister Sonnino, was inclined to caution because of public opinion formed by Catholic groups under the leadership of the Vatican and by the socialists, opposing Italy's entry into the war. Uncertainty as to the outcome of the military operations on the western front led to a further postponement of the choice. Italy's final decision to join the Allies was based on their favorable military position in the spring of 1915, as well as on the handsome prizes which she was offered. Such concessions as the Central Powers could make had to come either from Austria herself or from the Balkan countries that the latter hoped to dominate after the war. In the secret treaty signed in London in April, 1915, Italy received from the Allies, in addition to financial assistance, the promise of the Austrian territories of Trentino and the seaport of Trieste with its hinterland, as well as part of the province of Dalmatia and certain Adriatic islands. Italy was also promised, upon the successful completion of the war, rights in the newly created state of Albania, and full ownership of Turkey's Dodecanese Islands, which Italy had occupied three years earlier. In case Turkey should be partitioned and Germany's African colonies redistributed, Italy was to receive compensation. The price of all this for Italy was entrance into the war within thirty days. She declared war on Austria in May, 1915, but on Germany not until August, 1916. Italy occupied strategic points in Albania immediately, and also launched an attack against Austria in the region of the Isonzo River north of Venice. This latter area was to be the main scene of Italy's military efforts, which were neither vigorous nor fruitful. Four battles were fought here in 1915 and they all ended in stalemates [see map, pp. 62–3].

An important factor in bringing Italy into the war was her knowledge that the Allies were planning for the spring of 1915 a major campaign to seize Constantinople, secure the Balkan peninsula, and thus complete the ring around the Central Powers. The principal objection raised to this plan, of which Churchill was one of the chief proponents, was that it would require the removal of troops and equipment from the front in northern France, which many military leaders believed to be the only place where a military decision could be reached. It was nevertheless admitted that a victorious campaign against Turkey might have far-reaching results. Serbia had not yet been successfully invaded by the Central Powers, and if Rumania, Bulgaria, and Greece could also be brought into the war on the side of the Allies, the military position of the latter would be greatly enhanced. Moreover, a blow at the Turkish capital would in all probability take Turkey out of the war and release the Allied troops in the Near East for duty elsewhere. The decision was therefore reached to launch a combined naval and military attack on the Dardanelles, a narrow channel between the plains of Asia Minor and the rocky and well-fortified peninsula of Gallipoli. The Allies opened their attack in February, 1915, with a bombardment of the Gallipoli fortifications by British and French warships in the mined waters at the entrance to the Dardanelles. The initial bombardment was successful and was followed a month later by landings on the Gallipoli beaches, but due to inexperience and poor leadership the Allied troops were unable to overcome the difficulties presented by the rough terrain and the resolute resistance of the Turkish forces. A second costly series of landings was attempted in August, 1915, but they likewise failed to dislodge the Turks and in December the campaign was abandoned. Although it was a failure as a military effort, the Dardanelles campaign was long remembered for the valor of the Australian and New Zealand Auxiliary Corps, popularly known as the Anzacs, and for the brilliant military record of Mustafa Kemal, who later organized the Turkish Republic.

As the Dardanelles campaign was progressing, both of the contesting groups made strenuous efforts to win over the Balkan states. Of these, Greece was the most interested in the outcome of the Allied effort against Turkey. Many Greeks were still living under Turkish rule, and only two years earlier, at the end of the Balkan wars, Greece had annexed important Turkish territories. Opinion within Greece was divided, however, as to what course to pursue. King Constantine, whose wife was a sister of the German Kaiser, believed in the likelihood of German victory and advocated a policy of neutrality, at least until Greece's interests could be more clearly ascertained. Venizelos, the prime minister and popular nationalist leader, favored immediate participation in the war against Turkey. This controversy led to the resignation of Venizelos in the spring of 1915.

In the summer he returned to power and assisted the Allies to the extent of permitting the establishment of a military base at the northern Greek port of Salonika in October. The establishment of this base was of particular importance to the Allies in view of the developments in Greece's three northern neighbors—Bulgaria, Serbia, and Albania. Bulgaria was still smarting from her defeat in the Second Balkan War, and felt particularly bitter over the controversial province of Macedonia in southern Serbia. Victory at the Dardanelles might well have brought Bulgaria in on the Allied side, but now Bulgaria signed up with the Central Powers in September, 1915, and a month later joined them in a general attack on Serbia.

In 1914 the bravery and endurance of the Serbs had won universal admiration, but this time the odds against them were too great and their country was soon overrun. The Serbian army, nevertheless, managed to avoid annihilation and retreated over the mountains to the Albanian seacoast, from which it was evacuated in Allied ships. Except for Rumania, the Central Powers now dominated the entire Balkan Peninsula north of Greece and had a direct land route for the supply of Turkey. Austrian troops soon occupied the strategically located state of Albania and the small Slavic state of Montenegro, nestled in the mountains of north Albania. Rumania had been set somewhat apart from the main military developments by her geographical location. Her statesmen were thus able to avoid the immediate pressure of circumstances, and it was not until the latter part of 1916 that they decided to join the Allies.

The War of Attrition

MILITARY DEADLOCK. The German offensive on the eastern front in the spring of 1915 was a great success, and the Russians were pushed out of both Poland and Lithuania with huge losses. Grand Duke Nicholas was removed from his post as commander in chief by his nephew Emperor Nicholas II, who himself now undertook to supervise military operations. In 1916 the Russians under Brusilov launched a counteroffensive against Austria-Hungary, but achieved only limited gains despite great losses of men. One consequence of the Brusilov offensive was the entry of Rumania into the war on the side of the Allies in 1916. Hoping to seize the two Habsburg provinces of Bukovina and Transylvania with Russian aid, Rumania declared war on Austria-Hungary in August. The Rumanians miscalculated, however, on the amount of help they could get from Russia. Instead of marching into the Habsburg provinces, the Rumanians saw the greater part of their own country—including the capital city of Bucharest—overrun by a joint German-Bulgarian army. The Rumanian army was not captured, however, and with the aid of the Russians a front was established in northern Rumania. Only on the southernmost front did the Allies make important gains in 1916. At the military base established at Salonika in the preceding year the Allies built up an international force, of which an important element was the reconstituted Serbian army, under the French general Sarrail. This force now advanced into southern Serbia

T.R. MILLER

250 MILES

Aberdeen

**GREAT
BRITAIN**

Hull

London

Yarmouth

Dover

NORTH

SEA

NORWAY

Christiania
(OSLO)

Göteborg

DENMARK

Copenhagen

HELIGOLAND

KIEL
CANAL

Hamburg

Bremen

GERMANY

Berlin

Leipzig

Dresden

SWEDEN

Stockholm

BALTIC SEA

BORNHOLM
(DEN.)

FARTHEST
RUSSIAN ADVANCE
1914

Danzig

Stettin

Tannenberg

Posen

Breslau

SILESIA

Amsterdam

NETH.

GERMAN
FRONT LINE
NOV. II, 1918

GERMAN
ADVANCE
JULY 18, 1918

Ypres

Brussels
Liége

BELG.

Arras

FRONT
LINE
AUG., 1918

GERMAN
ADVANCE
SEPT., 1914

Compiegne

Paris

Orléans

LOIRE

Reims

Verdun

Essen

Cologne

Koblenz

Frankfurt

Mainz

LUX.

Metz

LORRAINE

Toul

RHINE

Strassburg

ALSACE

Belfort

Basel

FRANCE

SWITZERLAND

Lyons

Turin

Milan

Genoa

Bologna

Florence

Marseilles

Toulon

ITALY

Rome

Naples

Nürnberg

BOHEMIA

Prague

MORAVIA

Vienna

AUSTRIA

SLOVAKIA

DANUBE

Budapest

HUNGARY

TYROL

AUG.
1917

Klagenfurt

DRAVE

MARCH
1918

Venice

Trieste

Fiume

Agram

CROATIA

SAVE

BOSNIA

Sarajevo

MONTE-
NEGRO

Cattaro

Bari

Taranto

Valona

ALBANIA

SE

Belg

WEST
FRONT

ELBE

ODER

VISTULA

PO...

EAS

Craco

ADRIATIC SEA

THE
CENTRAL
POWERS

AREAS
OCCUPIED BY
CENTRAL POWERS

ITALIAN
FRONT

BALKAN
FRONT

WORLD WAR I IN EUROPE

MAP 3

and established firm positions for a later offensive. It also assisted Venizelos
in forming a provisional Greek government in Salonika which declared
war on the Central Powers and forced the abdication of King Constantine
in the following year.

In the west the two opposing groups of armies settled down to the dis-
mal trench warfare well described in Remarque's famous novel *All Quiet
on the Western Front*. In four great battles in 1915 the Allies tried to break
through the enemy lines, but no appreciable gains were made. By the end
of that year French casualties were 2,000,000, and British, 500,000. In the
spring of 1916 the Germans made a tremendous effort to capture the
famous French fortress at Verdun, but without success despite great loss
of life. A similar Allied effort later in the year in the region of the Somme
River was equally costly and futile.

It was not difficult for the Allies to organize a blockade of Germany.
The blockade of contraband war materials was permissible under international law, but when it came to such noncontraband goods as foodstuffs
the interests of many countries were involved. The neutrals bordering
on the North Sea—Holland and the Scandinavian states—were affected;
and the United States wished to exercise its right to trade in noncontraband goods with both sides. For Germany the problem was to break
through the blockade and impose a counterblockade on the British Isles by
means of mines, submarines, and sea raiders. Germany was likewise embar-
rassed by international law, which restricted the use of submarines. But
whereas British efforts to interpret international law in their favor only affected neutral property, those of Germany affected neutral lives as well.
Even in the relatively restricted submarine campaign in 1915, the sinking
without warning of the British liners *Lusitania*, in May, and *Arabic*, in August, with the loss of a number of American lives, had given rise to considerable feeling in the United States and had led to vigorous protests by President Wilson. An even stronger stand, amounting to an ultimatum, was
taken by the American government after the sinking of the *Sussex* in the
spring of 1916, and the Germans finally decided to suspend unlimited submarine warfare for the time being.

In the North Sea both the British and the German fleets maintained
their cautious policy throughout 1915. This relative inactivity was relieved
only by a series of skirmishes in the winter of 1914–15 between the battle-
cruiser squadrons of Beatty and Hipper. After two successful raids by Hipper on the British coast, he was finally caught by a superior British force.
The ensuing battle was inconclusive, however, and the two squadrons retired to their respective bases to await further developments. It was not
until the spring of 1916 that the two great fleets finally made contact. The
series of engagements in the North Sea on May 31, 1916, constituting the
battle known to the Allies as Jutland and to the Germans as Skagerrak,
was the only occasion on which the two main fleets under Jellicoe and
Scheer joined in combat, and it confirmed the supremacy of the British
in the North Sea for the duration of the war. The Germans showed, on

the whole, superior technical skill and inflicted on the enemy approximately twice the damage in tonnage and human casualties that they themselves sustained. While the British failed to destroy the German fleet, they nonetheless maintained their supremacy in the North Sea; and the Germans did not make any further serious attempt to challenge it.

THE WAR BEYOND EUROPE. While the main battles were being fought in Europe, the Allies were also engaged in a number of small campaigns around the fringes of the Ottoman Empire which were ultimately to bear fruit out of all proportion to the size of the forces engaged. The British navy had come to depend heavily on the oil produced by a British concession in Mesopotamia where the Tigris and Euphrates rivers flow into the Persian Gulf. Fearful lest the resources of this Turkish province be cut off by enemy action, the Allies took steps to occupy it. Encouraged by an easy capture of Basra in November, 1914, a British and Indian force moved northward the following spring with the objective of seizing the key city of Baghdad and thus seriously crippling Turkey. It almost reached Baghdad in November, 1915, after a series of rapid victories, but was finally stopped by the Turks and surrounded at Kut-el-Amara. After a dramatic siege lasting all winter, the entire force surrendered to the Turks in April, 1916. To the north of this theater, in Turkish Armenia, the Russians succeeded in making small but important gains after a bitter struggle with the Turks in the course of 1916 [see map, p. 69].

Another strategic position of importance to the Allies was the Suez Canal. A good-sized force was built up in Egypt in 1915 to defend the canal against what turned out to be a relatively weak Turkish attack. In the course of 1916 the Allies occupied the Sinai peninsula and by 1917 they were ready to invade the Turkish province of Syria, of which Palestine was then a part. As in the case of the Mesopotamian campaign, it was felt that the occupation of a large Turkish province and the capture of a major city such as Jerusalem would be a step towards weakening the position of the Central Powers. Here again, however, the strength of the Turks was underestimated and the Turks repulsed the Allies in June, 1917.

In Africa the greater part of the German colonies were occupied by one or another of the Allies during the first year of the war. England and France both participated in the occupation of Togoland and the Cameroons. German Southwest Africa was conquered by the forces of the Union of South Africa, with some British assistance, in the summer of 1915. Only German East Africa offered any sustained resistance. Here a remarkable German force under Lettow-Vorbeck outmaneuvered until the end of the war the British, Indians, and South Africans sent against him. Not until the armistice was declared in Europe was he finally brought to terms.

THE IMPACT OF THE WAR. Throughout Europe the war had started in a spirit of national enthusiasm. Both military and civilian leaders thought of the conflict in terms of the wars that Europe had known in the past two or three generations, and such plans and supplies as existed were based on the assumption of a short conflict. As the prospect of a brief war faded away and, especially after the disillusionments of 1915, the likelihood of a conflict of Napoleonic dimensions loomed ahead, the spirit on all the home fronts changed from enthusiasm to grim determination. As the realization came to the various peoples that they were entirely unprepared for the problems they faced, and as their governments were confronted with huge losses of manpower and vast shortages of munitions and supplies, drastic changes were introduced in the traditional political and economic methods of administration. Party governments were reorganized on a more representative basis, economic life was readjusted to entirely new patterns, and the full resources of each country were thrown into the struggle for survival. Of all the changes which the war imposed on the participants, doubtless the most important for the future development of Europe was the great increase that took place in the power of the state to exercise control over all aspects of political, economic, and social life.

France suffered as much as any of the principal participants from the initial effects of the war, and this strain was soon reflected in the political scene. As president of the French Republic, Poincaré remained throughout the war a symbol of national unity. The cabinet under prime minister Viviani did not fare so well. In 1915 parliamentary criticism of the war effort was sharpened by the military defeats, and relations between the military and political leaders became tense. Finally, in October, Viviani resigned and was replaced by Briand, who formed a cabinet uniting all leading political groups and re-established full co-operation between the government and the high command.

The British government passed through a similar crisis, when revelations of munitions shortages and the differences over the Dardanelles campaign shook the Liberal cabinet of Asquith. In May, 1915, Asquith reorganized his cabinet, dropping the controversial Churchill and adding a number of Conservatives and a Laborite. This coalition government weathered the bitter experiences in France, the North Sea, and Mesopotamia, as well as a rebellion in Ireland in the spring of 1916. A demand was nevertheless felt for more vigorous leadership than that of Asquith, and in December, 1916, Lloyd George succeeded him as leader of the Liberals and formed an even more broadly based government of national union.

The government of Goremykin in Russia responded to the impact of the war not by broadening its representative character but by placing greater reliance on intrigue and autocratic methods. While the threatening internal breakdown forced the government to accept the assistance of the middle class and provincial gentry organizations in mobilizing the resources of the country, Emperor Nicholas II and his wife came more and more under reactionary influences. Whatever the personal motives of such intriguers as the mystic Rasputin, who opposed the whole war effort, and Stürmer, who was believed to be pro-German, the result of their efforts was to undermine the dynastic regime. The assumption by the Emperor himself of the command of the armies in September, 1915, and the appointment of Stürmer to replace Goremykin in February, 1916, had the effect of alienating large groups in the Duma (Parliament). In November an even more repressive regime was established with Trepov as prime minister. The assassination of Rasputin a month later by a group of aristocrats was an indication of the extent to which the country had become demoralized by the strain of war.

The Habsburgs in Austria-Hungary fared no better than the Romanovs in Russia, although their problems were of a different character. The stability of Austria-Hungary depended on the support of Germany without and of the ambitious Magyars within. The Poles, the Czechs and Slovaks, the southern Slavs, and the Italians, were all in a state of active discontent. Some negotiated with the government in the hope of getting special privileges, while others—such as the Czechs and Slovaks under the leadership of Masaryk—made plans for independence at the end of the war. The Magyars contributed to the weakening of the empire by their reluctance to sacrifice any of their privileges. The assassination of prime minister Stürgkh by a socialist in October, 1916, and the death of Emperor Francis Joseph a month later, after a reign of sixty-eight years, symbolized the end of the old regime. As defeat followed defeat, the bonds which held the empire together were loosened and broken. The new emperor, Charles, did his best to carry on the traditions of his dynasty with a cabinet in Austria headed by Clam-Martinitz and supported by Tisza in Hungary, but the complicated multinational structure of the empire could not stand up under the strain of the war.

Of the major powers, only Germany started the war with a government that concentrated in its hands full authority and at the same time had broad popular support. The Social Democrats, the only large political group whose support of the government might have been in doubt, combined with the other parties in August, 1914 to provide a unanimous vote in favor of war credits. Four months later, on a similar occasion, all but one of the Social Democrats again supported the government. As discussions of war aims developed in 1915 and 1916, divisions between the Social Democrats and the middle-class parties began to appear, but in the first years of the struggle they were united in the idea that it was a defensive war in which the interests of all the German people were involved. The socialists took advantage of their position to press upon the chancellor, Bethmann-Hollweg, claims for the democratization of the Prussian electoral system and other reforms, but did not insist on more than vague promises for the postwar period. Relying on this solid backing, the German government went further than the other participants in reorganizing the domestic economy for war ends. Industry was mobilized by the brilliant Rathenau, and food production, the labor draft, and rationing were imposed with relentless vigor.

WAR AIMS AND SECRET TREATIES. At the start of the war, the immediate defense of national security was uppermost in the minds of all participants. Russia and Austria-Hungary each considered itself to be defending its interests against the encroachments of the other. Germany was believed to be threatened with encirclement, and France and England by German aggression. After the first months of the war, the inadequacy of these initial sentiments became evident, and public opinion began to center around more positive objectives. The needs both of morale at home and of propaganda abroad required the elaboration of war aims commensurate with the huge sacrifices being made. Austria-Hungary hardly had time to worry about any war aims beyond her Balkan interests, but in Germany there was wide discussion of the problem. While the Social Democrats remained loyal to their conception of a defensive war, the middle-class parties developed grandiose plans for the future. They saw a victorious Germany extending its frontiers permanently over Belgium and part of France in the west, and over Poland in the east. In partnership with Austria-Hungary, Germany would dominate the Balkans, while her economic influence would be extended through the Ottoman Empire to the Persian Gulf.

In England, the Liberal government of Asquith should be given credit for formulating British interests in terms of the re-establishment of a European system based on law in which large and small nations alike would be able to enjoy independence and peace. This noble and sincere aim was finally achieved in some degree with the founding of the League of Nations, but in the meantime practical considerations and the growth of a deep feeling of hatred against the enemy led the Allies to make their own plans of territorial aggrandizement. France in Alsace-Lorraine and Russia in Eastern Europe had immediate frontier demands that had played an important role in the outbreak of the war and that now served as basic war aims. The Allies also soon discovered that by arousing the minority peoples of the Austrian and Turkish empires they could seriously undermine their unity, and freedom of nationalities thus became a popular slogan.

As the war progressed, these territorial war aims were formally incorporated in the famous secret treaties which were to plague Wilson at the peace conference in 1919. Two of these have already been mentioned: the treaties by which Italy in April, 1915, and Rumania in August, 1916, were promised extensive territorial concessions in return for their participation in the war on the side of the Allies. Another group of secret agreements involved the partition of Turkey at the end of the war. In March, 1915, England and France conceded to Russia the city of Constantinople and the Turkish Straits, along with adjacent territory, on condition that Constantinople be established as a free port and that freedom of commerical shipping in the Straits be guaranteed. Compensation for England and France was arranged in April, 1916, when the former was assigned a sphere of influence in Mesopotamia and Palestine, and the latter in Syria, Adana, Cilicia, and southern Kurdistan. At the same time, Russia was granted an additional zone of influence in Armenia, part of Kurdistan, and adjacent territories in northeastern Anatolia. In the Sykes-Picot agreement of May,

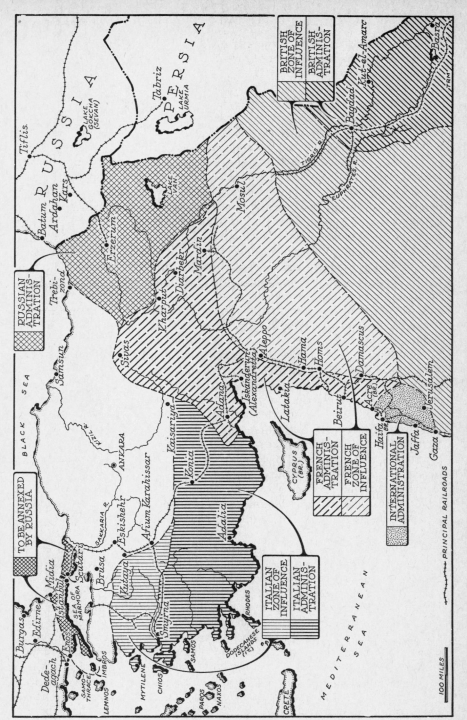

MAP 4 *Ottoman Empire: Allied Partition Agreements, 1915–17*

1916, a more precise definition was made by England and France as to which of Turkey's Arabic territories they would administer themselves and which they would turn over to an independent Arab state or federation of states. In April, 1917 (St. Jean de Maurienne Agreement), Italy was granted a sphere of influence in the Anatolian districts of Smyrna and Adalia. As though these treaties did not make the eventual partition of the Turkish Empire sufficiently complicated, in the course of 1915 the British had made vague and general promises to the Arab leader Husein, the Sheikh of Mecca, regarding the independence of the Arab peoples after the war. This commitment was kept secret even from the French. At the same time a national home in Palestine was offered to the Jewish people on condition that the rights of the existing non-Jewish population be respected, in a public declaration made by Balfour, the British foreign secretary, in November, 1917 [see map, p. 69].

There should also be mentioned two further secret treaties, the terms of which comprised the war aims of the signatories. In February, 1917, in return for certain naval assistance, the British promised to support the Japanese claim to the German rights in Shantung and to the German Pacific islands north of the equator, which Japan had already seized. In an analogous agreement a month later, Russia offered to support the French claims in Alsace-Lorraine, the Saar, and the Rhineland, in return for French assistance in achieving Russia's territorial claims with regard to the Central Powers. All of these secret treaties, concluded under the stress of war and at times in contradiction to publicly proclaimed ideals, became an integral part of the aims for which the war was fought.

Closely associated with the question of war aims was the position of the United States, the most important of neutrals. Both the Allies and the Central Powers, in their bitter struggle for the control of the trade routes, carefully watched its reaction. As was the case with many of the other neutrals, opinion in the United States was seriously divided and confused as to what should be done about the European war. The emotions of the large groups of recent immigrants were deeply involved, and the tradition of American aloofness from European affairs exerted a powerful influence. The Allied blockade and German submarine warfare served further to divide public opinion. The best indication of how people felt, however, was the fact that Wilson won the election in November, 1916, on his record of having kept the country out of war.

While public opinion continued to favor neutrality, the statesmen responsible for American policy were profoundly troubled by the prospect of a possible Allied defeat. In 1916 Wilson made two attempts to sound out the belligerents, having in mind the possibility of mediating in an effort to achieve a negotiated peace. Wilson sent his trusted and influential adviser Colonel House to Europe in January and February, 1916, to study the situation. House's investigation resulted in a suggestion to England that the United States call a peace conference as a means of reaching a compromise favorable to the Allies. German refusal to participate in

the conference or to agree to reasonable terms would be an indication of
her aggressive intentions, although it would not necessarily cause the
United States to join the Allies. The House proposal was rejected by the
British government, however, on the grounds that such a conference would
weaken the position of the Allies without offering them any real hope of
acceptable terms.

A more serious effort to achieve a negotiated peace was launched in
December, 1916. On December 12 Germany proposed, in a mood of confidence and without mentioning her terms, that negotiations for peace be
undertaken. This offer was turned down by the Allies at the end of the
month, because it looked to them more like an offer to accept surrender
than an offer to negotiate. In the meantime, on December 18, Wilson
came forward with the proposal that both sides frankly state their war
aims, in the hope that a compromise might turn out to be feasible. An
early reply was received from the Central Powers, who again refused to
offer any terms but suggested that direct negotiations among the belligerents would be the proper course to pursue. The Allies, deeply hurt that
Wilson should have made his proposal at a time when Germany's military
preponderance placed the Central Powers in a favorable position, met in
Rome to discuss their terms. The terms that they transmitted to Wilson
on January 10, 1917, included restoration of the territories occupied by the
Central Powers with suitable reparations, liberation of the minority peoples of Austria-Hungary and Turkey, and guarantees for the security of
the small states of Europe after the war. Wilson was somewhat taken
aback by these demands, but the balance was restored by the end of the
month when the Central Powers finally agreed to submit their claims.
They agreed to restore the territories occupied in Western Europe but
held out for a strengthened position in Eastern Europe as well as additional colonies. While in both cases the proposed terms doubtless contained much propaganda, it was clear that in the winter of 1916–17 both
contestants felt that military action still held out better prospects for
them than diplomatic negotiations.

The Turn of the Tide

During the winter of 1916–17, what amounted to a deadlock had
been reached between the two contesting groups of states. In the east,
after great efforts, the Central Powers had broken up the Russian offensives and had occupied most of Rumania. Though this was indeed a success it had been a costly one, and a great line of Russian troops stretching
from the Carpathians to the Baltic was still there to pin down large numbers of German soldiers. In the south, if Italy represented no great menace
to Austria-Hungary, the Italian Army was still active and required its
share of attention. In the west, Verdun and the Somme had taken their
terrific toll of men, and even the most optimistic on either side were beginning to doubt whether the enemy's line could ever be breached.

In the political sphere the negotiations of the past several months had shown that neither side was as yet willing to make any serious concessions in exchange for peace. For both groups of contestants the war had been so costly, and the possibilities of a compromise peace were so limited, that a continuation of the struggle seemed to be the only possible course. The question was: how was victory to be achieved? For the Allies the pattern was already set: a relentless tightening of the blockade, accompanied by steady military pressure on all fronts, with ultimate American assistance in prospect. For the Central Powers the decision was more difficult, since the military authorities had reached the conclusion that the armies alone could not hope for a victory over the enemy. It was under these circumstances that the German government took the fateful step of proclaiming unrestricted submarine warfare.

UNRESTRICTED SUBMARINE WARFARE. The decision to renew the full-scale submarine campaign which had been suspended in May, 1916, under pressure from Wilson, was a calculated gamble. The German experts believed that by sinking an average of 600,000 tons of shipping per month for five or six months they could reduce the shipping available for the supply of the British Isles by some 40 per cent. This was considered to be sufficient to bring England to her knees, before she could get any extensive assistance from the outside. Already toward the end of 1916, during the period of limited submarine warfare, the Germans had been sinking an average of 300,000 tons of shipping per month. With their constantly growing number of submarines, they were confident of doubling this figure after the removal of restrictions. The Germans recognized the likelihood that the United States would enter the war on the side of the Allies, but calculated that in its state of unpreparedness the United States could not send sufficient aid to affect the outcome of the war during the five or six months which they expected it would take to reduce England. It was with these expectations in mind that, in the latter part of January, 1917, Germany notified the United States government that it was planning to renew unrestricted submarine warfare on February 1. Wilson promptly broke off diplomatic relations with Germany, but he did not declare war. Still hoping that Germany might spare neutral shipping, Wilson adopted a policy of arming merchantmen pending the further development of events.

INTERVENTION OF THE UNITED STATES. The formal American declaration of war on Germany, voted by Congress on April 6, 1917, is to be explained principally by the growing conviction in the United States that a victory of the Central Powers would run counter to American interests and that this could be prevented only by active American participation in the war. While England and France had a natural advantage over the other European countries in winning American support, their success in this effort could never be taken for granted, nor was it an easy accomplishment. The historical and cultural associations of the United States with Western Europe were indeed a powerful factor in influencing American opinion, but they alone would not have been enough to overcome the desire to stay out of the war which predominated until 1916.

It is significant that the position of the United States as a maritime power brought it into almost exclusive contact with the Allies and also made it particularly sensitive to its commercial rights on the seas as a neutral. The control that the Allies were soon able to establish over German overseas trade by means of the blockade cut it off almost entirely from the United States. American trade with the Allied countries increased fourfold between 1914 and 1916, while that with the Central Powers almost disappeared. American private loans extended to the belligerents during the period of neutrality, which amounted to some 2.3 billion dollars, likewise went almost exclusively to the Allies. Moreover, Allied control of communications extended not only to commercial shipping but also to the news cables. American news reports regarding the European war were required to pass through Allied censorship, or came directly from Allied sources, and thus tended to place particular emphasis on the brutalities of the Central Powers, all of whose armies were in occupation of Allied soil. For these reasons and for many others the dependence of the United States on maritime communications tended to give it a more direct interest in the success of the Allies and brought it to a degree under their influence.

An even more important consequence of the maritime position of the United States was its involvement in the efforts of the two belligerent groups to strangle each other by means of blockades and submarine warfare. Initially, the British blockade had caused as much concern to the American government as the German submarines, and it was the subject, as has already been seen, of a long and bitter exchange of notes between the American and British governments. By its very nature, however, since it involved the lives of noncombatants as well as their property, German submarine warfare before long became a greater source of controversy than the Allied blockade. In the spring of 1916 American pressure had been sufficient to force Germany to suspend unrestricted submarine warfare. It was only as a last resort that Germany again unleashed her submarines at the start of February, 1917, and this led immediately to the rupture of relations with the United States. Wilson's slender hope that the neutrals might yet be spared the full fury of the submarine soon vanished, for American property and lives went down with those of the Allies. It was specifically on this issue that Wilson recommended and obtained a declaration of war by Congress on April 6. War was not declared on Austria-Hungary until the following December. With Turkey diplomatic relations were maintained.

While war was indeed declared over the issue of unrestricted submarine warfare, most Americans had come to believe by the spring of 1917 that this was merely the technical aspect of a much larger issue: that of the autocratic government and militarism of the Central Powers. From the initial invasion of Belgium to the indiscriminate use of the submarine, the Central Powers had given evidence of their ruthlessness. Likewise, in the diplomatic exchanges of the preceding year, the Central Powers had shown little inclination to make peace. This impression was greatly sharpened by the publication by Wilson on March 1 of a deciphered note from Zimmermann, the German foreign minister, to his diplomatic representative in Mexico. This note instructed him, in case the United States intervened, to attempt to bring Mexico into the war by urging her to undertake the conquest of New Mexico, Texas, and Arizona. The possibility of including Japan in this arrangement was also envisaged in the note.

While the idea of the inherently autocratic and militaristic character of the Central Powers was widely held in 1917, the democratic character of the Allied governments was not so widely accepted. It was a matter of particular concern to the important group of American liberals led by Wilson that Russia should share to so large a degree the same characteristics of autocracy and militarism which had become identified with the Central Powers. The news of the abdication of Nicholas II on March 15, following as it did the German declaration of unrestricted submarine warfare and the Zimmermann note, served to remove the last doubts from the minds of many Americans as to the democratic character of the Allied cause, which their interests demanded that they support. On March 20, the United States became the first state to recognize the Provisional Government in Petrograd [see below, pp. 177–79].

THE CRITICAL MONTHS. While the March revolution in Russia must certainly be regarded as a setback for the Allied military effort, the intervention of the United States more than compensated for it. The latter could not for the time being send a large number of divisions to the front lines to replace the rapidly disintegrating Russian forces, but it could and did make available large credits that permitted the Allies to obtain raw materials and munitions in almost inexhaustible quantities. The United States could also use economic pressure to bring the shipping and other resources of the remaining neutrals into the service of the Allied cause. Moreover, a number of other neutrals soon followed the example of the United States, including China and many Latin American states.

In the course of these events the Allies made new plans for an offensive on the western front. A major attack was mounted in April, 1917, by the French general Nivelle, but such gains as were made fell far short of the objectives and were achieved at great sacrifice. Nivelle was replaced by Pétain, who now faced the difficult task of handling widespread mutinies among the French troops. The British under Haig launched a vigorous attack in the autumn of 1917 on the Belgian sector of their front, but the campaign was a disastrous failure.

Even less successful were the efforts of the Italians, whose main objective was the important Austrian seaport of Trieste. In the period from her entry into the war until the latter part of 1917, Italy fought no less than eleven battles in an effort to cross the Isonzo River, which barred the road to Trieste. The Italian armies finally crumpled under a joint German-

Austrian attack in October, 1917, at Caporetto (the disastrous retreat across the Venetian plain has been well described by Ernest Hemingway in *A Farewell to Arms*). The Italians rallied just north of Venice, and within a year were strong enough to force the enemy into a general retreat.

The one important Allied success in 1917 was the defeat of the German submarine. The Germans had gambled that they could starve Britain out before adequate countermeasures could be taken against the submarine, and at the start they came within striking distance of their objective. In April, May, and June, 1917, they sank a monthly average of some 700,000 tons of Allied shipping, and at one point a grain reserve of only six weeks was left in Britain. But the Germans underestimated not only the resolution of the Allies but also their ingenuity in combating the submarine. On the home front, a vigorous effort was made by rationing and planning to reduce to a minimum the import needs of the population. With the use of detection devices, depth charges, and mines, and especially with the development of the convoy system in co-operation with the American navy, the British regained control of the seas. The rate of sinkings was reduced by the end of 1917 to one half of its high point in April, and it continued to decline throughout 1918. The Germans, on the other hand, lost half of their submarines during the entire duration of the war. In the end, their gamble with unrestricted submarine warfare also cost them the war itself.

The third year of the conflict, which saw the great turning point in the fortunes of the war, also marked the nadir of the morale of the contestants. The nationalists' enthusiasm and their certainty that they were fighting for a just cause, which had inspired such unprecedented sacrifices by the peoples of Europe, turned to doubt and disillusionment as the cost of victory seemed to outweigh by so great a margin any possible gains.

While the Allied countries were the first to show outward signs of fatigue, the peoples of the Central Powers were in many respects under an even greater strain. In Germany, the popular discontent took the form of demands for reform of the rationing system and of the Prussian three-class electoral law, and more particularly of criticism of the annexationist war aims. In the spring of 1917 a majority group in the Reichstag, led by the Catholic Erzberger and the Socialist Scheidemann, proposed that a resolution be passed favoring a compromise peace without annexations. The military leaders, headed by Hindenburg and Ludendorff, opposed this movement and in July convinced the Kaiser that he should dismiss the chancellor, Bethmann-Hollweg, and appoint in his place the subservient bureaucrat Michaelis. They also got the political leaders to amend their resolution so as to give the government greater leeway in eventual negotiations. The sentiments of the Reichstag were, nevertheless, clear enough. When in October a new crisis arose over a mutiny in the navy, the Reichstag forced the resignation of Michaelis as chancellor. In his place was appointed Hertling, an elderly statesman who was not under military influence. His foreign minister was the vigorous and moderate Kühlmann.

GERMAN WAR LEADERS *Emperor William II of Germany, flanked by Generals Hindenburg and Ludendorff, studying the military situation during World War I.*

In a far greater need of a compromise peace than Germany was her ally Austria-Hungary, and it was from Emperor Charles that the first serious peace feelers came. Using as an intermediary his brother-in-law Prince Sixtus, an officer in the Belgian army, he approached the French and British in the spring of 1917. An early peace was essential if Austria was to survive, and Charles was prepared to offer limited concessions to Italy on a reciprocal basis and to urge his German ally to adopt a reasonable attitude as regards Alsace-Lorraine and Belgium. It is not certain, however, whether Charles was prepared to make a separate peace or was merely trying to find a compromise basis for a general peace. The Allies were greatly interested in the possibilities offered by these suggestions, for they had long entertained the ambitious aim of making a separate peace with Austria and turning her against Germany. As it turned out, the Austrian proposal was quite unacceptable to Italy and, for that matter, to Serbia and Rumania. When the Germans learned of these negotiations they were not averse to following them up in order to sound out the Allies. In drawing up their own proposals, the Germans thought in terms of extending their influence over Russian Poland and the Baltic provinces and of giving Austria a greatly strengthened position in the Balkans. No important concession would be made in Alsace-Lorraine, and Belgium would not have its full independence restored. These terms are of interest only as a gauge of the views of the German government at this time, however, as the Allies decided not to discuss the matter any further.

The idea of a compromise peace did not die easily. It was shortly taken up by Pope Benedict XV who, after preliminary consultations, sent a note to the belligerents in August, 1917, proposing a peace without annexations or reparations. This note led to further negotiations within each of the two groups of allies, but the results did not differ greatly from those of previous efforts at compromise. The Central Powers were not prepared to withdraw unconditionally from all the territories they had occupied, particularly from Belgium. The Allies, on the other hand, were not prepared to give up the territorial claims, such as Alsace-Lorraine and Trentino, for which such great sacrifices had already been made. A compromise peace along somewhat similar lines was urged by a socialist conference of the Second International which met in Stockholm in May, but it did not receive serious consideration on the part of the warring governments.

COLLAPSE OF THE EASTERN FRONT. The Provisional Government which came to power in Russia when Emperor Nicholas II abdicated in March, 1917, was pledged to continue the war. It made a systematic attempt to reorganize the army, and in June and July a new offensive was launched against Germany and Austria. Significant gains were made at first, but the Russian army had neither the weapons nor the morale to sustain a long campaign. Unlike the Provisional Government, the Bolsheviks who seized power in Russia in November, 1917, had no interest in continuing the war. Their antiwar propaganda had in fact won them wide political support, and had contributed significantly to undermining the morale of the Russian armed forces [see below, pp. 176–89, for an account of the Russian revolution]. The disintegration of the Russian armies and the Bolshevik encouragement of the self-determination of peoples soon led to the breaking away of the numerous national minorities living along Russia's western frontiers. Before the end of 1917, movements favoring autonomy or independence had been proclaimed in Finland, Estonia, the Ukraine, Bessarabia, Latvia, and Transcaucasia. Moreover, the Germans were in occupation of Lithuania and Poland, which had been organized provisionally as independent states. Faced with this situation abroad and with the full demoralization of Russia's armed forces at home, Lenin decided to continue the policy of peace which had served as so useful a rallying point during the months preceding the revolution. For the Central Powers, similarly, there was every reason to seek a settlement in the east so that they could devote greater attention to the crucial western front.

Under these conditions representatives of Russia and the Central Powers met in the town of Brest-Litovsk early in December, 1917, and by the middle of the month armistice terms had been agreed upon. The negotiation of peace terms proved to be more difficult, however. The Bolsheviks were willing enough to relinquish Russian sovereignty over the provinces occupied by the Central Powers, but they wanted to see them established as independent states and not governed as part of a new German empire. The Germans, on the other hand, were well aware of Russia's internal weakness and saw no reason to make concessions in regions where they were already in occupation. For the time being neither side was willing to give in, and the peace negotiations were broken off in January, 1918.

A great debate now developed in Petrograd as to what policy was best suited to the principal objectives of the Bolshevik leaders: their maintenance in power within Russia, and the furtherance of civil war and revolution without. Some felt that extensive concessions to the Central Powers would undermine the prestige of their regime at home and spell doom for the revolutionary forces in Central Europe. Lenin, on the other hand, felt that peace at any price was necessary and that the revolution abroad could be left to follow its own course, until the Bolsheviks could consolidate their position at home. Unable to reach an agreement on this issue, the leaders accepted an expedient proposed by Trotsky which called for a declaration that the war was over without the conclusion of peace terms. It was hoped that the Central Powers, eager to use their troops elsewhere, would now come to terms rather than face the uncertainties of a long armistice or a revival of the fighting. However, the Germans called the Russian bluff and resumed the offensive, moving rapidly through Latvia and Estonia towards Petrograd. The other Bolshevik leaders now agreed with Lenin that peace was essential and decided to accept the enemy's terms.

The peace treaty that was concluded between Russia and the Central Powers at Brest-Litovsk on March 3, 1918, marked the final collapse of the eastern front. Russia renounced her sovereignty over Finland, the Baltic provinces, and Poland, and recognized the independence of the Ukraine. It also ceded to Turkey the Transcaucasian territories of Kars, Ardahan, and Batum in the region of the Black Sea. The German forces now moved forward rapidly and established their influence in all the European provinces abandoned by the Russians. The Bolsheviks, for their part, transferred their capital to Moscow from the strategically exposed city of Petrograd.

An immediate consequence of the peace of Brest-Litovsk was the surrender of Rumania. Perilously lodged in the northernmost corner of their occupied country, the Rumanian forces could not continue fighting once the Russians had abandoned them. In May a peace treaty was signed in

Bucharest in which territorial concessions were made to Austria-Hungary and Bulgaria, while Germany received a lease of Rumania's important oil resources. Significant for the future of Rumania was the tacit recognition by the Central Powers at this time of her annexation of the Russian province of Bessarabia. This province, which for many years had been a source of controversy between Rumania and Russia, had declared its independence, as the Moldavian Republic, in December, 1917, and its mixed population now welcomed the association with Rumanian people.

Victory of the Allies

VICTORY IN THE WEST. More as a measure of desperation than as one calculated to achieve victory, Ludendorff—who was now in full charge of Germany's war effort—decided to launch a great new offensive in the west in the spring of 1918. By this time it was recognized that the submarine campaign had failed to affect Britain's position decisively. Of similarly limited effect had been the German air raids. Between 1915 and 1917 a mounting number of raids by airships, commonly known by their German name of Zeppelins, had been directed against England, primarily against London. While these raids had been disturbing and had in some cases created panic, they had caused negligible casualties and had finally been stopped by teamwork between airplanes and searchlights. By the winter of 1917–18 raids by German airplanes had become a more serious menace to London and the channel towns, causing greater casualties than the airships and imposing a heavier strain on the civilian population; but even these attacks had proved to be an annoyance rather than a menace to the Allied home front. The final German offensive on the western front was launched by three armies in March, 1918, and reached its climax in May. The Germans made important initial gains and attained again some of the most advanced positions they had reached in 1914. The strength of the Allies proved too great for the exhausted Germans, however, and their offensive soon ground to a halt. It was as part of this successful resistance to the last German offensive that the American troops participated in their first important engagement at Belleau Wood near Château-Thierry in June, 1918. By the middle of July, the initiative had passed for the last time to the Allies.

Against the Ottoman Empire the Allies had already by this time achieved important victories. Baghdad fell in the spring of 1917 to a British army, which a year later moved north to protect Allied interests in the Caucasus region of Russia. After the peoples of Armenia, Azerbaijan, and Georgia declared their independence of Russia, this British force spent the summer of 1918 in a struggle against a joint German-Turkish force sent to take control of the region upon the collapse of Russian authority. This action was taken in accordance with the secret Anglo-French agreement of December, 1917, which provided that in case it should be found necessary to fight the Central Powers in southern Russia, the British forces would occupy the Caucasus region while the French would occupy the region north of the Black Sea to the Don River.

In the meantime, the British captured Jerusalem in 1917 and moved on into northern Syria in the following year to take Damascus. The Turks were now prepared to admit defeat, and on October 30 they signed an armistice. A month before the Turks, on September 29, the Bulgarians had signed an armistice in the face of a vigorous attack launched by the Allies from Salonika. The Serbs advanced rapidly into their own country from the Salonika front, reoccupying their capital city of Belgrade at the beginning of November and proceeding on into the territory of Austria-Hungary. Other Allied troops overran Bulgaria and crossed the Danube into Rumania in time to permit that country to re-enter the war just a day before Germany's final surrender.

The stage was now set for the final test of strength on the western front. The task of co-ordinating the Allied armies was given to the French general Foch, and by the late summer he had the Germans under Ludendorff in full retreat. On October 4, Germany and Austria-Hungary appealed to President Wilson for an armistice, and the negotiations were initiated which led to Germany's surrender five weeks later. On November 3 the Austrians capitulated, and on the 11th the Germans signed the armistice documents.

There can be little doubt that the principal cause of the defeat of the Central Powers lay in the superior military strength of the Allies. The western and southern fronts had held against the most vigorous efforts of the Central Powers, and the intervention of the United States more than compensated for the collapse of the eastern front. The great pressures of the war were reflected in the economic and social disintegration that undermined the strength of Germany and Austria-Hungary, and to a lesser degree of Bulgaria and Turkey as well. In Germany, the economic strain and the growing lack of confidence in the Kaiser and his advisers was shown by the mutinous state of the soldiers, the revolt of the sailors at Kiel and other seaports in October and November, and the socialist uprising in Bavaria on November 7. The Social Democrats had formed one of the largest German political parties on the eve of the war, and it was to their heirs—now split into groups ranging from moderate socialists to communists—that the political power passed when the abdication of the Kaiser was announced on November 9. In Austria-Hungary, on the other hand, it was the subject nationalities rather than the leftist parties which emerged first upon the collapse of the hereditary monarchy. In the middle of October, Emperor Charles made a last-minute bid to the minorities by proposing a federal state, but with the cessation of hostilities the empire broke up rapidly into its component parts. In the course of October and November, the Czechs and Slovaks declared themselves an independent state, Austria and Hungary were proclaimed as separate republics, Croatia and Slovenia joined with Serbia and Montenegro to form a new South Slav state, and Transylvania went over to Rumania. In Bulgaria and Turkey pro-Allied monarchs and governments likewise took the place of the ones that had lost the war, but more fundamental social and political changes did not occur immediately.

ARMISTICE. The German appeal to President Wilson for an armistice early in October raised important issues concerning the treatment of the defeated countries. A starting point was provided by the program for peace which the American president had outlined in January, 1918, in his famous Fourteen Points. In this important statement of American policy, Wilson proposed that the new international order should be based on "open covenants openly arrived at" (I), freedom of the seas (II), the reduction of tariff barriers (III) and armaments (IV), and the formation of "a general association of nations" (XIV). In regard to the territorial aspects of a future peace settlement, Wilson's program proposed that colonial claims be adjusted with due consideration for the interests of the peoples concerned (V), that the territory of Russia be evacuated and that she be welcomed into the family of nations "under institutions of her own choosing" (VI), that Belgium, France, Rumania, Serbia, and Montenegro be evacuated and restored (VII, VIII, XI), that Italy's northern frontier be adjusted to include all Italian-speaking peoples (IX), and that the subject nationalities of Austria-Hungary and Turkey, as well as the partitioned Polish population, be encouraged to establish autonomous or independent states along national lines (X, XII, XIII). In February and September Wilson made supplementary statements of policy which, without altering the substance of his program, emphasized the necessity for following popular wishes in the final settlement and the desirability of making a peace without rancor [see Appendix II].

When Wilson received the German plea for an armistice on October 4, his first consideration was to make certain that the enemy accepted the principles enunciated in the Fourteen Points. One of the German motives in turning to Wilson for an armistice had been to gain time to withdraw their forces to the Rhine frontier, where they might re-establish the front and still be able to bargain for peace terms. When Wilson informed the Germans, however, that the Allies would not treat with them until they had surrendered their ability to fight, they had no alternative but to give in, and on October 20 they accepted Wilson's terms. The American President now turned to his Allies, who had not yet been brought into the negotiations. Wilson's peace program had had an enormous influence throughout Europe, both in the enemy camp and among the subject nationalities. Yet it had not been accepted by the Allies who had done most of the fighting, nor had it even been submitted to them for their approval. While their high moral tone had won wide support among Allied statesmen, Wilson's Fourteen Points contained many vague statements and generalizations that had little meaning until their application to concrete situations had been agreed upon. Moreover, in the course of the war the Allies had undertaken a number of secret engagements that were in conflict with some of the principal points of Wilson's program [see above, pp. 67–71].

Wilson consequently entrusted to Colonel House the task of winning the support of the Allies for his program, and discussions on this subject were initiated.

In discussing the Fourteen Points with the Allies in Paris, House obtained Wilson's approval for a number of interpretations that went part way toward meeting the point of view represented by the French, British, and Italian statesmen. In regard to the distribution of colonies and the partition of the Ottoman and Habsburg empires, the traditional interests of the Allies as expressed in the wartime agreements were in the main allowed to take precedence. It was also conceded that "open covenants openly arrived at" did not necessarily preclude secret negotiations, nor did the removal of economic barriers mean the abandonment of protectionism. More important, upon British insistence it was agreed that the use of the blockade was not to be excluded by the acceptance of the principle of the freedom of the seas. At the same time, in regard to the Allied territory to be evacuated and restored, it was understood that Germany was to compensate the civilian population for damage done "by land, by sea, and from the air." Even after these interpretations of the Fourteen Points, House found it necessary to threaten a separate American peace before he could secure the agreement of the Allies. Upon the conclusion of these negotiations, the Allies notified Germany on November 5 that they were prepared to discuss armistice terms on the basis of the Fourteen Points. The Germans were informed at this time of the two principal reservations of the Allies regarding the freedom of the seas and the extent of reparations expected, but not of the important interpretations of the other points which Wilson had approved.

The Germans now realized that their complete defeat was only a matter of days, and they hastened to comply with the severe military terms of surrender laid down by Foch. Under the terms of the armistice of November 11, the German troops were required to evacuate their own territory on the left bank of the Rhine and to give the Allies three bridgeheads over that vital river so as to prevent any renewal of German resistance. They also agreed to surrender large quantities of guns, airplanes, and railroad equipment, as well as all of their submarines and most of their surface warships. Of similar scope and severity were the armistice terms concluded shortly before by Bulgaria (September 30), Turkey (October 30), and Austria-Hungary (November 3), although in the case of these countries the Allies undertook no specific engagement regarding the Fourteen Points.

Thus ended the great conflict which had cost the lives of ten million men and had thrown the whole world into turmoil. By virtue of stubborn fighting and the careful organization of their superior resources, the Allies had finally defeated the Central Powers. It now remained for them to achieve the more difficult task of building a world in which individuals, peoples, and states could live together in productive harmony.

CHAPTER

4

The Treaty of Versailles

The Paris Peace Conference

I N 1919 and after there was much criticism of the delay in assembling
the Peace Conference. Yet actually, in the perspective of the great peace
treaties over the centuries, and especially in view of the World War II
settlement, the speed with which decisions were reached appears mar-
velous.

When Wilson decided—contrary to the counsel of many of his advisers—to attend the Peace Conference in person, the meeting had to be postponed until after the President had delivered his State of the Union message to Congress at the beginning of December. In England political
developments also called for time. The British had held no election since
December, 1910, and Lloyd George wanted to be backed by a new mandate from the people before he undertook to make peace. He therefore
scheduled what has become known as the "khaki election" for December
14. As was generally expected, war fervor gave him and his government a
new lease on life. The disfavor with which this election came to be viewed
in later years played no small part in defeating Churchill when he tried a
similar election in 1945. In the election Lloyd George and other party leaders were carried away by their oratory. They promised, if re-elected, "to
hang the Kaiser," to make Germany pay the whole cost of the war (not
only reparations for damages), and to "squeeze the lemon until the pips
squeak." These election promises were later to plague the British delegation at the Peace Conference, particularly when they tried to oppose the
exorbitant demands of other powers.

Paris was Wilson's choice as a meeting-place, but it turned out to be
anything but neutral ground, and Gallic ridicule in the ensuing months
bore heavily on the spirit of the American President. He arrived in France
on December 13, 1918. The following weeks were spent on visits to Rome
and London which turned into grand triumphal processions and actually
did little to put the President in touch with public opinion. Conversations
with the leading allied statesmen did give him clearer ideas of their plans
for Europe. The English, French, and Italian premiers had already
sounded each other out at a conference in London on December 1–3, a
meeting which Colonel House was unable to attend because of illness.

Meanwhile the delegations of thirty-two states that had been at war
with the Central Powers were establishing themselves in Paris. In England
and the United States, and to a lesser extent in France and other countries,
commissions had long been preparing material for use in the forthcoming
negotiations. The United States group, known as The Inquiry, had been
established in September, 1917, and so for over a year this group of distinguished scholars had been gathering data on all sorts of peoples, geographical areas, and problems of the world. The result of all this was that the
United States delegation was in general one of the best informed. Unfortunately much of the material and expert opinion that was at hand was
not used when the treaty was actually formulated.

President Wilson and Robert Lansing, Secretary of State, headed the United States delegation. The other great powers, all parliamentary states, were represented by their premiers and their foreign secretaries: Lloyd George and Balfour for the United Kingdom, Clemenceau and Pichon for France, Orlando and Sonnino for Italy, Saionji and Makino for Japan. Some of the representatives of the smaller states were as distinguished as their more influential colleagues. Among them certainly should be mentioned Smuts from South Africa, Pašić from Serbia, Beneš from Czechoslovakia, Bratianu from Rumania, Venizelos from Greece, and the famous pianist, Paderewski, from Poland.

The march of time and democracy can be demonstrated by the conspicuous absence of royalty from the deliberations. At the Congress of Vienna in 1815 royalty was much in evidence, and a constant round of festivities testified to the social character of a gathering of princes. At Paris only King Albert of Belgium put in a brief appearance. Nor were the defeated states permitted a Talleyrand to plead their cause. Russia was not represented at all, although various statesmen of the tsarist regime who were in Paris attempted to exert their ounce of pressure. Lenin and Trotsky were engaged in the weighty business of building Russia into a communist state, as yet unrecognized by the Allies. There was still a homogeneous character to the conference, and the peace was to be made by men who adhered to the Western parliamentary tradition, undivided by ideology.

The Drafting of the Treaty

PROCEDURE AT THE CONFERENCE. On January 12 an informal meeting of the chief delegates of the four great European powers took place, and on the following day they were joined by the Japanese representatives. A Council of Ten, made up of two representatives from each great power, was the guiding and controlling group until the middle of March. The great powers had difficulty in finding a method of giving the small powers some show of participation in the negotiations, while actually retaining control in their own hands. It was finally decided to call a plenary session of the Conference on January 18, 1919. This date was the anniversary of the proclamation of the Kingdom of Prussia on January 18, 1701, and of the German Empire in the Hall of Mirrors at Versailles on January 18, 1871. The first plenary session was a purely formal one. Of the six meetings held before the treaty with Germany was signed, only one, in which the Covenant of the League was debated, had any significance. The small powers were allotted representation on various commissions, but these too were dominated by the great powers.

The decisions of the Conference were made by the Council of Ten, in whose actions the Japanese played only a passive role. This council was soon bogged down by the multitude of things to be dealt with. Not only was it burdened with the problems of the various peace treaties proper, but also it had to contend with the everyday task of running Europe. Revolu-

THE BIG FOUR AT PARIS Orlando of Italy, Lloyd George of Great Britain, Clemenceau of France, and Wilson of the United States, conferring in Paris during the Peace Conference, 1919.

tionary movements were shaping events in different parts of the continent; and in addition, each of the chief delegates had to keep a weather eye on political developments and domestic problems in his own country. From February 15 to March 14, for example, Wilson was absent from Paris to be in Washington for the opening of the new session of Congress on March 4. He took with him the draft of the Covenant of the League of Nations in order to put it informally before the members of the Senate.

To hasten decisions, meetings of the Council of Ten were discontinued on March 24. In its place the Big Four—Wilson, Clemenceau, Lloyd George, and Orlando—began to hold private sessions. Although consultation with advisers formed a running background to the discussions, the main decisions were made by this group. Closeted in a small room with only an interpreter or two present, these four men settled the fate of Europe. It was not without significance that Lloyd George and Wilson spoke English, Orlando spoke French, and only Clemenceau knew both languages and therefore could converse directly with all his colleagues. As topic after topic came up for decision, while Wilson offered principles, it was more often the other men who came forth with concrete proposals. Thus it was usually a British, Italian, or French proposal which became the starting point for discussions. Meeting as allies and friends these men could not keep on for days opposing each other even if vital matters of principle were at stake. For Wilson to have offered violent objection would have been to lay himself open to the charges of being pro-German and unmindful of the sacrifices the war had cost. It was more than expediency that led to the compromises between what has often been labeled Clemenceau's hard-headed realism and Wilson's idealism.

The Council of Five, consisting of the foreign ministers of Great Britain, France, Italy, Japan, and the Secretary of State of the United States, was organized at this time to deal with subsidiary questions. Their decisions, however, always had to be ratified by the Big Four. The share of the small powers in drawing up the treaty with Germany can be gauged by the fact that they received its text only at a plenary session of the conference on May 6, the day before the treaty was handed to the German representatives.

Having made substantial progress on the German treaty, at the end of April the Big Four began to study the Adriatic settlement, which led to difficulties. Wilson undertook to oppose Italy's exorbitant demands, and a crisis was at hand. On April 24 Orlando left in a huff for Rome, and for the next few weeks the Big Three made decisions. It was not until May 6 that Orlando returned to the Peace Conference to take part in the presentation of the German treaty. The Adriatic questions remained an issue for the Austrian settlement.

GERMAN ACCEPTANCE OF THE TREATY. The German government had been asked to send plenipotentiaries to Versailles to receive the treaty on April 25. The Germans, injured by the word "receive," at first were not inclined to send anyone accredited with power to negotiate. In their next note the Allies were more conciliatory in tone and spoke of "negotiating" the treaty. Having made their protest, the Germans gave way and sent a delegation headed by Count Brockdorff-Rantzau, foreign minister of the new Republic and an able professional diplomat. The delegation reached Versailles on April 29, well staffed with experts, translators, and a mass of data. At three o'clock on May 7, Brockdorff-Rantzau, accompanied by ten members of the German delegation and two interpreters, made his slow way to the Hotel Trianon. Here they found the delegates of the Peace Conference assembled. Clemenceau, with Wilson and Lansing on his right, and Lloyd George and Bonar Law on his left, presided and opened the meeting with a short address.

Brockdorff-Rantzau had decided to use the one occasion when he had the opportunity to meet the representatives of the Allies at the conference table to answer some of their charges. When Clemenceau had finished speaking, the Secretary General of the Conference handed over the treaty in its official English and French texts. Brockdorff-Rantzau rose to receive it, sat down again, and, as if on equal terms with his accusers, set forth his defense of Germany. It was a dramatic moment, not the less so because of the resentment the speech and the manner of giving it aroused. Brockdorff-Rantzau was a practiced diplomat and well aware of the niceties of protocol. The French press apparently had nettled him by printing a plan for the seating of the delegates which designated the place of the German delegation as the "bench of the accused." Brockdorff-Rantzau considered that it was beneath his dignity to stand before his judges as a common criminal was forced to do in court. He spoke quietly, but not submissively:

We are under no illusions as to the extent of our defeat and the degree of our powerlessness. . . . The demand is made that we shall acknowledge that we alone are guilty of having caused the war. Such a confession in my mouth would be a lie. . . . In the past fifty years the imperialism of all European states has constantly poisoned the international situation. . . .

He went on to point out that the principles announced by President Wilson and accepted as a basis for peace negotiations were binding for both parties. Upon this basis Germany was ready to examine the terms of peace which had been submitted. He hailed the idea of a League of Nations and in his closing words ventured into the realm of prophecy, declaring that only a just peace would be a lasting one.

The Germans were given fifteen days to prepare their written reply, which was to be submitted in writing in English and French. They immediately plunged into the task of translating the 200-page treaty into German. Afraid of the possibility of secret microphones being planted in their quarters, they at first added to their difficulty by keeping a pianist hard at work to drown out any stray bits of conversation. Anxious to expedite matters, they chose to submit replies dealing with separate sections of the treaty as soon as they were prepared. To these the Allies promptly drafted replies, but made only two small concessions, one in regard to the repurchase of the Saar mines, the other a promise to admit Germany to the International Labor Office before her entry into the League of Nations. In the end the Germans were granted a seven-day extension. On May 29 their comprehensive reply, which contained a whole list of counterproposals, was submitted. The Allies were haunted by the possibility that the Germans would refuse to sign the treaty unless major concessions were made. The French were determined to stand pat. In the American delegation there was some inclination to make changes, although in general it was considered that the time for major alterations had passed. The economic experts urged that a fixed sum should be set for reparations, but this was not done. In the end it was Lloyd George who was responsible for the only major revision that was made, a provision for holding a plebiscite in Upper Silesia.

The Germans received the Allied note on June 16 with a seven-day time limit for the answer. The chief delegates immediately left to discuss the final treaty with the German cabinet. They studied the treaty again en route to Weimar and agreed to oppose signing the document. The issue was then put up to the cabinet, which was divided in opinion and subsequently resigned office. Forming a new cabinet proved difficult and was accomplished only a day before the answer was due. The problem was then put before the German National Assembly, which voted 237 to 138 to sign the treaty, but with a so-called honor reservation:

> *The Government of the German Republic is ready to sign the Peace Treaty without thereby acknowledging that the German people are the responsible authors of the World War, and without accepting Articles 227 and 231 (trial of the Kaiser, trial of other war criminals, and war guilt).*

When the German reply was submitted to the Allies an answer was immediately returned, saying no reservations were acceptable. If the German government did not agree to sign within twenty-four hours the Allied troops would march into Germany. Again the question was placed before the National Assembly at Weimar. An hour and a half before the time limit expired, the German representatives at Versailles could announce that Germany accepted the treaty without any reservations; they were bowing to superior power.

On June 28, 1919, the fifth anniversary of the murder of Archduke Francis Ferdinand, the German treaty was signed in the great Hall of Mirrors at Versailles. The Germans had some difficulty in finding men willing to undertake the unwelcome and unpopular task. Only China, which was opposed to the provisions in regard to Shantung, refused to sign the treaty.

END OF THE PARIS PEACE CONFERENCE. The conclusion of the treaty with Germany was the main task of the Peace Conference. The treaties with Austria and Bulgaria were pushed through, but by that time the Peace Conference was in the doldrums, and the leading delegates had already departed. The Treaty of Versailles was to go into effect as soon as Germany and three of the major Allied powers had ratified it. Although the Senate of the United States refused to accept the treaty, Germany, France, Italy, and Great Britain exchanged their official ratifications on January 10, 1920, and the treaty came into force. The Peace Conference of Paris officially came to an end on January 21, 1920, with the peace treaties with Hungary and Turkey still to be concluded.

Here it might be added that the Congress of the United States passed a joint resolution on July 2, 1921, declaring the war with Germany at an

THE TREATY OF VERSAILLES *Signature of the German Peace Treaty in the Hall of Mirrors in the Palace at Versailles, June 28, 1919.*

end. The final treaty of peace with Germany was concluded on August 25, 1921, and in it Germany awarded to the United States "all the rights and advantages stipulated for the benefit of the United States in the Treaty of Versailles which the United States shall fully enjoy notwithstanding the fact that such Treaty has not been ratified by the United States."

The Basis of the Peace

The history of the drafting of the Treaty of Versailles is important in explaining its fate in subsequent years. In contrast to the great treaties of the past it was not a negotiated peace; the victors had meant to dictate the peace and had been successful. The Germans made political capital out of that fact, and Hitler was not alone in denouncing the *Diktat* (imposed peace) of Versailles. But if it was a dictated peace from the German point of view, it was most certainly a negotiated peace so far as relations among the Allies were concerned. The Allies were obliged to make many compromises, because they were not in real agreement as to the basis on which the peace was to be made.

It was only after Colonel House had threatened that the United States might make a separate peace with Germany, that Lloyd George and Clemenceau accepted the Fourteen Points as a basis for the armistice and subsequent peace negotiations. Even then they refused to accept the second point, which dealt with the freedom of the seas. In addition to the Fourteen Points there were the "Four Principles" of Wilson's address of February, 1918, and the "Five Particulars"—as they came to be called— of his address of September 27, 1918. These constituted an ideal and broad peace program and they formed what came to be known as the "pre-armistice agreement." As Brockdorff-Rantzau had pointed out in his speech, contractually they were binding on both parties. The whole peace program, in popular opinion at least, was summed up in the phrase, "self-determination of nations." [See Appendix II.]

There were, however, other principles, agreements, and promises, which the delegates brought with them to the Peace Conference. These were the various secret treaties and agreements made during the war, which have already been reviewed [see above, pp. 59–61; 68–70]. Although President Wilson did not feel bound by them, claiming ignorance of their terms, the other leaders were in a different position. A great deal had been said during the war about fighting for the preservation of international law, and about the sanctity of treaties. Were these perfectly valid treaties also to become "scraps of paper"?

In addition the statesmen were plagued with old frontier ambitions and fear of the future. This was notably true in respect to the French demand for the left bank of the Rhine, a demand that both England and the United States refused to sanction. To the French such a border change was a safety measure, but to the other Allies it was too crass a violation of the self-determination of nations which had been set up as a guiding principle for the conference. Wilson had stated as one of his four principles: "Peoples and provinces must not be bartered about from sovereignty to sovereignty as if they were chattels or pawns in a game." Yet most of the powers wanted something either from Germany or from one of the other defeated states. To grab for oneself it was necessary to let others have their share, and the treaty was not without its logrolling.

The statesmen also brought with them to Paris various promises made to their peoples during the war. These were a conglomeration, running the gamut from "hang the Kaiser" to "making the world safe for democracy," and seeing to it that this was really to be the "war to end wars." Attention to these promises became if nothing else a matter of political expediency, with public opinion always a concern of the negotiators. A genuine fear of a resurgent Germany that might try to undo the work of the Peace Conference gripped the hearts of many. Germany would have to be weakened to a point where she could never make such an attempt. The delegates did not have to look far to see the devastation of war. With passions still hot, a natural desire to punish was understandably at hand. Unfortunately it takes only a little mental gymnastics to convert vengeance into justice.

On the other hand there was present at Versailles a great deal of hope and some confidence that the foundation had been laid for a just peace. The treaty itself provided instruments through which adjustments and revisions could be made. Much in the treaty was provisional and depended on later decisions of the great powers; the whole reparations question was left to be worked out and administered by a Reparations Commission. More than once Wilson had accepted certain provisions that contravened his ideals, because he believed that they could and would be rectified later. He saw in the establishment of the League of Nations the greatest guarantee that such changes would be made. He saw in it the hope of the world.

The idea of the postwar world organization had been much debated before the Peace Conference met. In the United States, England, France, and Italy, not to mention other states, plans were formulated. In the end it was a combination of the British and American plans which was used as the starting point for discussions. As early as January 25 it had been decided to incorporate the Covenant of the League into the peace treaties. The French were no doubt the most critical of the whole idea, for to hard-bitten Clemenceau it seemed to offer little guarantee for the security of France. The French delegates pressed for the creation of an international army to enforce the decisions of the League, but this proposal was considered impractical and undesirable by the United States and Britain. When Japan pressed for an expression of racial equality in the covenant, the Americans were only too glad that the British delegation, on the insistence of Australia, had this demand set aside. Finally, on his return to Paris, Wilson advanced amendments to safeguard the Monroe Doctrine and to meet certain objections that had been raised in the United States. With some difficulty—largely because Great Britain and France withheld their consent for tactical purposes—these were adopted. But even these amendments did not go far enough to appease the United States Senate, which voted down the League and with it the whole Treaty of Versailles. How much the adherence of the United States to the League would have aided in developing an international organization capable of dealing with the imperfections of the peace can be a matter only for conjecture.

Although Germany was denied membership in the League, the Covenant was inserted as Part I of the Treaty of Versailles. This was indeed incongruous, but it was one method of getting a large group of nations to accept the League without delay. The Germans objected, but not to the idea of the League. In fact their delegation had brought plans for such an organization along with them to Versailles, assuming that Germany would be at once included in Wilson's "general association of nations." [For a discussion of the League, see Chapter 6.]

The Boundaries of Germany

THE WESTERN BOUNDARIES. In his Fourteen Points, Wilson had stated that the wrong done in Alsace-Lorraine should be righted. This was interpreted to mean prompt return of the area to France without any thought of a plebiscite. From that point on, the drawing of the western frontier caused difficulties. France demanded the whole west bank of the Rhine, but had to content herself with a fifteen-year military occupation of this territory.

An even more specific French demand was for a small part of the Saar valley centering about Saarbrücken. Historically, this territory was part of Germany and was only for a brief period (1792–1815) in French possession [see map, p. 94]. Its population of 650,000 was German and consisted largely of miners who worked the rich coal mines. Here a compromise was adopted. France was ceded outright the mines of this 742-square-mile territory as part payment for war damage to French mines. The territory technically remained under German sovereignty but was incorporated into the French customs zone and administered by an International Commission under the League of Nations. At the end of fifteen years the people were to decide whether they wished to continue under the League or be joined either to Germany or France. In case they voted to be reunited with Germany (as they did in 1935), Germany should have the opportunity of purchasing the mines from France (which was done).

Farther north three tiny bits of territory, in all 384 square miles, were joined to Belgium. Moresnet, an area of some 1400 acres containing a valuable zinc mine, had been administered jointly by Prussia and Belgium since 1815. This territory was annexed outright to Belgium. In Eupen and Malmedy public registers were set up in which anyone objecting to the transfer of the territory to Belgium could sign his name. As a true plebiscite, this was a mockery. Eupen and Malmedy became Belgian.

In 1864 Austria and Prussia had fought Denmark and severed the connection of the Danish royal house with the provinces of Schleswig and Holstein. It was now proposed to return at least Schleswig to Denmark, but with remarkable restraint the Danes turned down the offer. It was agreed that a new boundary between Germany and Denmark should be fixed "in conformity with the wishes of the population." Accordingly, two plebiscite areas were arranged and in 1920 the vote was taken. The southern zone voted to stay with Germany, while the northern zone (1,538 square miles), which contained a large number of Danish-speaking people, voted to join with Denmark. It was an equitable settlement and in accord with the principle of self-determination of nations.

THE EASTERN BOUNDARIES. The eastern frontier of Germany involved even more difficulties. The Poles were busily expanding their state, and there seemed to be no end to their demands for territory from Germany,

GERMANY
AFTER THE
TREATY OF VERSAILLES

MAP 5

Legend:
- Territory lost without plebiscite
- Territory lost after plebiscite
- Territory retained after plebiscite
- Demilitarized zone

Callout labels:
- ALLENSTEIN, 1920
- MARIENWERDER, 1920
- UPPER SILESIA, 1921
- SCHLESWIG 1920
- SAAR BASIN, 1935
- MORESNET EUPEN MALMÉDY
- DANZIG FREE CITY

Places / features:
LITHUANIA · Memel (Klaipeda) · NIEMEN R. · Königsberg · EAST PRUSSIA · WARSAW · POLAND · RUMANIA · HUNGARY · BUDAPEST · DANUBE R. · Bratislava · VIENNA · AUSTRIA · Berchtesgaden · CZECHOSLOVAKIA · HULTSCHIN · Prague · Pilsen · Munich · Ulm · Strasbourg · ALSACE · LORRAINE · MOSELLE R. · SWITZ. · FRANCE · PARIS · Lille · BRUSSELS · BELGIUM · Liège · Aachen · LUX. · Cologne · Coblenz · RHINE R. · Mainz · Frankfort · MAIN R. · Nuremberg · DANUBE R. · Essen · RUHR R. · Bremen · WESER R. · NETHERLANDS · THE HAGUE · NORTH SEA · ISLAND OF HELIGOLAND · DENMARK · COPENHAGEN · SWEDEN · BALTIC SEA · Lübeck · KIEL CANAL · Hamburg · ELBE R. · Stettin · ODER R. · BERLIN · Leipzig · Dresden · Breslau · Weimar · Danzig · POLISH CORRIDOR (POMORZE) · Posen (Poznan) · VISTULA R.

G E R M A N Y

T.R.M.

the former Austria-Hungary, and Russia. The French were inclined to support them. If Foch could have had his way all of East Prussia would have gone to Poland, and the French foreign minister kept insisting that Poland should be "great and strong, very strong." It was Lloyd George who acted as a moderating influence in this area. He was responsible for the plebiscite in Upper Silesia to regulate the boundary between Poland and Germany, and it was largely because of his insistence that Danzig with its overwhelming German population was returned to its ancient status of a Free City. The city was to be self-governing under the general supervision of a High Commissioner representing the League of Nations. As Danzig was the great harbor of the Vistula valley, it was only natural that Poland should be accorded special privileges there; it was incorporated into the Polish customs system and in foreign affairs was represented by Poland. A treaty of November 9, 1920, which subsequently was modified at various times, regulated affairs between the Free City and Poland.

When Napoleon created his Grand Duchy of Warsaw, he made it a landlocked state. This time, in order to assure Poland that "free and secure access to the sea" demanded in the Fourteen Points, it was decided to create a Polish Corridor along the Vistula to the Baltic, connecting with Danzig. Germany was called upon to cede the province of West Prussia, which joined East Prussia to the rest of Germany. In 1308 this province had been seized from the Polish kings by the Teutonic Knights, who held it until 1466. It was again a part of Poland from 1466 until the First Partition of Poland in 1772, when it went to Prussia [see map, p. 126]. Although population statistics are disputed, it seems clear that Poles outnumbered Germans in the district as a whole. What the results would have been had a plebiscite been held is questionable. People do not always vote on linguistic lines, as is amply demonstrated by the many postwar plebiscites.

Much can be said both for and against the creation of the Corridor. The question was asked whether it was "to be argued that the interest of the 2,000,000 Germans in East Prussia in having a land connection with Germany ought to outweigh the interest of 25,000,000 Poles in having assured access to the sea?" On the other hand, the Corridor was difficult to defend militarily, and the Poles had real reason to be uncertain of using Danzig freely, where they had to rely on German dock-workers. It was an unfortunate thing for the new Poland that it had lasting boundary disputes with all its neighbors, with the exception of Rumania and Latvia. The Germans felt keenly the division of their state, and this was the one item in the settlement that no German statesman ever accepted. The matter remained a burning issue in Germany under every regime. The Polish Corridor came to take a place in German emotions similar to that of Alsace-Lorraine in France after 1870.

In addition to the Polish Corridor, called Pomorze by the Poles, Poland was granted other territories outright. These were the greater part of the old German province of Posen (Poznan) and small bits of East Prus-

sia and Middle Silesia. The following table summarizes what these transfers meant in terms of nationality and religion.

TABLE 6

POPULATION IN GERMAN TERRITORIES CEDED TO POLAND

WITHOUT PLEBISCITE *

DISTRICT	TOTAL POPULATION	POLES	GERMANS	CATHO-LICS *(Approx.*	PROTES-TANTS *per cent)*
West Prussia	913,000	528,000	385,000	57	42
East Prussia	25,000	15,000	10,000	25	75
Posnan	1,955,000	1,273,000	682,000	75	25
Middle Silesia	38,000	28,000	10,000	40	60
	2,931,000	1,844,000	1,087,000		

* H. W. V. Temperley (ed.): A *History of the Peace Conference of Paris* (6 vols.; London, 1920–24), Vol. II, p. 214.

Plebiscites were held in the Marienwerder and Allenstein areas of East
Prussia on July 11, 1920. Many of the inhabitants of this area spoke Polish
but were Protestant in religion and preferred to remain with Germany. In
the Marienwerder areas 96,923 votes went for Germany and 8,018 for Poland, while in the Allenstein section the totals were 362,209 against 7,980.

The plebiscite in Upper Silesia was not held until March 20, 1921.
Here it had been decided that the vote should be taken by communes
and that an international commission would then settle the boundary.
Some riotous political agitation on both sides preceded the balloting, but
the election itself went off peacefully enough. This time Germany received
707,605 votes and carried 844 communes to Poland's 479,359 votes and
675 communes. The French, British, and Italian delegates on the International Commission could not agree on a frontier line, and so the problem
was handed to the League of Nations. The League Council appointed a
committee of representatives from Belgium, Spain, China, and Brazil,
who hit upon a line which actually pleased no one. Perhaps this is the best
thing which can be said for it. It divided, often in a seemingly needless
way, the economic life of communities. Factories were on one side of the
boundary and the labor supply or materials on the other. Sometimes even
parts of the same plant were on different sides of the line. It was a source
of continual local exasperation.

Germany was awarded about two thirds of the territory, while Poland
obtained the greater share of mineral wealth. Both countries received substantial minorities, 350,000 Germans being transferred to Poland and
572,000 Poles remaining in Germany. To protect these people and to regulate a host of other questions, an "Upper Silesian Convention" was concluded between Germany and Poland on May 15, 1922. Adding the
Silesian figures to the table given above, it may be seen that the Polish set-

tlement, while awarding Poland only 8.53 per cent of the area of prewar Germany, left in Poland a German minority of well over a million.

Germany lost two additional bits of territory to the east. The city of Memel and adjoining districts totaling 976 square miles were turned over to the Allied powers, who reserved to themselves its future disposition. In 1923 Lithuania took the city by a *coup d'état*. The seizure was acquiesced in by the powers with the stipulation that the Memel territory be given a great measure of local autonomy. Of its population of 145,000, about one half were German-speaking, the rest Lithuanians. To Czechoslovakia, Germany had to cede 122 square miles of Silesia.

Germany lost 13.05 per cent of its territory as a result of these boundary revisions. Her plans for union with German-speaking Austria—which the Austrians also favored at this time—were explicitly forbidden by Article 80 of the treaty.

The Colonial Settlement and Mandates

The disposition of German colonies was a difficult problem for the Peace Conference. England and France had secretly agreed to partition certain ones, and Japan had also been promised certain regions in return for helping to protect convoys in the Mediterranean. The whole question was also tied up with the division of Turkish lands in Asia Minor. Yet imperialism had been denounced during the war, and it was proclaimed again and again that this war was being fought for nobler motives. Doubts were cast on these assertions by the stream of proclamations and documents which the Bolsheviks sent out from Petrograd. Wilson attempted to face the issue in his Fourteen Points, urging "a free, open-minded and absolutely impartial adjustment of colonial claims based upon a strict observance of the principle that in determining all such questions of sovereignty the interests of the populations concerned must have equal weight with the equitable claims of the government whose title is to be determined."

THE MANDATE SYSTEM. It was General Smuts of South Africa who hit upon a way out. He suggested that certain peoples were not yet capable of self-government and that for a time they should be placed under the guidance of some more advanced nation. Wilson was taken with the idea, and in Article 22 of the Covenant provision was made for the establishment of a system of mandates. It was recognized that "the character of the mandate must differ according to the stage of the development of the people, the geographical situation of the territory, its economic conditions and other similar circumstances." Accordingly three types of mandates were set up which later were labeled A, B, and C. The A mandates were devised primarily for those peoples of the Turkish Empire who were considered almost able to run their own independent states. The B mandates were especially for the people of Central Africa. Here the Covenant stated: "The Mandatory must be responsible for the administration of the territory under conditions which will guarantee freedom of conscience

MAP 6 *Africa: Colonies and Mandates, 1935*

and religion, subject only to the maintenance of public order and morals, the prohibition of abuses such as the slave trade, the arms traffic and the liquor traffic, and the prevention of the establishment of fortifications or military and naval bases and of military training of the natives for other than police purposes and the defense of territory, and will also secure equal opportunities for the trade and commerce of other members of the League." This makes a difficult sentence but does define a B mandate. Other territories such as South-West Africa and the Pacific islands could "be best administered under the laws of the mandatory as integral portions of its territory." These were to be classed as C mandates. Each "advanced nation" to which a mandate was assigned was to make an annual report to the Council of the League for the territory in its charge, and this was done in later years.

AWARDING OF MANDATES. No one was disposed to leave Germany in possession of any of her colonies, and under Article 119 Germany renounced in favor of the victors "all her rights and titles over her oversea possessions." It was now a question of assigning the different colonies to various mandatory states. This task the great powers reserved to themselves; the League and the smaller Allies had no part. Togoland and the Cameroons were made class B mandates and divided between France and Britain as mandatory powers [see map, p. 98]. France was allocated the larger portion of each colony. Great Britain received German East Africa as a B mandate, although a small portion in the northwest (Ruanda and Urundi) was later turned over to Belgium. South-West Africa went to the Union of South Africa as a C mandate. The secret Treaty of London of 1915 had promised Italy compensations if France and Great Britain acquired the German African colonies. In recognition of this obligation both of these countries in the next years turned over some portions of their African possessions to Italy.

The German islands south of the equator, including German New Guinea, went as C mandates to Australia with two exceptions. German Samoa was assigned to New Zealand, and Nauru with its rich phosphate deposits went to Great Britain [see map, p. 568]. The islands north of the equator (the Marianas, Palau, Carolines, and Marshalls) were assigned to Japan. This aroused a dispute with the United States over the small island of Yap, which was strategically important as a cable center. In a special treaty of February 11, 1922, Japan assured the United States of rights and privileges in the use and working of cables on the island.

If altruism and genuine trusteeship had been the true foundation of the mandate system, it is unlikely that the powers would have been in such haste to be assigned as "mandatory powers."

NON-MANDATE GERMAN COLONIAL CESSIONS. Three bits of German colonial territories were not placed under the mandatory system. France received outright that portion of the Cameroons which she had ceded to Germany in 1911 at the time of the Second Morocco Crisis [see map, p. 98]. Portugal added to Mozambique the Kionga Triangle, an area of about a hundred square miles which had been a part of German East Africa. Germany since 1898 had held a 99-year lease on the port of Kiaochow in China and had been accorded certain special rights in the province of Shantung [see map, p. 489]. The disposition of these German rights had played a part in the acrimonious discussions between Japan and China in 1915 and 1918, centering around the Japanese Twenty-one Demands. By the secret agreements of 1917, Great Britain, France, and Italy had promised Japan these former German concessions. When China declared war on Germany in August of 1917, she specifically denounced all treaties and conventions made with Germany. At the Peace Conference Japan concentrated on two points, the inclusion of a statement on racial equality in the Covenant, and the acquisition of the German rights in China, which had been promised her. When she gave way on the first point the other great powers recognized the necessity of meeting her wishes on the second. To help them to this decision, Japan threatened that unless her views were met on the Shantung question she would withdraw from the Conference, refuse to sign the treaty, and would not join the League of Nations. In spite of the support of China's views by the American delegation, Japan acquired all of Germany's rights and privileges in Shantung. Japan, it is true, promised to return the territory in full sovereignty to China, retaining only certain economic privileges, but this agreement was not written into the treaty. It was this Shantung settlement which so incensed the Chinese delegation that they refused to sign the Treaty of Versailles.

Disarmament of Germany

. The opening paragraph of Part V of the treaty was later to plague the powers, for it indirectly made reference to an obligation on their part. It stated:

> In order to render possible the initiation of a general limitation of the armaments of all nations, Germany undertakes strictly to observe the military, naval and air clauses which follow.

In these clauses the negotiators did their best to see that German military power was broken. Instead of having a conscript army, Germany in the future was to be limited to a force of 100,000 to "be devoted exclusively to the maintenance of order within the territory and to the control of the frontiers." Afraid that Germany might train reserves through a period of short enlistment, the period of service was set at twelve years for enlisted and noncommissioned men, and at twenty-five consecutive years for officers. The German General Staff and all similar organizations were dissolved, the number of rifles, machine guns, rounds of ammunition strictly limited, and the manufacture of all arms and munitions of war restricted to certain factories under Allied supervision. No German military missions were to be sent abroad, and Germans were not permitted to enlist in foreign armies with the exception of the French Foreign Legion—this last provision being actually a concession to France. All German fortifications in the territory west of a line drawn fifty kilometers to the east of the Rhine were to be destroyed. This area was to constitute a demilitarized zone and even the small German army was barred from it.

The German navy was limited to six battleships, six light cruisers, twelve destroyers, and twelve torpedo boats, with a personnel of not more than 15,000 recruited on a long-term basis. Germany was to have neither naval or commercial submarines. The rate of and categories for replacements were carefully regulated. The rest of the Kaiser's erstwhile pride and joy was to be turned over to the Allies. Most of the German High Seas fleet had been surrendered in November, 1918, and interned at the great British naval base of Scapa Flow. Here on June 21, 1919, the German crews scuttled all the battleships and cruisers, except for the battleship *Baden* and five light cruisers. This was a last gesture of defiance and was taken as such.

While the armed forces of Germany were forbidden any military or naval air forces, civil aviation was placed under restriction only for a period up to six months after the treaty came into effect. The remnants of Germany's air force were to be turned over to the Allies.

Three Inter-Allied Commissions—military, naval, air—were established in Berlin to supervise the execution of this section of the treaty.

Reparations

In his Fourteen Points Wilson had stated that Belgium, France, Rumania, Serbia, and Montenegro would have to be evacuated and restored. Just what this implied was somewhat clarified in Lansing's note to Germany of November 5, 1918, in which he stated:

> [*The Allies*] *understand that compensation will be made by Germany for all damage done to the civilian population of the Allies and their property by the aggression of Germany by land, by sea, and from the air.*

The armistice itself spoke of "Reparation for damage done."

THE QUESTION OF PENSIONS. No sooner had the reparation problem been raised at the Peace Conference than Lloyd George and Clemenceau pressed for the collection of the total cost of the war, i.e., all military expenditures, and not only for civilian damages. This the American delegation refused as being contrary to the pre-armistice agreement. The idea of collecting total costs was dropped, but almost immediately Lloyd George broached the idea that war pensions should be classed as civilian damages and not as war costs. The American experts pointed out that this was illogical, but Wilson felt that the comparatively war-immune United States could not refuse to meet the wishes of the British and French. He overrode his advisers with the oft-quoted words: "Logic! Logic! I don't give a damn for logic. I am going to include pensions." Keynes, the noted British financial expert and a member of the British delegation at the conference, cites this capitulation as "perhaps the most decisive moment in the disintegration of the President's moral position. . . ."[1] It is usually estimated that the inclusion of pensions more than doubled the charge which would be placed on Germany. England had suffered comparatively little direct war damage outside of shipping losses. Unless pensions were included, Lloyd George could have no hope of collecting the vast sums which he had promised the British electorate.

TOTAL AMOUNT. The American delegation wanted above all two

[1] John Maynard Keynes: *The Economic Consequences of the Peace* (New York, 1920), pp. 52 ff.

things: an agreement on a definite sum that Germany should be forced to pay, and a recognition that this sum must be based in part on Germany's ability to pay. The French at one time spoke of $200,000,000,000, while two British representatives spoke of $120,000,000,000. It should be said at once that the best financial experts in these countries never supported such astronomical figures. Official prewar figures of the total wealth of France and Belgium, e.g., farms, buildings, factories, etc., did not begin to approach the total figures that were now asked for damages. It was soon clear that the amount which could be collected would never be anything like the amount promised by politicians and expected by the public in the victorious countries. Largely for political reasons Lloyd George and Clemenceau insisted that no definite figure be set in the treaty, and Wilson finally agreed. Under the treaty a Reparations Commission was established with vast powers. Part of the duty of this Commission was to determine by May 1, 1921, the total amount of Germany's obligations.

While the treaty did not set a total figure, it was not lacking in a multitude of directives that applied to reparations and German economic life in general. First of all it provided that by May 1, 1921, Germany would pay in cash or kind $5,000,000,000. This was to include the cost of the army of occupation. The Reparations Commission had the power to remit portions of this sum in return for bonds if it should prove necessary. Germany was also required to deliver at once $10,000,000,000 in bearer bonds which were to pay an interest rate of 2½ per cent from 1921 to 1925 and thereafter 5 per cent plus 1 per cent amortization charges. This meant that Germany would have to face an annual charge after 1926 of from $600,000,000 to $900,000,000 depending on how much of the original $5,000,000,000 she had succeeded in paying by 1921. The Commission was given the right to demand a further issue of $10,000,000,000 in bearer bonds at 5 per cent if they found Germany could meet this obligation.

REPARATIONS IN KIND. The treaty also prescribed a long list of things that had to be turned over and credited to the reparations account. The armistice terms had already required the delivery of vast amounts of materials both military and civilian. These were confirmed and other items added. For example, there were to be delivered to France 500 stallions, 30,000 fillies and mares, 2,000 bulls, 90,000 milch cows, 1,000 rams, 100,000 sheep, and 10,000 goats. A similar list was set up for delivery to Belgium. All German merchant ships over 1,600 gross tons, one half of the ships between 1,000 and 1,600 tons, and one quarter of her fishing boats were to be turned over. In addition Germany was to surrender 20 per cent of her inland navigation tonnage, and was also to construct in German yards 200,000 ships' tonnage annually for the next five years, to be handed over as reparations. In spite of the fact that she lost the important coal fields in the Saar and Upper Silesia, Germany was called upon to deliver to the Allies approximately 40,000,000 tons of coal annually over a period of ten years. Keynes in his excellent book, *The Economic Consequences of the Peace,* indicated within a few months of the signature of the treaty how impossible it would be for Germany to make these deliveries, particularly if she was to develop enough industry to enable her to make any reparation payments. Events proved him to be right.

ADDITIONAL ECONOMIC PROVISIONS. It is impossible to mention here all the provisions of what Churchill has called "the absurd and monstrous economic and financial chapters of the Treaty of Versailles. . . ." [2] Some articles were not especially onerous but hurt German pride because they were not reciprocal. Thus Alsace-Lorraine was to export to Germany duty-free for five years an amount of goods equal to the average amount sent annually between 1911–13. Germany, on the other hand, had to meet the French tariff. Similar provisions extended to Poland and Luxembourg. Certain restrictions were placed on German railways for the benefit of the Allies. The most important German rivers were placed under the control of International Commissions, on which Germany could easily be out-voted. Where these rivers formed boundary lines or served two or three countries, internationalization was reasonable. On the other hand, the Germans never were reconciled to the fact that Italy and Belgium were given seats on the Elbe Commission. It was, however, an admirable provision that created Czechoslovakian Free Zones in the ports of Hamburg and Stettin.

Breaking Germany's industrial capacity was not an avowed peace aim in 1919, as it was (for a time at least) after World War II. Yet Keynes writes: "Thus the Economic Clauses of the Treaty [of Versailles] are comprehensive, and little has been overlooked which might impoverish Germany now or obstruct her development in future." No one has yet devised a scheme for killing the goose and still managing to collect the golden eggs. The further fate of reparations can best be related in connection with the history of postwar Germany.

The "Honor" Clauses

When the German National Assembly was confronted with the Treaty of Versailles, the party caucuses hesitated to authorize signature of the treaty. When the German acceptance with reservations of the "honor" clauses was refused by the Allies, there was some clever parliamentary maneuvering in the National Assembly. The signing of the treaty was authorized, although the whole treaty was not brought up again for a vote Thus the issue underlying these articles was side-stepped.

THE "WAR GUILT" CLAUSE. The most violent objections of the Germans to the treaty were leveled at Article 231, which has subsequently been labeled the War Guilt Clause. The importance it attained in later years and the part it played in the rise of Hitler warrants its quotation in full:

The Allied and Associated Governments affirm and Germany ac cepts the responsibility of Germany and her allies for causing all the loss and damage to which the Allied and Associated Govern-

[2] Winston S. Churchill: *The Aftermath* (New York, 1929), p. 221.

*ments and their nationals have been subjected as a consequence
of the war imposed upon them by the aggression of Germany and
her allies.*

On January 25, 1919, the Peace Conference had appointed a Commission on "Responsibility of the War" under the chairmanship of the American Secretary of State. Basing its decisions largely on the document collections issued by the various governments at the start of the war, the commission reported back that "the war was premeditated by the Central Powers together with their allies, Turkey and Bulgaria, and was the result of acts deliberately committed in order to make it unavoidable." This was, of course, what was generally held to be the case in the Allied states at this time. Had the commission members evaluated properly the documents in the new *German White Book* that was placed before them, they would hardly have reached this verdict, which most historians have since decried.

When the reparations sections of the treaty were being formulated, Lloyd George and Clemenceau insisted upon a clause that would "assert at least the moral right of the Allies to recover the cost of the war forced upon them by Germany." Wilson, always adhering to principles, had no objection to a statement of Germany's responsibility for starting the war. The result was that Article 231 became the first article in the section on reparations. The article was meant to state the theoretical obligation of Germany to pay the costs of the war. What the treaty actually demanded in the way of reparations was stated in the next article. This was on a contractual basis, and was in accord with the pre-armistice agreement with Germany, as interpreted by the Allies. Unfortunately the introduction of Article 231 seemed to make the war guilt of Germany the only justification for reparations; at least it was so construed in Germany. Hence the feeling in Germany was strong that if Germany was not solely responsible for the war, there could be no justification for reparations. Some historians have maintained that Article 231 never was meant to convey an idea of German war guilt. Whether it was meant to or not, it did convey such an idea to the Germans and to many scholars throughout the world.[3] Article 231 became the very cornerstone on which those who sought to revise and overthrow the Treaty of Versailles built their edifice. No one will ever be able to evaluate to what extent the Versailles system was undermined when historians, as the result of the publication of countless documents and memoirs, were able to get nearer to the truth about the origins of the war than was possible for the men who drafted Article 231.

TRIAL OF "WAR CRIMINALS." The other so-called honor clauses dealt with the trial of the Kaiser and other "persons accused of having committed acts in violation of the laws and customs of war." The American

---

[3] For various interpretations of Article 231 see Philip Mason Burnett: *Reparation at the Paris Peace Conference from the Standpoint of the American Delegation* (2 vols.; New York, 1940), Vol. II, pp. 142–57.

delegation felt that such trials were not covered by existing international law. Lloyd George, however, had promised his electorate to hang the Kaiser, and the attempt was made to persuade the government of the Netherlands to extradite him. Since none of the Allies had a treaty of extradition with the Netherlands covering political offenses, the Dutch government lived up to the best traditions of liberalism and refused to deny asylum to William II. The powers actually found this a rather welcome solution to the whole episode.

In 1920 a provisional list of some 900 names was submitted to the German government of the persons whom the Allies wished to bring to trial. On it were many names of the foremost leaders of Germany. As it was, the German government stated that it was politically impossible to turn these men over to the Allies for trial, but it offered to try them before the German Supreme Court at Leipzig. Again a welcome way out of the impasse was found in the discovery that this procedure might be condoned under an obscure clause of Article 228. The inter-Allied commission in charge of this work now picked out forty-six so-called test cases presented by various Allied powers. Of these, twelve were finally prosecuted and there were six convictions, five of them being British cases. The sentences were light, the maximum being four years' imprisonment, and in line with the German attitude towards the whole proceedings.

In 1924 a case closely related to "war criminal" trials was brought before a Belgian-German Arbitral Tribunal that had been established under Article 304 of the treaty. The Belgian workmen who had been deported to Germany during the war brought suit for damages, and the German government acted as defendant. Finally a test case was singled out and the plaintiff won. In July, 1925, an agreement was signed under which the deportees were to receive 24,000,000 francs.

Final Provisions

Scattered through the treaty here and there, obligations were imposed on Germany which do not lend themselves to any classification. Some of these are important, others are not. Yet often the small things in life are among the most irritating. Smuts foresaw this when he wrote in a letter to Lloyd George: "The Treaty is full of small, comparatively unimportant provisions which serve no useful purpose but must be unnecessarily galling. . . ." Thus Germany had to restore all the astronomical instruments that her troops in 1900–01 carried away from China when an international force ended the Boxer Rebellion. Flags and war trophies that Germany had conquered in 1870–71 were to be returned to France. The original Koran that Turkey had reputedly presented to William II was to be given back to the King of Hejaz. Within six months Germany was to "hand over to his Britannic Majesty's Government the skull of the Sultan Mkwawa which was removed from the Protectorate of German East Africa and taken to Germany."

The economic and financial sections, as already indicated, are replete with details defying briefer enumeration. Germany was furthermore required to renounce the Treaties of Brest-Litovsk and Bucharest and to agree beforehand to any settlement the Allies might arrange for Eastern and Central Europe. Elaborate provisions attempted to define the status and rights of nationals in the various ceded territories and laid down the principles on which the minority treaties were based. This shows that, while the Treaty of Versailles was a treaty of peace with Germany, it was also much more. Not only through the League Covenant and the International Labor Statute, but also in many other provisions, it laid the foundation for a new public law of Europe and the world.

ENFORCEMENT OF THE TREATY. In addition to numerous commissions to supervise the execution of the various parts of the treaty, military sanctions were provided for. For fifteen years German territory west of the Rhine, including several important bridgeheads over the river, was to be occupied by Allied troops. If the conditions of the treaty were faithfully kept, at the end of five years Cologne was to be evacuated, at the end of ten years Coblenz, and after fifteen years Mainz and Kehl. If, before or after the expiration of the fifteen-year term, the reparations commission should ever find that Germany was in default, the whole territory would "be reoccupied immediately by the Allied and Associated powers." A separate annex to the treaty regulated the details of the military occupation.

At the insistence of the French, treaties in which Great Britain and the United States promised to assist France in the event of unprovoked aggression by Germany were officially annexed to the Treaty of Versailles. These treaties were an additional guarantee to France that the Treaty of Versailles would be enforced, particularly in respect to the demilitarization of the Rhineland. The British-French agreement was contingent on the ratification of the American-French treaty; since the United States failed to ratify, Annex I and Annex II were among the first provisions of the treaty to go by the board. Failure of the United States to ratify the Treaty of Versailles did not immediately lead to the recall of the American Army of Occupation. In fact, the last American troops were not withdrawn from Coblenz until January 10, 1923, at the time when France, in an effort to collect more reparations payments, occupied the Ruhr.

An Evaluation of the Treaty

The Allies and Germany had agreed to make peace on the basis of the Fourteen Points and of the principles advanced in Wilson's subsequent speeches. The latter should not be forgotten, for they were more of a design for the future than the famous Fourteen Points, many of which did not apply to Germany directly. It was not an impossible or impractical basis on which to negotiate a peace. Unfortunately, some of the Allied statesmen never adhered wholeheartedly to this program. They came to the peace table with an entirely different program outlined by their secret agreements and their secret ambitions. Many of the decisions of the Treaty of Versailles were influenced by problems that were more closely related to the other peace settlements. Italy, for instance, always viewed the German treaty with eyes that were focused on the North Adriatic region. Also, the establishment of new states in Eastern Europe always had to be kept in mind by the peacemakers. It is perhaps surprising not that the Wilsonian program failed to be honored completely, but that so much of it was written into the settlement.

No doubt Wilson made serious mistakes and gave way on vital issues. It is often stated that he should never have gone to Paris, that he should have remained in Washington where he might have made his influence count for more. Yet Birdsall, in an excellent volume on the treaty, states as his considered judgment: "The record clearly shows that on every major question but that of Reparations, the Treaty of Versailles would have been a worse treaty had Wilson remained in Washington. With all his mistakes, he emerges as the only man of real stature at Paris." [4]

The Treaty of Versailles has always had its very severe critics. Premier Smuts in signing it protested against many of its terms. China refused its signature, and the United States Senate withheld its ratification. Within a few months after its conclusion Keynes pointed out the impossibility of carrying out its economic clauses and labeled it a "Carthaginian Peace." It was a hard peace. Treaties of peace are always drawn up by the victors and give expression to wartime passions. Punishment and retribution are their stock in trade. They are likely to be one-sided documents, as is illustrated by the assumption that only the defeated states are guilty of breaking the rules of warfare or producing war criminals. To all this the Treaty of Versailles is no exception.

On the other hand, it was a treaty which brought peace rapidly to a war-torn Europe. Prisoners of war were promptly exchanged and there was no thought of using them for long terms of forced labor. Many of the boundary rectifications were in accord with the principle of national self-determination. Provisions in regard to minorities attempted to right age-old habits of oppression and inequality. Although Article 231 was inadvisedly drawn, it did serve the purpose of advancing the idea that war is a crime and that there is such a thing as "war guilt." Whether it can truly be assigned or adequately apportioned is another matter. Moreover, the treaty anticipated a general reduction of armaments. Labor in all countries was to benefit through the work of an International Labor Organization. A new era in world co-operation was intended by the establishment of the League of Nations. Many of the provisions of the peace treaty were looked on as provisional, and at least some of the men at Versailles thought they had established a procedure for peaceful revision of any wrongs that might have crept into the treaty. Unfortunately, later statesmen broke faith with them, and the League became an instrument for maintaining the Versailles system as it was, not for its peaceful alteration and evolutionary development.

[4] Paul Birdsall: *Versailles Twenty Years After* (New York, 1941), p. 295.

CHAPTER

5

The Eastern Peace Treaties

Victors and Vanquished.

The Habsburg Settlement: *Disintegration of Austria-Hungary; Treaty of St. Germain; Treaty of Trianon; Czechoslovakia, Rumania, and Yugoslavia; The Little Entente.*

The Borderlands of Russia: *Liberation of Poland; The Baltic States; Independent Finland; Russia and the Peace Conference.*

Bulgaria and the Treaty of Neuilly: *Aftermath of Defeat; Peace Treaty.*

Dissolution of the Ottoman Empire: *Treaty of Sèvres; Turkish Nationalism; Greek-Turkish War; Treaty of Lausanne; The Arab World.*

Victors and Vanquished

THE POLITICAL settlement in Eastern Europe and the Near East was in many respects the most significant result of the war. One of the principal causes of the conflict had been the striving of the minority peoples of the three eastern empires—the Habsburg, the Romanov, and the Ottoman—to achieve a more modern way of life by means of national self-determination. For many in Western Europe and in the United States, the war had seemed like a colossal and futile waste of human beings and of wealth, but for the minority peoples further east this was not the case. Many achieved as a result of the war the goal for which they had been fighting for generations—national independence. In no case was the victory total, unsullied by compromise and hardships, but for most the gains of the war outbalanced by far the costs.

For the Finns, for the Baltic peoples in Estonia, Latvia, and Lithuania, for the Poles, for the Czechs and Slovaks, for the Rumanians, for the Yugoslavs, for the Albanians, and for the Greeks, a new world was born and they exulted in it. The victory of the Arab peoples in Syria, the Lebanon, Iraq, Palestine, Transjordan, the Arabian peninsula, and Egypt was not as clear-cut, but they too saw national independence within their grasp in most instances, and were soon to participate as equals in the European community of nations. All these peoples now looked forward to the rapid transformation of their societies along the lines already pioneered by Western Europe. Even for the dominant nationalities of the three empires, the war resulted in a form of national liberation. The Russians and the Turks each underwent a national rebirth, and Austria entered upon a new statehood that was sufficiently vital to re-emerge after a second world war. For the Hungarians, however, and for the minorities remaining in Russia, no such transformation took place.

For the vanquished, the results of the war were equally clear-cut. The most complete defeat was suffered by the three European dynastic empires, which now disappeared from the European scene. The privileged gentry class, whose extensive political power had been based on their landed holdings, experienced a defeat almost as complete, although they survived for a generation in Hungary and in the Near East. In a political sense, Hungary was indeed vanquished and was forced to sacrifice in fact if not in principle the territorial integrity of the Crown of St. Stephen. Bulgaria was also vanquished, although its losses were less in territory than in pride.

The Habsburg Settlement

DISINTEGRATION OF AUSTRIA-HUNGARY. The breakup of the Habsburg empire, which was formalized in the peace treaties, was not merely the product of the victory of the Allies. It was the outcome of processes that had been generating for a long time and that were greatly accelerated by the pressures of the war itself. The stresses of the war magnified the tensions between the two constituent members of the Dual Monarchy—Austria and Hungary—and greatly intensified the nationalism of the minority peoples. As the rule of the Austrian and Hungarian governments became more harsh, amounting virtually to a military dictatorship, the desire for national independence became greater. The economic burden of the war, accompanied by a spiraling inflation, further stimulated the unrest.

A major crisis was reached at the end of 1916. In October Count Stürgkh, premier of Austria, was assassinated by a young Radical Socialist; and one month later Emperor Francis Joseph died. His long reign had started amid the furor of the Revolution of 1848, and closed with revolution again threatening his domains. His successor, Charles, now attempted by last-minute measures to save his empire. He dismissed some of the more uncompromising leaders, including Chief of Staff Conrad von Hoetzendorff, the man who had really run the country through a military dictatorship. He also called a meeting in May, 1917, of the Austrian parliament, which had not met since the spring of 1914. This parliament now became a forum of the leaders of the national minorities, many of whom had been emprisoned until recently. The position of the minorities was thus greatly strengthened, and in October, 1918, while the armistice was being negotiated, Emperor Charles announced that the monarchy was to be transformed into a federal state. It was too late, however, to save the empire. By now the minorities wanted complete self-determination, while the Hungarian government was still unwilling to accept any change at all.

Much of the strength of the national minorities came from the influential national committees that had been established abroad during the war. The most effective of these committees was that of the Czechs. Thomas G. Masaryk, professor of philosophy at the University of Prague and a member of the Austrian Reichsrat, was a true liberal and a keen student of the nationality problem in Austria. A European scholar of the first rank, he had acquired an admiration and understanding of America along with an American wife. He was soon joined in exile by Eduard Beneš, a professor of sociology and economics, who was to become one of the leading statesmen of Europe. A third name was less well known. Milan Štefánik, son of a Slovak Lutheran clergyman, had gone to Paris, where he made a reputation as an astronomer and explorer, became an aviator in the war, and came to have considerable influence in military circles, particularly in France and Italy. His voice was also important as representing the cause of the Slovaks.

A Czechoslovak National Committee was established in Paris, and the cause had been advanced so far by January, 1917, that the Allies in a note to President Wilson specifically included as one of their war aims the liberation of the Czechoslovaks from foreign domination. After the overthrow of the Tsar, Masaryk went to Russia to organize a military force out of the large number of Czechs and Slovaks who had become prisoners of war after surrendering to the Russians on the eastern front. A force of some 40,000 was soon transformed into an army. After Lenin took Russia out of the war, plans were made to evacuate these Czech legionnaires to the French front, and Masaryk himself had to return via Vladivostok and the United States. This in a way was most fortunate for the cause he was pleading, for he was received with open arms by the large groups of Czech and Slovak immigrants in the United States.

On May 30, 1918, a Slovak Convention was held in Pittsburgh, where a declaration was drawn up which approved of a union of Slovaks and Czechs, but stipulated that Slovakia should have its own assembly, administration, and courts of justice, and that Slovak should be the language for schools and public administration. Masaryk signed this declaration, and the Slovaks in America thought that by it they had made sure that the future Czechoslovak state would be organized on federal lines. This Declaration of Pittsburgh was not only important in furthering the cause of Czechoslovak independence; it was also to lead to many postwar recriminations between Czechs and Slovaks. When independence came, the Czechs favored a centralized state, while the Slovaks demanded their local autonomy. Masaryk was able to gain favorable recognition at Washington, and between May and September, 1918, the various Allied powers extended qualified recognition to the National Committee headed by Masaryk and Beneš. Czechoslovakia was now considered an ally, and its armies were recognized as belligerents. On October 18, 1918, Masaryk, Beneš, and Štefánik proclaimed the independence of Czechoslovakia in Paris, and organized themselves into a government.

While the Czechs and Slovaks had no foothold from which to start their independence movement, the South Slavs, or Yugoslavs as they were commonly known, could look to leadership from Serbia. The Yugoslavs faced a great obstacle, however, in the attitude of Italy. The Allies had made great concessions to bring Italy into the war on their side, and the territorial promises made to her by Britain, France, and Russia, in the secret Treaty of London (April 26, 1915), were not reconcilable with a large, free, and united Yugoslavia. A Yugoslav Committee was nevertheless formed in London in 1915 by Šupilo and Trumbić, representing the Croats and Slovenes of the Habsburg empire. Another notable advance was made in July, 1917, when Trumbić, as president of the Yugoslav Committee, and Pašić, as premier of Serbia, signed the Pact of Corfu. In this agreement the two statesmen rejected any partial unification and agreed that the future Yugoslav state should be a democratic monarchy headed by the Serbian dynasty. Thus were ended the political ambitions of King Nicholas of Montenegro. Equality of religion, the use of both Cyrillic and Latin alphabets, and a certain degree of autonomy for Croatia were promised.

The Pact of Corfu was displeasing to the Italians, but the course of events was against them. After the Bolsheviks took over the Russian government in November, 1917, they published the secret Treaty of London. This was a godsend to Austria because it served to increase the combat valor of Croat and Slovene soldiers, who were indignant at Italian ambitions. Then came the proclamation of the Fourteen Points with their emphasis on national rights. Severe Italian military reverses in the spring of 1918, along with an increasing amount of anti-imperialist agitation in Italy, also helped to make the Italian government ready for compromise. After a preliminary agreement was reached between the Italian ambassador at London and Trumbić of the Yugoslav Committee, a Congress of Oppressed Austrian Nationalities was called to meet in Rome in April, 1918. Here the Italian, Polish, Rumanian, Czechoslovak, and South Slav representatives proclaimed the right of self-determination, denounced Austria-Hungary as an instrument of German domination, and recognized the necessity of common action against the oppressor. Most important, however, was the accord reached between Italy and the Yugoslavs, by which Italy finally consented to the formation of a Yugoslav state. Boundary problems between the two were to be settled amicably on the "basis of the principle of self-determination" in such a fashion as not to prejudice the vital interests of either nation. The last was an escape clause recognizing that the boundary would not be drawn strictly according to the wishes of the people concerned. The "Pact of Rome," as the agreements were called, was a tremendous stimulus to Yugoslav agitation within Austria-Hungary. When the Habsburg monarchy collapsed in October, 1918, the Croatian Diet in Hungary adopted a resolution to the effect that: "Dalmatia, Croatia and Slavonia with Fiume are . . . a state completely independent of Hungary and Austria and . . . join the common national sovereign state of the Slovenes, Croats and Serbs. . . ." It now remained only for the peace conference to determine what the frontiers of the new state would be.

The government of Austria-Hungary signed the armistice on November 3. On the 11th, Emperor Charles withdrew from Austrian affairs, and two days later he laid down his powers as king of Hungary. He did not abdicate, however, in view of the possibility that either Austria or Hungary might choose a monarchical form of government. In the Austrian portion of the former empire, the immediate task of organizing new governments was accomplished with surprisingly little difficulty thanks to the co-operation of the old bureaucracy. In Hungary, on the other hand, the conclusion of hostilities was followed shortly by a bitter civil war. The conservative leaders turned to a liberal aristocrat, Michael Károlyi, to pull them out of their difficulties. As minister of nationalities in the new cabinet, Professor Oscar Jászi adopted a program of equal rights designed to retain the loyalty of non-Magyar Hungarians. The armistice soon brought the occupation of southern Hungary by the Serbs, however, and of the large province of Transylvania in eastern Hungary by the Rumanians. This occupation of Hungarian soil now undermined the Károlyi government. In March, 1919, it was overthrown by a Socialist-Communist coalition under Bela Kun, recently returned from revolutionary Russia, and soon attempts to carry out a complete communist program were in full swing. Events now moved swiftly. With French support, Rumanian forces invaded Hungary and overthrew Bela Kun in Budapest in August. The Rumanians in turn were replaced by a conservative nationalist government in November under Admiral Horthy. Thus within a single year Hungary went through the whole gamut of political doctrines, and the White Terror administered by Horthy in the months after he came to office matched the Red Terror of the communists in the preceding summer.

TREATY OF ST. GERMAIN. Although various commissions were appointed to study peace problems of the Danubian basin, it was not until after the main decisions of the German treaty had been reached that the Big Four turned their attention to Austria. The consideration of Italian claims produced a crisis, and Premier Orlando temporarily withdrew from the conference. In this case the dispute was not over what territories should be taken from Austria, but how Italy and Yugoslavia should divide the spoils. The Treaty of London (1915) had promised Italy the Brenner Pass, which was far beyond the Italian ethnic boundary line, a line which can be drawn with marked precision in this mountainous area. The Italians insisted on the necessity of a good strategic frontier, and no one was willing to oppose them. Wilson early agreed to the Brenner line in spite of the fact that it transferred some 250,000 German Tyrolese to Italy. Having so agreed, Wilson was determined to oppose some of Italy's far-reaching demands for territory along the eastern coast of the Adriatic. It became necessary to pass over this question for the moment, in order to settle the treaty with Austria. Two other major decisions were quickly reached: first, that the Germans in Bohemia and Moravia should be incorporated into Czechoslovakia, and second, that Austria, primarily out of deference to French wishes, should be denied the right to join Germany. The Austrians were even forced to change the name of their state from "German Austria" to Austria. This made it somewhat easier to tie up the new republic with the old Austria and thereby saddle the new state with the burdens of the old.

The Austrian delegation, however, headed by Dr. Karl Renner, maintained that Republican Austria was as much a new state as Czechoslovakia and the other states that were being established out of former Habsburg lands. Republican Austria had not been at war, and there was no more need for it to sign a peace treaty than there was for Czechoslovakia to do so. The war had really been an affair of the Habsburgs; to ask the smallest of the new states, and by far the poorest, to assume heavy reparation burdens because of the damage done by the old Imperial Army seemed to the Austrians a marked injustice. The Austrians had a good argument, but it was brushed aside. Someone had to make peace and pay reparations, and the lot fell to the German-Austrians and the Magyar-Hungarians who had been the core of the old state. The Austrian delegation further demanded adherence to the Wilsonian doctrine of self-determination and asked for plebiscites in all disputed territories. They pointed out that only some six million of the ten million Germans in the former Habsburg domains were to be permitted to join in forming the new Austria. Compromises were reached on a number of these issues, and on the whole, the Austrians obtained more concessions than the Germans. The Treaty of St. Germain was signed on September 10, 1919, and it went into effect in the following July after the exchange of ratifications. Representatives of the United States signed the treaty, but it was never accepted by the Senate. In its place a separate peace treaty was signed on August 24, 1921. By this treaty the United States obtained all rights that would have been awarded to her had she ratified the Treaty of St. Germain.

The great powers never entered into a definite pre-armistice agreement with Austria-Hungary, as they did with Germany, concerning the basis of the peace. In fact, Austria-Hungary made an unconditional surrender. Yet it has generally been held, both then and later, that the Wilsonian principles applied to all peace treaties. Actually, involved also were the secret treaties and partitions arranged during the war, notably for the benefit of Italy and Rumania, as well as the promises made to the Polish, Czechoslovak, and Yugoslav leaders. Sometimes these latter arrangements were in conflict with the Wilsonian program; at other times they were a direct implementation of it. In any case, the quarrels among the Allies over conflicting claims were considerably more difficult to deal with than the problem of how the new Austria should be treated.

In form the Austrian treaty was patterned on the one with Germany—which was no doubt a mistake, for the peace problems were not the same. Thus, Part I (the League Covenant) and Part XIII (the Labor Statute) are identical. The same arrangement is followed in regard to boundaries, disarmament, and reparations; clause after clause in the Austrian treaty parallels the Versailles treaty. For example, the section on reparations is introduced by an article on war responsibility which is a replica of Article 231 of the Versailles pact. The so-called war criminal articles are the same with the exception that the Allies made no claim on the person of Emperor Charles. There were, of course, a few differences. Among the most important of these was the addition of clauses dealing with minorities. These were similar to the special minority treaties that the other succession states were required to sign; Germany had not been required to sign such clauses.

The territorial problem was settled by carefully defining the future frontiers of Austria. Some of the former Austrian territory thus excluded was definitely awarded to certain states, as for example the Bukovina to Rumania, Bohemia and Moravia to Czechoslovakia, and South Tyrol to Italy [see map, p. 115]. The territory not definitely assigned to any state was reserved to the Principal Allied and Associated Powers for future distribution; in this fashion the Allies temporarily got around making certain thorny decisions, such as those regarding the northern Adriatic, Teschen, or Galicia. A plebiscite was ordered for the Klagenfurt district of Carinthia. Severe fighting had taken place in this area between Austrians and Slovenes, and the powers were forced to step in. They divided the territory into two parts. Zone A, the largest and most southerly section, was inhabited predominantly by Slovenes; Zone B, containing the City of Klagenfurt, was inhabited mostly by Germans The plebiscite was to be held first in Zone A, and if the vote went in favor of Austria there was to be no further balloting. The plebiscite was run off in orderly fashion on October 10, 1920, with 95 per cent of the qualified voters in Zone A participating. The result was 22,025 votes for Austria as against 15,279 votes for Yugoslavia, and the matter was thus settled.

Austria received one small bit of new territory. The powers awarded her outright a portion of German West Hungary. This district, usually re-

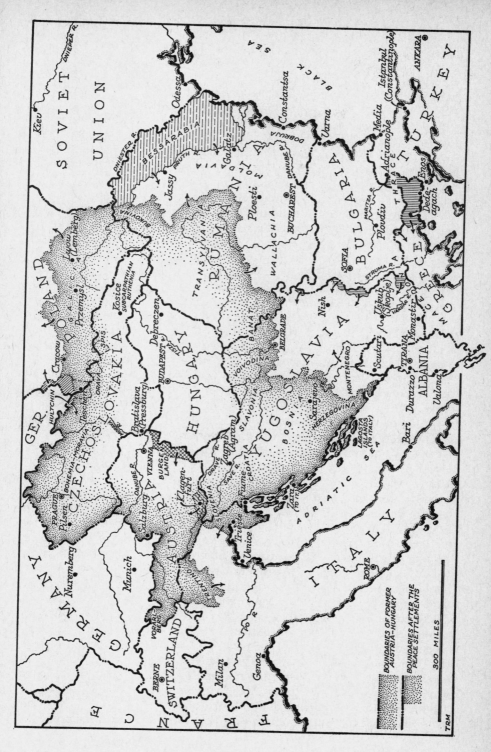

MAP 7 *Danubian Peace Settlement*

BOUNDARIES OF FORMER
AUSTRIA-HUNGARY

BOUNDARIES AFTER THE
PEACE SETTLEMENTS

300 MILES

TRM

ferred to by its postwar name of "Burgenland," is inhabited for the most part by Germans, and from it Vienna has always received its supply of vegetables and milk. Hungarian irregulars, however, refused to clear the territory. Finally, under Italian mediation a plebiscite was arranged for the city of Odenburg (Sopron) and eight adjoining villages, which constituted, of course, only part of the territory. An international commission supervised the plebiscite, which was held December 14–15, 1921, but since the Hungarians were in control they had the advantage conferred by favorable town and county officials. The vote went against Austria (15,334 to 8,227), and the plebiscite area was thereupon awarded to Hungary. Austria received in all only 1,558 square miles of territory from Hungary.

The Allies did not get around to making their final partitions and awards until months after the Treaty of St. Germain was signed. These were the end results: 26.63 per cent of the area of the old imperial Austria went to the new Republic, 26.48 per cent to Poland, 26.21 per cent to Czechoslovakia, 9.34 per cent to Yugoslavia, 7.86 per cent to Italy, and 3.48 per cent to Rumania. As will be seen below, all of these states also received portions of the former Kingdom of Hungary.

As with the Treaty of Versailles, severe restrictions were placed on Austrian armaments and her armed forces were limited to a professional army of 30,000. Similarly, reparations were required of Austria, although Vienna was starving and Allied relief agencies had to rush food to the city. As a matter of fact, Austria was able to make only modest payments and deliveries up to 1930, when all liability for further reparations was canceled.

One of the greatest mistakes of the Austrian treaty was that it was modeled too closely on the Treaty of Versailles. Had there never been the German reparation clauses, for example, the financial section of the treaty would no doubt have been cast quite differently. The decision to define Austria's borders and leave final disposition of various territories until later was certainly wise. On the other hand, more attention might well have been paid to the principle of self-determination. No boundary can be drawn so as to cut cleanly along lines of nationality. Yet not only as a matter of justice, but also with a view to expediency, one can question the wisdom of turning so many Germans, Slovenes, and Croats over to Italy, and of including so many Germans in Czechoslovakia and so many Ukranians in Poland. In all these matters the Peace Conference did not really have a free hand, for past agreements and the march of events gave the delegates little leeway. On one issue they had a free choice, and their decision not only was questioned then but has been ever since. In 1919 social-democratic Austria and democratic Germany wished to unite. This they were forbidden to do. France and Italy in particular were opposed to an extension of German power toward the Balkans, but besides this, there was a general feeling among the Allies that a defeated Germany should not acquire territory as a result of the war. Europe insisted on the creation of an independent Austria, an Austria that from the very beginning was financially a liability and politically one of the most disturbing factors in Europe.

THE TREATY OF TRIANON. The peace terms were not handed to the Hungarian delegation until the end of 1919. While the Austrians had claimed that theirs was a new state, the Hungarians insisted on the historical character of Hungary, which embodied the lands of the Crown of St. Stephen. While the Austrians asked only for a national state, the Hungarians spoke of historical provinces even if they were not racially homogeneous. They cited to the Allied statesmen the words used when it was decreed that historical Bohemia should remain intact, even if it involved denying self-determination to three and a half million Germans. If Bohemia was a unit, why not Hungary? Historical Hungary was to be broken up because it was not racially homogeneous, and yet a new Czechoslovakia was being set up which had large groups of five different nationalities. Three and a half million Magyars were being cut off from Hungary, and of these about 1,800,000 lived in lands contiguous to Hungary. In addition there were many Germans in the Old Kingdom who might feel more at home in Hungary than in Rumania, Yugoslavia, or Czechoslovakia. The Hungarian delegation concentrated on an attempt to have plebiscites held in the various territories they were being asked to cede. To this demand they returned time and time again, but it was always refused.

In presenting the final terms in May, 1920, the Allies added a covering letter that was of great importance, because it held out some slight prospect of boundary rectification. If the Frontier Delimitation Commissions should find that in any given area there existed an injustice contrary to the general interest, they might make a report to the Council of the League of Nations, which might then undertake to arrange amicable rectification of the boundary. This provision, it is true, did not go far toward satisfying Hungarian protests on the boundaries settlement; it was not even part of the treaty. Yet this covering letter did have an influence on the Hungarian delegation, partly because for some time the Hungarians had been conducting unofficial negotiations for a *rapprochement* with France. Some influential Hungarian businessmen had made contacts with French financial interests desiring concessions in Hungary. Paléologue, undersecretary of the French foreign office, was behind these, and soon the discussions had reached the government level. The Hungarian leaders considered the covering letter an expression of French good will, and they believed that with active French backing some real concessions might materialize.

On June 4, 1920, the Hungarians signed the Treaty of Trianon, but it took some sharp urging on the part of the great powers before the Hungarian Parliament could bring itself to ratify the treaty. (The United States concluded a separate peace with Hungary in August, 1921.) In form the Treaty of Trianon resembled the Treaties of Versailles and St. Germain. The League Covenant and the International Labor Statute were again parts of the treaty. There was again the clause on war responsibility, and the reparations settlement corresponding to that in the Austrian treaty. Disarmament was decreed, and the Hungarian army was set at 35,000. And like Austria, Hungary had to accept provisions in regard to minorities.

The treaty also laid down the frontiers of Hungary. All the lands of the Old Kingdom not included in the new country were either ceded directly to Czechoslovakia, Rumania, or Yugoslavia, or given to the Allies jointly for final distribution [see map, p. 115]. Of the Old Kingdom, only 28.6 per cent made up the new Hungary. The remaining lands were divided as follows: 31.5 per cent went to Rumania (primarily Transylvania and two thirds of the Banat); 19.6 per cent to Yugoslavia (primarily Croatia-Slavonia and one third of the Banat); 18.9 per cent to Czechoslovakia (primarily Slovakia, Sub-Carpathian Ruthenia, and the city of Pressburg); 1.2 per cent to Austria (Burgenland); .2 per cent to Poland (part of Orava and Spis); and less than .004 of one per cent to Italy, an area of five square miles of the city of Fiume. Hungary thus lost 71.4 per cent of its territory, containing about 60 per cent of its former population.

What has been said of the Treaties of Versailles and St. Germain can in large part be said of the Treaty of Trianon. All were drawn up in the same fashion and handed over to the defeated powers. Two points should perhaps be added. First, the refusal to grant plebiscites in any of the ceded territories was deeply resented by the Hungarians, and their resentment was not lessened when they were victorious over Austria in the one plebiscite that was later arranged for the city of Odenburg (Sopron). The second point is that the boundaries were not always well drawn. No one expected a boundary that would separate exactly the mosaic of national settlements which exists in some of these areas; yet, the exclusion of 1,800,000 Magyars who lived in compact settlements in territory bordering Hungary was in some cases an unnecessary violation of the principle of self-determination. The Allies believed that Czechoslovakia and Rumania should have a common frontier, partly in order to keep Poland and Hungary from being neighbors. To prevent, as far as possible, established railways from meandering in and out of one country, it was held that some lands had to be ceded regardless of population. The Hungarians, however, could never see that there was any justice in such a radical partition of the old Hungarian state. Soon, everywhere placards appeared reading, *Nem, nem, soha:* "No, no, Never" would Hungary accept the Treaty of Trianon.

CZECHOSLOVAKIA, RUMANIA, AND YUGOSLAVIA. In both the Austrian and Hungarian treaties, some of the lands taken from these countries had been definitely assigned to various states, while others had been reserved for a later decision of the great powers. In an inter-Allied treaty signed at Sèvres on August 10, 1920, certain of these decisions were officially stated and the boundary lines set forth. This treaty was supplemented by the Treaty of Rapallo of November 12, 1920, in which Italy and Yugoslavia settled their boundary differences. These agreements were not reached without some dispute, and, indeed, the inter-Allied treaty was never ratified by all the powers.

Czechoslovakia had been forced to take up arms to make good her claims against both Austria and Hungary. She also came into armed conflict with Poland over the rich Silesian mining district of Teschen, and two other small territories, Spis and Orava, all of which were claimed by both Poland and Czechoslovakia on historical, economic, and ethnical grounds. In each of these territories the populations were very mixed and included a considerable group of Germans. Lloyd George added fame to the Teschen dispute when in a flight of oratory he asked in the House of Commons: "How many members have heard of Teschen? I do not mind saying I had never heard of it, but Teschen very nearly produced an angry conflict between two allied states, and we had to interrupt the proceedings [of the Peace Conference] to try and settle the affairs of Teschen." Through the intervention of the powers an armistice line was drawn on February 5, 1919, which defined Czech and Polish zones in Teschen. Disputes followed, and in September 1919, the Supreme Council decided to hold a plebiscite not only in Teschen but also in Spis and Orava. Because of continuing unrest in these regions, however, the plebiscite was never held. Instead, the Conference of Ambassadors at Paris on July 28, 1920, laid down a decision, according to which each of the three territories was divided. Czechoslovakia was given most of the mines and the important railway, while the Poles received the town of Teschen and some mainly undeveloped coal deposits. The northeast part of Orava and the northwest part of Spis went to Poland, the latter boundary not being settled until 1924. The net result was that both Poland and Czechoslovakia remained dissatisfied.

Although Rumania had been defeated by the Central Powers and forced to sign a disastrous separate peace in May, 1918, she emerged from the Paris Peace Conference with double her previous size and population. Rumania received the Bukovina from Austria and Transylvania from Hungary without getting into any serious dispute with the Allies. In the Banat her claims, however, came into conflict with those of Yugoslavia. Here the large settlement of Swabians added to the ethnic confusion. In the end the Peace Conference drew the boundary line in such a way as to balance the number of Serbians awarded to Rumania against the number of Rumanians allotted to Yugoslavia. Little attention, however, was paid to railway lines in the Banat. A last-minute decision to give Vršac and Bela Crkva to Yugoslavia cut the main line of communication of the territory that went to Rumania.

Bulgaria was again forced to turn back to Rumania the southern part of Dobruja (which Rumania had first obtained in 1913), although this territory was inhabited almost completely by Bulgars, Turks, and Tartars. Rumania also acquired Bessarabia from Russia. On the overthrow of the Tsar in 1917 this province had declared itself an autonomous Moldavian Republic within the Russian state. In January, 1918, its government invited Rumanian troops to enter the country. Subsequently the Moldavian Diet declared itself independent and voted for union with Rumania. In order to regularize the situation, Great Britain, France, Italy, and Japan, in a treaty of October 28, 1920, recognized Rumania's right to annex this region, generally known as Bessarabia. This was done over Russian protests, and the Russian government never recognized this transfer of territory.

As regards Yugoslavia, Bosnia-Herzegovina and most of Croatia-Slavonia were able to join Serbia without any dispute. A serious boundary difference, however, arose over Italian claims in Dalmatia, at Fiume, and on the Istrian peninsula. Italy had been promised extensive territories in this region by the secret Treaty of London. Now in one or two places, particularly Fiume, the Italians demanded territory beyond what had been promised them. Wilson was determined not to agree to these cessions, and a crisis ensued at the Peace Conference. For over a year the great powers attempted to reach a settlement, but without success. In Istria there were three proposed boundary lines: that of the Treaty of London, a line proposed by Wilson, and another proposed by Tardieu of France. After the end of hostilities an inter-Allied government had been established at Fiume. This was brushed aside when the poet D'Annunzio, at the head of a group of Italian adventurers, seized the city on September 12, 1919, and issued flowery appeals to Italian patriotism, which did nothing to ease the political difficulties of the Italian cabinet. The progress of the powers was slow, but Italy was persuaded to give up her far-reaching demands on Dalmatia; finally, in March, 1920, it was decided to leave the working out of details to direct negotiations between Yugoslavia and Italy. In these negotiations the Yugoslavs were hardly a match for the Italians. Failure in the Klagenfurt plebiscite, along with the results of the American election, where Wilson's Democratic party was defeated, took some of the intransigence out of the Slav negotiators. A settlement was finally drawn up in the Treaty of Rapallo in November, 1920. Italy obtained the port of Zara on the mainland and some islands off the Dalmatian coast, along with an Italian-Yugoslav boundary more favorable than the line of the Treaty of London. This meant that the entire Istrian peninsula, with its predominant Slavic population, was to go to Italy. Italy also received valuable quicksilver mines and control over important railway centers. Fiume with a small surrounding territory was to be made into a Free City.

D'Annunzio's ardent nationalism rejected this solution, and he even formally declared war on Italy. He was forced to evacuate Fiume, but on March 3, 1922, a Fascist coup overthrew the government of the Free City and thereupon Italian troops took over. The *de facto* situation was regulated by a new Italian-Yugoslav treaty of January 27, 1924, whereby Fiume was ceded to Italy, while Yugoslavia received the neighboring suburb and port of Porto Baros with special port facilities in Fiume.

Yugoslav claims to Albanian territory, which were to make trouble later, had been part of the complicated Italian negotiations. The new

Yugoslav state obtained some territory from Bulgaria in the Treaty of Neuilly, and its territories were rounded out by the incorporation of Montenegro.

During the war a Montenegrin Committee for National Union had been formed in Switzerland. Representatives of this body participated in the Pact of Corfu of July 20, 1917, which called for the creation of a united South Slav State. At the close of the war King Nicholas was in southern France and out of touch with his people. When the Austrian and Bulgarian forces withdrew from Montenegro, Allied (mostly Serbian) troops took over. A national assembly was elected and it proclaimed the union of Montenegro with Serbia. This union was bitterly protested by King Nicholas, who did his best to assert his rights at the Peace Conference. For a while a Montenegrin Legion was subsidized by Italy, but with the death of King Nicholas in 1921 the movement to restore Montenegro as an independent state collapsed. Later elections to the Yugoslav National Assembly are fairly convincing evidence that at this time the Montenegrins favored union with their fellow Slavs.

THE LITTLE ENTENTE. Beneš, as foreign minister of Czechoslovakia, was the first to try to bring closer co-operation among the principal heirs of the Dual Monarchy. He made gestures to Rumania and Serbia as early as October and November, 1918, but these were ineffective because of complications arising out of the Hungarian revolution. In January, 1920, a Polish-Russian war broke out. Soon, possible Magyar aid to Poland became a part of the secret French-Hungarian negotiations being carried on at this time. Hungary permitted arms to pass through its territories to Poland and sent some of its own supplies. There was even talk of sending Hungarian troops, but in return Hungary naturally expected favorable frontier rectifications. The Czech leaders did not relish the idea of Magyar troops marching through Ruthenia to help the Poles. Continued rumors of a French-Hungarian accord led Beneš to push through an agreement with Yugoslavia to forestall any revision of the Treaty of Trianon. On August 14, 1920, Czechoslovakia and Yugoslavia signed an alliance laying the foundation for the Little Entente. Each pledged itself to come to the aid of the other in case of an unprovoked attack by Hungary. The obligations were thus very limited and did not cover attacks by other powers. Negotiations between Czechoslovakia and Rumania were unsuccessful at this time because Rumania wanted to extend the agreement to cover a possible attack by Russia and Bulgaria.

In the spring of 1921 Emperor Charles went to Budapest in an effort to resume his throne. The powers asked him to leave, but to make sure he would go, Beneš sent an ultimatum. This episode helped to further the formation of the Little Entente. In an alliance concluded on April 23, 1921, Czechoslovakia and Rumania promised not only to aid each other in case of an attack by Hungary but also to consult on all questions of foreign policy relating to that country. On June 7, 1921, the Entente was completed when Yugoslavia and Rumania also signed an alliance. This was a broader agreement, directed against both Hungary and Bulgaria. A series of military conventions signed within the next eight months supplemented the alliance ties. Although the alliance obligations were not fundamentally altered, the Little Entente was expanded during the next years by co-operation in matters of foreign policy and foreign trade. The original Czechoslovak-Yugoslav treaty of alliance had been concluded without aid from France, but soon France became one of the most ardent patrons of the Little Entente. This friendship rested on a sound basis, for all four states were set against any revision of the peace treaties.

The Treaties of St. Germain and Trianon left many questions for future settlement among the succession states, and when these came up for discussion the Little Entente tended to follow a common policy. A conference was held at Portorose on the coast of Istria in November, 1921, in which all the succession states, including Austria and Hungary—as well as France, Great Britain, Italy, and the United States—were represented. The main object was to promote economic reconstruction in Central Europe. For instance, each of the succession states had seized as many of the freight cars belonging to the old Austro-Hungarian railways as possible. These cars could not be sent across the frontier because there was every possibility that they would never be returned. With such problems the Portorose Conference dealt. In all, some twenty protocols were signed. These were not ratified by all the states, but nevertheless most of them were carried out, at least in part, with the exception of a proposed general tariff union

The peace treaties had split the central Danubian basin into many parts, yet there were also some provisions that, had they been carried out, would have assured a measure of economic unity. Unfortunately the Portorose Conference was only a beginning, and much more was needed to attain the international order which many of the statesmen of 1919 had in view.

The Borderlands of Russia

As in the case of Austria-Hungary, the liberation of the peoples of Russia was the culmination of a century-long struggle for national independence. The various national minority peoples within the Russian state, and in particular the Baltic peoples and the Ukrainians, had been given great encouragement for their nationalist movements by the policies of the Provisional Government. While the liberal regime had never gone so far as to establish a working state corresponding to the ideas it professed, the minority peoples had been led to believe that they would receive substantial autonomy within a Russian federation. This idea was also taken up by the Bolsheviks. Eight days after they came to power they issued a Declaration of the Rights of the People of Russia, promising self-determination and the abolition of national and religious disabilities for all the peoples of Russia. Although the Bolsheviks favored the granting of minority rights, they desired that the federal units should be under their own party control. This naturally brought them into sharp conflict with the nationalist leaders who had hitherto been active among the minority peoples, and the latter soon became one of the major sources of opposition to the Soviet regime. Situated as they were on the periphery of Russia, the subject nationalities were encouraged to believe that they could break away from the mother country. Finland, the Baltic states, and Poland actually succeeded in this; but the Ukraine, the Caucasus provinces, and Russian Central Asia were brought back under Russian control after the protracted agony of the civil war and intervention had impressed their influence on the entire settlement [see below, pp. 182–87].

LIBERATION OF POLAND. Divided between Prussia, Austria, and Russia since the end of the eighteenth century, the Poles never gave up hope of the eventual reunion of their state. Their hope for the future was constantly reiterated in the title of their national anthem: "Poland is not lost forever," and the uprisings of 1830, 1848, and 1863 testify as to the persistence of the Poles in their efforts to regain their independence. Nevertheless, the obstacles to Polish political activity in the decades before World War I were very great, and there was no unity of thought or organization in the three parts of Poland. After 1905, Russia, which had some 13,000,-000 Poles as opposed to about 4,000,000 each in Prussia and Austria, was the country where Polish political organizations were most active. Here the moderate National Democratic party was built up by Dmowski as the leading exponent of Polish nationalism; by election to the Russian Duma its leaders gained both experience and recognition. Pilsudski's Polish Socialist party was also founded in Russia, but it did not achieve fame until the war period. In Germany a Polish party was represented in the Reichstag. In Austria-Hungary, on the other hand, the Polish aristocrats played a more important part in domestic politics; in return for their support of the Habsburg dynasty they won extensive rights of local government in the Polish province of Galicia, with its capital at Cracow, and also held many high posts in the central government. Under this system many Poles gained experience in politics and administration, and Polish culture in Galicia flourished. But the price for this freedom was that political activity was directed more towards Austrian issues than to the development of an independent Poland [see maps, pp. 126 and 127].

With the coming of the war, the situation changed overnight. The so-called Eastern Front ran through Polish territory almost in its entirety, and the prospects of Polish independence oscillated as the armies of Russia and the Central Powers pushed each other back and forth across Eastern Europe. After the capture of Warsaw by the Central Powers in August, 1915, the greater part of Poland soon fell into their hands, and at first they treated it merely as occupied military territory. When they realized the advantages to be gained from winning the support of the Polish population, they made vague promises in 1916 of an independent state under a constitutional monarchy. The Poles were never won over to this plan, however, and the elusive "kingdom" disappeared in 1918 together with

German military power. Russia also made vague promises to the Poles after 1914, but it was not until the March revolution of 1917 that they received the encouragement for which they had been waiting so long. The Provisional Government recognized their independence in "all the territory where the Polish people constitute a majority of the population," and took immediate steps to implement this decision in so far as was possible within the limits of the territories they still held.

This decision of the Provisional Government, which followed by two months a firm statement favoring Polish independence on the part of President Wilson, gave a decisive turn to the work of the Polish political groups. From 1914 to 1916 Pilsudski, who had transferred his activities to Austrian Galicia because of Russian persecution, met with considerable success in organizing a legion of Polish soldiers to fight with the Austrian armies. He finally resigned because of disagreements with the Central Powers over their occupation policy in Poland, and he spent the last year and a half of the war in jail. The Polish leader who received widest recognition in the West was Dmowski, who established in Paris the Polish National Committee, which was to serve as the nucleus of the future independent Poland. This committee engaged not only in propaganda, in which it was greatly aided by Wilson's advocacy of Polish independence in the thirteenth of his Fourteen Points, but also organized a force of 50,000 men which fought on the Western front.

Despite this activity on the part of Polish patriots, the collapse of Germany still found the Polish independence movement in a state of disorganization. In Warsaw, Pilsudski early in November, 1918, took over the remnants of the political structure left by the Central Powers, while parts of Prussian and Austrian Poland were still under occupation. As a socialist and an anti-Russian, Pilsudski had little in common with his chief rival Dmowski, who was a moderate in politics and had favored the Russian Provisional Government. However, they both realized that with a peace conference in the offing they would have to present a common front. As a symbol of Polish unity, Paderewski—the world-famous musician who had been active in Polish affairs during the war—was chosen in January, 1919, to head the Polish cabinet, and Dmowski served with him as delegate to the peace conference. Meanwhile Pilsudski remained in Warsaw as chief of state of the Republic of Poland. Thus a unified Poland was present at the peace conference to defend its territorial and political claims, and it took part in the negotiations as a recognized Allied Power.

The principle upon which the Polish delegation to the peace conference based its claims was that of including in the new Poland all territories inhabited primarily by Poles. In general, this principle was acceptable to the Allies, and they gave early approval to the greater part of the territories claimed by Poland. There were a number of areas that the Poles claimed, however, where the population was very mixed or where the Poles justified their demands by economic rather than by ethnic considerations. This was particularly true in the frontier with Germany, where it was difficult to draw a clear ethnic line; here plebiscites were stipulated in the Treaty of Versailles. In the rich industrial region of Upper Silesia, after a controversial plebiscite held in 1921, a compromise line was finally found by a League of Nations committee which left substantial minorities in both countries and gave the bulk of industry to Poland [see above, pp. 93–7] The Polish claims in East Prussia were settled more easily. Here plebiscites held in 1920 showed that the population was overwhelmingly pro-German in sentiment, and the League permitted itself to be guided by the popular vote [see map, p. 94].

In the question of the East Prussian port of Danzig, on the other hand, the ethnic principle was forced to give way to the need of Poland for a commercial outlet to the Baltic. Judged by the nationality of its population, East Prussia had always been separated from the rest of Germany by a broad belt of Polish population stretching to the Baltic Sea. The application of the ethnic principle now gave this corridor to Poland, but it did not provide it with an adequate seaport. Danzig, situated at the mouth of the Vistula and adjacent to East Prussia, was largely German-inhabited. The Allies felt that the economic requirements of twenty million Poles were a more important consideration than the national preferences of some 170,000 Germans in Danzig, and decided to make that port a Free City under the League of Nations, to be supervised by a High Commissioner. According to this arrangement the Germans of Danzig would not be under direct Polish rule, although the Poles would control the commercial relations and communications of the port. This same principle of placing economic considerations ahead of ethnic was applied against Poland in the controversy between that country and Czechoslovakia over Teschen. This small territory with less than half a million population was of great importance as a rail center and as a source of coke and coal. Its population was Polish by a small majority, but its economic and strategic character were such that it was judged by the Allies to be more important to Czechoslovakia than to Poland. In the final award made in 1920, some three fourths of Teschen went to the former, along with a considerable Polish minority. Poland and Czechoslovakia after much dispute also divided the two small areas of Spis and Orava along the Polish-Slovakian border [see above, p. 119]. These territorial settlements continued to cause troubled relations between the two countries. From what had been the empire of Austria-Hungary, Poland also annexed the two large provinces of Western and Eastern Galicia. The former, with its capital at Cracow, was clearly Polish and aroused no controversy. However, Eastern Galicia, with its capital at Lwow (Lemberg), was the scene of bitter dispute between Poles and Ukrainians in the troubled years of 1919–20. The victorious Allies hesitated to assign it to Poland because its population was predominantly Ukrainian, although the city of Lwow was Polish. This issue was settled by the Polish victory over the Russians in 1920, and the incorporation of Eastern Galicia in Poland was recognized by the Allies three years later.

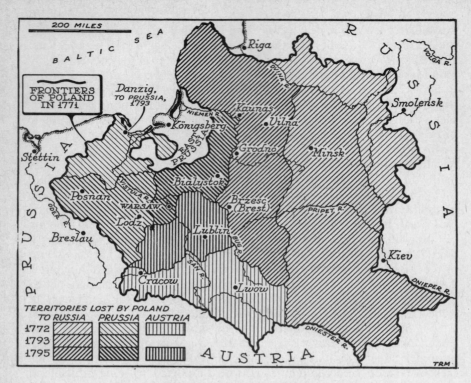

MAP 8 *Partitions of Poland, 1772–95*

The Treaty of Versailles and the plebiscites carried out under its provisions fixed the western boundaries of Poland for the next generation. While they left somewhat over one million Germans under Polish rule, the settlement proved as satisfactory a compromise as could have been expected given the mixed character of the population. To the east, the situation was entirely different. Here, the as yet unconsolidated power of the Bolshevik regime and the unstable existence of a Ukrainian state prevented the peace conference from taking any definitive action. A commission appointed by the conference did, however, recommend a provisional frontier in 1919 which gave to Poland all the districts it regarded as indisputably Polish in character. This frontier, which was later known as the Curzon Line, lay considerably to the west of the old frontier of 1772 which Polish nationalists claimed. While the Poles admitted that many Lithuanians and Ukrainians lived within the frontiers they claimed, they advanced historical and cultural arguments to support their position. Taking advantage of the civil war in Russia [see below, pp. 182–87], the Polish forces under Pilsudski, in alliance with certain Ukrainian groups, made great progress in the spring of 1920 and occupied Kiev in May. A counter-

Within the map:

100 MILES

BALTIC SEA

GERMANY

Gdynia • Danzig

Königsberg

EAST PRUSSIA

Memel

LITHUANIA

NIEMEN R.

Kaunas

•Vilna

•Minsk

DVINA R.

SOVIET UNION

ODER R.

•Poznan

VISTULA R.

•Lodz

•WARSAW

BUG R.

Bialystok

NIEMEN R.

CURZON LINE, 1920

Brzesc (Brest)

PRIPET R.

GERMANY

•Breslau

•Kielce

•Lublin

•Katowice

VISTULA R.

SAN R.

•Cracow

•Lwow

•Tarnopol

CZECHOSLOVAKIA

DNIESTER R.

RUMANIA

TRM

||||| Republic of Cracow, 1815
///// Kingdom of Poland, 1815
‐‐‐‐‐ Republic of Poland, 1921
•••••• Curzon Line, 1920

MAP 9   *Frontiers of Poland, 1815–1921*

attack by the Russians soon turned the tide, however, and by the summer the Poles were appealing to the Allies for assistance. The Allies made a proposal for an armistice based on the Curzon Line, but no agreement could be reached and the trial by arms continued.

By the middle of the summer the Red Army had come to within twelve miles of Warsaw, the Polish capital. With French technical assistance, Pilsudski now launched a counterattack that broke the advance of the Russians and started them on a long retreat. The Russians finally decided to negotiate, and in October, 1920, signed a preliminary treaty at Riga granting Poland a far more generous frontier than that provided by the Curzon Line. After further details had been elaborated, the definitive Treaty of Riga was signed in March, 1921, thus settling for the time being the question of the Polish-Russian frontier. There remained the controversial area around the city of Vilna, which was in dispute between Poland and Lithuania. The population was predominantly Polish, but the military events had left it in Lithuanian hands. The Poles were confident that a plebiscite would assign the territory to them, and appealed to the League of Nations asking that one be held. The Lithuanians refused to accept a plebiscite, however, and the Poles resorted to arms. In 1923 the Allies finally recognized the Polish claim [see map, p. 127].

The Poland which emerged from the war, while only half as large as the Poland of the eighteenth century, was nonetheless the sixth state in Europe in area and population, with almost 150,000 square miles of territory and over 27,000,000 inhabitants. While greatly devastated by the wars, it was rich in agricultural and mineral resources and had a population with remarkable recuperative capacities. At the same time, Poland's position between the two large and restless states of Germany and Russia was never secure. This insecurity was due not only to its geographical position, but also to the fact that Poland's postwar frontiers included substantial minority peoples of both her neighbors. While the German minority amounted to less than 4 per cent of the entire population, the one million Germans were located close to the German frontier and were acutely aware of their national rights. In the east, a minority of some 4,850,000 Russians lived in Poland, constituting about 18 per cent of the population. Of this minority, about four-fifths were Ukrainians.

THE BALTIC STATES. As a border population, the peoples of the Baltic states have been ruled by all the neighboring powers. In Estonia and Latvia, the Teutonic knights left a landowning class of barons, and Swedish rule strengthened the Lutheran faith introduced by the Germans. Polish influence was predominant in Lithuania, and the Catholic religion survived under Russian rule despite persecution by the Orthodox church. Russian rule was extended to all three provinces in the eighteenth century, but initially local conditions were left unchanged. Only in the latter half of the nineteenth century did the native population, spurred by reforms within the Russian Empire, begin to assert their rights; and after the revolution of 1905 the national leaders in Estonia and Latvia were able to organize.

During the war the Baltic provinces, like Poland, were the scene of almost constant warfare. It was not until the fall of the monarchy in March, 1917, however, that they had an opportunity to work for the establishment of independent states. Under the Provisional Government they were encouraged to establish National Councils preparatory to deciding on a form of government, and in Estonia and Latvia independent administrations were set up. Lithuania, under German occupation after 1915, formed a National Council in Petrograd which was wracked by internal conflicts. These developments came to a sudden end in November,

1917, and for two years German and Bolshevik troops, as well as various national groups, fought bitterly in this area. In 1920 the Soviet Union recognized the independence of the Baltic states and signed peace treaties with them. The Allies, however, delayed recognition in the hope that a liberal government might yet replace the Bolshevik regime in Russia. Wilson took the lead in urging this attitude, which was based on the consideration that, since the Provisional Government was the only regime in Russia recognized by the Allies, no territorial changes affecting former Russian provinces should be encouraged without its consent. As a result, the Allies at first granted only *de facto* recognition to the new governments. But as it became clear that the Russian Provisional Government had seen its last days, the Allied states shortly granted *de jure* recognition as well. In the meantime, any doubt as to the status of these three new states was removed by their admission as members of the League of Nations in 1921. At the same time the Baltic states were busy organizing their domestic regimes. Estonia in 1920, and Latvia and Lithuania in 1922, adopted republican constitutions and set out on a course of parliamentary government in the manner familiar to Western Europe.

INDEPENDENT FINLAND. Conquered by Russia in 1809, after some six centuries of Swedish rule, Finland had always occupied a privileged position in the great Slavic empire. The Russians regarded it as a buffer state that they found wise to keep contented by the concession of political autonomy. Thus, at a time when the rest of the Russian Empire was ruled by an iron hand from St. Petersburg, in Finland the Swedish nobility enjoyed home rule. The reform movement that swept Russia in the 1860's brought to Finland a number of political gains, including the regular meeting of the Diet, and was accompanied by a great upsurge of native Finnish national feeling and the further development of popular education. This flowering of Finnish nationalism coincided, however, with the reactionary policies of Alexander III and Nicholas II. During two periods, 1899–1905 and 1909–17, the traditional rights of the Finns were suspended in varying degrees and a policy of direct rule from St. Petersburg was instituted which met with great opposition in Finland and prepared the way for that country's eventual independence. The issue that initiated the policy of Russification was the requirement that the small Finnish armed force should henceforth be integrated into the Russian army. This was a violation of one of the traditional Finnish rights, and in 1909 Russia finally agreed to receive an annual payment of some $2,000,000 from the Finnish government in lieu of military service. The Finns thus escaped participation in World War I and actually enjoyed a period of great economic prosperity. Both their agricultural and their industrial resources were developed to the utmost, and they received high prices for their produce.

The March revolution in Russia brought with it new opportunities and new problems. By now there was a strong movement for independence, but at the same time Finland was wracked by domestic strife. In the winter of 1917–18 civil war broke out between the nationalist White

Guards, led by Mannerheim, and the socialist Red Guards, and to this struggle was added German and Russian intervention. The Whites were victorious only after a conflict that was carried on with extreme brutality on both sides, and that left deep scars only time could heal.

Considering the crisis through which it had passed, Finland made a remarkably quick recovery. In 1919 a constituent assembly drafted a republican constitution providing for a strong president to be checked by an assembly elected by universal suffrage. The elections held in 1919 showed that the political balance was held by the two moderate parties: the Progressives and the Agrarians. In the same year the Diet passed a law granting amnesty to the socialists arrested at the end of the civil war. The Social Democrats now freed themselves from the communist wing of their party, and participated in the government of the country with the other parties.

The course of events in Finland was such that the constitutional structure of the state was established before its frontiers had been fixed. Finland's long land frontier with Russia, stretching from the Arctic Ocean to the Gulf of Finland, was bound to remain in a state of flux until the Bolshevik regime had established its authority in northern Russia. The chief territory in dispute was Eastern Karelia, which lay along the frontier on the Russian side. The Finns of Eastern Karelia had been under Russian rule since the Middle Ages and had not formed a part of the Grand Duchy of Finland after 1809. In the course of 1918 and 1919, this frontier region was under the influence of the White Russians and the Allied forces based at Murmansk and Archangel. The Allied forces finally withdrew, and the White Russians were defeated by the Soviets. In October, 1920, Finland signed at Dorpat a peace treaty with Soviet Russia. Under the agreement Eastern Karelia remained in Russia, and Finland received a narrow corridor to the Arctic Ocean and the ice-free port of Petsamo. Russia also recognized the Finnish Republic and promised that the Karelians would be given autonomous rights [see map, p. 131].

This settlement with Russia removed the principal obstacle to Finland's peaceful development, but there remained still the question of the Aaland Islands, which were in dispute between Finland and Sweden. Geographically and historically a part of Finland, these islands were of great strategic importance to Sweden and were, moreover, inhabited entirely by Swedes. In view of the unrest in Finland after 1917, the Swedish government had encouraged the Aalanders to declare for union with Sweden, and the Finns had replied by using military force on the islands. Danger of war between the two countries was averted by action on the part of the League of Nations Council. A commission investigated the question and in 1921 decided that the islands should remain under Finnish sovereignty. The Swedish complaint was met with the provision that the islands should be demilitarized and that the Aalanders should have self-government and the right to appeal directly to the League in case the Finns violated their local rights. In one of its earliest actions, the League thus provided a satisfactory solution to a small but troublesome problem.

MAP 10 *Eastern European Peace Settlement*

RUSSIA AND THE PEACE CONFERENCE. While the Bolsheviks were gradually extending their authority over the greater part of the former Russian Empire and defeating one by one the confused and divided forces of the opposition, a separate drama was being played in Paris between the victorious Allies and the representatives of the former governmental authorities of Russia. The latter, who included such prominent statesmen as Milyukov and Sazonov, were thinking primarily in terms of finding some means of overthrowing the Bolsheviks. The Allies, on the other hand, were divided in their counsels. The American and British attitude was that every effort should be made to encourage a compromise among the contesting groups in Russia, while the French were reluctant to make any move that might imply recognition of the Bolsheviks. On Wilson's initiative, it was finally decided in January, 1919, that an invitation be issued to representatives of all Russian points of view, including the Bolsheviks, to meet at some neutral point to search for a basis of agreement. The White Russians rejected this offer, although the Soviet government declared its willingness to enter into negotiations.

The general Soviet attitude during this period was that it was worth making considerable concessions to obtain the withdrawal of all Allied assistance to the White Russians, with whom they felt confident that they could deal at a later date. This point of view was reflected in the Soviet reply to a direct approach made by Wilson through one of his aides, William C. Bullitt. The Soviet note was received in Paris in March, 1919. It stipulated that if the Allies would withdraw all aid to the anti-Bolshevik regimes, lift the blockade of Russia, and enter into diplomatic relations with the Bolsheviks, the latter would agree to negotiate with the White regimes on the basis of the territory they then held. In addition, both the Soviet and the White regimes were to recognize their responsibilities for the financial obligations of the former Russian Empire. Wilson and Lloyd George regarded these terms as unsatisfactory because they would grant the Bolsheviks their main objective, the withdrawal of Allied aid to the Whites, before the negotiations began. The Bullitt report was therefore suppressed and, except for various halfhearted efforts, no serious attempt was made to obtain Russian participation in the Peace Conference. This policy, which was based on the assumption that the Bolshevik regime would soon collapse, resulted in the absence of the Soviet government from some of the basic decisions regarding the future of Europe. As a consequence these decisions had a tentative and conditional quality, a fact that tended to increase the political and economic instability of Europe. The Soviet Union was not recognized by the leading powers of Western Europe until 1924, and it joined the League of Nations only in 1934.

Bulgaria and the Treaty of Neuilly

AFTERMATH OF DEFEAT. The political forces active in Bulgaria at the end of World War I may be divided into two categories: the parties supporting a nationalist program, and those stressing primarily social aims.

The nationalists stood for the economic development of the country with the aid of foreign loans, a modest social program, and above all the national unification of all the territories traditionally considered to be Bulgarian. In more or less permanent opposition to the nationalist parties were the Agrarian Union and the Social Democrats. Both groups had been organized at the end of the nineteenth century, but they had never held office. The members of the Agrarian Union believed that the country should be governed in the interests of the peasantry, which formed some 80 per cent of the population. While they thus should have had a permanent electoral majority, the Agrarians had hitherto lacked trained leadership and adequate organization. Stambolisky, the head of the Agrarian Union, had been in jail since 1915 because of his opposition to Bulgaria's participation in the war. The Social Democrats drew their support from the much smaller group of urban workers and civil servants. For almost a generation the party had been split into two wings. The moderates, like the revisionist socialists of Western Europe, favored parliamentary methods and co-operated with the nationalist parties within certain limits. The extremists, on the other hand, adhered to a narrow interpretation of Marxism, and in 1919 they came out officially as a Communist party and joined the Third International.

When the Allies launched their decisive offensive from Salonika in the middle of September, 1918, the Bulgarian government realized that the end had come. The Bulgarian armies soon began to disintegrate under the vigorous Allied blows, and the government sued for peace. The armistice signed on September 29 provided that a substantial body of Bulgarian troops captured in southern Serbia should be held as prisoners of war, and that with the exception of a few units the remainder should be demobilized. The Allies were to be given transport facilities through Bulgaria and use of her military supplies. Bulgaria was thus forced to terminate all resistance promptly.

While the armistice was being arranged, the Bulgarian army was in a state of full demoralization. As most of the soldiers were peasants, tired of the war and eager to return to their farms, the Agrarian leader Stambolisky decided to capitalize on their discontent. Recently released from prison, he hastily organized several regiments of returning troops into a revolutionary army and on September 27 he proclaimed a republic. The uprising was ill-conceived and poorly executed; the government managed to capture or disperse the rebels, and Stambolisky went into hiding.

This uprising, along with the humiliating armistice terms, marked the end of King Ferdinand's reign of thirty-one years. Crafty rather than wise, but domineering and in many respects very able, Ferdinand had exercised a determining influence on the policies of his country since the turn of the century. By manipulating the leaders of the nationalist parties and cultivating the chiefs of the army, he had succeeded to a large extent in getting around the parliamentary institutions provided by the constitution and in asserting his personal will. But since his policy during the war consisted of little more than following the lead of Germany and Austria-Hungary, his prestige was bound to decline with their collapse. At the insistence of the party leaders, he abdicated on October 4 and went into exile in Germany. He was succeeded by his 24-year-old son, who ascended the throne as Boris III. Elections were held in August, 1919, and over one third of the votes went to the Agrarians, while the nationalist parties re-

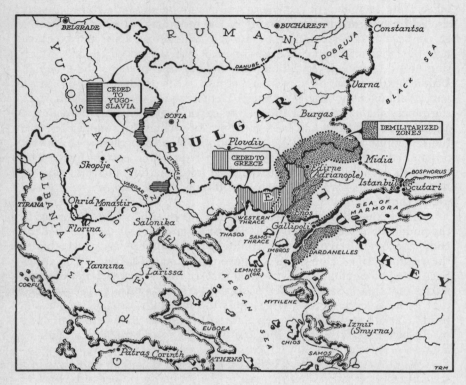

MAP 11   *Bulgaria and European Turkey: Peace Settlement*

ceived some two fifths and the communists one fifth. When the Assembly met in October, a new coalition government was formed under Stambolisky. It was this government that signed the peace treaty at Neuilly on November 27, 1919.

PEACE TREATY. In drawing the new Bulgarian boundaries in the Treaty of Neuilly, the Allies were influenced primarily by the role of that country in the recent war. In order to reduce the ability of Bulgaria to wage another offensive war, that country was required to cede territory in two areas: on the frontier of the new Yugoslav state, and in the province of Western Thrace in the south. To Yugoslavia, Bulgaria lost four strategic salients that she had found advantageous when she attacked the Serbian army in the rear in 1915. These four strips totaled some 975 square miles in area and had a population of 100,000, the greater part of which was Bulgarian. In the south, Bulgaria lost its Aegean coastline, an area of 3285 square miles and 260,000 inhabitants, among whom Bulgarians were in a minority. This territory was initially ceded to the Allies, and they transferred it to Greece in 1923. Greece later offered to make available a trade outlet at a suitable Aegean port equipped with appropriate harbor and rail facilities, but this offer was turned down by Bulgaria. Since its interest in Western Thrace was a matter of prestige and strategy rather than of commerce, the Bulgarian government feared lest the territorial claim it wished to keep alive be weakened by the acceptance of a trade outlet [see map, p. 134].

In addition to their complaints about the territories recently lost, Bulgarian nationalists claimed that some 600,000 Bulgarians still lived in Yugoslavia, 200,000 in Greece, and 135,000 in Rumania. The constant reiteration of these claims tended to have an inflammatory effect on domestic public opinion, and in the years following the war redress of these grievances was a prime political concern. An important factor in keeping this issue alive on such an exaggerated basis was that from 1913 to 1925 some 250,000 Bulgarian-speaking refugees had immigrated from the neighboring countries. The majority of these were from Greek and Yugoslav Macedonia, and they exerted a powerful political influence. The bulk of them joined the nationalist parties, and so many rose to cabinet positions that the Macedonians seemed almost to have taken over the government. Others, however, who in seeking adjustment to the new conditions were not satisfied with the nationalist doctrine, joined the Communist party, where they likewise achieved leading positions.

The effort of the Allies to reduce Bulgaria's aggressive potentialities by making territorial changes thus had its negative consequences. The chief security of the victors lay in the relative increase in their own territories. Whereas in 1914 Bulgaria had been as large or larger than any of its neighbors excepting Turkey, as a result of the peace treaties its area and population declined slightly, while Serbia's tripled, Rumania's were doubled, and Greece's were increased by about one third. At the same time, this gain in Allied security from the point of view of territory and population was in some degree offset by the extreme and unreasoning nationalism it provoked in Bulgaria.

The main provision of the Treaty of Neuilly in regard to military affairs was the prohibition of compulsory military service. In a primarily agricultural country it is difficult to attract soldiers for long periods of enlistment, and the Bulgarian delegation at the Peace Conference attempted to get this restriction lifted; but the Allies firmly held Bulgaria to the same terms regarding compulsory service which were applied to the other Central Powers. The total number of armed men permitted to Bulgaria was limited to 33,000. Strict limitations were also placed on military schools, munitions factories, and other military establishments.

It was recognized by the Allies that Bulgaria would not be able to pay for all the damage she had done to her neighbors, but reparations were to be exacted to the extent that Bulgaria was considered able to pay. The principal charge was a fixed sum of about $450,000,000 (2,250,000,000 gold francs), payable over a period of thirty-eight years. Supervision of the payments was to be made by an Inter-Allied Commission, which was to be given specified rights of inspection and control in Bulgaria. In addition, Bulgaria was required to return in kind any articles, or their equivalent in value, which she had removed from the occupied countries.

Dissolution of the Ottoman Empire

TREATY OF SÈVRES. Of all the problems that the victorious powers at the Peace Conference had to face, none offered more complexities and controversies than the disposition of the Ottoman Empire. This vast and strategically important area had been a source of rivalry among Russia, England, France, and Italy, and the secret treaties they concluded during the war for the partition of Turkey have already been mentioned [see above, pp. 67–71]. The Bolsheviks not only repudiated the agreements but published them, and this resulted in a good deal of opposition to their terms in Western Europe. The Peace Conference thus was not only faced with the secret treaties, and by wartime promises to Arabs and Zionists, but also with a vigorous demand by Venizelos that Greek sovereignty be extended over approximately half a million Greeks who lived in and around the port of Smyrna in Anatolia. In May, 1919, the Big Three (Lloyd George, Clemenceau, and Wilson), in an effort to bring pressure on Turkey, secretly authorized Venizelos to occupy this region. Greece thus accepted the responsibility of enforcing Allied decisions in the heart of Turkey. At the same time, the Kurds, the Armenians, and the Arab-speaking peoples, all demanded independence from Turkish rule.

While the peace treaty was being drawn up, Arabia, Syria, Palestine, and Mesopotamia were under occupation by Allied troops pending their final disposition. In Egypt the British retained their dominant position. Anatolia itself, which was inhabited predominantly by Turks, was partially occupied by small French and Italian forces, as well as by the Greeks. It was on the assumption that Turkey was entirely at their mercy that the Allies drew up their terms of peace at Sèvres. In European Turkey, the Greeks were granted—and occupied in advance—the province of Eastern Thrace, which extended almost to the suburbs of Constantinople. They also received Western Thrace, which had been ceded to the Allies by Bulgaria in 1919. There was some doubt as to the population of these two areas, but the figures at the disposal of the Allies indicated that the Greek inhabitants were in a majority in the former province, although Turks predominated in the latter. Greece also received from Turkey most of her Aegean islands. Constantinople and the Turkish Straits (the Bosphorus, the Sea of Marmora, and the Dardanelles), which had been under Allied military and naval occupation since the end of the war, were left under

Turkish sovereignty. A plan had been considered for depriving Turkey of this vital region and placing it under an American mandate. Wilson rather favored this plan, but the project was dropped because it was not well received by the American public. Instead, the important waterway of the Straits was internationalized and placed under the jurisdiction of a commission, to be composed of the representatives of six great powers and four interested small powers (including Turkey). This commission was to operate within the framework of the League of Nations; it was to see that the Straits were open to vessels of commerce and war at all times, and that Turkey maintained no fortifications or armed forces that could be used to obstruct traffic through the waterway [see map, p. 134].

In western Anatolia, the port of Smyrna with its hinterland was to be administered by the Greeks for five years, after which the final disposition of this region was to be decided by a plebiscite. In eastern Anatolia, Armenia was to become an independent state within frontiers to be fixed later on the recommendation of President Wilson, whereas Kurdistan was granted an autonomous government. Of Turkey's Arabic possessions, Syria was to become a French mandate, and Palestine and Mesopotamia British mandates, while in Arabia proper an independent Kingdom of Hejaz was recognized and was granted custody of the Mohammedan Holy Places (Mecca and Medina) [see map, p. 140].

These terms were signed at Sèvres on August 10, 1920, by the Allies and by representatives of the Turkish Sultan, but the treaty was never put into effect and a binding settlement of the Turkish territories was not reached until 1923. The assumption that Turkey was an occupied country and that Greek troops could enforce the decisions of the powers with regard to the central portions of the former Ottoman Empire proved to be unsound. By the time the treaty was signed Turkish spirit was undergoing a powerful national revival and the Greeks had started an advance from Smyrna into Anatolia which proved to be beyond their means.

TURKISH NATIONALISM. Mustafa Kemal, the leader of the Turkish national revival, was a prominent member of the Young Turk movement who had played an important role in the events of 1908–09 and had distinguished himself during the World War as a military commander at the Dardanelles and in Syria. He had early come to question the policies of the government, however, and his independent outlook had prevented him from obtaining positions of the highest responsibility before 1918. The defeat of Turkey fulfilled his darkest predictions, but it did not destroy his confidence in the spirit of resistance of the Turkish people. While he recognized that the Arab-speaking subjects of the empire must be relinquished, he opposed his government's policy of acquiescing in the Allied projects for partitioning Anatolia. Kemal's attitude was thus one of determined nationalism, and as such it had a wide appeal among many Turkish military and political leaders. Having failed to influence the government in Constantinople, Kemal obtained an appointment as inspector of the army in Anatolia. He began his tour of inspection in May, 1919, a few days after the Greeks landed in Smyrna. He arrived in Anatolia nominally as a representative of the government in Constantinople, but his activities in organizing a movement of national resistance soon brought him into sharp conflict with his superiors.

Kemal devoted the summer of 1919 to rallying Turkish opinion. In two large congresses, which brought together representatives from all the districts of the country, resolutions were passed that asserted the independence of Turkey within its national frontiers and called upon the Turkish people to vote for delegates supporting Kemal's program in the next elections. The nationalist forces were, in fact, successful at the polls, and when the Parliament met in Constantinople in January, 1920, they obtained the adoption of the National Pact. This document was a restatement of the principles of national independence elaborated by Kemal during the previous summer; it became the cornerstone of his political movement. At this point the Allies, sensing that their plans for Turkey could not be enforced if the nationalists obtained control of the government, sent additional forces into Constantinople in March. As a consequence the Parliament was dissolved. This action of the great powers was calculated to strengthen the conservative groups around the Sultan, but it actually had the opposite effect.

Kemal's reply to the Allies was to call a new parliament of the nationalist deputies to meet in the central Anatolian town of Ankara in April, 1920. The Sultan, while protesting, signed the Treaty of Sèvres on August 10, 1920; Kemal denounced it. With the convocation of the nationalist assembly at Ankara and the refusal to accept the peace terms, Kemal broke with both the great powers and the Sultan and thereby changed the course of Turkish history. In the course of the next two years Kemal laid the foundations of a new Turkish state, and the regime at Constantinople came to an end in 1923 with the deposition of the Sultan.

Working under difficult conditions Kemal reorganized the army and through it maintained Turkish unity and reasserted Turkey's position in international affairs. In April, 1920, a military agreement was negotiated with Soviet Russia under which Kemal received essential military supplies. By October of that year the army was strong enough to subdue the Armenians on the northeastern frontier of Turkey. This event was followed in March, 1921, by a peace treaty with the Soviet Union in which Turkey returned to Russia the port of Batum, which it had obtained by the treaty of Brest-Litovsk in 1918, but retained the adjacent Kars-Ardahan salient.

Kemal's main task, however, was to push back the Greek armies that since June, 1920, had been advancing into Anatolia. The Greeks, although they initially had the blessing of Italy, France, and Great Britain, received little help from them. Dissension developed among the Western Allies about Near Eastern affairs. In March, 1921, Kemal was able to reach an agreement with Italy, to be followed in October by one with France; under these agreements the two Western powers agreed to withdraw their troops from the small sector of southern Anatolia they had occupied. Great Britain was dominant in the region of the Straits, but failed to furnish the Greeks much material support. The Greeks were also torn by bitter internal political strife, a factor clouding its relations with the Western Allies and disrupting Greece's military efforts.

GREEK-TURKISH WAR. The lieutenants left behind by Venizelos, while he was away at the Peace Conference, had been guilty of serious mismanagement of Greece's affairs. Moreover, the country, greatly strained by having to support a mobilized army since 1912, desired a return to normalcy. The issue that upset the political stability was provided by the accidental death of King Alexander, who in October, 1920, succumbed to blood poisoning after being bitten by a pet monkey. After calling for the return of King Constantine [see below, pp. 393–94], the Royalists were themselves surprised when the Liberals, in the elections held the following month, won only 120 seats in the chamber out of 370. A Royalist government was now formed, and in December, 1920, King Constantine returned.

The return of the Royalists was followed by political change in the high command. The army, which was poorly equipped and dispirited, was now beset with increased dissension in the officer corps. In the spring of 1921 the Greeks met with their first serious reverses in Anatolia. The following autumn, after they had advanced some 400 miles from Smyrna, they were thrown back by the Turks at the Sakkaria River. From then on the Greeks were steadily pushed back until finally, a year later, in September, 1922, the Turkish army reoccupied Smyrna. A great conflagration broke out as the Greeks were evacuating the city, and fire and pillage were added to the disasters that the peaceful Greek tradesmen of the region had already undergone. The blame for this castastrophe now fell on the Royalists, and King Constantine promptly abdicated and was succeeded by the crown prince as George II. Constantine died peacefully in Sicily a few months later, but his leading supporters did not fare so well. An anti-Royalist military revolt under Colonel Plastiras broke out in the wake of the retreating army, and a Revolutionary Committee was established in Athens. Unable to win the support of Venizelos, the Revolutionaries took matters into their own hands. In November, after a court martial, they executed five Royalist ministers and one general. This act aroused consternation and hostility throughout Europe, particularly in Britain; as a result, no one was prepared to coerce the Turks for the sake of Greece.

TREATY OF LAUSANNE. The military victory against the Greeks was the cornerstone of the Turkish success at the Conference of Lausanne, where the powers gathered to work out new peace terms. But if Kemal was responsible for the military success in Anatolia, great credit must be given Ismet, his chief lieutenant and his successor as president of the republic in 1938, for the diplomatic victory by which Turkey's achievements were formally conceded by the great powers. Faced by the haughty and somewhat scornful Lord Curzon, who headed the British delegation, and by

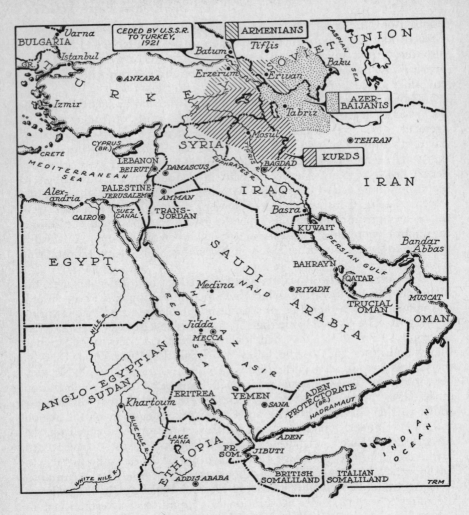

MAP 12 *Asian Turkey: Peace Settlement*

the representatives of the other powers, who, although divided on many issues, were united against the Turks on the main points, Ismet stood his ground firmly. Aided by his deafness, which at times enabled him to ignore proposals he considered unfriendly, Ismet won the maximum gains possible. Largely because of the grim realism of the negotiations that preceded it, the Treaty of Lausanne was the most lasting settlement to emerge from the war. Its terms can best be studied by distinguishing between the settlement as it affected Turkey proper, and as it concerned the successor Arab states.

From the point of view of the great powers, the most controversial issue raised at the Lausanne Conference concerned the administration of the Straits, which connected the Black Sea with the Mediterranean. While conditions had changed greatly since the Allies had conceded Constantinople and the Straits to Imperial Russia in 1915—an agreement subsequently denounced and rejected by the Soviet regime—Russia still had a vital and continuing interest in the fate of this region. Having recently defeated in a bitter civil war the armies of Denikin and Wrangel which had been supplied through the Straits and had later retreated through this waterway, Russia was eager to see it closed to all foreign warships. She therefore proposed at Lausanne that the Straits be closed to the fleets of all countries except Turkey. In order to secure her supremacy of the Black Sea region, Russia was willing to sacrifice her right to send her own fleet out into the Mediterranean. This was a concession Russia could easily make since her own Black Sea fleet, never a powerful force, was now completely outclassed by the naval tonnage available to the Western powers in the Mediterranean.

The point of view of Britain and France was, naturally, quite different from that of Russia. For several centuries they had had important political and commercial interests in the eastern Mediterranean region. At Lausanne they therefore proposed that in peacetime the Straits be opened to the warships of all nations, although with the restriction that the warships of any one power entering the Black Sea should not exceed in tonnage the fleet of the strongest Black Sea power. They also made proposals regarding the demilitarization of the two shores of the waterway and the creation of an international commission to enforce the provisions of the agreement.

In this test of strength between the Western powers and Russia, the former had all the advantages, since they had been in occupation of the Straits since 1918 and were at the height of their naval power. Russia, on the other hand, had hardly recovered from the civil war and had no naval power to speak of. Important also was the attitude of Turkey. Desirous of obtaining as full control as possible over the Straits, the Turkish government objected to the restrictions the Allies wished to place on its sovereignty. At the same time, it was well aware that unilateral Russian domination of the Black Sea would not be to Turkey's interest in the long run. In the end, the deadlock that had been developing at Lausanne over this issue was broken when the Turks accepted a modified version of the Allied proposal. In the regime for the Straits which was finally agreed upon, and which lasted until 1936, the waterway was declared free to commercial vessels at all times except when Turkey was at war, and even then the Turks could interfere only with enemy shipping. As for warships, no one power was to be permitted to send into the Black Sea naval tonnage larger than that of the Russian fleet stationed there, and a maximum limit of 30,000 tons was placed on the amount of naval shipping permissible at any one time to states not bordering on the Black Sea, such as Britain or

France. If Turkey were at war, only neutral naval vessels would enjoy these rights. It was further provided that the Turks were to demilitarize the European and Asiatic shores of the Bosphorus, the Sea of Marmora, and the Dardanelles, and the size of the garrisons permissible at Constantinople and other strategic points was strictly limited. The administration of these provisions was placed in the hands of a Commission of the Straits acting under the League of Nations. The Turkish representative was to be the permanent chairman of this Commission, which was composed of the five great powers (France, Great Britain, Italy, Japan, and Russia) and five neighboring interested states (Bulgaria, Greece, Rumania, Turkey, and Yugoslavia). Thus a compromise was reached which on the whole favored the Allied point of view, but which took into consideration also the territorial rights of Turkey and the security interests of Russia [see map, p. 134].

The Treaty of Lausanne also made provision for the boundaries of the new Turkey. In Thrace a settlement was reached which even a second World War did not change. Having been defeated by the Turks, the Greeks were now forced to give up Eastern Thrace, which they had occupied in 1919 and which had brought them to the very suburbs of Constantinople. This cession restored Turkey's frontier in Europe to what it had been on the eve of the war, with the exception of a small strip of territory that Turkey had ceded to Bulgaria in 1915. Western Thrace remained in Greek hands. Once again, various projects were discussed for providing Bulgaria with an economic outlet to the Aegean, but for reasons which have already been mentioned [see above, p. 135] nothing came of them. As to the Greek-inhabited islands of the Aegean, the Greeks also had to make some concessions. There were four principal islands that had been granted to Greece in 1920. Now Greece was required to return to Turkey two of them located near the mouth of the Dardanelles. Turkey, for her part, agreed to demilitarize them and to respect the rights of the local Greek population. Farther to the south, but in a somewhat similar relation to Turkey, were the Dodecanese Islands, of which Rhodes was the most important. While these islands were not specifically dealt with in the Treaty of Lausanne, their final settlement took place at the same time. Under Turkish sovereignty until 1912, they had been occupied by Italy in that year as a part of the settlement following the Italian-Turkish war. Since almost 90 per cent of their population was Greek, Italy had promised in 1920 to cede them to Greece in return for Greek support of Italian claims to Southern Albania. Following the collapse of that treaty and the decline in Greek fortunes, as well as a change in policy on the part of Italy, the Italian government denounced this agreement in 1923 and kept the islands. Mention should also be made of the island of Cyprus, of which about 80 per cent of the population was Greek. Occupied by the British in 1878, it was formally annexed by them at the start of the World War. In 1915 the British government offered Cyprus to Greece in partial compensation for the latter's entry into the war on the side of the Allies, but the offer was rejected. The Treaty of Lausanne now confirmed British sovereignty over Cyprus, which became a crown colony in 1925.

It has already been noted that in eastern Turkey the frontier with the Soviet Union was agreed upon in a separate treaty in 1921. A more controversial problem was the southeastern border of the new Turkey, inhabited by the turbulent Kurds. The key city in this region was Mosul, which was a center of oil production as well as a junction of river and land communications. Only a temporary settlement could be reached at Lausanne, and not until 1926 did Great Britain and Turkey agree on a frontier. Mosul was left within the frontiers of British-mandated Iraq, while Turkey received a modest financial compensation.

While it did not come within the scope of the Treaty of Lausanne, the status of the some 10,000,000 Turkish-speaking citizens in Russian Central Asia should be mentioned here. Conquered by Russia in the latter half of the nineteenth century, these peoples had taken advantage of the revolution and civil war to set up several autonomous principalities. As the danger of reoccupation by the Soviets grew, a movement developed for the creation of a vast Moslem and Turkish-speaking empire which would embrace Turkey, Persia, and Afghanistan, as well as Russian Central Asia. At the head of this visionary project emerged the exiled Young Turk leader Enver, who set up headquarters in Bokhara in the autumn of 1921. The movement was nevertheless built on slim foundations; during the following summer the uprising was put down by the Bolshevik army, and Enver was killed on the battlefield.

Another problem that was settled at Lausanne, although not in the treaty itself but in a separate agreement, had to do with the repatriation of the many Greeks who had found it impossible to continue living in Turkey in view of the bitter situation created by the war. The greater portion of them had already fled as refugees, and the exchange agreement signed at Lausanne made provision for regulating questions of property, transportation, and law. Under this agreement, some 400,000 Turks, living in the Balkan territories Greece had acquired since 1912, were returned to Turkey in return for approximately 1,300,000 Greeks. This exchange was carried out in an orderly fashion, and the whole settlement is frequently cited as a model solution for situations of this sort. Yet it should be remembered that for the persons concerned, the exchange was little short of disaster. Populations of whole towns were uprooted from regions where peaceful and prosperous trades had been built up over generations and, in the name of the principle of nationalism, were resettled in barren and inhospitable localities where they had to recapture their way of life in the face of many obstacles. It must be said, nevertheless, that the Greek government, which had by far the more difficult problem, made a valiant effort to assist the newcomers. In addition to the 1,300,000 Greeks from Turkey, some 100,000 others had come to Greece since the war from the Russian Black Sea region and from Bulgaria and Albania. With the aid of foreign loans, Greece managed to find homes, provide sanitation and housing, and re-educate the refugees. This work was carried on under the supervision of a Settlement Commission, whose first chairman was Henry Morgenthau, a former United States Ambassador to Turkey.

The victory of nationalist Turkey was reflected not only in the territorial settlement, but also in the final abolition of the special legal privileges of foreign governments and individuals in Turkey, known as capitulations. The capitulations had long been a source of grievance to the Young Turks, and upon entering the war in 1914 they had abolished them. The Allies, during their occupation of Constantinople, had returned to the system of capitulations, although Germany had recognized their abolition in 1917. They now became a major issue at Lausanne. The foreign governments feared that the property and persons of their nationals would be without legal protection if the capitulations were removed, whereas the Turks claimed that under the new government the judicial system would not differ from that existing in European countries. The controversy became so bitter that at one point the conference broke down because of the Turkish refusal to make concessions on this matter. When the conference reconvened, the Turks won a signal victory. Capitulations were permanently abolished, and in return Turkey admitted a few foreign jurists who were to serve for a limited period in an advisory capacity in the Turkish ministry of justice.

On the question of the public debt of the Ottoman Empire, estimated at some $623,000,000, a solution was reached which very largely freed the Turks from foreign economic control. It was agreed that Turkey would assume about three fifths of the debt, while the rest would be divided among the successor states. Moreover, the foreign-dominated Council of the Ottoman Public Debt, which had formerly exercised considerable authority over Turkish domestic financial administration, was henceforth to sit in Paris. The collection of revenues and other aspects of financial administration were now entirely in Turkish hands.

THE ARAB WORLD. The World War had found the Arab possessions of the Ottoman Empire in a state of considerable ferment. While the northern coastal province of Syria was under fairly strict Turkish administration, the lands to the south and east were only loosely held. The province known historically as Mesopotamia, and to the Arabs as Iraq, had been ruled through the local landlords. In the Arabian peninsula the northern province of the Hejaz, in which were located the Moslem holy places, had been controlled by the Hashim dynasty headed by Husein. Husein and his three sons, Ali, Faisal, and Abdullah, represented at that time the most prominent Arab ruling family and had great ambitions for the future. The province of Nejd in the south was controlled by Ibn Saud, leader of the fanatical Moslem Wahhabi sect. The coastal regions bordering on the Persian Gulf and Indian Ocean, on the other hand, were ruled by a number of minor Arab sheiks who for almost a century had been under strong British influence.

The movement for Arab independence dated from the late 1870's, and it developed rapidly through secret societies and the periodical press. The desperate disciplinary measures of Sultan Abdul Hamid, and the vigorous efforts at centralization on the part of the Young Turks after 1909, only served to re-enforce the desire of the Arab peoples for independence. The World War gave them the opportunity they needed, and the Allies gladly provided the military assistance and the organization. In advancing under British military leadership into the Ottoman Empire through the Arab provinces, the Allies used Mesopotamia and Egypt as their principal approaches [see above, p. 65]. The first prerequisite of a successful Allied campaign was the support of the Arab peoples themselves, and this was obtained in 1915–16 in an exchange of letters between the British government and Husein. The Arab leaders had jointly drawn up a formal proposal for the independence of all the Arab lands of the Ottoman Empire. In return for British assistance in achieving this goal, the Arabs were to grant Great Britain special military and economic rights. When presented with this proposal by Husein, the British accepted its general terms but made reservations regarding the exact extent of Arab territory that would gain independence. Excluded from the area of Arab independence was the northern portion of Syria bordering on Anatolia and a region on the Mediterranean seacoast vaguely defined as "lying to the west of the districts of Damascus, Homs, Hama, and Aleppo." Whether the territory later delimited as the mandate of Palestine was included in this reservation has since been a matter of bitter dispute between the Arabs and the British. At the time, while Husein was not entirely satisfied with the territorial terms of the agreement as he understood them, he decided to carry out the military part of the bargain and to leave to future developments the achievement of the full Arab claims.

By the end of 1917, the Allies had thus made three important commitments as regards Arab lands: the British engagement with Husein, the Sykes-Picot Agreement on British and French spheres of influence, and the Balfour Declaration on the subject of a national home for the Jews [see above, pp. 68–70]. Of these, the first remained secret and vague, the full text of the relevant correspondence not being published by the British until 1939. The Balfour Declaration, on the other hand, was from the start a public document. Whatever the Allied interpretation of these two commitments may have been, the Arabs regarded them as contradictory. Serious concern and distrust was aroused among their leaders when the concessions to the Zionists in Palestine were made known. This Arab unrest was greatly increased in December, 1917, when the Bolsheviks published the terms of the hitherto secret Sykes-Picot Agreement. The news of this document brought consternation to the Arab world, and the Allies were forced to take quick measures to regain Arab confidence. In a communication to Husein early in 1918, the British gave a general assurance, which nevertheless avoided any specific commitments, that the Arabs would be freed from Turkish rule. A few months later, in a declaration issued to seven Arab leaders, the British gave a further assurance that territories liberated by the Arabs themselves would receive full independence, while those liberated by Allied arms would have governments based on the consent of the governed. Finally, in November, 1918, a formal Anglo-French Declaration was issued which referred to "the setting up of national governments and administrations that shall derive their authority from the free exercise of the initiative and choice of the indigenous populations."

This was the status of Allied policy in the Arab lands when the war came to an end. The inconsistencies it reflects should be attributed more to indecision than to deceit. Under Wilsonian principles of self-determination, and in the light of certain Allied commitments, there can be little question but that the Arabs had a very strong claim to the entire area they considered to be theirs. Apart from this claim, however, there were other factors to be considered. The British did not, in fact, make any clear and unequivocal promises as to either the precise territories that would fall to the Arabs, or the exact form the new governments would take. On these points all of the commitments, including the Anglo-French Declaration, were capable of varying interpretations. They were doubtless purposefully vague. The Arab peoples had had little experience in self-government and they were, moreover, divided among a number of rival leaders. The French and the British had for many generations played an active role in the life of this region, and the newly developed oil fields added a further incentive for their continued intervention. In the face of these interests, there was little that the Arabs could do. Only if they had won full military control of their lands in the face of Allied opposition, as Kemal had done in Turkey, could the Arabs have gained their ends—but this was far beyond their capacity. Faisal, son of Husein, was active at the Peace Conference in pleading the Arab cause, but the compromise that was finally reached fell short of the Arab demands. At the San Remo conference in April, 1920, the Allied Supreme Council agreed that while the Arabian peninsula was to be given its independence, the remaining Arab territories were to be formed into mandates assigned to France and Great Britain. The old Turkish province of Syria was divided into a smaller province of Syria (including the territories which later became Lebanon) in the north, which was assigned to the French, and a southern province assigned to Great Britain and soon divided into two territories: Palestine and Transjordan. The British also received the mandate for Mesopotamia (Iraq). Under the system set forth in Article XXII of the Covenant of the League of Nations these were to be "A" mandates [see above, pp. 97–8]. This status involved the provisional recognition of the independence of the mandated countries and the rendering of no more than "administrative advice and assistance by a mandatory until such time as they are able to stand alone." Under this settlement the Arab provinces that were politically the most mature and culturally the most advanced fell under French and British tutelage, while most of the sparsely settled and politically backward Arabian peninsula received its independence.

II

THE
GREAT POWERS
AND THE
SEARCH FOR AN
EQUILIBRIUM

CHAPTER

6

Experiments in International Organization

The League of Nations: *Membership; Assembly and Council; Secretariat and Commissions; Settlement of International Disputes.*

The International Labor Organization.

The Permanent Court of International Justice: *Jurisdiction; Advisory Opinions.*

Other International Organizations.

The Minority Treaties: *Drafting of the Treaties; Procedure Under the Treaties.*

Attempts to Improve the League's Security System: *Geneva Protocol; Locarno Pact; Paris Peace Pact; Other Efforts.*

Disarmament: *Disarmament of Germany; Naval Disarmament; The League and Disarmament.*

Security Through Alliances: *The French Alliance System; The Italian Bloc.*

THE LEAGUE OF NATIONS was burdened, as part of the general peace settlement, with a number of obligations by the various treaties. Simultaneously with the League certain inter-Allied bodies, which had been established earlier, continued to function. Most of the frontier and disarmament commissions were supposed to report, not to the League, but to the "Conference of Ambassadors," which was simply a meeting of the chief Allied ambassadors resident in Paris. The "Supreme Council," which was a meeting of the heads of the chief Allied governments, also continued to exist and was mainly responsible for the series of conferences of the postwar years. If one examines the chief topics on the agenda of the twenty-four conferences sponsored by the major powers between 1920 and 1923 and the matters taken up by the League in the same period, no clear-cut line of demarcation is discernible. It would scarcely be worthwhile, even if space and patience allowed, to try to distinguish between activities of the League, of the Conference of Ambassadors, or of the Supreme Council. Their concurrent activities add confusion to the terminology of postwar international relations, but it was the great Allied powers who dominated the decisions wherever they were reached.

The League of Nations

MEMBERSHIP. The thirty-two Allied states signatory to the treaties of peace plus thirteen neutral states were invited to join the League of Nations. Any fully self-governing state, dominion, or colony not on the original lists could obtain membership upon the approval of two thirds of the League Assembly. On January 10, 1920, when the League was officially inaugurated, there were only twenty-three members, but by November, 1920, membership had risen to forty-two. Egypt was the sixty-third and last nation to join in 1937. By that time, however, various countries had taken advantage of their right to withdraw from membership. Never were all the great powers members at the same time. The United States, of course, never joined; Germany was admitted only in 1926 and resigned in 1933; Russia was admitted in 1934, only to be expelled in 1939; Japan held membership from 1920 to 1933, and Italy from 1920 to 1937. Of the great powers, only France and England held membership from the beginning until the end (1946), but as Viscount Cecil, one of the best authorities on the League, states: ". . . though they joined, [they] declined to carry out their obligations. In England," Cecil continues, "it is no exaggeration to say no Prime Minister who held office between the years 1920 to 1939 really believed in the League. Not one of them was prepared to put the whole strength of the United Kingdom behind it as they would have done to protect the independence and integrity of the British Commonwealth. That is the standard by which international collaboration for peace must be judged." [1] Failure of the United States to accept membership in the

[1] Viscount Cecil: "The League's Legacy to the United Nations," *The New York Times Magazine*, April 7, 1946. Arthur Henderson as foreign secretary (1929–31) was a striking exception to this attitude.

League was, of course, a severe blow to the effectiveness of the organization, and certainly another loss of great importance to the League resulted from the refusal to admit Germany and Russia for so many years. But the lukewarm support accorded to the League by those who did join was equally disastrous.

ASSEMBLY AND COUNCIL. In the Assembly, which met at least once a year at Geneva, all members were represented, and it became a great debating forum where every country, however small, could air its views. Its powers were broad, for it could "deal at its meetings with any matter within the sphere of action of the League or affecting the peace of the world." Yet the major decisions were taken by the League Council, which was made up of the representatives of certain great powers that held permanent seats, plus a varying number of representatives elected for a definite term by the Assembly. The latter were usually representatives of middle-sized powers. In addition, any member of the League might be asked to send a representative to sit as a full member whenever a matter especially affecting its interests was before the Council. The Council met at least four times a year, usually at Geneva, and in the course of time took over many tasks from the Council of Ambassadors or the Supreme Council. Its decisions were, with a few exceptions, to be made by unanimous vote, and it bore the chief responsibility for the maintenance of peace.

THE SECRETARIAT AND COMMISSIONS. To arrange for meetings, to receive reports and complaints, to register treaties, to supervise numerous publications, and to carry on all the other multiple activities of the League, a Secretariat was established. Headed by a Secretary-General and staffed by a group of assistants, secretaries, translators, and experts, this body soon numbered over five hundred. It constituted a real international civil service recruited from all parts of the world.

To describe the Assembly, Council, and Secretariat is a simple task. To complete the picture and discuss the great number of commissions, committees, and bureaus, either projected by the Covenant or created by the action of the League itself, is more than can be done in this brief account. These bodies did much splendid work and performed many tasks essential for the reconstruction of war-devastated Europe, from extending loans to various small countries or building up an international health organization to the suppression of the opium traffic and the care of refugees.

SETTLEMENT OF INTERNATIONAL DISPUTES. In spite of the accomplishments of League agencies in many and varied fields, in the end the League was bound to be judged by how successful it was in maintaining peace. Articles X–XVII of the Covenant laid down the procedure for pacific settlement of disputes. Should "the territorial integrity and existing political independence" of any member of the League be threatened by external aggression, the Council of the League was authorized to advise what measures should be taken to halt such aggression. Any member of the League could call the attention of the Council or the Assembly to "any circumstance whatever which threatens to disturb international peace. . . ." The Council was bound to meet at once to study the situation. Members of the League agreed to submit all disputes that could not be settled by diplomacy to arbitration, to judgment before the Permanent Court of International Justice, or to inquiry by the Council. "In no case would they resort to war until three months after the award by the arbitrators or the report by the Council. . . ." If a member, however, did go to war in defiance of its obligations under the Covenant, it was to be subjected to an economic blockade by the other members of the League. No international police force was provided, but these economic sanctions were a powerful weapon and if applied in good faith gave the League sufficient force to see that its decisions were respected.

While both the Council and Assembly had competence to deal with matters affecting the peace of the world, only seven of the sixty-six political disputes that came before the Council of the League between 1920 and 1939 were considered by the Assembly as well.[2] The Council followed no one procedure in dealing with disputes, and its machinery undoubtedly functioned more smoothly and with greater dispatch when no one of the great powers was a party to the dispute or considered its interests directly involved. For example, the Bulgarian-Greek clash of 1925 over a border incident was quickly settled, and arrangements were made to avoid further incidents of the sort and to remove sources of friction between the two peoples [see below, p. 398]. On the other hand, Italy's precipitate use of force in the Corfu incident (1923), remained uncensured [see below, p. 400], and Italy's view of the dispute dominated the proceedings. The affair was kept in the hands of the Conference of Ambassadors, despite a Greek appeal to the League Council. At least the incident did not lead, as might well have been the case formerly, to Italian annexation of Corfu. Thus the League, despite its limitations, did provide a convenient means of dealing with the numerous disputes of the postwar period, and its investigations and reports, even if a satisfactory settlement was not always reached, had a beneficial effect on public opinion and a salutory influence on the action of governments.

The International Labor Organization

The preamble of the ILO is a remarkable summation of the purposes of the organization, as these excerpts show:

> . . . the League of Nations has for its object the establishment of universal peace, and such a peace can be established only if it is based upon social justice;
> . . . conditions of labor exist involving such injustice, hardship, and privation to large numbers of people as to produce unrest so great that the peace and harmony of the world are im-

[2] For a list of the disputes that came before the League in the years 1920–39 see Wright: *A Study of War*, Vol. II, p. 1430; see also Myers: *Handbook of the League*, pp. 298–364.

perilled; and an improvement of these conditions is urgently required: as, for example, by the regulation of the hours of work, including the establishment of a maximum working day and week, the regulation of the labor supply, the prevention of unemployment, the provision of an adequate living wage, the protection of the worker against sickness, disease and injury arising out of his employment, the protection of children, young persons and women, provision for old age and injury, protection of the interests of workers when employed in countries other than their own, recognition of the principle of freedom of association, the organization of vocational and technical education and other measures;

. . . also the failure of any nation to adopt humane conditions of labor is an obstacle in the way of other nations which desire to improve the conditions in their own countries. . . .

The climate of opinion which is here indicated had already produced attempts at international organization for the improvement of labor conditions; an International Association for Labor Legislation existed as early as 1900, and the new organization had the benefit of a considerable body of precedents. Germany and Austria were members from the start, but the United States joined only in 1934, with the express stipulation that membership "shall not involve any obligations under the Covenant of the League of Nations." In all, 64 states joined the ILO and it is notable that some states, as for instance Japan, on withdrawing from the League retained membership in the labor organization.

Each member state sent four delegates to the International Labor Conference, which met regularly once a year at Geneva; two of these delegates represented government, one the employers, one the workers. Since voting was not by delegations as a unit, division on non-national lines was possible; i.e., workers' representatives might vote together. A so-called Governing Body was to act as a general executive. This Governing Body supervised publication of the official bulletin, the *International Labor Review,* and other publications of the office. It also appointed and instructed the Director, who recruited a permanent secretariat to undertake the collection of data, prepare agenda for meetings, and draft recommendations and reports. The secretariat made reports based on questionnaires sent to member governments on any subject on which action was contemplated (hours of work, child labor, unemployment of seamen, weekly rest, etc.). These reports served as a basis for discussion at the meetings of the General Council, which drew up a Draft Convention for which a two-thirds vote was necessary. The Draft Convention was then submitted to the governments for ratification. The Conventions as a rule set only minimum standards, and ratification by a state in no way lessened existing protection of workers anywhere. Ratification did make the Convention part of the domestic law of a state, just as any treaty becomes a part of a state's laws.

The ILO developed into a very active organization and was on the whole a successful attempt at international co-operation. It tackled practically every one of the subjects mentioned in the preamble. The data it gathered and the studies issued under its auspices were a great aid to governments in drawing up domestic legislation. If the League was intended to prevent war, the ILO in a less spectacular fashion struck at the very roots of war. It is to the credit of the ILO that after World War II, when the League and Permanent Court of International Justice were transformed into new institutions, it was not necessary to dissolve the ILO and start afresh. When the League was dissolved in 1946, the ILO, after some adjustments in its constitution, became one of the Specialized Agencies of the United Nations, with headquarters in Montreal.

The Permanent Court of International Justice

The need for rules to regulate conduct between states was long recognized, and gradually over the centuries, particularly after the seventeenth century, a system of international law was formulated. Actually, the acceptance of general laws advanced faster than devising a method of enforcing them. Yet even here progress was made. The refinement of certain rules and procedures in regard to diplomacy was of some assistance. The Conference system as developed after 1815 and the growth of the idea of the Concert of Europe were further steps along the path. When the United States and Great Britain agreed (1872) to submit their dispute over the "Alabama Claims" to arbitration, a landmark was set in the long attempt to devise peaceful means for settling differences between states.

In 1899 at the First Hague Peace Conference a Permanent Court of Arbitration was established. The name is misleading, for what the forty-some nations that eventually became signatory to the convention agreed upon was that each state should nominate four distinguished and able jurists to the Court. This list of men formed a Panel of Judges, and whenever two states wished to settle a dispute by arbitration they could turn to this panel and from it select the men who were to act as their board of arbitration. A permanent headquarters was established at The Hague to take care of correspondence and maintain a set of archives. Rules of procedure were also drawn up. In 1907 at the Second Hague Conference an attempt was made to create alongside the Court of Arbitration a Permanent Court of International Justice with a regular bench of judges. A statute was drawn up, but in the end it failed of adoption because no method could be devised for the election of judges. The great powers insisted on being represented on the bench, while the lesser powers demanded equality in position.

Up to World War II twenty-one cases had been submitted to arbitral decision under the Hague procedure. The Permanent Court of Arbitration is still in existence, and states can make use of its services if they wish to arbitrate a dispute.

Article XIV of the League Covenant charged the Council with the duty of formulating and submitting to the members of the League plans for the establishment of the Permanent Court of International Justice, commonly called the World Court. The statute of the court, drawn up by a committee of distinguished jurists and approved by the Council and Assembly, provided for a number of judges (eventually fifteen) to be elected for a term of nine years. Nominations were to be made by national groups in the Permanent Court of Arbitration or by national groups created in similar fashion by states not represented on that body. A majority in both Council and Assembly was required for an election. The statute, having been ratified by twenty-eight states, came into force in September, 1921, and the court met for its first session at its headquarters in The Hague on January 30, 1922.

JURISDICTION. Jurisdiction of the court was optional, for states were not bound to submit their disputes to it; yet the jurisdiction of the court was rapidly extended. This was achieved by two methods: first, states in drawing up treaties inserted clauses stating that any dispute arising under the terms of the treaty should be submitted to the Court for settlement, and second, the statute itself provided a so-called "optional clause" which states could sign with varying reservations. This clause stated that the signatory states bound themselves to submit their disputes to the court for adjudication. This was usually referred to as accepting "compulsory jurisdiction of the court." It should be noted that in most instances states accepted such jurisdiction on condition of reciprocity by other states, and only for a limited period of time. Also, very often specific exceptions were made, such as disputes relating to the territorial status of a country. Nevertheless, the increased willingness of states to bind themselves to accept the jurisdiction of the court was a significant step toward more and better world government.[3]

The court was open to all signatories of the statute, and by special arrangement non-member states could make use of the court if they desired. In this case they were expected to meet part of the expenses of the court, which were a regular charge on the budget of the League of Nations. Only disputes between states came before the court. Between 1922 and 1942 the court gave thirty-two judgments. There was no armed force available to enforce the court's decisions, but this was not necessary, for in each case the parties accepted and honored the verdict.

ADVISORY OPINIONS. The court was also enjoined by Article XII of the Covenant with the task of giving "an advisory opinion upon any dispute or question referred to it by the Council or by the Assembly." In practice these advisory opinions were requested for the purpose of establishing the exact legal status of a certain law or treaty involved in a dispute. In giving an advisory opinion the court did not decide an issue but only

[3] For a list showing when and under what conditions fifty-four states signed the optional clause see Manley O. Hudson: *The Permanent Court of International Justice 1920–1942* (New York), pp. 681–705.

stated what the law was. The Council or Assembly could use this statement as the point of departure in reaching a decision.

Early in its history the court exercised laudable restraint and refused to give an advisory opinion unless both parties involved in an issue appeared before it. This prevented the court from being involved in disputes in which one party refused to recognize the jurisdiction of the court, and it also discouraged the Council and Assembly from attempting to dodge their responsibilities.

In all, the court gave twenty-seven advisory opinions between 1922 and 1942. One of the most famous was the one centering about a proposed Customs Union between Austria and Germany in 1931. France, as well as other countries, was opposed to the Customs Union and brought the case before the Council of the League. The League then asked the Court to decide whether such a customs union was contrary to Austria's obligation under the Treaty of St. Germain and under a protocol signed at Geneva, October 4, 1922, in connection with an international loan. It was thus a legal question that the court was called upon to decide. In a sharply divided opinion, which included various concurring and dissenting statements, eight judges held the proposed Customs Union was illegal, seven held it was not. Austria and Germany thereupon announced that they would not press the negotiations, and the Council was relieved from dealing any further with the dispute.

In spite of the support which the United States gave to the idea of a World Court at the 1907 Hague Conference—indeed, an American jurist, Elihu Root, played a leading role in drafting the statute of the Court—and although Americans were always on the panel of judges, the United States never joined the Permanent Court of International Justice. The Senate consented to the ratification of the Statute of the Permanent Court on January 27, 1926, but with five reservations. These were unacceptable to the members of the Court. Every president of the United States after 1922 favored joining the Court, and there was widespread support of such a step among the public at large. Yet, when the question came before the Senate again in January, 1935, the Court again went down to defeat 52–36, the vote following no party lines. It is notable, therefore, that when the Permanent Court of International Justice was officially dissolved April 16, 1946, the United States was very ready to become a charter member of its successor, the "International Court of Justice," which was established under the United Nations Charter.

Other International Organizations

The League, the ILO, and the World Court were the three great organizations for co-operation on the governmental level. There were others that were classed as affiliated bodies of the League. There were also some organizations, such as the Universal Postal Union, which continued on their own independent way. All these governmental organizations were supplemented by a host of private international societies. The rapid increase in popular international conferences and congresses is perhaps an indication of awareness among the general public of the advantages of doing things on international rather than on national lines.

In 1922 the League Secretariat thought it wise to volunteer to act as a sort of international headquarters for some three hundred private organizations. It started a *Quarterly Bulletin* in which announcements of forthcoming meetings and short accounts of meetings held could be published. Looking over an index of such a volume one feels that everything possible had been organized, with no room for new societies. Yet new ones appeared regularly, while some dropped out and some were sparsely attended.

Only a sampling of the organizations can be listed: International Academic Union, International Association of Recognized Automobile Clubs, International Congress of Dealers in Art, The World's Poultry Science Association, World's Student Christian Federation, International Student Service, International Federation of University Women, Rotary International, and World Youth Congresses. Nor can an attempt be made to evaluate their work. The important thing, however, is not to forget their existence when speaking of international co-operation and friendship, for they have played a significant role in building up international-mindedness.

The Minority Treaties

DRAFTING OF THE TREATIES. In 1919, when an attempt was being made to establish a "just" peace and to organize Europe on national lines, it seemed only logical that those minorities which remained should be guaranteed basic rights. There was plenty of precedent for incorporating clauses into peace treaties protecting religious minorities, and at the Peace Conference it was the Committee of Jewish Delegations, in search of religious as well as more general guarantees, that provided the driving force behind the movement for the minority treaties. Because of the large Jewish minority in Poland, the committee was particularly anxious to get some guarantees from that state. To the powers also this seemed a good place to begin, because so many Polish problems were involved in making the peace with Germany. In the Treaty of Versailles Poland obligated herself to embody in a treaty with the Allied Powers "such provisions as may be deemed necessary . . . to protect the interests of inhabitants of Poland who differ from the majority of the population in race, language, or religion." This Minority Treaty, as well as the Treaty of Versailles, was signed on June 28, 1919.

In the Treaties of St. Germain, Trianon, and Neuilly, Czechoslovakia, Rumania, Yugoslavia, and Greece agreed to draw up similar minority treaties, but only after bitter protest. The small powers were indignant because none of the great powers was asked to undertake any minority guarantees. Italy, France, Germany, Great Britain (with the Irish) all had minorities within their borders. Bratianu of Rumania, speaking for the smaller powers, was particularly vehement in his denunciations. Their countries were civilized and had been Allies; their respective constitutions

MAP 13 States Under Minorities Obligations

guaranteed the citizens their civil rights; should these states have limita-tions imposed upon their sovereignty which the great powers did not im-pose upon themselves? All this was true, but Wilson in a remarkable an-swer to Bratianu on May 31, 1919, placed the situation in its proper perspective.

> *We are trying to make a peaceful settlement, that is to say, to eliminate those elements of disturbance so far as possible which may interfere with the peace of the world, and we are trying to make an equitable distribution of territories according to the race, the ethnographical character of the people inhabiting these terri-tories. . . . We cannot afford to guarantee territorial settlements which we do not believe to be right, and we cannot agree to leave elements of disturbance unremoved, which we believe will dis-turb the peace of the world. Take the rights of minorities. Noth-ing I venture to say is more likely to disturb the peace of the world than the treatment which might, in certain cases, be meted out to minorities. And therefore if the Great Powers are to guar-antee the peace of the world in any sense is it unjust that they should be satisfied that the proper and necessary guarantees have been given?* [4]

Wilson's statement shows clearly that although humanitarian considera-tions were part of the picture, the great powers were primarily con-cerned with insuring the tranquillity of Europe.

The states that accepted special obligations towards their minorities constituted a vertical belt across Europe to Asia Minor, from Finland to Iraq, for it was in this region that it was most difficult to fix boundaries on ethnological lines [see map, p. 158]. Obligations similar to those stated in the special minority treaties were accepted by Austria, Hungary, Bul-garia, and Turkey in their peace treaties. On entering the League, Albania, Estonia, Latvia, Lithuania, and Iraq made declarations that they would accord similar privileges to their minorities. Finland also undertook obli-gations in respect to the Aaland Islands. In a separate Convention signed at Geneva on May 15, 1922, Germany and Poland regulated the treat-ment of minorities (along with other problems) in Upper Silesia. This treaty was to last for fifteen years, and the rights guaranteed to the re-spective minorities went further than in the other minority treaties. The Upper Silesian agreement as well as all the other treaties provided for certain supervision by the League of Nations.

All these minority treaties and declarations were similar, but they were by no means identical. For example, in Turkey and Iraq the provi-sions were worded so as to apply primarily to non-Moslem minorities. In

---

[4] Quoted in Nina Almond and Ralph H. Lutz: *The Treaty of St. Germain: A Documentary History of Its Territorial and Political Clauses* (Stanford University, 1935), p. 569.

Greece and Yugoslavia the educational clauses applied only to the newly acquired territories, and in the Polish treaty the "Germans were entitled to their own educational facilities only in those territories which had belonged to Germany in 1914." [5] There were elaborate provisions for equality of rights before the courts and in the political, economic, and religious life of the state. Many specific provisions were inserted in regard to the use of native languages in schools, in the courts, and in the conduct of everyday affairs. Minorities were usually assured "an equitable proportion of state and communal expenditures for educational, religious and welfare purposes." Special provisions were often inserted for the protection of the Jewish Sabbath. For example, no electoral registrations or elections were to be held on Saturday.

PROCEDURE UNDER THE TREATIES. Since most of these states provided for the protection of civil rights in their own constitutions or laws, a member of a minority group whose rights were infringed had two means of redress, either the domestic courts, or an appeal to the Council of the League through the Secretary General. With the aid of a Minorities Commission, the latter determined whether the petition had substance and was receivable. If it merited investigation, the petition was referred to the government of the state concerned. Very often the head of the Minorities Commission let it be known that he would welcome an invitation to talk things over. If no action was taken by the state, the petition then went to the Council, which appointed a committee to investigate and work out a settlement. Sometimes these committees were successful, although often they gained only promises of reform not lived up to subsequently. There was another method by which a case might be brought before the Council. Any member of that body could ask for an investigation of a particular minority problem. This meant that a government had to press charges formally against another, an action that might well have grave political consequences, and the powers were loath to undertake this risk. The German government was the first to employ this direct method when in December, 1930, it questioned the conduct of Polish elections in Poznan and Pomorze. It has been observed that without the procedure of petition by the aggrieved minority itself the protection of minorities by the League might well have become a dead letter.[6]

Up to 1929 the Council never permitted publication of the number of petitions it received or the settlements reached. It had been estimated that up to that date about 300 petitions were received of which 150 had been declared acceptable. From 1930 to 1939, 585 petitions were presented, of which 338 were declared receivable, and examination of 298 of these was completed. The system of permitting the Secretary General to

    [5] Jacob Robinson and others: *Were the Minorities Treaties a Failure?* (New York, 1943), pp. 36–9.
    [6] Pablo de Azcarate: *League of Nations and National Minorities* (Washington, 1945), p. 99; C. A. Macartney: *National States and National Minorities* (London, 1934), pp. 324–40.

decide which cases were receivable has been severely criticized, but some sifting of cases was necessary. More fundamental was the criticism of the Council committee system. It is true that the method was slow and was often hampered by inadequate evidence, and that, like all international efforts, it tended to place expediency before abstract justice. Certain countries that had seats on the Council, notably Poland, did their best to obstruct minority proceedings. The fact that France was building up a system of alliances with the minority states also tended to diminish the effectiveness of League action. From the very start the minority states themselves, particularly those that had accepted the obligations under duress, did their best to sabotage the system. The treaties irked their national pride as an infringement of their sovereignty.

In 1934 the USSR joined the League. Poland, fearful that Russia might take the opportunity to bring many minority problems before the Council, denounced her minority treaty. This was a definite rejection of the Versailles system, just at the time when Hitler was taking action to the same end. However, in neither case did the League or anyone else take steps to uphold the established order. From then on the whole minority system went into a rapid decline. Instead of reason and consultation, force became the arbiter.

The minority system as established in 1919 was assuredly a forward-looking procedure. It attempted to make it possible for peoples of different races, nationalities, and religions to live together in one state and still enjoy life, liberty, and the pursuit of happiness. Unfortunately, persecution of minorities continued in most states, not, to be sure, because of the treaties but in spite of them; without them the minorities would undoubtedly have fared worse. That the minorities did not receive the protection which was their due is not so much a reflection on the treaties as upon the men who administered the affairs of the world.

Attempts to Improve the League's Security System

GENEVA PROTOCOL. While the League performed a multitude of useful functions, it was always viewed primarily as an instrument for the preservation of peace. Various efforts were made to strengthen this aspect of the League as a preliminary to disarmament. A draft treaty of mutual assistance, proposed in 1923, provided for military assistance to an attacked party through regional agreements under the aegis of the League Council. Britain, because of her far-flung empire, regarded this as too large a commitment, and led the movement to reject the proposal. Another formula proposed by the Assembly and known as the Geneva Protocol seemed to offer better possibilities of preventing a war before it started. Under this agreement the states would bind themselves to submit their disputes either to the World Court or to arbitration. Refusal to accept the decision reached would be considered an act of aggression. Thus all recourse to aggressive war would be banned and an objective means of defining an aggressor established. On first reading this sounds good, but it did little to alleviate many of the burning political problems of Europe. For instance, the problem of the Polish Corridor was not a legal question that could be decided by a court. Poland controlled this territory by virtue of incontestable treaty rights. Nor was it likely to be settled by arbitration, for this would mean a compromise that the parties were not willing to accept. Clearly the Geneva Protocol tended toward maintaining the *status quo*, and "to identify security with the maintenance of the 1919 settlement." [7] The Protocol was to go into effect when ratified by a majority of the powers having permanent seats on the Council, plus ten other members of the League. Again it was Great Britain that dealt the death blow. The Commons objected strenuously to the scheme because they were afraid of becoming too easily involved in economic sanctions, and in March, 1925, Britain turned down the proposition. The Geneva Protocol marks the end of attempts to strengthen the League through multilateral action. A host of bilateral nonaggression pacts and treaties of friendship, of neutrality, of arbitration, of conciliation, or of mutual assistance now came into being.

LOCARNO PACT. The Locarno Pact, which was concluded immediately after the failure of the Geneva Protocol, is a good example of a series of bilateral treaties that, taken together, form a regional agreement. This attempt to achieve security requires as a background a brief sketch of political affairs. French fear of Germany always constituted the very root of all security problems. In 1922 Germany and Russia concluded a treaty of friendship, known as the Treaty of Rapallo, by which provision was made for diplomatic recognition of Russia and the rapid expansion of Russian-German trade. The old fear of a German-Russian alliance again gripped the French foreign office, for no one could tell what these two non-League states might do. France immediately undertook an even firmer policy toward Germany than she had been following, and Germany was declared in default on reparations. Despite opposition from the United States and Great Britain, France in January, 1923, occupied the Ruhr [see below, pp. 221–22] and again made an attempt to establish small separatist German states along the Rhine. The German government ordered passive resistance and put the printing presses to work to pay the necessary expenses, which led to a spectacular and catastrophic collapse of the mark. The Germans had no recourse but to submit. A new government with Gustav Stresemann as foreign minister put an end to passive resistance in September, 1923, and launched a "policy of fulfillment"; Germany would do her best to meet her treaty obligations.

Collecting reparations by force had not been very successful, and France agreed to a general overhauling of the Reparations Settlement in the Dawes Plan of April, 1924. When France withdrew most of her troops from the Ruhr in November, 1924, and the rest in August, 1925, a certain stability was attained in Western Europe. In February, 1925, Germany had made a renewed effort to conclude a Rhineland Mutual Guaranty

[7] Walter R. Sharp and Grayson Kirk: *Contemporary International Politics* (New York, 1940), p. 546.

THE SEARCH FOR SECURITY: LOCARNO *Conference Delegates assembled after signature of Locarno Treaties, December, 1925. Statesmen in the front row are: Vandervelde (Belgium), Briand (France), Luther (Germany), and Baldwin (Britain); and, in the rear, Beneš (Czechoslovakia), Austen Chamberlain (Britain), Scialoia (Italy), Stresemann (Germany), Skrzynski (Poland), and Churchill (Britain).*

Pact. Shortly thereafter Briand, who had a broader conception of European politics than some of his predecessors, came to power in France. The advantages of such an agreement with Germany appealed to him as well as to Austen Chamberlain, the British foreign secretary. Not only would the Rhine frontier be settled, but in addition it might undermine the German-Russian Treaty of Rapallo, provide a welcome opportunity for Franco-British co-operation, and in some ways compensate for the failure of the Geneva Protocol. A conference was called for October 5–16, 1925, at Locarno, Switzerland, and here agreements that have since been known as the Locarno Pact were drawn up. They consisted of:

1. A treaty of mutual guarantee of the German-Belgian and German-French frontiers, signed by Germany, Belgium, and France, with Great Britain and Italy as guarantors.
2. German-French and German-Belgian arbitration treaties.
3. German-Polish and German-Czechoslovakian arbitration treaties.
4. Treaties of mutual assistance in case of aggression by Germany between France and Poland, and France and Czechoslovakia.

Under the treaty of mutual guarantee Great Britain and Italy agreed to come to the aid of Belgium or France in case Germany violated their common frontier, or to the aid of Germany if Belgium or France were the guilty parties. Except in the case of a "flagrant violation" apparent to anyone, the Council of the League was to decide which was the aggressor.

France would have liked to have had similar guarantees of the eastern frontiers of Germany, but Great Britain and Italy assumed no obligations in regard to Eastern Europe. While Germany was willing to sign arbitration treaties with Poland and Czechoslovakia, she steadfastly refused to give a guarantee to accept the eastern frontiers as definitive. France, by her treaties of mutual assistance, however, promised aid to Poland and Czechoslovakia should Germany attempt through force to change their common boundaries. Poland and Czechoslovakia of course each assumed a similar obligation to France, but not to each other.

The Locarno Pact was not warmly received by those states in Eastern Europe which revolved in the French orbit. French interest in Eastern Europe was believed to be in direct relation to her sense of insecurity with regard to Germany. Poland never liked the differentiation between the Rhine and the Vistula frontiers, which the great powers had conceded by guaranteeing the one and not the other. Russia also viewed the agreements with suspicion. A new trade treaty headlined by the Russian press as the Anti-Locarno Pact was concluded between Russia and Germany four days before the Locarno treaties were signed. This was followed by a Russian-German nonaggression treaty in April, 1926, in which each promised to remain neutral in case either should be attacked by a third power. Other provisions indicate that the Russian statesmen were making sure that Germany would not participate in any economic sanctions the League might direct against Russia.

It had been generally understood that the Locarno Agreements would be climaxed by Germany's entry into the League. But a delay was caused by a dispute over permanent seats on the Council, and it was not until September, 1926, that Germany was admitted to League membership. In Western Europe and the world at large the Locarno Pacts were hailed as inaugurating a new era of good feeling. Writers spoke of the Locarno spirit hovering over Europe. Tension did decline, and Europe entered upon a brief moment of relative prosperity. Whether this was because of Locarno, or whether Locarno was the result of the increased stability and security (which seems more likely) is unimportant. They came and departed together.

PARIS PEACE PACT. In April, 1927, Briand, desiring to commemorate the American entry into the war, suggested a pact between France and the United States renouncing war as an instrument of national policy. Since the chances of a war between France and the United States were remote, such a pact would be merely a friendly gesture. When Secretary Kellogg suggested in December of 1927 that the proposed treaty be made multilateral, it acquired new significance. To Briand's credit, he agreed. On August 28, 1928, the great powers (excluding Russia), the British Dominions plus India, and the three Locarno powers—Belgium, Czechoslovakia, and Poland—signed the agreement to outlaw war, and invitations were at once issued to forty-nine other governments to accede to the treaty.

The "Paris Peace Pact," also sometimes referred to as the Briand-Kellogg Pact, is one of the shortest treaties on record:

> *The High Contracting Parties solemnly declare in the names of their respective peoples that they condemn recourse to war for the solution of international controversies, and renounce it as an instrument of national policy in their relations with one another.*

> *The High Contracting Parties agree that the settlement or solution of all disputes or conflicts of whatever nature or of whatever origin they may be, which may arise among them, shall never be sought except by pacific means.*

The treaty was signed and eventually ratified without reservations. Its language is apparently simple and direct, yet many meanings were attached to it. In the diplomatic exchanges that preceded the signing, several governments stipulated conditions. Great Britain declared "that there are certain regions of the world the welfare and integrity of which constitute a special and vital interest for our peace and security. . . . Their protection against attack is to the British Empire a measure of self-defense. It must be clearly understood that His Majesty's government in Great Britain accept the new treaty upon the distinct understanding that it does not prejudice their freedom of action in this respect." [8] No enumeration was made of the areas of the world covered by this "British Monroe Doctrine," as it came to be called, but clearly the British foreign office was not binding itself too closely. The French statesmen emphasized the rights of self-defense and reserved freedom to act under previous treaty obligations. In a note sent to other powers on June 23, 1928, the United States declared that there was nothing in the treaty which "impairs in any way the right of self-defense" and each nation "alone is competent to decide whether circumstances require recourse to war in self-defense. If it has a good case, the world will applaud and not condemn its action." Secretary Kellogg,

---

[8] Toynbee: *Survey of International Affairs, 1928*, p. 21.

testifying before the Senate committee, stated: "I have said over and over again that any nation has the right to defend its interests anywhere in the world." Senator Borah was even more specific and declared: "We would have a perfect right to send an expedition anywhere, into Mexico or China, if it were necessary, in order to protect the lives and property of our citizens against actual threatened attack." The Japanese foreign minister made a similar declaration in Parliament in 1929 to the effect that Manchuria and Mongolia were of course within the sphere where Japan's "right of self-defense can be exercised. . . ." [9]

Apparently the great powers meant only to ban wars of aggression and reserved to themselves the right to determine whether their actions were offensive or defensive. Wars in support of obligations under the League, under the Locarno treaties, or under the French alliance system were also permitted. As one eminent political scientist put it: "Considering these reservations it would be difficult to conceive of any wars that nations have fought within the past century, or are likely to fight in the future, that cannot be accommodated under these exceptions. Far from constituting an outlawry of war, they constitute the most solemn sanction of specific wars that has ever been given to the world." [10] It should also be mentioned that the Pact of Paris only pledged the powers to seek a peaceful solution of their disputes, without making any attempt to define how this was to be done. Nor was any means set up for enforcing the pact. It remained a statement of policy and a convenient point of departure for castigating aggressively-minded states. After World War II it was used to bolster the legal basis for the prosecution of war criminals.

The Pact of Paris was eventually ratified by sixty-three states. It had at first been thought that Russia would spurn the invitation to join. Instead, within four days the Russians had agreed to the pact, although they took occasion to point out its shortcomings and particularly to criticize the "British Monroe Doctrine." Litvinov even persuaded the states on the Russian borders to apply the terms of the pact locally before it went into general application. The Litvinov Protocol was signed early in 1929 by the USSR, Poland, Rumania, Estonia, Latvia, and Lithuania.

OTHER EFFORTS. The Assembly adopted other measures to improve the League security system, such as the General Act of Geneva (1928), which established a recognized procedure for the appointment and work of Conciliation Commissions and reaffirmed the use of available pacific means of settlement. A League "Commission of Inquiry for European Union," sponsored by Briand, performed some valuable work in studying and holding conferences on certain pressing economic problems. Unfortunately the impact of the great economic depression was to diminish interest in such experiments in international or even regional co-operation.

[9] American and Japanese statements quoted from Raymond D. Buell: "American Policy toward the Sino-Japanese Dispute," *Foreign Policy Reports* (1938), 8:283 ff.

[10] Edwin M. Borchard as quoted in "The Anti-War Pact," *Foreign Policy Information Service* (1928), 4:365.

THE SEARCH FOR SECURITY: GENEVA   *French Foreign Minister Briand, British Premier Macdonald, German Foreign Minister Stresemann, and British Foreign Minister Henderson, discussing the possibility of a European federation, in Geneva, 1929.*

Disarmament

DISARMAMENT OF GERMANY. While the peace treaties made a start toward establishing a system of collective security, they also proposed general disarmament. "In order to render possible the initiation of a general limitation of the armaments of all nations . . . ," the defeated states (except Turkey) were required to accept a drastic limitation on their armed forces. The Germans held that this implied an obligation on the part of the powers to reduce their armaments to the German level. While this was not legally the case, the Allied intention may be seen from the reply to a question of the German peace delegation in June, 1919. "The Allied and Associated Powers wish to make it clear that their requirements in regard to German armaments were not made solely with the object of rendering it impossible for Germany to resume her policy of military aggression. They are also the first steps towards that general reduction and limitation of armaments which they seek to bring about." [11] Article VIII of

[11] Toynbee: *Survey of International Affairs*, 1928, p. 50.

the Covenant of the League charged the Council with formulating plans for disarmament.

The first step in this direction was, of course, the disarmament of Germany, which was completed under the supervision of technical experts responsible to the Inter-Allied Control Commission. This Commission was dissolved on January 31, 1927. Whatever can be said about German rearmament in later years, there can be no doubt that, for a period at least, Germany was disarmed in line with the policy laid down at Versailles. That some caches of small arms were made, however, is true. Of more importance were the secret agreements with Russia, carried on in the twenties chiefly by the German army authorities, but not entirely without the knowledge and co-operation of the civilian authorities. For a time, Russia was furnished financial and technical aid in industrial production for military purposes, some of this on German order, and certain German firms had establishments on Russian soil. Later German personnel (on inactive status) received training in Russia, there was some participation in poison gas experiments there, and military missions were sent to the Russian annual maneuvers. Nevertheless, the German government never trusted the Russians and feared the political repercussions in the West, were these activities made known. No military alliance was formed, and the government in general acted as a brake on the military.[12]

While Western statesmen were aware of these dealings, they did not take alarm. The German army in the twenties, expert as it was, did not constitute an offensive force; it could not even have defended the frontier against the well-equipped French and Polish armies. It was not German armament that prevented the other countries from disarming. On the other hand, her manifest desire for a revision of the Treaty of Versailles, her rising population, her industrial potential, and her insistence on equality were reasons enough to eye her with distrust. It was not strange that many of the powers were loath to surrender their military advantage.

NAVAL DISARMAMENT. Armament on sea, land, and in the air is all part of the same problem, but naval disarmament involved only the great powers and had a global rather than a European character. A series of independent conferences in this field was undertaken largely outside of the direct supervision of the League.

The war had brought a shift in naval power. For the first time the United States' fleet approached the size of Great Britain's, and the expanded Japanese fleet now ranked third among the navies of the world. In all three countries wartime building schedules threatened to continue. Indeed the Japanese program would give that state a dominant position in Far Eastern waters. Under these circumstances the United States government invited Great Britain, France, Italy, and Japan to a conference in Washington in November, 1921. Belgium, the Netherlands, Portugal, and

[12] Hans W. Gatzke: "Russo-German Military Collaboration During the Weimar Republic," *The American Historical Review* (1958), 73:565–97.

China were to be drawn in later, when certain matters in regard to the Far East were discussed.

At the Washington Conference an agreement was reached which in effect recognized the existing naval strength of the powers. Henceforth capital ships were fixed at a ratio of 5 for Great Britain and the United States, 3 for Japan, and 1.67 for France and Italy. No new replacements were to be laid down for ten years, and the life of a battleship was set at twenty years. In addition to this program, Great Britain, the United States, and Japan agreed to scrap seventy ships built or building, with a total of 1,644,839 tons. It fell to the lot of the United States to scrap thirty-two ships. The program was loyally carried out by all three powers by 1925. Great Britain, the United States, and Japan were also prohibited from acquiring any new bases in the Far East, or from increasing fortifications or facilities at bases already established.

Along with the disarmament treaty, two other political treaties were signed at this time bearing on the question of security in the Pacific. In a Four Power Pact the United States, Great Britain, France, and Japan agreed to respect each other's rights in the Pacific and to confer, should controversy arise between them or their interests be threatened by another power. In a Nine Power Treaty the five great powers plus China, the Netherlands, Belgium, and Portugal agreed to respect the sovereignty, independence, and territorial integrity of China and accepted the Open Door. Thus the principles which had guided United States policy in relation to China were generally recognized. Collateral negotiations carried on at the Washington Conference were also designed to bring greater stability to the Far East. In view of the Four Power Pact, the Anglo-Japanese Alliance was abrogated, and China and Japan supposedly settled their outstanding difficulties, largely through Japan's surrender of Shantung under some pressure from the other powers.

It had not been possible at Washington to restrict the building of submarines, because of the determined opposition of France. Without this, Great Britain was unwilling to limit cruisers, which were necessary for antisubmarine defense. Soon all the naval powers began to authorize large building programs calling for numbers of cruisers of greatly increased size. Just as the dreadnought had made many older battleships obsolete, so these newer and larger cruisers upset what balance there was in naval armament. Clearly an expensive building competition was on the way, and President Coolidge decided to call another conference, to be held at Geneva in the summer of 1927, to deal specifically with naval disarmament. A limited number of nations was invited to participate and two of these—France, who objected to separate naval discussions, and Italy, whose geographic position made her especially vulnerable—refused to attend. Japan played pretty much the role of spectator, but Britain and the United States were soon at loggerheads on the question of cruiser strength, and no agreement even on total tonnage could be reached.

Another attempt at a solution of naval competition was the London

Conference of 1930, but although difficulties between the United States and Great Britain were fairly well ironed out here, both France and Italy refused to accept the treaty. Britain thereupon insisted upon the so-called "escalator clause," which enabled any of the three signatory powers after due notice to alter their respective building programs if national security demanded it. At the time this clause was thought of chiefly as a safeguard against a possible French building program, but it gave an equivocal character to the whole agreement. Nevertheless the London Conference of 1930 marked the peak of the attempts to achieve naval disarmament. In December of 1934 Japan officially gave two years' notice for the termination of the Washington Treaty. A second London Conference of December, 1935, attended by the five powers signatory to the Washington Treaty, found Japan demanding parity with Britain and the United States, and led to no agreements of any significance.

Naval disarmament was a restricted and relatively simple matter. Only five states, all former Allies, were directly involved, and it was not intended to do much more than discourage big building programs. No one dreamed of cutting navies down to the limit imposed on Germany. In this light the Washington Treaty was a real achievement, but since it was based on a set ratio between powers, it could not be sustained in view of Japanese ambitions and British commitments. Efforts at parity even in limited measure were doomed to failure.

THE LEAGUE AND DISARMAMENT. It was the Assembly of the League that prodded the Council to begin its task of formulating plans for the reduction of armaments. As a result a Temporary Mixed Commission of experts was appointed on February 25, 1921. This Commission studied the question of private manufacture and traffic in arms, as tending to increase rivalry and danger of war, and other armament questions. After the Locarno Pacts were signed, more direct action seemed warranted, and the Council in December, 1925, set up a Preparatory Commission for a disarmament conference. This Preparatory Commission was charged with determining what arms should be limited and how the limitation should be accomplished. Thirty-two states, including the United States and Russia, were represented on the Commission, which actually was a Disarmament Conference in miniature.

The Preparatory Commission labored for five years to draw up a draft treaty to serve as a basis for the deliberations of a formal Disarmament Conference. All kinds of differences and difficulties arose. Limitation of the size of land armies brought with it the question of how to evaluate a conscript army (France, Italy, and others) in relation to a professional one (Great Britain, Germany, United States, and others). Here the question of counting reserves became a paramount issue. Limitation of war materials might be direct, i.e., based on the number of tanks, aircraft, artillery, and other weapons, or budgetary, i.e., determined by the amount of money spent. Budgetary limitation was held by the United States to apply unequally since professional armies are expensive and costs of production vary between states. Here too, for obvious reasons, the United States and France took opposing positions. It was soon evident that France and its allies—Belgium, Poland, Czechoslovakia, Rumania, and Yugoslavia—formed a united bloc on most questions. The most difficult problem was that of equality. Germany, supported by the other defeated states, steadfastly maintained that the victorious states should disarm down to their level. When the Russian delegation began its participation in 1927, Litvinov made a spectacular proposal that all armies, navies, and air forces be immediately abolished and all war material and arms factories destroyed. It was a safe proposition to make, for it was obvious no one would take him up. Germany was the foremost exponent of radical disarmament, supported on most points by Great Britain, the United States, and Russia, and some of the smaller states. France throughout insisted that nothing should be done to overthrow the disarmament provisions of the peace treaties. In the end, partly out of a desire to arrange a compromise, and partly because of the new international situation, Great Britain changed sides and agreed to support the French position. Italy, on the other hand, by 1930 was often siding with Germany. The final draft was a victory for French tenacity.

The Draft Treaty as finally drawn in December, 1930, and submitted to the Council was but a skeleton agreement for the limitation of land, sea, and air armaments. No figures were set and the treaty had by no means the unanimous approval of the states represented on the commission. Indeed it contained an article reaffirming all existing agreements that limited armament. While this included the Washington and London Naval Treaties, it could also be interpreted to mean that the defeated states were perpetually to be held at a much lower level of armament than their neighbors.

By the time the Disarmament Conference finally met, in February of 1932, economic and political conditions were even less favorable to agreement between the powers. France had been concerned about her security even when Germany lay prostrate at her feet. Naturally she feared for her safety if Germany were now released from the bonds of the Versailles Treaty. Germany was determined not to sign another agreement that recognized her status of inequality, and so withdrew from the Conference in September, 1932. More and more statements appeared in Germany (many for internal political reasons) to the effect that if the world would not disarm, then Germany would have to arm up to the level of the other states.

At this time there was a great campaign for the cancellation of war debts. It did not seem logical to the people of the United States that the states of Europe could not pay their debts yet could find enough money for large armament programs. Premier Herriot was anxious to get a financial agreement with the United States and therefore did not want to see the Disarmament Conference entirely collapse. In December, 1932, he consented to a formula stating that one of the guiding principles of the Disarmament Conference should be to see that Germany and the other defeated states were granted "equality of rights in a system which would provide security for all nations." What this meant exactly was not clear, but on the basis of this declaration Germany agreed to return to the Disarmament Conference.

When the Conference reassembled Hitler had become chancellor of the German Reich, and now more than ever there was a reluctance on the part of some powers to disarm, corresponding to the increasing determination within Germany to achieve equality. The promise of "equality of rights" which had lured Germany back to the Conference was clearly not going to materialize. Therefore, on October 14, 1933, Hitler withdrew from the conference and a few days later gave notice of his withdrawal from the League as well. By that time he had already begun to rearm Germany. Officially the Disarmament Conference was never closed, but it ceased to meet after May 1, 1937. Disarmament had failed, but even this brief account has indicated some of the difficulties which a limitation of armaments entails.

Security Through Alliances

Exactly what constitutes security and how it is to be obtained were problems confronting each of the states of Europe in this period. To Germany and the other defeated states, logically enough, security meant the overthrow of many of the servitudes placed upon them by the peace treaties. The USSR feared the united intervention of capitalistic states, and the latter in turn felt themselves vulnerable to communist upheaval. Italy feared that Germany or Yugoslavia might challenge her possession of lands inhabited by Germans or South Slavs. And so the round could be continued. In France, however, the memory of invasion was still fresh, and France made security the focal point of international relations.

THE FRENCH ALLIANCE SYSTEM. To France security came to mean not only protection from invasion, but the maintenance of all the peace settlements, for they seemed to be the sole guarantee of the stability of Europe. The eastern frontiers of Germany were nearly as important to France as the western and, never having great confidence in the League, France attempted to insure her position by a two-fold policy.[13] First she tried to build up her strength (*garanties physiques*) by a request for the Rhineland, insistence on a large French military and naval establishment, and somewhat later by a strong system of fortifications—the Maginot line. She also tried to bolster her strength by a policy of alliances and friendships (*garanties supplémentaires*). In 1919 she negotiated treaties with Great Britain and the United States, which promised their assistance in the event of unprovoked aggression by Germany. Although these treaties never went into effect because the United States Senate refused its consent, they indicated an early reluctance on the part of France to rely on the security system of the League. As time passed some of the Allies began to see advantages in altering certain provisions of the peace settlement, but found France stubbornly insisting on the sacredness of the settlement of 1919.

[13] Arnold Wolfers: *Britain and France between Two Wars* (New York, 1940), pp. 22 ff.

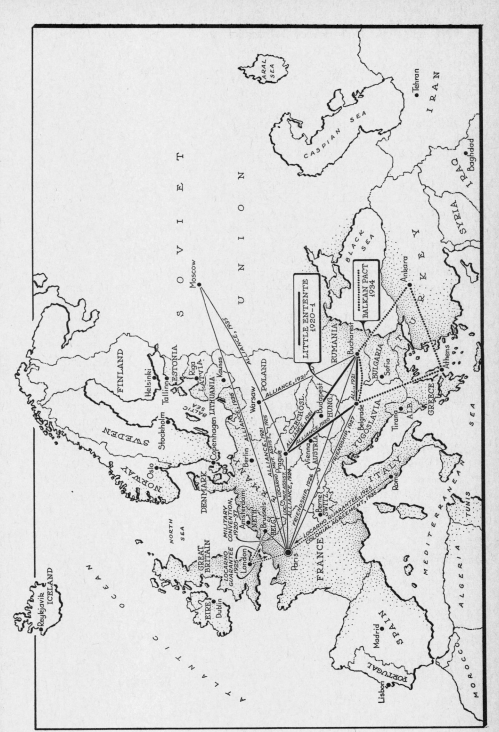

CHART III *The French Alliance System Between the Wars*

Although this policy tended to weaken the wartime coalition, the old friendship remained, and it was considered that the British and Italian guarantee of the Locarno Pact (1925) was more for the protection of France than of Germany. The United States, on the other hand, tended to withdraw from active participation in the political affairs of the continent.

The agreements, under a variety of titles, which France concluded with many continental states, taken together came to constitute the postwar French security system. Usually their stated object was the maintenance of the peace treaties with specific reference to certain problems. Thus the French-Czechoslovakian Treaty of Alliance and Friendship of January 25, 1924, had clauses specifically directed against the union of Austria and Germany and the possible restoration of the Hohenzollern dynasty in Germany. All, of course, were cast as defensive agreements.

The first agreement made was in the nature of a military convention between Belgium and France, signed on September 7, 1920 (see chart, p. 173). Only the exchange of letters approving the agreement, not the Convention itself, was registered with the League. Belgium on the whole co-operated closely with France in the next years and was associated with her in the Locarno Pact. The cornerstone of the whole French system, however, was the alliance with Poland of February 19, 1921, which was reaffirmed by the Locarno Treaty of Mutual Assistance. By this alliance Poland took the place that Russia had occupied before 1914 as the ally of France on Germany's eastern flank. Poland itself was allied to Rumania.

France early became a supporter of the Little Entente. The treaties that bound Czechoslovakia, Yugoslavia, and Rumania together have already been discussed [see above, pp. 121–22]. Although these treaties were aimed particularly at the maintenance of the Treaties of Trianon and Neuilly, they were important in regard to all Central European problems. France now established direct ties with each of the Little Entente states. She concluded a Treaty of Alliance and Friendship with Czechoslovakia on January 25, 1924, and confirmed it at the time of Locarno with a Treaty of Mutual Assistance. A Treaty of Friendship was concluded with Rumania on January 10, 1926, and with Yugoslavia on November 11, 1927.

France thus attached to herself a group of powers some of whom were technically only "friends" but actually might well be called "allies." To Belgium, Poland, Czechoslovakia, Rumania, and Yugoslavia, France granted financial and military assistance. Not only did this group come to have military predominance in Europe, but through their co-operation they held a commanding position in the League of Nations. They were in a position to impose their idea of security upon the League. The French Alliance System constituted a dominant bloc within Europe, and there was in the twenties no combination which attempted to balance it in power. Great Britain and the United States continued to maintain a friendly attitude toward their wartime associate. Russia's efforts to establish friendship with Germany and China were only partially successful, and she remained isolated until the thirties.

THE ITALIAN BLOC. Italy alone gradually assumed a more unfriendly attitude. It is true that Italy and France agreed in opposing the union of Austria with Germany, but Italy resented French dominance in Central Europe and the Balkans. In 1926 Italy concluded a pact with Albania which became an alliance the following year, and, more important, signed a Treaty of Friendship with Hungary in 1927. By this treaty Hungary hoped to break through her encirclement by the Little Entente, and Italy, if she wished to make anything out of the agreement, was forced to sponsor the cause of treaty revision. Mussolini, in a speech before the Italian Senate in June, 1928, came out openly for revision of the treaties. Mussolini thus opened a wide breach between Italy and the states of the Little Entente. The latter, he seemed to imply, were simply the tools of a reactionary France.

Although it never brought great results, Italy with some fanfare established connections with a second defeated state when she concluded a treaty of neutrality, conciliation, and judicial settlement with Turkey in 1928. A similar treaty was even signed with Greece that same year. In 1930 Italy concluded with Austria, another former enemy, a Treaty of Friendship that, at least for a period, had real significance. The Italians established ties with a fourth defeated state when King Boris of Bulgaria married Princess Giovanna of the House of Savoy on October 25, 1930. Italy climaxed her alliance system by establishing intimate connections with Germany, the most important of all the defeated states, some years later. Thus the treaties of alliance which France had negotiated with the powers of Central Europe in the hope of assuring security and the maintenance of the peace treaties slowly engendered a counteralliance system which came to stand for revision of the treaties.

The search for security in the twenties failed. It was not found in the League, nor in disarmament, nor in alliances. No one can tabulate the reasons. Certainly the lost cause that had the greatest prospects of achieving the desired end was the League of Nations and its kindred agencies. That most states still saw their chief safeguard of security in armaments and alliances is evidence of how the weight of the past burdens the future.

CHAPTER

7

The Soviet Union, 1917-28

The Revolution: *March Revolution; November Revolution; Civil War and Intervention; Victory of the Bolsheviks.*

Ideology of the Soviet State: *Political Heritage; Marxism; Leninism; Third International.*

From War Communism to NEP: *Seizure of the Commanding Heights; Disposition of the Land; The Process of Nationalization; New Economic Policy.*

Institutions and Policies: *Constitution of 1924; Communist Party; Social Changes; Postponement of World Revolution.*

The Revolution

THE REVOLUTION that swept Russia in 1917 was among the most fateful political consequences of the World War, and it had a lasting impact on the European scene. To some, including the Bolsheviks themselves, it was a turning point in history similar in magnitude to the French Revolution of 1789, and was destined to usher in a new era in which poverty and war would not be known. To others it was an evil cancerous growth on the European body politic, to be excised if possible by military surgery or at least to be confined to the frontiers of Russia. While the former view was kept alive by the Communist party in Russia, most of the world came to adopt a more moderate interpretation of this important event. The significance of the Russian revolution was acknowledged, in so far as it was a serious attempt to build a modern industrial state on the ruins of a dynastic empire. At the same time, the character of the Bolshevik regime, and the methods it used to achieve its ends, were recognized as peculiar to the traditions and problems of the Russian political heritage. It was thirty or forty years before Soviet Russia, now strikingly different from what the Bolsheviks had dreamed of in 1917, was prepared to offer new ideas and institutions to the rest of the world.

MARCH REVOLUTION. The collapse of the Russian empire in March, 1917, preceding by eight months the more decisive Bolshevik revolution, resulted not from a planned uprising but from the disintegration of the autocratic government of Nicholas II, which had been growing more arbitrary as the strain of the Russian war effort increased. The crucial breakdown came in the distribution of food in the capital city of Petrograd (before 1914, St. Petersburg; after 1924, Leningrad), which led to the outbreak of riots of city workers on March 8, 1917. The government called out the troops, but they mutinied and joined the rioters. By March 14 the disorganization became so great that political leaders in the Duma and outside of it, after some negotiation, formed a Provisional Government in an effort to restore order. Emperor Nicholas, who was at the front, made a vain effort to return to his capital, but found that neither his generals nor his troops were inclined to follow his orders. After negotiating with Rodzyanko, president of the Duma, the Emperor finally abdicated on March 15 in his own name and in that of his son and heir (who was incurably ill) in favor of his brother Grand Duke Michael. Fully aware of the unpopularity of the Romanov family, the Grand Duke decided on the following day not to accept the throne.

During the reign of Nicholas II a number of political parties and movements had developed which offered alternatives to his autocratic regime. These may be divided into two broad groups, designated roughly as liberal and socialist. The liberal group represented the interests of the city middle class and of the landowning gentry, and included the conservative Octobrist party and the somewhat more liberal Constitutional Democrats. The liberal group desired to limit the powers of the emperor by establishing a parliamentary form of government as understood in Western Europe. It favored moderate land reforms and government policies that would permit the development of transportation and industry under a free-enterprise system with the assistance of local capital and foreign loans. The Octobrists and the Constitutional Democrats had predominated in the four Dumas that had met since 1906, but they had never shared the confidence of the emperor. The socialist group included the Socialist Revolutionaries and the Social Democrats, the latter being divided into two wings: the moderate Mensheviks and the extremist Bolsheviks. Their program advocated radical land reforms, and a republican government dominated by workers and peasants which would to a greater or lesser degree control the banks, transportation, and industry. The socialists also differed from the liberals in that they had a well-established tradition of political terrorism and opportunism, which the latter found difficult to combat by parliamentary methods.

With the abdication of Nicholas II, political power passed on March 16 to the Provisional Government, which was dominated by the liberal parties and headed by Prince Lvov, a prominent advocate of parliamentary government. Milyukov, leader of the Constitutional Democrats, was minister of foreign affairs. Guchkov, who headed the Octobrist party, served as minister of war. The one representative of the socialist group in the new cabinet was Kerensky, a Socialist Revolutionary, who after some negotiation was given the post of minister of justice. The Provisional Government proceeded immediately with the announcement of a broad reform program. Autonomous rights were granted to the Finns, Poles, and other minority nationalities. Promises were also made regarding political liberties and land reform. Because of its insistence on constitutional procedure, however, the Provisional Government did not institute these changes immediately but left their final determination to an elective Constituent Assembly. A commission was appointed to draw up plans for the election of this assembly, and it proceeded with its work at a leisurely pace.

Side by side with the Provisional Government there was established in Petrograd a Soviet (council) representing the socialist party organizations headed primarily by middle-class leaders but including also many peasants, workers, and soldiers. The Petrograd Soviet had some three thousand members, but it was in fact controlled by an executive body of twenty-four which took upon itself considerable authority. On its own initiative the Soviet issued decrees, sent out commissions, received petitions, and exercised powers of censorship. A network of Soviets was established in other leading cities, and steps were taken to prevent a counterrevolution. The Soviets set to work immediately creating fighting brigades of workers and peasants, and winning over the regular units of soldiers and sailors stationed around Petrograd and at other important points. They also seized upon the political and economic unrest to advocate a number of policies calculated to win popular support away from the government. At the start the Petrograd Soviet supported the efforts of the Provisional Government to continue the war, but it also acted as a pressure group with the aim of imposing its own program on the government. The socialists were interested in the war only as a defensive measure and favored the renunciation of Russia's war aims. Their principal concern was with domestic affairs and, although they were at first divided and without firm leadership, it soon became clear that in pressing for a socialist republic they would be engaged before long in a bitter struggle with the Provisional Government. The March revolution, while it sought to eradicate the corruption and inefficiency of the old regime, was thus soon followed by civil strife that undermined Russia's contribution to the Allied war effort and within a year led to a separate peace.

The overthrow of the Romanov dynasty had not been a part of the program of the Russian liberal leaders, and they were ill prepared to exercise the political power to which they unexpectedly fell heir. At no time, as a matter of fact, did they possess any more than the outward forms of authority. The bureaucracy through which the Provisional Government had to work was inherited from the old regime, and the new government had few new loyalties to offer in place of the traditional ones that had vanished with the monarchy. Moreover, the principles of parliamentary government based on civil liberties and free economic enterprise—which the liberals professed—had never enjoyed wide support among the Russian people, and they had little appeal in face of the miseries and dislocations brought about by the war. With the army practically in a state of mutiny, and the peasants and workers prepared to satisfy their demands by direct action, the Provisional Government could do little more than issue statements of principle and make appeal to such feelings of patriotism as had survived the disasters of the last several years.

The socialist parties organized in the Petrograd Soviet likewise had been largely unprepared for the collapse of the monarchy. Initially, the Petrograd Soviet was dominated by the Socialist Revolutionaries and the Mensheviks, led respectively by Chernov and Chkheidze. Of the established Bolshevik leaders, Stalin and Kamenev were among the first to appear on the scene after the March revolution; and, of the younger party members, Molotov was in the vanguard. In the middle of April Lenin arrived from Switzerland, with a number of other prominent Bolsheviks. Their return was facilitated by the German General Staff, which hoped thus to encourage an early peace on the eastern front. Trotsky, a socialist but not yet a Bolshevik, returned to Russia in the middle of May and joined Lenin's party a month later.

NOVEMBER REVOLUTION. The duel between the Provisional Government and the Soviets was fought under conditions of great turmoil and confusion. Both groups consisted of loose, and in many respects discordant, political coalitions. Both were faced with a rapidly deteriorating economic and military situation. Under such circumstances, the advantage lay with those who could adjust themselves most rapidly to changing conditions, select the issues most likely to win favor at the moment, and use the military forces available at the right time and place. By both training and character, the socialists were better suited to this type of political struggle than the parties represented in the Provisional Government. Lenin in particular proved to be unsurpassed in adapting means to ends, and it was he and his Bolshevik associates who were responsible for the final victory of the socialists despite the fact that they never enjoyed a majority in the Soviets before November.

The first crisis in the struggle was provided by a Bolshevik demonstration in May against the moderate ministers Milyukov and Guchkov, nominally over the issue of war aims and military discipline. The two ministers resigned because of differences of opinion within the government, and Kerensky—who now represented the more moderate elements of the Soviets in support of the cabinet—was moved to the important post of minister of war. Under his leadership an offensive against the Germans was launched in June, but it failed completely. Taking advantage of this setback, the Bolsheviks tried to seize power in the middle of July without the assistance of the other socialist parties. The attempt failed, and Trotsky was arrested while Lenin fled to Finland. Lvov now resigned as prime minister, and his place was taken by Kerensky. Thus within the brief period between March and July, the most radical member of the Provisional Government had become its head. Within the Soviets a similar movement to the left had occurred, and the struggle between the two groups continued.

The final blow to the Provisional Government came from an effort to save it. General Kornilov, who now commanded the Russian armies and who feared that the Soviets would get control of the government, launched an attack on Petrograd in an effort to dislodge Kerensky and transfer the political leadership to more conservative hands. In self-defense, Kerensky called upon the Soviets for assistance and released the Bolshevik leaders from jail. Even though Kornilov was defeated in September, Kerensky's position was weakened by the fact that the Bolsheviks and their associates had now made themselves indispensable.

The army had been the last bulwark of the Provisional Government, and after the defeat of Kornilov the cabinet headed by Kerensky was an easy target for the Bolsheviks. Despite this fact, the idea of a second revolution did not have the full support of the Socialist Revolutionaries or the Mensheviks, and even among the Bolshevik leaders there was some doubt as to whether the time had yet arrived to take over power. Lenin nevertheless insisted that only if they seized power could the extremists hope to impose their ideas, and he carried the day. On November 6, 1917, well-organized civil and military units seized the government buildings and arrested most of the members of the cabinet. On the following day, at a congress representing Soviets from different parts of the country, the Bolshevik leaders received a vote of confidence, although their action did not have the approval of the moderate socialists. On the same day a council of commissars was set up under Lenin; both Stalin and Trotsky participated in it as prominent members.

In so far as their regime was based on popular support, the Bolsheviks had won it by appealing to the desire for peace on the part of the soldiers and to the economic demands of the peasants and workers. Now that they were in power, they set to work to translate their slogans into concrete policies. On the very first day of the revolution Lenin decreed the distribution of the large estates, and three months later the state took nominal title to all land while leaving it in the hands of those who cultivated it. In succeeding weeks the workers were encouraged to take over the factories, the banks were nationalized, the property of the church was confiscated, and other measures of a similar character were initiated.

The council of commissars was equally active in the political field. Late in November, in implementation of arrangements made earlier by the

LENIN   *The Soviet Prime Minister making a speech in the Red Square, Moscow, on November 7, 1918, the first anniversary of the Bolshevik revolution.*

Provisional Government, elections were held for the Constituent Assembly which was to have worked out the constitutional order for the future Russian state. In these elections the moderate socialists defeated the Bolsheviks by a majority of almost two to one, and when this assembly convened in the middle of January, 1918, it was dissolved by force after its first session. But while they vigorously suppressed groups that showed signs of opposing them, the Bolsheviks also held out advantages to important elements of the population whose support they desired. Thus, only a few days after coming to power, the Bolsheviks issued a Declaration of the Rights of the Peoples of Russia, in which minority groups persecuted before the revolution were promised self-determination and the abolition of national and religious disabilities. Within a few weeks, the abolition of class privileges and the granting of equal rights for women were also announced. In January, 1918, a Declaration of the Rights of the Toiling and Exploited People was issued, making further concessions to the national minority groups.

It was not until July, 1918, that the constitution was announced which set the pattern for the government of what was then called the Russian Socialist Federated Soviet Republic, usually referred to as the RSFSR. This constitution formalized the pyramided system of district, county, provincial, and regional Soviets. At the head of this structure of representative bodies was placed an All-Russian Congress of Soviets, meeting twice a year, which in turn elected an All-Russian Central Executive Committee. This constitution made provision for an electoral system giving the franchise to all citizens over the age of eighteen and weighted in favor of the city workers. The council of commissars, or ministers, was elected by the Central Executive Committee and was responsible to it. Thus the system of government by Soviets, or councils, established informally during the months following the March revolution in 1917, was officially adopted for what was left of the Russian state after the signature of peace with the Central Powers in the spring of 1918. The driving force behind this constitutional structure was provided by Lenin's well-organized Bolsheviks, who, after March, 1918, officially called themselves the Communist party.

CIVIL WAR AND INTERVENTION. The seizure of the government by the Bolsheviks in November, 1917, after the eight stormy months of revolutionary effort, proved to be only the beginning of their struggle for power. They established themselves in the capital and in the principal cities, but, owing to the resistance their policies and methods aroused, it was not until 1921 that they were able to extend their authority over the greater part of the extensive territories of the former Russian Empire. The opposition was never unified or even held together by a single purpose; it consisted principally of two groups: the national minorities, and the rival Russian political movements.

The leaders of the national minorities were motivated by a conviction, bred of many years of oppression, that only under conditions of political independence could they hope to make rapid progress towards a modern society. This attitude on the part of the minority peoples proved to be one of the underlying weaknesses of the old regime, and it became one of the principal concerns of the new. Equally bitter in their opposition to the Bolsheviks, although without the same geographical basis and popular support as the national movements, were their political rivals. Many members of the Tsarist army and bureaucracy, although they had been greatly demoralized by the defeats and gross mismanagement that had characterized the conduct of the war, did not accept the victory of the Bolsheviks—which they regarded as temporary—and immediately began to organize a counterrevolution. Led by generals of the imperial army, the White Russians, as they were called to distinguish them from the "Red" Bolsheviks, established three main centers of opposition—the Ukraine, southern Russia, and Siberia. Lesser fronts in the Baltic provinces and in the Arctic regions of Murmansk and Archangel also occupied the attention of the Bolsheviks. While this opposition was widespread, it was poorly organized and disunited. The aims of the various leaders were as diverse as their geo-

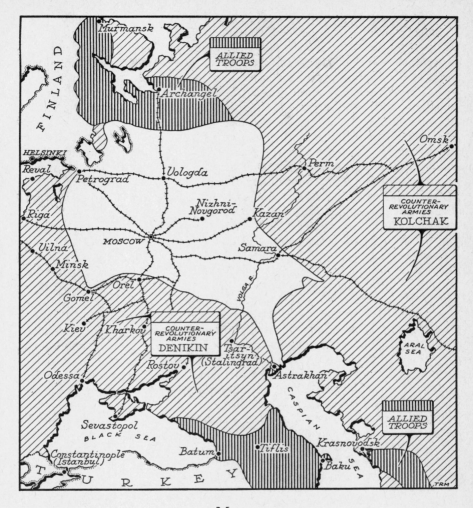

MAP 14

Russian Civil War: Furthest Advance of the Counter-Revolutionary Armies

graphical centers, and the halfhearted aid they later received from the Allies encouraged them to continue the struggle without substantially increasing their fighting capacity. Moreover, in addition to the opposition groups mentioned above, the civil war in all its theaters also had the aspect of a class struggle, with peasants fighting each other as well as their landlords, and with rural areas trying to resist control by the urban organizations of the workers. While all the developments of this bitter struggle cannot be followed here, some idea of the origins of the civil war can be had from a brief survey of its three principal centers.

The nineteenth century had seen the development of an active nationalist movement among the Ukrainian peoples, of whom some 3,000,000 lived in the Eastern Galician province of Austria-Hungary and 25,000,000 in southwestern Russia. On the tenuous foundation of a dialect closely related to Russian, a slender geographical relation to medieval Kievan Russia, existence as a separate administrative district of the early Polish-Lithuanian kingdom, and a brief period of autonomy under the Cossacks in the seventeenth century, the Ukrainian nationalists had built up a movement of considerable proportions by the end of the nineteenth century. Suppressed in its natural Russian centers of Kiev and Kharkov, this movement had found a more hospitable home in Lwow (Lemberg), capital of Austrian Eastern Galicia. With the disintegration of the Russian empire in 1917, the Ukrainian nationalists were prepared to organize an autonomous or independent state and to this end to play off the Germans and White Russians against the Bolsheviks.

Receiving the cautious approval of the Provisional Government, the Ukrainian nationalists established a Rada, or assembly, which gradually increased its authority as the government in Petrograd lost control of the situation. In the course of the struggle between the Germans and the Bolsheviks, the Rada proclaimed Ukrainian independence in Kiev in January, 1918. The Ukraine now signed a separate peace with the Central Powers, and the new state, headed by the conservative Cossack General Skoropadsky, was launched on its precarious existence with German support.

In Southern Russia, the Cossacks in the Black Sea region, and the peoples of Georgia, Armenia, and Azerbaijan in the Caucasus, were also in a state of unrest after the liberal revolution in the spring of 1917. It was in this region, in the lower reaches of the Don river, that the leaders of the imperial army assembled in the last weeks of 1917. First under General Kornilov, and later under General Denikin, they organized a volunteer army. In 1918 this force presented a common front against the Bolsheviks with the Ukraine on its left flank and, on its right, the peoples of Georgia, Armenia, and Azerbaijan, who had now declared their independence.

Until the defeat of Germany by the Allies in November, 1918, the position of the Cossacks and the White Russians in southern Russia was relatively stable. They did not make serious inroads into Soviet-controlled territory, but in the main the White Russians held the areas that served as the base of their operations and provided them with such food, equipment, and manpower as they were able to scrape together. For the Bolsheviks, this was a period of organization and training for the great effort to follow. Under the unified leadership of Trotsky, the Red Army had many advantages over the opposition. Apart from holding the inner lines of communication and possessing the bulk of the war industries of the old regime, the Bolsheviks also kept in the regular army by one means or another a considerable portion of the former imperial officers. By the end of 1918 Trotsky was able to organize an army of almost half a million men. In addition to its material strength, the Red Army also had powerful weapons

TROTSKY *Leon Trotsky (center), People's Commissar for War, reviewing the Red Army during the Russian Civil War.*

of propaganda to use in undermining the positions of its enemies. The mere encouragement of the peasants to seize the land, for instance, won the Bolsheviks many supporters in the areas controlled by the White Russians.

In Siberia, a variety of civil and military forces were active in 1917–18. One of the most important was the Czechoslovak legion of some 40,000 prisoners of war captured by Russia from the Austrian army. This force was now established as an independent army under the direction of the Czech nationalist movement in the West. There was also a government formed in Omsk primarily by the Socialist Revolutionary leaders who opposed the Bolsheviks. This government was soon overthrown by a more conservative regime headed by Admiral Kolchak.

It was in connection with these events in Siberia that the former Emperor Nicholas II and his family were executed. In August, 1917, they had been removed from the vicinity of Petrograd because of the proximity of the fighting, and after several changes of residence they were sent to the town of Ekaterinburg (later renamed Sverdlovsk) in the Ural mountains. Here they were under the custody of the local Bolshevik authorities and, when the town was threatened by anti-Bolshevik forces in July, 1918, the Emperor and his wife, children, and immediate entourage were shot for fear lest they be captured by the Whites. The execution took place without trial, although it later received the approval of the Soviet officials in Moscow.

In the first year after the Bolshevik revolution, Allied policy was based on two assumptions: that the Bolsheviks were in a conspiracy with the Germans and had brought Russia over to the side of the Central Powers, and that the power of the new regime was based on weak foundations and would soon collapse. The first assumption led to a desire to bolster the eastern front by sending aid to any group which would continue to fight the Germans. It also led to a move to occupy the principal Russian seaports where the Allies had been building up stocks of war supplies, to prevent them from falling into German hands. The belief that the Bolshevik regime was bound to be temporary, on the other hand, led to the establishment of relations with the various White governments. As 1918 passed into 1919 and 1920, the fallacy of these initial assumptions became apparent, and the Allied forces of occupation were gradually withdrawn. At the same time a new motive came to the fore, namely the fear of the spread of Bolshevism into Eastern and Central Europe. In the course of 1919 there was increasing evidence in such countries as Germany, Hungary, and Bulgaria that the extremist forces might be able to establish themselves on a long-term basis. This fear was encouraged by the pronouncements of the newly organized Third International in Moscow, which openly strove to arouse the peoples of Europe against their governments. Of all the attempts at intervention, however, only that of the Japanese in Siberia can be said to have had the purpose of permanently annexing an important part of Russia. None of the other expeditionary forces went prepared to stay, although most of them remained longer than they had originally intended.

The first Allied intervention occurred in North Russia in April, 1918, when a few British troops landed at the ice-free Arctic port of Murmansk. To this port the Russians had in 1917 built a railroad that soon became an important supply center. The British who landed there were joined before long by French, American, and Serbian detachments. At first they co-operated with the Soviet authorities against the Finns and Germans, but by the summer of 1918 the Bolsheviks began to consider the Allied force at Murmansk a source of danger to themselves. In August, the White Sea port of Archangel was also occupied by the Allies.

The Allied expedition to Siberia via the port of Vladivostok was a somewhat larger venture. The idea of striking at the Germans through

Siberia had arisen early in 1917, but the question of finding men and shipping for the venture was a difficult one. While the Japanese were eager to send troops to Siberia, Wilson was opposed to any Allied intervention there. A joint Allied intervention was finally agreed to in July, 1918, on condition that the territorial integrity of Russia would be respected. The ostensible reason for American participation was the guarding of military stores and the evacuation of the Czechs, but the American government was also interested in preventing the establishment of a Japanese sphere of influence in Siberia. Japanese motives were regarded as suspect because, while like the other Allies the Japanese feared the spread of Bolshevism, their principal object was one of aggression. Despite these rivalries among the Allies, the regime eventually established in Siberia by Admiral Kolchak became the principal hope of the White cause. It was generally recognized by the other White regimes, and in 1919 it was represented in Paris by Sazonov, who had served as Russian foreign minister from 1910 to 1916.

The Allied intervention in southern Russia was regulated by an Anglo-French convention concluded in December, 1917, immediately after the Bolshevik revolution. Under this agreement, the region of the Don river and the Caucasus mountains was to be a British sphere, and the Crimea, the Ukraine, and Bessarabia a French sphere. The oil fields of the Caucasus thus went to the British, who already had heavy investments there, while the Ukrainian coal and iron mines, in which French capital was invested, were to be protected by that country. The British occupied their zone immediately after the armistice with Germany and supplied extensive assistance to the White Russian forces under Denikin. The French landed in Odessa in December, 1918, and soon faced the confusion of the overlapping claims to authority of the Ukrainian nationalists, Denikin, and various revolutionary groups. In this venture the French made use of troops and equipment that they moved from Salonika, but the men were too war-weary to take a very active part in operations.

VICTORY OF THE BOLSHEVIKS. The year 1919 was the great turning point in the civil war, marking the time during which the Bolsheviks converted a possible defeat into a certain victory. Taking advantage of their shorter lines of communication and their unified command, the Bolsheviks strained every effort to secure a decisive military position. Under Trotsky's direction, the Red Army grew to 3,000,000 during 1919, and despite many desertions and widespread civil strife within the areas it controlled, it accomplished its purpose with great vigor. At the height of the civil war the Bolsheviks had as many as sixteen armies in the field at the same time, and Trotsky traveled from one front to another in an armored train with his advisers. While a shadow has been cast over Trotsky's career in recent years as a result of differences within the Communist party, most foreign observers at that time and since have shared the view that his organizing ability was an important factor in the Bolshevik victory.

The small Allied forces at Murmansk and Archangel in North Russia were the first to be withdrawn. They had assisted in the establishment of a

White Government of Northern Russia, in the hope that it might eventually be joined with the White regime in Siberia to form a continuous front against the Bolsheviks. This action represented a diversion of the original intent of the expedition, and public opinion in the Allied countries strongly favored the withdrawal of these forces. A definite decision to withdraw was made in the summer of 1919, and by October all Allied forces had been evacuated. Without the Allies, the Whites were unable to resist the Bolsheviks more than a few weeks, and in January, 1920, the entire region was in the hands of the Soviet government.

The White regime in Siberia, in which the Allies had for a while placed such great hopes, was defeated a few months later. With the Trans-Siberian railroad in the hands of the friendly Czech Army, and with the assistance of the Allied military forces, Admiral Kolchak made substantial headway in the winter and spring of 1918–19 as the head of the White Russian armies in Siberia. Admiral Kolchak was a moderate and patriotic Russian, but he was a poor administrator and had had little experience with land warfare. At the same time, he had great difficulty in getting along with the Japanese, American, and other foreign groups under his jurisdiction, who were constantly at odds with each other and whose points of view he did not understand. A vigorous Bolshevik offensive developed in the summer of 1919 and overran the Ural region, and in November the capital of Kolchak's regime at Omsk was captured. Shortly thereafter Kolchak himself fell into enemy hands and was shot. The various Allied groups now made haste to leave Siberia, and the long railroad line leading to Vladivostok was so crowded that many of the less fortunate refugees died from hunger and cold. The American forces under General Graves withdrew in the spring of 1920, having irritated the other Allies and the White Russians by their lack of enthusiasm for the venture. Only the Japanese stayed on for a longer period, hoping through the support of local White leaders to carve out a sphere of influence for themselves. They too finally withdrew from Vladivostok in October, 1922, and full Soviet sovereignty was established over the whole of Siberia.

Of all the territories from which the Bolsheviks finally drove out their enemies, the Ukraine undoubtedly had the most turbulent and exhausting experience. With the defeat of Germany in the West, the German occupation forces—which had given the Ukraine a warmly hated although relatively stable regime—withdrew. The government of Skoropadsky, which the Germans had sponsored, fell at the same time. The Ukraine was now at the mercy of a variety of conflicting groups that proceeded to fight a bloody series of battles on its territory. The rival bands of peasant anarchists under Petlyura and Makhno, reflecting the pent-up passions and prejudices of the oppressed agrarian population and yet opposed to Soviet rule, were active throughout 1919 and committed many outrages. Denikin's Whites also attempted to extend their sway over the Ukraine and for a brief period held Kiev. The French intervention force that arrived shortly after the armistice with Germany was never strong enough in material power or in morale to exert any great influence on developments in the Ukraine; by the spring of 1919 the French understood that nothing could be accomplished and withdrew their force of some 70,000 men from Odessa.

The British, like the French, were under pressure from domestic public opinion to send their soldiers home, and at the same time they became increasingly impressed by the poor prospects which intervention offered. They therefore withdrew from the Caucasus region in the summer of 1919 and left Denikin in southern Russia to his own devices. The latter had, in fact, launched a successful campaign against the Bolsheviks in 1919 and by the end of the summer, after capturing Kiev and Kharkov, he advanced to within two hundred miles of Moscow. This effort exhausted his power, and in the spring of 1920 Denikin suffered a complete rout. The command of the White armies in southern Russia now passed to General Wrangel, who made extensive gains in the summer of 1920 fighting from his bases in the Crimea. He too was defeated, however, and in November, 1920, the last White Russian armies were evacuated from the Black Sea ports under his command. The Red Army had in the meantime occupied the Caucasus region and by the end of 1920 had established full control over southern Russia.

A dramatic aftermath of the defeat of the White Russians was provided by the escape of about a million refugees from Russia. Of these, some 400,000 finally settled in France; the Balkans, Germany, Poland, and China made homes for over 100,000 each. In these countries the Russians found jobs ranging from those of common laborers to positions as scholars and businessmen, awaiting the day when they could return to their homeland. As the years passed and the Soviet regime showed no signs of collapsing, the older refugees gradually settled down to a way of life which was made to resemble as much as possible that of prerevolutionary Russia. For the younger generation, many of whom could scarcely remember the old regime, this type of existence had little to offer. They were assimilated by the countries of their adoption and eventually retained little that was Russian except their names.

Ideology of the Soviet State

POLITICAL HERITAGE. In considering the character of the state established in Russia after World War I, it is important to remember that Russia had never known other than an authoritarian form of government, or one dominated by a very small oligarchy. As early as the reign of Peter the Great (1682–1725), the Russian state had many of the characteristics that are associated today with the Soviet regime. Not only was the emperor accepted as the supreme authority in all political matters, but the sovereign exercised the right to compel service to the state on the part of all Russian citizens, including the landed gentry. Under Peter, the Russian state participated actively in industrial production, the colonization of the eastern lands, public works and communications, and domestic and foreign trade, in addition to dispensing justice, maintaining order, and caring for the security of the state. All of this activity required a sizable administrative staff, which was firmly centralized under the direction of the emperor himself.

A number of circumstances explain this tendency toward a centralized and authoritarian system of government in Russia. Russian political development had undoubtedly been molded to a considerable degree by the constant preoccupation with the conquest, organization, and defense of the great land mass which constitutes present-day Russia. The Russians may be said to have regarded this task as their "manifest destiny." It involved not only innumerable wars against Mongols, Turks, Poles, Lithuanians, Swedes, and Germans, but also a constant search for a stable frontier and for warm-water ports permitting Russia to trade freely with the outside world. It was not until the end of the eighteenth century that the western land and water frontiers of Russia were stabilized. The great effort this required helps to explain the traditionally centralized and militarized character of the Russian state.

Russia's agrarian economy must also be considered, apart from her preoccupation with problems of conquest and defense, when seeking an explanation for her authoritarian tradition. In 1800, some 95 per cent of the people were peasant serfs, while 4 per cent were townspeople and 1 per cent were landed gentry. As late as the revolution of 1917 some 80 per cent of the population lived on the land—about the same proportion as in France in 1789. The great mass of peasants, who remained serfs until 1861, had no opportunity to participate in the political life of Russia. Moreover, illiteracy on the eve of World War I was only a little under 60 per cent for Russia as a whole and somewhat higher among the peasantry. To the difficulty of introducing representative government in a country so largely agrarian in character was added the circumstance that most of the foreign influences that had made themselves felt in Russia were of an autocratic character. The Byzantine Empire, for example, which had exerted such a great influence on medieval Russia, transmitted to it highly autocratic political traditions. Likewise the Mongols, who ruled Russia from the thirteenth to the fifteenth centuries, stimulated the centralizing and militarizing tendencies in Russia. Thus, while Western Europe was experiencing the Renaissance, the Reformation, and the Counter Reformation—with all that they meant to Europe in the spread of knowledge, the development of new political forms, and the greater understanding of the relationship of man and society—the Russians were preoccupied with a much more elemental struggle for the liberation and unification of their principalities.

For these many reasons the political traditions of Russia differed considerably—in degree if not in kind—from those of Western Europe, and little experience was gained in representative government. Not until 1906 did Russia have a national assembly representing more than a small oligarchy. The assembly established in that year was elected on a broad franchise, although by an indirect system of voting. The emperor retained a veto on legislation, and cabinet ministers were responsible to him and not to the assembly. Within a year the franchise was again restricted and the government largely freed itself from serious interference on the part of the assembly. Under these circumstances, it is not difficult to visualize the enormous handicaps under which the Provisional Government labored in 1917 when it tried to apply liberal democratic methods in the midst of the wartime crisis, or by contrast the relative ease with which the authoritarian institutions favored by the Bolsheviks could be established.

Side by side with the authoritarian political institutions in Russia, and in many respects functioning as their inevitable corollary, was the tradition of revolutionary action on the part of those opposed to the government. Under a system in which it was difficult to criticize the government openly, it was not unnatural that political reformers should turn to revolutionary methods. Apart from peasant uprisings, which fall into a somewhat different category, the first effort to overthrow the central government was made in 1825 by a group of young members of the gentry who had come into contact with Western ideas during the Napoleonic wars. This attempt failed miserably and was followed by a period of reactionary government under Nicholas I, but Russia continued to be an active center of revolutionary thought. While a writer like Herzen might be regarded as nothing more than an advanced liberal in Western Europe, Bakunin was a leader of the anarchist movement and advocated the most extreme measures for the destruction of governmental authority. Thus, before the middle of the nineteenth century the Russian revolutionary tradition contained elements both of radical social doctrines and of extremist political methods. The former trend is exemplified by the Nihilists, the Populists, and the Social Democratic party. The ruthless and opportunistic methods advocated by Bakunin and his disciple Nechaev found expression in the People's Will society, which organized the assassination of Alexander II in 1881; and in the organization known as the St. Petersburg Terrorists, one of the leaders of which was Lenin's elder brother, executed by the government in 1887. The various Russian revolutionary groups drew their inspiration from many sources and were divided by many controversies as to doctrine and method. Of the frankly revolutionary organizations which survived into the twentieth century and participated actively in the events of 1917, the Socialist Revolutionaries and the Social Democrats were the most important. The former, interested primarily in a radical solution of the peasant question, was led by such men as Chernov and Kerensky and probably had the deeper roots in Russian political soil. The Social Democrats, on the other hand, had a more imposing ideology and a leadership prepared, in the Russian revolutionary tradition, to make use of any means necessary to attain their goal.

MARXISM. For almost two centuries before the Bolshevik revolution, progressive Russian opinion had been combing the resources of Western political thought for ideological and theoretical assistance in its struggle to supplant the semifeudal autocracy of the Romanov dynasty with a system better suited to the needs of the Russian people. During this process almost every prominent school of European thought found its Russian adherents at one time or another: the French *philosophes,* the German Idealists, the Utopian Socialists, and the English Liberals, to mention only a few. These systems of Western thought all exerted some influence on the Russian autocracy, but they never succeeded in supplanting it. They all assumed the existence of a strong middle class, which Russia did not possess, and until 1917 they constituted no more than minority efforts to apply the conclusions of Western theory to the problems peculiar to Russia. Only Marxism relied on a highly centralized state for the initiative in social change. This circumstance goes a long way to explain why Marxism was the first Western social doctrine to be fully applied in Russia despite the many contradictions between Marx's assumptions and the Russian reality.

Marxism offered not only a plausible explanation of the economic and social inequities of society, but also a specific cure for these ills within the framework of a challenging philosophy of history. Starting with the theory that the value of a commodity is proportional to the amount of labor required to produce it, Marx argued that under the capitalist system the worker does not receive a fair share of the income derived from selling the commodity. The surplus value, or the difference between the market price of a commodity and the value of labor required to produce it, is kept by the employer who, according to Marx, consequently exploits the worker. The employers who own the means of production are thus able to accumulate capital, and hence Marx predicted that a great growth would occur in large-scale business enterprises. This actually did take place, but Marx made a further prediction that has not been borne out by experience: namely, that in the course of time the economic status of the workers would greatly deteriorate in relation to that of the employers.

While many aspects of Marx's analysis of capitalism have since been shown to be inaccurate, he incorporated his analysis in a broad interpretation of society which has had great influence on subsequent thinkers. His study of the society of his own time led him to the conviction that under capitalism two classes were engaged in a struggle for the control of the means of production: the working class, or the proletariat, and the middle class of employers, or the bourgeoisie. This class struggle he believed to be merely a continuation of an age-old conflict between exploiters and exploited which for him provided the key to the understanding of historical development. Adapting the work of such leaders of Western thought as Hegel and Feuerbach, Marx and his colleague Engels elaborated the system known to philosophers as dialectical materialism. This system offers both an explanation of historical change and an economic interpretation of society. Marx's dialectic explains history in terms of the clash of opposing economic classes which, according to him, has occurred at each stage of history, and of the syntheses or resolutions of the conflicts which have emerged from these clashes. Since each new synthesis eventually develops its own conflicts, society is in a state of constant change. Thus in ancient times slaveholder and slave were engaged in a bitter struggle, while in the feudal period landlord was pitted against serf.

According to Marx, the conflict between the bourgeoisie and the proletariat, which he saw going on around him in the nineteenth century, was bound to end in the seizure of the means of production by the workers themselves and in the common ownership of all means of production. Once this occurred, Marx believed, the dialectical process of change through conflict would come to an end, since with the emergence of the proletariat in the dual capacity of owner and worker there would be only one class and hence no further class struggle. Marx's system also held that all social and political institutions—while subject to human will, chance, geographical environment, great personalities, and many other factors— were in the last analysis determined at any given stage in history by the relations of men engaged in production. In primitive times, according to this theory, the exigencies of hunting and fishing determined the character of social and political institutions. In the classical period, when the slaveholder owned both the worker and the means of production, these institutions reflected the requirements of the agriculture, handicrafts, and trade of the time. Production under feudalism, when the serf was partly free and the techniques of agriculture and industry were on a considerably higher level, necessarily required quite different institutions and beliefs from those prevalent during classical times. Under capitalism, finally, when workers are personally free but, according to Marx, do not receive the full benefits of their labor, institutions are molded by the demands of large-scale industry and mechanized labor producing under the free enterprise system. Since Marx believed that in each stage of history the prevalent social and political institutions reflected the interests of the dominant class, he predicted that only after the establishment of full-fledged communism would it be possible to have institutions adapted to the needs of the vast majority that constituted the working class.

Communism then, in Marx's view, was the goal toward which mankind was of necessity moving. Yet while this trend was assumed to be inevitable, Marx believed that the organization of the workers into a political party for the purpose of seizing power would hasten the process of change. Once the government, an instrument of the bourgeois class, was in the hands of the proletariat, a dictatorship would have to be established to rule the new society until all vestiges of capitalism had been destroyed. In the Communist Manifesto, published in 1848, Marx therefore proclaimed the slogan "Workingmen of all countries, unite!" and insisted that their freedom could be obtained "only by the forcible overthrow of all existing social conditions."

The teachings of Marx, elaborated by his colleague Engels, were widely read and discussed in the latter part of the nineteenth century and influenced a variety of people and groups. The inaccuracies and flaws that characterize both the analysis of capitalism and the system of dialectical materialism prevented the great majority of scholars and thinkers from accepting Marx's theories without reservations. Of the various aspects of Marx's system, only the economic interpretation of history can be said to have been generally accepted, and this only in a greatly modified form. A number of political leaders, nevertheless, accepted Marxism more or less literally, and by the end of the nineteenth century practically every country in Europe had an active Social Democratic party that participated in politics and worked for the establishment of socialism. The Marxist group in Russia, formed in 1882 and established formally as the Social Democratic party in 1898, was in close touch with the socialists of Western Europe and in general followed a parallel line of development. However, one of its leaders, Vladimir Ilich Ulianov, better known by his revolutionary name of Lenin, was opposed to this evolutionary trend. Starting with a small following in 1903, he became the dominant force among Russian Marxists in 1917 and shortly thereafter he and his followers were ruling the whole of Russia.

LENINISM. That the first socialist state should have been established in Russia, a relatively backward country in regard to capitalist development, is not as surprising as it may seem at first. As early as the middle of the nineteenth century, the revolutionary Herzen had observed that the very weakness of capitalism in Russia would make the introduction of socialism just that much easier. The relative weakness of the Russian middle class, which was well demonstrated by the irresolute policies of the Provisional Government in 1917, was not the only advantage which the Marxist leaders had in Russia. There was also a greater disparity than in Western Europe between the small number of large industrial enterprises and agricultural estates and the large mass of peasants and workers living in poverty. This contrast between the wealth of the few and the poverty of the many, which was always commented on by foreign observers in Russia during the generation before World War I, was greatly increased by the deterioration of the Russian economy during the war itself. Moreover, Russia was the one major country in Europe in which the proletarian dictatorship required by the Marxist doctrines could be introduced without a serious break in the political traditions of the country. In Western Europe the practice of parliamentary government had by and large been sufficiently well established at the beginning of the twentieth century to make a return to authoritarian methods seem reactionary in theory and difficult in practice. In Russia, by contrast, the great majority of the people normally looked to the government for leadership. The dictatorship established by the Bolsheviks, while more ruthless than that which Russia had known under Tsarism, was nevertheless in a tradition which the Russian people understood.

Despite these various ways in which Marxism was appropriate to conditions in Russia, it is doubtful whether the Bolsheviks would have succeeded as they did, had it not been for the leadership provided by Lenin. Born in 1870 of a middle-class family, Lenin was strongly influenced by the execution of his elder brother in 1887 and devoted himself to the study of socialism from his youth. Before the end of the century he was recognized by the Marxists of St. Petersburg as an up-and-coming revolutionary. Lenin will probably be remembered in history chiefly as the tactician of the Bolshevik revolution of 1917 and of the consolidation of Soviet power, but he was also a theoretician of note. In the field of general socialist theory he is best known for his interpretation of imperialism as the highest stage of capitalism, in which he carried a step further the teachings of Marx and Engels. The age of imperialism, by which Lenin meant the years between 1871 and 1914, he characterized as a period in which capital had ceased to obtain a sufficient return in the principal industrial states and had gone out into the less developed parts of the world in search of new markets and cheaper labor and raw materials. By this means Lenin explained the active competition for colonies on the part of the great powers in the Near East, Asia, and Africa. This competition for markets, Lenin claimed, led inevitably to the World War that broke out in 1914. On the basis of this analysis Lenin predicted that World War I would mark the end of the capitalistic system, which would be uprooted by a series of socialist revolutions all over Europe. While this did not in fact occur, the belief in the imminent spread of the revolutionary movement was a powerful factor in encouraging the Bolsheviks in the difficult years between 1917 and 1921.

More immediately connected with the Bolshevik victory in Russia were Lenin's views regarding the organization of the revolutionary party and the timing of the proletarian revolution. The central issue—whether the Russian Social Democratic party should aim at wide membership among the working classes, like the socialist parties in Western Europe, or should be a small and compact revolutionary group prepared to impose a proletarian dictatorship—came up at the party congress held in London in 1903. Lenin led the fight for a small party of revolutionary leaders, and since he won a majority support in these debates his faction came to be known as the Bolsheviks, from the Russian word for majority. The Mensheviks, or minority group, led by Martov, agreed with Lenin on most general issues of policy but interpreted Marx's writings to mean that the socialist ideology should be a natural growth among the workers as a class. Despite Lenin's victory in London in 1903, the Bolsheviks soon lost their majority in the Social Democratic party and it was not until the late summer of 1917 that they again assumed the leadership in party decisions.

While Lenin's interpretation of imperialism may be regarded as an extension of Marx's system, most students agree that his views on the timing of the proletarian revolution in Russia represent a departure from Marxism. Most Marxists, and for that matter most Bolsheviks, believed that the proletarian revolution could not occur until the bourgeois state had reached a high stage of development. Since the Provisional Government marked the start of middle-class rule in Russia, most socialists in 1917 were prepared for a long period of political activity under the bourgeois regime. Although Lenin until the eve of the revolution had held similar views, he soon perceived the weakness of the Provisional Government and by dint of persistent argument won his followers over to the idea of an immediate revolution. In adopting this course, Lenin substituted the dictatorship of the proletariat for the more gradual political education of the working class under a bourgeois government which Marxist theorists had hitherto considered inevitable. This idea of the dictatorship of the proletariat was developed by Lenin in his *State and Revolution* (1918). It envisaged a transitional period of indefinite duration during which the newly established proletarian state would ruthlessly employ all power available to it for the purpose of crushing domestic opposition. No pretense of political democracy would be made, and only at a much later date, after it had trained the masses in the way of communism, would the dictatorship be relaxed. The Bolsheviks were thus acting on the basis of a carefully rationalized theory when they seized power in November, 1917, dissolved the newly elected Constituent Assembly two months later, and decreed a broad program of socialist measures.

THE THIRD INTERNATIONAL. One factor which influenced the relations of the Bolshevik regime with the Allies and the border states throughout the latter part of the civil war was the persistent Russian effort to promote revolutions. Just as all the decisions of the Western states were colored by their mistaken belief that the Bolshevik regime could not survive for many months, so the new Soviet government made many concessions in the expectation that revolution would soon engulf Europe. Especially in Germany, the collapse of the army and navy had been accompanied by considerable extremist sentiment. The Western leaders themselves were acutely aware of the opportunities for revolutionary activity which the economic instability of the immediate postwar period offered, and this possibility strongly colored their attitude toward the Soviet state.

Under these circumstances, the Soviet leaders might have adopted a policy of lulling the apprehensions of the West and thus obtaining from them more favorable treatment. Instead, and this was typical of Lenin's aggressive tactics, Moscow decided to proclaim the world revolution immediately and to encourage the Communist parties all over the world to seize power as soon as possible. To this end a conference was held in Moscow of representatives of many foreign Communist parties, and in March, 1919, the Third, or Communist, International was founded. Following in the footsteps of the First International (1864–76), founded by Marx, and of the Second International (founded in 1889), which had become a loose federation of nationally-conscious socialist parties, the new organization set out to provide a central direction for workers' movements outside of Russia. The Communist International not only was founded in Moscow, but also bore the stamp of the Russian interpretation of Marxist doctrine. Although the Bolsheviks had until 1917 played only a secondary role in the European revolutionary movement, they now became its directing force. The effort was thus made to apply on an international scale the tactics that had brought the Bolsheviks to power in Russia, despite the different conditions existing in Western Europe. The success of the Russian revolution also presented the Communist International with another problem, which was to remain with it for the next generation. This was the fact that, as the giant among Communist parties, the Bolsheviks tended to dominate the International and to give it the appearance of being an arm of Russian policy rather than an international movement without any national bias. This was strongly resented by many leftists who might otherwise have been loyal followers of the movement, and it proved to be a major handicap to the efforts of the International all over the world.

Nevertheless, the International was born amidst great fanfare, and the prospects for its success seemed good in 1919. That proved to be the last good year for revolutions, however, and the Communist uprisings that broke out in Berlin, Munich, and Budapest all died an early death. A second conference of the International met in Moscow in 1920 with representatives from thirty-nine countries, and rules were drawn up to increase the revolutionary discipline of the movement. A direct outcome of this conference was the "First Congress of Peoples of the East," held in Baku in September, 1920, in which the effort was made to arouse the national self-consciousness of the Asians, as a first step toward revolution. Apart from increasing the determination of the Western States to make no concessions to the Bolsheviks, these activities had no marked effect on the European situation. It was only twenty-five years later, and as a result of very different circumstances, that the first state beyond the borders of Russia got a Communist government.

From War Communism to NEP

SEIZURE OF THE COMMANDING HEIGHTS. The period of crisis between the assumption of power by the Bolsheviks and the final consolidation of their authority over the entire territory of Russia was no time for the systematic implementation of the untried Marxist theories that guided the Communists in their general policy. At the same time, the chaos of the civil war period offered a unique opportunity to destroy some of the fundamental institutions of imperial Russia, such as large estates and private ownership of industry, and thus to clear the way for the changes the Communists planned to introduce. Moreover, for purely political purposes the Bolsheviks were eager to let the peasants seize the land and the workers take over the factories. The propaganda that had given them such success during the war had been based on this program, and to have proceeded immediately with the construction of a state-controlled economic system, even if the Bolsheviks had had the power to do so at the time, would have lost them the support of their largest following.

This delay in organizing a socialist state along Marxist lines was further necessitated by other practical considerations. The Bolsheviks were as yet relatively few in number, yet they required for their success the smooth functioning of industry, agriculture, and banking. Just as the Red Army

would have had a far more difficult time of it in the civil war if a large
number of former imperial officers had not been available to command the
troops, so in the economic field it was necessary to retain the services of
the great body of technicians without whom the system could not be operated. Furthermore, the Bolsheviks did not yet have a definitive economic
blue-print for society, and in their theoretical discussions they had assumed
that a period of experimentation would be necessary before they could devise in practice the institutions appropriate to their Marxist principles.
Lenin therefore elaborated a transitional program in which the aim of the
Bolsheviks was to seize the "commanding heights" of the old system—the
larger banks, the heavy industry, the principal means of communication,
and the large estates—while retaining the old administrative personnel.

As it turned out, no such smooth transition was possible during the
civil war and instead a series of measures were taken which have come to
be known as "war communism." The commanding heights were indeed
seized, but production declined rapidly in the midst of the conflict, and
the government had to adopt a policy of wholesale nationalization in an
effort to arrest the economic disintegration. In the end, the inflation of
currency and the decline of agriculture and of industrial output were so
great that the government's efforts amounted to no more than emergency
measures, and by the end of the civil war period Russia was left with a
ruined economy.

DISPOSITION OF THE LAND. Although Russia had had a sizable industrial plant for many years, and one which had been growing rapidly during
the generation preceding the revolution, it was still primarily an agricultural country. The great mass of the citizens and of the soldiers were peasants, and their status was in many respects the primary economic factor
any government had to consider. While serfdom had been abolished in
Russia in 1861, the great majority of the peasants lived under very difficult
conditions. Under the terms of the liberation decree they had not received
title to the land, but only its use on the condition that they kept up the
installments on the compensation due to the state. The payment of compensation had in fact broken down before the end of the nineteenth century, and after 1905 the government embarked on a policy of encouraging
the development of a class of conservative peasant landowners by assisting
them through Peasants' Banks. This movement had not proceeded very far
by the time of the revolution, however, and the great majority of the peasants did not have the use of sufficient land to feed their own families, and
so had to earn additional income as laborers. Of the 13,000,000 agrarian
families in the period immediately before World War I, no less than
10,000,000 fell into the category of the poorest peasants. On the other side
of the scale were the 30,000 big landowners, who owned approximately the
same amount of land as the 10,000,000 poorest. The solution of the land
problem was a complicated and technical matter concerning which there
were many opinions and which in any case depended on the development
of industry, the export trade, and the other elements of the economy. As a

political problem, however, the land question was much simpler. The desire of the great majority of the peasants to own their own farms was the central political fact, and—although private ownership ran counter to their principles—the Bolsheviks did not hesitate to favor it in order to win the support of the peasants.

The initial Soviet decrees on the land question, issued immediately after the November revolution, provided for the liquidation of the large estates by the local authorities, who were to hold title to them pending their final disposition by the government. The actual course of events was far different from that which the decrees prescribed. The land was in fact distributed locally to the peasant proprietors in a disorganized and inequitable fashion, in the course of which much livestock and property was destroyed. When in the course of 1918 the government nationalized the land and tried to organize collective farms, it met with almost complete failure. At the same time, because of the inflation the peasants refused to sell their grain at the designated prices, and the establishment of a state monopoly in grain failed to solve the food problem. In the summer of 1918 the government established committees of poor peasants to seize the grain from those who had a surplus. This method caused more confusion than it was worth and was abandoned by the end of the year. This disorganization, added to the confusion caused by the civil war, resulted in a marked decline in agricultural production and thus by 1921 led to severe famines in several heavily populated districts.

THE PROCESS OF NATIONALIZATION. In industry, the process of seizing the "commanding heights" was much simpler than in agriculture. Much of the heavy industry was located near the large cities that first came under Bolshevik control, and the workers had already come within the scope of the Soviet organization. Nevertheless, great difficulties were encountered both from lack of raw materials and fuel and because of the refusal of owners and managers to co-operate with the workers. Nationalization of the key industries at first resulted in the organization of workers' committees that were supposed to control the factories while the former administration stayed on the job. Over-all control was vested in a Supreme Council of the National Economy, which for a long time had only remote contacts with the concrete developments. The inefficiency of these early methods led to the general nationalization of all industry in the summer of 1918, with centralized direction under the Economic Council. Despite this centralization no effort at general planning was made. Industry was in a state of disorganization that had started before the revolution, and all that could be done was to concentrate on the heavy industries directly connected with the conduct of the civil war. As a result, by 1920 the output of all industry had declined to 20 per cent of what it had been in 1913. In the heavy industries the index was just below 13 per cent, and in the case of such basic commodities as iron ore, pig iron, and steel, production was proportionately even lower.

In the confusion of the civil war, internal trade collapsed almost entirely. Depending as it did to so large an extent on agricultural production and on the private commercial institutions of the prerevolutionary period, internal trade could not survive the period of disorganization which accompanied the civil strife. The Bolsheviks made various efforts to assert state control over trade and to introduce a system of rationing. Within the limits of the supplies at their disposal they were able to institute a certain control, but the lack of production and the refusal of the personnel trained before the revolution to co-operate with the Bolsheviks resulted in an almost complete standstill in internal trade. Foreign trade was nationalized in 1918 after various experiments in licensing had failed, but in the face of the Allied blockade it dwindled almost to the point of extinction. Moreover, the Bolsheviks tended to regard trade as a means of foreign intervention in their affairs, and discouraged any commercial relations except on their own terms.

The chief influences on the economic life of Russia during the period of war communism were of circumstance rather than of policy. In no field was the new regime more completely the victim of circumstance than in that of public finance. It inherited a large budgetary deficit and an inflationary situation, for prices had tripled between 1913 and February, 1917, and by the end of the year of revolution prices were over twelve times higher than they had been on the eve of the war. The Bolsheviks seized the principal banks as soon as they came to power, hoping to operate them with the co-operation of the private bankers. This measure failed, and soon all credit institutions were nationalized. The mere nationalization of the banks was, nevertheless, of little significance in view of the rapid deterioration of the entire economic system. Throughout this period the state had to rely increasingly on the issue of money in order to cover its expenditures, as revenue from taxes almost disappeared. In 1921 the state was issuing a thousand times more rubles than in 1917, although by the end of this process the value of the new money hardly covered the expense of printing it. Under these circumstances barter was largely resorted to, and the establishment of a new economic system was left for a later date.

NEW ECONOMIC POLICY. The curtailment of socialization and the official sanction of considerable free trade and uncontrolled economic activity was one of the most difficult and controversial decisions the Bolsheviks had to make. Yet the collapse of the economy by the end of the experiments in war communism was so extensive that there was no course open except to inaugurate a period of convalescence. It had been hoped at first that the state would be able to restrict free enterprise to a minimum, but once the decision was taken, it was found impossible to apply controls in most sectors of the economy. Lenin justified the New Economic Policy, or the NEP as it was known, as a concession necessary to win over the peasants who constituted the vast majority of the Russian people. If during this process the government could keep no more than the "commanding heights" of the economy in its hands, it would be able in a few years to take the initiative in imposing socialism.

In the field of internal trade, the NEP was very successful in increasing the volume of trade by encouraging the small businessmen, known as Nepmen. In 1923 the discrepancy between agricultural and industrial prices had been so great that while the former had fallen to 89 per cent of the 1913 level, the latter had risen to 276 per cent. This discrepancy was gradually reduced by 1927, to the relief of the peasants, and at the same time internal trade was gradually brought under extensive state control through an increase in planned purchases. Foreign trade was kept in the hands of the state throughout this period, and served both to keep out foreign competition and to mobilize in the interest of its domestic policy such bargaining power as the government possessed abroad. In the industrial field the state kept in its own hands the major industries, employing 85 per cent of all workers, but it had great difficulty with an administrative system that tried to combine management by technicians with administrative participation on the part of trade union and party representatives. The recovery of industrial production was slow, and it did not reach the 1913 level until 1927.

Throughout this period agriculture remained Russia's principal concern. While a return to a normal production of food was essential, this could only be accomplished by making concessions to the peasants' desire to own their farms. As a result, during the period of the NEP the number of peasant farms increased by 65 per cent over the prewar period. At the same time, wide differences developed in the size of the farms; the richer peasants, or kulaks, who owned only 4 per cent of the total number of farms, possessed almost one half of the seeders and harvesters in the country. Thus, although in trade and industry the government had progressed far towards restoring normal activity by the end of the NEP while keeping the essential control in its own hands, in agriculture it had obtained its successes only by granting unprecedented freedom to private enterprise. Russia had gone a long way from the famines of 1921, when Hoover's American Relief Administration had fed millions of starving peasants, but it had done so at considerable sacrifice of its socialist principles.

Institutions and Policies

CONSTITUTION OF 1924. As the Bolsheviks gradually defeated the various enemies in their territory, they established three socialist republics in addition to the RSFSR: the Ukrainian, the Byelorussian, and the Transcaucasian. Each of these republics was given a constitution similar to that of the RSFSR of 1918, and in 1922 these four states joined to form the Union of Soviet Socialist Republics, or USSR, as the Russian state has been known since that time. The relations of these four republics were formalized in a new federal constitution which was formally ratified in January, 1924 [see map, p. 479].

The Soviet Constitution of 1924 set forth the institutions of government under which Russia was ruled until 1936, and its principal interest from a formal point of view is the manner in which authority was shared between the All-Union organs and those of the component republics. Under this constitution, all power was concentrated in an elected All-Union Congress of Soviets that topped the pyramid of Soviets through which Russia was governed. This Congress of Soviets, which was a body of over two thousand members meeting every two years, in turn elected a bicameral Central Executive Committee comprising a Council of the Union and a Council of Nationalities. The former represented the people of Russia on a geographical basis while the latter represented the union republics, and the autonomous republics and regions into which the latter were subdivided. In addition to the four original union republics, the Uzbek and Turkmen republics were established in 1924 and the Tadjik Republic in 1929.

The executive power was vested in the Council of People's Commissars, or cabinet, appointed by the Central Executive Committee. Of the twelve commissariats, six were concerned with All-Union affairs and had separate administrative organs. These were the commissariats of foreign affairs, defense, foreign trade, railways, water transport, and communication. The remaining six dealt with matters of primarily local interest and worked through the corresponding commissariats in the individual republics whose activities they co-ordinated. These were the commissariats of national economy, agriculture, labor, supplies, finance, and workers' and peasants' inspection. While certain alterations were made in this distinction between All-Union organs and those of the individual republics, its principal features remained unchanged during the twelve years of the constitution's existence. Two other All-Union institutions for which the constitution made provision were the Supreme Court and the United State Political Department. The Supreme Court, in the European tradition of Roman law, had as its chief functions the review of cases sent up from the lower courts, the interpretation of All-Union legislation and of that of the separate republics, the adjudication of legal disputes between the republics, and the trial of high officials. It could also sit as a tribunal of first instance for certain categories of cases. The United State Political Department, better known as the OGPU, was established for the purpose of co-ordinating the police authorities of the individual republics in their efforts "to combat the political and economic counterrevolution, espionage, and banditry." The OGPU thus took the place of the Extraordinary Commission, or Cheka, established by Lenin in December, 1917, to combat the enemies of the Bolshevik regime.

In evaluating the representative character of this constitution, the relative size of the seven republics, the electoral procedure, and the role of the Communist party should all be taken into account. While formally a federation, the USSR was, in fact, dominated by the Russian Republic. Taking population figures of about 1930, the RSFSR had 116 million inhabitants, which was about 68 per cent of the total. By comparison, the Ukraine had 33 million inhabitants; Byelorussia, Transcaucasia, and Uzbekistan between 5 and 7 millions each; and Turkmenistan and Tadjikstan just over 1 million each. The elected Congress of Soviets was thus overwhelmingly Russian in its composition, and the representation of the other states, with the possible exception of the Ukraine, was largely nominal. This discrepancy was compensated for to some extent by the Council of Nationalities. The representative character of the Congress of Soviets was also affected by the electoral procedure. Not only were important categories of the population disfranchised by virtue of their middle-class origin, but the urban proletariat was given a preponderance through the provision that there be one deputy for each 25,000 city electors and one for every 125,000 of the rural population. Elections were held by show of hands rather than by secret ballot. Moreover, since the system of elections was indirect, with local Soviets electing representatives to the next higher Soviet, there was plenty of opportunity to weed out undesirable persons before they could be elected to the Congress of Soviets. While these factors all played an important role in the operation of the Soviet government, the key to the whole structure was the Communist party.

COMMUNIST PARTY. The discipline and unity of purpose that characterize the Soviet government stem not so much from its constitution or from the character of the Russian people as from the structure of the Bolshevik organization. Reorganized after the revolution as the All-Union Communist Party of Bolsheviks, it set as its goal "the leadership of the proletariat, the toiling peasantry, and all toiling masses in the struggle for the dictatorship of the proletariat for the victory of socialism." In line with the principles of Lenin, even after the Bolshevik victory the party was kept small in numbers and strict in discipline. During the critical year of 1917 party membership rose tenfold from 20,000 to 200,000, and by 1920 it had over 600,000 members. By 1930 the membership had risen to 1,182,600 regular members, with 492,600 candidates for membership. In a country with a population of somewhat over 150,000,000 inhabitants in the latter year, party membership was thus kept down to about one per cent of the population. In social structure the party membership in 1930 consisted of some 65 per cent workers, 20 per cent peasants, and 15 per cent state employees. About 14 per cent of the members were women, while over 22 per cent of the entire membership came from the two cities of Moscow and Leningrad. Admission to the party was difficult, and required the sponsorship of several regular party members of five years' standing, as well as a probationary period of several years.

The strength of the party was derived from its internal organization. The party congresses, of which ten were held between 1918 and 1930, formed the basic governing body of the party, but real control was vested in the Central Committee chosen at each party congress. Whereas between one and two thousand members were present at the party congresses, the Central Committee in 1920 had no more than nineteen members. It remained in permanent session. Even more important than the Central Committee were its three executive groups: the Political Bureau or Politburo, the Organization Bureau or Orgburo, and the Secretariat. The Politburo was the governing body of the party and in fact, if not in theory, of

Russia as well. In 1920 it was composed of seven members: Lenin, Stalin, Trotsky, Kamenev, Bukharin, Preobrazhensky, and Serebriakov. The Org-buro handled matters of party organization and in particular the appointment of party members to government positions. As a result of its activity, not only did party members hold all key political positions in Russia, but their work was co-ordinated to meet the requirements of the policies decided on by the Politburo. The Secretariat had initially the secondary task of administering the work of the Central Committee, but after Stalin's appointment as General Secretary in 1922 its functions were rapidly increased to include the general organization of party personnel. There was also a party control commission that enforced party discipline and ethics.

The form of political leadership which emerged in Russia was thus the small and well-disciplined oligarchy of professional revolutionaries advocated by Lenin since 1903. Lenin was well aware that size did not make for strength in a political organization, and warned in 1920 that "to a ruling government will inevitably gravitate careerists and scoundrels who deserve only to be shot." And shot they were if any failed to pass the various tests by which party members were periodically screened. While the Constitution of 1924 thus provided formally for a representative assembly in which all powers of government were vested, the decisions were in fact made by the hierarchy of the Communist party. As Lenin himself said: "Not only were all former adherents of the imperial regime and of the Provisional Government banned from political activity, but so also were the socialists who did not hew to the Communist party line." Zinoviev announced in 1922: "We have taken away political freedom from our opponents; we do not permit the legal existence of those who strive to compete with us. We have clamped a lock on the lips of the Mensheviks and the Socialist Revolutionaries." If all the members of the Soviets from the local to the All-Union level were not Communists, they were at least persons who had been passed on by the local party organization as being reliable.

This determination of the party to suppress all opposition was reflected in the legislation affecting civil liberties. With a view to rallying the support of persecuted minority groups to the new regime, the Declaration of the Rights of the Peoples of Russia, issued only eight days after the Bolsheviks came to power, promised self-determination and the abolition of national and religious disabilities for all the peoples of the new state. The establishment of equal rights for men and women and the abolition of class privileges were also accomplished by special legislation before the end of 1917. A further proclamation of rights was made in January, 1918, in the Declaration of the Rights of Toiling and Exploited People, in which the establishment of "a free union of free nations" was announced. The same declaration decreed universal labor service, which was introduced frankly as a means of "abolishing the parasitic strata of society." As a means of further guarding the security of the proletarian state, the "exploiters" were disenfranchised.

It was not until the promulgation of the Constitution of the RSFSR of July 10, 1918, that a full list of civil rights in the accepted sense of the term was adopted. These rights were kept, with a few changes, in the revised RSFSR constitution of 1925 and in the constitutions of the other republics of the USSR, and presumably for this reason were not included in the federal constitution of 1924. This list of civil liberties included the freedom of religious and antireligious propaganda, as a corollary of the separation of church and state; the freedom of the press, to be achieved by turning over to the workers the printing presses and the necessary raw materials; the freedom of assembly, including access to meeting halls, furniture, heat, and light; the freedom of organization; and the freedom of education. Work, later regarded as a right, was here listed as an obligation, as was military service. The equality of races and peoples was reiterated. Underlying these rights was the condition implicit in their terminology and explicitly stated in Article 23 of the 1918 constitution, and repeated in Article 14 of the 1925 constitution, which "In the interests of the workers . . . deprives individuals or groups of individuals of rights which they exercise to the prejudice of the socialist revolution." Soviet citizens were free to support the government, but if they opposed its policies they were deprived of their rights by the above-cited provision. Under the guise of extending civil liberties, the Soviet regime thus established a rigid censorship of press and assembly, forbade religious instruction, and imposed economic and political restrictions on certain "disfranchised" groups.

No provisions for party discipline could have been more carefully drafted or more vigorously enforced than those which governed the Bolshevik organization. This discipline was applicable, however, only if the party leaders were in full agreement as to what policy they wished to pursue. Even Marxist doctrine, as Lenin himself recognized, provided "only general guiding principles," the development and application of which was a matter of day-to-day interpretation and decision. The Bolshevik leaders had been divided in such a vital decision as the organization of the revolution in November, 1917, and throughout Lenin's period of leadership serious controversies arose from time to time. For instance, a group of Left Communists objected to the treaty of Brest-Litovsk in 1918, whereas in 1921 a group known as the Workers' Opposition criticized the party leadership for not taking adequate steps to combat bureaucracy. In the same year more serious opposition was provoked by Lenin's decision to postpone the immediate introduction of socialism and to embark on the New Economic Policy. This was the last major decision Lenin made, for in the spring of 1922 he was stricken by paralysis resulting from a cerebral hemorrhage. He rallied briefly in 1923, but finally died in January, 1924.

During the last two years of Lenin's life, a split developed among the leaders of the Politburo, and later it almost broke up the party. The chief contenders for leadership in 1922 were Trotsky, commissar of war; Zinoviev, president of the Communist International who had just re-entered the Politburo after a period of disagreement; and Stalin, general secretary of the party. At this time the issues were largely personal, and the seven-member Politburo was seriously divided. Lenin was by this time too ill to participate actively in party affairs. Trotsky, the brilliant war leader, had a vain and domineering character and was without support. Zinoviev had a large personal following in the Politburo, including Kamenev and Bukharin. Stalin himself had little support in the top body, but as organizer of the party he was in a strong position by reason of his power to appoint local party officials and thus to gain control of the party congress. Lenin was aware of the dangers of this situation and from his sickbed he dictated a memorandum in which he criticized Trotsky's "self-confidence" and called Stalin "rude" and recommended his removal from the key post he held. But Lenin was no longer able to implement his views. When Lenin died, it was Stalin who addressed the Congress of Soviets and vowed in the name of his colleagues to work for the unity of the party, and for the strengthening of the dictatorship of the proletariat and of the Red Army.

Stalin emerged victorious as Lenin's successor before the end of the 1920's, and his policies henceforth determined the course of Russian history. Stalin was born in 1879 of a humble family in the province of Georgia as Iosif Vissarionovich Djugashvili and assumed his revolutionary pseudonym later. He played only a secondary role in the revolution of 1905, but his position in the party rose steadily, and between periods of exile he attended party congresses in Stockholm and London. In the winter of 1912–13 he spent several months with Lenin in Cracow and Vienna, where he wrote his principal prerevolutionary theoretical study on *The National Question and Social-Democracy*. By 1917 Stalin had reached the top rank of party leadership, and sat on the twelve-member Central Committee that organized the revolution in November. Throughout his career Stalin was more a party organizer in Russia than an international revolutionary, and he always thought in primarily Russian terms. Trotsky, Zinoviev, and Kamenev talked in doctrinaire fashion of the impossibility of building socialism in Russia until capitalism had been abolished in Europe. Stalin, on the other hand, while still believing in the inevitability of the spread of socialism, recognized that it was not likely to take place immediately and urged that Russia do what it could in the meantime to strengthen itself through industrialization. Lenin can be quoted on both sides of this issue, but in the main he was dubious as to the prospects of socialism in Russia if it continued to be surrounded by capitalist states. Nevertheless, Lenin's policy was always flexible, and no one can say what he might have done had he lived. In any case, with the failure of the Communist uprisings in Central Europe and in the Balkans, in addition to the spectacular defeat of the Chinese Communists at the hands of Chiang Kai-shek in 1927, the advocates of the primacy of world revolution lost all support. Through his thorough manipulation of the party organization Stalin had the party congress, and hence the Central Committee with its Politburo, under his full control. The lively party debates of the early 1920's now gave way to a disciplined unanimity. By 1927 industrial and agricultural production had once again reached the 1913 level, and in the following year the first Five Year Plan was inaugurated.

SOCIAL CHANGES. Vast changes had been taking place in the Russian way of life since the liberation of the serfs in 1861, and Russia had made considerable progress under the Tsars in developing a modern society. Under the Bolsheviks this process of modernization was continued, although it followed a different pattern from that of the earlier years. The population of the Tsarist empire was about 165 million on the eve of the war, but due to the territorial losses arranged in the peace treaties, the area later occupied by the USSR probably had a population of about 140 million at the end of the war. The census of 1926 reported a population of 147 million. The peasantry continued to comprise some three fourths to four fifths of the population, while the working class remained at a little over one tenth.

The great change was in the third group, which may be called the upper or governing class for want of a better name. It grew perhaps as much as from 8 to 12 per cent of the population in the years between 1917 and 1927, and its membership underwent revolutionary changes. In the last years of the empire, the upper class, in the broadest sense of the term, embraced many groups. At the top were the government officials, the nobility, and the officer corps of the armed forces. To these must be added the clergy, members of the liberal professions, and managers in industry and commerce. This upper class was widely dispersed by the revolution. Some were killed and many more went into exile, while some remained in Russia as workers or peasants. Perhaps as many as one-half of the imperial upper class, however, survived to become a part of the similar group in the new Soviet state. It was officially reported in 1930, for instance, that 41 per cent of the higher officials of the Commissariat of Finance were former imperial civil servants, nobles, clergy, and businessmen. Members of the old upper class thus formed a significant segment of the new, but of course they did not in any sense dominate it. It was the members of the Communist party who headed the new upper class, supported by an army of government officials which at the end of the decade was four times the size of the imperial bureaucracy. While the leaders of this new elite had great power, in the early years they did not use it for their personal benefit. The political leaders, as distinct from the Nepmen during their brief period of affluence, tended to be hard-working and ascetic.

Other areas of Russian society went through a period of rapid change now that the lid of censorship on which the Tsarist regime had been sitting for so many years had suddenly been released. In matters concerning education, the family, the church, and general culture, the first years after the Russian revolution were a period of unbridled experimentation. Most of the impressions the outside world received of the new society were derived from the vast series of changes instituted in the prerevolutionary, or "bourgeois," social institutions. Thus in the field of education, homework and examinations were abolished in elementary schools, and instead of a curriculum emphasizing the three R's the pupils were taught sociological concepts and participated in "projects" for the study of the society in which they lived. In the universities, academic degrees were abolished and professors were subjected to discipline by the Communists in the student body. The family was also greatly altered in its legal position, with civil marriage and easy divorce introduced, along with legalized abortions and the abolition of inheritance. More ambitious plans of raising all children in state institutions were abandoned for lack of means. The church was separated from the state, the priests were persecuted, and widespread antireligious propaganda was inaugurated. In the fields of scholarship and art, likewise, prerevolutionary concepts were abandoned and new approaches were tried. The theoretical basis for all of these experiments was provided by the Marxist doctrine that the institutions of a country should reflect its social structure. In this instance, however, the institutional changes were rushed through before the social structure of the country had been altered by the Five Year Plans.

Some of these changes were no more than experiments, while others produced lasting results. The number of pupils in elementary schools grew from eight million in 1915 to over ten million in 1928–29, and literacy was increased from an estimated 40 per cent in 1914 to 51 per cent in 1926. In respect to these and to other features of education, the new society thus continued the steady progress that had been achieved in the last years of the empire. In scholarship and the creative arts the Soviet regime permitted some freedom to "bourgeois" artists, as they called the non-Marxists, but it gave its main support to the Communists. In architecture, music, and literature new talents were developed and Soviet achievements received wide acclaim abroad. The leading literary figures were fellow-travelers rather than party members. A few soon lost their enthusiasm and found escape in suicide or exile, but many of the ablest made their peace with the new society and retained considerable freedom throughout this period.

POSTPONEMENT OF WORLD REVOLUTION. Grounded in the doctrines of Marx, the Russian Communist party believed firmly in the inevitability of world revolution and kept a watchful eye on the international political barometer with a view to taking advantage of any opportunities that might arise to hasten and guide the development of events. In countries already well developed industrially, they looked forward to early revolutions and made preparations accordingly. Asian states still under the domination of the Western powers received assistance from Russia in their movements of national liberation, for in these countries the Communists believed that socialization would have to wait. The gauging of Soviet policy decisions was at best a delicate matter, and the Soviet leaders made many miscalculations. Moreover, their domestic policy was closely related to foreign developments, and one of the major controversies within the Bolshevik party was concerned with this very issue: was a European revolution requiring Russia's participation imminent, or would Russia have a breathing spell to strengthen itself for a more distant conflict? It was not until the later 1920's that a decision in favor of domestic reconstruction was taken, and before the issue was finally settled it cost the lives of many leading Bolsheviks.

In pursuing their policy the Russian Communists made use of two disciplined and frequently contradictory instruments: the Third or Communist International, generally known as the Comintern, and the Commissariat of Foreign Affairs. The former, headed by Zinoviev from 1919 to 1926, and from then until 1929 by Bukharin, had the task of mobilizing the various labor parties in other European states for the task of revolution. The foreign office, headed from 1918 to 1930 by the former monarchist diplomat Chicherin, conducted Russia's official relations with foreign countries in a more or less traditional fashion. Although the foreign office eventually emerged as the principal organ of Russian foreign policy, the Comintern was more active in the early years. In 1919 and 1920 Zinoviev was still expecting a revolution in the near future and proceeded vigorously with the organization of a network of parties. His principal aim was to require the absolute discipline of all member parties under the leadership of the Russian Bolsheviks. For this purpose he obtained the agreement of the second Comintern congress in 1920 to a series of conditions with which all member parties had to comply. These conditions required the existing socialist parties to break with all labor groups that refused to submit without question to the Moscow line. This split was in fact carried out in Germany, France, and other countries. It resulted in the formation of minority parties under rigid communist discipline, and hence in the division of each national labor movement into two warring factions. The same type of division occurred in the trade unions when the Communists set out to win membership for their own federation of trade unions.

Still hoping for a general revolution, the Comintern now embarked on a series of individual ventures that one by one ended in failure. The theory on which these movements were based was that the industrial and agrarian socialist groups that refused to follow the Communist line were all enemies of the proletariat and belonged in the same category with the various liberal, nationalist, reactionary, and fascist parties then active in Europe. In failing to make a distinction among the various non-Communist parties, the Comintern antagonized them all, and as a result in many countries the Communists were all but wiped out.

Turning now from Europe to the peoples of the Near and Far East who were still fighting Western imperialism, the Comintern hoped to win there the successes it had failed to obtain in Europe. The Comintern congress at Baku in 1920 had offered Russian aid to all peoples engaged in a struggle with imperialism, and in Afghanistan, Iran, Turkey, and Morocco some Russian assistance had been made available. The Moslem countries had withstood Communist infiltration, however, and they accepted the aid while closing their ears to the propaganda that accompanied it. In the Dutch East Indies and in China, on the other hand, the Com-

munists made considerable headway, although in the end they met with
much the same fate as did their European counterparts. In Java a premature Communist uprising was suppressed in 1926. The Chinese picture
was somewhat more involved. Here the Communist party after its founding in 1920 had won an influential position in the nationalist Kuomintang
party. Founded in 1911 by Sun Yat-sen, the Kuomintang was led after his
death in 1925 by General Chiang Kai-shek. The Communists had been
useful in rallying mass support for the Kuomintang and had gradually
worked themselves into a position where they might have taken over the
whole organization. Perceiving this possibility, General Chiang suddenly
turned on his Communist allies in 1926 and, after a series of skillful political maneuvers, attacked and destroyed them in the course of the following year.

This series of failures on the part of the Comintern led to a change
both of leadership and of policy. As head of the organization, Zinoviev
was replaced by Bukharin. Henceforth, the Comintern was to play a less
active role abroad and to serve primarily as an instrument of Soviet policy. In this role it continued, as before, to make few distinctions among
the various non-Communist parties; in Germany on occasion it co-operated
with the Nazis in the belief that their advent to power would bring Germany closer to revolution.

Having finally concluded that adventures in world revolution had
little to offer for the time being, the Bolsheviks decided that the building
of socialism in one country would require peaceful relations with the outside world. "Those who want peace and seek business relations with us
will always have our support," Stalin reported to the seventeenth Communist party congress in 1934, "but those who try to attack our country will
receive a crushing repulse to teach them not to poke their pig snouts into
our Soviet garden." After 1926 the Soviet foreign office thus had new opportunities to pursue the search for friends which it had started shortly
after the revolution. The first moves Russia made to assure its security in
a hostile world were directed towards Germany, which was similarly isolated and desired to increase its bargaining power with the Western states.
An agreement between the Bolsheviks and the German army in 1921 had
permitted the manufacture of certain armaments by the Germans on Russian soil, in an effort to avoid the restrictions of the Versailles treaty. Then
in 1922, Russia and Germany had succeeded in concluding a political
treaty at Rapallo, Italy, which had strengthened their respective positions
without winning them any immediate gains. After the Soviet Union had
been recognized by most European states, a more concrete approach to
Russian security was initiated in 1925 with the conclusion of a treaty of
neutrality and nonaggression with Turkey. In the next two years similar
treaties were concluded with Germany, Lithuania, and Iran, and they
helped to counteract the effect of the Locarno agreements signed in 1926
and interpreted in Moscow as creating a Western bloc against Russia.

After 1926 the atmosphere of Russian foreign policy changed considerably. A period of relative economic and social stability in Europe was now taken for granted, and the decline in activity of the Comintern was accompanied by an increasing effort on the part of the Soviet foreign office to reach understandings with the Western powers. The League of Nations, which had at first been castigated as "the Holy Alliance of the bourgeoisie for the suppression of the proletarian revolution," was now regarded with greater favor. This change in the Soviet outlook was accompanied and influenced by a similar softening of the attitude of the Western powers, whose confidence in their ability to deal with communism at home had been largely restored. Under these circumstances Litvinov, who served as principal Soviet representative in Europe during these years and succeeded Chicherin as foreign commissar in 1930, was able to participate actively in European diplomacy. At the disarmament conferences held in Geneva in 1927–30, Litvinov achieved fame by championing complete and immediate disarmament. This was a sound policy for the Soviet Union at a time when it was militarily weak and was engaged in building up its heavy industry, and Litvinov's proposal bore a striking resemblance to the initiative of the imperial government under similar circumstances, which had led to the calling of the first Hague Peace Conference in 1899. More constructive—and less sensational—was the Litvinov Protocol of 1929 providing for the immediate application of the Kellogg-Briand pact for the renunciation of war to the countries bordering Russia. Poland, Latvia, Estonia, and Rumania adhered to this Protocol immediately, and were soon followed by Lithuania, the Free City of Danzig, Turkey, and Iran. The military weakness of Russia, combined with the failures of the Comintern, had thus created conditions which resulted in an atmosphere of mutual confidence between the Soviet Union and its neighbors. The Russian network of nonaggression treaties was now extended to include Afghanistan, Estonia, Latvia, and Finland, as well as France and Italy. The final acceptance of Russia as a member of the family of nations came with its recognition by the United States in 1933 and its admission to the League of Nations in the following year.

While still believing that the Soviet Union could not remain at peace with the noncommunist states over a long period of time, the Bolshevik leaders calculated that during the process of intensive industrialization at home Soviet interests would best be served by a policy of reconciliation with the other powers. In pursuing this policy the Bolshevik leaders tended to treat all noncommunist governments alike, and only after the victory of the Nazis in Germany did they come to believe that some capitalists were worse than others. But this was a problem for the future and was met by another change of policy. In the meantime a temporary balance had been established between the communist and noncommunist worlds, and the Bolsheviks were able to cultivate their "Soviet garden" without interference.

CHAPTER

8

The
Weimar Republic

The German Constitution: *Election of the National Assembly; Work of the Assembly; The German Government; Political Forces in Germany.*

Reparations: *Setting the Reparations Bill; The Occupation of the Ruhr; The Dawes Plan; The Young Plan; War Debts and Reparations; The End of Reparations.*

Economic Development: *Collapse of German Currency; Results of the Inflation; Foreign Loans; Industrial Expansion; Labor Policy; Housing; Agricultural Policy.*

Religion: *Church and State; Church and Education.*

Political Development: *Swing Away from the Left; Presidential Elections; The Rise of National Socialism; The Collapse of Parliamentary Government.*

To discuss the drafting of all the new constitutions that made their appearance in Europe in the twenties would not be practical in a general treatment of European history. Yet the formulation of these fundamental laws was an important event in the history of each state. The method used in drafting the constitution of Germany was fairly typical of the procedures followed in other states. This constitution was also the first to be drawn up and, because of the advanced political theories it incorporated, greatly influenced the others. To describe its formulation will, therefore, serve as a means of studying the general problem of constitution-making in this period. It also will serve as a striking contrast to the procedure of establishing a democratic government in Germany after World War II.

The German Constitution

ELECTION OF THE NATIONAL ASSEMBLY. On November 9, 1918, Prince Max of Baden, last chancellor of the German Empire, turned over the government to Friedrich Ebert and Philipp Scheidemann, leaders of the powerful Social Democratic party. The Kaiser had abdicated the previous day and fled to Holland, and the ruling houses in the German states soon laid down their powers. Everywhere republics were proclaimed. At Berlin Ebert created a directory of six men—three from the majority and three from the more radical minority wing of the Socialist party. This Directory set about governing Germany, and on November 30, 1918, it issued a general electoral law providing for the election of a National Assembly, according to the principle of proportional representation, by all men and women over twenty years of age. Field Marshal von Hindenburg consented to remain as Chief of Staff and was able to prevent the outbreak of widespread civil war, the army being demobilized peacefully.

In many of the states, the revolutionary governments had a distinct socialist tendency. In some, attempts were made to establish Workers' and Soldiers' Councils on the Russian model, and in Berlin the extreme leftists, who took their name from the pseudonym "Spartacus" used by their leader Karl Liebknecht, seized control of the government of the city for a week in January, 1919. Ebert, who had been forced to flee, recruited a corps of volunteers with the aid of General Groener and Gustav Noske and successfully ended the "Spartacist Rebellion." In these confused days, certain volunteers took matters into their own hands, seizing and killing without trial the socialist leaders, Rosa Luxemburg and Liebknecht.

The elections held on January 19, 1919, were preceded by an ardent political campaign. Some of the measures imposed by the socialistic governments in parts of Germany caused a reaction to their rule. Education had always been left to the various state governments. In Prussia and in Saxony, as well as in one or two other states, a socialist minister of education took steps against the continuation of religious instruction in the public schools. The fear of what socialist governments might do in the way of curbing established religious practices was a real issue in the elections for the National Assembly; it was probably more important than fear of socialistic economic practices. Monarchy was discredited, and there were few who thought seriously of its return. Since no one party or political philosophy obtained a majority in the elections, it was necessary to form a coalition. The Social Democrats, who were the largest party (165 out of a total of 421), were forced to work together with the Democrats (75) and Catholic Center (91).

WORK OF THE ASSEMBLY. On February 6, 1919, the National Assembly met at the small Thuringian town of Weimar. It was the city of Goethe and Schiller and was associated with the best traditions of German liberalism. The Assembly had three main tasks: to govern Germany, to conclude peace with the victorious Allies, and to draw up a new federal constitution. The Assembly elected Ebert president and adopted a provisional law for the governing of Germany. A coalition cabinet soon lost the cooperation of the Democrats, who refused to share the responsibility of signing the unpopular Peace of Versailles. The Social Democrats and Catholic Center were thus forced into an unholy alliance, for the two parties had for years been enemies; they were miles apart ideologically on many issues, and the Papacy continued to issue pronouncements against the theories of socialism. However, there were points on which they did agree. Both supported the Republic, both favored individual rights, both were willing to go far towards giving the state control over economic questions, and both were opposed to communism. The one issue on which they split and which nearly wrecked the whole work of the National Assembly was the position of church and schools in the new state. Eventually they agreed on a compromise that left the basic issues unsettled. The vexed question of federal vs. state control over education was to be settled by a future law drawn up by the national government. So bitter was the political strife on this issue that every attempt to pass this law in the twenties failed.

A draft of a proposed constitution was hammered into shape first by representatives of the state governments, then by a committee of the National Assembly, and finally in a long plenary session. It was approved by a vote of 262–75, the Social Democrats, Center, and Democrats voting for it. On August 11, 1919, the constitution was promulgated by President Ebert and it went into effect three days later without ever having been approved by a national referendum.

THE GERMAN GOVERNMENT. The legislature consisted of an upper chamber, the Reichsrat, and a lower chamber, the Reichstag. The former was modeled on the old Bundesrat of the German Empire and represented the eighteen state governments. Each state was to have at least one representative with an additional representative for each unit of 1,000,000 (later reduced to 700,000) inhabitants. In order to limit the predominance of Prussia it was decreed that no one state could hold more than two fifths of the total seats. Furthermore, half of the Prussian delegation were to be controlled by the local provinces within Prussia, and only one half by the Prussian state government. As constituted, the Reichsrat had sixty-six members. It exercised important administrative functions, and its consent was necessary to legislation. If the Reichsrat failed to agree with the lower chamber, the latter body could impose its will by passing the law a second time with a two-thirds majority. Actually the cabinets, because of a provision in the constitution (Art. 69), regularly submitted their proposed legislation first to the Reichsrat. The result was that the upper chamber developed into a body far more important than one would gather from a reading of the constitution. It became one of the best upper chambers in Europe, and conflicts between the upper and lower house did not materialize.

The Reichstag was elected by men and women twenty years of age or older, according to the principles of proportional representation. Proportional representation means party representation in the legislative bodies according to *party strength* among the voters. The Germans adopted the so-called Baden System, which is one of the simplest of all the proportional representation schemes adopted after World War I. Not only is it important to understand how proportional representation works, but the German system in particular must be understood to appreciate one of the methods by which Hitler at a later period achieved power.

Germany was divided into thirty-five electoral districts in which each party nominated a list of candidates. The position of the candidates on the list was of real importance and was one of the ways in which party discipline was maintained. Each party was given a representative for each 60,000 votes the party received in an election. The number of seats won went to the candidates in the order in which their names appeared on the list. The unused votes could then be combined with the unused votes of the party in an electoral union—which was a combination of two or more districts. Here the additional seat was filled from the list that contributed the largest quota towards meeting the required 60,000 votes. The ballots remaining after this distribution were united with the party remainders from all over the Reich. These seats were filled from a Reich list nominated by the party, where the names of the leaders of the party were usually found. This made certain that the chief men of the party would always be returned. A final residue of over 30,000 entitled the party to another seat. A provision that no party could win more seats on the Reich lists than it had won in the primary election districts was directed against so-called "splinter parties," which might win many scattered votes but never poll 60,000 votes in any one district.

In practice this system brought a very close correlation between the popular votes accorded to different parties and the seats that these parties held in the Reichstag. It strengthened but did not create the multiple-party system. This had existed in Germany long before proportional representation was adopted and no doubt would have continued to exist under the Republic had the old single-member districts been retained. The striking thing about the Baden System was that the size of the Reichstag fluctuated according to the size of the vote in a given election. This was originally thought to be desirable because it would encourage people to go to the polls to support their party. The German system has suffered undeserved condemnation because Hitler captured new voters, got out the stay-at-home vote, and thus built up the numerical representation of his party in the Reichstag while the strength of the other parties remained stationary [see table on Reichstag elections, p. 448]. The arguments for and against proportional representation are numerous. Here our interest, however, lies simply in pointing out that it was one of the instruments of democratic government provided in many of the new constitutions of postwar Europe. When it went into the discard, so did free elections and democracy in general.

Whereas the Reichsrat proved more successful than had been expected, the Reichstag did not fulfill the position designed for it by the constitution. The Reichstag was intended to be the ruling body of Germany. It controlled the cabinet, it passed all laws, and it had the power to repeal presidential decrees. It could amend the constitution by a two-thirds vote of two thirds of its membership. But the party system effectively undermined its position. The strong party discipline abetted by the rules of the Reichstag made that body really a conference of parties rather than an assembly of representatives. There was little independent voting on the part of representatives, and the party caucus reigned supreme. When the extreme parties of the right (Nazis) and left (Communists) became so strong that they could combine to outvote the parties of the middle, which were the only ones willing to assume the responsibility of governing through a coalition, the Reichstag was unable to continue to play its given role in the government.

The German president was elected by a direct vote of the people. If a candidate did not receive a majority of the votes at the first election, a second election—in which new candidates could also present themselves—was held, and this time only a plurality of votes was required. The words of the constitution seemed to grant the president only the usual powers accorded the titular head of a state in all parliamentary governments. The real executive was meant to be the cabinet, and one of its members had to countersign all acts of the president. There were, however, two special provisions or interpretations that gave an opportunity for a president to exert his influence if he wished. These must be explained, for both provisions play a part in the events leading to Hitler's assumption of power.

The constitution provided in Article 53 that "The chancellor and, upon his recommendation, the national ministers, shall be appointed and removed by the president of the Reich." This was taken to mean that the chancellor was responsible not only to the Reichstag but to the president as well. In 1932 Hindenburg forced Chancellor Bruening to resign when the latter still had the confidence of the Reichstag. It is true that a new cabinet appointed by the president would, according to the terms of the constitution, sooner or later have to win the confidence of the Reichstag, but the provision did enable the president, at least for a period, to exercise full powers through a ministry that had only his support.

The president was granted further extraordinary power under Article 48 of the constitution. Here the president, working through the cabinet, was granted power (1) to force a state "to carry out the duties imposed upon it by the national constitution or national laws," and (2) "if the public safety and order be seriously disturbed or threatened," to set aside certain rights enumerated in the constitution and enact by decrees "the necessary measures to restore public safety and order." The latter provision was meant to establish a temporary constitutional dictatorship, a practice that had been provided for in the old German constitution and was common in European constitutional practice. The president was obligated to communicate to the Reichstag all decrees issued. Although it was not necessary for the Reichstag to approve such decrees, they might be abrogated by the Reichstag if it so desired. To some this last distinction might seem a fine point, but actually it was important. Very often some weeks or months intervened between the time when the president issued a decree and the time when the Reichstag (which might have been adjourned) was presented with this decree. By that time it would have had little effect to repeal the decree, which had long since been put into operation and had served its purpose. To approve decrees, however, very often would have led to difficulties because such action would have meant a vote in direct conflict with party principles. The result was that the decrees were passed over in silence. Thus the Reichstag failed to assume one of the responsibilities imposed upon it by the constitution. It abdicated in favor of government by the executive.

In practice the president was given wide leeway in deciding what constituted a threat to public safety. Up to 1925, 135 decrees and ordinances were enacted under this clause. Then for a period the use of such emergency powers went into abeyance, only to be revived with a vengeance in 1930. From then on, emergency decrees practically supplanted all legislation by the Reichstag. Budgets were even enacted by decree. True legislative government had disappeared from Germany long before Hitler took over on January 30, 1933.

Germany was renowned before the war for its excellent civil service and its system of municipal government. Both of these were practically untouched by the revolution. Municipalities expanded their services and continued to serve the people in admirable fashion. The civil service was on the whole nonpolitical, and this tradition was worth preserving. Old civil servants went over into the employ of the new Republic, and the new regime was able to continue without a violent wrench in services. School teachers, tax collectors, policemen, judicial officers—all carried on. This had definite advantages, for a new personnel cannot be recruited over night. Yet, as a result many people went over into the service of the Republic, particularly in the judiciary and in the university faculties, who were more attached to monarchical than republican ways.

Although the old practice of enforcing national laws through state officials was continued, there was such a great shift of powers to the national government that political scientists debated whether Germany was not in fact a unitary state in spite of its apparent federal organization. A national court had jurisdiction in disputes between the national and state governments, and the constitution specifically stated that national law breaks state law. New republican constitutions were adopted in each of the German states (*Länder*), the number of which had declined through voluntary consolidation to seventeen by 1928. As in most European countries, the courts did not exercise the power of declaring a law unconstitutional, and therefore did not serve as guardian of the elaborate bill of rights incorporated in the constitution.

POLITICAL FORCES IN GERMANY. Germany started the twenties bravely with a democratic framework of government, and it should not be believed that this was all façade. Admittedly there were antidemocratic forces at work. Germany was not an egalitarian state; there was still a worship of rank and position, and each person liked to be called *Herr Doktor, Herr Regierungsrat*, or what not. Something of that social democracy which is concealed under the term "Citizen" of the French Revolution, "Mr." in the United States, or "Comrade" in Russia was lacking. A belief that one man is as good as the next strengthens political democracy, but it was not very widespread in Germany. There was also a tradition of authoritative procedure and a veneration of the virtues of militarism. On the other hand, while the landed Junkers exercised an influence beyond what their numbers warranted, they were by no means so powerful as is often believed. The great landed gentry in Hungary and Poland exercised far greater influence, and this might also be said of the "ruling class" in Great Britain. In Prussia, where the Junkers supposedly held sway (although Mecklenburg would be a better example), the government from the beginning to the end remained under the control of the Social Democrats, and Prussia had one of the most liberal governments in all Germany. The industrialization of Germany had brought a shift of power to the wealthy capitalists and in part to the working masses. It was a twentieth- and not an eighteenth-century Germany that experimented with democracy.

Moreover, there is a real liberal and democratic tradition in Germany that is often overlooked. The memory of the Revolution of 1848 and what it stood for never died out. The Paulskirche which was the seat of the famous Frankfurt Parliament in 1848 later became a national shrine. Germany, it should also be remembered, had the strongest labor organizations of all Europe and also the strongest Social Democratic party. It had a well-organized and strong Catholic Center party. It had a literate population; its educational system was well established and reached all sections of the populace. There was also an appreciation of individualism and freedom of thought that is rooted in the Protestant Reformation. In no place in continental Europe did a Jew feel more at home than he did in Germany in the early twenties.

Unfortunately, democracy in Germany was inextricably bound up with Germany's defeat and the Peace of Versailles. The peace treaty had been imposed by the democratic powers and they had acted as godfathers to the German Republic. To the end, they remained more interested in enforcing the treaty than in strengthening the Republic. And that is understandable. But liberal and democratic Germany was also nationalistic and had in years past been the spearhead in the struggle for German unity. All Germans were opposed to the Versailles Treaty, particularly to the settlements of the eastern frontier. The Republic was saddled with the sins of the Empire. It was called upon to carry the burdens and solve the economic problems resulting from the four-year holocaust. Many of these problems were much the same but not so acute in the other states of Europe. All governments had to face perilous tasks, and democratic Germany was by no means the first or the only one to succumb to the temptation of meeting them by recourse to dictatorship.

Reparations

SETTING THE REPARATIONS BILL. Under the Treaty of Versailles the Reparations Commission was charged first of all with collecting five billion dollars in Germany before May 1, 1921, mainly to cover the cost of the armies of occupation. On May 1, 1921, the Reparations Commission was also to announce the total reparations bill. To guide the Reparations Commission ten categories of damages were established in the treaty, pensions being one of the most important. During 1920 the Reparations Commission asked the Allied governments to submit a list of damages. The Commission was also busy with many other tasks, such as evaluating the deliveries Germany was making and supervising the restitution of identifiable property that Germany had seized.

The chief Allied powers also held various conferences where they discussed the problem of reparations. One of the most important of these was held in July, 1920, at Spa, where certain percentages were agreed upon for the division of reparation payments. The restitution of livestock, industrial material and rolling stock, cash, securities, works of art, furniture, river shipping, etc., while it came to involve large sums of money, was not a part of reparations. Table 7 on page 220 shows the percentage distribution of reparations made by the powers at Spa, and subsequent distributions of 1929 and 1931. Half of the Austrian, Hungarian, and Bulgarian reparations payments were also to be allotted according to these ratios, but 40 per cent of the other half was to go to Italy and the rest to Greece, Rumania, and Yugoslavia.

Having divided the pot it was still necessary to set the sum it was to contain. In January, 1921, the Allies suggested a figure of fifty-six billion dollars as total reparations liability. Germany replied with an offer of seven and a half billion dollars. The Germans maintained that they had delivered more than the five billion dollars due May 1, 1921, and were going to stop deliveries until the total bill was presented. The Reparations

TABLE 7

DIVISION IN PERCENTAGES OF GERMAN REPARATIONS PAYMENTS *

	SPA AGREEMENT, 1920	REVISION OF 1929	FINAL DISTRIBUTION, 1931
British Empire	22.00	23.05	23.58
France	52.00	54.45	56.14
Italy	10.00	10.00	8.06
Japan	.75	.75	.66
Belgium	8.00	4.50	5.60
Portugal	.75	.75	.66
Yugoslavia		5.00	3.92
Rumania	6.50	1.10	1.00
Greece		.40	.35
Poland			.03

* Compiled from *Paris Peace Conference*, Vol. XIII, p. 442; see also Toynbee: *Survey of International Affairs*, 1920–1923, pp. 120 ff.

Commission, however, evaluated German deliveries at approximately two billion dollars, and thus Germany was in default. The Allies promptly issued an ultimatum on March 3, and five days later occupied the cities of Duisburg, Ruhrort, and Düsseldorf. They also took over German customs collected on the external frontiers of occupied territories, which meant practically all the western borders of Germany. Time was running short and the Reparations Commission was faced with bewildering estimates of damages. The figures of different countries and different experts did not agree. Fortunately the Commission was not forced to present a breakdown of its figures when on May 1, 1921, it produced a sum total. Germany was to pay $33,000,000,000, plus the total Belgian war debt and the cost of the armies of occupation. The Belgian war debt was estimated at $1,403,096,456 and, along with Belgium's share of general reparations, was always given a priority in reparations payments. The German experts had long maintained that it would be impossible to pay anything like such a sum, and it was feared that now Germany would refuse to sign on the dotted line. The Allied governments presented an ultimatum and made military preparations for the occupation of the Ruhr. The German government resigned, and a new cabinet was constituted just in time to accept the Allied dictum before the deadline was at hand.

Germany was required to issue immediately three series of bonds covering the thirty-three billion dollars; these bonds were to bear 5 per cent interest and a sinking fund of 1 per cent. Only twelve and a half billion would go into circulation until more funds were available to meet the interest and sinking-fund charges. Germany was to pay within twenty-five days $250,000,000, and thereafter $500,000,000 annually plus a variable annuity equivalent to 26 per cent of the value of German exports. Just what Germany's total bill, counting the heavy interest charges, would add up to in the end and when payments would cease was an open question under this system of reparations payments.

To obtain gold and foreign exchange, Germany had to sell her products abroad. It was soon clear, however, that the biggest problem about reparations would be the question of transfers. Unemployment began to appear in Great Britain as well as in other countries, and no one wanted to accept German-manufactured goods. German coal, timber, and a few other products were acceptable, but these could never be sufficient to fulfill the total reparations bill. Germany's industrial plant was also in bad shape, and before she could export finished goods she had to buy large quantities of raw materials. All this was a heavy drain on Germany's monetary and credit system.

As Germany was forced to meet the payments, the mark began to decline sharply in value. This decline was hastened by a certain export of capital from Germany by individuals who wanted to get their wealth out of reach of taxation and possible confiscation for reparations. The mark continued to decline until at the end of 1921 it was worth only about 2 per cent of its prewar value. At the Conference of Cannes in January, 1922, the Allies granted Germany a partial moratorium. In July the situation had deteriorated to such an extent that the Allies were faced with granting a full moratorium. Sharp differences now arose between Great Britain and France. The former was more inclined to show leniency to Germany, for in Britain hopes were fast vanishing of ever making large collections. British industrialists were eager to restore the German market, which before 1914 had taken about 25 per cent of British exports. In France, Poincaré was at the helm and he was determined to recover immediately some of the vast sums that his government had just paid out for the reconstruction of devastated areas. All through the remainder of 1922 the question was debated back and forth. No one seemed able to devise a scheme for making the cash payments, and so these were not the issue. Instead, Poincaré concentrated on getting the Reparations Commission to declare Germany in default on timber deliveries. The British were inclined to give Germany more time and to accept the German explanation that private contractors had refused to deliver timber to the German government in return for marks that really had no value. The French, however, pressed their point home and won the support of Italy and Belgium. By a vote of three to one (Great Britain) the Reparations Commission declared Germany in default.

THE OCCUPATION OF THE RUHR. Over the protests of Great Britain and the United States, France, with Belgian and Italian support, now undertook to occupy the Ruhr. This episode aroused tremendous feeling in Germany. The occupation of the Rhineland had been much resented in Germany, and the French occupation army was hated more than any other. The French made use of North African and Senegalese troops, and they became a favorite target for newspaper items. When the Ruhr was occupied this hatred rose to a red-hot pitch. It was during this occupation that Adolf Hitler, in collaboration with the well-known General Ludendorff, made his abortive attempt (Beer Hall Putsch) to take over the government of Bavaria and of Germany.

For an explanation of the French position one has not far to seek. French losses in the war had been tremendous, not only in devastated territory but in the terrific loss of manpower. France was governed by a very strong fear of Germany, coupled with resentment at the difference between the prospects held out by the peace settlement and actual conditions. She felt herself deserted by her allies, which tended to make her even more intransigent. Nevertheless, the occupation of the Ruhr acted as a boomerang for France, who was considered to be turning the thumbscrews on a prostrate enemy. The United States chose this time to withdraw its armies of occupation, and Britain was definitely hostile to the whole French procedure. Actually nothing did more to rehabilitate Germany in the eyes of the world than did the Ruhr occupation. France's clumsy attempt at this time to create small independent Rhineland states also did not help Gallic prestige.

True, the attempt of the German government to defeat the French occupation with a program of passive resistance failed. There was some violence, and over seventy Germans and twenty Allied soldiers (French, Italian, and Belgian) lost their lives. Between 140,000 and 150,000 Germans were deported from the Ruhr. Heavy fines and prison sentences were imposed on others, and much property was confiscated. It was at this time that the German mark lost all value in the most spectacular inflation of modern times. Deprived of her main industrial centers and with her currency worthless, Germany had to submit. Officially the French had again asserted their leadership in Europe, but in a Europe that was going nowhere. The expected reparations payments did not materialize.

THE DAWES PLAN. Even before the occupation of the Ruhr, American Secretary of State Hughes had proposed that an international committee of experts should examine the question of Germany's capacity to pay. After much diplomatic dickering it was finally agreed to do this. The so-called "Dawes Plan" called for the evacuation of the Ruhr and annual reparations payments starting at $250,000,000 and gradually increasing over four years to a standard payment of $625,000,000. These payments could be raised or lowered according to Germany's prosperity. Specific sources of revenue (income of German railways, etc.) were pledged as security for payments, which were to be made through a special bank to be under the direction of seven Germans and seven foreigners. As a beginning Germany was to receive a loan of $200,000,000. An "Agent General of Reparations," resident in Germany, was to supervise the execution of the plan.

The inauguration of the Dawes Plan, the establishment of a new currency, and the conclusion of the Locarno Agreements [see above, pp. 162–65] ushered in a period of prosperity in Germany. German municipalities and businessmen obtained huge loans, primarily from the United States. Factories were renovated, a new merchant marine was built, and "Made in Germany" again became a familiar stamp in the channels of world commerce. Although much of the foreign exchange came from foreign loans, Germany made its reparation payments as scheduled. From 1924 to 1930 she paid a total of $1,994,566,695.

THE YOUNG PLAN. The Dawes Plan provided only a schedule of payments. It did not say when they were to cease, or what the total amount of payments would be. The figure of thirty-three billion dollars, plus interest, plus Belgian war debt, plus cost of armies of occupation, still stood. No one any longer had any hopes of collecting this sum. By 1928 prosperity had begun to ebb somewhat in Europe. Germany began to feel the pinch of the full annuity payments, to which had to be added a heavy interest charge on all her foreign loans. A committee of experts under the chairmanship of Owen D. Young of the United States was now charged by the interested governments with "drawing up proposals for a complete and final settlement of the reparation problem." The committee consisted of representatives of Belgium, Great Britain, France, Germany, Italy, Japan, and the United States. From February to June 1929, the committee wrestled with the so-called "Young Plan."

The main feature of the new scheme was that it set a definite limit to reparations payments. For the next thirty-seven years Germany was to pay certain set sums which fluctuated from year to year but averaged about $512,500,000. For the following twenty-two years the average was to be somewhat less. Germany could thus look forward to ending her payments in 1988. The annual payments were less than under the Dawes Plan, and the total expected was not quite one third of the thirty-three billion set in 1921. Deliveries in kind were to be stopped after ten years, and payments were to be made through a new "Bank of International Settlements." It was hoped that this bank would solve the difficult problem of transfer. Germany's control over her economic system was increased by abolishing the Reparation Commission, the Agent-General for Reparation, and certain other supervisory agencies.

WAR DEBTS AND REPARATIONS. The Young Plan also recognized the interrelation of war debts and reparations. For years the European powers had sought to establish a connection between them. The United States had refused to listen to proposals made at the Peace Conference for an all-round cancellation of war debts, for it was felt that this would burden the citizens of the United States with an undue share of the cost of the war. In 1922 Lord Balfour added another facet to the problem when he informed Great Britain's debtors that Britain would seek to collect from them only an amount equal to the sum that she had to pay to the United States. At that time these powers together owed Britain four times the amount Britain owed to the United States, and they insisted they could pay their debts only if they received reparations. Thus, what all the other nations combined could not pay was somehow to be collected from Germany alone. At the other horn of the dilemma was the United States, which was thus maneuvered into a position where it was easy for others besides cartoonists to picture Uncle Sam as Shylock. A few people in the United States urged the cancellation of war debts, and the issue was a favorite topic for college debates. The mass of the people were opposed to cancellation, and politically it was a settled issue. The United States government in the twenties entered into funding agreements bearing varying rates of interest with the different debtor states. These agreements were scheduled to run for sixty-two years.

The Young Plan now recognized the connection between Reparations and War Debts by dividing the annual payments made by Germany into (a) reparations and (b) "outpayments." The payments under reparations were to remain constant, while the "outpayments" (which constituted the bulk of the annuities) were to be tied to the debt obligations of Germany's creditors. If these obligations should be modified, Germany's payments in this category were to be reduced proportionately. The payment of reparations under the Young Plan was thus definitely tied to the United States' policy of debt collection.

THE END OF REPARATIONS. Putting the matter in what is, no doubt, an oversimplified way, the issue came to be whether the American or the German taxpayer was to pay the war debts. This was partly the result of the high tariff that the United States laid on foreign imports, making it impossible for Germany or any other state to meet debt payments. Not only in the United States, but everywhere, national economic systems were considered more important than a sound international economic structure, and it was a world-wide depression that brought an end to reparations through the Hoover Moratorium (1931) and the Lausanne Settlement (1932) [see Chapter 12].

The problem of reparations had its effects on all aspects of life and culture. Some of the political repercussions of the Ruhr occupation have been pointed out. The payment of reparations acted as a millstone on all the German cabinets. That there was a reluctance to pay is clear, but it is also equally clear that economically it was not feasible to collect the huge sums that the Allies expected. Taking the Allied evaluation figures, up to 1930 Germany had paid $4,600,996,045. The German figures were much higher. Whether Germany could have paid appreciably larger sums will forever remain a moot question.

Economic Development

While Germany retained the core of its industrial establishment, the Versailles Treaty necessitated some fundamental adjustments. This was not only because of reparations payments but also because Germany lost some 14.6 per cent of its arable area, 74.5 per cent of its iron ore, 68.1 per cent of its zinc and 26 per cent of its coal production.[1] The loss of the

[1] Gustav Stolper: *German Economy, 1870–1940: Issues and Trends* (New York, 1940), p. 135.

merchant marine was also a heavy blow to German economy. Rolling stock on the railroads had deteriorated, and repairs and replacements had not been maintained in the factories.

The Social Democrats talked a great deal about socialization of industry. This did not cause much alarm, for the people of Germany were used to a great amount of state participation in industrial undertakings. The railroad, telephone, and telegraph systems, as well as public utilities like municipal traction systems, gasworks, electricity, and waterworks, had for years been owned either by the states or the municipalities. Now cities and other local government areas continued to expand their program of municipal socialism, and the railway network was nationalized.

In 1919 some autonomous governmental authorities (public corporations) were established for the coal, potash, and steel industries, but it proved impossible to socialize completely any of the so-called key industries. Consolidations took place, and great cartels were formed over which the government exercised a major degree of regulation and control. Cartels, however, were not considered harmful, and the attitude of the German government towards them did not correspond to that of the American government towards trusts. The German state, of course, regulated industry not only directly by law but also indirectly through its currency, taxation, trade, and wage policies. It also increased its participation in industry by establishing government-owned or controlled companies and corporations, which were run by private business methods and competed with private capital groups. Such a system of "mixed economy" was not unique in Germany, but it was developed there more than in most countries. Many of the wartime industries that had been built by the state constituted an important segment of this type of economic organization.

COLLAPSE OF GERMAN CURRENCY. Although depreciation of currency occurred throughout Central Europe, the situation in Germany was worst of all. In 1913 a mark was worth 23.8 cents. It depreciated considerably during the war and after, but was fairly stable through 1920 and part of 1921, at the rate of 60 or 70 to the dollar. It began to plummet in July, 1922, and with the occupation of the Ruhr in January, 1923, the printing presses were really set to work. "In the last months before the collapse more than 300 paper mills worked at top speed to deliver notepaper to the Reichsbank, and 150 printing companies had 2,000 note presses running day and night to print the Reichsbank notes." [2] But even this was not enough. Private business concerns and municipalities issued "Emergency Currencies" (*Notgeld*), which had a local circulation. Waiters found it cheaper to use currency as a scrap-pad to figure up their accounts than to go out and purchase blank paper. Wages of course did not keep up with the rise in prices. Money burned in the pocket, and everybody tried to buy something before it lost all value. By November 12, 1923, the dollar was worth 840,000,000,000 marks. By November 20 it was quoted at 4,200,000,-

[2] Stolper: *German Economy, 1870–1940*, p. 154.

000,000 marks and at this point a halt was called. A new *Rentenmark* was finally issued. 1,000,000,000,000 paper marks were equal to one gold mark or one *Rentenmark*. The *Rentenmark* was supposedly based on Germany's landed and industrial property. Actually the new currency had little real backing. The people, however, had confidence in it, and that, with the let-up in reparations payments, was sufficient to carry it through. Today economic historians speak of the "Miracle of the Rentenmark."

RESULTS OF THE INFLATION. Some money speculators and big industrialists made huge profits out of the early inflation, although much of their wealth disappeared with the final currency collapse. The process was simple enough. An industrialist obtained credit, purchased real goods, and then later repaid his debt with marks that had depreciated further in value. That worked well in 1921 and 1922, but failed when the mark hit astronomical figures. Hugo Stinnes built up a big industrial empire in this period, but lost much of it later because he carried over into the period of stabilized currency debts from the previous period, which he had been unable to unload. Property held at fixed money values—such as bonds, mortgages, and savings-bank deposits—became worthless. People who had saved a small sum for old age were left destitute, since even insurance policies were worthless. Later the government attempted to salvage something by revaluating long-term indebtedness. Various rates were set, the highest being 25 per cent on mortgages. Some attempt was made to equalize the burden by setting special tax levies on property and by regulating rents.

The inflation had important political repercussions. Many always held the Republic to blame for it, and it became a fine point of attack for anti-republican demagogues. It was an excellent political issue, for everyone knew the results, but no one knew for certain why it had come about. The inflation particularly weakened the middle classes, and old ideas of property values came to be discarded. It also caused many white-collar and middle-class employees to seek government employment. Many private pension systems had been wiped out, but old government servants, including teachers, soon were drawing their pensions again because the state could recoup its finances through its power of taxation. The right to a government pension seemed the greatest security a person could obtain. The experience of the inflation left such a bitter imprint on the minds of the people that no government ever dared enter on an inflationary policy again. When the great depression struck, other powers abandoned the gold standard and devaluated their currencies, but Germany refused to follow in their footsteps. According to economic theory it probably would have been the thing to do, but politically it was impossible. Instead, Germany tried to obtain similar benefits by devious forms of currency manipulation. This accounts at least in part for the "travel mark," "export mark," etc., of the Hitler regime [see below, p. 458].

FOREIGN LOANS. During the period of comparative prosperity following the establishment of a sound currency system, the Dawes Plan, and the Locarno Pacts, confidence in Germany's future returned to Western capitalists. Loans were pumped into the German economy. Of the $5,150,-000,000 that Germany received up to 1931, exactly half was on short-term credit. The banks, which were coming increasingly under the control of the state, took these short-term loans and extended credits to industries on a long-term basis. The same practice was followed by the big banks in Austria and other countries, with the exception of Czechoslovakia, where there was much less need for foreign capital. When the banks in the United States failed to renew their short-term loans, the Central European banks were caught short because they could not call their own long-term loans. This led to the great banking crisis that was part of the big depression. In order to stop further withdrawal of short-term money (about ten billion marks remained), the German government at the end of July 1931 (a month after the Hoover Moratorium), proclaimed its own moratorium on short-term credits.

INDUSTRIAL EXPANSION. With the foreign loans Germany not only met reparations payments but rebuilt its industry along American lines. The use of assembly lines (*Laufender Band*) was among the most widely adopted innovations. Industrial consolidation took the form of cartels, one of the most important of which was the *Interessen Gemeinschaft der Farben Industrie*, literally "Community of Interests of the Dyestuff Industry." Usually referred to as "I. G. Farben," this organization—formed in 1925—came to control some 400 firms in Germany and 500 abroad, and had cartel arrangements with others. It dominated the important chemical industries and accounted for all of Germany's production of synthetic gasoline and rubber. The modernization of Germany's industrial plant and methods enabled her to regain her pre-eminence in the chemical, electrical, and optical industries. Her merchant fleet was rebuilt and the two giant liners, the *Bremen* and *Europa*, set the standards in luxury and speed for the Atlantic crossing. Exports increased, which made imports possible. This was essential, for normally there was hardly a food staple, except sugar, or a raw material, except coal, coke, and potash, of which Germany had a sufficient domestic supply. By 1929 exports took approximately one third of the total industrial output. This meant that one out of every three industrial workers was dependent on the export trade. When exports were curtailed by two thirds during the years 1929 to 1933, unemployment mounted in the same proportion (2,258,000 March, 1930, to 6,031,000 March, 1932). To meet this crisis Chancellor Bruening extended state control over German economic life to a point from which the transfer to the totalitarian state of Hitler could be made only too easily.

LABOR POLICY. Ever since Bismarck had pioneered with the creation of a social insurance system, the German worker has been relatively well protected against industrial accidents, sickness, and destitution in old age. The Republic had but to round out the system by introducing unemployment insurance in 1926. Proclamation of an eight-hour maximum working day was the first decree issued by the revolutionary government in 1918.

Strong unions existed and were even strengthened by the Republic.

Under the Empire, collective labor contracts had been a private affair between the unions and employers. The government now undertook the task of mediating when no agreement could be reached by employer and union. In such a case, the government as mediator issued its decision, and if it was accepted by one of the parties it became binding on all. The authorities had power to declare a collective contract binding for all employers and employees in a respective industry and district, even if they were not directly represented in the negotiations. This was particularly important in Germany where there were three main groups of trade unions—the Free Unions, Christian Unions, and Hirsch-Duncker Unions—often competing for membership in the same industry or shop. Originally it had been expected that government mediation would be the exception. Instead, it was relied upon more and more, and the government came to wield great power over the wage and price structure of Germany. The system was admirably devised to enable the government to carry through its radical deflationary policy (lowering of prices and wages) after 1930, but it also had its unfortunate aspects. The compromises and adjustments that had formerly been achieved directly between industry and labor were now transferred to the governmental level. The government was blamed for all the ills of the economic system, a situation that did not add to its prestige and security. The producers blamed the government for low prices; the employees blamed it for low wages.

In addition to a far-reaching system of collective bargaining, the government in 1920 introduced a system of shop councils, which negotiated with each individual employer within the terms of the general union contract. Some sharing in management was also envisaged for the shop councils, but this never became an important part of their work.

HOUSING. The government also participated very directly in the building of houses. Reich, states, and municipalities all shared in this activity, sometimes building housing projects outright, more often providing the necessary credit to private individuals or associations. Germany established a very good record in actually getting the houses built and not just talking about them; the lowest income groups found quarters and conveniences unknown to similar wage earners in many other countries. Strict rent control was also practiced. This was particularly necessary because the inflation wiped out the wealth of many families, while real estate values remained. Tenants obtained a vested right to their apartments and could not be ousted as long as they paid the rent set by the state.

The state was forced to participate in housing as well as in establishing many industries, simply because private capital was not available. The scarcity of funds literally forced the state to be the builder. Here mention should also be made of the many public stadiums and athletic fields erected throughout Germany by municipalities. Germany in this period produced some of the most advanced examples of modern functional architecture, a field in which the name of Walter Gropius was outstanding.

AGRICULTURAL POLICY. Germany under the Republic continued to be a food-importing country. In western and southern Germany small individual proprietorships were the rule, while in the northeast over 50 per cent of the agricultural lands belonged to large estate owners. As a rule these owners administered their own estates and did not sublet to tenants. Although there was talk about breaking up the large estates, land distribution was not a great part of the revolution. By 1931, 1,500,000 acres had been transformed into some 50,000 settler farms out of approximately 13,800,000 acres held as large estates before the war. Such resettlement was one device for meeting the problem of unemployment.

In the northeast, potatoes and rye were the big staple products. The agricultural depression of the late twenties hit this rye belt particularly hard. As in all countries, the government endeavored to provide agricultural relief. A special fund called *"Osthilfe"* was established. It developed into a typical political "slush fund," and its manipulation played a tragic part during the last days of the Republic. The government did much toward furthering agricultural research and helping the farmers to farm more scientifically. Great use was made of chemical fertilizers, and the yield per acre increased. The farmers were also strong supporters of the co-operative movement. In 1930, out of the more than 50,000 co-operative societies in Germany, 77 per cent belonged to agriculture.

Religion

CHURCH AND STATE. Although the Weimar constitution declared that church and state were separated, that, indeed, no state church existed, the state governments continued to collect church taxes on behalf of the major denominations—Roman Catholic, Lutheran, Reformed, and Jewish. These bodies had the privileges of public corporations. The so-called free churches (Methodists, Baptists, Christian Scientists, Jehovah's Witnesses, etc.) went their own way and did not receive state money. This procedure continued an established practice in Germany. Likewise the church authorities maintained close relations with certain state agencies. About two thirds of the population was Protestant, and a third Catholic, while the Jews numbered only half a million.

Religious liberty was the rule in Germany long before 1919, yet the new constitution brought new freedom to the churches. The Jesuits, for example, were permitted to return, and the unlimited right to form religious associations brought about a great increase in the number of religious orders. This meant that Catholics could expand their activities and services. On the whole, Jews were well treated in Germany, and many Jews from "the East" migrated to what seemed to them a promised land. They benefited by the educational opportunities that were now freely opened to them. Many entered government employ and other professions that had been effectually closed to Jews before the war. The German government up to the time of Hitler did not discriminate against them by legislation. Reformed Jews gained headway over the Old Orthodox bodies.

Political clericalism was inherited by the Weimar Republic. The strong Center party was a member of all German cabinets up to the advent of Hitler. In Bavaria there was even a rival Catholic party—the Bavarian People's party. Protestants as a whole were more diverse in their political affiliation, although the National People's party was closely connected with Protestant church groups. The existence of clerical parties had its unfortunate aspects. It often brought about a real conflict of conscience. How could a man be a Social Democrat or even a member of other parties and still be a good Catholic? On the other hand, many people came to take their religious obligations lightly, although they did not actually withdraw from the churches or object to paying the church taxes.

CHURCH AND EDUCATION. While relations between church and state were on the whole friendly, the problem of religious education in the schools was one that nearly wrecked the Weimar Assembly. On this issue the Protestant and Catholic churches were united.

The German constitution left the regulation of church and educational affairs to the respective state governments; not only this, but in some of the states there were several systems. Prussia, for instance, had permitted historic provincial church and school systems to continue when it annexed different provinces in the nineteenth century. Public schools were mainly differentiated on religious lines. The two main types were the confessional school, which was staffed by teachers of one confession and attended largely by pupils of the same confession, and the *Simultan* school, to which pupils of all confessions came and were separated only for religious instruction.

Educational authorities had long stressed the need for overhauling and unifying Germany's educational system. With the greater mobility of population that is part of modern civilization, it was important to facilitate transfer from one school to another. The party that tried to push a revised educational code was, however, the Social Democratic party, which was on the whole hostile to religious education in the public schools. It was true that this subject was a primary cause of the complexity of the German school system. Their attempts to force through a revised educational code always failed because the Center party could enlist the aid of Protestant groups on this issue. It did appear that most German parents wanted religion as part of the regular curriculum. Nevertheless, a tendency under the Weimar Republic towards greater secularization of education was evident, and professional educators took over from clergymen as inspectors of schools.

Political Development

SWING AWAY FROM THE LEFT. The political trend in Germany was similar to that in the other states of Central Europe. In June, 1920, the Social Democrats had to surrender the chancellorship to the Catholic Center party. From then until 1928 they were represented for very brief periods in only two of the nine cabinets. In 1928 Hermann Müller, a Social Democrat and a signer of the Versailles Treaty, became chancellor and held the office until 1930. His cabinet was the last that functioned in a normal parliamentary manner. Never did the Socialists control the government outright, and for only three years in the history of the Republic did they head the coalition cabinets. The Center party was a member of practically every cabinet, and in general the middle-class parties controlled the federal government. This was not true of the governments of the states. In some the Social Democrats never held power, but they held the leadership continually in Prussia, which comprised roughly three fifths of the area and population of Germany.

The important post of minister of foreign affairs was held by Gustav Stresemann of the People's party from November, 1923, until the time of his death in October, 1929. He was responsible for the Pact of Locarno, for taking Germany into the League in 1926, and in general for a policy of Western orientation. He was, however, explicit in his refusal to recognize the eastern frontiers of Germany and was a warm supporter of *Anschluss* with Austria. Moreover, he kept alive the contacts with Russia created by the Treaty of Rapallo in 1922 and subsequently strengthened by numerous trade pacts.

PRESIDENTIAL ELECTIONS. In 1925 the death of President Ebert, who had been elected by the Weimar National Assembly, made it necessary for the German people to hold their first presidential election. In hopes of defeating the rightist candidate, the Socialists agreed to support the leader of the Center party. The rightist parties, on the other hand, drafted Field Marshal Paul von Hindenburg—the hero of Tannenberg and a Protestant —to be their standard-bearer. The election was bitterly fought. Hindenburg was charged with favoring a monarchist restoration, and a remilitarization of Germany. Opposition to his candidacy in the foreign press did him no harm so far as the German electorate was concerned. The religious question also entered into the picture, for many Protestants, even if they carried their religion lightly, did not wish to see a Catholic occupy the highest elective office. The election was so close that the Communists, who polled almost two million votes, could have swung the election the other way had they gone along with the Socialists in supporting the Center party leader.

Hindenburg took seriously his oath to uphold the constitution. He performed his duties so satisfactorily that when he was up for re-election in 1932 the Social Democrats and Center party furnished him his greatest support. This time much of the rightist and nationalist vote went to Adolf Hitler, the leader of the relatively new National Socialist German Workers party. The Communist candidate doubled his previous vote and polled over four million ballots.

THE RISE OF NATIONAL SOCIALISM. In March, 1918, Anton Drexler, a locksmith in Munich, formed a "Committee of Independent Workingmen" whose object was the conclusion of an honorable peace. The end of the war led him to organize his group into the German Workers party. The formation of new parties was a common event in the Germany of that period, when there were also many volunteer armed bands (*Frei-korps*). There were, for example, Ehrhard's Brigade, the Baltic *Landwehr*, Heydebreck's Wehrwolves Corps, the Pfeffer-Rossbach-Lützow-Epp-Corps. As these were forced to disband, many of their members transferred their activity to more legitimate political parties. In 1919 Captain Ernst Roehm, a member of Epp's Corps, joined the German Workers party and brought with him many of his friends. Roehm had organizing ability and soon came to play an important part in building up the party. Another early recruit was Gottfried Feder, a young civil engineer, who had taken to writing on economics. He had a theory of productive and unproductive capital, most of the latter being supposedly controlled by Jews and big business. Soldiers were now active in politics, and Feder gave some lectures to the Reichswehr units stationed in Munich. Here Adolf Hitler, at that time a so-called lance corporal (private first class), heard him and was impressed by his economic theories. Hitler spoke frequently himself, and his commanding officers, recognizing his oratorical abilities, appointed him lecturer to the troops. The soldiers were to be taught to feel and think nationally.

Adolf Hitler was born on April 20, 1889, at Braunau, in Upper Austria, where his father was a lesser customs official. Hitler received the usual elementary education and customary Catholic religious instruction. In 1903 he went to Vienna, where he earned his livelihood as a painter and acquired many of his political and social views. His anti-Jewish phobia dates from this period. Two years before the war he migrated to Munich. By this time he had acquired some skill as an artist and he supplemented his income by doing sketches and hand-painted postcards. With the opening of hostilities in 1914 he enlisted in the Bavarian army and fought throughout the war. There was nothing fictitious about his combat service and he won the "Iron Cross," the German army's award for bravery. He was wounded in 1917 and severely gassed in 1918. His slow recovery from the latter and Germany's defeat left him at loose ends and emotionally unsettled.

As part of his "educational" work with his company, Hitler was detailed to attend a meeting of the German Workers party. Here he entered into the discussion and so impressed Drexler that the latter invited him to become a member of the inner political cell. After great hesitation, so he relates in his autobiography, he decided to join the party. His membership card bore the number seven. For nine months he continued in the army, but withdrew in April, 1920, to devote his entire time to politics.

At this time the party headquarters in Munich was in touch with the old National Socialist party in Vienna, which was debating adding the word "Worker" to its name. The upshot was that Drexler's group changed its name and henceforth was called the National Socialist German Workers party (*National Sozialistische Deutsche Arbeiterpartei*; NSDAP), in the hope that this name would appeal to broad strata of society. Great care was also given to the design of a new party flag. Red was chosen the basic color, partly in order to irritate the Communists and Social Democrats. By placing the black swastica on a white circle, the old colors of the Empire—black, white, red—were restored. The party did not adopt the old flag in its entirety because, as Hitler states, its purpose was not to resurrect the old Empire with all its faults, but rather to build anew.

The party now had not only a new name and a new flag, but also a new program. In February, 1920, it adopted a twenty-five-point statement drawn up by Feder as the unalterable program of the party. Here are set forth its basic racial philosophy of anti-Semitism, the necessity for control of "exploitive capital," the rehabilitation of the middle classes and an economically prosperous peasantry, and the strong centralization of state power.[3]

Hitler threw all his energy into building up the party. He developed his oratorical skill and soon discovered that he had the ability to sway large audiences. Denunciation of the Versailles Treaty was always a good starting point, and the Jews furnished a convenient scapegoat for all of Germany's ills. They had been responsible for the German revolution, that "stab in the back" which undermined the resistance of the German army. They were responsible for the high interest rates that sucked the life blood out of the small shopkeepers and peasants. With money furnished by General von Epp the party in December, 1920, acquired a paper, the *Völkischer Beobachter*. It was during 1920–21 that they found it advantageous to form special patrols to preserve order at meetings and to lend a hand in militant political agitation. These Storm Troops (*Sturmabteilungen;* SA) adopted a distinctive brown shirt and soon developed into a large organization. Although he was not its official leader at this time, Ernst Roehm stood back of the whole SA. He would have liked to turn it into a secret army, as a replacement for the forbidden conscript levies. Hitler, who by July, 1921, had won complete control over the party, was opposed to this. He wanted to use the SA primarily for political affairs, and he felt that a volunteer organization lacking real coercive power could never be welded into a disciplined, efficient military force. Hermann Goering, a well-known aviator in the war, joined the party and became leader of the SA. Hitler still felt so insecure that he recruited a special bodyguard, which ultimately developed into the famous Elite Guard (*Schutzstaffel;* SS). A black shirt and a dagger became characteristic parts of the uniform of this small and highly disciplined organization.

The occupation of the Ruhr and the complete collapse of German currency led Hitler, with the help of General Ludendorff, to attempt the Munich Beer Hall Putsch of November 9, 1923, which was an effort to take over the government of Bavaria. Contrary to expectations the Reichswehr remained loyal to the government. A volley dispersed the swaggering revolutionists, but made a number of martyrs whose graves became a Munich shrine in later years. Now the property of the party was confiscated. Goering, who had been seriously wounded, was smuggled into

---

[3] A more detailed discussion of National Socialist theory is reserved for Chapter 18.

Austria and reached Sweden via Italy. An amnesty was granted to him in 1926. Hitler was sentenced to five years' imprisonment. While in prison, which was not an ordeal of hard labor, he dictated the first volume of his autobiography, *Mein Kampf*, to Rudolf Hess, one of his devoted party supporters. Henceforth, this book became the authoritative statement of the party philosophy and program of action.

On being released from prison in February, 1925, Hitler began reorganizing his party. It was not an easy task. The ban against his speaking in Bavaria was not lifted until 1927, and in Prussia not until 1930. It was in this period of reorganization that Goebbels was given the task of building up the party organization in Berlin. He was an excellent organizer and soon became a leading member of the party hierarchy. Roehm, who spent 1928–30 as a retired former German officer training the Bolivian army, was appointed head of the SA in January, 1931.

Hitler and his other key party men—Frick, Feder, Gregor Strasser, Darre, Ley, Rosenberg—worked hard at building up the party. They campaigned in out-of-the-way hamlets that had usually been by-passed. A brass band, lots of bright flags, and impassioned oratory won many votes. A tremendous amount of sheer hard labor went into building up the party. The National Socialists were responsible for staging a plebiscite on the adoption of the Young Plan in 1929. Although they lost the campaign, they showed they had grown tremendously in strength.

In order to strengthen the German democratic parties which were in power, France, in the spring of 1930, agreed to withdraw her armies of occupation. This was five years ahead of schedule, but the concession did not forestall the growth of Hitler's influence. The mounting unemployment and economic distress made the people willing to listen to anyone who promised relief. In the September, 1930, elections Hitler won 108 seats in the Reichstag, a gain of 96 seats over the 1928 poll.

THE COLLAPSE OF PARLIAMENTARY GOVERNMENT. The election of 1930 was a turning point in German history. Chancellor Bruening, head of the Center party, formed his coalition out of rightist parties, but it was a minority government. In a Reichstag of 577 members neither the National Socialists (108), the Social Democrats (143) or the Communists (77) were represented in the cabinet. This failure to command an absolute majority in the Reichstag explains, in part, why Bruening abandoned the normal procedures of parliamentary practice. He governed by presidential decrees issued under Article 48 of the constitution; and the Social Democrats, the largest party in the Reichstag, tolerated the procedure. It is true that these were difficult times. Bruening undertook a sharp deflationary program to combat the depression. Since this meant a cutting of wages and prices, it was not popular, and members of Parliament with an eye towards re-election were glad they did not have to vote on the various measures dealing with such controversial problems.

On April 14, 1932, Bruening took his first strong measures against the National Socialist party, when he ordered the Hitler SA and SS disbanded.

Special uniformed party organizations were no longer to be permitted. On May 12 the Reichstag defeated a vote of "no confidence" in this ministry by thirty votes. Yet on the last of May the Bruening government resigned, for the cabinet had lost the support of Hindenburg.

Bruening's dismissal was undoubtedly the result of political intrigue by a group of men around the President. Officially the President charged Bruening with having ministers with Bolshevist ideas in his cabinet, because they wanted to undertake a large scale land settlement program in East Prussia. To this President von Hindenburg and other big landholders were opposed. The President also maintained that the recent state elections indicated that Bruening's government no longer represented the will of the people. Bruening's fall was generally regretted in the West because he was considered an ardent republican. This he was not. In fact, he liked to govern too well by decree, and he had definite plans for the restoration of the monarchy. It is the chain of political events culminating with Hitler's accession to power which has magnified the importance of Bruening's dismissal.

Franz von Papen, the new chancellor, formed another minority government of the right, the so-called "Cabinet of Barons." He reaped the benefit of Bruening's careful diplomacy when the Lausanne Conference abolished the payment of reparations. On the plea that the Prussian state government was no longer able to carry out its duties, Papen took over the administration of that state under Article 48 of the constitution. This gave him, and the chancellors who succeeded him, control over the Prussian state police. The Reichstag was dissolved, but in the July, 1932, elections the National Socialist representation jumped from 108 to 230 seats in a Reichstag of 608 members. The election was honestly run, and there was no undue coercion, although Papen had permitted the SA and SS to don their uniforms again. Hitler, as leader of the largest party, demanded that he be given sole power. Hindenburg refused, insisting that if Hitler wished to be chancellor, there would have to be a coalition government that had the support of the Reichstag. This Hitler refused and again Papen formed a government. Like his predecessor, Papen governed by decree, but in the new Reichstag, a combination of National Socialists and Communists could repeal every decree he issued. By their united action they could also prevent any law whatever from being passed. Since both these extreme parties expected to benefit by the collapse of the Weimar regime, they were willing to co-operate to this end. As a last resource another election was held with no better results, and regretfully Hindenburg accepted Papen's resignation.

The Nationalists were the most conservative party, formed largely of army officers, the civil service, conservative landholders and men of vested interests, who were loud in criticism of the Republic yet laid claim to an extreme patriotism. To this congenial group Hindenburg turned, making General von Schleicher his new chancellor. The latter was an arch intriguer who for years had been pulling strings from his *Reichswehr* office, but his

Nationalist-dominated cabinet lacked the majority support of the Reichstag. He made surprising bids for support from the labor unions and announced a program of increased settlement of the unemployed on the big eastern estates. An investigation of the *"Osthilfe"* was also rumored to be in the offing. This program appealed neither to the great industrialists nor to the Junkers. Papen now arranged a meeting between Hugenberg, the leader of the Nationalist party, and Hitler. A working program was arranged between the two groups, providing for a coalition cabinet with Hitler as chancellor. By this agreement the Nationalist party deserted Schleicher's government, and when the president refused another dissolution of the Reichstag his resignation was in order. On January 30, 1933, Hitler became chancellor of Germany with Papen as vice chancellor. In the cabinet Nationalists outnumbered the National Socialists. Germany, like most of the other states of Central Europe, had gone from Social Democracy through varying stages of liberal and conservative party rule to a dictatorshop of the right.

CHAPTER

9

The Establishment of Fascist Italy

Postwar Italy, 1919–22

IT was a divided Italy which had entered the war and the strife between "interventionists and neutralists" carried over into the postwar years. Great dissatisfaction with the treaties prevailed, and the years 1919–22 were truly a time of disillusionment, unrest, and turmoil. The value of the lira declined, and the cost of living increased by leaps and bounds. The two million demobilized Italian soldiers had difficulty in finding any jobs at all, while industrial workers sought to maintain their wartime economic status in the face of an industrial slump. Agricultural workers were discontented with their status on the great estates and in some sections began to seize lands for themselves. This was a movement that ran its course quite apart from the series of strikes and lockouts plaguing Italian industry at this time.

Meanwhile, the government exerted no leadership and advanced no clear-cut policy. What many Italians felt, was expressed in deeds by D'Annunzio. Gathering a group of vociferous nationalists, ex-soldiers, and adventurers, he led them in a spectacular descent on the city of Fiume; this city was desired partly as compensation for Italy's failure to receive Dalmatia [see above, pp. 87; 120]. D'Annunzio now thumbed his nose at the Italian government and issued grandiloquent manifestos on Italian destiny and Italian history. Many of the political devices, symbols, and ideologies first elaborated by this Italian poet in his government of Fiume were later adopted by Mussolini's Fascist party. When Italy concluded the Treaty of Rapallo with Yugoslavia on November 12, 1920, recognizing the establishment of Fiume as a free city, D'Annunzio declared war on the government. Three well-placed shots from an Italian warship led him to surrender, and Italian troops took over the policing of the city. This ended the immediate issue, but did not do away with the dissatisfaction and restlessness which had produced it.

ELECTIONS OF 1919 AND 1921. The parliamentary elections of November 16, 1919, the first since 1913, were held under a new electoral law that established proportional representation. There was a decided swing to the left, and the Socialists won about one third of the seats. The Populists, a new party led by a priest, Don Luigi Sturzo, ran second to the Socialists. They stood for more decentralization of government, guarantees for religious schools, labor reforms, the establishment of peasant farms on the great landed estates of the South, and far-reaching social reforms. Had the Socialists and Populists come to an agreement they might have worked out an adequate liberal program of reform through parliamentary action. The Socialists refused to enter a coalition government and instead of working through Parliament concentrated on direct action. The leaders of the party were under the spell of events as they were shaping themselves in Russia. Eventually in January, 1921, the extreme left wing of the Socialist party became the Communist party. The remaining Socialists split into two groups in 1922—the Italian Socialist party, and the right wing group known as the Reformist Socialist party, with Giacomo Matteotti as one of its leaders.

The failure of the Socialists to assume any parliamentary responsibility led to a continuation of Italian cabinets based on factions rather than on party support. So great was the dearth of leaders that the king was obliged to call upon Giolitti, now seventy-eight years old, to form a cabinet. Neither he nor two succeeding premiers were able to control a parliamentary majority despite new elections. Finally, in October, 1922, King Victor Emmanuel III asked Mussolini, the leader of a parliamentary delegation of only thirty-five members, to form a cabinet.

During the war Parliament had seldom been called into session and the government was carried on by decree. This abdication by Parliament of its proper functions did not cease with the end of the conflict. New bills granting the cabinet full power to carry on legislation by decree were enacted from time to time. Parliament never reasserted its full legislative powers and never assumed a dominant role in governmental affairs. When Mussolini took over, he simply applied the axe to a Parliament that had long been withering away.

The Rise of Fascism

IL DUCE. Benito Mussolini was born in 1883 near Forli, in the province of Romagna, in north central Italy. His father was a blacksmith and his mother had for some years taught school. Largely self-educated, Mussolini was for a short time a village schoolmaster. He early became interested in socialism. Earning his living as a manual laborer, he visited Switzerland, southern France, and the Austrian Tyrol, but because of his socialist agitation was excluded from all these territories. Upon returning to Italy he soon got into difficulties with the authorities because of his opposition to the Tripolitan War of 1911–12. As a doctrinaire Socialist he was against imperialism. By 1912 he had won his way to the editorship of *Avanti*, the official Socialist daily. When war broke out in 1914, he advocated a policy of absolute neutrality at first, but soon left this program and began to advocate intervention in the war on the side of the Allies. This led to his expulsion from the Socialist party, an action which nettled him forever after. It has been charged that French money was finding its way into Mussolini's hands at this time. Be that as it may, within three weeks he founded a new paper, *Il Popolo d'Italia*, which until 1919 carried the caption "A Socialist Daily."

Mussolini now became the spokesman for the left wing of the interventionist movement, a heterogeneous group held together only by the common desire for active participation in the war. Soon these men, regardless of party, organized themselves into small groups or *fasci*. Similar revolutionary *fasci* had been organized among the Socialists of Sicily in the nineties and since then the term *fasci* had retained a certain vogue in left wing circles. Mussolini, as head of the Milan group, was instrumental in calling a national convention of the various *fasci* scattered about Italy. A national organization, the *Fasci d'azione revoluzionaria* (bands for revolutionary action), was formed at Milan in January, 1915. By the end of February there were over one hundred local organizations affiliated with the national group, making the total membership about 9,000. They were very vocal, and organized street demonstrations in favor of intervention. Mussolini always considered this the start of the Fascist movement.

FOUNDING OF THE FASCIST PARTY. Soon after Italy's entrance into the war in 1915, Mussolini was called to the colors. He attained the rank of corporal, a distinction also associated with Napoleon and Hitler. In the spring of 1917, he was wounded by the explosion of a trench mortar. Demobilized, he returned to his paper and became a bitter critic of the politicians who were doing nothing to stop the spread of defeatism. If his agitation to enter the war can be considered the first step in the organization of the Fascist movement, Mussolini's campaign against defeatism and a subsequent campaign against the peace treaties may be considered the second and third steps. These were climaxed by the formation in March, 1919, of new postwar political groups, the *Fasci di combattimento*. A hierarchy of officials was established, and agents were sent out into the provinces to contact various groups and bring them under the control of the Milan organization.

In this period Italy abounded in local political groups, each with its own axe to grind. Among them were militant socialist and communist formations that were extremely critical of the war veterans. The returning soldiers, instead of being honored, were often jeered at as tools of imperialist oppressors. War veteran groups naturally organized in defense of their rights and honor, such groups being called *arditi*. They were small armed squads of young nationalists and ex-soldiers, who after the war retained their arms and a form of military organization. They never were so firmly knit together as some of the *Freikorps* that made their appearance in Germany at this same period, but it was these *arditi* who first wore the black shirt and carried a black banner, and it was from them that D'Annunzio recruited many of his volunteers for the descent on Fiume. There were also blue-shirted groups affiliated with the Nationalist party, and grey-shirted liberal squads.

Out of this melee of local organizations and squadrists, Mussolini slowly recruited and built up his Fascist party. There was no common policy except perhaps that of nationalism and super-patriotism. Whenever it raised its head in other countries in later years, fascism was always to manifest the same loud-voiced 100-per-cent chauvinism. The Fascist groups resorted to a policy of intimidation and terror, beating up opponents and using such tactics as forcibly administering large quantities of castor oil.

The Fascists have always claimed that they saved Italy from communism. In the postwar period, workers began to take over factories in sit-down strikes, but after a few months these seizures stopped, when the government promised that workers' councils would be established. Antifascist writers believe that by the time fascism came to power, the danger that Italy would become communist was long past—if indeed there had ever been such a possibility. Yet the general belief in such a danger undoubtedly aided the growth of the fascist movement. It certainly led many industrialists to lend their support to the Fascists, and it also accounts for the good press that Mussolini received in many foreign countries, not only in 1921–22, but in later years also. Sir Percival Phillips, special correspondent of the London *Daily Mail*, was responsible for a series of articles declaring that the Black Shirts had slain the Red Dragon of Communism. Fascism was considered "a democratic force in the field stronger than the socialism and communism of Marx." [1]

It was in this period of squadrist action that fascism gradually acquired most of its rites and ritual. The uniforms, songs, symbols, and organization of the *arditi* passed over into the Fascist party; the Roman salute came into use, and the lictor's rods and fasces were adopted as symbols of the unity which the party professed to bring to Italy.

Politically the Fascists did not fare very well. In the November, 1919, elections Mussolini's followers did not win a seat, and the Socialists celebrated somewhat prematurely his passing into oblivion. In the 1921 elections Mussolini was returned to the Chamber of Deputies with thirty-four of his supporters, but the party really had no policy or platform, and there was considerable division among the leaders as to what direction the party should take. This internal conflict was eventually compromised, and in November, 1921, Mussolini appeared as the unquestioned leader of the *Partito Nazionale Fascista*.

During the fall and summer of 1921–22 the Fascists ousted the Socialists from many of the communal councils, particularly in northern Italy, and railway and telegraph offices were often taken under Fascist "protection." Against this renewed policy of direct action the government did nothing. On October 24, 1922, a big Fascist party congress was held in Naples, where Mussolini cast aside his former republican policy and came out openly for the monarchy. For some time he had been courting closer relations with certain army generals, and this open declaration for the monarchy strengthened these ties.

THE MARCH ON ROME. From Naples, Mussolini returned to his editorial offices in Milan, but about 30,000 Fascist party members adjourned to the vicinity of Rome. Under the leadership of the Quadrumvirs General de Bono, Captain de Vecchi, Lieutenant Italo Balbo, and Michele Bianchi, plans were made to stage a big demonstration and take over control of the municipality of Rome, much in the same fashion as they had taken over many northern Italian cities. Premier Facta attempted to obtain the signature of the King to a decree declaring a state of siege in Rome and establishing martial law, but the King refused his signature, whereupon the Facta cabinet resigned on October 28, 1922. This decision of the King gave Mussolini his golden opportunity, for no one else was able to form a government under these conditions. Victor Emmanuel III, on October 29,

[1] Sir Percival Phillips: *The "Red" Dragon and the Black Shirts. How Italy Found Her Soul. The True Story of the Fascisti Movement* (London, 1922), p. 7.

telephoned Mussolini in Milan asking him to head a cabinet. Within twenty-four hours the new cabinet was created by forming a coalition in which the Fascists held less than half the posts, and on the evening of October 30 the Fascist militiamen began to withdraw from the city. The "March on Rome" had been successful, but few people dreamed what was in store for Italy. The old-line politicians expected that soon another political crisis would ease Mussolini out of office.

Fascist Theory

PRAGMATISM. Mussolini and his followers had been agitating for years, yet when they took office they had elaborated no systematic platform or theory. As Mussolini wrote later, in what has since become the authoritative statement of fascist doctrine: "Fascism was not the nursling of a doctrine worked out beforehand with detailed elaboration; it was born of the need for action and it was itself from the beginning practical rather than theoretical. . . ." [2] Fascism is empirical and pragmatic. That program is followed which is most likely to succeed in reaching any given end. As a Fascist theorist put it: "The party has pretended to go to the left, the government has pretended to go to the right; but in fact both go zig-zag according to the dictates of the moment." [3]

THE STATE. In spite of this opportunism, there is a core of fascist doctrine which rests on the conception that the state has a reality and existence over and apart from the individuals who compose it. The organic unity of the state was an idea not really new, for it had been an accepted part of nineteenth century theory ever since Hegel gave modern formulation to a concept which is very ancient in political thought. That the state is a source of liberty no one denies. For example, it is plain that everyone has more liberty on the highway because the state makes traffic regulations and enforces them. The Fascists, however, carried this idea to an extreme and maintained that individuals had no rights against the state, enjoying only such liberties as the state provided. They denied, for instance, that there were any inalienable rights of individuals, an idea which in theory, at least, democracies uphold. The Fascists also made much of what they called the futurity of the state. As they put it, the state is not the present generation but "the recapitulating unity of the indefinite series of generations." The Fascists demanded sacrifices for the future, and charged that democracies were concerned with only the citizens living at a particular moment. Democracies refute this charge by pointing to educational policies, programs for the conservation of national resources, and the popular will to defend the heritage of freedom.

In fascism, since the purpose of the state is something apart from the

[2] Mussolini's article in the *Enciclopedia Italiana* on "The Political and Social Doctrine of Fascism" as translated by Jane Soames in *The Political Quarterly* (1933), 4:342; see also *International Conciliation*, No. 306.

[3] Misuri as quoted by Herbert W. Schneider: *Making the Fascist State* (New York, 1928), p. 77.

individuals who compose it, the question arises, who is to determine the end of the state to which everything must be subservient? Fascism insists "that the government be entrusted to men capable of rising above their own private interests and of realizing the aspirations of the social collectivity considered in its unity and in its relation to the past and future." [4] The doctrine of popular sovereignty is, therefore, repudiated in favor of state sovereignty. While the masses might be given a consultative voice, the control and direction of the state must be placed in the hands of the elite. The elite must be organized and disciplined to constitute an efficient governmental hierarchy. Instead of Liberty, Equality, and Fraternity, the watchwords were Responsibility, Discipline, and Hierarchy. At the top stood the leader, *Il Duce*. In practice he, more than anyone else, determined the immediate policies, which were always directed towards the one great end, increasing the power and glory of the Italian state.

The means through which the end was to be attained varied from time to time, in line with the opportunism that is part of fascism. Thus Mussolini came to champion an extreme conception of nationalism, open adherence to the doctrines of imperialism, a contempt for pacifism, and a glorification of war. "Above all fascism," according to Mussolini, ". . . believes neither in the possibility nor the utility of perpetual peace. It thus repudiates the doctrine of pacifism—born of a renunciation of the struggle and an act of cowardice in the face of sacrifice. War alone brings up to its highest tension all human energy and puts the stamp of nobility upon the peoples who have the courage to meet it."

FASCISM VS. LIBERALISM. From the basic acceptance of the philosophy of a totalitarian state, certain corollaries followed. The general doctrines of liberalism and democracy were spurned, although strangely enough the Fascists often reiterated that only through fascism could the historic democratic values be achieved. This claim to be the only "true" democracy which is a part of both fascism and communism indicates that historic democratic rights and values, being fundamentally sound, have a universal appeal. Fascists condemned socialism and communism along with democracy. Indeed, no small part of fascist doctrine was made up of being antidemocratic, antisocialistic, anticommunistic, anti-Freemason, anticlerical, in fact anti-anything that was not fascistic.

Aside from a glorification of the Italian nation which included an ardent Italianization of German and Slav minorities, racial doctrines were not in the beginning a part of fascism. However, in the middle thirties, no doubt as a result of the growing friendship with Nazi Germany, Italy too adopted a policy of anti-Semitism [see below, p. 429]. In Italy, however, the anti-Semitic laws were never strictly enforced.

The Fascists discarded freely elected representative bodies and resorted to a one-party state. The representative bodies that they established

[4] Alfredo Rocco: "The Political Doctrine of Fascism," *International Conciliation* (1926), No. 223, p. 405.

were actually only bodies to provide a sounding board for governing officials. Theoretically Parliament could and did enact laws, but actually fascism called for government through executive decree. Instead of political authority rising upward from the people, it descended on them from the party and state hierarchy. Officials were appointed rather than elected; ordinary civil liberties were greatly curtailed if not abolished; education and the press became largely a state monopoly and were used as agencies of propaganda. In fact, the control of men's minds through an elaborate and highly varied system of propaganda was one of the essential features of the fascist state in operation. This was coupled with arbitrary use of force and violence as a means of stamping out opposition to the state. Secret police and special courts alongside a regular police and court system were the order of the day.

CORPORATIVE THEORY. To replace the old form of state organization, fascism required that the state should be organized along corporative lines, which means, briefly, according to the main productive groups. This end was not achieved in Italy until well into the thirties and even then it never was fully completed. Although the theory of the corporations viewed an industry as a whole, the Italian system never gave up the separate organizations (syndicates) of employers and employees. This system thus differed from that in Germany, where employees were merged in the "Labor Front." In general, the corporative theory involved consolidation of many private enterprises, whether they were willing or not, and government control of all large-scale enterprise, with national power and self-sufficiency the aim. It also implied state control over labor and employment, and in all phases of the corporative economy the Fascist leaders were to hold the initiative. While the corporative system was primarily a means of organizing the economy of the state, it was also made to serve as a basis of political reorganization. As will be pointed out later, a body recruited from the corporations eventually replaced the Chamber of Deputies and along with the Senate performed what few functions were allotted to this revised Parliament.

One of the chief ends of corporative economy was to make Italy independent of foreign countries, and the word *autarky* came to be applied to this endeavor to attain self-sufficiency. It led Mussolini to build up agriculture, reclaim lands, wage his "battle for wheat," develop industry and armaments, advocate large families, and demand the acquisition of new territories. It should be stated at once that general world trade policies, tariff barriers, trade quotas, etc., helped to force the Italians along this path of economic nationalism. The cry, "Buy American," "Buy British," or "Buy Italian," has much the same effect on international trade, whether it is shouted in a democratic or a fascist state. Before World War II there was not much difference in the economic nationalism of states, no matter what their ideology. Yet wide control over the economic life of the country and great restriction on the freedom of employer and employee are part of fascist corporative theory.

ORIGINS OF FASCIST THEORY. A study of the sources of fascist ideas, theories, and practices must move over uncertain ground. Similar ideas had been held by early political writers, but we cannot be sure how the contemporary exponents came by them. When a movement attains success the tendency is for its supporters to give it prestige and standing by tracing it back—giving it footnotes, so to speak, in order to bolster its validity. But with all these limitations, it is worthwhile pointing out some of the historical antecedents of fascism.

It is obvious that fascist philosophy of the state was influenced by Hegel. Fascist writers like to quote Machiavelli, particularly passages from *The Discourses*. As Rocco put it, "Fascism learns from him not only its doctrines but its action as well." From Vico, it is said, fascists obtained their condemnation of pacifism, but a more immediate source would be the agitation that led to Italy's entrance into World War I. We know that Mussolini attended the lectures of Pareto at Milan, and his early training as a Socialist must have had considerable influence on his thought. Fascism turned especially to the teachings of the French syndicalist Georges Sorel for an economic philosophy. More than on any individual, the Fascists drew heavily upon the awakened spirit of Italian nationalism. They sought inspiration and guidance from the grandeur and glory of Ancient Rome, the Renaissance, and above all from the *Risorgimento*. It was to this latter period, when Italy achieved unification and became one of the great powers of Europe, that the Fascists looked for the idealization of patriotism.

It was the age in which it was nurtured that produced the specific theories and practices of fascism. It was a carrying over into peacetime of much of the philosophy and practices of the war, for fascism with its dictatorship was most assuredly a product of the war. In no small sense, it developed out of a defensive spirit among the veterans and a desire to see that their sacrifices had not been made in vain. It was also a militant reaction to bolshevism. Economic distress in all its ramifications—closely related to the destruction of the war—not only played a great part in the evolution of fascism itself but also accounted for the wide acceptance of fascist doctrine within Italy.

The Reorganization of the Government

When Mussolini and his coalition cabinet took over the government on October 30, 1922, there was a rush for the bandwagon, and many local politicians brought their followers into the party. In the spring of 1923, however, the Populist Party Congress passed a resolution condemning the action of the Fascist squads in particular and fascism in general. Mussolini thereupon forced the Populist members of the cabinet to resign, thus narrowing the base of the coalition. Convinced that he needed a more docile parliament, Mussolini prepared for new elections.

CHANGE IN THE ELECTORAL LAW. The old liberal and conservative members, believing that the gains made by the leftist parties in the 1919 and 1921 elections were the result of the new proportional representation law, supported Mussolini's demands, and with some coercion the "Acerbo Election Law" was passed. Under it the party receiving the largest vote, providing it was at least 25 per cent of the total, would be awarded two thirds of the seats in the Chamber of Deputies. The remaining seats were to be distributed to the other parties in proportion to the number of votes they received. Parliament was now dissolved and new elections set for April 6, 1924. The Fascists prepared their election lists with great care and were able to get many old political leaders to run under their banners. They improved on traditional methods of electoral coercion and won an overwhelming victory.

THE MATTEOTTI INCIDENT. Mussolini now had a parliament that seemed made to order, but quite unexpectedly the opposition began making trouble. Above all, the Socialists began to use the parliamentary sessions as a forum for the denunciation of fascism and all its works. Matteotti, leader of the Reformist Socialist group, was particularly vehement in his denunciation of Fascist electoral methods. Even before this he was on the Fascist black list because of his book, *The Fascisti Exposed*, in which he presented hundreds of cases of illegal violence perpetrated by the Fascist party. Such opposition was not to be countenanced, and Matteotti was waylaid in an alley behind the House of Parliament and murdered. The assassination aroused a tremendous sensation, and it was soon clear that high Fascist party officials were involved in the plot. Confidence of the people in the regime was shaken, and the opposition members of parliament, harking back to a practice of the plebeians in Roman times, withdrew and assembled by themselves on the Aventine Hill. Here they vowed to remain until the complicity of the government in the Matteotti affair had been disproved. In fact, this Aventine Secession never ended, and in 1926 Mussolini declared the seats of the secessionists vacant.

In 1924 Mussolini was still not in absolute control of either state or party, despite his own statement: "In internal affairs whatever happens, happens through my precise and direct volition and on my express order, for which I naturally assume full and personal responsibility." [5] The next months were a period of great decisions as to what the future organization of the party was to be. In the end those who wanted a highly centralized authoritarian party won. On January 3, 1925, Mussolini in a bold speech took upon himself the responsibility for the murder of Matteotti and defied parliament to impeach him. There was, of course, no danger of this, since after the Aventine Secession parliament consisted entirely of Mussolini's henchmen.

FRAMEWORK OF GOVERNMENT. Mussolini now began to organize his dictatorship on a legal basis. By two basic laws, one on the "Powers and Prerogatives of the Head of the Government" passed on December 24, 1925, and the other enacted on January 31, 1926, giving the executive power to draft decrees having the force of law, parliament formally abdi-

<hr />

[5] As quoted by Schneider: *Making the Fascist State*, p. 126.

cated its legislative function in favor of Mussolini and his ministers. The next years saw measures enacted, either by decree or by parliament, which provided for fundamental reorganization of labor relations, the police and security system, local government, education, etc.

The constitution of Italy, known as the *Statuto* of 1848, had no provision for amendment, and Mussolini was content to leave it alone. The king remained and his position was not very different from what it had been previously; Mussolini was responsible to him alone [see chart, p. 250]. The king technically named new ministers, and in case Mussolini's post became vacant, was to appoint his successor from a list of names submitted by the Fascist Grand Council, which was the highest party organization. This procedure was, in fact, duly followed in July, 1943. The cabinet, presided over by Mussolini as chief of state, consisted, as formerly, of the heads of various departments—foreign affairs, war, interior, and so on. Often Mussolini presided over four or five of these departments, in addition to maintaining his position as premier. The Italian civil service was purged of opposition elements and greatly expanded because of increased governmental functions. New appointees, of course, were recruited largely from the Fascist party membership. All, including teachers, had to take an oath of loyalty to the regime.

The Italian Senate was an appointive body and, although many pronouncements were made in regard to its abolition, it was retained. The new appointees were, naturally, men who accepted fascism. Another electoral law made a farce of parliamentary elections, since there was only one list of candidates, but it was not until December, 1938, that the Chamber of Deputies voted itself out of existence; on March 23, 1939, the Chamber of Fasces and Corporations became the new lower chamber of parliament.

The first measure affecting the judiciary was one intended to rid the various judicial benches of judges who were considered politically untrustworthy. This was part of the general purge of the civil service. In 1926 a "Special Tribunal for the Defense of the State" was established and it was destined to receive permanent status. Its procedure was similar to that of courts-martial and it was headed by Fascist militia and army officers. There was also an immediate increase in summary justice on the part of police courts and a tremendous expansion of the police system. Concentration camps were established on the Lipari Islands, but these prisons were not comparable in size or brutality to the prison camps in Nazi Germany or Communist Russia. New criminal codes with the re-introduction of the death penalty were put into operation in 1932, and progress was made on the formulation of new civil codes. A new Labor Court was established in 1926 to provide a means of settling disputes between employer and employee organizations.

In local government an appointive official, the *podesta*, replaced the old elected communal council and syndic. He was appointed by royal decree and in practice was supported by the central government when he came in conflict with local party politicians. In some larger communes, appointed consultative chambers were instituted to advise the *podesta*. Appointed officials also took over the direction of affairs in the ninety-two provinces into which Italy was divided.

The Party Organization

PARTY FRAMEWORK. Entwined in all these governmental bodies, as well as in most other Italian organizations, was the Fascist party [see chart, p. 250]. Although the party became a state organ, it always retained its separate organization, its own officials, its own militia, and its own treasury. At the head of the party stood Mussolini as *Il Duce* (the leader). The directory headed by a Secretary General supervised the financial and administrative affairs of the party. It had supervision of many party organizations such as the Association of Fascist Teachers, Association of Fascist Railway Workers, Association of University Students, the National Leisure-Time Organization (*Dopolavoro*), the Press, Propaganda, and so forth. The most important party organization, and really the policy-making group, was the Fascist Grand Council. By law and practice, in normal times all important measures and policies came before this body. It was dominated by Mussolini and was composed of the surviving Quadrumvirs who led the March on Rome, certain officials who held important government posts, such as the presidents of the two legislative chambers, the ministers of foreign affairs and finance, the president of the Royal Academy, and others appointed by Mussolini for three-year terms. In all it was a body of about thirty members.

A National Council (of about 120 members) consisting of the provincial party secretaries and certain other party leaders was created to hear what decisions the party hierarchy had made rather than to deliberate on party policy. In each province there was a party secretary and a directory of seven members. The primary party units were the *Fasci di Combattimento*, headed by a secretary and an appointed directorate. The local directorate fixed the dues, but at least two lire for each member had to go to the provincial and national party headquarters. The whole party was controlled by appointed officials, and local units were subject to constant supervision by higher party officials. There was no intraparty democracy so far as the rank and file were concerned.

AUXILIARY ORGANIZATIONS. The method of recruiting members for the party varied from time to time. In 1926 it was decreed that only graduates of the Fascist youth organization would be admitted to membership, but this policy was not always adhered to. The youth organizations consisted of the Sons of the Wolf, for boys 6–8 years old; the more important *Balilla*, for boys 8–14 years of age; and the Young Fascists, 18–21 years. A parallel organziation existed for girls but this never enrolled as large a membership. There were also auxiliaries for women.

A part of the party and of the army, but also an auxiliary of the party with its own distinctive organization, was the Fascist Militia. On January 14, 1923, the "Volunteer Militia for National Safety" was organized. It had its own general staff, its own officers, and its own arms, and formed a special Fascist police force. Most of the members of the militia were not in active service and were mobilized only for parades and occasional exercises. The units in active service were given the job of policing the railways, patrolling the ports, and in general lending authority to the party. The army and militia did not get along well, for the regular army officers refused to accept the militia officers as equals and resented the favoritism awarded the militia in pay, advancement, and award of decorations. A compromise was finally reached, and the members of the militia had to take an oath of loyalty to the king. In time of war the militia was to be incorporated into the army, but it always retained its distinct organization and its distinct Black Shirt garb.

Among the other auxiliary party organizations one more needs to be mentioned: The *Opera Nazionale Dopolavoro*. This National Leisure-Time Organization provided all kinds of recreational and cultural activities for the laboring classes. It sponsored sports events and competitions of all kinds, workers' libraries, lectures, theatrical performances, excursions, and various types of adult training. It had a membership of over three million and its work constitutes one of the brightest spots of Fascist Italy.

The Corporative State

A fascist organization of labor gradually took place, replacing the old labor unions. Both employers and employees were organized into so-called Syndicates (although these were hardly exponents of syndicalism as taught by Georges Sorel), which in 1926 were grouped into nine National Confederations [see chart, p. 250].

THE SYNDICATES. The syndical organizations all nominally elected their officials, but actually these were chosen by higher officials and were ultimately controlled by the government. The workers' syndical organization concluded the collective labor contracts with representatives of the employers' syndicates. The conditions of work and wages were then binding on all workers in that industry in the area. Collective disputes arising out of these contracts, if not settled by arbitration of a special board under the Ministry of Corporations, could then be appealed to a special Labor Court. Individual disputes were submitted to the appropriate syndical authorities, and if a settlement was not obtained, appeal could be made to the courts. There were many such disputes. In 1935 the Confederations of Agriculture and Industry alone were faced with 219,000 disputes. Of these 198,000 were dealt with by the syndical authorities, and in about two thirds of the cases the decision was in favor of the workingmen. It is often charged by anti-Fascists that the workers won the unimportant cases, and the employers the important ones. However that may be, it is clear that the worker had a chance to air his grievances and often did obtain redress. Strikes and lockouts were forbidden, and few actually occurred.

THE CORPORATIONS. The term "corporation" is likely to lead to confusion, for it was used in various senses under Fascism. Before 1925 it was

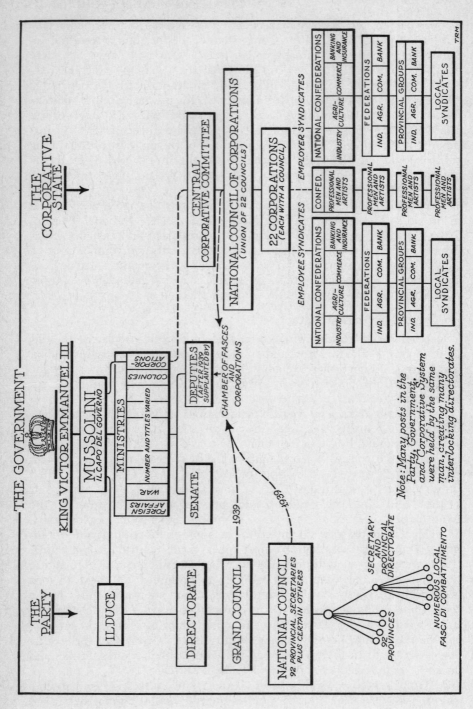

CHART IV *Italian State Organizations*

Note: Many posts in the
Party, Government,
and Corporative System
were held by the same
man, creating many
interlocking directorates.

used as a designation for unions of syndicates (later called federations). In 1926, when the National Syndical organizations were established, the law provided for the possibility of creating liaison organizations between the employer and employee organizations. These were to be called corporations. Eventually in February, 1934, twenty-two corporations were established. These were to be based on cycles of production, which meant, for example, that the Textile Corporation Council would have representation from the sheep raisers, flax growers, the textile manufacturers, and others, including those who sell the textiles. The Council would consist of representatives drawn from both employer and employee syndical organizations, certain technicians, representatives of co-operatives, the Fascist party, and even other groups. These Corporation Councils usually numbered less than fifty members. The twenty-two Corporation Councils were then brought together into a National Council. The work of the National Council, which had about five hundred members, was guided and co-ordinated by a Central Corporative Committee of about fifty. The whole system was under the supervision of the Ministry of Corporations, for many years headed by Mussolini.

The corporations did not accomplish world-shaking changes, but they did have some things to their credit. They provided consultative bodies for working out marketing agreements, production standards, etc. The officials were regularly supervised from the top and the Corporative System became an important means of controlling the totalitarian state. The Italian Corporative System was the most elaborate and highly developed of the many schemes that were evolved during the thirties to organize the economic life of the state within a capitalistic economy. But a good part of it was mere organization. With less governmental and administrative paraphernalia, other states have exercised perhaps as great an influence on their economy.

When this rather complex corporative organization was finally functioning, the Chamber of Deputies in December, 1938, voted itself out of existence. Its place was taken by the Chamber of Fasces and Corporations, made up of the National Council of Corporations, the Grand Council of the party, and the National Council of the party. This did not produce any real change in the method of enacting law, which was still done largely through decrees.

ECONOMIC POLICY. From the beginning the Fascists launched a program of public works. Many of these were costly and were carried on more for prestige than for economic utility. The program of land reclamation that had been carried on by previous governments was taken up with renewed vigor; the draining of the Pontine marshes was one of the most spectacular achievements. The Italian merchant marine was even more heavily subsidized, and the protection of industries increased. The production of wheat was pushed in the so-called "Battle for Wheat." The stabilization of the lira in 1927 at a rate somewhat higher than conditions actually warranted (Mussolini wanted the lira to outvalue the French franc) soon made difficulties for the export industries. Yet the active intervention of the government in private economy came largely after 1930 and was the result of the great depression. Here, as in so many other countries, the economic collapse forced the government to step into business, something in better accord perhaps with Fascist theory than with generally accepted conceptions of democratic doctrine.

Cultural Policy

CIVIL RIGHTS. The Fascists were relatively slow to enforce their control over the press. The papers, for example, gave full publicity to the charges made by Matteotti and to the events connected with his death. But soon after that crisis was passed (1924–25) the freedom of the press was sharply curtailed. Scientific and learned publications, which did not reach the masses, were even permitted to print critical articles long after all other publications were brought into line. Yet these too eventually came under the "Axe of Fascism." A secret police system gradually established its hold over Italy, with the resulting inevitable loss of personal liberties. No one, however, regrets that Mussolini was able to break the hold of the Mafia (1927–28) over Sicily. His campaign against Freemasonry at least had the support of the church authorities. In all this it should be borne in mind that the Fascists moved more slowly than did the Bolsheviks in Russia or the National Socialists in Germany. Nor did they have special classes or groups that they attacked, to compare with the aristocrats in Russia or the Jews in Germany. The arbitrary and harsh policy pursued against the German and Slav minorities in the North should be mentioned here, but even these measures were not so severe as those imposed by the Communists or Nazis. The curtailment of liberty and civil rights, however, always involves brutality, and there was plenty of this in Italy.

EDUCATIONAL REFORM. In 1923 a far-reaching reform of the educational system was inaugurated. It was the work of the philosopher Giovanni Gentile, who had been made minister of education. Compulsory education was extended from twelve to fourteen years and attendance laws were made stricter. The curriculum was liberalized, and more advanced methods of instruction were introduced. Religion continued to be taught in all public schools. Along with increased subsidies from the national treasury, however, went increased state control over local officials in educational matters. Schools in all countries are used as places to teach loyalty, patriotism, and support of the state. It is not surprising, then, that the Italian schools became firm exponents of fascist doctrines. Private schools remained untouched, as a whole, by the Gentile reforms, although their graduates had to take state examinations in order to secure diplomas and certificates.

For some years the twenty-one universities were not subject to much interference. In 1929 it was decreed, however, that all rectors and deans had to be Fascist party members. In 1931 university professors along with all other teachers were forced to take an oath of loyalty to the regime. Only eleven professors refused to take the oath and they were dismissed. Benedetto Croce, world-renowned historian and philosopher, and a few others took this occasion to resign their posts.

RELIGIOUS POLICY. Ever since the unification of Italy the Vatican had lived in official enmity with the Italian state. It had refused to accept the offer for a settlement of differences which the government had set forth in the Law of Papal Guarantees in 1871. But there was no strict separation of church and state; the Italian treasury still continued to pay the salaries of the Italian clergy, church schools continued, and religious education was regularly given in state schools. In 1868 the Pope had promulgated his decree *non expedit* stating that it was not expedient for Catholics to vote in parliamentary elections. This decree had been confirmed repeatedly, and under Leo XIII (1878–1903) the papacy went a step further and expressly forbade what hitherto had been pronounced simply inexpedient. But in spite of these formal Papal pronouncements, many Italians continued to vote in the parliamentary elections and at the same time adhered to Catholicism and considered themselves to be loyal sons of the church. This ability to go against clerical pronouncements and still remain within the church has been one of the outstanding characteristics of Italians of all ages. A good number of Italians also began to vote Socialist in spite of all the pronouncements of the church against Marxist doctrines. It was largely this fact which led the Pope in 1905 to state that since a rigid application of *non expedit* might lead to the triumph of the enemies of society and religion, on the request of the Bishop and with the sanction of the Holy See, Italians could now vote in parliamentary elections. The formal hostility between the Vatican and the Italian government continued, although repeated efforts for a settlement were made. It was not until 1919 that *non expedit* was entirely repealed.

In the postwar decade the Vatican launched on a policy of negotiating concordats with many states, with a view towards assuring the position and privileges of the church. Thus, among others, concordats were negotiated with Latvia in 1922, with Bavaria in 1924, with Poland in 1925, with Lithuania in 1927, with Czechoslovakia in 1928, with Italy, Portugal, and Rumania in 1929, with Germany in 1933, and one with Yugoslavia in 1935 which, however, never went into effect. In these agreements the Pope's free appointment of bishops was confirmed, the right to give religious instruction was safeguarded, and the church was given freedom to carry out its policy of social action. On the other hand, the Vatican usually had to agree to restrict the political activity of the clergy.

Thus the Lateran agreements, which were agreed to by the Italian government and by the Pope on February 11, 1929, were in line with the general policy of the Papacy in this period. These agreements were drawn up in three parts. Under the first the Pope's temporal power over a limited area was restored. Henceforth he was to rule over Vatican City, which was a district of 108.7 acres within Rome, centering about St. Peter's and the Vatican. He was also to rule over Castel Gandolfo, a summer residence outside the city. In a second pact the Italian government agreed to pay an indemnity as a settlement for church property which had been confiscated during the Unification of Italy (1859–70). The third agreement was a concordat not unlike the concordats with other states mentioned above. Catholicism was recognized as the religion of the state, the appointment of the clergy was regulated, church property was exempted from taxation, and the state agreed to provide state funds for the payment of salaries for the clergy. Monasteries were granted a legal personality, which made it possible for them to acquire property again. The state agreed to recognize the rules of canon law in regard to marriage. This meant that Catholic marriages were legal without the necessity of an additional civil ceremony, and that dissolution of such marriages was left to the church. Priests were to have the privilege of giving religious instruction in the elementary and secondary schools, and Catholic societies (Catholic Action) were not to be molested.

There has been much dispute as to which side obtained the better deal. That argument is really beside the point, for each gained substantial advantages. The ending of the long dispute with the church was a real feather in the cap of the Fascist leaders, and it did much to increase their standing, both in Italy and in the world at large. The Pope was no longer a "prisoner within the Vatican," and the peoples of Rome rejoiced when on July 25, 1929, for the first time since 1871 a Pope left the confines of the Vatican. Although difficulties soon developed between the church authorities and the Fascist officials, notably over the control of youth organizations, the disputes led to no serious conflict. The financial, as well as most of the other provisions of the agreements, were lived up to by the state.

Foreign Policy

The Fascists nourished the idea that Italy had not received its full share of the spoils of war. This led to strained relations with Yugoslavia over frontier questions, and also with France and England. The latter countries were reluctant and tardy in awarding to Italy the colonial compensation due under the Treaty of London. In addition, Mussolini felt himself destined to build an empire, to dominate the Mediterranean, and to convert the Adriatic into an Italian lake (*Mare Nostrum*). These policies, along with the stronger navy that was a necessary concomitant, clashed with the interests of Yugoslavia, Greece, France, and Britain, all of which had definite Mediterranean policies of their own.

COLONIES AND FRONTIERS. Italy's colonial empire was a relatively recent acquisition. Largely desert, it contained little mineral wealth, and above all was not well adapted for settlement by Europeans. In the eighties of the last century Italy had acquired the African colonies of Eritrea on the Red Sea and Italian Somaliland on the Indian Ocean. Her attempt in 1896 to link these two together by the conquest of Ethiopia was an abysmal failure. As a result of the Boxer Uprising Italy obtained (1901) an unimportant concession in Tientsin, China. In 1911–12 she fought a successful war against Turkey and acquired the North African territories of Cyrenaica and Tripolitania, later united in the colony known as Libya. At the same time Italy occupied the Dodecanese Islands. This had raised delicate international questions and in the years 1913–14 was a matter of much negotiation among the European powers.

On July 29, 1919, Greece and Italy had made an agreement under which Greece was to support Italian claims to Albania and portions of Anatolia, and Italy was in return to support Greek claims to Thrace and Epirus, and also cede the Greek-inhabited Dodecanese Islands to Greece. Italy cancelled this agreement in October, 1922, on the ground that the whole Near Eastern settlement had been overthrown by the failure to ratify the Treaty of Sèvres. This naturally irritated the Greeks and brought loud protests from England. In fact, England used this as an excuse to delay until 1924 the cession to Italy of Jubaland, which had been promised her as compensation for England's acquisition of German colonies. Italy had long ago withdrawn her troops from Albania (August, 1920), and the Treaty of Rapallo with Yugoslavia (November, 1920) had supposedly established the boundary line between the two countries. By this treaty Fiume was to become a Free City, but Italian troops were not withdrawn after they had driven D'Annunzio out of the town. Nevertheless, on October 23, 1922, Italy and Yugoslavia in another treaty reaffirmed the Treaty of Rapallo and again solemnly affirmed that Fiume was to be a Free City.

This, in brief, was the situation inherited by Mussolini when he became premier on October 31, 1922. He was not slow to proclaim that Italy was going to assert her position in international affairs. He scored his first success when the Treaty of Lausanne in 1923 finally recognized Italy's possession of the Dodecanese Islands. Mussolini next set out to settle differences with Yugoslavia. In January, 1924, it was agreed that the Free City of Fiume was to go to Italy while Yugoslavia retained the neighboring town of Porto Baros. Even this arrangement did not establish friendly relations between the two countries. The Slovenes and Croats particularly resented the Italianization of their nationals in Italy, although the Germans in Tyrol were in even worse straits. Yugoslavia also charged Italy with stirring up the Macedonian Revolutionary Organization in Macedonia. The Yugoslavs resented the growing patronage of Austria and Hungary by Italy, and even more the Italian policy in Albania. Here, Yugoslavia had supported Ahmed Zog in his bid for power (1924), but it was Italy that in a series of agreements (1925–27) with Zog won a kind of protectorate over Albania.

ALLIANCE POLICY. The Italian attempt to establish a system of alliances in Central Europe and the Balkans has already been outlined [see above, p. 175]. Italian support of the demands of some of the revisionist powers was eventually to bring difficulties with France, which was determined upon maintaining the Peace Settlement of 1919. There were other points of difference between the two countries. Paris soon became a haven for anti-Fascist Italian refugees. France also tended to support Yugoslavia and Greece when they got into controversies with Italy. Naval rivalry became acute between the two, for France did not want to accord Italy dominance in the Mediterranean. In 1919 France ceded some strips of desert to Italy on the border of southwest Libya, which the Italians never considered adequate compensation for the valuable German colonies France had received. Furthermore, the French in 1918 had unilaterally cancelled an agreement of 1896 under which the Italians resident in Tunis could retain their Italian nationality. These problems continued to disturb French-Italian relations for some time.

While there were many differences between Italy, France, and Britain, it should be underlined that throughout the twenties this core of the victorious wartime coalition remained on the same side of the fence. All were friendly to the United States, none was intimate with the USSR. The critical point was of course their relations towards Germany and Austria. Even into the thirties Mussolini's foreign policy continued to be based primarily on co-operation with France against Germany, in spite of growing connections with revisionist states.

CHAPTER

10

France During the Twenties

FRANCE had emerged from the war the leading power on the continent. Alsace-Lorraine with its valuable iron and potash deposits and its great textile industry was reunited with France, and important colonies came under French control. Germany was disarmed and at least partially dismembered. Under the reparation clauses of the treaty the Germans agreed to pay practically any bill that the French and their allies might present to them. But Clemenceau did not have his way on all points. Although not so widespread as in Italy, there was a great deal of dissatisfaction in France with the treaties. Notably the Rhineland settlement was open to severe criticism. The fear of Germany was far from stilled. A passion for security gripped all Frenchmen and came to dominate French policy in the next years.

The longing for a return of normal conditions was particularly intense in France. Normal conditions to most people meant prewar conditions, a chimera that could only lead to disappointment and political instability. In addition the soldiers clamored to be demobilized; they wanted nothing to do with restoring order in Eastern Europe. In 1919 a rather serious mutiny occurred in the French Black Sea fleet. French forces not only were withdrawn from Odessa, but soon thereafter French armed intervention in Turkey was cut short.

The revolution in Russia shattered the prewar pattern of alliances, and the League of Nations was no substitute in French eyes. It was necessary to create a friendly bloc in Eastern Europe which not only would serve to check Germany but would act as a dam against communism. The French had a special grievance against the Bolsheviks, for the latter had canceled the many Russian bonds which patriotic Frenchmen had bought before the war to aid an ally. Bad faith in financial relations has soured many a friendship, and thousands of individual Frenchmen felt a personal grievance against the Bolshevist government. Antagonism to communist Russia became an important issue in postwar France and added another element to an already complicated political scene.

Political Development

ELECTIONS. Clemenceau in November, 1917, had organized a strong cabinet and felt no need of calling an election before undertaking negotiations for peace, as Lloyd George had done in England in the so-called Khaki Election. Once the peace treaties were made, however, elections could no longer be postponed.

The great leader of the Socialist party, Jean Jaurès, had been assassinated on July 31, 1914. No new leader of like stature appeared to pull the party together and to make good the inroads which war inevitably makes on a doctrinaire anti-war group. The war had also affected the labor unions, particularly the great *Confédération Générale du Travail* (CGT). The latter had shifted from revolutionary syndicalism to nationalistic patriotism, although a group remained attached to their old principles. Now both the Socialists and Trade Unionists were torn by the problem of what their stand should be toward the Russian Revolution. Right and left wings strove for power, and controversy was at its height when the elections were held in November, 1919. The danger of communism became a leading issue in the electoral campaign. A famous poster depicting a Bolshevik as a man with a knife between his teeth appeared everywhere.

In May, 1919, parliament had enacted a hybrid proportional representation law. Under it the party that received the majority of the votes in a given district was to receive all the seats from that district. Only if no party won a majority did the proportional system begin to function. Under these circumstances the election resulted in an overwhelming victory for the Nationalistic Bloc.

THE HORIZON BLUE CHAMBER. Over half of the Chamber, it is often remarked, were practicing Catholics, which was a far cry from the membership of previous Chambers, which had enacted (1901–05) and aggressively supported the laws separating church and state. Known as the Horizon Blue Chamber because of the color of the uniforms of the many officers who were elected to it, the parliament was definitely right center. The leaders held to the philosophy of the strong hand, particularly in foreign affairs.

One of the first tasks set the new Chamber was to participate with the Senate in electing a new French president. Clemenceau had hopes of being chosen and he richly deserved this highest honor the Republic could bestow, but he had made too many political enemies during his long career and was too staunchly anticlerical. Instead, Paul Deschanel, the dapper president of the Chamber of Deputies, became the next president. Within a few months Deschanel lost his mind and Alexandre Millerand was elected to succeed him. Although at one time a Socialist, Millerand was at this time an ardent nationalist, firm in his anticommunist views. Traditionally, the French president was supposed to perform numerous useful public functions such as laying cornerstones, cutting ribbons on new bridges, and attending banquets. It was a fixed rule of constitutional practice that affairs of state were to be decided by the cabinet. Millerand, however, began to interfere in political matters. This aroused the ire of the left parties, and when they won the elections in 1924 he was forced to resign. Gaston Doumergue, who succeeded him, was "unassertive and self-effacing" and held the office until 1931.

CARTEL DES GAUCHES. The victory of the left parties in 1924 came about in part because of the thorough-going reorganization of these parties. A definite cleavage took place in 1920 among the Socialists. The left wing now openly proclaimed its adherence to the Third International and became the French Communist party (*Section française de l'Internationale communiste*; SFIC). Thus the Socialist party (*Section française de l'Internationale ouvriere*; SFIO) was free to build along reformist lines. The term "Socialist," instead of being considered a political liability, was viewed as an asset in France, and a number of groups added it to their name. Thus, the well-established Radical Socialist party was hardly what its name implies but would in most countries be considered a liberal party, standing to the right of the Socialist party proper. It did, however, frequently combine with the Socialist party against the right.

The labor unions also fought out the question of relationship to Moscow. A general strike in 1920, which turned out to be a fiasco, discredited the whole labor movement. Membership in the unions, over 1.8 million in January, 1920, declined by over half during the year as the struggle between right and left wings in the labor unions continued. Finally in 1922 a definite separation occurred. Those inclined towards communism formed the *Confédération Général du Travail Unitaire* (CGTU) while the more moderate socialist *Confédération Général du Travail* (CGT) set about rebuilding on moderate lines. This split in labor ranks was not healed until 1936 when the two federations united into a reorganized CGT. Of lesser importance was a Confederation of Catholic Trade Unions.

Not only did the left reorganize itself, but some of the policies of the National Bloc aroused much opposition. The renewal of diplomatic relations with the Vatican and a lax enforcement of anticlerical laws in general brought back to the left some of their lost supporters. Then too, France was none too successful in foreign affairs. The proposed Anglo-American Treaties of Guarantee were not ratified, the collection of reparations did not go well, and the occupation of the Ruhr (1923) proved unpopular even in France. Particularly the more liberal groups did not like the strained relations that were developing with England and the United States. Among the parties of the left, notably among the Socialists, many believed in the Weimar Republic, were opposed to the use of force in international affairs, and stressed peace and friendship rather than a rigid enforcement of the Treaty of Versailles.

The victory of the left (*Cartel des Gauches*) in 1924 brought a new tone to French policy. Relations with the Vatican became less intimate, although there was no fundamental change in policy. Briand came to the fore in this period, which is marked by the Locarno Pact and numerous attempts to strengthen the League; these have already been reviewed [see above, pp. 161–66]. In 1926 a severe financial crisis occurred. A National Union government made Poincaré premier and gave him great powers in a valiant attempt to save the franc. In this he was successful, and France benefited by the general economic prosperity of the period.

RIGHT CENTER VICTORY. In 1927 the proportional representation law was repealed and single-member constituencies were again established. This, it was generally thought, would benefit the left, but instead a rightist chamber was returned in the 1928 elections. This was no doubt the result of the achievements of the rightist National Union cabinet of the past two years. Poincaré having retired for reasons of health in 1929 after three strenuous years in office, his supporters favored such men as Tardieu and Laval. The impact of the depression came later in France than in other countries, and her leaders were correspondingly slow to adjust to the changing situation. They tended to insist on the same old demands in foreign affairs, declaring that nothing was to be conceded. By the end of the four-year term of the rightist chamber (1932) prosperity had also ended in France, and a period of political instability was at hand.

THE PARLIAMENTARY SCENE. In this rapid account of French political development no attempt has been made to name all the different premiers who headed the many cabinets. From the close of the war until January, 1933, which is approximately the period here surveyed, France had twenty-seven different cabinets, Germany fourteen, and England seven. Political scientists offer various reasons for the many cabinet changes that were part of the political pattern under the Third Republic. One factor was the existence of many political parties and the resultant necessity of always having a coalition cabinet. The lack of party discipline was important, for the deputies were prone to vote against policies advocated by their leaders who sat in the cabinet. The premier had no control over the Chamber, for there was no effective power of dissolution, and he could not send the deputies back to face their electorate. The rules of the Chamber, particularly the way committees were constituted, the manner in which bills were steered through the Chamber by a *rapporteur* of the committee rather than by the responsible minister, and the system of interpellations which often led to snap votes overturning the ministry—all these played a part. In general, the tendency was for the Chamber of Deputies (and in ever increasing measure the Senate) to dictate to the cabinet. Such was not the case in England, where the House of Commons follows the leadership of the cabinet. Yet when the over-all picture is viewed, French policy, in spite of the many cabinet changes, was as consistent and stable as that of any country in those postwar years. In France a new cabinet usually means not a basic change in policy but only a change in personnel. Cabinet posts are shuffled about and the same parties are likely to be represented in the new coalition. The permanent civil service officials are the ones who actually conduct affairs and give permanency and stability to the government. Thus it is possible to speak generally of French policy in various fields during this period in spite of the number of changing ministries.

Economic Development

RECONSTRUCTION. The most urgent task in France after the war was to reconstruct the war-devastated areas. This devastation was largely confined to the ten northern departments. Over 800,000 buildings had been destroyed, thousands of miles of railways, canals, and highways disrupted, and thousands of acres of farm lands laid waste. The Germans were expected to pay for all this damage, but reparations payments proved inadequate. The French government had to raise the money to carry on the work and by 1925 had spent over 80 billion francs on reconstruction. Agriculture can be considered to have recovered its prewar status by 1925, and reconstruction in general to have been completed by 1926. This was a real achievement and redounds to the credit of France.

INDUSTRY. To the Briey iron deposits of French Lorraine were now added the deposits of that portion of Lorraine taken by Germany in 1870, a transfer which gave to France the greatest single European iron field. In spite of the possession of the Saar coal mines, France still lacked adequate coking coal, and so it was necessary to re-establish connections with the coal owners of the Ruhr. French steel production expanded tremendously in these years, and a sound basis was laid for the development of her heavy industries. France was also the possessor of the largest European deposit of bauxite. To manufacture aluminum from this ore requires large amounts of electricity; and France and Italy led the European states in the development of hydroelectric power. The great Alsatian potash field was another valuable addition to France's mineral wealth. Comparatively, her coal fields were not so valuable as those of Germany, Poland, or England, and practically no oil was produced.

The rebuilding of industrial centers in the north furnished France with a new and modern industrial plant. The addition of the textile industry of Alsace ranked France as the third cotton-manufacturing country in the world in the early twenties. Silk was an even more valuable export. Many new industries were started, and Renault and Citroën became famous names in the world's automotive industry. Yet France remained predominantly a country of small industrial enterprises, where nearly two thirds of the registered industries had no paid employees, and only one half of one per cent employed one hundred or more. The few big enterprises were, however, very important, since they employed about 45 per cent of the total number of wage earners.

AGRICULTURE. Agriculture had been and continued to be important in France, and the peasantry exercised great influence on French political life. Nevertheless, as in all countries, there was a shift of population to urban areas. Whereas before the war about 45 per cent of the laboring population of France were engaged in agriculture, by 1931 the figure had dropped to 35 per cent. Many farmers turned to cattle raising, and the acreage devoted to cereal production fell. Yet increased use of machinery and greater use of artificial fertilizers kept French agricultural production on a high level in spite of the decrease in the number of workers. Rural electrification made great headway. The French peasant spent more money on "store clothes" and varied his diet by purchases at the local markets. Although they continued to live on the land, the French peasants were rapidly becoming urbanized in their way of living.

France remained a land of peasant proprietors. About 25 per cent of the holdings were less than 2½ acres, and 47 per cent were between 2½ and 25 acres. Many of these holdings were too small to be farmed economically. Only 2 per cent of the holdings were over 125 acres, but these accounted for nearly one third of the cultivated area. Although most of the big estates had been liquidated during the French Revolution, these last figures show that large landed estates had not entirely disappeared from France. Yet land distribution was no great problem here, as it was in the states of Eastern Europe.

TARIFFS. The peasantry were an important political force. Even many of the inhabitants of the cities maintained a rural outlook, for to many of them their most cherished possession was a small place in the country. It is not surprising, then, that French agriculture was protected by a high tariff. In fact, France in general was a strong protectionist state and her postwar tariffs were well above the level of 1913. During the war outright prohibition of the importation or exportation of various products had been in force. The government lost the power to proclaim such prohibitions in

1920, but it was not until 1927 that all such bans on the export of food were removed.

It was difficult to adjust tariff rates to the varying depreciated currencies of other countries. In addition, the franc was far from stable, and the years 1924–28 were one continued financial crisis. When the franc declined from a prewar value of 19 cents to 2 cents in 1926, Poincaré was made premier in order to save the franc and France. Parliament gave him the power to enact financial measures by decree, particularly to adjust custom duties to the new value of the franc. Among other measures, Poincaré set aside revenues of the tobacco monopoly as a sinking fund for the retiring of short-term loans. To insure confidence that the sinking fund would not be looted later, he did not have it set up through ordinary legislation but had it made part of the French constitution. In 1928 the franc was put on the gold standard with a par value of 3.93 cents, making it possible to adjust French tariff schedules accordingly.

France in 1927 concluded its first important postwar trade treaty by negotiating an agreement with Germany containing the "most favored nation" clause, the principles of which were incorporated into trade agreements with other countries. Thus, by 1929 France had finally straightened out her tariff policy—only to have it upset by the dislocation of trade which was part of the depression. France reacted to this crisis, as did other countries, by raising her tariff rates, and was also the first to make wide use of quantitative restrictions by introducing the quota system. Applied first of all in 1931 to lumber and wine, by July, 1932, quota restrictions had been placed on 1133 items. While it is always theoretically possible to overcome a high tariff, it is impossible to surmount a quota barrier, since this means that a state will import just so much goods and no more. The allocation of quotas to various countries became an important function of government and offered great possibilities for political maneuvering.

GOVERNMENT AND BUSINESS. The French government, like that of most modern states, was deeply involved in the problems of the new industrial era. Immediately after the armistice the eight-hour day and forty-eight-hour week were established by law for industrial, mining, and commercial unions. French social legislation, however, was still far behind that prevailing in the newly acquired provinces of Alsace-Lorraine, and this contrast stimulated further French legislation. In 1928 night work for women and children was prohibited in factories, mines, quarries, and workshops. In the same year the old patchwork social-insurance laws were overhauled and a broad unified scheme of social insurance covering old age, sickness, disability, death, and maternity benefits was enacted, to go into effect in 1930. Under the law, worker and employer contributed equal shares, and the state contributed a proportionate amount and assumed the responsibility of making up deficiencies. There was only one contribution to cover all risks, and payments in turn were made from the one fund. Although the law extended compulsory social insurance to new groups, many wage earners were still outside the fold, but many of these—small artisans, tradespeople, farmers, artists, journalists—could enter the system voluntarily.

The increasing interest of the government in improving health standards was manifested by the establishment of a Ministry of Public Health in 1930. Research centers were maintained, and hospitals for the deaf, dumb, blind, and insane were improved. Housing projects were not extensive aside from the reconstruction of devastated areas. Since France in the twenties was not plagued with great numbers of unemployed, the government did not find itself called upon to engage in large public building programs. In fact, there was a shortage of workers in France during the thirties. With emigration to the United States restricted, more than three million imported workers, particularly from Italy, Spain, Poland, and North Africa, helped to rebuild France. It was not until 1932 that the French government closed her doors to this influx of foreign workingmen.

In France the postal, telegraph, and telephone services were state owned. The government also had radio broadcasting stations, but some private stations were permitted. In 1921 there were two state-operated railway systems (*Chemins de Fer de l'Ouest* and those of Alsace-Lorraine) and five major privately operated systems. In 1937 provisions were made for the consolidation of all the railways into one national system. That the French were not opposed to government in business is shown by the old established tobacco, match, and powder monopolies, which were all state owned and controlled. In 1926 the importation and sale (but not manufacture) of industrial alcohol was added to the list of state monopolies. In 1919 the government greatly extended its control over mining and increased the share of mining profits which went to the public treasury.

The government also took a benevolent attitude toward the co-operative movement. It helped establish co-operative societies in the devastated areas and in the first years after the war furnished machinery and supplies at nominal cost. The government often discussed proposed legislation on co-operatives with the Supreme Council of Co-operatives. In 1922 there were 4,790 consumers' co-operatives with two and a half million members. There were also many agricultural co-operatives, in which the dairy groups were the strongest. Credit and banking co-operatives also existed. The co-operative movement as a whole gained in strength during the postwar years and closer relations were established between the consumer and producer societies.

Alsace-Lorraine

A few weeks after the armistice of November 11, 1918, French troops had occupied Alsace-Lorraine, where for a period things went well. As in 1870, this transfer of territory placed these provinces on the winning side of the fence. There would be no reparations payments for these people to make, and in addition the French government set a very favorable rate of exchange for the conversion of German marks into French francs. Yet, it was soon evident that the "Lost Provinces" could not easily be slipped back into the niche from which they had been torn in 1870. In many ways the provinces had benefited from connection with a prosperous Germany. To ease the economic consequences of breaking established trade agreements, the Versailles treaty provided that Alsace-Lorraine could send goods into Germany for five years without tariff restrictions. The advanced German schemes of social insurance had also been in operation in the provinces. At this time France had nothing to compare with the German insurance system. The workers wanted social insurance continued, and this was done, although the employers complained that it placed them at a disadvantage in relation to other French industrialists. This situation was remedied when parliament enacted the broad social-insurance law of 1928 referred to above.

On the other hand, many changes had also occurred in France, and fifty years of French development could not be enforced on the provinces overnight. The general trend in France had been toward centralization, a fact which made adjustment even more difficult. The main subjects about which differences arose were language, religious policy, and local autonomy.

LANGUAGE DIFFICULTIES. Many American students have read in their French language courses a description of "La dernière classe." It is a story full of pathos and centers on the imposition of the use of German in the schools of Alsace-Lorraine after 1870. From this account one would never realize that only a minority of the population spoke French and that this minority was mostly concentrated in Lorraine. The overwhelming majority had always spoken a South German dialect, while the literary language of press and church was High German. Many people, particularly of the upper middle classes, were more or less bilingual. Before 1870 the French government never had a linguistic census of the provinces, and the wording of the French censuses after 1919 proved to be confusing. French scholars on the whole accept the German census figures, which showed in 1910 a German-speaking population of 1,634,260 and a French-speaking population of 204,262.[1]

With the hatred of all things German that prevailed in France in 1919 it is perhaps understandable that the French authorities began to impose a French linguistic regime in the returned provinces. French became the language of instruction in elementary schools; German signs were replaced by French; the state railways were taken over by the French government and French-speaking officials were installed; German-speaking judges, local government functionaries, and teachers, were dismissed. The railroad workers in Lorraine were the first to protest by a strike in 1919, and as a result more native Lorrainers and Alsatians were appointed to office. To still the rising discontent some concessions had to be made to local demands, but nevertheless the government did not go very far. In spite of many demands by the old teaching staffs, church authorities, and the popu-

---

[1] A. Meillet: *Les langues dans l'Europe nouvelle* (Paris, 1928), pp. 370–78; Paul Levy: "La langue française en Alsace et en Lorraine," *Le Français moderne* (1933) 1:144–59; (1934) 2:130–53.

lace, only a very limited amount of German instruction a week was permitted in the schools. The regular language of instruction for all subjects was to be French in elementary schools and—as the older pupils finished their courses—also in secondary schools. German was to be taught only as a foreign language, although in some cases religious instruction in German was permitted. At the University of Strasbourg all courses, even those in German language and literature, were to be given exclusively in French.

RELIGION. Alsace-Lorraine was three fourths Catholic, and it was the Catholics who were at the center of the controversy over the language question. Within Alsace and Lorraine, as in most of Germany, the schools were organized on confessional lines—Catholic, Protestant, Jewish [see above, p. 230]. The elementary school system had been largely under the control of the church authorities. Since the people and their churches were largely German-speaking, the clergy naturally wanted the children to learn to read the language in order to be linguistically equipped for religious instruction. Furthermore, Germany had never abolished the Concordat of 1801, which Napoleon I had negotiated with the Vatican. It still regulated for Alsace-Lorraine the relationship between the church and the governmental authorities. Under it the state paid the salaries of the clergy, an arrangement that had long been ended in the rest of France. The priests also held a rather distinctive position within the provinces. After 1870 they had often been the leaders in local opposition to German rule, which in the early years was dominated by Protestant Prussians. The priests came to be regarded locally as patriotic leaders. They can be compared in this respect to the priests in Ireland or Poland. The whole religious-educational controversy in Alsace-Lorraine came to a head in 1924 as a result of the victory of the leftist parties in the French parliamentary elections.

Herriot, the new premier, undertook to extend to Alsace-Lorraine the French laws separating church and state. To do this meant abrogation of the Concordat of 1801 and incorporation of the schools into the centralized secular school system of the rest of France. This program aroused so much opposition in the provinces, at a time when the government was beset by serious financial difficulties, that it seemed wise not to enforce the separation laws in Alsace-Lorraine. The policy of gradually extending the control of the state over the schools was, however, continued.

CENTRALIZATION VS. LOCAL AUTONOMY. The religious controversy stimulated a movement for autonomy among the Alsace-Lorrainers. This goes back to differences in historical development, particularly to the fact that the people were accustomed to the German concept that municipalities should be free to undertake many functions on their own initiative. They were willing to raise funds locally and were liberal spenders for local government projects. In this they were unlike the rest of France, where the general idea in local government is to save money by doing nothing. Then too, in 1911 the German government had granted to Alsace-Lorraine a great deal of local autonomy, and the local diet had become a real functioning body with power. Now all this was ended. The Alsatians and Lorrainers did not like the constant control from Paris that goes with a centralized state. For years representatives had defended their rights in the German Reichstag, and the local politicians were not long in assuming the same role in the Chamber of Deputies at Paris.

The autonomy movement became particularly strong after the attempt of the leftist governments (1924–26) to integrate the provinces into the religious and educational system of the rest of France. In 1928 fifteen of the leading autonomist leaders were arrested; others fled the country. The people reacted to this "persecution" by electing three of the defendants to the Chamber of Deputies. The Communists, welcoming an opportunity to embarrass the French government, joined with the Catholic parties in backing the autonomist movement. When later French governments lived up to their promises of respecting local customs, languages, and religious arrangements, the autonomy movement subsided. Also, the economic depression caused most of the autonomists to put a higher value on their ties with France. The advent of Hitler furthered this development, for only the small group of people who desired reannexation to Germany looked at all favorably on the National Socialist Revolution in Germany. Indirectly too, the rise of Hitler aided the reconciliation, for the French government found it advisable to treat this important frontier province with greater consideration.

Alsace-Lorraine has played a part in both German and French history; it lies deep in the traditions of both cultures. The great University of Strasbourg has enriched the culture of both peoples. It symbolizes what the provinces as a whole are and would prefer themselves to be—a link between the two countries.

Religious Policy in France

Alsace-Lorraine did not provide the only religious problem in France. Protestants within France number about one million and as a whole have exercised a political influence out of proportion to their numbers. The Masonic Society is strong and has been active in furthering anticlerical laws. But Protestants, Masons, and atheists could never account for the popularity of the laws separating church and state in France, if the overwhelming majority who are Catholics were obedient and devout followers of the Pope. The Church itself is the first to admit that many of the French are what is usually termed nominal Catholics. This is particularly true among the men. The greater preponderance of devout Catholics among the women of France affected the woman-suffrage movement adversely. Even the leftist parties, who doctrinally were supporters of women's rights and woman suffrage, opposed granting the ballot to them in France. It was felt that women would be more likely to vote as the priests told them, which would probably accrue to the benefit of the conservative parties.

THE PAPACY AND THE THIRD REPUBLIC. The church—by its support of the monarchists, the anti-Dreyfusards, and others—had in the past gained the reputation of being against the Third Republic. The fact that the extreme right-wing royalists, whose views were expressed in the *Action Française*, won support in clerical circles damaged the church in the eyes of the other political parties. This support went to great lengths. The Pope in 1914, for instance, had placed certain novels of M. Maurras (the rabid leader of the monarchist *Action Française*) on the Index, but refused to publish this ban as it would reflect on an ardent opponent of the anticlerical groups. Suddenly, in 1926, this policy was reversed. The Pope published the original ban of 1914, placed the *Action Française* also on the Index, and by this action officially gave his support to the Third Republic.

This action of the Pope was the result of more friendly relations between the Vatican and the French government. The National Bloc cabinets (1920–24) had followed a conciliatory policy, and in 1920 the French government was even officially represented at the canonization of Joan of Arc. That St. Joan was canonized at this particular time might also be interpreted as a conciliatory gesture on the part of the Church. In 1921 the French government and the Vatican exchanged diplomatic representatives. In 1924 an accord was reached over the old question of the custodianship of church property, which had been in dispute ever since the separation laws of 1904. National monuments and the great cathedrals were to be under the custody of the French government, while smaller buildings (local churches) were to be handed over to diocesan associations. When the leftist parties came to power after the election of 1924, they not only tried to enforce the separation laws in Alsace-Lorraine but also withdrew the French diplomatic mission from the Vatican. This led to a tremendous outcry in France, and within a month a petition of protest received over a million signatures. The government gave way and the embassy at the Vatican was retained.

THE CHURCH AND SOCIAL ACTION. The church in France was also undergoing a gradual reformation, which made it more acceptable to the people politically. Not only was open papal approval of the Third Republic popular, but the church increased in influence by adding to its range of activity, as for example, supporting the Boy Scout movement, which spread rapidly throughout France. Many of the younger clergy were also socially minded and sympathetic to the demands and aspirations of the working class. They again displayed real missionary zeal in their work in some of the "Red" industrial centers. Many of these young priests, having experienced the horrors of war themselves, were sympathetic to the antiwar views held by the parties on the left. The ties between Conservatism, Nationalism, and Catholicism were weakening.

The Empire

HISTORICAL DEVELOPMENT. The French colonial empire in the twenties was the second largest in the world and comprised an area of about five million square miles with a population of around sixty-eight million. Most of the vast holdings of the first French colonial age were lost to England in the wars of the eighteenth century. The colonies in the Western

Hemisphere (Guiana, Guadeloupe, Martinique, St. Pierre, and Miquelon), the five trading stations in India [see map, p. 650], and a few other scattered posts were remnants of the first French colonial empire. These old colonies (*Anciennes Colonies*) always had a status and administrative regime apart from the newer colonies. Their peoples, for example, were French citizens and for years had the privilege of the franchise, although in practice there was considerable manipulation of the vote. In the nineteenth century France launched on her second colonial era by intervening in Algeria in 1830. It was some years before this most important of all French overseas territories definitely came under French control. This was followed by the acquisition of Cochin China, in 1861, to which additions were made later [see map, p. 660].

The Third Republic after 1870 followed an active policy in the opening of Africa, which led to disputes with Italy (Tunis), England (Upper Nile Valley), and, particularly in the first decade of the present century, with Germany (Morocco). After World War I, France received back the portion of the Congo which she had ceded to Germany in 1911, and shared with England the mandate over the Cameroons and Togoland [see map, p. 98]. Although the King-Crane Commission at the time of the Peace Conference reported that the Syrian people were loath to be under the French, the mandate over Syria was given to France, which for centuries had claimed special protective rights over Christians in the Near East [see map, p. 140].

Frenchmen never settled in large numbers in the overseas territories and, in general, constituted there only the governing and entrepreneur class, while the great bulk of colonial population was native. Various types of colonial government were devised, but there was little self-government. Colonial assemblies existed, but in most cases these were controlled by nominated members, or by members elected by the French governing classes within the colony. Where the natives did possess the franchise, it was so managed from above that it meant very little.

For years the *Anciennes Colonies* were represented in the French parliament at Paris, and such representation was granted to one or two other territories. There seemed to be little logical reason in the selection of colonies for this representation. Part of Algiers, for example, was organized into departments and sent representatives to sit in the Senate and Chamber of Deputies at Paris. This principle of giving colonies representation in the parliament of the controlling power is a unique method of bringing a measure of self-government to imperial possessions. Actually, because of the suffrage requirements, the few representatives from the colonies represented the French and not the native element. Even so, their few votes were overwhelmed by the votes of the representatives of Metropolitan France. Although there was some discussion about associating more of the overseas territories with France after 1920, not much was done about it at that time.

French politicians were wont to proclaim that France was not a nation of 41 million souls but one of 110 million. The population of the colonies indeed came to be considered as one of France's greatest defensive assets. France expanded her colonial forces and made great use of them in garrisoning various parts of the Empire. Regiments of Senegalese as well as troops from other areas were even stationed in France. The virtual lack of a color bar was one of the strongest points in French colonial policy. The French spoke fully as much of their *mission civilisatrice* as the English did of the "White Man's Burden." They did make notable contributions to improving standards in various colonies; impressive modern cities were built in various far-off spots, hospitals and schools were founded. But at the same time they contravened regulations for mandates in using forced labor in the Cameroons and in recruiting natives for armed forces. The basic concept of French colonial rule, both politically and economically, has been one of centralization and subordination. The old mercantilist concept that colonies exist for the benefit of the mother country remained the underlying philosophy of the French Empire. This is amply demonstrated by the tariff arrangements between France and her various colonies.

COMMERCIAL POLICY. The most important of the French overseas possessions (Algeria, Tunis, Indochina, Madagascar, Guadeloupe, Martinique, Guiana, and Réunion) were among those where an "assimilated" tariff policy was followed. Under this scheme the French tariff rates were applied to imports into the colonies, and free trade existed between France and the assimilated colonies. A great advantage to such colonies was that their goods were not subject to quota restrictions on being exported to Metropolitan France, but there were, however, quotas for imports into the colonies from foreign countries. The French tariffs were, naturally, fixed primarily with reference to conditions in France and often entailed hardships in the colonies. For example, the high tariff on textiles made cheap cotton goods unavailable to the natives of Madagascar.

Such a policy of tariff assimilation cannot be practiced in all areas without ruining the colony involved. A scheme of tariff preference was, therefore, devised for West Africa, New Caledonia, Oceania, Somaliland, St. Pierre, and Miquelon. These territories had varying tariff rates, but France and the other territories of the French Empire were given a preference usually amounting to about 10 per cent.

By international agreements France was bound to observe the Open Door in some of its colonies. Among these agreements were the Congo Basin Treaty of 1885 growing out of the Berlin Conference on African Affairs, the Act of Algeçiras of 1906, and the restrictions on mandates. This meant that the same tariff rates were to be applied to imports from France and her Empire as were levied against imports from foreign states. Morocco, Equatorial Africa, Cameroons, Togo, Syria, were such open-door territories, to which should be added the French stations in India.

That the Empire as a whole continued to be of increasing economic importance to France is shown by trade figures. By 1936 the colonies were taking about one third of French exports, and sending to France an only slightly smaller proportion of French imports.

POSTWAR DEVELOPMENTS. During the war France had made promises to her colonies, which were hard to keep, while still retaining a strong hand in colonial affairs. Moreover, the spirit of Arab nationalism, which received great stimulus during the war, caused trouble for France not only in Syria, but also in Tunis, Algeria, and even Morocco. The revolutionary movements in China led to unrest in Indochina. France found it difficult to maintain peace in this far-off colony, and repeated uprisings were put down with an iron hand. These uprisings were the forerunners of the serious rebellion that confronted France in this colony at the close of World War II.

In Syria and Lebanon France was forced to concentrate an army of 90,000 men before she was able to assert her position as mandatory power; the difficulties which this involved will be discussed in a later chapter [see below, pp. 414–16]. Although Lebanon was declared a republic in 1926 and Syria in 1930, it was France that dominated the formulation of the new constitutions, and both states continued to be French mandates. Tunis was a French protectorate technically governed by the Bey of Tunis, but French advisers told him what to do. In the postwar years the Nationalist party, with little success, began to make demands for more native control of affairs. In 1918 the French government canceled the treaties that gave special rights to Italian nationals in Tunis, an action that caused more difficulties with the Italian government than it did with Italians resident in Tunis [see below, pp. 493–94]. It was Arab nationalism that caused French difficulties here and in other parts of North Africa.

Northern Algeria, divided into three departments, was governmentally a part of France, and sent representatives to sit in the parliament at Paris. Even these departments could not be considered an integral part of France, for they retained many colonial characteristics, while the four southern Algerian territories were governed outright as a colony. It was always maintained that citizenship could not be granted to the Arabs in Algeria because of the conflict between the Koran and French Civil Law. In 1919 it was made possible for some classes of natives to acquire French citizenship, but the mass of native Algerians had no right to vote, and Algeria remained a territory run by Frenchmen and a few naturalized Arabs and Jews. The Arab nationalists clamored for representatives in the local government bodies and for more power for these bodies. Algeria was one of the most important of all French overseas territories. It was a key post for France's position not only in the Mediterranean but in all Africa. From Algeria modern transportation routes led across the Sahara to French colonies in Equatorial Africa. Algeria was rich in iron and in addition had zinc, lead, and coal deposits. Its agricultural products were even more valuable. It produced wheat, barley, oats, tobacco, and a variety of garden vegetables and tropical fruits that found a ready market in France. Algerian wine, which was cheap in price, was an important article of export.

Morocco was technically a protectorate. Here General Lyautey, one of the greatest colonial administrators France has produced, did a remarkable job. He paid scrupulous attention to native rights and prejudices, being careful to accord the sultan all the splendor and vestments of power, but actually he expanded tremendously French control over Morocco. An example of his methods is to be seen in the modern city of Casablanca, where he was careful also to build a new native city in native style to satisfy the local populace.

The Spaniards, who controlled a small section of northern Morocco opposite Gibraltar, also nominally ruled by the sultan, had difficulties with the mountain tribes in 1921. Abd-el-Krim, the chieftain of the Riffs, continued his successes in the following years, and soon was encroaching on French controlled areas. France considered the danger serious enough to dispatch Marshal Pétain, the great hero of Verdun, to deal with the Riffs. A combined Spanish-French campaign was successful; Abd-el-Krim was captured and exiled to the island of Réunion in the Indian Ocean, where he was to remain until after World War II. At that time, on promises of good conduct he was granted permission to return to France, but he escaped from his ship in Egypt and was soon engaged in furthering national movements among the peoples of Northern Africa.

Foreign Policy

To discuss the foreign policy of France in the twenties would be to discuss the policy of all Europe, for France as the leading European power was involved everywhere. All the issues—negotiation of peace treaties, reparations, war debts, colonial conflicts—cannot be reviewed again here. The French statesmen—consumed with a passion for the maintenance of the peace settlements, the prevention of German resurgence, and the restriction of communism—built up an elaborate system of alliance among the powers of Central-Eastern Europe. This attempt to achieve security by France and her allies was part of the general quest for peace and has been discussed in the chapter on the League of Nations and disarmament.

THE STRONG HAND. During the years 1920–24, when rightist governments were in control, French leaders followed a policy of the strong hand. This is well illustrated in their policy towards German reparations, which culminated in the occupation of the Ruhr. The aggressive policy followed in the Ruhr occupation led to a growing estrangement with Great Britain and the United States. No less definite was the determination of the French leaders to contain Bolshevism. They actively supported Poland and came out on top in this venture [see above, pp. 126; 172–74]. Less successful were their imperialistic policies in southern Russia and Turkey, where French troops were withdrawn. Colonial difficulties in Indochina, Syria, Tunis, and other places were dealt with firmly. Relations with Italy did not run smoothly, because France was reluctant to grant Italy adequate colonial compensations and also curtailed the rights of Italian nationals in Tunis.

CONCILIATION. The elections in May, 1924, brought new men of the left into power. They found it easier to co-operate with the Labour government of Ramsay MacDonald in Great Britain and with a Germany whose foreign policy was being directed by Gustav Stresemann. It must be remembered that Stresemann attempted to fulfill the terms of the peace treaty, and on this basis French statesmen could and would be co-operative. The Dawes Plan was accepted, the Locarno Treaties negotiated, and Germany was admitted into the League. Aristide Briand, the great conciliator, became France's foremost League statesman, and one of the outstanding figures of the period. He joined with Secretary Kellogg in proposing the outlawing of war. While his plans for the creation of a federation of Danubian states never reached the signature stage, they were no more utopian than those of outlawing war. It was an era of good feeling, if indeed such a name can be applied to any postwar years, and Briand contributed largely to it.

But throughout this period France did not depart from her basic policy of opposing any revision of the peace treaties, which seemed to all Frenchmen to be the very foundation of future security. Her leaders still depended upon a strong army and navy, coupled with alliances among the smaller states of Central-Eastern Europe. Despite a general policy of conciliation, there was no relaxing of the ties with the Little Entente, which became even firmer as time went on.

INACTION. Thus the policy of holding the line was maintained, and it was continued by the right center parties which took over after the 1928 elections. Now, if ever, some adjustments were necessary because of the great depression that struck the world in 1929. France was no more fortunate than other states in possessing men who had the vision to see what the times demanded. Tardieu and Laval, who dominated French policy in these years, did make some concessions. It was not a small matter that the Young Plan was accepted. In order to undercut the growth of the Nationalist Socialist party in Germany, France belatedly made a gesture to the German government by withdrawing her forces of occupation on June 30, 1930. This was well ahead of the time table set by the Versailles Treaty. Yet French opposition to German demands for revision of the Treaty of Versailles remained as adamant as ever. This is borne out by the French attitude toward the problem of disarmament. France also led the successful fight to prevent the proposed Austro-German customs union of 1931.

SUMMARY. To maintain the peace settlement that France considered the anchor of her whole security program, she retained her armaments, created an elaborate alliance system in Central-Eastern Europe, manipulated the League of Nations, and above all strove to preserve intact the victorious coalition of the Great War. Disputes and rivalries occurred with each of her former allies, but the cornerstone of her policy was to retain the friendship of Great Britain and Italy in Europe, of Japan in Asia, and of the United States in America. Although there were no mutual guarantees of protection, none of these powers was ever close to being classified as an actual enemy of France until after 1935. French policy suffered a real setback when the Anglo-French bid for Italian friendship was spurned by Mussolini after the Italian conquest of Ethiopia. It was, nevertheless, true that France through Briand took a leading part in a number of international efforts to forestall the possibility of another war. However misguided or futile some of these efforts may have been, they **were no** less than the French system of alliances, an expression of the depth of the French dread of another war.

CHAPTER

— 11 —

The United Kingdom
and the Empire

Political Development: *The War Period; Khaki Election; Shifting Party Strength; Summary.*

Economic Policy: *Financial Situation; Foreign Trade; Tariffs; Labor Policy; Social Insurance.*

Religion and Education: *The Anglican Church; Disestablishment in Wales; Education Act of 1919; Universities.*

Ireland: *The War; Civil Conflict; The Irish Free State; Ulster.*

The British Empire: *Definition of Dominion Status; Dominion Developments; India.*

Foreign Policy.

◆

REBUILDING war-devastated areas was no problem in England, but even there reconstruction of another sort was badly needed. Under various Defense of the Realm Acts (DORA) severe censorship and restrictions of personal liberty had been enforced, and the whole economy of England had come under government regulations. Rationing, import licenses, wage and labor controls, all had to be liquidated; and many vested interests both in the government bureaucracy and in industry resisted this procedure. Factories had to be reconverted to peace-time production, and old established trade connections not only in Europe but also in South America had to be reknit, if Britain was to recapture her export market. The demobilized soldiers wanted jobs and homes, and there was a real housing shortage. Women who had flocked into industry during the war were reluctant to give up their jobs especially as rising living costs required that family incomes be supplemented by the earnings of wives and daughters. Great Britain had borne a large share of the financial burden of the war, and budgetary problems plagued the postwar governments. The war had also brought new relations between the mother country and the component parts of the British Empire. An overhauling of these connections, particularly in the case of Ireland and India, was long overdue. Nor should it be forgotten that, as one of the great victorious powers, Great Britain had many responsibilities in regard to the peace settlement. Her armies and her fleet in the months after the armistice still played an active role all the way from the Baltic to the Near East.

Political Development

THE WAR PERIOD. August, 1914, brought a party truce in Great Britain. Controversial issues were to be shelved, and everyone was to throw his support to the prosecution of the war. But dissatisfaction with the Liberal government mounted steadily, and in order to create more solidarity a coalition cabinet was appointed in May, 1915, although Premier Asquith remained at the helm. The war effort in the next months was far from being spectacularly successful, and several ministers resigned. Finally in 1916 a sweeping reorganization of the government took place with Lloyd George taking the position of premier. A section of the Asquith Liberals was not in sympathy with the change, and this division in their ranks marked the beginning of the end of the supremacy of the Liberal party.

Certain governmental innovations followed. A small inner circle of cabinet members—at first four in number—was designated as a War Cabinet. These men were relieved of heavy departmental duties and could devote their entire attention to war affairs. Previously no records had ever been kept of cabinet meetings. Now a secretary was provided whose duty it was to prepare the agenda, keep the minutes of cabinet meetings, and to see that all decisions were dispatched to the proper officials. This secretariat, originally designed as a wartime device, proved so valuable that it became a permanent institution. Its records when made available will be a most illuminating historical source. In 1917 the King decreed that all princes of his family who were British subjects and bore German titles should adopt British surnames. The family of Teck became Cambridge, and that of Battenberg, Mountbatten. The royal family itself was henceforth to be known as the House and Family of Windsor instead of the House of Hanover.

Lloyd George as prime minister drew much of his support from the Conservatives or Unionists, as they called themselves at this time, whose leader was Bonar Law. With the conclusion of the armistice these two leaders decided to hold a parliamentary election. It was long overdue, for the Parliament then sitting had been elected in December, 1910, for a five-year term. During the war it seemed best to extend the mandate of Parliament from time to time, rather than to risk the disturbances of an election.

THE KHAKI ELECTION. In the spring of 1918 Parliament passed a Representation of the People Act which ranks in importance with the Reform Bills of 1832, 1867, and 1884–85. It was a very broad act, that redistributed seats, changed the system of registering voters, improved the system of absentee voting, restricted plural voting somewhat, legislated against corrupt practices, and above all widened the suffrage. Now all men over twenty-one could vote under a residence qualification in one district and in addition might have a second vote in a different constituency, if they were occupiers of land or property of an annual rental value of £10 in that constituency. If they were graduates of a university they might also vote for the university representatives to Parliament. However, no man could vote more than twice, and one vote had to be by virtue of a residence qualification. Women over thirty were given the vote if they or their husbands could meet the requirements for voting in local affairs. This was based entirely on occupancy of property of a rental value of £5. Therefore, women could not vote by virtue only of a residence qualification. This excluded primarily daughters living at home and women in domestic service. These differences in suffrage requirements between men and women were held to be necessary in order to preserve a certain equality in numbers between male and female electors. The death toll among men had been heavy during the war, and the armed services still claimed many. It was not until 1928 that suffrage requirements for men and women were placed on a par, but even then plural voting for both men and women remained a possibility.

No one knew what effect the electoral law of 1918 would have. The addition of some 8,500,000 women, plus additional male voters made a total electorate of about 21,300,000. Holding the election so soon after the close of hostilities seemed bound to favor the government. Lloyd George and the other coalition leaders called for a popular mandate to strengthen their hands at the coming Peace Conference. Elaborate promises were made to the electorate about making Germany pay the cost of the war. The remnant of Independent (Asquith) Liberals, the Labor party, the majority of whose members had withdrawn support from the coalition government in the summer of 1918, and the Irish Sinn Feiners constituted a weak opposition. The coalition forces won an overwhelming victory. Although the Coalition Conservatives (Unionists) outnumbered the Coalition Liberals 334–136, Lloyd George remained premier, but he now governed on sufferance of the Conservatives.

After the signature of the peace treaties in 1919 there was no longer one great common cause to hold the coalition together. The problem of the budget, the advisability of continuing armed intervention in the Near East, and especially the question of protection or free trade—all this brought out increasing differences between the two coalition parties. Nor were the party men content any longer to follow the rather high-handed leadership which Lloyd George exercised. In October, 1922, the Conservatives voted to withdraw their support from the government, and there was nothing for the little Welshman to do but resign.

SHIFTING PARTY STRENGTH. It was up to Bonar Law, the new premier, to conduct the ensuing parliamentary elections (November, 1922). He led his Conservative party to a resounding victory on a platform of "tranquillity and stability." The Liberal party, hopelessly split into two factions—the Asquith Liberals and Lloyd George Liberals—had to surrender its place as the opposition party to the rapidly rising Labor party. The new government was beset by increasing unemployment and the failure of prosperity to materialize. Stanley Baldwin, who had replaced the ailing Bonar Law as premier, decided that a protective tariff was necessary. Since this involved a fundamental change in British policy, he dissolved Parliament and put the question to the people in a general election in accordance with the best English democratic tradition.

The election of December, 1923, resulted in a Conservative defeat, but no one party held a clear majority. It is true that the issue of free trade had been enough to unite the Liberals, but even so they ran a weak third. Ramsay MacDonald, leader of the Labor party, formed a cabinet which was dependent on Liberal support. He granted the USSR *de jure* recognition and set out to expand Russian-British trade. His proposal for a Russian trade treaty and a loan to the Soviets aroused the ire of both Conservatives and Liberals. The upshot was that MacDonald dissolved Parliament, and for the third time in two years the British were faced with a parliamentary election.

In 1924 the Conservatives campaigned on a platform of economy. Costly governmental spending programs were censured, and socialism and communism became an issue. A few days before the voters went to the polls the *Daily Mail* published a letter allegedly written by the Bolshevik leader Zinoviev to British Communists, inciting them to overthrow the British government by force. The people were naturally indignant, and the Labor party suffered from its socialist connections. The election resulted in a Conservative majority of 209 over the combined votes of the other parties. Such a landslide had not taken place in England for many a decade. Even Asquith was defeated, but he was awarded a peerage and as the Earl of Oxford and Asquith took his seat in the House of Lords.

Stanley Baldwin again became prime minister. His square face, pipe, heavy watch chain strung across his vest, and high shoes typified the solid unexciting government he gave England during the next four and one-half years. Labor showed its dissatisfaction in 1926 by staging a general strike, which was highly dramatic but unsuccessful. Diplomatic relations with Russia were severed. An important Imperial Conference worked out a basis for the future status of the dominions within the British Commonwealth of Nations [see below, pp. 290–91]. But Baldwin was unable to keep his pledges to reduce public expenditures, trade did not expand as expected, and unemployment grew steadily. The elections of 1929 gave Labor 288, Conservatives 260, and Liberals 59 seats in the House of Commons.

Ramsay MacDonald formed a Labor government which had Liberal support, but had been in power only a few months when the crash which set off the great business depression occurred on the New York stock market. Its ever widening effects soon engulfed the British government with new difficulties. Mounting tariff barriers in other countries again raised the problem of protection in Britain, and it was a budgetary and financial crisis that led to the resignation of the MacDonald cabinet in August, 1931. Instead of dissolving Parliament, the King prevailed upon MacDonald to form a National coalition government composed of Labor, Conservatives, and Liberals. The majority of the Labor party opposed the coalition, and read those Labor leaders (MacDonald, Snowden, Thomas) who co-operated with it out of the party.

When the National government attempted to inaugurate various economies, riots occurred in many cities. Unemployment figures stood at unprecedented heights (2,825,772), although they were still to go higher. A mutiny in some of the fleet units indicated perhaps better than anything else the temper of the times. To meet the grave financial situation the government was forced to abandon the gold standard, and the pound sterling fell from a par of $4.86 to $3.49. It did not take much oratory to bring home the seriousness of the situation and the need for a united front to meet this new crisis in Britain's history. The National government won a resounding majority of 500 seats in the general election which was held in October, 1931.

SUMMARY. Between 1914 and 1931 coalition governments had been in power in Britain most of the time. Only from 1922 to 1924 and from 1925 to 1929, when the Conservatives held the reins, did a single party constitute the government majority. Labor had displaced the Liberals as the other party in what is traditionally taken to be England's two party system. Its rising strength rested on a wise combination of trade unionism and Fabian Socialist doctrine. It also had close connections with the widespread co-operative movement. Labor had taken office twice but never had sufficient power to put over its program. In creating a National government in 1931 Britain was but following the European fashion of the time. Parliamentary leaders sought to accomplish by less drastic means and under other forms what dictatorially minded persons sought through the creation of single party states. It meant that normal party government ceased to function, and it was the resurrection in peacetime of the techniques of war government.

The postwar years thus brought an extension of the power of the executive. More and more measures were dealt with by Departmental Orders, and Orders in Council based on statutory authorization. These can be compared to executive orders in the United States or presidential decrees in Germany and France. Most of these orders were theoretically subject to scrutiny and approval by Parliament, but in actual practice they were regu-

larly approved in batches. It was no doubt a necessary device to deal with
the many problems that face a modern state. Yet the danger exists that
such government by administrative decrees may turn into a new despotism.
More and more the cabinet governed England, and the House of Commons
followed its lead.

The House of Lords remained and, dominated by its hereditary members, influenced the government more indirectly than directly. The Labor
cabinets always had to consider a possible veto by that body. Under the
Parliament Act of 1911 it would have taken two years to circumvent such
a veto, and that is a rather long time when a severe economic crisis is at
hand. Had it not been for the House of Lords, it is generally conceded that
the Labor governments might well have launched a bolder program.

Economic Policy

FINANCIAL SITUATION. The war brought a rise in Britain's national debt
from £650 millions ($3,149,000,000) in March, 1914, to £7,828 millions
($38,044,080,000) in March, 1920. Only then was it possible to halt its up-
ward spiral. Unlike other European countries, England did not rid itself
of any part of this debt through a policy of currency inflation. In 1925
Winston Churchill, as Chancellor of the Exchequer, restored the gold
standard and established sterling at its prewar parity.

Britain had covered much of its debt by floating war loans at relatively
high rates of interest, and these constituted a heavy carrying charge on the
budget. The government also was faced with the interest and repayment
of the large loans advanced by the United States. In 1923 this debt, which
at that time stood at $4,600,000,000, was funded so that England would
pay an average of 161 millions for ten years and 184 millions for the next
fifty-two years. Over against her indebtedness Britain credited the loans to
her allies, made during the war, and her share of the reparations. From
neither source did she ever receive any substantial amounts. Such a debt
burden required heavy taxes, although some relief was granted after 1922.
It also seemed to call for economies in government and this was a recurring
issue in elections. If there were differences of opinion in regard to tax reductions and restriction of government expenditures, all Englishmen were
agreed that foreign trade must be expanded, a problem closely related to
England's general financial position.

FOREIGN TRADE. About 80 per cent of Britain's population is urban,
and normally in the neighborhood of 60 per cent of its food is imported.
This means that Britain had to export goods if its people were to live. In
the twenties she continued to be the largest single exporter of manufactured
goods, but the United States, and later Germany and Japan, gained rapidly on her. Britain's strength still lay in her old established industries,
notably textiles. In none of the great new twentieth century industrial
fields, such as automobiles, did she lead. The result was inevitable. Whereas
in 1913 Great Britain accounted for 13.93 per cent of the world's exports,
by 1929 her share had dropped to 10.84 per cent.

The relative decline in exports was all the more a problem since Britain's imports, always larger, increased more rapidly than her exports. The differences had to be covered by income from foreign investments and payments from services (shipping, insurance). This left smaller sums available for investment at home or abroad. Unless the volume of exports was increased, British industries could not prosper, unemployment would mount, and this in turn would curtail the home market. It is not surprising that under these conditions Britain decided that at long last her policy of free trade must be sacrificed. This would not only build up the home market but it would make possible a system of preferential rates within the Empire, which might well go a long way toward stimulating exports. It would also prove a valuable bargaining weapon in negotiating trade agreements with other countries.

TARIFFS. In 1914 Great Britain enjoyed free trade. It is true there were revenue duties on a whole list of imported products (coffee, tea, cocoa, sugar, dried fruit, tobacco, wines, beers and spirits), but if these products were produced at home a corresponding excise duty was placed on them. These duties, therefore, were for revenue and did not constitute a protective tariff. At various times during the war the duty rates on these products were raised. In 1915, supposedly in order to save cargo space, a tariff of 33⅓ per cent *ad valorem* was set on automobiles, motorcycles, clocks, watches, music instruments, and films. These McKenna duties, named after the Chancellor of the Exchequer, continued after the war. They constituted the first break in England's free trade system. In 1921 a Safeguarding of Industries Act accorded a 33⅓ per cent tariff protection on a whole list of so-called key industries (chemicals, optical glass, precision instruments, etc.). A protective duty was placed on hops, and revenue and excise duties on silk in 1925, followed in 1928 by duties on additional items.

Such tariffs were only minor because England, with its dense population, was heavily dependent upon imports in almost all fields. The British still regarded themselves as on a free trade basis in 1931. Actually, as a revenue producer their various duties were as important as the high tariffs imposed by the United States. In 1929–30, customs revenue amounted to $586,893,000 in Britain and to $587,100,000 in the United States.

When the National government won the elections in 1931, it was generally held that tariffs would be imposed, for the Conservatives dominated the coalition. Manufacturers rushed to import goods, and in order to forestall this an "Abnormal Importations" Act was rushed through Parliament. Under this law orders could be passed by the President of the Board of Trade levying up to 100 per cent duties on imports of manufacturers. Three such general orders were issued within the next months. Under a Horticulture Products Act the minister of agriculture could impose similar duties on certain classes of fresh fruits and vegetables. This was followed by an Import Duties Act of 1932 imposing a 10 per cent *ad valorem* duty on all imports except those on a specified free list, which included most raw materials. The rates under this act were subsequently raised.

It should be pointed out that these tariffs applied only to what is officially known as the United Kingdom of Great Britain (England, Scotland, and Wales) and Northern Ireland (Ulster). Each of the dominions and different possessions within the Empire had its own system of duties. In the mandates Britain was obligated to follow an open-door policy. In most of the Crown Colonies free trade existed. India had a separate tariff system of her own.

The dominions had tariff autonomy and imposed various degrees of protection. Most of them granted a preferential rate to imports from Britain, at least on some products. Britain in turn granted preferences to their products. Thus after 1919 the McKenna duties on Empire imports were only 22½ per cent, while the rate was 33⅓ per cent on imports from other states. To take advantage of this rate many American automobile manufacturers established branches in Canada. The 1921 key industry duties also did not apply to Empire products. How far preference had advanced is shown by the fact that "in 1930 over half the sales of Canada and Australia to the British market received preference, and over 30 per cent of the sales of other British countries. . . ." [1]

Under the Ottawa Agreements of August, 1932, Britain negotiated special preferential agreements with Canada, Australia, South Africa, Newfoundland, India, and Southern Rhodesia. These countries also concluded some agreements among themselves, and concessions made by one did not necessarily apply to another. Above all it was maintained that the trade preferences granted to members of the Empire or to the United Kingdom did not have to be extended to foreign powers which had treaties containing the most favored nation clause. At the Ottawa Conference the British colonies were invited to give preferences to Empire products. This most of them did in the next years, although the rates of preference varied greatly. The result was to complicate even more the bewildering system of rates and tariffs that exist within the Empire.

The imposition of a protective tariff in Britain and the extension of imperial preference under the Ottawa Agreements was in line with the general trend all over the world toward nationalistic tariff policies. Each country attempted to become more self-sufficing. To buy more pork and wheat from Canada meant that Britain could buy less from Denmark and the countries of Eastern Europe. These small countries had to sell and so they turned more and more to Germany, which was attempting to unite Central and Eastern Europe into one great economic unit. With the United States under the Smoot-Hawley Tariff of 1929, Russia under its system of planned foreign trade, the French Empire and now the British Empire tending to become more closed trading units, it is not surprising that world trade as a whole languished.

LABOR POLICY. Trade unions were legalized in Great Britain in 1824 and since then have grown tremendously in membership and power. There

---

[1] Frederic C. Benham: *Great Britain Under Protection* (New York, 1941), p. 90.

has been no uniform pattern of trade union organization, and industrial unions, such as the Miners' Federation and National Union of Railwaymen, exist alongside of a host of craft unions. In 1868 a co-ordinating body, the Trades Union Congress, was formed and since then has represented most of the union membership. In 1900 a Labor Representation Committee was organized which in 1006 became the Labor party. The English worker was now organized to achieve the ends of labor through direct political action.

The war brought a rise in the trade union movement. By 1920 there were 1360 unions with a membership of 8,346,000. Wages were at unprecedentedly high levels, and the workingmen were determined not to return to the low prewar levels. Serious mine strikes occurred in 1919 and again in 1921, when government control of the mines ended. The government appointed a commission to investigate and agreed to pay a subsidy so that wages would not have to be cut. The mine owners, however, did nothing to improve the mines through modernization, and in 1925 serious trouble again broke out. Another government commission was appointed and, on the whole, made recommendations favorable to the miners. The miners accepted, the owners did not. This time the Trades Union Congress backed the miners by calling a general strike (1926) which involved primarily the transport workers, printers, and the iron, steel, and building trades. The government, aided by volunteers, undertook to transport food and other necessities. The strike was stigmatized as a manifestation of class war, and public opinion was against it. On promise of further negotiation, the Trades Union Congress called off the strike. The government claimed that the strikers had surrendered unconditionally, which was not true, yet the episode weakened the unions. In 1927 Parliament passed a Trades Union Act, which declared all sympathetic strikes illegal and restricted the collection of levies from union members for political purposes. Now such levies could be legally collected only if each individual union member specifically authorized it.

By 1932 trade union membership had declined about one-half from its peak of 1920, yet the power and influence of the unions on the whole increased. Trade unions were recognized in practically all industries by the employer associations. Collective bargaining was the rule, and the labor contracts regulating wages, hours, etc. were increasingly negotiated on a national rather than a local basis. The decline in trade union membership was chiefly due to the vast amount of unemployment that plagued England throughout the twenties. The number of unemployed never fell below a million and in 1930 the number stood at two and one-half million. Such colossal unemployment called for direct government aid to keep people from starving. It required a complete overhauling of England's social insurance system.

SOCIAL INSURANCE. In 1908 England adopted its first Old Age Pension Act. This was followed three years later by a far-reaching sickness and unemployment insurance act, based upon contributions by the employer, employee, and the state. Subsequently expanded, by 1920 it covered two thirds of the employed people in Britain. In 1925 widows, dependent children, and orphans were protected by another insurance act. Whereas Germany had led in old age, sickness, and accident insurance, England pioneered in the field of unemployment insurance. This is the most difficult of all problems to deal with on an insurance basis; systems so far devised are not designed to take care of all unemployment. They are at best meant to take care of temporary periods of unemployment and to cushion the effects of long-time unemployment.

Under the English system a person was entitled to receive unemployment benefits for a certain number of weeks each year if he had been contributing to the fund for a certain period. The amount paid and the periods of payment were altered several times during the twenties. However, many people reached maturity without ever having held a regular job and hence could not draw benefits. In most cases additional aid was required after the insurance payments had ceased. To take care of the latter a system of transitional benefits paid by the government was devised. At first these went on almost indefinitely, but in 1931 there was an effort to set some limits. After the regular insurance payments had been made, no person was to receive additional payments if he had property or other means. This so-called "means test," which led to extensive inquiries into the private affairs of the unemployed, was variously administered. It did not work well and was very unpopular with the working class.

Many people were thrown on local poor relief, which was still being administered largely under a system set up in the early nineteenth century. Gross inequalities existed in practice, and Poor Law rates (taxes) varied greatly in different sections of England. Finally in 1929 a thorough reorganization in Poor Law administration was made. The historic Poor Law Unions were done away with, and local relief was entrusted to the regular urban and rural areas of local government. Britain had to make great relief payments, but during the twenties did not institute a large system of public works to combat unemployment. The technique of priming the pump of prosperity by large building programs was a feature of the thirties that was never popular in Britain.

Religion and Education

The established church of England is the Protestant Episcopal, and that of Scotland, the Presbyterian. In both countries full religious liberty exists, and there are no longer civil disabilities because of religion. These two churches, however, do enjoy special privileges and receive financial support from the state, much of this in the form of special endowments or as payments for services rendered.

The so-called Nonconformist churches—Congregationalists, Methodists, Baptists, Quakers, etc.—and the Roman Catholic church, have no special connections with the state. In actual membership, these churches combined outnumber the established churches, yet such statistics account for only a small proportion of the total population of the British Isles. What nominal allegiance the large unchurched group favors is pretty much anyone's guess. It varies in sections of England but probably in general favors the historic established bodies. Marriage statistics at least would indicate this.

THE ANGLICAN CHURCH. The king is by law the supreme governor of the Anglican church. He appoints, with the consent of the prime minister, the archbishops and bishops, and names as well many other church officials whose offices are in the gift of the crown. In actual practice the appointments are usually made by the government after consultation with the responsible church authorities. Nevertheless, ecclesiastical appointments still constitute an important source of political patronage. The right of appointing clergy to many benefices—livings, as they are commonly called—often rests in the hands of lay patrons. This is largely the result of the dissolution of the monasteries in the sixteenth century, when ecclesiastical lands passed into lay hands and the right to appoint clergy on this land went with the transfer.

In 1919 an important Church of England Assembly (Powers) Act was passed, designed to make the church more self-governing, although Parliament still retained ultimate authority. The Church Assembly was to consist of three houses, one composed of the bishops, the other two representing the lesser clergy and the laity. When this assembly passes a measure, it is submitted to a joint committee of Parliament, consisting of fifteen members each from the House of Commons and the House of Lords. This committee examines the measure and reports to Parliament, which must either approve or disapprove, for it cannot amend the act.

In 1928 the House of Commons was unwilling to accept the *Revised Prayer Book* and refused its approval. This meant that a lay body, in which Catholics, Jews, nonconformists, atheists sat alongside Anglicans, decided a matter of doctrinal import for the established church. The action of the Commons aroused much dissatisfaction, and the bishops authorized the use of the revised prayer book without parliamentary sanction. This was undoubtedly not entirely legal but did conform to prevailing practice, since for years the clergy had not been following strictly the authorized prayer book. Various proposals were subsequently advanced to make it impossible for Parliament to legislate on matters of faith and to give the church more complete control over its own affairs. This was difficult to do, because there was no disposition to disestablish the church or curtail its privileges. Some reassessment of the financial arrangements between church and state seemed desirable, but the riots against payment of tithes during the thirties (particularly in 1936) produced no basic reforms.

DISESTABLISHMENT IN WALES. In September, 1914, the King gave his approval to a bill for the disestablishment and disendowment of the Anglican church in Wales and Monmouthshire. This had been forced through by the House of Commons over the veto of the House of Lords under the Parliament Act of 1911. A Suspensory Act passed at the same time postponed the bill from taking effect until after the close of the war. In 1919 the disestablishment act was amended, and a grant of one million pounds was made to the Anglican church in Wales to cover the additional value of the tithes which it was surrendering. After the official disestablishment (March 31, 1920) the Welsh Anglican church was organized under its own archbishop; it has no special connection with the government, but continues to enjoy the possession of many endowments and vested funds. Its official position is now on a par with the large nonconformist churches in Wales.

EDUCATION ACT OF 1918. In comparison to the United States and some of the continental countries, Britain was slow in adopting a compulsory and free educational system. The acts of 1870, 1891, and 1902 laid a foundation for such a system, and it was furthered by a new Educational Act passed in 1918. Attendance at school was made compulsory for children up to fourteen years of age. No longer could they be exempted after the age of twelve, although this practice was continued in Scotland, which had its own school system with somewhat different regulations. Children who left school at fourteen were supposed to attend continuation schools for 320 hours a year until they were eighteen years of age. Those that continued their regular schooling until they were sixteen were under no further obligation. Of more importance, the act prohibited all employment of children under twelve, and employment of children between the ages of twelve and fourteen on school days was limited to after school hours and before 8 p.m. This provision hit at the practice of the Lancashire textile mills of employing children as "half-timers." Provision was also made for nursery schools, holiday and school camps, playing fields, physical training, and medical inspection. Elementary education was to be free, and greater provision was made for public scholarships for secondary education. Under the act the national government expanded its financial aid to local authorities who still supervised the schools. The measure was a real step forward; but unfortunately adequate funds were not made available, and well into the twenties a good part of the educational reform program remained unrealized. Above all the continuation schools were slow about getting under way.

UNIVERSITIES. Oxford and Cambridge still held their ancient place of pre-eminence among the British universities. Oxford admitted women to full membership in the University with the privilege of taking degrees in 1920. In the same year scholars who were not members of the Church of England at long last were admitted to Oxford theological degrees. Cambridge had taken this latter step before the war. The postwar years brought great expansion and progress at the other English universities, particularly at the University of London. Among its many excellent branches the School of Economics and the newly established School of Slavonic Studies should be mentioned.

Ireland

In 1912 the Liberal government in England introduced a Home Rule Bill for Ireland. This was passed three times over the veto of the House of Lords and received royal assent in 1914. It was promptly suspended for the duration of the war, with the understanding that it would not go into effect without additional amendments to protect the wishes of Northern Ireland. The northern six counties (commonly referred to as Ulster) are predominantly Protestant and industrial. Sentiment in these counties was definitely against severing ties with Great Britain. The men of Ulster feared being swamped in a Catholic-controlled Home Rule Parliament and between 1912–14 organized a volunteer force to oppose Home Rule as then planned by the London government. Armed clashes would certainly have occurred had the government ever attempted to carry out its plans.

THE WAR. With the opening of hostilities leaders of both Northern and Southern Ireland pledged their co-operation to Great Britain. Although Ireland furnished a substantial number of volunteers in the first months, there soon developed a strong anti-British republican group known as Sinn Fein. This organization, whose name means "Ourselves Alone," established connections with Germany through Irish-American channels. The Germans promised to land arms, and a rebellion was planned for Easter 1916. Plans miscarried, and the ship carrying munitions to the rebels had to be scuttled to prevent capture. Great Britain rushed additional troops to Ireland, and the rebellion was suppressed without difficulty. The British tried and executed fifteen of the leaders who had surrendered, among them Sir Roger Casement. An additional 3,000 Irishmen, seized more or less at random, were interned in England.

This British method of dealing with Irish rebels, tried so often before, had its usual effect. The Sinn Fein movement grew. America's entrance into the war made it politically unwise to attempt any further Irish-German connections. Yet when Britain tried to enforce a draft in Ireland in the spring of 1918, the attempt had to be given up. In the parliamentary elections held that fall Sinn Fein won seventy-three seats to the old Nationalist party's seven. Only Ulster elected men favorable to maintaining the ties with England. The Sinn Feiners refused to go to London and instead met as a National Assembly (Dail Eireann) at Dublin. They proclaimed Ireland a republic and elected De Valera president. He was at that time in an English prison, but before long escaped to the United States, where he was hailed as president of Ireland.

CIVIL CONFLICT. The British were bound to take cognizance of the new Dublin government, which started out to extend its control over all Ireland. The newly organized Irish Republican Army carried on guerrilla warfare with the British "Army of Occupation," as the Irish called it, and the British-controlled police. Many discharged English soldiers (dressed in khaki) were recruited for the police (dressed in dark green) and because of their medley of uniforms were nicknamed "The Black and Tans." The

Irish Republican Army considered all those who co-operated with the British as traitors and spies and took ruthless measures against them. The British revenged the killing of their comrades by an equal policy of terror. It soon became clear that no forcible methods could pacify Ireland outside of a full scale war.

In 1920 a new Government of Ireland Act was passed in London, by which separate parliaments were to be established in Northern and in Southern Ireland. A Council in which each part was to be equally represented was to deal with common Irish affairs. These parliaments were duly elected and then each went its own way, but the common Council was never established. The upshot was that there were now two more or less recognized governments in Ireland, but their relations to Britain were far from settled. Civil conflict continued. In 1921 Lloyd George offered Ireland dominion status and persuaded the government at Dublin to confer on this basis. Arthur Griffith and Michael Collins were the leaders of the delegation that went to London to negotiate, De Valera remaining behind. On December 6, 1921, a treaty was signed granting Southern Ireland dominion status as the Irish Free State. Ulster was to continue under the existing arrangements.

THE IRISH FREE STATE. De Valera insisted that the delegation had gone beyond their instructions, and led a fight against the treaty when it was placed before the Dail Eireann for ratification. Griffith and Collins maintained that the treaty granted Ireland all its essential freedoms, and the remaining ties with Britain were only such as to maintain those friendly relations which all Irish professed they wanted. Besides they were convinced that Britain would fight rather than make further concessions. The main targets of the opposition were the division of Ireland into two parts, the oath of loyalty to the crown, and Britain's continued possession of certain military defenses. Nevertheless, the treaty was ratified 64–57. De Valera resigned, and a provisional government was established with Griffith as president.

New elections were held in June, 1922, which resulted in a great victory for the government forces. William T. Cosgrave supervised the drawing up of the new constitution, for Griffith died in August and Collins was assassinated ten days later. De Valera and his followers continued in opposition and refused to take their seats.

The Free State under President Cosgrave was torn by internal strife, but was eventually stabilized and admitted to the League of Nations in 1923. As a dominion it participated in the Imperial Conferences of the British Commonwealth. In 1925 the boundary with Northern Ireland was finally established along the lines drawn in 1920. When a new electoral law required all candidates at an election to pledge that they would take their seats if elected, the opposition tactics of De Valera's followers were ended. After the 1927 elections De Valera's *Fianna Fail* became the leading opposition party. He did not let up his agitation against the oath to the

British crown or his demand for an entirely independent Ireland. He also was opposed to the continuation of land annuities. These were payments to Britain owed by Irish tenant farmers in repayment on loans advanced under various acts of Parliament from 1891 to 1909. Largely on this campaign platform De Valera won the elections of 1932. He was subsequently elected president by the Dail, and a new era was at hand for the Irish Free State.

ULSTER. Under the Government of Ireland Act of 1920 as amended in 1922, a separate government of Northern Ireland was established at Belfast. The executive consists of a governor representing the king, and of a cabinet of ministers responsible to a bicameral legislature. This government has competence to deal with its own affairs, save a list of matters of imperial concern (foreign affairs, defense, treaties, etc.) which are reserved for the government in London. Northern Ireland sends thirteen representatives to sit in the House of Commons at London. This arrangement for Home Rule has apparently worked satisfactorily.

The British Empire

England, Great Britain, the United Kingdom, the British Commonwealth of Nations, the British Empire—are names which correctly or incorrectly are often used interchangeably. Nor are foreigners the only ones to err in this regard. In fact, Britishers themselves are among the worst offenders. The word "Empire" is no longer so fashionable as when the special Christmas issue of Canadian stamps in 1898 carried the caption "We hold a vaster Empire than has been." The Empire is not so large today, and the term British Empire is going into disuse. In its stead people use the term Commonwealth, which has a more democratic connotation. A few words of definition may clarify these overlapping terms. England conquered and incorporated Wales into its system of government, although Wales has always retained its historic identity and its own Welsh language. In 1707 the Union with Scotland took place which gave rise officially to the term Great Britain (England, Wales, and Scotland). In 1801 the legislative union of Great Britain and Ireland was consummated under the name of the United Kingdom. Ireland now sent its representatives to sit with those from England, Wales, and Scotland in the Parliament at London. When the Irish Free State was established in 1922 the name became the United Kingdom of Great Britain and Northern Ireland.

The term British Empire was meanwhile used to cover the vast conglomeration of territories subject to the British crown no matter if they happened to be called colonies, chartered companies, protectorates, dependencies, mandates, or dominions. After the war, with the growth of self-government in the dominions, the term British Commonwealth of Nations came into general usage. As Professor Keith, the great authority on the British Empire, states, "It is now usual to group the self-governing Dominions with the United Kingdom . . . as the British Commonwealth of

Nations, thus constituting a distinct position within the larger conception of the British Empire." [2] This was to be further modified in deference to India in 1949 by the omission of "British" from the title.

DEFINITION OF DOMINION STATUS. Ever since Queen Victoria's golden jubilee in 1887 there have been periodic conferences of representatives of the colonies with the government in London. At the Colonial Conference of 1907 the name dominion was officially bestowed on the self-governing colonies. These consisted of Canada, Newfoundland, Australia, New Zealand, and the Union of South Africa. Henceforth, there were to be Imperial Conferences of the dominions and the mother country every four years. The war interrupted the series, although Imperial War Conferences which dealt with war problems were held in 1917 and 1918. The great part which the dominions played in that struggle, along with the individual recognition granted them at the Peace Conference and as members of the League of Nations (except for Newfoundland), enhanced their position as independent sovereign states. Although an unofficial meeting was held in 1921, the first official postwar Imperial Conference was not held until 1923. It was devoted mainly to discussion of a system of imperial preference, which was not adopted at this time.

The Conference of 1926 finally got down to defining the legal status of the dominions. It suggested a reform of the title of the British king, largely to accord with the changed status of Ireland. This was carried out the next year by striking out an "and" between Great Britain and Ireland, thus it became "George V, by the Grace of God, of Great Britain, Ireland, and the Dominions Beyond the Seas, King, Defender of the Faith, Emperor of India." The last phrase of this title was to disappear in 1948 with the independence of India. The Conference agreed that the governor general in each dominion was to hold a position in relation to all administration essentially the same as that of the king to the government in Great Britain. This meant that the king as represented by his governor was to follow the advice of the prime minister of the dominion. The Irish Free State was concerned with abolishing the right of appeal from dominion courts to the Judicial Committee of the Privy Council, but no clear-cut decision was made on this issue. Later, Ireland repealed this privilege, and it has been curtailed in other dominions, although not abolished. The Conference suggested the following definition of a dominion:

> *They are autonomous Communities within the British Empire, equal in status, in no way subordinate one to another in any respect of their domestic or external affairs, though united by a common allegiance to the Crown, and freely associated as members of the British Commonwealth of Nations.*

The suggestions of the 1926 conference were discussed again at later meetings and finally were incorporated into the Statute of Westminster, passed

[2] Arthur Berriedale Keith: *An Introduction to British Constitutional Law* (Oxford, 1931), p. 163.

by the Parliament in London in 1931. Under its provisions no change in the law of succession to the British throne can be made without the consent of the dominions. Parliament in London can pass a law applying to the dominions only when requested by them. No law passed by a dominion parliament can be declared void because it is repugnant to the law of England or to any existing or future act of the British Parliament. Nor can the king disallow an act of a dominion parliament, following the advice of his British ministers; in dominion affairs he must act on the advice of the dominion ministers.

In some respects the Statute of Westminster went farther than some of the dominions themselves desired. Amendment to the Canadian, Australian, and New Zealand constitutions previously required an act of the British Parliament. The provinces and states of these areas, fearful of losing their "states' rights" to the central government, have insisted that this procedure be continued. Parliament's consent to such an amendment would no doubt be a formality if requested, yet the fact remained that states that were becoming more and more independent every day still did not have sole authority to amend their own constitutions. This provision, along with a common sovereign, and the continued right of appeal to the Privy Council were some of the legal ties which still bound the dominions to the mother country after the Statute of Westminster. They were and are insignificant in comparison to the ties of sentiment, loyalty, and self-interest. The British fleet and the power of the British Empire as a whole protect the dominions as individual states, although the latter have begun to share this burden.

DOMINION DEVELOPMENTS. The problems of the postwar years were not so acute in the dominions as in the mother country, but they were problems common to all states that had been at war. Soldiers had to be demobilized, there was debt and some currency inflation. All of the dominions are predominantly rural, and they suffered from the decline in agricultural prices. Their interest in preferential trade has already been discussed. On the whole the dominions increased their tariffs and launched on a policy of industrialization; this was above all true of Canada where many American concerns opened branches. In Australia and New Zealand the government took a more direct hand in industrial development. New Zealand developed an advanced system of co-operative enterprise and services.

The dominions, along with other states, followed a policy of restricted immigration although all of them (with the exception of Ireland) were far from overpopulated and had many undeveloped lands and national resources. Australia and New Zealand followed a definite white supremacy policy and excluded all Japanese and Chinese. In South Africa the race question was also acute, although here it was more of an internal problem. The one and a half million whites were determined to maintain their supremacy over the five and one-half million blacks. The war slogans about democracy and self-determination had reached some of the more advanced colored people, and the twenties presented plenty of evidence that the "native problem" was mounting. Political strife between the "English" and the Dutch (Afrikanders) heightened. There was considerable sentiment in South Africa for breaking the few remaining ties with Great Britain. In Canada the problem of the French minority also increased. As a whole French Quebec had been least enthusiastic in its war effort and had vigorously resisted the draft. The entrenched position of the Catholic church in this province and its control over education and politics aroused disfavor in other sections of Canada.

Economically Newfoundland prospered the least. Its government literally went bankrupt, and in 1934 it voluntarily relinquished its status as a dominion. A group of civil service experts was appointed by the crown to straighten out its affairs, and for some years Newfoundland was governed as a Crown Colony.

The Irish Free State, as pointed out above, was established in 1922 with all the privileges of a dominion. It co-operated in the Imperial Conferences of the twenties, but its development and history ran such a separate course, particularly after De Valera became president in 1932, that it constantly occupied a position apart from the other dominions.

INDIA. English interests in India date from the founding of the East India Company in 1600. In the course of the eighteenth century this Company, with the active aid of the English government, defeated the French, and India passed under English control. As a result of the Sepoy Mutiny (1857) the governing powers of the East India Company were abolished, and the Government of India Act of 1858 became the basis of India's government. In 1876 Disraeli proclaimed Queen Victoria Empress of India, which flattered her and added luster to the British crown, but brought few changes to the inhabitants of India.

More than a third of India's territory lay within the boundaries of some 600 native states. These varied in size from properties of a few acres to Hyderabad, which was larger than England and Scotland combined. These native states were not a part of British India, although the princes who ruled over them were under the suzerainty of the British crown. Britain named advisers to reside at their courts and exercised control over their foreign affairs. To describe these rather vague but real rights of the crown the British invented the word "Paramountcy."

India's population of 319 million (1921), constituted about one-sixth of the population of the world, and of this number about 72 million lived in the native states. There were many religions, the Hindus numbering about 217 million, and the Mohammedans with 70 million constituting the second largest group. Rich in mineral resources, with tremendous possibilities for future development, India constituted a real jewel in the British crown. It has often been called the key to the British Empire, since so much imperial history has been centered about its possession, and maintaining the routes to India has been for many years a chief concern of British foreign policy.

During the war India had been loyal in spite of attempts by Germany and Turkey to create difficulties. The Indian Moslems never responded to the Turkish sultan's proclamation of a Holy War. In all, India sent 1,338,628 combatant and non-combatant auxiliaries to various battlefronts. This was more than was furnished by all the dominions combined. Her losses were 73,432 killed and a slightly larger number wounded. She contributed £150 million ($729,000,000) to the Empire's war chest and subscribed even more to loans. As a means of encouragement and as a reward, Britain promised that after the war governmental reforms would be instituted.

Supposedly to carry out these promises a Government of India Act was passed in 1919. It established a system of national government, democratic in form but leaving the British still in control. The viceroy representing the king had extensive powers of legislating by decree. He also controlled the executive council of ministers and nominated a large number of the members of both the upper and lower chambers. The other members were elected by a restricted suffrage. Questions of defense, of the budget, of foreign affairs were particularly under executive control. In spite of suggested reforms, this system of national government in India as established in 1919 remained in existence until 1947.

The provincial governments were also overhauled. There was to be an appointive governor, an executive council, and an elective legislative council. The British revived the term "Dyarchy" to describe the strange distribution of powers granted to the provincial governments. The "reserved powers" (defense, police, etc.) were under the direct control of the governor and council, but the transferred powers (education, sanitation, public health, etc.) were under the direction of ministers elected by the provincial legislative council and responsible to it. In other words, in regard to some questions there was to be executive government, in regard to others there was to be self-government in the provinces.

It is not surprising that this system of government did not satisfy the people of India. The great National Congress party under the leadership of Mohandas K. Gandhi carried on ceaseless agitation for further reform. In September, 1920, Gandhi launched his first non-co-operation campaign. English goods were boycotted, and Gandhi advocated a revival of village industries and the weaving of homespun cloth. Not all restricted themselves to non-violence as advocated by Gandhi, and many clashes occurred in 1921. With his arrest in 1922 and sentence to six years' imprisonment the campaign of passive resistance collapsed. Two years later Gandhi was released because of the serious state of his health.

The act of 1919 was admittedly only a stop-gap measure, and finally in 1927 a Statutory Commission headed by Sir John Simon was appointed to investigate and report on conditions in India. Unwisely, no Indians were appointed to serve on the commission. The Congress party refused to co-operate and in 1928 voted to revive the policy of non-co-operation unless dominion status were granted by December 31, 1929.

When January 1, 1930, dawned, dominion status had not materialized.

Instead the British government had issued a call (October, 1929) for Round Table Conferences to study the question of dominion status. The Congress party answered by declaring for complete independence. In March, 1930, the second civil disobedience campaign was started. This time Gandhi led a demonstration march to the sea, as a protest against the salt taxes. This was an example of his unusual ability to make use of symbols with dramatic significance; the idea that salt should be free to all was linked up with the unlimited expanse of the sea. The spinning wheel he used as a homely symbol of resistance to industrialization. He was a leader whose power did not cease when he and many of his followers were jailed.

In November, 1930, the First Round Table Conference was held, attended by the Indian princes and some Indians who were willing to co-operate with the English government. The princes accepted the principle of federation and agreed that the national government should have an extensive measure of self-government. The conference made so much progress that Gandhi was inclined to negotiate on this basis. He swung the Congress party to a policy of co-operation and even agreed to attend the Second Round Table Conference himself.

In all, three such conferences were held. The results of these discussions were laid before Parliament in a White Paper and formed the basis of the India Government Act of 1935. Under this act Indian local government was reorganized, abolishing dyarchy, and extending democracy considerably in this field of government. This section of the act was accepted by the Indians and put into operation. In the elections of 1937 the Congress party won a governing majority in eight out of eleven provinces. The proposed national constitution, however, had so many undemocratic features that the Indians refused to accept it. The constitution would have introduced into the central government the principle of dyarchy, now discarded in local government. Furthermore, it planned to give the Indian princes—who were to join in the government under special Acts of Accession still to be negotiated—the power to nominate large blocs of representatives. The viceroy was also to be accorded many special powers under this national constitution that never went into effect.

This bare outline of the measures taken in India necessarily omits many angles of the problem, but does serve to show that during the twenties and into the thirties no satisfactory regulation of India's position within the British Empire had been achieved. The reluctance of the British, particularly of many members of the Conservative party, to grant India dominion status is clear. Winston Churchill was largely responsible for placing many of the so-called safeguarding clauses in the Government Act of 1935.

Foreign Policy

British foreign policy has been a complex of many principles and aims. Four traditional and historic ones were: maintenance of the Balance of

Power, prevention of any great power from obtaining control of the Lowlands (Belgium and the Netherlands), control of the seas, maintenance of the road to India. Around these main points rotated many regional policies, such as maintaining Turkey in control of the Dardanelles, and the support of Arab States in the Near East. The latter was definitely connected with another tenet of British foreign policy, namely the encouragement of foreign trade. Her liberal policy toward Germany, as contrasted with France, was largely motivated by a desire to re-establish a market for British goods in Central Europe. Her attitude toward South America has been practically entirely governed by trade considerations. Indeed, with governments all taking a more direct part in economic affairs, questions of foreign trade began to assume an ever-increasing importance in British foreign policy. In the postwar era Britain also was forced to pay attention to the special interests of her Dominions. The problem of maintaining the British Empire required skill and finesse. The British statesmen were also determined to cultivate friendly relations with the United States. These aspects of Britain's policy are strikingly illustrated by her treatment of Japan. Certainly her renunciation of the Anglo-Japanese Treaty of Alliance at the time of the Washington Conference (1922) was due to consideration of United States' and Australian feelings. It is true a certain remnant of her old days of splendid isolation remained after the war. There was a general reluctance to make commitments either through the League (Draft Treaty of Mutual Assistance, Geneva Protocol) or to individual countries. While France and Italy negotiated a host of different treaties and pacts, Britain failed to make definite commitments except in the case of the Locarno Treaties (1925), and even these were given to both Germany and France. She was particularly averse to making any commitments in Eastern Europe. When in 1939 Chamberlain made definite promises to Poland, Rumania, Greece, and Turkey, it was a reversal of many years of British practice.

Many incidents illustrating the general tenets of British policy have already been presented in this book and more will follow. Throughout the period of the twenties Britain maintained her friendship with France as the cornerstone of her continental policy. Differences arose between them, and France often felt Britain did not collaborate closely enough; yet British policy was more in the nature of a restraining influence than any rupture of loyalty. Britain also was friendly with Italy. Italian-British colonial difficulties were settled amicably when Britain turned over a section of Jubaland, to compensate Italy for the German colonies which Britain received. In fact, in many circles of Britain there was rather widespread admiration for Mussolini, which was, however, definitely not shared by the Labor party.

Although England was one of the first to grant Russia *de jure* recognition and was willing enough to trade with her, hostility to communism and a traditional fear of Russian imperialism made England follow on the whole an anti-Russian policy. In the immediate postwar years Russian policy in China clashed with British interests. Britain did not raise serious objection to Japanese expansion in Northern China, partly because of a desire to maintain Japanese friendship, partly in order to have a counter to Russia in Northern Asia.

Britain's German policy also clearly had the object of preventing a possible German-Russian alliance. On the other hand, friendship to Germany never reached such a stage that Britain was willing to turn over the mandate of any of the former German colonies to the government at Berlin. Good luck and strong-armed tactics had given Britain her Empire, and there was no disposition to surrender any part of it. That too was a cardinal point of British foreign policy.

CHAPTER

12

The World Depression

The End of an Era

POSTWAR READJUSTMENTS. The end of World War I found almost all the countries of Europe suffering from the economic strain of the military effort. Russia had suffered the most serious maladjustment as a result of war and revolution, and its production of goods was only a fraction of what it had been. Germany had likewise strained its economy, and its agricultural and industrial production in 1920 was less than two thirds of what it had been in 1913. The Italian economy was functioning at about three fourths of its prewar productivity. French industry and Belgian agriculture had also suffered seriously, while in England production stood at about 90 per cent of its prewar level. The economic maladjustment was reflected even more sharply in Europe's foreign trade. The total trade of Germany had been reduced to one quarter of its prewar volume, and that of Sweden to one half. French and British exports had likewise been reduced to one quarter and one half, respectively, although their imports had been maintained at a much higher level. The temporary decline of trade as a result of wartime conditions was to have been expected, but it soon became apparent that important overseas markets might never be recovered. Whereas the share of the leading European states in world trade had declined somewhat as a result of the war, that of such non-European states as the United States, Canada, and Japan, had risen substantially.

Adjustments in production and finance were difficult to make at the end of the war, and a great deal of disorganization inevitably resulted. The industries which had been most vigorously expanded during the war were frequently those which were of little importance in time of peace. At the same time it was not always possible to manage the demobilization of the huge armies in such a way as to provide a smooth transition. The removal of the severe rationing systems which the war had brought to most European states was also a delicate operation. Moreover, it was the general practice to make the reconversion to peace with a minimum of government interference, and the conflicting trends which characterized the postwar period of readjustment frequently resulted in profound social unrest. In most countries the first year or two after the war saw a brisk prosperity, with rising production, high prices, and relatively full employment. This boom, however, broke as soon as the initial postwar demand for commodities had been met, and was followed in 1921 by a swift collapse of profits and employment.

A more profound symptom of the economic dislocation resulting from the war was provided by the currency inflation that took place in most European states. In some countries, like France, a relatively moderate inflation occurred which reduced the value of savings and fixed incomes but which also reduced the public debt and gave the French franc an advantage over rival currencies in the realm of foreign commerce. In Germany, by contrast, inflation swept through the country like a hurricane, wiping out all values and temporarily reducing the country to chaos. Persons holding tangible property in the form of real estate and industrial plants survived the storm, and the national as well as private debts were wiped out. Industrial production and exports were considerably stimulated by the inflation. However, these gains were more than offset by the financial ruin of all persons who had accumulated savings, the suffering of workers whose wages lagged behind the rise in prices, and the general social unrest resulting from the universal feeling of insecurity bred by inflation.

Throughout Europe the destruction wrought by the war had been serious, but in the long run, it was the dislocation of economic institutions as a result of the military effort that proved most difficult of readjustment after the war. Demobilization of manpower, the reallocation of markets and raw materials, and the regrouping of the various elements of the economy in new political frontiers and sovereignties, could not be accomplished overnight. Moreover, the effort on the part of each state to achieve an ever-greater control over all factors affecting the national economy, tending in its more extreme form towards the unattainable goal of self-sufficiency, was greatly accentuated as a result of the war. The great struggle had illustrated the helplessness of a state which depended heavily on imports, and this lesson was taken to heart after the war with results which only increased the difficulties of economic readjustment.

MIRAGE OF NORMALCY. Despite all of the difficulties that the European states faced in trying to regain the prosperity which they had known before the war, there remained nevertheless a strong inclination on the part of most European leaders to believe that the maladjustments were only temporary and that before long Europe would get back on the normal road of political and economic development, abandoned so blindly in 1914. Economic developments in the individual European states during the decade following World War I have been discussed in other chapters of this book, but certain common characteristics of the European economy between the war and the depression deserve to be emphasized.

The mirage of normalcy was greatly encouraged, for instance, by the fact that by 1926 all the major European countries had regained their prewar level of production and looked ahead to the achievement of new goals. They all had to face the fact, of course, that the postwar world was different from that left in 1914. Non-European countries had expanded their productive capacity out of necessity during the war, and in most cases had introduced new machinery and methods making them less dependent on the industrialized European states. Similarly, many of the less industrialized European states that had depended on their more advanced neighbors for industrial products had been forced during the war to develop their own infant industries and were reluctant to abandon them now that the war was over. The war had also upset the agricultural system. Food production had been greatly increased during the war thanks to blockades and other abnormal conditions, and a return to prewar conditions was not easy.

The optimism with which most Europeans faced the future in the middle 1920's was derived from their confidence that by adopting more efficient methods and by introducing new industries, the prospects for another era of industrial expansion would be greatly brightened. The introduction of more efficient methods into industrial production, the process known as rationalization, received a great impetus during the 1920's. Equipment of all sorts was standardized, from simple shovels to complex machinery. Research in the use of raw materials made it possible to obtain several times as much heat or horsepower from a given amount of coal or gas, and industrial chemistry rapidly opened up entirely new possibilities in the development of synthetic materials. Industries that had been in their infancy at the start of the war, such as the manufacture of automobiles, artificial cloth, and many items of household equipment, now assumed a major role. Production in these new spheres, as well as in such ancient handicrafts as the manufacture of shoes, was greatly expanded by the adoption of assembly-line methods. At the same time, technological improvements were matched by a new efficiency in industrial organization. The

sharp competition which had characterized the earlier stages of industrialism now gave way to amalgamations of banks, consolidation of industrial
corporations, and the concentration of economic control in the hands of
relatively few groups. Expansion and optimism was thus tempered by a desire for stability and security.

Generally speaking, the normalcy so ardently desired in the 1920's was
only partly achieved in the realm of industry. In Eastern Europe, where
industry had lagged before the war, significant gains were made. The newly
organized states launched many new enterprises and registered important
gains in terms of their own standards. In Russia, where entirely different
conditions existed, the Five Year Plans got under way in 1927 and soon
produced significant results. In Great Britain, on the other hand, the production of many basic industries declined, although pig iron and steel continued to show substantial gains. Similarly in Italy, the prosperity of the
later 1920's produced very mixed results and the country never shook off
the feeling of economic instability. France and Germany, by contrast, and
most of the smaller states of Western Europe, enjoyed a brief period of
prosperity which gave many informed persons the illusion that Europe
would soon be able to work its way out of the postwar maladjustments.
The difficulty of the situation was that economic institutions were so interrelated, that purely national solutions had relatively little meaning. Russia
tended to isolate itself from the rest of the world, while France and Germany revived their ailing economies by vigorous leadership. On the other
hand, difficulties encountered by Britain and Italy, and the general uncertainty that underlay the small successes of their neighbors, must be traced
to the slow revival of international commerce. In an age when Europe's
banks, industries, and mines had set the pace for the rest of the world, the
national policies of the European great powers had indeed exercised an important influence. In the 1920's, however, it was world-wide economic
forces which exerted the determining influence.

INTERNATIONAL ECONOMIC FORCES. The close interrelationships of the
national economies, so greatly upset by the war, were soon restored in a
different form. One of the principal connections was provided by the interlocking war debts and reparations. The initial decisions regarding reparations had been made with little thought for the long-term interests of Europe. The payments made were very far from those expected even under the
revised plans, but they required borrowing on the part of Germany since
only one third could be paid in the form of exports [see above, pp.101–3].
As a result, by 1930 Germany had incurred foreign debts in the amount of
15,000,000,000 gold marks, of which about one half was owed to the
United States, and the rest to Great Britain, the Netherlands, Sweden,
Switzerland, and France.

The significance of the problems involved in financing the German
reparations lies in their relation to the inter-Allied debts. These amounted
to a total of some twenty billion dollars at the end of the war, of which
$9,450,000,000 was owed to the United States, $8,700,000,000 to the United

Kingdom, and the remainder to France. The key countries in this complex relationship were the United States and Germany. It was the United States to which the largest block of inter-Allied debts was due from the United Kingdom, France, and Italy, and these were the very countries which expected to collect the bulk of German reparations. The insistence of the United States that the debts owed to it by the Allies be paid in full thus served to strengthen the determination of the latter to collect reparations from Germany. Since Germany could not pay reparations without in turn borrowing from the United States and elsewhere, a vicious circle was created that substituted for the healthy exchange of goods in international trade an artificial and in the end disastrous transfer of credits. Economic nationalism reached new extremes during these years, and, while some countries were willing to consider the cancellation or reduction of debts owed to them, few were willing to lower their tariffs sufficiently to permit the imports which were the only way in which the debts could be paid. Moreover, the United States, which emerged as the principal creditor of both Germany and the Allies, was the most adamant in insisting on the payment of debts while refusing to lower tariffs. The American financial system thus became one of the cornerstones upon which the economic stability of Europe rested.

Economic nationalism, unstable currencies, high tariffs, and unsettled debts, were fortunately not the only characteristics of the economic picture in the 1920's. Many efforts were made in this period to achieve greater economic co-operation among the European states, and in this the League of Nations played a leading role. This was accomplished through its various organizations dealing with labor conditions, transportation, restrictive economic practices, and other matters. International interchange in the economic field also took place at conferences organized by various bodies. Outstanding among these was the conference organized by the Allies which met at Genoa in 1922, and that convoked by the League of Nations at Geneva in 1927. Labor and business also had international bodies representing their respective interests. Despite these various forces which tended to encourage economic co-operation, the spirit of economic nationalism and competition continued to be preponderant. Each European state struggled to build up its position at the expense of the others, yet all were bound to the powerful financial structure of the United States by the intricate network of reparations and debts.

Impact of the Depression

THE AMERICAN CRASH. The United States did not in any sense dominate the European economic scene, despite the great relative increase in its standing as a result of World War I. Nevertheless, its relations with Europe as creditor and as a participant in world trade were such that any sudden change in the American economic tempo was bound to have worldwide repercussions. Such was the case with the stock-market crash which occurred on Wall Street on October 24, 1929.

That the American boom preceding the crash was limited primarily to the stock market and to real estate is indicated by the fact that neither in industrial production nor in factory employment did any great expansion occur between 1926 and 1929. Capital construction started falling off as early as June, 1928, while the peak of industrial production and employment was passed just one year later. During the period between June and October, 1929, the prices of securities on the stock market, nevertheless, continued their inflationary rise, but when the panic finally occurred it was reflected immediately on production and employment. A brief revival of trade and production took place in the first months of 1930, but after May of that year the decline continued with increasing momentum.

The American crash was reflected all over the world in the steady fall of prices during 1930. The index of wholesale prices during that year fell 16 per cent in the United States, 18 per cent in Great Britain and Italy, 13 per cent in Germany, 6 per cent in France, and 21 per cent in Japan. Industrial production also declined heavily during 1930, to the extent of 21 per cent in the United States and 14 per cent in Great Britain. Capital likewise moved much more slowly in 1930 than it had during the previous year, despite a great reduction in interest rates. Most characteristic perhaps of all the initial effects of the American crash was the readjustment of world trade. While the total volume of trade declined appreciably, the debtor countries had a favorable balance of exports as against imports during 1929–30, while the creditor countries had an unfavorable balance.

The strictly economic repercussions of the American crash were accompanied by widespread social and political consequences. While salaries and wages did not fall nearly as rapidly as prices, unemployment increased by about one half in most European countries during 1930. This immediately confronted the various governments with the question of the care of unemployed, and in turn a series of political issues were raised that served to crystallize the conflicts among the political parties. Nevertheless, despite the severe shock European economy experienced in 1930, the nature of the maladjustment remained predominantly that of a commercial slump until the spring of 1931. Rallies in prices and production occurred here and there despite the increasing gloom of the outlook. It was not until the commercial slump was followed by a financial crisis in May, 1931, that political and social repercussions on a larger scale became inevitable.

THE EUROPEAN CRISIS. The chain reaction which had been started by the American crash in the autumn of 1929 now produced a further explosion in Central Europe. The financial structure of Austria and Germany had been precarious ever since World War I, despite the superficial prosperity of the later 1920's, and the initial tremors of the depression in 1930 were sufficient to bring ruin. The first bank to collapse was the *Kreditanstalt* of Vienna, which held over two thirds of all Austrian assets and liabilities. During May, 1931, the *Kreditanstalt* found it impossible to cover its losses, particularly those incurred abroad, and all the resources of the Austrian government were rallied to its support. A loan from the Bank of England in

June finally prevented the complete collapse of Austrian finances, but in the meantime a political crisis had started in Austria, and the entire structure of Central European finance was called into question. The fears aroused by the Austrian failure were soon reflected in Germany, whence foreign investors began to withdraw their capital. When a large German industrial concern failed in July, the banks which were its chief creditors were unable to take the loss. The German government made frantic efforts to obtain foreign assistance, but it met with lack of confidence and uncertainty on all sides. A bank holiday was accordingly declared in the middle of July, and by the time the banks reopened a few days later the government had taken a series of measures designed to stem the tide of financial collapse.

Great Britain's economy was in a much stronger position than those of the states of Central Europe, but it soon gave signs of reacting to the crises in Austria and Germany. British investments had, in fact, played an important part in the reconstruction of Central Europe, and the economic distress in this region had an adverse effect on these investments. A moratorium on intergovernmental debts was negotiated by President Hoover in July, 1931, which suspended inter-Allied and reparations payments and served to soften the blow of the collapse in Central Europe. Further steps were then taken by European states to promote the economic stability of Germany. British financial interests were so widespread, however, and the balance of trade and loans on which the economic stability of Great Britain depended was so delicate, that a decisive readjustment of British finances could not long be postponed. Great Britain finally went off the gold standard in September, 1931. This move was necessitated by the heavy withdrawals of foreign holdings in London and by the unfavorable balance of British trade. Its effect was to reduce the value of the pound by almost one third in terms of other currencies or of gold, and this served both to stabilize the pound at its new level and to reduce the cost of British products on the foreign market.

The fall of the English pound had immediate international repercussions, for the currencies of many other countries had been based on it. Over twenty countries suspended the gold standard in the year following the British action, although it was retained during 1932 by the United States, France, Italy, Germany, Poland, and almost twenty other countries over the world. The general effect of this irregular monetary depreciation was to cause wide variations of prices and a sharp rivalry for trade, as between countries on the gold standard and those with devalued currencies. In this competition the latter inevitably had the advantage, and between 1933 and 1936 the United States, France, and most of the other gold standard countries devalued their currencies or adopted strict currency controls. In the years following 1931 a general depression settled down over Europe and influenced almost every branch of economic activity. Industrial production in Europe, exclusive of the Soviet Union, declined to 92 per cent in 1930, 80 per cent in 1931, and 72 per cent in 1932, of the 1929 level. Employment had declined by 1932 as much as 40 per cent in Germany, as compared with 1929, although in the United Kingdom and Italy the decline was only 15 and 21 per cent, respectively. In France the effects of the depression were delayed by about two years, but by 1934 a decline in employment of about 23 per cent had been registered. The upswing of production and employment was not as rapid as the decline, but by 1936 most European states had returned to the 1929 level in terms of domestic production and employment.

The most important result of the collapse of the international economic structure was that it threw each country back on its own resources. Where before the depression a high standard of living had been sought by means of the international exchange of goods and services, now the chief concern of each state was to protect its own incomplete resources from the uncertainties of the ailing international system. High tariffs were the first measure to which each state resorted. Yet while tariffs assured the protection of industrial products and raw materials, they also served to maintain artificial prices in each country. Currency regulation was also widely resorted to as a means of securing domestic economic stability. The international financial system was further weakened by the cancellation of reparations and debts, thus encouraging each country to rely even further on its own resources. All of these restrictive measures served to encourage domestic stability, but their effect was to deal a lasting blow to world trade. While world trade declined fully as rapidly as domestic production and employment, falling by 1934 to 34 per cent of the value of trade in 1929, it failed to rally after the depths of the depression had passed. The domestic economies of most European states had in large measure returned to normal by 1936, but world trade had by the eve of World War II not yet returned to one half of its value in 1929. This failure of world trade to revive was due primarily to the persistence of restrictive practices on the part of the individual states, long after the crisis which had provoked them had passed. Having seized control over foreign trade, the European governments were for a variety of reasons unwilling or unable to relinquish it.

European agriculture likewise suffered seriously as a result of the depression. The stage for a catastrophic agricultural slump had been set during World War I, when abnormal conditions led to the doubling of food prices in Europe. These declined steadily during the first postwar decade, although in 1929 they were still well above the 1913 price level. This decline was now greatly accelerated by the crisis, and in 1934 food prices stood at 61 per cent of the level in 1913. As with the other sectors of the economy, the European states tried to meet the agricultural crisis on a purely national basis. Domestic agricultural prices were artificially supported, and the intensification of agriculture was encouraged in order to make each country as free as possible of imports. A variety of other remedies was tried, ranging from a quota system in England to collectivization in Russia. The one element common to all of these measures was that they placed increasing economic power in the hands of the national governments and created almost insuperable obstacles to a return to an international system of exchange.

CONFERENCES AND REMEDIES. The economic and political issues raised by the crisis, which in most respects were no more than an intensification of problems Europe had faced for a generation, were considerably clarified during the early 1930's. The unbalanced economic structure inherited from the peace settlements, the excesses of American investors, and the chain reaction of financial catastrophes which linked New York with Vienna, Berlin, London, and later Paris, were clearly enough understood. Obvious also was the extent to which national governments had of necessity assumed the responsibility for economic activity, and had concentrated in their own hands the power to make decisions that had formerly been left to the wide variety of private individuals in the international system. The paradox which now confronted Europe was that even after production and employment had returned to normal, most national governments found it politically inexpedient to give up the extensive powers they had assumed in the economic field. Once national governments had taken responsibility for the personal economic welfare of the voters on whom they depended for support, they could not again expose the material security of the electorate to the vagaries of the free economic system without risking their political lives.

It was thus in an atmosphere of jealous economic nationalism that remedies were sought which might alleviate the international crisis. A movement for the settlement of outstanding international debts was initiated at the Lausanne Conference in 1932 by an agreement that in effect terminated German reparations payments. In the following year the Allied debts to the United States were settled either with token payments, to which most countries resorted, or, as in the case of France, by defaulting. Only Finland paid its debt in full. During the depths of the depression some progress was also made in reviving international trade by means of bilateral treaties. Such agreements were in each case severely limited in scope by the cautious protectionism of the countries involved. Nevertheless they served in some measure to encourage the resumption of international trade. A number of multilateral efforts were also made in the early years of the crisis to affect the reduction of tariffs, and they likewise had only limited results. The most important of these multilateral efforts were the Ottawa Agreements of 1932, which sought to stimulate world trade by reducing tariffs within the British Commonwealth. While the immediate aim of increasing trade within the British Commonwealth was certainly achieved as a result of the Ottawa Agreements, there is good reason to believe that the cost of this achievement was a further increase in barriers to trade relations with countries outside of the Commonwealth. In the long run, a more important contribution to the revival of commerce was made by the reciprocal trade treaties initiated by the United States in 1934.

The principal effort to find remedies for the economic crisis by international negotiation was the World Economic Conference held in London under the auspices of the League of Nations in the summer of 1933. The immediate objects of the conference were to lower tariffs, to restore satisfactory international monetary standards, and to reduce other restrictions on commerce and loans which had been imposed during the crisis. Sixty-four countries, including the United States and the Soviet Union, participated in the conference. It was preceded by extensive studies on the part of economic experts, and by negotiations among the principal participating states. The United States had refused to agree to placing the question of war debts on the agenda, but free discussion was anticipated on all other aspects of the crisis. Moreover, the first signs of domestic economic recovery were in sight in Europe, and there was some reason to believe that the conference could find means of encouraging this trend. Nevertheless, the conference failed to achieve the desired results. The view was generally held that no progress could be made in the reduction of tariffs until satisfactory international monetary standards had been restored through the stabilization of currencies. Such stabilization depended in the first place on the establishment of a fixed rate of exchange between the British pound and the American dollar, and the inability to stabilize exchanges lay at the bottom of the failure of the conference as a whole.

It is the general consensus that the failure to achieve currency stabilization was due more to American policy than to that of the other countries concerned. President Roosevelt had only recently assumed the duties of his office, and his prime concern was still the promotion of domestic recovery. To stabilize the dollar in terms of European currencies, which most of the delegates at the World Economic Conference desired, would have meant to surrender the useful weapon of currency manipulation in dealing with American domestic problems. President Roosevelt was unwilling to do this and his decision, made during the course of the negotiations in London after considerable hesitation, contributed powerfully to the failure of the Conference. However, currency stabilization was by no means the sole issue on which the states of the world were unable to agree. No compromises could be reached on such problems as tariff reductions, the co-operation of central banks, and the resumption of international lending, and there is every reason to believe that this widespread refusal to surrender national controls in the hope of achieving a revival of international trade would have persisted even if the question of currency stabilization had been settled.

Economics and Politics

PREDOMINANCE OF ECONOMIC NATIONALISM. A good case can be made for the view that the World Economic Conference of 1933 was the last chance which the European states were given to abandon the trend towards purely national solutions of their economic problems and to return to a policy of international economic co-operation. As has already been pointed out, the immediate pressures favoring the retention of national controls were very great indeed. A return to a system of greater international ex-

change would have meant a wide variety of sacrifices on the part of each
state of the short-term benefits which accrued from government regulation
on a national basis. If the national governments had offered to make the
necessary concessions in international negotiations, they would have risked
alienating important domestic groups that might in many cases have combined to overthrow them. This attitude is well illustrated by American policy in 1933. To President Roosevelt, the advantages to the domestic economy of a flexible currency, that could be manipulated with a view toward
encouraging economic recovery, appeared to outweigh possible gains as a
result of a stabilized currency in the realm of international trade. The economic nationalism of the United States during the depression thus closely
resembled that of the European states, and stemmed from the same general causes.

Compromises on the part of a wide variety of conflicting interests,
which a return to normal economic relations would have required, could
have been made only if there had existed a clear realization of the dangers
economic nationalism entailed. In the early 1930's no such realization existed on the part of Europe's statesmen. The general view expressed at the
end of the World Economic Conference was that national policies would
have to settle down to some sort of stability before international economic
exchanges could again be undertaken on a large scale. This view assumed
that new opportunities would arise for a general conference such as that
which was being disbanded in London, and that time would work in favor
of compromise. Yet the contrary proved to be the case. The renewed reliance on national economic measures, which resulted from the failure of the
World Economic Conference, led not to a gradual equalization but rather
to greater competition.

Glancing back over the period since World War I, it is not difficult
to see how rapidly the trend towards economic nationalism had gained momentum. The disintegration of the Austro-Hungarian, Russian, and Turkish empires had indeed corresponded to the demands of the minority peoples and had represented an essential step in the direction of democracy.
What was not clearly understood at the time, however, was that disaster
would ensue if economic frontiers were reduced to the limits of the new
political frontiers. Similarly in Western Europe, conditions tending towards economic nationalism had been in evidence during the first postwar
years. In the continent as a whole, only those countries with fully balanced
domestic economies or with well-established international connections
were able to survive for a few years the trend towards protectionism. In
Eastern Europe, Czechoslovakia was probably the only country which was
able to participate extensively in international trade. In the West, a return to the general international exchange of the prewar period was the
rule rather than the exception. Yet even there, such countries as Italy and
Germany never fully regained their earlier position in international commerce. Victory or defeat was less a factor in this trend than the economic
dislocation caused by the war.

In the field of international trade, the world depression thus served to strengthen a trend that had already started as a result of World War I. What had once been an exception now became almost universal practice, and a knowledge of the nature and variety of national economic controls is essential to an understanding of political developments in Europe since the depression. Each state approached the problem in the light of its own traditions and possibilities, and a wide variety of state economic policies emerged. Yet they all had the common characteristic of increasing the powers of the state in the economic field and of making each state as independent as possible of the international economy. The trend towards economic nationalism had a further consequence that was not anticipated by European statesmen. This was to drive many states towards political authoritariansm and to confront them with the apparent dilemma of economic disaster or war.

NATIONAL ECONOMIC POLICIES. The measures taken during the early 1930's by the various national governments naturally varied widely, depending on the political traditions, economic conditions, and special problems of each country. Certain general tendencies are, nevertheless, apparent in all of the European countries, for all faced the common problems of increasing over-all production, maintaining a balance among the various elements of the national economy, keeping as large a number of persons employed as possible, and finding means through purchase or barter of procuring the commodities that could not be produced at home. Thus, high tariffs, and quotas and embargoes on certain exports, were common to all countries. Similarly, most countries sought to reduce the value of their currency in order to lighten domestic indebtedness and to increase exports. Controlled currencies, frequently with differing values for varying uses, were also common. At home, all governments went to the assistance of essential elements of the economy by means of loans and protective legislation. In some countries only shipping required such aid, while in others industry and mining also received assistance. In the agrarian countries, the first concern of the state was to support the price of grain. The responsibility assumed by the state for the economic welfare of the entire population also led the European governments to take a variety of measures to protect those sectors of the population which were particularly affected by the depression. Whether the government was fascist, socialist, or liberal, care was taken to provide full employment or relief for the unemployed. Special care was also taken to adjust wages in relation to the cost of living.

Despite the common problems most European governments faced, a wide variety of solutions were applied. Countries with a strong parliamentary tradition, such as France and Great Britain, and for that matter most of the smaller states of northwestern Europe, did not find it necessary to sacrifice political democracy in order to regain economic stability. In these countries enterprise remained in principle free from state control, and the government exerted its influence only when public policy or political pressure made this necessary. Likewise, full freedom was tolerated in the discussion of economic ideas and problems, and in the organization of workers, producers, and consumers in a wide variety of associations. The measures adopted by these governments were frankly experimental, and for a number of years it was assumed that the initiative of the state was a temporary matter. Even in the later 1930's, when state enterprise in certain fields came to be regarded as a matter of course, private property and free enterprise were in principle maintained. This was particularly the case in the important matter of prices. Here liberal governments generally found means of exerting their influence to regulate prices without challenging in principle the free adjustment of supply and demand.

In such states as Italy and Germany, quite different methods were adopted. Defeat or disappointment in World War I had greatly increased the pressure of national feeling in these countries, and economic weakness had also contributed its share to the almost unchallenged authority with which the state was soon to become endowed. In Italy, the fascist regime had established a firm control over labor and capital by the middle 1920's, but it was not until after the depression that this economic control was changed to direct management. Although the corporate state was established in Italy in 1927, only in 1934 were the twenty-two corporations finally created which were to serve as the basis for the full regimentation of the national economy. Through these bodies the state exerted a far more rigorous supervision over all phases of economic life than was the case in France or Great Britain. Moreover, the Italian government managed to acquire most of the power accruing to the state under socialism, without taking on all of the responsibilities which go with government ownership of the means of production. In Germany the government had gone a considerable way in the direction of state socialism during the 1920's, but this had been done within the framework of a democratic, though turbulent, political system. After 1933, events followed an entirely different course. The government now took steps to abolish all independent political parties and labor unions, and gradually brought all sectors of the economy under a system of rigid regimentation. Private property was retained in name only, and even the industrialists who had at first supported the Nazi regime eventually lost control of their own properties.

The agrarian countries of Eastern Europe also moved steadily in the direction of state economic intervention in the years after the depression. As in the case of Italy, economic difficulties had combined with political instability in such countries as Poland, Lithuania, and Yugoslavia, to bring about authoritarian regimes even before the depression. Moreover, only the state was able to supply sufficient capital for many of the needs of industrialization. In almost all the other countries of Eastern Europe the state assumed a determining voice in economic affairs during the middle 1930's. In the case of these countries the export of foodstuffs was the backbone of the economy, and the prices of these commodities determined the standard of living of the great majority of the population. The governments, therefore, concentrated on the support of agricultural prices, either by direct subsidy or by negotiating barter agreements with food-importing countries. This operation soon led to a general program of currency control and economic regimentation, which placed all elements of the economy under the direction of the state.

It is customary to think of Russia as a country relatively unaffected by the great depression and pursuing an independent policy within an almost autarkic economic framework. It is true that the Five-Year Plans which got under way in the 1930's were fulfilled almost without regard to the great depression, and that such economic relations as Russia maintained with the outside world were of a secondary character and rigidly limited by the state. It is nevertheless clear that the general conditions which made Russia an easy prey for the Bolsheviks at the end of World War I, were in many ways similar to those prevalent in such countries as Italy and Poland. Economic weakness thus provided an opportunity for authoritarianism throughout Europe, while the nature of the groups which seized this opportunity varied widely. Russia was the first country where totalitarian economic doctrines were applied, and an explanation of the nature and direction of Soviet economic policy must be sought as much in Russian economic conditions at the end of World War I as in the leadership and ideology of the Bolshevik movement. Even in the Soviet Union, serious doubts were entertained in the 1920's as to whether the rigid application of a socialist program should be attempted in the hostile atmosphere of postwar Europe. Stalin finally won the argument at the end of the decade, with his slogan of "socialism in one country," but by this time conditions in Europe as a whole were beginning to change. The significance of the world depression for Soviet economic development is that it produced conditions favorable to the implementation of the Five-Year Plans. The European states could no longer afford to be so hostile towards the Soviet Union, and in particular they were more amenable in trade negotiations. Moreover, they were rapidly becoming divided into rival groups by the political consequences of economic nationalism.

POLITICAL EFFECTS OF THE DEPRESSION. The first effect of the depression in the great majority of European states, was to necessitate what was generally regarded as a temporary resort to state power. Only in those countries which had come out of the World War with seriously undermined political and economic stability, such as Italy, Germany, and some of the states of Eastern Europe, did the depression serve immediately to encourage authoritarian tendencies. The first impression of political thinkers was that it was a slump like other slumps, and that Europe would emerge on an even keel after the necessary administrative steps had been taken.

As the depression deepened, however, and especially when government initiative in economic affairs continued even after domestic production and employment returned to normal, many began to doubt whether the economic liberalism of the early 1900's would ever return. In the light of the events of the world depression, the period of prosperity after World War I began to appear more as an ephemeral phenomenon than as the return to normalcy it had seemed at the time to be. Once the increased role of the government was accepted as a reality, political thinkers began to look around for new concepts with which to define the relations of state and society. The ideas underlying the measures of Roosevelt's New Deal and of MacDonald's National coalition in England represented the most moderate forms taken by this trend of thought. Such measures were considered to involve the application to social and economic problems of government authority under full democratic responsibility and to provide a basis on which new relationships of state and society could be developed without sacrifice of political democracy. A similarly moderate development, going somewhat further in the direction of social democracy, was represented by the "middle way" of the Scandinavian states in which the co-operatives played a major role.

In contrast to this moderate approach to state authority was the more radical program of the Socialists. The ideas of Marx and Lenin had commanded the respect of many European intellectuals, and the events of the great depression appeared to them as a fulfillment of their prophesies. The contradictions which Marx had predicted would confront capitalism as it became more complex, and in particular the dangers inherent in the intense competition among the advanced industrial states which Lenin had described in his *Imperialism: The Highest State of Capitalism* (1917), appeared to many Europeans to fit the situation in which they found themselves in the 1930's. Moreover, the widely advertised success of the Five-Year Plans in the Soviet Union gave the appearance of providing an answer to the questions which many were raising as to the outcome of the European crisis.

Socialist parties grew rapidly in most European countries, and in Germany, France, and parts of Eastern Europe, the Communists achieved a position of strength which they had not known since the early postwar years. Recalling their defeats of a decade earlier the Communist parties, under the guidance of the Communist International, adopted a policy of forming the so-called Popular Front coalitions with other leftwing parties. Such a Popular Front coalition was formed in France in 1935 and came to power after winning parliamentary elections in the spring of 1936. A Popular Front of similar scope won the Spanish elections in 1936 and guided the destinies of the republic during the greater part of the Spanish civil war (1936–39). The stated purpose of the Communists in sponsoring the Popular Front tactics was to seize the leadership of the proletarian political movements, which they regarded as having been betrayed by the Socialists. In no country during this period were the Communist parties able to gain a predominant position, but the Popular Front experiment was a fruitful one from their point of view and brought them greater political prestige and influence than they had hitherto possessed.

Closer than communism to the temper of the 1930's were the authoritarian doctrines, which won the adherence of so many Europeans. Mystical and romantic in its approach to political problems, and looking to Fascist

Italy as the pioneer totalitarian state in postwar Europe, this authoritarianism relied on national feeling and on the power of an efficient bureaucracy
and police to inspire confidence and hope among Europe's desperate peoples. German National Socialism was the most characteristic of these authoritarian doctrines, but numerous alternate formulations were to be developed in the 1930's by such leaders as Codreanu in Rumania, Georgiev
in Bulgaria, Metaxas in Greece, and Franco in Spain. Authoritarian theorists found many European advocates of nationalism and violence from
whom they could borrow ideas. In the more popular view, no writer met
with greater favor than the German historian Spengler, whose widely read
Decline of the West (1918–22) predicted that the age of capitalism would
end in a glorification of military power. By a combination of exhortation
to violence, the popularization of heroic myths, and the astute use of the
political power of the state, the various authoritarian regimes managed to
win a broad basis of support and to tide over the worst years of the depression. The ultimate goals of their doctrines were vague as compared
with communism and socialism, however, and they relied for their influence more on the satisfaction of immediate needs than on a rational consideration of Europe's problems.

This ferment of political thought, so greatly stimulated by the world
depression, took place in an intellectual atmosphere in which many of the
fundamental verities of the early 1900's had already been undermined. The
mechanistic physical universe accepted at the start of the century as a matter of course had been upset by Planck's Quantum Theory as early as 1900,
and by the even more disconcerting Theory of Special Relativity which
Einstein published in 1905. While it was a generation before the full impact of these revolutionary concepts was felt in political philosophy, they
posited a universe which was far more complex and dynamic than that
which had formed the basis for informed thought at the turn of the century and provoked many new fields of speculation. Similarly, the earlier
view of human nature was greatly changed between World War I and the
depression by the researches of psychologists, among whom Freud achieved
the widest renown. The new psychology emphasized man's impulses more
than his reason, and described the limits of human behavior in terms of
the emotional energies that require satisfaction. In these and many other
fields of knowledge the stable outlook of the older generation was shattered, and the resulting intellectual unrest played an important role in the
political ferment of the 1930's. It is difficult to avoid the conclusion that
the world depression was as important as World War I in changing the
face of Europe. The war wrought vast destruction and accelerated many of
the inherent tendencies of European society. It was, however, the depression that dealt the final blow to the way of life which Europe had known
at the start of the century.

III.

THE SMALLER POWERS IN THE INTERWAR PERIOD

CHAPTER

13

The Lowlands, Scandinavia, and Switzerland

The Lowlands: *History; Political Development; Economic Development; Education and Religion; Colonial Empires; Foreign Policy.*

The Scandinavian Countries: *History; Political and Economic Development; Education and Religion; Colonial Possessions; Foreign Policy.*

Switzerland: *History; The Swiss Militia; Political Development; Economic Development; Education and Religion; Foreign Affairs.*

I N Western Europe before World War I a considerable number of small states were already well established, in most of which democracy was firmly rooted. The old states of Portugal and Spain, on the other hand, stood somewhat apart and had not kept pace with general Western progress. The postwar domestic history of these two states furnishes the background for the Spanish Civil War (1936–39) and will be discussed in connection with that general European crisis. Here the Netherlands, Belgium, and Luxembourg will be grouped as the Lowlands; Sweden, Norway, and Denmark as the Scandinavian States, and Switzerland will be accorded the separate treatment that its unique position in Europe merits.

Of these seven small states only one, Belgium, was actively involved in the war. Luxembourg was so rapidly overrun that although under enemy occupation it could hardly be considered a belligerent. Reconstruction problems in Belgium were immense, and she was not only accorded special German payments aside from reparations but also received generous aid from her former allies, notably the United States. The other states had in various ways suffered restrictions caused by the war. This was notably true of the Dutch, Norwegian, Danish, and Swedish fleets which were depleted not only by submarine sinkings but also by the allied policy of requisitioning. Their foreign trade had been seriously curtailed by Britain's blockade policy. Yet as a result of an expansion of wartime trade with both Germany and the Allies, these countries enjoyed an economic boom. They escaped not only the heavy casualty lists, the physical destruction of their cities, the heavy indebtedness, but also much of the immediate postwar political turmoil that afflicted those countries that fought.

The war also brought greater prestige to the small states. The creation of the succession states in the east seemed a guarantee that small states would not be swallowed up by the expansion of the great powers. Needless to say, all the small western states became ardent supporters of the League, for it offered them a standing in international affairs such as they had never enjoyed before.

The Lowlands

HISTORY. At the Peace of Westphalia (1648) the northern provinces of the Lowlands achieved independence but the southern provinces remained under Spanish control until 1713, when they passed into the possession of Austria. The Congress of Vienna (1815), which had to reorganize Europe after the Napoleonic upheaval, restored the king of the Netherlands to his throne and awarded him the former Austrian provinces as well. This union was not a happy one. The southern provinces spoke a different language, were different in religion, and had experienced two centuries or more of different historical development. In 1830 the provinces revolted and proclaimed an independent Belgian state. This state was recognized by the Dutch king only in 1839, in which year the great powers mutually guaranteed to respect the neutrality of Belgium.

Belgium was dissatisfied with the award of certain small territories to the Netherlands and with Dutch ownership of both banks of the mouth of the river Scheldt. There were, however, provisions for joint control of the river, and the Belgian port of Antwerp, about fifty miles up the Scheldt, prospered and more than doubled in population. Belgium also had claims on Luxembourg, but only the Walloon portions (1725 square miles) were assigned to Belgium by the powers in 1839. The remainder (999 square miles), known as the Grand Duchy of Luxembourg, was subject to the Dutch king personally, but was a member of the Germanic Confederation. In 1867, after the dissolution of the Confederation, it was, like Belgium, placed under a guarantee of neutrality by the powers, and in 1890, on the accession of a woman to the Dutch throne, passed legally to the next male heir. In 1917 the rule of succession in Luxembourg was changed, making it possible for a Grand Duchess to rule.

The Belgian insurrection of 1830 thus laid the foundation for the future political development of the Lowlands. Not counting large water areas, the Netherlands (about the size of Maryland) was only a thousand square miles larger than Belgium. In population Belgium outnumbered Holland, although in the third decade of this present century the population of the Netherlands rose to exceed that of Belgium slightly, both numbering about nine million. Luxembourg today has a population of about 300,000.

So far as ethnography goes one cannot truly speak of minorities, although in each state there were and still are distinct linguistic groups. Belgium is approximately equally divided between the Teutonic Flemings whose dialects are related to Dutch, and the Latin Walloons who speak French. The former are concentrated in the northern provinces, the latter in the south. In the Netherlands the people are all of related stocks. There are a number of Friesians in the northern provinces and some Flemings in the south, but in contrast to Belgium, ethnographical differences have never been an important issue in Holland. The people of Luxembourg generally speak a South German dialect, but their literary and church language is High German; some French is spoken, and many of the better educated people are bilingual. Luxembourg and Belgium are overwhelmingly Catholic, although the Walloons of Belgium are not so firmly attached to the church as the more devout Flemings. The Netherlands is predominantly Protestant, although slightly over a third of the population is Roman Catholic. During the last century the Catholic church there has grown rapidly in numbers and in influence.

POLITICAL DEVELOPMENT. Without altering the basic features of their governments all these states revised their constitutions in the early postwar years. Among various changes the most important was the enfranchisement of women, although in Belgium this was greatly restricted. As in most of the countries of Europe there was also a marked growth of Socialist parties. These were troubled by the usual conflict of that period between right and left wings, but the Communists exercised little power. Of more importance was the continued development of Clerical parties. Holland has one Catholic and two Protestant church parties, all essentially conservative. In all three countries the Clerical parties outnumbered the Socialists. Only Belgium had parties based on what might be called a linguistic basis. The old Liberal party was essentially a Walloon party, and after 1919 a Flemish Nationalist party made its appearance. There was also a distinct Flemish Clerical group.

In the Netherlands Queen Wilhelmina, who had started her reign as a ten-year-old girl in 1890, continued on the throne. There was a brief bit of violent socialist-labor agitation in 1919, but the elections of that year returned the Conservatives to power. The Dutch government remained true to the old liberal practice of granting political asylum. There the former

German Emperor granted interviews, wrote his memoirs, and acquired some fame as the wood-sawyer of Doorn.

The acquisition of Eupen, Malmedy, Moresnet, as a result of the Treaty of Versailles, brought valuable timber and zinc resources to Belgium. Popular King Albert (1909–34) returned to rebuild his country and in 1926 was given dictatorial powers to solve a severe financial crisis. He devalued the Belgian franc and introduced a new currency unit, the Belga, with a ratio of five for one. The most persistent problem which plagued Belgium politically was the Flemish question.

The establishment of Belgium in 1830 had been engineered by leaders from the Walloon provinces, who instituted French as the official language of the entire kingdom. By limiting the electorate through property and professional qualifications, political power was placed in the upper middle class, which even in Flanders was sympathetic to the use of French. The universities, the secondary schools, most of the primary schools, the army, the courts, all were French. It was not long before the Flemish half of the population began to demand reforms. They obtained some concessions, but it is really remarkable that no more were forced upon the government before World War I. The Germans during their occupation (1914–18) gave the Flemings many of the linguistic privileges which they had been demanding for years. A group of so-called Flemish "Activists" who co-operated with Germany during the war were later tried for treason. Forty-five were condemned to death (later commuted), and one hundred and twelve were given sentences ranging up to life imprisonment. This action by the government only strengthened the Flemish movement, for in the eyes of many the condemned men were martyrs. All the Wilsonian talk about the rights of small nations and self-determination stimulated the Flemish agitation, and when the new suffrage law of 1919 gave more power to the masses, their wishes could no longer be ignored. In 1921 Belgium was divided into two linguistic sections, in one of which Flemish was to be the language of administration, in the other French; and a bilingual regime was established in Brussels. This arrangement was only a step, so far as the Flemings were concerned. Other laws followed, notably the law of 1928 which divided the army into French and Flemish regiments and put the two languages on a par in the military schools. In 1930 the University of Ghent finally was recognized as a completely Flemish institution. Two years later new language regulations extended the use of Flemish in administration and above all in education. It was the educational demands of the Flemings which always gave the movement its liaison with the church. It was the old French-dominated Liberal party which in the nineteenth century had fought for a system of state schools.

Although the Flemish question still continued to play a great role in political affairs, by the middle of the thirties most of their important demands had been conceded. It is true that a small Flemish fascist group developed, which favored creating a large State of Flanders by uniting the Flemish provinces with the Netherlands since they spoke a similar language. However, this was only a small group, and throughout the long agitation for Flemish rights, there was no significant movement against the Belgian state. Like Switzerland, Belgium seemed destined to be one of the rare examples of a peaceful, democratic, non-national state.

Fascism was to change all this. In 1935 Leon Degrelle founded his Rexist Fascist party, which drew its support from the Walloon sections and soon struck up close co-operation with some of the small Flemish fascist groups. The Rexists received support from Hitler, but more so from Mussolini, who placed a radio station in Milan at their disposal. The Belgian government opposed these Fascists, forbidding the formation of military units and the wearing of uniforms by political groups. Fascists were also barred from speaking over the Belgian state radio. Although the Fascists were far from taking over the state, the growth of extremist movements on the right and left made it increasingly difficult to maintain the cabinets, which had to be based on an unnatural alliance of Socialists and Clericals.

Luxembourg was an illustration of the advantages and disadvantages of living in a small state. There had been no compulsory military service in Luxembourg since 1881. The armed forces of Luxembourg consisted of one company of volunteers with 170 men and 6 officers, along with a slightly larger force of gendarmerie. It was industrially very strong, thanks to the great iron ore deposits that continue into Luxembourg from Lorraine. Nevertheless, Luxembourg was not important enough to make many decisions freely. Grand Duchess Adelaide was forced to abdicate in January, 1919, because of her Germanophile policies during the war; she was succeeded by her sister Charlotte. The Treaty of Versailles had forbidden Luxembourg to continue as a member of the German tariff union. In a plebiscite held in September, 1919, the people voted for a tariff union with France, but out of consideration for French relations with Belgium, France refused to go through with this arrangement. Luxembourg was forced to conclude a monetary and tariff union with Belgium.

ECONOMIC DEVELOPMENT. The Lowlands—lying athwart the mouths of the Rhine, Meuse, and Scheldt—have from the early Middle Ages served as the great European entrepôt. Today these rivers have been connected with a system of canals so that water-borne commerce from much of Germany, Switzerland, and northern France finds its cheapest and best outlet via Dutch and Belgian ports; barges loaded in Lowlands ports even find their way down the Danube. The Lowlands can truly be said to be the transit center of Europe. Rotterdam and Antwerp take their place alongside of New York, London, and Hamburg as the great ports of the world. The Netherlands has always had an important ocean-going fleet. This, together with their rich East Indian possessions, has made them the center for Europe's imports of spices and other colonial goods. Belgium through its development of the Congo basin has added African tropical products to those of the Dutch East Indies. Although greatly expanded after the war, Belgium's merchant fleet was of less importance than her large fleet of barges which plied the European network of canals. Since the Lowlands are so important commercially, particularly in regard to transit trade, they have traditionally been "free traders." The Netherlands has had fewer and lower duties even than Belgium, but there too with the coming of the depression, tariffs, particularly on agricultural products, and also import quotas, were imposed.

The Lowlands have also always taken an important part in Europe's industrial life. Many were the battles which were fought to control the lucrative wool trade of Flanders during the Middle Ages. Wealthy burghers symbolize the Dutch, quite as much as landed aristocrats do Hungary or Poland. The old interest in textiles has continued to this day; wool has given way to linen and to cotton, and in recent years to rayon, but textiles have always remained an important article of export from this region. Belgian laces are world famous. The nineteenth century brought the full impact of the industrial revolution to all three countries. Belgium and Luxembourg, with coal and iron deposits, developed important heavy industries. Along with this went a general industrial development until Belgium came to rank as the third industrial country of Europe. Although predominantly a rural country in 1830, a hundred years later only 17 per cent of the Belgian population was engaged in agriculture, 10 per cent in the extractive industries, and over 50 per cent in manufacturing. There were many small industries, but the majority of the workers were engaged in large industrial enterprises. By 1925–26 most of Belgium's industrial plants had not only been restored but had been modernized. Her mines were mechanized, and a new important coal field in the region of Antwerp was developed. This brought many important industries to this area. There was in general more economic advance in the Flemish than in the Walloon sections of Belgium.

Holland, even more than Belgium, has always imported many of the raw materials for its industries. The well-administered government coal mines in the province of Limburg constituted its only mineral resources. Agriculture had occupied an important place in export, yet in the postwar years the percentage of industrial exports increased until they approximated 60 per cent of the total. Cut diamonds continued to be an important trade item. More foods were processed than in earlier years and hence were classed as manufactured exports. An important new concern manufacturing radio and electrical equipment established its position among European competitors. The great colonial areas which Belgium and Holland controlled helped to cushion the economic crisis of the thirties in these countries. In Luxembourg as in Belgium, the iron and steel industries benefited by the general European rearmament program which brought a measure of prosperity.

Both Belgium and the Netherlands have a large supply of skilled labor. They rank first and second in population density among the states of Europe, and their population has steadily increased. In general, Belgium has been the more conservative in her labor policies and only in 1921 permitted the free development of trade unions. The effect of World War I was to create a much broader democratic base for the Belgian state, which was reflected in increased strength in the Socialist parties and more liberal labor legislation. During the twenties and thirties a progressive social insurance system was established. Holland had effective union organizations long before Belgium. Before World War I her system of labor and social insurance laws was also more advanced than that of Belgium. This program too was extended after the war.

EDUCATION AND RELIGION. After many years of dispute regarding the relationship of state and church schools, Belgium and the Netherlands emerged in the twenties with similar systems. In the Netherlands Catholics and Protestants united in demanding state support for their privately run schools. This was ultimately granted, the state, of course, having the right of inspection and supervision of the curriculum. This system has also been adopted in Belgium. The amounts of the subsidies to be granted not only for instruction but for building programs were perennial points of controversy in parliament. Beside the confessional schools, which receive state subsidies, there is a system of state schools in which religion is usually given as an elective subject. There are also purely private schools, often of a specialized nature and many of them run by clerical orders, that receive no state aid.

For the most part, the Netherlands had a more advanced educational system than Belgium, because its roots went back farther. Compulsory education was not introduced in Belgium until 1914 and in that year there was not as yet a single state secondary school for girls. On the whole there was real educational advance in both countries in the postwar period. In curricula the schools were very conservative; Greek and Latin dominated the secondary schools and were basic requirements for admission to the universities.

Mention has already been made that the churches were active in politics, in organizing labor unions, and in education. This holds true of other social and cultural spheres. Belgium has more than any other country become the testing ground for "Catholic Action." This is a great modern movement in the church aiming to arouse the social, civic, moral, and religious conscience of the people. The conferences at Mechlin in Belgium have furnished a world-wide impetus to this movement. In the Netherlands the Protestant majority has given to that country a combination of liberalism and conservatism, which seem to be the characteristic components of Calvinism.

COLONIAL EMPIRES. In the early nineteenth century two of the smallest countries in Europe, the Netherlands and Belgium, ranked among the great colonial powers of the world. The Dutch possessions dated from early sixteenth and seventeenth century European colonial expansion. A few figures will bear out the statement that the prize possession was the Dutch East Indies. These fertile islands (c. 1936) "produced 91 per cent of the world's Peruvian bark, 75 per cent of the world's kapoc, 53 per cent of the pepper, 37 per cent of the rubber, 23 per cent of the cocoanut products, 19 per cent of the agava fiber, 16 per cent of the tea, 10 per cent of the sugar, and 20 per cent of the tin." [1] Although maintaining a commanding position herself, the Netherlands shared the trade of the East Indies with other nations. Only late in the thirties were discriminatory regulations enforced against Japan. In spite of native protests and a serious revolt in 1926–27 in Java, the Dutch made few concessions to the native population. The East Indies remained a governed and not a self-governing group of territories.

Thanks to the personal enterprise and avarice of King Leopold II (1865–1909), Belgium came to play a leading part in the opening of Africa. He established the Congo Free State in 1884 and ruled over it with a high hand. His administration marked the apogee of modern colonial exploitation. In 1908 Leopold ceded his sovereign rights in the Congo to Belgium, and it became a Belgian colony. Much Belgian capital flowed into the territory, and it steadily advanced in importance in Belgian trade figures. Although great improvements were made in dealing with the natives, the Congo remained a colony exploited mainly for the benefit of Belgium.

FOREIGN POLICY. Belgium, as a greatly publicized participant in the war, was forced to be more active in foreign affairs than her northern neighbor. There was no longer any talk of an international guarantee of Belgium's neutrality, although Britain and France did not officially cancel their obligations until 1926. Belgium naturally considered her best guarantee of safety to be close co-operation with France, and in September, 1920, an alliance in the form of a military convention was concluded between the two countries. Belgium participated in the occupation of the Ruhr and was a party to the Locarno treaties [see above, pp. 162–65]. These treaties were popular in Belgium, since in these agreements Germany publicly renounced all claims to the territory awarded to Belgium in 1919 and the Belgian frontiers were guaranteed. France and Belgium at this time by identical declarations limited their alliance to obligations arising under the Locarno treaties. With the Netherlands, Belgium had various disputes over waterways, but finally in 1925 long-standing difficulties over the navigation of the Scheldt were settled.

After Hitler reoccupied the Rhineland, Belgium on October 14, 1936, denounced her military alliance with France. This was generally interpreted as an expression on the part of Belgium of her desire to remain strictly neutral in any possible conflict between Germany and France. To lend emphasis to this policy, Belgium in April, 1937, obtained a release from her obligations under the Locarno pacts. France and Britain, nevertheless, promised unilaterally to help Belgium defend her territories should she resist an attempted invasion. Hitler at the same time guaranteed to respect the inviolability of Belgium, except if Belgium should participate in military action against Germany. Belgium also sought to strengthen her security by a policy of rearmament. In 1936 the term of military service was lengthened and a larger number of troops was retained under arms; many forts were built, and the Albert Canal, begun in 1930, was completed

[1] Bartholomew Landheer (ed.): *The Netherlands* (Los Angeles, 1943), p. 174.

and strongly fortified. It seemed that Belgium had erected sufficient safe-guards against being used as a corridor for either German or French armies.

In the postwar years, because of proximity, trade, and historic con-nections, the Netherlands had to tread a wary course between Great Brit-ain and Germany. With Germany disarmed and friendly to Great Britain, this was not too difficult. Holland had always had to consider that her colonial empire was subject to the good will of those who commanded the British fleet. Increased Japanese activity in the East raised new problems, which only made the Netherlands more friendly to the United States and Britain. Nevertheless, the Dutch always believed that a policy of neutrality, friendship to all, and co-operation through the League was the best way to maintain their independence.

The Belgian fortifications of the thirties actually made Holland's mili-tary position weaker, for now the least-defended approaches between Ger-many and France seemed to be across her lands. The Dutch also increased their armaments and built fortifications, but not on the Belgian scale. Their main defenses were still based on plans to flood certain areas by the opening of dikes. The Dutch leaders were not inclined to negotiate with any powers in regard to special guarantees, for they considered the inviola-bility of their territory as axiomatic. Their policy remained one of inde-pendent and impartial neutrality. They therefore welcomed the adherence of Belgium to this platform and her consequent rejection of entangling alliances. There were traditionally many irritating differences between the two countries, but influential circles in both Belgium and Holland began to point out the advantages of a defensive bloc that would unite the eco-nomic and military forces of the two countries. This unity was not achieved, although co-operation between Holland and Belgium was very close in the months preceding their being drawn into World War II.

In 1930 the Netherlands, Belgium and Luxembourg joined with Nor-way, Sweden, and Denmark in the so-called Oslo agreements, which were designed to increase trade and co-operation among the small states. Al-though Finland joined the group in 1933 and the agreements were broad-ened in 1937, they never had great commercial significance because of the hostility of the great powers. Of more importance was the Convention of Ouchy of 1932, which provided for a reduction of tariff barriers between the three Lowland states. Britain's insistence on benefiting from all these tariff reductions because of her most-favored-nation agreements practically nullified the Convention. Yet it was the beginning of a trade policy that, after World War II, was to lead to a tariff union among the three coun-tries of the Lowlands.

The Scandinavian Countries

HISTORY. The three Scandinavian countries—Denmark, Norway, and Sweden—have a similar historical background. Their peoples are of Teu-tonic origin and in the Middle Ages often shared the common name of Norsemen or Vikings. In 1397, by the so-called Union of Kalmar, Norway and Sweden were brought under the suzerainty of the ruler of Denmark. Each kingdom, however, retained its own laws and organs of government and at times had a separate ruler. The Swedes revolted in 1523, and gradually gained in strength until in the seventeenth century Sweden was one of the leading powers of Europe.

By the early twentieth century, historical development had led to the establishment of three independent Scandinavian states. As to size, Denmark was the smallest, but even Denmark was a quarter larger than the Netherlands. Norway came next in size but was the smallest in population, numbering not quite three million, while Denmark approached the four-million mark. Sweden, with its six million, was still well behind the population of either Belgium or Holland. The three states had all been swept by the Protestant Reformation, and in each there was an established Lutheran State Church. Over 97 per cent of the population gave allegiance to this church; Scandinavia can be considered as staunchly Protestant as the Iberian peninsula is Catholic. Ethnographically, Scandinavia has no important minorities. A few Lapps cross indiscriminately over Norwegian and Swedish frontiers in the far north. The only important Scandinavian minority living outside of the state boundaries are the Swedes in the Aaland Islands and in other sections of Finland. Many Scandinavians have also emigrated to the United States, where the 1930 census listed 1,122,576 as having been born in Denmark, Norway, or Sweden.

POLITICAL AND ECONOMIC DEVELOPMENT. The Scandinavian countries have enjoyed such a reputation in recent years for being progressive democracies that it is hard to realize that this is a relatively modern development. Throughout the nineteenth century Denmark remained an autocracy, where the king not only reigned but actually governed. In Sweden, too, the king exercised great influence. Cabinets and ministers existed, but it was not until after 1914 that parliamentary government really became a part of constitutional practice. The new Danish constitution of 1915 brought universal suffrage and other liberal reforms. Democracy in Norway evolved as part of the struggle against the Danish and Swedish kings. Norway has always been somewhat more advanced and liberal than either Denmark or Sweden. In the latter two countries more vestiges of the royal power of bygone days remain. Partly because of tradition, but largely due to the respect and love felt by the people, the monarchs still exercise a real influence on state affairs.

The postwar decades brought a growth of socialist parties bearing various labels, although communists were never able to make much headway. There were no distinct clerical parties as in most of the other countries of Europe. Some of the more conservative parties did carry as part of their platform the continued maintenance of the state church and religious education in the schools. Yet the Scandinavian countries were religiously so homogeneous and practiced such genuine religious toleration that religion did not form a real basis for political cleavage.

In Scandinavia the people were used to a certain amount of paternalism on the part of their governments. Paternalism is usually an attribute of well-run monarchical states, and the Scandinavian rulers were on the whole able and conscientious sovereigns. Although starting from a different ideological basis, the socialist parties, too, urged the governments to undertake more and more services for the people. The result was that in the interwar years the Scandinavian states developed into our best examples of social service states. This was not a system of complete state ownership, but rather a system of mixed economy with private and state enterprises helping but also checking each other. Co-operatives of all sorts—producers, credit, retail, manufacturing, wholesale—were expanded tremendously. The governments have undertaken services on their own (health, care of the sick and aged, etc.); they have gone into business, sometimes sharing with private capital (mixed corporations), and at other times establishing 100 per cent government-owned-and-operated concerns. In Sweden, for example, there are government-owned and privately-owned railways, electric generating plants, and forests, each meeting the competition of the other. There are a variety of housing schemes, some undertaken by private initiative, others managed through co-operatives; in some the government furnishes a large part of the finances, while in others the government itself does the construction. There has been, on the whole, no doctrinaire problem as to whether this or that is, or is not, a proper sphere of governmental action. If there is need, and the government seems best suited to carry on a certain project or new development, it has taken over the task. The states have also gone far in appropriating and developing natural resources (waterfalls, mines) for the benefit and profit of all the people.

After the war, the governments began to extend various provisions of social insurance previously established. The state now takes its part in unemployment insurance by subsidizing unemployment benefit societies, which were originally organized by the trade unions. In 1934 Sweden established a separate state system to function alongside the old benefit funds. On the whole, the Scandinavian states have adopted a system of work relief rather than direct relief to help solve the problem of unemployment. Sweden worked out a system of planning projects in advance of the need, so that there would be no unnecessary leaf-raking projects when unemployment became acute.

All three states have exercised a very stringent control over liquor. In Denmark chief reliance has been placed on heavy taxation of spirits. Norway attempted a system of prohibition from 1919 to 1926, and since then has instituted a state monopoly for both the manufacture and the sale of spirits and wines. Sweden established a National Liquor Control Board, under which liquor was dispensed through publicly controlled but privately managed stores with limited dividends. Sales were restricted through a system of passbooks, which were withdrawn in case of abuse. This system of liquor rationing, after a long period of trial, was repealed in 1955.

While there has been much government in business, it should be emphasized that the three Scandinavian states operate very much on the basis of a capitalistic economy. Ivar Krueger, who started out by dominating the Swedish match trust, soon cornered the match monopolies in a great many of the states of Europe. He built up a fabulous international financial empire that crashed in 1932 and resulted in Krueger's suicide. There were plenty of other Scandinavian industrialists who amassed great fortunes. They were in line with that great Swedish inventor and industrialist, Alfred Nobel (1833–96), who built a fortune from manufacturing dynamite and smokeless powder and from the exploitation of the Baku oil fields. He established the Nobel Foundation, which gives awards each year on the recommendation of the different Swedish academies to individuals of international pre-eminence in the fields of physics, chemistry, medicine, and literature. He also established the Nobel Peace Prize, which is awarded by five persons nominated by the Norwegian Parliament.

While great industrialists and shipping magnates exist, the many farmers with small holdings are more typical of Scandinavian economy. Denmark is renowned for its dairy products, which have for years set standards for the agricultural export trade of Europe. Agriculture is, in fact, the leading occupation in each country, although only 2.2 per cent of Norway and only 9.3 per cent of Sweden is arable land. There are of course much larger grazing areas, and dairying is very important. Fishing and shipping run agriculture a close second, particularly in Norway. Sweden and Norway both have important resources of timber, and much wood pulp is exported. Sweden's very high quality iron deposits are the only mineral resource of special note. Much of this iron reaches the international market through the far northern Norwegian port of Narvik. This port is ice-free, while the Swedish ports in the Gulf of Bothnia are ice-bound the greater part of the year. Of the three, Sweden has the most important manufacturing industries. Swedish steel has a world-wide reputation; in the interwar period its Bofors armament industries ranked with Creusot in France, Krupp in Germany, Vickers-Armstrong in Britain, or Skoda in Czechoslovakia. As trading and commercial countries the Scandinavian states have followed a low-tariff policy. Normally the largest volume of foreign trade has been with England, followed by Germany and then by the United States. Next, as a rule, comes trade with one of the other Scandinavian states.

EDUCATION AND RELIGION. Educationally the Scandinavian states have been ahead of most of the states of Europe, and illiteracy is almost unknown. For more than a century elementary education has been compulsory in all three states, and in all three the state administers the school system, which is free. Religion is a regular subject of instruction, although parents have the privilege, rarely exercised, of getting their children excused from these classes. Private and parochial schools are permitted, but their numbers are insignificant. The Danish system of Folk High Schools, which are continuation schools for adults, deserves special note. They have been very successful and have placed Denmark ahead of the rest of the world in this difficult field of adult education.

In each country the king is required by the constitution to be a Lutheran. The Lutheran church, as the established church, is the only one to receive subsidies from the state; the clergy are paid partly from the income of lands and forests belonging to the church and partly from parish rates. The churches are governed in part by their own assemblies, under the supervision of the Minister for Church and Education, and of parliament.

COLONIAL POSSESSIONS. Denmark sold her possessions in the West Indies (the Virgin Islands) to the United States in 1914, although the transaction was not completed until three years later. The Faeroe Islands have been incorporated directly into Denmark and are governed as an integral part of the kingdom. Iceland in 1918 was recognized as an independent sovereign state united with Denmark only through a common king. Of her once vast territories, only unexplored and thinly settled Greenland remained in her hands. Denmark's possession of Greenland was always challenged by Norway, and the dispute flared up again in the twenties. Finally, in order to protect some settlements of Norwegian fishermen, Norway on July 10, 1931, proclaimed the annexation of certain sections of the east coast of Greenland. Denmark protested, and the two countries agreed to submit their dispute to the Court of International Justice. It was a sensible and civilized method of settling the problem. When the court held in favor of Denmark, the Norwegian government accepted the decision.

Norway was able in 1919 to obtain recognition by the Allied and Associated Powers of her sovereignty over Spitzbergen, although the status of this island has since been disputed by the USSR. Spitzbergen has important coal deposits, and the ice pack permits free navigation to its ports about four months each year. In 1928 Norway annexed Bouvet and Peter Island in the South Atlantic. Both are important as bases for whaling ships. She also increased her Arctic holdings by annexing Jan Mayen Island. Judged by past standards the Arctic holdings of the Scandinavian states are unimportant. The air age, however, has added to their significance since they may afford strategic bases.

Sweden has no colonial possessions. In 1917, following the Bolshevik revolution, the people of the Aaland Islands voted to join with Sweden. This action led eventually to a dispute with the new Finnish Republic. In 1921 the League Council assigned the islands to Finland with the proviso that they be given an autonomous regime. Sweden accepted the verdict, although most of the inhabitants of the islands were racially Swedes [see above, pp. 130–31].

FOREIGN POLICY. Geographic position, trade, and dynastic ties are factors that have given Great Britain a particularly favorable place in Denmark and Norway. Sweden, with its close ties to Finland and its position on the Baltic, always has to orient her policy with a view towards Russia. Particularly friendly relations were maintained by Sweden with the new Baltic republics of Estonia, Latvia, and Lithuania. With republican Germany all the Scandinavian states were on friendly commercial terms. But their chief desire was to establish closer ties among themselves; many tripartite conferences were held and each country made special trade concessions to the others. In 1930, as mentioned above, they entered into the so-called Oslo Agreements with the Netherlands, Belgium, and Luxembourg, but this new grouping was unable to achieve any great importance.

In 1934 Norway, Sweden, Finland, Denmark, and Iceland established a loose sort of organization for the promotion of economic co-operation among the Northern Countries. They made it a practice to insert "neighboring countries" clauses in their trade treaties, which exempted any concessions they might make to each other as neighbors from the application of the most-favored-nation principle. The foreign ministers began to hold regular conferences and there was far more cohesion in the "Scandinavian bloc" than in the larger grouping of "Oslo States."

The Scandinavian states were not bound by any alliances to aid one another. It was rather in pursuing similar policies that they sought unity. Thus they all adopted a strict policy of neutrality and in a joint declaration on May 27, 1938, announced that they would follow a common set of neutrality rules. They also recognized that each had certain obligations in regard to maintaining neutrality. Like all the other European states they, too, strengthened their armaments after 1936–37. This was a real change for Denmark, which for years had followed a policy of demilitarization. Sweden, having great supplies of high-grade ores and unsurpassed armament factories, was in a position to take care of her national security requirements except for airplanes. In fact, armaments came to be one of the chief exports of Sweden. Norway counted on her rugged terrain and placed chief emphasis on her navy to protect the long coast line.

Neutrality, friendship to all, ardent determination to maintain their independence, support of the League with all its allied agencies of international co-operation—these policies summarize the foreign policy of the Scandinavian states. Despite their self-respecting independence, they might be considered the most truly international-minded of any modern states.

Switzerland

HISTORY. In 1231 Emperor Frederick II of the Holy Roman Empire purchased the territory of Uri and established it as a self-governing canton whose freedom depended directly upon him. Frederick did this in order to protect the route between his Swabian and Italian possessions. His action marks the real beginning of a self-governing Switzerland. Two other territories, Schwyz and Unterwalden, soon won similar privileges. In 1291 these three cantons joined in a perpetual pact for a common defense against the Habsburgs, who laid claim to their territories. This pact was the beginning of the Swiss Confederacy, and in the following centuries other cantons joined the union. The Swiss often had to fight to preserve their freedom, and their ties to the Holy Roman Empire were not completely broken until the Peace of Westphalia (1648), when the independence of Switzerland was recognized.

The old Swiss Confederation (1291–1798) came to an end with its conquest by France during the French Revolution. At this time a strongly centralized state, tributary to France, was established. The new constitution brought recognition of equality, freedom, abolition of privileges based on birth, restriction of the powers of the church, and other doctrinaire revolutionary principles. The people nevertheless resented the curtailment of their local cantonal rights. Napoleon I reorganized Switzerland on a federal basis (1803–15) and added six cantons, one of them being the predominantly Italian-speaking canton of Ticino. The city of Geneva was annexed to France in 1798, but at the Congress of Vienna (1815) the powers revoked this and added the French-speaking cantons of Valais, Neuchâtel, and Geneva to Switzerland. Since then Switzerland has had no territorial changes. The Vienna Congress also arranged for international recognition of the future neutrality of Switzerland.

The Swiss, jealous of their local liberties, again established a very loose Confederacy (1815–48). In 1843 seven Catholic cantons united in an agreement (*Sonderbund*) to protect their very special interests. This led to a brief civil conflict and a reorganization of the Confederacy (1847–68). This time the national government was given somewhat greater powers. In 1874 a new constitution, which is still in force, carried this trend towards centralization even farther.

Switzerland as thus established through the centuries is a small country about half the size of the state of Maine. It is larger than any of the Lowland states but smaller than Denmark. About a quarter of its territory is usually classed as unproductive, although the mountains account largely for its great tourist trade, by no means a small business. It is divided into twenty-two cantons. Since three of these are for governmental purposes divided into half-cantons, the total number is often given as twenty-five. Nineteen of these twenty-five are predominantly German, five French, and one Italian. Of the total population of about four million, 72 per cent speak German, 21 per cent French, 6 per cent Italian, and less than 1 per cent Romansch, a local language allied to Latin. Since 1937, when Romansch was added, all four languages have been considered national languages. Switzerland sets the example for the rest of the world by demonstrating that it is not necessary for all the people of a country to speak one language in order to achieve a common nationality.

Historically Switzerland played an important part in the Reformation. Here Zwingli and Calvin carried on their work. Yet some of the cantons were never won over by the reformed doctrines and have remained staunchly Catholic. About 57 per cent of the Swiss are Protestant and 41 per cent are Catholic, with the rest adhering to other religions. Of the twelve predominantly Protestant cantons, nine use the German language and three the French; of the ten predominantly Catholic cantons, seven speak German, two French, and one Italian. Catholic or Protestant minorities, as the case may be, exist in all the cantons, which makes for mutual toleration.

THE SWISS MILITIA. Historically the Swiss took part in many European wars. In the heyday of mercenary armies (the fifteenth to the eighteenth centuries), many of the princes of Europe vied with each other in hiring their services. The rise of mass national armies ended all this, and the constitution of 1874 definitely prohibited the hiring-out of mercenary contingents. Only the Pope by special arrangement still is permitted to recruit his picturesque Swiss bodyguard.

The maintenance of a standing army is definitely forbidden by the constitution. At the same time it imposes an obligation of personal military service on every Swiss male citizen. There are few exceptions, and all those excused must pay an extra tax; this applies even to Swiss citizens living abroad. When called up, a recruit receives an initial three months' training course. He then takes his uniform and rifle home with him, which is a historical reminder of the ancient right of all free men to bear arms. Very often he keeps up his marksmanship by joining a shooting club. For twelve years he is a member of the *Elite*, or first-line division, and during this time he has to undergo seven refresher courses of thirteen days each. From thirty-three to forty years of age he is enrolled in the *Landwehr* and has to take one repetition course. From forty to forty-eight he is a member of the *Landsturm* but is not required to take additional training. The Swiss officer corps is recruited from the ranks, for everyone must start out as a private. In peacetime no officer ranks higher than a colonel, but in time of crisis a commander in chief with the rank of general is named. World War II brought the fourth general since 1815.

While the Swiss accept the necessity for their military establishment, this does not mean they are enthusiastic about it. There is considerable grumbling about its costs both in time and money. The government's use of the army to suppress the general strike of 1918, while it gained favor in some circles, brought increased dissatisfaction among the workers. Yet the mobilization of the army in both World Wars showed morale to be high and the populace willing to bear this burden that their neighbors placed upon them. That Swiss troops were on guard at the frontier, determined to resist all aggression, was no doubt a factor in persuading the warring powers to respect Swiss neutrality, but Switzerland's best defenses are her impassable mountains and her difficult terrain.

POLITICAL DEVELOPMENT. During World War I the Swiss government was forced to undertake rigid control over currency, foreign exchange, and banking, and to intervene by regulation and subsidy in many other spheres of the economy. All this continued the general shift of power from the cantons to the national government, a shift that had been going on throughout the nineteenth century. The trend continued in the postwar years. This does not mean that the cantons lost their significance; as members of a federal state the cantons are woven into the Swiss framework of government and only a major revolution could alter these arrangements. It simply indicates that the Swiss have chosen to do more and more things on a national rather than on a local level. They are not afraid of the state, for in a true democratic sense they consider themselves the state.

Already possessing an advanced system of democratic government, the Swiss continued to push forward. In 1919 a scheme of proportional representation was introduced for elections to the lower house of parliament. In 1921 a plan was adopted for optional referendum on international treaties. Although there was already wide use of the initiative and referendum on domestic questions, this extension of the referendum into the international sphere was a new venture in direct government by the people. For local affairs, one canton and four half-cantons have retained a general gathering of all citizens as their representative bodies. Like the New England town meetings, these Swiss *Landsgemeinden* are pretty much managed and directed by permanent officials. In one respect the Swiss did not keep pace with many of the other states of Europe: they failed to introduce women's suffrage.

After World War I three major political parties shared about equally the support of three fourths of the electorate. The Radical party was the one that really made Switzerland; and it is essentially a liberal party. It lost ground somewhat to the Socialists, who are by no means pure Marxists. They are primarily a working-class party combining political liberalism and some Marxist economics with adherence to planning schemes. In 1922 a group of left-wingers broke from the Socialists and formed the Communist party; it never gained many recruits and was proscribed in 1940 because of Switzerland's bad relations with the USSR. As in most countries with a large Catholic population, there is a Catholic Conservative party. It dominates in the Catholic cantons, while the Protestant cantons show much more political diversity. In the United States the national party organization has pretty well absorbed state parties, but in Switzerland it is the cantonal party organizations that are most important.

The change in party strength did not bring an immediate corresponding shift in the Federal Council (cabinet). This body consists of seven men elected for four-year terms, who preside over the different departments and constitute the executive. The Councilors are elected by the Federal Assembly, which is a combination of the upper chamber (representing the cantons) and the lower chamber (representing the people), and it is customary to re-elect them as long as they will serve. This means that the Federal Council does not reflect exactly the political complexion of the chambers. It has taken a long time for the Socialists to get their men into executive positions. The Federal Council as an executive is unique among the governments of the world. It is a permanent executive, which is responsible to the elected chambers but does not resign if measures advocated by the Council are defeated in the legislature. One member of the Federal Council is elected by the Assembly to act as president of the Confederation. His term is for a year, and he cannot succeed himself. He has no special powers, but does serve the purpose of a titular executive, which seems to be a necessity when it comes to accrediting foreign representatives. Even a democracy needs a first citizen.

The Swiss have never hesitated to extend the activities of the state into economic fields. Long before the war, the state had nationalized the railways. Telephones, telegraph, and radio are now run by the government; and gunpowder, alcohol, and tobacco have long been government monopolies. As early as 1908 the state extended its jurisdiction over water-power resources. Although many of the wartime regulations were abolished, the government in the twenties continued to expand its activities in the economic sphere. A constitutional amendment in 1929 gave the federal government power over agriculture. A policy of aid to farmers through price fixing and subsidies followed. Back of the whole program was a desire to make Switzerland less dependent on imported foods. Twice during the twenties the Swiss by referendum refused to adopt a system of prohibition. There was, however, a very ardent prohibition movement, and in 1930 the reformers were able to get a constitutional amendment adopted giving the federal government control over the production and sale of fruit brandies. Previously, the production of fruit brandies had been unregulated; peasants considered it a right to do what they wished with their fruit, and there were many local stills. Under the present system they can continue to distill for their own use tax-free, but are obliged to sell their surplus to the government. Formerly, Swiss brandy was cheap and consumption averaged about seven liters a year per head of population, accounting for much of the "alcohol problem." Because of the need of regulation, the Swiss injected their government into the brandy business.

ECONOMIC DEVELOPMENT. Switzerland has long ceased to be primarily a rural state, although the yodeling cowherds still exist, and Swiss cheese is as famed an article of export as ever. Actually Switzerland is one of the most industrialized states of Europe. This is all the more remarkable since Switzerland has no important mineral resources. Industrially, her water power and her highly skilled labor supply are her greatest assets. Since most of the raw materials for manufacturing have to be imported, the Swiss have multiplied their value by expending much labor on them. Watches, precision instruments, laces, silk ribbons, pharmaceuticals—all of which absorb much labor and relatively little material—have long been basic articles of Swiss manufacture. More than a third of the population works for export.

Switzerland, anxious to protect both her agriculture and her manufacturing industries, has been a rather high-tariff country. The general decline in world trade in the early thirties was nearly catastrophic for Switzerland. In 1932 exports fell to less than half the value of imports. To cope with this situation Switzerland raised her tariffs and instituted a wide system of quota restrictions. Production of wheat was subsidized. In September, 1936, in line with French currency reforms, Switzerland devalued her franc. This led to a stimulation of exports, and, benefiting also from the general world trade revival, Swiss trade figures rose steadily in the following years. Thanks to her relatively stable currency as well as her stable political and economic life, Switzerland in the years between the wars increased in importance as an international financial center. The Bank for International

Settlements under the Young Plan was established at Basel. Income from foreign investments and from the expanding tourist trade has always helped to balance Switzerland's foreign trade accounts.

In the interwar years labor unions were permitted and collective bargaining was practiced. The federal government was empowered to regulate employment of women and children and conditions of work in factories. Accident insurance was compulsory. It was not, however, until 1947 that a system of federal old age and unemployment insurance was enacted. Before the adoption of the 1947 measure, chief responsibility for dealing with unemployment rested with the communes, which were aided by grants from the cantonal as well as the federal treasury.

EDUCATION AND RELIGION. Each canton during the course of history has developed its own school system, and since there is such great diversity among cantons because of language, religion, and economic development, the school system of Switzerland is extremely varied. The schools on the whole are excellent. Stress is laid on language instruction, and most Swiss know in addition to their mother tongue something about one or more of the other languages of their country. Private schools are permitted, and ever since the days of the great Pestalozzi there have been some famous private academies. Most of the Catholic private schools are of a specialized nature, and there are not many elementary parochial schools.

The main religious statistics of Switzerland have been presented in the section on history, for religious diversity is part of the historical background of Switzerland. Although in the past there has been much religious strife when only Protestants could attain full citizenship in the Protestant cantons and Catholics in Catholic cantons, this situation has long since ended. The period of French dominance during the Revolutionary Era did much to bring about the breaking of old religious restrictions. The declaration of Papal Infallibility at the Vatican Council in 1870 led to a minor *Kulturkampf* in Switzerland (1872–74) and the separation of a small group from the Catholic church. Known as the "Christian Catholics," they are similar to the "Old Catholics" in Germany. Religious-civil controversies account more than anything else for certain provisions of the Constitution of 1874 which seem to strike at the privileges of the Catholic church, such as the provision banishing the Jesuits and affiliated orders.

Outside of these restrictions the constitution guarantees full religious liberty and freedom of worship. A few remnants of historic anti-Semitism have cropped up now and then, but happily, this feeling has lessened and Jews now enjoy complete equality. No one is obligated to pay church rates if he makes a formal withdrawal of his church membership. Regulation of church affairs is left to the jurisdiction of the cantons, so that there is a great variety of procedures. Some cantons have two or even three established churches (Protestant, Catholic, Christian Catholic), in others there are only two or one. Geneva alone has at present no established church. Thus, only here where once the church ruled the state under the iron hand of Calvin is there complete separation of church and state.

FOREIGN AFFAIRS. In November, 1918, partly as a repercussion of the revolution in Germany, a general strike occurred in Switzerland. The Swiss government charged the Soviet government with subversive propaganda in connection with the strike and broke off diplomatic relations; these were not resumed until after World War II. In May, 1923, a Soviet representative at the Lausanne Conference was assassinated and this event led to a bitter diplomatic dispute that was not settled until 1927. But even then Switzerland did not recognize the government of the USSR, and in 1934 Switzerland opposed strenuously the entrance of Russia into the League. Strained relations continued between the two countries, as is indicated by Russia's refusal to attend the Civil Aviation Conference in 1944, because such "a fascist state" as Switzerland was going to attend.

In April, 1919, the Austrian province of Vorarlberg voted by a large majority to join Switzerland. The Swiss ignored this opportunity to enlarge their state. The Protestants were not anxious to see the addition of such overwhelmingly Catholic territories, and no one was anxious to shoulder a part of the old Austrian debt, which would have come along with the province. Switzerland did, however, negotiate (1920–23) a currency and customs union with the Principality of Liechtenstein. Other agreements were also concluded, and after 1920 Switzerland undertook the representation in foreign countries of this minute territory of sixty-two square miles and twelve thousand German-speaking inhabitants. The only member of the Liechtenstein diplomatic corps is a representative at the Swiss capital.

Membership in the League of Nations raised a problem for Switzerland. She was determined to retain her status as a neutralized state, and yet it was obvious that this was not consistent with the obligations that a League member assumed under the Covenant. Nor were the powers at first disposed to make an exception, for that might well open the door for all kinds of qualifications on the part of other states. By some clever diplomacy and with the aid of France, Switzerland was able to get a clause inserted in the Treaty of Versailles that recognized the Act of 1815, establishing Swiss neutrality, as being an international engagement for the maintenance of peace. No provision of the Covenant was supposedly to contravene any article of the treaty, and hence the powers had suddenly agreed that Swiss neutrality and membership in the League were not incompatible. Nevertheless, the people of Switzerland were not completely convinced, and the referendum for joining the League barely carried. Since a referendum must be carried by a majority of cantons, a change in one hundred votes in one canton might have reversed the decision.

Closely connected with the problem of the continued recognition of Swiss neutrality was the continuance of the free-tariff zones in France in the vicinity of the city of Geneva, which had been established in 1815. France wanted to abolish them, as well as certain neutrality rights that Switzerland had in Savoy. The two countries made an agreement, but a dispute developed when they came to carrying it out. This was submitted to the Court of International Justice, which allowed the claim of Switzerland to free zones in Haute-Savoie and the Pays de Gex.

In May, 1935, Hitler, in a speech in the Reichstag, declared that the German-speaking cantons of Switzerland were not *Reichsdeutsch* and did not constitute a "lost" German territory. But, as was the common practice, the Nazis established a National Socialist organization for German nationals residing in Switzerland. The assassination of the leader of this group in February, 1936, by a young Jewish Yugoslav student led to the abolition of National Socialist organizations on Swiss soil. This was followed by some diatribes in the press of both countries, but Germany continued to be Switzerland's best customer, and many German tourists eagerly sought the curative benefits of the rarefied and free air of the Alps.

Switzerland was in a precarious position, lying between imperialist fascist regimes to the north and to the south. Swiss leaders noted Mussolini's pronouncements about a greater Italy and his occasional references to the Italian section of Switzerland. In view of this, and the general deterioration of the international situation, Switzerland in 1936 undertook to strengthen her armaments. New fortifications were built and equipment modernized. No one doubted that if any country attempted a serious violation of Swiss soil there would be determined opposition by a united and indignant Swiss citizenry. Yet Switzerland sought safety chiefly in attending strictly to its own affairs and by making its international banking and commercial facilities available to all the powers. In order to emphasize this position, Switzerland in 1938 petitioned the Council of the League to recognize her unconditional neutrality. This the Council did, thereby freeing Switzerland from the obligation of participating in economic sanctions. Germany and Italy, at that time no longer in the League and bound together by Axis agreements, likewise agreed to respect the historic neutrality of Switzerland.

Thus Switzerland was generally successful in maintaining her traditional policy of neutrality. Political exiles flocked to her from many states of Europe. In spite of this she was able to establish and maintain friendly relations with all states except the USSR. It was not until 1946, after the close of World War II, that Switzerland resumed the diplomatic relations with Russia which had been broken by the October Revolution in 1917.

CHAPTER

— 14 —

Danubian Europe

The New Governments: *Legislatures; Executives; Administrative Services; Judiciaries; Bills of Rights; Federalism vs. Centralization.*

Economic Reconstruction: *Reparations; Commerce and Industry; Agriculture.*

Religious Problems: *Education; Clerical Political Parties; Religious Situation in Czechoslovakia; Religion and Nationality.*

Political Development: *Austria; Czechoslovakia; Hungary; Yugoslavia; Rumania; Bulgaria; Albania; Summary.*

Postdepression Economic Problems: *International Action; Currency Regulation, Quotas, Clearing Agreements; Regional Economic Agreements.*

International Relations.

———◆———

ONCE established, the Danubian states had to lay the basis of government by formulating new fundamental laws. In all the states—except Bulgaria, where the old constitution was continued—National Assemblies met. The political complexities of these bodies and the various leaders who directed affairs have their significance for the history

of each country; but while there was diversity there was also much simi-
larity.

The New Governments

LEGISLATURES. The various constitutions established democratic parliamentary governments incorporating many of the most advanced political devices of the time. Male suffrage was universal; in some states women
voted, but often under special qualifications. Proportional representation
was the rule. The lower chambers of the bicameral legislatures were always
elected directly by the people. Hereditary upper chambers vanished; some
were now elected directly (Czechoslovakia), others indirectly since they
represented governmental subdivisions such as provinces or states (Austria,
Hungary, Rumania). In some, representatives of special groups—churches,
universities, chambers of commerce, etc.—found seats alongside elected
representatives (Hungary, Rumania). At first Yugoslavia, Bulgaria, and
Albania had unicameral legislatures, but Yugoslavia later adopted a bicameral system.

EXECUTIVES. Ministries responsible to the parliament, and in some
cases also to the head of the state, constituted the executive. The universal
adoption of the parliamentary form of government modeled on those of
England and France was, of course, in line with democratic tradition in
Europe. Some interesting adoptions were also made from practices in the
United States and Switzerland. Among them the use of initiative and referendum was the most important, although in actual practice it was seldom
used. Austria and Czechoslovakia became republics and invested parliament with the power of choosing their president. Hungary became a kingdom without a king, Admiral Horthy acting as regent (1920–44). In Yugoslavia the Serbian Karageorgevich dynasty took over; in Rumania the
Hohenzollerns remained on the throne; and in Bulgaria the House of
Saxe-Coburg-Gotha was continued when King Boris III replaced his father.
Albania, officially established in 1913 as an "autonomous principality under international guarantee," set up a government under a regency in
1918, became a republic in 1925, and was transformed into a kingdom
in 1928.

ADMINISTRATIVE SERVICES. The increased activity on the part of the
new states necessitated a large administrative service. In this regard the
traditions and personnel of the old Austria-Hungary proved a real boon to
some of the new succession states. Some purging was done, but to a remarkable degree the old civil servants (in so far as they could speak the
necessary languages) found employment in the new states. There was
much petty graft and arbitrariness inherent in the Eastern administrative
systems, which were still greatly influenced by Turkish ways. Unfortunately, the ruling groups of old Serbia and Rumania were addicted to
Eastern methods, and the administrative services of western Yugoslavia
and of western Rumania were pulled down to a lower level.

The state bureaucracy became the haven for the majority of university graduates. In the early years there was such a need for educated personnel that practically all graduates could be easily absorbed. In the later twenties they became a pressure group demanding places, and the number of governmental servants increased out of all proportion to the size of the state. There was also a reluctance on the part of many of these civil servants to accept positions in the provinces. They all sought employment in the capital cities, where they could play a more direct part and share in the spoils of party politics. Salaries were small, but a government position carried prestige among the home folks. Then too, by resorting to more or less recognized devious practices, plenty of money could still be made in politics.

JUDICIARIES. An independent judiciary was established, usually modeled on the previous judicial system. Only Czechoslovakia adopted a modified form of judicial review, which was so hedged about with restrictions as to be hardly comparable to American practice. Since no cases were ever brought before the court, this part of the constitution was obsolete from the start. The rule in all the states was the general continental one, that a law once passed was not open to challenge as to its constitutionality. In a sense the question of judicial review was academic, for the relative ease with which all constitutions could be amended would have made it easy for legislatures to re-enact an invalidated law as part of the constitution.

BILLS OF RIGHTS. All the constitutions had either elaborate bills of rights or many provisions scattered throughout the constitution to serve the same ends. Here perhaps more than anywhere else could be found the difference of emphasis between nineteenth-century liberalism and the newer socialism. True to the old tradition of the Declaration of the Rights of Man, many things were listed which the government should not do. The government should not restrict freedom of religion, speech, the right to vote, etc. Had at least these sections of the bills of rights been put under the special protection of the courts, had there been some peaceful recourse when the government violated these rights, democracy and liberty might be a brighter memory to the people of Danubian Europe.

Important as judicial review is in restraining improper governmental action and enforcing the traditional rights of man, it is not so significant when it comes to enforcing the newer socialistic concepts of human rights which the bills of rights also contained. Courts cannot coerce a government if it fails to act. Such social rights were not entirely new to constitutions, but never before had they received such widespread recognition or such elaborate formulation. While the older rights seem to echo Jefferson's refrain, "That government is best which governs least," the newer rights charge the government with a whole list of obligations and duties. The government must assure the right to work; the health of the citizens, particularly the laboring man, must be safeguarded; the aged must be cared for; the family must be protected, etc. To implement all these "rights" the government would of necessity have to provide a far-reaching social-service program, regulate trade and industry, and become in truth the very nur-

turer of the whole population. Most of these fine promises remained a
dead letter, a fact that helped to discredit governments in the eyes of the
people.

FEDERALISM VS. CENTRALIZATION. The trend in all the Danubian states
was toward greater and greater centralization. Czechoslovakia never got
around to implementing the autonomy foreseen for Slovakia and Ruthenia;
the state was run from Prague. Yugoslavia, where antagonism and bitter
political strife arose between the Serbians and Croatians, might well have
done better to adopt a federal form of government. But here, too, the
Serbians wished to direct affairs from Belgrade. Rumania also was highly
centralized. Intense nationalism on the part of dominant groups, along
with the planning that goes with a highly developed social service state
and a controlled economy, favored the establishment of unitary states.

There was also the problem of creating national unity among peoples
of differing historical backgrounds and cultural levels. What d'Azeglio said
of Italy in 1860—"We have made Italy, we must now make Italians"—
might well be said of Czechoslovakia, Rumania, Yugoslavia, and Albania.
Bohemia-Silesia-Moravia, which had been part of Austria, was on a higher
cultural and economic level than Slovakia and Ruthenia, which had been
part of Hungary. Yugoslavia had a variety of levels and standards; some
provinces were characteristically Western (Carniola and parts of Croatia);
others, like Bosnia-Herzegovina and Macedonia, bore the heavy imprint of
long years of Turkish administration. Rumania obtained not only Transylvania and the Bukovina from Hungary and Austria, but also Bessarabia,
which was one of the most backward of Russia's European provinces. The
Albanians remained organized largely along tribal lines, and little respect
was paid to the central government. Instead of recognizing these differences by organizing the state on a federal basis, the tendency was to enforce uniformity through the creation of a unitary state. There is little
time to wait in the modern age, and so thousands of years of different historical development were to be wiped out overnight. This attempt did not
work even when backed by force. The decline of federalism after World
War I meant a sacrifice of democracy and of individual rights, especially
for the minority groups.

Economic Reconstruction

REPARATIONS. One of the most urgent and difficult problems with
which the new states had to deal was the establishment of sound financial
systems. The League of Nations had to arrange loans for Austria, Hungary,
Greece, and Bulgaria. The depreciated currencies were usually stabilized at
a level well below the prewar par, thus cutting the value of all private savings. This stabilization also had the effect of wiping out a large part of the
state debt, but nevertheless all the Danubian states were weighed down
by heavy financial burdens. Austria, Hungary, and Bulgaria were charged
with reparations payments, while Yugoslavia, Rumania, and Czechoslovakia had to make so-called Liberation Payments and assume their share

of the old Austro-Hungarian internal debt (the so-called Liquidation Payments). It was a web of financial obligations which the Hoover Moratorium put on the shelf in 1931.

Although the Treaty of St. Germain had long sections on reparations, the section of the Reparations Commission which was established in Vienna June 18, 1920, was chiefly concerned with obtaining loans to help Austrian economy on to its feet. Here the League of Nations furnished valuable aid.

The city of Vienna, which had served as a financial center and capital for a large economic empire, was particularly hard hit. A city of its size—two million inhabitants out of a total Austrian population of six and one-half million—was bound to throw the economy of a small mountainous state out of kilter. By the time the Young Plan went into effect Austria could not even meet the interest charges on her loans, and no one thought of setting up a schedule of reparations payments. In June, 1930, Austria, credited with only something over one and a half million dollars in payments and deliveries, was formally discharged of all financial obligations arising out of the armistice or peace agreements.

The Reparations Commission was likewise forced to seek the help of the League of Nations in reconstructing the finances of Hungary. Except for deliveries of coal, Hungarian reparations payments were suspended until 1926. From then on for a period of twenty years, the annual payment was to be ten million gold crowns. Aided by a large influx of foreign capital, Hungary made some reparations payments. When the Young Plan went into effect, Hungary was assigned a schedule of annual payments gradually rising from seven to thirteen and a half million crowns.

Bulgaria failed to meet any of her payments on reparations up to 1923. In that year the Inter-Allied Commission negotiated an agreement with the Bulgarian government under which payment of three fourths of the debt was indefinitely postponed. On the remaining quarter Bulgaria was to make annual payments, which were duly made in the period 1923–28. In October, 1928, Bulgaria was granted a postponement because of a severe earthquake. A revised schedule of payments was set up under the Young Plan, but payments were suspended by the Hoover Moratorium and later canceled. Actually Bulgaria made reparations payments amounting to about .025 per cent of the sum demanded by the treaty. She paid about four times this amount by deliveries in kind or as charges for the armies of occupation, etc. Here, if ever, can be seen the folly of trying to collect reparations payments from a country so completely impoverished by war.

COMMERCE AND INDUSTRY. As an expression of sovereignty and independence, each of the states in Danubian Europe erected its own tariff system. Attempts to avoid this had failed at the Portorose Conference in 1921. Neither did the five-year preferential tariff arrangements materialize between Czechoslovakia, Austria, and Hungary as planned in the peace treaties. Austria, the only one of the smaller states which had to import large quantities of foodstuffs, had the lowest tariff of all. But even Austria introduced a high protective system in 1930. However, in most of the countries in the early twenties the unstable currency constituted a greater hindrance to trade than any tariff system. Recourse was also made to quota and licensing systems.

The imposition of tariff systems not only complicated trade but also disrupted old manufacturing procedures. Semifinished goods were often produced in various parts of the old Austria-Hungary and then assembled in one spot to be finished. For example, in the manufacture of textiles Austria retained 25 per cent of the spindles but only 9 per cent of the looms of the old monarchy. Many of the big concerns had central offices in Vienna and were directed from there. Now these offices had to be moved, which left many a white-collar employee in Vienna without a job. Czechoslovakia, which inherited better than 75 per cent of the old industrial plant of Austria-Hungary, was the most industrialized of all the succession states. These industries were concentrated in Bohemia and were balanced by the rural economies of Slovakia and Ruthenia. Czechoslovakia, however, always had a surplus of manufactured goods to export. Its glass, machinery, armament, textiles, shoes (Bata), and Pilsener beer were world-famous. Austria, like Germany, had to export manufactured articles in order to pay for good and necessary raw material. On the other hand, Hungary, Yugoslavia, Rumania, and Bulgaria had agricultural surpluses.

The small states of Central Europe cannot be censured for trying to create a rounded national economy when the whole world was doing the same thing. For example, it might be good in theory for Hungary to receive its manufactured goods from Czechoslovakia and remain a rural state, but—considering the bad blood between the two—it is not surprising that restrictive trade practices were used. In the twenties a satisfactory trade developed between these two states, but it practically disappeared when a bitter commercial war broke out with the expiration of their trade treaty in December, 1930. It soon became difficult for all the agricultural exporting states to sell their products abroad at a profitable price, particularly when the products of the peasants had to compete with the crops of the mechanized farms of the United States. The simple answer seemed to be to manufacture goods at home. Raw materials and a sufficient labor supply were at hand. Private individuals in Western Europe and the United States were eager to supply the necessary capital, for interest rates were high and profits seemed assured. Establishing industries would also furnish employment for the excess population of rural areas while producing a greater domestic market for foodstuffs. Only through industrialization could the standard of living be raised. Progress, civilization, in fact the whole modern world seemed keyed to industry, leaving little room for the peasant state.

The passion for advancement, for an equal status with the more developed states of the Western world, was also a real motivating force in the Danubian countries. This trend was particularly to the advantage of the enterprising businessman, who came to wield great political influence. The governments, especially in Yugoslavia and Rumania but in other countries as well, catered to industry. The resulting high prices for consumer goods, induced by a high tariff, were burdensome for the many small peasants who barely eked out a living. The highest price levels for industrial goods in all Europe were to be found in the agricultural exporting states of Southeastern Europe.

This growing industrialization of Danubian Europe meant a certain dislocation of old trade channels. Then too, economics was made to serve political ends. Definite attempts were made to weld the states of the Little Entente together by establishing close economic ties between them, but these were not entirely successful. Had there been more friendship, there would have been more trade. Had there been more belief in peace or in the possibility of peaceful change, there would not have been such an urge to make each state as self-sufficient as possible. But all this is simply saying that Danubian Europe was part of the world, and the same tendencies existed here as elsewhere.

Not all was chaos; indeed, real progress was made in all the states after the dislocations of the first years were overcome. Industrial production distinctly increased. It is by no means certain, as is so often supposed, that economically the Danubian basin was worse off when it was divided into a number of small states than when it had been a part of one large sovereign state. Better relations did develop among the succession states. Trade treaties were negotiated, and intra-Danubian trade still played an important part in the trade of all the states. The table below shows that this trade was relatively more important in the early twenties than it was after the depression. It was always least important to Czechoslovakia, whose well-developed industry competed in a world-wide trade. That old prewar regional trade connections sometimes held over is indicated by the important part Danubian trade played in the economy of Austria and Hungary. Economy of transport was an important factor. For example, because of cheaper transportation by barge on the Danube, it was better for Austria to buy her wheat from Hungary or Rumania even if the price of wheat was much lower on the Rotterdam market.

In 1913 Germany accounted for approximately 40 per cent of the exports and imports of Austria-Hungary, and after the war she continued to play an important part in Danubian trade as a whole, affecting the economy of all the states.

AGRICULTURE. Agricultural reform in Danubian Europe called first of all for a redistribution of land to the peasantry. Bulgaria and portions of Yugoslavia (notably old Serbia and Montenegro) had many small peasant proprietorships. In Austria the amount of agricultural land held in big estates was insignificant and no large-scale distribution was carried out. The large estates were mostly forests. Large agricultural estates were, however, numerous in Czechoslovakia, Hungary, and Rumania. All the revolutionary governments announced a program of redistribution which was

TABLE 8

TRADE AMONG THE DANUBIAN STATES IN PERCENTAGE OF TOTAL
IMPORTS AND EXPORTS OF EACH COUNTRY*

	EXPORTS AVERAGE OF			IMPORTS AVERAGE OF		
	1924	1928–30	1935	1924	1928–30	1935
Bulgaria	36.8	37.9	31	41.4	36.6	38.5
Austria	68.4	30.9	20	18.98	17.9	43.7
Hungary	39.25	58.2	37.3	60.21	48.9	18
Czechoslovakia	39.9	30.9	19		31.7	23
Rumania	46.8	37.9	32.2	44.94	43.9	28.1
Yugoslavia		20			29.6	

* Compiled from Antonin Basch: *The Danube Basin and the German Economic Sphere* (New York, 1943), p. 29; Gerhard Schacher: *Central Europe and the Western World* (London, 1936), p. 215.

carried out with varying degrees of thoroughness and impartiality. Rumania was one of the first states to inaugurate a radical land-reform law. This measure was applied most completely in Bessarabia, where the influence of communism was strongest, but also in Transylvania and in the old Rumanian provinces. About 50 per cent of the land was transferred, and many new peasant proprietors were created. In Hungary a start was made at distribution in the first year of independence, but with the return to power of the conservative groups this distribution was largely cancelled. Hungary remained a land of great estates, the only effective distribution being to small groups of war veterans.

The motives leading to land reforms "were political, social, and national, not economic." [1] To break up large estates into small holdings meant almost universally a decline in yield. The small farms were not managed so well as the large estates had been. Neither did the small farms have the necessary machinery or tractive power.

Distribution had its political aspects in all countries. Liquidation of the old landed classes was a popular move; it seemed a matter of social justice. The landed estates of alien or minority groups were fair game. Lands held by German or Magyar nobility in Rumania or Czechoslovakia were likely to be sequestered first of all; also the land was frequently turned over to favored groups within the states. All too often landless laborers who had formerly worked a great estate received no part of the land when it was distributed. The Germans in Czechoslovakia with justification charged that a disproportionate share of the land in German-inhabited areas was sequestered and that peasants of German nationality did not receive their share. On the other hand, it is equally true that most of the large estates were German-owned and that "the Czech and Slovak farmers who profited

[1] Hugh Seton-Watson: *Eastern Europe Between the Wars 1918–1941* (Cambridge, 1946), p. 79.

most largely in the distribution of land . . . had the least." [2] Land distribution was also used as a means of colonizing certain areas with favored "national groups." In Czechoslovakia, Czech and Slovak colonies were settled in what had formerly been predominantly German and Ruthenian areas. Rumania also favored peasants of Rumanian nationality, especially in the Dobruja. Serbs were colonized in the newly organized border regions of Yugoslavia. This resettlement brought with it all sorts of minority problems. These new groups had to have schools where instruction would be in their own language. This meant, for example, that the government had to build a new school building for the Czech or Slovak groups in the Sudetenland, while the old buildings served the German pupils.

The usual procedure was to permit the owner of an estate to retain a certain acreage. In Czechoslovakia, for example, this was set rather high—at 360 acres (150 hectares) for arable land and 560 acres for diversified (wooded, grazing) land, while an owner might be permitted to keep as much as 1200 acres under certain circumstances. About half of the 96,519,-808 acres subject to redistribution in Czechoslovakia was left in the hands of the original owners. Many of the forest lands were retained by the state and operated as state enterprises. Some of the lands were granted to neighboring peasants to round out their holdings, while others were transferred to previously landless groups. All too often the cry for land was so incessant that too many small holdings of a few acres each were established. Many of the peasants were not able to contract for more, although the payment they were asked to make for the land was very low.

Endless disputes also arose over valuation of the land and payments. Since many of the owners lived in other countries (notably in Hungary or Austria), the question of payment soon reached the level of international governmental negotiations. In any case, the depreciation of currency made compensation largely a matter of theory, although some payments actually were made.

In most of Central Europe the custom prevails that on the death of the owner his lands are divided equally among all his sons. As a result, in the years subsequent to the original distribution, the land was parceled into even tinier plots of land. If the land was of unequal quality, it was customary to give each son a strip of the good and a strip of the poorer land. Thus a peasant's holding of five or ten acres would be divided into many strips, to each of which roads and paths had to be left. Few of these strips were large enough for agricultural machinery to be used efficiently, even if a peasant possessed such tools. Many of the small owners, who formed by far the larger group, did not even possess a horse or a yoke of oxen. This meant that they had to hire "power," usually from more wealthy neighbors. In some instances governments and co-operatives provided machinery that could be leased. This had to be paid for either from the peas-

---

[2] Lucy E. Textor: "Agriculture and Agrarian Reform" in R. J. Kerner (ed.): *Czechoslovakia* (Los Angeles, 1940), p. 227; see also Elizabeth Wiskemann: *Czechs and Germans* (New York, 1938), pp. 147–60.

ants' meager cash income or by exchanging hand labor. The net result was that in many sections agriculture was carried on by very primitive means. The yield per acre was low, and poverty was the rule among the mass of the peasantry. Their miserable huts of one or two rooms equalled the squalor of the slums of big cities. Actually the "sturdy peasants" of song and story were not a healthy lot.

Land distribution and the agricultural problem as a whole were complicated by overpopulation of rural areas. Denmark, which was a highly developed industrial and agricultural state, had 36.6 people per square kilometer of arable land, while the corresponding figures were 80.6 for Hungary, 116.3 for Rumania, 119 for Bulgaria, and 157.4 for Yugoslavia. When the average yield of wheat per acre is put over against these figures, some indication of relative conditions will be apparent. In Denmark the average yield for 1933-37 was 31.3 quintals per hectare, while in Hungary it was 13.9, in Rumania 9.1, in Bulgaria 11.9, and Yugoslavia 11.1. Much more manpower went into producing a bushel of wheat in Eastern Europe than in the West.

Population rose rapidly in all of Central Europe, partly because of increased medical care and sanitation and partly through curtailment of emigration. From 1900 to 1910, 2,100,000 persons emigrated to the United States from Austria-Hungary alone, a stream that ceased to flow with the imposition of immigration quotas by the United States. Remittances sent home by emigrants, always an important factor in the economy of these regions, took a corresponding fall. The economic pressures and ills that the New World had for a time siphoned out of Central Europe were now left there to increase and fester.

The problem of overpopulated Danubian Europe was the subject of much discussion. Much might have been done to improve conditions through an industrial development adapted to local needs and supplies, through diversification of agricultural products and the development of canning factories, by the expansion of a program of state aid, or through an extension of already well-established co-operatives. The tragedy of the situation was the prevalence of undernourishment in countries that exported large agricultural surpluses. The governments as a whole did little for agriculture after the initial land reforms. The economic depression of the thirties was as deep and as far-reaching in its effects in agricultural Danubian Europe as in any other part of the world.

Religious Problems

Although the period of religious wars is long past, religion is still an important political issue. The growing power of the state and its secularization affected many fields formerly dominated by religion. For instance, in all the Danubian states a form of civil marriage was recognized by the state, and in some it was required before a church service could be performed. As in all Central Europe, the churches received financial support from tax funds. This was usually granted to the major denominations, although not always on an equal basis; in Czechoslovakia, for example, the Roman Catholic church, because of its political strength, received special treatment, and in most of the states Jewish synagogues did not get their proper share.

EDUCATION. The Catholic church had exercised great control over the educational system of Austria-Hungary, and these rights were not radically curtailed in the new states, since most of them were predominantly Catholic or had large Catholic minorities. Nevertheless, the establishment of non-Catholic schools was made easier, and the trend toward more secular education continued. All states had publicly supported school systems, but private schools were also permitted.

With the exception of Albania, each country had its state universities, its agricultural and technical schools, its music academies, and its normal schools. The University of Vienna still maintained its international reputation and was the particular mecca for medical students from all the Danubian countries. Charles University, now with only a Czech faculty, and the German University at Prague also deserve mention. In Bulgaria an American College at Sofia—associated with the Near East College Association—brought American practices and standards. This college was the outgrowth of activity of the American Board of Missions, which had begun work in Bulgaria and Macedonia when these territories were still under Turkish rule. There was also an American-staffed Agricultural Secondary School at Kavaja in Albania which was subsidized by the Albanian government.

CLERICAL POLITICAL PARTIES. Political parties were often divided along religious lines. The Communists tended to be aggressively antireligious, while the Social Democrats, as a rule, did not press the issue. Politically, most Protestants took the stand that the church should ally itself with no one political party. This was, however, not the case with the Roman Catholics. Wherever Catholicism was strong—Austria, Czechoslovakia, Hungary, and Yugoslavia—the clerical political parties were supported by the church as a means of protecting its interests. Often these parties were specifically directed against communism and socialism. This does not mean that the Catholic parties were opposed to legislation on behalf of labor; in fact, they often favored far-reaching policies of social legislation which were to be enacted within the existing capitalistic framework of society. In some cases the clerical parties were associated with particular national groups, as in Czechoslovakia and Yugoslavia. In the latter country the Croatian clerical parties opposed the Serbian-dominated parties, which were closely allied with the Orthodox church.

RELIGIOUS SITUATION IN CZECHOSLOVAKIA. Although Czechoslovakia remained predominantly Roman Catholic and the Catholic parties were very strong, this was the one country in Europe where Roman Catholicism lost ground. John Huss (1369–1415) had always been revered both as a national and religious leader, and the creation of a new state revived a traditional spirit of religious independence. Even the members of the Czech hierarchy who remained loyal Catholics observed a certain autonomy, as is exemplified in their disputes with the nuncios sent from Rome. The Catholic church lost one sixth of its members, mostly to a newly organized "Czechoslovak Church" and to the Protestant groups, who utilized their newly won religious freedom to strengthen their organizations.

The "Czechoslovak Church" resulted from a movement of some two hundred priests who in 1919 undertook to wrest reforms from the Papacy. They wanted "use of the vernacular in the liturgy, democratization of the parish organization, modifications in the training of theological students, lay representation in the governing bodies, abolition of compulsory celibacy, establishment of an autonomous Czechoslovak patriarchate, and a number of other items." [3] These demands were of course condemned as heretical. The rebelling clergy attempted unsuccessfully to establish relations with the Orthodox Church of Serbia. Nothing remained but to organize their own church, and in the end it "developed into a modernist communion, Unitarian in theology, strongly anti-Roman as well as anti-Orthodox." Whole parishes went over to this communion, and in 1937 its membership comprised over 850,000 communicants.

The Lutheran and Reformed Churches of Bohemia, Moravia, and Silesia united to form the Evangelical Church of Czech Brethren. Its membership doubled between 1918 and 1935, when it had 320,000 members. The strongest Protestant body, however, was the Lutheran church in Slovakia with a membership of 586,000. Here also there was a Reformed church (219,000) whose members were largely Magyars. The Lutherans on the whole gave strong support to the concept of a united Czechoslovakia, while the Catholics, who were the largest group in Slovakia, were the most ardent supporters of "Slovak autonomy." This was particularly true of the Slovak People's party under the leadership of Father Andrej Hlinka. To him there were no Czechoslovaks but only Czechs and Slovaks. The distinction is important. This conservative clerical group wanted as little as possible to do with liberal free-thinking Prague. The latent opposition between Slovaks and Czechs which had distinct clerical undertones aided Hitler's disruption of the state in 1939. It was then that Father Josef Tiso led the movement for an independent Slovakia.

Before the war Slovakia had been part of the Archdiocese of Esztergom in Hungary. The new Czechoslovakia wanted all dioceses to be limited to national boundaries. This the Cardinal-Primate of Esztergom was able to hold off, and the new dioceses were not yet fully organized when the political unity of Czechoslovakia was shattered in 1938. This question complicated Vatican-Czechoslovak relations. The bitterest dispute, however, came when the government in 1925 officially participated in a nationwide celebration in commemoration of the death of John Huss. The Papal nuncio left Prague in protest, and in turn the Czechoslovak representative at the Vatican was recalled. A wave of anticlericalism swept through Czech

[3] Matthew Spinka: "The Religious Situation in Czechoslovakia" in R. J. Kerner (ed.): *Czechoslovakia*, p. 293.

lands, where it was easy to identify Catholicism with the hated German-Austrian domination. The fact that the Sudeten Germans were rather strict Catholics also was a factor behind the internal Czech-German antagonism that plagued Czechoslovakia from the very start of its political career.

In Ruthenia—the most eastern section of Czechoslovakia—there were many so-called Uniates (sometimes called Greek Catholics), who were Roman Catholic in faith but followed Eastern rites of worship. Many of the Uniate clergy were sympathetic to Hungary and the ecclesiastical connections that had existed for so many years with dioceses in that state. The Uniates were on the whole supporters of the Ruthenian autonomy movement, and within three years after the close of World War I some seventy villages involving 100,000 people had turned Orthodox. This movement was largely a nationalistic expression of a desire to be united with the Ukraine, which was at that time attempting to establish its independence.[4]

RELIGION AND NATIONALITY. The case of Czechoslovakia illustrates the fact that religious differences tended to complicate the relation of national groups within a state. This was likewise true of Yugoslavia, where the Slovenes and Croats as Roman Catholics had long been in contact with the centers of Western civilization. They tended to think of their culture as more advanced than that of the Serbians, who in turn were nationally self-conscious and militant defenders of their Orthodox faith. The Moslems in Yugoslavia had their own political party. In Rumania, too, religion complicated minority problems. The Germans and Magyars of Transylvania were predominantly Protestant, while the Rumanians were Orthodox. Here, as in Czechoslovakia, there were many Uniates, who were mainly Ruthenians.

Although about two-thirds of the Hungarians were Roman Catholics, the large Protestant group of over two million exercised a political influence out of proportion to its size. Much of the Hungarian tradition of patriotism was associated with opposition to Catholic Habsburgs, and modern Hungary was extremely nationalistic.

Albania, where tribal and clan organizations were still strong, was 71 per cent Moslem. The northern tribes (10 per cent) were largely Roman Catholic, while most of those Albanians (19 per cent) who adhered to the Orthodox church were in the south. Greece claimed that the Orthodox Albanians were really Greeks and that southern Albania (northern Epirus to the Greeks) should belong to Greece. The Greek Patriarch at Constantinople strove to retain his spiritual as well as temporal jurisdiction over Albania and refused to recognize the Albanian Orthodox Church, which was declared autocephalous in 1922.

The tendency of the Greeks to claim all adherents of the Orthodox church in disputed population zones as Greeks also complicated Bulgarian-Greek relations. When the Bulgarian Orthodox Church declared itself autocephalous in 1870 and was so recognized by the Turkish sultan, the

---

[4] Donald Attwater: *The Catholic Eastern Churches* (Milwaukee, 1935), p. 93.

Greek Patriarch at Constantinople declared the church to be in schism and outside the Orthodox Communion. The Bulgarian church went its own way, but being branded as schismatic rankled many churchmen even if it did not bother the laity. Instead of being a tie between Bulgaria and Greece, a common Orthodox faith was a divisive influence.

Certainly the new regimes brought increased liberty to the Jews everywhere. Their rights were supposedly guaranteed by the special minority treaties and by the bills of rights of the new constitutions. Yet new excuses were invented and grafted on age-old prejudices. Very often conservative and clerical groups adopted anti-Jewish measures because they associated the Jews with radical left-wing political philosophies. Austria had its traditional small amount of anti-Semitism, but in the twenties this was not a serious problem. In Hungary many of the Jews had become thoroughly Magyarized and were accepted as the ardent patriots they were. Historically, Rumania was the most anti-Semitic country of all. While the lot of the Jews was improved and they now could become Rumanian citizens, they undoubtedly were worse off here than in any other country except Poland. Czechoslovakia, Yugoslavia, Bulgaria, and Albania, on the whole, have had a good record in this matter. The growth of anti-Semitism in the postdepression period and the part it played in the rise of various dictatorships, particularly in Austria, Hungary, and Rumania, was in marked contrast to the freedom of the twenties.

Political Development

In 1919–20 all the states of Central Europe were organized on a democratic basis. In most of them Social Democrats played a leading if not predominant role. In less industrialized Yugoslavia, Rumania, and Bulgaria, rather advanced peasant parties took the part that the socialists played in Austria or Czechoslovakia. Gradually, however, the radical or liberal groups who made the revolutions were replaced by more conservative rightist parties. Very often this change was the result of the natural political reaction that political scientists refer to as the swing of the political pendulum. The new states were faced with colossal difficulties; the promised land did not appear, and, instead of pushing forward, people preferred to stop, if not indeed to turn back to the good old days. Besides, specific problems complicated the political life of each of the states. In Austria it was the problem of accommodating the life of a city of two million inhabitants to the economy of a small mountainous state; in Hungary it was the refusal to accept the dismemberment of the historic lands of the Crown of St. Stephen; in Bulgaria it was the strong Macedonian irredentist movement sponsored by the Internal Macedonian Revolutionary Organization; in Albania it was the creation of a central government; in Yugoslavia, in Rumania, and even in Czechoslovakia it was the task of welding into one nation diverse national groups with different historical and cultural traditions.

In all these countries there was a weakening of democratic governments during the twenties. By about 1930 dictatorships were either already established or well on the way towards taking over, with the exception of Czechoslovakia, where economic prosperity and the wise leadership of President Masaryk eased many problems.

AUSTRIA. The 1920 elections brought an end to the rule of the Social Democrats in Austria, although they retained control of the city government of Vienna. Henceforth, they became the leading opposition party, and the clerical Christian Socialists led most of the coalition cabinets. The Christian Socialists drew much of their support from the provinces and were ably led by a Catholic priest, Ignaz Seipel. A German Nationalist party, under Johann Schober, usually sided with the Christian Socialists. Political strife was keen, and extrapolitical organizations soon sprang up. The first was the *Heimwehr*, which recruited most of its followers from rural districts and was conservative in outlook. Prince Ernst Rudiger von Starhemberg built the *Heimwehr* into a fairly efficient private army. Although the political nature of the *Heimwehr* was unpredictable, it can be considered in general a Christian Socialist organization. Later, in some provinces the *Heimwehr* came to be an arm of the National Socialist (Nazi) party. To hold their own, the Social Democrats formed the *Schutzbund*; it was well organized and drew its members largely from Vienna and other industrial centers. Clashes between *Schutzbund* and *Heimwehr* could always be counted upon to enliven every political campaign.

The economic rehabilitation of Austria was the great problem, and here the League of Nations provided vital assistance. Austria spoke out boldly—but with little effect—against Italian treatment of the Germans in South Tyrol. The big question of foreign policy, however, was union (*Anschluss*) with Germany. This had been denied by the Allies in 1919, but the issue never died out. In 1926 there was a revival of *Anschluss* agitation, certainly far more in Austria than in Germany. Finally, in 1931, Germany and Austria projected the formation of a customs union. Because of the sharp opposition of France, Czechoslovakia, and Italy, the project had to be dropped [see above, p. 156]. In order to bring pressure on Austria to abandon the planned customs union, France withdrew some of its short-term credits from the Austrian banks. This action played a part in the collapse on May 11, 1931, of the Austrian *Kreditanstalt*, one of the biggest international banking houses in Central Europe. Its bankruptcy brought with it bank failures in most of the other Danubian states. The economic crisis led to an increase of political unrest, enhanced by the success of the National Socialist party in Germany.

Engelbert Dollfuss, a protegé of Monsignor Seipel, was small of stature but full of energy. When he became chancellor in May, 1932, as head of a Christian Socialist-Agrarian cabinet, the depression was at its height. He scored an immediate success by obtaining a loan of three hundred million schillings through the League of Nations. In return he had to promise not to enter into political union with Germany before 1952, and this condition caused a storm of protest in Austria. On the other hand it brought him favor with Mussolini, who soon was acting as his godfather and counselor. Ever since 1930, when Italy and Austria had concluded a treaty of friendship, Mussolini had encouraged fascist elements in Austria, and the Dollfuss regime now became an outpost of Italian fascism.

In March, 1933, Dollfuss suspended parliament and launched his private brand of dictatorship. Within a month the Communist party was outlawed, and this was followed by a decree, aimed at the Nazis, forbidding the wearing of uniforms by all political parties. Hitler struck back by charging all Germans a thousand marks for a visit to Austria—a crippling blow to the Austrian tourist business. In June the National Socialist party within Austria was officially dissolved, but this did not end the political agitation.

Already officially rid of the Communists and Nazis, the Austrian chancellor was determined to end the power of the Social Democrats. In February, 1934, he dissolved all political parties except his own Fatherland Front, a coalition of Christian Socialists, Agrarians, and the *Heimwehr* led by Starhemberg. He had already curbed by various means the Socialist-controlled government of Vienna. The Socialists retaliated with a general strike, whereupon Dollfuss promptly arrested many of the Socialist leaders, and soon full-scale civil war broke out. When the Socialists barricaded themselves in some of the great municipal housing projects, Dollfuss did not hesitate to order the army to bombard the buildings that had been the pride of Social Democratic Vienna. With only a few small arms at their disposal, the Socialists had to capitulate. After this blood bath, which also was carried on in some provincial cities, Dollfuss was supreme. The Socialists never forgave him for this act of violence. It left the chancellor a very narrow basis of support, for now he had alienated the entire left as well as the Nazis.

In May, 1934, Dollfuss issued a new authoritarian constitution. Ideological inspiration was supposedly derived from the Papal Encyclical *Quadragesimo Anno* of 1931, in which the Pope had advocated the corporative organization of society. The Austrian constitution provided for a complicated arrangement of five corporative councils but these never were actually put into operation. Meanwhile the government was carried on by decree. A concordat with the Vatican (signed June 5, 1933; ratified May 1, 1934) assured the Church of control over Austrian education and abolished divorce.

A *Putsch* of July 25, 1934, carried out by Austrian Nazis, but inspired from Berlin, led to the assassination of Dollfuss. Mussolini at once sent some divisions to the Brenner Pass, and it was clear to Hitler that if he undertook to bring about *Anschluss* at this time he would have an Italian-French-Little Entente coalition to face. For the time being, Austrian independence was recognized and Kurt von Schuschnigg, a lawyer who had taken an active role in Catholic political activities, became the new chancellor-dictator. Starhemberg, the leader of the *Heimwehr*, was vice chancellor. Within a year the Austrian army was incorporated into the Fatherland Front, which meant that this potential source of opposition was thoroughly co-ordinated. Schuschnigg soon broke with Starhemberg, and, with the reintroduction of military conscription, the *Heimwehr* was disbanded. Many of its members struck up ties with the Nazis, and on the advice of Mussolini, Schuschnigg found it expedient to make his peace with Hitler.

In an agreement of July 11, 1936, Hitler promised to respect the independence of Austria, and Schuschnigg agreed to pursue a policy friendly to Germany. As Mussolini became deeply involved in Ethiopia and in Spain, where he was working together with Germany, his interest in an independent Austria declined. The Austrian dictator, realizing his precarious position, began to cultivate closer ties with the Little Entente. To this Hitler objected, and an invitation was issued to Schuschnigg to visit Berchtesgaden in February, 1938. Schuschnigg under duress agreed to reform his government and to make Arthur Seyss-Inquart, the leader of the Austrian Nazis, his minister of interior. Nazis were also to be permitted to join the Fatherland Front. Back in Vienna, Schuschnigg decided to stage a plebiscite on the issue of Austrian independence. It was to be run in true dictatorial fashion: ballots in favor would be supplied, but all opposed would have to furnish their own. Hitler, realizing the whole affair was aimed at him, demanded that the plebiscite be cancelled. Meanwhile the Austrian Nazis were causing many disturbances. Rather than throw the country into civil war Schuschnigg turned his power as chancellor over to Seyss-Inquart, who promptly appealed for German troops to restore order. They entered Austria on March 12, 1938, and the following day the union of Austria and Germany was proclaimed.

Austria now became the Ostmark with Seyss-Inquart as *Statthalter* (governor). The process of co-ordinating Austrian life and economy proceeded rapidly. The vast *Hermann Göring Werke* absorbed most of the mines and metallurgical establishments of Austria. German machines were relatively cheap and a great mechanization of Austrian agriculture took place. A favorable exchange rate for converting schillings into marks was established which helped to assuage the feelings of many. As they saw it, the new arrangement meant merely the exchange of one dictatorship for another, and incorporation into Germany brought more prosperity. The change of regime did bring great hardship to the Jews, but the Austrian people as a whole were not inclined to take a stand for them. The church, too, only belatedly made protest, when Hitler brought about certain changes, such as permitting divorce again in Austria. In 1939 the former nine Austrian provinces were rearranged into seven *Reichsgaue*, which were increasingly governed directly from Berlin.

CZECHOSLOVAKIA. The Socialists had played an important part in the formation of the Czechoslovak state, but from 1922 to the end of the Republic in 1938 Agrarian parties always dominated the coalition governments. At first the German parties presented a united opposition, but after 1925 the German Agrarians and German Socialists began to co-operate with their Czech counterparts. Svehla, the Agrarian leader, managed to stabilize the currency, to pass advanced social insurance laws, and to encourage industry while at the same time protecting agricultural interests.

Thomas Garrigue Masaryk served as president of the Republic until 1935. His unfaltering belief in democracy, his impartiality, and the great esteem and prestige he enjoyed among all the national groups helped immensely to keep democracy functioning. Eduard Beneš, the perennial foreign minister, was greatly concerned with insuring Czechoslovakia's international position. He conceived and watched over the Little Entente and maintained close alliance ties with France, but he was never successful in establishing friendship with Poland; the division of Teschen, Spiš, and Orava proved to be a wound that did not heal. Beneš was one of the strong supporters of the League of Nations and played an important part in its activities.

While Czechoslovakia continued to enjoy a democratic government, it had by no means solved all of its problems. The Slovaks and Ruthenians resented the fact that the autonomy which they believed had been promised to them was never granted. They resented the program of centralization originating in Prague, even if it did bring certain reforms and a large amount of good government. The Ruthenians benefited from new roads, many new schools, and other material advantages, but they resented the influx of Czech officials which came with the enlightenment.

The Czechs, like the Serbs in Yugoslavia, considered themselves the true upholders of the State idea. They tended to look upon the millions of Germans, Magyars, Ruthenians, and even at times the Slovaks, as "minorities" and not as Czechoslovakians. Many of these people had opposed being incorporated into Czechoslovakia in 1919 and had never been fully reconciled. Although tensions were not so acute as in other countries, democratic Czechoslovakia also had not solved its nationality problems.

The advent of Hitler in Germany led to the growth and activity of a National Socialist party among the Sudeten Germans. In October, 1933, a law was passed against subversive parties. Seeing what was coming, Konrad Henlein dissolved this Nazi party and organized a new one, the *Sudetendeutsche Heimatfront*, which officially was in favor of the democratic republic and the frontiers as established in 1919, and against the restoration of the Habsburgs. He demanded, however, more decentralization of administration and more local government for the German districts. Most of the three and a half million Germans were settled in a relatively narrow fringe bordering the German Reich and known as the Sudetenland. These districts were highly industrialized and consequently were hit by the depression harder than many of the other sections of Czechoslovakia. There was constant complaint that the government at Prague did not do enough to alleviate unemployment.

In the 1935 parliamentary elections, the first to be held since 1929, Henlein's party polled the largest popular vote of any party. It cut decidedly into the vote of the other German parties which had co-operated with the cabinet. Henlein now commanded only one seat less in parliament than the Czechoslovak Agrarians, who for years had been the backbone of all cabinet coalitions. The old governing parties compromised their differences, and a coalition headed by Milan Hodža, a Slovak, took over. Beneš had been foreign minister since the founding of the republic, and when he succeeded to the presidency on the retirement of Masaryk in December, 1935, Krofta, a well-known Czech historian, became foreign minister. Beneš, Hodža, and Krofta, then, were the three who had to face the storm that was engulfing the state.

Increasing political agitation caused the government to issue in May, 1936, a drastic "Act for the Defense of the State." Grave objections were raised against its constitutionality, for it abolished ". . . to a large extent, under wide discretionary powers of the government, constitutional guarantees and constitutional rights." [5] The Czech government took measures to suppress extremist parties, but the attempt to abolish and suppress is not always successful, especially if the agitation is supported by powerful neighbors. Henlein constantly raised his demands, and at the same time the Ruthenian, the Magyar, and some of the Slovak parties voiced their dissatisfaction with the policy of the central government.

The annexation of Austria by Germany brought the resignation of the German Agrarians and German Christian Socialists from the Hodža cabinet. Only the German Socialists continued to co-operate, and the issue between Czech and German became more clearly drawn. Finally the long German-Czech strife, which had been an issue ever since 1919, came to a head in September, 1938.

From the resulting Munich settlement, which gave the Sudetenland to Germany, and other concessions to Hungary and Poland (which will be discussed in detail in connection with the outbreak of World War II), Czechoslovakia lost 29 per cent of its territory, 34 per cent of its population, and most of its strategic defenses in the West [see map, p. 530]. Yet to some the future of Czechoslovakia did not seem utterly hopeless. Hitler always said he wanted only Germans in his Reich and there were people who still believed him. On October 4, 1938, the British government announced that the Franco-British guarantee of the new frontiers of Czechoslovakia was in effect. A British loan was granted to the Czechoslovakian government.

Beneš resigned the presidency on October 5, 1938, and was succeeded by Emil Hacha. His cabinet made a real effort to satisfy the minorities. Slovakia and Sub-Carpathian Ruthenia were given autonomy, with their own ministers—except for foreign policy, defense, and national finances. Even the spelling of the name was changed from Czechoslovakia to Czecho-Slovakia.

Hitler continued to make demands. There still remained 400,000 Germans to be "protected," and by a treaty they were accorded the privilege of becoming German citizens although remaining in Czecho-Slovakia.

[5] Karl Loewenstein: "Militant Democracy and Fundamental Rights, II," *American Political Science Review* (1937) 31:643.

This meant they would be under the protection of German law. Germany also obtained (November 30, 1938) the right to build an extraterritorial German highway across Moravia to Vienna and a canal connecting the Oder and Danube rivers.

At Bratislava, the capital of Slovakia, Mgr. Tiso began to develop his own governmental system. Both his cabinet and the one in Sub-Carpathian Ruthenia threatened to become too friendly to the Germans. As a consequence, in early March 1939 President Hacha dismissed both cabinets. Martial law was proclaimed in Bratislava. Appeals were at once made to Hitler by both of the ousted governments. Under pressure from Hitler, President Hacha reconvened the Slovak parliament, which, after three negative polls, on March 14, 1939, finally voted for the complete independence of Slovakia. Sub-Carpathian Ruthenia was now isolated and there was little for Premier Volosin to do but proclaim its independence. As a state it lasted twenty-four hours, for Hungary immediately sent in troops and proclaimed its reunion with the other lands of the Crown of Saint Stephen. Hungary also obtained a small portion of Slovakia at this time.

Tiso asked Hitler to take the new state under his protection. This was arranged by treaty, and Germany was even given the privilege of stationing troops in the country. Tiso drew up a new Slovak constitution, providing for a Christian National Republic, which was to be a single-party state organized on corporative lines. Power was concentrated in the hands of a president elected by parliament, and Tiso took over this office. Slovakia was under German dominance and its independence might well be considered a fiction, but the lot of the Slovaks during the next years was not as hard as that of the Czechs.

On the day that Slovakia was voting its independence, President Hacha went to Berlin for an interview. Here the Czech president was coerced in the early morning hours of March 15, 1939, into signing a document creating the "Protectorate of Bohemia and Moravia." Even before the document was signed, German troops were on the march to occupy the Protectorate, which was formally proclaimed on the next day. Although President Hacha continued to hold office and the fiction of a separate Czech government was maintained, Hitler appointed a "Protector," and power and control swiftly passed completely into the hands of the Nazis. After the outbreak of war ex-President Beneš established a Czechoslovakian government-in-exile that was recognized in July, 1940, by Britain and subsequently by other Western powers.

HUNGARY. After the defeat of the Communist regime under Bela Kun, Admiral Horthy, a member of the lesser gentry, became regent, but the old aristocracy dominated the government. For ten years (1921–31) Count Stephen Bethlen acted as premier and directed Hungarian affairs. He ended the policy of land distribution and in other ways preserved the privileges of the old feudal aristocracy. One of his first acts was to issue a decree changing the suffrage system by reintroducing public voting in the rural districts. Only the towns retained the secret ballot. Although the facade of democratic government remained, the heart and soul was taken out of it, for the government could always swing the periodic elections. In foreign policy Bethlen was an ardent revisionist, and in 1927 he was able to break through the encirclement of the Little Entente by concluding a treaty of friendship with Italy. Lord Rothermere, the English newspaper magnate, became a warm supporter of Bethlen's policy of treaty revision.

The economic crisis, however, proved too much for Bethlen's control. He won the 1931 elections, to be sure, but in the cities where there was a secret ballot the vote went against him. The opposition concentrated on his rather shaky financial policy, and when the depression closed the Hungarian banks, he had to resign. He turned the government over to an aged aristocrat, Count Gyula Károlyi, whose recognized personal integrity carried him through a year of perilous government. His cabinet marked the end of the control of the old aristocrats and the advent to power of the lesser landed gentry and middle class. It also brought into greater prominence the "Arrow Cross," the Magyar Fascist party.

Under General Julius Gömbös (premier 1932–36), a man of reactionary and anti-Semitic views, Hungary took on many of the trappings and techniques associated with fascist states. Gömbös had distinct dictatorial leanings, but was never strong or skillful enough to overthrow the well-established system of government. The nature of Hungary's electoral system, however, is indicated by the 1935 parliamentary elections. Whereas the opposition groups won 1,041,000 votes to the government parties' 908,000, they obtained only 51 seats to 166 seats for the government. Gömbös was an ardent revisionist and successfully enlisted Italian aid. The Rome Protocols of 1934, signed by Austria, Hungary, and Italy, marked a new era [see below, pp. 368; 428]. Hungary was slowly breaking through the encirclement of the Little Entente.

Kálmán de Darányi (1936–38), who succeeded Gömbös, followed much the same policy. In 1938 a sweeping anti-Jewish law was passed inaugurating a *numerus clausus* of 20 per cent (reduced to 6 per cent later) for Jewish employment in business and the professions. Any Jews baptized before August, 1919, and any who had fought in the war were not affected by this legislation. A United National Socialist party ("Hungarists") was formed in August, 1938, by the union of Count Ferenc Szálasi's National Will party with the Arrow Cross group.

Bela Imredy, who followed Darányi, instead of merely making promises actually introduced a measure calling for gradual redistribution of land. He also tightened the anti-Semitic legislation. This, however, was not enough to save him when the opponents of land reform discovered that one of his grandfathers was a Jew who, it was true, had been baptized before the age of seven. Even by the letter of the law, Imredy was no Jew, but he had to resign. Count Paul Teleki, a distinguished professor of geography and a friend of Count Bethlen, now became premier (February, 1939). He dissolved various fascist parties, on the grounds of terrorist activities and plots to establish a dictatorship, but he did not change fundamentally the policy of the state, and the anti-Semitic legislation remained. He co-operated with Hitler in the dismemberment of Czechoslovakia, and in 1940 was instrumental in getting the Axis to force Rumania to cede the northern part of Transylvania. He nevertheless realized the danger of becoming a mere instrument of Nazi Germany, and negotiated a pact of friendship between Hungary and Yugoslavia on December 12, 1940. When he was unable to prevent the Hungarian cabinet from joining in the German attack on Yugoslavia in April, 1941, he committed suicide. It is said he preferred death to breaking his pledge of friendship. He also no doubt was opposed to turning Hungary over in this fashion to the Nazis, yet it was the logical result of the collaboration between Berlin and Budapest.

Yugoslavia. The Serbians always intended that the new Serb-Croat-Slovene State, as it was then called, should be governmentally an expansion of old Serbia. In their eyes Serbia was to play the same role as Piedmont had played in the unification of Italy. Serbia had been an independent state and the dynasty was Serbian in origin. Serbians dominated the foreign service, the central government departments, and the higher posts in the army. The Croats and Slovenes had a different concept, for they expected that the new state would allow them a great deal of local autonomy. The Croats and Slovenes resented the Serbian officials and troops sent into their midst while their own sons had to do army service in Macedonia. A disproportionate share of taxes seemed to be collected in Slovenia and Croatia, but the money was spent to repair war devastation in Serbia, to erect imposing government buildings in Belgrade, or to develop the backward regions of Macedonia. Under all the real and petty grievances lay the feeling of the Slovenes and Croats that they were culturally superior to the Serbians.

Stephen Radić had been the only Croat leader to oppose the union of Croatia and Serbia when the question was put in the Yugoslav National Council in November, 1918, and it was he who led the Croatian opposition in the parliament at Belgrade and constantly fought the centralizing tendencies of the government. His Peasant party was outlawed (1924) but was rehabilitated when Radić was lured into accepting a cabinet post, which he soon resigned (1926). There can be no question about Radić's devotion to the cause of the peasantry. He was an agrarian like Stambolisky in Bulgaria and supported the latter's policy of South Slav co-operation on the basis of a genuine Peasant party collaboration. In June, 1928, Radić opposed the ratification of a Yugoslav-Italian agreement because he felt it sacrificed Croatian interests. While speaking in parliament he and two of his followers were shot by a Montenegrin deputy. All Croatian members immediately seceded from parliament and threatened to set up shop in Zagreb. Feeling ran high in Croatia, where Vladko Maček took over the leadership of the Croatian Peasant party. When King Alexander called him in for consultations, he demanded the federalization of Yugoslavia into five units (Slovenia, Croatia, Vojvodina, Serbia, and Montenegro), each having its own local army. These conditions Alexander would not accept, and—since parliamentary government without Croatian participation was impossible—on January 6, 1929, he undertook to rule by royal decree.

The royal dictatorship was carried on with the aid of cabinet officials who continued to enjoy the old democratic title, but that was as far as democracy went. Rigorous censorship was introduced, all political discussion ended, and political parties dissolved. The vexed question of federalism Alexander sought to solve by officially changing the name from "Serb-Croat-Slovene State" to the customary one of Yugoslavia. Nine new provinces (*Banovinas*), presided over by a governor named by the king, were to replace the old provinces. General Peter Živković, a Serb, was Alexander's strong man, and Maček, the new leader of the Croats, was imprisoned. The peace and quiet of a police-ridden country descended upon the people.

After two years Alexander announced the end of the dictatorship and proclaimed a new constitution. Electoral procedure was regulated so that the governing parties were always sure of a victory, but in spite of all the official fixing, opposition parties were able to maintain a precarious existence. The façade of a parliamentary government was maintained. Between 1931 and 1935 Yugoslavia had five premiers; after them came Milan Stojadinović, who remained in office for four years. In spite of official corruption the Croatian party was so successful in the December, 1938, elections that Stojadinović was forced to give way to Dragiša Cvetković.

The establishment of the dictatorship in Yugoslavia gave concern to French statesmen, and the return to democratic forms with the 1931 constitution, even if it brought no real democracy, was definitely approved at Paris. In 1933–34 Alexander accepted an invitation from French foreign minister Barthou to make a state visit to France. It was this visit which was so abruptly terminated by the assassination of both Barthou and King Alexander in Marseilles on October 9, 1934. The assassin was a Macedonian working in connection with a Croatian revolutionary society. This organization had its headquarters in Hungary, and some of the leaders had excellent protection from Italy. Recriminations were exchanged between Yugoslavia and Hungary and there was even talk of war. However, a settlement was finally arranged through the good offices of the League. Since Alexander's son, Peter II, was not of age, a three-man regency was appointed. A cousin of the dead king, Prince Paul, became chief regent and in the next years exercised important influence on Yugoslav affairs.

All through the thirties Yugoslavia was disturbed by antagonism between Croats, Slovenes, and Serbians. Maček, the Croatian peasant leader, was in and out of prison. The Yugoslav government negotiated a concordat with the Papacy in 1935 which aroused the ire of the Orthodox Serbians. Orthodox clergy organized protest demonstrations and threatened to excommunicate every member of parliament who voted for ratification of the treaty. The controlled parliament did ratify the agreement (1937), only to have the government announce later that it would not be put into effect. Finally, in an effort to end the civil conflict, the government entered into serious negotiations with the Croatian leaders. There can be no doubt that events in Czechoslovakia and Poland helped to induce the Serbians to make concessions. On August 26, 1939, the restoration of a democratic government in Yugoslavia was announced. Henceforth the state was to be organized on a federal basis and the Croatians were to have full autonomy in cultural and economic matters. Free elections with a secret ballot and free political parties were restored. Maček and five other Croatians immediately entered the cabinet at Belgrade. As war broke out in Europe, Yugoslavia was closer to internal political peace than it had been since the first years of its foundation.

RUMANIA. At the Peace Conference Rumania benefited from the panic over bolshevism. The successful expedition against Bela Kun in Hungary netted her more Austro-Hungarian territory than had been promised by the secret treaty of 1916. In addition, she acquired from Russia the province of Bessarabia, which, however, brought with it the lasting antagonism of the USSR. King Ferdinand and his more famous Queen Marie occupied the throne until 1927. Affairs were actually directed by Ion Bratianu, the son of the great Liberal party leader of the same name, and later by Iuliu Maniu, leader of the Peasant party in Transylvania. A man of integrity, schooled in political opposition in the old Hungary, Maniu soon exercised great power over the Peasant parties of Rumania. From 1928 to 1930 he was premier, and his administration marked the peak of good government and civil rights in Rumania. However, the economic depression soon began to plague the government; prices for agricultural products dropped; business interests clamored for relief. The people all objected to the taxes which were necessary to implement the government's program of social reform. In order to circumvent political opposition, Maniu decided on a bold stroke—a change of kings. Prince Carol, who had been married to Princess Helen of Greece, had renounced his rights to the throne in 1925 and gone off to live in exile with his red-headed mistress Magda Lupescu. On the death of King Ferdinand in 1927, Prince Carol's son, a boy of six, ascended the throne as Michael I, making a regency necessary. In 1930 Maniu agreed to Carol's return on condition that he end his affair with Mme. Lupescu and effect a reconciliation with Queen Helen, whom he had divorced in 1928. Such a restoration would not only be popular among wide sections of the Rumanian populace, but seemed to bring advantages in foreign relations. Once on the throne Carol II refused to keep his promise. Mme. Lupescu was esconced at Bucharest and soon was the center of a court camarilla. In gay Bucharest, Maniu did not get far with his so-called bourgeois morality, and when he insisted that Lupescu had to go he was promptly relieved of his office.

Carol had returned with visions of being the Mussolini of Rumania but with this difference: in Rumania the king was to be boss while the premier was to be the tool. He began to lay the foundation of his royal dictatorship, and one cabinet crisis followed another. For a time, Professor Iorga, Rumania's most distinguished historian and a man of worldwide reputation, was induced to act as premier. Carol carefully maintained a semblance of democracy, and a sort of cabinet dictatorship ensued. Cabinets were constantly changing, and general elections were held periodically. It was in this period of political instability and economic crisis that Codreanu built up his fascist organization, the "Iron Guard," which was militantly anti-Semitic and highly nationalistic. Its members could be paid to break up political meetings or strikes with equal ease. At least in the early years, the King even subsidized the Iron Guard.

When, much to the surprise of everyone, the government parties suffered a resounding defeat in the December, 1937, elections, King Carol turned to Octavian Goga, whose National Christian party had received only 10 per cent of the vote. Even before parliament had a chance to meet, the King dissolved it and ordered new elections for March, 1938. Goga meanwhile enacted by decree a whole series of stringent anti-Semitic laws. Jews were forbidden to own land and were barred from professions, and all those who had been naturalized since 1920 were deprived of their citizenship. Since practically no Jews were citizens of Rumania before that date, this meant that about 5 per cent of the total population were now classed as non-citizens. This rabid anti-Semitism led to protests from England and France based on Rumania's minority obligations under the League. Goga also sent his armed party guards into all sections of Rumania. Martial law was proclaimed and a strict censorship of the press instituted. There was well-grounded fear that Goga was preparing to establish an out-and-out fascist dictatorship.

In a very few months Goga had thoroughly discredited himself. His anti-Semitic program was too extreme even for most Rumanians. The business world was thrown into turmoil and a general economic crisis threatened. King Carol seized this opportunity to appear as the saviour of the state from fascism. The constitution was suspended and all political parties suppressed. A hurriedly arranged plebiscite gave overwhelming approval to the new constitution Carol announced. The cabinet was to be responsible to the king; a bicameral parliament was retained, the senate being made up largely of appointive members and the lower chamber elected proportionately from various professional groups. Carol had now legally secured all power in his own hands.

As the heralded bulwark against fascism, the King took steps to rid the country of the Iron Guard, the most virulent pro-Nazi group. Many members were arrested and Codreanu, the leader, was first imprisoned, then shot "while trying to escape." Carol did introduce some important reforms and the anti-Semitic measures were relaxed. In a wise and far-reaching new nationalities statute, all minorities were given an equal right with Rumanians without distinction as to race, language, or religion. To help implement this policy Rumania was divided into ten new provinces, an arrangement that broke up some of the old racial groupings. Carol was not able to stamp out all fascist elements, not even the Iron Guard, although it was officially dissolved. The King, however, remained definitely outside of the Axis camp and he was rewarded by receiving a guarantee of

Rumanian independence from Great Britain and France on April 13, 1939. Unfortunately, by his dictatorial methods he had alienated not only the fascists but many of the old Liberal and Peasant party leaders. He sat on a shaky throne, and, when the fortunes of war brought German ascendancy in Southeastern Europe, he was forced to flee the country, leaving the throne to his son Michael, who on September 6, 1940, again became King of Rumania.

BULGARIA. The last days of the war brought the abdication of Ferdinand and the accession of Boris III to the Bulgarian throne. In the parliamentary elections of August, 1919, an overwhelming victory was won by the Agrarian party, led by Alexander Stambolisky. A member of Parliament since 1908, the latter had been an opponent of King Ferdinand's war policy and in 1915 was imprisoned. Now, as premier of Bulgaria, he undertook to rule the state in the interest of the peasants, who constituted about 80 per cent of the population.

Stambolisky took revenge on the cabinet officials who had led Bulgaria into the war; trials were held, and the men convicted and imprisoned. Crown lands and estates of over seventy-five acres were broken up, while a heavy income tax was levied on all except the peasants. Freedom of the press was curtailed, and instruction at the University of Sofia restricted. Stambolisky had the unpleasant task of signing the Treaty of Neuilly. His foreign policy was on the whole conciliatory and sensible; he developed a plan for co-operation among the Eastern European countries based on a common rule by Agrarian parties. This so-called "Green International" never materialized, but it was at least a constructive, forward-looking plan. His policy of conciliation with Yugoslavia roused the ire of the many Macedonians living in Bulgaria. The leaders of the Internal Macedonian Revolutionary Organization (IMRO) united with old Bulgarian nationalist leaders to overthrow Stambolisky's government by a *coup d'état* (June 9, 1923), and a few days later he was assassinated.

Bulgaria was now plunged into a period of bloody reprisals. The Communists staged an insurrection (1923) which was put down with vengeance. Alexandrov, the leader of the IMRO, was killed (1924), whereupon this organization was split into two factions. The factions fought each other, at the same time carrying on raids in Greek and Yugoslavian Macedonia. Some 200 recorded assassinations took place in 1924. In April, 1925, one of several attempts was made on the life of King Boris. Later in the same month most of the government officials were in attendance at the funeral of an assassinated general, when a bomb was set off by a dissident Communist group; it badly damaged the Sofia Cathedral, killed 123 persons, and wounded 323. The government immediately outlawed the entire Communist party.

Clearly, politics was not only a serious but a dangerous business in Bulgaria. Back of much of the strife lay the fact that Macedonia had been divided between Greece and Yugoslavia. The exchange of nationalities between Greece and Bulgaria brought many Macedonians to reside in Bul-

garia. Landless and embittered, they were easily won over to violent political methods. The Macedonians agitated supposedly for the creation of an
independent Macedonian state, but as a practical objective most of them
favored annexation of Macedonia to Bulgaria. The Bulgarian government
at times encouraged them and furthered their policies. It is true that the
IMRO was so strong in Bulgaria and its cause so popular that it was difficult for the Bulgarian government to take action against it. The IMRO
was in large part responsible for the tense relations that existed between
Bulgaria and its neighbors Yugoslavia and Greece during the twenties. An
armed boundary clash between Bulgaria and Greece in 1925 was settled
through the mediation of the League of Nations [see above, p. 398].

In 1930 King Boris married Princess Giovanna, daughter of the King
of Italy. The marriage alliance brought a closer connection with Italy,
which began to champion Bulgarian claims. Both countries had their difficulties with Yugoslavia and Greece, and this was a friendship based on
mutual antagonisms.

The formation of the Balkan Conference in 1930 laid the basis for
greater inter-Balkan co-operation. In 1933 there was an exchange of visits
among the sovereigns of Bulgaria, Yugoslavia, and Rumania. It was clear
that if Bulgaria was not to be entirely isolated, an end would have to be
made of the IMRO agitation. On May 19, 1934, a *coup d'état* established
what amounted to a military dictatorship, with Kimon Georgiev as premier. Parliament was dismissed, censorship was imposed upon the press,
and the political parties were dissolved. Drastic measures were taken
against the IMRO and its power was broken. Within a year, King Boris
was able to ease the military men out of control and to entrust civilians
with the direction of affairs. From that point on King Boris dominated
affairs, and after April, 1935, Bulgaria, like the other Balkan states, could
be classed as a royal dictatorship.

King Boris was in many respects an able politician. He balanced one
group against the other and kept the ship of state on a relatively even keel.
Adroitly he shifted from one premier to another and managed to include in
each cabinet men who represented various political views. In 1936 he dissolved the Military League and also clipped the wings of a so-called National and Social Movement.

In 1937, in answer to a petition presented by some of the old political
leaders, Boris promised a return to constitutionalism. A new electoral law
was issued, which granted suffrage to all men over twenty-one and to all
married women and widows. Elections were to be on a nonpartisan basis,
and candidates were expressly forbidden to run as representatives of the old
political parties. In spite of these restrictions and a good deal of coercion
on the part of those in power, about one third of the 160 members of parliament could definitely be classed as belonging to the opposition. This
parliament was actually only a consultative body, but it did provide a
tribune for members of the opposition to air their views and they were not
prevented from doing so. It cannot be compared to the submissive Reich-

stags that Hitler produced. On the other hand, the restrictions on the formation of political parties prevented any real restoration of democratic government.

In foreign affairs Boris had to steer a difficult course. The Communist party, along with all other political parties, was outlawed, but he resumed diplomatic relations with Russia in 1934. Better feeling developed towards Yugoslavia, but Bulgaria never went so far as to accept her curtailed frontiers, and the demand for revision was kept alive. Trade relations with Germany grew, until in 1938 Greater Germany took 59 per cent of Bulgarian exports and furnished 52 per cent of her imports. Nevertheless, it was an Anglo-French loan of $10,000,000 which provided the money for the now-permitted rearmament program. At the outbreak of hostilities in 1939 Bulgaria was not ranged on either side, and it was Russian demands for bases and, on the other hand, German successes, which eventually gave Boris no alternative but to join the Axis in March 1941.

ALBANIA. As Turkish power weakened in the nineteenth century, neighboring Serbians, Greeks, and Bulgarians began to cast longing eyes at Albanian-inhabited provinces. Albanian revolts and demands for autonomy plagued the Turkish rulers in the years before the Balkan Wars of 1912–13. On November 28, 1912, when it was already clear that there would be a general territorial reorganization in the Balkans, Albanian independence was proclaimed. Austria-Hungary and Italy wanted to prevent Serbian expansion to the sea, and it was primarily due to their efforts that the other great powers were induced to recognize the new Albanian state. In tortuous negotiations centering in an ambassadorial conference in London, the boundaries of Albania were agreed upon. The powers also supervised the establishment of an international *gendarmerie* and an Albanian government.

Prince William of Wied was elected as the ruler of the new state. He landed at Durazzo on March 7, 1914, but from the outset his rule was beset with insurmountable difficulties. There was little internal unity and Greece, Montenegro, and Serbia constantly caused border difficulties. Austria-Hungary and Italy, who were largely responsible for the establishment of Albania, were so jealous of each other that neither was able to lend strong support to the Prince of Wied. He left the country on September 3, 1914, the first European prince to lose his throne as the result of the World War.

The fortunes of war led to the occupation of large portions of the country by various armed forces. The Albanians, alarmed over this partition of their country, drew together. A National Assembly met December 25, 1918, and a government under a regency was set up at Tirana. The Italian occupation forces soon lost all stomach for fighting and were not supported by the strife-torn Italian government. In August, 1920, Italy withdrew from Albania. On December 17, 1920, Albania slipped into the League of Nations and thereby was assured international protection. Yugoslavia and Greece continued to make difficulties along the northern and southern frontiers, but the great powers working under the League were able to re-establish Albania within the boundaries of 1913. Only a few very minor boundary rectifications were made in favor of Yugoslavia. The final act fixing the borders of Albania was signed by the powers in 1926.

Albania was unique among all the states of postwar Europe, and different standards must be used in judging its progress. In many ways Albania was the most backward and primitive state of Europe. By way of contrast, the return from America of many Albanian immigrants, who proceeded to build modern homes, brought new standards and new ways of life. Political democracy in Albania had no substance, and it is not surprising that Albania was one of the first of the states to succumb to the general pattern of dictatorship which spread over Eastern Europe. Ahmed Bey Zogu, a member of one of the most important Moslem clans, became the strong man of the government. Although exiled for a time, he was able, with Yugoslav support, to return in 1924, and in 1928 he had himself proclaimed King Zog I.

At first Zog turned to Italy for aid, and a pact of friendship was negotiated in 1926, followed by a 20-year treaty of alliance in 1927. Italian loans increased and Italian experts supervised a rather extensive internal-improvement program, including the development of an oil field and a 45-mile pipeline to Valona. Italian officers organized and trained the army; in short, Albania came under Italian protection.

By 1932 Zog began to try to shake off Italian control. In that year a customs union was rejected and a year later he closed Italian schools in Albania. In 1934 he attempted to check Italian immigration and lessen Italian influence in the Albanian army. This was going too far for Mussolini, and when the Italian fleet appeared at Durazzo, King Zog took the hint. Nevertheless, Italy did show herself more accommodating in the trade and financial agreements negotiated in the following years.

Zog attempted to modernize his country and there was some material progress. Roads were built and modern buildings began to appear in various cities. The freedom-loving Albanians did not all take kindly to his dictatorial rule nor to his reforms. In May, 1937, he had a serious insurrection on his hands when some of his Moslem subjects objected to a decree forbidding the veiling of women. But this too was put down like many previous uprisings.

Shortly after Hitler took over Prague, Mussolini decided to end Albanian independence. On April 7, 1939, troops were landed at Durazzo, where more than a token resistance could scarcely be made. King Zog, his wife, and their two-day-old son fled over the difficult overland route from Tirana to Greece. Five days later a hastily convoked Albanian Constituent Assembly offered the Albanian crown to King Victor Emmanuel III of Italy, who only recently had extended his list of titles by becoming Emperor of Ethiopia. A new constitution subsequently vested all legislative and executive power in the King's hands. Italy took over control of foreign affairs, and Albania lost its status as a sovereign state in the family of nations. A separate administrative system remained, and Albania had its own legal code, church organization, and schools.

SUMMARY. The Danubian states did not start out by denouncing democratic and liberal values. They retained in most cases the old forms of government. In the kingdoms the king or regent shifted power from one man to another, and cabinets were regularly made and unmade. Nowhere did a dictator-premier arise to compare to either Mussolini or Hitler. But freely elected parliaments that determined the policy of the state vanished. The more or less old-fashioned dictatorships in the Danubian states adhered to no particular ideology. Dollfuss in Austria with his "Christian Corporative State" was, perhaps, the exception, for his plans were based on certain papal encyclicals. Some fascist ideas, of course, crept into the various regimes as Italian fascism and German national socialism gained in stature. Above all, various techniques were copied—such as armed political party groups, elaborate secret-police systems, and censorship. Yet many of these were not new devices, and the Danubian peoples were accustomed to them from previous regimes.

Conditions resulting directly from the war, minority strife, and the economic depression were important factors in bringing about these governmental changes. The various plans that were devised to combat the depression all seemed to concentrate power in the hands of the few. Currency regulation, allotment of quotas, and other trade controls all gave the executive a tremendous hold over the entire nation, for parliaments, with their numerous parties, were hardly the best instruments to make decisions on complicated economic agreements.

Postdepression Economic Problems

The great drop in world agricultural prices which began in 1929 disrupted the economy of all the Danubian states. Germany and Austria, which had been heavy importers of agricultural products, and Czechoslovakia, which imported a lesser amount, raised their tariff rates as a means of bringing relief to their own farmers. The price of wheat in Berlin, Prague, and Vienna rose to twice what it was in Budapest or Belgrade. The agricultural exporting states retaliated by raising their tariffs on industrial imports. The result was that industrial prices were well above world levels in all these states. The total volume of foreign trade declined, poverty increased, and the standard of living sank. The peasant in Eastern Europe was faced with destitution, for he received a low price for his produce and had to pay a high price for the few articles he was able to buy.

Something could have been done to alleviate the problem by building up purchasing power within the state, although this was only a partial solution and a very difficult one to accomplish. The basic problem was how to sell food, which many were starving for in the industrial states, at prices which would assure a livelihood to the peasants of the rural states. This objective obviously required the expansion of foreign trade. Statesmen in every country sought to bring this about, and attempts were also made to work out a solution through international action or by the negotiation of regional pacts. In the end, however, each state, seeking its own advantage, went its own way, which only led to more national and imperialistic rivalries.

INTERNATIONAL ACTION. In 1930 Poland organized an agrarian bloc consisting of Poland, Estonia, Latvia, Czechoslovakia, Rumania, Yugoslavia, Bulgaria, and Hungary. At a series of conferences it was decided to ask the Western powers to grant these countries preferential tariff treatment on agricultural products. "Most-favored-nation" clauses and preferential tariffs in the British Commonwealth of Nations were obstacles to such a scheme. Nevertheless the granting of preferential tariffs to help the export of agricultural products remained a cardinal point in all plans for bringing relief to the Danubian states. In the spring of 1932 Premier Tardieu of France proposed a Danubian Federation, which was to be knit together by preferential reciprocal tariffs between Austria, Czechoslovakia, Hungary, Rumania, and Yugoslavia. It was a limited and concrete plan that really amounted to the beginning of a Danubian customs union. Not even all of the five small powers favored the proposal, and it never had the support of Germany, Italy, or Britain. It was generally considered a French-Little Entente device for controlling the Danubian basin. Discussion continued at a conference of the great powers at Stresa in 1932 and at the ill-fated London Economic Conference in 1933. No definite results were obtained, and the Danubian states were left to work out their own foreign trade problems as best they could. In fact, by that time a whole complicated bilateral trading system had already come into existence in Southeastern Europe.

CURRENCY REGULATION, QUOTAS, CLEARING AGREEMENTS. When the Vienna *Kreditanstalt* went bankrupt in May, 1931, it set off a chain reaction in the whole Danubian basin. Everywhere short-term and medium-term loans were called. Foreign exchange vanished. To prevent the sudden devaluation of the external value of the national currency and to assure a certain degree of monetary stability, the Danubian states all introduced foreign exchange control between August, 1931, and February, 1932.

The methods and devices for currency control varied in each state, but all required governmental permission before payments could be made abroad. Blocked accounts rapidly accumulated to meet the payment of recent imports. Since Germany had an export surplus to Austria, Czechoslovakia, Hungary, and Yugoslavia, she was one of the first to feel these new trade restrictions. Special German agencies were established to make purchases in these states so as to liquidate these blocked accounts. Later, with the advent of Hitler, the tables were turned and the Danubian states became the ones who held large blocked accounts in Berlin banks. Soon differing exchange rates for the same currency developed in most of the Danubian lands. Governments having to buy certain products, or anxious to throw trade to certain states, subsidized exports. Hungary became perhaps the most famous of all for its varying pengö rates. This was long be-

fore the German mark had achieved its many values under Hjalmar
Schacht's astute manipulation.

Currency regulation leads to a quantitative restriction of trade, for the
allotment of exchange indirectly leads to the establishment of quotas, and
it is but a short and inevitable step for the government to establish quotas
directly by law. The administration of the quota system in turn gives the
government a further means of controlling the economic life of the state.
It also provides an effective bargaining weapon in conducting foreign trade
discussions.

Currency regulation and establishment of quotas, instead of increasing
the volume of foreign trade, tended to decrease it. The problem of how to
pay for goods remained. In 1931 a conference of the Central Banks convened in Prague. Here the president of the Austrian National Bank proposed the introduction of clearing agreements. Instead of following the old
direct method of payment between exporter and importer by transmitting
foreign exchange, cumulative accounts were to be established in the central
bank of each state. An importer would then pay for his goods by depositing
money in the central bank of his country, and the exporter would be paid
by the bank of his own country. The scheme seemed to offer many advantages, for it did away with the necessity for foreign exchange. Payment
would become a bookkeeping matter involving transfer of funds within a
given country to different accounts. In the end, of course, the sum total of
exports and imports would have to be equal if the accounts were to
balance.

Clearing agreements altered old established international trade methods. They encouraged the conclusion of bilateral trade agreements and
eventually became an important means of expanding Germany's trade to
the east. They came into existence before Hitler was in power, at a time
when gold and foreign exchange had disappeared from the economy of the
Danubian states. It was a method which enabled these states to carry on
foreign trade among themselves, and did not preclude them from trading
with other countries. Austria, Czechoslovakia, Hungary, Yugoslavia, Rumania, Bulgaria, Greece, Turkey, Germany, Italy, Spain, Latvia, and Estonia all entered into such clearing agreements. The rest of the European
states managed to get along without them although many adopted exchange control.

REGIONAL ECONOMIC AGREEMENTS. The proposed German-Austrian
Customs Union of 1931 had been knifed by France, and Germany in turn
had done her bit to help destroy the Tardieu Danubian Federation in
1932. Yet efforts to conclude such regional pacts continued. A series of
Balkan Conferences carried on between 1930 and 1933 by Yugoslavia, Rumania, Albania, Bulgaria, Greece, and Turkey, aimed toward more economic co-operation, bore little fruit. In February, 1933, immediately after
Hitler's assumption of power, the Little Entente concluded a Pact of Reorganization. The states that constituted this group were to have a permanent Council of Foreign Ministers with a Secretariat, and an Economic

Council was created for the purpose of co-ordinating more closely the economy of the three states. Unfortunately the hoped-for results were not achieved, for the trade of the three states was in most cases similar and not complementary. Czechoslovakia had considerable trade with both Rumania and Yugoslavia, but Rumania and Yugoslavia exchanged very little and even Czechoslovakia was unable to take many agricultural products. The Little Entente statesmen expressed the pious hope that the other Danubian states would join their pact, but they consistently refused to make any political concessions that might have acted as an inducement. In justice, however, it should be added that Bulgaria and Hungary, for their part, made no pretense of abating their territorial claims, for the sake of friendly relations with the Entente.

Mussolini also set about at this time to lay an economic basis for more influence in Central Europe. In 1931 Austria and Hungary under the so-called Brocchi agreements had arranged for *de facto* preferential treatment on certain commodities, notably wheat and flour; in 1932 this arrangement was extended to Italy. These agreements were designed to avoid formal conflict with most-favored-nation clauses by granting concealed tariff preference under the guise of export credits and preferential freight rates. On March 17, 1934, the Rome Protocols were signed, preparatory to an expansion of trade between Austria, Hungary, and Italy. Austria and Italy, both food-importing countries, were in a position to take Hungarian wheat. Trade did increase somewhat between the three states in the next years, partly because Austria and Hungary did not apply sanctions against Italy during the Ethiopian campaign [see below, pp. 495–97]. The significance of the Rome agreements ended when Italy in 1937 granted to Yugoslavia equal preferential treatment on timber and cattle.

In the fall of 1934 Germany launched a new trade plan to connect Central and Southeastern Europe into one great regional economic unit under German dominance. Basically the plan called for Germany to supply manufactured goods and for the other states to furnish food and raw materials. The plan of *Grossraumwirtschaft* (Large Territorial Economy), as it developed, had important political and strategic considerations behind it. In case of a future war Germany was to be able to supply her own needs or obtain them from states not subject to blockade. These would supply them voluntarily, but if need be they could be easily overrun.

Germany now began to negotiate bilateral agreements with all the Danubian states to take their agricultural exports at higher prices than the level of the world market. This served to bolster domestic prices. For example, Germany's agreement to purchase wheat came just in time to save the Yugoslavian wheat-subsidy program from total collapse. Payments were arranged through clearing agreements, for the Danubian states were as short of foreign exchange as were the Germans. Soon the Danubian states began to accumulate large blocked accounts in Berlin banks. This was only partly due to the inability of Germany to deliver goods. The accounts rose with the seasonal sale of agricultural products, and many of the products Germany was called upon to deliver in return were articles of heavy industry which in the normal course of manufacture are not turned out overnight. When the balances in Berlin got too high, the Balkan states cut exports. Yugoslavia, for example, refused to sell copper to Germany against marks, and Rumania required that at least 75 per cent of the payment for her oil exports had to be in free foreign exchange.

The Danubian states benefited materially by the increase in German trade. Germany paid high prices and in return on the whole charged competitive prices for the goods she sold. In many cases, in fact, they were well below the high industrial prices normally prevailing in these countries. Nor did her exports consist only of cameras, mouth organs, and tooth paste. She had to supply the items desired by these states, unfortunately often armaments. Sometimes the quality was not up to standard and deliveries were delayed. Germany also entered into contracts to purchase all available soy beans, rape seed, and sunflowers, all three oil-producing crops. This is often cited as a German attempt to control and plan minutely the economy of Rumania or Bulgaria. Yet this shift to soy beans was going on at an even more rapid rate on the farms of the United States. The farmer in both Rumania and Iowa discovered that he could make more money by growing soy beans than by growing wheat.

The small states had been experimenting with exchange control, quotas, and other regulatory measures from "the days before Hitler," and as yet were not at his mercy. They were shrewd and hard bargainers, but in the end Germany, as the more powerful, was bound to gain the advantage. The small states were at a disadvantage, having to sell agricultural products in a market so glutted that farmers in the United States were plowing under crops. Germany was willing to buy these products and in turn had the manufactured goods to sell which the peoples of the Danubian states wanted. Trade with Hitler did not preclude these Danubian states from trading with other countries. In fact, they were able on the whole to maintain their trade with the Western states. They would have preferred to expand this trade, for it brought free foreign exchange, but the United States and France had agricultural surpluses of their own, and Britain was bound to get most of her food from the dominions. League sanctions also cut off Italian trade for a vital period (November, 1935 to July, 1936) from some of the states. The actual trade with Western states remained static, while the increase in amount of trade that came with economic recovery was captured by Hitler. With the absorption of Austria and parts of Czechoslovakia, Germany took over that trade as well, and Greater Germany definitely held first place both as to exports and imports in the trade of the remaining Danubian states.

International Relations

The successful trade drive in Southeastern Europe brought to Hitler prestige and a certain dominance in the area. The members of a farmers cooperative society in Yugoslavia or Bulgaria, which received a favorable con-

STATESMEN OF THE LITTLE ENTENTE *Stoyadinovich, Premier of Yugoslavia, with his colleagues Titulescu of Rumania and Beneš of Czechoslovakia, addressing a Little Entente conference at Bled, Yugoslavia, in August, 1935.*

tract in Germany, were not likely to be very anti-German or too concerned over what Hitler did in Austria. Then too, during the thirties all these states except Czechoslovakia were under dictatorship of one sort or another. In some there were important groups who ideologically were very sympathetic to national socialism. The failure of the Western powers either directly or through the League to check Hitler's piecemeal disintegration of the Versailles system also gave the statesmen in the small states cause to ponder. If France did not fight to stop the remilitarization of the Rhineland, would she move to prevent Hitler's march eastward?

Although Hitler slowly gained influence in the Danubian basin and sapped the blood of the old alliance groups, officially these groups remained intact. The reorganized Little Entente continued as the dominant alliance group along the Danube. By means of the Balkan Pact of 1934 two of the partners (Yugoslavia and Rumania) were pledged with Greece and Turkey to maintain the *status quo* in the Balkans. Over both groups France placed her benevolent shield and supplied military credits.

The attitude of the Danubian states toward Russia became generally less hostile, although basic antagonism remained. In 1934 both Rumania and Bulgaria finally recognized the USSR, but Yugoslavia was to delay doing this until May 11, 1940. In 1935 Czechoslovakia negotiated a mutual assistance pact with the USSR. This to a certain extent weakened the Little Entente, for neither Rumania nor Yugoslavia was ready for any such intimate ties with Russia.

Yugoslavia, meanwhile, struck out on new foreign-policy paths in the thirties, making treaties with Bulgaria (where the Macedonian Revolutionary Organization had been suppressed) in January, 1937, and with Italy in March of the same year. Her boundaries had thus been secured by a series of agreements, including the pledges of Rumania and Greece in the Balkan Pact, and the Little Entente guarantee of the Hungarian border, which was reinforced by a Yugoslav-Hungarian Friendship Pact of December, 1940. The only frontier that had no specific guarantee was the one with Austria, and this was the first to be changed.

Italy's abandonment of Austrian independence and the gradual development of Hitler's Austrian policy, culminating with the annexation of Austria in March, 1938, were of the greatest significance in the process of reorganizing the Danubian basin. The disappearance of Austria as an independent state changed the entire international position of the Danubian states. The events that followed in rapid succession—the seizure of the Sudetenland in 1938, the occupation of Prague in March of 1939, the establishment of an independent Slovakia under German auspices—brought an end to any possible Danubian co-operation. Hungary moved quickly to get her share of the spoils of Czechoslovakia; Yugoslavia and Rumania did not dare to act, and the Little Entente was at an end.

Now it was Britain that hastened to rescue what still might be saved. With unprecedented haste Premier Chamberlain announced in the House of Commons on March 23, 1939, an Anglo-French guarantee of aid to Poland in the event of aggression. On April 13 these same two powers guaranteed the independence of Poland's ally, Rumania, and of Greece. Five days before, Albania had gone the way of Austria and of Czechoslovakia, but this time it was Mussolini who preened his feathers. Hungary, Yugoslavia, and Bulgaria remained without formal alliance ties with the Axis, the Western powers, or Russia. They were hostages to fate.

CHAPTER

— 15 —

The New States of the Baltic Region

Republican Finland: *Economic Adjustments; Problems of Democracy; Finland and Europe.*

The Baltic States: *New Governments; Economic Reorientation; Regional Problems; The Baltic States and the European Crisis.*

Poland: *Heritage of Partition; Political Regime; Economic Reconstruction; Between Two Worlds.*

———◆———

THE COUNTRIES on the eastern shores of the Baltic Sea—Finland, the Baltic states (Estonia, Latvia, and Lithuania), and Poland—shared not only a similar geographical location but also a series of political and economic problems that were closely related in their origin and, ultimately, in their consequences as well. They faced above all the task of adjusting their political relations at home and abroad to the new Europe of the 1920's and orienting their economies away from the Russian system to which they had hitherto been adjusted and towards the trade structure of Central and Western Europe. While experiencing many common problems, these countries also differed in numerous respects. Lithuania, for instance, had no common frontier with the Soviet Union, although it shared with its neighbors the dangers of communist infiltration. Finland, Estonia, and Latvia, on the other hand, were not contiguous with Germany and avoided the acute frontier disputes that Hitler later pressed against Lithuania and Poland. Moreover, these countries always tended to be drawn into relationships with other states and groupings. Thus Finland had both common interests and traditional ties with the Scandinavian states, although these did not reach the point of formal alliance or federation. Similarly Poland was drawn by common interests towards Rumania.

Republican Finland

ECONOMIC ADJUSTMENTS. Finland emerged from World War I independent and self-confident but handicapped by memories of the recent civil war and by proximity to revolutionary Russia. Finland's foreign trade was firmly founded on its timber industry, which accounted for over three fourths of its exports. During the immediate postwar period there was a boom in wood products, which were being used increasingly for matches, paper, plywood, and cellulose, as well as for general construction. In the five years between 1922 and 1927 the export of wood products increased by over one half. This increase helped not only business, which was able to import increasing amounts of manufactured goods, but also the agricultural population, which supplemented its income with winter work in the lumber camps. The boom in timber nevertheless proved to be shortlived as immediate postwar construction tapered off. As early as 1928 manufacturers found it necessary to reduce production in order to maintain prices, and Finland underwent a small local depression before it was struck by the larger wave of European economic dislocation in 1931. Since it was forced to rely to so large an extent on a single export, Finland was more sensitive to world economic trends than most countries.

The distribution of land, unlike the export trade, was within the power of the government to handle. Four fifths of the Finnish people were rural inhabitants, although on the eve of World War I only one quarter of them owned the land on which they lived. Of the approximately half a million rural families, about one third were tenant farmers while two fifths were agricultural laborers. The violence of the civil war and the constant stream of propaganda coming from across the Russian frontier had impressed all the Finns with the urgency of agrarian reform if only as a measure of political pacification. The means by which land distribution should be achieved was nevertheless a delicate political issue. The Communists naturally favored the nationalization of the land, but this solution had no support outside of their small group. On the other side of the political spectrum, the Swedish and Concentration parties, representing the interests of the landowners, made strenuous efforts to prevent a solution by violence. It was a credit to Finnish democracy that a compromise solution to the land question was finally worked out in 1927 by the Agrarian leader Kallio with the support of the Social Democrat and Progressive parties. The agrarian law provided state financing both for small farms and for cottage sites for workers, with compensation for landowners. The larger estates were protected against expropriation, while a large new class of small landholders came into being.

As a result of the agrarian reform, some 120,000 additional families were able to purchase their own land or cottages. By the time the reform had been fully applied, one third of the families in Finland were landholders. During the first years of independence, the agricultural position of Finland was improved by a great expansion of the area cultivated and by improvement in the methods of cultivation. As a result of increased production, Finland was raising by 1934 most of the cereals required for domestic consumption. The production of dairy products was also greatly increased. In this expansion of agricultural production, government assistance played an important role, but the initiative lay with the farmers themselves.

The Finnish practice of organizing economic life with a minimum of government regulation is also illustrated by the rapid growth of the co-operative movement, which eventually enlisted as members over one half of the adult population of the country. Producer and consumer co-operatives played a dominant role in Finnish economic life, and co-operative banks provided credit for the peasant. In the agricultural field, dairy products and farm equipment in particular came within the scope of the co-operative movement, while in the cities foodstuffs and restaurants were extensively handled by the co-operatives. The co-operatives were also active in the field of popular education, conducting lecture courses on subjects of public value and editing periodicals with a wide circulation. One aspect of the co-operative movement which reflected political divisions within Finland was the split during World War I between organizations serving the rural districts and those active in the cities. The former, known as the Neutral Society, developed a more conservative political outlook adjusted to the views of the agrarian population. The urban districts, on the other hand, supported the Progressive Movement, which was particularly strong among the Social Democrats. Nevertheless, this division of the Finnish co-operative movement did not prevent the two groups from working side by side nor did it lead them to deviate from their economic function into political channels.

PROBLEMS OF DEMOCRACY. Finland established a parliamentary system based on universal suffrage, but the republic was born in a spirit of bitter civil strife, and only time and a spirit of compromise could bring the people together in full support of their political system. The most difficult problem Finnish democracy had to resolve, and one which stemmed directly from its bitter experiences of the civil war, was that of the continued existence of extreme left-wing and right-wing political movements. The Communist party had been disbanded after the civil war, but it continued to exist under other names that permitted it to evade the laws directed against it, and in 1922 it won 27 out of the 200 seats in the Diet. The close connection of the Finnish Communists with the Comintern in Moscow led to a renewed effort to dissolve the party in 1923, but in the following year it reappeared under a new name and won 18 seats in the Diet. In the elections of 1927 and 1929 its representation in the Diet rose to 20 and 23. As fanatical as the Communists, although without the powerful backing the latter possessed, were the Finnish nationalists. Representing primarily the conservative farming population, and led by the Lutheran clergy, the nationalists were sensitive to Communist activity. When the Communists inaugurated a propaganda campaign in a conservative district of western Finland in the autumn of 1929, the nationalists rose to the challenge and proposed that the Diet pass a series of anti-Communist measures including suppression of the Communist press. This latter measure failed to win a majority in the Diet, and the cabinet resigned. Relander, who had succeeded Stahlberg as president in 1925, now called on the aging conservative leader Svinhufvud to form a coalition government. The latter proceeded to put into effect a series of rigorous anti-Communist measures which succeeded effectively in crushing the Communists for the time being, although not without violating the constitution. In the face of the opposition of the Social Democrats, the legalization of these measures required a two-thirds majority in a new Diet. Elections were held in October, 1930, and the new Diet approved the anti-Communist measures by a margin of one vote. By a similar margin, the conservative Svinhufvud was elected to the presidency in the following January on a nationalist program. On this major issue involving both civil liberties and political violence, the Finns thus found themselves seriously divided.

Two other less important but at the same time controversial issues the Finns managed to solve by parliamentary methods. These were the language question and prohibition. The constitution of 1919 had provided in somewhat ambiguous terms for the use of both Finnish and Swedish in administrative matters, but the implementation of this provision led to a sharp social conflict. The small Swedish-speaking minority represented the former ruling class of the period before the rise of Finnish nationalism at the end of the nineteenth century. In the new Finland, this group felt that its language was the last vestige of its former privileged position, and it fought bitterly to preserve it. The language law passed in 1922 provided a compromise that defined as bilingual for administrative purposes any district with a language minority of over 10 per cent. Under this arrangement, out of a total of over 600 communes, 36 were identified as Swedish-speaking and 64 as bilingual, in addition to the Aaland Islands, which were entirely Swedish-speaking. The higher educational status of the Swedish-speaking minority of some 11 per cent was, moreover, recognized by the granting of school appropriations larger than its proportional share.

Another problem that tested Finnish democracy, and one that had tried the capabilities of countries far more experienced in self-government, was that of the legal prohibition of the sale of alcoholic beverages. An active prohibitionist movement had aroused Finnish opinion on the question of alcohol early in the twentieth century, although the problem was not a particularly acute one in Finland. This movement led to the adoption of a prohibition law in 1919 which had wide public support. The experience of the first decade of its operation, however, showed an increase of alcoholism and lawlessness which the government found itself unable to check despite rigorous police measures. The controversy over prohibition had also its political side, in so far as the moderate and left-wing parties favored it, whereas the conservative parties gave it no support. It was nevertheless primarily a social issue, and the repeal of prohibition in 1932 marked the recognition that the solution did not lie in legislation.

FINLAND AND EUROPE. Finland appeared on the scene in 1919 without traditions in foreign policy, and the developments of the immediate postwar era presented the Finns with a number of alternatives. A very attractive one was that of associating with the Western democracies under the leadership of France, as the Finns considered themselves close to the West in their political outlook. Other possibilities were those of co-operating with the Scandinavian states, or with the Baltic states of Estonia, Latvia, Lithuania, and Poland, whose problems were in many ways similar to those of Finland. Both of these alternatives were, nevertheless, rejected on the ground that Finnish interests could best be preserved by an independent policy, and the course of neutrality was finally chosen.

A corollary of Finnish neutrality was active participation in the work of the League of Nations, and from 1927 to 1930 Finland filled one of the elective seats on the Council of the League. Finland was one of the countries for which the League represented a means of achieving real security without identification with one or another of the European coalitions, for unlike other small countries Finland did not supplement its membership in the League with outside political agreements. For reasons beyond Finland's control, the League nevertheless failed to offer the political security it seemed to promise.

The slump in foreign trade which affected Finland in the years after 1928 had prepared it to a degree for the more serious depression which was to follow. The fall of the English pound in the autumn of 1931 nevertheless dealt a severe blow to the Finnish economy, for Britain took about one half of Finland's exports. The reduction in trade and the rise in unemployment were met by the government with a variety of makeshift measures, but only by a revival of the export trade could Finland hope to regain its prosperity. The government's export program was in a large measure accomplished in 1933 when a new trade agreement was concluded with Great Britain. The principle of reciprocal trade, which the treaty with Britain incorporated, led within a year to a marked decrease in trade with Germany. The restrictions imposed on trade by the Nazi regime were such as to give disproportionate advantages to Germany, and Finland was now able to retaliate through her increased trade with Britain. By 1937 Finland had in most aspects of its economy attained or surpassed the high level of 1928.

The accomplishments of the Finnish republic during the first two decades of its independence were generally regarded as equal or better than those of any comparable country. In spite of a rise in population from 3,250,000 to 4,000,000, it became 85 per cent self-sufficient from the point of view of agriculture. During this period the volume of industrial production more than doubled, and great advances were made in social legislation, education, and the extension of the co-operative movement. In the political field the most aggravating problem was the bitter antagonism of the Communists and the extreme nationalists. The suppression of the former in 1930 did not put an end to the activities of the latter. In 1932 an uprising was staged by the extremist Civil Guard, a holdover from the civil war period, led by the nationalist Wallenius. The swift action of the government brought an end to the uprising within a few days, although the point of view it represented was perpetuated in the right-wing Lapua movement. Yet if the political sentiments of the Finnish people were judged by the views of the majority, moderation was their chief characteristic. In the free Finnish elections, the Communists never had more than 27 seats (1922–24) in a Diet of some 200, whereas the largest number of seats won by the Lapua movement was 14 (1933–36). In the years after 1930 the Social Democrats and the Agrarians shared a steady majority in the parliament, and in 1937 the nationalist Svinhufvud was succeeded in the presidency by the Agrarian leader Kallio.

In foreign policy, the decline of the League of Nations finally led Finland to abandon its neutral position in favor of co-operation with its neighbors who shared similar interests. In 1932 it adhered to the Oslo Convention in support of closer economic relations among the Scandinavian states along with Holland and Belgium, and after 1935 this movement was extended to the field of military security and the inclusion of the Baltic states was envisaged. However, these regional arrangements remained at best halfhearted efforts to find shelter in face of the approaching storm.

The Baltic States

New Governments. Unlike Finland, the three Baltic countries started out on their careers as independent states with no political experience beyond that acquired in the independence movement after 1905. Moreover, the end of the war had been followed by serious social readjustments resulting from the overthrow of the former ruling class and extensive changes in land distribution. This political inexperience was reflected in the constitutions adopted by Estonia and Latvia in 1920 and by Lithuania in 1922, as well as by the stormy course pursued by their numerous political parties.

The constitutions of the three states, which were broadly similar in structure, represented an effort to balance the power of the elective assemblies against that of the executive organs. In all three cases unicameral legislatures based on universal suffrage were established, and representation was further extended by provisions for initiative and referendum. Civil liberties were scrupulously protected in these constitutions, and every effort was made to provide for popular control over both the legislative and the executive branches of the governments. In the case of Latvia and Lithuania the chief executive was a president elected for a term of three years and subject in most matters to the will of the legislature either directly or through the cabinet. In Estonia the prime minister was himself the chief executive and therefore changed with each new cabinet. In all three countries the cabinets were responsible to the legislatures in accordance with customary parliamentary practice, and in Estonia the ministers were elected by the assembly. While little objection could be raised to these constitutions as documents based on the most advanced thought of Western political scientists, experience soon showed that they were not suited to Baltic conditions. The great proliferation of political parties and the frequent changes in cabinet gave evidence of considerable instability, and the regimes that started out with such bright hopes declined into authoritarianism within four years in Lithuania and within fourteen in Estonia and Latvia.

From the start, the backbone of political life in these three countries was formed by the agrarian and center parties. These parties represented the peasants, in many cases recent beneficiaries of the land reforms, as well as the churches and certain urban groups. Estonia and Latvia were predominantly Lutheran by religion, while the population of Lithuania was largely Roman Catholic. The peasant populations of these countries were, moreover, strongly nationalistic in their sentiments. In Estonia and Latvia this nationalism had been stimulated by the independence movements and was kept alive by the proximity of the Soviet Union and the constant threat it represented to their security. In the problems of Vilna and Memel, Lithuania had additional issues around which nationalist sentiment could rally. The position of these agrarian and center parties was threatened both from the left and from the right. In Lithuania, where representative government met with its first defeat, it was the nationalists who overthrew the government. Taking advantage of discontent aroused by concessions the moderate regime had made to the socialists and to certain minority groups, the Nationalist party established a government with Smetona as president and Voldemaras as prime minister. With the use of authoritarian methods Smetona remained in power until World War II, and leaders of the moderate parties as well as of the trade unions and the Socialists were persecuted during his regime.

In all three Baltic states the domestic problems of a social and economic character which they had inherited were doubtless irritated by the insecurity resulting from the presence of restless minority groups. Lithuania, for instance, had minorities totaling over 16 per cent of its population of some two million, and the question of providing schools and other minority rights for these groups was a source of great controversy. Latvia, similarly, had minorities totaling 20 per cent of its population, and of these about one half spoke the language of neighboring Russia. Estonia had a minority population of only 12 per cent, of which three fourths was Russian. These minority questions, when added to religious issues, economic unrest, and political insecurity, resulted in problems that even countries with larger resources and greater political experience would have found difficult to handle.

ECONOMIC REORIENTATION. Before the war the three Baltic states had formed an integral part of the Russian economy, deriving much of their prosperity from the manufacture of goods destined for Russian markets. The independent status they acquired, as well as the change of regime in Russia, brought this relationship to an end and forced the Baltic states to seek new markets. The economies of these countries were further affected by the widespread destruction that occurred during the war and the civil strife that ensued. In the field of agriculture, an even more important factor was the drastic land redistribution, which not only placed political power in new hands but also altered the organization of agrarian production.

In Estonia and Latvia, about three fifths of the land was formerly in large estates owned either by the German aristocracy or by the church. In Lithuania about one half of the land was held by large landowners, generally of Russian or Polish nationality. These estates were almost all divided up at the end of the war, and in the case of Latvia and Lithuania with little or no compensation for the owners. The political effects of this reform lay in the removal of the foreign landowning aristocracy from its dominant position and the emergence of native middle-class leaders. Its effect on agriculture was to dislocate the traditional economic system. The small holdings into which the land was now divided were at first less efficient than the larger estates, and this inefficiency was reflected directly in a decline in production. The principal effort to resolve this dilemma took the form of an extension of the co-operative system, which eventually compensated to a considerable degree for the effects of the land reform. In Lithuania agriculture had been in such a backward state that the improvement of agricultural methods alone went a long way towards solving its problems. In Estonia and Latvia the solution lay less in an intensification of agriculture than in the introduction of new interests, and of these, dairy farming proved to be the most remunerative in terms of exports.

Even more than agriculture, industry in the Baltic states had been closely related to the needs of prewar Russia. Especially in Estonia and Latvia, where industry played a relatively important role, manufactured goods had been supplied to the Russian market in exchange for raw materials. Textiles and shipbuilding had been the leading industries working for the Russian market, while Baltic timber had found an outlet in the West. The first problem was to restore the factories destroyed during the war, and this was done gradually with the aid of foreign capital. The next step was to readjust production to new markets. The metallurgical industry found it impossible to compete with the West, but timber and, to a lesser extent, textiles offered opportunities that permitted Estonia and Latvia to recapture something of their former importance as industrial centers. Lithuania, where industry was far less developed than in the two northern states, was preoccupied chiefly during the first decade of its independence with the reconstruction of industry to supply its local needs.

The key to the establishment of a sound economy in all three countries lay in the reorientation of foreign trade, for only by exporting their timber and agricultural products could they hope to purchase the manufactured goods which they required. Although Estonia and Latvia were more industrialized than their southern neighbor, the economies of the three countries were essentially similar and therefore offered no basis for complementary regional trade. In the case of all three countries it was with Great Britain and Germany that first postwar ties were established, and only later were the countries able to diversify their foreign markets.

REGIONAL PROBLEMS. Estonia and Latvia concluded in 1923 a defensive alliance providing for mutual diplomatic and military assistance. Unlike Lithuania, these two countries had a common frontier with the Soviet Union and consequently a sense of insecurity which provided their primary motivation in foreign policy. The agreement between Estonia and Latvia, which Lithuania refused to join, was the one concrete achievement of the many efforts during this period to provide for greater co-operation among the countries of northeastern Europe, although tentative arrangements were made to include Lithuania in some of its provisions. The development of the League of Nations and an appreciable decrease in the propaganda emanating from the Soviet Union served to reduce the sense of insecurity of the Baltic states. By 1925 they abandoned their efforts to build a strong regional bloc and sought to stabilize their relations on an individual basis.

This trend was encouraged by the Soviet Union, which had strenuously opposed the conclusion of any regional arrangement in northeastern Europe and now embarked on a program of negotiating separate nonaggression pacts with the Baltic states. The Soviet statesmen regarded a regional bloc as necessarily directed against their own country, and consequently preferred to deal with each state separately. This approach was greatly facilitated by the conclusion of the German-Soviet treaty of neutrality and nonaggression in 1926, which removed for the time being the danger that the Baltic countries would again become the scene of a struggle between the two larger powers. The conclusion of a nonaggression pact with Lithuania in 1926 demonstrated the validity of the Soviet approach, as it caused considerable uneasiness among Lithuania's neighbors and definitively terminated the faltering efforts to construct a northeastern bloc. Lithuania was glad to conclude the agreement with the Soviet Union, because it thus received an ally in its bitter struggle with Poland over Vilna. Estonia and Latvia had no similar reasons for desiring to win Russian friendship, however, and they hesitated to conclude agreements with the Soviet Union when the latter rejected certain terms they proposed. The adherence of the three Baltic states to the Litvinov Protocol outlawing war in 1929, which at the time appeared to represent a considerable achievement for the Soviet government, had little actual effect on the course of their relations. It was not until 1932 that Estonia and Latvia finally concluded non-aggression pacts with Russia.

In addition to sharing the regional problems of her two northern neighbors, Lithuania's political leaders were almost continuously preoccupied during the first postwar decade with the controversial issues of Vilna and Memel. The Polish seizure of the city of Vilna [see above, pp. 127–28] had been recognized by the powers in 1923 and by the Vatican two years later, but Lithuania refused to accept this solution. This controversy affected the entire postwar development of Lithuania, and support of the grievance provided an entering wedge for Soviet influence. Despite sustained efforts, Lithuania proved unable to bring about any change in Vilna's status and finally in 1938, on the eve of a new war, agreed under duress to establish regular relations with the Polish government.

Lithuania was more successful in pressing its claim to Memel. This strategic territory, which afforded Lithuania its best outlet to the sea, had been ceded by Germany to the Allies at the end of the war, and the latter had considered various plans for it, including the establishment of a free city. In 1923 the Lithuanians precipitated a crisis by seizing the Memel territory and establishing a provisional government. The Allies recognized the validity of the Lithuanian case and proceeded to seek for an equitable settlement. The problem was complicated by the fact that while about half of Memel's 140,000 inhabitants were Lithuanian-speaking, they were predominantly Protestant in religion and pro-German in sentiment. In 1924 the Allies signed a convention with Lithuania assigning Memel to that country and giving the territory a limited degree of autonomy. A governor was to be appointed by the Lithuanian government, but there was to be a locally elected assembly and an administration responsible to it. While in form this settlement appeared to offer a compromise between the interests of Lithuania and those of the inhabitants of Memel, in practice the assembly and the governor were in almost constant disagreement and the territory enjoyed no political stability. Various attempts at compromise were made, but the problem remained unsettled until the eve of World War II.

THE BALTIC STATES AND THE EUROPEAN CRISIS. The adjustment made by the Baltic states during the first postwar decade, from their position as an integral part of the Russian economy to their new status as independent states trading primarily with Central and Western Europe, was rudely upset by the depression of 1931. This economic crisis soon produced political repercussions that profoundly altered the constitutional structure of these countries. Their prosperity had been built on a vigorous foreign trade and some use of foreign loans for domestic development. The fall of prices which accompanied the depression knocked the props out from under this system and forced the Baltic peoples to fall back very largely on their own resources. By 1934 prices had fallen to about one half their level of five years earlier. As this decline in prices affected agricultural products even more than industrial, the Baltic farmers were severely hit and the state turned its attention to their relief. Through subsidies and other forms of encouragement, a substantial increase in agricultural production was achieved and the purchasing power of the farmers was proportionately raised. In these two countries the state also took an active interest in the encouragement of industry. After the initial slump, the indices of industrial production by 1937 exceeded the 1930 level by 40 per cent in Estonia and 47 per cent in Latvia. The expansion of industry in Lithuania was less rapid, but its problems were similar to those of its two northern neighbors. The general effect of the depression in the Baltic states was thus to increase very considerably the role of the state in economic life and to drive the governments of the three countries towards measures designed to increase their economic self-sufficiency.

Foreign trade provided the connecting link between the economic system of the Baltic states and that of the rest of Europe. During the depression, the exports of Estonia and Latvia fell to less than one third of their value before the crisis, while those of Lithuania fell to less than one half. Imports were reduced proportionately. Moreover, the earlier level of commerce was never regained in terms of value. The policy of self-sufficiency which the three governments adopted during the depression freed them to a considerable degree from reliance on the outside world for foodstuffs, and their imports consisted very largely on raw materials for their growing industries. Their exports underwent less change, and timber and dairy products continued to play the major role. The adaptation of foreign trade to the policy of self-sufficiency brought with it not only an increased participation of the three governments in commercial affairs, but also involvement in the active Anglo-German competition for trade. In the case of Estonia, Germany and Great Britain each retained their one-third share in its exports. Their share in Latvian exports likewise remained equal, but rose from a quarter to a third each. In the case of the imports of the two countries, Germany retained a considerable lead over Great Britain. In Lithuania, on the other hand, political relations intervened to give Britain a great advantage over Germany between 1930 and 1936. In the latter year German-Lithuanian relations were improved, however, and a trade agreement was concluded permitting Germany to regain its position.

While in commercial relations the Baltic states were involved in a rivalry between Germany and Great Britain, their geographical position placed them directly in the path of the struggle between Germany and the Soviet Union. Between the signature of the German-Polish nonaggression pact of 1934, and the conclusion of similar pacts between the Soviet Union and Czechoslovakia and France, respectively, in 1935, numerous efforts were made to negotiate a security pact for Eastern Europe. When this failed, the three Baltic states implemented plans that they had been considering for the establishment of a neutral bloc representing their own interests alone. The Baltic Entente of 1934 was the result of a series of agreements providing among other things for the co-operation of the three states in international affairs. This policy was greatly furthered in 1936 when Latvia received a nonpermanent seat on the League Council as the representative of the three states. By choosing a course of neutrality rather than adherence to either the German or the Soviet groupings, the Baltic states managed to preserve a degree of independence in international affairs until the fateful summer of 1939.

The political strain caused by the depression and the subsequent rise of an aggressive Germany was more than the immature parliamentary systems in Estonia and Latvia could bear, and the advent of authoritarian regimes in these two countries in 1934 may properly be attributed to the European crisis. In Estonia the regime established by Paets in the face of threats from the extreme nationalist Liberators consolidated its political power through the Patriotic Front organization. This one-party regime drew up a new constitution in 1937 providing for a strong president and a Chamber of Deputies elected by universal suffrage but somewhat restricted in power. The Chamber was counterbalanced by a National Council, partly representative of municipalities and public institutions and partly nominated, which shared its power. Elections held in 1938 confirmed the position of the Patriotic Front, and Paets was elected as president. The regime established by Ulmanis in Latvia in 1934 was a product of conditions similar to those in Estonia, although it was of a somewhat more conservative character. No new constitution was introduced in Latvia, and Ulmanis governed under martial law. There was discussion of reorganizing the state along corporative lines, but only a few steps were actually taken in that direction. In Lithuania the breakdown of parliamentary government had occurred as early as 1926 with the establishment of the Voldemaras dictatorship, which promulgated an authoritarian constitution in 1928.

While the constitutional developments in the Baltic states in the 1930's represented only the formal aspects of the crisis, the political trend they reflected was clear enough. The position of each of these small countries had been so shaken by the collapse of their foreign trade and the intensification of the German-Russian struggle that they all sought security in the increased authority of their governments. In economic affairs, the governments undertook to regulate foreign trade, to guide the development of industry and agriculture, and to provide for the economic security of individuals whom the economic system of the 1920's had failed to protect. In political affairs the government suppressed the extremist parties and minority groups that sought to gain power, often as agents of Germany or Russia. Similarly in foreign affairs, the Baltic peoples placed their faith in the co-operation of their three authoritarian governments in a policy that sought to avoid foreign commitments.

Poland

HERITAGE OF PARTITION. The reconstruction of Poland after World War I was a unique achievement if only because it involved the consolidation of territories that for a century and a half had been partitioned among the three powerful and autocratic states of the Romanovs, the Habsburgs, and the Hohenzollerns. While the Polish people rejoiced in the reunion of their lands, it soon became apparent that they would have to cope with the problems inherited from all three sectors. This diverse heritage, combined with a geographical location between two potentially powerful rivals, confronted the Polish people at the end of World War I [see maps, pp. 127 and 130].

The problems presented by this heritage of partition were amply reflected in the diversity of political groupings that struggled for dominance during the first years of the Polish Republic. It has been estimated that during the first constitutional period, which ended in 1926, eighty political parties existed and fourteen cabinets were formed in an effort to create a stable government. During this period no unifying idea or political philosophy was developed around which the Polish people could rally. Nationalism was indeed a political outlook common to all Poles, and one that was all the more fervent because of the persecution it had undergone for so many years. In Poland nationalism nevertheless did not prove to be a force for unity because opinions differed as to Polish national interests, and the wartime differences among Polish national leaders continued to make cooperation difficult [see above, pp. 123–25].

Poland's political leaders also differed as to the form the republican government should take. The Roman Catholic church exerted a powerful influence in Poland, and an important group of nationalist parties favored a strong centralized government in which the interests of the church and the landowners would be safeguarded. At the same time there was a strong movement of peasant radicalism which, although under church influence, favored land reform and a regime with the interests of the underprivileged peasants at heart. There was also a socialist trend of thought which desired to introduce Marxist principles into the government of Poland despite the predominantly agrarian character of the country. Finally there were the national minorities, each of which had its own special interests but which were able at times to make their influence felt by allying themselves with the larger parties.

Of the many political parties that emerged from this complex pattern in 1919, the largest was the rightist National Democratic party of Dmowski. This party had been built up in Russia during the years of relative freedom after 1905 and was characterized both by its conservative outlook and by its attachment to pro-French policies after the war. Many Polish national leaders, including Paderewski, were attracted to it. Along with several small like-minded groups, Dmowski's party formed the Christian League of National Union, which rallied around its conservative representatives of all three sections of Poland. This Christian League brought together all of the conservative nationalist forces and presented the country with a vigorous program favoring a centralized state, with an emphasis on military strength and on commercial and industrial development. This coalition also favored the union of church and state and firm measures against the minority groups.

Less influential at first, but potentially with greater popular appeal, were the parties representing the interests of the peasants. Peasant movements had arisen before the war both in Russian Poland and in the Austrian province of Galicia, and by 1919 they had a well-developed program of agrarian and social reform based on a redistribution of the land, and with it of political power, in favor of the smaller landowners. Along with this tradition of agrarian radicalism, these groups also exhibited a tendency towards emotional nationalism which is common among agrarian peoples. As a consequence, the peasant parties were constantly torn between support of the nationalists and co-operation with other moderate groups, and as a result much of their political influence was dissipated. The principal agrarian political group was the Peasant party led by Witos. An important influence during the first years of the republic, it gradually abandoned its reform program in favor of nationalism. A more extreme branch of agrarianism was represented by the Populist or Liberation party led by Thugutt. While Thugutt co-operated with Witos on some issues, the Populists adhered more consistently to their reformist principles and generally voted with the leftist parties.

Socialism was another influential force in Polish politics. In the days before Poland's liberation, socialism had exerted a powerful influence in both Russian and Austrian Poland and had brought forward the dominant personality of Pilsudski. Upon the liberation of Poland a Socialist party was organized, but it failed to gain the prominent position that might have been expected. Pilsudski himself moved rapidly towards the nationalist camp and before long found himself in direct opposition to the Socialists. Moreover, Polish socialism was not a force capable of uniting the various minority groups, as it was organized along national lines. This narrow approach to socialism, in an agrarian country predominantly Catholic in sentiment, deprived the Socialist party of much of its potential strength.

Another aspect of the Polish heritage was the existence of minority groups amounting to almost one third of the population. While these had a common interest in protecting their rights and were for the most part opposed to the very existence of the Polish state as then established, each minority was at the same time divided by many issues. The Ukrainians, for instance, supported as many as ten political groupings ranging all the way from conservative nationalism to left-wing socialism. The Byelorussians, or White Russians, were divided into almost as many groups. The Jewish minority, on the other hand, was split between the Zionists, who wished to migrate to Palestine and establish a new homeland, and those who wished to make a permanent home for themselves in Poland. Only the one million Germans found it possible to reconcile their differences and present a common front to their Polish rulers.

POLITICAL REGIME. The first efforts to establish the political structure of Poland took place between 1918 and 1922, which were years filled with fateful events. The Peace Conference with its accompanying frontier problems, the Russian-Polish war, and the accession of Poland to the French alliance system all took place during this period [see above, pp. 93–7 and 123–28]. Polish political leaders nevertheless found time to proceed with the organization of the state, and by the spring of 1921 they had a constitution that made provision for a parliamentary system based on universal suffrage.

The membership of the Constituent Diet which convened in February, 1919, was largely elected by universal suffrage, but also contained appointed members from districts where it was not possible to hold elections. This body was dominated by the conservatives and the moderate peasant forces, both of which were strongly nationalist, and they combined to defeat the Socialists, who had until recently held the initiative under the leadership of Pilsudski. At first the victory of the nationalists was not pressed to the limit, but instead took the form of a series of provisional constitutional measures that attributed all sovereign powers to the Diet, and required the chief of state to obtain its approval in both civil and military matters. This attitude on the part of the Diet was perpetuated in the Constitution finally drawn up in the spring of 1921. It provided for a president elected for a seven-year term by the two houses of the National Assembly, but like the French presidency with powers strictly limited by the legislative body. While this predominance of parliament might work well in a country like England which had a tradition of political stability based on two or three parties, it was difficult to operate in a country with as wide a variety of political trends as Poland. The National Assembly was elected by universal suffrage and consisted of a lower house, or Diet, and a Senate. The Diet was distinguished from the Senate both by lower age qualifications for voting and membership, and by the sole right of initiating legislation. The National Assembly was elected for a five-year term, and could be dissolved by the president only with the consent of three fifths of the upper house. Under this system the executive power was in the hands of the prime minister, whose function it was to implement the measures agreed to by the Diet and the Senate. The Constitution of 1921 also made provision for the civil liberties common to Western democracies.

Elections under the new constitution were held in November, 1922, and a month later the new Diet and Senate held a joint session to choose a president of the republic. The period of the Constituent Diet (1919–22) had been one of stormy political controversies, and the attitude of the conservative nationalist assembly had greatly embittered the forces with a revolutionary tradition which had Pilsudski as their leader. The latter expressed openly his dissatisfaction with the new constitution because it failed to give the executive adequate authority. The elections in 1922 revealed that neither the conservatives nor the socialists could command a clear majority in the bicameral legislature, and for the first time the parties representing the national minorities held the balance of power. The Socialists, in alliance with the minority parties, were thus able to obtain the election of one of their members as president. The president was assassinated by a rightist within a few days after his election, however, and the political atmosphere did not calm down until a member of the more moderate Peasant party had been chosen to succeed him. Wojciechowski, the new president, managed to win the confidence of all factions, and Poland now embarked on a brief period of relatively normal political life.

The political instability during these years only served to reaffirm the conviction of Pilsudski that under the Constitution of 1921 the president had inadequate powers. With the aid of part of the army, he overthrew the government in the spring of 1926 and arranged for Moscicki, a prominent scientist, to be elected president. Pilsudski obtained the passage of amendments to the constitution which gave the president the power to dissolve the National Assembly and, under certain circumstances, to issue decrees having the force of law. Pilsudski himself now became prime minister, and for two years (1926–28) ran the government with the support of a coalition of nationalist groups. When this coalition failed to gain a majority in the elections of 1928, Pilsudski resigned and left the government in charge of his supporters. The latter, faced with the powerful opposition of the moderate Peasant party of Witos, the Socialists, and other groups of the center and the left, adopted increasingly dictatorial tactics. As a result of this open persecution of the opposition leaders, the supporters of Pilsudski won full control in the elections of 1930. With Pilsudski himself remaining in the background, the government was conducted along authoritarian lines by a group of army officers.

ECONOMIC RECONSTRUCTION. As in the political field, the century and a quarter of partition made it very difficult to create a coherent economy out of the three parts of Poland which were brought together in 1918. All three sections had been primarily agricultural in character, and as territories inhabited by minority peoples they had not been developed as rapidly as other parts of the Russian, Austrian, and German empires. Moreover, they had suffered greatly during the war. For four years the armies of Russia and the Central Powers had fought on Polish soil, and few districts had been left untouched. To the destruction of World War I was added almost immediately the great strain of the war with Soviet Russia. During the first postwar years, when many European states were able to get an early start on their problems of economic reconstruction, Poland continued to be engaged in the elementary processes of adjusting its frontiers. In addition to these security problems, Poland was also held back by the necessity of creating some unity out of the variety of currencies, taxes, and systems of communication it had inherited.

The reconstruction of the Polish economy was further hampered by the tendency of all countries in postwar Europe to strive for greater self-sufficiency. It was only with the greatest difficulty that Poland was able to attract sufficient investments and to acquire adequate markets to make possible the development of the country's natural resources. Nevertheless, in most spheres of economic activity Poland made substantial progress between World War I and the depression. Poland's economic difficulties are well illustrated by the development of the coal industry, one of its greatest assets. The coal mines, which were distributed in all three sections of prewar Poland, were seriously dislocated by the war. Their prewar markets in the three great empires were to a great extent cut off, and new outlets had to be found. In addition, the mines were located about three hundred miles away from the Baltic ports through which some 90 per cent of the coal was shipped. Despite these handicaps, production of Polish coal reached the prewar level by 1928 and continued to increase after a brief slump during the depression. A similar development took place in the iron and steel, textile, paper, and other industries. Of the capital required for the expansion of Polish industry, a little over one third came from abroad. A considerable proportion of the remainder was provided by the Polish government, which found in state capitalism the most efficient means of promoting industrial development.

Polish foreign trade was extensively reorganized after the war, although it continued to depend to a considerable extent on the area with which Poland had formerly been associated. In 1928, for instance, some 40 per cent of its imports came from Germany, Austria, and Czechoslovakia, while 58 per cent of its exports went to those three countries. Trade with Russia, on the other hand, was almost completely discontinued. By 1928 Poland had in addition begun to develop a healthy exchange of goods with Great Britain, France, and Belgium, which together provided 19 per cent of Poland's imports and took 13 per cent of its exports. Poland also engaged in commercial relations with the United States, which supplied some 14 per cent of its imports by 1928 although it failed to take more than a small fraction of Poland's exports. Coal and wood were Poland's most important exports, while its imports were divided almost equally between raw materials and manufactured goods.

Despite the considerable development of industry, Poland was in 1930 still a predominantly agricultural country with some two thirds of the population living on the land. Moreover, the growing agrarian population was larger than the land could support. This was due partly to the backward agricultural methods of an ignorant peasantry that produced one of the lowest yields per acre in Europe. The hardships of the agricultural population were also due to some degree to the unequal distribution of the land. In 1921, 65 per cent of the farms were barely large enough to support a family, another 32 per cent were of medium size, while approximately one half of the farm land was divided among the remaining 3 per cent of large landowners. In addition there were some four million landless peasants.

Confronted with this agrarian problem, the Polish government attacked it from several angles. An attempt was made to regulate agricultural prices through protection and subsidy, but the pressure of world prices was too powerful a force to be stemmed by local measures. An effort was also made to increase the yield of Polish agriculture, and this met with greater success. Agricultural production, nevertheless, could not be dealt with independently of the question of land tenure. With at least two thirds of the peasantry living at a bare subsistence level, and with their farms frequently divided into numerous and widely dispersed small strips, there were very narrow limits to what could be accomplished by intensive cultivation.

There remained the redistribution of the land, to provide farms for the landless and increase the holdings of the poorer farmers. Redistribution had long been demanded by the various peasant parties, but it was opposed not only by the large landowners but also by experts who held that the subdivision of the large farms would reduce their yield by making mechanization impossible. The pressure in favor of dividing the large estates was nevertheless irresistible, and during the first years of independence a series of laws was passed providing for the division of the large estates and the consolidation of the smallest holdings. Despite vigorous opposition on the part of the large landowners, some 800,000 peasant families received farms in the course of two decades. However, this reform failed to keep pace with the growing population, and the agrarian crisis deepened. As a result, the opinion was widely held that redistribution in itself could not relieve the population pressure and would have to be accompanied by some form of co-operative agriculture if a substantial rise in the standard of living was to be achieved.

BETWEEN TWO WORLDS. Situated between two powerful but temporarily weakened states, and possessing territories and minorities claimed by each of them, Poland was bound to seek allies on which it could rely in case either of its two neighbors again became aggressive. By skillful maneuvering Polish statesmen could preserve their country's security against either one of its two neighbors independently, but when the two agreed to co-operate, no combination of allies could save Poland. Until the eastern frontier was stabilized in 1920 Poland's entire effort was devoted to the struggle against Russia, for during these early years Germany represented no danger. With the initiation of friendly Russian-German relations in 1922, Poland took special pains to find friends both through the League of Nations and through bilateral agreements that would help to guarantee its security. Not until 1932, however, with the conclusion by the Soviet Union of nonaggression pacts with both France and Poland, did the latter gain a temporary respite from its exposed position.

Throughout this period Poland's chief friend was France, with which it concluded an alliance in 1921. Both countries were particularly interested in preventing the revival of German power, and in addition France was able to use its influence in the League of Nations to assist the new state. Although it had deep roots in the historic friendship of the two countries, this alliance was for Poland primarily one of practical advantage, the value of which varied in direct proportion to the influence of France in European affairs. During the first postwar decade France's influence was paramount, and Poland relied on it heavily. Rumania was in a position similar to that of Poland, and the two countries established friendly relations immediately after the war. A mutual-assistance pact was concluded between them in 1921, and until the opening of World War II Polish-Rumanian relations continued to be close and friendly.

With the Baltic states Poland never arranged a full working agreement despite many efforts. The dispute between Poland and Lithuania over

Vilna, and the preoccupation of the former with the German danger, prevented them from having any more than formal relations. In the case of Czechoslovakia also, the frontier disputes which arose during the Peace Conference prevented the countries involved from enjoying cordial relations for a number of years. Not until 1926 did Poland and Czechoslovakia sign a treaty providing for close commercial and political co-operation, and this era of good feeling turned out to be of relatively short duration. Polish policy was preoccupied very specifically with its position between Germany and Russia, and such groupings as the Little Entente with its Danubian orientation had little interest for Poland. Poland's relations with Germany during the first postwar decade were of almost unrelieved hostility. The problems created by Silesia, the Polish corridor, Danzig, and the German minority provided an inexhaustible supply of controversial issues which kept the two countries constantly at loggerheads.

The pressure of foreign affairs played a significant role in the decline of the parliamentary system in Poland, and after 1930 the legislative and executive power was gathered increasingly into the hands of a small clique of army officers. Headed until his death in 1935 by Marshal Pilsudski, and subsequently by Marshal Smigly-Rydz, this group of officers used authoritarian methods to obtain the degree of political unity they regarded as necessary for national security. The effect of the world depression was to increase discontent and unrest both at home and abroad, and the army regime believed that by placing itself above the parties and by restraining political antagonisms it was rendering the country a service. As it became increasingly difficult to mobilize public opinion behind the officers' regime, the government proceeded to organize its own party. Known as the Camp of National Union, this organization was founded in 1937 and met with some success in bringing together a variety of political groups.

The army regime strengthened its position in 1935 by obtaining the adoption of a new constitution greatly increasing the powers of the executive. Under the Constitution of 1935 the president could on his own authority appoint the prime minister, the chief justice, and the commander in chief of the army. He also appointed one third of the members of the Senate and played an important part in selecting his own successor. The Assembly, by contrast, had its powers greatly curtailed. It could force the resignation of a cabinet only with difficulty, and it could be dissolved at any time by the president. Moreover, although universal suffrage was maintained, the minimum voting age was raised for both the Diet and the Senate, and the electorate was thus restricted. At the same time, a new electoral law was introduced under which the government obtained substantial control over the nomination of candidates; and as a result the electoral process became little more than a formality.

Despite the increased authoritarianism the new constitution introduced, Poland under the army regime was not a totalitarian state. Civil liberties were not fully respected, yet an opposition press existed and considerable activity was carried on by the traditional political parties in opposition to the government's policies and methods. If these parties were unable to play an effective role in politics, it was less the result of government regimentation than of the wide differences among the parties themselves. To the right of the government were the National Democrat and the National Radical parties. The former maintained a conservative attitude in politics and nursed its traditional rivalry with Pilsudski and his followers; the latter was a more extreme group with fascist tendencies that found favor among the middle-class youth after 1934. Both of these parties nursed strong feelings against the minorities in Poland, and tended to devote more attention to this issue than to constructive statesmanship. To the left of the army regime were the Peasant and the Socialist parties. Witos, the leader of the Peasant party, went into exile, but the work of organizing the peasants was carried on by his lieutenants. After breaking completely with Pilsudski, the Socialists co-operated actively with the Peasant party in the struggle against the authoritarian regime. A number of smaller liberal groups were also active. By the time of the last national elections in 1938 the government party was so well organized that it was able to win three fourths of the seats in the Assembly. That this vote did not represent the true sentiments of the country was demonstrated later in the same year in the municipal elections, which were less strictly supervised. Here the opposition parties won two thirds of the seats on municipal councils, and it was only the deep cleavages among them that permitted the army regime to stay in control.

Poland was as badly hit by the depression as any other European country and registered a decline in national income of 55 per cent between 1929 and 1933. In contrast to most of the neighboring countries, Poland did not at first try to meet the crisis with a policy of rigid self-sufficiency, but continued to encourage foreign trade with a minimum of government regulation. The country had barely recovered from the war when the depression struck, and it had little reserve strength to fall back on. It was not until 1937 that industrial production passed the 1928 level, and this was achieved only as a result of the government's belated intervention in domestic affairs. The turning point in this development was the year 1936, when the government embarked on a heavy program of internal investment. By this means Poland liberated itself very largely from dependence on foreign capital and was able to revive industrial production independently of its lagging foreign trade. Recovery was nonetheless very slow. Lacking a solid middle class, burdened by heavy military expenditures, and handicapped by an inefficient bureaucracy, Poland did not fully overcome in the economic sphere its heritage of partition and backwardness.

In the period after the depression, the international position of Poland was powerfully influenced by the rise of an aggressive Germany. Since the period of the Locarno agreements of 1925, Poland had been increasingly impressed with the danger that France and England might be inclined to secure their position in Western Europe by countenancing German expansion eastward. It now embarked on a policy of dealing directly with Germany in an effort to guarantee its security without depending on the Western powers. Germany, on the other hand, was as yet in no position to assert its will in Eastern Europe and welcomed the opportunity to drive a wedge between Poland and its former Western allies. The German-Polish non-aggression pact of 1934 was the outcome of this situation, and for a brief period the relations of the two traditional enemies were most cordial.

The German-Polish agreement was at best only a temporary measure, and upon the German occupation of the Rhineland in the spring of 1936 the Polish government tried to renew its contacts with the West. But this was the era of appeasement, and France and England were not in a mood to resist the Germans. Thrown back on its own resources, Poland derived what advantage it could from its German connection while awaiting the development of events. Its principal immediate gain from this policy—one that was soon shown to have no substance—was the annexation of the Teschen region from Czechoslovakia in September, 1938, after the Munich agreement. During this period Poland all but lost sight of the Soviet Union. The Soviet-Polish nonaggression pact of 1932 had indeed been renewed two years later, but it was not until the frantic summer of 1939 that a working agreement between the two countries appeared feasible. In April an alliance between Poland and Great Britain was concluded. As the alliance with France was still in force, Poland was now firmly committed to the anti-German camp and became involved in the negotiations with the Soviet Union. The failure of these negotiations sealed Poland's fate, and in September the country found itself partitioned between Germany and Russia.

CHAPTER

— 16 —

The Eastern Mediterranean Region

◆

Europe and the Eastern Mediterranean Region

THE EASTERN MEDITERRANEAN region, which for so long formed the center of Classical and Christian civilization, was in large measure cut off from Europe for many centuries. Arab rule in parts of this area, and later the establishment of Ottoman Turkish rule over the entire region, provided a barrier to close relations with Christian Europe. This barrier was finally broken at the start of the nineteenth century by the rapid expansion of the European states, and the Ottoman Empire was confronted with the choice of adapting itself to a new way of life or of suc-

cumbing completely. Both Greece and Egypt acquired a substantial degree
of independence early in the nineteenth century, and by the time of the
World War little more than the Arab lands were left under Turkish rule,
apart from the province of Anatolia which formed the Turkish heart of
the empire.

France and Great Britain—followed shortly by Russia, and only later
by Austria, Germany, and Italy—reached into this region in the natural
course of their commercial and political expansion. The search for secure
routes to India, and their rivalry for the control of that wealthy empire,
had been originally the principal concern of France and England; they
were now motivated primarily by commercial interests. Russia's motive was
the protection of her southern frontier and later of her important grain
trade with the West, which was carried by the water route through the
Turkish straits. The opening and maintenance of these great highways
across the Ottoman Empire soon led to acrimonious rivalries among the
great powers and, on several occasions, to war. Yet, what in the long run
characterized this activity far more than the wars was the gradual subjugation of this region to direct or indirect rule by the European powers. In
some cases this rule was effected by direct acquisition, as in the case of
Britain in Egypt and Austria in Bosnia and Herzegovina. In other instances it involved a joint guarantee by several powers, as was the case with
Greece after its liberation, or merely a sphere of commercial and cultural
influence, such as France had in Syria. With the Ottoman Empire itself,
the powers had a more complex set of arrangements including capitulations, administration of the Ottoman debt and railroad, oil, and banking
concessions, and the instruction of military and naval personnel.

All this comes under the heading of what is generally termed imperialism, and along with some humiliation it brought many benefits to peoples of this region. In its efforts to stave off a full partition, the Ottoman
Empire put through many reforms that improved the administration of the
country and gradually extended education. While the interference of the
European powers was resented, the permanent investments they made, especially in railroads, contributed greatly to the material welfare of these
peoples at little expense to themselves. At the same time the peoples of this
region went to Europe in ever-increasing numbers to study and observe.

Whenever the European powers entered a new region of the world to
establish political control and to invest their capital, a stage was always
reached at which the subject peoples were sufficiently mature—as to resources, organization, and ideology—to revolt against their masters. This
achievement was in a very real sense a coming of age, for it signified that
the apprentice had acquired sufficient skills to compete with his master as
an equal. Moreover, there were many stages through which each people
had to pass before it could claim full and sovereign independence. Greece,
for instance, had revolted against Turkish rule in 1821 and developed under the guardianship of the Western powers—with substantial freedom—
for the rest of the nineteenth century; but it was only in 1923 that almost

all the Greek people who so desired were able to live in a Greek state which was as independent as any small power can be. Similarly Egypt had been able in 1841 to gain freedom from Turkish rule only under the guardianship of the powers; but it did not obtain a substantial degree of independence, signified by admission to the League of Nations, until 1937.

Unlike Greece and Egypt, Turkey and the Arab successor states remained an integral part of the Ottoman Empire until 1918. With them and with Egypt the process of Westernization had been greatly complicated by the fact that Islam is both a religion and a form of government. Unlike the Balkan peoples, the Moslems faced the problem not only of learning the lessons which the West had to teach but also of reconciling them with their all-embracing faith. To the end the Moslem religion remained a force opposed to change, and the Young Turks after trying several compromises finally embarked on a policy of frank secularization. Only in Turkey, however, was nationalism accompanied by a full subordination of the Moslem church. In Iraq, Syria, Transjordan, and Egypt, varying degrees of compromise were achieved, while in Saudi Arabia the religious enthusiasm of the Wahhabi sect was harnessed in the service of Westernization and nationalism.

The increased adoption of Western ways was accompanied by an opposition to Western rule throughout the Near East. One ideological element that was a cornerstone of Near Eastern nationalism was the revival of the national historical tradition. In Turkey, Kemal cultivated a historical school that not only recalled the great days of the Ottoman Empire but went so far as to trace the origins of the Turkish people back to the Sumerians, the Phoenicians, and the Hittites. The Arabic leaders, for their part, emphasized the achievements of Arab literature and science and urged their peoples to regain the standing their forefathers had attained. Nationalism, however, is a matter not only of history and tradition but also of organization and political skill. Only the Turks, among the Moslem peoples of the Near East, possessed the ability at the end of World War I to forge a national program and command respect for it. Egypt had no truly independent army or administrative system. The Arab successor states, on the other hand, were still apprentices in the art of government and for a generation continued to be seriously divided by dynastic and regional differences.

Postwar Greece

THE REPUBLICAN EXPERIMENT. Greece emerged from the war both victorious and defeated, for the reverses in Anatolia in many ways more than counterbalanced the earlier victories in the Balkans [see above, pp. 139–44]. In a situation in which the constitutional structure of Greece depended to a great extent on its international position, issues of foreign policy took precedence over institutions and individuals and became a determining influence on domestic affairs. The monarchy had been established in 1832 by the decision of Great Britain, France, and Russia, and it was maintained until World War I as appropriate to a country of Greece's status. But its roots were not deep, and when the European system disintegrated, the position of the monarch depended on his ability to identify himself with the successful prosecution of Greece's main objective: the political unification of all Greek-speaking peoples. The king had come as a representative of the great powers, and to survive he must use his international connections to serve Greek ends; for by the end of the nineteenth century the Greek parliamentary system had developed to a point at which a president could serve as chief of state as well as a king. The decline in prestige of the Greek monarchy at the end of the war was thus due to its failure to promote Greek national interests. The German sympathies of King Constantine had made his position untenable during the first period of his reign (1913–17), when the Allies controlled the Eastern Mediterranean region, and the failure of the campaign in Turkey brought disaster to the second period (1920–22). The reign of Constantine's second son, Alexander, was cut short by his untimely death (1917–20), and after his eldest son came to the throne in 1922 as George II the monarchy survived only one year longer.

With the departure of George II in 1923 after the military disaster in Anatolia, it was natural that the Greeks should turn to a republican form of government rather than seek a new dynasty. There was a strong republican movement in Greece, inspired both by classical traditions and by the early aspirations of the revolutionary movement of the 1820's. By the 1920's it had at its service several generations of lawyers and political leaders who had been trained in French republican traditions. The republic was proclaimed by the national assembly in March, 1924, but the new constitution was not ratified until 1927. Presumably with a view to giving the republic greater stability, this constitution reintroduced a bicameral assembly, which Greece had not known since 1844. The Chamber was elected by universal manhood suffrage, and three fourths of the members of the Senate were elected by popular vote, with a forty-year age requirement for eligibility to vote in the election. The remaining fourth was selected by chambers of commerce, the national university, and certain other public institutions. The president was elected in a joint session of the two houses for a five-year term. As compared with the monarch under the previous constitution, the president had less control over the convocation and dissolution of the assembly, and no vestige of the veto power.

This period saw the growth of two new political forces that remained outside the party structure but that exerted a strong influence on Greek affairs: the refugees and the military groups. The settlement in Greece of some 1,400,000 refugees from Turkey, Russia, Bulgaria, and Albania between 1922 and 1925 introduced into the political scene a large number of new voters with strong views on the issues of the day. The process of resettlement had imposed great economic hardships on them, especially upon the great majority who came from Turkey, and they bore a strong resentment against the monarchy whose failure to achieve Greek national aims had resulted in their displacement. As a result, the refugees tended to support the republican parties. They also contributed an important element to the membership of the Communist party. As for the military groups, they comprised the officers of the army and navy, who were in theory outside the realm of politics, but whose professional duties kept them in close touch with the affairs of the nation. Their revolts were usually brief and bloodless, and their motives were patriotic within the limits of their understanding of Greek national interests. The first of these revolts took place in 1909 and resulted in substantial civil and military reforms, carried out by Venizelos two years later. In the postwar years this type of pressure on the government became more frequent, with rebellions by republican officers in 1922, 1925, 1926, 1933, and 1935. Similar pressure was exerted in favor of the restoration of the monarchy in 1935 and helped establish an authoritarian regime in 1936.

THE ERA OF VENIZELOS. The two leading political parties contending for popular support during the republican period were the Liberal and the Populist. From 1924 to 1932 the preponderance of political power was in the hands of Venizelos' Liberal party and of the smaller groups that supported the famous wartime leader. Although the Liberal majority in the Chamber was at times slender, and although the more extreme republicans in the army resorted to a dictatorship in 1925–26 under General Pangalos, Greece made rapid progress during these years towards solving its political and economic problems. In this period the pro-royalist Populist party led by Panagis Tsaldaris headed a vigorous and persistent opposition coalition. In the elections of 1926, 1928, and 1932, the royalist parties received between 33 and 40 per cent of the popular vote, and in 1933 they received a parliamentary majority. A Communist party was formed in 1918, but only after the depression did the Communists begin to exert an influence on the political life of Greece, and then less by virtue of their popular support than because they held the balance of power between the two major parties.

The principal domestic problem of Greece during this period was to care for its rapidly increasing population. Quite apart from the refugees, the natural increase in population brought the number of inhabitants up from six to seven million between the years 1925 and 1937. In 1931 the density of population in relation to the cultivated land was about double that of neighboring countries in Southeastern Europe. Greece, nevertheless, possessed certain crops—such as tobacco and olives—which brought in a large export profit, and these helped to compensate for her agricultural poverty. Moreover, Greece possessed one of the largest merchant marines in the world, and its earnings helped the home country. At the same time, there were large and prosperous groups of Greek immigrants in a number of foreign countries, particularly in the United States, who contributed to the support of their relatives in the old country, and whose total annual remittances amounted to an important item in Greece's balance of trade. This rather unusual economy resulted in no more than a modest standard of living for Greece. It also brought its people into closer contact with the outside world than was the case in neighboring countries, a circumstance that placed Greece somewhat at the mercy of economic conditions abroad. In 1928, 42 per cent of the industrial products, 43 per cent of the raw materials, and almost half the grain consumed in Greece came from abroad. A strong movement, therefore, developed during the republican period to make Greece more self-sufficient. Efforts were made to increase the industrial output and make more land available for cultivation. Extensive irrigation works were built in the recently acquired province of Macedonia, where most of the refugees had been settled. This work was carried on with the assistance of international loans, which were sponsored by the League of Nations.

GREECE AND ITS NEIGHBORS. The great program of national expansion undertaken during and after the World War left Greece with enemies on all sides. It is to the great credit of Greek statesmanship that within a decade almost all of the remaining controversial issues had been settled by arbitration and conciliation. Turkey had been the principal enemy, and by 1930 a full settlement was reached of all the issues dividing the two countries. Apart from the exchange of populations agreed upon in 1923 [see above, p. 143] there were property questions resulting from the exchange, controversies regarding the status of Greeks and Turks who had not been exchanged, and issues concerning naval strength and commercial relations. The solution of all these issues was not easy, and Great Britain played an important role in bringing the two countries together. When they finally resolved their difficulties in 1930, in a series of pacts and treaties, the reconciliation was complete. The new friendship was sealed by an exchange of visits between Venizelos and Ismet, Kemal's prime minister. In recording this friendly exchange, it is not inappropriate to recall that Kemal was born in Salonika, now an important Greek seaport, whereas Venizelos was born in Crete while it was still under Turkish sovereignty.

Hardly less bitter than the rivalry with Turkey, and far more fraught with difficulties for the future, were the controversies between Greece and its northern neighbors. Inherited from the World War and from the Balkan wars that preceded it, these differences were both territorial and economic in character. Bulgaria never gave up its claim to the province of Western Thrace and the territorial outlet to the Aegean Sea which this region would give it. While Bulgaria was in no position in the 1920's to press the territorial issue, it seized upon the status of the some 80,000 Macedonian Slavs still remaining in Greek Macedonia as an issue with which to keep its claims alive. Although Bulgaria's claim to these Slavs was questionable, and they had in fact chosen to remain in Greece, the years after the war saw numerous frontier incidents provoked largely by Slavic nationalist groups. One of these incidents in 1925 led to the invasion and occupation of a portion of southern Bulgaria by elements of the Greek army. Bulgaria then appealed to the League of Nations, and after an investigation, the Greek government was required to pay an indemnity of $225,000.

GREEK–TURKISH RECONCILIATION   *Premier Venizelos of Greece
(left) visiting President Mustafa Kemal (later Atatürk) of Turkey, in Ankara, 1930.*

While this particular incident was thus settled peacefully, the larger issues
between the two countries continued to aggravate the unsatisfactory character of their relations.

    In contrast to Bulgaria, Yugoslavia had been an ally of Greece during
the latter part of the war, and it was from Salonika that the Serbian army
advanced when it finally liberated its home country. A controversy nevertheless developed after the war over the use by Yugoslavia of the Greek

port of Salonika, which was the only convenient outlet for Yugoslav exports to the Mediterranean region. This extended controversy was finally settled in 1929, when Greece established a Free Zone in Salonika where Yugoslav commerce could be transshipped without being subjected to Greek customs regulations [see map, p. 134].

Italy and Albania remained rivals of Greece throughout this period. As Albania was under the protection of Italy, so was Greece in a somewhat different sense under that of Great Britain. The frontier dispute over Southern Albania was the focus of this rivalry, and when five Italian members of the frontier commission were assassinated inside the Greek border in 1923, Italy countered by bombarding and occupying the Greek island of Corfu. Greece took the case to the League of Nations; the Italians were required to withdraw their troops from Corfu, and the smaller country agreed to pay a stiff indemnity for failing to provide for the security of the Italian officials. Even with Albania, its bitterest foe, relations improved in the course of time, and in 1928 Greece concluded political and commercial treaties with both Albania and Italy.

England, as the predominant great power in the Eastern Mediterranean, remained Greece's principal friend and supporter. Britain had had a leading part in Greece's struggle for liberation from the Ottoman Empire in the 1820's, in which Lord Byron had played a well-publicized and tragic role, and the centennial celebrations of the events connected with Greece's independence served as appropriate occasions for a reaffirmation of the traditional friendship of these two countries. At the same time, Greece's nationalist program led to serious difficulties with Great Britain over the island of Cyprus. In 1931 Greek nationalists on the island, aroused by an issue involving control over elementary education, organized an uprising that resulted in the burning down of the residence of the British governor. Public opinion was aroused in both Greece and England, but a peaceful settlement was reached without any change in the status of Cyprus.

DECLINE OF THE REPUBLIC. As was the case with so many other European states, the world depression provided Greece with a crisis that precipitated important political changes. To a greater degree than most countries, Greece depended for its well-being on a vigorous foreign trade and the maintenance of prices on the world market for its principal exports, such as tobacco, fruits and wine. The fall in prices after 1930 was soon reflected within the country. The sale of tobacco, which accounted for over half of Greece's exports, had fallen over 50 per cent by 1932 and did not return to its normal predepression volume until 1936. The value of Greek foreign trade as a whole fell by about one third between 1929 and 1932 and recovered only slowly. The effects of the depression within Greece threw the burden of relief on the government, which now attracted criticism for maladministration that had gone unheeded during the more prosperous times. Discontent was directed particularly against Venizelos, who had held power as prime minister since 1928 at the head of a strong coalition. Venizelos had made a brilliant reputation for himself in the international field during and after World War I, but was less of a success in domestic affairs, where his dominant personality tended to annoy his subordinates and exasperate his opponents.

The effects of the depression, accompanied by party strife, were reflected in the election of 1932, in which the Venizelists were able to obtain no more than a plurality. New elections in the spring of 1933 produced more definite results, however, and gave a clear majority to the Populists, who traditionally favored a monarchy but were pledged at this time to support the republic. The advent to power of a prodynastic party for the first time since 1924 had immediate repercussions, in the form of an attempted military *coup* led by republican officers. It cast a long shadow on Greek politics by introducing a note of violence in what was soon to become an era of authoritarian government. Suppression of the republican *coup* led to the rise within the army of a strong monarchist group which soon made its influence felt. The Populists, in the meantime, were making use of their newly acquired political position to bring about changes to their own advantage in the electoral law and in the organization of the army. The political struggle finally came to a head in the spring of 1935 with the outbreak of a new republican military revolt, in which Venizelos himself played an important role. This proved to be a turning point in Greek affairs, for the monarchist military group was now able to assert itself. By means of martial law, new elections, and finally a plebiscite, the monarchy was re-established, and at the end of 1935 George II returned to the throne after twelve years of exile.

The brief reign of George II in 1922–23 had given him no opportunity to establish himself as a controversial personality, and his return was characterized by a general political reconciliation. Even Venizelos, from his exile in France, issued a statement urging tolerance and a return to constitutional methods. The king, on his part, reduced the influence of the rightist officers who had brought him to power, amnestied leading members of the opposition, and took the initiative in preparing impartial elections. Conditions were not propitious, however, for a return to political normalcy. The elections of January, 1936, returned royalists and republicans in almost equal numbers and gave the balance of power in parliament to the small but vigorous Communist party, which won 15 seats out of 300. No sound regime could be established on this basis, and the king appointed General Metaxas, leader of a small rightist group, to head a nonparty government. Meanwhile economic unrest and strikes were increasing, and parliament decided to grant wide powers to Metaxas for a five-month period in an effort to restore stability.

THE METAXAS REGIME. In August, 1936, Metaxas suspended the constitution and dissolved parliament, giving as his excuse the threat of a general strike allegedly being prepared by the Communists. He thus established a virtual dictatorship, and by accepting the consequences of these acts King George identified himself increasingly with the new regime. The form of government imposed by Metaxas was in no sense peculiar to

Greece, but rather resembled the regimes established in most countries of
Eastern Europe during the later 1930's. It was characterized by a full reliance on the police for its authority and could claim little popular support.
A systematic and almost laughable effort was made to remove from Greek
life vestiges of political democracy, including the chair of constitutional law
at the University of Athens and the teaching in the public schools of those
parts of the Greek classics which might be considered as favoring democracy. At the same time, a determined effort was made to indoctrinate the
population with a national discipline by the institution of youth and labor
organizations along fascist lines. The Greeks are a politically sophisticated
people, however, and while they could not resist the power of the police
they did a great deal to undermine the efforts of the government through
ridicule and passive resistance. For the average citizen the regime was nevertheless not entirely without its advantages. A social program including
minimum wage regulation and unemployment insurance was inaugurated,
and the trend towards a social-service state which Metaxas sponsored was
in certain respects parallel to developments in the more democratic countries of the West.

An important factor in the relative stability of the Metaxas regime was
that it came to power just as general economic conditions were beginning
to improve again. By 1937, both imports and exports surpassed the 1929
level by a wide margin. Similarly, the production of foodstuffs, after a renewed slump in 1936 owing to a severe drought, rose to unprecedented
heights in the following year. Metaxas took full advantage of the favorable
conditions to encourage the trend towards self-sufficiency which had been
started under Venizelos. A ten-year program of economic expansion was
inaugurated with the aid of government financing, and both agriculture
and industry were brought within the scope of the plan. Rapid progress was
made in the increase of the area under cultivation, and in the late 1930's
Greece was for the first time producing more than half of the grain it consumed. Greece became almost self-sufficient with regard to cotton and
greatly increased the production of other crops. Industrial production,
which had not been seriously affected by the depression, rose from an index of 100 in 1929 to 140 in 1935 and 163 in 1938. While both in agricultural and in industrial production the gains made under the Metaxas regime represented primarily an acceleration of trends that had been under
way in the 1930's, the regime received considerable credit for concentrating
its efforts in these fields.

It was more difficult for the government to influence developments in
foreign trade, but gains were made in this field also. The improvement in
Greece's trade position was due primarily to the increase in domestic production, but credit should be given also to the strict controls placed by the
government on all foreign exchange and trade transactions. In addition,
Greece relied increasingly on bilateral trade agreements as a means of directing its foreign commerce along the lines desired by the government.

One result of government control over Greek foreign trade was an increase in commercial relations with Germany. Normally about half of Greece's exports by value consisted of tobacco, and in the 1930's Germany was the only country willing to purchase this commodity at favorable prices. As a result of this situation, Germany's share in Greece's exports rose from 14 to 38 per cent between 1932 and 1938, while its share in Greece's imports rose from 10 to 30 per cent in the same period. This position as Greece's most important market and supplier was an important source of German influence in Greece.

In its approach to foreign policy, as with its handling of internal affairs, the Metaxas regime diverged very little from the trends of the times. The peculiar problem faced by Greece in trying to defend its security was that its traditional enemies—Italy, Albania, and Bulgaria—were gradually becoming more closely associated with the one country that was willing and able to trade with Greece, namely Germany. How to maintain the close relations with Germany which were essential to Greek prosperity, without at the the same time making important political concessions to the other states associated with Germany, was a dilemma to which Metaxas never found a satisfactory solution.

The one policy Greece was able to pursue in its effort to counterbalance the influence of Germany and its associates was to strengthen its relations with friends and prospective allies. Already in 1933 the establishment of friendly relations with Turkey had been confirmed by a treaty, provoked by a fear of Bulgarian aggression, which guaranteed the common Greek-Turkish frontier in Thrace. Then in 1934 Greece—together with Turkey, Yugoslavia, and Rumania—signed the Balkan Pact, which bound the signatories to consult with each other in case their security was threatened. The Balkan Pact was clearly directed against possible attempts by Bulgaria or Albania to revise the peace settlements, attempts that would almost certainly have Italy as a sponsor. The Balkan Pact was defensive in character, and it contained a rigorous definition of the conditions under which the signatories would consider that aggression had occurred. The danger of an early disturbance in the Balkans was greatly reduced in the summer of 1935, when Italy's attention was withdrawn from that region and turned almost exclusively for the time being to the conquest of Ethiopia.

This was the situation in foreign affairs which Metaxas inherited when he assumed office in 1936, and Italy's successful defiance of the League system and Germany's growing share in Greece's foreign trade were the principal factors influencing his subsequent policy. By 1937 Germany had Yugoslavia and Bulgaria, both neighbors of Greece, well in hand. This was a serious blow to Greek security, for it nullified in practice the Balkan Pact of three years earlier. As a gesture of appeasement, the signatories of the Balkan Pact signed an agreement with Bulgaria in the summer of 1938. In return for a Bulgarian promise to refrain from attempting frontier changes by force, recognition was granted of Bulgaria's right to rearm and to fortify its frontiers. The victory of the Axis powers at Munich a few months later dealt the final blow to the hopes of most Greeks that their country could find a means to counterbalance the Axis.

Events now moved rapidly from negotiation to aggression. The Italian occupation of Albania in April, 1939, evoked a pledge on the part of Great Britain and France of assistance to Greece in case its independence should be endangered. The scene of conflict moved away from the Balkans for the time being, however, and during the winter and spring of 1939–40, Axis military efforts were directed towards the West. When the defeat of France freed Italy's forces during the summer, that country's attention again turned to the Balkans. Desiring to assert its position as a Mediterranean power while Germany was still preoccupied with events to the north, Italy now attempted to establish control over Greece. Using the pretext of Greece's refusal to comply with certain of its demands, Italy invaded that country from Albania in October, 1940.

The Turkish Republic

IDEOLOGY OF REPUBLICAN TURKEY. In the generations before the war, Turkish intellectual leaders searched widely for ideas in Western political thought in their efforts to modernize the rapidly disintegrating Ottoman Empire. In the course of this process a number of schools of thought developed, but they all followed the same general lines in adhering to the dominant trends of contemporary European thinking. Kemal inherited this reformist ideology; after changes had been duly made to meet the new geographical and political circumstances of postwar Turkey, it was formally adopted as the doctrine of the Turkish Republic. This ideology is summarized in one terse statement in Article 2 of the amended Turkish constitution: "The Turkish State is republican, nationalist, populist, 'etatist,' secular, and revolutionary."

In this single sentence the principles of Kemal's Turkey are set forth, and the vast difference between the new and the old Turkey is clearly delineated. As a republic, Turkey was to be freed from the Ottoman dynasty, which had ceased to be an efficient institution of government. In the last years of the empire, especially during the long reign of Abdul Hamid (1876–1909), the court had become the center for the intrigues of all the most reactionary forces in the country. As a republic, Turkey would henceforth rely for its political leadership entirely on men trained and tested in public life. The principle of nationalism which accompanied that of republicanism had its origin in the collapse of the empire. The Young Turks themselves, at an earlier stage, had favored the development of an Ottoman rather than a Turkish citizenship, thus encouraging the loyalty of non-Turkish minorities. The World War, however, and the great outburst of nationalism which preceded and accompanied it, had a determining influence not only on the minority peoples of Turkey but also on the Turks themselves. After the war, and especially after its bitter struggle against the Greeks on Turkish soil, Kemal's regime drew heavily on the Turkish national tradition in rallying popular feeling.

Within this republican and nationalist framework, the new Turkey strove to implement the other four principles of its creed. Populism means the enjoyment by all citizens of equal social, economic, and judicial rights. It means, in short, the development of a legal system similar to those gradually adopted by Western Europe after the French Revolution, in place of the previous system, based on religion and custom, which had permitted many inequities. The principle of "etatism," or the assumption by the state of the primary responsibility for the social and economic development of the country, was a natural outgrowth of the situation and the times. In a country such as Turkey there was relatively little private capital or enterprise apart from peasant agriculture. Any rapid development of the country under the existing system would have to come from continued foreign investments, and this would bring the very interference by foreign powers which Turkey was now trying to avoid. As a consequence, the new leaders decided that the state must take the initiative in the development of communications and industry as well as in such matters as health and education. A program such as this was bound to meet with firm opposition from all the conservative forces in the country, and these forces were concentrated principally in the Moslem churches, since in the tradition of Islam most branches of the legal system were administered by the religious authorities. Kemal therefore adopted the principle of secularism, under which there was brought about a separation of church and state even more complete than that existing in most European countries.

Finally, the new Turkish state considered itself to be revolutionary. By this it was meant not that Turkey would follow any particular European revolutionary doctrine, but rather that social and economic changes would be initiated from above by the introduction of vigorous reforms, and that no attempt would be made to wait for the slower processes of evolution. While the new Turkey was thus in a sense in violent opposition to Western political influence and interference, the principles that guided its leaders were in the main those of progressive European thought.

POLITICAL STRUCTURE. Shortly after peace was finally signed at Lausanne in 1923, Kemal and his associates undertook to develop a permanent political structure for Turkey. The abolition of the office of Sultan by the Ankara regime in 1922 had cleared the way for a new form of government, and in the following year the National Assembly declared Turkey to be a Republic and elected Kemal as its first president. The constitution drafted in 1924 vested full authority in a National Assembly elected for a four-year term. The consent of this assembly was necessary for the enactment of all laws, and it supervised the different ministries and elected the president of the republic. In addition to the assembly, the president, and the cabinet, the constitution provided for a council of state. This body, elected by the assembly, had the technical function of passing on administrative matters and of handing down opinions concerning draft laws, contracts, and other business before the assembly. The capital of the Republic was established at Ankara, deep in the heart of Anatolia and free from the taint of foreign influence with which Constantinople was associated.

The form of the Turkish Republic, then, was very similar to that of governments in Western Europe, but its operation was naturally handicapped at first by the political inexperience of the Turkish people. From the very start the initiative in political matters was in the hands of the People's party founded by Kemal in 1922. It was destined for many years to be the sole political party, although Turkey was a one-party state more out of necessity than by choice. In a country that had a literacy rate of under 20 per cent and that had just emerged from fifteen years of constant wars, the new ruling group stressed reforms and modernization rather than free discussion. The People's party was therefore organized on a national basis and provided a unified leadership for those active in the reform movement. It should also be noted that propaganda rather than policing was the chief weapon used to mobilize opinion. The two purges that occurred during Kemal's long presidency (1923–38) were of limited scope and played a small part in the reform movement, in comparison with the vast efforts at education and propaganda carried on by the People's party. This effort to win support for the social and economic reforms was made not only by press and radio, which were monopolized by the People's party, but also through Folk Houses, scattered all over the country, which served as meeting houses and as headquarters of the various branches of party activity.

Social and Economic Reforms. In contrast to the other successor states of the Ottoman Empire, whose principal concern during the first postwar decade was their struggle for national independence against the European mandatory or protecting powers, for Turkey this was a period rich in social and economic reforms. From the start, the principal obstacle to modernization had been the legal and customary lore of the Moslem church. As a first step, in 1924, the assembly voted the separation of church and state and the replacement of the religious schools by a secular state school system. In the following year the monastic orders, which had played an important role in nurturing the Moslem tradition, were likewise abolished. At the same time, the Moslem fez was discarded as the accepted headgear and replaced by the Western hat. The removal of the veil, which Moslem women customarily wore outside their homes, took place more gradually.

The Moslem faith had represented not only a set of customs but also a legal system covering a wide variety of matters. The problem of replacing this body of law with modern legal codes was attacked in 1926 when the assembly adopted civil, penal, and commercial codes based on Swiss, Italian, and German models. Perhaps the greatest reform of all, however, was the adoption of the Latin alphabet in 1928. The Arabic alphabet, in which the Turkish language had hitherto been written, was so complex that it had been largely responsible for the delay in reducing illiteracy. The adoption of the Latin alphabet was accompanied by a large-scale educational effort that within seven years quadrupled the number of those who could read and write. Finally, between 1934 and 1936 all Turkish families were required to adopt surnames, thus discarding another Turkish custom in favor of Western practice. Kemal took the family name of Atatürk (meaning Foremost Turk), and his prime minister, Ismet, took that of Inönü (after one of his victories over the Greeks in Anatolia).

On the economic side the principal goal of the reform movement, in application of the principle of "etatism," was to expand industrial operation under state control. To this end a number of state banks were established after 1924, and by purchase and construction they gradually extended their control over the mining, manufacturing, and shipping industries. One of the most significant state enterprises, which of necessity preceded the others, was the development of the railroad network. Existing international lines were purchased by the state, and new construction was pushed to such an extent that railroad mileage was almost doubled in the next twenty years; by 1939 all but 6 per cent was owned and operated by the Turkish government. These economic reforms were greatly facilitated by the adoption of the Western measurement of time and the metric system.

Relying as it did on taxes and local resources for its economic program, Turkey was less affected by the world depression than were most countries. In fact, Turkey emerged in 1930 from a long period of trade deficit and with the exception of a brief period in 1938 was able to maintain a favorable balance of trade. While the 1920's were for Turkey years of rapid social and political change and readjustment, in the 1930's Turkey settled down to a period of consolidation and expansion along the lines formulated during the previous decade.

Industrialization was one of the principal goals of Atatürk's regime, and was pressed vigorously during the 1930's. The initiative was originally taken by a private bank in which Atatürk and other members of the government owned an important share, but after 1933 several banks were formed by the government to take charge of investments. There has developed, as a result, a form of state socialism. Without attempting to institute a fully planned economy along Soviet lines, the Turkish government indirectly administers all of the transportation and most of the larger industries within the country. A wide variety of industrial establishments were launched during the 1930's, and Turkey's valuable mineral resources were likewise developed. In the years between 1936 and 1941 the number of employees in industry and mining increased by 60 per cent, and the value of production by 120 per cent. By the end of the decade, industry and commerce together accounted for about one third of the national income. Agriculture, which continued to engage four fifths of the population, also underwent many changes. The area of land under cultivation was doubled between 1927 and 1936, and special attention was devoted to such industrial crops as cotton and sugar beets. Most of the land was tilled by small farmholders, and the government devoted special attention to the improvement of agricultural methods.

Atatürk's reform movement devoted itself as much to the cultural advance of the people as to the material development of national production. Even more than in the case of industry and agriculture, a great many ideas and inhibitions had to be changed before progress could be made along Western lines. The separation of church and state, the reform of the alphabet, and the emancipation of women laid the foundations for later developments. Between 1928 and 1946, the number of boys in primary schools rose from 300,000 to 900,000, and the number of girls from 100,000 to 500,000. A similar expansion took place in the professional schools and universities. At the same time, the youth of the country was for the first time encouraged to engage in sports, and an extensive health program was inaugurated.

The regime under which these changes took place was the one-party system in which Atatürk's People's party held a monopoly of political power. Although a nominal parliamentary system was in operation, criticism of the government was limited to arguments within the People's party. That the regime was generally acceptable to the Turkish people, however, was demonstrated by the lack of widespread popular discontent and the absence of the flagrant use of repression which characterized most of the authoritarian regimes in Europe. The stability of the regime was illustrated by the smooth transition of power which took place upon the death of Atatürk in 1938. In his place, the Assembly elected his close collaborator Ismet Inönü, who had served as prime minister from 1923 to 1937. The dignity and restraint with which this change occurred and the course of subsequent events left the lasting impression that the legacy of Atatürk, unlike that of so many other dictators, was the achievement not of a single dominating personality but of a generation of Western-minded leaders.

One traditional Turkish problem, with which less progress was made, was the treatment of minorities. There had remained in Turkey approximately 1,000,000 Kurds in Eastern Anatolia, and some 125,000 Greeks, 78,000 Jews, and 50,000 Armenians, located in Istanbul and the other coastal cities. While technically these minorities possessed all the rights of Turkish citizens, in practice there was considerable discrimination against them. The Kurds are an unruly mountain people who on several occasions were repressed by force and were finally brought under relative control by a policy of resettlement. The other minority groups had traditionally been the businessmen of Turkey, and their interests suffered as commerce and industry were gradually brought under the control of the nationalist government. Feeling against the minorities was popular rather than official, however, and the government intervened more than once to prevent outright persecution. More questionable, in the light of the avowed principles of the government, was the capital tax levied in 1942. Whereas the ostensible purpose of this tax was to raise revenue, it was administered by local officials in such a way as to bring ruin to most Christian and Jewish businesses. The minorities never recovered from this blow, although within a year the government administered partial redress.

TURKEY AND THE WORLD. Although the West is accustomed to think of Turkey chiefly as an object of rivalry of the European powers, it had in fact long occupied a position of leadership in the Moslem world. In the latter part of the nineteenth century the Islamic title of Caliph (or successor to the Prophet Mohammed), which had fallen into disuse, had been taken up by the Ottoman sultan. Thanks to his position as head of the largest independent Moslem state and to the vigorous propaganda he conducted, the Sultan had received general recognition as the leader of Islam from many of the 300,000,000 Moslems living in India, Russia, the Dutch East Indies, China, Egypt, and other countries, who hoped that in union through religion they could find the strength to better their political position. The influence of the Caliphate was limited, however, by the military strength of the Ottoman Sultan, which was not great. Nevertheless, even after the war the Caliphate, if promoted vigorously, might again have become a force in the Moslem world. By abolishing this institution in 1924, the Kemalists explicitly abandoned the idea of playing a role in the Moslem world; and since no other Moslem sovereign ruler had the power to succeed to the role of Caliph, that institution once more fell into disuse. The new Turkey not only abolished the Caliphate; it also abandoned any claim to leadership of the Islamic peoples in general or of the Arab successor states. While this policy earned the resentment of some Moslem groups that sought to advance their position with Turkish assistance, it permitted Turkey to concentrate entirely on its domestic program without foreign entanglements.

With the Soviet Union, Turkey's relations continued correct but cool. Turkey and Russia had a common problem in their opposition to the peace settlement, and Russia's weakness during the first postwar years relieved Turkey of any fear that its sovereignty would be violated by Russia. Their relations were formalized first in a treaty of peace in 1921 and then in a treaty of friendship and neutrality concluded in 1925, which was due to last for twenty years. Relations with Greece, another traditional enemy, also improved rapidly once the exchange of populations had been accomplished. Turkey's final return as a regular member of the European family occurred in 1932, when it was admitted to the League of Nations.

No event illustrates more clearly the change in the international prestige which Atatürk's regime brought to Turkey than the revisions made at Montreux in 1936 in the regime of the Straits, which the Turkish government had unwillingly accepted in 1923 [see above, pp. 141–42]. The Turks had been hoping for some time to obtain the removal of restrictions on their sovereignty, and an opportunity was provided when the threat of Italy and Germany to the Western powers greatly increased the value of Turkey as a potential ally of the latter nations. Under the new regime negotiated in a conference at Montreux in which Great Britain, France, and the Soviet Union played the leading roles, important changes were made in Turkey's position at the Straits. The International Commission of the Straits was abolished, and its duties were transferred to the Turkish government, which was to report annually to the League of Nations. Turkey, moreover, was now permitted to militarize the Straits. In time of war, Turkey as a neutral nation was required to prevent the passage of belligerent warships unless they were passing through the Straits in fulfillment of their obligations under the League Covenant. In case Turkey itself was at war, or was threatened, the regulation of warships was left to its discretion. Finally, the position of the Black Sea fleets, of which Russia's was the most important, was made more secure by virtue of new restrictions placed on the passage of non-Black Sea ships through the Straits. As compared with the 1923 treaty, the Montreux Convention was a recognition that Turkey had attained a new position of prestige and responsibility in international affairs. This agreement also marked a change in Russia's position in the Near East, and an acknowledgment by France and Great Britain that the role of victors which they had occupied in the Eastern Mediterranean since 1923 was now a thing of the past.

In strengthening its independent position during the 1930's, Turkey's first problem was to place its relations with its smaller neighbors on a friendly basis. In the Balkans this was accomplished by a treaty of friendship with Greece in 1930, and was further cemented by the Greek-Turkish treaty of guarantee in 1933, and by Turkish co-operation in the Balkan conferences and in the Balkan Pact of 1934. A similar agreement was concluded in 1937 with Iraq, Iran, and Afghanistan to the East. This non-aggression treaty, known as the Saadabad pact, pledged the signatories to consult one another in all international conflicts affecting their common interests. Still outstanding, however, was the controversy over the Syrian province of Alexandretta on the eastern frontier of Turkey. Some 40 per cent of the population of this province was Turkish, and it was feared that when the French mandate in Syria came to an end the Arab nationalists would discriminate against the Turks. With the assistance of the League Council, Turkey obtained a separate political regime for Alexandretta in 1937. In the following year, in co-operation with the French, a predominant position was secured for the Turkish element in the province, which was given the Turkish name of Hatay. Finally in 1939, by political arrangement with the French and against the vigorous protests of the Syrians, Turkey annexed the province.

More delicate were Turkey's relations with the great powers. While Atatürk and İnönü could firmly reject the Italian claim to a dominant position in the Eastern Mediterranean, they had to treat with great respect a Germany whose share in Turkish exports rose from 13 to 43 per cent between 1929 and 1938, and in Turkish imports from 15 to 47 per cent during the same period. Turkey's relations with the Soviet Union were based on the treaty of friendship of 1925, and Russia did not appear to object to the firm repression of Communism in Turkey, so long as that country did not become a satellite of an unfriendly power.

To counterbalance the potentially menacing proximity of conflicting German and Russian interests, Turkey tended to rely increasingly on the more disinterested friendship of Great Britain and France. Thus, after the dismemberment of Czechoslovakia in the spring of 1939, Turkey concluded a provisional mutual-assistance pact with France and Great Britain. This agreement, following the Turkish acquisition of the province of Hatay, was concluded on the assumption that the Western states would find a common basis of action with the Soviet Union, but when the Nazi-Soviet pact was signed in August, 1939, the Turks decided to explore the situation further. The Turkish foreign minister went to Moscow with a view to concluding a pact further defining relations with Russia. The latter was in no mood for compromise at this time, however, as the treaty with Germany had opened up the prospect of Soviet domination of Eastern Europe from the Baltic to the Black Sea. Russia, therefore, demanded that Turkey abandon its pact with the Western states and close the Straits to non-Black Sea powers. These were terms which Turkey could not accept, and in October, 1939, the formal treaty of mutual assistance was signed with Great Britain and France.

The Independent Arab States

EGYPT. When Great Britain terminated its protectorate over Egypt and declared that country to be an independent state in 1922, it reserved the guarantee of its special interests for negotiation in a separate treaty. These interests consisted of the security of British communications in Egypt, the defense of Egypt against foreign interference, the protection of foreign interests and of minorities in Egypt, and the security of the Sudan. Prime Minister MacDonald stated in 1924 with refreshing candor: "It is no less true today than in 1922 that the security of the communications of the British Empire in Egypt remains a vital British interest and that absolute certainty that the Suez Canal will remain open in peace as well as in war for the free passage of British ships is the foundation on which the entire defensive strategy of the British Empire rests." To implement their policy the British had not only extensive military and civil power within Egypt but also the ability to bar the admission of that country to the League of Nations, and both of these weapons were used before a settlement was finally reached.

The question of how British interests were to be defined and guaranteed was to plague British-Egyptian relations for the next fifteen years. Under the parliamentary form of government established in 1923, three main trends of opinion emerged. The most moderate was that of the Liberal party, representing among others a majority of the former Turkish governing group that had stayed on in Egypt as part of the upper class. The Nationalist party, founded in 1907, was the traditional representative of the Egyptian striving for independence. The most extreme group of the nationalists now emerged as the Wafd party, headed by Zaghlul. The extremists predominated between 1924 and 1930, and relations with the British in this period were marked by continual strife, culminating in several assassinations. In 1930 King Fuad took advantage of this strife to impose an authoritarian regime that succeeded in suppressing the extreme nationalists and made some progress in evolving a settlement with the British. The restoration of parliamentary government in 1935 produced conditions favorable to a return to domestic political stability and a definitive settlement with the British. Upon King Fuad's death in 1936, these efforts were continued by his young son and heir Farouk. Moreover, both parties recognized that the revival of Italian imperialism in Ethiopia, which raised the whole question of the status of the Suez Canal, required their immediate attention.

The principal object of the Anglo-Egyptian treaty concluded in 1936 was to grant full independence to Egypt while retaining the minimum requirements for the strategic security of the British Empire. This was accomplished by the conclusion of a defensive alliance for an initial period of twenty years, during which time British land and air forces would be maintained in the Canal Zone but not in the rest of Egypt. The British Mediterranean fleet, on the other hand, would have the use of the harbor of Alexandria. In case of war, Egypt was to permit the use by British forces of its transportation and other facilities. In the Anglo-Egyptian Sudan, the Egyptian army and civil-service personnel were to be put on an equal status with the British, and it was hoped that the native Sudanese would take an increasing share in the administration of their country.

The achievement of full Egyptian independence also required the relinquishment of the responsibilities Britain had assumed for the protection of foreigners and foreign interests in Egypt. The capitulations, under which Egypt had been required to grant privileges to twelve foreign governments and their citizens, involved a variety of special courts and a separate regime protecting foreign investments amounting to some two billion dollars. The British now took the initiative in calling a conference of the capitulatory powers, and in 1937 it was agreed that the extraterritorial privileges would be abolished at the end of twelve years. Final recognition of Egypt's status as a full-fledged state came also in 1937, when that country was admitted as a member of the League of Nations.

One of the issues that exerted a steady influence on Egyptian affairs was the status of the Anglo-Egyptian Sudan. This extensive colonial province, which stretched south to Ethiopia, Kenya, and Belgian Congo, had been conquered by the British at the end of the nineteenth century. The population of the Sudan was Moslem by religion and Arabic by language, and, what was more important, the Sudan controlled the upper regions of the Nile River, on which Egypt's very existence depended. Egypt's political connection with the Sudan was by now of a century's duration, and during the period of British domination the Egyptians had paid the major share of the military and irrigation expenses of the Sudan. So long as the British maintained a military force at Khartum and could exert a determining influence on the allocation of the Nile waters for irrigation projects, the Egyptians would feel that the destiny of their country was in foreign hands. In fact, no issue had a wider appeal to all levels of Egyptian opinion than that of the control of the Nile waters, and the demand for full Egyptian sovereignty over the Sudan played a major role in the long negotiations that preceded Egypt's independence [see map, p. 140].

SAUDI ARABIA. During the five years following the end of the war, King Husein of the Hejaz declined from a position of recognized leadership in the Arab world to that of a homeless exile. The astuteness that had led him to co-operate with the British during the war in order to advance the fortunes of his dynasty and of the Arab peoples deserted him when he became embittered by his failure to achieve the full extent of his ambitions. In 1921 and again in 1923 the British approached him with a view to placing their postwar relations on a permanent basis, but Husein persisted in refusing to come to any agreement that involved recognition of the regimes established in Palestine and Syria. In refusing to accept the peace settlement as an unpleasant reality and to be satisfied with the establishment of his two sons in Iraq and Transjordan, Husein sacrificed not only a considerable British subsidy but also the military assistance which would have guaranteed the Hejaz from attack by its neighbors.

Husein was thus isolated and friendless when Ibn Saud, ruler of the Wahhabi dynasty in central Arabia, attacked him in the autumn of 1924. Within a little over a year he was in exile and his kingdom had disappeared. Ibn Saud's victory now gave him control over the Moslem holy places at Mecca and Medina, and this control made him a central figure in the Moslem world. At his invitation an Islamic Congress met at Mecca in the summer of 1926, and it succeeded in reconciling the interests of the various Moslem sects in the regulation of the holy places. In the following year the British formally recognized Ibn Saud's independence as the "King of the Hejaz and of Nejd and its Dependencies." The degree of authority that Ibn Saud had by this time achieved is demonstrated by the fact that the British did not ask for special interests; nor did they require Ibn Saud's adherence to the Balfour Declaration as regards Palestine. Similar treaties were shortly signed by Ibn Saud with the other European powers possessing extensive Moslem interests—France, the Soviet Union, Italy, and the Netherlands.

The formal adoption in 1932 of the name of Saudi Arabia for the territories unified under the leadership of Ibn Saud marked the end of the period of expansion. One final frontier adjustment, made in 1934 with neighboring Yemen, left that state chastened but independent under the rule of Imam Yahya. The chief purpose of Ibn Saud now was to provide for the security of his state rather than for its territorial growth, and to this end he issued a general pardon to political exiles from his kingdom. After long negotiations, he also concluded important political agreements with Iraq and Egypt in 1936. These treaties settled the outstanding political rivalries that Ibn Saud's rise to power had engendered, made provision for pilgrimages to the Moslem holy places at Mecca and Medina, and laid the basis for closer political co-operation among the Arab states in defense of their common interests.

Ibn Saud's program of domestic reform was at first held back by lack of adequate revenue, but this handicap was removed by the development of Arabian oil reserves. The exploitation of these resources had been delayed in part by uncertainty as to their location and extent, and in part by rivalries among the oil companies. In 1933 Ibn Saud finally took the decisive step of granting a concession to two American companies, organized as the Arabian American Oil Company. This concession, extending over an area of some 400,000 square miles in eastern Arabia, won for the Arab state large loans and technical assistance in a wide variety of fields, even before the oil wells began to produce. The development of these resources did not get under way until 1938, but within ten years Saudi Arabia was second only to Iran among the countries of the Middle East in oil production. Almost as important as the economic benefits of this arrangement were its political consequences. While the United States government had not taken the initiative in obtaining the Arabian concession, the participation of American capital in so large an undertaking implied a new interest in the political problems of this region. British, French, and Russian influences continued to predominate in the Middle East, but the statesmen of that region were alive to the possibilities inherent in the presence of an additional great power with few political demands and great economic and technical resources.

The Arab Mandates

SYRIA AND LEBANON. Upon the formal establishment of French authority in Syria with the occupation of Damascus in 1920, the mandatory power found itself faced not only with the opposition of Syrian nationalists but also with a heritage of civil and religious strife within the country. While most of the population of almost 3,000,000 were Arabic in language, about a quarter were Christian by faith; there were, moreover, some ten Christian and five Moslem sects. Of the Christian sects, the most important were the Maronites, who owed their allegiance to Rome. Among the Moslems the Sunni were by far the most numerous, but the bellicose Druse mountaineers, who numbered about 100,000, were also an important factor. Confronted with this variety of religious groupings—each with its own geographical location and cultural tradition—and doubtless also desiring to counteract hostility by fostering political decentralization, the French had divided the country by 1925 into four almost autonomous subsidiary states. In addition, a certain administrative autonomy was granted to the coastal district, which included the towns of Alexandretta and Antioch and had a large Turkish population.

Of these provinces the two most important were Syria, with its capital at Damascus, and Lebanon, with its capital at Beirut. The former was largely Moslem by faith and was the strongest center of Arab nationalism. The latter had a slight Christian majority and tended to lean somewhat on the French for support. It was not long before a large majority of the population had accumulated serious grievances. The mandatory was blamed not only for the political subdivision of the original mandate, but also for drawing the boundaries of the various autonomous units in such a way as to favor one or another of the religious groups. In addition, the Arabs objected to a number of policies adopted by the French in the exercise of their administrative authority. The introduction of a currency based on the depreciating French franc was exasperating to a population that had enjoyed the relative stability of the Egyptian pound. Similarly, the insistence on the use of the French language on a par with the Arabic met with great disfavor. Most important of all, the French imposed serious restrictions on civil liberties, affecting all those who supported the Arab nationalist movement and desired to work for Syrian independence.

These controversies came to a head in 1925 with the arrival of General Sarrail as French High Commissioner. During the latter part of the war Sarrail had commanded the Allied army based at Salonika. He was a controversial figure in French politics, and in Syria he promptly justified his reputation by running into difficulties with both the Christian Maronites and the Moslem Druses. It was the latter who first challenged French authority, by revolting in the summer of 1925, and the uprising spread to the whole of the mandate. The series of French punitive measures which followed served only to irritate the Arabs, and the bombardment of Damascus in October, with the loss of several hundred civilian lives, brought the entire situation to the attention of European opinion. The aim of the insurgents was now frankly independence, so that the replacement of Sarrail by a civilian had little effect on the development of Arab feeling. In the spring of 1926 the French again shelled Damascus, this time with an even greater loss of life, and an investigation was instituted by the Permanent Mandates Commission of the League of Nations. The League itself was unable to intervene in the administration of the French mandate, but by this time French opinion had been adequately impressed by the seriousness of the situation so that steps were taken to find a solution which would serve to implement the principal purposes of the mandate system and at the same time conciliate the Arab nationalists.

In Lebanon a republican constitution was promulgated in 1926, providing for a partially elected assembly. While a number of modifications were made in this structure during the subsequent years, it provided for a substantial degree of self-government and took care to respect the delicate balance of religious groupings on which the stability of the country rested. In the other three autonomous units comprising the mandate, now reunited as Syria, the resentment that had been fanned by the French punitive measures made conciliation more difficult. When the French in 1928 finally permitted an elected assembly to draft a constitution, it included territorial and political conditions that conflicted with French rights under the mandate system. This assembly was dissolved by the High Commissioner in 1930, and he now promulgated a modified constitution providing broad opportunities for self-government. The first assembly under this arrangement did not meet until 1932, and while the more extreme nationalists were returned in a minority, the French continued to meet with only a moderate success in finding a working agreement with the Arabs. The more extreme nationalists refused to accept the French offer in 1933 of independence within four years, on condition that France be permitted to retain certain military, political, and financial privileges for twenty-five years. The nationalists blocked ratification of this agreement in the Syrian assembly, and in the prevailing atmosphere of acute political strife extremist groups of both rightist and leftist tendencies grew rapidly in influence.

The rise of Italian power in the Eastern Mediterranean served to emphasize the necessity for an orderly transition from mandate to independence, and the victory of the Popular Front government in France led to a more conciliatory approach on the part of the mandatory. In 1936 treaties were finally negotiated with both Syria and Lebanon which appeared to satisfy the requirements of the situation. It was agreed that all the provinces of the mandate excepting Lebanon were to form a unitary state of Syria, and provision was made for the minorities that would fall under Arab rule under this arrangement. The large Arab minority in Lebanon was dissatisfied at being separated from Syria, but was unable to alter the settlement. Under the 1936 treaties, independence was to be provided for both states after a transitional three-year period. France was to retain a privileged position for another twenty-five years, but its rights were stated in more moderate terms than in earlier drafts and were regarded as acceptable in Syria and Lebanon.

Despite the bright prospects for an early peaceful settlement which the 1936 treaties offered, new difficulties soon arose. One of the most serious was the antagonism aroused among the Arabs by the French agreement, under Turkish pressure, to establish a special regime in the Syrian province of Alexandretta. The final transfer of this province to Turkish sovereignty in 1939 was regarded by many Arabs as a betrayal by France of its responsibilities as a mandatory. Moreover, the difficulties of the Arabs in neighboring Palestine aroused great sympathy, and a Pan-Arab conference was held in Syria in 1937 to organize the defense of Arab interests. At the same time, in France there was great criticism of the 1936 treaties on the ground that French interests were inadequately protected. Attempts made in 1938 to obtain revision of the terms in favor of France nevertheless found no support among the Arabs. With the approach of war the possibilities of a compromise settlement diminished, and when World War II finally broke out, it found the 1936 treaties still unratified and widespread discontent prevailing in the French mandate.

PALESTINE. The relatively friendly relations that had existed between the Arabs and the Zionists at the Peace Conference deteriorated rapidly once Palestine was definitely assigned to Great Britain as a mandate. Within an independent Arab state, the Arab leaders were willing to cooperate in the settlement of a limited number of Jewish refugees. When independence was denied them, they were determined to resist British efforts to implement the Balfour Declaration. While the Moslems constituted some 80 per cent of the population in 1922, they feared that the continued large-scale immigration of Jews would rapidly reduce their predominance. An anti-Jewish disturbance in Tel-Aviv in May, 1921, which while not on a large scale was nevertheless indicative of prevailing Arab opinion, led to a renewed effort on the part of the British to reinterpret the Balfour Declaration in such a way as to reduce friction. In 1922 the British Colonial Office, which at that time was headed by Winston Churchill, issued a document known as the Churchill Memorandum stating explicitly that Great Britain did not contemplate the subordination of the Arab population or the conversion of the whole of Palestine into a Jewish National Home. The memorandum stated that, on the contrary, such a Home should be founded in only a limited area of Palestine and that immigration would be regulated by the economic capacity of the country and the economic interests of the Arab population. This policy was accepted by the Zionist Organization but was rejected by the Arab leaders, who refused to cooperate with any solution not based on the wishes of the majority of the population. Arab intransigence was further reflected in a refusal to participate in the elections for the Legislative Council set up in 1922 or in the deliberations of the Advisory Council established in the following year. The British, therefore, abandoned these efforts at partial self-government and fell back on a system of administration based on informal consultation with the various interested religious and national groups.

Although the Arabs did not alter their point of view in the years immediately following these first disturbances, during most of the 1920's the likelihood of large-scale Jewish immigration appeared to be far less than they had at first expected. The pressure of Jewish immigration depended to a large extent on the treatment of Jewish minorities in Europe. In the 1920's, while there was a steady flow of settlers from Poland and the Soviet Union, the pressure was not great. At the end of the war no more than 5 per cent of Palestine's population was engaged in industry, and in addition the economic absorptive capacity of the agricultural regions was regarded as very low unless extensive irrigation projects were undertaken. As the early immigrants from Eastern Europe did not in most cases bring with them any large amount of capital, the mid-1920's saw an economic depression in Palestine. This relative lack of economic activity on the part of the Zionists is generally believed to have been the cause of the political stability that characterized this period. This calm was so encouraging that the British were able to organize a degree of local self-government on the municipal level, and the municipal elections held in 1927 were regarded as a great success.

The Arabs were not satisfied with these local reforms, however, and both in 1928 and 1929 petitioned the British for the application of the principle on which they had always insisted: an assembly based on popular representation. The British were unable to grant this concession, which would have undermined both the system on which the mandate was based and the commitment implicit in the Balfour Declaration; and disturbances began to break out anew. In August, 1929, a bitter struggle developed over a controversy concerning the Wailing Wall in Jerusalem, which was a sacred place for both Jews and Arabs. In the resulting skirmish, over one hundred lives were lost on each side. In reviewing the situation created by this latest outbreak, the British now found themselves confronted by new demands on the part of both parties. The Zionist Organization requested the enlistment of Jews in the security force in order to insure the protection of Zionist settlements. It also urged that steps be taken to increase Jewish immigration and colonization. The Arabs, for their part, demanded the cessation of all immigration, assurance that land settled by Arabs would not be transferred to the Zionists, and a system of representative government. Before any plans could be developed to reconcile these conflicting demands, the growing persecution of Jews in Central and Eastern Europe introduced a new and, as it turned out, decisive factor into the situation.

The late 1920's and early 1930's was a period of relative stability in Arab-Jewish relations in the British mandate of Palestine, but the political consequences of the economic depression in Europe soon exerted a determining influence on the balance of forces. This influence was indirect and took the form of Zionist pressure for increased immigration into Palestine of Jews fleeing from the growing wave of persecution in Central and Eastern Europe. From an average of little over 5,000 a year between 1927 and 1932, the rate of Jewish immigration rose to an annual average of some 34,000 between 1933 and 1940. The following are the total population figures for Palestine during these years:

TABLE 9

POPULATION OF PALESTINE, 1922–40

YEAR	MOSLEMS	JEWS	OTHERS	TOTAL
1922	589,177	83,790	79,081	752,048
1932	771,174	180,793	100,905	1,052,872
1940	947,846	463,535	133,199	1,544,530

It was the Zionist point of view that transfer to Palestine was the only acceptable solution for Jews who were not allowed to live in peace in Europe, and the Zionist Organization was able to exert great pressure in London to prevent Great Britain from adopting a policy that might in the long run be prejudicial to Jewish immigration. The Arabs, on the other hand, feared that they would eventually find themselves in a numerical minority and that they would be forced by economic and political pressure to abandon their villages. Caught between these two points of view, the British government found it difficult to adopt a firm policy. Certain previous commitments, such as the Balfour Declaration in 1917, as well as political pressures in England and on the continent, recommended a policy favorable to Jewish immigration. At the same time, the large Moslem populations of the Near East and India were becoming excited over the issue and were able to exert influence which the British government could not overlook.

Moreover, explicit pledges had been given in the past that due consideration would be accorded to the economic interests of the Arab population.

The difficulties inherent in this situation are well illustrated by the
obstacles encountered when the British tried to extend self-government in
Palestine. Proposals published in the spring of 1936 made provision for a
constitution under which certain functions of the British High Commissioner would be transferred to a Legislative Council, to be partly appointed
and partly elected. Zionist leaders protested that under this constitution
the Arabs would be able to prevent further immigration. The Arabs, on the
other hand, felt that these proposals left too great authority in the hands
of the High Commissioner and deprived them of their rights as the majority national and religious group in the population. Arab feeling now took
the form of widespread strikes during the summer of 1936, which aroused
the sympathy of neighboring Arab states and impressed world opinion
with the vigor of Arab sentiments. The economic hardships resulting from
the strikes nevertheless prevented their indefinite prolongation, and a great
increase in the British military forces in Palestine returned the initiative
into the hands of the mandatory.

The widespread unrest had the effect of reopening the entire question
of British policy in Palestine, and a Royal Commission was appointed to
investigate the situation. The report of this Commission, which was published in the summer of 1937, made the unexpected proposal that efforts
to find a compromise under the mandate should be abandoned in favor of
the partition of Palestine into an Arab and a Jewish state. The British government had some hopes that this proposal would offer a way out of its
difficulties, but the reactions of the other interested parties were not favorable. The League of Nations was skeptical regarding the partition scheme,
but authorized its further investigation. The Zionists were encouraged by
the acceptance for the first time of the idea of an independent Jewish
state, but preferred to explore further the possibilities of a compromise
within the larger frontiers of Palestine before accepting partition. The
Arabs, on the other hand, were almost unanimous in opposition to partition. In 1938 they organized a full-fledged revolt against British authority,
which was suppressed only after the loss of several thousand lives. The
British government, for its part, now dispatched a Partition Commission
to Palestine to examine the various partition schemes. It finally decided in
1938 that partition would not provide political and economic conditions
conducive to a peaceful settlement.

The British government, fully cognizant that the approach of war on
the continent necessitated the greatest possible stability in the Near East,
now fell back on direct negotiations among the interested parties. A Round
Table Conference was convoked in London to which were invited representatives of the various Arab and Jewish organizations in Palestine and
abroad. Long and stormy negotiations ensued, in which the almost irreconcilable antagonisms between the two groups were once more thoroughly
aired. From this conference emerged a new statement of British policy,

known as the White Paper of 1939. This document envisaged the creation of an independent state of Palestine at the end of a ten-year period. During the first five years a total of 75,000 Jews would be permitted to immigrate, and after that period immigration would be subject to Arab consent. While many regarded this solution as favorable to the Arab viewpoint, their leaders found it unacceptable. The Zionists, for their part, rejected the White Paper unconditionally. The British thus entered World War II with a problem on their hands in Palestine which was not only unresolved but was in a more explosive state than ever before.

TRANSJORDAN. As the balance of forces developed in the Arab countries after the war, Transjordan and Iraq grew in importance for the British. The defeat of King Husein by Ibn Saud had resulted in a striking decline in British influence in the greater part of the Arabian peninsula, while the controversies in Palestine made that mandate a source of irritation rather than of influence. As a consequence, British influence in the Arab countries came to rely more and more on the two mandates of Transjordan and Iraq, where Husein's sons Abdullah and Faisal were installed as rulers. The British, therefore, made broad concessions of independence to these two rulers, while keeping in their own hands the essential policy-making authority. In 1923 the existence of Transjordan as an independent government was recognized, while the British retained sufficient authority to fulfill the international obligations they had undertaken in the mandate. Since the Balfour Declaration did not apply in Transjordan, the basic controversy that existed in Palestine between the British and the Arabs did not develop in the neighboring territory. To conciliate the Arabs on this score, the British even went a step beyond the letter of the law by forbidding the purchase of land in Transjordan by Jews. The status of Transjordan was further clarified in 1928 in a treaty with Great Britain, in which the latter transferred to Abdullah's government the powers of legislation and administration entrusted to the British under the mandate. In return, Abdullah agreed to follow the guidance of British advice in matters relating to foreign relations, financial policy, and jurisdiction over foreigners. King Abdullah evolved a satisfactory working relationship with the British under this arrangement. Six years later the scope of his activities was extended when he appointed consular representatives to the other Arab states, and his personal qualities and family connections gave him a position of leadership among Arabs which extended beyond the frontiers of his state. Although no more than a handful of British officials remained in the country, it proved to be a haven of relative stability during the troubled years that World War II brought to the Near East.

IRAQ. In the years between 1920 and 1931 the number of British and Indian officers in the Iraq government was reduced from 2,906 to 196, and the full independence that the Arabs desired gradually came into sight. Despite this progress, however, the balance of forces within the country was so delicate as to make the task of the High Commissioner very difficult. King Faisal, himself an outsider, was placed in the position of choosing between the nationalist Iraqi parties, which desired the immediate declaration of full independence, and the more moderate Iraqi, who favored cooperation with the British. In August, 1922, Faisal and the nationalists were able to overthrow the moderate cabinet on the issue of ratifying the treaty that confirmed Britain's special position in Iraq. A sudden illness of the King, however, gave the High Commissioner a pretext for taking up the reins of government himself, and the crisis passed without need for any drastic action.

The nationalists nevertheless continued to exercise a steady pressure on the British, and the broadening of Iraqi responsibility can be traced in the constitution promulgated in 1925. This tendency was also encouraged by the strong body of opinion in England in the early 1920's which favored the complete withdrawal of Great Britain from Iraq. The constitution declared Iraq to be an independent state and guaranteed to its citizens equality before the law regardless of race or creed, as well as freedom of conscience. These guarantees, along with the other civil liberties, were particularly important in view of the religious differences in Iraq. The king, who shared the legislative power with the bicameral parliament, was given broad powers of government when the legislature was not in session, but the latter remained as the final authority. Cabinet ministers were explicitly made responsible to the lower house, which also had the final word on financial matters. The separate electoral law provided for an indirect system of election, special provision being made for the representation of non-Islamic minorities. In the spring of 1924 a constituent assembly was called to ratify the three documents on which Iraq's future independent existence was to be based: the British-Iraqi treaty of 1922, the constitution, and the electoral law. Iraqi nationalist opinion had already obtained a reduction of Britain's special status from twenty years to four, but it still objected to the broad controls over policy which the treaty and the constitution gave to Great Britain. After the exercise of great pressure by Faisal and the High Commissioner, including the threat of dissolution, the nationalist-dominated assembly finally voted the three documents in June, 1924. After this point the extension of practical self-government continued more rapidly, although never with sufficient speed to satisfy the more extreme nationalists. A new treaty in 1930 made the provision for Iraq's full independence and admission to the League of Nations within two years. At the same time, the British took care to assure a continuance of their special position in Iraq for a period of twenty-five years. This treaty provided for firm British guidance in matters of foreign affairs, and use of Iraqi transportation and communication facilities by the British in case of war. Air bases were also leased to the British on favorable terms. On this basis, Iraq was admitted to the League of Nations in 1932.

Iraq was of particular interest to British policy not only because of its strategic position in relation to India and Britain's commitments in the Near East, but also because of its important oil resources. On the eve of World War I, British and German interests in Mesopotamia had reached a working agreement with the Turkish government in regard to the exploitation of the oil. In 1920 Germany's oil interests were assigned to France, and five years later a new oil consortium was founded, known as the Iraq Petroleum Company. Apart from a 5-per-cent interest owned by an individual financier, ownership was divided equally among four great oil companies. Two of these, the Anglo-Iranian Oil Company and Royal Dutch Shell, were controlled by British policy. The other two represented French and American interests. Through the Iraq Petroleum Company and its subsidiaries, these interests operated concessions in all the Near Eastern countries with the exception of Saudi Arabia, which was not opened up until the later 1930's—and then under different auspices. While there was no extensive commercial production of oil in these countries, except in Iran, until the later 1930's, control over these resources was regarded as of great importance and exercised a significant influence on British policy.

In domestic affairs British policy was less successful, for the mature exercise of political independence demanded qualities the Iraqi had not yet acquired. With illiteracy at some 90 per cent, it could not be expected that a parliamentary system along European lines would be possible for a good many years. In actual practice, political power was wielded by a relatively small group of influential families and interests. Civil service, the administration of justice, and the collection of taxes were all attempted under conditions of great difficulty, and the methods applied evolved very slowly from the relatively lax system of the Ottoman Empire. The mediator between the British and the influential Iraqi, who included both moderate and extreme nationalists among their number, was King Faisal. He proved to be very skillful in preventing the nationalists from going too far beyond the limits of common sense in pressing their claims. He also recognized the advantages of British friendship and at times overstepped the bounds of his constitutional prerogatives to fulfill the requirements of the mandatory power.

The death of Faisal in 1933 brought an end to this era of relative stability. His son and successor, Ghazi, was still in his early twenties and had little of his father's political skill. Iraqi politics had always possessed an element of restlessness, with fifteen cabinets following each other in rapid succession between 1921 and 1933, but under King Ghazi the system ceased to function effectively. At the same time, the country was swept by a wave of nationalism which fed on minority problems at home and Arab reverses abroad. This excitement reached its climax in 1936, when General Bakir Sidqi overthrew the cabinet and established a military dictatorship. The assassination of the dictator in the following year terminated the direct intervention of the army in politics, but it established a precedent of forceful and unconstitutional action. The death of King Ghazi in an automobile accident in 1939 added a further element of instability. His son was only in his fourth year when he ascended the throne as Faisal II, and Iraq entered the war era without firm and experienced leadership.

IV

THE
SECOND WORLD
CRISIS

CHAPTER

17

Italy, France, and Great Britain in the Thirties

Italy: *Italian Economy; Foreign Policy; The Empire; Racial Policy; The Vatican.*

France: *The Political Scene, 1932–36; Formation of the Popular Front; The French New Deal; Foreign Affairs.*

Great Britain: *Political Developments; Economic Changes; Ireland; The British Commonwealth; Foreign Policy.*

WESTERN EUROPE during the thirties lay under the spell of the economic depression and the rise of Hitler. To combat the depression, somewhat similar policies were followed in all the states. Currencies were openly depreciated or the same results obtained through other methods. In general there was an upsurge of economic nationalism which involved imposition of numerous trade restrictions and often the subsidy of domestic production. Various efforts were made to raise the price level of agricultural products, for farmers everywhere found that prices were actually below a reasonable cost of production. Unemployment was general, and governments resorted to direct relief as well as to a variety of measures designed to provide work. Governments were forced to intervene in economic affairs, not because they wanted to, but because it was necessary to start the wheels of industry turning again.

The resurgence of Germany was only the most spectacular aspect of a general change in world affairs. The depression had wiped the slate clean of reparations and actually also of war debts, although there were some die-hards in the United States who refused to recognize this fact. With this a great segment of the postwar settlement was swept into oblivion, and it was clear that more changes were to follow. Western Europe comprised the core of the victorious coalition. The Manchurian Crisis of 1931–33, the Italian-Ethiopian War of 1935–36, and the Spanish Civil War of 1936–39 were to weaken that coalition seriously. Everywhere tension mounted, and one political crisis followed another. Whether democracies could carry on under prevailing conditions was a seriously debated question even in well-established democratic states, where extremes on both right and left began to challenge the very basis on which societies and governments were organized.

This confusion and doubt was particularly marked in France in the thirties. France had changed less in the decade following the war than had either Italy or Britain. The path for Italy was already set in the twenties, and the thirties brought only a continuation and extension of the same policies. Britain, true to her policy of slow evolution, had begun to shape new trade and colonial policies immediately after the war, and these were amplified. The widespread acceptance in England of the National government of 1931 showed that the British people were still agreed on the basic principles and forms of government. No one seriously challenged the monarchy or the parliamentary system. In France some of the political reorganization that had already been accomplished by Italy and Britain was still to be undertaken. Conflict between right and left continued, and there was no agreement on the basic forms of government. Large groups challenged the Third Republic and its institutions. All too many tried to graft either communist or fascist theories and practices on a traditional acceptance of democracy and liberty. Many shouted for change but in their hearts wished to keep their innumerable personal vested interests and a great deal of the *status quo*. No real solution was ever found.

The revival of German nationalism, with its openly avowed aim of upsetting the peace settlement established by the Treaty of Versailles, and the growing weakness of the League brought new problems of security. Before long each state frantically sought protection through an increase in armaments. Thus a much larger role for national governments, with a corresponding readjustment of democratic ideas and faiths, was the result of economic troubles and insecurity.

Italy

ITALIAN ECONOMY. The final establishment of the corporative system, begun in the twenties, was achieved in the mid-thirties [see above, pp. 249–

51], but the general lines of Italian policy were not so much altered by this development as by the depression, which forced the government to grant further aid to many industries. An Industrial Reconstruction Institute, which served much the same function as the Reconstruction Finance Corporation in the United States, was founded in January, 1933, to provide long term loans for many hard pressed businesses. No widespread policy of nationalization was adopted, but step by step the government increased its participation in and control of the nation's economy. By 1940 the Industrial Reconstruction Institute alone, through its financial holdings, controlled about 20 per cent of the economic life of the country.

By the end of 1933, unemployment figures were well over a million. The social insurance program had to be supplemented by public grants, for even the few who were eligible for these short-term insurance benefits could not live on the small payments, ranging from twelve to thirty-six cents a day. The government expanded its public works program and encouraged internal migration so as to bring relief to certain areas. In October, 1934, an eight hour day and a forty hour week were adopted. Hourly wages were not increased, so the take-home pay was correspondingly smaller. Nevertheless, artificially high prices for such products as wheat were maintained in order to encourage production.

In her export industries Italy faced the crisis which was common to all countries of the world. Her chief exports were silk, rayon, and cotton goods —industries that suffered particularly from the depression everywhere. Italy entered into a host of bilateral trade agreements, and new and higher tariffs were imposed. The economic sanctions imposed by the League of Nations (October 1935–July 1936), as a protest against the Ethiopian War, resulted in further control of foreign trade by the Italian government through counter-sanctions aimed at the countries concerned in the League action. War economy, with its drain on the little foreign exchange available, forced the government to undertake an increasingly minute policy of trade control. Italy and Germany were the two great powers that resorted to the policy of clearing agreements in these years [see above, pp. 366–67].

The enormous expense connected with military ventures in Ethiopia (1935–36) and in Spain (1936–39) weakened an already shaky Italian economy [see below, Chapter 20]. Taxes reached unprecedented heights, and in 1935 the government resorted to a forced loan. All real estate owners were forced to purchase 25-year bonds equal to 5 per cent of the assessed valuation of their property. In October, 1936, the lira was officially revalued.

FOREIGN POLICY. In March, 1933, Italy proposed a four-power pact between England, France, Italy and Germany. Under it the four great powers would co-operate on deciding the political questions of Europe and could counter the influence of the small states in the League of Nations. France, under obligations to her allies in Central Europe, demanded extensive changes in the treaty draft, and the Four Power Pact as signed on July 15, 1933, was a most innocuous document. Even so it never was rati-

DANUBIAN STATESMEN IN ROME *Premier Mussolini of Italy, Chancellor Dollfuss of Austria (second from right), and Premier Gömbös of Hungary at the signing of the Rome Protocols, March, 1934.*

fied, yet it bears testimony to Mussolini's ambition to elevate Italy to a more important position in world affairs.

The Rome Protocols of 1934 brought closer trade ties with Austria and Hungary, but their chief importance lay in the political field. For a brief period Mussolini became the great champion of Austrian independence. He supported the Dollfuss dictatorship in Austria (1933) and when Dollfuss was assassinated at the time the Nazis attempted their Austrian coup in July, 1935, Mussolini ordered extra troops to the Brenner Pass. France was particularly grateful for this assistance in checking Nazi expansion. But the events of the Ethiopian and Spanish crises caused Italy to forsake her championship of Austria, and the way was cleared for a rapprochement with Germany. One of the most significant events in European history in the thirties was Italy's break with Britain and France, her shift in alignment from Western to Central Europe.

The formation of the Axis was brought about by a German-Italian agreement of October 25–27, 1936, the signature by Italy on November 6, 1937, of the German-Japanese Anti-Comintern Pact, and the conclusion of the Pact of Steel of May 22, 1939 [see below, pp. 512; 534]. The latter was a hard and fast military alliance. In addition to conquering Ethiopia, Italy had on April 7, 1939, invaded Albania and ended the independence of that state. Victor Emmanuel III was now King of Italy, Emperor of Ethiopia, and King of Albania.

THE EMPIRE. In 1934 Italy officially united Tripolitania and Cyrenaica into one colony of Libya (see map, p. 98). The reorganization of the empire continued in 1936 when Eritrea and Somaliland were joined to Ethiopia to form a new colony of Italian East Africa. In 1937 a Six-Year Plan for East Africa was announced. Italy undertook to build a highway system and to spend millions of lire on public works. Plans were made for the exploitation of Ethiopian resources, especially cotton, rubber, and other tropical products. This would reduce the need for foreign exchange, since both East Africa and Libya were within the Italian controlled currency area.

RACIAL POLICY. The conquest of Ethiopia led to the adoption of a series of racial laws. It is generally assumed that this was the product of the new ties with National Socialist Germany although Mussolini always denied this. Whatever the reason, between July and November, 1938, a number of decrees against the Jews were issued. There were in all only about 70,000 Jews in Italy and up to this time they had gone unmolested. At first the measures were directed at foreign Jews, but soon they were directed at all the Italian Jews as well. Jewish students and teachers were banned from the schools and universities. Marriage between an Italian and a Jew was absolutely forbidden, no Jew could employ an Aryan house servant, no Jews could be employed by the state or by any private institutions supported by the state. In the end no Jew could own or manage an establishment affecting national defense or employing more than one hundred persons. They were also prohibited from owning land with a taxable income of more than 5,000 lire or residential property with a taxable income of more than 20,000 lire. On the whole the Italian legislation went very far and in general followed the anti-Semitic pattern enacted in Germany, Hungary, or Rumania. Its one saving grace was that the Italian laws were not strictly administered. Yet persecution did follow, and Italy ceased to be a haven for the Jewish exiles of other states.

THE VATICAN. In general the relations of the state and the Vatican were amicable. The Vatican was circumspect in its utterances, but various statements showed clearly that the Pope favored the Italians in their imperialistic venture in Ethiopia. It meant a whole new field for missions, and definite plans were made to expand the Ethiopian churches which were affiliated with Rome. The Pope was even more outspoken in favor of the Italian position in the Spanish Civil War. The anti-clerical position taken by the Spanish Republic and the communist support given to the Loyalists in the Civil War caused the papacy to take sides openly in this conflict.

The papacy, however, not only issued general statements denouncing the Italian racial laws but attacked them more particularly because they violated the Concordat of 1929, according to which the state had agreed to recognize and register all marriages performed by the church. The new laws prohibited the civil registration of marriages between Italian "Aryans" and "non-Aryans." This challenged the rights of the church over marriage, but in spite of formal and informal representations by the Vatican the decrees remained.

The Vatican continued its policy of concluding concordats with various governments. The two most important ones of this period were with Germany in 1933 and Yugoslavia in 1935. While there were encyclicals and papal pronouncements that condemned policies of various fascist states, the bitterest denunciations were reserved for Marxist socialism and communism, which were held to be incompatible with Christianity. On the other hand, in an important encyclical *Quadragesimo anno* issued in 1931, Pope Pius XI decried the existing maldistribution of wealth and called again for economic and social reforms that would give the worker a fair share of the wealth he produced.

On the death of Pius XI in 1939 Cardinal Eugenio Pacelli, who had served as nuncio to Berlin and for years had been papal secretary of state, was elected to the papal chair as Pius XII. His diplomatic skill was to stand him in good stead during the coming troubled years.

France

THE POLITICAL SCENE, 1932–36. In the election of 1932 the parties of the left won a clear-cut victory with 350 seats, of which the Radical Socialists held 160, the Socialists 131, and the Communists only 10. But the left was far from united. The Socialists refused to enter a cabinet with the Radical Socialists, and the latter were forced to form a series of coalitions with various minor left and center groups. Within nineteen months France was presented with six cabinets.

The basic cause for this political instability was the economic depression that had, after some delay, reached France. Other countries devalued their currencies to meet the situation, but for political reasons the French clung to the gold standard. The cabinets adopted a policy of deflation. This involved cutting government expenses through reducing the number of office-holders as well as by lowering salaries and pensions. These were highly unpopular measures and brought the concerted opposition of powerful civil service organizations, which have always exerted considerable pressure on the nerve centers of French politics. Then, too, international affairs presented extremely controversial matters. The Hoover moratorium and the cancellation of reparations were burning issues in France, whose war damages had been by far the most severe. Outside of parliament a rising group of fascist leagues poured vituperation on the politicians and the government in general.

On the extreme right was the royalist *Action Française*. A movement as well as a political party, it aroused a stir far greater than its small membership warranted. Its youth organization, the *Camelots du Roi* (King's

Companions)—made up largely of students—became expert at disrupting meetings. This, and a number of other such groups, all placed an exaggerated emphasis on youth. Of greatest importance was the *Croix de Feu*, led by Colonel de La Rocque. The name of this group was derived from the fact that originally it was an organization of war veterans who had been decorated for courage in active service. It soon expanded by recruiting a group of National Volunteers (*Volontaires Nationaux*) from among the sons of these men, and then a more extensive group of sympathizers (*Regroupement National autour des Croix de Feu*). Membership rose rapidly from 200,000 in 1934 to over 700,000 by the end of 1935. Strongly disciplined, the *Croix de Feu* delighted in holding frequent secret mobilizations. Its stock in trade was denunciation of the parties in power and a call for a stronger executive form of government. It claimed to be the only group which really put the national welfare of France above partisan ends. To left sympathizers, the *Croix de Feu* was nothing but an out-and-out fascist party.

In January, 1934, one of the internal scandals which periodically disturbed French politics broke into the headlines. Serge Alexander Stavisky, a clever financial manipulator, had succeeded in being made director of the municipal pawnshop of Bayonne and had issued about $25,000,000 worth of bonds on behalf of the enterprise. To help their sale he was able to induce the minister of public works to write letters recommending the bonds to insurance companies. He was about to be arrested after a long period of immunity from investigation of his unusual business practices, when found a suicide. The press had been largely responsible for the intended arrest, and now made the most of the chance to charge corruption in high political circles, for Stavisky clearly had "connections" there.

Premier Chautemps was forced to resign, and Daladier, who formed a new minority cabinet, announced the appointment of a parliamentary commission of inquiry. Meanwhile he dismissed the popular prefect of the Paris police, to the disgust of the populace who believed that the guilty individuals were in the government. On February 6, 1934, when Daladier was to meet parliament for the first time, the extremist parties summoned their members to demonstrations. Riots ensued, the most serious since the Commune of 1871. Mobs threatened to storm the Chamber of Deputies, and the police found it necessary to use firearms. After giving Daladier a vote of confidence, the deputies slipped quietly away to safety. Popular indignation found expression in a rash of lapel buttons which read "I am not a Deputy."

The Stavisky scandal seemed to justify the charge of the extremists that the politicians were all thieves and crooks. Something had to be done to restore confidence. Ex-President Doumergue was called out of retirement to form a Government of National Union, made up of Radical Socialists and representatives of the center and right. Everybody expected Doumergue to undertake a bold policy. The Chamber of Deputies, glad to escape popular wrath, granted the new premier full powers for a limited time (February 28 to June 30, 1934), to take all measures to balance the budget. Briand had asked for decree power in 1916 but it had been refused him. Poincaré had been granted it in 1924 but never used it, although he did exercise such powers under a similar grant in 1926. This grant of power in 1934 marks a new procedure in French political practice, one that was followed with increasing regularity in the succeeding years. Unable or unwilling to legislate, parliament abdicated its responsibility in favor of decree legislation. These decrees ultimately had to be approved by parliament, but they were regularly submitted all together weeks after they had gone into effect separately. Actually France, like many other countries of Europe in this period, was governed by decrees rather than by the regular legislative process.

Doumergue continued the deflationary policy, but his proposal to amend the constitution giving the executive power to dissolve the Chamber was voted down. Doumergue was followed in rapid succession by Flandin, Bouisson, Laval, and Sarraut. Each of these headed a so-called National Union cabinet with a gradual shift to the right in evidence up to the parliamentary election of 1936.

FORMATION OF THE POPULAR FRONT. Soon after Hitler took power in Germany the Communist International changed tactics. It began to advocate the co-operation of Communist parties with any group that was willing to unite in an anti-fascist front, and this policy was later officially approved by the 1935 World Congress of the Third International. One of the first such united fronts to be established was in France. Between the traditional fear of Germany and the growing rightist leagues within France, the French left was forced to seek union. In July, 1934, the Socialists and Communists made an agreement for common action against fascism. The Socialist and Communist dominated trade unions began to co-operate in strikes. The two parties, instead of knifing each other as had been their previous practice, lent mutual support in the municipal elections in the spring of 1935. The consequent success of the left not only alarmed the parties of the right, but also brought the Radical Socialists into the leftist fold. The Popular Front—as the coalition of Communists, Socialists, Radical Socialists, and several lesser groups, came to be called—first came to light in the great anti-fascist demonstrations of Bastille Day, July 14, 1935. A few months later the two labor federations, which had split in 1921 on the issue of communism, again united to form one *Confédération Générale du Travail*. The fusion of the two federations was completed in 1936. Finally an electoral agreement preceding the April, 1936, elections gave concrete form to the coalition. French law required that if no candidate for deputy received an absolute majority of the vote in a district, there should be a run-off election in which a mere plurality would be sufficient to elect. The parties of the Popular Front now arranged that, in the first balloting, each of the three coalition parties would run its own candidate. If a second balloting proved necessary, the two candidates with the least votes would withdraw, throwing their support to the candidate who had received the most votes. This electoral agreement worked out successfully, for the right did not counter by a similar arrangement. With the addition of a few minor groups the Popular Front now commanded 389 out of 618 seats in the Chamber.

The Socialists had always previously refused to join in a ministerial coalition with bourgeois parties. Now, however, as the largest party of the majority group they could not well decline to assume responsibility. An agreement with the Radical Socialists was easily worked out, but the Communist party still preferred to remain outside the government, although it did promise support. Léon Blum, an intellectual disciple of the great French Socialist Jaurès, became premier. That he was a Jew was not without importance, for it intensified the hostility of certain rightist groups.

The French New Deal. Directly after the elections of May, 1936, a wave of strikes swept over France. In most cases the workers occupied factories, and Premier Blum refused to use force to evacuate them. Instead he prevailed upon the General Confederation of Labor and the leading employers organization (*Confédération Générale de la Production Française*) to sign an agreement. This Matignon Accord, as it was called, became the cornerstone of the whole New Deal program which Blum inaugurated. The employers agreed to grant workers complete freedom to organize and to conclude collective labor contracts with the unions. Wages were to be increased on an average of 12 per cent. The workers' delegates on the other hand agreed to persuade the strikers to go back to work as soon as each management had accepted the general agreement.

Blum pushed through a series of laws to implement the Matignon Accord, and these are often considered a part of the agreement, although strictly speaking they were not. (1) Employees in commerce, industry, and the liberal professions, were guaranteed a minimum vacation of fifteen days with pay after one year's continuous employment. (2) A forty hour week was to be introduced over the next few months. (3) The procedure for negotiating labor contracts and the points to be covered were defined. (4) All labor disputes were to be submitted to compulsory conciliation or arbitration without resorting to strikes or lockouts. (5) To take care of extra leisure on the part of the workers a special Under Secretariat of Sports and Leisure was created. One of the most popular measures in this connection was a 40 per cent reduction in railway fares to all workers on holiday travel. Special excursions, similar to the popular "Strength Through Joy" trips in Germany, were also organized. (6) To relieve the burden that was placed on industry by the new laws, the government provided more liberal credit terms to hard pressed enterprises. (7) To ease unemployment, school children were to stay in school a year longer, that is, to the age of fourteen. (8) A public works program calling for an expenditure of twenty billion francs over a period of three years was adopted. This was to be in addition to the modest programs of previous governments. Blum, along with Roosevelt in the United States, accepted the principle of priming the pump of prosperity through a spending program.

The above measures all applied primarily to industry and labor. A new deal was also outlined for agriculture. A moratorium was enacted to apply to certain classes of rents and to farm mortgages. The most important bit of legislation, however, was that establishing a National Wheat Office. This office had complete control over domestic marketing as well as foreign trade in wheat. Farmers had to declare the acreage sown to wheat and were allowed a certain quota which they could sell at a price set well above the world market figures. Any excess amounts were to be sold to the wheat office at a lower price. Milling restrictions established the amount of native wheat which millers and bakers had to use. This made it impossible to use hard North Dakota wheat which French bakers preferred and which actually cost them less than the native product. There was no thought of importing Danubian wheat. The French peasant was such a power politically that even more than in other countries the farmer had to be mollified.

Several other popular measures were adopted. Among these was the nationalization of arms factories. Not only did this strike a blow at "the merchants of death" who had profited out of the last war, but it also enabled the government to co-ordinate and supervise arms production and sale. With the Spanish Civil War just over the borders of France, this was important. Aviation companies were not nationalized, but the state came to their relief by taking over two thirds of their capital stock. Veterans' pensions were restored. Restrictions and reductions on salaries of civil servants were removed. The Bank of France, which dominated French finances and even at times dictated to the government, was reorganized. Management of the bank was now vested in a small board, some members of which were now elected by all the stockholders, but the majority consisted of either government appointees or government officials, and public opinion considered this a blow at the French Wall Street.

Steps were undertaken to reform France's antiquated and ill-adjusted tax system. Economies in collection and new accounting systems were devised, but a thorough reform of the tax structure was not achieved. New loans had to be floated, and an effort was made to make these attractive to the small investor. The financial situation, however, remained very unsatisfactory. In terms of gold, French prices were about 25 per cent higher than British and American prices, when compared to the standard of 1930. In order to stimulate exports and also achieve a new stability for the franc, the government in September, 1936, devaluated the franc by about 30 per cent.

Financial difficulties closely related to general world financial and trade policies nevertheless continued to plague the government. It was also difficult to enforce the forty hour week, particularly in some of the great retail stores, hotels, and restaurants. Strikes ensued and a cry went out that the tourist trade was suffering. The government was also criticized because the buildings for the great international exposition, which was scheduled for the summer of 1937, were not completed on time. The forty hour week seemed clearly to be the cause of the delay in construction. So great was the uproar that in March, 1937, Blum announced a "breathing spell" during which the reforms were to be assimilated. Conservative and traditional financial methods were again the order of the day, and business circles hailed the respite. The franc continued to slip downwards as it had been detached from gold and permitted to seek its own level. In July, 1937, what amounted to a new devaluation of 14 per cent was undertaken. Further devaluations occurred in May, 1938 and in March, 1940, cutting the 1935 value of the franc well over 50 per cent.

The financial situation never ceased to cause difficulties, although the stimulus given to industry by a program of rearmament eased the economic crisis on other fronts. Increased tension in international affairs also caused the general public to look askance at the effort of labor to further its demands by a series of strikes. Thus an attempt at a general strike on November 30, 1938, in protest against decrees of a new premier curtailing the "New Deal" legislation, ended in failure.

FOREIGN AFFAIRS. French foreign policy in the thirties continued along the lines previously laid down. An attempt to strengthen the bonds of the French security system followed the advent of Hitler in 1933. Foreign Minister Barthou in the summer of 1934 made a grand tour of European capitals. To help cement French-Yugoslav ties, King Alexander was invited to make a state visit to France. Upon his arrival at Marseilles on October 9, 1934, he was met by Barthou, and a few moments later both were assassinated while riding together through the city. Barthou had hoped to bring about a Yugoslav-Italian rapprochement, thus tightening the circle about Hitler. Unfortunately for this plan, investigations soon disclosed that Italy, which for years had followed an anti-Yugoslav policy, had been connected with the Croatian-Macedonian groups who were responsible for the assassinations. Although the matter was smoothed over, better Yugoslav-Italian relations could hardly materialize at this time.

The French foreign office continued to woo Mussolini, and on January 7, 1935, a general French-Italian agreement was signed. France ceded to Italy some 44,500 square miles of desert on the southern border of Libya [see map, p. 98]. Both countries agreed to follow a common policy directed towards maintaining the independence of Austria [see below, pp. 493–94]. Throughout the Ethiopian and Spanish crises the French leaders followed a tortuous policy to retain Italian friendship, a policy that failed in the end. Closely related to the policy towards Italy was the attempt of the French leaders to strengthen their control over their North African colonies, which had become increasingly important in relation to French security. In Morocco a developing nationalist movement was checked, and a new railway between Tunis and Algeria strengthened the defenses of these regions. The Popular Front governments attempted to win native support by making some concessions to demands for reform.

The French attempt to complete their security system by negotiating an alliance with Russia was not entirely successful [see chart, p. 173]. The move chilled French relations with some of the powers in Eastern Europe, notably **Poland** and Yugoslavia. Nor did it help French-British or French-Italian relations. Moreover, it added to the internal political conflict in France, which in turn shackled French foreign policy. While the Russian-French Mutual Assistance Pact seemed to be generally well received when it was projected in December, 1934, and when it was signed on May 2, 1935, it ran into unexpected opposition when the time came for ratification in the Chamber in February, 1936. Although ratification was pushed through, it was clear that wide sections of French opinion were bitterly hostile to this agreement. The opposition to close connections with Communist Russia was not confined to the clerical parties. The Russian purges did not inspire confidence either in army circles or elsewhere, and the bourgeoisie was naturally suspicious of communism. A considerable section of French public opinion was willing to accept the treaty so long as it was administered by a rightist government, but became critical, to say the least, when a leftist cabinet was to interpret it. They breathed a little easier when Blum was replaced by a Radical Socialist, Chautemps, although the cabinet was still Popular Front. The French Senate twice refused to grant full powers to Blum, but did consent to granting power of decree to his more conservative successors.

In spite of all this, very few French rightists sought a solution to the communist danger in an alliance with Hitler. Germany was still the enemy. At the same time the average Frenchman was strongly against waging a preventive war. The French leaders have often been criticized for not forcing Hitler to withdraw in March, 1936, when he set aside the clauses of the Treaty of Versailles demilitarizing the Rhineland. Yet at the time this seemed hardly an issue on which to take a stand that might mean war. The aim of the French authoritarians was close collaboration with Mussolini and a French government modeled somewhat on that of Italy, a sister Latin state.

The Popular Front governments of Blum and Chautemps lasted from June, 1936, to April, 1938. When Daladier, a Radical Socialist, took over in 1938 the immediate issues and incidents that culminated in World War II were already in evidence. Daladier's policy at the time of the Munich crisis (September, 1938) was opposed by the Communists and not supported by the Socialists. The decisions of Munich ignored Russia, appeased Hitler, and sacrificed a democratic ally of France [see below, pp. 524–30]. It became necessary to shift the cabinet somewhat to the right, and this meant the end of the Popular Front. Indeed, after the outbreak of the war (September, 1939) the Communist party was officially dissolved, its members expelled from the Chamber, and its leaders arrested.

Daladier remained in power until March, 1940, when Reynaud took over, promising a more aggressive prosecution of the war. Parliamentary elections that were due were postponed. The German victory over France led to Reynaud's resignation (June 16, 1940), which marked the end of the Third Republic and the establishment of a new regime under Marshal Pétain with its capital at Vichy in Central France.

Great Britain

POLITICAL DEVELOPMENTS. The election of October, 1931, gave an overwhelming majority to the coalition known as the National government. MacDonald remained as premier, but his small group of National Labor supporters was swamped by the Conservatives, who held 471 seats out of a total of 615, and thus in their own right commanded an absolute majority in Parliament. Even before the elections the cabinet had been given far-reaching power to carry out financial reforms by order-in-council. A series of tariff measures culminating in the Ottawa Agreements were written into law [see above, pp. 281–82]. This shift to protectionism led the free trade Liberals to resign from the cabinet (September 28, 1932), and the Liberal party, like the Labor party, was divided between those who supported and those who were opposed to the National government.

MacDonald continued to head the cabinet, and in theory the National government had only been reconstructed. Actually the Conservative majority more than ever before called the tune, and England shifted back to old time party government. But it was not a return to the former Tory conservatism. Many measures to combat the depression were inaugurated, involving broad economic planning schemes. In foreign affairs the government had to reckon with the collapse of the World Economic Conference held in London (June–July, 1933), the failure of the Disarmament Conference, and the rise of Hitler in Germany. Finally, after presiding over the festivities connected with the Silver Jubilee of George V, MacDonald resigned as premier (June, 1935). Physically he was a sick and weary man, but his mental weariness must have been as great in view of the gyrations that had led him from being the leader and spokesman of the Socialists to a position where he was the tool of the Conservatives. His old friends were no longer with him, and in Labor party rooms his picture was turned to the wall.

The new premier, Stanley Baldwin, a Conservative, continued the fiction of a National government. A few weeks after he assumed office the results of a much-publicized "Peace Poll" were announced. For some months protagonists of the League of Nations had been conducting a carefully organized poll on specific questions relating to international peace. Conservative leaders had denounced the poll, even attacking it on the floor of the House of Commons. Baldwin himself while a member of the MacDonald cabinet had come out against the poll, and at the same time against collective security in general. He stated that without Germany and Japan— not included in the League at this time—and without knowledge of United States policy he would be unwilling to pledge the services of the British navy in any coercive measures for peace. The total number of votes cast in the Peace Poll represented over 37.9 per cent of the electorate, an astonishing achievement for the private organizations which conducted the poll. It showed beyond a doubt that the mass of the English people favored the League. The Conservative leaders were not slow to follow the trend, and

Baldwin soon was to be heard hailing the League as the "sheet-anchor" of British policy.

Few observers doubt that the results of the Peace Poll led the British government to push the policy of sanctions when Mussolini invaded Ethiopia. This strong support of the League was very popular, particularly with the Labor party. Shrewdly capitalizing on this sentiment Baldwin ran a general election in November, 1935, in which he called for approval of his foreign policy. The result was a foregone conclusion, and the National government was returned to power with 431 seats. The Conservatives, with 387, again had a majority, although Labor had doubled its representation by winning 154 seats. The small but vocal British Union of Fascists led by Sir Oswald Moseley cut no figure in the elections.

During the campaign Labor representatives charged that the government would lose its ardor for the League after the elections. Attempts to work out a compromise Italian-Ethiopian settlement did follow, and certainly within the next few years the British leaders made many attempts to patch up their relations with Mussolini. The parliament elected in November, 1935, extended its mandate after the outbreak of World War II in September, 1939, and it was not until July, 1945, that another general election was held. Numerous shifts and reconstructions in the cabinet were made, but it always remained a coalition National government. Stanley Baldwin was replaced as prime minister by Neville Chamberlain on May 28, 1937, who in turn gave way to Winston Churchill on May 10, 1940.

George V, a conservative and traditional English monarch, died in January, 1936, and was succeeded by his son Edward VIII who, as Prince of Wales, like his grandfather Edward VII, had achieved a reputation as a rather gay blade. Edward had carried out many ceremonial missions to various parts of the Empire and for years had been in the international spotlight. Since he was considered one of the most eligible bachelors in the world, it was, therefore, headline news throughout the world when it became known that he intended to marry an American, Mrs. Warfield Simpson, whose second divorce was pending. Stanley Baldwin, as premier, with the backing of the Archbishop of Canterbury and with the consent of the governments of the dominions, made the question of marriage a constitutional one. He refused permission for the King to marry Mrs. Simpson, even though Edward proposed that the marriage should be on a morganatic basis and that children, if there be issue, should not inherit the throne. Edward VIII had already on several occasions shown that as king he had a will of his own, notably in regard to social and foreign policy. This no doubt added to Baldwin's determination to see to it that, while the king might reign, the prime minister ruled. On December 10, 1936, Edward made a farewell broadcast which was heard around the world announcing his abdication to his peoples.

The first act of the younger brother, who succeeded him as George VI, was to create Edward Duke of Windsor. For a time the Duke served as governor at Nassau, but no post of importance has ever been found for him within the British service. Neither has his wife ever been received within the royal family circle. George VI resembled his father, and the people expected him to follow in his father's footsteps. They were not disappointed; the English crown as shaped in the nineteenth century remained a symbol of the past in a rapidly changing modern world.

ECONOMIC CHANGES. The economic policies of the National government were not unlike those of other states, for the problems were much the same: agricultural depression, declining foreign trade, mounting unemployment, and the steadily rising demand of the people for more governmental services. Real progress was made in dealing with all these problems before 1935, but here again as in other countries it was only the rearmament program of the later thirties which brought great stimulus to industry.

In Britain only slightly more than a million out of a working population of over twenty-one million are engaged in agriculture. The number of people adversely affected by the low prices of agricultural products was, therefore, relatively small. Yet agriculture was still a very important industry, in some sections the dominant one, and the World War had taught the British public the importance of home production. The British farmer could not compete with the mechanized agriculture of the United States and the dominions, nor for that matter with the low-income peasant agriculture of Eastern Europe. In a vigorous effort to protect agriculture tariffs were imposed, and, even more important, on most competing products import quotas were set. Wheat growers received a subsidy from a fund which was raised by a processing tax levied on all millers. Production of beet sugar had been subsidized since 1924, and after 1932 milk, bacon, pigs, beef cattle, potatoes, and hops were rapidly added to the products which were subsidized by grants from the treasury. From time to time new products were added, and in 1933 the whole fishing industry was given direct government aid. Guaranteed prices for barley and oats were fixed by the agricultural act of 1937. Most of the subsidy schemes required that the producers should agree to certain acreage allotments or other regulations.

England's system of agricultural planning had beneficial results for the farmers. Prices rose and more acreage was brought under cultivation. Whether the great stimulus to wheat growing (the acreage sown to wheat increased from three million in 1930 to four and one-half million in 1935) was wise is certainly a debatable point, considering that wheat could be imported so much more cheaply from abroad. As economic conditions improved some of the planning schemes were dropped and others modified, but Britain never abandoned the idea that agriculture should receive governmental aid. No longer was the farmer to be subjected to the rigors of an unfettered *laissez-faire* program. In the last analysis the British agricultural program was a national defense measure, and it was always regarded as such. The program also gave the government valuable bargaining power in negotiating foreign trade treaties designed to encourage British exports.

The increase of exports remained the chief aim of British statesmen. In this they were successful, and after 1933 both import and export figures mounted. As a consequence of the Ottawa Agreements the share of the British Empire in Britain's trade went up, although not so much as had been expected. In 1930 the Empire furnished 29 per cent of Britain's imports and this increased to 40 per cent in 1936. As for Britain's exports the Empire received 43.5 per cent in 1930 and 50 per cent in 1938. During these years Britain was very active in negotiating trade agreements. While these all contained the most-favored-nation clause, actually many were so framed that they were little more than bilateral barter agreements. For example the Baltic states agreed to buy 70 to 85 per cent of their coal from Great Britain, and in turn Britain promised to buy certain amounts of bacon, butter, and other dairy products. Between 1931 and 1937 Britain negotiated some twenty commercial treaties, of which those with the Scandinavian and Baltic countries, the Argentine, and the Soviet Union, were the most important. Britain also successfully opposed the attempt of the Oslo Powers to conclude special trade agreements, which might have been the beginning of a customs union between the Low Countries and the Scandinavian countries. Some slackening of the bitter tariff war with Ireland took place in 1935–36, but it was not until 1938 that Britain, in return for concessions, accorded Ireland the same preferences as the rest of the dominions.

After long negotiation the United States and Britain signed a Reciprocal Trade Agreement on November 17, 1938. Since the British agreement included her colonies, and on the same day a United States-Canadian trade treaty was signed, this series of agreements brought a reduction of tariffs which affected trade in all parts of the globe. Along with other concessions Britain abolished her special wheat duties and reduced the tariff 10 per cent on lard and fruits. The United States conceded tariff reductions on textiles, china, glass, leather goods, and a variety of other items.

Unemployment reached its peak in 1932, when the average of wholly unemployed numbered 2,136,052. In 1937 this figure had almost been cut in half, but it moved up again temporarily because of the trade recession in 1938. The government stimulated export industries in every conceivable fashion. It subsidized the erection of factories, particularly in certain depressed areas where unemployment was especially high and long lasting. Shipbuilding received some very important assistance, and it was only through government subsidies that the mammoth luxury liner *Queen Mary* was ever built. When war came she was to ferry many a soldier to far-flung battle lines. Some grants were made for slum clearance, but the policy of granting subsidies to private builders, which had been followed in the twenties, was virtually abandoned. Cheaper building costs and the low interest rates which followed the abandonment of the gold standard did, however, stimulate the building trades. In general the British statesmen did not initiate a large public building program like that of President Roosevelt in the United States. Government employment agencies, an old institution in Britain, increased their services. Aid was forthcoming to help a man move himself and family to a new job. Various acts were passed in the thirties extending the scope of the social insurance laws and increasing the benefit payments. These social insurance services did much to ameliorate the hardships arising from unemployment, accidents, and old age.

IRELAND. Technically still a dominion and part of the Commonwealth, the Irish Free State had nevertheless a unique status. With the elections of 1932 De Valera took over control in Ireland. As prime minister he introduced a measure in the Dail abolishing the oath of allegiance to the king, but the Irish Senate, where the opposition parties still dominated, refused its consent. More important, he stopped the land annuity payments, still owed to the British government as a result of loans advanced to Irish farmers for the purchase of lands. These loans had been made before the war, and in 1926 an Anglo-Irish agreement had set the total at £5,000,000 a year. The Cosgrave government, then in power in Ireland, had never submitted this agreement to the Dail. De Valera held that it was therefore invalid and that the annuities had been cancelled by the Government of Ireland Act of 1920. The British leaders, as a means of collecting the annuity payments in another fashion, retaliated by levying a special 20 (later 40) per cent *ad valorem* duty on the chief imports from Ireland. Since about 90 per cent of Ireland's exports went to Britain this was a serious blow. The Irish government countered by raising its own tariffs and using the withheld annuity payments to subsidize exports. Ireland was not spared the depression, and as in other countries this policy of protection and subsidy was part of the recovery program.

De Valera constantly pushed forward his program of breaking off the remaining legal ties with Britain. Appeal of judicial cases to the Privy Council in London was forbidden. The office of governor-general was abolished. Finally in 1937 a new constitution was accepted by a national plebiscite. It changed the name of the Free State to Eire but, although it contained many provisions asserting the independence of Eire, did not go so far as to declare a republic. The position of the king in Ireland, however, was not clearly defined, and the office of the governor-general, traditionally the representative of the king in a dominion, was to be held by the Irish president. In May, 1938, Dr. Douglas Hyde, a Protestant and a long time professor of Gaelic at University College, Dublin, was elected president in a popular vote, but De Valera continued as prime minister.

In April, 1938, an overall agreement between Ireland and Britain was negotiated which ended the long dispute over land annuities and put a stop to the tariff war. Britain agreed to surrender its rights under the Treaty of 1921 over the Irish naval bases at Cobh, Bere Haven, and Lough Swilly. Winston Churchill objected strongly to this surrender, and when Eire remained neutral during World War II the British admiralty looked with regretful and covetous eyes on these bases. Eire agreed to make a £10,000,000 payment in return for a cancellation of all claims to land annuities. Thus the tariff war was ended and Eire was treated like the other dominions.

In spite of continual agitation on the part of De Valera, Northern Ireland showed no inclination to join with Eire. In fact the determination of the predominantly Protestant counties to retain their connection with Britain seemed stronger than ever.

THE BRITISH COMMONWEALTH. The extension of Imperial Preference that resulted from the Ottawa Agreements (1932) was not so popular as might be assumed. In the colonies it resulted in higher prices since it restricted the importation of cheaper goods from Japan and other countries. In Britain the farmers complained that meat and dairy produce from the dominions came in free. British manufacturers complained of high duties in the dominions. In fact, one result of the agricultural depression was an increased emphasis on industrial development in the predominantly rural economy of the dominions. By the appointment of additional diplomatic representatives to represent their special interests abroad, and by the conclusion of separate trade treaties, the dominions advanced their position as independent states.

In Canada the depression increased the rivalry between the provincial and federal governments. The depression, along with modern large scale industrial developments, called for action by the federal government, since these problems could not be dealt with on a local basis. In 1935 one tenth of the Canadian population was dependent on public relief. At the same time the Canadian courts, by a series of decisions interpreting the rigid distribution of powers in the Canadian constitution, cut down the scope of federal activity in favor of the provinces. The problem became so acute that in 1937 a Royal Commission (Rowell-Sirois Commission) was appointed to study the financial relations between the dominion and the provinces. Its report favoring an extension of federal powers was not adopted because each province saw some of its vested interests jeopardized. The only change agreed upon was to give the dominion control over unemployment insurance.

Sectional and provincial feeling mounted in Canada. In Quebec the Catholic church continued to foster the cultural integrity of the French-Canadians. Prices, wages, incomes tended to be lower in Quebec than in neighboring provinces. Sentiment developed that the French were "hewers of wood and drawers of water" for English and American industrialists, who withdrew their profits from the province. Maurice Duplessis capitalized on such sentiment, and it did much to sweep his new *Union Nationale* into power, ending a forty-year domination by the Liberal party. His views on economic measures had the strong support of the Catholic hierarchy. In Alberta a "Social Credit Party," whose financial platform was far from orthodox, took over. A new socialist farmer-labor party—the Cooperative Commonwealth Federation—won some seats in the federal parliament and more in various provincial legislatures.

Newfoundland, which had been forced to relinquish its status as a dominion in 1934, continued for the time being under the supervision of royal commissioners. In Australia the extension of the financial powers of the commonwealth government led to a flare-up of states rights sentiment. In 1933–34 West Australia attempted to secede from the Commonwealth, but the British Parliament refused to pass the necessary legislation. In the end financial adjustments were made and the demands of the states were satisfied. The government of New Zealand extended even further the participation of the state in economic affairs. In South Africa the general world crisis led in 1934 to a fusion of the two parties led by Smuts and Herzog into a United South African National party. This attempt to create a National government like that in Britain in turn led to a resurrection of the Nationalist party under the leadership of D. F. Malin. This party drew its largest support from the Dutch (Afrikander) section of the populace. It was frankly republican in outlook and strenuously opposed the slight amount of representation that was accorded to the natives by the government in 1936. Next to Ireland there was more sentiment in the Union of South Africa for breaking the ties with Britain than in any other dominion. Nevertheless, co-operation with the British Commonwealth of Nations was advisable in view of the threat to control of South-West Africa which Hitler's demand for colonies implied.

The constitution which was granted to India in 1935 did not settle the Indian problem [see above, pp. 292–94]. While the provisions in regard to provincial governments went into effect, the new central government scheme was never accepted by the Indian people. The Indians continued to demand dominion status, if not complete independence. The National government in London with its Conservative majority was not willing to grant either of these demands. When World War II broke out the Indian Empire was thrust into the conflict by executive action, without consultation with any Indian legislature.

FOREIGN POLICY. Under the weight of the grave domestic problems of the depression, the British were inclined to pursue a cautious foreign policy. They showed great reluctance to restrain Japanese aggression in China so long as it was restricted to the north. Towards Germany the policy was in form correct, but this does not imply that there was approval of the philosophy of national socialism or of Hitler's policies. The British would have preferred to have the *status quo* maintained. When faced with a Germany that was arming, the British did not force the issue but instead negotiated a naval treaty (1935) under which the Germans agreed not to build more than 35 per cent of the British tonnage, a limitation that did not apply to submarines. This treaty must be viewed in the light of a steady undercurrent of opposition to Russia that prevailed at the foreign office. It found expression particularly in the hands-off attitude of the government during the Spanish Crisis. Against their real inclinations the British conservative leaders were forced by British public opinion to take a sharp stand against Italy during the conquest of Ethiopia. The desire of the government, however, was to maintain the British-French-Italian coalition against Germany. In spite of repeated attempts on the part of Britain to re-establish friendly relations (British-Italian agreements of January 2, 1937, and April 16, 1938), Mussolini turned more and more towards Germany.

In a world that was rearming, Britain only gradually moved toward preparedness. In 1934 after the failure of the Disarmament Conference, a comprehensive five-year plan for rebuilding the Royal Air Force was undertaken. In February, 1936, a new cabinet office was created by establishing the Ministry for the Co-ordination of Defense. In 1936–37, thirty-seven new ships were laid down, including two 35,000 ton capital ships, which was in marked contrast to a previous ten year average of 12.8. A mechanization program for the army was put into effect. Whereas in 1930, 10.8 per cent of the national budget was devoted to military expenditures, by 1937 this proportion had increased to 20 per cent and the figures continued to mount. In April, 1939, Britain for the first time introduced peace-time conscription for men of twenty to twenty-one years. In relation to other countries Britain's armament program was perhaps conservative, but it was not a totally unprepared Britain which accepted Hitler's challenge in September, 1939.

Britain traditionally was reluctant to undertake alliance obligations in regard to Eastern Europe. She accommodated herself to Hitler's annexation of Austria and to the dismemberment of Czechoslovakia in 1938. Hitler's seizure of Prague on March 15, 1939, was another matter. It was this act that caused Prime Minister Chamberlain to reverse British policy and to give Poland, Rumania, and Greece a guarantee of their independence. This was seconded by France, but Britain now took the lead against further expansion of Germany under Hitler.

18

National Socialist Germany, 1933-39

Factors Underlying the Collapse of the German Republic: *The War; Economic Conditions; Political Deficiencies; Nazi Propaganda and Organization.*

National Socialist Theory: *Terminology; The State; Sources of National Socialism.*

National Socialism in Action: *New Elections; Gleichschaltung; Reorganization of the Government; Racial Policies; Economic Reorganization; Church and Education; Foreign Policy.*

———————◆———————

THE RISE of national socialism was part of the history of pre-depression Germany [see above, pp. 231–36]. To understand Germany under the National Socialists it is necessary to review some of the factors which underlay the collapse of democracy in Germany. To do so is not to tear apart the web of history, nor to give precedence to one cause over another, but to focus attention on the conditions accounting for Hitler's rise to power.

Factors Underlying the Collapse of the German Republic

THE WAR. The dictatorships of Europe were all closely associated with conditions resulting from World War I. In many ways dictatorship was merely carrying over into times of peace the controls and techniques of government that had been devised during the war. In times of emergency it has often been thought necessary to resort to quick dictatorial action. Germany in the twenties passed from one crisis to another and it was not difficult to arrive at the conviction that the crises of peace were as serious as those of the war years. People were ready to accept an authoritarian government, thinking of it as a temporary expedient.

If war was an underlying factor in producing all dictatorial governments it was especially important in Germany, for here the war had brought military defeat. The Germans had been required to change their political system by the victorious Allies, and the Republic was always associated with defeat. It was also inextricably tied up with the onerous Treaty of Versailles. This treaty not only brought loss of territory and heavy financial payments, but in the eyes of most Germans an impairment of German honor, for they refused to recognize the so-called war guilt clauses of the treaty [see above, pp. 103–04]. German honor also seemed challenged because Germany was not considered civilized enough to act as a mandatory power under the League and was forced to accept a policy of unilateral disarmament. The financial burdens exacted by the treaty weighed down every cabinet from the moment it came to power. Nor were the Allies inclined to make any concessions in order to strengthen the hands of the supporters of the Republic. When concessions were made, they came late and usually as the result of an extreme stand or threat by Germany. Had Chancellor Bruening obtained the changes in reparations for which he begged and which were eventually made, and had the Allies granted to him the slightest measure of equality in armament, many observers believe that he might have been able to stay in office.

ECONOMIC CONDITIONS. Coupled with the defeat in the war and all that it entailed were the bad economic conditions that came to prevail in the Reich after 1928. The collapse of the mark had wiped out the wealth and security of most of the middle class. Taxes were heavy and interest rates ran from 8 to 10 per cent or even higher. Unemployment mounted, partly because of new technological developments. It is calculated that from 1926 to 1931 a million men lost their positions although production increased 20 per cent. It is not intended here to discuss all the aspects of the correlation between the economic depression and the rise of dictatorship, but only to underscore the fact that such a relationship existed. Unemployment and employment figures are perhaps as good an index of general economic prosperity as exists, and the table on p. 447 will show that conditions were becoming desperate. It also indicates that Hitler was successful in lessening unemployment, a fact which accounts for much of his popular support after he took office.

POLITICAL DEFICIENCIES. None of the political parties in Germany seemed capable of dealing with the many problems which confronted the Republic. The Communists, who did have a program, did not have the power to take over the government. The Social Democrats were more dem-

TABLE 10
AVERAGE MONTHLY FIGURES FOR UNEMPLOYMENT
AND EMPLOYMENT IN GERMANY
1929–34

YEAR	UNEMPLOYMENT	EMPLOYMENT
1929	2,121,200	17,597,000
1930	3,139,400	16,321,800
1931	4,573,200	14,245,700
1932	5,579,700	12,499,000
1933	4,733,000	13,070,000
1934	2,657,000	15,106,900

ocrats than socialists and refused to take any major steps without the support of the majority of the Reichstag. Party complexity and the growth of extreme political parties of the right and left made it difficult if not impossible to obtain the necessary parliamentary majority to carry out any strong policy. The leaders were all too ready to give up the struggle and resort to government by decree under Article 48 of the German constitution [see above, p. 217]. Decree government can be dated back to 1930 in Germany, about two years before Hitler took power on January 30, 1933. Under the Weimar Republic there was little change in local government, the judiciary remained much as it had been under the Empire, and the old officials in the civil service continued to carry on affairs. The result was that many officials were not loyal supporters of the government or of the democracy they were called upon to serve. They believed in other forms and theories of government. A good number were monarchists if not authoritarians at heart.

A point might well be made that the Weimar Constitution attempted to establish too advanced a form of democracy. It did not contain the numerous checks and balances which serve to restrain popular will and direct government in the United States. The constitution promised many things in its bill of rights which the government could not live up to and consequently brought discredit to democracy as a whole. There was also lacking in Germany some of that social democracy which helps a democratic government to function smoothly.

Political scientists with the wisdom of hindsight have picked out certain defects in the Weimar Constitution and pointed out that other constitutional provisions might well have forestalled the rise of Hitler. While there may be some truth in this, it overlooks the fact that dictatorships arose in many other states in Europe, which were governed under quite different constitutions. The German system of proportional representation is often singled out for attack [see above, pp. 215–16]. Hitler, it is true, never substantially cut down the vote of the left parties, but by appealing to new voters and getting stay-at-home voters out to the polls he built up the size of his party in the Reichstag. The following table [p. 448] indicates

TABLE 11

PARTY REPRESENTATION IN THE REICHSTAG

	NATIONAL ASSEMBLY	I JUNE 6 1920	II MAY 4 1924	III DEC. 7 1924	IV MAY 29 1928	V SEPT. 14 1930	VI JULY 31 1932	VII NOV. 6 1932	VIII MAR. 3 1933	IX NOV. 12 1933	X MARCH 29 1936	XI APRIL 10 1938
Right												
National Socialist					12	108	230	196	288	661	740	813
German Nat. Peoples	44	71	95	103	78	41	37	51*	52			
German Peoples	19	65	45	51	45	30	7	11	2			
Economic	4	4	10	17	23	23	2	1				
Other Parties	3	5	51	26	23	53	9	12	7			
Middle & Moderate Left												
Catholic Center	91	64	65	69	61	68	75	70	74			
Bavarian Peoples		21	16	19	17	19	22	20	18			
State (Democrats)	75	39	28	32	25	15	4	2	5			
Left												
Social Democrat	163	102	100	131	153	143	133	121	120			
Independent Socialist	22	84										
Communist		4	62	45	54	77	89	100	81			
Totals	421	459	472	493	491	577	608	584	647	661	740	813

* Schwarz Weiss Rote Front.

how Hitler won power without ever really taking away supporters from the left.

NAZI PROPAGANDA AND ORGANIZATION. Factors such as these help to explain the downfall of democracy in Germany, but equally important were the efforts of Hitler and his cohorts, by skillful propaganda and much hard work, to build a party organization. Every speech of Hitler's started out with a denunciation of the Treaty of Versailles. He appealed to all classes except the Jews whom he saddled with all that was wrong in Germany. By connecting Jews with communism Hitler gave a new, and in many circles a very popular twist to anti-Semitism. No one, least of all Hitler, could hope to explain the intricacies of foreign trade or inflation to a mass audience of thousands, but it could be made crystal clear to them that it was Jewish capitalists who were at fault. It was an exaggerated version on a lower level of the practice of some American politicians of putting the blame on Wall Street for everything that is wrong in the United States.

Hitler made a place for all of his followers. He set them to work in his Storm Troops (SA), his Elite Guards (SS), his youth groups, and in countless other special organizations. He had his special appeal to veterans, to mothers who had lost their sons in the war, to students, to the lower middle classes, to the peasants, to the workers, to the women, and even to the churchmen. He promised the latter that he would clean up some of the extreme "liberalism in morals" that arose in postwar Germany and came to be associated in many minds with the Republic. Nudism, the gaiety of Kurfürstendam in Berlin, the art magazines, the freedom of the Youth Movements, all were to be rejected. His attack on communism found favor among many groups. He promised everybody a revitalized Germany, strong and prosperous, where everyone would have a job. Germany would no longer have to pay tribute to the rest of the world and would once again take its rightful place among the great powers of Europe.

It is not surprising that voters were willing to turn out the old politicians and give one so full of promises a chance. What many of them did not realize was that they would not be given the opportunity to do the same to Hitler in his turn. It should always be remembered that, following methods scarcely more highhanded than those of his opponents, Hitler built up his party to a point where it controlled 44 per cent of the electorate and in a coalition with the Nationalists controlled 52 per cent of the mandates in the Reichstag. On the surface at least, the Nazis were but another political party, not a new political philosophy bent on organizing the state on entirely different lines.

National Socialist Theory

Many of the appeals which Hitler directed to the people were a product of existing conditions. As in Italian fascism there was much pragmatism about German national socialism. Yet unlike fascism, national socialism developed most of its theories and formulated many of its ideas and programs before actually achieving power. In this national socialists resembled democrats, socialists, and communists, who first formulated their doctrines and then proceeded to establish governments.

In a nation where theorizing and speculating is often considered a national characteristic it is not surprising that many writers came to expound and formulate nationalist socialist theory. Yet the list of most important sources can easily be restricted to three books. First chronologically would come the famous twenty-five point program adopted in February, 1920, which became the unalterable program of the party. This program was drawn up by Gottfried Feder, and his commentary on the various articles (*Das Programm der NSDAP*) remains the classic exposition of the program. While this program went somewhat into eclipse in later years, it never was repudiated. The second source would be Hitler's *Mein Kampf,* and the third Alfred Rosenberg's *Myth of the Twentieth Century.* While Hitler's book is verbose and repetitious, it is clarity itself compared to the confused and turgid exposition of Rosenberg's volume.

TERMINOLOGY. An explanation of some terms associated with national socialism will introduce its basic theories. The Nazis called their state the Third Reich, beginning in 1933. In their reckoning the First Reich was the Holy Roman Empire (962–1806), and the second was the Empire created by Bismarck (1871–1918). They thus wiped off the slate the periods of German history which they considered inglorious transition arrangements: the period of Napoleonic domination 1806–15; the German Confederations 1815–71; and the Weimar Republic 1919–1933.

Officially the party was known as the *Nationalsozialistische Deutsche Arbeiterpartei* (National Socialist German Workers Party). National, they maintained, was derived from the Latin root *nasci* and meant, to be born. National, therefore, was to be understood biologically and racially, and a nation was a unity of people established by birth. The same blood makes a common people, and similar descent was the important factor. Socialist was derived from the root *soci* and was held to mean the community (*Gemeinschaft*) of those people who were joined by a common tie of blood. It had nothing to do with Marxian doctrines. Their slogan *Gemeinnutz vor Eigennutz* (good of the community above individual good) expresses this concept. The Nazis were strong German nationalists and always advocated a greater Germany. They made a special appeal to the workers and stressed the need for every one to work for the good of the nation. They instituted a labor service which was to act as a great leveling and indoctrinating medium. "Through this school" they maintained the whole nation had to pass. While they constantly spoke of the party they also referred to it as a movement (*Bewegung*). By the leaders it was always conceived as far more than an ordinary political party.

THE STATE. In theory the National Socialists did not place the state at the pinnacle as did the Fascists in Italy. In fact they held that the party commanded the state, and both state and party were but a means of enhancing the German *Volk* (nation). In order to serve the *Volk* best, however, the National Socialists demanded the creation of a totalitarian state.

This was to be based on the concept of *Blut und Boden* (Blood and Soil). It was to be administered on the basis of leadership; it was to be a *Führerstaat*. The elite were to govern, and authority descended from the leader down through an elaborate appointive hierarchy, specially trained and tested for loyalty. They retained a Nazified Reichstag, created various other assemblies, and called together many conferences of one sort or another. Yet these bodies did not even merit being called consultative chambers. They were rather cheering sections, and acted as bodies before which the governing officials might announce policies. They also served as a means of compensating and honoring loyal party followers. Members of the Nazi Reichstag could not be classed as legislators, but they always drew their salaries and took advantage of other perquisites pertaining to office.

The National Socialists were legalistically minded. They started out by giving the Führer and his cohorts power to legislate by decree. The result was that laws, administrative orders, and decrees were issued without end. All their acts had a legal basis, no matter how arbitrary they often were. To challenge them, it becomes necessary to go back and question the legality of the original National Socialist assumption of power. To the very end the Weimar Constitution was never formally repealed.

SOURCES OF NATIONAL SOCIALISM. It is impossible to say definitely where Hitler and others obtained many of their ideas. As the movement developed they naturally were influenced by the example of Mussolini, although it should not be forgotten that the National Socialist party antedates the Fascist Revolution in Italy. They were of course greatly influenced by Germany's past history, and conscientiously tried to resurrect what they considered were ancient German virtues. They cited the days when the Germans were organized on a tribal basis to strengthen the idea that blood ties determined who was a German. The glories of Prussia at the time of Frederick the Great were extolled. Many national socialist ideas were merely revivals of patterns that existed in Germany before the war. The party framework, with the supreme leader, the descending hierarchy of officials and the authoritative position of these officials, was patterned on the organization of the Catholic church. Similarly, the unalterable twenty-five point program has been considered analogous to the unchangeableness of the dogma of Roman Catholicism. Nazi concepts of the state were influenced by the teachings of Hegel and Treitschke that the state is power and all institutions and practices must be directed towards this goal. Schopenhauer's emphasis on the will to live became a favorite teaching, while Nietzsche's idea of the superman was grist for the Nazi mill.

In a philosophy where race plays such an important part it is not surprising that the influence of Darwin and Mendel was great. The idea of the struggle for existence and the survival of the fittest was easily incorporated with a few distortions into national socialist theory. Mendel's conclusions, that through a mixture of races not new races but rather mixed groups (bastards) are created, became a call for "racial purity." The Nazis became ardent disciples of eugenics, which Webster defines as "the science which deals with the influences that improve the inborn or native qualities of a race or breed, especially the human race." The theory that race is the determining factor in history was not original with the Nazis. Various writers in the nineteenth century had been concerned with this thesis. Two of them should be mentioned here. One was a Frenchman, Count Joseph Arthur de Gobineau who in his *Essai sur l'inégalité des races humaines* (1854) stated that racial problems overshadowed all other problems in history. He upheld the superiority of the Aryan race and maintained that racial degeneration was the inevitable result of the mixture of Aryans with inferior races. The other was Houston Stewart Chamberlain, a Germanized Englishman, who published in 1899 a ponderous volume entitled *Grundlagen des Neunzehnten Jahrhunderts*. Chamberlain came to much the same conclusion as Gobineau but tended to stress the superiority of the Teutonic race. There can be no doubt that Hitler was greatly influenced by his ideas.

Aside from these literary sources it did not take much searching to come in contact with anti-Semitic ideas in postwar Europe. Hitler himself states that he developed a fanatical hatred for Jews while spending some years in Vienna. He came to believe that the Jews controlled the labor unions and the Social Democratic party, that they were international and not nationally minded. Jews, therefore, could not be for a national Germany. Since the National Socialists insisted that race and nation were to be one and the same, it followed that there could be no room for the Jews. The fallacies in this thinking are obvious, especially to Americans who are themselves the product of the "melting pot."

National Socialism in Action

NEW ELECTIONS. When President von Hindenburg appointed Hitler chancellor of Germany in January, 1933, the latter presided over a coalition cabinet consisting of National Socialists, Nationalists, and certain non-party men. He could not command a clear majority in the Reichstag and therefore decided to hold a new election. A bitter election campaign followed which was highlighted by the burning of the Reichstag building on February 27, 1933. The Communists were charged with the deed, but at a later trial the attempt to implicate Georgi Dimitrov, a Bulgarian Communist resident in Berlin, failed. He was freed and went to Russia where he soon was elevated to important office in the Communist International. The actual firing of the building was charged to a half-witted Dutchman, van der Lubbe, and he no doubt in an innocent way was implicated. He paid the death penalty, while the Nazi plotters, who were responsible for the fire, went unscathed.

The fire, however, served its purpose. President von Hindenburg issued far-reaching emergency decrees restricting constitutional guarantees of freedom of speech, of the press, of assembly, of association, and of the mails—decrees which were never repealed. Many Communist leaders were arrested, and the country was flooded with propaganda about the danger of a Communist *coup*. In spite of highhanded Nazi tactics, the elections were

THE NEW GERMANY AND THE OLD *Adolf Hitler, Chancellor of Germany, greeting President Hindenburg during a ceremony in Berlin, 1933.*

run off by old election officials in a remarkably orderly fashion. The Communists were even credited with winning 81 mandates, although they were never permitted to take their seats in the Reichstag. In the election the Nazis obtained 44 per cent of the seats, their allies the Nationalists 8 per cent, the Catholic Center 11 per cent and the Social Democrats 18 per cent. The Nazis and Nationalists thus could command a majority of the Reichstag, but to amend the constitution they needed a two thirds vote. With the Communists excluded, the support of the Center party would be sufficient to enable them to obtain this percentage.

Probably as a result of Hitler's promise to conclude a concordat with the Papacy, the Center party agreed to vote with the National Socialists and Nationalists in passing the all important Enabling Act of March 24, 1933. It seemed as if there were safeguards enough in the act. Neither the Reichsrat or the Reichstag were to be abolished or their power to legislate taken away; the powers of the president remained untouched, and the act was passed for a limited time. Yet this Enabling Act gave Hitler the power to enact ordinary legislation by decree. Then in January, 1934, Hitler was specifically granted the authority to decree constitutional changes.

GLEICHSCHALTUNG. The reorganization of Germany on which Hitler now embarked goes by the name of *Gleichschaltung*, variously translated as co-ordination or regimentation. An exact word in English for this process is hard to find, but its avowed purpose was to bring everything and everyone into line with the theory of national socialism. It meant the introduction of the principle of leadership, the end of democratic election procedures, the suppression of so-called Jewish and Marxist influences, and public adulation of the Führer and the Third Reich.

While the overall pattern of this *Gleichschaltung* did not change, the procedure varied. Sometimes laws had to be enacted as was the case in the reorganization of the state governments. Sometimes the regimentation could be achieved simply by changing the directing personnel. Old organizations were not always abolished, but were transformed by judicious appointments or supervised "election" of trusted Nazis to important posts. In some cases, as for example the labor unions, it was necessary to create entirely new organizations. Variations also occurred in different parts of Germany and according to the ardor of subordinate officials. This may have been partly responsible for the fact that no united opposition developed, for all the people did not feel the heavy hand of the Nazis in the same way or at the same time.

There were also certain benefits and tangible advantages which the Nazis could offer. It should not be forgotten that while dictatorships bring about curtailment of many liberties, they also bring certain new liberties in exchange—the freedom that comes with cheap excursions on the state railroads, the right to lord it over persons hostile to the regime, or perhaps the official endorsement of certain new standards of morality. Above all the Nazis were also able to engender a wave of enthusiasm among the majority of the populace. Not all this was the result of brass bands, flying flags, and torchlight processions. The concerted attack on unemployment was most significant. There was a widespread feeling that at last something was being done, and people did not stop to ask whether all the changes were improvements. Germany became a beehive of activity and the people liked it.

REORGANIZATION OF THE GOVERNMENT. The Enabling Act was basic to all governmental changes, for it sidetracked parliament as the legislative body. Hitler soon deprived the state governments of their democratic features, and the states became largely administrative units. The national authorities appointed "Reich Regents" to head the various state governments, and there were plans to devise a new territorial division of Germany. This was never accomplished, however, and some diversity among the states remained to the end. The disappearance of self-government in the states led to the logical abolition of the Reichsrat in January, 1934. By that time all political parties except the National Socialists were dissolved, and the Reichstag was continued as a one-party representative body. It was called into session now and then to hear important pronouncements and pass a law or two. On the death of President von Hindenburg on August 2, 1934, Hitler combined the offices of president and chancellor, but retained the title "Der Führer," an action which was approved by a popular plebiscite.

A civil service law of April, 1933, retired all Jewish officials except those who were in service before August 1, 1914, or those who had been front soldiers, or whose fathers, sons, or husbands fell in the war. If they had been in office for ten years they were granted a pension. Two years later additional decrees abolished the few privileges remaining to the Jews so far as state service was concerned.

The Nazis not only changed over governmental procedures but also strengthened their party organizations. Party offices parallel to governmental departments and bureaus were established. For example, there was a party cabinet to correspond to the national cabinet, a party office dealing with foreign affairs, and often leading Nazi officials headed both party and state departments. Marshal Goering seemed able to hold an almost unlimited number of offices. Many of these top Nazis were able and hardworking officials. To class them as fools or sycophants would be to misunderstand the Third Reich. There was plenty of rivalry, but on the whole this was checked by a common loyalty to Hitler. In June, 1934, the so-called Blood Purge occurred, when officially 77 persons—some party leaders, others more or less innocent bystanders—were summarily executed because of an alleged plot. At that time General von Schleicher, Ernst Roehm, and Gregor Strasser were killed. Papen, the Nationalist leader who had engineered Hitler's assumption to power, narrowly escaped to continue his service to the state as Hitler's most able foreign ambassador, first at Vienna and then at Ankara.

Auxiliary party organizations, among them the youth movements, were expanded. Great annual party congresses came to be held at Nuremberg where party pageantry and oratory were at their height. The "People's Welfare Organization" of the party alleviated much distress among war victims, the aged, and the very poor sections of the populace with its large Winter Help collection. No one was to go hungry in the New Germany and the largesses of the party (like those of Tammany Hall) produced many loyal supporters.

The influence of the Storm Troops (SA) on the whole gradually declined within the party, while that of the Elite Guards (SS) increased. The latter developed its own secret service alongside of the *Gestapo* (*Geheime Staatspolizei*) and also formed special units within the new German army. These were recruited from volunteers, had a distinct uniform, and enjoyed not only special privileges, but special duties, becoming one of the chief instruments for the enforcement of Nazi terroristic policies.

RACIAL POLICIES. Many observers had thought that the anti-Semitic features of national socialist policy would be sidetracked once the party was in power. Instead anti-Semitism slowly and surely increased until it culminated in a dreadful policy of extermination, characterized by mass deportation, forced labor, inhuman concentration camps, and lethal gas chambers, during the war (1942–45). In September, 1935, the Nuremberg Laws were issued, defining a Jew as a person with three or four Jewish grandparents, or a person with two Jewish grandparents provided he professed the Jewish religion or was married to a Jewess. Marriage between Jews and Aryans was prohibited. Half or quarter Jews were classed as "mixed offspring," who might with special permission marry Aryans, and were freed from most of the restrictions which were placed on those classed as Jews. Most Jews soon lost their positions not only in public service but also in private industry. All kinds of measures, reminiscent of the medieval ghetto, were instituted to mark out and isolate the Jews. In 1938, following the assassination of a German diplomat by a Polish Jew in Paris, a pogrom was instituted, synagogues and other Jewish property were attacked, and a fine of a billion marks was placed on the Jewish community. Jewish children were removed from regular German schools and crowded into special classes or separate Jewish schools supported by the Jewish community. Even these schools were to disappear later. Jews were free to migrate, but this involved finding a place to migrate to and usually selling what property they had at great sacrifice. The officially sponsored anti-Semitic measures even before the more drastic decrees issued during World War II make a sordid record. That many individual Germans did not approve of this policy is true, but this does not excuse the state for such a reversion to barbarism.

ECONOMIC REORGANIZATION. There can be no question of the success of the National Socialists in dealing with the unemployment problem, and at least for the first year or two this was not directly due to the remilitarization of Germany although this became important later. When the National Socialists took over they found already in existence a program of voluntary Labor Service. Many useful projects such as reforestation, draining of swamps, and road building were undertaken by these battalions, and the Nazis made such labor service compulsory. They instituted an extensive housing program, concentrating chiefly on small one or two family dwellings with a garden, and in 1937 over three hundred thousand dwellings were erected. They also built stadiums and swimming pools, and laid out a trunk line system of super-highways, the much advertised *Autobahnen*, which of course had distinct military value.

The last of the twenty-five points in the party program had called for the creation of professional and trade chambers or "estates." These did not develop into a corporative system and were never used, as in Italy, as a basis for the political reorganization of the Reich. They remained merely a scheme for the co-ordination of various segments of the nation's life and economy.

The Nazis began by evolving an overall scheme for labor. The old unions were abolished and their funds confiscated. Employees and employers —except for peasants and civil servants—were then enrolled in a common Labor Front which became one of the most important of the estates and for years was headed by Dr. Ley. Strikes and lockouts were a thing of the past, and government-supervised collective bargaining was the rule. Special bodies made up of representatives of labor and management were instituted along with special courts to settle disputes.

The Labor Front of course collected dues, and it became one of the richest and most powerful organizations within the state. One of its departments was the "Strength through Joy" organization. Patterned somewhat on the lines of Italy's *Dopolavoro*, it arranged all kinds of entertainments, athletic events, and excursions for the workers. "Strength through Joy" bought its own excursion steamers and took large groups of workers at very low rates on cruises to the Mediterranean or along the fiords of Norway, trips such as workers had never dreamed of before. A scheme was also devised to enable German workers to purchase a cheap automobile, but World War II came before the much-talked-of *Volkswagen* got into production. There were also plans to aid the worker to buy a home, as for instance the scheme by which a tenant paid 300 marks on occupancy and acquired possession after paying a rent of twenty marks a month for three years. Undoubtedly "Strength through Joy" provided many valuable services, and it did much to increase the popularity of the Nazis.

An estate of Trade and Industry was set up in 1934 to control industrial and commercial activities. This was a cover organization to bring together the thousands of existing business organizations and concerns. There was no attempt on the part of the National Socialists to nationalize industry; indeed they turned some of the banks which had come into state hands back to private management. On the other hand they were not opposed to intervening in private industry or to establishing state-owned and managed concerns where they thought it was necessary. Private property remained the foundation of German economy, but it was subjected to ever increasing regulation. The government taxed heavily, it regulated new investments, it controlled foreign trade through its currency policies. This was not so much because of any specific Nazi economic theories, but rather because of the general world economic situation and the determination to create a strong totalitarian state.

In 1936 a Four Year Economic Plan was announced which was to be under the direction of Hermann Goering. This plan was to implement a policy of autarky that was to make Germany as self-sufficient as possible. Coupled with this was the idea of *Grossraumwirtschaft*; what could not be produced in Germany was to be purchased from neighboring regions which would not be subject to blockade in time of national emergency. Germany in turn would supply these neighboring regions with manufactured goods, and an integrated economy comprising a large area of Europe would result.

Much of this trade between Germany and Southeastern Europe had to be on a barter basis for neither party had the necessary free exchange to conduct it along customary lines. Germany, because of political reasons and a fear of repeating the inflation of 1923, refused to devalue the mark and officially remained on the gold standard. What other powers sought to gain for their economy through a policy of devaluation, the Nazis tried in part to obtain through establishing marks of different values for different purposes. Export marks varied in value from country to country, and blocked accounts were regularly established. The Yugoslavians, for example, were paid for their wheat by marks sent to a Berlin bank, which could only be spent for German goods. Tourists were also lured to Germany by selling special travel marks at a reduced rate. One need not understand all the ins and outs of currency regulation to realize that through it any government can obtain a strangle-hold on the nation's economy. The Nazis had such a hold.

Under a policy of self-sufficiency the peasants naturally were favored, for Germany never raised enough food of its own. Besides, the peasants were the bulwark of that "Blood and Soil" policy which played such an important part in the theory of the National Socialist state. A special estate of Agriculture, organized into regional associations, was established as the instrument for performing important functions in regard to land tenure and general social policy. A basic inheritance law declared that holders of properties up to 125 hectares (309 acres) could not have their land mortgaged or sold. These hereditary farms were to pass intact to one heir, usually the eldest or youngest son, according to the custom of the area, the other children being entitled to a vocational training at the expense of the farm. Holders of such property were even given an official title, *Erbhofbauer* (Hereditary Estate Peasant), which pleased them no end.

A Reich Chamber of Culture was created, embracing seven subdivisions: films, radio, theater, musicians, artists, professional writers and authors, and journalists and editors. Since membership was compulsory for anyone engaged in these fields of activity, control could be exercised by excluding persons who were considered undesirable. Censorship of books, plays, films, was a reality. Public bonfires were stoked not only by pornographic material from the newsstands, but also by the best of books by Jewish and Socialist authors, or by anyone who happened at a particular moment to be in disfavor. Modern abstract art was pilloried because Hitler, who considered himself an expert in this field, condemned it. Music by Jewish composers disappeared from concert programs, while Wagner, one of Hitler's favorites, was glorified. It was an artificial and regulated Nazi culture over which Propaganda Minister Joseph Goebbels extended his skillful and malevolent rule.

CHURCH AND EDUCATION. In Germany churches were organized on state lines, but there were in some states several established churches—so that in all Germany there were twenty-nine such self-governing Protestant bodies deriving their income from tax funds. In addition, there were many small denominations usually referred to as Free Churches—the Methodists, Baptists, Moravians, Mormons, Christian Scientists, Jehovah's Witnesses, and others. In line with their policy of centralization, the National Socialists advocated the unification of the twenty-nine "established" churches into one United Protestant church. As in the whole Protestant world, there was much talk in Germany of the desirability of church union, and German church leaders were not opposed to such action. If the German states were to be done away with as Hitler promised, some sort of regrouping of the churches would obviously be necessary. Church leaders met with Hitler's representative, and a general agreement was reached. A new church constitution was to be drawn up and a national bishop was to be head of the new United Protestant church.

The church authorities, without consulting the government, announced their choice of Dr. Bodelschwingh, a man renowned for his mission work within Germany, as the new national bishop. This angered the Nazi leaders and the Nazi wing of the church, the so-called German Christians, who were in favor of one Pastor Müller, a former army chaplain and Hitler's confidant. Other differences developed, and Bodelschwingh, finding he could not exercise the duties of his office, resigned June 24, 1933. The government now began to appoint Nazi-minded officials to various administrative posts in the church, but unlike the representatives of the political parties, labor unions, and countless other organizations, many of the Protestant leaders resisted. The old church authorities designated July 2, 1933, as a day of penance and prayer, while the Nazi-appointed minister of church affairs proclaimed the same day as one of peace and thanksgiving for the reorganization of the church. The average parish minister was in a dilemma. Should he remain true to his old church leaders or to the new orders from Berlin? At this point President von Hindenburg stepped in and requested Chancellor Hitler to see that peace was restored in the Protestant church. Some of the most ardent Nazi appointees were thereupon removed, and more moderate personages placed in charge.

Elections were now held for a National Synod. Since practically all Protestants were legally church members whether they took an active part in church affairs or not, it was easy for the National Socialists to get out a

large enough vote to swing the elections. When the Synod met, it elected
Müller bishop and adopted a constitution. Many of the old church authorities refused to accept the new bishop or the new constitution. For example
the bishops of Bavaria, Württemberg, and Hanover, as well as others, had
enough courage, insight, and ability to retain control over their own groups.
Their churches remained intact and went pretty much their own way, but
many of the church bodies, particularly in North Germany, were deeply
divided. Some accepted the new church regime, others went into opposition and became known as the "Confessional Church" because they took
their stand on the historic confessions of the Protestant churches. Martin
Niemöller, former submarine captain and pastor of an influential church in
a fashionable suburb of Berlin, became one of the outstanding leaders of
this Confessional Church movement. He paid for his opposition by being
placed in a concentration camp in 1937 from which he was not released
until 1945.

The Nazis were often in a position to coerce the opposing "Confessional" ministers. In some cases they were able to cut off salaries. On the
other hand, at least in the first years, some of the ministers were able to
obtain redress in the courts. Gradually the influence of the Nazis was able
to infiltrate into the administrative offices of the various churches, where
men who were able to reconcile themselves with the regime received appointments as vacancies occurred. Governmental interference varied greatly
in different sections of Germany. The plight of the church in Thuringia or
sections of Prussia was quite different from that of Bavaria. A second
church constitution was promulgated in 1937, but it too did not receive
general acceptance. While the Nazis gained ground and the goal they
sought became more clearly marked, they never were able to co-ordinate
the church completely. This is a remarkable tribute to the courage, devotion, and faith of many churchmen.

Those members of the old established churches who accepted the new
church regime were known as "German Christians." They saw no basic
conflict between Christianity and national socialism. They never went so
far as to abolish the Old Testament, or make Hitler into a God—things
which were often attributed to them—yet they were able to accept the
racial and other radical programs of the Nazis. The Nazis permitted and at
times even encouraged some extreme so-called religious movements. The
German Faith Movement did its best to revive the celebration of ancient
Teutonic festivals such as May Day, and the Solstice. If Woden and Thor
were not worshiped, they at least received a lot of publicity, but the neo-pagan groups never numbered many followers. The government on the
whole dealt leniently with the so-called free churches, such as the Methodists and Baptists. There was no attempt to draw them into the United
Protestant Church; for the moment Hitler was out for bigger game.

Under the Weimar Republic the Roman Catholic Church had an almost ideal situation for a country which was predominantly Protestant. It
had freedom to organize as many religious orders as it wished, it could make

use of the tax system for financial support, it received state subsidies for building purposes, it received tax funds to run Catholic-managed schools. These privileges, it should be pointed out, applied to established Protestant churches as well. To assure the continuation of this favorable position in the Third Reich, the conclusion of a concordat was desirable. Such an agreement was in line with the general Vatican policy of postwar years.

Hitler was glad enough to make an agreement with the Catholic church, for a concordat would pave the way for the peaceful capitulation of the Center party. On July 20, 1933, the document was signed. Three existing concordats which the Pope had concluded with German states (*Länder*) were confirmed; the property of the church and its buildings were safeguarded; Roman Catholic religious instruction in the schools was guaranteed, and Catholic youth organizations were permitted; existing financial arrangements for state support were continued. In return the Pope promised that the clergy would not engage in political activity.

In subsequent years there were many instances of violation of the concordat by the state, but there were some provisions which were fairly consistently carried out. Church taxes and subsidies were continued. There were as many Protestant as Catholic clergymen in concentration camps. Masses continued to be said throughout Germany, and the number of Catholic churches closed did not begin to reach the number that were suspended during the Bismarckian *Kulturkampf* of the seventies of the previous century. This is not to say that there were no difficulties. Cardinal Faulhaber in Munich obtained fame for his denunciation of the regime in a series of lenten sermons. The Hitler youth groups made serious inroads on Catholic youth organizations. Currency restrictions prevented transfer of funds, and much publicity was given to the arrest and trial of some members of religious orders who were caught smuggling funds out of the country in order to pay debts. The church could not endorse the extreme Nazi doctrines on race and marriage, but the greatest difficulty developed over restriction of the rights of the church in education.

Private schools were abolished, and that closed a good number of Catholic institutions. Members of religious orders were no longer permitted to teach. The Nazis aimed to abolish public confessional schools also, and in this they succeeded, despite the opposition of both Protestant and Catholic churchmen. Nevertheless, to the last, religious education was a regular part of the instruction in most German schools. Hitler did not abolish religion or drive religious education out of the school system. Many of the old teachers of religion continued to instruct, and, as convinced Nazi teachers withdrew from religious instruction, they were replaced in many instances by local clergy. Hours were reduced, and what the religion teacher tried to teach in one hour was often countered by classes in racial theory during another. As the hold of the Nazi regime grew stronger, restrictions on religious instruction increased, and it was further curtailed during the war.

Much variety remained in the school system of Germany, and it was only in 1937–38 that Hitler ventured to adopt a national education law. English was made the first modern language to be studied, and other changes were made which on the whole were improvements, but the law also provided ample school time for indoctrination in racial and other Nazi theories. Special schools existed for the training of future Nazi leaders, the *Adolf Hitler-Schulen* and the more advanced *Ordensburgen*.

The universities were rapidly co-ordinated. Many distinguished professors were dismissed or resigned. The rectors and deans, formerly elected by the faculty, were now appointed by the government and made responsible to the minister of education. Theological faculties were permitted to continue, and technical and scientific research advanced. The universities cannot be said to have become sterile institutions, yet the burning of books in the first days of the new order symbolized the respect of the Nazis for free inquiry.

FOREIGN POLICY. In *Mein Kampf* Hitler laid down the principles of his foreign policy. Germany was to be made strong and its position in Europe restored; the fetters of the Treaty of Versailles were to be broken. Germany was to have additional territory, but this was not to be sought in overseas colonies but rather by the extension of German territory in Europe which meant expansion eastward. Germans living outside the Reich were to receive the protection of a strong national German state. Hitler advocated an alliance with England and was determined not to let the fate of a few hundred thousand Germans in South Tyrol spoil his relations with Italy. France he considered an eternal enemy of Germany, but his special wrath was reserved for communism and its supporters. Above all Hitler insisted that Germany must avoid ever again becoming involved in a two-front war.

More detailed accounts of different phases of Hitler's ventures in foreign policy are presented elsewhere in this book. It will serve as a summary here to note a number of instances when Hitler followed the line indicated in *Mein Kampf*. He dramatically withdrew from the Disarmament Conference and the League of Nations (October, 1933), when it seemed clear to him that neither of these bodies would disarm other powers or grant Germany the right to rearm. He shifted German industry over to the manufacture of armaments and in March, 1935, boldly announced the creation of a German air force and the reintroduction of compulsory military service. He also started to build a fleet, but the conclusion of a Naval Treaty with Great Britain (June 18, 1935) indicated his desire not to permit naval rivalry to becloud Anglo-German friendship. A year later on March 7, 1936, he sent his troops into the demilitarized sections of the Rhineland. All this, of course, not only was a violation of the Treaty of Versailles, but the latter involved a denunciation of the Locarno Pacts.

Hitler constantly maintained that he had no thought of attacking France, but was only seeking to prevent Germany from being overrun. Equal right to armament gave both countries the same status in a sphere which is closely related to national sovereignty. The return of the Saar

Basin to the Reich as a result of an internationally controlled plebiscite held on January 13, 1935, removed one cause of friction between the two countries. In return for a payment of 900,000,000 francs France ceded its rights of ownership over the mines, railways, customs stations, and other immovable property in the Saar. France, however, always considered her security bound up with maintaining the *status quo* in Eastern Europe. Here Hitler soon began to make changes.

He started out by concluding a non-aggression pact with Poland on January 26, 1934. To end even temporarily the long disputes with Poland over frontiers, over Danzig, over the treatment of minorities, and over tariffs, was a real achievement. His attempt to engineer a Nazi *Putsch* in Austria failed in 1934 but *Anschluss* was achieved in 1938. This brought "home" about seven million German-speaking peoples. His campaign to build a strong national Germany was continued by the annexation of the Sudeten Germans in September, 1938. That he would not be satisfied by annexing territory inhabited by Germans, but had definite plans for eastward expansion was shown by the seizure of Prague in March, 1939, and the final dismemberment of Czechoslovakia.

All this could not be accomplished without a shift in the alignment of the powers. Ties with Italy grew more intimate when the League imposed sanctions on Italy at the time of the Ethiopian Crisis (1935). Soon Hitler and Mussolini were co-operating in the Spanish Civil War, and in 1936 the Rome-Berlin Axis was formed. The hard and fast military alliance that Hitler always wanted was not concluded until May, 1939. Meanwhile, on November 16, 1936, Hitler had concluded the Anti-Comintern Pact with Japan, carrying out his anti-communistic policy [see below, pp. 512–13]. In November, 1937, Italy signed the Anti-Comintern Pact which presaged the future coalition of World War II.

Britain's guarantee to Poland in April, 1939, indicated to Hitler that he not only had failed to obtain his much sought Anglo-German agreement, but that he now also faced the danger of a two-front war. This he always had said must be avoided at all costs. The conclusion of the pact with Russia on August 23, 1939, was at least in line with this postulate of his policy, although it ran counter to much of what he had written in *Mein Kampf*. The partition of Poland which this agreement involved was also in direct line with his oft-repeated statement that Germany must be territorially united and achieve its living space (*Lebensraum*) by expanding eastward.

CHAPTER

19

Russia Under the Five-Year Plans, 1928-41

Socialism in One Country

THEORY AND PRACTICE. Russia's road to modernization was marked by many upheavals. The liberation of the serfs in 1861 was only the first of these upheavals, and in significant respects the most important. It was the primary step that Russia had to take on its road from an agrarian to an industrial way of life, and Russian society was very largely transformed in the next four decades. The second upheaval, in 1905, was more political in character. It resulted in a partial transfer of political power from a bureaucracy dominated by the dynasty, the gentry, and the army, to representatives of the new groups that had emerged as a result of Russia's social transformation. These new groups may be called, for want of a better name, the middle class. The third upheaval in March, 1917, completed this transfer of political power, and henceforth the struggle in Russia was to be between the varied elements comprising this new and as yet inexperienced middle class. At the beginning of the revolutionary year political power was in the hands of the moderate and conservative members of this new class, but in the chaos of war and economic distress they failed to hold on to their power and in November, 1917, a fourth upheaval occurred when the Bolsheviks seized power. The Bolsheviks spoke in the name of the working class, but they were in fact no more than another group of middle class leaders, the most radical, inspired by the doctrines of Marx.

That this most radical of the groups of middle class leaders should have seized and held on to power at the end of 1917 was not inherent in the situation. It was due to some extent to the indecision of their rivals, but more particularly to the tactical skill and opportunism of Lenin. He led his party to power not by following Marxist doctrines, but by abandoning them or reinterpreting them to fit the changing needs of the situation. Following Lenin's guidance, the Bolsheviks made a determined effort to create a new society, but by the end of the first revolutionary decade they had not achieved a great deal. By 1928 industrial and agricultural production, as well as the standard of living, had no more than reached the level of the eve of the war fifteen years earlier. There had been revolutionary changes in the composition of the ruling class, and radical innovations were introduced in the urban areas in education, religion, and culture, but so far as the larger organization of society was concerned these innovations were neither profound nor were they particularly characteristic of Marxism.

The relative failure of this first decade of revolution must be attributed less to any lack of ability on the part of the Bolsheviks than to the inadequacies of the doctrine which they were seeking to implement. Marx and Engels had made important contributions to the study of the central problem of modern society, the transition from an agrarian to an industrial way of life, but their interest had been primarily in England, France, and Germany in the latter half of the nineteenth century. Moreover the generalizations which they set forth in such sweeping terms were intended more as tentative conclusions than as binding laws or blueprints for a future society. Lenin himself had recognized this in considerable measure, and had exercised much opportunism in adapting Marx's generalizations to Russian reality. He died, however, while Russia was still recovering from the throes of civil war. The recovery of the Russian economy by 1928, confronted his followers with the problem of how to proceed from there. The path which was finally chosen, that of the five-year plans accompanied by collectivization, marked the fifth great upheaval of Russian society. In importance it almost rivalled the first upheaval, the liberation of the serfs in 1861.

The problem which Lenin's heirs faced was threefold: (1) how to stimulate rapid industrialization, now that production had been stabilized at the pre-war level; (2) how to pay for this industrialization out of a primarily agrarian economy; and (3) how to achieve these goals within the framework of a Marxist philosophy which advocated world revolution. The first two problems alone would not have been difficult to solve, for not only all the Western states but Russia itself under the empire had made good progress with industrialization starting from an agrarian society. The difficulty was how to do this in a communist fashion, using the state as the sole accumulator and investor of capital, avoiding the use of foreign capital or assistance so far as possible, and keeping all aspects of the operation under the strict control of the Communist party. Two contrasting policies were initially proposed by party leaders for accomplishing this difficult assignment. The Rightists, led by Bukharin and Rykov, wished to proceed cautiously with industrialization, making extensive economic concessions to the peasants so that they would continue to raise food for the growing cities, and postponing world revolution for the time being. The opposing view was that of the Leftists, led by Trotsky and Zinoviev. Their program, which went by the name of "permanent revolution," involved a vigorous attack on all three fronts: rapid industrialization, bringing the peasants forcibly under strict state control, and at the same time maintaining a vigorous effort abroad to stimulate world revolution.

Although for political reasons Stalin was allied at different times in the middle 1920's with both Bukharin and Zinoviev, his own policy favored neither Right nor Left but combined elements of each. Stalin opposed the Rightist policy of making concessions to the peasants, on the ground that they would soon have so much bargaining power that the state would lose control of them. At the same time he opposed the Leftists because he believed that promoting world revolution under the conditions existing in the 1920's would jeopardize industrialization at home. Stalin's solution, which went under the name of "socialism in one country," thus favored rapid industrialization, forcible collectivization of the peasants, and postponement of world revolution. The central theme of Stalin's thought was that unless Russia was industrialized rapidly the cause of socialism both at home and abroad would be endangered. "We are fifty or a hundred years behind the advanced countries," said Stalin in a prophetic speech before a Conference of Managers of Socialist Industry in February, 1931. "We must make good this distance in ten years. Either we do it or they crush us." It was in June, ten years later, that Stalin's Russia was to face its greatest crisis.

STATE PLANNING. In the course of the first three five-year plans (1928–32, 1933–37, and 1938–42), the Soviets practically achieved their aim of socializing both the agricultural and the industrial sectors of their economy. They also made considerable progress in expanding the output of consumption goods, while still placing the greatest emphasis on production goods. Under the State Planning Commission, or Gosplan, which was instituted in 1920 and took over full direction of the economy from the Supreme Economic Council in 1928, a network of national, republic, and local planning institutions was developed to assist in drawing up the plans and in observing their execution. The methods and techniques for accomplishing this operation were evolved only slowly and they required the training of a new generation of Russians who remembered little of the old regime and could be relied upon to co-operate rather than to criticize. According to the Soviet concept planning meant not only drawing up plans but executing them as well, and the technicians learned to keep their task within manageable limits by observing and controlling key points in the economy through which the remainder of the economic system could be planned. The over-all five-year plans were not meant to be rigid, but could be altered from year to year to meet changing conditions.

An important step in the development of Soviet Russia's planned economy was taken in 1935 when rationing was abandoned, and this was accomplished without reducing the state control over trade and prices. Private trade, which had constituted almost 60 per cent of all trade in 1923–24, was practically eliminated by 1931, and the various organizations which clothed and fed the population were gradually gathered into the hands of the state as well. The highly centralized rationing system through which the state administered its controls resulted in many inequities, however, and it was discontinued as soon as conditions permitted. Its abolition was facilitated in particular by the gradual increase in agricultural production and the reduction of the export of raw materials and agricultural products necessary during the early years of industrialization. Henceforth some three fifths of all internal trade was conducted directly by the state, and the rest by the collective farms, co-operatives, and other local organizations. Volume and prices remained the object of central planning, and the vast gap which continued to exist between the net cost of all consumption goods and the prices paid by the public was the result of the high rate of the taxation. The day when consumption goods would be available in proportion to the demand was still some distance in the future.

A very important consideration in Soviet planning throughout this period was foreign trade. With the restoration of the Russian economy as a result of the NEP the foreign trade interrupted by the civil war again became active and, under the state monopoly, it was harnessed to serve the objectives of the domestic program. During the years of Russian recovery the expansion of foreign trade was handicapped by the fact that agricultural products, which comprised the chief export, could barely keep up with the domestic demand of a growing population. In terms of Russian foreign trade in 1913, on the basis of figures adjusted for changes in prices and territory, foreign trade in 1931 reached only 69.5 per cent of the prewar figure. Soviet imports and exports decreased steadily after the peak year of 1931, due largely to the world depression but also because Russia had become better able to satisfy its domestic needs.

Insofar as the three five-year plans did require imports, the Soviet authorities were constantly faced with the difficulty of exporting food and other products which were sorely needed at home. This difficulty was relieved only in part by the export of gold bullion. Moreover, the changes in the Russian economy resulting from the five-year plans were soon reflected in the pattern of foreign trade. Whereas 67.7 per cent of Russia's exports were agricultural in 1913 and 57.2 per cent in 1926–27, only 36.4 per cent of Russia's exports consisted of agricultural products in 1938. The export of industrial products and raw materials rose proportionately from 32.3 per cent in 1913 to 63.6 per cent in 1938. Production goods occupied a consistently larger place in imports than consumption goods, representing 70 per cent of the total in 1913 and 88 per cent in 1938. Foreign trade served the Soviet Union not only as a means of supplementing the domestic economy but also as an instrument of foreign policy. Although Russian foreign trade amounted to no more than 2 per cent of the world total, the proportion was much higher in certain key products.

EXPANSION OF INDUSTRY. Between 1928 and the coming of World War II the productive capacity of Russian industry grew at a rapid pace. Official Soviet figures tend to exaggerate this growth, claiming an index figure of 768 for 1940 as compared with 100 for 1927–28. Western economists believe that the index figure should be closer to 400 for 1940, and they can support their estimate by detailed analyses of Soviet statistics. In either case the expansion of Soviet industrial production was rapid, for an increase of four times in twelve years is very substantial indeed. On the eve of World War II, Russian production of pig iron and steel was less than half that of the United States and somewhat lower than that of Germany, although well ahead of British production. At the same time, Russian production of coal remained well below that of either of the principal free enterprise countries.

Many factors account for this achievement. The Russian economy was relatively slack in 1928, as its level of production was no higher than it had been fifteen years earlier, and consequently it had considerable resources of manpower and technicians to draw on. Also the population grew rapidly during this period, from 147 million in 1926 to 170 million in 1939, and this natural growth was supplemented by an influx of workers from the countryside to provide an ample supply of labor. Capital was somewhat tighter, as the Soviet government relied as little as possible on foreign credits and investments. This meant that capital had to be raised internally, and this was accomplished by a harsh husbanding of domestic resources which bore heavily on the country. Foreign skills were freely borrowed, however, and technicians from abroad, including many Americans, were employed to assist the Russian engineers. Foreign machinery was also imported, and many Russians were sent abroad to study. At the same time, technical education was rapidly developed within the Soviet Union to supply the ever-increasing demand for accountants, draftsmen, and engineers. Finally, the Russians were able to develop further the very extensive raw material resources of their own vast country.

The most significant feature of Soviet industrialization has been its primary emphasis on heavy industry: steel mills, chemical factories, power plants, mining equipment, heavy machinery, and armaments. Relatively little of the increased production under the five-year plans was devoted to consumer goods, such as clothing, home furnishings, automobiles, and other commodities. Another feature of Soviet industrialization was that the stress in the volume of production inevitably led to considerable waste as well as a great sacrifice in quality. Industrial managers were given credit for filling the quotas assigned to them, and every possible saving in material, design, and workmanship was made in order to reach the quantitative goals. Moreover, the lack of engineers and of skilled workmen contributed to the low quality of the product. The relatively poor quality of many Soviet goods was due also to difficulties inherent in a system of planned economy. The controls which demand exercises over quality in an unregulated economy are absent from the Soviet system and must be replaced by the same precise standards in the national plan in which the volume of production is expressed. Unless the plant managers are held to such qualitative standards by devices similar to those used to encourage the fulfillment of the quantitative quotas, little improvement in workmanship can be expected. In the third five-year plan such qualitative standards were finally worked out and were accompanied by the usual schedule of penalties and benefits. The motive of personal incentive was thus maintained in the Soviet economy, although in a somewhat different form than in other countries.

Collectivization of Agriculture. The course of industrialization was greatly dependent on the policy toward agriculture. In countries which modernized earlier than Russia, the peasants and farmers had sold their produce to the cities in exchange for clothing, farm machinery, and other consumer goods. Such was the policy that the Rightists had proposed for Russia, as a temporary expedient to ease the dislocations caused by industrialization. But this policy had a price. It meant that an important segment of the new industry would have to be devoted to satisfying the peasant consumer. This involved slowing down the pace of development in heavy industry in order to satisfy the needs of the Russian people. This was a policy of moderation, and it was rejected by Stalin. The alternative to buying food from the peasants with consumer goods was to seize it from them by force, and this in substance is what Stalin's regime proceeded to do by means of collectivization.

Agricultural co-operatives or collectives are of course not in principle harmful to the interests of the peasant or farmer. Their purpose is to pool the resources of small agricultural holdings so as to permit the use of large-scale machinery, planning, and marketing, and under the right conditions this makes farming more efficient. Indeed, the Soviets expected that collectivization and the accompanying mechanization would make Russian agriculture more productive, but their main purpose was to control agricultural production and to assure a supply of food to the cities at minimum cost. There were also theoretical reasons for collectivization, as Marxism required that all means of production should be owned and operated by the state. This theory could be interpreted in a variety of ways, however, and Stalin's was the one that most benefited the state at the expense of the peasant. Of the total agricultural acreage in Russia in 1927–28, 98 per cent was held by individual peasant holdings, 1.1 per cent by state farms, and 0.9 per cent by a few experimental collectives. Collectivization struck the Russian peasants like a whirlwind in 1930, and the initial destruction and confusion which it provoked were without precedent. While general orders came down from Moscow, the new policy was implemented by local officials and Communist party members who were prepared to stop at nothing to coerce the peasants. The result was a disorganized scramble in which several million peasants lost their homes and were either killed or deported to work camps in Siberia. The peasants regarded collectivization as theft of their private property which would deprive them of their economic independence and their prospects of prosperity, and they resisted it bitterly. As a by-product of this struggle, there was a wholesale slaughter of farm animals. The number of horses and cattle was reduced from 34.6 million and 67.1 million respectively in 1929, to 16.6 million and 38.4 million in 1933. A decade later Stalin admitted the cost of collectivization. "Tell me," Churchill inquired during a wartime visit to Moscow in August, 1942, "have the stresses of this war been as bad to you personally as carrying through the policy of the collective farms?" "Oh, no," Stalin replied, "the collective farm policy was a terrible struggle."

By 1940, over 90 per cent of the peasants had been collectivized. After some experimentation, Soviet collectives finally took an intermediate form between a co-operative owned by the peasants and a completely communized agriculture. The form of collective farm, or *kolkhoz*, which then was adopted is known as an *artel*. Under this system the land is owned by the state and leased to the collective, which owns farm animals, buildings, and equipment apart from heavy machinery. In addition, each peasant family is allowed his own cottage, garden plot, and farm animals and equipment in limited quantity, for private use. The property owned by the collectives, and more particularly the land and possessions of the peasants, form the largest segment of property in the USSR not formally administered by the state. The collective operates under a charter which sets forth the rights and obligations of the members. In theory it is self-governing, but in practice the state and the Communist party determine its policies. Vital to the work of collectives at this stage were the Machine Tractor Stations, or MTS which owned and operated the tractors, combines, and heavy agricultural machinery for the collectives, and also provided them with technical and financial services. Each MTS serviced several collectives, and in 1940 there were over 7,000 MTS for some 250,000 collectives. The MTS were an arm of the state, and soon became one of its chief instruments for coercing the collectives.

Apart from the collectives and the MTS there were also state farms, or *sovkhozy*. These were owned and operated by the state, and some 4,000 had been established by the eve of World War II. These state farms were generally devoted to specialized crops, and were in most cases operated at a loss. As late as 1940 some 6 per cent of the peasants were as yet uncollectivized. Their holdings constituted no more than 1 per cent of the arable land, however, and they were subjected to many restrictions.

The measure of success of this system was its result in terms of agricultural production. Contemporary Soviet statistics were modest in this regard, claiming slightly over 50 per cent increase in gross agricultural production between 1928 and 1940. Western estimates for this period, largely substantiated by Soviet revelations in the 1950's, were even more modest. It appears that Soviet agricultural production in 1940 was only 15 per cent higher than in 1928. Several factors explain the ability of the Soviet government to feed its rapidly growing urban population with such a modest increase in agricultural production. Far less grain was exported than in the earlier period, and also much less grain was needed to feed the livestock population which had been depleted as a result of collectivization. Most important, however, was the fact that the system of collectivization enabled the state to obtain a much larger share of agricultural production, particularly grain, for its own use. The share of the total grain production distributed by the state, for instance, increased from 15 per cent in 1928 to 40 per cent in 1939. Moreover, collectivization permitted the state to obtain this grain at a lower price than under the earlier system. While the revolutionary step of collectivization accomplished little to increase food production, it gave the state a much greater control over the food that was produced. The loser was the peasant, some 54 per cent of the population in 1940, who paid the bill. The peasants now received a much lower price for the grain that the collectives delivered to the government, and had less left for themselves. It appears reasonably certain that by 1940 the Russian peasant was not only bearing the principal burden of the cost of industrialization, but that he was relatively worse off than at the end of the Tsarist regime. While 11 or 12 per cent of the peasant income was taken in taxation in 1912, according to one estimate, the state received some 15 to 18 per cent in 1937.

The Transformation of a Society

COST OF THE FIVE-YEAR PLANS. The rapid growth of heavy industry under the five-year plans called for a massive investment of capital by the state. The only way to raise this capital was to divert it from other sectors of the economy—from agriculture, from light industry, from wages, from housing, and from the standard of living in general. Only the totalitarian controls exercised by the Soviet government permitted it to extract this price without provoking a widespread reaction. It has already been noted how the system of collectivization enabled the government to obtain a large return from agriculture. Another major means of raising capital was the turnover tax, which accounted for 40 to 60 per cent of government revenue. This is a form of sales tax which bears particularly heavily on articles of common consumption including food. In addition to this indirect taxation, there was a personal income tax as well as a provision, nominally voluntary, for the purchase of state bonds.

It has been estimated that the average wage-earner in the USSR paid some 60 per cent of his income in taxes, direct and indirect, and in the purchase of state bonds. This cost of the Soviet method of industrialization is reflected in the real wages of the Soviet worker, that is to say the value of goods and services that can actually be purchased with the wages received, after deducting direct taxes and bond purchases. It appears that after a sharp slump in the early 1930's, real wages in 1937 were still only 80 per cent of the 1928 level. Indeed, due in part to the ravages of World War II, it was not until the 1950's that the average Soviet wage-earner could purchase as much with his wages as he could in 1928. The 1928 level, in turn, approximated that on the eve of World War I. The effect on the individual worker was nevertheless not as great as these statistics would seem to indicate. The working class in this period absorbed many millions of peasants who had enjoyed a very low standard of living, and were now relatively better off. At the same time, a great many women joined the labor force, thus increasing the earnings per family. Throughout this period the peasant was in a considerably less favorable position than the worker.

In addition to the economic cost of the five-year plans, what may be called the social cost must also be considered. The several millions of citizens in the concentration camps, and the many who were executed in the course of the great purges, are a part of the cost. How was it possible for the government to extract such a price from the Russian people? Two methods in particular were used. One was the concentration of power in the hands of the government, that was thus enabled to force the Russian people to do its will. The police was one of the principal instruments of the state, and it had special troops equipped with tanks and planes to help it carry out its tasks. The second method was a system of discipline and incentives. Generally speaking, most substantial gains accrued to a new upper class which was now given a variety of financial and honorific rewards calculated to make it loyal to the state as a matter of self-interest. Before examining this system of discipline and incentives in more detail, however, it is necessary to take a look at the position of labor, the group most affected by the five-year plans.

THE POSITION OF LABOR. As a regime officially dedicated to the welfare of the proletariat, the Soviet government expressed great concern for the status of the worker. In practice, however, the needs of industrialization took precedence over all other considerations. The relatively free position of labor under the New Economic Policy was now replaced by strict controls. Labor unions became instruments employed by the state to increase the discipline and productivity of the workers. Wages were henceforth fixed by the state, and along with various speed-up devices were used to get the most out of labor. In the period between 1928 and 1938, the non-agricultural population rose from 31 million to 66 million.

The real earnings of this large new class declined during this period, as has already been noted, but in other matters the state paid its respects to the proletariat. The guarantee of the "right to work" in Article 118 of the Constitution of 1936, that assures to Soviet citizens "the right to employment and payment for their work in accordance with its quantity and quality," represented the latest development in Soviet labor policy. The "right to work" had not been mentioned in official Soviet documents since 1918, when it had been prematurely introduced, and it was now re-established on the ground that with the success of the five-year plans Russia was in a position to guarantee full employment. As the expansion of industry kept well ahead of the growth of the labor supply, industrial unemployment had in fact disappeared after 1930. While the seven-hour day and the social insurance provisions were maintained, wage incentives were combined with increased labor discipline. In the 1930's the principal emphasis was placed on improving the quantity and quality of labor production. Workers were sent to technical schools in hundreds of thousands, and many incentives were offered them to increase production. Particularly successful was the movement initiated after the example of the widely advertised coal miner, Stakhanov, which encouraged workers to raise their incomes by surpassing their quotas. By these methods labor productivity was increased 82 per cent during the second five-year plan and 38 per cent for heavy industry during the third, according to Soviet statistics. By 1939 there were some thirty million workers, who with their families comprised about one-third of the population.

The coming of World War II brought further changes in the labor picture. Decrees issued in 1940 gave factory foremen new responsibilities, including that of hiring and firing workers, and granted them wages three to five times those of workers. Workers were prohibited from changing jobs, and absenteeism was punished by compulsory labor at the place of employment with reduced wages. The eight-hour day again replaced the seven-hour day, with no change in wages. A labor reserve was also established into which up to a million youths could enlist voluntarily, or if necessary be conscripted, for technical training of six months to two years.

A discussion of Soviet labor relations would not be complete without mention of the rapid growth in size of the Corrective Labor Camps after 1930. Under the Commissariat of Internal Affairs, known as the NKVD from 1934 to 1946, sentences to hard labor became increasingly common for a wide variety of offenses. Political prisoners rated more severe treatment than criminals, and large numbers of the more prosperous farmers who resisted collectivization (*kulaks*), political opponents including disaffected Communists, and various minority peoples, were sent to these camps. Statistics on sentences were not published after 1930 and only general estimates by critics of the Soviet system exist as to the number of prisoners in the camps on short or long-term sentences. The number of prisoners rose from about half a million in 1930 to several million by the end of the 1930's. Lack of information prevents an accurate estimate of the population of these camps, but it is clear that the status of labor was somewhat different from that indicated in the statutes which regulated conditions of work. These camps were scattered all over the country and made the NKVD the largest employer of labor in the Soviet state. Projects like the White Sea-Baltic canal were constructed by forced labor, used also in such enterprises as building highways and railroads, and mining coal and gold. Inmates who escaped or survived their sentences, reported living and working conditions of the greatest misery.

DISCIPLINE AND INCENTIVES. One of the most characteristic features of Soviet society is the many ways in which the state manipulates the system of discipline and incentives by which it forces and cajoles the Russian people into the great effort of industrialization. Some of the most important forms of discipline are mentioned elsewhere in this chapter: the discipline of the peasants imposed by collectivization and the forced delivery of grain; the discipline imposed on labor by low wages and the deprivation of all bargaining power with the state-employer; and the discipline imposed on all society by the institutions euphemistically known as Corrective Labor Camps to which several millions were sentenced in the 1930's.

Other forms of discipline affected intellectual and social life. One often thinks of the revolution of 1917 as ushering a period of unfettered freedom from traditional restraints in art and literature, family life, and education, and indeed for a number of years in these areas there was radical experimentation at least in the urban centers. This experimentation was short-lived, however, and did not survive the five-year plans. What was needed in an era of forced industrialization, as Stalin saw it, was the subordination of all forms of expression to the service of the state. The idea of art for art's sake, or of literature as a mirror of human emotions and of social change, was quite alien to Stalin's conception. Instead, artists and writers were herded by the Communist party into national organizations, and required to devote all their energies to extolling the virtues of the regime. Under this system art tended to become poster art, depicting idealized peasants, workers, and civil servants. Literature became a form of propaganda in which only the most unconditional praise of Soviet society was permitted. Religion, which could not be distorted to serve the ends of the state, was rigidly suppressed.

In the case of family life, the easy divorce and abortions permitted in the 1920's were abolished, and it was proclaimed that stable family life was essential to a disciplined society. Marriage was popularized, abortions were prohibited except for reasons of health, and divorce was made cumbersome and expensive. Marriages were still registered without a wedding ceremony in the same drab office in which births and deaths were registered, but every effort was now made to give the family a sense of permanence. Similarly in education, radical experimentation gave way to regimentation. In the 1920's much attention had been paid in the schools to class discussion and social projects, and students were encouraged to follow their own inclinations and even to ignore their teachers. Now the state emphasized such solid subjects as language, history, mathematics, and natural sciences, and put the students in uniform and under semi-military discipline. At the same time there was a great expansion of education during this period. Between 1920 and 1940, enrollment in primary and secondary schools rose from 10 to over 30 million, and illiteracy declined from 50 to 20 per cent. In the same period, enrollment in institutions of higher education increased from 200,000 to 600,000. The expansion of education was much more rapid in the 1930's than in the 1920's, and it contributed significantly to the creation of a serious-minded and disciplined class of urban employees.

Counterbalancing these various forms of discipline, were a series of incentives which encouraged hard work and loyalty to the regime. The principal of these incentives took the form of salary differentials, as a result of which the civil servants and managers rapidly achieved a status vastly superior to that of the average worker or peasant. It has been estimated that this new privileged class grew in size from about 2 million in the early 1920's to perhaps 10 or 12 million by 1940. Their monetary income was several times that of the workers and peasants, and on a proportional basis they paid lower taxes. At the same time the civil servants and managers were given better living and working conditions, and had access to food and other consumer goods which were not available to the population at large. They also had more ready entry to institutions of higher education, and their children had better opportunities for training and careers. The more important members of this new class could afford to employ servants, and enjoyed the use of chauffeur-driven cars and villas in the country. Thus all those occupying positions of influence in Soviet society had good reason to support the government and to co-operate in the enforcement of a system in which the great mass of the population was kept forcibly at a relatively low level of income.

Apart from the incentives in privilege and income explicitly provided for this new class, there were incentives of a more general character that affected a somewhat larger sector of the population. A rapidly industrializing society has the need for people trained in many new skills. Russia needed hundreds of thousands of accountants, schoolteachers, mechanics, technicians, and engineers, and the bulk of these had originally been children of unskilled peasants. Thus, while their material well-being in terms of food, clothing, and housing in most respects showed little or no improvement in the generation after the revolution, they had a personal sense of moving up the social ladder. If their new skills did not bring them much more bread, they at least felt that they were helping to create a society in which their children or grandchildren would be better off.

The Communist party and the Soviet government made every effort to capitalize on this sense of progress. The basis of Soviet propaganda was the Marxist philosophy, that maintained communism was an ideal of human prosperity towards which all mankind was inevitably moving. This was a very vague and general outlook, however, and in the 1920's it had often taken a rather negative form so far as Russia was concerned. It was assumed that the more industrialized countries of the West were ahead of Russia in most respects, and all of Russian history before 1917 was regarded as deplorably backward. In the 1930's all this was changed. Under the guidance of the Central Committee of the Communist party, Russian historical scholars graphically described in textbooks, popular articles, and lectures the rise of Russia from a group of small principalities located on the river network between the Black Sea and the Baltic in the early middle ages to a vast and unified empire in the twentieth century. This interpretation stressed in particular such great figures as Ivan the Terrible and Peter the Great, who had conquered new territories and had suppressed domestic opposition. By combining this long historical tradition with the recent achievements of socialism, the molders of Soviet opinion drew a vigorous picture of the Russians as a people steeled in the furnace of history and now chosen to lead the world to an era of socialism which according to the Marxists was to be the culminating achievement of mankind.

While non-Soviet observers may take exception to such a view of history, it can hardly be doubted that this blending of socialism and nationalism, that developed out of the transitional Stalinist doctrine of "socialism in one country," exerted a powerful influence on the Russian mind. When the great depression temporarily slowed down economic growth in the United States and Europe, the Soviet propagandists maintained that these countries had gone into a permanent decline. By contrast, they depicted the Russian people as being in every way better off than those of the rest of the world. Ludicrous as it frequently appeared to outsiders, this propaganda played a significant role in concealing the hardships of Soviet industrialization and in spurring the Russian people on to greater efforts.

The Victory of Stalinism

CONSTITUTION OF 1936. The Constitution of 1924 was replaced twelve years later by a new federal constitution. It registered the changes that had been made in the body politic and introduced certain new principles of government. The principal change that had occurred since 1924 was the abolition of private enterprise in agriculture and industry, and this was reflected in the system of representation introduced in the new constitution. The Bolsheviks believed that they had won the battle against private enterprise and were well launched on the first stage of socialism. In Marxist terminology, the class structure of Russia had been altered, and in place of property owners and proletariat there now existed under a system of collective ownership three strata of society: the workers, the peasants, and the intelligentsia or educated class. A new electoral system was therefore adopted in which direct elections were substituted for the earlier system of indirect representation through the pyramid of local soviets. Officially, there were no longer any disenfranchised classes.

SOVIET LEADERS *Bulganin, Zhdanov, Stalin, Voroshilov, and Khrushchev at the first session of the Supreme Soviet, Moscow, January, 1938.*

The new representative system required a change in the highest organs of state authority. The Congress of Soviets of the 1924 constitution was abolished, and the former Central Executive Committee was replaced by the Supreme Soviet. The two chambers of the Supreme Soviet were elected for a four-year term by universal suffrage with a minimum voting age of eighteen. The Soviet of the Union was elected on the basis of one deputy for every 300,000 people. In the Soviet of Nationalities, on the other hand, there were 25 deputies from each union republic, 11 from each autonomous republic, 5 from each autonomous region, and 1 from each national district. The two bodies comprising the Supreme Soviet exercised jointly the legislative power and elected a permanent Presidium, or steering committee, which among other functions convened the two chambers and wielded their powers between sessions. The president of the Presidium was nominally the chief of state, thus occupying a position comparable in form to that of the president of the United States or the king of England. This post was occupied by Kalinin, who had served as chairman of the Central Executive Committee under the previous constitution; he was succeeded upon his death in 1946 by Shvernik, former head of the trade unions. In addition to electing the Presidium, the Supreme Soviet appointed the Council of People's Commissars, or cabinet.

The new provisions for direct and universal suffrage in the Constitution of 1936 did not alter the fact that the control of all political activity by the Communist party was as absolute as ever. The new constitution formally described the Communist party as "the vanguard of the working people in their struggle to strengthen and develop the socialist system and . . . the leading core of all organizations of the working people, both public and state" (Article 126). In elections to the Supreme Soviet only one candidate was nominated for each position, and he was invariably elected. Nomination of candidates, under Article 141 of the new constitution, was controlled by "Communist party organizations, trade unions, co-operatives, youth organizations and cultural societies." Since the last four of these bodies were all guided by the first, the nomination of candidates—and hence the composition of the Supreme Soviet—was firmly in Communist hands. This identification of the Communist party with the state was carried so far that by the eve of World War II, most members of the Supreme Soviet and all high executive officials were Bolsheviks, and the more important ones were generally members of the Communist Central Committee and of the Politburo as well. Moreover, as before, civil liberties were strictly limited. Personal rights, such as the right to work, to rest, to security, and to education (Articles 118–21), were in principle available to all those not sentenced by the courts. Civil liberties, on the other hand, such as the freedom of speech, press, assembly and demonstrations, were specifically granted only "in conformity with the interests of the working people, and in order to strengthen the socialist system" (Article 125). Other rights (Articles 122–4, 127–9) were granted in the same spirit. At no time did the Soviet state claim to grant civil liberties to its critics, nor was freedom of political opinion regarded as a necessary or even desirable right.

The Constitution of 1936 retained the federal aspects of the Soviet state. To the seven republics existing in 1929, four were now added by a process of subdivision. The former Transcaucasian Republic was again divided into its three constituent republics of Azerbaijan, Armenia, and Georgia. In Soviet Central Asia, in addition to the Turkmen, Uzbek, and Tadjik republics previously established, territory was taken from the RSFSR to form the Kazakh and Kirghiz republics. The Russian Republic, thus reduced, as well as the Ukrainian and the Byelorussian, remained as before. Some of these eleven republics constituting the Soviet Union also included subordinate autonomous republics and regions, and national districts. Each republic had certain rights of local government and linguistic independence, and even the right of secession (Article 17), but these were again subject to Communist approval. Moreover, the republics remained vastly disproportionate in size. The RSFSR had some 64 per cent of the entire population, thus dominating the Soviet of the Union, while the Ukrainian had another 21 per cent. In the Soviet of Nationalities, the

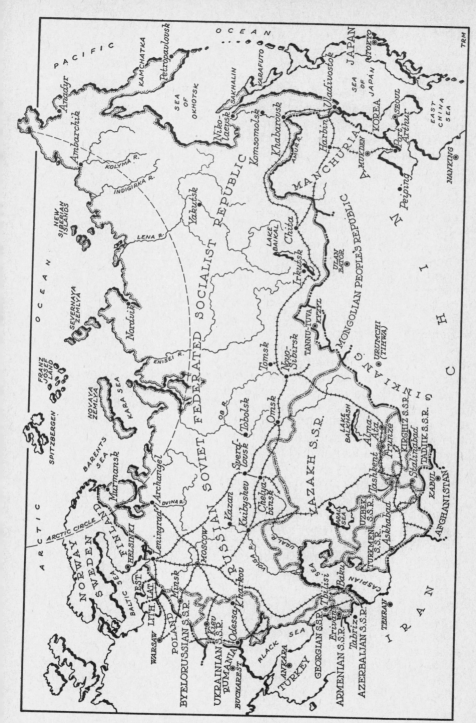

MAP 15 *The Soviet Union in 1936*

RSFSR was to be sure in a minority, but it occupied over one third of the seats by virtue of the representation of its numerous sub-divisions. As in the earlier constitution, the Commissariats were divided between all-union and republic, depending on their function.

THE GREAT PURGES. Elections were held under the new constitution in 1937, and the result, which was known well in advance by the published list of unopposed candidates, was an unqualified success for the Stalin regime. This ability to organize elections did not reflect any party unity, however, for during this period the Communists were undergoing the greatest upheaval in their history. The controversies of the first decade of the Bolshevik revolution did not disappear with the relative success of the five-year plan, but instead were augmented. The Left opposition of Trotsky, Kamenev, Zinoviev, Radek, Rakovsky, and Piatakov, who considered that Stalin was not revolutionary enough, and the Right opposition of Bukharin, Rykov, and Tomsky, who thought that he was too revolutionary, continued to nurse their discontents. That these various groups were opposed to the Stalin regime was a matter of public knowledge, but the exact form which their opposition took is a question that the great purge trials of 1935–38, with their sensational confessions, did not fully reveal. The confessions of the accused did not ring true to outside observers in most cases, and the documentary evidence produced at the trials was not impressive. The assassination in 1934 of Kirov, a man close to Stalin and a member of the Politburo, was one of the few overt acts attributed to the oppositionists, and most of their activity allegedly consisted of negotiations with each other and with foreign agents. Supporters of Stalin undoubtedly felt that the existence of opposition in high quarters might become fatal to the regime in case of war. Most Western observers believed, on the other hand, that whether in war or in peace a purge was the only method available to a dictatorship in dealing with those who disagreed with it.

Whatever history may finally reveal to have been their true nature, the great purges swept like wildfire through the party ranks. Under the vigorous supervision of state prosecutor Vyshinsky, almost all the leading oppositionists were tried and executed. Yagoda, head of the NKVD police system after 1934 was himself arrested in 1937 and subsequently executed. His successor, Yezhov, was replaced two years later by Beriya. From top leaders in military and civilian life, the purge was extended to include thousands of lesser officials who were either shot or sent to labor camps. Trotsky, himself exiled since 1929, was finally assassinated in Mexico in 1940. Of the seven members of the party's Politburo in 1920, all but Lenin were in the end purged by Stalin. Yet the party survived this experience. About a million members and candidates were expelled from the party between 1934 and 1939, and some 650,000 members and candidates were admitted in their place. In the latter year the party thus had some 1,588,900 members and 888,800 candidates, or a total of 2,477,700. Representing about 1.5 per cent of the population of Russia, the party was now composed very largely of younger persons who had joined after Stalin's rise to power and who were loyal to him.

By 1939 the Politburo had a relatively stable membership of eleven including Stalin and in addition two alternate members, each of whom had some important post in the government as well as in the party organization. These Russian leaders, with the year they became regular members of the Politburo, deserve to be listed: Andreyev (1932), commissar of transport, and later of agriculture; Voroshilov (1926), commissar of defense for many years; Zhdanov (1935), political boss of Leningrad; Kaganovich (1930), commissar of railways, heavy industry, etc.; Kalinin (1925), president of the Presidium of the Supreme Soviet; Mikoyan (1935), commissar of food industry, foreign trade, etc.; Molotov (1926), chairman of the Council of Commissars, 1930–41, and commissar of foreign affairs after 1939; Khrushchev (1939), head of the Ukrainian Communists; Beriya (alternate member), commissar of internal affairs after 1939; and Shvernik (alternate member), head of the trade unions. Throughout the period after 1922 Stalin remained as secretary general of the party and, while keeping the real power in his own hands, occupied no position in the Soviet state. Only after the coming of World War II did he abandon this purely party role to become chairman of the Council of Commissars and commissar for defense in 1941. Behind the façade of the Constitution of 1936, the Communist party thus continued more than ever to dominate the scene. Through its power of nomination the party saw to it that its members or persons sympathetic to it filled all elective positions, while the party chiefs occupied the leading appointive posts in the government.

RUSSIA AND THE RISE OF FASCISM. While the diplomatic events of this period are discussed elsewhere, the impact of the rise of fascism in Germany, Italy, and Japan on general Soviet policy deserves special attention. This development did not alter the underlying principles of Soviet foreign policy, for Moscow continued to regard all non-communist countries as potential enemies. Differences of degree were recognized, however, and the type of regime built up by Hitler in Germany was soon publicly condemned as far more dangerous both to the Communist parties abroad and to the Soviet homeland than were the Western democracies. The Soviet Government now initiated an active campaign of associating itself with the enemies of the three principal fascist powers. The admission of the Soviet Union to the League of Nations in 1934, its treaties of mutual assistance with France and Czechoslovakia in 1935, and its treaty of non-aggression with China in 1937, were all a part of this pattern. This period also saw the active participation of the Soviet Union in the drafting of the Montreux Convention of 1936 which revised the regime of the Turkish Straits, in the political and economic campaign against Italy during its war with Ethiopia, and in the abortive efforts of the Non-Intervention Committee with regard to the Spanish Civil War.

The Comintern likewise participated in this campaign against fascism.

From a policy of considering all non-communist parties as enemies of equal value, the Comintern now veered around to the view that the Communist parties should co-operate with all political groups which opposed fascism. The Bulgarian Communist leader Georgi Dimitrov, who had made a name for himself by defying Goering at the Reichstag fire trial in 1933, was now appointed to head the Comintern. This appointment not only brought to the fore a personality already well identified with the immediate issue of anti-fascism, but also tended to dissociate the Soviet state from the Comintern by placing a non-Russian at its head. At the seventh congress of the Comintern in 1935, Dimitrov elucidated the new policy by stating explicitly that "in the face of Fascist danger, Communists may, while reserving for themselves freedom of political agitation and criticism, participate in election campaigns on a common platform and with a common ticket of the anti-fascist front, depending on the growth and the success of the united-front movement, also depending upon the electoral system in operation." Thus was born the policy which resulted in support by the Communists of the Popular Front government in France between 1936 and 1939, and in similar united-front movements in other countries. This policy likewise led to the intervention of the Comintern in the Spanish Civil War, after an initial period of non-interference. In Spain it was the non-Russian Communists who played the principal role in the international brigades, although Soviet military experts were also present along with political commissars who carried on a ruthless campaign against left-wing deviationists in the midst of the civil war. The fascists won the struggle in Spain, but the general result of the Comintern's united-front policy there and elsewhere was to win for it general approval amongst those groups that feared fascism more than communism. The Comintern thus rendered an important service to the Soviet state, of which it remained the instrument.

Despite the relative success of the Soviet policy of rapprochement with the democratic powers, it was one of limited possibilities. The governments of the Western powers were aware that the Soviet leaders regarded the united front against fascism as a tactical device, and the Western statesmen were divided in their counsels as to whether Germany or Russia represented a greater danger to them. While the greater immediate military menace of Nazi Germany was recognized, no firm decision was taken by Great Britain or France; both were still inclined to place economic recovery above military preparedness. Faced with the indecision of the Western states and with the increasing isolation of Russia, Hitler played them off against each other in a manner which postponed the complete isolation of the Axis until 1941. By forcing the Western powers to partition Czechoslovakia at Munich in 1938 Hitler aroused Moscow's suspicions of the West, and in 1939 he reaped the rewards of this maneuver by concluding the non-aggression pact with Russia which gave him a temporary predominance in Eastern Europe.

The Soviet attitude during the last years before World War II was in many ways parallel and complementary to that of the Western states, which Moscow distrusted only less than it feared the Germans. To avoid isolation, the Russians sought to prevent what they regarded as an imminent anti-Soviet agreement between the Western states and the Axis. Russia could offer to the former an agreement directed against the Nazis, and to the latter security from attack in the East. In either case, the Russians were determined to obtain for themselves a security zone of influence extending as far into the Baltic region, Eastern Europe, and possibly the Near East, as bargaining conditions would permit. Faced with these terms in the summer of 1939, the confused statesmen of the West could not see their way either to consent to an extension of Soviet influence or to obtain a reformulation of the Soviet terms. The Nazis, on the other hand, had no scruples against making territorial concessions as a temporary maneuver, and in August, 1939, the Nazi-Soviet agreement was concluded. In Soviet eyes this pact was preferable to isolation, although less desirable than an agreement with the Western states on Russian terms. Speaking in 1941, Stalin justified the Nazi-Soviet pact as giving Russia two more years in which to prepare for the inevitable war with Germany. Whether Russia or Germany gained more in strength during these two years, was the standard by which this maneuver would in the long run be judged.

STALINISM. Just as Leninism is the term used to describe the adaptation of the Marxist doctrines of proletarian revolution and dictatorship to the Russia of World War I, the Soviet system which emerged in a relatively stabilized form in the later 1930's is generally referred to as Stalinism. While Leninism was concerned first of all with the seizure and maintenance of political power in a world racked by war and revolution, the main task of Stalinism was the building up of a strong Russian state along Marxist lines in an era of relative peace.

The principal characteristic of Stalinism was its solution of the fundamental problem of Marxism, the nationalization of all means of production. Nationalization was carried out by an over-all program of planning which touched all phases of the economy. The success of Stalinist socialism was assured not only by the establishment of specific institutions but also by the relentless energy of the Communist party. The party was retained as the single source both of policy and of personnel, and its position of exclusive privilege was explicitly formulated in the Constitution of 1936. The diligence of the Russian people in implementing Communist policies was guaranteed on the one hand by incentives of wages and power which offered wide opportunities to men of ability, and on the other by a system of censorship, police terrorism, and labor camps, which tended to discourage the organization of any opposition group.

The tremendous sacrifices in human lives and liberty which the policies of Stalinism cost were justified by its supporters as necessary for the accomplishment of the mission of the Soviet regime. This belief that the end justified the means was greatly strengthened by the Russian record in World War II, when the political unity achieved by the purges and the industrial strength built up by the five-year plans appeared to be important factors in the Russian victory. In this view the execution or imprisonment of the peasants who resisted collectivization in the 1930's and of the hundreds of thousands of political opponents of the regime constituted the sacrifice demanded by the inevitable unfolding of the Marxist dialectic. The reality of the Soviet tyranny was frankly admitted, but to the Stalinists it was a small sacrifice in comparison with the great benefits which they expected communism eventually would bring.

Opponents of Stalinism abroad directed their criticism against the means which it employed as much as against its goals. While admitting the gains made in the development of heavy industry and in the modernization of society, they claimed that these achievements did not justify the great expenditure in human lives and liberties with which they had been purchased. They demonstrated that if industrial production during the period after 1913 had increased at the same rate as in the quarter of a century before that year, the results would not have been greatly different from those achieved under Stalinism. They also pointed out that the per capita production of grains showed only a slight increase between 1913 and 1937. Critics of Stalinism were also impressed by the fact that, apart from the increase in the proportion of industrial workers, the principal change in the social structure of the Russian people in the years after the revolution was the growth of the bureaucracy. Whereas the nobility, officers, middle class, intellectuals, and clerical workers, had together constituted some 9 per cent of the population in 1914, Soviet statistics indicated that by 1940 the number of state and party officials and employees had risen to about 14 per cent.

The arguments of the supporters and critics of Stalinism were, however, only the extreme opinions among many which were expressed with regard to the Soviet regime. The vast gulf which separated Russian political and economic traditions from those of the rest of the world made comparison and hence evaluation very difficult. To most observers the survival of the Soviet regime after numerous crises indicated that it had achieved more than a minimum of efficiency and stability, and that its accomplishments could best be judged in the light of Russian conditions and standards.

CHAPTER

— 20 —

The Failure of the League System

Revolution and Aggression

THE PROBLEM of maintaining peace after a war is not so much one of keeping down the defeated and disarmed nation as it is a problem of holding together the victorious coalition. After 1919 Germany made no real progress in her campaign for the revision of the peace treaties until after the victors had ceased to work together. Many complex factors interact—among them jealousies, unfulfilled national desires, conflicting imperialistic demands, insistence upon equality—to break up a victorious coalition. These differences are often brought to a head when somewhere a revolution occurs, bringing new officials, bent on new policies, to the fore. The League of Nations devised no method of dealing with revolutions, for these were a matter of internal concern. Yet revolutions were one of the most disturbing events in international affairs, for they affected seriously not only the state involved, but also the relations of the other states among themselves. To get a proper perspective on the events which broke up the victorious coalition after World War I it is useful to recall the major revolutions as well as the major territorial aggressions of these years.

CHRONOLOGY OF REVOLUTION. The Bolshevik revolution had already divided the anti-German coalition as early as 1917. Russia was, in fact, the first of all revisionist powers. Lenin was denouncing the Treaty of Versailles and demanding its overthrow at the very time when Germany was being forced to accept it. The Turkish revolution can no doubt be classed as the second major postwar upheaval. It overthrew the Allied schemes for the partition of Asia Minor and led to profound inter-Allied differences. While not a revolution, of course, the Republican victory in the United States election of 1920 should also be mentioned, for it brought a gradual withdrawal of America from European affairs. The United States did not join the League of Nations or the World Court, nor did she ever ratify the Treaty of Guarantee on which France counted so much. So complete was her withdrawal that separate peace treaties were negotiated by the United States with the defeated states. The Fascist regime which was established in Italy in October, 1922, was accepted by Italy's friends, but Fascist imperialistic demands and policies soon brought Italy into conflict with her former allies. Reaction to the Rivera Dictatorship in Spain in 1923, the Republican revolution in 1931, and the Franco Civil War in 1936 led to further differences among the Western powers. When the army engineered what amounted to a revolution in Japan in 1931–35, Japan could no longer be counted on the side of her former allies.

In Central and Eastern Europe there was in the late twenties and early thirties a general swing from democratic to dictatorial governments. The most significant of these changes was of course the National Socialist domination of Germany in 1933. These new regimes as a whole were less ardent supporters of League procedures than the democratic governments which preceded them. New political philosophies and new men in power account, in part at least, for the shift in political alignments that took place in the thirties.

MARCH OF AGGRESSION. Closely associated with these revolutionary changes were the major territorial aggressions of the interwar period. It is a matter of opinion whether communist revolutionary action in China in the twenties, together with the establishment of a communist dominated Outer Mongolian state, constituted Russian territorial aggression or not. There is, however, no dispute about the imperialist nature of Japanese policy in Manchuria after 1931. This was followed a few years later by the Italian conquest of Ethiopia in 1935–36. By the time Hitler began expanding the boundaries of Germany through the annexation of Austria in 1938, the inability of the League to stop aggression, whether it was in China or in Ethiopia, or foreign intervention, as in Spain, was a patent fact. Actually Hitler was only the last and the greediest of the territorial aggressors of the interwar period.

Failure to stop aggression undoubtedly was the biggest blow to League prestige, but other things contributed to its decline. Pledged to a policy of disarmament, the League lost ground with the failure of the disarmament conference. Many states withdrew from membership for one reason or another, and by 1939 the weight of power and influence in the world might be said to lie outside the League. The United States, Brazil, Japan, Germany, Italy, Spain, and a number of lesser states were by this time not members of the League. The three great League powers were Great Britain, France, and Russia, and they were far from united on what League policy should be.

The Manchurian Crisis

ESTABLISHMENT OF THE REPUBLIC OF MANCHUKUO. The important Chinese province of Manchuria opened to Japan all the usual rewards of imperialistic venture. By modern standards it was an undeveloped country and offered a profitable field for capital investment. As the economic depression descended, the conquest of Manchuria offered prospects of returning prosperity to Japan. Barred from emigrating to the United States, Australia, or New Zealand by the stringent immigration laws of these countries, the Japanese saw in Manchuria a haven for Japan's surplus population. Strategic considerations also entered into the picture. Manchuria not only would become a bulwark in Japan's defense against Russia, but would also provide important outposts for the domination of northern China.

Immediately after World War I Japan began to invest large sums in this region. It was Japanese capital that built the new railways in Manchuria until about 1927. At that time Chinese authorities began to build a number of railways which were soon competing with the Japanese-controlled network. The Japanese protested against this new construction,

declaring that it was contrary to their Railway Agreement of 1905, a treaty
the Chinese did not recognize as binding. The climax came on September
18, 1931. Japanese forces serving as railway guards under treaty arrangements were out on maneuvers when a section of track was blown up. It
was a minor explosion, but the Japanese generals held the Chinese responsible and took over the city of Mukden, including the barracks with 10,000
Chinese soldiers. Within the next few days Japanese forces occupied the
leading cities along the South Manchurian railway, thus placing all of
South Manchuria under Japanese control. The cabinet in Tokyo opposed
sending additional troops into Manchuria and announced that the occupation troops would be withdrawn as soon as the "riots" had ceased. The Japanese military authorities, however, went ahead on their own, moving additional forces from neighboring Korea (annexed by Japan in 1910) into
Manchuria. On March 9, 1932, the Independent Republic of Manchukuo
was proclaimed under the presidency of Pu Yi, the former emperor of
China. Little attempt was made to disguise the Japanese control of the
new state.

LEAGUE ACTION. Immediately after the occupation of Mukden China
appealed to the League of Nations, invoking Articles X, XI, and XV of
the Covenant. Under these articles, it was the duty of the League to investigate, report, and make recommendations for a settlement of the dispute.
The Council obtained the promise of the Japanese civil authorities to
withdraw their troops into the Railway Zone, but this was never carried
out. Further attempts to mediate peace led to the appointment on December 31, 1931, of a Commission headed by Lord Lytton and made up of
nationals of Great Britain, France, Italy, Germany, and the United States,
to investigate the situation on the spot.

Meanwhile, fighting broke out in Shanghai, where Japanese troops,
stationed in the International Settlement, had been re-enforced. Upon a
renewed appeal from China a special Committee of Nineteen was appointed by the Assembly of the League to study the situation and report.
The immediate crisis in Shanghai passed when the Committee of Nineteen
was able to arrange an armistice that provided for the withdrawal of Japanese troops (May 5, 1932). As to the other questions in dispute between
China and Japan, it was decided to wait for the report of the Lytton Commission. This report was not forthcoming until October, 1932. It recognized
that Japan had special interests in Manchuria, but recommended that this
territory should remain under Chinese sovereignty. A local gendarmerie was
to maintain internal order and all other forces were to be withdrawn. Recommendations based on the Lytton report were adopted by the League in
February, 1933, with only Japan casting a negative vote.

By this time Japan had officially recognized Manchukuo as an independent state and had entered into an alliance with it. Since the League's
recommendations struck squarely at this arrangement, Japan gave notice
of its withdrawal from the League. At the same time hostilities were renewed in China, and the important province of Jehol was overrun. When

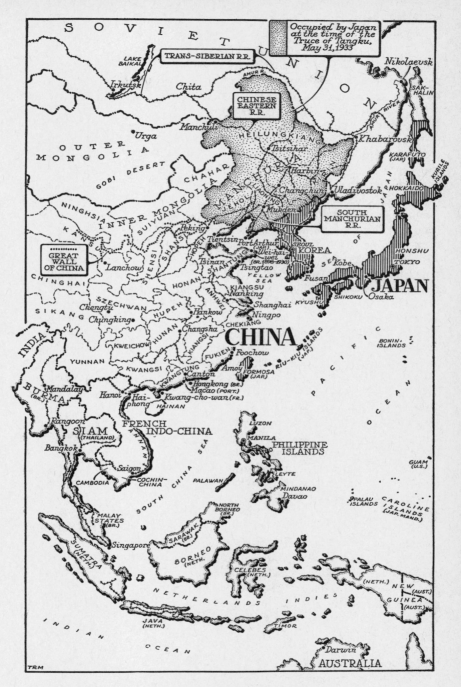

MAP 16 *Japanese Expansion in China*

the City of Peiping was threatened the Chinese government signed an armistice at Tangku, May 31, 1933.

The League had been unable to change the situation in Manchuria, but at least the fighting had stopped, and the powers contented themselves with refusing to recognize the new state of affairs. The United States had publicly proclaimed on January 7, 1932, that it would follow a policy of nonrecognition in regard to "any situation, treaty or agreement which may be brought about by means contrary to the covenants and obligations of the Pact of Paris." In this belated attempt to put teeth into the Pact of Paris, the United States now called on all nations to refuse to recognize the results of aggressive action, but this suggestion was received with little enthusiasm. More realistic than some of the other powers, the USSR in May, 1933, offered to sell its interests in the Chinese Eastern Railway to Japan. After two years of bargaining the sale was made to the Republic of Manchukuo for 140 million yen. By this transaction the USSR simply withdrew from an exposed front to more easily defended positions in Mongolia.

MONGOLIA. Outer Mongolia had been controlled by the Manchus only through alliances with native rulers. Under the Chinese Republic this system collapsed, and Tibet and Outer Mongolia broke away from the Republic. From 1912 to 1918 a regime dominated by Tsarist Russia held sway in Outer Mongolia. This was followed (1919–20) by a "White" Russian government which was ended by Red Army action, whereupon a Revolutionary People's Government (1921–24) was established. In a treaty concluded in 1924 Russia recognized that China's sovereignty extended to Outer Mongolia, and Soviet troops were withdrawn. Soviet advisers replaced the troops and established the Mongolian People's Revolutionary Government, which has controlled Outer Mongolia ever since. In 1934 this government concluded a Mutual Assistance Pact with the USSR. The Japanese expansion into Manchuria soon led to clashes where Manchuria bordered on Russia and on Outer Mongolia. No one spoke of war, but some of the engagements went well beyond the usual border squabbles common to these areas. The conflicts of 1935–36 were especially serious. In 1935 Japan also moved southward into the Inner Manchurian provinces of Chahar and Hopei.

NEW ALIGNMENTS. Chiang Kai-shek, the head of the Chinese National Government, had long been battling Communist leaders in various sections of China. Many accused him of being more interested in fighting Communist Chinese than in halting Japanese expansion. In December, 1936, he was captured under rather mysterious circumstances by one of his own generals who was in touch with Chinese Communist forces. An agreement was now negotiated between Chiang Kai-shek and the Communists for a common front against Japan. Just how much the Russians were behind these negotiations is not clear, but a Chinese-Russian Entente was established for the time being.

On her side, Japan concluded the Anti-Comintern Pact with Germany (November 25, 1936). This was not an alliance for mutual aid against Russia but rather an agreement to co-operate in combating communism [see below, pp. 512–13]. It did, however, mark the existence of better relations between Japan and Germany. As Germany had concluded the Axis agreement with Italy on October 25, 1936, the Anti-Comintern Pact was the beginning of closer ties between these three great powers.

The Ethiopian Crisis

HISTORICAL BACKGROUND. In tracing the history of an episode such as Italian aggression in Ethiopia,[1] it is important not to lose sight of the setting within which these events occurred. It should not be forgotten that the Italian conquest of Ethiopia climaxed years of imperialistic fascist utterances, that it came when all industrial states were desperately combating the depression, that the League had just shown its inability to cope with the problem of disarmament or to stop Japanese aggression in Manchuria, and that, as a result of two years of energetic policy, Hitler seemed to most statesmen of Europe to be the major threat to the peace of the world. On every hand there was the greatest reluctance to alienate Mussolini or to lose his aid in checking Hitler.

Ever since 1889, when an Italian-supported chieftain signed a compromising treaty on becoming Emperor of Ethiopia, the Italians had built up claims to a protectorate over that country. A severe defeat by the Ethiopians at Adowa in 1896 did not discourage Italy from continuing to negotiate at various times with England and France for a free hand there, or at least an agreement as to spheres of influence. Nevertheless Ethiopia, with the active support of the three great allied powers, was admitted to the League of Nations in 1923. In 1928 Mussolini changed tactics, negotiating a pact with Ethiopia, by which trade was to be encouraged, Ethiopia obtained a free zone in the Italian-controlled port of Assab, and Italy was granted the concession of constructing certain important roads. The Italians hoped that the treaty would lead to further concessions, but these did not materialize. Haile Selassie, who had served as regent since 1916, was crowned king on October 7, 1928, and emperor in 1930, launched an extensive reform program. Of the many experts who were called in for technical assistance, only one was Italian, for the emperor was well aware of the Italian plan for gradual political infiltration into Ethiopia. Meanwhile the Italians continued their intrigues to detach various tribes from allegiance to the central government. They also continued their efforts to straighten out colonial differences with Britain. In July, 1934, for example, protocols were signed with Britain and Egypt which delimited the boundary between Cyrenaica and the Anglo-Egyptian Sudan.

ITALIAN PLANS. By this time Mussolini's plans to take over Ethiopia were far advanced. Like the other imperialist powers in their time, the Italian government found the highest motivation for its Ethiopian policy. When Ethiopia entered the League in 1923 it agreed, along with all other

---

[1] Ethiopia is the official name of the state that includes most of the region often referred to as Abyssinia.

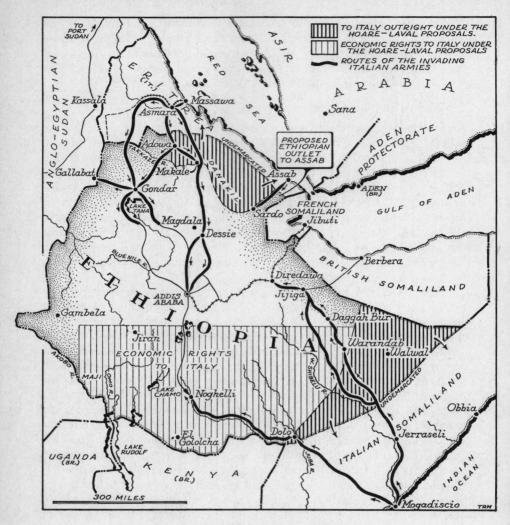

MAP 17   *Italian Conquest of Ethiopia*

African powers (1) to prohibit the acquisition of arms by unauthorized persons, and (2) to suppress slavery and the slave trade. Slavery in Ethiopia was officially abolished the following year, but there is no question that it continued among many remote tribes. It is also true that various tribes acquired arms, as is attested by numerous border raids along the ill-defined boundaries. Italy now was disposed to carry the torch of civilization, bringing peace and the end of slavery to Ethiopia. The Italians maintained that Ethiopia's failure to stamp out slavery forfeited her right to protection by the League.

WALWAL INCIDENT. On December 5, 1934, at the oasis of Walwal near the border between British and Italian Somaliland, a clash occurred between the Ethiopian escort of an Anglo-Ethiopian boundary commission and Italian troops. Ethiopia claimed that the oasis was sixty miles inside the Ethiopian frontier and had been illegally occupied by the Italians. Most maps did show the region as belonging to Ethiopia, although it was generally recognized that boundaries in these regions had never been well defined. The Italians in turn claimed they had been in occupation of the oasis for some years and that Ethiopia had recognized that lands used by tribes subject to Italy should belong to Italy. About one hundred Ethiopians and some thirty Italian colonial troops were killed in the clash. The Italians, backed by some tanks and planes, retained possession of the oasis.

The Italian government at once demanded an apology, the payment of 200,000 Ethiopian thalers and the punishment of the responsible Ethiopian officers. This Ethiopia refused, proposing conciliation or arbitration under the 1928 Treaty of Friendship. Italy insisted that this was not a question suitable for arbitration and reiterated her demands. Realizing the seriousness of the situation, Ethiopia brought the matter to the attention of the League of Nations and on January 3, 1935, made a formal appeal under Article XI, paragraph two, of the Covenant. Before the deliberations got under way, France and Italy concluded a far-reaching understanding which they had been negotiating for some months.

FRENCH-ITALIAN COLONIAL AGREEMENT. Although Italy had arranged various colonial agreements with Britain, not much progress had been made in settling affairs with France. The small territorial cessions made by France in southeast Tunisia in 1919 were never recognized by Italy as adequate compensation for the important German colonies which France obtained. Deep-seated resentment also existed over the treatment of Italians in Tunisia. Prudence clearly called for a settlement with France before Italy launched on new colonial ventures. It was an opportune moment, as the French statesmen had been much pleased by the anti-German attitude of Mussolini, when Hitler attempted an Austrian *Putsch* in July 1934 [see above, pp. 351–52].

A general settlement of the differences between the two countries was reached when the French foreign minister, Laval, signed a treaty at Rome on January 7, 1935. France ceded about 44,500 square miles of desert to the south of Libya and about 309 square miles along the border of French Somaliland and Eritrea. In addition France granted to Italy 2,500 shares of the French-owned Jibuti-Addis Ababa Railway. Italy in turn recognized that all questions of compensation under the Treaty of London were now settled. It was agreed that in Tunis all children born of Italian parents before 1945 should be Italian citizens, those born between 1945 and 1965 should have the right of option, while those born after 1965 were to be French nationals. Italian schools were to maintain their existing status until 1955. The Austrian problem was thoroughly canvassed, and the two signatories promised to consult with one another and Austria if a threat to

Austrian independence should arise. It was a thrust at Hitler when they condemned modification of armament obligations by unilateral action, promising to act in concert should this occur. Henceforth, all differences between the two states were to be settled by diplomatic negotiations or through the existing League agencies.

Outward manifestations of French-Italian friendship soon made their appearance in the form of ceremonial visits. There can be no question that Italian-French relations were on a better footing in the spring of 1935 than they had been for years. Laval always insisted that the agreement of January 7, 1935, did not affect the sovereignty, independence, or territorial integrity of Ethiopia. According to the letter of the agreement he was no doubt correct. Nevertheless, Mussolini was justified in believing that the treaty with France left him free to carry out an active African policy, a claim which Laval's statement in the Chamber of Deputies bears out.[2]

THE LEAGUE AND THE GENERAL EUROPEAN SITUATION. The Council of the League in January, 1935, was able to induce both Italy and Ethiopia to arbitrate the Walwal incident. Italian shipment of troops and supplies to the East African colonies, however, continued while Italy delayed appointment of arbitrators, which brought renewed protests from Ethiopia. The arbitrators met with frequent interruptions from June to September, when they came to the unanimous decision that neither side had been proved guilty of aggression. The problem of ownership of the oasis was not touched upon, as the arbitrators had been instructed not to deal with questions of sovereignty. These arbitration negotiations served to free the Council from the necessity of dealing directly with the problem.

Other events occupied the interest of most European statesmen in these months. In January Hitler had scored a big victory in the Saar plebiscite. This was followed, on March 16, by his denunciation of the clauses of the Versailles treaty providing for German disarmament. It was the first direct repudiation of that treaty and could not be passed by without notice. A conference was held in April 1935 at Stresa, where England, France, and Italy jointly protested against German rearmament. Although Italian transports were moving to East Africa in a steady stream, the circumspect conferees did not mention Ethiopia, at least so the published record stands. A series of events followed which seemed far removed from Africa and yet greatly influenced the developing Italian-Ethiopian crisis. On May 2, the Russian-French Alliance was signed, to be followed on June 18, 1935, by the Anglo-German Naval Treaty. If the former aroused apprehension in England, the latter caused consternation in France. Italy loomed more than ever as the balance-weight in world affairs and both English and French statesmen were anxious to keep her friendship.

Italy seemed determined to make war as soon as the rainy season in Ethiopia ended. To forestall this, Anthony Eden, British minister for

[2] Maxwell H. H. Macartney and Paul Cremona: *Italy's Foreign and Colonial Policy 1914–1937* (London, 1938), p. 299.

League affairs, visited Rome in June, but came away emptyhanded. At the suggestion of the Council of the League, representatives of France, Italy, and Britain held a tripartite conference in Paris on August 14 in an attempt to reach a direct settlement of Italy's African demands, but this too proved fruitless.

Meanwhile the results of the Peace Poll had been published in England, making it clear that the people of Britain were strong supporters of the League [see above, pp. 437–38]. Naturally the government leaders became more League-conscious. When the regular session of the League of Nations assembled in September, Sir Samuel Hoare, British Secretary for Foreign Affairs, electrified the Assembly by a speech in which he promised that England would live up to her obligation for collective resistance to all acts of aggression. No one knew that he had on the previous day discussed the situation with Laval and come to an understanding that there should be no naval blockade, that the Suez Canal should not be closed, that military sanctions were not to be imposed, nor any other action taken which might lead to war. Whether the wily Frenchman relayed this information to Mussolini is uncertain, but to do so would have been in line with the policies he was accustomed to follow.

IMPOSITION OF SANCTIONS. On October 3, Italy, without a declaration of war, launched its long expected attack on Ethiopia. The forces advancing from Eritrea by the speedy capture of Adowa removed the blot of 1896 from the escutcheon of the Italian army. Those coming northward from Italian Somaliland had a less spectacular campaign. Soon both Italian armies found it necessary to take time out to build roads and bring up supplies.

The League now acted with unprecedented speed. On October 7, the Council declared Italy to be the aggressor and four days later the Assembly voted to impose economic sanctions, which were to become effective November 18. President Roosevelt had already put into effect the American neutrality legislation and in a proclamation had enumerated the items on which trade was restricted, mainly arms and munitions. The League added a few items to this list, but no sanctions were placed on oil or coal. Austria, Hungary, and Albania, all bound to Italy by special trade treaties and other agreements, refused to apply sanctions. Switzerland, in view of her special position as a neutralized state, refused to apply sanctions unconditionally, especially in regard to the restriction of imports. Germany, as a nonmember of the League, introduced a licensing system under which exports to Italy were prevented from increasing much over previous exports. Although the neutrality legislation forced the United States to restrict trade on some items to both belligerents, Italian trade with the United States increased in other categories, notably in oil.

Italy protested bitterly against the League-sponsored measures and answered with a plan of counter-sanctions. A strict licensing system was established for imports not on the sanction list from countries imposing sanctions. Italian exports to these countries were also restricted. One effect of this was to make it easier for Hitler to expand his trade drive into Southeastern Europe [see above, pp. 368–69; 458–59].

Britain was largely responsible for pushing League action. It was the British fleet which was most ostentatiously shifted to the Mediterranean, and it was the British foreign office which negotiated a series of agreements with France, Spain, Yugoslavia, Greece, and Turkey, providing for mutual support in case war should arise. Mussolini protested the formation of this Mediterranean bloc and reserved his bitterest invectives for the British statesmen. In France the rightist groups were definitely antisanctionist. They maintained that the English were more interested in protecting their imperial interests than in backing the League. Heretofore it was France that had tried to push League action, particularly when it was a question dealing with Germany. Now the roles were reversed. The French leaders who had just established the long-coveted closer relations with Italy were loath to see these placed in jeopardy by a policy of sanctions.

HOARE-LAVAL AGREEMENT. On November 14, 1935, the British elections were held and the National government won a resounding victory, thanks to widespread support of its foreign policy. But the British leaders never gave up the idea of a compromise settlement. Hoare, bound for a Swiss vacation, stopped off in Paris and with Laval cooked up a scheme for a pacific settlement between Italy and Ethiopia. Ethiopia was to cede outright to Italy some 60,000 square miles along the borders of Italian Somaliland and Eritrea in return for a corridor of about 3,000 square miles connecting Ethiopia with the port of Assab in Eritrea. Further, England and France were to use their influence at Addis Ababa and Geneva to secure for Italy a zone of 160,000 square miles in southern Ethiopia for her exclusive economic exploitation (see map, p. 492). This plan of settlement was officially communicated to the Italian and Ethiopian governments and also to the League. Somehow these secret proposals leaked out, and when a map appeared in the London press showing that about two thirds of Ethiopia was to be turned over to Italy, public indignation flared up. The opposition parties had charged in the election campaign that, once the balloting was over, the cabinet would make a deal with Mussolini. The Hoare-Laval proposals now gave many a government opponent the occasion to chant, "I told you so." Many influential men of all political faiths wrote letters to the press denouncing this betrayal of the League. Individual resignations are a rare occurrence in English parliamentary practice, but Prime Minister Baldwin had no recourse but to replace Hoare by Anthony Eden, who was well known for his pro-League and anti-fascist views. British public opinion truly killed the Hoare-Laval proposals, and they were officially buried when the League, on December 19, thanked the British and French delegates for submitting their proposals but did nothing about them.

THE QUESTION OF OIL SANCTIONS. The League had appointed a Committee of Eighteen to consider further sanctions, which was bound to mean an embargo on oil shipments. Laval wished to prevent this. He was able, apparently, to convince Hoare that oil sanctions would lead to an Italian attack on the British fleet, and that the French fleet was not at that time in a position to lend aid. This was what lay behind the Hoare-Laval agreement.

The opponents of further sanctions argued that it was useless to put an embargo on oil if the United States were free to send in supplies. No definite promises were made by the United States, but there were indications that the United States would at least have limited oil exports to normal quantities if the League had taken action. There was even some reason to believe that the United States would have stopped all shipments. Since the United States supplied only 6.3 per cent of Italian imports, a normal flow of United States oil would not have upset the sanction policy. A committee of experts appointed by the League found the imposition of oil sanctions feasible, but, thanks largely to the delaying tactics of the French foreign office, they were never applied.

END OF THE CRISIS. Indeed the question of whether to impose oil sanctions or not faded away before German reoccupation of the Rhineland on March 7, 1936, and Italian victories. The Italian troops had the advantage of modern mechanized equipment and air power, and they did not refrain from using poison gas. The terrain and weather, more than the Ethiopian army, delayed their advance. Finally on May 5, troops based in Eritrea captured Addis Ababa. Emperor Haile Selassie had fled a few days earlier, and on May 9 the Italian government formally proclaimed the annexation of Ethiopia. King Victor Emmanuel III was hailed as Emperor of Ethiopia. Within a month Ethiopia, Eritrea, and Somaliland were organized into Italian East Africa and Marshal Badoglio was proclaimed viceroy. The League Council recognized the *de facto* situation and voted to abandon sanctions as of July 15.

For two hundred and forty-one days sanctions had been in effect, and Italy marked the League's surrender with a great celebration. The League had failed to prevent aggression, and the policy of sanctions was discredited. Yet it should be noted that a complete program of sanctions had never been applied. All items of trade were never covered and certain very important products, notably oil and coal, were on the exempted list. Many League members were not wholeheartedly behind the policy, and some openly refused to participate. From the start the whole action was weakened by the fact that the four great nonmember states—the United States, Germany, Japan, and Brazil—were not subject to the limitation of sanctions. Although some trade restrictions were imposed by some of these nonmember states, this was not so effective as it would have been, had these powers been obligated to support the League's program. Many a trader or statesman in sanction-supporting countries feared that rivals were capitalizing on his sacrifices. What started out as an attempt to bolster the League's authority through effective collective action ended in undermining it seriously. A spirit of resentment against England and France came to dominate the minds of Italian officials. Although for a year and a half

EMPEROR IN EXILE   *Haile Selassie, exiled Emperor of Ethiopia, addressing the League of Nations in June, 1936.*

longer Italy remained within the League, it was clear that she would not support vigorous collective action sponsored by that body. More great powers were without than within the League, and power politics still were the order of the day.

The Spanish Crisis

HISTORICAL BACKGROUND. The roots of the Spanish conflict reached back to Spain's failure to undertake reforms that had been enacted into law in most of Western Europe before World War I. Not only was Spain plagued by problems associated with increased industrialization, which all modern states encountered in varying degree, but it still had not solved the issue of clerical or state control of education, marriage, or divorce. Although religious toleration supposedly existed, Protestant churches were far from free and were burdened by many restrictions. The agrarian question remained practically untouched as late as 1931. Spain was still primarily a country of large land-holding grandees and impoverished peons.

Even before the war the Spanish cabinets had come in conflict with the church. In 1909, as an outgrowth of an attempt at a general strike, convents were burned and members of the clergy were killed. Over great opposition by the clerical parties a so-called Padlock Law was passed in 1910 that forbade the establishment of more religious houses without the consent of the government, taxed industrial enterprises controlled by religious orders, and permitted public worship by non-Catholic bodies. The premier who had pushed through this law was later assassinated by an anarchist, and existing practices were not greatly altered. Spain remained under the control of an oligarchy consisting of the nobility, the clergy including the religious orders, big business men, army officers, and a section of the upper middle class. It is estimated that this group comprised about 500,000 men, women, and children, which amounts to about two per cent of the total population.

With the outbreak of war in 1914 Spain declared her neutrality. The sympathies of the working-class, the intellectuals, and commercial circles were on the whole pro-Ally, while the clergy, nobility, and bureaucracy were pro-German. All factions united however in their desire to keep Spain neutral. The war brought a tremendous expansion of mining and manufacturing industries, and the consequent prosperity lent strength to the workers' movement.

With the end of the war the tide of prosperity ebbed in Spain, while expenses for the pacification of Morocco mounted. For years Spain had been trying to subdue the tribesmen in Spanish Morocco, but with little success. In 1921 disaster struck: a Spanish army 20,000 strong was defeated by the Riffs under Abd-el-Krim, with a loss of over half their number. Spain had to retreat from the entire eastern zone which had been laboriously taken bit by bit since 1909. Bad generalship, and lack of supplies and equipment were in part responsible, and the people clamored for a parliamentary investigation of army graft and corruption.

Just before a parliamentary committee investigating this situation was to issue its report, which the army wished to suppress, General Primo de Rivera raised the banner of revolt in Barcelona on September 13, 1923. King Alfonso XIII, who had witnessed twelve cabinets since 1918, readily consented to the demand of the Madrid garrison to appoint Primo de Rivera as head of the government.

THE RIVERA DICTATORSHIP AND THE END OF THE MONARCHY, 1923–1931. With the approval of the king, Rivera dissolved the Cortes, suspended jury trial, and established a strict censorship of the press. He publicly styled himself a dictator and was not averse to being compared to Mussolini. With King Alfonso he paid a state visit to Rome, and pictures of the two kings with their dictators beside them were spread over the face of the globe. In 1925, it is true, Rivera officially ended the dictatorship and became a prime minister with a cabinet, but no elective Cortes was called into being. He rebuilt the army and had the good fortune of securing French assistance against Abd-el-Krim, who attacked the French in Morocco. A joint campaign against the Riffs was successful in 1926.

Relieved of the nightmare of campaigns in Morocco, Primo de Rivera could turn his attention to domestic policy. His motto was: "Country, Religion, Monarchy." He launched on an extended public works program and in the end he accomplished a good deal in this field. Many paved roads were built; railroads were extended and their rolling stock improved, thanks to government subsidies; expositions at Seville and Barcelona displayed what great advances were being made. The administrative service was purged of some of its incompetents, and the cost of collecting taxes declined from ten to four per cent. In educational matters Rivera surrendered to the clericals. He enforced uniform textbooks for the nation, which in practice meant a clerical point of view in the books of all schools. The clergy had long been campaigning for this measure. University faculties were subjected to many vexatious measures, and, to stop the student riots, one university after another was closed.

These educational policies along with strict censorship laws aroused the opposition of the intellectuals, and many of them found means of agitating against Rivera. Efforts to do away with seniority as the basis of promotion in the artillery corps roused opposition from another quarter. The depression ended what little success had been achieved in the economic sphere, and with this the support of the industrialists was lost. The king, sensing the way the wind was blowing, decided to improve his own standing by forcing Rivera to resign, January 28, 1930. The erstwhile dictator fled to France, where he died three months later.

General Berenguer, who now took over the direction of affairs, undertook a policy of conciliation. Some of the Rivera regulations were canceled, although many onerous ones remained. Amnesties were granted, and within a few months censorship was ended. The result was an avalanche of criticism of the monarchy and of conditions in general. As the depression deepened, strikes increased in violence. In December, 1930, a garrison in the Pyrenees mutinied, and martial law was again clamped down on the whole country. Two officers, who were ringleaders in the mutiny, were shot and immediately became transfigured into republican martyrs. So widespread was the opposition that Alfonso was forced to announce the restoration of the constitution and to set a date for elections. The municipal elections which were held on April 12, 1931, resulted in a victory for the republican parties. King Alfonso was persuaded to depart for Paris two days later. He left without abdicating, supposedly to await the results of the national election, but he was never to return and died in exile in 1941.

FOUNDING OF THE REPUBLIC. Alcala Zamora, an old liberal leader, organized a provisional government and supervised the election of a constitutional assembly on July 28, 1931. This body adopted a progressive democratic constitution, elected Zamora president, and named Azana, a man of more radical views, prime minister. Under Azana's leadership a policy of separating church and state was carried out, the Jesuit order in Spain was dissolved, a system of state schools was established, large estates were expropriated, and a beginning of land distribution was made. Catalonia was conceded an extensive degree of autonomy. However, the left-wing leaders pushed things more rapidly than the people were prepared to go, and the elections of May, 1933, were carried by the right-wing parties.

The reform program which had been inaugurated was now not so much repealed as circumvented. The Catholic church regained much of its control over education, and the Jesuits continued to teach. The machinery for land distribution was thrown out of gear, and reaction went so far as to require full compensation for all land taken from the grandees. Since the government appropriated only fifty thousand pesetas for this purpose, this meant that the nobility retained their lands. When Catalonia declared its complete independence, the government intervened with arms and put an end to its extensive autonomy. A succession of rightist cabinets at no time commanded a strong majority in parliament, and the severe economic crisis of these years added to the difficulties of governing Spain. When it eventually proved necessary to dissolve parliament, the rightist parties formed an anti-Marxist alliance, while the parties of the left, following the French example, joined in a popular, or united front. The latter swept the elections held on February 16, 1936.

Azana again became prime minister and immediately began to carry forward the reforms which had been cut short by the rightist reaction. An amnesty was granted freeing thousands of political prisoners; Catalonian autonomy was restored; the distribution of lands was resumed; various anti-clerical policies, notably the development of lay schools, were again inaugurated. The people pressed for more radical measures, and a rash of strikes developed. On the other hand, the Spanish Fascists (known as the Falange or Phalanx) added to the turmoil by their aggressive actions. The government dissolved the Falange and imprisoned many of its leaders. Associations of army officers became restive, for they considered Premier Azana an arch enemy of the army. Certain officers, in March, 1936, attempted to bring pressures upon Azana to stop the strikes. Violence and counter-violence increased. On July 12 three Fascists shot Lieutenant Castillo, a member of the Republican Guards. That evening Calvo Sotelo, an able rightist political leader who had made some very critical speeches in the Cortes, was assassinated in retaliation.

OUTBREAK OF CIVIL WAR, 1936. A group of army leaders, who had been planning a *coup d'état* ever since the elections, seized upon this moment when public opinion was shocked by the murder of a prominent member of the Cortes. On July 18, the banners of revolt were unfurled by the army chiefs in Spanish Morocco. On the second day of revolt General Francisco Franco flew from the Canary Islands to Morocco in a British plane which had been chartered by some wealthy Spaniards.

The revolt spread to the garrisons in the chief towns of Spain, and within a few days the rebels were in control of most of the regular army, the air force, and about half the navy. It was a purely Spanish affair and in essence an army revolt against the program of the Spanish Popular Front. No foreign power was behind the uprising, but when the government did not collapse as expected, each side sought supplies and aid. The rebel cause seemed to be in jeopardy in the first days, as failure to win over the fleet made it dangerous, if not impossible, to ferry the contingents from Morocco to Spain. These were scheduled to act as the spearhead in the attack. At this critical moment the local National Socialist leader of the few hundred Germans resident in Morocco appeared at Franco's headquarters, offering to procure some German airplanes. On July 28, 1936, thirty Junker transport planes arrived in Morocco. They were soon set to work ferrying troops and supplies to Spanish cities where the situation was critical. By July 30 Italian planes were also at hand. German and, especially, Italian aid to Franco increased steadily as time went on.

THE POSITION OF PORTUGAL. To many it seemed that Spain was now passing at an accelerated tempo through the same cycle that Portugal had followed in recent years. After the overthrow of the monarchy in 1910 Portugal had been the scene of frequent revolutions until a military coup under General Carmona in 1926 restored order. Oliveira Salazar soon took over the guidance of affairs, first as finance minister, then as prime minister (1932), from which position he supervised the adoption of a new constitution in 1933. He was a professor of economics and an expert in finance and was able to put Portuguese finances on a sound basis. He was also a devout Catholic and the losses experienced by the church in Portugal at the time of the overthrow of the monarchy were more than made up under his regime. The new government excluded the free functioning of political parties and, although there was not much talk of political philosophies and Salazar remained in the background, the dictatorship was very real. It was a paternalistic government, to which communism was anathema, and Salazar hailed Franco as a brother knight in the crusade to remove communism from the Iberian peninsula. Nevertheless the old ties with England were never broken, for this alliance was to Portugal's advantage in retaining the vast Portuguese colonies in Africa.

POSITION OF THE POWERS. If Franco denounced his opponents as Communists, they in turn were not slow to pin the Fascist label on him. What in origin was a Spanish civil crisis became a world conflict of ideologies, a battle between fascism and communism. In Russia the Central Council of Trade Unions "invited" all workers to contribute one half of one per cent of their monthly wages to a fund for the "Loyalists" as the supporters of the Spanish government were called. Stalin maintained that ". . . the liberation of Spain from the yoke of Fascist reactionaries is not the private concern of Spaniards, but the concern of all advanced and progressive humanity." [3] Supplies were slow to reach Spain from Russia, but this aid was of vital importance in stiffening the resistance of the Loyalists. They were also greatly helped by large numbers of volunteers from many countries who flocked to Spain, lured by the opportunity to strike a blow at fascism.

---

[3] As quoted in Vera Micheles Dean: "European Diplomacy in the Spanish Crisis," *Foreign Policy Reports* (1936) 12:230.

The Vatican, along with the Catholic hierarchy in most countries, was definitely on the side of the rebels. Yet here and there a Catholic bishop or some leading Catholic organization spoke with favor of the Republican cause. In Spain the Basque provinces, traditionally very loyal to the church, established their own autonomous state and fought loyally on the Republican side. In France and England leftist and liberal opinion favored the Republic. The British leaders, perhaps more than the French, banked on a nationalist Spain emerging from the conflict that would turn to Britain for support in throwing off the domination of Italy, Germany, or Russia. Economically, Britain held high stakes in Spain.

Premier Blum, as head of the Popular Front government in France, did not wish to alienate completely the parties of the right by becoming involved in the Spanish Civil War. It was he who led the way to an agreement among the powers on a so-called policy of non-intervention; military supplies were not to be sent to either side. Finally, an international "Non-intervention Committee," representing twenty-seven European states, set up headquarters in London in September, 1936. It was not until the end of the month that Portugal satisfied herself about certain technicalities and took her place on the committee. Meanwhile supplies had been pouring across her frontiers to Franco. Some aid was also reaching the Loyalists from France and Russia.

The establishment of this committee was one of the arguments used by Geneva officials to dissuade the Spanish government from officially placing its difficulties before the League. It was, after all, a civil war, and therefore not strictly an affair of the League, although there were League articles which might have been interpreted to cover it. The League was never asked to end hostilities or to intervene directly in Spain, but it was requested on several occasions to consider the problem of foreign intervention. In December, 1936, the Council, which was called into special session because of the crisis, passed a resolution to the effect that all states were under obligation to refrain from intervening in the internal affairs of another state.

Since this was a civil war, the American neutrality laws did not apply. President Roosevelt, in order to co-operate with the policy of the Non-Intervention Committee, appealed to American citizens not to sell arms and ammunition to either side. This policy of moral suasion was fairly successful at first, but in December, 1936, a shipment of some four hundred airplane engines to Loyalist forces received a great deal of publicity. It was a rather brazen flaunting of President Roosevelt's policy, and the latter asked Congress to amend the neutrality law so that it could be applied to the Spanish civil strife. It is usually held that he was under severe pressure by Catholic religious circles to take this step, but it is likewise true that in 1936 the people of the United States in overwhelming numbers believed that the way to avoid getting involved in war was not to sell supplies to either party. The bill to extend the neutrality law was rushed through Congress with a vote of 81 to 0 in the Senate and 406 to 1 in the House of Representatives. Representative John T. Bernard of Minnesota, who cast the

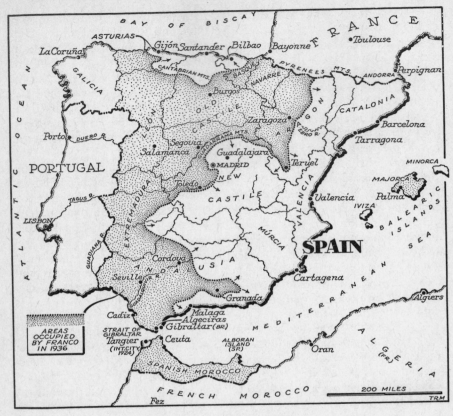

MAP 18 *Spanish Civil War*

sole negative vote, believed that the United States should sell arms to the Loyalists. He maintained: "The facts are clear. A popularly and democratically elected government of Spain has been treasonably and rebelliously attacked by a handful of its wealthy privileged classes, urged on and openly supported by the two most militaristic and predatory governments of Europe. . . . Fascism is engaging in the open rape of Spain." [4] On the passage of the bill President Roosevelt immediately issued a list of war materials which could not be sold to either side. Trucks and oil were not on this list and these were sold, with the Franco forces benefiting most. The German and Italian bombers which blitzed Loyalist towns were powered by American gasoline.

THE WAR. Despite this foreign aid General Franco had not been able to continue his rapid conquests. Madrid was not captured and the Civil

[4] *Congressional Record* (1937) 81: Part 9, Appendix, p. 65.

War dragged on. The bitterness and cruelty of the conflict knew no bounds. Hostages were taken and shot. Tortures were devised that outdid the cruelty of the courts of the Spanish Inquisition. No one knows how many were killed in this fratricidal carnage, but conservative estimates range from one to one and a half million. The inhumanity of Spaniard to Spaniard was a bitter reality.

It is impossible to state the exact amount of foreign aid which reached the two sides, but it was very large. Italy gave the greatest support, and the number of Italian soldiers fighting in Spain was at times over a hundred thousand. Motor vehicles, artillery pieces, and equipment of all kinds were furnished. There were never so many Germans in Spain as Italians, but their technical and aviation forces were of superior quality. Spain served as a proving ground for techniques which were later used in Poland. Moreover, Hitler saw in Spain an ideal situation for keeping Mussolini involved, so that the Italian dictator could not check Germany's expansion eastward. The foreigners fighting for the Loyalists, it is estimated, numbered about 40,000, including three thousand Americans. Many of these volunteers were idealists from all parties, but Communists and fellow travelers accounted for the largest number. Russia furnished the Loyalists with valuable aid, but the total number of Russians in Spain during the Civil War is not supposed to have exceeded six thousand.

Aware that war materials were being furnished to both belligerents in spite of official denials, the Non-Intervention Committee in March, 1937, evolved a scheme for naval blockade of the coast and for international supervision of the French and Portuguese borders of Spain. That part of the coast which was held by the Rebels was to be patrolled by French and British ships, the remainder under Loyalist control by German and Italian. Within a few weeks a German cruiser on patrol was bombed, and in retaliation a town held by the Loyalists was shelled. Temporarily Italy and Germany withdrew from the naval patrol. Portugal, which had never taken kindly to an international supervision of her frontier, now canceled that arrangement, which in turn led to the abandonment of the French border patrol.

Submarine attacks on ships destined for the Loyalists now developed. These ships were supposed to be carrying noncontraband supplies, and the attacks were labeled as piracy. France and England took the lead in calling a conference on the naval blockade, which met at Nyon, Switzerland, in September, 1937. Nine powers sent representatives, while Germany and Italy abstained. The conference authorized an Anglo-French naval patrol to attack any submarine, surface vessel, or aircraft, which illegally attacked a non-Spanish vessel. This resolute action at least put an end to the indiscriminate sinking of ships.

The International Blockade was never effective. The powers soon made no attempt to hide what they were doing in Spain. In Italy casualty lists were publicly posted. It was generally accepted that a Loyalist victory would mean a Communist-dominated Spain, and this the leaders of West-

*SPANISH INSURGENT   General Franco, with his cabinet at Burgos,
Spain, in August, 1939, after his victory.*

ern Europe did not want. Statesmen in France and England, in spite of
Mussolini's Spanish policy and his agitation among the Arab tribes in
North Africa, still sought to maintain friendly ties with the Italian government. In January, 1937, England and Italy signed an innocuous gentle-
man's agreement in which each power recognized that the other had vital
interests in the Mediterranean. This was followed in April, 1938, by a more
important treaty in which England recognized Italy's conquest of Ethiopia,
while Mussolini promised to withdraw Italian troops from Spain immediately after the close of hostilities. Opposed to this policy, Eden resigned as
British foreign minister and Lord Halifax was appointed to succeed him.

In the summer and fall of 1938 Franco gained one hard fought victory
after another. There was also dissension within the Loyalist ranks, and various minor civil wars within the Civil War took place. Italy and Germany
had recognized the government of General Franco as the legitimate government of Spain as early as November 18, 1936, but it was not until February 27, 1939, that France and England took this step. Finally on March
28, 1939, the Civil War came to an end with the surrender of Madrid.
Thousands upon thousands of refugees crossed the border into France dur-

ing the last months of the fighting. Gathered into large concentration camps, they led a miserable existence and constituted a serious problem for the French government. Meanwhile, somewhat to the surprise of many, the German and Italian legions were promptly withdrawn from Spain.

FASCISM VICTORIOUS. The Civil War had started out as an army revolt. Not only did the army leaders ally themselves with the great fascist states of Europe, but early in the revolt they took over the small Fascist party which had slowly been establishing itself in Spain. The paraphernalia of fascism was adopted, but it was the special characteristic of fascism in Spain that it meant continued rule by the same privileged groups as before: the army, the church, and the upper classes. With the end of the Civil War Franco dealt ruthlessly with all opposition that remained. Estimates as to the number of political prisoners run all the way from one half to two million. He repealed much of the legislation passed by the Republic. The Catalans and Basques lost their autonomy. Their land was returned to the grandees, and the process of breaking up large estates was halted. Labor unions were abolished and syndicates formed on the Italian model. The Catholic church regained many of its old privileges. Catholicism was re-established as the state religion, salaries of priests were again paid by the state, and all confiscated church property, including that of the Jesuits, was returned. Civil marriage and divorce were prohibited. The church also regained its dominant control over education.

The new regime did achieve a certain prosperity. Much was accomplished in rebuilding bridges, roads, railways, and buildings destroyed in the conflict; agricultural reforms, notably irrigation projects, were inaugurated and business relations with foreign states re-established. German and Italian influence remained dominant in Madrid, and on April 7, 1939, Franco adhered to the Anti-Comintern Pact. In May he followed the example of his friends in giving notice of Spain's withdrawal from the League of Nations.

The Chinese Incident, 1937

REOPENING OF HOSTILITIES. The Italian Conquest of Ethiopia, 1935-36, and the Spanish Civil War, 1936–39, took the spotlight away from Far Eastern affairs for a while. In the spring of 1937 North China was apparently calm, although rumors of increased Japanese troop movements began to reach the outside world. Then on July 7, 1937, occurred the Lukouchiao or, as it is more often called, Marco Polo Bridge Incident. The Japanese charged that their forces, which were out on night maneuvers near Lukouchiao, an important railway junction a few miles to the south of Peiping (Peking), were fired upon by Chinese troops. Japanese reinforcements were immediately moved in from Manchuria, and the War Office announced that troops were being sent from Japan. By the end of July, Tientsin and Peiping were in Japanese hands. War was never declared, because to do so would almost certainly have forced President Roosevelt to apply the United States' neutrality legislation cutting off military supplies to both belligerents. The armed conflict continued as an "incident" and was not ended until V-J Day, August 15, 1945.

LEAGUE ACTION. China again appealed to the League under various articles, which normally should have set in motion the League's machinery for peaceful settlement with the possibility of sanctions. The latter, however, were in disrepute as a result of the failure to enforce them against Italy in the Ethiopian Crisis, and none of the great powers wanted to get involved in such a program again. The Chinese appeal was referred to the Far Eastern Advisory Committee of Nineteen, which had been dormant since May, 1933 [see above, pp. 488–90]. This Committee found that the Japanese action was contrary to the Pact of Paris of 1928 as well as to the Nine Power Treaty of 1922, and recommended consultation by the signatories of the latter treaty. This report was adopted by the League Assembly (October 6, 1937) along with a resolution calling upon all League members to refrain from any action which would weaken China's power of resistance. The day before, President Roosevelt in a speech in Chicago had caused a sensation by referring to the necessity of quarantining certain powers as a means of stopping the spread of "world lawlessness." These remarks had been made without consultation with the Department of State, and a week later the President modified his position somewhat, speaking of co-operation with both China and Japan in seeking a solution by agreement.

Representatives of the signatories of the Nine Power Treaty and those other states which subsequently adhered to it met in Brussels on November 3, 1937. Germany and the USSR were also invited to attend, but Germany refused on the grounds that she had not signed the treaty. In all, nineteen states were represented. Since Japan absented herself, Italy was regarded as the Japanese mouthpiece at the Conference. The Italian statesmen derided the application of coercive measures. They maintained that the conference should limit itself to bringing the two parties together. This was in line with the policy of the United States, Britain, and France, who promptly made it clear that their watchword was peace by mediation on a basis acceptable and fair to both parties. What the specific points of such a settlement would be they never divulged.

The conference formulated a report which upheld the principles of the Nine Power Treaty and by implication the doctrine that any changes made contrary to these principles should not be recognized by the powers. It held that questions of law, orderly processes, and world security were involved and denied the contention that the conflict concerned Japan and China alone. The delegates elaborated no settlement and, having fulfilled their obligation of a full and frank discussion, adjourned.

The League likewise produced no solution. It followed the course of hostilities and at various times passed resolutions favorable to the Chinese cause. When China renewed her appeal for aid in September, 1938, the League invited Japan to assume temporary membership to co-operate in settling the dispute. Japan, of course, refused, and the Council urged all member states to apply individual sanctions against Japan. This request was repeated in May, 1939, but the results can be considered nil.

REACTION OF THE GREAT POWERS. League action had been hampered immensely by the general weakening of that agency during the thirties. In the Far East it was particularly ineffective because of the divergent interests of the great powers. The United States, Germany, Japan, and after December, 1937, Italy, were not members of the League. During a great part of the crisis England and France were not basically opposed to Japanese action in the north of China, although they naturally would have preferred peace and the *status quo*. Britain felt that the United States should take the lead in restraining Japan, but the United States, while willing to co-operate with the League, as a nonmember could not press League action.

Gradually the lines began to be drawn. Despite former ties with China, the Anti-Comintern states came to side with Japan, while the Russians consistently supported the Chinese government. German and Italian military advisers and instructors were withdrawn from China, while Soviet military supplies flowed in. Hitler recognized the Repubic of Manchukuo in February of 1938, and an Italian-Japanese-Manchukuo tripartite trade pact was signed that July. Meanwhile a serious dispute with Japan over the Amur River frontiers in June, 1937, confirmed the identity of Russian and Chinese interests.

In December, 1937, two British gunboats on the Yangtze River were damaged by Japanese bombers, and a few days later the American gunboat Panay was sunk. The Japanese government declared that this was a mistake, apologized and agreed to pay the United States $2,214,007.36 as indemnification for deaths, injuries, and property loss suffered by Americans. Meanwhile both Britain and the United States pushed their rearmament programs. Britain completed her naval base at Singapore and increased the fortifications at Hong Kong. In March, 1938, Britain, France, and the United States invoked the escalator clause of the 1936 naval treaty as Japan refused to reveal her building program. The following June, in a statement which makes rather strange reading today, Secretary of State Hull emphatically condemned the bombing of civilian populations or its material encouragement, and urged the restriction of the sale of bombing planes. Various other protests were made, but the United States government refused to apply its neutrality legislation lest supplies should be cut off from China. As a matter of fact, more military goods were being sent from America to Japan than to China.

On November 3, 1938, Japan announced that the purpose of her military campaign was the establishment of a New Order in Asia based on mutual tripartite co-operation of Japan, Manchukuo, and China. This was officially rejected by the United States and of course never was recognized by the Chinese government. Only a few quisling governors of provinces held by the Japanese accepted the idea. Fighting continued in China, which eventually became one of the major theaters in the far-flung battle fronts of World War II.

INTERESTS OF THE UNITED STATES IN THE FAR EAST. The United States was a relatively late comer in China and as such became the advocate of the Open Door Policy there. Under this policy Secretary Hay in 1899 secured assurances from the great powers that henceforth no special trading privileges were to be sought in China, and all powers were to trade on an equal basis. Later the United States also asked the powers to agree to maintain the territorial integrity of China. Missionaries and students benefiting from Boxer indemnity scholarships also tended to multiply the friendly contacts between the United States and China. With Japan, however, American relations were less cordial, partly because the Philippines lay too close to Japan, and partly because of the stringent American immigration laws which bore heavily on both Japanese and Chinese, but were more bitterly resented in Japan.

The economic stake of the United States in the Far East was much less than it was in Europe, and relatively far less important than that of other powers. American trade with the Far East during 1931–35 amounted to about one half of its trade with Europe, and the United States exported as much to Canada as it did to the whole Far East. Of American trade with the Far East in 1935, 43 per cent was with Japan, 24 per cent with the Philippines, and only 14 per cent with China and Hong Kong. In all respects American economic interests were greater in Japan than in China. Of all the foreign investments of the United States in 1935 only 6 per cent were in the Far East, and of these three times as much was invested in Japan as in China. American investments were small compared to the British. In 1931 only 6 per cent of the total foreign investments in China were owned in the United States, as compared with 36 per cent owned in Britain, and 35 per cent in Japan.

These figures would indicate that it was not primarily economic considerations which produced the pro-Chinese and anti-Japanese policy of the United States government, a policy which was unquestionably in line with the sentiment of the people. It is true that in relation to the Philippines, American defensive interests favored an anti-Japanese attitude. But on the whole a traditional policy of maintaining the territorial integrity of China, plus a certain amount of American idealism seem to account more than anything else for American policy during the Japanese-Chinese conflict.

Shifting Alliances

The hopes which had been placed in disarmament plans went glimmering after the failure of the disarmament conference. Armament programs in all countries, seemed necessary not only for national defense, but also because in a period of economic depression they stimulated industry, cut unemployment, and at least temporarily brought prosperity. The thirties also saw the diminution of League prestige and authority as a result of its failure to deal satisfactorily with the problems in Manchuria and China, Ethiopia and Spain. With these two main avenues to peace closed it was inevitable that alliance systems, as another road to security, would take on greater importance [see above, pp. 172–75]. Two major alliance systems, centering in France and Germany respectively, were the outstanding development of the thirties.

EXTENSION OF THE FRENCH SECURITY SYSTEM. France was the great exponent of seeking security through alliances in the twenties, and this policy was continued in the next decade. The advent of Hitler tended to strengthen the ties which bound the Little Entente together and attached it to France. In the Balkans in 1934, Yugoslavia, Rumania, Turkey, and Greece concluded a pact designed to maintain the *status quo* in this region, which was definitely in line with French policy. French-Italian relations reached a new peak of intimacy with the conclusion of their colonial agreement of January, 1935. France also entered into friendly negotiations with Russia, and after Hitler's reintroduction of military service (March 16, 1935) a French-Russian mutual assistance pact was signed on May 2, 1935. Czechoslovakia became a direct party to this agreement two weeks later, when it concluded a similar pact with Russia, which contained the very significant reservation that the pledge of mutual assistance would become effective only if the victim of aggression received aid from France. Neither Russia nor Czechoslovakia was thus bound to aid the other unless France acted.

Although the Russian agreement caused some misgivings among France's friends and among Frenchmen themselves, the French alliance system was at its strongest in the summer of 1935. Hitler was still isolated, except for a ten-year nonaggression pact with Poland of January, 1934, and a naval agreement with Great Britain of June, 1935. By this latter treaty Germany agreed to limit her fleet to 35 per cent of the total British tonnage. No limit was set on submarines, which Germany was again building, despite their prohibition in the Treaty of Versailles. This Anglo-German treaty caused uneasiness in Paris and many of the other capitals of Europe —nowhere more so than in Russia. A German fleet of such proportions meant a German-controlled Baltic Sea, to which the British at this time did not object. Russia, admitted to the League in 1934, became even more aggressively anti-Nazi as Hitler's vituperative speeches against communism showed no signs of abatement. In Paris the anti-fascist policy of Russia was welcome, for French leaders always saw in Germany the greatest threat to their security and continental leadership.

RUSSIAN POLICY. At the Seventh World Congress of the Communist International that met in Moscow in July, 1935, resolutions were passed condemning Japanese imperialism in the East and Hitler's actions in the West. In order to combat fascism the Congress advocated the establishment of the united front with socialist organizations. One of the first manifestations of this change of party tactics was the electoral agreement in France and Spain that led to the victory of the "Popular Front" as the coalitions were known in these countries. Whereas Communists had usually fought so-called liberal and "reform" organizations, they now began to co-operate with them and, by a policy of peaceful penetration, to take them over. The Congress also authorized the entry of Communists into all fascist mass organizations which had a monopoly of legal existence in any country "in order to counterpose the interests of the masses in these organizations to the policy of fascism, and undermine the mass basis of the latter." [5]

THE ANTI-COMINTERN AND THE ROME-BERLIN AXIS. The World Congress of the International was not slow in arousing a counterreaction. As early as August, 1935, the United States protested officially to the Russian government against the activities of the Congress, which, it was held, interfered with the internal affairs of the United States. The meeting of the Congress was considered a violation of the Russian promise to end international communist activity, made in November, 1933, at the time when the United States accorded the USSR diplomatic recognition. While the United States was content to protest, Germany and Japan acted. On November 25, 1936, they concluded the so-called Anti-Comintern Pact. The Russian leaders always made a fine distinction between the Russian government and the directing body of the Communist International (Comintern), and the German-Japanese agreement was carefully worded with this distinction in mind. The pact was therefore not specifically directed against Russia, but only against the spread of communism, and the two signatories agreed to collaborate to this end. Ribbentrop, the German negotiator, called the signature of the agreement "an epoch-making event," "a turning point in the struggle of all law-abiding and civilized nations against the forces of disintegration."

A short time before the signature of this Anti-Comintern Pact, Germany and Italy had laid the foundation for the Rome-Berlin Axis, as it came to be called, in the October Protocols of 1936. These sealed the friendship which had grown up out of the events of the Ethiopian Crisis and the Spanish Civil War. These protocols were informal, but it was clear that in return for Hitler's acceptance of Italy's Ethiopian conquests, Mussolini had withdrawn his objections to annexation of Austria by Germany. Mutual co-operation in opposing communism was the keynote, but it was not until November, 1937, that Italy adhered to the Anti-Comintern Pact, and this marked the first signature by Germany, Japan, and Italy of a common agreement. It was only in May of 1939 that Germany and Italy contracted a more formal alliance, both political and military, known as the Pact of Steel, and a formal tripartite pact between Germany, Japan, and Italy was not signed until September of 1940 [see below, pp. 545–46].

Germany and Italy also established good relations with Yugoslavia by trade agreements. The leaders in Belgrade had leanings toward dictatorship, and in general anti-communist sentiment was very strong in the ruling circles there. Yugoslavia had not as yet resumed diplomatic relations

[5] *Documents on International Affairs 1936*, p. 452.

with the Russian government, and emigré Russians still retained residence in the old Tsarist embassy in Belgrade.

REACTION TO HITLER: A SUMMARY. This period, then, was one marked by the emergence of a new coalition of powers, known as the Rome-Berlin Axis, to which may be added Japan, as a signer of the Anti-Comintern Pact. It had its origins in the dissatisfaction of these powers with their position at the close of World War I and in their desire for expansion. The latter did not bring them into conflict with each other, but rather served to unite them as "have-nots" against the "have" powers, whose imperialism was of an earlier date. The various steps by which these states strove to break out of their narrow confines were separately hardly important enough to push France and Britain to war, but in their sum they constituted a direct challenge to the *status quo* and the leading position of these two states.

Germany under Hitler defied the conditions placed upon her by the Treaty of Versailles, by rearming, at first secretly, then openly. England preferred to make a naval accord to insisting upon the letter of the treaty, but this only served to weaken English ties with France. The remilitarization of the Rhineland (1936) was an issue on which England was unwilling to take a stand and France reluctantly gave way. Hitler was so encouraged by this success, that many observers have considered this the crucial moment of the interwar period. The Little Entente was definitely weakened when Austria's independence was threatened after the formation of the Axis. Some Austrians, among them Chancellor Schuschnigg, were not opposed to a Habsburg restoration. This the statesmen of the Little Entente feared even more than the extension of Germany's borders to Hungary. As 1938 dawned, nowhere in Europe was there a country, not even Austria itself, which was willing to risk a war to prevent the union of Austria and Germany.

In the East also, Britain and France were slow to take a definite stand. They were never disposed to take the lead in opposing Japanese expansion so long as it was confined to the north of China. The territorial integrity of China was not of paramount importance to them. Their own stakes lay to the south, and in the north they believed that Japan and Russia would sooner or later collide. The Anti-Comintern Pact was the common tie between Germany, Italy, and Japan, and thus its main accent seemed to be eastern and anti-Russian. Lingering distrust of communism and a not unnatural willingness to see German expansionism turning to the east tended to immobilize British and, to a certain extent, French opinion.

The British reluctance to trust the Soviet government was not entirely shared by the French, who looked to Russia for aid in isolating Hitler. This seemed about to materialize with Russia's anti-Nazi policy, her active support of the League after becoming a member in 1934, and her alliance with France in 1935. But all this did not pave the way for complete cooperation with Britain or even with France. Whether communism or fascism constituted the greater threat presented a real problem to British statesmen. In the middle thirties they were more disposed to grant Hitler his demands for the creation of a German national state than to ally with Communist Russia, whose imperialism was always feared in London. Thus there was a basic weakness in the French chain around Hitler. Yet it was the French network of alliances that was entrusted with the task of maintaining the peace in a Europe which was arming again and had lost faith in international agencies.

CHAPTER

21

Immediate Background
of World War II

Germany and Europe: *Hitler's Plan; The Indecision of the Western Democracies; The Soviet Attitude.*

The Austrian Crisis: *The Annexation of Austria; Expansion of Nazi Political Influence.*

The Czechoslovak Crisis: *The Sudeten Germans; Munich; Dismemberment of Czechoslovakia.*

Prelude to War: *The Great Issues; Frustration of the Grand Alliance; The Nazi-Soviet Pact; Poland and the Outbreak of Hostilities.*

Germany and Europe

HITLER'S PLAN. By the end of 1937, Hitler's success in militarizing Germany, occupying the Rhineland, and asserting German initiative in Central Europe without provoking any serious countermeasures on the part of the victors of the recent war, brought him to a turning point in his career. The attention of Hitler and his lieutenants had been devoted thus far to rebuilding the foundations of German national power and to testing the strength and intentions of the states whose policies had dominated the European scene since World War I. During this period Hit-

ler had frequently stated the aims of his foreign policy both in *Mein Kampf*
and in his numerous speeches, but even his own followers were not certain
how much of what he said was to be taken literally and how much was
propaganda designed to arouse the passions of his listeners. It is possible
that Hitler himself may not have made up his mind before this time just
how he would carry out the program that he had been promoting with
such fanatical zeal for so many years.

However this may be, on November 5, 1937, Hitler held a solemn conference with his five principal advisers on state affairs, and in a four-hour
session made a fundamental statement of policy which he asked them to regard "in the case of his death as his last will and testament." [1] The problem of German policy he once again defined at this conference as one of
acquiring a larger living space for the 85 million people comprising the
German nation, of whom only 66 million then lived within Germany. He
reviewed the efforts that Germany had made to find food and raw materials within its own frontiers, and he demonstrated that only in a few essential products could Germany ever be self-sufficient. He then went on to
assert that commercial agreements did not offer a solution to Germany's
problem, since a dependence for essential products on distant countries
and on long routes of supply would place Germany at the mercy of its
suppliers. The creation of a large overseas empire would not be a sound
solution either, he asserted, even if colonies were readily available. The
conclusion which Hitler, as always, drew from this reasoning was that the
proper course for Germany was to conquer "agriculturally useful space"
on the European continent itself. He did not refer explicitly to Poland and
the Ukraine, but there can be no doubt that those were the territories
which he had in mind.

Before Germany could hope to achieve this ultimate objective, which
he regarded at this time as possibly requiring a generation or more, Hitler
considered that the Germans living in Central Europe must first be consolidated. This meant that the immediate task of German policy was to
annex the almost seven million Germans of Austria and the three and a half
million German-speaking inhabitants of the Sudeten territories of western
Czechoslovakia. Hitler was convinced that this must be accomplished before 1942, when Germany would begin to lose the head start which it possessed in armaments. The question then was one of selecting the proper
time to strike at Austria and Czechoslovakia. Hitler believed that the two
circumstances most likely to favor his scheme were either an outbreak of
civil strife in France, which would immobilize that country and hence England as well, or else the development of an open conflict in the Mediterranean between Italy, and France and England. Hitler asserted at this conference in November, 1937, that Germany must in any case be prepared
to strike vigorously when the right moment arrived. He resolutely rejected

[1] U.S. Chief of Counsel for Prosecution of Axis Criminality: *Nazi Conspiracy and
Aggression* (8 vols., 2 supp.; Washington, 1946–48), vol. III, pp. 295–305, Document
386–PS.

the counsels of caution advanced by such military advisers present at the conference as the minister of war and the commander-in-chief of the army, who stressed the relative lack of preparation of the German armed forces and pointed to the size and training of the French army. Hitler brushed aside these arguments less on military grounds than on political. The disunity of France and the caution of Britain were to him sufficiently valid reasons for seizing the initiative at this time. On the military side Hitler realized that Germany's armament production was reaching its peak, for it was approximately two or three times that of Britain and France combined during the year 1938–39, and this was a superiority which could not be maintained for long.

Such were the nature and extent of Hitler's plans in 1937. The larger war was not yet envisaged, and indeed he doubtless hoped to avoid it. His immediate task was to absorb the Austrians and the Sudeten Germans at the lowest possible cost. The ostensible reason for these steps, and one which carried considerable weight with the Western democracies, was that of unifying all German-speaking peoples. Hitler's real purpose, however, was to use these gains as stepping stones to further conquests. The acquisition of Austria would give Germany an assured predominance of the Danubian region, which could be used for both economic and political ends. The annexation of the Sudeten Germans, moreover, would make Germany clearly the first power on the continent by eliminating Czechoslovakia as a military factor, and would thus pave the way for future conquests.

THE INDECISION OF THE WESTERN DEMOCRACIES. Underlying the irresolution with which France and Great Britain met the resurrection of German military power was the memory of the untold suffering caused by the great war which had been fought only twenty years earlier. Great Britain, and more especially France, had never overcome the feeling that nothing could be solved by war and that almost any compromise was preferable to another conflagration. This feeling was intensified by the continuing after-effects of the economic crisis which led in Britain to extreme caution and in France to extensive social changes.

In France in particular, the domestic political situation was hardly conducive to a vigorous foreign policy in the winter of 1937–38. The controversial social legislation of Blum's Popular Front regime during the twelve months after it came to power in June, 1936, had failed to gain a solid majority in parliament. Four cabinets succeeded each other between June, 1937, and April, 1938, when Daladier finally formed the moderate Radical Socialist ministry that was to survive until the spring of 1940. Moreover, the policies of the Socialists and Communists had brought to the surface powerful rightist and royalist forces in France, that were inclined to regard Hitler as possibly less dangerous to their interests than Blum's coalition regime. At the same time the military position of France was rapidly declining, for the production of armaments was affected by the social unrest. A more important cause of French weakness, however, was the attitude of the military leaders. Since 1930 they had constructed a chain of

CEMENTING FRENCH–POLISH TIES   *Marshal Pilsudski of Poland, Louis Barthou, French Foreign Minister, and Colonel Beck, Polish Foreign Minister, conferring in Warsaw in 1934.*

fortifications of unprecedented size and design, known as the Maginot Line, along the French-German frontier. Having made this heavy investment, the general staff convinced itself that the security of France was guaranteed. The development of airplanes and tanks was deliberately neglected, for only a small minority of staff officers led by De Gaulle believed in the striking power of the armored divisions and air fleets that Germany was developing at this very time. This almost mystical reliance on the Maginot Line spread from the military leaders to the politicians, and permitted them to believe that they could neglect with no damage to France's position the network of alliances in Eastern Europe that had formed the cornerstone of their security system since the war.

The situation in Great Britain differed from that in France, but its consequences for international relations were for the time being much the same. Chamberlain, who had succeeded Baldwin as prime minister in May, 1937, was firmly convinced that every effort should be made to reach an agreement with Hitler and Mussolini by means short of war. He considered that their objectives were limited in scope and believed that if the two dictators received a hearing on the part of Great Britain and France and were granted reasonable colonial and other concessions they would settle down peacefully. Chamberlain was so convinced of this point of view, that in appeasing the dictators he was even willing to neglect the basic principle of British policy which consists of not permitting a single power to dominate the European continent. A corollary of appeasement was the isolation of Russia, for while Chamberlain rarely attacked the Soviet Union in public he consistently ignored it in his efforts to create a stable Europe. Chamberlain's approach to foreign policy was not merely a personal matter, for he reflected the attitude of British public opinion at this time and was backed by a solid majority in Parliament.

In Eden as foreign secretary, Chamberlain inherited from Baldwin a man who clearly differed with him in his outlook on Europe. Equally desirous of avoiding war, Eden believed that this could be achieved not by appeasing the dictators but by rallying together all the nations of Europe, including Russia, in firm resistance to the demands of the Axis. In his view, Germany and Italy would only be encouraged by conciliatory gestures, whereas if they were faced by a united and defiant Europe they might well be stopped in their tracks. This was in substance the traditional British policy of maintaining the balance of power, and it received the vigorous support of Churchill who, as an independent Conservative, remained outside the government. The differences between Chamberlain and Eden did not immediately come to the surface, for on many points they were in agreement. This was particularly true as regards the need for rebuilding Britain's defenses, in which both ministers believed. Unlike the French, the British were active in the development of planes, tanks, and anti-aircraft artillery, and were conducting research that was soon to put them in the forefront in numerous technical fields. Nevertheless, this armament program, despite the constant prodding of Churchill, developed slowly. Not until 1937 was the large-scale expansion of British war production inaugurated, and even this effort was far smaller than that of the Germans although in quality it was a close rival.

The unstable relationship of Chamberlain and Eden was upset in the winter of 1937–38, when the issue of appeasement finally presented itself in an unavoidable form. The difficulty of Eden's position had been that few countries could summon sufficient determination to stand with Britain in a crisis. The French desired in principle to co-operate with the British, but they were for the time being involved in domestic problems. Belgium and the Netherlands, on the other hand, whose security was closely connected with that of Britain, had adopted a policy of neutrality. The Scandinavian states were likewise eager to avoid becoming involved in any firm action with regard to Germany. Under these circumstances Eden greeted with enthusiasm the proposal of President Roosevelt, made in secret to the British government in January, 1938, that a conference be called in Washington to seek a solution to Europe's difficulties. Chamberlain rejected this suggestion, on the ground that it might displease the dictators and therefore interfere with the negotiations for a general settlement with Italy that he was about to undertake. Over this issue the rift between Chamberlain and his foreign minister widened perceptibly. One month later, when Chamberlain decided that negotiations with Italy should be initiated immediately, Eden resigned [see above, p. 506]. A minister who had consistently served as a brake on the policy of appeasement thus left the cabinet, to be replaced by Lord Halifax whose views coincided with those of Chamberlain.

THE SOVIET ATTITUDE. It has already been pointed out that the political philosophy of the Soviet Union assumed that all the states of Europe were bound sooner or later to succumb to the contradictions of the political and economic system known in Marxist terminology as "capitalism." The Russians nevertheless recognized that the fascist dictatorships, while they might in theory represent nothing more than "capitalism" in an advanced state of decay, were in fact a far greater menace to Soviet security than were Great Britain, France, and the smaller states of Europe. As they saw Britain and France progressing along the road of appeasement, the Soviet statesmen tried to halt the trend that they feared might lead to an anti-Russian coalition. It therefore became their policy to emphasize constantly in public statements the desirability of close co-operation between Russia and the Western democracies in dealing with the Axis powers. Molotov as premier, Litvinov as commissar for foreign affairs, and Maisky as ambassador to Great Britain, all reiterated the theme that Russia was a powerful and determined state without whose participation no effective decisions could be taken in European affairs.

From the Soviet point of view this was a sound approach. Its immediate aim, comparable in a sense to Britain's traditional policy, was to restore the balance of power in Europe which had been upset by the rapid growth of militarism in Germany and Italy. Such statesmen as Churchill and Eden, despite their strong reservations concerning the Bolshevik regime, considered the German menace to be so immediate that every effort should be made to reach a working agreement with the Soviet Union. They were in a minority, however, for the Soviet approach had failed for two reasons to win the confidence of the Western leaders holding political office.

In the first place, Europe had not freed itself from the deep-seated conviction that Soviet actions were impelled by ulterior motives. For a generation Soviet propaganda had been asserting the inevitability of another war in which the destruction of "capitalism" would be accomplished under Soviet leadership. Western apprehensions had been lessened to a degree, indeed, by Stalin's doctrine of "socialism in one state." The united-front policy of co-operation with non-fascist states, that brought Russia into the League of Nations in 1934 and led the Communist parties in Europe to seek co-operation with other leftist political groups, had also tended to reconcile Western opinion. These policies had even confused Communists in Russia, and Stalin found it necessary to clarify the situation in a widely publicized letter dated February 12, 1938, in reply to the questions of a perplexed member of the Young Communist League named Ivanov. In this letter Stalin explained that Soviet socialism was not secure so long as Russia was surrounded by inevitably hostile "capitalist" states. The way to achieve this security, he asserted, was "to strengthen and consolidate the international proletarian ties between the working class of the USSR and the working class of the bourgeois countries." This assertion that the Soviet Union intended to work in collaboration with the working classes abroad, which meant in substance with the Communist parties and associated groups, was not calculated to win the confidence of Western political leaders. Neither was their enthusiasm aroused when Voroshilov, the Soviet commissar for defense, referred to the soldiers of the Red Army in a speech on February 22, 1938, as "the champions of the workers of the world to free them from the yoke of capitalism."

A second weakness in the Soviet policy of attempting to work more closely with the Western democracies was the fact that the prestige of Stalin's regime had been seriously undermined by the political purges which reached their climax during the years 1936–38. While some observers might rejoice that many of Lenin's most prominent collaborators had been liquidated, many feared that a European system that had as its cornerstone the collaboration of the Western democracies with the Soviet Union was not likely to be a very stable one. Moreover, the execution of many top Russian military leaders created the impression that the fighting ability of the Red Army had been undermined. Suspicion and distrust thus dissolved much of the effectiveness of the Soviet plan for co-operation with the Western states, and a working agreement was finally reached only under the pressure of war itself.

The Austrian Crisis

THE ANNEXATION OF AUSTRIA. Early in February, 1938, Hitler consolidated his position at home by removing some of the most prominent officers of the German army who opposed his foreign program, including the minister of war and the commander-in-chief. To assure his personal control over the army, he created over the general staff a supreme command of the armed forces headed by General Keitel, who could be trusted to follow Hitler's instructions. Thus reassured as to his domestic position, and confident that the rest of Europe would not interfere, Hitler now went ahead with his plan for annexing Austria by force. Now began the series of events, starting with Schuschnigg's visit to Berchtesgaden, which ended with the invitation from Hitler's agent, the new Austrian chancellor, Seyss-Inquart, for German troops to occupy Austria. On March 13 the union of Austria with Germany was announced by Seyss-Inquart, and on the following day Hitler made a triumphal entry into Vienna [see above, p. 352].

The annexation of Austria was a great victory for Hitler since, at no cost to Germany, he seized the key to Danubian communications, isolated Czechoslovakia, neutralized what was left of the pro-French Little Entente coalition, and demonstrated to the world once again that he could defy the

Versailles system without fear of reprisals. The reaction of Europe to these events provided abundant evidence of political paralysis. France was in the midst of a cabinet crisis. In Britain the House of Commons was informed by Chamberlain that the *Anschluss* could only have been prevented by war and implied that he would not alter his policy of appeasement. The Western democracies, therefore, reacted unfavorably when the Soviet Union proposed on March 18 that a conference be held to discuss means of collective action in case of a threat to the peace by Germany. This proposal resembled in some respects the one made in secret by Roosevelt two months earlier, and also pointed towards the Franco-British-Russian "grand alliance" that Churchill had been urging for some time. After due consideration, however, Chamberlain rejected the Russian proposal on the ground that "the establishment of exclusive groups of nations" would be "inimical to the prospects of European peace." By this he meant that he still considered direct negotiations with the dictators as the best means of assuring peace, and he now proceeded to demonstrate his theory by concluding an agreement with Mussolini on April 16 which recognized the Italian position in Ethiopia and Spain in return for a general assurance of Italian friendship. Hitler, in the meantime, organized a plebiscite in Germany and Austria on April 10 in which both countries accepted union by overwhelming majorities.

EXPANSION OF NAZI POLITICAL INFLUENCE. The contribution of the annexation of Austria to Germany's commercial penetration of the Danubian region lay in two spheres. From the strictly economic point of view, Germany was able to benefit by the extensive commercial contacts and investments which Austria possessed in these countries. Austrian investments in Yugoslavia, for instance, were some six times as large as those of Germany. By a systematic exploitation of these various advantages, the German policy of commercial expansion was able to make distinct gains. Apart from the economic benefits, Germany also gained an important psychological victory in the Danubian region. The attitude of the Western democracies at the time of the Austrian crisis made it apparent that they were not willing to take any serious steps to meet the German policy. The trade offensive which France and Britain developed in the spring of 1938 did not offer any real alternative to the Danubian states, and the view was widely held that Germany was deliberately being encouraged by the Western democracies to develop the Danubian region as an exclusive economic sphere for its own purposes.

All the states of southeastern Europe had been moving in the direction of authoritarian regimes since the world depression for reasons closely resembling those that had influenced the development of events in Italy and Germany. Despite this trend, however, these countries had not adopted totalitarian philosophies and were, in fact, very jealous of their freedom from political control by Germany and Italy. The German economic drive was indeed accompanied by strong political pressure, but the latter met with far less success than the former. The weakness of the Danubian states lay in the fact that their domestic stability depended primarily on their ability to obtain a good price for their agricultural exports, and Germany provided the only market which was willing to take their exports on a systematic basis. Metaxas of Greece, whose country was under somewhat less economic pressure from Germany than its neighbors to the north, stated the situation succinctly when he declared: "Greece is not 'pro-German'; it is a question of finding a market for her tobacco crop." Despite these difficulties, the states of southeastern Europe managed to retain a considerable degree of independence until the war was actually upon them.

While Hitler thus found it difficult to gain a determining voice in the domestic affairs of the countries of southeastern Europe, he at least succeeded in breaking up any efforts on their part to join forces against the Axis. The Balkan Entente was weakened when it found itself under compulsion in July, 1938, to recognize Bulgaria's right to rearm. Some of the Balkan states continued to discuss their common problems in conferences, and in this they were encouraged by the Western democracies, but Germany managed to keep them effectively divided by playing on their differences. Moreover, what was left of the Little Entente was destroyed when an independent Czechoslovakia disappeared from the scene early in 1939. The states of southeastern Europe were thus rendered defenseless against Nazi aggression when it finally presented itself in a decisive form in the spring of 1941.

The Czechoslovak Crisis

THE SUDETEN GERMANS. The ease with which he took Austria encouraged Hitler to proceed immediately with his plans against Czechoslovakia. He recognized, however, that this time he would have to overcome more serious obstacles before he could annex the Sudeten Germans and eliminate the Czech state. Not only did Czechoslovakia have a strong line of fortifications in the Sudeten mountains defended by some thirty-five well-equipped divisions, but it also had binding commitments from France and Russia. Under the mutual assistance treaty with France, dating from 1925, the two countries promised to lend each other immediate aid and assistance in case one were attacked. This treaty was to apply even in the event that the machinery provided for in Article 16 of the League Covenant failed to come into operation. Similar mutual assistance treaties were concluded by the Soviet Union in 1935 with both France and Czechoslovakia, thus binding the three states to take action in case of aggression against one of them. At the same time, the obligations of the Soviet-Czech treaty were to take effect only after the implementation of the French-Czech treaty. The question as to when aggression had actually occurred, of course, would in doubtful cases have to be decided when the occasion arose. For the time being, however, Czechoslovakia was reassured by firm statements made in the middle of March, 1938, by both France and the Soviet Union that they would honor their treaty commitments.

The case of Great Britain was somewhat different, since it was not bound by any commitments apart from the general guarantee of assistance provided by Article 16 of the League Covenant. Britain's attitude was no less important for this reason, however, since in the last analysis France could not be expected to take a firm position without strong British backing. The Czech government could therefore not fail to be disappointed when Chamberlain elucidated his policy before the House of Commons on March 24, 1938. While he indeed pledged his country's support of the machinery provided by the League Covenant, he explicitly refused to give assurances that Britain would support France in case the latter were called upon to assist Czechoslovakia against German aggression. The substance of Chamberlain's policy, even after the union of Germany and Austria, was thus one of continuing his efforts to reach a direct settlement with the Axis dictators. This was to be accomplished at the expense of collective efforts either through the French-Russian-Czech mutual assistance system or by means of joint consultation between the Western powers and Russia such as had been proposed by Roosevelt in January and by Molotov in March. Chamberlain feared that collective action would provoke the dictators to war, whereas he believed that appeasement would lead to a workable peaceful settlement.

Encouraged by the British attitude, Hitler now pressed forward with his plans for using the Sudeten Germans as a Fifth Column for destroying the Czech state. Henlein, the Nazi leader of the Sudeten Germans, was called to Berlin and briefed for his role. Returning to Czechoslovakia, he announced at Karlsbad on April 24, 1938, the Nazi proposals that called for nothing less than setting up an autonomous German province within the Czech state. President Beneš and prime minister Hodža saw clearly that acceptance of this plan would make their country a satellite of Germany, and they promptly rejected it. Instead, they offered to grant the Sudeten Germans minority rights of a more limited character. France, which had now achieved a degree of political stability with Daladier as prime minister and Bonnet as foreign minister, consulted with the British government at the end of April. Chamberlain again asserted that his country could not commit itself to backing French action in support of Czechoslovakia, and proposed instead that the Czech government be urged to make more liberal concessions to the Sudeten minority. Before this line could be pursued further, however, a brief crisis occurred in connection with the Czech municipal elections on May 22. Henlein's Nazis used the election as a pretext for a great campaign, and it was widely feared that Germany might give him armed support. Beneš replied by ordering partial mobilization, however, and France and Russia rallied to his support. Chamberlain, who feared nothing worse than the sudden outbreak of hostilities, sought to restrain Hitler with the cautious warning that Britain also might become involved. Impressed by this collective action, Hitler advised Henlein to moderate his tone, and the crisis passed without further trouble.

MUNICH. The May crisis produced important reactions in both camps. Hitler was determined that he should not be frustrated again and gave

MUNICH AGREEMENT *Signatories of the Munich Agreement relaxing after their work: Field Marshal Goering, Hitler, Schmidt (interpreter), Ciano, Mussolini, Daladier, Chamberlain, François-Poncet, at Munich, September 30, 1938.*

orders that the detailed plans which General Keitel had drawn up for military aggression against Czechoslavokia should be ready for implementation by October 1. The appeasers in the West, on the other hand, had been appalled by the proximity of war and were eager that such a crisis should not be repeated. Their method was to conciliate the Nazis by urging upon the Czech government broader concessions to the Sudeten minority. To this end Chamberlain obtained the agreement of the French that his friend and associate Lord Runciman be sent to Prague to mediate between the Czechs and the German minority, whose relations had by now reached a deadlock. The vacillating Daladier was reluctant to accept this proposal, but his foreign minister Bonnet was a leader of the appeasers in France, and the premier permitted himself to be convinced that the Runciman mission was a good idea. Runciman was therefore sent to Prague at the beginning of August, 1938.

While the issue at stake was the very existence of the Czechoslovak Republic, the negotiations leading up to the Munich crisis concerned the secondary but closely associated question of the status of the Sudeten German minority of three and one half million within Czechoslovakia. In the negotiations at Prague following the arrival of the Runciman mission the Czechoslovak government went very far indeed in making concessions, for the Plan No. 4 advanced early in September granted practically all that Henlein had demanded at Karlsbad in April. Henlein rejected all of these offers, however, for what the Nazis desired was not autonomy but a pretext to crush the Czechoslovak state. By the middle of September Henlein had broken off negotiations, and Hitler had hurled his threats at Czechoslovakia from the Nazi party rally at Nuremberg. Britain and France now consulted with each other and agreed that Chamberlain should make a personal appeal to Hitler in an effort to obtain the best terms possible.

When Chamberlain went to visit Hitler at Berchtesgaden on September 15, 1938, his purpose was to find terms on the basis of which Germany and Czechoslovakia could reach a peaceful settlement of their differences. If such terms could be found Nazi aggression would be unnecessary, and all the embarrassing questions connected with French and Russian assistance to Czechoslovakia would be avoided. Thus far such terms had concerned the degree of autonomy to be granted to the Sudeten Germans, but when Chamberlain's plane landed in Germany he was informed that Hitler now demanded that the territories inhabited by Sudeten Germans be ceded to Germany. This proposal was discussed during the three-hour interview between the two statesmen. Chamberlain was irritated that he should thus be confronted by new terms, but he was now convinced that Hitler was willing to go as far as war and so he agreed to consult with the British cabinet with regard to Hitler's new terms. The latter, in turn, agreed to take no action until he had heard again from Chamberlain. There followed several days of critical negotiations between the British and French cabinets, and on September 19 the two governments presented to President Beneš their final decision that Czechoslovakia must cede to Germany all territories with over 50 per cent Sudeten German inhabitants.

The Czechoslovak government was now faced with the most difficult of all decisions. To accept this demand meant to give up the Czechoslovak line of fortifications, to relinquish some 800,000 Czechoslovakians in addition to the greater part of the German minority, and in substance to surrender the independence of the Czechoslovak state itself. The only alternative seemed to be to resist the Germans alone. Consulted once again, both the French and the British governments replied that they considered their proposal to be a reasonable one and would not consider themselves responsible for the consequences if Czechoslovakia rejected it. The Soviet government agreed to come to the support of Czechoslovakia unilaterally as soon as the case was brought to the attention of the League, but few Czechoslovakian statesmen were willing to go to war with Germany if Russia were their only ally. After considering all the alternatives, Beneš and Hodža finally decided on September 21 to accept the proposals of Britain and France. On the following day Hodža resigned and was succeeded by a coalition government under General Syrovy. With the Czech surrender in his hand, Chamberlain now proceeded to a second meeting with Hitler at Godesberg on the Rhine. At their opening session on September 22, he informed Hitler of his success and proposed a plan for the transfer of the Sudeten territories which was considerate of Czechoslovakian sensibilities. Hitler, eager to press his advantage, rejected Chamberlain's proposal and demanded an immediate occupation of the territories by the German army. This attitude astonished Chamberlain, but on the following day he succeeded in working out a compromise. He took away from Godesberg a German memorandum demanding that the territories in question be completely evacuated by October 1, and that plebiscites in certain additional areas be held in November.

For a few days war now appeared to be inevitable. Although Chamberlain was somewhat inclined to accept the Godesberg memorandum as a basis of negotiation, his cabinet and British public opinion had finally been provoked by Hitler's naked reliance on force. France was equally aroused, while in Prague the Czechoslovak government resolutely rejected the new terms. Thus by September 26, Hitler was faced with the firm rejection of his terms by Britain, France, and Czechoslovakia. Chamberlain even went so far as to give assurances to Daladier of British support in case France went to war with Germany over Czechoslovakia. Hitler appeared to have no intention of changing his course, and in a savage speech in Berlin he poured out his hatred against Czechoslovakians. Yet despite their newly found resolution Chamberlain and Daladier were still seeking a solution short of war, whatever the cost to Czechoslovakia. In a final appeal on September 27, Chamberlain proposed to Hitler that a four-power conference composed of Great Britain, France, Germany, and Italy meet to seek a solution to the crisis. An immense sigh of relief was heard on the following day in London and Paris, when Hitler consented to this proposal upon the urging of Mussolini and invited representatives of the four states to Munich.

The conference at Munich was a brief affair, and the agreement that was drawn up on September 29 and signed in the small hours of the following day represented no more than a slight modification of the terms demanded by Hitler at Godesberg. The Sudeten territory was divided into four zones which the German army was to occupy progressively between October 1 and 7. The determination of a final fifth zone, to be occupied by the 10th, was left to an international commission on which Czechoslovakia would be represented along with the four signatories. The four powers agreed to guarantee the new frontiers of Czechoslovakia once they were established. Having made these decisions, the four powers at Munich communicated their agreement to the Czech government on the morning of September 30. The latter now had no recourse but to accept, and by noon the Sudeten phase of the Czechoslovak crisis was over. Peace had been preserved for the time being, and Czechoslovakia had paid the bill.

DISMEMBERMENT OF CZECHOSLOVAKIA. While Hitler may have been somewhat disappointed at having been denied a brief military campaign against Czechoslovakia, Munich was in every sense a complete victory for him. It made Germany undeniably the first power on the continent, and definitively upset the security system under which France and Britain had held the initiative since 1919. The humiliation of Czechoslovakia was complete. Not only its entire line of fortifications but in addition some three quarters of its industrial resources went to Germany, along with over 10,000 square miles of territory and a population of 3,600,000 including 800,000 Czechoslovakians. The occupation policy of the Germans was ruthless to the minority who opposed the Nazi regime, and the Czechoslovakians obtained no support from the French and British in their efforts to temper the details of the transfer. On October 5 Beneš resigned as president, and Syrovy added the duties of chief of state to those of prime minister. On November 30 the Czechoslovakian Parliament elected the jurist Hacha as president, while Beran became prime minister. In the meantime Poland and Hungary, both of which possessed minorities in Czechoslovakia, stepped in to claim their share of the spoils. The former immediately seized the small territory of Teschen [see above, pp. 118–19], while the latter obtained by negotiation a very sizable strip of southern Slovakia. By the end of November, Czechoslovakia had thus lost about one third of its population and two fifths of its territory. It had ceased to be a factor in European affairs, and was now little more than a satellite of Germany.

Almost equal in significance to the gains which Hitler obtained at Munich for Germany as a European power, was the victory over his critics at home. While Hitler had long since eliminated the liberals and the leftists as a factor in domestic politics, he had never fully won over the military leaders to his program. Patriotic in the traditional sense, many staff officers regarded Hitler as an unbalanced rabble-rouser who was bound sooner or later to lead Germany to destruction. While they conceded his success in the Rhineland and in Austria, they had not believed that France and Britain would be willing to sacrifice Czechoslovakia. Under the leadership of General Halder, the chief of staff, and of his predecessor General Beck, they were prepared to challenge Hitler at the first moment he showed signs of losing his grip. There is even some reason to believe that only the surrender of the Western democracies at Munich prevented Halder and Beck from carrying out their plans at the end of September, 1938. Whatever the details of the plot, it was forestalled by Hitler's triumph and it was not until the ill-fated attempt in July, 1944, that the dissident army officers summoned the determination to assert themselves.

In the Western democracies the news of the Munich agreement was greeted with tremendous relief and appeared for a time in the light of a great victory. Particularly was this the case in Britain, where public opinion hailed Chamberlain as a hero. Nevertheless, in Parliament the Munich agreement was subjected to very severe criticism during the great debate on October 3–6, for many recognized Munich immediately as a great defeat for the Western democracies. Chamberlain himself was satisfied that he had the situation in hand and placed great reliance on a written agreement to which he had obtained Hitler's signature at Munich on September 30, in which the two statesmen "resolved that the method of consultation shall be the method adopted to deal with any other questions that may concern our two countries." France signed a similar agreement with Germany in December, 1938. Daladier, who lacked both Chamberlain's naivete and his energy, realized that France had suffered a defeat but could not summon the strength to stand up to the powerful pressure of public opinion. The appeasers within his cabinet, led by Bonnet and a powerful majority in the Chamber of Deputies, gave their support to the Munich agreement. From the Soviet Union and the United States little was heard during the Munich crisis. The Soviet statesmen remained consistent in their advocacy of collective action in support of Czechoslovakia, but once the Czechoslovak government agreed to the initial Anglo-French surrender on September 21, it did not seriously consider accepting unilateral Soviet support. One of the most significant features of the Munich agreement was the absence of the Soviet Union, and this forcible isolation accounts for much of the subsequent Russian policy. President Roosevelt's approach, substantially like that of Churchill and Stalin at this time, favored collective action. He led a nation, however, which was determined to avoid war, with no army or air force to speak of, and with a navy which was directed more towards the Pacific than the Atlantic. On September 26, Roosevelt sent a message to the interested countries urging that they reach a peaceful settlement of their differences, and on the following day he sent an additional appeal to Hitler, but there is no evidence that these notes had any appreciable effect on the outcome of the negotiations at Munich.

As 1938 passed into 1939, the Munich agreement began to appear as less of a victory even to the appeasers. Hitler was now in full control of Central Europe and in no mood to compromise. The fierce anti-Jewish pogrom which he carried out in November warned the world that there would be no relenting of the Nazi philosophy. Hitler was only encouraged by the moderation with which his various insults were accepted in London and Paris, and he proceeded rapidly with his plans for the final subjugation of Czechoslovakia. Early in March he encouraged the autonomist movements in the provinces of Slovakia and Ruthenia to break their ties with the Czech state. He then called President Hacha to Germany and on March 15 compelled him to sign a treaty which turned what was left of his country into a German protectorate. The German army occupied Prague, and Czechoslovakia ceased to exist. Under the leadership of Father Tiso, Slovakia was established as a nominally independent state. Hungary immediately moved in to occupy the easternmost Czechoslovak province

of Ruthenia, that on the previous day had proclaimed its independence
[see map below]. Mussolini, in a pale imitation of the man who had once
been his pupil and was now his master, sent troops into Albania on April 7.
Albania was annexed to the Italian Empire, after King Zog had fled into
exile.

MAP 19   *Partitions of Czechoslovakia and Poland, 1938–39*

Prelude to War

THE GREAT ISSUES. Chamberlain said on one occasion, with reference
to the fateful decision of going to war, that "we must be very clear, before
we embark upon it, that it is really the great issues that are at stake." Chamberlain had really believed that Hitler was sincere in his oft-repeated promise that he had no claim in Europe beyond the unification of all the
German-speaking peoples of Central Europe. He was, therefore, profoundly
shocked when Hitler seized the rest of Czechoslovakia in March, 1939, and
thus revealed in an incontestable fashion his aim of dominating Europe.
Chamberlain's appeasement was not calculated to permit the Western democracies to improve their bargaining position, and it actually served to
strengthen Hitler. It is the conclusion of no less an authority than Churchill that, in terms of military strength, "the year's breathing-space said to be

gained' by Munich left Britain and France in a much worse position compared to Hitler's Germany than they had been at the Munich crisis." [2]

It should be said, however, that the final dismemberment of Czechoslovakia in the spring of 1939 revealed to Britain and France "the great issues" that were at stake. Up to this point it had been assumed that Hitler had limited aims, and the policy had been adopted of making concessions to these aims. Now it was clear that the very existence of all the free states of Europe, including France and Britain, was at stake. Chamberlain and Daladier shifted their policy from appeasement to one of building up a coalition to oppose Hitler. Where they had earlier rejected Russian and American suggestions of a joint approach to Germany lest it provoke the Nazis to war, they now turned to the idea of a "grand alliance" of Britain, France, and Russia, that the critics of the policy of appeasement had been advocating for some time. At the same time this change of policy was at best halfhearted, for many uncertainties were entertained with regard to co-operation with Russia.

The relative position of the Soviet Union had in the meantime undergone a great change during the winter of 1938–39. At the end of September, 1938, when the four powers met at Munich to seal the fate of Czechoslovakia, Russia was alone in Europe. What the Soviet leaders feared most of all was that the four at Munich might form a coalition which would place Russia at a permanent disadvantage. In his significant speech on March 10 before the Eighteenth Congress of the Communist Party, Stalin accused the Western states of predicating their appeasement policy on war between Germany and the Soviet Union. He warned them, moreover, that they should not base their plans on a Nazi-Soviet conflict and recommended collective security as the best means of handling the problem of Germany. Within a week after Stalin's speech, the entire atmosphere changed. The German seizure of Prague destroyed the Munich agreement and led the Western democracies to come out clearly in opposition to the Axis dictators. This change now left the Soviet Union holding the balance of power, for neither Britain and France nor Germany and Italy could under the altered circumstances feel secure without an understanding with Russia. The Soviet statesmen by this time distrusted the two groups almost equally, but they recognized the strength of their bargaining position and were prepared to make the most of it in defending the one great issue which they had at stake: the security of the Soviet Union.

FRUSTRATION OF THE GRAND ALLIANCE. In the consultations that took place after the fall of Prague the Soviet Union promptly proposed, on March 18, that the situation be examined in a six-power conference of the Soviet Union, Great Britain, France, Poland, Rumania, and Turkey. This was a broader approach than the Western states were prepared for at the moment, and Chamberlain suggested instead that of the smaller states Poland alone be brought into the picture at this juncture. When Poland,

---

[2] Winston Churchill: *The Gathering Storm* (Boston, 1948), p. 339.

which feared Russia as much as it hated Germany, refused to accept a guarantee with which the Soviet Union was associated, action was taken on a more restricted basis. On March 31 Britain pledged aid to Poland in case its independence was threatened by Germany, France had a treaty of mutual guarantee with Poland dating from 1925. Anglo-French pledges of aid were extended to Rumania and Greece on April 13, and Britain and France concluded separate mutual assistance agreements with Turkey in May. Moreover on April 27, the British government took the unprecedented peacetime step of introducing military conscription.

It was thus in a somewhat friendlier atmosphere that negotiations between Russia and the Western states were resumed in April, 1939. When Great Britain suggested on April 15 that the Soviet Union make a unilateral guarantee of assistance to any neighboring state which expressed a desire for such a pledge, Litvinov replied with a proposal which made perfectly clear the price which the Western democracies would have to pay for their grand alliance. The Soviet proposal of April 17 stipulated that in addition to concluding a mutual assistance pact and a military convention, the Soviet Union, Great Britain, and France, should guarantee all the states between the Baltic and the Black Sea. For Russia this was not an illogical price to ask, since it would provide a defensive barrier against Nazi aggression not only in the immediately threatened states of Poland and Rumania, but also in Finland and the Baltic States to the north and in Bulgaria, Yugoslavia, and Greece, to the south. This was a price which such advocates of the grand alliance as Churchill were prepared to pay, but Chamberlain and Daladier considered it to be more than the situation required. Not only were the smaller states of Eastern Europe opposed to receiving Soviet assistance, but the Western statesmen felt they would be placed in the position of granting to Russia in the extensive zone between the Baltic and the Black Sea a sphere of influence that they were convinced would soon be occupied by Soviet troops. To push these countries towards Russia against their will, under circumstances in which the Soviet Union might still in the end choose to remain inactive in case of Nazi aggression in the West, did not appeal to Chamberlain. On May 8 the Soviet proposals were rejected as being too comprehensive. In the meantime Litvinov, who was believed to favor a Western orientation, was dismissed on May 3, and Molotov was appointed in his place as Soviet foreign minister.

The Soviet-Western negotiations never proceeded much beyond the exchange of proposals which took place in the middle of April. Additional exchanges of views took place in May, and in June Molotov invited Halifax to visit Moscow to explore further the possibilities of agreement. The British government did not regard the chances of success as sufficiently great to warrant a visit by the foreign minister, however, and secondary officials were sent instead. Discussions continued throughout June and July, but the area of agreement did not widen perceptibly. The Russians insisted that the Baltic states should be included in the guarantee, and that under certain circumstances Soviet troops should be stationed in those countries, while the British and French were unwilling to extend the scope of joint assistance beyond Poland and Rumania. An Anglo-French military mission, which went to Moscow early in August to explore the possibilities of a three-power military convention, made equally slow progress. The Soviet statesmen were disconcerted not only by the persistent reluctance of the Western negotiators to meet their terms, but also by what appeared to them as distinct signs that the policy of appeasement had not really been abandoned. The Russian suspicions were particularly aroused by the visit to London in the middle of July of an impressive German economic mission, and by subsequent rumors of a large British loan to Germany. Convinced that the British and the French had no serious intentions of meeting their terms, Stalin and Molotov proceeded to bring to a head the negotiations with Germany which they had been secretly conducting since May.

THE NAZI-SOVIET PACT. In turning to Germany rather than to the Western states for an agreement, the Soviet statesmen were doubtless making what was for them a second choice. While they had no great trust in Britain and France after Munich, the mutual assistance pact and military convention that Stalin proposed might have developed into a grand alliance that would have changed the course of European diplomacy. Combined as it was intended to be with guarantees to the states bordering on Russia, this alliance offered the maximum security which the Soviet regime could obtain against a Germany that it recognized as its principal enemy. The arrangement that it now negotiated with Germany, by contrast, was no more than a non-aggression pact which offered Russia a breathing spell before the inevitable conflict with Germany, and a security zone which increased the depth of Russia's defenses.

The agreement with Germany was more easy to negotiate, however, since the Nazis felt no inhibitions in paying the price which the Western states had considered to be too high. Where the latter refused in the end to associate themselves with guarantees which Russia's neighbors were unwilling to accept, Germany saw no difficulty in assigning to Russia the Baltic states and parts of Poland and Rumania. To Chamberlain and Daladier, it appeared to mean sacrificing the independence of the small states established after World War I, and with them the principles of sovereignty upon which the postwar European system had been founded. To Hitler, however, it was a concession that he expected to take back by force of arms within a few years. The Russian-German negotiations grew out of discussions concerning a trade agreement that started as early as May, 1939. It was not until later, however, that the possibilities of a political agreement were seriously explored and the Germans became convinced of Russia's willingness to conclude a non-aggression pact. Once this willingness was ascertained events moved rapidly, since Hitler was concerned for his timetable with regard to Poland while Russia was apprehensive lest the Western states revert to a policy of appeasement.

The treaty of non-aggression which Molotov and Ribbentrop signed in Moscow on August 23, 1939, was essentially a simple document. The two parties pledged to refrain from aggression against each other, either individually or in alliance with other powers. Each party also pledged to remain neutral in case the other became the object of belligerent action by a third party. Issues arising between the two parties were to be settled by arbitration, and the treaty was concluded for a period of ten years. This much was immediately published to the world. The price paid by Germany was described in a "Secret Additional Protocol" signed on the same day. Under its terms, an assignment of spheres of influence was made "in the event of a territorial and political rearrangement" in Eastern Europe. Russia was to have Finland, Estonia, and Latvia, on the Baltic Sea, the eastern part of Poland with a population of some thirteen million, and the Rumanian province of Bessarabia. To Germany fell Lithuania and the rest of Poland.

POLAND AND THE OUTBREAK OF HOSTILITIES. For Hitler, the pact with Russia was the last of a long series of measures that he had taken since March in preparation of the "territorial and political rearrangement" that he was planning for Poland. As early as March 21 he informed the Polish government that Germany must have the Free City of Danzig, and that the German minority in Poland must be given better treatment. The German occupation of Memel on the following day, which deprived Lithuania of most of its coastline, served notice that Hitler was now going to concentrate on the northern sector of his eastern front. Hitler replied to the Anglo-French guarantee of Poland by denouncing on April 28 the German-Polish non-aggression pact of 1934 and the Anglo-German naval treaty of 1935. On May 22 he further strengthened his position by concluding the military alliance with Italy, christened the "Pact of Steel." A week later he concluded non-aggression pacts with Estonia and Latvia. All of these moves were part of a carefully prepared plan aimed at the destruction of Poland. The blueprints for the military campaign had been completed early in April, and on May 23 Hitler informed his chiefs of staff at a memorable meeting that they must not expect another Munich but should be prepared for war with France and Britain and perhaps with Russia as well.

The die was cast, and Hitler's task was now that of isolating Poland so that the war might be fought under the best possible circumstances. Within the framework of these plans the non-aggression pact with Russia of August 23 played a capital role, for it permitted Germany to proceed against Poland with no immediate concern for the Soviet army. Hitler even hoped in the last days of August that the Nazi-Soviet pact might induce Britain and France to renounce their guarantee of Poland, but in this he was disappointed. Chamberlain immediately wrote Hitler a letter which stated Britain's determination to fight in unmistakable terms, and on August 25 this stand was formally incorporated in a mutual assistance pact with Poland. This pact had reference to aggression by "a European Power," which in a secret protocol was defined as Germany. During the last days of peace,

Hitler occupied his time with a series of conciliatory gestures towards Britain and France, and a mounting propaganda campaign against Poland. At dawn on September 1, 1939, the German army invaded Poland, thus starting the war which Hitler considered essential to his plans for a greater Germany.

22

World War II

Predominance of the Axis

BALANCE OF FORCES. At the start of the war, Germany had many advantages that contributed to Hitler's belief that the conquest of Europe lay within his grasp. The most carefully husbanded of these advantages was the military power that had been built up since 1933 on the foundation of the small army permitted to Germany by the peace treaty of 1919. Germany's military advantage was not merely a question of numbers and weight, but also of quality. After their defeat, the German military leaders had given serious thought to the errors made in World War I and had evolved equipment and techniques that they believed could bring them success where they had failed a generation earlier. The essence of the German military reform was a reliance on speed and movement, in place of the exhausting and fruitless trench warfare of the earlier war. To obtain the desired speed and movement, Germany developed advanced types of tanks and planes and trained its soldiers to use them in close co-ordination. The military thinking of the Western allies, by contrast, had learned from the earlier war only that well-fortified positions were impregnable to assault. Their victory in 1918 had convinced them that the methods used to achieve that victory could not be improved on, and as a result they placed their faith in such massive permanent fortifications as the Maginot Line which stretched from the Belgian frontier to Switzerland.

In addition to the superiority of his armed forces, Hitler also enjoyed the advantage of disunity among his many enemies. While he had made clear his intention of establishing a German hegemony in Europe, the threat he represented appeared to his enemies to be less immediate than their mutual rivalries and controversies. In politics as in war, Hitler was thus able at the start to pick the time and place of his attack, and to deliver it with greater force than his victim of the moment was able to cope with. The negotiations in the summer of 1939 had shown how divided were the various countries which Germany had marked for conquest, and the skill with which Hitler played them off against each other contributed as much to his victory as did his military machine. Nevertheless all this had its limits and, as his conquests grew in number, the unity and preparedness of his remaining enemies increased until they were finally able to turn him back. This turning point was not reached until 1942, however, and during the first two years of the war the Axis possessed a distinct predominance. Poland, Denmark, Norway, Holland, Belgium, France, and the Balkans, all fell before the German onslaught, and only when he attacked England and Russia did Hitler's war machine grind to a halt. Even these two powerful countries did not find the strength to defeat the Germans until the United States added its resources to theirs.

EASTERN CAMPAIGN. The opening campaign of the war provided a striking exhibition of the new methods of warfare developed by the German army. In the brief period of one month, forty-four German divisions crushed a nation of thirty-five million inhabitants. The Germans achieved many objectives during this rapid operation, destroying Poland, establishing a temporary working relationship with the Soviet army, and thus freeing the bulk of Germany's armed forces for action in the west. It was nevertheless the technique of the *Blitzkrieg*, or "lightning war," which caught the immediate attention of the onlooking world.

The Polish campaign now provided the Soviet government with the opportunity for which it had been waiting, and it proceeded promptly to extend its power in several directions. The first step was to occupy the portion of eastern Poland that had been assigned to Russia in the Secret Additional Protocol of the treaty of August 23. This occupation was started on September 17 and completed within a few days, the reason given being

GERMAN–SOVIET AGREEMENT *Molotov signing the German-Soviet agreement for the partition of Poland, with Ribbentrop and Stalin in the background, Moscow, September 28, 1939.*

the desire to rescue the oppressed Ukrainian and Byelorussian minorities of eastern Poland. Ten days later, a final adjustment of the new German-Russian frontier was made by Ribbentrop and Molotov in Moscow. Under the settlement of September 28, the important Lublin province in eastern Poland was transferred from the Soviet to the German zone. In return, the Soviet Union received almost all of Lithuania as its sphere of influence, in addition to Latvia, Estonia, and Finland which had been assigned to it by the earlier agreement. The Soviet Union thus annexed some 76,500 square miles of Polish territory with a population of 12,800,000, including some 7,000,000 Ukrainians and Byelorussians.

Russia turned next to the Baltic states, which had thus far been passive but uncomfortable observers of the catastrophic demise of Poland. Agreements known as "mutual assistance pacts" were now negotiated between the Soviet Union and Estonia (September 29), Latvia (October 5), and Lithuania (October 10). In each case the two countries agreed to assist each other against aggression, and each of the three Baltic states granted the use by Soviet armed forces of naval and air bases on their territory. Of the three states, only Lithuania received compensation, and this was in the form of the Vilna district that was ceded from the Soviet zone of Poland. While all this was accomplished with the full agreement of Germany, the latter's estimate of future developments may be judged by the arrangements which it made for the evacuation of the German minorities from the three Baltic states.

With Finland, Russia found it more difficult to negotiate. In routine fashion a Finnish delegation was called to Moscow early in October, but it returned home without having come to any agreement with the Russians. The latter had demanded territorial concessions on the Karelian Isthmus, where the frontier was at some points as close as twenty miles from Leningrad, and in the Arctic region near the ice-free port of Petsamo, as well as the lease of the harbor of Hangö and of certain islands in the Gulf of Finland. In return, the Russians offered Finland some territory along the central portion of the Russian-Finnish frontier. The Finns were willing to make some concessions, but they would not lease the bases in the Gulf of Finland that the Russians considered essential for their security. The failure of these negotiations was followed at the end of November by a full-scale Soviet military campaign against Finland. The Russians underestimated the Finnish will to resist, and the initial Soviet effort was poorly planned, resulting in large Russian casualties but no decision against the small Finnish army.

This Russian aggression was condemned throughout the world, although not by Germany. Finland appealed to the League of Nations, which took the unprecedented action of expelling Russia from membership. In England and France there was a demand that direct military assistance be given to Finland and an expeditionary force was readied for this purpose, but Norway and Sweden refused to grant permission for the transit of troops. Sweden, fearing military involvement, was particularly ac-

tive in furthering Finnish-Russian peace negotiations. Delayed for a time
by the fierce northern winter, it was not until February that the Russians
were able to resume their attack. On March 12, 1940, a peace treaty was
signed under which Finland had to cede considerably more territory in the
Karelian Isthmus than the Russians had originally demanded, in addition
to leasing the Hangö peninsula. The Finns had preserved their independence and the poor showing of the Russian troops had disclosed weaknesses
in the equipment and leadership of the Soviet army. These made a strong
impression on German military minds, while at Moscow strenuous efforts
were made to remedy the deficiencies.

In the balance, however, Russia's strategic position had greatly improved as a result of the territorial changes in Poland and the Baltic. The
Soviet Union now controlled most of the territories that it deemed essential for its military security, and that had been the stakes of the negotiations in the summer of 1939. A considerable price had been paid for these
gains in terms of prestige, and concurrent efforts to neutralize Turkey and
the Balkans had met with no success, but Soviet statesmanship was in large
measure satisfied with the results of its efforts.

While these great changes were unfolding in the east, the military
situation was relatively quiet in Western Europe. On the western front in
particular, where the great struggle had centered during World War I,
there was no activity at all. This period has been referred to by Chamberlain as the "twilight war," and the American press frequently called it the
"phony war." It is probably most accurately described, however, by the
German term of *Sitzkrieg,* or the "sitting war."

Yet things were not so quiet as they seemed, for Great Britain and
France took important steps during this period to strengthen their position. Apart from the rapid production of armaments of all types that was
pressed with utmost vigor, the Western Allies made substantial gains in
their efforts to control the sea lanes. As in the first war, the German submarines presented a problem. The British were better equipped to handle
the situation than they had been a generation earlier, while the Germans
had not yet given this phase of the war their full attention. As a result
some 340,000 tons of British shipping were lost during the first six months
of the war, a relatively modest figure, and almost half of this loss was made
up by current shipbuilding. The Germans, during the same period, lost
almost one third of their submarines. Moreover, all of the German commercial shipping was driven from the seas, and the successful campaign
against the naval raiders culminated in the scuttling of the pocket battleship *Graf Spee* in the harbor of Montevideo in the middle of December,
1939, after an unsuccessful encounter with three British cruisers.

In the diplomatic field, the position of Great Britain and France was
strengthened by the conclusion on October 19 of mutual assistance pacts
with Turkey. These agreements specifically exempted Turkey from joining
under any circumstances in a war against Russia, but they nevertheless
served as an indication that Turkey would not be drawn into the Nazi-

Soviet orbit. While the morale of the Western Allies was not very high during this period, they firmly rejected several invitations to peace negotiations made by Hitler in public speeches during October and November, 1939.

AGGRESSION IN THE WEST. The success of his campaign in Eastern Europe accomplished Hitler's initial purpose of freeing the bulk of his forces for the task which now became his major objective: the subjugation of France and Great Britain. Hitler was as fully aware as Stalin that the settlement in Eastern Europe was no more than a temporary arrangement between two mortal enemies, but at least it was an arrangement which could be considered reliable for the time being. A number of German divisions remained in the east throughout the western campaigns, but they represented no substantial drain on the aggressive strength of the German army in what was now the main theater of the war.

The war in the west was launched by Hitler on April 9, 1940, with an attack on Denmark and Norway. This action had been contemplated for some time as a means of preventing possible allied intervention in this area, which would have cut off the indispensable supplies of Swedish ore and ended German control of the Baltic. The allied plans for aiding Finland, and the probability that the waters along the Norwegian coast would be mined as they had been in World War I, hastened German action. In fact England, over the strong protest of Norway, did mine Norwegian waters the day before Hitler attacked. Germany suffered serious naval losses in this campaign, but in a few weeks it won important strategic positions for use against England. Indeed, this campaign was such a blow to British prestige that on May 10 Chamberlain's Conservative government was replaced by a National government under Winston Churchill, including the leaders of the Labor and Liberal parties. For five years this government was to bear the burden of directing Britain's powerful forces. Churchill appeared before Parliament offering nothing but "blood, toil, tears and sweat," and received a unanimous vote of confidence. It was sufficient for Parliament that he had but one policy: "to wage war, by sea, land, and air, with all our might and with all the strength that God can give us"; and one aim: "Victory."

On May 10, 1940, the same day that Churchill took office, Hitler delivered his main attack against the Western Allies through Belgium and the Netherlands. Although there was a rough equality in manpower between the opposing forces, the Germans completely outclassed the allies in their use of parachutists, tanks, and planes in closely co-ordinated teams to open up gaps which the infantry could exploit. The Dutch army capitulated in five days and the Belgian in eighteen. By May 20 the Germans had reached the English Channel after cutting off from the main body of French troops, many French divisions, and all of the British and Belgian forces. Between May 27 and June 4 almost 340,000 British and French troops were evacuated by sea from the channel port of Dunkirk, as Britain's Royal Air Force gained temporary superiority over the Germans in this area. Mussolini, rushing to the aid of the victor, declared war on France and launched a feeble offensive across the French-Italian frontier on June 10.

Its armies already broken, France's final surrender came as an anticlimax after the whirlwind battles north of the Somme. An attack launched on June 5 once more broke through the French lines, and on June 14 the Germans entered Paris. The end had now come for the French government, and in its temporary capitals, first at Tours and later at Bordeaux, it attempted to reach a settlement with its British ally. Reynaud, who had succeeded Daladier as prime minister on March 21, was firmly resolved to continue fighting. In this resolve he was supported by numerous Frenchmen including General de Gaulle, who as under-secretary for national defense was just beginning to play an important role in French affairs. Many prominent Frenchmen had by now decided, however, that neither France nor Britain could hope to survive the German onslaught and that the only reasonable course was to surrender and make whatever bargain they could with a Nazi Europe. Marshal Pétain, the hero of World War I, who was now a member of the government, was the leading exponent of this point of view. During this crisis Churchill made every effort to support Reynaud, obtaining cautious words of encouragement from President Roosevelt and sponsoring a scheme for an Anglo-French Union drafted by a group of French and British leaders. Yet none of these expedients was able to affect the issue, and on June 16 Reynaud resigned and was replaced by Pétain with General Weygand as minister of defense. On the following day the French asked for an armistice, and on June 22 they signed the terms offered by the Germans. Approximately two fifths of the country was to be left unoccupied under French administration, while France was to pay the costs of the German occupation of the larger northern sector that extended along the coast to the Pyrenees. The French prisoners of war were to remain hostages in Germany, and the navy was to be disarmed and left in French ports [see map, p. 543].

For Britain the fall of France was a disaster, but not quite a catastrophe. As Weygand had remarked a few days earlier, the English Channel was "a very good anti-tank obstacle," and Churchill went to work to save what was possible of the French legacy. While Britain continued to maintain relations with Pétain for a short period, it recognized as "Leader of all free Frenchman" General de Gaulle who had left France with a small group of leaders. At the same time, fearing that the Germans would not honor their armistice pledge to disarm the French fleet, the British navy sank or damaged a number of French war vessels in African harbors after they had refused an offer to go to England or to neutral ports.

BRITAIN FIGHTS ALONE. Isolated and crippled in the face of an enemy who had conquered much of Europe, the peoples of Britain now put up a fight which Churchill has appropriately called "their finest hour." The German army was indeed at the height of its power and prestige in the summer of 1940, but its leadership was now uncertain and divided. The campaigns

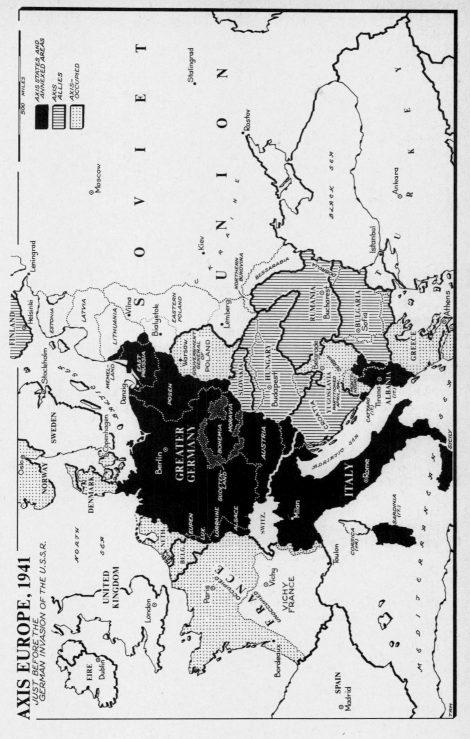

AXIS EUROPE, 1941

JUST BEFORE THE GERMAN INVASION OF THE U.S.S.R.

AXIS STATES AND ANNEXED AREAS

AXIS ALLIES

AXIS-OCCUPIED

500 MILES

MAP 20

thus far had been fought in vindication of the defeats in World War I. It was these campaigns for which Germany had prepared, and they fitted clearly into the pattern of Hitler's thought and propaganda. England was a different matter, for Hitler viewed the British with a strange mixture of admiration and hatred. The German army was not equipped or trained to cross the English Channel, yet Hitler hoped that the mere threat of invasion would bring Churchill to terms. Hitler directed on June 16 that preparations be made for the invasion, but his plans were never systematic or thoroughgoing. The German air force had never been stronger, but it could not decide whether to concentrate on radar stations, shipping, air fields, or population centers.

The British made careful plans to meet the expected attack and were prepared, as Churchill described it, "to drown as many as possible on the way over and knock the others on the head as they crawled ashore." It was the battle in the air, however, that was decisive. It started in July and reached its climax on September 15, when the Germans made their last great effort to break the RAF. This attempt failed, and in October Hitler abandoned his invasion plans and turned his attention to the east. During the two critical months of August and September, 1940, the British destroyed 1244 German planes at a cost of 721 RAF fighters, and this was a loss which the Germans could not afford to take indefinitely. The bombing of London and the industrial cities extended through the winter. The destruction of the manufacturing town of Coventry on November 14 and the great fire in the center of London on December 29 were hardly more than routine episodes in this ferocious air campaign. Yet here again the Germans failed, and after May, 1941, the raids lost their persistence. Hitler had discovered that in addition to the RAF he had to contend with the unbreakable spirit of the British people. Not only were the British not cowed by the German raids, but by the spring of 1941 they were already beginning to drop bombs in large numbers on Germany.

In the midst of the battle of Britain, a struggle developed for the control of North Africa and the Middle East. Italian forces in Libya moved into Egypt in the autumn of 1940, but in a remarkable campaign in the following winter the British drove the Italians 500 miles westward to the port of Benghazi, putting ten divisions out of commission. This effort overtaxed the British resources, however, and they were forced to withdraw to Egypt. In the course of 1941 the British nevertheless greatly strengthened their position in this strategic area. They defeated pro-Axis elements in Iraq and helped the Free French to do the same in Syria. They organized a joint Anglo-Russian occupation of Iran, to prevent it from falling into Axis hands and to make it secure as a route of supply to Russia. In a remarkable campaign in East Africa two British columns, one from Khartoum in the Sudan and the other from Nairobi in Kenya, advanced on the Italian colonial possessions of Eritrea, Ethiopia, and Italian Somaliland. In less than four months they subdued the Italian forces and brought East Africa under British control. Only in the Mediterranean did the British fail to secure their positions in 1941. Land-based Axis aircraft continuously harassed the convoys to the eastern Mediterranean, and strained the over-taxed British resources to the limit.

Expansion of the War

NAZI-SOVIET RELATIONS. The Nazi-Soviet agreements of 1939 were based on the assumption by the Russian statesmen that the armies of Germany and the Western democracies would be engaged in a long and costly conflict before either side would be able to achieve victory. There can, therefore, be little doubt that the rapid German success in the west in the spring of 1940 placed the Russians in a position which they had hoped to avoid, namely that of being faced alone by a greatly strengthened Germany. Russia now took a series of measures calculated to strengthen its position. As early as June, 1940, Soviet troops occupied Estonia, Latvia, and Lithuania, where they had hitherto only stationed limited forces. The governments of these countries were promptly overthrown, and pro-Soviet regimes were established, which in August requested incorporation in the Soviet Union. This request was granted with alacrity, and the three Baltic states thus became constituent republics of the USSR. The German government raised no objection to this procedure, although it was clearly directed against the Nazi threat.

The Nazi-Soviet rivalry now turned to the Balkan states, which had thus far managed to stay out of the war. In June, 1940, the Soviet Union resumed diplomatic relations with Yugoslavia after a lapse of over twenty years, thus emphasizing the Russian interest in Balkan developments. In the same month, after a summary ultimatum, Russia occupied the Rumanian provinces of Bessarabia and Northern Bukovina. This act encouraged Rumania's other neighbors to make territorial demands. King Carol besought the aid of Hitler and Mussolini, but to no avail. When the Axis representatives met in Vienna towards the end of August to consider the plight of Rumania, they agreed that it should cede Northern Transylvania to Hungary. After making this concession, Rumania also found it necessary to give in to the Bulgarian demand for the cession of Southern Dobruja in September. These successive territorial losses were more than the prestige of King Carol could support, and he abdicated in favor of his son Michael. At the same time, an authoritarian regime was established in Rumania under General Antonescu [see maps, pp. 543 and 549].

The significance of these developments was that they permitted Nazi Germany to pose as the protector of the Balkan states. While accepting the Soviet raid on Rumanian territory, Germany had now guaranteed the integrity of what was left of Rumania and had gained decisive influence in Hungary and Bulgaria. Having thus blocked Soviet aspirations in the Balkans, Germany further strengthened its position by negotiating with Italy and Japan the Tripartite Pact of September 27, 1940. This pact required the three powers to assist each other in case another power became involved in the war in Europe or in the Far East. Although a separate article

RUMANIA JOINS THE AXIS *General Antonescu (at right), Premier of Rumania, presenting himself at Berlin in November, 1940, before the Nazi leaders: Ribbentrop, Hitler, Hess, Ley, Admiral Raeder, Goebbels, and General Keitel.*

affirmed that its terms did not apply to the Soviet Union, it in fact provided the basis for a new series of Axis political agreements in Eastern Europe. In November, 1940, Hungary, Rumania, and Slovakia adhered to the Tripartite Pact, and what amounted to an anti-Soviet bloc of states was thus formed. Germany further strengthened its position in the Baltic by making arrangements, in September, for the transit of military personnel through Finland to Norway.

Both Nazi Germany and Soviet Russia now recognized that the time had come to review their relationship. The former was reaching the height of its military power and political influence, and Hitler and Ribbentrop were in no mood to make concessions to an isolated Russia. The latter, on the other hand, was still uncertain as to the outcome of its policy, and Stalin and Molotov were eager to discover just how firm the German position was. It was therefore arranged that Molotov should go to Berlin in November, 1940, to discuss the situation. After considerable discussion, interrupted by a British air raid, Ribbentrop came forward with a proposal that the Soviet Union associate itself with the Tripartite Pact and accept as its sphere of influence the region of Iran and India. If this were acceptable, a separate agreement would be concluded with Turkey to provide a preferred treatment for Soviet naval vessels in the Straits. Molotov took this offer back to Moscow with him, aware that it did not satisfy his basic requirement that Germany should not have exclusive influence in the Balkans. After consultations in Moscow, a reply was therefore drafted that accepted the German offer but only on condition that German troops be withdrawn from Finland, that Soviet security be protected by a mutual assistance pact with Bulgaria, and that Russia receive naval and air bases within range of the Turkish Straits. As regards the separate agreement concerning the Turkish Straits, Molotov demanded in addition that efforts be made to obtain for Russia a long-term lease to bases on the Straits themselves. These Russian conditions represented nothing less than a direct challenge to German predominance in the Balkans, and Hitler never carried the negotiations any further. It was now clear to the Russians that Germany would accept an extension of Soviet influence only in the direction of Iran and India.

INVASION OF RUSSIA. The failure of the negotiations of November, 1940, marked the end of the co-operation of Germany and Russia. Hitler now made explicit provisions for the attack on Russia and issued a directive on December 18, 1940, ordering that final preparations for an invasion be completed by May 15, 1941. In the meantime, it was necessary to secure Germany's position in the Balkans before such an extensive operation could be undertaken. As early as October, 1940, Mussolini had attacked Greece from Albania in the hope of winning a rapid victory in conjunction with the African campaign, that would assure to Italy a predominant position in the eastern Mediterranean region. But the Italian attack did not go according to plan. While the Greece of Metaxas had in many respects pursued a pro-German policy, submission to an Italian army of occupation was another matter, and the small Greek army fought bravely under the skillful direction of General Papagos. Instead of moving rapidly towards Salonika and Athens, as they had expected, the Italians found themselves being pushed back by December deep into Albanian territory.

The spring of 1941 thus found this feeble Italian campaign still in progress, and Germany now moved swiftly to secure its Balkan positions. German influence was already firmly established in Hungary and Rumania, and it required little argument to convince the Bulgaria of King Boris to adhere to the Tripartite Pact on March 1, 1941. On the same day, a substantial number of German troops entered Bulgaria. Yugoslavia, however, did not come willingly into the German camp. The Yugoslav government under the regent Prince Paul, did indeed sign the Tripartite Pact on March 25, but this decision was not accepted by influential elements within the government and army. This discontent culminated in the overthrow of the government on March 27, and young King Peter was installed as chief of state in place of his uncle Prince Paul.

Throughout this tense period, the Russians had been able to offer no effective resistance to the German measures. The one gain to which Soviet statesmanship could point during this period was the neutrality pact concluded with Japan on April 13, 1941. The agreement pledged each state to neutrality in case the other became involved in the war and made provision for the integrity of the Japanese-controlled territory of Manchukuo and the Soviet-dominated Mongolian People's Republic. By this treaty both Russia and Japan sought to protect their rear lines in the event of an extension of hostilities the full measure of which they could hardly as yet foresee.

In the meantime, the Nazi campaign in the Balkans was proceeding "according to plan," as the characteristic phrase of the press releases described the situation. Attacking with overwhelming power on April 6 from Hungary, Rumania, and Bulgaria, the German army overran the greater part of Yugoslavia in less than two weeks. Striking simultaneously at Greece with Bulgarian support, it soon isolated the northern Greek forces which had been fighting bravely in Albania since October, and pressed hard on the small British expeditionary force which had been sent to the aid of Greece. By June 1 Germany was in full control of the Balkan peninsula, as well as of Crete and the Aegean islands, and free to direct its entire attention to Russia. As a final measure calculated to protect his southern flank, Hitler concluded a treaty of friendship with Turkey on June 18, 1941, in which the latter gave renewed assurances of its neutrality.

The time had come for Hitler to carry out his fateful decision to attack the Soviet Union. After carefully avoiding until now the dangers of a war on two fronts, he finally decided that the risk was no longer a serious one. This decision was based on two assumptions: that the British would not be able to menace the German rear, and that the back of the Soviet army could be broken in 1941 before the arrival of winter. This step was taken against the advice of many of his military experts, but Hitler's intuition had proved so successful in the past that all the uncertainties of this calculated risk were brushed aside and the date for the attack was finally set for June 22.

The Russians were not unprepared for the German blow. While they were willing to make many concessions in order to avoid the test of arms, they had placed great emphasis on the important territorial gains in Eastern Europe in 1939–40 and had not concealed their bitter opposition to the Nazi Balkan campaign in the spring of 1941. Moreover, the Soviet statesmen had ample warning from various quarters that a German attack was in the offing, although the final certainty of such an attack could never be fully determined. During their almost two years of neutrality, the Russians had bent every effort to equip and train their large armies in the light of the lessons of the war in the West. For a generation, tank warfare, artillery, and paratroops, had been the special concern of the Red Army, and during the 1920's their experiments in this field had gone hand in hand with those of the Germans. If the quality of Russian equipment and training was not up to that of the Germans at this time, as Stalin was later to

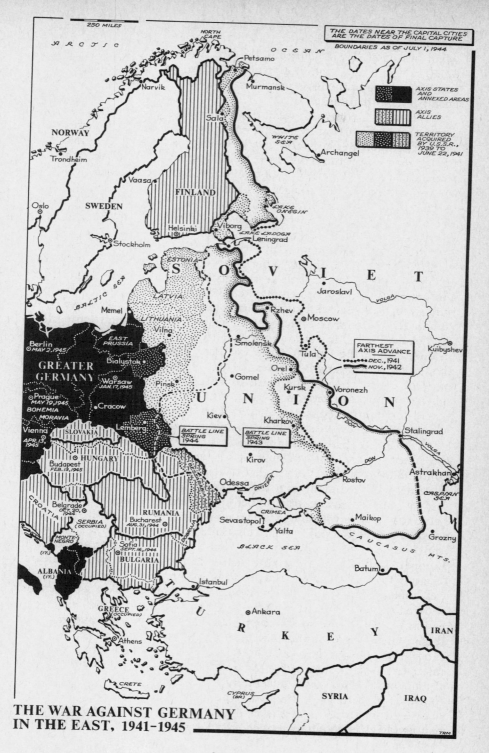

250 MILES

THE DATES NEAR THE CAPITAL CITIES
ARE THE DATES OF FINAL CAPTURE
BOUNDARIES AS OF JULY 1, 1944

ARCTIC   NORTH   OCEAN
                CAPE
Narvik   Petsamo
                Murmansk
                Sala

AXIS STATES
AND
ANNEXED AREAS

AXIS
ALLIES

TERRITORY
ACQUIRED
BY U.S.S.R.,
1939 TO
JUNE 22, 1941

NORWAY

Trondheim

Oslo   Vaasa

SWEDEN   FINLAND

                Helsinki   WHITE SEA

Stockholm   Viborg   LAKE ONEGA
                Leningrad   LAKE LADOGA   Archangel

                ESTONIA   S O V I E T

                LATVIA   Jaroslavl   VOLGA

Memel   LITHUANIA   Rzhev   Moscow
                Vilna   Smolensk
Berlin   EAST   Tula   Kuibyshev
MAY 2, 1945   PRUSSIA
                Bialystok   FARTHEST
GREATER   AXIS ADVANCE
GERMANY   Warsaw   Pinsk   Gomel   Orel   DEC., 1941
                JAN. 17, 1945   NOV., 1942
Prague   Cracow   Kursk   Voronezh
MAY 19, 1945
BOHEMIA   U N I O N
MORAVIA   Lemberg Kiev   Kharkov
Vienna SLOVAKIA   Stalingrad
APR. 13,   BATTLE LINE   BATTLE LINE   DON   VOLGA
1945   SPRING   SPRING
        HUNGARY   1944   1943
Budapest   Kirov
FEB. 13, 1945   Rostov   Astrakhan
                        Odessa
CROATIA   DNIEPER
                RUMANIA   CASPIAN
Belgrade   Bucharest   SEA
OCT. 20, 1944   AUG. 31, 1944   CRIMEA   Maikop
SERBIA   Sevastopol   Grozny
(OCCUPIED)   Sofia   Yalta
MONTE-   SEPT. 16, 1944   CAUCASUS MTS.
NEGRO   BULGARIA
(IT.)   Batum
ALBANIA   BLACK SEA
(IT.)   Istanbul

GREECE   Ankara   IRAN
(OCCUPIED)   T U R K E Y
Athens

CRETE   CYPRUS   SYRIA   IRAQ
                (BR.)

THE WAR AGAINST GERMANY
IN THE EAST, 1941–1945

TRM

MAP 21

admit to Roosevelt and Churchill, the Red Army could rely on its superior numbers, the great expanse of territory over which they could maneuver, and the training of the Russian soldiers and civilians to operate behind the enemy lines as partisans.

When the Germans struck at dawn on June 22 it was with a weight of armor and accumulation of manpower rarely if ever before assembled for such an enterprise. The swiftness and force of the blow were almost certainly greater than the Russians had anticipated. By December the Germans reached points within 30 or 35 miles of Leningrad and Moscow, but they no longer had the strength to press further. On December 5 the last German offensive near Moscow came to a halt, and on the following day the central Russian army under General Zhukov launched a vigorous counterattack [see map, p. 549].

ROAD TO PEARL HARBOR. In certain respects the American attitude towards World War II did not differ greatly from the Russian. At the start, the desire to keep out of the war was very widely felt in both countries. As the Axis threat grew, both the United States and Russia took steps to secure strong outposts which would have to be seized by the enemy before the homeland could be attacked. While the Russians were securing Eastern Poland, the Baltic states, and Bessarabia, and were angling for influence in the Balkans, the United States was busy strengthening its outposts in the Pacific, establishing new bases in the Caribbean and Iceland, and winning the co-operation of the Latin American states in a scheme of hemispheric defense. Similarly, both the Soviet Union and the United States waited to be attacked, rather than taking the initiative into their own hands, and thereby suffered grievous defeats during their first year of war.

Yet despite these striking parallels, there were profound differences in the American and Russian approach. The strong sympathy felt in the United States for the Western democracies in no way compared with the relatively detached manner in which the Soviet statesmen bargained with the West in the summer of 1939 before concluding a pact with the Nazis. Faced with an overwhelmingly isolationist electorate, and until 1939 nearly as convinced as the public that the United States could keep out of the war, President Roosevelt moved cautiously to adjust American policy to European reality. The Neutrality Act of 1937, which placed an embargo on arms to any belligerent state, clearly worked to the advantage of the well-armed Nazis. In November, 1939, a new Neutrality Act was therefore adopted which permitted the sale of arms, ammunition, and implements of war to belligerents on condition that they could pay for and transport them. This feature of the new act was popularly known as "cash and carry," and it amounted to an official indication that the United States was interested in the victory of the Western democracies. During the battle of Britain, on the eve of a national election in which neutrality was a keynote, Roosevelt took further steps to aid the British. In June, 1940, arms were released from United States arsenals for purchase by Britain, and in September the United States traded fifty over-age destroyers for long-term leases of bases on British possessions in the western Atlantic and the Caribbean. After his re-election for a third term, Roosevelt secured the adoption of his most momentous proposal with the passage by Congress of the Lend-Lease Act in March, 1941. This law gave the president the right to place American resources at the disposal of any state the defense of which he considered necessary to American security, although Congress retained the power to authorize the necessary appropriations. Lend-lease credits were promptly made available to Great Britain and other countries, and in November, 1941, they were extended to the Soviet Union as well.

Steps were now taken to secure one additional base. Iceland, hitherto a Danish possession, had proclaimed its independence in April, 1941. Three months later, American, Canadian, and British troops occupied the island in order to protect the flow of shipping to and from Great Britain. Having agreed to all of these measures, Roosevelt and Churchill met off the coast of Newfoundland in August, 1941, in the first of their wartime conferences. Here they drafted a general statement of policy known as the Atlantic Charter in which they pledged allegiance to democratic principles and, in cautious phraseology, promised to work for a world in which political and economic equality would prevail among nations "after the final destruction of the Nazi tyranny" [see Appendix III]. The United States was still at peace, however, and it might have continued almost indefinitely in its role of "arsenal of democracy" had it not been suddenly brought into the war by the Japanese attack at Pearl Harbor.

American public opinion was inevitably turned toward Europe during the momentous years of 1939–41, and had little appreciation of the equally important events which were unfolding in the Pacific area. It knew that Japan was rapidly coming under the control of a ruthless group of militarists who wished to organize the whole of the Far East under their leadership, much as the Nazis wished to dominate Europe and the Near East. It nevertheless believed that the vast extent of China was a much larger area than the Japanese could ever hope to conquer, and that the combined strength of the American, British, and Dutch navies represented a force which no Japanese government would dare to challenge.

While these general considerations contained many elements of truth, they represented only a part of the picture. What was less fully realized was that during the 1930's the Japanese had been building up a navy formidable in size, equipment, and training, which by 1941 was more powerful than the combined American, British, and Dutch forces stationed in the Pacific. The Japanese army and air force were similarly of high quality, and had profited by their years of training on the Asian mainland. The conclusion of the Nazi-Soviet pact in August, 1939, was a temporary setback for the Japanese since it left Russia neutral and able to keep an eye on Far Eastern developments. The defeat of France in the spring of 1940, however, offered an opportunity that Japan was not slow to seize. In the late summer of 1940 Japan was permitted by Vichy France to occupy northern Indochina, and less than a year later it seized the whole of the

French colony. This acquisition gave Japan airfields within striking distance of Singapore, an additional base from which to increase its stranglehold on China, and an important supply of rice. In the meantime, Japan's adherence to the Tripartite Pact in September, 1940, and its conclusion of a non-aggression treaty with the Soviet Union in April, 1941, gave it further assurance that it need expect little interference from the dominant European powers for the time being. Whatever doubts the Japanese may have had as regards Russian neutrality were finally removed in June, when the Nazi attack on the Soviet Union absorbed the full energies of the Red Army.

The summer of 1941 brought the crisis in the Pacific to a head. For the Japanese imperialists the time had come to strike, and they hoped that the United States would remain a source of essential raw materials. In 1938 and again in 1940, the United States had placed restrictions on the raw materials and manufactured goods available to Japan, but in 1940–41 Japan was still obtaining four fifths of its oil and substantial amounts of scrap iron from the United States. These supplies had not been cut off for fear of provoking the Japanese militarists to attack the oil resources of the Netherlands East Indies before the United States was ready to defend its interests. The United States was thus using the sale of oil and scrap iron in order to buy time until it was ready to meet a Japanese challenge. This was only a makeshift arrangement, and when the Japanese finally seized control of French Indochina in July, 1941, Roosevelt promptly replied by freezing Japanese assets in the United States. Similar measures were taken by the British and the Dutch, and had the effect of cutting Japan off from all available purchases of oil and other raw materials. The issue was now clearly defined: either Japan had to bring its aggressive expansion to a halt, in which case it would be granted the right to purchase raw materials for peacetime needs, or else it could strike at the available sources of raw materials and challenge the United States, the British Commonwealth, and the Netherlands East Indies to a full-fledged war.

These alternatives were quite apparent in Tokyo and a bitter controversy developed between the Western-minded statesmen, headed by prime minister Konoye, and the war party led by General Tojo, the minister of war. In October, 1941, Konoye resigned and was replaced by Tojo, and the imperialists had their way. The surprise Japanese attack on the naval base and adjacent army air fields at Pearl Harbor, on the Hawaiian island of Oahu, on the morning of December 7, 1941, soon achieved its primary purpose of immobilizing the United States Pacific fleet. America was now helpless in the face of Japanese aggression for the time being, but this Japanese victory had been bought at a high price. On the following day the United States, the United Kingdom, Canada, South Africa, the Netherlands, and Luxembourg declared war on Japan. Within a few days the exiled governments of Greece, Yugoslavia, and the Free French, as well as Australia and New Zealand, also entered the conflict. On December 11 Germany and Italy declared war on the United States, and the Axis satellite states of Hungary, Bulgaria, and Rumania soon followed suit. During the six months following Pearl Harbor all the Latin American republics, except Argentina and Chile, severed relations with or declared war on the Axis powers.

Measureless consequences were to flow from the attack on Pearl Harbor, for what had started out as a series of carefully-timed attacks by Nazi Germany on its neighbors in 1939 had now become a great conflagration enveloping the entire world. Yet there was little sign at this time of the great weight of ships, armor, and manpower that was eventually to be thrown against Japan, and during the winter of 1941–42 its forces were able to advance almost without hindrance. The Philippines, Hong Kong, and Malaya were attacked on the same day as Pearl Harbor, and the American garrisons on the islands of Guam and Wake were hit on the following day. Within less than a month the Japanese had scored successes everywhere, although the small Philippine island fort of Corregidor held out until May under the command first of General MacArthur and later of General Wainwright. The government of Thailand (Siam) made a settlement with Japan in January, 1942, and during the following month Malaya was overrun and the British stronghold of Singapore fell. By the end of March the Japanese were also virtually in control of Burma, and of the Netherlands East Indies with their vast wealth. These were indeed extraordinary gains, and there was little the great coalition that had just been formed could do except to bring small forces to bear around the perimeter of the Japanese-controlled area. Like the Russians, however, the Pacific Allies were not crushed but had merely retreated with heavy losses before overwhelming odds. Like the Russians also, they reorganized their forces during 1942 and prepared to strike back with ever increasing power [see map, p. 569].

EUROPE AT WAR. During the years of Axis predominance Hitler talked a great deal about a "New Order" that he was going to establish, but the treatment received by the peoples overrun by the Axis armies resembled much more the old disorder. Territories producing supplies needed by the Axis war machine were provided with a strict but orderly military administration, while those that incurred Nazi disfavor were treated with unbelievable brutality. Some territories were annexed by Germany or by one of its allies, while others were held for eventual autonomy in an Axis Europe. Some peoples were marked for extermination and others were sent to German factories, while the majority were left at home to live as best they could.

Of all the occupied states Poland suffered the most. While the western portion of the country was incorporated into Germany, the central provinces, including Warsaw, Cracow, Lublin, and later Lwow, were established as the Government General of Poland under German administration. In both sections the Germans attempted systematically to kill off all of Poland's political and intellectual leaders, in addition to the large Jewish population of the country. Here German rule reached depths of brutality that no previous war had known. In the Balkans the pattern of Axis occupation did not differ greatly from that in the rest of Europe. In Yugoslavia a much more ruthless regime was established by the Axis in 1941. Large sections of the country were annexed by the neighboring Italian, Hungarian, and Bulgarian states, and the province of Croatia was established as an autonomous state under a fascist regime. The Serbian puppet state embraced little more than a quarter of the original population of Yugoslavia. Similarly in Greece, the Axis ruled with a heavy hand. The Italians and Bulgarians were allowed to occupy northern Greece, annexing certain provinces, while the Germans held the southern section with the aid of a puppet government. In Yugoslavia and Greece the resistance of the population was particularly fierce, and the regime of the occupying powers was correspondingly heavy.

Eastern Europe was just behind the German battle lines in 1941, and the occupied peoples suffered accordingly. The rich territories under German rule in Western Europe, however, were relatively distant from the Nazi-Soviet struggle and were less brutally repressed. The little state of Luxembourg was incorporated into Germany, but the control of the neighboring states took diverse forms. While Denmark was permitted to keep its government since it was technically not at war, the Netherlands was administered by a Reich Commissioner, the Austrian Nazi Seyss-Inquart. In Norway a native fascist movement lent support to the German Commissioner, and the name of its leader, Major Quisling, soon became a synonym for traitor and fifth-columnist. Belgium and northern France, because of their strategic importance, were administered jointly by a military commander. The eastern French provinces of Alsace and Lorraine, on the other hand, were given a civil administration which envisaged their eventual incorporation into Germany. In the south of France, a small zone came under Italian control.

There remained also the unoccupied portion of France with its government at Vichy under Marshal Pétain, which posed a difficult problem for Great Britain and the United States. It was the American viewpoint that breaking off relations with the Vichy regime would mean throwing it into the arms of the Nazis, along with the important overseas possessions which remained under its administration: North and West Africa, Indochina, Madagascar, French Guiana in the Caribbean, and the tiny islands of St. Pierre and Miquelon off the coast of Newfoundland. Vichy was regarded as an important listening post in Axis-occupied Europe, and the success of the Allied landings in North and West Africa in November, 1942, was generally attributed to the careful preparations on the spot which the Vichy government had permitted.

The British view was quite different. In the crucial summer of 1940 Churchill was not prepared to take a chance on Pétain's being able to pursue a policy independent of Nazi control. He therefore immediately took the action which resulted in the sinking of major units of the French fleet at Oran in July, 1940, and the Vichy regime promptly broke off relations with Great Britain. The British government now gave increasing support to General de Gaulle. Having recognized him as "leader of all free Frenchmen" as early as June, 1940, it gave him a semi-official position in London. With this support, De Gaulle set in motion the Free France movement, later known as Fighting France, and won the loyalty of the French possessions of Equatorial Africa, the French Cameroons, French India, French Oceania, and New Caledonia. The De Gaullists later obtained possession also of the French mandates of Syria and Lebanon, and in a controversial act seized the islands of St. Pierre and Miquelon without obtaining the previous consent of the British and American governments. In 1941 De Gaulle established a National Committee which had at its disposal important French military and naval forces, and which exercised a powerful influence within occupied and Vichy France. The United States never gave De Gaulle the degree of support which he received from Great Britain, but it extended Lend-Lease aid to him in 1941 and recognized the authority of his National Committee in French Equatorial Africa, the Cameroons, and New Caledonia.

One factor which helped to keep alive the hope of the peoples in Axis-occupied Europe was the knowledge that their former governments, while defeated, were maintaining in exile a framework of organization which would permit them to re-establish their authority upon the defeat of Germany. Eight such governments-in-exile were established in London by 1941: Belgium, Czechoslovakia, Greece, Luxembourg, the Netherlands, Norway, Poland, and Yugoslavia. In some cases, as with Belgium, Czechoslovakia, Luxembourg, and Norway, constitutional provisions or precedents existed permitting their governments to carry on abroad. The Netherlands, on the other hand, had made no provision for such an eventuality and its government simply assumed the necessary authority. Since the governments of Greece, Poland, and Yugoslavia, were already authoritarian to a greater or lesser degree, they could make the transition without difficulty. These governments all received recognition in due course as members of the coalition, issued legislation, and conducted active foreign policies. Some of them had substantial armed forces at their disposal, but in most cases their influence was psychological and was exerted through broadcast propaganda and underground communication with the occupied states.

The Great Coalition

THE UNITED NATIONS. The involvement of the United States in World War II resulted in the amalgamation into one great coalition of almost all of the states whose security was threatened by the Axis powers. Although Hitler, Tojo, and Mussolini rejoiced in the Japanese victory at Pearl Harbor, this event in fact marked the beginning of the end for the predominance of their military machines. The Axis powers had thus far enjoyed the advantages of strategic initiative, fanatical zeal, and well-knit internal lines of communication, but these advantages were crucial only when they could keep their victims divided and annihilate them one by one. Once their opponents united, the Axis could not crush each one separately with a sudden surprise blow. Moreover, the fanaticism of their soldiers was worn down by long campaigns, and the short lines of communication were counterbalanced by the overwhelming superiority of matériel which the coalition could assemble. The Axis leaders did not foresee all of these eventualities in December, 1941, but by the end of another year only the most shortsighted among them could hope for anything better than a compromise peace.

The threatened states recognized that their great resources would be of little value unless they could achieve some degree of political unity, and they acted promptly to this end. Churchill arrived in Washington before the end of December 1941 to consult with Roosevelt, and with the ambassadors who represented the views of the other besieged or occupied states, including Litvinov from Russia and Soong from China. From these consultations emerged the United Nations Declaration, signed on January 1, 1942, which formally inaugurated the coalition established to defeat the Axis. Apart from the big four, twenty-two nations signed this document, including five members of the British Commonwealth and Empire, eight European states, and nine Latin American republics. The Declaration pledged each government "to employ its full resources, military or economic, against those members of the Tripartite Pact and its adherents with which such government is at war," and "to co-operate with the governments signatory hereto and not to make a separate armistice or peace with the enemies" [see Appendix IV]. These pledges were faithfully adhered to, for the propaganda of the Axis powers was never able to offset their record of aggression and destruction.

Having formed their coalition, the United Nations also found it desirable to make some reference to war aims. The informal statement known as the Atlantic Charter, that Roosevelt and Churchill had issued after their first meeting in August, 1941, was now subscribed to by all the United Nations as their "common program of purposes and principles." The eight-point program of the Atlantic Charter, which was reminiscent in many respects of Wilson's Fourteen Points, attempted to state in very broad terms such principles as would command the loyalty of all friendly peoples. Roosevelt and Churchill denied for their own countries any claim of territorial or other aggrandizement (Point 1), and expressed the desire to see no other territorial changes which were not agreed to by the peoples concerned (Point 2). Reference was also made to the right of peoples to choose the form of government under which they would live, and to the restoration of the sovereignty of states overrun by the Axis (Point 3). Greater access for all states to trade and raw materials after the war (Point 4), and international collaboration in the economic field (Point 5), were also proposed. Finally, hope was expressed for the postwar security of all states (Point 6), freedom of the seas (Point 7), and a disarmament program in combination with a "permanent system of general security"

(Point 8). Vague and noncommittal as this program was, it not only served to bolster the morale of the United Nations but also had a perceptible impact on the peace settlement [see Appendix III].

INTER-ALLIED CO-OPERATION. Before any postwar program could be tackled the war had to be won. The Russians were devoting their entire attention to the struggle with the Nazis, therefore the initiative for planning the strategy of the war beyond the Eastern European front lay with the British and American leaders. A tentative program had already been developed in staff conferences that had been secretly under way since the autumn of 1940 between the two countries, and the principal strategic decisions were reached by Roosevelt and Churchill at Washington in January, 1942, without serious disagreement. The most significant of these was the decision that the bulk of American manpower and supplies should be thrown first against Germany. This meant making the Pacific a secondary theater for the time being, a decision which was not easy for American public opinion to accept, since Japan was generally regarded as the major enemy. Both the American and the British chiefs of staff, nevertheless, recognized that only in Europe could a decisive campaign be fought. Not only was Germany the most powerful of the Axis states, but the Russian and British armed forces were already on the spot, and American men and equipment could be moved there more rapidly than to the Pacific.

Once this basic decision was reached, means had to be found for its implementation. It was agreed that air bombardment of Germany from England was to be expanded as rapidly as possible, and supplies were to be rushed to the Soviet Union. The blockade of Germany, it was expected, would serve to wear down German resistance, and also that the peoples in the Axis-occupied countries could be stimulated to revolt. A large-scale invasion of the European continent was believed to be beyond the range of immediate possibilities, however, and alternative plans were made for a landing before the end of 1942 on the relatively unprotected coasts of West and North Africa. At the same time a unified command was established for American, British, Dutch, Australian, and New Zealand forces in the South Pacific, where the Japanese advance was shortly to encompass the British and Dutch possessions in that area and to threaten Australia itself.

By the middle of January, 1942, these decisions had been agreed upon, and Churchill returned to Great Britain. This series of discussions marked the beginning of one of the most successful examples of close military collaboration in modern times. The success of this venture was due in no small degree to the personalities of the leading statesmen of the two countries. Churchill, and Roosevelt to a somewhat lesser degree, had held important posts during World War I and were fully aware of the needs of the situation. Hull in the United States and Eden in Great Britain had both had long experience in foreign affairs, while Lord Halifax and Winant ably represented their respective countries in Washington and London. On

ALLIED STATESMEN IN LONDON Representatives of the Allied Governments-in-Exile meeting in London with British Foreign Minister Eden (center on far side of table) in February, 1943. Seated at table, starting on Eden's right, are Spaak (Belgium), Milanovich (Yugoslavia), Law (British Parliamentary Undersecretary), Beck (Luxemburg), Van Kleffens (Netherlands), Masaryk (Czechoslovakia), Lie (Norway), Pleven (Fighting France), Cadogan (British Permanent Undersecretary), Tsouderos (Greece), and Raczynski (Poland).

the military side, Generals Marshall and Arnold headed the American army and air force staffs, and Admiral King was chief of naval operations, while all three services met as the Joint Chiefs of Staff under the chairmanship of Admiral Leahy as deputy of the President. In the United Kingdom, Field Marshal Brooke served as Chief of the Imperial General Staff, while Air Marshal Portal was in charge of the Royal Air Force, and Admiral Pound served as Chief of the Naval Staff until he was succeeded upon his death in 1943 by Admiral Cunningham.

The work of the two national military establishments was co-ordinated by a Combined Chiefs of Staff in Washington. Subordinated to this body was the Munitions Assignment Board, under the authority of which all the munitions produced in the British Commonwealth and the United States were pooled and allocated to the various war theaters. Harry Hopkins served as head of this Board, among his many other activities, and the remarkable energy and devotion with which he promoted the Allied war effort contributed to his premature death. The American-British wartime co-operation was a subtle and complex alliance, requiring the reconciliation of many diverse interests and personalities. Certain advantages accrued to the British by virtue of their earlier involvement in the war and greater experience in European affairs. In the long run, however, the preponderance of American wealth and manpower made itself felt, and when differences of opinion arose between the two powers Roosevelt's views generally won the day.

Military co-operation between Russia and the Western states did not develop so rapidly. In May, 1942, Molotov visited London and Washington to explain the Russian military situation and to request the formation of a second front by the Western Allies in order to relieve the pressure on the Soviet army. During the Soviet minister's visit in London, a twenty-year Anglo-Russian alliance was concluded, in which the two powers agreed to fight to the end against Germany and made provision for co-operation in the postwar period. At the time this treaty was being negotiated Molotov pressed for recognition of the Soviet annexation since 1939 of Estonia, Latvia, and Lithuania, and of parts of Finland, Poland, and Rumania. Churchill found it difficult to resist this pressure until Roosevelt came to his aid by expressing the firm belief that the United Nations coalition would only be weakened by attempts to obtain recognition of boundary changes before the end of the war. The question of a second front on the European continent was taken up by Molotov and Roosevelt in Washington. The problems involved in shipping supplies were explained to the Soviet statesman, and it was pointed out that preparations for a landing in Europe would inevitably mean reducing the amount of supplies shipped directly to Russia. Molotov was, nevertheless, informed that the solution of these difficulties was envisaged and that the formation of a second front in Europe might be expected before the end of 1942. This expectation proved to be too optimistic, however, and the landings in West and North Africa were carried out instead.

BATTLE FOR SUPPLIES. An essential element of the coalition was the material assistance given by the United States to the peoples already engaged in fighting the Axis powers. The main categories of supplies were lend-lease goods, and the materials shipped to the American forces overseas. Lend-lease alone amounted to some 50 billion dollars between 1941 and 1945. Of this amount, about 3.6 billion was in services, 6 billion in food, and the remainder in war materials. Of the total, 31 billion dollars worth of lend-lease went to the members of the British Commonwealth, 11 billion to the Soviet Union, 3 billion to France, and 1.5 billion to China. The United States received some 7.8 billion dollars worth of reverse lend-lease, of which 6.7 billion was from Great Britain.

The first problem in the shipment of supplies, and for a long time the major one, was that represented by the German submarines. The general character of the problem was not greatly different from what it had been during World War I, although numerous technological improvements had been made in both the offensive and the defensive aspects of this highly developed type of warfare. The Germans early developed an aggressive submarine campaign against North Atlantic shipping, and it was all the British could do to keep the convoys moving. After Pearl Harbor the Germans carried the battle to the Caribbean and to the American coastwise routes, and for a number of months the United States entry into the war brought little relief to Britain. Before the submarines were conquered allied losses on several occasions went over 600,000 tons of shipping per month, and at the height of the crisis the Germans had over 100 submarines on the seas. March, 1943, was the last bad month. After that date the United Nations rapidly gained mastery of the sea lanes. The increased use of destroyer escorts, of land and carrier-based aircraft, and the systematic bombing of submarine bases in Europe, were the principal new features in the campaign against the submarine. During the entire five and a half years of the war the Germans sank over 23 million tons of allied shipping, and lost 782 submarines. In the same period, however, the allies built over 42 million tons of new shipping.

Many other problems in addition to those presented by the submarine had to be solved before supplies could flow smoothly. Airplanes, which had initially been shipped by sea, were eventually flown to their destinations wherever possible. This required the construction of airfields in Nova Scotia, Newfoundland, Labrador, and Iceland, on the North Atlantic route, and across Africa to Egypt for the supply of the Near East. The sea route to Murmansk and Archangel in northern Russia was so menaced by the German planes, submarines, and surface vessels, operating off the coast of Norway, that very extensive steps were taken to develop a supply route through Iran. The Trans-Iranian Railroad from the Persian Gulf to the Caspian was repaired, and large numbers of freight cars and locomotives were sent to increase its capacity. New highways and assembly plants for trucks and planes ultimately made Iran one of the main routes for supplying the Soviet Union.

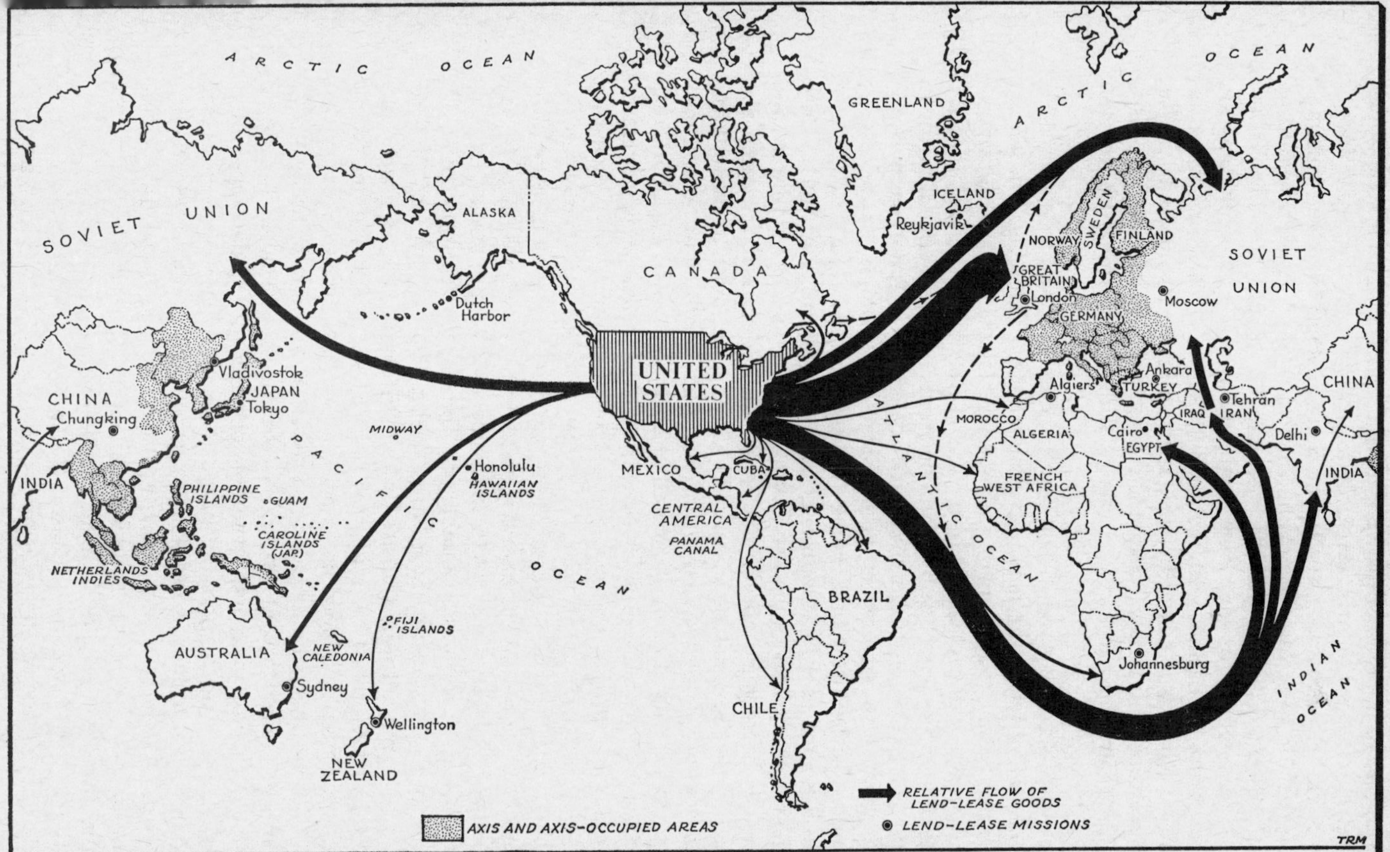

LEND-LEASE SUPPLY ROUTES

Map 22

In the Pacific, Russian ships were neutral, since Japan and the Soviet Union were still at peace, and were able to maintain a substantial flow of goods to Soviet Far Eastern ports. In the South Pacific, however, Australia and New Zealand were for a long time the only countries which could receive supplies by shipping directly from the United States. The supply route to China, which for some time had gone from the port of Rangoon in Burma by rail to Lashio, and thence by truck into China over the famous Burma Road, was closed by the Japanese in the spring of 1942. Karachi, in western India, now became the principal port of entry for Asia, and supplies moved by rail and air across India to northern Burma and China.

WAR AND SCIENCE. One of the few benefits that war contributes to mankind occurs through the rapid development that takes place in science and technology, for progress made in these fields is generally applicable to peacetime pursuits. Moreover, World War II illustrates the fact that the use made of scientific research by the belligerents can be a crucial factor in the outcome of the war. Churchill's friend Professor Lindemann supervised the various research activities in Great Britain which were co-ordinated under the Ministry of Defense. In the United States an Office of Scientific Research and Development, established in 1941 with Dr. Bush as its director, was given general supervision over a variety of military and civilian research organizations. In the Soviet Union, scientific research was supervised by the Academy of Science. The Axis states never competed successfully with their opponents in the organization of scientific research. While national research councils existed in both Germany and Japan, they were given little authority and few resources. At first the Axis powers relied on obtaining a quick victory on the basis of the weapons which they had already developed, and by the time they realized that this would be impossible it was too late to organize the intensive and well-integrated research programs which are an essential prerequisite to important advances.

Among the variety of projects embraced by the war research of the belligerents, one of the most valuable was the use of electronic tubes for radio detection and ranging by means of the device known as "radar." Radar was first put into general use by the British in 1939 as a defensive measure against German air raids, where it proved to be of invaluable service. It was later developed as an offensive weapon used to detect and identify enemy targets at night or at great distances, and in this capacity it soon revolutionized war at sea and in the air. In the field of weapons one of the most important improvements occurred in the development of rockets. From the small, portable bazookas to the fourteen-ton German V-2's which began to fall on London at 3400 miles per hour in September 1944, rockets introduced a new element into the science of war. In addition to the innumerable electrical and mechanical devices which were developed, great strides were made in medicine. The mass production of penicillin for the cure of infectious diseases, the development of atabrine as a substitute for quinine in the treatment of malaria, and the increased use of plasma for blood transfusions, may properly be attributed to the demands of the war.

Of all the results of wartime science, however, the most sensational occurred in the field of atomic research. For a generation the scientists of many nations had been attempting to split the atom with a view to harnessing the energy which this fission would release, but it was not until the eve of the war that two German scientists succeeded in producing atomic fission with the use of uranium. This development in pure science set many minds speculating as to its practical applications, and in the summer of 1940 studies of uranium were initiated with a grant of a few hundred thousand dollars from the United States government. From these small beginnings research projects grew by leaps and bounds, and before the end of 1942 a chain reaction produced under careful control at the University of Chicago pointed the way towards a solution of the principal problems which were still puzzling the scientists. In 1943 a greatly expanded organization with vast manufacturing facilities was established under U. S. Army supervision, concealed behind the innocent name of "Manhattan District," and scientists of many nationalities worked together in secret in a closely integrated network of American, Canadian, and British research bodies. This vast project, which before long required the investment of some $2,000,000,000, came to a successful climax on July 16, 1945, when the first atomic explosion was produced in the vicinity of Albuquerque, New Mexico. This development amounted to nothing less than a turning point in the history of mankind, and opened up as yet incalculable possibilities of progress and destruction.

Initiative of the United Nations

The winter of 1942–43 was the turning point of the war. Up to this time the Axis had suffered few defeats and had retained the strategic initiative. Henceforth it was the United Nations which had the initiative, and with increasing strength they pressed on to victory. The Anglo-American landings in North Africa, the British victory in Libya, the defeat of the Germans at Stalingrad, and the halting of the Japanese advance in the Southwest Pacific with the battle of the Bismarck Sea—all these fateful events took place between November, 1942 and March, 1943.

NORTH AFRICA. The first step in the advance of the Western Allies towards the heart of Germany was in North Africa. On November 8, 1942, three Anglo-American landings under the command of General Eisenhower were successfully made at Casablanca on the Atlantic and at Oran and Algiers on the Mediterranean. Extensive negotiations with some of the Vichyite administrators of these French possessions had helped prepare the way for the invasion, and the controversial decision to work with the Vichy officials rather than installing a De Gaullist regime proved on the whole to be justified. Shortly before the landings in North Africa the Axis suffered an equally grave reverse in Egypt, where the British under Montgomery were finally able to strike back at the German-Italian army under Rommel.

Starting from the strong El Alamein line, Montgomery broke through the Axis positions and started the long pursuit of Rommel across the Libyan desert to Tripoli, 1400 miles away, which he reached in January 1943.

Pressed by Montgomery from the east and by Eisenhower from the west, the German and Italian forces under Rommel now resolved to make a last stand in Tunisia. German headquarters, which had promptly ordered the occupation of Vichy France in November, 1942, made arrangements to send supplies and reinforcements to Rommel by air. Inadequate preparations and poor weather prevented the Anglo-American forces in the west from making much headway against the Germans before the end of the winter, but in March, 1943, after initial reverses, the Allied forces attacked vigorously from the west and the southeast. A general rout of the Axis armies took place during April, and on May 12 the remaining 250,000 Germans and Italians surrendered. Africa was finally cleared of the enemy, and the British and American land and air forces had proven that they could co-operate successfully against the Axis [see map, p. 565].

EUROPEAN THEATER. The main concentration of Nazi troops throughout this period was in Eastern Europe. Having failed to destroy the Russian armies in 1941, the Germans now attempted to take over the vast economic resources of the southern Ukraine and the Caucasus. In their summer campaign in 1942 the Germans pressed far into the Caucasus region and reached the Volga River at Stalingrad. By this time they had already conquered about one third of the population of Russia, one third of its chemical industries, one half of its coal and electric power, and over one half of its resources in a number of vital minerals. A victory at Stalingrad would have permitted the Germans to isolate Moscow and Leningrad, and to secure strategic positions and economic resources which might have enabled them to take decisive action in 1943. This became impossible when the Russians under Zhukov succeeded in encircling the Germans after a bitter winter struggle. In January, 1943, they captured a German army of some 300,000 with its commanding general and his staff [see map, p. 549].

By the spring of 1943 the Russians were finally in a position where they could attack the Germans with full vigor. With the enemy now on the defensive, the Russian armies rolled forward with few setbacks and reached Berlin in the spring of 1945. Until the latter part of 1942 the Russians had fought with little foreign assistance. Now Lend-Lease supplies began to arrive in quantity, and the large number of planes, tanks, trucks, and jeeps from the United States played an indispensable role in subsequent Russian offensives. By the autumn of 1943 the Russians had recaptured Kiev and crossed the Dnieper at several points; during the winter Leningrad was freed. In the spring of 1944 Odessa was recaptured and the Germans were driven out of the Crimean peninsula.

In the meantime the Anglo-American forces under Eisenhower in North Africa moved on into Italy. The strategic aim of this campaign was to obtain the southern part of Italy for the twin purposes of using the excellent network of airfields around Foggia for the bombing of Central and

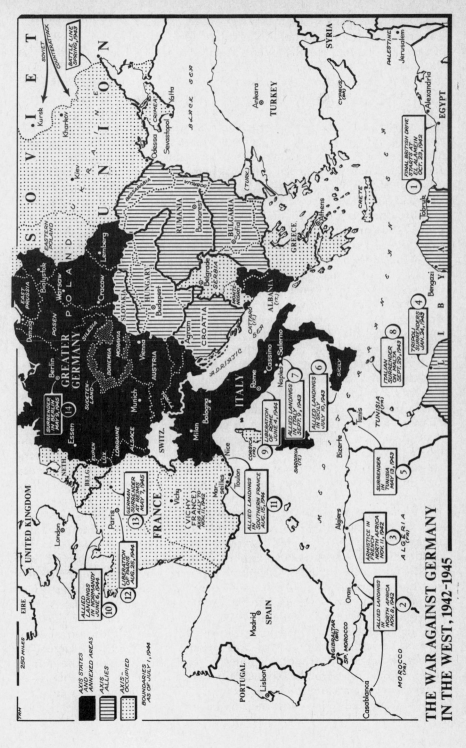

**THE WAR AGAINST GERMANY
IN THE WEST, 1942-1945**

MAP 23

Eastern Europe, and of establishing a base for the invasion of the Balkans or southern France, as policy might dictate. This was a poor substitute for the direct invasion of France, for which the Western Allies still lacked sufficient strength, and it was one of the slowest and clumsiest campaigns of the war. Sicily was invaded in June 1943, and the Axis forces under German command fought and retreated so skillfully that it was not until June 4, 1944, that the Anglo-American forces entered Rome. Early in the campaign, in July, 1943, Mussolini fell from power and was succeeded by Marshal Badoglio who promptly sued for armistice terms. Although Badoglio himself had long been a Fascist hero, and had directed the Italian conquest of Ethiopia in 1935–36, he headed a group of responsible leaders who had the confidence of King Victor Emmanuel III and who believed that the time had come for Italy to change sides. Thus during the greater part of this campaign the Italian government co-operated with the Western Allies as a co-belligerent, while remnants of Mussolini's regime in the north continued to fight under German command. In the later stages of the Italian campaign, a significant contribution was made by Polish, Greek, and Brazilian contingents.

At the start of the war Germany possessed a great preponderance of air power, and this played a decisive role in its *Blitzkrieg* victories in Poland, Scandinavia, the Lowlands, and France. The German use of air power was very largely tactical, that is to say in close conjunction with land or sea operations, and relatively little attention was given to the development of a force of heavy bombers which could operate independently. Even in the bombing of England in 1940 the Germans directed their attention initially to such tactical objectives as ports and airfields on or near the Channel, and the heavy bombing of cities such as London and Coventry came only later. While these attacks on large cities did considerable damage, they were light as compared to the raids which the British and American air forces later sent over Germany. Moreover, the bombing planes used by the Germans were not as up-to-date as their fighters or dive-bombers, and were very vulnerable to attack.

The Anglo-American plan of strategic bombing attacks on Germany had two main objectives: to cripple or destroy German war industry, and to break the German morale by war-weariness and apathy and by terrorizing the civilian population. In implementation of the first objective, systematic raids were carried out against specific key industries producing such essential war materials as ball bearings, steel, airplanes, synthetic gasoline, and so on. The British tended to bomb at night when their planes were less vulnerable to attack, while the Americans made a specialty of high altitude daytime bombing made possible by the use of "precision" bombsights. The raids on the civilian population took the form of large-scale attacks on big cities, without any objective other than breaking the morale of the population. Some 61 German cities of over 100,000 population were attacked in the war, and some 300,000 persons were killed while over 7 million are estimated to have lost their homes.

THE PACIFIC THEATER. As a secondary theater pending the defeat of Germany, the Pacific did not receive a quota of manpower and supplies proportionate to the tasks at hand, and the allied commanders were forced to adopt an approach described in military terminology as a strategic defensive and a tactical offensive. This meant that for the time being the principal allied effort in the Pacific would be directed not towards a general attack on Japan, but towards a wearing down of the Japanese forces by the exertion of unremitting pressure. This strategy would also permit the acquisition of bases for a conquest of Japan proper which could be attempted only after men and supplies were released from the European theater.

It was soon recognized that the United States would have to assume responsibility for the conduct of the war in the Pacific, and the region was divided into two theaters that operated under the direction of the Joint Chiefs of Staff in Washington. The Southwest Pacific theater, under General MacArthur, included the Philippines, the Netherlands East Indies, New Guinea, and Australia. The Pacific Ocean Areas, under Admiral Nimitz, was a larger theater which extended from New Zealand and the Solomons in the south to the Aleutian Islands in the north, and embraced the important central Pacific island groups of the Gilberts, the Marshalls, the Carolines, and the Marianas. A separate China-Burma-India theater, under General Stilwell, was established for the American forces on the Asiatic mainland. While these three theaters were under American command, they were allied in character, and despite the preponderance of American power a significant role was played by the British, Australians, and Chinese in the theaters adjacent to their bases. In Washington a Pacific War Council was established for the consideration of general policy problems, on which sat representatives of New Zealand, the Netherlands, Canada, the Philippines and India, in addition to the United States, the United Kingdom, China, and Australia.

The first task of the allied forces was to stem the tide of Japanese aggression, and this was accomplished gradually during 1942–43. In May, 1942, an important Japanese task force was caught in the Coral Sea, northeast of Australia, and decisively repelled by an allied fleet. In June a powerful Japanese fleet advancing on Midway Island, presumably with the central island of Oahu in the Hawaiians as its ultimate objective, was turned back after losing four aircraft carriers with a large number of trained pilots, two cruisers, and other vessels. Both the Coral Sea and Midway were fought almost entirely by carrier-based planes, and American shipbuilding facilities soon gave the allies a permanent preponderance in aircraft carriers. A final task was to save Port Moresby in New Guinea, which the Japanese wanted as a base for use against Australia. The occupation by American forces of Guadalcanal in August, 1942, and the destruction of a large Japanese convoy in the battle of the Bismarck Sea early in March, 1943, marked an end to Japanese aspirations in this area. In the meantime the Japanese received a foretaste of what was to come when sixteen planes under Lt. Col.

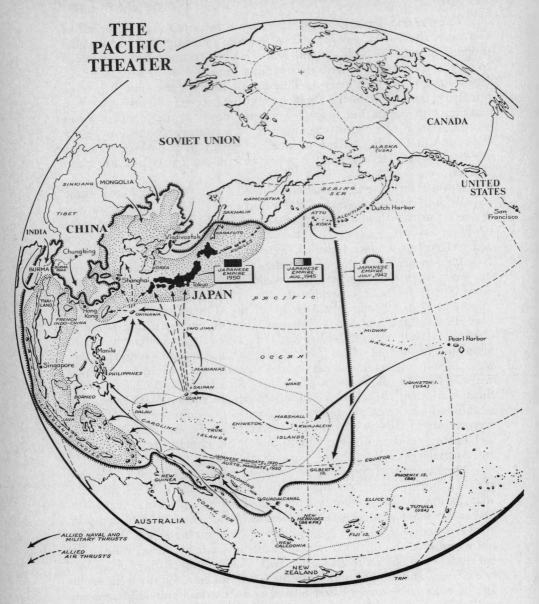

THE PACIFIC THEATER

CANADA

SOVIET UNION

UNITED STATES

SINKIANG   MONGOLIA

TIBET

KAMCHATKA

BERING SEA

ALASKA (USA)

ATTU   ALEUTIANS   Dutch Harbor

KISKA

San Francisco

INDIA   CHINA   SAKHALIN

Vladivostok   KARAFUTO

Chungking   KURILES

BURMA   BURMA ROAD   KOREA

JAPANESE EMPIRE 1950   JAPANESE EMPIRE AUG., 1945   JAPANESE EMPIRE JULY, 1942

Shanghai   Tokyo

JAPAN

P A C I F I C

THAILAND   Hong Kong   OKINAWA

FRENCH INDO-CHINA   IWO JIMA

MIDWAY

HAWAIIAN

Pearl Harbor

Manila   MARIANAS

Singapore   PHILIPPINES   SAIPAN   WAKE

O C E A N   IS.

JOHNSTON I. (USA)

BORNEO   GUAM

PALAU   CAROLINE   TRUK   ENIWETOK   MARSHALL

JAVA   ISLANDS   ISLANDS   KWAJALEIN

JAPANESE MANDATE, 1920   EQUATOR

AUSTR. MANDATE, 1920   GILBERT IS.   PHOENIX IS. (BR)

NEW GUINEA   SOLOMONS

CORAL SEA   GUADALCANAL   ELLICE IS.   TUTUILA (USA)

AUSTRALIA   NEW HEBRIDES (BR & FR)   FIJI IS.

NEW CALEDONIA

⟶ ALLIED NAVAL AND MILITARY THRUSTS

⟶ ALLIED AIR THRUSTS

NEW ZEALAND   TRM

MAP 24

STILWELL AND CHIANG   *General Stilwell, U.S. Commander in the China-Burma-India Theater, presents the Legion of Merit to Generalissimo Chiang Kai-shek, at Chungking, China, in August, 1943.*

Doolittle, launched from the aircraft carrier *Hornet,* dropped bombs on Tokyo in April, 1942.

It was now possible for the United Nations forces to start on the long road that led to Japan. In the Southwest Pacific, MacArthur used heavy land-based planes for bombing and transport, and was able to cut off and bypass strongly fortified Japanese bases such as Rabaul. In the course of 1944 he advanced from New Guinea to the island of Morotai, which was only 300 miles southwest of the Philippines. In the theater of the Pacific Ocean Areas, Nimitz had a somewhat different problem. His task was the destruction of Japanese naval power and the complete strangling of the lanes of shipping on which Japan depended for its existence. This involved the seizure of the smaller islands of the central Pacific by means of amphibious landings, and the use of carrier-based planes. Nimitz seized Makin and Tarawa in the Gilbert Islands in November, 1943, and moved on via the Marshall Islands to Saipan and Guam in the Marianas in June and July, 1944. With the defeat of the Japanese in the battle of the Philippines Sea in June, and the occupation of the Palau Islands in September, Nimitz secured MacArthur's right flank for the advance into the Philippines.

Stilwell's Burma-China-India theater was regarded as the least important of those in the Pacific, but he was kept busy with many assignments. His mission here was to keep the Chinese armies fighting with the aid of supplies and technical advice, which involved maintaining the difficult air route known as "The Hump," between bases in eastern India and Kunming over 17,000-foot mountains. He served as commander of the American forces in this theater, as well as chief of staff to Chiang Kai-shek, as field commander in northern Burma, and as distributor of Lend-Lease supplies in his theater. When a separate Southeast Asia Command was established in India under Vice Admiral Mountbatten in August, 1943, Stilwell served also as his deputy. In January, 1944, a combined attack was launched against the Japanese in Burma, employing British, Indian, Chinese, and American forces. After months of bitter fighting the important railhead of Myitkyina on the Irrawaddy River was captured, and this served as a base for the reconquest of Burma in 1945. In the course of this campaign Stilwell became involved in an irreconcilable controversy with Chiang because of the latter's refusal to sanction the co-operation of Chinese Nationalist and Communist troops, and in October Stilwell was recalled from the front.

The Defeat of the Axis

STRATEGY AND POLITICS. While the first concern of the statesmen of the United Nations was the winning of the war, they could not forget that the purpose of the war was, after all, to establish peace. The efforts at collaboration of the members of the United Nations coalition were never as successful in the political field as in the military, and the defeat of the Axis was followed almost immediately by the revelation of wide divergencies of outlook in political matters. In general, it may be said that the members of the coalition co-operated most successfully in the political field when dealing with problems of a long-range and theoretical character, and least successfully in handling immediate, practical questions. Thus the problem of world organization was handled in a systematic and dignified fashion, and the Charter of the United Nations adopted at San Francisco on June 26, 1945, provided what was probably as good a compromise solution as could have been hoped for. As regards the terms of surrender and armistice, a superficial unanimity was maintained at least until the termination of hostilities, despite profound differences concerning the interpretation and application of these terms. The question of the establishment of a second front, on the other hand, was the subject of an intense and very public dispute which had serious political implications. Matters of immediate practical importance came to be handled increasingly on a unilateral basis by the authorities within whose direct field of operations they fell. Each of the leading members of the United Nations coalition thus developed a regional preponderance in the territories overrun by its armies or navies. By the end of the war the world therefore found itself with both an over-all United Nations organization, and at the same time a system of *de facto* spheres of influence confirmed by vague but nevertheless binding wartime agreements. This situation was destined to have a lasting effect on the postwar settlement.

The origin and fate of the unconditional surrender doctrine is a good example of the methods employed by the United Nations coalition in the initiation and implementation of policy regarding common political problems. The question of the terms of surrender is a critical one, since such terms provide an important propaganda instrument both for undermining the morale of the enemy and for rallying the members of the coalition. Wilson's Fourteen Points represented a similar propaganda instrument in World War I, although after the war it boomeranged when the leaders of the defeated states made great political capital out of the failure of the victors to carry out the promised terms in every detail. The Atlantic Charter did not contain specific terms regarding the treatment of enemy territory, and its use did not go beyond that of providing a general common program for the United Nations.

The question of terms of surrender was thus still an open one when Roosevelt, after only brief consultation with Churchill, announced to the press during the Casablanca conference in January, 1943, that the objective of the war was to obtain the unconditional surrender of Germany, Italy, and Japan. This gesture was not unpremeditated on the part of the President, for he was sensitive to the mistakes made by Wilson a generation earlier and was also aware of the extensive criticism that his dealings with the Vichy government had aroused in connection with the recent landings in North Africa. The term which he selected, associated as it was with General Grant and the American Civil War, indicated that it was intended primarily for American public opinion. To Roosevelt unconditional surrender did not mean that the occupation policy of the victors would be ruthless, but rather that they would make no commitments before surrender that the defeated states might use against them as Hitler had earlier used the Fourteen Points.

Strong criticism of the unconditional surrender doctrine was soon heard from American and foreign propaganda experts. The objection was not to the intrinsic character of unconditional surrender as understood by Roosevelt, but rather to the probable effect of this uncompromising term on the enemy peoples. It was believed that this term would give the impression to the Axis countries that a United Nations victory was greatly to be feared, and that the cost of defeating the Axis would therefore be greater in lives and matériel. A lively controversy ensued in which Roosevelt refused to modify his doctrine, although the prolonged negotiations preceding the armistice signed with Italy in September, 1943, revealed that unconditional surrender was not meant to be taken too literally. Under these circumstances, Hull, Molotov, and Eden adopted this term at their conference in Moscow in October, 1943, although until the end of the war renewed efforts were made to obtain a definition of unconditional surrender that would make it appear less fearful to the enemy peoples if not to their governments. No change was made in the doctrine as it affected the major Axis powers, but in the case of the satellite states of Hungary, Rumania, Bulgaria, and Finland, a joint statement was finally issued in London, Moscow, and Washington on May 12, 1944, that in substance offered these states easier terms if they took the initiative in breaking away from the Axis. The Potsdam Declaration of August 2, 1945, had a similar purpose with regard to Japan.

Far deeper in its ultimate political implications than the controversy over unconditional surrender was that which developed around the Russian demand for a second front on the European continent. The greatest menace to any coalition is the suspicion on the part of one of its members that it is bearing more than its share of the burden of the fighting, and if the British were left to fight alone in 1940, it was the turn of the Russians in 1943 to question whether their allies were doing all they could in Western Europe. While no formal charges of disloyalty were lodged at the top level during the war the Russians were, nevertheless, most desirous of seeing a substantial body of German troops attracted away from the eastern front by a landing in France. Molotov presented a formal request for a second front early in 1942, and the Soviet government and its friends within the Allied countries conducted a vigorous publicity campaign to this end.

To Roosevelt and Churchill the first difficulty was the shortage of shipping, the strain on which was greatly increased by the crises in the Pacific and in the Near East in 1942. There was also the problem before Stalingrad of whether matériel could not be used more effectively if shipped to the Russian front than if stockpiled in England in preparation for an eventual invasion. At the Roosevelt-Churchill conference at Casablanca in January, 1943, to which Stalin turned down an invitation because of the crisis on the Russian front, the chiefs of staff saw no possibility of seaborne operations in Europe in 1943 beyond those planned for Sicily and Italy. A cross-channel invasion was finally agreed to, however, for the spring of 1944 at the next meeting of Churchill and Roosevelt which was held in Washington in May, 1943, and this plan was further developed when they met again with their staffs at Quebec the following August. At the Tehran meeting of Roosevelt, Stalin, and Churchill in November, 1943, the Russians were fully informed as to these plans, and shortly thereafter General Eisenhower was appointed to head the operation with the title of Supreme Commander, Allied Expeditionary Force.

The controversy over the second front was further complicated by the vigorous campaign which Churchill conducted for strategic reasons in favor of an invasion of the Balkans. Since the days of the Dardanelles campaign in World War I, the British prime minister had been an ardent sup-

CONFERENCE AT TEHRAN *Stalin, Roosevelt, and Churchill at Tehran, Iran, in December, 1943.*

porter of the idea of attacking the Germans from the southeast rather than from the west. During World War II he pressed for a Balkan campaign as an alternative first to the cross-channel invasion and later to the invasion of southern France from Italy, but his views were consistently opposed by the American military authorities. The Russians also expressed vigorous opposition to the idea, and drew the conclusion that Churchill's real aim was the political one of preventing Soviet domination of southeastern Europe. Churchill was not particularly inclined to submit to Russian pressure on this subject, however, for he well remembered that in the bitter spring of 1940, "without premonition of their own future, the Soviet Government watched the destruction of that 'Second Front' in the west for which they were soon to call so vehemently and to wait in agony so long."

It is difficult to determine at what point in the war unilateral action began to gain preponderance over joint determination of policy. The conditions conducive to the formation of permanent spheres of influence were created early in the war with the establishment of distinct military theaters. As between the United States and Great Britain, it was agreed as early as January, 1942, that the Pacific theater should be under American command, while a Southeast Asia theater was set up later in India under a British commander. An American general commanded the North African campaign in 1942–43, and continued in command in Sicily and Italy until the end of 1943 when Eisenhower was transferred to England to take command of the Normandy invasion. When this change was made, Italy and the eastern Mediterranean came under British command.

The Russians, for their part, established a very distinct predominance in Eastern Europe before the end of the war. Having failed to obtain recognition of the boundary changes made in Eastern Europe during 1939–41 in connection with the Anglo-Soviet treaty of May, 1942, they continued to urge their point of view. In May, 1944, Churchill offered to recognize a controlling Russian influence in Rumania in return for Soviet recognition of a similar British position in Greece. When informed of this scheme, Roosevelt objected that a balance-of-power system based on spheres of influence was not likely to form a sound basis for peace. Only after a personal appeal from Churchill did Roosevelt consent to withdraw his objections for a trial period of three months. In October the matter was pressed further by the British, and the Russians were conceded predominant influence in the three states of Rumania, Hungary, and Bulgaria. In return the Russians recognized the special British position in Greece, and agreed to a fifty-fifty division of influence in Yugoslavia. Similarly in the Far East, the Russians were granted a sphere of influence in Manchuria tentatively at the Tehran Conference and explicitly at the Yalta Conference of February, 1945.

The tendency of these military theaters to become political spheres of influence became clear when the armistice terms with the various defeated Axis states were agreed upon. In Italy, the Russians had only a small say. In the Axis satellite states of Finland, Rumania, Bulgaria, and Hungary, on the other hand, the Soviet army with explicit Anglo-American consent was given a predominant voice in political affairs until the termination of hostilities with Germany. Similarly in Germany and Austria, a division into exclusive spheres won the day over joint occupation, and the latter form of co-operation was limited to the cities of Berlin and Vienna. Likewise in the Far East, American influence was predominant in defeated Japan, while the conquered Japanese islands eventually became a trust territory under the United Nations administered by the American Navy. While it may have been sincerely intended that these zones of military command should bear no relation to the postwar settlement, the fact of their concrete existence and the inability of the allies to find any alternative solution gave these zones of command a determining influence in that settlement.

CONFERENCE AT YALTA *Roosevelt presenting the American case at the conference table at Yalta, U.S.S.R., in February, 1945. Seated at the table, starting at Roosevelt's right, are Secretary of State Stettinius and Admiral Leahy, for the United States; Gromyko, Maisky, Stalin, Molotov, and Vyshinsky, for the U.S.S.R.; and Churchill and Eden, among others, for the United Kingdom.*

CONQUEST OF GERMANY. The critical moment of the war against Germany in the west came on June 6, 1944, when five divisions under the command of General Eisenhower were landed on the beaches of Normandy. The port of Cherbourg fell three weeks later, and by the beginning of July the Allies had about 1,000,000 men in Normandy. These forces were divided into two armies, the American First Army under General Bradley and the British-Canadian Twenty-First Army Group under General Montgomery. These were soon joined by General Patton's Third Army. For a few weeks the Allies were held up by strong German opposition, first under Rundstedt and Rommel and later under Kluge, but soon they broke through and on August 19 some ten German divisions were encircled and forced to surrender. In the south, American and French forces landed on the Mediterranean coast of France on August 15, and moved rapidly north against light German opposition. Paris was liberated on August 23 and Brussels on September 3, and six months after the landings in Normandy the Allied armies were drawn up on the German frontier in a line stretching from the Maas River in the Netherlands to Switzerland.

On the eastern front, the summer and autumn of 1944 saw a rapid advance of the Russians, directed primarily towards southeastern Europe with Budapest and Vienna as objectives. While the Soviet army had from the start of the war outnumbered the Germans on the eastern front, its superiority was now about three to one—or approximately 4,500,000 Russian troops to 1,500,000 Germans. The political content of Soviet strategy became increasingly clear as they entered the territory of their neighbors in Eastern Europe. The Russians had already pressed their political advantage to the full in the Eastern European countries which were fighting on the side of the United Nations: Czechoslovakia, Poland, and Yugoslavia. With the Czechoslovak government-in-exile headed by Beneš, Russia maintained friendly relations and signed a twenty-year treaty of alliance in December, 1943. Against the exiled Polish government, however, the Soviets conducted a vigorous political campaign. When the Poles pressed for an impartial investigation of the execution of over 10,000 Polish officers, some of whose remains were discovered at Katyn near Smolensk in 1943, the Soviet government severed relations with the government-in-exile and transferred its attentions to the Communist-dominated Union of Polish Patriots established on Russian soil earlier in the war. At the end of 1944 the latter group was established in the city of Lublin as a Provisional Government, after the Russians had delayed their entry into Warsaw until the large Polish underground movement under General Bor, that was loyal to the exiled regime in London, had been destroyed by the Germans. In Yugoslavia the Soviet Union supported the Communist-controlled partisans under Tito against the nationalist guerillas led by Mihailovich, and since the Western Allies hesitantly supported both leaders Tito eventually gained the upper hand. A parallel situation existed in Albania, where the Communists under Hoxha succeeded in defeating their opponents.

While much could thus be accomplished by political warfare, the decisive steps in the military sphere were taken by the two Ukrainian armies that swept into southeastern Europe in the late summer of 1944. The Russians were aided by the bombing raids of the Fifteenth Air Force with bases in southern Italy. Rumania surrendered on August 23, after the Antonescu regime was overthrown by King Michael, and two days later Rumania declared war on Germany. Bulgaria, the only Axis satellite state which was not at war with Russia, tried to negotiate an armistice with the Western Allies on whom it had declared war in 1941. The latter were uncertain as to what they should do about Bulgaria, however, and before they could make up their minds Russia declared war on September 5. This maneuver permitted the Russians to accept Bulgaria's surrender four days later, and to occupy the country with all the rights and influence of a conqueror. The Soviet armies now continued westward, passing through Belgrade in the middle of September with the assistance of Tito, and obtaining the surrender of a dissident Hungarian government in January, 1945.

The end of 1944 found Hitler's regime in circumstances that would have brought any less fanatical leader to the point of suing for an armistice.

In both the east and the west enemies of superior strength were standing on Germany's frontiers and were girding themselves for a final onslaught in the spring of 1945, while in the south the German forces in Italy were steadily being pressed back. Already serious rifts had appeared within the ranks of the German army, where there were no doubts as to the proximity of German defeat. For some time certain anti-Nazi political leaders headed by Goerdeler and Hassell, and a group of Prussian noblemen known as the Kreisau circle, had been plotting the overthrow of Hitler. The latter, led by Stauffenberg, Moltke, and Yorck, were either officers or were closely associated with such army leaders as General Beck, a former chief of staff, who had long been seeking reasons of principle as well as of policy to rid Germany of Nazism. After numerous setbacks the plot was finally sprung on July 20, 1944, when Stauffenberg arranged for the explosion of a bomb during a conference at Hitler's headquarters. The bomb went off, but neither Hitler nor his chief aides were killed. Himmler's Gestapo immediately conducted a purge of the army in which some 5,000 persons were killed, and the full authority of the Nazis over Germany's war machine was thus restored.

Hitler now decided to make one last attempt to frustrate his enemies. He still retained the complete loyalty of his old party lieutenants, Goering, Goebbels, and Himmler. To these was added Admiral Doenitz, the creator of Germany's submarine fleet, who in the last years gained great influence with Hitler. Moreover, the German army, despite its many defeats since 1943, was still able to fight with determination. The German counter-measure in the west took the form of a vigorous thrust against the Allied line with over twenty divisions on December 16, 1944, in the Ardennes region of northern France. After a bitter battle the Germans were finally brought to a halt, but it was over a month before the Allies straightened out the "bulge" created by the initial thrust. In the east, a comparable diversion against the Russians was created by the determined German defense of the region of Budapest and Vienna, where the Soviet armies were held up from January to March, 1945. Meanwhile, a last, desperate effort was made to terrorize Great Britain from the air with the V-1 and V-2 bombs. The former, a jet-propelled flying bomb, was used between June and September, 1944, and about 7400 fell on the British killing almost 6,000 persons. The V-2's, on the other hand, were rockets. Over 1,000 crossed the Channel during the seven months after September, 1944, killing some 3,000 persons.

These last gestures of Hitler had little effect on the termination of hostilities, for once the Allied offensives got under way in the spring of 1945 nothing could stop them. In the west the first crossing of the Rhine was made on March 7, over a bridge at Remagen captured by good fortune, and by the middle of April the Ruhr industrial area was encircled. In the east the Russians advanced with equal speed. Starting in January from a line extending from East Prussia, through Warsaw, to Budapest, the main armies under Rokossovsky, Zhukov, and Konev, moved rapidly across Poland

CLOSING THE GAP IN GERMANY *American and Russian troops meeting for the first time at Torgau, Germany, on the Elbe River, in April, 1945.*

and crossed the Oder river by March 1. Further south, Vienna fell early in April. The collapse of Germany was now imminent. On April 25 American and Russian troops met at Torgau on the Elbe River, conflicts resulting from the juncture of the Soviet and Western armies having been minimized by a pre-arranged agreement regarding zones of occupation. On the 29th, the German armies in Italy surrendered. Mussolini, who had escaped to northern Italy after his fall in 1943, was captured and killed by partisans on the same day. Hitler committed suicide in Berlin on April 30 after naming Admiral Doenitz as his successor, and the latter immediately proceeded to arrange for the surrender of all the German armies. On May 7 the surrender instrument was signed by Field Marshal Jodl at Eisenhower's head-quarters in Reims, France, in the presence of American, Russian, French, and British military authorities. The surrender was to take effect within forty-eight hours, and the victory of the United Nations forces in Europe was celebrated on May 8 as V–E Day. On the 9th a final act of capitulation was ratified in Berlin under Russian auspices by the heads of the German army, navy, and air force, in the presence of representatives of the four lead-ing Allied states.

CONQUEST OF JAPAN. The fanaticism of the Japanese militarists was certainly equal to that of the Nazis, although the former suffered a greater loss of prestige at home as a result of the uninterrupted series of defeats after 1942. Upon the loss of Saipan in July, 1944, General Tojo resigned as prime minister and was succeeded by General Koiso. The latter proved un-able to rally Japan's military leaders to a firm policy, and he was suc-ceeded in turn by Admiral Suzuki in April, 1945. Suzuki fully realized that there was no longer any hope of victory and was prepared to negotiate a compromise peace. This road, however, proved to be barred to him by the Allied doctrine of unconditional surrender, and so the war in the Pacific continued.

The American, British, and Australian forces, with the aid of Chinese and Indian troops, bore the brunt of the fighting in the Pacific theater. They were at the height of their strength and full redeployment from Eu-rope was beginning to get under way. An attack was launched on Burma in August, 1944, which ended with the capture of the port of Rangoon the following May. In the main theater, MacArthur and Nimitz decided in September, 1944, that they would proceed directly to the central Philippine islands of Leyte and Luzon, by-passing and cutting off the strong Japanese forces on the southern islands. Leyte was the first target and the most criti-cal, since the Japanese were determined to cut off the invasion force under General Krueger. Admiral Toyoda called out all available forces, and in the largest naval engagement of the war challenged the two American fleets under Admirals Halsey and Kinkaid on October 23–25 in what has come to be known as the battle of Leyte Gulf. The heavy Japanese losses spelled an end to their naval power, and the occupation of Leyte proceeded unmo-lested. When MacArthur and Krueger moved on to the main island of Luzon in January, 1945, the bitter Japanese resistance on land was not matched by any comparable activity at sea or in the air. The destruction of Japanese air power and the Allied air initiative against Japan itself were greatly facilitated by the conquest of the islands of Iwo Jima and Okinawa in the spring of 1945. From the main air bases on the Marianas and from these islands a tremendous air attack was launched against the enemy's homeland. Thousands of tons of explosives and incendiaries were dropped on Japan by the Twentieth Air Force, and the country was rapidly being reduced to ruins.

Despite these rapid and overwhelming Allied successes, the military conquest of the Japanese mainland might have required a long and costly

JAPANESE SURRENDER *Japanese Delegation aboard the U.S.S. Missouri in Tokyo Bay, September 2, 1945, being presented with the surrender documents. General Percival (Britain), General Wainwright (U.S.), and General MacArthur (U.S.), are in foreground.*

campaign, which was in fact in full preparation, had it not been for the use of the atomic bomb. President Roosevelt had done everything possible to develop this weapon before his death on April 12 and, upon learning of the successful experiment in New Mexico, President Truman and Churchill promptly authorized its use against Japan. The first bomb was dropped on Hiroshima on August 6 with catastrophic results. Seeing that Japan would soon have to surrender, the Russians declared war two days later and invaded Manchuria. A second bomb on Nagasaki convinced the Japanese that further resistance was useless, and on August 14 they accepted the Allied terms. The surrender document was formally signed in Tokyo Bay on the USS *Missouri* on September 2, 1945, in the presence of American, British, Chinese, Russian, and other Allied representatives.

V

POST
WORLD WAR II
EUROPE

CHAPTER

23

The United Nations Organization

Drafting of the Charter: *Beginning of the United Nations; The San Francisco Conference.*

Structure of the United Nations Organization: *Membership; General Assembly; Security Council; Economic and Social Council; Specialized Agencies; International Atomic Energy Commission; Other UN Organizations; Trusteeship Council; The Secretariat; Amendment.*

Pacific Settlement of Disputes: *Charter Provisions; Use of Armed Forces; Regionalism.*

The International Court of Justice: *Membership; Election of Judges; Jurisdiction.*

◆

Between the day of its founding and the outbreak of war in 1939 twenty-one states had been added to the list of original members of the League of Nations. This meant that most of the nations of the world were, a one time or another, affiliated with that body. But over against this gain in membership must be set fifteen withdrawals, among which were some of the leading powers of the world. By the start of the war Japan, Germany, and Italy were no longer members; Hungary had served notice of withdrawal and was to be followed by Rumania a few months later (July 11, 1940). Only Finland and Bulgaria among the so-called "Axis Powers and Their Satellites" retained their membership in the League. On the other hand, the opponents of the Axis at the start of the war were all members of the League and continued to support that institution; in fact, for a time they infused new life into it. When Finland called on the League for aid after being attacked by the USSR, the League with unprecedented zeal expelled the Soviet Union from membership (December 14, 1939). This meant that Russia in the future would hold a special grudge against the League. When the fortunes of war brought both the USSR and the United States into the anti-Axis coalition, the balance of Allied power lay with these two states that were not members of the League. It seemed far easier to build a world organization anew than to rehabilitate the old in view of all the existing prejudices against the League.

Drafting of the Charter

BEGINNING OF THE UNITED NATIONS. If the aggressive policies of the Axis powers tore the old League apart, its successor, the United Nations, grew out of the anti-Axis war coalition. Immediately after the United States entered the conflict, the twenty-six states then at war with the Axis drew up a statement of policy. This "Declaration by United Nations" was signed at Washington on January 1, 1942, and was subsequently adhered to by twenty-one states as they were drawn into the war on the side of the Allies. In fact it was this group of states, with a few additions, which constituted the charter members of the United Nations organization [see Appendix IV].

The Declaration of 1942 as a reaffirmation of the principles of the Atlantic Charter and a promise not to make a separate armistice or peace with the enemy. From time to time leading statesmen made statements pointing toward a future world organization, but it was not until the Moscow Conference of October, 1943, that an official communiqué dealt with the subject. Here the representatives of the USSR, the United Kingdom, the United States, and China proclaimed ". . . the necessity of establishing at the earliest practicable date a general international organization. . . ." A month later at the Tehran Conference, Churchill, Stalin, and Roosevelt confirmed this declaration.

As a step toward implementing the Moscow declaration, Secretary Hull invited representatives of the USSR, the United Kingdom, and China to join in exploratory conversations at a conference to be held at an estate called Dumbarton Oaks, in Washington, D.C. Ostensibly the Soviet authorities did not want to jeopardize their neutrality policy toward Japan, and so they refused to participate at the same conference table with the Chinese. It was not an auspicious beginning for an organization aimed at establishing co-operation among all nations. The Dumbarton Oaks Conference, therefore, was run in two shifts. From August 21 to September 28, 1944, representatives from the USSR, the United Kingdom, and the

United States discussed a draft plan. Then the Chinese replaced the Russians and discussions continued until October 7. By the end general agreement had been reached, except for the matter of voting procedure, and the "Dumbarton Oaks Proposals" were made public for discussion and study.

At the Yalta Conference in February, 1945, three important decisions in regard to the future world organization were reached. First, a plan was made for voting procedure which caused much debate when it was subsequently written into the Charter. Secondly, Roosevelt and Churchill promised Stalin that they would support separate membership in the organization for the Byelorussian and Ukrainian Soviet Socialist Republics. The Russians felt that, in view of separate representatives from each of the dominions of the British Commonwealth of Nations, the member states of the USSR should receive a separate vote. On a similar basis the United States might have claimed forty-eight members, and therefore Stalin settled for representation for only two of the more important members of the Soviet Union. In return he was willing to allow the United States two additional votes, a concession that was never used. Finally, it was decided to call a conference to meet at San Francisco on April 25, 1945, to prepare a Charter along the lines suggested by the Dumbarton Oaks Proposals. On Russian insistence, only those states which had declared war on either Germany or Japan by March 1, 1945, and had signed the "Declaration by United Nations" were to be invited to attend. Thanks to this pressure, Turkey, Egypt, Saudi Arabia, and various other nations declared war on Germany so that in the future they too might be classed among the "peace-loving nations" [see Appendices IV and VI].

THE SAN FRANCISCO CONFERENCE. Neither pressure from the closing campaigns of the European War nor the sudden tragic death of President Roosevelt (April 12, 1945) prevented the San Francisco Conference from opening as scheduled. In spite of previous agreement as to what states should be invited, the problem of membership caused some difficulty. The Russian delegation wanted representatives from the Lublin Polish Government to be seated, but this was refused by the United States and Britain, as that government had not yet been broadened according to the agreement reached at Yalta. Poland, which had been fighting the Axis longer than any state, was the one member of the United Nations which was to have no part in drawing up the Charter. In line with a decision reached at a Pan-American Congress held at Chapultepec, Mexico, a few weeks earlier, the United States and the Latin American states supported the admission of Argentina to the Conference. The USSR finally agreed and was rewarded by official recognition of Byelorussia and the Ukraine as members of the United Nations. Denmark was welcomed to membership after Germany's surrender. Sweden, Switzerland, Spain, Eire, and Portugal had no one to plead their cause and, along with the enemy states, were the notable absentees. The Charter was thus the work of the victorious nations, and various articles are directed specifically against their former enemies.

The Conference divided into numerous commissions and committees. The delegates worked hard and furiously with the aid of an able staff of experts. English and French were the working languages, and in addition many documents were published in Russian, Chinese, and Spanish. On an average about a half million sheets of paper were used daily to document the proceedings. The surrender of Germany brought many new urgent problems to the fore which demanded the attention of the leading statesmen. There was little chance for extended debate, and the decisions of the great powers carried the day. But in spite of all this, the Charter which was adopted in a plenary session and signed by the various delegations on June 26, 1945, is generally held to be a real improvement over the Dumbarton Oaks Proposals. It was, as all such documents are, the result of compromise. With the war still going on in the Far East and the atom bomb still a secret, some of the points seemed less important than they proved to be at a later date.

Structure of the United Nations Organization[1]

The Charter of the United Nations begins by stating the purposes and principles of the organization to be: (1) the maintenance of peace and security; (2) the development of friendly relations between nations; (3) the furtherance of international co-operation in solving problems of an economic, social, cultural, or humanitarian character; and (4) the establishment of a center for harmonizing the actions of nations. The organization is definitely declared to be based on the sovereign equality of its members; it acts through states, not directly on the peoples of the world. While the terms of reference under which a matter may be brought before the United Nations are broad, there is one very important limitation. Under Article 2, paragraph 7, the organization is forbidden "to intervene in matters which are essentially within the domestic jurisdiction of any state" nor can the members be required "to submit such matters to settlement under the present charter." This leaves great latitude for debate as to what matters fall within domestic jurisdiction. It has led to bitter disputes over agenda, but it may have served a purpose by making it possible to sidestep irreconcilable differences.

MEMBERSHIP. The original members of the United Nations constitute those fifty countries which participated in the San Francisco Conference, with the addition of Poland which signed the Charter in October, 1945. Membership in the organization "is open to all other peace-loving states" on recommendation by the Security Council and a two-thirds vote of the Assembly. In the Security Council a recommendation for membership requires a total of seven votes with all five of the great powers which have permanent membership either approving or abstaining from voting. This gives to each of the major powers an absolute veto on new members, a

[1] The authors have drawn heavily on the excellent volume by Leland M. Goodrich and Edvard Hambro: *Charter of the United Nations: Commentary and Documents* (2nd and rev. ed., Boston, 1949).

power they have repeatedly used. Up to 1955 nine states were admitted to membership, while the applications of twenty-one states were refused. Unfortunately the ability of each state to assume its obligations under the Charter was hardly considered, for membership became involved in the conflict for and against communism which divided the world. Finally in December, 1955, a package deal was arranged under which sixteen states were admitted to membership, the number being about equally divided among protégés of the USSR and of the Western powers. Having reached an agreement with Japan on ending the state of war (1956), Russia no longer vetoed Japan's application, and Japan as well as various new African and Asian states were subsequently admitted to membership. Switzerland, which has never applied for admission, the Chinese People's Republic, and the two Republics in Korea, in Vietnam, and in Germany are among the most notable absentees from the roster of the world organization. [See Appendix IV for list of members and the dates of admission to the UN.]

Any member state that has persistently violated the principles of the Charter can be expelled from membership by the Assembly on recommendation of the Security Council. On the other hand, no definite provision was made for a state to withdraw from membership although it was generally held that the right to do so was implied. Nonmember states can become affiliated with the specialized agencies of the United Nations and seven of them (German Federal Republic, Liechtenstein, Monaco, South Korea, South Vietnam, San Marino, and Switzerland) have done so.

Indonesia was the first to resign from the United Nations. It had strenuously opposed the establishment of the state of Malaysia (1963) and, when this state was given one of the elective seats on the Security Council, Indonesia made good its threats by formally withdrawing on January 21, 1965, from the United Nations and from the specialized agencies of which it was a member, the resignation to be effective March 1, 1966. It soon resumed membership, however, with the consent of the Assembly in September of the same year.

GENERAL ASSEMBLY. Each member of the United Nations can send not more than five representatives to the General Assembly but in all cases has only one vote. "On important questions," such as recommendations in regard to peace and security, a two-thirds majority of members present and voting is required, while on lesser issues a mere majority suffices. The Assembly has been given broad powers, and under Article 10 "may discuss any questions or any matters within the scope of the present charter." It can make recommendations to member states or to the Security Council, but the right to make such recommendations does not apply to any dispute that is on the agenda of the Security Council. Recommendations of the Assembly are not binding; there is no power to carry them out, except the force of public opinion and the willingness of disputing powers to co-operate.

The General Assembly meets in regular annual session the third Tuesday in September and in special sessions as occasion requires. It meets at

UNITED NATIONS GENERAL ASSEMBLY *The seventh session of the General Assembly opens in October, 1952, with a moment of silence.*

the headquarters of the United Nations in New York City unless the Assembly at a previous session decides on another place of meeting. The assembly appoints many standing, as well as temporary *ad hoc*, committees. With the Security Council hamstrung by mutual hostility and frequent use of the veto by the permanent members, the Assembly has gained in stature. Its activities have increased beyond expectations; to enable it to fulfill its obligations, the United States delegation proposed in 1947 the establishment of an Interim Committee to be made up of one representative from each state. This committee would deal with matters referred to it by the General Assembly and in general would represent that body when it was not in session. This "Little Assembly" plan was strongly opposed by the USSR and other East European states as an attempt to circumvent the Security Council. The Committee however was established and has been helpful in some instances.

More important in strengthening the Assembly was the "Uniting for Peace" resolution adopted in November, 1950. Under this resolution, when the Security Council has failed to act because of a veto by one of the permanent members, an emergency session of the Assembly can be called on twenty-four hours' notice at the request of seven members of the Council or a majority of the Assembly. The Assembly was authorized to make "appropriate recommendations to members for collective measures, including, in the case of a breach of the peace or an act of aggression, the use of armed force." The significance of the Uniting for Peace resolution is that no deadlock can arise because of the negative vote of one of the great powers; recommendations in the Assembly are carried by a two-thirds vote. A Peace Observation Commission was also established to report on international tension anywhere in the world.

SECURITY COUNCIL. The Charter made no pretense of granting each state equal power within the United Nations. This is brought out most clearly in the provisions establishing the Security Council. The United States, Britain, Russia, France, and China were made permanent members, with six other members (increased to ten in 1965) elected by the Assembly for two-year terms [see below under Amendment, p. 598]. The latter were to be chosen with reference to their contribution to the maintenance of peace and security and also with a view to providing geographical distribution. The procedure for voting, as decided upon at Yalta after much debate and many explanations, was written into the Charter. Each member of the Council was to have one vote. On procedural matters a vote of any seven members (nine after 1965) sufficed, but on all other matters decisions were to be "made by an affirmative vote of seven members [nine after 1965] including the concurring votes of the permanent members." This meant that in these matters each of the great powers had the right of veto, a right which at that time was as much desired by the United States and Britain as by Russia. The Charter heads Articles 28–32 with the word "Procedure," and, therefore, questions arising under these particular articles and dealing with organizational issues were considered to be "procedural matters." In practice there has been much debate as to what comes under these articles. Since deciding what is "procedural" is considered a substantive matter (that is, nonprocedural), not many things of importance have escaped the necessity of an affirmative vote of the great powers.

As voting developed in practice, some rather technical interpretations have been made. A great power may abstain from voting without defeating a measure if there are seven other affirmative votes. This enables a power to withhold its approval, although it does not exercise its right to veto. A difference of opinion has also developed over the interpretation of the veto. The Western powers claim that a veto is a negative vote by a permanent member that defeats a motion that would otherwise pass. If enough powers vote in the negative to defeat the measure, no one vote can be considered a veto. Under this interpretation the United States, for example, did not cast a veto until March 17, 1970, when it joined with the United Kingdom in voting against an African-Asian sponsored resolution which would have condemned the British government for not using force to oust the "rebel" regime of Prime Minister Ian D. Smith in Rhodesia [see below, pp. 847–48].[2] Russia, on the other hand, considers that many negative votes by the United States have contributed to the defeat of a measure and therefore constitute a veto. Since Russia has often cast the sole negative vote among the great powers, the Western interpretation has led to widespread criticism of the so-called veto power. Again, when it comes to a pacific settlement of disputes, a party to a dispute must abstain from voting. This apparent limitation of the veto, however, is set aside by the fact that technically both "situations" and "disputes" come before the Council. In a "situation" a power involved in the disagreement is not required to abstain from voting, and it is a substantive question (subject to veto) for the Council to decide whether a particular issue is a "situation" or "dispute." All this might seem like a mere technicality, but because of phraseology it is impossible under the Charter to charge a great power or its protégé as an aggressor state and to take punitive action against it, if that great power chooses (as may be expected) to exercise its veto.

The Security Council was designed to be the most powerful agency of the United Nations. It is predicated on the assumption that the great powers of the wartime coalition must co-operate in the maintenance of peace and that without such co-operation no world government can succeed. Whatever the shortcomings of the United Nations may be, this represents a more realistic attitude toward the prerequisites of peace than the League of Nations Covenant.

ECONOMIC AND SOCIAL COUNCIL. Perhaps of more important in preserving peace than some of the agencies specifically devised to deal with aggression is the Economic and Social Council. It is empowered to get at some of the roots of war by initiating studies and reports "with respect to international economic, social, cultural, educational, health and related matters" and to make recommendations to the General Assembly, to individual members of the United Nations, or to specialized agencies. Its essential function is to facilitate voluntary co-operation, and the Council itself can make no decision that binds a member. The Council is made up of eighteen (twenty-seven after 1965) members elected by the Assembly

---

[2] On this particular vote there were 9 in favor, 2 against, and 4 abstentions. The vote of either the United Kingdom or the United States would have been sufficient to kill the resolution, but it is the United Nations practice to record the votes as a veto by each. Up to March 17, 1970, the permanent members of the Security Council had cast the following number of vetos: the Soviet Union, 105; the United Kingdom, 4; France, 3; Nationalist China, 2; and the United States, 1.

for three-year terms, one-third being elected each year. A retiring member is eligible for immediate re-election, but there is no provision assuring the great powers of representation on the Council. All decisions are taken by a majority vote of members, and the great powers have no veto.

The Economic and Social Council is empowered to appoint such commissions, standing and *ad hoc* committees, and such other bodies as are necessary to carry on its work. Among some of those appointed are the Economic and Employment Commission, Transport and Communications Commission, Statistical Commission, Commission on Human Rights, Social Commission, Commission on the Status of Women, Commission on Narcotic Drugs, Fiscal Commission, Population Commission, Economic Commission for Europe, Economic Commission for Asia and the Far East, and Economic Commission for Latin America. These commissions with their subcommissions hold public meetings, initiate studies, and submit reports. Unfortunately, the commissions are staffed by representatives appointed by states, rather than by experts selected by the Secretary-General of the United Nations. Not all are political appointees, however, and many competent men, fully conversant with the work of the commission, are named to serve.

SPECIALIZED AGENCIES. During the war the Allied powers had established organizations to deal with certain problems. Thus, a conference in Hot Springs, Virginia, in 1943, gave rise to an International Food and Agricultural Organization, and the Bretton Woods (New Hampshire) Conference of 1944 led to an International Fund and Bank. In the Charter it was provided that the Economic and Social Council should conclude agreements with these organizations and other similar international bodies. One such body, the United Nations Relief and Rehabilitation Administration (UNRRA) was liquidated in 1947. The Council can also supervise the establishment of new organizations, and the World Health Organization is the result of such action. These bodies, when they are brought under the United Nations, are technically known as Specialized Agencies and their relationship to the United Nations varies according to the negotiated agreements. Membership in these specialized agencies does not result from belonging to the United Nations, and some members cooperate in only a limited number of them. On the other hand, states which are not members of the UN can, and often do, join the specialized agencies. Each agency has its own charter, its own administrative organs, and its own budget, the latter being subject to review by the General Assembly. Staffed by experts, the specialized agencies have made a signal contribution to the accomplishments of the United Nations.

The International Telecommunication Union (1865), the Universal Postal Union (1874), and the International Labor Organization (1919) are three old organizations which have now been tied to the United Nations as specialized agencies. The former International Meteorological Organization (1878) was transformed into a new World Meteorological Organization in 1951 as a specialized agency. Other international bodies,

THE UNITED NATIONS SYSTEM

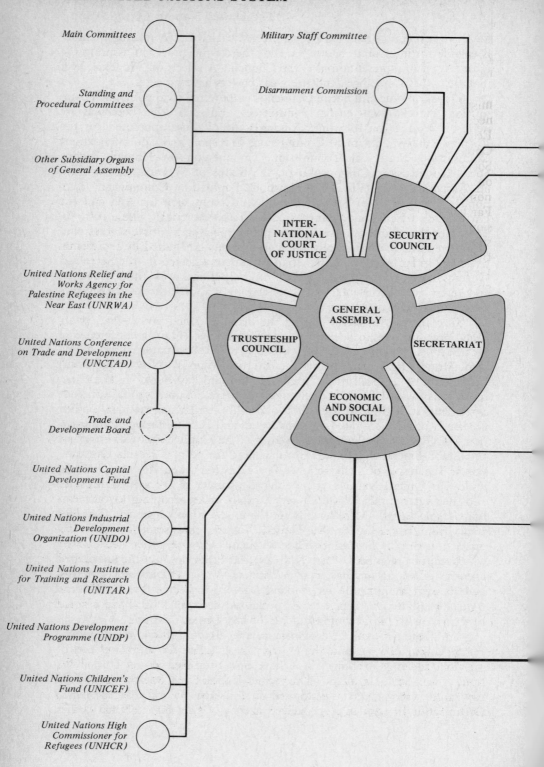

Main Committees

Standing and
Procedural Committees

Other Subsidiary Organs
of General Assembly

Military Staff Committee

Disarmament Commission

INTER-
NATIONAL
COURT
OF JUSTICE

SECURITY
COUNCIL

GENERAL
ASSEMBLY

TRUSTEESHIP
COUNCIL

SECRETARIAT

ECONOMIC
AND SOCIAL
COUNCIL

United Nations Relief and
Works Agency for
Palestine Refugees in the
Near East (UNRWA)

United Nations Conference
on Trade and Development
(UNCTAD)

Trade and
Development Board

United Nations Capital
Development Fund

United Nations Industrial
Development
Organization (UNIDO)

United Nations Institute
for Training and Research
(UNITAR)

United Nations Development
Programme (UNDP)

United Nations Children's
Fund (UNICEF)

United Nations High
Commissioner for
Refugees (UNHCR)

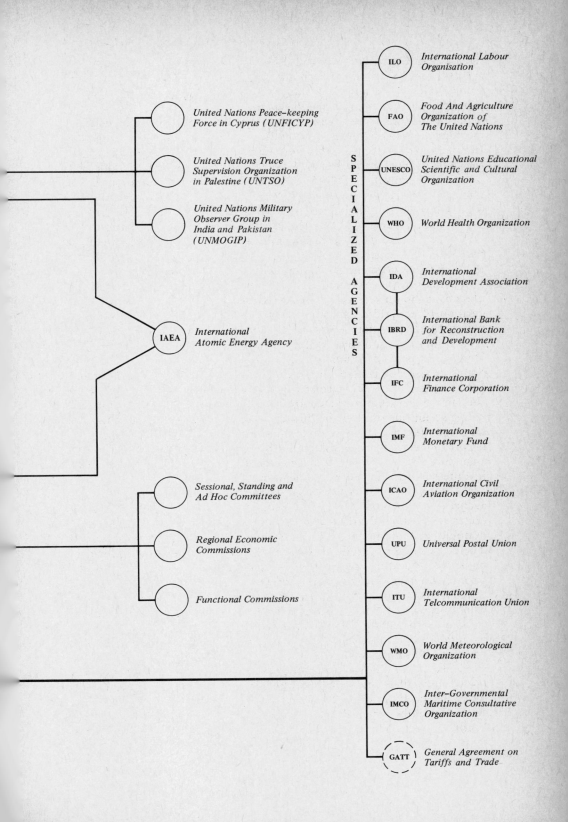

United Nations Peace–keeping
Force in Cyprus (UNFICYP)

United Nations Truce
Supervision Organization
in Palestine (UNTSO)

United Nations Military
Observer Group in
India and Pakistan
(UNMOGIP)

IAEA · International
Atomic Energy Agency

Sessional, Standing and
Ad Hoc Committees

Regional Economic
Commissions

Functional Commissions

**S
P
E
C
I
A
L
I
Z
E
D

A
G
E
N
C
I
E
S**

ILO · International Labour
Organisation

FAO · Food And Agriculture
Organization of
The United Nations

UNESCO · United Nations Educational
Scientific and Cultural
Organization

WHO · World Health Organization

IDA · International
Development Association

IBRD · International Bank
for Reconstruction
and Development

IFC · International
Finance Corporation

IMF · International
Monetary Fund

ICAO · International Civil
Aviation Organization

UPU · Universal Postal Union

ITU · International
Telcommunication Union

WMO · World Meteorological
Organization

IMCO · Inter–Governmental
Maritime Consultative
Organization

GATT · General Agreement on
Tariffs and Trade

such as the *Office international d'Hygiène public* and the International Institute of Agriculture, which for many years had its headquarters in Rome, have been absorbed into the newly created organizations. To complete the list of specialized agencies will indicate what a far-reaching field the Economic and Social Council touches through these bodies. They include: the International Bank for Reconstruction and Development; the International Finance Corporation (established in 1956 and affiliated with the Bank); the International Monetary Fund; the International Civil Aviation Organization (ICAO); the United Nations Educational, Scientific and Cultural Organization (UNESCO); the Intergovernmental Maritime Consultative Organization (ratified 1958); and the International Trade Organization (ITO). The ratification of the draft charter for the latter agency was delayed, but in the meantime an Interim Commission for the ITO undertook to administer an international commercial treaty, the General Agreement on Tariffs and Trade (GATT).

INTERNATIONAL ATOMIC ENERGY COMMISSION. As a follow-up of President Eisenhower's speech to the UN General Assembly in 1953 for the creation of a world organization to promote the peaceful uses of nuclear power, the International Atomic Energy Agency (IAEA) was established. Its statute came into force in July, 1957, and headquarters were set up in Vienna. A pool of fissionable materials was established, and the United States at the first general meeting of the agency promised to match the contributions of all other countries through July 1, 1960. It still remains the largest contributor among the approximately 90 member states, providing about one-third of the budget. The IAEA is not one of the specialized agencies but is an autonomous international organization with a negotiated working relationship with the United Nations to which it makes an annual report. The working agreement between the two bodies provides in different ways for close co-operation.

OTHER UN ORGANIZATIONS. There are a bewildering number of agencies, commissions, boards, and committees that have been established under the United Nations and are entirely its creatures. There are, for example, five international organs dealing with the regulation of narcotics. There is also an important Technical Assistance Board, which provides on request technical assistance to undeveloped countries in economic affairs, public administration, or social welfare.

TRUSTEESHIP COUNCIL. To supervise the administration of territories whose peoples have not yet attained a full measure of self-government, an elaborate Trusteeship System was established. It was intended to provide an intelligent and enlightened basis for the administration of non-self-governing territories with a view toward rendering them capable of independence. It covers such territories from the following categories as are placed under it by individual agreement: (1) former mandates, (2) territories detached from enemy states, and (3) territories placed under the system by states responsible for their administration. The trustee system is headed by a council made up of representatives from governments which administer trust territories and an equal number of representatives elected by the Assembly from nontrustee states. Each of the five permanent members of the Security Council must be represented in one or the other category. Decisions in the Trusteeship Council are taken by majority vote, and no power has a right to veto. This Council hears reports from the administering authorities, accepts and examines petitions from the natives, and provides for periodic visits. Its duty is also to formulate a questionnaire on the political, economic, social, and educational advancement of the inhabitants of each trust territory. This has the great advantage of providing comparative information, for the answers to these questionnaires are the basis of the annual report to the General Assembly by the administering authority.

A territory comes under the trustee system only after an agreement is negotiated, and there is no compulsion for an administering state to do this. Three of the Class A mandates under the League of Nations—Lebanon, Syria, and Iraq—became members of the United Nations and so were specifically exempted from the trusteeship system by Article 78 of the Charter. Two erstwhile Class A mandates, Palestine and Transjordan, have been reorganized into the states of Israel and Jordan, both now far beyond the state of trusteeship. Of the eleven territories held under B and C mandates, ten were placed under the trusteeship system by the administering states: United Kingdom (Togoland, the Cameroons, Tanganyika); France (Togoland, the Cameroons); Belgium (Ruanda-Urundi); Australia (the mandate covering Northeastern Guinea, New Ireland, New Britain, and the Solomon Islands); New Zealand (Western Samoa); Australia with the United Kingdom and New Zealand (Nauru); United States (the mandate covering the Mariana, Caroline, and Marshall Islands). In the trusteeship agreement negotiated by the United States for the former German islands mandated to Japan, these islands were declared a strategic area. Under the Charter this brings the areas under the supervision of the Security Council rather than the General Assembly. The United States is thus able to exercise its veto if any proposals contrary to its wishes are made in respect to these territories. The Union of South Africa steadfastly refused to negotiate a trusteeship agreement for South West Africa, over which it held a mandate, and soon took steps toward uniting this former German colony with the Union. This led to difficulties for South Africa within the United Nations.

Outside the former mandated areas no other territories except former Italian Somaliland were placed under the trusteeship system (1950). The agreements negotiated with the trustee states varied greatly, as for that matter did the provisions of the League mandates. On the whole they provided for an intelligent and enlightened legal basis for the administration of non-self-governing territories. A practice was also established for members of the UN responsible for administering non-self-governing territories to submit regularly to the Secretary-General information on economic, social, and educational conditions in these territories.

THE SECRETARIAT. To coordinate the work of the United Nations Organization and perform the necessary day by day tasks, the Charter provides for a Secretariat to act as an administrative staff. The Secretary-General is appointed by the Assembly on the recommendation of the Security Council. The Charter makes no mention of the term of the Secretary-General, but a precedent was established when Trygve Lie, a Norwegian appointed as the first incumbent of this office, was named for a five-year period. As the chief administrative officer of the organization the Secretary-General has to do with directing all meetings of the various UN bodies; he draws up an annual report to the Assembly and can on his own initiative bring to the attention of the Security Council any matter that he considers dangerous to international peace and security. In making appointments to the staff of the Secretariat, the Secretary-General is authorized to give paramount consideration to securing the highest standards of efficiency, competence, and integrity, due regard being paid to recruiting the staff on as wide a geographical basis as possible. Examinations have been devised and a real basis has been laid for establishing an International Civil Service system. Staffs are assigned to the various organs of the United Nations on a permanent basis, but they constitute a part of the Secretariat and remain under the direction of the Secretary-General.

AMENDMENT. The Charter can be amended, but that process is so difficult to achieve that it seems unlikely that the structure or scope of the organization will be radically changed in the future by this method. More can perhaps be expected in this line from a liberal interpretation of the document as it now stands. The Assembly has found it possible to pass "resolutions" on many issues and the Council has enacted "recommendations" that were not foreseen but have carried great weight. Amendments must be "adopted by two thirds of the members of the General Assembly and ratified in accordance with their respective constitutional processes by two thirds of the members of the United Nations, including all the permanent members of the Security Council." Provision is made for the possibility of calling a conference to review the present Charter, but all alterations so suggested would still require approval of two-thirds of the members including all permanent members of the Council. This means, of course, that any of the present great powers holds an absolute veto on Charter amendments. In 1955 the Assembly provided for a committee which was to fix a time, place, and procedure for a conference to review the Charter. The life of the committee was subsequently extended and in the fall of 1963 it reported to the General Assembly that ". . . there was a general agreement that the existing international circumstances were still not propitious for holding a general conference for the purpose of reviewing the Charter. . . ." It did draw the attention of the Assembly to the general feeling among member states that the ". . . Security Council and the Economic Council should reflect better the increase in the number of United Nations Members, in particular those from Africa and Asia. . . ." The committee was continued.

On December 13, 1963, the Assembly "bearing in mind the conclusions and recommendations of the committee" adopted proposals to amend the Charter so as to increase the membership of the Security Council from eleven to fifteen members and the Economic and Social Council from eighteen to twenty-seven members. Member states were called upon to ratify the amendments by September 1, 1965. The Assembly further decided, although it was not part of an amendment, that henceforth ". . . the ten non-permanent members of the Security Council shall be elected according to the following pattern: (a) five from African and Asian States; (b) one from Eastern European States; (c) two from Latin American States; (d) two from Western European and other States." Without prejudice to the previous distribution of seats in the Economic and Social Council, of the nine additional members, seven were to be allotted to African and Asian States, one to Latin America, and one to "Western European and other States." By September 1, 1965, 94 of the 114 member states, among them the permanent members of the Security Council, had ratified the amendments, which thus became effective.

Pacific Settlement of Disputes

CHARTER PROVISIONS. The Charter centers the maintenance of peace and security on the obligation of member states to seek a solution of their disputes "by negotiation, enquiry, mediation, conciliation, arbitration, judicial settlement, resort to regional agencies or arrangements, or other peaceful means of their own choice." If a dispute or situation is brought to the attention of the Security Council by a member state or by the Secretary-General, the Council will normally recommend that the parties follow one of the pacific methods of settlement. Without being subject to a veto of any power, the Security Council will "discuss" a dispute or situation, but an investigation or recommendation may be defeated by any of the permanent members. If no settlement is reached and the Security Council decides that international peace is endangered, it may, if agreement can be obtained, call upon members "to comply with such provisional measures as it deems necessary, . . . without prejudice to the rights, claims, or position of the parties concerned." To lend weight to its decisions the Security Council can recommend measures not involving use of armed force, such as "complete or partial interruption of economic relations and of rail, sea, air, postal, telegraphic, radio, and other means of communications, and the severance of diplomatic relations." Should such measures be thought inadequate the Council may take "such action by air, sea, or land forces as may be necessary to maintain or restore international peace and security."

USE OF ARMED FORCES. Each member state is obligated to furnish "armed forces, assistance and facilities, including rights of passage as determined" by agreements. The Security Council requested the Military Staff Committee, consisting of the chiefs of staff of the permanent members of the Security Council or their representatives, to study this problem and draw up a pilot agreement. This involved establishing the kind and quantity of the armed forces which were to be put at the disposal of the Security Council and where they were to be stationed. After over a year's work the Committee made a report formulated in forty-one articles. While unanimous agreement on many of these articles was not achieved and an International Police Force has not been created, the Military Staff Committee continues to meet regularly, but comes to no conclusions. The UN, however, soon found it necessary to organize special forces to act as truce observers and to carry out peace-keeping operations, as in Kashmir, in Palestine, in the Congo, and in Cyprus [see below, pp. 811–58].

REGIONALISM. It is expressly stated that until the Council has time to act, there is nothing in the Charter which impairs "the inherent right of individual or collective self-defense if an armed attack occurs." By this and other articles the formations of regional groups is not only recognized but encouraged. Members are urged to achieve pacific settlement of local disputes through regional arrangements, the Security Council being kept informed of all such actions.

Much can be said for and against the use of such regional groupings. For one thing, they have an historical background; in the past we have had alliances such as the Locarno Agreements, Balkan Ententes, Pan American Unions. Often these bodies can deal with local problems very successfully. On the other hand, very often these local groups are directed against some particular state, and they divide the nations of the world into power blocs. Instead of increasing the unity of a world organization, they split it into segments and make the pacific settlement of disputes more difficult than ever. Such early regional agreements as the Organization of American States seemed innocuous enough, but alliances such as the North American Treaty Organization (NATO) and the Warsaw Pact were less easily fitted into the UN system [see below, pp. 633–38 and Appendix VII].

The International Court of Justice

Before the San Francisco Conference there had been some question whether it was desirable to establish a new court or to continue the old Permanent Court of International Justice established in 1919. It was finally decided to create a new body, and the Charter expressly established the International Court of Justice as an organ of the United Nations. The Charter contains only a few provisions in regard to membership and jurisdiction, the detailed organization being left for elaboration in a separate statute. Actually there is little difference between the old and new courts, and, as in the past, the seat of the Court is at The Hague.

MEMBERSHIP. All members of the United Nations are *ipso facto* members of the Court. States that are not members of the United Nations may join the Court under conditions laid down by the Assembly and upon recommendation by the Security Council. In 1948, Switzerland became the first nonmember of the United Nations to join the International Court. The terms of admission required the Swiss to accept the provisions of the Court Statute and also Article 94 of the Charter which defines the obligations of member states to abide by decisions of the Court. Switzerland is also to assume its equitable share of the expenses of the Court. Liechtenstein and San Marino are the only other non-United Nations members who have joined the Court (1958).

States which are not members of the Court can bring cases before it under conditions laid down by the Security Council. The Council has required the deposit of a declaration expressing willingness to accept the jurisdiction of the Court as laid down in the Charter and in the Statute and Rules of the Court. For example, the Polish government, at that time (1946) represented on the Council, attempted to bar Franco Spain from appearing before the Court. This was defeated and indicates an intention to make access to the Court independent of political considerations.

ELECTION OF JUDGES. The Court consists of fifteen judges elected for a term of nine years, one-third retiring every three years. Nominations are made by the national groups in the Permanent Court of Arbitration [see above, pp. 154–55]. No group may nominate more than four members of whom only two can be of their own nationality. These nominees are then presented to the Security Council and Assembly, and any candidate receiving an absolute majority in both bodies is elected. Elaborate provisions are made for the selection of judges which apparently foresee every eventuality under which difficulties in election might occur.

Provision is made that not more than one judge from any national group shall sit on the bench at any time. Care is also to be taken that the main forms of civilization and the principal legal systems of the world are represented on the panel. If a dispute comes before the Court when the bench includes no judge of the nationality of the party concerned, that party may select one judge, preferably from among those persons who had been nominated as candidates for the regular elections. In 1965 there were on the Court six judges from Europe, three from Asia, three from North and South America, one from Australia, and two from Africa.

JURISDICTION. Only states and not individuals may bring cases before the Court. Jurisdiction of the Court extends to "all cases which the parties refer to it and all matters specially provided for in the Charter of the United Nations or in treaties and conventions in force." This latter phrase indicates clearly the close relationship between the new and the old world courts. In the years between the wars countless treaties and agreements had provided for reference to the Permanent Court of International Justice. All these cases will now come before the new International Court of Justice. The rule for Compulsory Jurisdiction remains the same and declarations made to the old court were transferred for the period which they still had to run.[3] It was largely due to the stand taken by the United States and Russia at the San Francisco Conference that acceptance of the Compulsory Jurisdiction of the Court was not written into the Statute. It therefore remains optional, and declarations accepting Compulsory Jurisdiction "may be made unconditionally or on condition of reciprocity on the part of several or certain states, or for a certain time." As in the past these declarations vary in content and scope. The United States in its declaration of August, 1946, specifically excluded "disputes with regard to matters which are essentially within the domestic jurisdiction of the United States of America as determined by the United States of America."

Like the old court the new International Court of Justice can also be asked by United Nations agencies to give advisory opinions on any legal question [see above, pp. 155–56]; no individual state can ask for such an advisory opinion. Decisions are made by a majority vote of the judges and are based on the generally accepted principles of international law.

[3] For a list of declarations currently in force see latest issue of the *International Court of Justice Yearbook*.

CHAPTER

24

Negotiations for Peace

Postwar Balance of Power: *End of the Coalition; Yalta and Potsdam; London, Moscow, and Paris; Division of Europe.*

The European Peace Treaties: *Italy and the Axis Satellites; The Problem of Central Europe; Austrian State Treaty; Toward a German Settlement.*

The Japanese Peace Treaty: *Principles of a Settlement; Occupation Policy; The Japanese Settlement.*

Postwar Balance of Power

 END OF THE COALITION. In considering Allied diplomacy during and after the war, what is remarkable is not that the Western democracies and the Soviet Union failed to reach any general agreement as to the postwar organization of Europe, but rather that they were able to maintain their coalition until the end of the war with so few alarms and disagreements. It is now clear that the success of the coalition must be attributed more to the immediacy and gravity of the common danger represented by the military might of Germany and Japan than to any harmony of opinion among the Allies regarding the political bases of a stable peace. During the long period since the winter of 1917–18, when the Bolsheviks had negotiated a separate peace with the Central Powers, agreement between Russia and the West had been the exception rather than the rule. Close cooperation had been achieved almost as a last

resort in the face of an immediate threat to their security, and once the
enemy was defeated the differences in political outlook that had been
temporarily overlooked inevitably reappeared. Indeed, the great sacrifices
the war had demanded from each participant made the complete fulfillment of the divergent political objectives appear all the more imperative to each of the victors.

The policy of the United States regarding the organization of the
peace was clear enough by the end of 1945, and the influence its power had
achieved by this time gave American views a determining position among
the Western democracies. The principal motive of American policy at
this stage appears to have been the desire to give up as rapidly as possible
the responsibilities acquired by the United States in Europe and to
transfer them to authorities which could handle them on a permanent
peacetime basis. Thus it was expected that the United Nations would
handle the larger problems of political security and economic rehabilitation. In the liberated countries of continental Europe, whether Allied or
defeated, it was assumed that the provisional regimes established at the
end of the war would shortly be succeeded by freely elected governments.
Only in the case of the major enemy states was a continuation of responsibility beyond the immediate future foreseen, and even here the prospects
of early peace settlements were regarded as bright. On the basis of this
optimistic view of the postwar settlement, the United States took two
critical steps that had the immediate effect of weakening American influence. The first was to terminate lend-lease aid, and the second was
to withdraw American troops from abroad with all possible speed. Faced
with this sudden relaxation of American influence in Europe, there was
little that Great Britain, France, and the smaller Western Allies could
do. Deeply concerned with their domestic problems, and uncertain regarding the future, they adjusted themselves as best they could to the
sudden withdrawal of American material support.

In contrast to the indecision of the Western democracies, the Soviet
Union pursued a firm and vigorous policy. Indeed, its leaders believed in
1945 no less than in 1939 that the Western democracies represented a
danger to Russia only second to that of fascism. Like all statesmen, the
Soviet leaders had the security of their country as their foremost objective.
They conceived of this security, however, in very special terms. It meant,
first of all, the regaining of the position of influence in Eastern Europe,
the Near East, and the Far East which Russia had lost in the declining
years of the empire. It also meant, moreover, that every effort should be
made to extend Soviet communism to all countries that had been weakened by the recent war. The Soviet leaders did not consider that their
way of life would be secure so long as any major area of the world
remained under an alien form of government. This was of course a theoretical outlook which did not necessarily require such immediate implementation as might provoke a new war, but in the conditions which
existed in Europe and in the Far East in the early postwar years the

Soviet Union had good reason to believe that it could extend its political influence without serious opposition.

YALTA AND POTSDAM. It was thus in a spirit of great dynamism and self-confidence that the Soviet statesmen approached the question of a postwar settlement. On the other hand, the Western leaders were still reluctant to abandon the assumption that something resembling the liberal Europe of the 1920s would arise from the ashes of the conflagration. Numerous signs of this divergence of views were evident in the relations of the Allies during the various stages of the war, but it was revealed most clearly during the last wartime conference of the Big Three held at Yalta, in the Russian Black Sea province of Crimea, in February 1945.

The war in Europe was now nearing its end, and Russia had already made important political gains in Eastern Europe. The principle had been firmly established that until the end of the war each great power would supervise political developments in those areas over which its armies passed as they pursued the foe. For Russia this meant all the territory north of Greece. Moreover, the armistice terms already agreed to for Rumania, Finland, Bulgaria, and Hungary, in the autumn and winter of 1944–45, had given the Soviet authorities almost unrestricted political powers and extensive economic rights. At the same time, the Russians took steps to gain influence with the governments of Eastern Europe which had resisted German aggression. The Czechoslovak government-in-exile, confident that it could form a bridge of understanding between East and West, had concluded a twenty-year treaty of alliance with the Soviet Union in 1943. With the Polish government in London, however, Russia had severed relations in the spring of 1943 and was promoting in its place a group of Communist leaders in Russia known as the Union of Polish Patriots. In Yugoslavia, Greece, and Albania, the Soviet Union was giving full encouragement to the Communist-led guerrillas who were in revolt against the recognized governments-in-exile of these countries, which were co-operating as best they could with the Western Allies.

In view of the degree of control now exercised by the Soviet Union in Eastern Europe, it was clear that the Western Allies could not expect to exert a determining influence in this region. The situation was correctly described at a later date by James F. Byrnes, a member of the American delegation at Yalta and shortly to become Secretary of State, when he said: "It was not a question of what we would *let* the Russians do, but what we could *get* the Russians to do." Apart from the important decisions taken at Yalta with regard to the organization of the United Nations, the treatment of Germany, and the settlement in the Far East, the principal work of this conference had to do with the postwar organization of Eastern Europe.

As regards territorial adjustments, it was agreed by the Big Three that Russia should receive, with certain very minor changes, that part of Poland lying east of the Curzon line [see above, pp. 126–28], and that Poland should be compensated with territory from Eastern Germany. In the case of both Yugoslavia and Poland, Stalin agreed that the Communist regimes established under Soviet supervision should be broadened by the admission of representatives from the Western-oriented governments-in-exile. Potentially more far-reaching in its consequences was the broad statement of policy known as the Yalta Declaration on Liberated Europe. In this document the three great powers agreed, after only brief discussion, to assist the liberated peoples of Europe "to form interim governmental authorities broadly representative of all democratic elements in the population and pledged to the earliest possible establishment through free elections of governments responsive to the will of the people."

On paper, this series of broad compromises regarding Eastern Europe represented a considerable achievement. Despite the fact that the Soviet Union was in almost full military control of this region, Stalin had not only agreed to admit non-Communists into the governments of Poland and Yugoslavia but had also consented to hold throughout Eastern Europe early elections which might well bring to power governments opposed to Soviet policy. The substance of these compromises, however, was very slight. Their interpretation and implementation after the defeat of Germany depended on the relative bargaining power of the parties to these agreements, and Russia soon discovered that she could assert her own point of view without effective opposition.

This was clearly seen when these problems were discussed further at the Potsdam Conference in July and August, 1945. Among the many issues taken up at this conference by Truman, Churchill (succeeded in the midst of the conference by Attlee, when the results of the British elections became known), and Stalin, were those related to the peace settlement in Italy, Germany, and Eastern Europe. As regards Poland's western frontier, it was agreed that pending the final peace settlement with Germany, three areas should be placed under Polish administration: the large area in Germany lying to the east of the Oder and Neisse rivers; the area of the former Free City of Danzig; and the southern portion of East Prussia. While no final commitment was made by Truman and Attlee as to the eventual determination of these frontiers in the German peace treaty, Poland and the Soviet Union treated the agreement as a permanent cession of territory. In consequence, two weeks after the end of the Potsdam Conference, in a treaty signed on August 16, 1945, Poland ceded to the Soviet Union the provinces of eastern Poland which the Big Three had agreed at Yalta should go to Russia.

Apart from this important decision, the powers made little headway at Potsdam in dealing with the many lesser issues which arose in connection with the peace settlement in Eastern Europe, many of which involved the implementation of decisions taken at Yalta. They did, however, agree to the establishment of a Council of Foreign Ministers that would have as its task the drafting of the peace treaties for Italy, Rumania, Bulgaria, Hungary, and Finland. It was to this body that the peace negotiations were now transferred.

CONFERENCE AT POTSDAM *Prime Minister Attlee, President Truman, and Marshal Stalin at Potsdam, Germany, in August, 1945. Standing behind them are Admiral Leahy, Foreign Minister Bevin, Secretary of State Byrnes, and Foreign Minister Molotov.*

LONDON, MOSCOW, AND PARIS. The new device of a Council of Foreign Ministers was first tried out in London in September, 1945, but its initial contributions to a settlement were slight. Confident that the Western Allies were not prepared to take a firm stand, Molotov promptly launched an offensive by demanding a share in the administration of Italy's North African colonies, the cession of Trieste to Yugoslavia, and heavy reparations from Italy. At the same time he denied that Russia was interfering in the affairs of Rumania, Bulgaria, and Hungary, and claimed that no violations of the Yalta Declaration on Liberated Europe had occurred. These and other issues were discussed with violence and without agreement, and in the end the conference reached a complete deadlock over the procedural issue of the right of French and Chinese representatives to participate in the discussions. Byrnes for the United States and Bevin for Great Britain refused to make the territorial and political concessions demanded by Molotov, and the conference ended in open failure. To the West it appeared that the Russians were deliberately making preposterous demands in order to postpone or avoid granting the concessions that a diplomacy of compromise would have required.

Three months later, in December, 1945, the Foreign Ministers met again, this time in Moscow. Byrnes and Bevin now made significant concessions with regard to the recognition of the Communist-dominated regions in Eastern Europe, sacrificing in considerable measure the substance of the Yalta Declaration although retaining it in form. The Russians, for their part, agreed to the calling of a peace conference in Paris to draft the five proposed peace treaties. In addition to the five great powers, the smaller states which had contributed to the victory in Europe were to be represented.

Working in London through the spring of 1946, the Deputies of the Council of Foreign Ministers resolved many of the disputed issues, but failed to solve the major differences of opinion. The Foreign Ministers themselves convened once more, this time in Paris, and in two long sessions, from April 25 to May 15 and again from June 15 to July 12, they finally worked out compromises on the issues that had been delaying their progress: the disposition of the Italian colonies; the Italian-Yugoslav frontier; and Italian reparations. The five members of the Council of Foreign Ministers and sixteen smaller Allied nations now convened in the Luxembourg Palace in Paris at the end of July. For ten weeks the conference dragged on in a disorganized and frequently comical fashion. Insofar as the draft terms had already been agreed to, the compromises they represented were supported by Great Britain and the United States as well as by the Soviet Union and the well-disciplined smaller states of Eastern Europe. The Western European states and the British Dominions took frequent issue with these decisions, however, and in debating the clauses not yet agreed upon by the Foreign Ministers the conference descended to the most flagrant forms of propaganda and bargaining. In the end, while the treaties bore little resemblance to the co-operative decisions which had not infrequently been achieved during the war, they at least represented a reasonably sound resolution of the political forces at work in the Europe of the postwar period.

DIVISION OF EUROPE. The negotiations leading up to the first peace treaties gradually revealed to the general public the extent and nature of the rift separating the Western Allies and the Soviet Union, a fact already known to those who had observed at first hand the rapid and ruthless consolidation of Soviet power in Eastern Europe during the first postwar year. This rift made even more difficult the task, that would have been awkward enough in any case, of transferring the conduct of international relations from the coalition of great powers that won the war to a system in which the organs of the United Nations and the point of view they represented could assume the initiative. The leading members of the victorious coalition had undertaken commitments during the war that were bound to have a continuing influence. They had in fact divided Europe for military reasons into two spheres of influence during the war, and the so-called "Iron Curtain" stretching from Stettin to Trieste represented no more than a continuation for political purposes of the line drawn before the conclusion of hostilities.

This division of Europe reflected underlying differences in policy between the Western democracies and the Soviet Union and was destined to influence the political affairs of Europe for many years. Regional political, economic, and military blocs were organized on each side of the Iron Curtain at the initiative of the Soviet Union and the Western democracies [see below, pp. 630–55]. Commercial intercourse and diplomatic negotiations between the two blocs came almost to a standstill, and relations were particularly tense during the Korean war. A situation thus developed in which Austria remained without a peace settlement for a full decade after the war, and the unification of Germany was indefinitely postponed. At the same time each bloc made vigorous efforts to integrate these uncommitted territories more effectively into its orbit. In turning now to a discussion of the peace treaties, it is important to bear in mind the atmosphere of tension and rivalry in which they were negotiated.

The European Peace Treaties

Italy and the Axis Satellites. The peace treaties with Italy, Bulgaria, Hungary, Rumania, and Finland, having been negotiated at the same time, were similar in their general structure and may be discussed together. Many of their articles were concerned with detailed technicalities of primarily legal importance. Of greater importance, however, were the territorial, economic, and political terms which were to have a significant influence in determining the future role of these countries.

With regard to the territorial settlement, the principal problems related to Italy. On Italy's eastern frontier, the greater part of the province of Venezia Giulia, including the city of Fiume, was ceded to Yugoslavia. The key city of Trieste, however, of which 80 percent of the population was Italian, was not assigned to either of the contestants. Instead, Trieste and a small hinterland were established as a Free Territory under the guarantee of the United Nations Security Council. The question of Trieste continued to be a major political issue between the Soviet and Western blocs for a number of years, but the gradual improvement of relations between Yugoslavia and the West paved the way for a compromise solution. A division of the Trieste territory which gave the city itself to Italy and a major share of the hinterland to Yugoslavia was finally reached in October, 1954. Yugoslavia also received Zara and several other Adriatic islands. In addition to the territory it lost to Yugoslavia, Italy was required to cede a small strategic area on its western frontier to France, the Dodecanese Islands in the eastern Mediterranean to Greece, and the Adriatic island of Saseno to Albania.

The disposition of Italy's conquests in Africa posed a difficult problem which taxed the ingenuity of European statesmanship. The independence of Ethiopia was immediately recognized but no satisfactory solution could be found for the former Italian colonies of Libya, Eritrea, and Somaliland. It was decided that they should remain under British military rule for the time being, and that if the four powers could not agree within a year as to their disposition, the matter would be referred to the United Nations General Assembly. It was soon recognized that the latter approach offered the best framework for a solution, and under United Nations auspices the former Italian territories have moved in the direction of self-government. Thus, by the decision of the United Nations and with its assistance, Libya became an independent kingdom with a federal constitution in 1951. Similarly under United Nations supervision, Eritrea was made an autonomous province federated with Ethiopia in 1952. Under this arrangement Eritrea retained self-government in domestic affairs, while its foreign relations were handled as a federal responsibility by the government of Ethiopia. Somaliland became a trust territory of the United Nations in 1950 under Italian administration, as part of a program that led to independence as Somalia in 1960 [see below, p. 766].

The remaining four peace treaties also confirmed certain territorial changes that had already been sanctioned under the armistice terms. Thus Finland ceded to the USSR the northern province of Petsamo, a strip of territory in the central portion of the Soviet-Finnish frontier, and the strategic area of the Karelian Isthmus in the south including the city of Viborg. These territories ceded to the Soviet Union amounted to some twelve percent of the area of Finland and included important economic resources. Finland was also required to lease for a fifty-year period the naval base of Porkkala-Udd on the Gulf of Finland, but this lease was terminated by Russia in 1955.

Rumania, for its part, confirmed the cession of Northern Bukovina and of Bessarabia to the Soviet Union and of Southern Dobruja to Bulgaria. These territories had originally been ceded in 1940, during the period of the Nazi-Soviet pact and had been reoccupied by Rumania during the war. At the same time Rumania was able to get back the province of Northern Transylvania, which it had ceded also in 1940 to Hungary. Finally, Hungary ceded to Czechoslovakia a small strip of territory on the Danube opposite the city of Bratislava. After wrestling with the Czechoslovak claim for an exchange of minorities with Hungary and considering the suggestion of the latter for territorial compensation, the powers decided to leave the question to bilateral negotiations between the two countries involved [see maps, pp. 611, 613].

Detailed provision was made in each of the five treaties for the reduc-

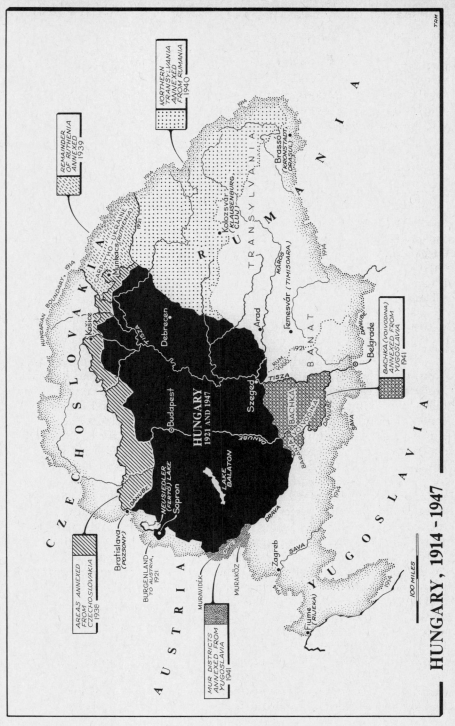

REMAINDER OF RUTHENIA ANNEXED 1939

NORTHERN TRANSYLVANIA ANNEXED FROM RUMANIA 1940

AREAS ANNEXED FROM CZECHOSLOVAKIA 1938

BACHKA (VOIVODINA) ANNEXED FROM YUGOSLAVIA 1941

MUR DISTRICTS ANNEXED FROM YUGOSLAVIA 1941

C Z E C H O S L O V A K I A

Hungarian Boundary, 1914

Košice

CARPATHO-UKRAINE Munkács (RUTHENIA)

1921

1914

R U M A N I A

Kolozsvár (KLAUSENBURG) (CLUJ)

T R A N S Y L V A N I A

Brassó (KRONSTADT, ORASUL)

Debrecen

TISZA

1914

Arad

MAROS

Temesvár (TIMIŞOARA)

B A N A T

HUNGARY 1921 AND 1947

Budapest

RUM. YUGO. 1921

Szeged

TISZA

Belgrade

DANUBE

BACHKA

BARANYA (VOIVODINA)

DANUBE

SAVA

1914

NEUSIEDLER (FERTÖ) LAKE

Sopron

LAKE BALATON

DANUBE

BURGENLAND TO AUSTRIA, 1921

A U S T R I A

MURAVIDÉK

MURAKÖZ

DRAVA

Zagreb

SAVA

1914

Y U G O S L A V I A

Fiume (RIJEKA)

1914

100 MILES

HUNGARY, 1914 – 1947

MAP 25

TRM

tion of the armaments and armed forces of the defeated states and for the restoration of the legal and property rights of the victorious states. The five states also promised to guarantee "the enjoyment of human rights and of the fundamental freedoms" to all their citizens, and undertook to dissolve Fascist organizations and to make persons accused of war crimes available for trial. They also undertook to pay reparations in the amount and to the countries indicated in the accompanying table:

TABLE 12

REPARATIONS OBLIGATIONS

(in millions of dollars)

TO	ITALY	RUMANIA	BULGARIA	HUNGARY	FINLAND
USSR	100	300	—	200	300
Yugoslavia	125	—	25	50	—
Czechoslovakia	—	—	—	50	—
Greece	105	—	45	—	—
Ethiopia	25	—	—	—	—
Albania	5	—	—	—	—
Totals	360	300	70	300	300

After a few further adjustments had been made by the Foreign Ministers, the first peace treaties following World War II were finally signed in Paris on February 10, 1947, and they were ratified by the powers in the following months. All the treaties except that with Finland contained a commitment on the part of the occupying Allied nations to withdraw occupation troops within ninety days of their coming into force. Russia retained the right, however, to maintain sufficient forces in Rumania and Hungary to safeguard its line of communications with Austria until a treaty was concluded with that country. In addition, all five treaties incorporated provisions for their interpretation by the diplomatic representatives of the great powers in the capitals of the treaty states, and for the settlement of disputes arising from the treaties by these representatives, assisted, if necessary, by an appointee of the Secretary-General of the United Nations. This last provision was little more than a formality, of course, for the terms of the treaties themselves had already demonstrated how firm was the line drawn between the Soviet sphere of influence and that of the Western Allies. At the same time, these first peace treaties reflected another factor in postwar international relations that was fully as important as the Soviet tenacity of purpose. This was the fact that the United States had not lost interest in European affairs after the defeat of Germany, but quite to the contrary was willing to exert considerable influence in support of the principles held by the Western Allies. This fact was clearly perceived during the negotiation of the peace treaties and was before long to become the dominant feature of the postwar settlement.

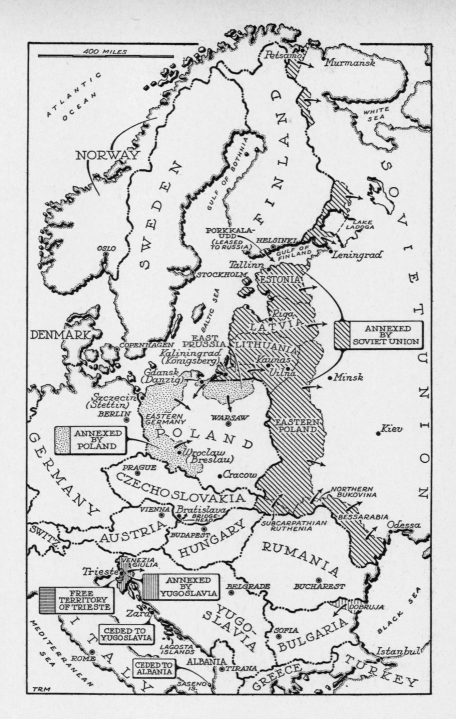

MAP 26 *Eastern Europe: Territorial Changes, 1939–1947*

THE PROBLEM OF CENTRAL EUROPE. Most divergent policies and interests had been compromised by the Allies with a view to amassing the military power necessary to defeat the armies of Hitler's Third Reich. Yet these compromises dissolved as soon as the military power of the Axis collapsed, for the very resources that gave Germany such strength as an enemy made it also the principal prize sought by the two rival blocs into which the victorious coalition soon disintegrated. Indeed, Germany formed in many respects the heart of Europe, and each of the rival blocs regarded control of Germany as essential to its security.

On only one aspect of the problem did the victors find a solution, reached at a stage in the war when their interests called for compromise. When the foreign ministers of the three major Allies met in Moscow in October 1943, they issued a declaration to the effect that Austria should be restored as an independent country. This declaration made no provision, however, for the actual transition period between occupation and independence or for the territorial and political terms under which the Austrian state should be re-established. These questions proved to be fruitful sources of disagreement after the war, yet the early decision as to independence and the relatively limited nature of its resources made a settlement with Austria less controversial than one with Germany.

The differences in approach of the victorious powers to the problem of Germany were soon apparent. This was a matter of immediate concern to the Soviet Union, which suffered the heaviest losses in fighting Germany. It is clear that the USSR desired to obtain as heavy reparations as possible from Germany, and that the methods for accomplishing this would include a removal of factories, a levy on current production, and the use for labor of German prisoners of war in Russia. The Soviet leaders did not wish to see a Germany associated with the Western democracies, and to prevent this they sought to create a large Communist party in Germany that might be called upon to seize control of the government in case Soviet policy should deem this desirable. A "Free German Committee" of Communist leaders had already been established on Russian soil as the nucleus for the future German Communist party.

The Western Allies were by no means in full agreement as to Germany's future. One important aspect of official American thinking was the plan elaborated by Secretary of the Treasury Morgenthau in the latter part of 1944. This plan envisaged the permanent reduction of German power by the destruction or removal of the heavy industry. It also involved the cession of certain German provinces to neighboring countries and the partition of the remaining territory into three states. In addition, long-term controls of Germany's domestic economy as well as of its foreign trade were to be established. Responsibility for implementing these various measures was to be divided between the United Nations and Germany's neighbors. This very extreme plan was soon modified when the difficulties of its implementation were more fully understood, but it continued for some time to exert a strong influence on American thinking. The United King-

ALLIED COMMANDERS AT BERLIN *The Big Four Commanders:*
Field Marshal Montgomery (Britain), Marshal Zhukov (Soviet Union),
General Eisenhower (United States), and General Koenig (France) at the
inauguration of the Allied Control Commission in Berlin, June, 1945.

dom and France were likewise deeply interested in finding a settlement
that would restrict the power of Germany once and for all, but their thinking ran along more moderate and traditional lines. They realized that the
German people would have to eat and that Europe's prosperity would depend in considerable measure on Germany's economic health, and their
policies were guided by this realization.

By the time the military forces of Russia and the Western Allies met
in the center of Germany, considerable progress had been made in agreeing
on the initial steps of a joint policy. The Moscow conferences in the fall of
1943 established certain general principles regarding the surrender and demilitarization of Germany, the punishment of war criminals, and the
powers to be exercised by the Allied Control Council. This conference also
established the European Advisory Commission, which met in London and
worked out many of the details regarding the treatment of Germany.
Further general decisions regarding frontiers and reparations were made at
Yalta, at which time it was also decided that France should participate in
the occupation of Germany. On June 5, 1945, the Americans, British,
French, and Russian governments were thus able to issue a joint statement
on "Arrangements for Control of Germany," which summarized the points
of agreement. The four occupation zones were announced, and the Allied
Control Council was established in a Greater Berlin that was to be jointly
administered. Supreme authority regarding all matters affecting Germany
was granted to the four commanders-in-chief who comprised the Control
Council. These arrangements satisfied the needs of the moment, but they
offered no answer to the broader problems of political and economic policy
that the Allies would have to face. It was in order to seek an agreement on
these important matters that the Big Three met in Potsdam.

The territorial settlement agreed upon at Potsdam assigned to Polish
administration the large agricultural area east of the Oder and Neisse rivers
and partitioned East Prussia between Poland and the Soviet Union. Under
this arrangement, which remained technically provisional until the terms
of the peace treaty had been agreed to, some nine million German refugees
from these territories were transferred to Germany. In addition, some
three million Germans were expelled from Czechoslovakia and another
half million from Hungary. These twelve million refugees were distributed unequally among the four occupation zones and added to the
problems of the German economy. The time had not yet come to settle on
the future form of the German government, but a loose decentralization
was agreed to as the guiding principle for provincial government within
each of the four zones. A vigorous denazification program was also adopted,
and arrangements were made for the trial of the major war criminals [see
below, pp. 660–61].

The economic problems represented by a defeated Germany could not
be postponed as easily as the political, and they soon became a major source
of disagreement. It was originally agreed that Germany should be treated as
an economic unit, that war industries would be prohibited, and that large

concentrations of economic power within Germany should be discouraged. Provision was also made for preventing the level of German industrial production from rising sufficiently to give Germany a higher standard of living than that of Europe as a whole. Reparations, which were the key to the economic settlement, were to be paid from the removal of Germany's plants and capital equipment and from its external assets. The Russian share of the reparations bill was to come from the Soviet occupation zone, and in addition one quarter of the industrial equipment removed from the three Western zones was to go to Russia. In partial compensation for the latter source of reparations, Russia was to supply the other zones with certain food and raw materials from its own sector. Furthermore, the German navy and merchant marine were to be divided among the principal victors.

Almost immediately, this broad compromise approach gave rise to numerous conflicts. France, which had not been invited to participate in the Potsdam Conference but could exercise its veto in the Control Council, held up the implementation of the economic program in an effort to get territorial and economic concessions in Western Germany. Russia interpreted the Potsdam Agreement as permitting removals for reparations from current production, while the Western Allies insisted that only capital equipment and foreign assets could be used for this purpose. Moreover, it soon became apparent that the level of German industry had to be regulated less on the basis of the needs of the German people than on those of the entire European economy. In the last analysis, it was the consensus among the Western Allies that the Soviet authorities were responsible for the failure of the Potsdam system because of their refusal to contribute food and raw materials from their zone, or to co-operate in the establishment of central economic institutions for Germany.

These various issues were debated at the meetings of the Council of Foreign Ministers in Paris in 1946 and in Moscow in the spring of 1947 and at even greater length by the deputies of the foreign ministers meeting in London, but to no avail. The American proposal of a long-term four-power treaty guaranteeing the demilitarization of Germany, first made by Secretary Byrnes in April, 1946, was rejected by the Soviet government. With equal stubbornness the Western Allies refused to accept the Soviet proposal for the four-power control of the industrial region of the Ruhr. The one thing which could be said in favor of the deadlock which now developed was that the objectives and determination of the Western Allies and the Soviet Union became quite clear. Both parties realized that the prize at stake was nothing less than the control of Germany as a whole and with it the control of Western and Central Europe.

Both sides now took steps to consolidate their hold on their respective occupation zones. Russia, with a unified zone to start with, had already gone a long way toward making its zone an obedient instrument of Soviet policy. The Western Allies, somewhat slower in getting started, now proceeded to unify their zones. A preliminary fusion of the American and

British zones went into effect on January 1, 1947; the Russians countered by further increasing German industrial production in their own zone. When no results were produced by the next meeting of the Council of Foreign Ministers, held in London during November and December, 1947, the Western Allies introduced a currency reform in their zones in June, 1948. The Russians replied by blockading the Western sectors of Berlin, and only the dramatic improvisation of the Anglo-American airlift averted the breakdown of the administrative establishment of the three Western Allies in Berlin. This resulted in a strengthening of ties between the Western zones and in plans for the creation of a Western German State [see below, pp. 664–76]. The Soviet blockade of Berlin was finally raised in May, 1949, in conjunction with a new meeting of the Council of Foreign Ministers in Paris. Again no agreement was reached on the broader issues, but the framework of four-power negotiations was re-established, and certain economic adjustments were made.

AUSTRIAN STATE TREATY. The position of Austria was anomalous at the end of the war, for it was considered neither a satellite nor a liberated state. Divided into four occupation zones, with the capital city of Vienna similarly administered except for a small zone in the center under joint four-power occupation, Austria was in no sense free. Yet Austria had not been at war as a separate state and therefore could hardly be expected to sign a peace treaty. This difficulty was circumvented by referring to the projected settlement as the "Austrian State Treaty," and at the Potsdam Conference a start was made in the protracted negotiations that finally resulted in the conclusion of an Austrian treaty in 1955.

At Potsdam the decision was reached that no reparations should be exacted of Austria, but under the German reparations clauses Russia was given the right to appropriate German external assets in the Axis satellite states and in eastern Austria. Later, at the meeting of the Council of Foreign Ministers in December, 1946, it was agreed that special deputies of the foreign ministers were to be named to draw up a draft treaty with Austria. These deputies soon found that they could come to no agreement on two major issues: the definition of German assets, and Yugoslav territorial claims against Austria. The Russians maintained that all property in Austria owned by German nationals at the end of the war constituted German assets, while the Western powers refused to count as German assets those which Germans had acquired "under duress." Thus, for example, property confiscated from Jews by the Nazis would not be subject to Russian seizure under the Western interpretation. Matters were further complicated by the attempt to distinguish between "assets" and war booty. The other major point of disagreement arose over Yugoslavia's claim to a portion of Carinthia and Styria, together with her demands for reparations. Russian rights to the important Zistersdorf oil fields and the control of the Danube Shipping Company were also points in dispute.

In the ten years following Potsdam the foreign ministers and their deputies held almost three hundred meetings to discuss the Austrian treaty, without making any substantial progress. It is clear from the circumstances of these negotiations that the obstacles to agreement lay not in the substantive issues under discussion but in the importance of Austria to the general European settlement. The problem of Austria was indeed subsidiary to that of Germany, and so long as no settlement was in sight on this issue the Soviets considered it to be to their advantage to delay the Austrian treaty. Under the terms of the peace treaties with Hungary and Rumania, the Soviet Union had the right to keep armed forces in these countries for the maintenance of the lines of communication with the Soviet zone of occupation in Austria, and this was a right which they wished to retain. At the same time, since the Western bloc felt strongly about Austrian independence, the continued occupation of Austria gave the Soviets valuable bargaining power in negotiating a German settlement. It was therefore not until the situation in Europe as a whole had greatly changed that the Soviet government found it advantageous to agree to a treaty with Austria.

Apparently the principal circumstance that led to this change in the Soviet attitude was the progress made by the Western bloc in incorporating the German Federal Republic into the Western defense system. This development called for extensive Soviet countermeasures, and these took the form of an effort to obtain the formal neutralization of such strategic countries between the two blocs as Yugoslavia, Austria, and Germany. In this scheme Austria played a particularly important role as a place where a spectacular demonstration of the new Soviet policy could be staged. In the spring of 1955 the Soviet government therefore made known its willingness to negotiate a settlement and invited representatives of the Austrian government to Moscow. Discussions were subsequently held with the other governments concerned, and on May 15, 1955, the Austrian State Treaty was signed. Judged in the light of Soviet demands over the past decade, the terms of this treaty were lenient. The Yugoslav territorial claims had long since been abandoned, and the principal price paid by Austria was the settlement of the Soviet claims to German assets. Austria was obliged to deliver $150 million worth of goods over a period of six years, to pay $2 million in cash for the Danube Steamship Company, and to deliver one million tons of crude oil annually for ten years. More important was the obligation of Austria to declare its neutrality, for this provision not only meant that Austria could not be brought into the Western defense system but also established with Western approval the principle of neutralizing the uncommitted countries between the two blocs. It remained for subsequent negotiations among the four great powers to determine the role that the idea of neutrality would play.

As it turned out, neutralization was not extended beyond the case of Austria and it proved to have limitations that the Austrian government had not anticipated. Austria was admitted to the United Nations without difficulty in 1955. When it applied in 1961 and again in 1963 for associate membership in the European Economic Community (EEC) [see below, pp. 647–49], however, the Soviet Union protested that a neutralized state should refrain not only from military ties with other states but also from political, economic, and cultural ties. The matter rests there pending the EEC's readiness to consider new applications for membership, but the incident has served to emphasize Austria's special position. Although Austria is self-neutralized, having declared its neutrality by means of a parliamentary law, it took this stand in fulfillment of a condition of Soviet acceptance of the Austrian State Treaty. Its future freedom of action is therefore affected by the Soviet interpretation of this agreement.

TOWARD A GERMAN SETTLEMENT. It was generally recognized that the significance of the Austrian settlement lay in its relationship to the negotiations regarding Germany, and indeed German opinion was greatly impressed by the relatively favorable terms accorded to Austria on condition that it declare its neutrality. After a decade of frustrating negotiations the agreement regarding Austria seemed to mark a turning point, for if the four powers were willing to compromise on Austria, they should also be able to reach agreement on Germany. The passage of time had nevertheless made a German settlement more difficult, for since the Berlin blockade of 1948–49 the two parts of divided Germany had become increasingly committed in both a political and an economic sense to the rival blocs of which they formed a part. The Soviet zone was transformed into a Communist state—the German Democratic Republic—and was fully integrated into the Soviet orbit in Eastern Europe. A German Federal Republic was created from the three Western zones, with somewhat more than double the area and triple the population of the Soviet zone, and this state rapidly developed close ties with Western Europe and the United States [see below, pp. 664–80].

During the five years following the Berlin blockade it became apparent that three issues were paramount in the propaganda and negotiations concerning the future of Germany. One was the question of German unity, generally desired by all elements of the German population. Her neighbors were naturally apprehensive about the resurgence of a powerful Germany, but it was recognized that in the long run the solution lay not in permanent partition but in the integration of Germany into some new form of European organization. Closely related to the unification issue was that of the political complexion of the future Germany. German opinion in the Western zone was overwhelmingly opposed to Communism, and it was generally believed that free elections in the Eastern zone would likewise result in a crushing defeat for the Communists. Associated with this was a third issue—whether the future Germany should be demilitarized and neutralized. This proposal met with considerable sympathy on the part of many Germans who had come to recognize the fallacies underlying the traditional militarism of their country, but it would also tie the hands of the government in a manner which no great power had previously accepted voluntarily.

In the contest over Germany, it was with these three major issues that the policies of the two blocs were concerned. Soviet policy recognized the inevitability of unification, but wished it to take place on Soviet terms. At one stage the USSR therefore proposed that a Constitutional Council be elected for the whole of Germany, but with equal representation from the Soviet and Western zones despite the fact that the latter was more than twice the size of the former. This proposal was designed to give the Communists assurance of one-half the votes in such a Council, thus permitting them at least to block proposals which they opposed. Associated with this scheme was the proposal that Germany be demilitarized and neutralized. Soviet policy had a particular advantage in negotiating on Germany, because it had effective control of the German territory east of the Oder-Neisse line which had been placed under Polish administration. Although this territory was never held out as bait to Germany at this stage of the negotiations, it was widely believed that the Soviets might arrange to have it returned if it suited their policy to do so.

The policy of the Western bloc had the objective of obtaining a unified Germany that would be free from Communist control and able to participate in the plans for the integration of Western Europe. The one great advantage of the West was the assurance that in any free election the Germans would vote against communism, and this assurance grew stronger as the political stability and economic prosperity of the Western zone rapidly outstripped the impoverished and terrorized Eastern zone. Western diplomacy was also aided by the fact that, however much demilitarization and neutralization might appeal to certain sectors of German opinion, it did not seem likely that a great power would in the long run voluntarily relinquish its freedom of action in foreign policy. Western policy therefore rested on a united Germany based on free elections, in the belief that such a Germany would become an active participant in the security and prosperity of Western Europe. It was recognized that a significant tradition in German policy favored playing the East off against the West, but the record of Soviet policy since the war was such that for most Germans the choice between the two blocs was clear enough.

When the four leading powers met at Geneva in July, 1955, conferring at the highest level of government for the first time since the Potsdam Conference ten years earlier, each side presented once again its views on a German settlement. The Western powers declared for a united Germany based on free elections and freedom to choose its allies after unification. In recognition of Soviet security interests, the Western powers also proposed that mutual security pacts be concluded and that a demilitarized buffer zone that would include the present Soviet zone in Germany be established between East and West. The Soviets, by contrast, maintained that Germany could not be unified until European security had been established and that this necessarily involved the liquidation of the Western European Union and the North Atlantic Treaty Organization. The problem of Germany was thus again subordinated to the larger strategy of the Western and Soviet blocs, neither of which was willing to risk losing its existing positions in Europe, and the negotiation of a German settlement was forced to await the further development of events.

For twenty years the policy of the German Federal Republic under Christian Democratic leadership adhered strictly to a policy of no negotiations with the Soviet bloc, and under the prevailing conditions this policy contributed greatly to the stability of German politics. A policy which was admired for its firmness in the earlier years, however, came to be regarded as rigid and inflexible by the end of this period. A new generation of Germans retained its belief in NATO as the cornerstone of German security, but desired a greater degree of maneuverability in other matters. By 1970 the permanence of the Oder-Neisse line and the reality of the German Democratic Republic as a separate state were widely acknowledged, and it no longer seemed practical to base Germany's Eastern policy on any alternative reality.

The opportunity to explore new possibilities came as a result of the election that brought the Social Democrats to office in October, 1969, as a dominant member of a coalition with the Free Democrats. As chancellor, Willy Brandt now took the initiative in organizing talks with Willi Stoph, the East German premier, looking toward recognition, and they met on March 19 and May 21, 1970, with a view to agreeing on a framework for negotiations. To Stoph's demand for the international legal recognition of his country, Brandt responded by proposing a series of steps leading toward normal relations. Although the two statesmen did not significantly narrow the gap between them at these initial meetings, they agreed to continue the dialogue and this was generally taken as a sign that reconciliation might be possible. At the same time, Brandt's government held talks with Poland and the USSR, looking toward an improvement of economic and political relations.

The Soviet-West German talks culminated in a treaty signed in Moscow by Kosygin and Brandt on August 11, 1970, which accepts the existing political frontiers in Eastern Europe as a basis for the normalization of political relations. This treaty involves the acceptance by West Germany of the Oder-Neisse line, its frontier with Poland, and the continued existence of two Germanies. The treaty is supplemented by two related documents: a letter from the West German to the Soviet government stating that the treaty does not stand in contradiction to the West German aim of achieving German unity by processes of free self-determination; and a West German note to France, the USSR, the United Kingdom, and the United States, informing them that the treaty does not affect their rights and responsibilities in regard to an eventual peace treaty. The treaty had to be ratified by the West German parliament, where it would be a political issue between the Social Democrats and the Christian Democrats, but few doubted that it reflected the views of a majority of West Germans. The effect of this settlement was to postpone indefinitely the question of a united Germany in favor of the more practical problems of reducing political tensions and barriers to trade.

SOVIET-WEST GERMAN TREATY *Brezhnev, Brandt, and Kosygin (left to right) at the signing of a treaty pledging to observe the current borders of the two nations as inviolable, August 11, 1970.*

The Japanese Peace Treaty

PRINCIPLES OF A SETTLEMENT. The defeat of Japan, unlike that of Germany, had been accomplished almost exclusively by a single great power. The immediate problems raised by the termination of hostilities were, therefore, a great deal simpler. In dealing with these problems, three general principles were adopted by the American government to provide a starting point for the elaboration of a permanent settlement. These principles were that the Japanese Empire should be dismembered, that the resulting Japanese state should be demilitarized and democratized, and that American occupation policy should be as free as possible from interference by the other Allies.

The idea of dismembering the Japanese Empire was readily acceptable to the United Nations coalition, and a declaration issued by Roosevelt, Churchill, and Chiang Kai-shek after the conference at Cairo in November, 1943, proclaimed this principle as a war aim. It was also specifically provided that Manchuria, Formosa, and the Pescadores Islands should be restored to China. In a secret agreement concluded at Yalta in February, 1945, the Russian share of the Japanese legacy was defined in anticipation of Soviet participation in the Pacific war after the defeat of Germany. It was agreed that Russia would annex the southern part of Sakhalin Island, which it had ceded to Japan in 1905, as well as the Kurile Islands to the north, which Russia had transferred to Japan in 1875. In Manchuria, Russia was to be granted the rights it had exercised before 1905, with regard to the joint operation with China of the Chinese Eastern and South Manchurian railroads and the lease of Port Arthur as a naval base. At the same time the adjacent port of Dairen was to be internationalized. Finally, it was agreed that the Chinese province of Outer Mongolia, which had enjoyed a separate existence as the Mongolian People's Republic since the 1920s, should be granted permanent autonomy. In return, Russia promised to declare war against Japan within sixty days after the end of hostilities in Europe. These agreements were made without the presence of Chiang Kai-shek. Since the arrangements regarding Manchuria and Outer Mongolia required the eventual concurrence of China, Roosevelt assumed the obligation of notifying the Chinese government of them at the appropriate time and, with Churchill, guaranteed that these Russian claims would in any case be fulfilled. As regards Korea, which had been a Japanese province since 1910, the Cairo declaration of 1943 had promised that it would be granted independence "in due course." At Potsdam, however, a provisional occupation by American and Soviet troops was agreed to with the 38th parallel as the line dividing the two zones.

OCCUPATION POLICY. The American occupation forces moved into Japan alone after the surrender in August, 1945, and the initial steps in the process of the demilitarization and democratization of Japan were handled directly by them. The Japanese emperor and government were subjected to the authority of the Supreme Commander, General Douglas MacArthur, and with their co-operation the Japanese armed forces and military installations were promptly brought under control. The process of "democratization" was a much more complex matter and could only be carried out by degrees.

The United States government regarded the problem of Japan as distinct from that of Germany, where the Big Three had contributed more or less equally to the victory. Both the British and the Russians, however, favored joint determination of policy in regard to Japan. In spite of pressure from its allies, the United States successfully resisted any real interference in American occupation policy but agreed to the establishment in Washington of a Far Eastern Commission representing the eleven states which participated in the Pacific war. At the same time an Allied Council was set up in Tokyo, representing the British Commonwealth, the Soviet Union, China, and the United States. Under this arrangement, policy would continue to be initiated by the United States, but if objections were raised to these policies by the Council in Tokyo, implementation would have to be delayed while the matter was referred to the Commission in Washington. Since the great powers exercised a veto on the Commission, the United States could prevent the adoption of measures to which it objected.

The Japan which the American forces occupied in 1945 was only a fragment of the empire which had attacked the United States in 1941. Extensive territories were ceded upon Japanese surrender to China and the Soviet Union as a result of the wartime agreements, and Korea was occupied jointly by the United States and the Soviet Union. In addition the North Pacific Islands, which Japan had held under a mandate from the League of Nations, as well as the Ryukyu and Bonin Islands, were administered by the United States separately from Japan proper. Arrangements were soon made for the United States to hold these islands as trusteeship territories for the United Nations. From an empire of 260,770 square miles with a population in 1940 of over 105 millions, Japan was thus reduced to an area of 141,529 square miles and a population in 1945 of some 72 millions. These figures tell only a small part of the story, however, for the former territories possessed many of the raw materials and markets that had made Japanese prosperity possible. The principle of dismemberment was thus rigorously applied, but this led to economic problems for which no solution was then in sight. The dismemberment of the empire was accompanied by a renunciation of war on the part of the Japanese government that was written into the new constitution and by a purge of the leading Japanese militarists. As a result, Japan lost not only its empire but also, for the time being, even the means of acquiring one.

The policy of democratization resulted in changes which gave evidence of a fundamental transformation of the Japanese way of life. The most drastic reforms were in the political sphere and were incorporated in the new constitution adopted in May, 1947. The traditional right of the emperor to exercise the powers of government, which in fact had rarely been exercised in recent years, was now replaced by a constitutional provision that the emperor could act only with the advice and approval of the cabinet. This significant change in political practice was accompanied by a separate declaration on the part of the emperor denying his own divinity. These measures transformed the emperor into a constitutional monarch and reflected a trend that had already made significant progress in Japan before the war.

The transformation of the role of the emperor was accompanied by several other constitutional measures designed to make the Diet more representative of the popular will and to subordinate the cabinet to the Diet and the armed forces to the cabinet. Both houses of the Diet were now to be elected by universal suffrage, broadened to include all adult women, and every effort was made to create a Diet that could function effectively as the highest organ of government. Political parties were also re-established. These measures were supported by a broad program of economic and social rights as well as the traditional civil liberties. To enforce these rights a judicial system was established that was independent of the executive, thus marking a sharp break with past Japanese practice. Plans were also made to decentralize Japanese administration by strengthening local government. Apart from the judicial reform, most of these changes were along lines familiar to the Japanese. The significance of the new measures was that they were adopted in a period of national transformation and were accompanied by constitutional guarantees of binding force. It was the hope of the Japanese leaders who drafted the new constitution, with American assistance, that the new democratic system was being established in such a manner that it could not be changed short of another major upheaval.

In the social and economic sphere the changes adopted during the occupation period were equally significant. In this sphere democratization was interpreted to mean the freeing of the individual from a traditional authoritarianism that took many forms. The destruction of the armed forces and the elimination of the military bureaucracy was only a first step in this direction. A variety of reforms were introduced with the general purpose of strengthening the sense of individual responsibility in society. Thus, for example, compulsory education was extended from six to nine years, women were given a legal status equal to men, the largest of the industrial combines (*zaibatsu*) were broken up, the trade unions were strengthened, and in a sweeping land reform the proportion of tenant cultivated lands was reduced to 10 percent from about 50 percent. The immediate result of this and other similar reforms was to create a Japan that at least in form and to a considerable extent in practice resembled the Western democracies. These reforms were introduced during the six and a half years of occupation, and it remained to be seen whether they would endure. The significance of the relationship between Japan's domestic and international position was widely recognized, for there would be no purpose in planning for a democratic Japan unless it could be assured of a reasonable opportunity for economic development and a position in international affairs commensurate with its real importance.

THE JAPANESE SETTLEMENT. As was the case with Germany, the conclusion of a Japanese peace treaty depended not on a settlement of the traditional issues between defeated and victorious powers but on the struggle between the Soviet and Western blocs. As soon as the success of the Communist revolution in China was assured, the Soviet government began to press for a peace treaty with Japan in a form that would tend to bring that country under the influence of the Soviet-Chinese orbit. Many of the Western states, and in particular Australia and the United Kingdom, adhered initially to the belief that Communist intentions were peaceful and that no stability was possible for Japan outside an Asian framework. Japanese leaders were likewise inclined to this view at the start. The Japanese view was based in part on economic considerations, for in 1949 Japanese imports exceeded exports by some 40 percent, and the deficit of some $400 million was borne by the United States. It was difficult for the Japanese to envision any long-term solution of this economic problem except through close commercial ties with the Asian mainland, and hence a peace settlement which included China and the USSR seemed essential. Equally questionable to most Japanese leaders was a solution that would tie Japan politically to the West, at a time when the West appeared to be weak and divided while communism was clearly on the upsurge in Asia.

In the face of this pressure for a general peace treaty, the United States at first had only confusion to offer instead of a policy. From a position of undisputed power and influence in 1945, American policy had declined to such a point that early in 1949 the Secretary of the Army expressed the view that Japan would have to be written off by the United States in the event of a war with Russia. Although a policy of withdrawing from Japan was vigorously denied by higher government officials, the impression of confusion and weakness in American policy was strongly conveyed to Japan and to the rest of the world. This confusion was temporary, however, and the view gradually took hold in Washington that the only solution for Japan was a separate treaty with the Western bloc. To implement this decision a long series of negotiations was started in 1950 with the countries concerned. At first there were many objections to the idea of a peace treaty based on terms drawn up by the West which the USSR would in all probability reject and which Communist China would not even be invited to sign. It was probably the North Korean attack on South Korea in June 1950, and the subsequent revelation of the aggressive policies of the Soviet Union and of Communist China, that in the long run turned the tide in favor of the American peace proposals.

The Japanese peace treaty was negotiated over a period of eleven months, and the invitation to Japan and its former enemies to attend a peace conference at San Francisco in September, 1951, was issued jointly by the United States and the United Kingdom after they had reached a compromise on the draft treaty. The essence of this compromise was that neither Nationalist China nor Communist China should be invited to sign the treaty, and that it should be left to Japan to decide on its relations with the two Chinas after the peace treaty had been signed. Unlike most peace treaties, the negotiations were concluded before the conference was held, so that the meeting at San Francisco was devoted primarily to the formal acts of agreement and signature. The Soviet Union attended the conference, but did not succeed in altering the peace terms and therefore refused to sign the treaty. India, on the other hand, refused to attend the peace conference in consequence of its policy of neutrality between the Western and Soviet blocs. With these exceptions, however, and in the absence of the two Chinas, the Japanese peace treaty met with general acceptance and was duly ratified.

Under the terms of this treaty Japan accepted the disposition of its territories that had been made at the end of the war. Japan also agreed in principle to pay reparations, although the treaty "recognized that the resources of Japan are not presently sufficient, if it is to maintain a viable economy, to make complete reparation" for war damage. As a matter of fact, the question of reparations was much disputed among the Allies, since the United States realized that any further deficit in Japan's trade balance would have to be made up by American aid. The treaty therefore avoided the issue to the extent of leaving the final adjustment of reparations to separate negotiations between Japan and the various powers concerned. It was further provided that the occupation forces should be withdrawn within ninety days after the coming into force of the treaty.

This provision nevertheless did not mean that United States armed forces would have to leave Japan, for at the same time that the peace treaty was signed a separate security treaty was concluded between the United States and Japan. This security treaty gave the United States the right for an indefinite period to base military forces in Japan in order "to contribute to the maintenance of international peace and security in the Far East and to the security of Japan from armed attack from without." Under this agreement United States forces could also be used at the request of the Japanese government to put down disturbances instigated by a foreign power within the country. At the same time Japan agreed not to grant without prior American consent any bases or other military rights to a third power. In 1960 this security treaty was renewed in a revised form for a ten-year period, despite popular demonstrations reflecting a fear that the treaty might involve Japan in new wars.

The treaty provided that it would continue beyond the ten-year period unless either country terminated it by giving one year's notice. In 1970 both countries decided to let the treaty continue in force, and this time the popular opposition in Japan was much less virulent than ten years earlier. The continued acceptance of the treaty by Japanese opinion was due in no small part to the agreement reached in November, 1969, that in 1972 the United States would return to Japanese sovereignty Okinawa and the other Ryukyu Islands which it had occupied in 1945.

The United States continues to administer the Trust Territory of the Pacific Islands, under the supervision of the UN Trusteeship Council. This territory includes the Marshalls, the Carolines, and the Marianas, which form the major portion of the island grouping known as Micronesia. These were former German colonies, mandated to Japan under the League of Nations, which were captured by the United States during World War II. It is proposed that this territory, with a population close to 100,000, be given a commonwealth status similar to that of Puerto Rico.

In 1956, after long negotiations, the Soviet Union finally agreed to a declaration ending a state of war with Japan. This declaration provided for a normalization of diplomatic and trade relations, but it was not a peace treaty and did not make provision for a territorial settlement since the USSR did not accept Japan's demand for the return of the four southernmost islands in the Kurile chain. The declaration did, however, promise

Russian support for the admission of Japan to the United Nations. Japan joined the United Nations in December, 1956, and has since played an active role in its deliberations. Under the peace treaty signed at San Francisco, Japan had renounced sovereignty over South Sakhalin and the Kurile Islands, which it had annexed from Russia in 1905, but a dispute remained over the four southernmost of these islands—Habomai, Shikotan, Kunashiri, and Etofuru. The Soviet Union agreed to cede Habomai and Shikotan, the two islands closest to Japan, but Japan claimed all four on the ground that they were settled by Japanese. The willingness of the United States in 1969 to return the islands it had occupied gave Japan an occasion to raise the question of the four Kurile Islands again. The Soviet Union would not change its position on this issue, but relations between the two countries continued to improve in other respects. A vigorous trade developed between them, and the periodic meetings of the Soviet-Japanese Joint Economic Committee formulated plans under which Japan played a significant role in developing raw materials and port facilities in Soviet Asia.

25

The Polarization
of Europe

The Cold War: *The Iron Curtain; Soviet Alliance System; North Atlantic Treaty Organization; Nuclear Weapons and Disarmament; The Summit.*

Consolidation of Western Europe: *Prospects for a United Europe; The Marshall Plan; Economic Integration; Council of Europe.*

Peaceful Coexistence: *Polycentrism; The Search for Alternative Solutions.*

The Cold War

THE IRON CURTAIN. In the course of the war it was generally believed in Western Europe that democratic solutions to postwar political problems could readily be found. Russia had been reasonably cooperative during the war, and the Charter of the United Nations was agreed to with no more than normal controversy. In this view, the problems of Germany and of the Eastern European states could be solved by free elections, and the resulting governments would participate in due course in the deliberations of the United Nations. There was no inclination to minimize the problems of economic recovery that Europe would face after the war, but the Internationl Bank for Reconstruction and

Development and the International Monetary Fund, which came into existence in 1945, seemed to offer an adequate framework for international co-operation in the economic sphere.

Perhaps to a greater extent than in Western Europe, opinion in the United States envisaged a world in which the application of force would no longer be necessary. After the defeat of Japan, the American government readily acceded to the popular demands for a rapid demobilization of its armed forces, which went from 8.3 million men in 1945 to 1.4 million in 1949, and for a reduction in the defense budget, which went from $81 to $14 billion in the same period. On two occasions during the war President Roosevelt had informed Marshal Stalin that he did not think the American public would support the maintenance of American forces in Europe after the defeat of Germany, and indeed the reduction was even more rapid than the President had anticipated. At the same time the United States discontinued lend-lease aid, a cornerstone of American wartime policy, and made other moves which reflected a belief that a stable Europe could be restored without major reliance on American influence.

No similar belief in postwar stability underlay Soviet policy. Judging from official pronouncements, it is clear that the Soviet leaders anticipated that World War II might be followed by a wave of revolutionary movements similar to those that had come in the wake of World War I. They were prepared to take advantage of such a situation so long as this could be done without risk to Soviet security and with only a modest expenditure of resources. It is also likely that Russian domestic instability was a factor in the intransigence of the Soviet government. Soviet leaders may have felt that only by evoking the image of a Russia surrounded by enemies could they demand of the Russian people the sacrifices required by the effort of postwar reconstruction under the methods employed by the Communist party.

These differing expectations soon became evident in the course of the negotiations for a postwar settlement, and they formed the basis for the controversies that soon ensued. The central issue then and since has been the question of how Europe would be organized, that is, who would control it. The Soviet Union, as the great power that had suffered most in the war, was concerned that Germany would regain control over Europe as it had after the First World War, and they were determined to prevent this at all costs. To the extent that this policy was expressed in the language of Marxism-Leninism, it projected an aggressive image of Soviet domination over Europe. The Soviet fear of the West was nevertheless real, and at the very least it motivated a policy of firm and continuing control over all the territories and peoples occupied by the Soviet army at the end of the war.

The fear of the Western countries, that the Soviet Union would gain control over Germany and would then seek to press its influence further west, was equally great. Although Soviet armed forces were reduced from 12 million to perhaps as low as 2.8 million between 1945 and 1948, this was not known at the time and even the latter figure was substantially higher than that of any of the principal Western powers. In both France and Italy, moreover, Communist parties were members of the governing coalitions until 1947, and their potential for subversion could not be ignored by Western statesmen.

Thus there developed what came to be known as the "Cold War"—cold, in the sense that it involved hostility but not fighting—which was to dominate the first postwar generation. It was a genuine conflict in the sense that the leaders on each side were convinced that the other side had aggressive intentions centering on the control of Europe through the control of Germany. At the same time, neither side recognized that the opposing leaders were motivated more by defensive than offensive considerations.

The intensity of the Soviet antagonism to the Western Allies was reflected in the election speeches of Stalin and Molotov in February, 1946, which described the Western states as enemies; and in November, 1947, Zhdanov formally characterized Europe as being divided between peace-loving Communists and aggressive imperialists. At the same time, many acts of Soviet policy conveyed an aggressive impression to foreign observers. The harsh oppression of Eastern Europe after 1945, the reluctance to withdraw from Iran in 1946, the threats to Greece and Turkey in 1947, and the coup in Czechoslovakia in 1948 all appeared to be part of a pattern, and it was generally believed in the West that Soviet power was prepared to move into any position that the Western states were not willing to defend.

As early as March, 1946, Churchill declared in a noteworthy address in Fulton, Missouri, that "From Stettin in the Baltic to Trieste in the Adriatic an iron curtain has descended across the continent." At the time many thought that Churchill was exaggerating the situation, but subsequent events appeared to support his view and the term "Iron Curtain" soon gained wide currency as an apt description of the political and ideological barriers separating East and West. The United States was somewhat slower than Western Europe to respond to the changed emphasis of Soviet policy, but by the time the Truman Doctrine was announced in 1947 the belief in Soviet hostility was widely accepted. The victory of the Communist party in China in 1949, and experience with aggressive Communist actions in Korea, Indochina, Malaya, the Philippines, and other areas in East Asia, served to strengthen the view that the Western countries were beleaguered.

Indeed, it came to be widely believed that Soviet-led Communist forces would strike in Europe if an appropriate opportunity were afforded, and Churchill expressed the view in 1948 that "the atom bomb alone stands between Europe today and complete subjugation to Communist tyranny." In retrospect it seems unlikely that the Soviet Union was planning aggression against Western Europe, but in the light of Soviet actions elsewhere, responsible Western statesmen felt at the time that they could not assume other than aggressive intentions. It was in this atmosphere that NATO was established, with a view to limiting Soviet power in Europe to the territories over which it had gained control at the end of World War II. These political attitudes on both sides resulted in the Cold War, in the course of which feelings ran so high that no meeting of the heads of state was held between the Potsdam Conference in July and August, 1945, and the summit meeting in Geneva in July, 1955.

SOVIET ALLIANCE SYSTEM. The Soviet alliance system in Europe was based initially on mutual assistance treaties concluded with the government-in-exile of Czechoslovakia in December, 1943, and with the postwar governments of Yugoslavia and Poland in April, 1945. To these were added a new series of treaties in the spring of 1948 with all the states of Eastern Europe. By 1948 an alliance system of similar bilateral treaties had thus been created in Eastern Europe, both between the USSR and the states of this region and among these states themselves. These treaties provided for collaboration and consultation among the signatories, mutual assistance in the event of aggression by Germany or any third state, and the strengthening of political, economic, and cultural ties. They were concluded for a twenty-year period, and it was stipulated that they would be implemented in the spirit of the United Nations Charter.

In January, 1949, this treaty system was supplemented by a Council of Economic Mutual Assistance (COMECON), which had the task of integrating and rationalizing the economies of the Eastern European countries. In the early postwar years each country had tried to imitate the Soviet system of encouraging the rapid development of heavy industry, but they had neither the resources nor the markets to justify such a program. As a result, their economies were extensively disorganized, and both agriculture and consumer goods were seriously affected. It was not until 1955 that the Soviet government, acting through COMECON, succeeded in bringing some order out of this chaos, and an effort was made to get the various states to agree on a division of labor. An attempt was also made to coordinate the economic plans of these countries and to relate them to the overall Soviet plan.

Underlying this treaty system was the reality of Soviet controls in Eastern Europe, exercised through the Communist parties, the Soviet police network, and a variety of political and economic pressures. Unlike the NATO structure later established in the West, the Eastern alliance system was dominated exclusively by a single power. The Soviet alliance system was nevertheless affected by the extent to which the loyalty of its lesser members could be relied on. It was in fact an uneasy union held together by the presence of the Soviet army, and after the death of Stalin it showed signs of weakness. The Warsaw Pact of May, 1955—which embraced Albania, Bulgaria, Czechoslovakia, East Germany, Hungary, Poland, Rumania, and the USSR—was widely heralded as a reply to NATO, although in fact it was no more than a confirmation of existing treaty relationships. A Soviet marshal was named supreme commander of the Warsaw Pact forces, and a Political Consultative Committee was established to formulate common policies. The unity of this structure was nevertheless soon undermined by the revolts against Soviet authority which took place in Poland and Hungary in October, 1956. Equally threatening to Communist unity in Europe was the growing controversy between the USSR and China, which cast even more serious doubts on the ability of the Communist countries to co-ordinate their policies. By 1965 the Chinese Communist leaders had reached the point of ridiculing the entire range of Soviet policies, and of referring to the Soviet leaders as "revisionists" who were betraying Lenin's revolutionary policies and were in fact collaborating with the United States to dominate the United Nations.

These Chinese accusations were a gross distortion of Soviet policies, arising as they did from a heated quarrel within the Communist family of nations, but they nevertheless reflected profound changes in strategic thinking that had been going on in Soviet military circles. The military strategy that guided Soviet leaders in the early postwar period was one of full and balanced development in all branches of the armed services. Atomic weapons, the air force, and missiles were developed rapidly, but not at the expense of the more conventional elements of military power. Under Khrushchev, however, attention was devoted very largely to nuclear and rocket weapons (to the exclusion of conventional forces). Using the threat of these powerful weapons, the USSR hoped to gain concessions from the West without resort to war. In June, 1961, Khrushchev sought to gain recognition of East Germany by insisting, under an explicit threat of direct action, that a German peace settlement be concluded before the end of the year. In October, 1962 the USSR prepared to install nuclear weapons in Cuba which were capable of reaching the major American cities. In both cases, however, the United States and its allies stood their ground and the USSR backed down. By the mid-1960s the initial Soviet advantage in rocketry had been more than overcome by the United States, and a relative balance between the forces of NATO and the Warsaw Pact was generally acknowledged. The Soviet Union was now much more cautious in engaging in policies that might lead to escalation, and it was this new caution that was the object of ridicule by a China that was still confident that peasant uprisings were capable of overcoming all odds.

NORTH ATLANTIC TREATY ORGANIZATION. The reaction of the West to postwar Soviet policy initially took separate forms in Europe and the United States, but the two movements were soon merged into a single defense effort. In Europe, Britain and France, on March 4, 1947, signed a treaty of alliance at Dunkirk. A year later, on March 17, 1948, they joined with Belgium, the Netherlands, and Luxembourg in agreeing to the Brussels Treaty for economic, social, and cultural collaboration and collective self-defense. This treaty, popularly known as Western Union, made provision for a consultative council of foreign ministers and a permanent commission of ambassadors meeting in London. Under the direction of these bodies,

DRAFTING THE ATLANTIC PACT *Representatives of the interested Western states in consultation at Washington, D.C., in March, 1949. Left to right are: LeGallais (Luxembourg), Van Kleffens (Netherlands), Silvercruys (Belgium), Morgenstierne (Norway), Secretary of State Acheson, Bonnet (France), Wrong (Canada), and Franks (Britain).*

a defense committee and a chiefs-of-staff committee, along with other bodies, were responsible for working out a common defense policy.

Perhaps of even greater moment was the decision of the United States to participate in regional and other collective arrangements, an action that was foreshadowed by the Truman Doctrine in 1947 [see below, pp. 807–8]. This departure from traditional American policy was reflected in the Vandenburg Resolution, adopted by the Senate in June, 1948, which expressed the determination to make use of "the inherent right of individual or collective self-defense" recognized in Article 51 of the United Nations Charter. The decision to establish regional defense organizations represented a recognition that the UN Security Council was not effective in handling disputes among the major powers, but at the same time American policy felt it was important to maintain the United Nations structure and to relate to it such regional groupings as might be set up.

These two developments in Western Europe and in the United States prepared the way for the acceptance of the North Atlantic Treaty, which was signed on April 4, 1949, by the United Kingdom, France, Belgium, the Netherlands, Luxembourg, Denmark, Iceland, Norway, Italy, Portugal, Canada, and the United States. Greece and Turkey acceded to the treaty in October, 1951, and the German Federal Republic was admitted in 1955. This treaty established the North Atlantic Treaty Organization (NATO), which soon became one of the most comprehensive and effective peacetime alliances that the West has known. NATO is headed by an executive body, the North Atlantic Council of Foreign, Defense, and Finance Ministers, which meets several times a year and is serviced by an international secretariat with headquarters in Paris. The central feature of NATO from the start has been its military command structure under the direction of the Supreme Headquarters Allied Powers Europe (SHAPE) in Paris, with General Eisenhower as the first Supreme Allied Commander (1949–52). Under this central direction, regional commands have been established for Northern Europe (Oslo), Central Europe (Fontainebleau), and Southern Europe (Naples). To each command are assigned contingents of land, sea, and air forces contributed by the member states, and these are under international command. This complex structure was elaborated over a period of years, and by 1958 some forty active army divisions were at least nominally assigned to NATO along with important naval and air forces.

The development of this defense force was in many respects a remarkable achievement, and NATO made a vital contribution to the security of its members. Yet it was beset by numerous problems and in many respects fell short of expectations. The central issue concerned the nature of the military threat and the means that should be used to counter it. Under the terms of the treaty an attack against one member of NATO was to be considered an attack against them all, and this meant that an integrated strategy had to be devised which would take into consideration the wide diversity of interests and capabilities of the member states. Particularly acute were the differences in outlook between the United States and Western Europe. The Europeans wished to see substantial American forces stationed on the continent, but it was the American view that European states with a combined population of some 190 million ought to be able to provide the bulk of their own forces. European concern was due partly to uncertainty as to the firmness of the American commitment in Europe, in view of the tradition of isolationism, and partly to the fear that in the event of Soviet aggression the United States might abandon Europe to the Russian armies and counterattack with nuclear air power. If this occurred Russia might ultimately be defeated, but Europe would be destroyed in the process. The solution finally reached by NATO was a strategy that regarded the NATO forces in Europe as a "shield" to deter Russia from easy conquests on the Continent, while American atomic weapons were to be a "sword" available in case Russia launched an all-out attack. This strategy emphasized the essentially defensive character of NATO, since its forces in Europe were entirely inadequate for an attack on Russia.

This strategy of "shield" and "sword" had a certain logic to it, but it met with many objections. One was that American strategic air power was not under NATO command, as the decision to use nuclear weapons rested with the president alone. It was also asserted that since American air power served as a deterrent to Russia in any event, there was little chance the Russians would attempt a general offensive. More likely was a series of limited attacks by Russia with conventional weapons in relatively unimportant areas. Such attacks could overwhelm the relatively weak ground forces available to the West, but might not be of sufficient gravity to justify a major nuclear reply. Further doubts were cast on NATO strategy by the rapid development of missiles, for by 1958 practically all of Europe was within range of Russian-based missiles. Many critics believed that for all practical purposes the West could checkmate Russia's nuclear power, but was much weaker than Russia in conventional forces. Under these circumstances, nuclear disarmament would tend to strip the West of its defenses while leaving Russia relatively strong.

When NATO was established it had as its goal the formation of a community of nations with integrated political, social, and economic institutions. Its membership soon proved too diverse to provide the basis for such a community, but when the problem arose of admitting Germany into NATO, France proposed that a European Defense Community (EDC) be formed, with more limited membership. Planned as a part of the movement for European integration, the EDC as a supernational organization had the particular aim of providing the means for Germany to rearm without threatening the security of its Western neighbors. Such an organization had many unforeseeable risks, however, and despite its French sponsorship the proposal was in the end defeated by the French parliament in August, 1954. The French wished to have a long-term guarantee that Britain would maintain its military contingents on the European continent at the existing level, in the belief that French and British force together would be adequate to counterbalance those of Germany. In the absence of such a British guarantee, the French felt that their security would be better served by keeping their defense forces independent than by pooling them with the other members of EDC. In place of EDC, a Western European Union (WEU) was formed in May, 1955, by adding the German Federal Republic and Italy to the Brussels Treaty group. The WEU was not a supernational authority, as had been envisaged in the case of the EDC, but it served as a means of permitting Germany to participate in the defense of Europe with adequate guarantees for its neighbors.

With the development of nuclear weapons, however, the solutions that met the needs of the 1950s were not adequate for the 1960s. As nuclear weapons began to dominate military thinking, the European countries were increasingly uneasy in a situation in which an American president (over whom they had no control) had a virtual monopoly on the use of nuclear weapons that might vitally affect Europe. The United States was reluctant to let European countries have control over American nuclear weapons stationed in Europe, lest they be used in local conflicts and trigger a major nuclear war. Even less satisfactory was a third alternative, however, namely the proliferation of nuclear weapons under national control such as had already begun in England and France. As a possible solution to this dilemma, the United States proposed the creation of a multilateral nuclear force (MLF) consisting of some twenty-five surface vessels, each equipped with eight Polaris missiles and manned by crews of mixed nationalities. France nevertheless opposed the MLF on the ground that it would in effect perpetuate the American military dominance of the alliance. Instead France favored the creation of a European nuclear deterrent, including England, which would permit Europe to become a third major nuclear power along with the United States and the USSR. At the same time both England and Germany leaned toward the American proposal and opposed the French proposal. This debate reflected the fact that NATO remained a coalition of independent sovereign states, and was not making significant progress in developing a system of political consultation that would serve to integrate national policies [see below, pp. 644–51].

NUCLEAR WEAPONS AND DISARMAMENT. As soon as the war was over it was recognized that the one major security problem underlying all others was the control of atomic energy. At this stage the United States was in the responsible position of being the only country that had succeeded in producing atomic bombs, although the scientific knowledge contributing to this achievement was possessed in varying degrees by a number of countries, including the Soviet Union. In November, 1945, the United States, in concert with the United Kingdom and Canada, proposed that a United Nations Commission be created to draw up regulations for the control of atomic energy and for the restriction of atomic weapons. The Russians accepted this proposal in December, and in the following months an Atomic Energy Commission was etablished. Its membership included the members of the Security Council, with the addition of Canada.

An American plan was now placed before the Commission, providing for the establishment of an International Atomic Development Authority that would have a monopoly over the dangerous uses of atomic energy and would supervise its scientific and technical uses through a system of licensing and control. Under this plan the Authority was empowered to inspect raw materials and production facilities in any country, in order to safeguard against the secret manufacture of bombs, and its actions in this regard would not be subject to the veto. The United States agreed to transfer to the Authority its own atomic energy facilities by stages as the plan was being put into effect. The Soviet representative objected to this plan on several grounds. While he was willing to accept a general system of control, he insisted that the great power veto be retained. At the same time, he refused to grant to an international agency full authority to supervise the development of atomic energy for peaceful purposes. Moreover, he demanded that the United States destroy its atomic bombs prior to the establishment of a control system. While the American plan was accepted by all countries except the members of the Soviet bloc, and was ultimately approved by the General Assembly by a vote of forty to six, with four abstentions, it was killed in the Security Council in July, 1948, by a Soviet veto. The announcement by President Truman on September 23, 1949, that an atomic explosion had occurred in the Soviet Union served to stress the gravity of the problem but contributed little to its solution.

The initial failure to control atomic energy led to a general arms race. In the field of nuclear weapons the United States maintained its leadership, exploding its first hydrogen bomb in November, 1952, nine months ahead of the Russians. Later Great Britain also developed nuclear weapons, and research reached an advanced stage in several other countries. In the field of long-range missiles, on the other hand, the Soviet Union took the lead in 1957 and gave evidence that it was a year or more ahead of the West. By the early 1950s it was clear that a sufficient supply of nuclear weapons was available to destroy all civilization, if they should be released in an all-out war. Moreover, there was evidence that the continued testing of nuclear weapons might seriously damage the health of future generations. By 1958 some $100 billion a year was being spent around the world on armaments, and as many as eighteen to twenty million men were being kept under arms. Even though none of the great powers appeared to be contemplating major acts of aggression, the danger always existed that a minor conflict might as a result of miscalculation rapidly develop into a major war. Since such vast damage could now be wrought at little more than a moment's notice, none of the major powers could rest assured that at some moment of crisis it might not be subjected to a surprise attack. Moreover, even the wealthiest of nations could find better uses for the immense resources that were being poured into armaments.

The issues and problems involved in proposals for disarmament were clearly reflected in the long and discouraging sessions of the UN Disarmament Commission that met in London in the summer of 1957. One important issue was that of preventing surprise attacks, for it was felt that if the great powers could be assured that no sudden aggression was being prepared they would be better able to consider other aspects of disarmament. On this issue President Eisenhower had already presented at the summit conference in 1955 an "open-skies" aerial inspection plan, under which all or major sections of the territory of the great powers would be open to aerial photography. No agreement could be reached at London, however, as to methods or areas of inspection. A second issue was that of controlling nuclear weapons and suspending nuclear tests. The Russians were willing to suspend tests, but rejected Western proposals for the enforcement of this measure by inspection teams. A third issue was the traditional one of limiting the size of conventional forces. How could the manpower under arms be reduced, what quotas of forces should be assigned to the various nations, and how would these quotas be enforced? Here again no solution was reached.

The disarmament discussions in 1957 nevertheless helped to clarify the issues, and in the following year considerable progress was made. In March, 1958, the Soviet Union announced that it would suspend nuclear tests. In August, a Conference on Detection of Bomb Testing held in Geneva brought substantial agreement between Soviet and Western specialists on the feasibility of a system of detection for the supervision of a ban on testing. Shortly thereafter the United States announced the suspension of tests for a year starting October 31. The moratorium on testing was broken in 1961, first by the USSR and shortly thereafter by the United States, but this continued testing of more sophisticated weapons only emphasized more strongly the need for controls.

The United Kingdom tested its first weapon in 1952 and France in 1960. This proliferation of nuclear weapons, and the knowledge that China also would soon possess an atom bomb—which was in fact tested in 1964—led the United Kingdom, the United States, and the USSR to agree in 1963 to a treaty banning nuclear weapons tests in the atmosphere, in outer space, and under water. This was a major achievement, and 107 states soon ratified the treaty. But France and China both refused to accept it, because they were still in the process of testing their new weapons.

In the meantime, a renewed effort was made in 1961 to press forward with disarmament. Agreement was reached in the United Nations on the formation of an Eighteen-Nation Committee on Disarmament, with five members each from NATO and the Warsaw Pact and eight representing nonaligned countries [see below, p. 870]. This Committee met annually starting in 1962 and has made some progress toward its goal. In 1963, it sponsored an agreement between the United States and the USSR to establish a direct communication link between Washington and Moscow. The "hot line," as it is called, is a teletype cable that passes through London, Stockholm, and Helsinki, and is expected to reduce the likelihood of a war occurring because of accident, miscalculation, or failure of communication.

The continuing work of negotiation now moved into more difficult areas, but a major turning point was reached in November, 1969, when the United States and the USSR signed the treaty on the nonproliferation of nuclear weapons. This treaty stipulated that the nuclear powers would not supply nuclear weapons or technology to other states, that nonnuclear states would not seek to acquire such weapons or technology, and that installations in the latter countries using fissionable material for peaceful purposes would be subject to inspection under procedures worked out by the International Atomic Energy Agency. This treaty would not go into effect until forty other countries had ratified it, but prospects for such ratification were good. At the same time, the United States and the USSR reached agreement on the draft of a treaty prohibiting the placing of nuclear weapons on the seabed or ocean floor beyond the twelve-mile limit.

The negotiations leading up to these agreements helped to create an atmosphere of sufficient mutual trust to enable the United States and the USSR to tackle the key problem of the limitation of the large stockpile of nuclear weapons that they had accumulated for possible use against each other. In June, 1968, the Soviet government announced its willingness to exchange opinions on this subject, and an American negotiating team was preparing to depart for Moscow in August when the occupation of Czechoslovakia occurred. Finally in November, 1969, the Strategic Arms Limitation Talks (SALT) were inaugurated in Helsinki. The first round of talks was concerned primarily with procedural matters, but by the end of the second session (April-August 1970) the prospects were good that a measure of agreement might in due course be achieved. It was expected that the process of negotiation might take many months, but the very fact that bilateral talks were under way was regarded as a hopeful sign.

THE SUMMIT. Not the least of the problems facing European statesmen was how to undertake the negotiation of the great issues that had to be solved. The United Nations was the most convenient arena, but in some respects its atmosphere was not suited to the discussion of matters of the highest importance. The Security Council was governed by rigid rules of procedure, while in the General Assembly the presence of over one-hundred delegations prevented easy and intimate exchanges of opinion. Committees of experts performed a useful service, but their members did not have the authority to make important concessions. Even meetings of foreign ministers tended to be conducted rather formally on the basis of a fixed agenda. With a view to breaking this deadlock and seeking a freer exchange of opinions on fundamental issues, Churchill proposed in 1953 that a meeting be held "at the summit," that is to say, by heads of state, without an agenda and simply as a means of exploring each other's views. Some criticized this proposal on the ground that little grass grows at the summit, and that discussions further down the slope by seasoned diplomats would be more fruitful, but the idea nevertheless seemed worth trying.

The first postwar meeting of heads of state took place in Geneva from July 18 to 21, 1955. Eisenhower, Bulganin, Eden, and Faure met every afternoon to discuss general principles, and in the mornings their foreign ministers—Dulles, Molotov, Macmillan, and Pineau—met to work out the details. These meetings produced some moments of genuine warmth, as when Eisenhower assured the Russians that NATO had no aggressive aims, and in general a spirit of friendship and sincerity prevailed. When it came to discussing specific issues, however, the heads of state did not go much beyond the positions their governments had set forth in the past. On the unification of Germany, the West again favored free elections in both parts of the country, whereas the Russians preferred to maintain the status quo [see below, pp. 620–22]. Various proposals were presented for a defense treaty linking all the European states, but before the German problem was solved no agreement was possible as to the terms of such a treaty. In the field of disarmament, as already noted, it was to be three years before a start could be made in reconciling Soviet and Western views. Only on the broad issue of improving East-West relations was some progress made in agreeing on measures to reduce barriers to travel and cultural exchange. All of these matters were referred for further discussion to the meeting of foreign ministers held in Geneva from October 27 to November 16, 1955, but little further progress was made.

In the ensuing years there was no change in the status of Germany or in the prospects for a general European security treaty embracing East and West. At the same time responsible leaders in the West turned over in their minds possible alternatives to the proposals that had already been made. At the heart of any new negotiations looking toward "disengagement," as the proposed relaxation of tensions was now called, was the question of what concessions either side could make. If the United States withdrew from NATO, as the Soviet leaders desired, the position of the Western European states would clearly be weakened. If the United States withheld from supplying nuclear weapons to Europe, again tension would be reduced but at the expense of European security. Similarly if Germany were encouraged to unite only on condition that it be neutralized, a condition that the government of the German Federal Republic did not accept, the Western position would be relatively weaker. The plan suggested in 1957 by Rapacki, the Polish foreign minister, for banning the production and stockpiling of nuclear weapons in the two Germanies and in Poland (to which Czechoslovakia later associated itself) like other Communist proposals, made no provision for inspection. Seen from the Soviet point of view, there was similarly no incentive for compromise, for Soviet leaders had no intention of giving up any of the territories over which they held sway east of the Iron Curtain. In the winter of 1957–58 an extensive public correspondence was exchanged between Soviet and Western statesmen on the subject of further discussion at the summit, and in August, 1958, as an aftermath of the Middle East crisis Khrushchev made a formal proposal for another summit conference. The Western statesmen agreed on condition that the meeting be held as a session of the UN Security Council, to assure an orderly procedure. At first Khrushchev appeared willing to accept this condition, but after consultation with Mao Tse-tung he decided against it on the ground that the Chinese People's Republic would not be represented. The Middle Eastern crisis was subsequently resolved without a summit meeting, but the feeling nevertheless prevailed that discussion by the heads of state might help things along.

A visit by Prime Minister Khrushchev to the United States was finally arranged in 1959, and in the course of a conference with President Eisenhower at Camp David it was agreed that the Berlin question and disarmament issues should be a matter of continued negotiation and should not be allowed to reach a crisis stage. This was essentially an agreement designed to improve the atmosphere of international relations and was not intended to lead to immediate practical results. This new atmosphere facilitated arrangements for a summit conference of the Big Four in Paris in May, 1960, and for a visit by President Eisenhower to the USSR in

SUMMIT MEETING AT GENEVA *The heads of state of the Big Four meet in July, 1955, for the first time in ten years. Clockwise from the upper right are President Eisenhower and Secretary of State Dulles of the United States; Premier Faure and Foreign Minister Pineau of France; Prime Minister Eden and Foreign Secretary Macmillan of the United Kingdom; and Communist Party First Secretary Khrushchev, Premier Bulganin, and Foreign Minister Molotov of the Soviet Union.*

June. On the eve of these new meetings, however, the USSR announced that an American U-2 aircraft engaged in photographing Soviet military installations had been shot down over the USSR. This event destroyed the hopes for any agreement at the summit, and President Eisenhower's visit was cancelled. A subsequent investigation by the United States Senate Foreign Relations Committee concluded that the U-2 affair had been seriously mishandled, but that it was not the primary cause for the breakdown of the summit conference. Most observers believed that Khrushchev had hoped to use the summit conference to divide the West over the German question. As the time for the conference approached he realized that this would not be possible, and he seized on the U-2 incident to cover his position. In June, 1961, President Kennedy held a brief meeting with the Soviet Prime Minister in Vienna, but it proved to be less a conference than an opportunity for Khrushchev to press vigorously his demands for an immediate conclusion of the German peace settlement on Russian terms [see above, pp. 620–22]. The record of summit meetings was thus not encouraging, and experience appeared to indicate that such encounters might serve as symbols of friendly relations but that complex issues could best be resolved by negotiations conducted by professional diplomats.

It was probably a measure of the relaxation of tensions that so much progress was made toward disarmament in subsequent years without resort to summit meetings. The relatively brief and informal meetings held by President Johnson and Prime Minister Kosygin at Glassboro, New Jersey, in June, 1967, were concerned primarily with the Middle East and Vietnam crises and served to demonstrate the continuing goodwill of the leaders even if they did not have any significant effect on the development of events.

Consolidation of Western Europe

PROSPECTS FOR A UNITED EUROPE. The decisive role that the Soviet Union and the United States played in European affairs during the war itself was of necessity continued during the peace settlement. If the United States felt a strong inclination to withdraw from European affairs at the end of the war, it soon realized that to do so would leave Europe completely at the mercy of the Soviet Union and that American security would thereby in the long run be endangered. As a result of this realization, the United States entered into active participation in European affairs; and this policy in turn led to a rivalry with Russia for influence which in the terminology of political science is generally referred to as the "bipolarization" of political power. With Moscow at the Eastern pole and Washington at the Western, the European states tended to gravitate toward one or the other sphere of influence. The frontier established between these spheres of influence was in the end no different from that set up for administrative purposes between the military forces of Russia and those of its Western Allies during the war, and attempts by either side to change this line of demarcation after the war only tended to harden it into an Iron Curtain.

The dangers of the bipolarization of political power, which in some respects resembled the two-coalition system of the Triple Entente and the Triple Alliance dominant in the European scene during the decade before World War I, lay in the possibility that during some critical test of strength a resort to war might appear to one or another constellation of states as preferable to compromise. The situation arising out of World War II thus appeared to offer a more precarious basis for peace than would exist in a political system composed of a larger number of states relatively equal in strength. At the same time these dangers were considerably mitigated by the fact that, while the frontier between the two spheres of influence ran through the middle of Europe, the centers of power were beyond the confines of the continent. A divided Europe was thus placed in the position of playing an important but nevertheless secondary role in the rivalry between the two great protagonists.

Many observers at the end of World War II were struck by the apparent political helplessness of Western Europe despite its very substantial potentialities. The heart of the difficulty clearly lay in Europe's political disunity. Although the countries of Western Europe had great potential resources, they were divided by many and frequently conflicting sovereignties each of which was proud of its national tradition and its individuality. European agriculture and industry were adapted to small, protected markets, which placed severe limits on productivity even when they produced substantial profits. Individual European economies could not support the vast investments and enterprises common to the American and the Soviet economies, which permitted more efficient production. In short, Europe as it emerged from World War II was unable to bring to its peoples the full benefits of modern science and technology, and it seemed likely that Europe would fall steadily behind if steps were not taken to remedy the situation.

There was no clear and simple solution to this problem, and indeed there was a good deal of controversy as to just what the facts were and how they should be interpreted, but most European leaders recognized that tariffs had to be lowered and that Europe should move in the direction of pooling resources and markets. A great boost was given to this movement by the Marshall Plan, which did much to set the European economy back on its feet after the war and to foster economic co-operation. Indeed, in the purely economic field, Europe took giant strides in the direction of economic integration in the next decade. In the political field progress was much slower, and the limited achievements of the Council of Europe testify as to the difficulties that had to be overcome.

THE MARSHALL PLAN. The United States took the lead in extending grants and loans to bolster the economy of the states of Western Europe. In an address at Harvard University on June 5, 1947, Secretary of State Marshall made a proposal for American support of a united effort of the states of Europe to achieve recovery and prevent the further disintegration of Europe. Leaders in France and Britain immediately sponsored a conference to meet in Paris to work out such a plan. The Soviet leaders, however, damned Marshall's proposal as an instrument of American imperialism and not only refused to co-operate but kept the Eastern satellite states from doing so. Spain was not invited, but representatives of sixteen other nations met in Paris in July, 1947: Austria, Belgium, Denmark, France, Greece, Iceland, Ireland (Eire), Italy, Luxembourg, the Netherlands, Norway, Portugal, Sweden, Switzerland, Turkey, and the United Kingdom. The conferees faced a difficult task, but by September 24 were able to sub-

mit to President Truman a plan for mutual aid and self-help as a counterpart to financial aid from the United States.

The European countries concluded that over the next four years they
would need $22.44 billion worth of food, fuel, raw materials, and capital
equipment over and above what they could pay for. About $3 billion of
this they expected to obtain from the International Bank and other sources;
but a staggering amount was left for the United States to provide. President Truman pared down the figure and asked Congress to provide $17
billion for the four years 1948–51. Congress passed an interim aid bill
and proceeded to debate the issue thoroughly. On April 3, 1948, the law
providing for the European Recovery Program (ERP, Marshall Plan) was
signed by the President. Instead of making a four-year grant, Congress
appropriated $6.8 billion for the first fifteen months and undertook to
make three additional annual grants later. The Act established an Economic Co-operation Administration (ECA) to carry out the program from
the American side, and Paul T. Hoffman was given overall direction of the
program.

In Europe the participating nations in April, 1948, established a permanent organization known as the Organization for European Economic
Co-operation (OEEC), with headquarters in Paris. It was headed by a
council representing the member states, and its technical work was carried
on by a secretariat and numerous permanent committees. It was charged
with presenting to ECA the detailed claims of each country for Marshall
Plan aid and elaborating a long-term plan for European co-operation and
recovery. The claims presented required the approval of Hoffman, who
then issued grants or in some instances authorized loans. Most of the
money was made available in the form of outright grants, and each country was required to place in a "counterpart fund" an amount of money in
its own currency equal to these grants. The European states obtained
these funds by selling to their own inhabitants the food and material sent
to them under the Plan. The counterpart funds accumulated and could be
spent by the different European countries only with the approval of the
American authorities, who were concerned with seeing that the funds were
used to bolster the nation's economy and encourage European recovery.
Each country receiving aid negotiated a special agreement with the United
States in which details in regard to the use of funds were dealt with. Often
a certain percentage of the counterpart funds (5 percent in the case of
Great Britain) was set aside for the use of the United States to pay its
expenses in that country, such as those of the embassy there. Provisions
were also inserted looking toward the acquisition by the United States
of stockpiles of scarce raw materials. The Marshall Plan was directed toward increasing the co-operation of European states among themselves,
and with this in view the latter drew up on October 16, 1948, an "Agreement for Intra-European Payments and Compensations." This provided
for clearing on a multilateral basis the differences in trade balances between any two states, for currencies were still not freely convertible.

In the entire period from 1945 through 1963, of a total American foreign assistance program of $96 billion, Western Europe received $39.3 billion. Of this amount $15.6 billion was in military grants and $23.7 billion in other grants and credits. In the same period the Near East and South Asia received $16.2 billion, and Eastern Europe and the USSR $1.5 billion. In the 1950s defense loomed large in the foreign assistance to Western Europe, but both military and economic aid served the common purpose of stimulating the European economy. This assistance was one of the central features of the European economic revival, which by the 1960s resulted in an unprecedented prosperity. Indeed, the policies initiated by the Marshall Plan are generally regarded as the most successful venture in foreign affairs ever undertaken by the United States.

ECONOMIC INTEGRATION. The Organization of European Economic Co-operation (OEEC), which continued after the Marshall Plan officially came to an end in 1952, soon became the cornerstone of the movement for the integration of the European economy. In 1961 the OEEC was reorganized as the Organization for Economic Co-operation and Development (OECD). The main task of the OEEC, as of its successor, was to reduce trade barriers and to facilitate the transferability of currencies among its members. This latter task was helped by the creation of the European Payments Union in 1950. Proposals are also under consideration for the creation of a Free Trade Area, and in 1958 a European Nuclear Energy Agency was established. These steps were a marked advance over the increasing autarky that had characterized the European states between the two world wars, but they were still a long way from the thoroughgoing economic integration that many regarded as the source of American and Soviet economic strength.

What could not be achieved by the members of the OEEC was nevertheless attempted by a smaller group of states—France, the German Federal Republic, Italy, Belgium, the Netherlands, and Luxembourg. In 1951 these six states formed the European Coal and Steel Community (ECSC), Europe's first fully federalized organization. Its structure includes a council of ministers, an assembly elected by the parliaments of the member states, an administrative authority, and a court to settle disputes regarding the interpretation of the treaty. The purpose of this Community is to stimulate the production of coal and steel by creating a free market through the reduction of trade barriers. During the first four years of operation the volume of production of the members of the Community increased 23 percent for coal and 145 percent for iron and steel, and this achievement demonstrated the advantages of economic integration.

Encouraged by these results the same six nations—now frequently known as the Europe of the Six—embarked on a much bolder venture. On March 25, 1957, they signed two further treaties: one setting up the European Economic Community, generally known as the Common Market, and the other establishing a European Atomic Energy Community, or Euratom. The former organization envisaged elimination of all trade

barriers between its members in three stages over a period of twelve to
fifteen years, involving not only freedom of movement of goods, but
also of labor and capital, as well as the standardization of social security
systems and wage benefits. This was indeed a bold venture, but experience
indicated that it was not only feasible but necessary if Europe was to
survive as a center of progress. Euratom was more specialized in its implications, in that it was concerned with creating a common market for
nuclear raw materials and equipment as well as a reservoir of nuclear
technicians available to member states. These two agreements, combined
with the ECSC, thus provide for the 185 million inhabitants of the Europe
of the Six a solid basis for economic integration. While all six states were
of course members of the OEEC, there were very significant differences
between the two approaches. In the case of the OEEC, the member
states retained their sovereignty and were free to disregard its recommendations. In the case of the Community, however, the member states surrendered their sovereignty for certain specific purposes and permitted the
Community to make decisions for them. While the Community was
economic in its functions, it thus called for the pooling of political authority and to this extent laid the foundations for a federated Europe.

The development of the European Economic Community was greeted
with considerable apprehension by other European countries insofar as
its policies tended to discriminate against nonmembers. Britain was
particularly concerned, since it faced the dilemma of maintaining its trade
with Europe without undertaking restrictions—such as those binding
members of the EEC—that would limit its wide-ranging commercial arrangements outside Europe. To meet this problem, a European Free
Trade Association (EFTA)—also known as the Outer Seven—was formed
in 1960 by Britain, Denmark, Norway, Sweden, Switzerland, Austria, and
Portugal. This group of seven countries also worked for tariff reductions,
but it did not accept the degree of internationalization favored by the
founders of the EEC. When Britain sought further to strengthen its
position by gaining admission to the EEC under special conditions that
it sought to negotiate, De Gaulle in 1963 announced France's refusal to
accept the British conditions on the grounds that this conditional membership would serve to increase American economic influence in Europe.
Europe thus remained divided between the Six (EEC) and the Seven
(EFTA), and hopes for further economic integration were placed on the
continuing negotiations in the mid-1960s of the General Agreement on
Tariffs and Trade (GATT) which sought on a worldwide basis to increase
trade by reducing tariffs and other restrictions.

The decision of the European Economic Community in December,
1969, to consider applications for membership by Britain, Ireland, Denmark, and Norway was followed by prolonged negotiations that finally
led in 1971 to agreement on terms for Britain's admission. It also offered
a prospect of further broadening the Community's membership to include

countries such as Austria, Sweden, and Switzerland, which sought a special status due to their policies of neutrality.

Common tariff policies were more easily achieved by the members of EEC in industry than in agriculture, but by the end of the 1960s policies in the latter area had reached a degree of equalization that envisaged a virtually free exchange of goods by 1975. At the same time, provisions have been agreed upon by which the proceeds of certain national taxes will be paid into the common EEC budget. It has been estimated that by the later 1970s the Community might have an annual revenue of some $4 billion from this source. In addition to making significant progress on matters of fiscal policy, the EEC has gone a long way toward the adoption of common social measures. Labor can now move freely from one country to another within the system, and social security benefits earned in any of the member countries can be credited to the appropriate fund in the worker's own country. The EEC is still a long way from establishing a new multinational sovereignty, but it is not difficult to envisage a Community of ten members by the later 1970s with a far greater degree of shared sovereignty than seemed possible in the 1960s.

The internal strengthening of the EEC has been accompanied by separate arrangements with associate members. Greece and Turkey became associate members in 1961 and 1963, and by 1970 another twenty-one overseas countries and thirteen overseas departments and territories still under European sovereignty shared an associate status. These associate members benefit from tariff advantages offered by the EEC, while protecting their own markets, and also have access to a development fund provided by the six European members.

COUNCIL OF EUROPE. The functional economic communities established by the Europe of the Six were by all odds the most important steps toward European integration after the war, but they were limited to rather narrow and specialized fields. At the same time these institutions were being created, a much more comprehensive movement for the consolidation of Europe was under way under the auspices of the Council of Europe. This organization was established in May, 1949, by ten of the Western European states, and by 1971 it numbered seventeen members [see Appendix VII]. Its headquarters are in Strasbourg, and its central organs are a Committee of Ministers composed of the foreign ministers and a Consultative Assembly of 147 elected by the parliaments of the member states. Representation in the Assembly is proportional to the size of the country, ranging from three for Cyprus, Iceland, Luxembourg, and Malta, to eighteen for France, the German Federal Republic, Italy, and the United Kingdom. The representatives sit in the Assembly alphabetically according to their own names, not by national groups, and each man votes according to his own convictions. The Assembly is not itself a parliament, for it has no authority to legislate for the member states. Its recommendations, which require a two-thirds majority of the representatives casting a vote, are made to the Committee of Ministers, which in turn may make recommendations to the member states. The work of the Council is carried on by a permanent secretariat.

In the course of a decade the Council of Europe has undertaken many activities in the interest of European unity. It had hoped originally to acquire political authority with limited functions but real powers—an area of activity with regard to which member states would delegate their sovereignty—but this is more than the members were willing to concede. This type of authority was granted only by the Europe of the Six to the three Communities. The Council of Europe has in fact established close relations with these Communities but has not made a significant contribution to their work.

Greater progress was made, however, in establishing the Council as a general policy-formulating body for Europe. It has, for instance, sponsored a number of treaties that have a significant bearing on the welfare of all Europeans. Of these the most important is the European Convention for the Protection of Human Rights and Fundamental Freedoms, signed in Rome in 1950. Unlike the Universal Declaration of Human Rights adopted by the United Nations in the same year, this convention provides legal guarantees of the rights in question. These guarantees are enforced by a Commission of Human Rights empowered to make a friendly settlement of complaints and a Court of Human Rights to handle cases the Commission is unable to settle. Steps have also been taken to give individuals as well as states the right to petition the Court, but this radical measure has met with strong resistance. Other conventions sponsored by the Council of Europe are concerned with social security, social and medical assistance, patents, and similar subjects.

The Council also receives reports from the wide variety of international bodies on which its members are represented, including the OEEC, the organizations of the Europe of the Six, and the various affiliates of the United Nations. These reports serve as the starting point of debates that help to crystallize the policies of the member states. The Assembly also conducts debates on major issues of European foreign policy and has helped in some measure to restore parliamentary influence in an area that has increasingly become the prerogative of the ministries of foreign affairs. In the cultural field, the Council has awarded research fellowships and sponsored conferences in furtherance of the European idea, and it supports a series of publications.

The Council of Europe is not a superstate, and in many respects it has failed to achieve the goals set by its founders. Its members have been reluctant to grant even the very limited authority the Council now possesses, and the leadership in integrating Europe has been assumed by such organizations as NATO and the Communities of the six West European states. The Council has nevertheless made significant gains in its role of reflecting the spirit of Europe on important issues, and its achievement of fostering interparliamentary co-operation is an essential step if European unity is eventually to be achieved.

Peaceful Coexistence

It is characteristic of the postwar era that "peaceful coexistence," like other terms in common usage such as "democracy," "socialism," "capitalism," "imperialism," and even "peace," has a Western meaning and an Eastern meaning. The Western meaning is living together in disagreement but in peace, solving international problems on a pragmatic basis without resort to war. The Eastern meaning is the transformation of all societies from "feudalism" through "capitalism" to "socialism" and "communism" without resort to war between the major states. The Western meaning is thus relatively static, implying that each side will retain its own ideology and social system more or less indefinitely. The Eastern meaning is more dynamic and implies that all societies will eventually be communist but that it is preferable in terms of the risks involved in a nuclear age for this to take place gradually. In this respect the Chinese view differs markedly from the Soviet, in maintaining that socialist revolutions should be strongly encouraged wherever feasible without regard to "coexistence" or to the risks involved.

"Peaceful coexistence" in its Western meaning, at least, was descriptive of the general trend of European diplomacy in the 1960s. In the preceding period the settlement of the German question and hence the security of Europe had been regarded as temporary, and at least the implicit aim of both the Western and the Eastern countries had been to change the balance of power by uniting both Germanies within the framework of their respective coalitions. In the 1960s the main emphasis was on regularizing the relations of the European states in their existing form, which meant accepting the partition of Germany for the foreseeable future. This regularization involved two somewhat separate developments: a decline in the relative dominance of the USSR and the United States in their respective treaty organizations, popularly known as polycentrism in regard to the Soviet orbit, and a search for alternative ways to organize the security of Europe without juxtaposition of the Warsaw Pact and NATO defensive alliances.

POLYCENTRISM. Although the decentralization of the two organizations did not significantly affect European politics until the 1960s, it had its origins in events that took place in the preceding decade: in the death of Stalin in 1953 and the subsequent criticism of his policies by Khrushchev in 1956 and in the accession to power in France of De Gaulle in 1958. These events were not in themselves the causes of the decentralization, but they were symbolic of developments which would in all likelihood have had the same effect in the long run.

Underlying these changes in the international relations of Europe was a decline in the mutual fear that had motivated the two coalitions in the first place. By 1960 it was evident to both sides that another European war over Germany was not in sight, and that such dangers to both protagonists as continued to inhere in the situation could probably be managed without resort to the threats that had been common in the preceding decade. It was in this context that the death of Stalin and the subsequent de-Stalinization was significant. His name and reputation had been associated since 1946 with the most unyielding aspects of Soviet policy, and it seemed likely that the collective leadership of his successors who denounced important aspects of his domestic policy would be more accommodating. This in fact proved to be the case. The relaxation of the East-West conflict within Europe was also affected by the development of military technology, which in significant degree transferred the emphasis of mutual deterrence from land forces and short-range missiles stationed within Europe to long-range missiles stationed outside the continent. Finally, at least in Western Europe, the rapid economic development of the major European countries in the second postwar decade, stimulated by the creation of the European Economic Community, made for less dependence on the United States.

The uprising in East Germany in 1953 and the more significant revolutionary movements in Poland and Hungary in 1956 marked the first important steps toward polycentrism in Eastern Europe. Although Soviet power was reasserted by military force in each case, the subsequent policies of the East European countries both at home and abroad exhibited far greater divergencies from the Soviet model than had been thought possible in earlier years. The possibility of differing roads to socialism was further emphasized by the Soviet efforts starting in 1955 to re-establish friendly relations with Yugoslavia. As it turned out, the Soviet-Yugoslav reconciliation was successful only within rather narrow limits and did not have significant consequences for developments in neighboring countries, but the effort was nevertheless indicative of Soviet attitudes. In the 1960s Rumania also developed a policy that was remarkable for its independence in foreign affairs. While retaining the firm control of the party in domestic affairs, Communist leader Ceaucescu remained neutral in the Soviet-Chinese struggle and sought with some success to industrialize his country on the basis of closer economic relations with the Western rather than with the Eastern countries. Even the occupation of Czechoslovakia in 1968 by Soviet forces, supported by Bulgarian, East German, Hungarian, and Polish contingents, did not essentially change the trend toward polycentrism. This move was accompanied by a strong affirmation of the Soviet intention to intervene whenever it thought a Communist party was losing its grip on a country, but it did not significantly affect domestic developments in neighboring countries. Hungary, Poland, and Rumania continued to go their separate ways in matters of domestic policy, while maintaining normal relations with the USSR.

The term "polycentrism" is normally employed with reference to Eastern rather than Western Europe, but somewhat similar developments

occurred there also. The leader in the movement of the West European
countries away from an American-dominated coalition was De Gaulle's
France, which sharply limited its NATO obligations in 1966 and in the
following year compelled the organization to move its headquarters, at
great expense, from Paris to Brussels. De Gaulle feared that a US policy
that relied on close relations with the United Kingdom, and possibly with
Germany as well, would be able to impose its will on Europe in domestic
as well as in international affairs. As a counterpoise to Anglo-American
influence, he proposed to develop as an independent third force a Western
Europe based on the European Economic Community. Such a grouping
would be able to negotiate independently with both the United States
and the USSR, although De Gaulle was fully aware of the differences
between American and Soviet policies and was firm in resisting Soviet
efforts to exploit his new policy for its own benefit. Thus De Gaulle's
visit to the USSR in 1966 was marked by pronounced cordiality, but it
did not bring West European policy any closer to the Soviet position.
Whatever such tendencies might have existed on the part of political
forces other than those led by De Gaulle were dealt a stunning blow
by the occupation of Czechoslovakia two years later.

The emergence of an independent French policy marked in some
respects a sharper break with the past than the more modest assertions of
autonomy in Eastern Europe, but the change in the West was not as
great in reality as it was in appearance. Since NATO, unlike the Warsaw
Pact, was a free association of nations, the reduction of France's role did
not challenge its underlying principles although it did reduce its battle-
ready forces in the event of a crisis. A majority of the French people
probably supported De Gaulle's resentment of American influence in
Europe, but they also joined with him in recognizing the importance of
American friendship. After De Gaulle's retirement in 1969, President
Pompidou sought to establish close relations with President Nixon, although he did not propose that France resume its earlier role in NATO.

THE SEARCH FOR ALTERNATIVE SOLUTIONS. The affirmation of an
independent French policy may be seen both as an aspect of polycentrism
and as a search for a new solution to the problem of European security,
for the new French policy was less anti-American than it was pro-European.
With the possibility that the European Economic Community might soon
be enlarged to include Britain, Ireland, Norway, Denmark, and possibly
other countries as well, the prospects for a stronger, more unified, and
more independent Western Europe were impressive.

By the late 1960s, three alternatives that had earlier been seriously
considered no longer seemed feasible. It was clear that neither the United
States nor the USSR would be able to unite both Western and Eastern
Germany under its own hegemony. It was equally unlikely that a re-
unified Germany could be integrated into an independent Europe extending to the Soviet frontier. The remaining possibilities involved some
form of reduction of tension within the existing framework, namely a

solution that acknowledged the division of Germany and the coexistence of two alliance systems. This point was not reached, however, until some of the earlier alternatives had been reviewed once again.

The initial Soviet aim in the search for alternative solutions was to encourage the dissolution of NATO and the withdrawal of American forces from Europe. This plan was set forth in a "Declaration on Strengthening Peace and Security in Europe," adopted by the Warsaw Pact allies at a conference in Bucharest in July, 1966. This declaration included six points: closer cultural, economic, and technological relations among the European countries; the dissolution of both NATO and the Warsaw Pact, as military organizations if not as alliances; a reduction in the level of European armaments; the barring of West German access to nuclear weapons; acceptance of the existing European frontiers; and an all-European conference to discuss European security and cooperation. Observers noted that the declaration had a strongly anti-American tone, and that it left out of account two critical factors: the USSR was preparing to renew with the Communist states of Eastern Europe its bilateral defense treaties, which existed apart from the Warsaw Pact; and the Soviet armed forces would remain on the border of Europe, whereas under this plan the American armed forces would be withdrawn across the Atlantic.

European leaders were well aware of these shortcomings of the Bucharest declaration, but they regarded it as a useful point of departure for the consultations that ensued. These consultations were profoundly affected, however, by the Soviet-led occupation of Czechoslovakia in August, 1968. A Soviet leadership which had in considerable measure established an image of itself as moderate and peace-loving now gave the impression of being unpredictable and in the last analysis ruthless. To a significant degree, these developments aroused once again the feeling of insecurity in the presence of Soviet armed forces in the center of Europe that had prevailed among West European leaders in the early postwar period.

The effects of the Czechoslovak crisis may be seen from the much more modest proposals for European security advanced by the Warsaw Pact countries after a meeting in Budapest in June, 1970. The emphasis was now on a European security conference in which the United States and Canada would also participate. This conference would concern itself with European-wide solutions to common cultural, economic, social, and particularly environmental problems. As regards military security, the Budapest formula simply proposed the reduction of foreign forces stationed on the territories of the European states.

This set of proposals was close to positions which the NATO countries had already adopted, and the prospects for a European conference including the members of both treaty organizations to discuss security and cooperation were now regarded as favorable. Among the Western leaders in the mid-1960s, only De Gaulle had favored a new approach to European security problems, but the election of a Social Democratic government in

Germany in 1969 and changes in United States public opinion led to a more flexible outlook.

American opinion in the late 1960s, reacting in particular to the demands of the war in Vietnam, had begun to question the value of NATO. The main concern was that American global commitments were overextended. South Vietnam was only one among forty-eight countries to which the United States had extended defense commitments and assurances, and the potential burden of these obligations did not seem to be matched by commensurate gains for United States security. The total cost of the American commitment to NATO, for example, was estimated in 1967 at $12 to $14 billion. If France did not find NATO essential, why should the United States maintain 350,000 troops (with over 250,000 dependents) in Europe?

In 1968 the American commitment of troops to NATO was reduced by 30,000, and in the following year Canada began a phased reduction of its 10,000-man force. Consideration of a further American troop cutback of 50,000 was suspended as a result of the occupation of Czechoslovakia, but the underlying desire to reduce foreign commitments persisted. When it became apparent that a joint reduction of armed forces in Europe might be undertaken by agreement with the Warsaw Pact countries, prospects for achieving a generally lower level of military forces improved.

The European solution that seemed most likely in the 1970s was thus one in which frontiers and alliance commitments would not be changed, but in which security would be maintained less by military force than by European-wide cooperation on common political, economic, and social problems.

CHAPTER

—— 26 ——

Germany:
West and East

———— ◆ ————

Germany Under Four-Power Control

TERRITORIAL CHANGES. The division of Germany which came with Allied Military Occupation [see above, pp. 614–18] not only disrupted many administrative areas that had been created by Hitler but also cut across very old established state and provincial boundaries. Baden, Bavaria, and Württemberg, for example, were divided between the American and French zones, and Prussia disappeared from the map. In the east, Russia appropriated the Königsberg salient (13,200 sq. km.) and incorporated it into the RSFSR except for the district of Memel, which was awarded to the Lithuanian SSR; the rest of the territory up to the Oder and Western Neisse rivers (55,887 sq. km.) was given over to Polish administration and thus became *de facto* a part of Poland. In 1945 Russia unilaterally handed over the city of Stettin on the left bank of the Oder to the Poles, who soon converted it into the completely Polish city of Szczecin. Berlin (890 sq. km.), an enclave in the Russian zone, was divided into four sectors, each administered by one of the occupying powers. In the four occupation zones the responsible authorities soon found it expedient to establish new states (*Länder*) so as to make possible some co-ordination of local government and some administrative centralization. The Russian zone (107,173 sq. km.; population 17,313,734 according to the 1946 census) was divided into five states; the British zone (97,699 sq. km.; population 22,304,059), containing the rich industrial Ruhr area, was partitioned into four states; the American zone (107,459 sq. km.; population 17,254,945) included three states in the southeast along with the city-state of Bremen in the north, which served as a United States port; the French zone (40,215 sq. km.; population 5,077,808), in the southwest along the upper Rhine, incorporated three states [see map, p. 658]. The Saar Basin, the boundaries of which were considerably extended, was joined economically to France in 1947. This territory, with its own autonomous government, was administered separately from the French zone proper. In April, 1949, the Western powers decreed some thirty-one minor border changes, involving 135 sq. km. and about 13,500 inhabitants, in favor of France, Luxembourg, Belgium, and the Netherlands. Russia protested against all these Western boundary changes, but they have remained in effect.[1]

STATE GOVERNMENTS. In general the United States took the lead in returning governmental functions to the Germans. In June, 1946, delegates were chosen for state constitutional conventions. These constitutions were approved by the people in a referendum, and state legislatures were chosen. The British, with their tradition of an unwritten constitution, proceeded with the establishment of state governments in their zone without formulating a written document. Both Russia and France favored drawing up formal constitutions. In most cases the new constitutions included much detail that would better have been left to ordinary legislation. All borrowed heavily from the state and national constitutions of the period of the Weimar Republic; in addition, those in the West incorporated American

---

[1] Some slight adjustments in these boundary changes have subsequently been negotiated. There have also been some changes in state boundaries. On December 9, 1951, Württemberg-Baden, Württemberg-Hohenzollern, and Baden decided by plebiscite to unite into a single southwest state, Baden-Württemberg, with its capital at Stuttgart. On January 1, 1957, the Saar was rejoined to Germany, becoming the tenth state in the Federal Republic. By a law of July 23, 1952, the five states of the Soviet zone (German Democratic Republic) were abolished and 217 counties were established, grouped into 14 districts.

and French practices, while those in the East showed Russian influences. Titular executives were dispensed with, and cabinets headed by premiers responsible to a popularly elected legislature were the rule. Judicial review made its appearance, particularly in the American zone. All constitutions provided for some socialization, those in the Russian zone going further in this respect than the rest. In all states many laws and regulations of former

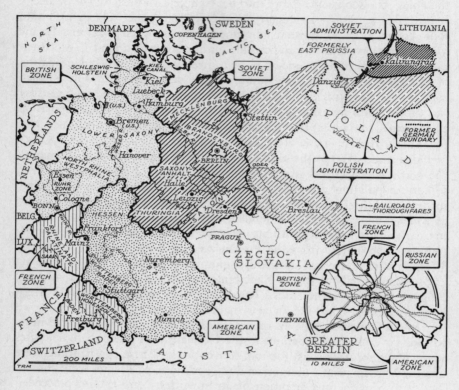

MAP 27   *Germany After World War II*

eras applying to a particular territory remained in effect; and since the new states were in some cases conglomerations of regions that had been under different states, a variety of laws prevailed. This diversity of law was particularly important in matters involving local jurisdiction, such as school legislation.

The form and letter of the constitutions are not as important as the freedom that exists under them. In the early postwar years the states could only do as much as the occupying powers were willing to have them do. Russia and France exercised the tightest control, while Britain came next. The re-establishment of even a limited amount of self-government necessitated the resurrection of political parties. These were not slow in appearing, but since they had to be licensed by the occupying powers it was always a controlled freedom which they enjoyed. In the Western zones the Social Democrats, the Christian Democrats—a predominantly Catholic party known as the Christian Social Union in Bavaria—and the Free Democrats—a conservative group standing for free enterprise—were the leading parties. The Communists never polled more than 10 percent of the vote in the Western zones. In the Russian zone in 1946 the Communist and Socialist parties merged to form a Social Unity party (SED), and this has been the party used by the Soviet authorities to carry out their ends. It was not, however, the sole party and did not always control the majority of the seats in all the state governments in the Russian zone. Some minor Peasant parties came to be closely allied with the SED. The Christian Democrats and Free Democrats in the early years of occupation always polled a strong vote, but because of control by the Soviet occupation authorities were never able to exercise great power.

Interzonal Relations. After the establishment of state governments the American and Russian authorities took the lead in establishing consultative bodies of German leaders on a zonal basis. Yet these zonal governments never achieved significance except in the Russian zone.

When the Allied Control Council failed to set up central administrative agencies for trade and industry, the United States invited the other three occupying powers to form an economic union of all four zones. Only the British accepted the invitation, and in the autumn of 1946 steps were taken to join these two zones economically into what was known as Bizonia. As the gulf between West and East widened, France came to co-operate more closely with Britain and the United States on occupation policy. These three powers, together with Belgium, the Netherlands, and Luxembourg, met in an extended Conference in London (February to June, 1948) and agreed to the establishment of a German government for the three Western zones. In order to satisfy France, all six powers were to share in controlling the Ruhr.

Up to this time a common currency, although its actual value varied in the four zones, had been a tie uniting all Germany. No agreement on currency reform could be reached with the Russians because they were unwilling to submit to joint supervision of the amount of paper money to be issued. The Western states finally proceeded on their own and instituted (June 18, 1948) the much-needed currency reform in their zones. The Russians thereupon countered with currency measures of their own. It was the currency question which brought the controversies between the occupying powers to a head and resulted not only in the Russian blockade of Berlin, necessitating a spectacular airlift on the part of the United States and Britain, but also in the cessation of all trade between the Western and the Russian zones (June, 1948, to May, 1949). These controversies centering about the Berlin blockade ended in fact if not in theory what little four-power government there had been for all Germany. There was nothing left to do but establish separate governments for West and East Germany. Berlin remained under four-power administration, but in effect was divided into two cities: West and East Berlin.

DENAZIFICATION. In the first days of occupation the United States army tried to enforce a strict antifraternization policy but this soon collapsed. Similarly, it soon became clear that it would be impossible to carry out the plan to punish all former Nazis. One example must suffice. Under Hitler practically all teachers were forced to join Teacher Associations, membership in which now classed them as Nazis. It is not hard to understand the impossibility of recruiting a whole new teaching force untainted by such Nazi ties. American authorities soon realized that the original denazification plans would have to be altered. The Russians from the start struck at only the top-flight men, and the British and French also never attempted such thoroughgoing denazification as did the United States. On June 1, 1946, the responsibility for further denazification in the American zone was passed over to German tribunals acting under United States supervision. Now various categories of offenders were established. Although the German tribunals were bombarded by criticisms from all sides, they ground wearily on. By the end of June, 1949, over thirteen million adults had filed questionnaires, of whom three and one-half million had been considered chargeable. Of these only 1,635 were judged major offenders, although over 600,000 received some punishment.

In addition to the general denazification procedures, the United States, Britain, France, and Russia collaborated in the establishment of an International Military Tribunal at Nuremberg which tried the surviving topmost Nazis. These men were indicted on various counts, the chief one being the crime of plotting aggressive warfare. After a long trial, in which many documents from the German archives were read into the record, sentence was meted out on October 1, 1946. Three of the defendants (Sahacht, Papen, and Fritzsche) were freed; seven (Hess, Funk, Doenitz, Raeder, Schirach, Speer and Neurath) were given terms from ten years to life; twelve (Goering, Ribbentrop, Keitel, Kaltenbrunner, Rosenberg, Frank, Frick, Streicher, Sauckel, Jodl, Bormann, and Seyss-Inquart) were sentenced to death. Goering escaped the hangman's noose by committing suicide, something Ley had accomplished early in the trial. Never before had such a tribunal been established, and there was great difference of opinion as to whether the trials were in accordance with International Law, or indeed with the laws of the respective victorious states. Critics of the procedure point out that even if there was a law that applied, it was being enforced only against the defeated countries. To overlook Russia's aggressive action in the Baltic states and Finland, for example, disturbed many judicial-minded observers. On the other hand, it was maintained that, although there was no precedent, it was high time to establish a procedure for trying "war criminals," and the trials were laying the basis for a new order in the world.

In December, 1945, the Allied Control Council further agreed that military tribunals should be established in each zone to try various top-ranking men and organizations. The United States established its tribunal at Nuremberg and conducted twelve important trials between April, 1947, and April, 1949. While the first Nuremberg trial was an international affair, the last twelve were entirely American. At one, officials of I. G. Farben were tried, at another, Krupp officials; one dealt with medical men, and another singled out various men who had held ministerial posts in the Nazi government. Of the 185 indicted in the American court, more than half received prison terms, some for life, and 24 were sentenced to be hanged. When these convictions are added to those of the military tribunals in the other zones and those of courts in other European countries, it should be clear that the wartime promise of punishing the guilty had not been overlooked. The German courts have also tried many war criminals, and prosecutions are still continuing. To prevent prosecutions from being cut off by Germany's twenty-year statute of limitations on murder, parliament in 1965 decided the statute should run from December 31, 1949, the date on which West German courts were completely freed from Allied control and not from 1945 when the Third Reich collapsed. In 1969 the statute of limitations was extended from twenty to thirty years, which means war criminals will be subject to prosecution until December 31, 1979. Soldiers of the four powers who have been guarding Rudolf Hess, the only remaining Nazi prisoner (removed to a hospital 1969), in the fortress at Spandau carry on one of the last acts of co-operation of the wartime coalition.

EDUCATION AND RELIGION. The first task in regard to education was to provide sufficient school buildings, equipment, and teachers. The schools that were not destroyed were overcrowded by the influx of refugees and expellees from Eastern Europe. Pencils and paper, not to mention textbooks or laboratory equipment, were lacking. Only after a more rational denazification policy made sufficient trained and experienced personnel available could the schools be properly staffed. A feeding program that centered in the schools was one of the most important projects undertaken.

The occupying powers also charged themselves with the reorganization of the whole German educational system. The Allied Control Council on June 25, 1947, issued a directive on "Democratization of Education in Germany." This was of course interpreted differently in each zone. In West Germany there was on the whole little zonal control, and schools were reorganized in the various states much as they had been before the Nazi era. Private schools were permitted, and the old pattern of interdenominational and confessional public schools reappeared. Everywhere religion continued to be a regular but not compulsory subject of instruction in elementary and secondary schools [see above, pp. 230; 459–62]. The Catholic Church, insisting on the validity of the Reich Concordat of 1933, concluded by Hitler, claimed the right to establish confessional schools throughout Germany. This right was, however, not recognized in some of the states, and the validity of the concordat was disputed. It was not until 1957, when school systems had long been re-established, that the Supreme Court of West Germany decided that the concordat was indeed valid, but that the provisions in regard to schools could not apply, since in the various constitutions of postwar West Germany it was recognized that education was a matter of state jurisdiction. In general the old system of attendance at an eight-year elementary school followed by continuation school, or four years at elementary school followed by nine years at a secondary school (Gymnasium), was restored.

In East Germany, although there was much talk about removing Fascist influence from the schools, the educational system continued to be developed along the lines set by the Nazis. The Russians as early as July, 1945, created a German Central Administration for People's Education. Under the supervision of its president, a law for democratization of German schools was drawn up and adopted in the spring of 1946 in almost identical form in each of the states of the zone. This law became the basis of the education articles in the state constitutions. From the beginning, therefore, a uniform educational policy existed in East Germany. Only interdenominational state schools were permitted and religion was not to be taught as part of the school curriculum. Such instruction was left entirely to the churches, which, however, were to be permitted to use school rooms for this purpose. In practice, disputes arose over the latter provisions, and state authorities assumed a hostile attitude towards the religious education programs that the churches—Protestant and Catholic—established. A unified school system with eight years of elementary and four years of secondary education became the rule.

In Berlin a few private (Catholic and Protestant) schools were permitted, but the regular schools were established entirely on a nonconfessional basis, with religious instruction left to the churches. The old University of Berlin lies in the Russian sector of the city, and in 1948 a "Free University" was established in the American sector. It is free from the universal compulsory instruction in Marxism which characterizes all educational institutions under Russian influence.

The loss of the eastern territories to Poland has brought about one of the first major changes in the religious map of Europe since the seventeenth century. As the Protestant Germans were moved out, they were replaced by Catholic Poles. Most of the Protestant expellees were settled in northern Germany, while the Catholic Germans from the Sudeten areas went mostly to southern Germany. However, the great interchange and resettlement of populations brought about by the war has done much to scramble the religious map of Germany. With the addition of Catholic Germans from Czechoslovakia and Southeastern Europe, Catholics almost equal Protestants in number. Jews number 20,000, and throughout Germany they enjoy a liberty comparable to that of the days of the Weimar Republic.

The Reformed and Lutheran churches, which had been organized on state lines before Hitler, and which he never could unite into one church body, have formed a Council of the Evangelical Church in Germany. It is a loose confederation, and the administration of the respective church bodies remains much as it was heretofore. So far the Iron Curtain has not been able to divide completely either the Protestant or Catholic churches, although in 1969 the eight regional Protestant churches in East Germany formed their own church federation.

ECONOMIC MEASURES. By turning the German territory as far as the Oder-Neisse line over to Russia and Poland, the Allied Powers deprived Germany of lands that normally supplied 25 percent of her food. Not only Germans from these lands but also German refugees from other areas of Eastern Europe were crowded into the rump German state, so that in spite of four million military and civilian dead, Germany was left with four million more people than in 1939. In the total population of about 66 million there were 13.5 million uprooted people (refugees, expellees, displaced persons) who for one reason or another could not return to their old homes. These people were not equally distributed throughout Germany and in 1952 varied from 9.4 percent of the population in Rhineland-Palatinate to 36 percent in Schleswig-Holstein. The expellees were able to bring little if any clothing or equipment with them, and the housing problem, intensified by the immense destruction of the war, defied description. In some sections the authorities were able to integrate the Eastern Germans rapidly into the community, but in others they were held in camps. The expellees, who in their old homes owned farms, shops, and factories, were at first lucky to find jobs as laborers, although gradually many have re-established themselves in business and in the professions. Actually the displaced persons provided a great labor reservoir, which has been important in the rebuilding of Germany.

Both in the first directive to the American Occupation Authorities and later in the Potsdam Agreement may be seen the influence of the Morgenthau Plan of turning Germany into an agricultural country. On April 1, 1946, the Allied Control Council published its plan for the collection of reparations and decreed what the level of the postwar German economy was to be. A whole list of prohibited industries—synthetic gasoline, oil, rubber, ammonia, heavy tractors, and so forth—was drawn up, and restrictions were placed on others, limiting them to a certain percentage of prewar production. Germany even in the best prewar years had been able to produce only from 70 to 85 percent of its food; now with a smaller area, a larger population, and a great lack of fertilizers (the nitrogen plants were closed) it could not even approach these figures. The United States and Britain were forced to pour in millions of dollars' worth of food and supplies. In the spring of 1947, President Truman asked Herbert Hoover to undertake an economic survey of Germany and Austria. Hoover recommended numerous changes in policy, above all the increase of German exports so that the American taxpayers might be spared the burdens of relief. On July 15, 1947, a new directive was issued to the American occupation authorities, and the United States launched on a policy of making the bizonal area self-supporting. Unable to get four-power agreement, Britain and the United States went ahead alone and on August 29 announced higher industrial levels for Bizonia.

The Potsdam Agreement called for the dismantling of many industrial plants, which were to be sent to various countries as reparations. On October 16, 1947, a list of 767 plants in the Western zone was published, comprising war plants forbidden to Germany and surplus peacetime factories. The dismantling program aroused much discussion and opposition and created resentment among the German workers as unemployment figures rose. The Congress of the United States passed a resolution of inquiry, for to dismantle a synthetic gasoline plant meant that American dollars would be needed to pay for imported gasoline, not to mention relief to the unemployed. On the other hand, some of the factories were clearly surplus if the level of German industry was to be controlled, and there was little chance that countries that had suffered destruction and looting by the Germans would in any other way receive reparation payments. The question had two sides, and while the United States came to oppose further dismantling, Britain and France held fast until November, 1949, when an agreement was reached which virtually halted this destruction of the German economy. Meanwhile the currency reform on June, 1948, was of inestimable value in stimulating recovery and laying a sound basis for the economy of West Germany.

In the East the Soviet authorities broke up the large estates, but the subsequent Soviet attempt to collectivize argriculture aroused much opposition and did not proceed according to plan. Many industries were nationalized, and socialized control and ownership of utilities were extended. The Russians carted off the machinery of many plants, yet, while continuing to do this, publicly opposed further dismantling when this was an issue among the other powers. Under the guise of collecting reparations the Soviet milked the East German economy and acquired part ownership of many key industries. The financial measures that Russia undertook at the time of the currency reform in the Western zone did not have a parallel economic effect, and economic recovery lagged. In 1949 Russia set to work to integrate East Germany further into the political and economic structure of Eastern Europe by sponsoring the establishment of the German Democratic Republic as a counter to the German Federal Republic established by the Western Allies.

The German Federal Republic

THE BONN CONSTITUTION. In accordance with the agreement reached by the Western Allies at the London Conference of 1948 [see above, p. 659] a Parliamentary Council composed of delegates chosen by the state governments of West Germany met at Bonn on September 1, 1948. By the time the four powers had reached an agreement to end the Berlin blockade (May 5–12, 1949) this Council had hammered and compromised together a "Basic Law for the Federal Republic of Germany." This went into effect on May 24, 1949, upon ratification by two thirds of the state parliaments in the Western zones. The Bonn Constitution is a lengthy document, which draws heavily on former German constitutions. Although there are elaborate safeguards to preserve states' rights, the distribution of power is such as to make possible the establishment of a strong central government, for federal law takes precedence over state law. The constitution provides for a president elected for five years by the lower house, which for this purpose is augmented by an equal number of delegates from the state parliaments. His powers are nominal, for the real executive power is vested in the chancellor and cabinet. Interesting attempts have been made to provide for cabinet stability; for instance, the lower house on its own initiative cannot dismiss the chancellor without immediately electing his successor. If the chancellor asks for but does not receive a vote of confidence, the president may at his request dissolve the chamber. The upper chamber (Bundesrat) with 41 members, represents the state governments, each state having three to five votes according to population, and the votes of each state delegation being cast as a block. Constitutional amendments and certain other types of legislation, enumerated in the constitution, require the consent of the Bundesrat, and it can exercise a suspensory veto even on ordinary bills. The lower chamber (Bundestag) with a membership of 496 (in 1970) is elected for a four-year term, with the electorate consisting of all persons who have reached the age of twenty-one, although nine states have so far (1970) lowered the age requirement to eighteen for state elections. The national electoral law has been amended several times since the constitution was adopted. Under existing (1970) procedure each voter has two votes and the ballot he receives has two columns. He casts his first vote in the first column for the candidate of his choice in his particular election district, and the candidate receiving the largest number of votes is the winner. His second vote in the second column is cast for a party which nominates a separate list of candidates in each state. Although the lists of second-ballot candidates are made public, not all of these candidates' names appear on the ticket. Parties can therefore afford to nominate second-ballot candidates who have no particular campaign appeal but are experts in certain fields such as finance, education, agriculture, or labor relations. This is an advantage, but, unfortunately, it is also a way of rewarding stolid party workhorses. The share of seats which each party receives from the second vote is determined according to the principles of proportional representation (D'Hondt system). In order to prevent many small splinter parties from winning seats under the system of proportional representation, which would add to the difficulties of the legislative process, the law provides that a party must win at least 5 percent of all second votes or carry three election districts to be able to enter the Bundestag. Half the seats are filled through the first vote, the other half through the second. This combination of direct and proportional electoral procedures is one of the most interesting features of Germany's postwar political development. A Constitutional Court was established to protect the constitution and decide controversies between state and federal governments. As in the past, state authorities have the chief responsibility of enforcing federal laws.

In 1968 parliament approved a bill providing for the establishment of an emergency government in time of war or national catastrophe. It will consist of a joint committee, two thirds of its members drawn from the Bundestag, one third from the Bundesrat. Among other powers, the committee would have the right to assign armed forces to police duty, to take over functions usually performed by civilian officials, to control transportation, and draft all men over eighteen into "defense units." The right to strike is guaranteed at all times, and any curtailment of an individual's civil liberties would lapse automatically after six months. The measure, reminiscent of the emergency procedures under the Weimar constitution, aroused much debate and protest, notably among the students. But the student riots in Germany, as elsewhere in the world at that time, seemed to threaten orderly government and were one of the very reasons for this legislation and for its general approval by the public.

Elections for the first Bundestag were held on August 14, 1949, with sixteen parties in the field, four of which elected no candidate. It was a right-center victory, and the Communists polled less than 6 percent of the total vote. A coalition government, representing the Christian Democrats, Free Democrats, and German party, was formed, and Konrad Adenauer became the first chancellor, holding that office continuously until his resignation in October, 1963. Dr. Theodor Heuss, a Free Democrat, was elected president and was re-elected in 1954. He was succeeded in 1959 by Heinrich Lübke, a Christian Democrat, who had served as minister of agriculture, but lacked the stature of Heuss. He was elected for a second term in 1964, and in 1969 was succeeded by Gustav Heinemann, the first Social Democrat to hold that office since Friedrich Ebert in the early 1920s.

ESTABLISHING FULL SOVEREIGNTY. In April, 1949, the three Western powers had negotiated a Trizonal Fusion agreement establishing an Allied High Commission as the chief Allied agency of control. Each power was represented by a High Commissioner, and various administrative departments and agencies were established. The three powers specifically reserved to themselves authority in regard to disarmament and demilitarization, reparations, control of the Ruhr, foreign affairs, foreign trade and exchange, displaced persons, refugees, protection of Allied forces of occupation, protection of the constitution, and a variety of other subjects. The plan was intended to give the prospective new German government wide authority, but it is hard to conceive of anything the occupying powers could not legally do under the rights they reserved to themselves. With the end of military government in September, 1949, Allied control passed into the hands of a civilian High Commission (HICOG), although military occupation continued. In November, 1949, this commission concluded the first negotiated postwar Allied-German agreement, the so-called

Petersberg Protocol. With this agreement West Germany entered the field of foreign policy, being given the right (1) to begin participation in international affairs, (2) to apply for membership in an International Authority for the Ruhr, and (3) to re-establish consular and commercial relations with foreign countries. The outbreak of the Korean war in June, 1950, led the Allies to re-examine the situation in Western Europe, with the outcome that in August the German Federal Republic was admitted as an associate member to the Council of Europe and in the following year was accorded full membership. However, it was not until the spring of 1951 that a revision of the Occupation Statute permitted Germany to re-establish a foreign office, and Chancellor Adenauer took over the duties of Minister of Foreign Affairs. That year also brought the formal termination of the state of war with Germany by Great Britain (July 9), France (July 15), and the United States (October 19).

The scheme for internationalizing the Ruhr envisaged at the London Conference in 1948 was never implemented; instead, plans for a European Coal and Steel Community were drawn up in April, 1951, and put into effect the following year. Adenauer took a leading part in these negotiations, and Germany became a full partner in the organization. Other changes were made in the Occupation Statute with the purpose of ending various servitudes, particularly limitations placed on German industry and ship-building. Negotiations meanwhile proceeded for the replacement of the Occupation Statute by a number of contractual agreements and a security pact. Churchill had been one of the first statesmen to call for German rearmament, and by this time the United States also was pressing for it. France was strongly opposed to anything like a purely German army and the problem resolved into the question of how German units could be integrated into a European army. Finally a series of conventions known as the Contractual Agreements were signed on May 26, 1952, by the three Western occupying powers and West Germany. These agreements, which were designed to restore virtual sovereignty to the Federal Republic, were tied up with the proposed European Defense Community (EDC). When France finally refused to ratify the EDC treaties in 1954 [see below, pp. 741–42] Britain called a conference in London, attended by Canada, the United States, France, Germany, Italy, Belgium, the Netherlands, and Luxembourg, at which new agreements were worked out. Germany and Italy were to join the Western European Union, which was to undertake the integration of the German forces into a common defense force. Unlike the EDC treaty, this arrangement provided that Britain would also place some troops at the disposal of the new West European army. West Germany was also admitted to NATO, and the whole new military organization was assimilated with the latter's defense schemes. Before these agreements could be signed on October 23, it was necessary for Germany to reach a bilateral agreement with France on the Europeanization of the Saar. The delay over EDC had been long, but this series of agreements was ratified by all the powers in record-breaking time, and on May 5, 1955, the Occupation Statute was revoked. The Federal Republic hereby regained full sovereignty and became a free and equal partner of the Western powers.

POLITICAL EVENTS. There was much hostility inside Germany to a policy of rearmament, which the Social Democrats maintained was unconstitutional. Adenauer was able to muster enough support to amend the constitution, thus setting aside any doubt as to the legality of German rearmament. It remained a highly controversial issue, and the government moved slowly from 1956 on in establishing a force based on compulsory service for a twelve- (after 1961, eighteen-) month period. Year by year the number called rose until the planned strength of about 500,000 was reached in 1965. A small navy and air force were also established. All these have been closely correlated in grouping and armament with Germany's NATO allies, particularly the United States. Germany has not attempted to establish a self-sufficient armament industry, but relies about equally on purchases at home and abroad. When the United States and Britain (December, 1962) proposed building a multilateral nuclear naval force within NATO manned by mixed contingents from the Allies, Germany at once expressed willingness to participate. The proposal aroused a great deal of opposition, not only on the part of Russia, but also from some of the NATO allies, notably France, and such a force was not established. Germany remains a non-nuclear power.

Politically there has been a decline in the number of small parties and a trend toward a two-party system consisting of the Christian Democrats (CDU) with its Bavarian branch, the Christian Social Union (CSU), and the Social Democrats (SPD), although a third party, the Free Democrats, has steadily maintained an effective minority position. An attempt to form a Refugee party in 1950 out of the refugee-expellee group, which totals approximately one-fifth of the population, had little success. After five years of litigation instigated by the Bonn government the Federal Constitutional Court on August 17, 1956, outlawed the Communist party and its affiliated front organizations, declaring that they were unconstitutional since they aimed to overthrow the constitution.

In 1957, for the first time in the history of monarchical or republican Germany, a single party (CDU) achieved an absolute majority of the popular vote and seats in a parliamentary election. The Social Democrats with one-third of the seats were, however, still in a position to block a constitutional amendment. The Free Democrats and the German party, the only other parties to obtain seats, shared about 11 percent of the vote. The German party, the most conservative of the groups, received representation in Adenauer's cabinet and subsequently was largely absorbed in the CDU. In the 1961 parliamentary elections only three parties won seats. Adenauer's party (CDU) lost heavily in this election and, although still holding the greatest number of seats, was forced to form a coalition government with the Free Democrats led by Erich Mende.

Their chief rivals, the Social Democrats, had as a rule shown more strength in state and local balloting than in the parliamentary elections. They had at times controlled the governments in Hesse, Schleswig-Holstein, and Bremen, and had been dominant in West Berlin. To win support the Social Democrats needed to widen their appeal. Gradually the party abandoned many of the distinct Marxist doctrines which characterized its position before 1933. For example, it no longer opposed religious instruction in the schools or advocated an extensive program of nationalization. What had already been the practice was officially made part of the party platform at the party convention in Bad Godesberg in November, 1959. Here the party dropped most of its traditional Marxist aims; socialism in Germany as in most other countries was simply transforming itself. On the death of its long-time party chairman, Erich Ollenhauer in December, 1963, the dynamic mayor of West Berlin, Willy Brandt, became chairman of the party.

Within the Christian Democratic party as well as in the Free Democratic party, the two coalition parties, there was considerable opposition to Adenauer's continuing as chancellor. A promise was extracted from him to resign far enough before the scheduled elections of 1965 to permit his successor to establish himself as leader of the governmental coalition. On October 15, 1963, he finally did so and was succeeded by Ludwig Erhard, the minister of economic affairs. Adenauer, who was eighty-seven years old, retained his position as chairman of the CDU. Chancellor of the Federal Republic ever since its establishment in 1949, he had led West Germany from the ruins of World War II and a position of isolation to a place of eminence, firmly allied with the great powers of the Western world.

Adenauer never hid his opposition to Erhard as his successor, but the position of the latter was so strong within the party and in Germany as a whole that he had to give in. Erhard was one of the few Protestant leaders of the CDU, which has always sought to achieve a broader confessional basis than that of the Center party of pre-Hitler days. Acclaimed as the architect of Germany's postwar economic miracle, the new chancellor was generally considered the party's best vote getter.

The election held in September, 1965, was a personal as well as a party triumph for Erhard. The CDU with its Bavarian affiliate (CSU) increased its representation from 242 to 245 seats. The Social Democrats gained as well, increasing the number of their mandates from 190 to 202. The Free Democrats on the other hand declined from 67 to 49 seats, but still held the balance and again entered into a coalition government with Erhard as chancellor.

In spite of his political triumph, Erhard's popularity declined, largely because of the economic recession and a severe budgetary crisis. There was also considerable in-fighting within the Christian Democratic party and Erhard lacked the will and political cunning of Adenauer. He and his party suffered a severe defeat in the July, 1966, provincial elections in North Rhineland-Westphalia, which was traditionally a Christian Democratic stronghold. Strong factions within his party demanded that Erhard surrender his leadership. The cabinet finally decided on significant tax raises which led the Free Democrats to withdraw from the coalition (October 27, 1966). They apparently hoped to join with the Social Democrats in a new government but the latter refused since such a cabinet would have only a bare majority. Instead the Christian Democrats and Social Democrats, despite considerable opposition within each party, decided to form a grand coalition under the leadership of Kurt Georg Kiesinger, the popular Christian Democratic governor of Baden-Württemberg, with Willy Brandt, the chairman of the Social Democrats as vice chancellor and foreign minister. For the first time since pre-Hitler days, Social Democrats again held cabinet posts. This left the Free Democrats with only 49 seats as the sole opposition party. In the electorate, voters turned to a new rightist National Democratic party. It was generally labeled as a neo-Nazi party, an affiliation which its leader Adolph von Thaden denounced. In 1966–68, this party gained 6 to 9.8 percent of the vote in various state elections, the high being in Baden-Württemberg.

The parliamentary elections in September, 1969, offered the first nationwide test for this new party. They conducted a vigorous campaign which led to some turbulent counterdemonstrations. In the end they received only 4.3 percent of the vote and consequently, because of the law restricting splinter parties, won no Bundestag seats, while the Christian Democrats and their allied Christian Social Union won 242 (245 formerly); the Social Democrats 224 (202); and the Free Democrats 30 (49). The Social Democrats were thus the only party to gain, and they entered into a carefully negotiated coalition with the Free Democrats. Willy Brandt became the first Social Democratic chancellor since 1930, with Walter Scheel, the leader of the Free Democrats, as Minister of Foreign Affairs.

ECONOMIC RECOVERY. As a result of initial grants under the Marshall Plan and other American assistance, the German economy had started to expand following the currency reform of 1948. It was a system of regulated free economy, with no nationalization of industry. A broad program of social insurance undergrids the whole economic and social structure of the state. The rebuilt cities present evidence of careful planning and provide many examples of modern functional architecture. Remarkable advances have been made toward meeting the housing shortage. Oil heat, hot water, refrigerators, and modern electric appliances of all sorts are in evidence, although the traditional feather bed holds its own winter or summer. Hitler's plan to build a small, durable, efficient, and relatively inexpensive automobile for the common man has been transmuted into the modern popular Volkswagen which has had wide success throughout the world. The Volkswagen Company has been denationalized and shares sold to the people. The proceeds of the sale went to the establishment in 1959 of the Volkswagen Foundation for the purpose of promoting research in science, engineering, and education. German exports again are to be found in all markets of the world. German civil aviation was restored in April 1955, and Lufthansa has re-established itself among the international airlines. A commercial fleet has been established, and German ships again are in the New York–European passenger and cruise service.

It would be easy to cite statistics without end to show Germany's phenomenal industrial expansion. After ten years of unprecedented growth, the economy slowed down in 1960–62, without, however, engendering a marked recession. In spite of the great influx of refugees and expellees, a labor shortage developed. Germany in 1965 was playing host to over a million "guest workers" recruited chiefly from Southern Europe (about 300,000 Italians, 161,000 Greeks, 157,000 Spaniards, 60,000 Yugoslavs) and the Near East (92,000 Turks, 6,000 Jordanians), but drawing some from as far away as Chile. The number has since declined, but these nonetheless are still a vital addition to the German labor force. Recruiting teams are sent out to work in co-operation with foreign governments. The workers are given physical examinations and their special skills ascertained. They usually contract to work for a three-year period, and at times are even joined by their families. The trade unions see that these workers receive the same pay and working conditions as native workers, although the long-term benefits from the social security system may be somewhat different. Postal authorities estimated that these workers sent home about $300 million in 1964. To evaluate the economic and social influence of this labor recruiting program both for Germany and for the countries from which the workers come could provide significant thesis topics for future Ph.D. candidates.

Important oil resources have been discovered, and German production equals about three-fifths that of the more famous Rumanian fields, supplying about one third of domestic needs. Natural gas fields along the North Sea coast are being developed. The coal industry, greatly expanded immediately after the war, has been heavily hit by the use of oil and other sources of energy. In 1969, twenty-four of the twenty-eight coal companies in the Ruhr, representing 85 percent of German coal production, formed a huge company (Ruhrkohle A.G.) as a step toward reviving the sick industry. The new company will be the largest in West Germany's heavy industry sector and will be exceeded only by the Siemen Communications and Electronics Works in the number of employees. Steel production has increased tremendously, and Germany plays a vital role in the European Coal and Steel Community. The canalization of the Moselle, completed in 1964, initially favored by France, in no way handicapped but rather enhanced Germany's economic position within the Community. West Germany has consistently furthered integration of European trade and has given its enthusiastic support to the establishment of the European Economic Community (EEC) and the European Atomic Energy Community (Euratom). It favored admission of Great Britain and eventually the other members of the European Free Trade Association to EEC. Germany has the highest, and France the lowest priced agricultural products of the six member states, and in December, 1964, Germany had to accept a real cut in its subsidized grain prices when it came to establishing uniform grain prices for the Common Market. Yet the agricultural issues were not all settled. Germany favored giving Common Market authorities greater control over the agricultural marketing funds than France was willing to grant; it was basically a matter of difference in views as to how fast and how far European integration was to go.

Even before the devaluation of the franc in August, 1969, speculators had been banking on the upward evaluation of the mark, and three days before the election of September, 1969, the German foreign exchange markets had to be closed. As a stop-gap measure immediately after the elections the mark was freed from a fixed exchange rate and allowed to fluctuate freely on the market. One of the first acts of the Brandt cabinet was to revalue the mark upward by 9.29 percent on October 24, making it equal to 27.3224 United States cents. The measure was generally hailed in world banking circles, but it necessitated some intense negotiations among the members of the Common Market to bring about adjustments, notably in regard to agricultural subsidies.

FOREIGN AFFAIRS. Although not admitted to the United Nations, the Federal Republic co-operates with all the specialized agencies of that organization and has made voluntary contributions to many of its activities. Under Konrad Adenauer's long and skillful leadership, Germany became an equal party in NATO and various other Western-oriented European organizations. He was convinced of the necessity of close co-operation with France, although he did not want this to jeopardize close ties with Britain and above all with the United States. His francophile policy found its climax in the conclusion of a Treaty of Reconciliation with France on January 22, 1963, providing for close co-operation in matters of diplomacy, defense, culture, and education. Some spoke of this as establishing a Paris-Bonn axis within NATO, as a counter to American-British leadership. This, so far as Germany was concerned, was not the intention; it was meant to end the age-long hostility between the two countries which was a *sine qua non* for European unity. Chancellor Erhard and his successor endeavored to follow Adenauer's French policy, but De Gaulle's singularly independent course made this difficult. Germany favors rapid European economic and political integration; De Gaulle sought to delay it. Germany favors retaining United States and British influence in Europe; De Gaulle wanted a Europe with Anglo-Saxon influence held to a minimum. Germany favors a multilateral (NATO) atomic policy; De Gaulle wanted an atomic striking force under his own control. Germany, at least officially, supported United States policy in Vietnam; De Gaulle opposed it. Numerous other such differences could be noted, but actually the policies of both Germany and France are firmly built on future co-operation rather than on enmity.

A cornerstone of Germany's foreign policy is the nonrecognition of the German Democratic Republic. After Adenauer's visit to Russia in September, 1955, which led to the establishment of diplomatic relations between Moscow and Bonn and the return of some additional but not all war prisoners, Walter Hallstein, state secretary in the foreign ministry, formulated the so-called Hallstein Doctrine. Under it the Federal Republic will break diplomatic relations with any state (with the exception of the Soviet Union) which recognizes the German Democratic Republic. Since then this doctrine has actually been enforced twice; against Yugoslavia in 1957 and against Cuba in 1963. The Bonn authorities have threatened to apply the doctrine on numerous other occasions; it has, however, also taken the position that the doctrine does not ban establishment of trade or even consular relations with East Germany or states which recognize it. Actually while *de jure* the existence of the German Democratic Republic is not recognized by the Federal Republic, all kinds of agreements, mostly involving trade, have been arranged between the two Germanies on a *de facto* basis. Likewise, while having no official relations with the other communist states which have recognized East Germany, West Germany has established numerous contacts with them. Trade with these communist states has increased over the years, although the major part of German foreign trade is with states outside the communist bloc.

By contributions to UN agencies, by funds designed to help countries which had formerly been colonies of the Common Market states [see below, pp. 865–69] and lately more directly through bilateral agreements, Germany has taken an active interest in foreign aid. It was a combination of such foreign aid agreements and the enforcement of the Hallstein Doctrine which led to an embarrassing Near Eastern crisis for Chancellor Erhard in the spring of 1965.

In 1952 Germany undertook to pay Israel a sum of $850 million as a debt of conscience for the treatment of Jews during the Nazi period. In addition to these annual "reparation" payments which were to extend until 1965, Chancellor Adenauer, when he met Premier Ben Gurion of Israel in New York in 1960, promised to supply Israel with $80 million of military aid. The United States, which had always refrained from giving direct military aid to Israel because of the repercussions on relations with the Arab states, instigated and blessed this action by Adenauer. The forwarding of this military aid was never publicly announced, although the Arab states, of course, knew of it. In 1964, as Israeli-Arab relations tensed over the diversion of the Jordan River, Israel approached the United States for armored tanks. Washington, in turn, brought heavy pressure on Germany to deliver to Israel 150 of the Bundeswehr's surplus Patton tanks, originally purchased in America. Chancellor Erhard, bound by Adenauer's promise, reluctantly agreed.

The promised delivery of tanks, soon known in Cairo, moved President Nasser to protest and retaliate. In the background Nasser cherished another grievance, for, at Israel's request, the German government was in the process of persuading German technicians and rocket experts to withdraw from positions they had accepted in Egypt. He invited Walter Ulbricht of East Germany to pay an official visit to Egypt. The Bonn authorities, taking the view that this was tantamount to the recognition of East Germany, threatened that if the visit were not cancelled, they would apply the Hallstein Doctrine and also cancel the substantial foreign aid being extended to Egypt. As an inducement to President Nasser, Germany cancelled further military aid shipments to Israel, amounting to 20 percent of the original $80 million grant. This led to denunciations of Germany by Israel and talk of boycotting German goods not only in Israel but also by Jewish firms in the United States.

The visit by Ulbricht to Cairo went off as planned, and East Germany promised Egypt economic aid to the extent of $100 million in long and short term credits. West Germany countered by cancelling her foreign aid to Egypt and announcing its intent to establish diplomatic relations with Israel. This move was not exactly welcomed with open arms by Israel, where anti-German feeling still ran high. The Arab states meanwhile had held a summit meeting to decide their course of action. When the exchange of ambassadors between Bonn and Israel was finally arranged, ten of the thirteen Arab states (Iraq, United Arab Republic, Syria, Lebanon, Saudi Arabia, Jordan, Kuwait, Yemen, Algeria, and Sudan) broke off diplomatic relations; Morocco, Tunisia, and Libya refused to go along with the majority and retained their relations with the Federal Republic.

None of the Arab states formally exchanged ambassadors with East Germany, nor were trade relations with West Germany severed. The latter also signified its intention to continue foreign aid to the Arab states. The whole crisis was most embarrassing to Chancellor Erhard's government, and confirmed in the minds of many Germans a feeling that their leaders were particularly inept in matters of foreign policy. As Willy Brandt, the head of the Social Democrats, remarked on Germany's policy in general: "[Germany] has become an economic giant but has remained a political dwarf."

Brandt did nothing spectacular to reverse his own judgment when he became foreign minister himself in 1966, but he did attempt to ease Germany's relations with the Eastern European states, and the Hallstein Doctrine was relaxed. On January 31, 1967, Rumania and Germany exchanged ambassadors and a year later diplomatic relations were resumed with Yugoslavia. German trade with the Eastern European countries increased, and German tourists flocked to their resorts. To stop the constantly improving relations with West Germany was no doubt one of the aims of Soviet intervention in Czechoslovakia in August, 1968. In spite of its friendliness toward Israel, Germany's relations with the Arab states improved slowly. Jordan was the first of the ten states which had broken with Germany in 1965 to resume diplomatic relations, doing so on February 27, 1967.   Less successful were Germany's relations with the United Arab Republic, which in 1969 granted diplomatic recognition to the German Democratic Republic.

When Brandt became chancellor after the September, 1969, elections the new government again emphasized its desire to better relations with Eastern Europe and lent substance to its words by signing the nuclear nonproliferation treaty.   It also reached an agreement with the Soviet Union under which the latter will sell natural gas from Siberia to West Germany.   Much to the chagrin of East Germany the pipeline is to be laid through Czechoslovakia and deliveries are to start in 1973.   Negotiations with Poland and East Germany were inaugurated.   Brandt also was able to carry the day at a meeting of the Common Market at the Hague in December when it was agreed that negotiations should be started in the spring of 1970 for the admission of the United Kingdom to the association.

Brandt's whole policy of bettering relations with Eastern Europe hinged on the attitude of Russia.   Persistent and difficult negotiations finally led to a treaty of reconciliation and peaceful cooperation which was signed at Moscow on August 12, 1970.   In this "Moscow Treaty" the Federal Republic and the Soviet Union pledged "themselves to respect unreservedly the territorial integrity of all states in Europe in their present frontiers."   Specifically West Germany accepted the Oder-Neisse line as the western frontier of Poland.   Both powers declared that their treaty in no way affected the rights and responsibilities of the four powers, that is, the United Kingdom, France, the United States, and the Soviet Union, concerning Germany as a whole and Berlin.   Thus, the final peace treaty with Germany remains a four-power responsibility.   The treaty was subject to later ratification and was generally regarded as a model for further treaties to be negotiated by West Germany with the other East European states.

Brandt's next major step was the conclusion of a treaty of reconciliation with Poland.   This was finally initialed on November 17 and signed in a formal ceremony in Warsaw on December 7, 1970.   Although West Germany does not border on Poland, the recognition of the Oder-Neisse line as the western boundary of Poland was easily the key provision of the agreement.   The use of force in the settlement of disputes was renounced, and the treaty specifically stated that it did "not effect bilateral or multilateral international agreements previously concluded by the parties or concerning them."   The treaty was supplemented by two letters.   One was addressed by the Bonn government to the United States, Great Britain, France, and the Soviet Union, saying the treaty in no way affected the rights and responsibilities of these powers for Germany as a whole and for Berlin.   The other was from the Polish government to West Germany recognizing the right of certain people "of indisputable German nationality and people of mixed families" residing in Poland to emigrate to either of the German Republics.   This had been one of the main concessions sought by the Bonn negotiators. Some opposition has appeared in Germany, and changes in the Polish government with the replacement of Gomulka in late December, 1970, may cause delay in the ratification of the treaty.

The German Democratic Republic

ESTABLISHMENT OF THE STATE. The Soviet authorities had even preceded the Western Allies in working out a central government. In December, 1947, they sponsored a German People's Congress in Berlin at which only the Communist party of the Western zones was officially represented. This congress elected a German People's Council and authorized it to draw up a constitution for all Germany. This document, completed in March 1949, was the issue in the election of the third German People's Congress in May, and was approved unanimously by that body on May 30, 1949. A reconstituted German People's Council officially proclaimed the German Democratic Republic on October 7, 1949. Berlin was named the capital of the new state, and the government offices were established in the suburb of Pankow.

The constitution provided for a president, a cabinet, and a popularly elected unicameral legislature (*Volkskammer*). It contained an elaborate bill of rights, but also provided in Article 49: "All basic rights shall remain inviolable, except where this Constitution authorizes their restriction by law or makes their further development subject to legislative action." Under this clause, considering the wide powers given to the government, the bill of rights is deprived of all safeguards. Wilhelm Pieck, one of the founders of the German Communist party, was elected president and served until his death on September 8, 1960. Instead of electing a successor the parliament amended the constitution, abolishing the presidency and creating a State Council of twenty-four members. Walter Ulbricht, chairman of the Politburo and the man who actually controlled affairs, was elected Chairman of the Council. The State Council can issue decrees with the force of law and has the right to make fundamental decisions in matters of defense and security of the country. It has become the directing and policy-making body. The head of the cabinet also acts as one of the six deputy chairmen of the Council. This office was held by Otto Grotewohl, an ex-Social Democrat, until his death in September, 1964, when he was succeeded by Willi Stoph, a talented administrator who had been serving as deputy premier during Grotewohl's long illness. A new constitution adopted in 1968, designed to stress the socialistic nature of the state, made no significant governmental changes and if anything restricted civil liberties still more.

The German Democratic Republic was increasingly organized on Soviet lines. Everywhere—in education, industry, trade—Russian patterns were followed. In order to increase control over the whole republic a policy of centralization was ruthlessly followed, the state governments being abolished in 1952. In place of the five states the Democratic Republic was organized into 217 counties (*Kreise*) and these grouped into 14 (15 in 1967) administrative districts (*Bezirke*). The district diets, meant to serve as deliberative and advisory bodies, are without true legislative functions according to Western constitutional concepts. All power rests with the central government, and the legislature is little more than a rubber stamp. The leaders of the Communist party from their positions in the State Council and cabinet determine policy. Parliamentary elections are held every four years and four so-called bourgeois parties are officially tolerated. They are, however, effectively submerged in a united National Front list in which the Socialist Unity party (Communist) dominates; voters are confronted with only this one list of candidates when they go to the polls. The tally of the October, 1963, *Volkskammer* elections are not only illustrative but also most instructive, for all elections are of the same pattern: total electorate 11,621,158; total votes cast 11,533,859 (99.25 percent); valid votes 99.96 percent, of which 99.95 percent were for the National Front list and 0.05 percent against it; invalid votes 0.04 percent. "The National Front list comprised 110 candidates from the Social Unity party (SED); 45 each from the East German Christian Democrats (CDN), the Liberal Democratic party (LDP), the National Democratic party (NDP), and the Democratic Peasant party (DPP); 60 from the Free German Trade Union Federation; 30 from the Democratic Women's League; and 19 from the Cultural League—a total of 434, or one for each seat."[2]

In area the Democratic Republic was about one-half the size of the Federal Republic with approximately one-third the number of inhabitants (18,793,000) of whom 80 percent were Protestant. The population declined steadily to 17,079,000 in 1961, when the trend was reversed. This loss was largely due to the flight of refugees to West Germany, which by June, 1961, had welcomed 3,099,000 persons from East Germany. In spite of mined and policed frontiers, people continued to escape, most of them crossing over from East Berlin. The Democratic Republic gradually extended its control over East Berlin and in 1960 declared it an integral part of the Democratic Republic. The Western powers have never recognized this, and their occupying forces in West Berlin strive to maintain what few rights they have in the eastern sector of Berlin. People of all classes fled, but the refugees included an extraordinarily large percentage from the professional classes. For example, between January 1 and August 31, 1958, a total of 813 doctors, veterinary surgeons, and dentists, 250 professors and lecturers, and 2,300 teachers fled to West Germany. In desperation the East German government erected a wall between East and West Berlin on August 13, 1961, and since then the exodus to the West has been held to a trickle.

The flight from the Democratic Republic bears witness to much dissatisfaction among the people and also of the police nature of the state.

---

[2] *Keesing's Contemporary Archives*, p. 20385; for 1967 election, see p. 22162.

On June 17, 1953, serious riots broke out in East Berlin and in other East German cities. These were suppressed only with the aid of Russian troops. It was clear that East Germany's large police force would not suffice to maintain internal order. In 1955 an East German army was established, although universal conscription was not introduced until January, 1962.

A law in 1959 reorganized the school system and provided for the extension of compulsory education to ten (formerly eight) years.

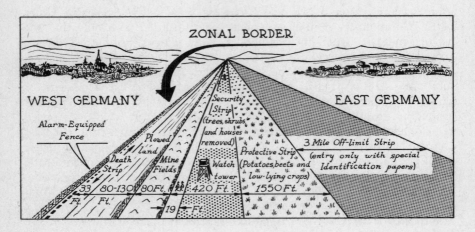

CHART VI   *The Iron Curtain. The zonal border between East and West Germany, 3½ miles in depth, was built by Soviet Zone Authorities to prevent East Germans from fleeing to the West. This "Iron Curtain" border runs for 830 miles through the heart of Germany. (Reproduced from* Berlin: Crisis and Challenge *by courtesy of the German Information Center, New York.)*

Religious instruction, no longer a part of the curriculum, is left entirely to the churches. The churches continue to receive certain aid from the state. For a time there was bitter conflict over state-sponsored Youth Dedication Services, which were designed to be a substitute or to replace the Confirmation services conducted by the churches. Contrary to their original position the churches have come to the decision that it is permissible for young people to take part in both services. Many problems remain in regard to schools and the churches, but it is not all conflict and state coercion. Here as in other realms the people have learned to live under the new conditions. In East Germany, in general, pride in accomplishments is noticeable, and a certain East German patriotism has made its appearance. Not only West Germany, but also East Germany has progressed.

Although Ulbricht has maintained firm control over the state, a certain amount of liberalization which manifested itself in all Eastern Europe after the death of Stalin also took place in East Germany. In the fall of 1964 an amnesty freed over 10,000 prisoners, many of them held for political infractions. A change in policy permitted East German men over 65 and women over 60 to visit relatives in West Germany once a year. The industrial expansion has brought a marked gain in the material well-being of the people and an increase in the comforts of daily life.

ECONOMIC POLICY. In line with their popular maxim: *Arbeite mit, plane mit, regiere mit* (Work with us, plan with us, govern with us) the Democratic Republic has instituted a planned economy. The first five-year plan, 1951–56, was followed by a second which was cancelled after three years in favor of a new seven-year plan, 1959–65. This synchronized it with the Soviet seven-year plan which also began in 1959. Each year the long term plan is implemented by a specific annual program. In 1950 the Democratic Republic was admitted to the Russian sponsored Council for Mutual Economic Assistance (COMECON) and since then has co-operated closely with the planning of this organization. East Germany has large deposits of lignite, potash, and salt, and rare elements such as uranium, cobalt, bismuth, arsenic, and antimony are exploited in the western Erzgebirge and in Thuringia. Its deficiency of oil has been remedied by the construction of a pipeline from the Russian fields, and large refineries have been constructed. The big industries have been nationalized, and these undertakings account for about 86 percent of the entire industrial output. The chemical, optical (Zeiss works at Jena), and machine goods industries have been greatly expanded, and East Germany is a chief exporter of these products to the other Communist states. About half its foreign trade is with the Soviet Union, while Czechoslovakia and West Germany each account for about 10 percent of the imports and exports. West Germany considers trade with East Germany as internal trade and therefore it is not subject to the quotas and other restrictions imposed by the Common Market. This gives the Democratic Republic a distinct advantage over other COMECON countries in trading with the West. East Germany has constructed shipyards on the Baltic, although its maritime activity is on a relatively small scale.

Immediately after the war the large estates of the Junkers, various war criminals, and Nazis were confiscated and distributed among the peasantry. A policy of collectivization was soon inaugurated which progressed slowly and has undergone various modifications. There are three types of collective farms, differentiation being based largely on whether pastures, orchards, and so forth, are part of the collectives, and on the degree of collective activity as well as ownership of the equipment on the farm. In all three types the acreage brought into the farm remains the property of the individual farmer. There are also some state farms. According to official figures, in 1950 5.7 percent of the arable land was in the collectivized sector; in 1960, 92.5 percent;[3] in 1967, 94.1 percent. East Germany is not self-sufficient agriculturally and must import a considerable amount of foodstuffs which account for about 25 percent of its imports. All indices show that East Germany's industry, agriculture, and trade have expanded. The increase has not been as spectacular as in the Federal Republic but East Germany is very much a going concern, thanks in no small part to Russia's economic and military support, but also to traditional German habits of work and industry.

FOREIGN AFFAIRS. In 1949 the other Russian satellite states immediately recognized the German Democratic Republic, and along with the Soviet Union exchanged diplomatic representatives with the new government. Since then, none but Communist-controlled governments have taken this step (twelve in all), although the republic has commercial representatives in over thirty "capitalist" countries.

On January 1, 1954, reparation payments to Russia were ended, but this did not bring much relief, for the trade treaty with Russia stipulated deliveries, prices, and exchange rates. The following March the USSR announced that henceforth relations with East Germany would be similar to those existing with any other sovereign state, although it was not until September 20, 1955, that a treaty was concluded in which Russia recognized the full sovereignty of the Democratic Republic. The Western powers have never recognized this sovereignty and continue to regard the Soviets as the responsible authority in East Germany. The Soviets—although they retain a large army in East Germany—shun this responsibility. They maintain that Russian troops are there only in accordance with a treaty agreement of March 12, 1957 with the Democratic Republic. It was only on January 1, 1959, that Russia exempted the Germans from making contributions to the maintenance of these troops. On June 12, 1964, during a visit to Moscow, Ulbricht signed a twenty-year treaty of friendship and mutual assistance. It was meant to bolster East Germany's international status and included a guarantee of its territorial integrity. Yet it fell short of being the peace treaty which Khrushchev had long been demanding of the Western Allies and which he threatened to sign alone.

East Germany's foreign policy is definitely linked to the Soviet orbit. In 1950 a treaty was signed with Poland in which the Oder-Neisse line was recognized as the eastern boundary. The Democratic Republic joined the Warsaw Defense Pact in 1954, and government leaders do not lack ardor in following the party line with denunciations of Western imperialists. In the ideological conflict between Moscow and Peking, the East Germans have tended to side with the Russians.

Berlin and the Issue of Reunification

THE DIVIDED CITY. Berlin, about 100 miles from West Germany, is an enclave surrounded by the Democratic Republic. Legally under the

---

[3] *Statistisches Jahrbuch der Deutschen Demokratischen Republik*, 1968, p. 255.

agreements made by the occupying powers it stands apart from the Germanies, and here the modicum of four-power control that remains is centered. In 1948 during the Air Lift crisis the government of Berlin, under Russian instigation, was split into a government of East Berlin (Soviet Sector) and a government of West Berlin (United States, British, and French sectors). Since then there have been two separate municipal governments.

In drawing up its constitution the Federal Republic wanted to consider West Berlin as one of its *Länder*, but this was vetoed by the Western powers. West Berlin, however, was permitted to send nonvoting members to the parliament of the Federal Republic, and in general correlates its practices and laws with those existing in West Germany. At times the parliament of the Federal Republic meets in West Berlin, thus paying respect to Berlin as the historic capital. The Federal Republic heavily subsidizes West Berlin, and their economies are closely linked. The same currency prevails, and although West Berlin has its own stamps they can, much to the delight of stamp collectors, be used throughout the Federal Republic. West German treaties, however, do not cover West Berlin; a special Berlin clause has to be added to each treaty if it is to apply to the city. This is particularly important in trade agreements. The Bonn authorities would like all their treaties automatically to include West Berlin, but this the Western powers have always vetoed, which is in line with their fixed intention of retaining Berlin as a separate entity until a general German peace treaty is concluded. This enables them to continue to exercise rights stemming from their victory in World War II and from the occupation agreements. Enclosed as West Berlin is by the Democratic Republic, its freedom is guaranteed by the continued occupation. Thus, while in respect to domestic law and public policy the Western powers have permitted West Berlin to be almost completely integrated into West Germany, in matters of defense and international relations they have been careful to retain control.

The Soviet authorities have followed a contrary policy and have encouraged the integration of East Berlin into the Democratic Republic. The city was immediately made the capital of the Republic and it became the center of government for all East Germany. The Municipal Council nominates sixty-six representatives to the Assembly of the Democratic Republic, but these, like the deputies from West Berlin in the West German parliament, have no voting rights. In general the East German authorities consider East Berlin as an integral part of their state and have come to class it as one of fifteen districts (*Bezirke*). The designations used for East Berlin in the *Statistisches Jahrbuch der Deutschen Demokratischen Republik* indicate rather interestingly the steady progress of integration: through 1957 it was listed as *Berlin, demokratischer Sektor,* 1958–59 as *Demokratisches Berlin,* and from 1960 on as *Haupstadt Berlin.*

The division of Berlin into two entities brought with it many anomalies. Police and economic barriers were erected, telephone service was broken off, yet for years the elevated railway continued to pass from one city to the other. So did the people, and West Berliners with their higher valued currency for a time found it economical to patronize the excellent theater and concert stages in East Berlin. Many East Germans crossed over daily to jobs in West Berlin; there were also the thousands of East Germans who deserted the Communist paradise as refugees. However, this intercity traffic was always subject to police intervention and this increased until on August 13, 1961, the East German authorities erected a wall between the two cities. Henceforth traffic was effectively restricted to seven checkpoints; few indeed escaped by crashing the well-policed wall or tunneling under it. What had been a partially controlled demarcation line was now considered by the Soviets as part of the state frontier of the Democratic Republic.

REUNIFICATION AND THE BERLIN CRISIS. The building of the wall was the climax but not the end of a long Berlin Crisis, which was only one aspect of the broader problem of German reunification. Statesmen in both camps have often expressed their desire for a united Germany, but, of course, under different conditions. West Germany refused until 1970 to recognize the Oder-Neisse boundary (which East Germany had long accepted) and has held that reunification should be on the basis of free all-German elections. This plan has the backing of the Western powers. The authorities of the Democratic Republic, backed by Russia, hold that reunification should be the result of a negotiated agreement between the two republics on the basis of a confederation.

From 1949 when the first major "Air Lift" Berlin Crisis was settled to 1954 it was impossible to hold a four-power meeting of foreign ministers to discuss the German problem. The Berlin Conference that met in January, 1954, produced no accord. The conclusion of the Austrian State Treaty in May, 1955, removed one issue that always complicated discussions on Germany and raised hopes that now perhaps progress could also be made on a German settlement. After much diplomatic sparring a conference of the four chiefs of state—the first such meeting since the Potsdam Conference of 1945—met in Geneva in July, 1955. Despite a temporarily friendly atmosphere, the summit meeting reached no decisions. For the next three years the tension lessened; only minor disputes, mostly about traffic regulations on the *Autobahn* to Berlin, kept issues alive. On November 28, 1958, in a note to the Allied powers, Khrushchev denounced the occupation agreements and demanded that West Berlin be made a free city. The free status would be guaranteed by the four powers, or possibly by the United States. If no agreement to this end was reached within six months, the Soviet Union would negotiate a peace treaty with the Democratic Republic and turn over to it full control of the land, water, and air approaches to Berlin. The setting of the time limit gave the Soviet note the tone of an ultimatum. The Western powers had no intention of acceding to the Russian demands which would have involved their withdrawal from West Berlin, and the surrender of their

KENNEDY AND KHRUSHCHEV *The two world leaders going to their first meeting in Vienna.*

occupation rights. This would have left them without a secure basis for future negotiations on the overall German settlement. It should be noted that Russia was demanding that only West Berlin be made into a free city; East Berlin would be part of the German Democratic Republic whose sovereignty was to be recognized by the Allies in the agreement. Yet the ensuing discussions did lead to a four-power foreign ministers conference at Geneva in the summer of 1959, at which delegations from both German states were present as advisers. By this time the Soviet Union had given up its demand that a solution be reached within six months, and the Geneva Conference was generally regarded as preparatory to a summit conference to be held in Paris in 1960. This conference did meet but was exploded by Khrushchev, ostensibly out of wrath against the United States for sending a reconnaissance plane (U-2 incident) over Russia.

The Soviets continued to press for a Berlin settlement. Shortly after President Kennedy took office, he expressed his willingness to meet with Premier Khrushchev and discuss outstanding issues. The two leaders met in Vienna on June 3, 1961, without coming to any agreement. In fact the Russians immediately issued an *aide memoir* threatening to conclude a peace treaty with East Germany that would end all Western rights in Berlin. Again the Western powers stood firm. Both Russia and the United States announced increased military expenditures and the strengthening of their armed forces. Although the Soviets did not conclude the threatened peace treaty with East Germany, they did sponsor the building of the Berlin wall on August 13, 1961. The Allies protested vigorously and sent high-level personages, among them Vice President Johnson, to assure the West Berliners that they intended to stay in West Berlin.

Since then the status quo has in general been maintained. There have been incidents, mostly involving interference with the flow of traffic on the *Autobahn* and canals from West Berlin to West Germany. On the other hand, in some years agreements have been reached permitting West Berliners to visit relatives in East Berlin for a brief period at Christmas, Easter, and Pentecost. Chancellor Willy Brandt's policy of establishing better relations with Eastern Europe did lead to direct negotiations with the East German government in the spring of 1970. On March 19 Chancellor Brandt and Premier Willi Stoph met at Erfurt, the first time the chiefs of government of the two German states had met in conference. Further meetings and negotiations were envisaged. The basic situation, while perhaps eased a bit, nevertheless continues unchanged; divided Berlin, divided Germany, remain the victims of a divided world.

CHAPTER

27

The Soviet Union

Evolution of Soviet Policy: *Aftermath of War; The Communist Party Line; The Role of the Party.*
Patterns of Soviet Change: *Economic Growth; Society and Culture; The Soviet Model.*

Evolution of Soviet Policy

A FTERMATH OF WAR. In the early years of the war the Communist leaders were profoundly apprehensive of its outcome, knowing as they did the deep distrust in which their leadership was held by the peoples of Russia. Indeed, in some areas of the Soviet Union overrun by the Germans, the invading troops were greeted by the populace as liberators. The Germans soon made it abundantly clear, however, that this welcome was not justified. They treated the peoples of the USSR with brutality and contempt and demonstrated that rule by the Nazis was worse by far than rule by the Communists. At the same time the Communist leaders changed their tactics to meet the new crisis and made broad concessions to public opinion. They stimulated national feeling wherever possible, ignoring for the time being the idea of class conflict, and the war was termed a patriotic struggle for the fatherland. In 1943 the Russian Orthodox Church was officially recognized again, and the war received religious sanction. There was also a return to tradition in the armed forces, with the re-establishment of ranks, medals, and a privileged status for officers. Moreover, the impression was given by the government that after the war a more humane policy would be adopted at home, and that special attention would be given to the production of food and consumer goods that had been so seriously neglected in the prewar five-year plans. During the war the peoples of the USSR were in a very real sense partners rather than servants of the Communist party, and they hoped that this new partnership would survive the war.

The vast destruction the German armies had wrought confronted the Soviet government with an almost overwhelming problem at the end of the war. In human terms, it has been estimated that as many as 7 million Russians lost their lives as a result of the war while another 20 million or more were left homeless. In economic terms, the losses in fixed and working capital and in private property equaled two thirds of the prewar wealth in the occupied territories. Since these were in most respects the most productive parts of Russia, the loss for the country as a whole may have been as much as one quarter of the total prewar wealth. Owing to the dislocations caused by the war, the decline in national production was fully as great as the destruction of fixed capital. The nonagricultural labor force similarly declined from some 31 millions in 1940 to 19 millions in 1943. It was thus a twofold task which faced the Soviet government in 1945: it had to make good the losses resulting from the war, and it also had to resume the program of industrialization which the war had interrupted.

In plotting their course in the postwar world, the Soviet leaders thus had to take into account an unprecedented situation. The very extensive war damage called for a massive program of reconstruction which would require great efforts. At the same time, the mood of the Russian people favored a continuation of the more relaxed policy that had been created to meet the needs of the war. Moreover, in the last year of the war many hundreds of thousands of Russians had seen what life was like in Central and Eastern Europe. Despite the wreckage left by the Germans, the Russian soldiers could see with their own eyes that life in the "capitalist" world was a good deal more comfortable than what they had known at home. Also, the Soviet government itself now enjoyed the confidence of the Western democracies, and the atmosphere was favorable to extensive American economic assistance.

The Soviet leaders were thus confronted by a difficult dilemma. If they returned to their prewar methods they would place a great strain on the Russian people and would again find themselves in conflict with the outside world. To adopt a moderate policy, on the other hand, would be to abandon the principles of Marxism-Leninism and to set in motion forces that might permanently weaken the grip of the party on Soviet affairs. Under these circumstances, the Soviet leaders decided against a policy of moderation and in favor of the traditional Stalinist methods. This decision was soon reflected in Soviet statements and actions.

THE COMMUNIST PARTY LINE. The "party line" is the term used to describe the general policy adopted by the Communist party in the achievement of its objectives. The broad objectives never change, but the party line is flexible and its twists and turns are a reliable guide to the Soviet interpretation of the development of events.

In the immediate postwar period the exposition of the party line was under the direction of one of Stalin's intimate colleagues, Zhdanov, until his death in 1948. The apathy of the Russian people in the first years after the conclusion of peace was met not by relaxation but by a renewed emphasis on Marxist-Leninist doctrine, combined with a continuation of the stress on national patriotism, which had reached a high point during the war. Much effort was devoted to showing that the Russian way of doing things was better than Western methods. The party claimed that the Soviet army had defeated the Germans practically single-handed. It also maintained that many modern applications of science, from airplanes to electric light bulbs, had originally been invented by Russians. In the cultural sphere, all recognition of non-Russian values and achievements was described as "objectivism," and dialectical materialism was asserted to be the only way of arriving at the truth. In practice, this meant that in peacetime all scholars and artists had to work enthusiastically on the tasks assigned to them by the party, and any lack of interest in such assignments was criticized as "formalism."

In the realm of foreign affairs an open ideological war was declared against the West and all it stood for, and every effort was made to press the cause of communism abroad. Within the Soviet orbit in Eastern Europe, Soviet policy gave full support to vigorous and occasionally independent-minded Communist leaders in their effort to establish and consolidate revolutionary regimes. It also supported the efforts of Albania, Bulgaria, and Yugoslavia to infiltrate northern Greece and to help set up a Communist government in that war-wracked country. In France and Italy the large Communist parties participated in coalition regimes, and did their best to infiltrate the essential organs of government. Similarly, in such Asian countries as Iran, Japan, China, Indochina, Malaya, Korea, and the Philippines, the Russians gave such assistance as they could to local Communist movements. In this fashion the Soviet leaders sought to maintain a fighting morale within their country and to take advantage of the many opportunities for extending their influence abroad which were available in the aftermath of a terrible war. When the United States announced its determination to stem the tide of Soviet influence in the spring of 1947, with the Truman Doctrine and the Marshall Plan, the Soviet government took up the challenge. A new propaganda weapon, the Communist Information Bureau (Cominform), was established in September, 1947, and Zhdanov announced that the world was now divided between the "imperialist" camp of the United States and the "anti-imperialist" camp of the Soviet Union.

Despite this defiant attitude, a significant change occurred in the party line in 1948 in regard to European affairs. The firm Western policy in occupied Germany, and the conclusion by the West European states of the Brussels Treaty in March, 1948, which formed the basis for the North

Atlantic Treaty Organization concluded in the following year, showed the Russians that the West meant business. In the light of this show of determination, Soviet policy in Europe now changed from general expansion to the consolidation of gains already made. In Eastern Europe the Russians ousted the more independent and national-minded Communist leaders, executing many of them on trumped-up charges. In the case of Yugoslavia, which was not directly under Soviet control, an effort was made to undermine Tito's position by charging him with numerous acts of disloyalty. This policy resulted in a tighter Soviet grip on the East European states already under its control, but a weakening of Soviet influence in Yugoslavia as well as in Western Europe. The retreat in Europe, however, was matched by a more active policy in Asia. The victory in 1949 of the Chinese Communists, with extensive Soviet aid, was now used as a springboard for aggression. In June, 1950, the North Korean Communists, trained and assisted by the Russians, attacked South Korea, which had been under American occupation, in an effort to take over the entire country. In the ensuing Korean war a massive propaganda effort was made throughout Asia to identify Russia with Asian nationalism and the United States with European imperalism.

Within Russia, in the period after 1948, the government continued to make maximum demands on the Russian people. It maintained that since Russia was encircled by "capitalist" enemies, the people must tighten their belts in a manner that almost resembled a wartime crisis. At the same time the party leaders moved to play down those aspects of Marxism-Leninism which gave the impression that political events were at the mercy of economic forces. With the active participation of Stalin, significant revisions were made in Communist doctrine maintaining, contrary to traditional Marxist teaching, that the state plays an active role in influencing both political and economic developments. Associated with this emphasis on the decisive role of the state was a very active anti-American campaign, which was carried on in the press, in the theater, on the movie screens, and over the radio. Thus by both positive and negative propaganda, a supreme effort was made to convince the Soviet people of both the correctness and the inevitability of the leading role played by their government.

Another turning point in the party line was reached in the spring and summer of 1953 with the death of Stalin and the conclusion of a truce in Korea. By now Soviet industry had more than regained the prewar level of production, and the strain on the Russian people was beginning to tell. Moreover, there was no statesman of Stalin's stature available to take his place, and some relaxation of the regime's centralized control was inevitable. This was accompanied by a somewhat lighter hand in the Eastern European states and a general effort to avoid controversial foreign policy issues in the world at large. This phase of the party line was associated with Malenkov, who succeeded Stalin as prime minister from 1953 to 1955, and went under the name of the New Course. In economic policy, the New Course called for a marked increase in consumer goods and more generous terms for agriculture. This was accompanied by a "thaw" in the cultural sphere, with wider freedom for writers and artists. In politics, there was a marked change from the unqualified glorification of Stalin which had characterized the party line in the last twenty years. Now the cult of personality was decried, and it was claimed that Russia had a "collective leadership" in which no single individual was dominant.

Malenkov's New Course lasted only two years. By 1955 Khrushchev had achieved the dominant position in Soviet policy-making that lasted until his enforced retirement in 1964, although Bulganin served as prime minister from 1955 to 1958. In this phase of the party line, heavy industry was again given precedence, but there was at the same time a steady improvement in the supply of consumer goods. For the first time, party policy now favored economic and social reforms that relaxed somewhat the bureaucratic centralization of Stalin's day and gave a new generation of party leaders around the country greater initiative. Public criticism of the government was now permitted within certain limits, and foreigners were permitted to visit the country under conditions similar to those that had existed in the early 1930s.

In the realm of foreign affairs, the Communist party formally adopted in 1956 the view that international war is not inevitable, and it proclaimed a policy of "peaceful coexistence." Such a policy meant not that the Soviet Union accepts the coexistence of other social systems on a long-term basis, but rather that it expects the worldwide victory of Communism to take place gradually by means short of international war. These other means especially include assistance to Communist parties seeking to gain power in other countries, by peaceful means if possible and by means of domestic revolutions if necessary, until the Communist countries achieve a preponderance in world affairs. This policy was successful in Cuba, but in other countries it was confronted by a growing determination on the part of the United States and its allies to support the forces of moderation. The Soviet approach also met an unforeseen obstacle in the form of the demand of Communist China for a more vigorous and aggressive support of Communist revolutions than was contemplated under the policy of "peaceful coexistence." This policy was nevertheless successful in winning friends among the uncommitted states. Khrushchev and his colleagues paid official visits to many countries in Europe and Asia in an effort to convince foreign opinion that the image of a relentlessly aggressive Russia current in Stalin's later years was a false one. Moreover, Soviet technical achievements, as evidenced by the launching of the first artificial earth satellite in October, 1957, contributed to the impression of a strong and self-reliant Russia that no longer had to resort to the type of bullying that characterized Stalin's regime. At the same time, there was no change in the underlying Soviet attitude. Khrushchev's Russia, like Stalin's, assumed that the victory of Communism all over the world was the ultimate goal. Certain "different roads to socialism" were permitted to the states of Eastern Europe, but when a Hungary revolted, or a Yugoslavia insisted on pursuing an independent policy, Khrushchev used all the means at his command to bring them into line. Thus the outside world had ample evidence that, while the methods of the Soviet Union had changed, its objectives had not.

The principal change in the party line introduced by Brezhnev and Kosygin when they came to power in October, 1964, was a new concentration of effort on the problems of agriculture. For the first time since the inauguration of the five-year plans, it was recognized that the long-term emphasis on heavy industry had resulted in critical imbalances within the Soviet economy. Khrushchev had dealt with these problems by means of temporizing measures and flamboyant administrative reorganizations, but the time had now come to make fundamental changes in the pattern of Soviet economic development. This concern with the domestic crisis was reflected in a cautious and conciliatory approach to foreign affairs that sought to prevent the hostilities in Vietnam and the continued antagonism of Communist China from distracting Soviet energies from internal affairs.

The results of the policies launched by Brezhnev and Kosygin did not come up to their hopes, and by 1970 they were facing a major crisis in the form of a serious stagnation of economic growth. The central problem appeared to be that the Soviet leaders were not able to make a satisfactory choice about the allocation of their resources among the various goals they were seeking to reach. The outer space program was cut back substantially, and Soviet scientists stood by glumly as the American astronauts made two landings on the moon in 1969.

The most difficult choice, however, was between investment in defense and investment in economic growth. On this issue the Soviet leaders were indecisive, and their record has revealed an alternation between the two goals which served to slow down economic growth without meeting the needs of military security. In a major report to the Central Committee at the end of 1969, Brezhnev announced that relatively lower rates of growth would continue to prevail for the immediate future.

THE ROLE OF THE PARTY. Since the Second World War the commanding position of the Communist party has continued to be the central feature of the Soviet political system. To an increasing extent the party has served as the brain of the USSR, stimulating a nervous system that reaches into every nook and cranny of Soviet life and also responding with considerable sensitivity to the needs and frustrations of a society in the throes of rapid change.

In the mid-1960s the membership of the Communist party, including candidate members, numbered about 12 million. This figure represents almost 5 percent of the entire population, about 10 percent of the population aged twenty-five and over, and almost one third of the specialists working on the national economy. The party was thus kept relatively small in proportion to the population as a whole, for reasons of discipline and cohesion, but was very strongly represented in all positions involving specialized knowledge and decision-making. By now the great majority of the members had joined the party during or after the 1930s, and few of them knew much about the Russia that had existed before the Stalin era. They were predominantly younger people, who took for granted the predominant role of the Communist party and were concerned primarily with economic and social development.

The war and the death of Stalin were serious crises for the party, but it survived them without any weakening of its ultimate control over the country. In the later years of Stalin's rule, however, the formal structure of the party bore little relation to its actual operation. Although Party Congresses were supposed to meet at regular intervals, the Nineteenth Congress did not meet until 1952, thirteen years after the Eighteenth. Stalin paid little attention to the Central Committee, supposedly the governing body of the party. The Politburo, at the apex of party authority, rarely met as a formal body. Instead, Stalin handed out assignments to the various members of the Politburo, who were the country's leading statesmen. He ruled as a dictator, permitting no one to oppose him. At the Nineteenth Party Congress in 1952, a year before he died, Stalin made important changes in the governing bodies of the party. The Central Committee was almost doubled in size. The size of the Politburo was also greatly increased, and it was renamed the Presidium. These changes were presumably made by Stalin with a view to bringing new and younger personnel into these bodies in order to dilute and counterbalance the influence of the party veterans, whose rivalry the old dictator still apparently feared.

The death of Stalin on March 5, 1953, brought to an end his thirty-one-year tenure as secretary of the party. He was initially succeeded both as prime minister and as party secretary by Malenkov, but his successor's hold on the latter position lasted only nine days. On March 14 Khrushchev began his dynamic career as party secretary, although at first he was generally regarded as a rather secondary figure. The new Presidium of the party included all of Stalin's principal associates in his later years, but significant changes soon took place in the method of government. Most important was the fact that, for the time being at least, there was no single individual who could take Stalin's place. His successors made much of the fact that they now had a "collective leadership," and indeed there can be little doubt that there was much more general discussion of policy among the top leaders. At the same time, with no single dictator available to give the orders, the police could not retain the arbitrary power over high party members which it had exercised in Stalin's day. In July, 1953, Beria, Stalin's chief of police, was removed from office, and five months later he and several of his principal subordinates were executed. Control of the police was placed in the hands of a Committee on State Security subordinated to the cabinet, and at least high party members were now free from the type of police supervision to which Stalin had formerly subjected them.

This relative relaxation in the relations of higher party officials was accompanied by more orderly procedures in the conduct of party affairs, as reflected in the proceedings of the Twentieth Party Congress in 1956. Indeed, in what was probably the most sensational speech ever made in Soviet Russia, Khrushchev denounced Stalin's methods of government in most decisive terms. He cited many examples of Stalin's arbitrary methods, and asserted that "Stalin acted not through persuasion, explanation and patient co-operation with people, but by imposing his concepts and demanding absolute submission to his opinion. Whoever opposed this concept or tried to prove his viewpoint and the correctness of his position was doomed to removal from the leading collective and to subsequent moral and physical annihilation." While much was thus said against the cult of personality which characterized Stalin's regime, the "collective leadership" soon began to look less collective. The elevation of Bulganin to the post of prime minister in February, 1955, in place of Malenkov, was clearly carried out at Khrushchev's initiative. In March, 1958, Khrushchev himself became prime minister, thus combining for the first time since Stalin's death the top executive positions of both party and government. Indeed, it had already become clear from his many speeches and pronouncements at home and abroad that he was the dominant personality in the government. Within the party, he had already consolidated his position in 1957 by dropping from the Presidium such veterans as Molotov, Malenkov, Kaganovich, and Zhukov. Even at the height of his power, however, Khrushchev's authority within the party was not comparable to that of Stalin. He had some difficulty in winning over the Central Committee when he was outvoted on policy issues in the Presidium in July, 1957, and there was much evidence of continuing discussion and disagreement on matters of policy among top leaders. In October, 1964, a majority of the Presidium again voted against Khrushchev, and this time they were supported by the Central Committee. The two key positions held by Khrushchev were once again separated, with Brezhnev becoming first secretary of the party and Kosygin being appointed as prime minister.

The position of the Communist party now combined the strengths of centralized and authoritative political leadership with the uncertainties of a system of government by men rather than by law. The party is headed by the Presidium of the Central Committee, an executive body of eleven members and eight candidate members. Its decisions are implemented by the Secretariat of the Central Committee, of which the first secretary, a Presidium member, is the head of the party. Only four men have held this position since its establishment in 1922 as the keystone of the party structure: Stalin (1922–53), Malenkov (March 5–14, 1953), Khrushchev (1953–64), and Brezhnev (since October 14, 1964). The Presidium is nominally elected by the Central Committee and acts in its name, but it is in fact self-appointed.

The Central Committee itself is a body of some 175 members and 140 candidate members, which is elected by Party Congresses. Party Congresses met irregularly under Stalin, but since his death the four Congresses, from the Twentieth (1956) to the Twenty-Fourth (1971), have been important landmarks in Communist policy-making. The Congresses are bodies of over 4,000 voting delegates, elected at meetings of party members. In a formal sense, the party has a democratic structure under which the members send delegates to the Congress that elects the Central Committee, which in turn elects the members of the Presidium and the Secretariat. In practice, the Presidium and the Secretariat designate the members of the Central Committee and the Congress through their control over the local party organizations. Since Stalin's death, however, the center of gravity of political power has shifted somewhat from the Presidium and the Secretariat to the Central Committee. In 1957 Khrushchev had to appeal to the Central Committee to overrule a Presidium that had voted against him, and he won his case. In 1964, for the first time in party history, the Central Committee voted a first secretary out of power. The evidence represented by these two instances of deference to the Central Committee on the part of the Presidium is too limited to constitute a trend. It nevertheless suggests that the dominant role of Lenin and Stalin between 1917 and 1953 must be regarded as exceptional, and that the party is still groping for a satisfactory means of conducting its affairs in the absence of a dominant personality. The new relationships are a far cry from the 1930s when Stalin ordered 70 percent of the Central Committee members arrested and shot.

The Communist party controls the Soviet Union by both direct and indirect methods. The most important direct methods of control are the appointment of key officials and the formulation and implementation of policy. All the major positions in the government are held by leading party members, and since 1941 the first secretary of the party has normally served also as prime minister. The leading positions in party and government are thus held to a very considerable degree by the same people, and to this extent the party may be said to govern the country directly. Direct party controls are also exerted by the Secretariat of the Central Committee which has some fifteen departments that are concerned with political, economic, social, and intellectual activities, and employs a paid staff, or "apparatus," of about 100,000. The Secretariat controls all appointments in the government and in public organizations, verifies the implementation of all policies, and censors all publications. In addition to its own staff, the Secretariat can draw on the services of 300,000 primary party organizations. These represent party members in all enterprises and institutions and constitute the nerve ends of the party's system of controls and communication.

The indirect controls available to the party are exerted through the various public organizations that nominally lead an autonomous life but in fact serve the purposes of the party and are regarded by it as "transmission belts" for the implementation of its policies. The most important transmission belts are the Supreme Soviet, the legislative branch of the Soviet government that is elected by universal suffrage on the basis of single-candidate constituencies; the Central Council of Trade Unions, with a membership of 68 million, which performs many public functions in addition to its responsibility for labor relations and welfare; and the Komsomol, or Communist Youth League, with 21 million members. These and other bodies serve to organize "the masses," as the party refers to nonparty members, and to educate and guide them in the direction desired by the party. The only organizations that do not serve as a transmission belt for the party are the Orthodox, Moslem, and other religious bodies. These are permitted to perform religious rites for the benefit of nonparty members, but are restricted to this function.

A brief description such as this of the party-dominated governmental structure may convey the impression that authority flows smoothly from party to government and from government to economic, social, and intellectual life, but this is not in fact the case. Once agreement as to policy is reached in the Presidium, there no doubt is a certain simplicity in the chain of command as compared with other forms of government. When it comes to reaching a decision as to policy, however, the degree of centralization of the Soviet system adds a further dimension of difficulty to the problems of decision-making inherent in any form of government. Soviet political life has always been fraught with controversies, and as the economic and social structures have become more complex the controversies have been more profound. In a fundamental matter such as the allocation of resources the party is confronted by the demands of a wide variety of interest groups: the armed forces, the various branches of heavy and light industry, the state and collective farms, educational and research institutions, and the various republics with their national subdivisions. Since the party permeates all enterprises and institutions, it is responsible for all of their needs, and each interest group has its advocates within the party. This association of party members with interest groups goes as high as the Presidium itself, and the controversies over consumer goods and capital goods, heavy industry and agriculture, and economic rationality and political control have been the source of the differences between Malenkov and Khrushchev, Khrushchev and Molotov, and Brezhnev and Khrushchev. When Stalin was the undisputed leader, these controversies were carried on at a lower level and resulted in the purge of many thousands of party members. Now these issues are brought out into the open in the public statements of political leaders and interest groups, but without resort to Stalinist purges. It is characteristic of the Soviet system, as compared with most others, that the entire range of conflicting interests common to modern societies must be resolved within the Communist party by bureaucratic methods in the absence of a stable constitutional order. The final decision lies with the Presidium of the Central Committee and the Central Committee itself, but their respective roles were in a state of flux in the 1950s and 1960s and the determination of policy rested with the changing and obscure relationships of a dozen party leaders.

The Communist party of the Soviet Union thus entered the 1970s with a continuing controversy between "dogmatists," who wished to maintain a tight centralized party control over all economic and social activity, and "pragmatists," who were prepared to experiment with alternative methods of control and organization in an effort to gain the benefits that might result from greater local initiative and spontaneity. Khrushchev had been a pragmatist in this sense, and probably the main reason for his downfall was that his efforts at decentralization had threatened the authority normally exercised by high officials in both party and state. Under the leadership of Brezhnev and Kosygin, the party moved toward a more dogmatic approach and this trend was reflected in renewed praise of Stalin. The anti-Stalinist trend of the later 1950s was criticized as excessive, and at the ninetieth anniversary of his birthday in December, 1969, Stalin was praised as a theoretician and for his view that the strength of the state, the police, and the army must not be challenged.

Most observers regarded this renewal of a dogmatic approach as a defensive measure against the threats which Soviet leaders perceived to their authority. The intensification of the controversy with China throughout the 1960s and the crisis in Czechoslovakia in 1968 challenged the authority of Soviet leadership in the Communist orbit. The contrast between the slowing down of Soviet growth and the relatively rapid advancement of economic and social institutions in Western Europe, Japan, and the United States, threatened the credibility of Soviet policies in the eyes of a younger generation of Soviet citizens that was better informed about developments abroad than ever before. The challenges anticipated by Soviet leaders in the 1970s were not from other political groups within the country, but rather from problems at home and abroad that they found increasingly difficult to solve by traditional means.

Patterns of Soviet Change

ECONOMIC GROWTH. Throughout the postwar period the primary concern of the Communist party has continued to be the industrial development of Russia. Indeed, it would not be too much to say that all other concerns were subordinated to this one overriding goal. Rapid economic growth requires heavy investments, and it is one of the principal achievements of the Soviet system that it has been able to enforce such heavy investments over a long period despite high human costs. This high rate of investment, of which heavy industry has been the principal beneficiary, has had as its consequence the draining of resources from other branches of the economy. Agriculture, housing, consumer goods, and the real income of workers have been greatly burdened by the emphasis on heavy industry. Looked at positively, on the other hand, the party can be proud of its success in keeping so much of Russia poor in order to make industry prosper. In Communist eyes, the goal of industrial strength justifies the means used to obtain it.

As the largest country in the world in area, and the third most populous, the USSR can draw on a wide range of physical and human resources in implementing its policy of rapid industrialization. In gross national product it has risen from fifth in rank before 1917 to second, following only the United States. In gross national product per capita, it ranks about twentieth among the countries of the world, and in some of the key indices of economic development it ranks well above the twentieth on a per capita basis. This single-minded concern with industrialization on the part of the Soviet leaders has nevertheless resulted in serious imbalances within the economy which by the beginning of the 1970s seemed likely to result in a serious crisis. This crisis is reflected in the fact that the annual rate of growth of gross national product declined from an average of 7 percent in the 1950s to 5.5 percent in the 1960s, and there were indications of the possibility of some further decline as the USSR moved from the eighth five-year plan (1966–70) to the ninth (1971–75). This growth rate in the 1960s is at about the same level as that of the West European and English-speaking countries, and is well below that of Japan and several other countries.

This failure on the part of the USSR to sustain a higher rate of growth than a considerable number of countries that employ much less drastic methods of government has led to a profound reassessment of their system on the part of Soviet leaders. This reassessment was in fact initiated by Khrushchev, and his denunciation of Stalin was a first necessary step in opening the debate. In his insistence on the predominance of heavy industry, however, Khrushchev remained much of a Stalinist himself. In criticizing those who favored a more balanced system, Khrushchev asserted that "these pseudotheoreticians try to claim that at some stage of socialist construction the development of heavy industry ceases to be the main task and that light industry can and should overtake all other branches of industry. This is profoundly incorrect reasoning, alien to the spirit of Marxism-Leninism—nothing but slander of our party. This is a belching of the rightist deviation, a regurgitation of views hostile to Leninism, views which Rykov, Bukharin, and their ilk once preached." Despite the main innovations sponsored by Khrushchev, his fall from power in October, 1964, must be attributed ultimately to his failure to solve the fundamental problems that plagued the Soviet economy.

These fundamental problems can be considered under two categories: management and allocation of resources. The extreme administrative centralization favored by Stalin served a useful purpose at a time when the economy was in a relatively early stage of development and when a first generation of managers was still being trained. As the economy became more complex, however, centralization became a serious handicap to development. Khrushchev recognized this and in 1957 reorganized the system of management, dissolving 141 industrial ministries at the union and republic levels. In their place he created 104 regional economic councils, each with the authority to regulate the fulfillment of the plan within its region. Overall supervision of the plan, as well as the coordination of the regional councils, was in charge of the State Planning Committee and the corresponding planning bodies at the republic level. This reform had the effect of giving Communist party agencies a greater influence in economic decisions. A further reform in 1962 reduced the number of regional economic councils to forty, and management was reorganized to conform more closely to the governmental pattern. At the same time, the Communist party was divided at its lower levels into separate industrial and agricultural hierarchies, as a mean of effecting a closer supervision of the economy. In 1963, finally, Khrushchev established a Supreme Economic Council as a kind of super-cabinet concerned with economic management. These reforms were essentially reorganizations of the party and government agencies, however, and did not mark a departure from the tradition of detailed bureaucratic supervision of the economy. There was some limited experimentation—known as Libermanism, after the economist who proposed the system—with planning production in consumer industries on the basis of market demand rather than on central plans. This orientation toward a market economy was not widely adopted, however, and did not mark a basic change in Soviet methods of planning and management. In the later 1960s, there was a general re-emphasis of central planning.

More frustrating than the problems of management were the choices involved in allocating resources. It would not be going too far to say that a central problem of Russian history has been the achievement of a West European level of economic development and national security on the basis of a substantially lower per capita level of production. This national effort at belt-tightening has inevitably led to some distortion, by West European standards, in the allocation of resources. A relatively high rate of industrial growth was achieved after 1928 at the expense of growth in agricultural production and consumer goods, and after forty years the problem has not been satisfactorily solved. A continued emphasis on heavy industry was necessitated not only by the philosophy of a system that regarded industry as the cornerstone of socialism but also by the development of a military technology which relied primarily on heavy industry. The rivalry with China, the continued restlessness of the East European countries in the Soviet orbit, and in particular the arms race with the United States added markedly to the normal pressures for maintaining a high allocation of resources to heavy industry. Such statistics as are available provide evidence that periods of high defense expenditures in the early and late 1960s corresponded to periods of low rates of growth in the gross national product. The Soviet economy could produce either guns or butter, but not both.

There was of course considerable validity to the argument that the production of consumer goods would benefit in the long run by the further development of heavy industry, even though most consumers did not see why these benefits should be delayed so long. In the case of agriculture, however, the point was reached in the 1960s when a change in the normally low allocation of resources for technological modernization could no longer be avoided. The extent of this problem was revealed by Soviet figures that showed that in the early 1950s the average grain yield was not as high as in 1913, and that the area sown to grain was only 2 percent greater. This was a remarkable admission for a country that claimed to be the most advanced in the world and whose population had risen from 140 to 190 million. The cause of this stagnation was the failure of the government, in the interest of rapid industrialization, to devote adequate resources to agricultural production. Two solutions were possible: to cultivate existing lands more intensively by means of fertilizers, irrigation, and machinery; or to extend cultivation to marginal lands where rapid increases in production might be achieved with very limited investments. Khrushchev chose the latter course, and by 1958 had planted in grain some 100 million acres of virgin lands in Central Asia and adjacent regions, increasing by one third the grain area of the USSR. At the same time, an effort was made to improve production on the existing farmlands by consolidating management into larger units. The number of collective farms had already been reduced by consolidation from 235,000 in 1945 to 93,000 in 1953, and now the number was reduced further to some 40,000. The number of state farms was increased from 5,000 to 9,000, partly by incorporating collective farms and by establishing new state farms in the virgin lands.

As a result of these reforms, particularly the virgin lands program, grain production increased from 82 million tons in 1953 to 125 million in 1962. In 1963 and again in 1965, however, the virgin lands suffered disastrous crop failures. Bread lines appeared in Soviet cities, and the USSR was compelled to make large purchases of grain abroad. These failures were caused less by climate than by inadequate farming methods. In the virgin lands, where rain is scarce, the land was ploughed by traditional methods without regard to the danger of erosion. Within a few years, wind erosion threatened to turn large areas of the new lands into dust bowls. Khrushchev had thus purchased a rapid increase in grain production by massive inputs of land and labor, but had sought to avoid the much more costly investment that the application of modern technology would have required. A comparison of Soviet and American agriculture illustrates the nature of this problem. In 1962–63 the USSR had 75 percent more sown crop land than the U.S., but employed seven and a half times more labor and only 31 percent as many tractors and 24 percent as much commercial fertilizer per acre. Khrushchev's successors sought to remedy this situation, and in 1965 Brezhnev issued a report on "Urgent Measures for the Further Development of Soviet Agriculture." The essential features of this proposal included a significant increase in state investments in agriculture, particularly in artificial fertilizers, and the channeling of a greater proportion of the receipts from agriculture into the incomes of individual collective farmers. This combination of investments and incentives led to an increase of almost one-fourth in the rate of growth of agricultural production in the later 1960s and temporarily relieved the crisis. These were only short-term measures, however, and a drought in 1969 led to further shortages of food in Soviet cities. A long-term solution of the agricultural crisis called for greater capital investments than could be made without raising fundamental questions about the direction of the entire economy.

SOCIETY AND CULTURE. In October, 1957, the Soviet government surprised the world with the announcement that the first artificial earth satellite, or "sputnik," had been launched. This was naturally a matter of great pride on the part of the Communist party. For the rest of the world it served as dramatic evidence of the level of development attained by science and technology in the USSR.

In exercising its all-embracing controls over Soviet life, the Communist party goes to great lengths to support and develop those aspects of society and culture which are essential to the development of a powerful state. The most striking feature of Russian society is the strong position established by the ruling elite, which embraces the bulk of the Communist party as well as nonparty technicians in many fields. The contrast between this "new class," as it is sometimes called, and the rest of the population gave every evidence of continuing as a fundamental feature of postwar Russia. Many members of this group lived very comfortably indeed, and they were the principal ones to enjoy television sets, refrigerators, and other household appliances when Soviet industry began to turn them out in small quantities. They also enjoyed significant privileges not available to the rest of the population. What was most important from the party's viewpoint, however, was that all persons having power and influence in Soviet society received benefits and prestige that assured their loyalty to the regime. The success of this system may be judged from the fact that only a handful of members of this group tried to escape from the system despite the stress under which they lived.

Education, and especially technical training, has also received strong support from party and state. Compulsory eight-year schooling has been established, and an important effort has been made to improve the conditions of study by introducing boarding schools. Great emphasis is also placed on higher education, which is the principal gate of entry into the privileged elite and is therefore highly prized. Soviet expenditures per student in higher education equal those in most Western countries, with special emphasis on the natural sciences and engineering.

The philosophy of Soviet education stressed the training of specialists for service to the state and the economy. Precedence was given to mathematics and the natural sciences, as well as to foreign languages, and in these subjects Soviet students received a very solid training. Discipline in the schools was strict, and in all programs of study there was a large dose of political indoctrination. Knowing the officially approved answer was stressed at the expense of freedom of discussion, and a loyal attitude was as important as a good scholastic record. Tuition fees, enforced in 1940, were dropped again in the 1950s. Scholarships were available in higher educational institutions for deserving students and varied in size from one institution to another. Only in exceptional cases did scholarships cover all the expenses of a student, however, and the parents were normally expected to pay a part if not all of the bill. At the same time, students admitted to higher educational institutions were exempted from regular military service. In general, higher education provided entry to membership in the ruling elite and as such was highly coveted by all Soviet students.

Strong government support is also given to research in all fields, and again, particularly to natural sciences and mathematics. Advanced research is organized under the Academy of Sciences of the USSR, with over 120 institutes and some 35,000 employees at all levels. The Academy gives special attention to scientific work applicable to national defense and economic development, and conducts research on a wide range of important problems. In the field of nuclear research, for instance, Soviet scholars kept abreast of Western science until World War II interrupted their work. In 1949 they made their first nuclear test, and in 1953 they develop thermonuclear weapons. Similarly, in such advanced fields as industrial atomic power stations, nuclear accelerators, earth satellites, and intercontinental missiles, they matched, and in some cases surpassed, the work of Western scientists. Not so much attention has been paid, however, to biology, medicine, and other fields of science less closely related to state power. Since the death of Stalin there has been little political interference in scholarship in the natural sciences, and there have been extensive contacts and exchanges of personnel and publications with the West.

Excellent work is also done in the performing arts, which are supported by a large network of training schools and theaters. The Russian ballet has retained its world-renowned quality since imperial days, and great attention is lavished on the production of classical works. Classical ballet techniques have also been adapted to folk themes, and the famous Moiseyev dancers who have toured the United States provide a striking example of this form of art. The performing arts, like the ornate architecture of Soviet public buildings, have served to stress the power of the state and to provide in some measure a substitute for the comforts which the masses lack in their private lives. In the creative arts, on the other hand, state support has been accompanied by very rigid party controls. Musical themes and forms have been dictated by the party, and compositions failing to adhere to them are severely criticized. In this atmosphere world-renowned composers such as Shostakovich and Khachaturian continued to work, but under conditions that restricted their creativity.

The Soviet achievement in creating a strong and generally loyal elite and in developing such fields as technical education, scientific research, and the performing arts has attracted wide approbation in other countries. At the same time the high price of these achievements has also been recognized. Particularly striking have been the material restrictions imposed on the great majority of the Russian people. Although a small proportion could hope to join the elite through the gate of higher education, the conditions of life for most of them have improved only moderately in the course of a generation of rapid economic growth.

Apart from the question of material welfare, there are sweeping restrictions on human rights which affect the entire population. In all fields of Soviet life the Communist party is supreme, and no views can be expressed in public unless they are within the rather limited framework approved by the party. In matters of property and administration, justice is available through recourse to the courts. In matters relating to politics, however, the interests of the state as perceived by the party take precedence over law. All forms of expression are regarded as instruments of party propaganda, and every effort is made to achieve a unified impact on people's minds.

After Stalin's death there was a significant "thaw" in the party's attitudes. Especially after the inauguration of the de-Stalinization campaign in 1956, intellectuals were permitted to criticize the harsher aspects of Soviet life and to voice hopes and ideals in a manner that would have led to certain arrest in Stalin's day. One of the most striking of the novels that sought to present Russian life as it really was, rather than in an idealized form, was Vladimir Dudintsev's *Not By Bread Alone* (1956). It told the story of the trials and tribulations of an inventor trying to deal with Moscow's self-satisfied bureaucracy. The inventor wins out in the end, but not before he has served a term in a concentration camp. "Now at last I have seen the 'invisible empire' of bureaucracy," he remarks at the end of the novel. The Communist party condemned Dudintsev's negative tone, but in post-Stalin Russia it was possible for the book and its author to survive. Even more revealing was Alexander Solzhenitsyn's *One Day in the Life of Ivan Denisovich* (1963), which describes in vivid terms life in a Soviet concentration camp. This book and its author also survived a storm of criticism, although it was published at a time when severe restrictions were again being imposed on Soviet intellectuals. The threat inherent in party controls was voiced most dramatically against *Doctor Zhivago*, published in the West in 1957, in which Boris Pasternak protested eloquently against the destructiveness of the revolution and the cruelty of the leaders who sought through unrestrained violence to reshape human life. When Pasternak received the Nobel prize for literature, he was reviled as a "Judas" and a "pig" by the Soviet authorities and was compelled to reject the honor which he had initially welcomed.

In the later 1960s party leaders began to fear that criticism of the Stalin era would get out of hand. Many of the "sons" had lost their fathers in Stalin's purges, and they were inclined to blame the entire generation of "fathers"—including the current party .leaders—for the excesses of Stalinism. Younger poets such as Andrei Voznesensky and Yevgeny Yevtushenko, who had received privileged treatment a few years earlier, were no longer in favor. Mikhail Bulgakov's widely admired *The Master and Margarita,* written in the 1930s, was finally published in 1967 but only in a censored version. The later novels of Solzhenitsyn, *The Cancer Ward* and *The First Circle,* could be published only abroad. Although Solzhenitsyn was considered by most critics as one of the greatest Russian writers of the twentieth century, and was frequently compared with Dostoevsky, he was finally expelled from the Union of Soviet Writers for refusing to accept the party's censorship. He accepted a Nobel prize in 1970, but did not go to Sweden for the ceremonies for fear that he might not be allowed to return to the USSR.

Restrictions on the freedom of expression increased significantly as the USSR entered the 1970s, but they did not match the harshness of the Stalin era. The sentences of five and seven years imposed on Yurii Daniel and Andrei Siniavsky in 1966 for maligning the USSR in books published abroad served as a warning as to the limits of permissible criticism. At the same time a considerable clandestine literature was circulated, and views critical of official policy were widely read and discussed even when they could not be published. A new generation was coming of age which took the Soviet system for granted, but which also asserted the right to view it with a critical attitude. The leaders of party and state did not welcome this development, but neither did they undertake to crush it completely. A process of accommodation between state and society was under way that seemed likely to lead to new forms of regulation and expression.

THE SOVIET MODEL. As the USSR rounded out a half century of development, the continuing international debate regarding the significance of the Soviet experiment reached a new maturity of understanding. The rapid recovery of the USSR from the terrible strains of war demonstrated the viability of the system and the success of the Communist party in organizing and co-ordinating the complex process of economic and social development. The central question that concerned international opinion was not whether the Soviet system would continue to exist, but rather what it had achieved, what these achievements had cost, and to what extent the USSR represented a model that other countries could follow.

It has already been noted that in terms of gross national product per capita the USSR ranks about twentieth among the countries of the world. In some areas of achievement, however, it ranked considerably higher than this. In its rate of economic growth, it ranked higher in the 1950s than any of the major countries except West Germany and Japan. In the 1960s, however, the rate of growth was significantly lower. The rate of social change, as measured by the shift of the labor force from agriculture to industry, was much more rapid than in most countries. Both enrollments and expenditures in higher education were also relatively high, although a similar record was not achieved in primary and secondary education. In public health, in the performing arts, and in the promotion of science and technology the USSR also ranks among the highest.

The costs of these achievements can best be measured in terms of the areas in which Russia ranked well below the twentieth country. In the 1960s its agriculture was still very inefficient. Real wages and household consumption were also among the important sacrifices that had been made to achieve a high rate of industrial growth. As late as the 1950s the average Russian was in important respects not much better off than before the revolution, and the significant gains in the standard of living made in the 1960s were of a very uneven character. A most important cost is also represented by the continuing and severe limitations on human rights. While these limitations no longer bear the stamp of Stalinist methods, they continue to restrict thought, expression, political opinions, and other forms of freedom in many fundamental ways.

At the culmination of the era of Stalin in the early 1950s there was some reason to believe that the Soviet model might be widely adopted. The thirteen countries governed by Communist parties, with almost one third of the world's population, looked to the USSR for leadership and appeared to constitute a monolithic "Soviet bloc" of states. Subsequent developments revealed, however, that this unity was more apparent than real. As the pressures of postwar tensions and of Stalin's personal influence were relaxed, each of the Communist countries adopted a somewhat separate path of development. All the countries of Eastern Europe with the exception of Bulgaria ceased to follow strictly Soviet guidance and sought more diversified patterns of domestic organization and international trade and relations. China, for its part, launched a major campaign against Soviet policies that marked a decisive turning point in the world Communist movement.

These developments fundmentally altered the international image of the USSR as the guiding spirit in a Communist commonwealth of nations, and led to a new evaluation of the significance of the Soviet model. Indeed, the monopoly of power on the part of Communist parties proved to be the one feature that all Communist countries have in common. Their methods of industrial and agricultural organization varied greatly, vital differences in skills and resources called for widely varying policies of development, and questions of theory aroused many controversies. Despite the divisions that wracked the Communist orbit, the qualities of leadership demonstrated by the ruling Communist parties nevertheless had their attractions for aspiring politicians in certain situations and countries. The international network of the Communist movement had built an organization of parties that extended to many countries, and in some they were the most active proponents of political and economic development.

For the great majority of the countries of the world, however, the Soviet model has come to be regarded as a significant but essentially unique example of political and economic development. The great majority of the countries of Latin America, Asia, and Africa have been attracted less by the Soviet model than by the radical republican model that traced its origins to the American and French revolutions. Thus Kemal Atatürk and Reza Shah after the First World War and Nehru, Nasser, Sukarno, Betancourt, and Azikiwe, among many others, after the Second World War, preferred the Western tradition of rapid development that matches vigor with restraint and seeks a balanced development in which agriculture, human welfare, and political rights will not in principle be sacrificed to industrialization. The advanced countries, for their part, evolved a more mature attitude toward the USSR. Both those who considered it the epitome of evil and those who had seen it as the realization of the liberal vision of freedom and justice, came to realize that the Soviet Union was a phenomenon with deep roots in the Russian past that was not likely to be copied in detail by others except under the compulsion of Soviet military occupation. In this view Soviet developments appeared less as an implementation of the theories of Marxism-Leninism than as a resultant of inherited policies and problems peculiar to Russia, of the limitations imposed by a one-party system, and of the personal decisions of Lenin, Stalin, and their successors.

CHAPTER

28

Eastern Europe

Postwar Governments: *United-Front Regimes; People's Democracies.*

The Soviet Orbit: *Consolidation of Soviet Controls; Revolts and Repression.*

Different Roads to Socialism: *Unity and Diversity; Tito's Yugoslavia.*

◆

Postwar Governments

UNITED-FRONT REGIMES. The establishment of the Soviet sphere of influence in Eastern Europe was by no means simply a matter of imposing an alien political regime during a period of military occupation. The presence of Soviet troops in these countries indeed played a vital role in this process, but one which was in the last analysis secondary to the political tactics employed by the Soviet regime. Three distinct stages may be distinguished in the establishment of this sphere of influence. The first involved obtaining the acquiescence, if not the explicit consent, of the Western powers to the establishment of such a sphere. The second stage was that of obtaining the participation of the local Communist parties in united-front governments in each of the countries concerned. The third and final stage involved the assertion of a predominant position by the Communists, after they had succeeded in eliminating or neutralizing their major opponents. In many cases these three stages overlapped, and the point of transition from one to another is not always clear, but they nevertheless represented the essential process through which Soviet influence passed before firm control could be asserted.

It has already been related how the United Nations coalition tended to settle immediate occupation problems on the basis of spheres of influence and how the advance of the Soviet armies toward Germany gave them the advantage of overwhelming military force in Eastern Europe which could be directed toward political ends. The Western states, for their part, had interests that they wished to secure in Italy and Greece. The first step toward acknowledging a Soviet orbit in Eastern Europe was taken during the autumn of 1944, when the Russians agreed to recognize the predominant British interest in Greece and to share an interest in Yugoslavia, in return for British recognition of a predominant Soviet interest in Rumania, Hungary, and Bulgaria. This policy was carried a step further when the armistice terms were agreed to for Rumania (August, 1944), Finland (September, 1944), Bulgaria (September, 1944), and Hungary (January, 1945). Here again, the Soviet high command was granted a position of almost exclusive influence in political as well as military matters. The Western states had already secured a similar preferred position in Italy.

In the case of the Eastern European states that were already members of the United Nations coalition, the situation was more complicated. Only in Czechoslovakia was Soviet influence established without a controversy with the Western states, since the government-in-exile was prepared to accept the establishment of a Soviet sphere of influence. The Czech-Soviet treaty of alliance of 1943 had already reflected the decision of Beneš and his foreign minister, Masaryk, son of the founder of the Czechoslovak republic, to rebuild their country as a bridge between East and West. The Yugoslav and Polish governments-in-exile, on the other hand, were determined to resist any Soviet interference in their affairs. The Russians countered this attitude by promoting alternative regimes, under Tito in Yugoslavia and Bierut in Poland, which by the end of the war were in physical control of their respective countries. Faced with this accomplished fact, Roosevelt and Churchill agreed at Yalta, in February, 1945, to transfer their recognition to new coalition governments in which certain members of the governments-in-exile would be admitted to the Soviet-dominated regimes. In return, they obtained from Stalin a pledge of "the earliest possible establishment through free elections of governments responsive to the will of the people." In the view of the Western states, none of these arrangements was intended as a recognition of a permanent Soviet sphere of influence. The duration of the armistice terms with the satellite states did not extend beyond the signature of peace, and it was expected that in the defeated as well as in the liberated countries excessive Communist influence would be moderated by the free elections which were to be held shortly after the termination of hostilities. As it turned out, however, the granting of these initial, and in general reluctant, concessions to Russia took the initiative out of the hands of the Western states.

The second stage of Soviet control, which involved obtaining key positions for Communist leaders in each government, was accomplished without great difficulty. Beneš voluntarily admitted Communists into the Czechoslovak cabinet, while in Poland and Yugoslavia they had a predominant position in the new coalition governments from the start, with the blessing of the Big Three. In Albania, the victory of the partisans under Hoxha after a civil struggle gave the Communists a leading role. In the former Axis satellite states—Rumania, Bulgaria, Hungary, and Finland—Communists were admitted as a matter of course to the coalition governments formed at the end of the war. In general they received key positions, such as the ministries of interior and justice, but at the start they did not have a free hand in political matters. The new postwar regimes in all these countries were known in Communist terminology as united-front governments, which meant flexible political coalitions within which the Communists could maneuver for position as a minority group until they were prepared to assume full power. It was a subtle technique of infiltration, which deceived the Western states for a while and even misled experienced non-Communist statesmen in Eastern Europe.

The transition of the Communist parties from minority participation in the united-front governments to a position of complete dominance, which formed the third stage in their assumption of power, varied in method and timing with each country. It was in this stage that the surviving monarchs—Peter of Yugoslavia, Simeon of Bulgaria, and Michael of Rumania—were deposed. Only in Yugoslavia and Albania did the Communists have unquestioned authority from the start. In Rumania and Bulgaria, the leading non-Communists were forced out of the government in the spring and summer of 1945. In Poland, on the other hand, it was not until January, 1947, that the Communists openly asserted their power. A similar process took place in Hungary in the following June. Most spectacular of all, to the extent that it revealed to Western opinion the methods and aims of the Communists more clearly than ever before, was their seizure of power in Czechoslovakia in February, 1948. Only in Finland did the Communists fail to make the transition to the third stage and remain without a determining voice in the government. The Russians were acquainted with the toughness of the Finns from past experience and were satisfied for the time being to let well enough alone.

PEOPLE'S DEMOCRACIES. While the united-front governments were the device used by the Communists to neutralize rival political groups before their final seizure of power, once they asserted their full authority they established new constitutional regimes known as "people's democracies." These new regimes were not meant to represent the final establishment of the Soviet form of socialism, but rather provided a framework within which the transition from a "capitalist" to a "classless" society

STATESMEN OF EASTERN EUROPE *Representatives of seven Communist states discussing their problems at Warsaw, Poland, in June, 1948. Left to right are: Kolarov (Bulgaria), Molnar (Hungary), Molotov (USSR), Modzelewski (Poland), Ana Pauker (Rumania), Clementis (Czechoslovakia), and Simich (Yugoslavia).*

could be made. The Communists thus foresaw that these countries would have to go through a phase similar to that which Russia experienced between 1928 and 1936, during which the governments would gradually take over all means of production in both industry and agriculture. The new constitutions, therefore, made provision for the liquidation of earlier political institutions and empowered the governments to muzzle all criticism and suppress all opposition parties. Special attention was also paid to appeasing the minorities in these countries, by making provision for federalism or for national rights that recognized local sentiment without sacrificing any of the centralized political power.

The new constitutions of the people's democracies thus reflected a system in which the commanding heights of the economy were in the hands of the state, while private property and private initiative were permitted to continue for the time being within certain narrow limits. As in the Soviet Union, the real authority was exercised by the Communist parties led by such vigorous figures as Georgi Dimitrov in Bulgaria (until his death in July, 1949), Ana Pauker in Rumania, Gottwald in Czechoslovakia, Bierut in Poland, Rakosi in Hungary, Hoxha in Albania, and

Tito in Yugoslavia. The party Central Committees in each case appointed all important officials and made all policy decisions. The absolute character of these dictatorships was camouflaged somewhat by an elaborate parliamentary system. Local party committees nominated candidates, who were not necessarily Communists, to the single electoral lists presented to the voters. The deputies met in unicameral legislatures (except in the case of Yugoslavia, where the federal structure required two chambers) and served for terms of four to six years. Each assembly was headed by a Presidium, or steering committee, which exercised all the powers of the assembly between sessions. The president of the Presidium was a secondary figure who, as in the Soviet Union, performed the functions of chief of state. The real power was exercised by the cabinet, however, which in form was appointed by the assembly but in fact represented the leadership of the Communist party. Several non-Communists might be found in each cabinet, but they were permitted to remain only in their personal capacity as experts or to appease sections of public opinion which had retained some influence.

Since the Communists were a minority in every country in Eastern Europe, and a very small minority in most of them, the opposition they had to overcome was considerable. The openly pro-Nazi elements were in most cases tried and executed, but there were many other political leaders who had suffered with the Communists under Axis rule. They were willing to share political power with the Communists, but they refused to submit to Communist dictation, and so a showdown was inevitable. In some cases, as with Beneš and Masaryk in Czechoslovakia, it was the prewar middle-class liberals who retained the majority. In Albania, on the other hand, rival groups of nationalist leaders competed for power. The situation was more complicated in Yugoslavia, where the leaders of the constituent nationalities joined in varying coalitions with the heads of the Peasant parties. In most of the countries of Eastern Europe, however, the parliamentary democrats had been discredited by the economic disorganization following World War I, while the nationalist leaders were tainted by collaboration with the Axis.

There remained, nevertheless, the Agrarians and the Socialists, who had behind them a full generation of political activity and who enjoyed a wide following, and they proved to be the chief opponents of Communist rule. With the exception of Czechoslovakia, between 50 and 70 percent of the population in these countries was engaged in agriculture, and the great majority were independent peasant proprietors. They had, moreover, developed a vigorous agrarian ideology stressing the consideration they felt the peasant should receive in the overall economic policy of the state. The Agrarians believed in a land reform that would divide up the remaining large estates, and in promoting the modernization of agriculture through the co-operative efforts of peasant proprietors. This program was in direct contrast to the ultimate Communist aim of collectivizing the small farms and turning the independent peasants into an agricultural proletariat. The Communist hatred of the Agrarians was less on theoretical grounds, however, than on the practical one that the latter had in most of these countries far greater electoral strength. As soon as they had the police and the machinery of government well in hand, the Communists therefore attacked the Agrarians relentlessly. In Yugoslavia, Šubašić was thrown out of the government and Jovanović was jailed, as were Maniu and Mihalache in Rumania. In Bulgaria, the Agrarian leader G. M. Dimitrov (not related to the Communist Georgi Dimitrov) was permitted to go into exile, while his successor, Petkov, was executed. Ferenc Nagy of Hungary and Mikolajczyk of Poland, who had served as prime ministers of their respective countries in the united-front governments, managed to escape with their lives. The Socialist leaders, who had a much smaller following and whose doctrines did not present a clear-cut contrast to those of the Communists, were either suborned or were forced out of political life.

The Soviet Orbit

CONSOLIDATION OF SOVIET CONTROLS. Within the framework of these essentially domestic developments, the Soviet Union exerted its control over Eastern Europe through many channels. While Western observers were inclined to see this development of a Soviet orbit in Eastern Europe as an aspect of Soviet expansionism and as evidence of the doctrine of the inevitable march of communism toward worldwide victory, the motive which probably loomed largest in Soviet policy was national security. In the view of the Soviet leaders the countries of this region would be controlled either by them or by their enemies, and they did not wish to see control of the region wrested from their hands after the sacrifices of the recent war. In this sense, the new sphere of influence provided the Soviet Union the very guarantee of security in Eastern Europe which it had sought with only partial and temporary success in its negotiations with France and England and with Germany in the summer of 1939.

The principal instrument of Soviet influence in Eastern Europe consisted of the local Communist parties, which in each country served as obedient agents of the Communist party of the USSR until 1948. In that year the Yugoslav party declared its independence in the face of Soviet efforts to subvert it, and rumblings of discontent began to be heard in other countries. Control was also exercised more directly, through the Soviet diplomatic officials in each country, and through agents of the Soviet secret police and of the Russian Communist party, who kept an eye on the local Communists as well as on each other. On a more formal level, the Soviet Union concluded mutual-assistance pacts with all these countries except Albania. The treaties with Czechoslovakia, Yugoslavia, and Poland were concluded before the end of the war, while those with the four former Axis satellites were not signed until 1948. The overt aim of these pacts in every case was to provide for a common defense against a revived and aggressive Germany. A more flexible form of control was created in September, 1947, with the establishment of the Communist Information Bureau (Cominform). Its purpose was to co-ordinate the activities of all the Communist parties in their efforts to combat "Anglo-American imperialism," and in many respects it resumed the work of the Communist International (Comintern), which was dissolved in May, 1943. When the pressure of the Marshall Plan began to be felt in Eastern Europe, Russia attempted to counteract it by sponsoring a Council for Economic Mutual Assistance in January, 1949 (COMECON).

The Soviet Union derived very substantial economic gains from its dominant position in Eastern Europe. By 1947, these countries were taking over one half of Russia's exports and supplying over one third of its commercial imports, whereas on the eve of the war they had shared less than 5 percent of its foreign trade. Russia's advantage in this trade was more than merely commercial, since it did not hesitate to use its bargaining position to obtain favorable prices. Moreover, it was able on occasion to re-export some of these products at considerable profit. At the same time, the Soviet Union received reparations payments from Finland, Hungary, and Rumania which practically equaled its commercial imports from the entire region. It also had a very advantageous political arrangement for the import of Polish coal. It has been estimated, in fact, that in 1947 Russian imports of all categories from Eastern Europe were just about double its exports to that region. This was of necessity a temporary advantage, since these countries could not continue indefinitely to support such an unfavorable balance, but in the decade while it lasted it was a very profitable relationship for Russia.

At the point where the Soviet sphere of influence took on many of the aspects of old-fashioned imperialism, even Communists began to question Soviet policy. In Eastern Europe, as elsewhere, many had joined the Communist party after the war because they thought it would provide answers to the social and economic problems that their countries had found it so difficult to solve under the various parliamentary and authoritarian regimes of the interwar years. What began to discourage them was not so much the fact that Russia sought economic benefits from its position in Eastern Europe as the Soviet insistence that all local problems be solved by the methods the Communists had developed in Russia. These countries had a wide variety of problems and interests that differed from those of the Soviet Union, and gradually important Communist leaders began to raise serious objections to Soviet policy. Many of them, like Kostov in Bulgaria, Xoxe in Albania, and Rajk in Hungary, were executed for treason. In Yugoslavia, although Tito was expelled from the Cominform, he successfully withstood its verbal onslaughts and the political and economic ostracism of the other countries in the Soviet orbit. That Tito was favored by geography and possessed an armed force built up during the war without Soviet interference did not diminish the fact that he had succeeded in delivering the most serious blow that the prestige of Moscow had received since the great purges of 1936–38.

An important consequence of the centralized Soviet controls in the Stalin era was that all these Eastern European countries pursued economic policies closely parallel to those of the USSR itself. In agriculture the first step was the breakup of the larger estates. In Poland, Czechoslovakia, and Hungary this measure involved one-third to one-half of all agricultural and forest land. In Bulgaria, Rumania, and Yugoslavia, where landholding was already very largely in the hands of the peasants, relatively little land was involved. Thereafter all the East European states moved initially toward collectivization, but in the 1950s Yugoslavia and Poland reversed their policies and returned to private ownership of land. These two countries now have dual economies, with socialized industry, trade, and services, but with over 85 percent of the land privately owned. Bulgaria, Czechoslovakia, East Germany, Hungary, and Rumania collectivized their agriculture, and in these countries less than 15 percent of the agricultural land is privately held. Western studies have reached the conclusion that the two countries with private agriculture have performed better than those with socialized agriculture. By 1970 the former had exceeded the prewar level of agricultural production by a considerable margin, whereas the latter had barely attained that level.

Industrial production, on the other hand, surpassed the prewar level in all these countries by 1950 and has since grown to several times that level. Industrial growth has been purchased at a high price in personal consumption and levels of living, however, and has not been matched by similar increases in labor productivity and general economic efficiency. By 1970 the economies of these countries had outgrown the rather simple methods of planning and control introduced initially by the Communist parties, and the question of how to provide the flexibility and local initiative required by more advanced economies remained largely unanswered. In Hungary and Yugoslavia, and to a lesser extent in Poland and Rumania, reforms in planning and management were undertaken in the 1960s which offered promise of greater efficiency.

REVOLTS AND REPRESSION. The Soviet system of forced industrialization produced great strains in Eastern Europe, and only by the most severe use of police measures were these countries kept under control. When Stalin died in 1953, and when within a short time Beria's position as head of the police was undermined, the pressure of discontent in this region could no longer be contained. The first effort to meet this discontent was Malenkov's "New Course," which promised measures to increase food and consumer goods. In Hungary and Poland, where the pressure was particularly great, agriculture was decollectivized. These and other measures brought few immediate benefits, however, and could not counterbalance the great demoralization that occurred in Communist ranks. Soon there was widespread criticism of the Stalinist system, especially in student and literary circles, and extensive riots occurred in Poznan.

Soviet leaders were now faced with the choice of reimposing Stalinism or trying to accommodate the needs of the individual countries. They chose the latter course. As a consequence of this new policy, the Cominform was dissolved in April, 1956. The policy soon had an impact in Poland and Hungary. In Poland the Communists favoring an independent policy, led by Gomulka, rapidly gained the initiative. In October, 1956, Gomulka became prime minister, and even though the great majority of the Poles were anti-Communist they believed that he was the only alternative to Stalinism. In the national elections of January, 1957, Gomulka therefore received a resounding majority.

In Hungary, events did not move so smoothly. Here the Communist party was weaker than in Poland, and public opinion was less accustomed to the restraints bred by living on the brink of disaster. Imre Nagy, like Gomulka a Communist who favored an independent policy, was unable to keep control over the situation. He became prime minister in October, 1956, but immediately found himself faced with a revolution against any form of Communist rule. Now the Russians stepped into the picture, and on November 4 they sent in an army of tanks, which re-established Communist rule after bloody fighting. Nagy was replaced by Kadar, the secretary of the party, who now attempted to build a new policy on the ruins left by the revolution. In the meantime a flood of refugees left Hungary, and the world was once again impressed by the brutality of Soviet methods.

All the countries of Eastern Europe felt the impact of the events in Poland and Hungary, but Soviet controls were sufficiently strong to make extensive concessions unnecessary. Throughout the region, however, economic planning was now adapted more closely to the needs of the individual countries. A division of labor among them began to emerge, with more attention devoted to consumer goods and agriculture, and the pace of industrialization slowed down. At the same time there was some lessening of police controls, and travel abroad became freer. Only in Poland was substantial freedom gained, however, for Poles were now free to criticize the Soviet system as well as their own. Poland also negotiated an American loan of $98 million and sent a number of students and scholars to the United States. Indeed, even this degree of freedom began to irritate the Russians after they recovered from the blow to their prestige of the events in 1956. Many factors, including the difficulty of bringing Tito back into the fold, led the Russians in 1958 to tighten up again on their Communist neighbors. The signal for this change was the execution in 1958 of Imre Nagy, who had been held in prison since 1956, and even Gomulka was compelled to issue a statement approving this act of revenge.

Despite these setbacks the trend toward independence from Soviet policy initiated in 1956 continued to evolve, and in the mid-1960s the

Communist countries of Eastern Europe exhibited many forms of diversity. Hungary was the country that had gone furthest in relaxing domestic controls, and under the leadership of Kadar its government sought, by balancing Eastern and Western influences, to pursue a policy of economic growth suited to its own particular needs. Kadar won the support of the population by raising the standard of living, dissolving most of the collective farms, and permitting greater personal freedom. Western travelers visiting Hungary were impressed by the success of these measures. Equally dramatic were the changes initiated in Rumania in the early 1960s, culminating in the declaration of April, 1964, which asserted the right of Communist countries to independent policies within a framework of common institutions and doctrines. Acting according to the declaration, Rumania succeeded in encouraging Western investments, in adopting a neutral position in the Sino-Soviet dispute, and in various other ways significantly loosening the close ties that had bound it to the USSR.

Czechoslovakia likewise, initially in a gradual and cautious fashion, sought opportunities to loosen the constraints of the Soviet straitjacket. The Communist leadership had followed the Soviet model as consistently as any country in Eastern Europe and shared with Soviet leaders a particular concern for the possible resurgence of German power. Czechoslovakia expelled some 3 million Sudeten Germans from its Western territories at the end of the war, and alone among the East European countries shares a common frontier with West Germany. At the same time, there were countervailing influences. Czechoslovakia had in effect been an occupied country since 1938, the only one in the region that had not experienced extensive domestic violence within its frontiers. This was a long period for even such patient peoples as the Czechs and Slovaks to remain passive, and it helps to explain the burst of vitality that occurred in 1968. In January of that year the leaders of the Czechoslovak party ousted the conservative Antonin Novotny as first secretary of the party and elected Alexander Dubček to replace him.

Such changes in top leadership frequently reflect rumblings that come from the depths of society, and on this occasion a large number of Czechs and Slovaks from all walks of life suddenly exploded with criticism of past policies and with proposals for political and economic reform. Press censorship was lifted, attacks on a whole range of Soviet-inspired policies were aired, decentralization of economic controls was advocated, and even the possibility of a two-party system was discussed. Western observers were inclined to interpret this outburst of reforming zeal as a step in the direction of a new form of democratic socialism, but to the Soviet leaders and also to the East Germans it looked more like the crumbling of party controls in the face of popular discontent. If Czechoslovakia were allowed to slip away from Communist control, what was to prevent Poland, Hungary, Rumania, and others from following its path?

Dubček was the popular hero of the day, and he was convinced that his party apparatus was in control of the situation. The Soviet leaders and

BRATISLAVA, 1968 *Soviet leaders meet with Dubček. Left to right: Podgorny, Kosygin, Brezhnev, Shelest, Dubček, and Suslov.*

likeminded colleagues in the neighboring countries met with Dubček in a series of high-level conferences and sought to convince him that he ought to tighten the reins. When persuasion failed, Soviet troops, accompanied by token contingents from Bulgaria, East Germany, Hungary, and Poland, occupied Czechoslovakia without warning on the night of August 20–21, 1968. This decisive blow was swift and virtually bloodless, but it produced a reaction resembling in many ways that following the repression of the Hungarian uprising eight years earlier.

The leaders of the Czechoslovak government were taken to Moscow virtually as prisoners, but after negotiations Dubček was allowed to remain as head of the party, and Soviet authorities sought to minimize the presence of their troops and to undertake only gradual changes in personnel. Throughout the transitional period Soviet policy was firm but relatively subtle, and there were no executions and few arrests. When Dubček was finally replaced by Gustav Husak as head of the party in April, 1969, the change was formally proposed by Dubček himself. Husak was a moderate who had been jailed by Novotny in the 1950s and who now sought to re-establish the degree of central control necessary to meet Soviet requirements without entirely alienating Czechoslovak opinion. It was by no means certain that such a policy could succeed, however, for citizens in all walks of life resented deeply the character of the Soviet occupation. When Jan Palach, a university student, died after setting fire to himself on St. Wenceslas Square in Prague in January, 1969, his sacrifice became the symbol of the defiant attitude of Czechoslovak opinion.

Different Roads to Socialism

UNITY AND DIVERSITY. When Khrushchev advanced the doctrine in 1956 that there were "different roads to socialism" and that all Communist states did not have to follow the Soviet pattern, he was recognizing that even under Stalin there had been considerable diversity among the countries of Eastern Europe despite an outward appearance of conformity. Khrushchev's new doctrine was designed in part to bring Yugoslavia back into the fold, but it also reflected an acknowledgment of a long-term trend which has survived the imposition of Soviet authority by military force in Hungary in 1956 and in Czechoslovakia in 1968.

As the countries of Eastern Europe entered the 1970s, it was apparent that the Soviet occupation of Czechoslovakia was an event of limited impact which did not portend a general reversal of policy. What had concerned the Soviet leaders was not so much the specific reforms under discussion, for other countries in the orbit had already gone a good deal further in the direction of many of the changes proposed in Prague, but rather a loss of control over the country by the Communist party. Ever since the Second World War the Soviet leaders had been very explicit in asserting that their national security depended on having "friendly" governments in power in Eastern Europe, and by friendly they meant governments controlled by Communist parties which saw eye to eye with the Soviet leaders on the main issues of policy. The occupation of Czechoslovakia in 1968 reasserted this position in a most forceful way, and two years after the event the available evidence tended to indicate that its objective was essentially this concern for security. As Brezhnev said in his formal explanation of the occupation in September 1968, "There is no doubt that the peoples of the socialist countries and the Communist parties have, and must have, freedom to determine their countries' paths of development. However, any decision of theirs must damage neither socialism in their own country nor the fundamental interest of the other socialist countries, nor the worldwide workers' movement, which is waging a struggle for socialism."

The occupation of Czechoslovakia was carried out in the name of the Warsaw Pact, which commits Bulgaria, Czechoslovakia, East Germany, Hungary, Poland, Rumania, and the USSR to a common security policy and parallels in some respects the North Atlantic Treaty Organization. This is one of the most important instruments available to Soviet leaders for the enforcement of common policies, and it is significant that the only times Soviet troops have fought in foreign countries since 1945 have been in East Germany, Hungary, and Czechoslovakia. Another instrumentality of Soviet control is the Council of Mutual Economic Assistance (COMECON). Through this organization the USSR has sought to integrate the economies of these countries, but this effort has not been very successful. Trade among the East European countries and between them and the Soviet Union has increased considerably since the establishment of COMECON, and efforts have been made to create a regional economic system. The economic development of these countries depended too much on trade with the more industrialized West to permit any substantial regional autarky, however, and the question has not yet arisen of seeking the degree of economic integration envisaged by the European Common Market.

The efforts to promote regional unity under Soviet auspices thus remained limited, and the trend toward diversity that is sometimes referred to as "polycentrism" continued after 1968. The underlying basis for this trend is that the countries of this region were pursuing quite diverse patterns of development before the Second World War and had economic and social institutions and values that differed very considerably. Three issues in particular tended to make for diversity: political centralization, economic growth, and national interest.

The criticism of political centralization was directed in particular against the curtailment of individualism and initiative in all walks of life, which placed enormous obstacles of bureaucratic red tape in the path of efforts to introduce innovations. Censorship was perhaps the most obvious instrument of political control, but the unwillingness of party leaders to delegate authority goes a long way to explain the stagnation that characterizes many aspects of life in these countries. When all economic and social decisions are controlled by relatively few persons, it takes a long time for awareness of new problems to reach the center and for changes to be implemented.

Problems of economic growth were closely related to political centralization, but also involved other issues such as the need for more consumer goods, for the diversification of foreign markets, and for the introduction of advanced methods of research and management directed toward higher productivity. Numerous experiments were made in freeing the managers of enterprises to permit them to give greater consideration to domestic and foreign markets in their decisions, but in economics as in politics the central authorities were afraid to risk the loss of control that might result.

A significant role was also played by traditional feelings of national interest. These countries had all gained independence in their contemporary form in the nineteenth and twentieth centuries after struggling against great odds, and they had confidence in their ability to solve their own problems. They resented the large role played by Soviet influence and interest in their national affairs just as much as they had resented the roles of Russian, Austrian, German, and Turkish overlords in earlier generations.

An important factor affecting all these issues in the 1970s was the fact that a new generation of leaders was beginning to gain access to positions of authority. The older generation had been molded by the experiences of the war and the early postwar period and were conditioned to place a high premium on the security of the Communist regimes from foreign and domestic enemies. Their principal task had been to establish the new governments in a hostile environment, and concern for the security of these governments was their highest value. The younger leaders, men and women in their forties who grew to maturity after the war, take the Communist system for granted and see the domestic and foreign environment as relatively friendly. For them the highest value is the development of their countries, the creation of more effective social and economic institutions, and the freedom to study models from the West as well as from the East in gaining for their countries the full benefits of the scientific and technological revolution.

Intellectual leaders in these countries have participated actively in the discussion of these issues. Indeed, some of the sharpest criticism of the traditional Soviet doctrinal approach has come from intellectuals who were influential in party affairs. Milovan Djilas, a close associate of Tito, represented an extreme point of view when he accused his Communist colleagues in *The New Class* of having created a ruling elite that was as privileged and isolated from the people as the one it had overthrown. This went beyond the criticism permissible even in relatively liberal Yugoslavia and earned him a long jail sentence. In Poland, Adam Schaff, long a member of the Central Committee, discussed in *A Philosophy of Man* his concern for problems of the individual, which were not met by the doctrines of Marxism-Leninism. Similarly his colleague Leszek Kolakowski, in *Toward a Marxist Humanism,* sought to reinterpret Marxism as part of the West European humanist tradition. In Czechoslovakia, even before 1968, the Academy of Sciences published a sophisticated discussion of the problems faced by modern societies under the title *Civilization at the Crossroads: Social and Human Implications of the Scientific and Technological Revolution*, which draws heavily on the findings of West European and American social scientists.

A new spirit was also reflected in the development of the social sciences. The dogmatic Marxism of the first postwar generation gave way to more scholarly and pragmatic work in economics and sociology, which drew extensively on work in Western Europe and the United States. Scholars, policy-makers, and managers of enterprises sought new ideas and methods from other countries that might be applicable to their own problems, and young people went abroad by the hundreds to study. Party leaders did not regard this activity as contradicting the Marxist ideology, but maintained rather that there was no conflict between the ideology and the objective methods of the social sciences.

Of the countries of Eastern Europe in the Soviet orbit, Hungary under the leadership of Kadar was the one that had gone furthest by 1970 in setting in motion extensive domestic reforms within the general framework of conformity with overall Soviet requirements. One of the virtues of Kadar's policies was that they were implemented in such a way as to avoid creating international excitement, but at the same time held out prospects for a significant transformation of economic and social institutions. Poland, despite considerable friction among party leaders and a policy of excluding Jewish leaders from positions of responsibility, was also moving in a similar direction. The younger generation of leaders was both nationalist and progressive, and sought to develop a more flexible and innovative approach to their problems. When the workers revolted at the end of 1970 due to the high cost of living, the aging Gomulka was ousted as leader of the Communist party and replaced by Edward Gierek, who promised to modernize the economic system.

Rumania took a daringly nationalistic attitude in defying Soviet efforts to mobilize the East European countries in a common front against China, although on the domestic scene its reforms did not match its rhetoric. The Czechoslovak reform movement was broken by the Soviet occupation, but the subsequent repression was relatively mild, and it seemed likely that the trend toward more dynamic institutions would be delayed rather than reversed. Of all the countries of this region, Bulgaria was the one that stayed closest to the Soviet model and was the most cautious in experimenting with new ideas. Albania, for its part, went so far as to change its allegiance from the USSR to China. This was apparently less for reasons of doctrine than as a means of protecting the Communist party hierarchy in Albania from the threats posed by a liberalizing Yugoslavia and USSR.

TITO'S YUGOSLAVIA. Among the "people's democracies" of Eastern Europe only Yugoslavia succeeded in pursuing a Communist policy free from Soviet domination, and Tito's success in developing an independent ideology has been a notable achievement. For a year or two after his expulsion from the Soviet orbit in 1948 Tito was barely able to maintain his position, but once he was assured of survival he embarked on a new course. In this he was greatly assisted by financial aid from the West. The United States alone contributed economic and military aid in the amount of some $2 billion.

The long-term significance of Tito's independent policy lies in the example to the other Communist countries of Eastern Europe of Yugoslavia's ability to defy Soviet pressures and to develop a distinctive form of Marxism-Leninism. In the political sphere, Titoism has sought to change the role of the Communist party from direct to indirect control without sacrificing its fundamental initiative in policy-making. The two principal steps in this direction have been the revision of the party statutes in 1952 and 1964 and the adoption of a new constitution in 1963. This latter document seeks to strike a balance between the six member republics and the federal government, and also to relate the legislative bodies more directly to the functioning institutions of society. A characteristic feature of the new constitution is the federal assembly, which consists of five chambers elected indirectly by corporate groups. A federal chamber is responsible for domestic and international political affairs, and the remaining four chambers are concerned with economic, educational and cultural, social, and administrative matters. Special provision is also made for the representation of the various nationalities. Chambers reflecting a similar corporate structure also exist in the 6 republics, 40 districts, and 581 communes into which the country is organized. The Communists retain a monopoly of political power, but the first federal assembly elected under the new constitution has already overruled the government on several occasions.

A parallel effort to decentralize the administration has been made in the economic sphere. A centrally-planned economy has given way to one that depends more on the market. At the same time significant powers within enterprises have been given to workers' councils, which are permitted within certain limits to plan production and allocate profits and investments. This experiment with decentralization has had many vicissitudes, and the rapid growth of the economy has been accompanied by serious problems of investment and emphasis. Yugoslavia has also suffered from a growing adverse trade balance, and the threat of the protective tariffs proposed by the European Common Market looms ahead as a major problem. Agriculture has remained uncollectivized, and market prices have been substituted for policy pressure in an effort to increase food production.

The establishment of workable forms of political and economic decentralization facilitated a healthy rate of economic growth and marked Yugoslavia as a unique form of accommodation between centralized Communist controls and a relatively open society. In 1958 the name of the Communist party was changed to Yugoslav League of Communists, as a means of emphasizing that the party would henceforth lead rather than command. Associated with the party is the much larger Socialist Alliance of the Working People, the membership of which overlaps with the League and serves to give it a popular base.

The degree of success achieved by Yugoslavia in mobilizing the resources of a country comprising six distinct national groups with conflicting traditions and widely differing levels of development is generally attributed to the personal skill of Tito, who by 1970 at the age of 74 had been head of state for a quarter of a century. Despite the elaborate administrative structure that he had devised, the fact remains that in the last analysis the critical decisions are made by the leaders of the Yugoslav League of Communists and that at the present time there exists no satisfactory way to find a successor to Tito when the need arises. The best solution the League could reach in 1969 on the occasion of the fiftieth anniversary of the establishment of the Communist party, was to tighten the central party structure. Provision was made for a congress to be held every four years, a conference every year, a Presidium of fifty-two members which exercised continuing supervision of the affairs of the party, and a new Executive Bureau of the Presidium of fifteen members. This last-named body, which included two members from each of the six republics, one from each of the two autonomous regions, and Tito as President of the League, was apparently designed to be the responsible authority when the time came to find a successor to Tito.

The underlying problem which these various arrangements were designed to meet was the same as that which had divided the country in the 1920s and 1930s—the problem of finding a formula that would satisfy Croatia and Slovenia, in the relatively advanced western part of the country, Bosnia-Herzegovina, Montenegro, and Macedonia, in the more poorly developed southeastern region, and Serbia, which was the largest republic and which formed the nucleus around which the federal state had been assembled. A Croatian by origin, Tito was a national hero of undisputed authority, but alternative leaders were identified to a much greater extent with one or another of the rival nationalities. The Croatians and Slovenes were reluctant to have their wealth siphoned off for investment in the southeast and sought increasing autonomy to run their own affairs. The Serbians, in whose republic the capital city of Belgrade was located, were more inclined to press for national unity. This issue reached a crisis in 1966 when it was discovered that the Serbian leader Rankovic, one of Tito's closest associates and longtime Minister of Interior and head of the police, had installed listening devices in Tito's office and private quarters, apparently in preparation for an attempt to seize power. Tito dealt with this challenge successfully, but the possibility of another effort by Serbian nationalists to gain control of the country during a time of crisis continued to haunt public life. The main consequence of these developments by 1970, however, was a general trend toward the assumption of greater authority by the republics at the expense of the central government.

Foreign and domestic policy in Yugoslavia are closely related, because concern for their common security is one of the principal bonds that hold the six republics together. The principal theme of Yugoslav foreign policy has been nonalignment, and Tito has condemned actions of the United States in the Dominican Republic and Vietnam as well as the Soviet occupation of Czechoslovakia. While seeking an independent policy, often in conjunction with India, Egypt, Indonesia, and other countries in a similar position, Yugoslavia has also sought to gain the benefits of association with the European Common Market. Yugoslavia is in principle nonaligned, but its leaders are well aware that the only foreseeable threat to their national security comes from the USSR, and that the best markets for their exports are outside the Soviet orbit.

CHAPTER

29

The United Kingdom:
Empire and Commonwealth

Political Developments: *Alternating Leadership; Constitutional Changes.*

Social Services: *Education; Extension of Social Security.*

Economic Developments: *Nationalization; Crisis in Foreign Trade.*

Empire and Commonwealth: *The New Commonwealth of Nations; Administrative Reorganization; Continuing Changes in the Empire.*

———◆———

THE AFTER-EFFECTS of war brought similar problems to both victorious and defeated nations. Some had been devastated, and others occupied, while those that had escaped these trials nevertheless had found their economy strained to the utmost. All governments were burdened with obligations that tended to lead them in varying measure toward more collectivization. Western Europe had become conscious of the need for unity, and this consciousness gave rise to experiments in economic co-operation. Colonial empires were undergoing great changes, some achieved peacefully, others leading to armed conflict. This colonial conflict was intensified by the great division in ideas between Communists and anti-Communists characteristic of the postwar period.

Political Developments

During the war the English national government, in which Conservatives played a leading role, made plans for the future. In 1942 there was issued a far-reaching report, drawn up by Sir William Beveridge, which was designed to bring freedom with security to all Englishmen by the elimination of "want, ignorance, idleness, squalor, and disease." The implementation of this program of social insurance to cover everybody from the "cradle to the grave" was left to further legislation, and in 1944 the government submitted a general scheme to Parliament. It met with general approval, but detailed legislation was postponed.

ALTERNATING LEADERSHIP. It was, however, not left to the wartime government to carry out postwar reconstruction. With the surrender of Germany, the question of the continuation of the coalition cabinet was raised. Labour representatives refused to participate further, which led to the dissolution of Parliament and a general election (the first in ten years) in July, 1945, in which Labour won a clear majority. The old Liberal party, which had dominated the scene after World War I, declined to such an extent that it held only twelve seats. As soon as the results of the election were announced, Churchill, who was attending the Potsdam Conference, resigned and was replaced by Attlee. Morrison, as Lord President of the Council and Leader of the House of Commons, Bevin, as Secretary of State for Foreign Affairs, and Bevan, as Minister of Health, held important cabinet posts and were key men in the new government.

While the House of Commons is elected for a five-year term, it is usually dissolved before its mandate expires. The Labour government, however, held such a comfortable majority and was so intent on pushing through its reconstruction plans that new elections were not held until February, 1950. The campaign was a spirited one in which the nationalization program was the leading issue. The Labour party again scored a victory, winning 315 seats as compared to the Conservative and allied parties' 297. The Liberal party was reduced to 9 seats, while the Communists lost the two seats they had formerly held.

A reorganized Labour cabinet was confronted with many problems. The Korean war, which brought Britain to the side of the United States in supporting the policy of the United Nations, was not popular among the people. Putting defense needs ahead of social services and production of domestic consumer goods caused a rift in Labour party ranks. The adverse trade balance created an acute financial situation, which was aggravated by the nationalization of the oil industry in Iran. The latter led to a bitter dispute and the forced withdrawal of English technicians from that country. The British opposition to nationalization virtually closed down the whole Iranian oil production, but this reduction cut both British profits and British oil supplies. Prime Minister Attlee decided to seek a new mandate from the people, and elections were held in October, 1951. This time the Conservatives and allied groups won a majority of 321 seats to Labour's 295, and Winston Churchill again became prime minister.

In February, 1952, George VI died and was succeeded by his daughter Elizabeth, who ascended the throne as Elizabeth II. The coronation services were held in June, 1953, with great fanfare amidst demonstrations of loyalty to her and to the unity of the Empire. Churchill (now Sir Winston Churchill) directed the policy of Britain until April 5, 1955, when he resigned and was succeeded as prime minister by his long-time foreign secretary, Anthony Eden. The new prime minister soon called for elections, and in May, 1955, the Conservatives again won a resounding victory, obtaining control of 54.8 percent of the seats in Commons. For some time the Labour party had suffered from division within its own ranks, Mr. Bevan on the left challenging the leadership of Mr. Attlee. Although the breach was nominally healed, this internal dissension hurt the Labour party in the election. The Conservatives also capitalized on the growing British prosperity and the easing of international tension which had resulted from the more conciliatory policy pursued by Russia.

The change from Labour to Conservative leadership did not alter the basic lines of British foreign policy, which centered in the retention of Commonwealth ties and in close co-operation with the United States and the countries of Western Europe. Although Britain recognized Communist China in January, 1950, it nevertheless co-operated with the United States in measures designed to stop the expansion of communism in both Asia and Europe. Pragmatists in foreign policy, the British no doubt were somewhat more ready to negotiate and trade with the Communist world than was the United States. Britain became a leading member of the Western European Union, the North Atlantic Treaty Organization, the Council of Europe, the Organization for European Economic Co-operation, the European Payments Union, and other Western European movements. In December, 1954, Britain also signed an agreement for close co-operation with the European Coal and Steel Community.

The American attitude toward British and French armed intervention in Egypt in October, 1956, led to a brief divergence of policy. Eden, his health shattered, resigned on January 9, 1957, and was succeeded by another Conservative, Harold Macmillan. In the spring of that year, Britain undertook a drastic revision of its defense forces, heralded as "the biggest change in military policy ever made in normal times." Over a five-year period there was to be a marked reduction in the size of the armed forces, and compulsory service was to be ended, while the forces remaining were to be modernized and adapted to the nuclear age.

Though originally opposed to a European free trade area, linking the European Economic Community (Common Market or Inner Six) with other members of the Organization for European Economic Co-operation (OEEC), Britain in 1957 changed its attitude. When negotiations to this end failed, the United Kingdom joined with Austria, Denmark, Norway, Portugal, Sweden, and Switzerland to form the European Free Trade Association (EFTA or Outer Seven). This agreement, which went into effect on May 3, 1960, originally planned that inter-EFTA tariffs should be gradually reduced and eventually eliminated on April 1, 1970. The process was speeded up and by December 31, 1963, tariffs had been reduced by 60 percent. The target date for complete abolition was set for December 31, 1966, when quantitative import restrictions were also to be eliminated. Agricultural products are not covered by these tariff reductions, but in order to increase trade in this field a series of bilateral agreements, notably one between the United Kingdom and Denmark, were negotiated. On July 31, 1961, the British government announced that it would seek membership in the Common Market. There was opposition at home and in some of the Commonwealth countries, but it was French President de Gaulle's veto which ended these negotiations in January, 1963. Repeated later attempts by Britain to gain membership in the Common Market finally met with success in the summer of 1971, when negotiations on terms of admission were successfully concluded.

Under Macmillan's leadership the Conservatives won the election in 1959, and he carried on as prime minister until illness forced his resignation in October, 1963. He was succeeded by his foreign minister, the Earl of Home, who had strong rivals in his own party. So traditional has it become that the prime minister should be a member of the House of Commons that Lord Home resigned his peerage and as Sir Alec Douglas-Home won a bye-election. The Conservative party was hard hit when War Minister John Profumo was involved in a morals scandal that furnished the British press with headlines for weeks. Adding to the dissension within the party there was a mounting trade deficit and general unrest in the country. In the election held in October, 1964, the Labour party, under its new leader, Harold Wilson, carried the day, but with a majority of only 4 seats: Labour 317, Conservatives 304, Liberals 9. After a precarious year and a half in office Wilson dissolved Parliament and in the election on March 21, 1966, achieved an absolute majority of 97 seats. This enabled him to survive in the troubled years ahead, although he had repeatedly to shuffle the membership of his cabinet. Economic progress was made and the balance of payments stabilized. In spite of a continuing inflationary trend the overall situation seemed so favorable that Prime Minister Wilson dissolved Parliament ahead of schedule and elections were held on June 18, 1970. Contrary to all opinion polls the Conservatives under the leadership of Edward Heath swept the election, winning a majority of 30 in a House of Commons numbering 630. The Liberals declined to an all time low of six seats.

CONSTITUTIONAL CHANGES. Some innovations have been made in British constitutional practice in the postwar years. The Representation of the People Act (1948) ended the university and business premise

THE ROYAL FAMILY AND HEADS OF STATE AT
CHURCHILL'S FUNERAL *January 30, 1965.*

franchises, and the United Kingdom finally joined those countries where
no person has more than one vote. In parliamentary elections only those
registered as residents or as service voters can vote. The act also effected
a redistribution of seats, and each constituency henceforth returns a single
member. On January 1, 1970, the voting age in parliamentary elections
(as well as the age of full legal capacity in general) was reduced from
twenty-one to eighteen years.

In December, 1949, in order to avoid delays in its nationalization
program, the Labour party revised the Parliament Act of 1911 so as to
restrict the House of Lord's power to hold up a bill favored by the House
of Commons to one instead of two years. In an effort to strengthen the
House of Lords by bringing in specially qualified people, the Conservative
government in 1958 sponsored a measure that permitted the appointment
of life peers and peeresses. For the first time women were to be admitted
to the upper chamber, although hereditary peeresses were still somewhat
illogically excluded. This was remedied by the Peerage Act of 1963 which
also admitted all Scottish peers to the House of Lords. Since the last
Irish representative peer died in January, 1961, this means the House of
Lords no longer has any elective peers. The Act of 1963 also permitted
peers to renounce their peerages for life; that is, a peer could resign his

peerage (which would not affect his heirs) in order to run for election to the House of Commons, from which English and Scottish peers are still barred. The Labour government announced legislation to abolish the hereditary basis of the House of Lords in 1967, but this was subsequently withdrawn.

Social Services

EDUCATION. Even before the close of hostilities Parliament enacted a far-reaching educational reform. The Education Act of 1944 struck a blow at ignorance and drastically reconstructed the primary and secondary educational system of England and Wales. The school-leaving age was to be raised from fourteen to fifteen not later than 1947, and eventually to sixteen, as sufficient buildings and teachers became available. For the first time all children over eleven were to receive a secondary education without charge. The school-meals plan dating from 1906 was extended, and all children in public primary and secondary schools were given subsidized lunches, free of charge if there was necessity. The amount of public funds that Britain has poured into education has steadily risen, nearly trebling between 1955 and 1965. Yet much remains to be done and additional educational measures are regularly enacted by Parliament. A Family Allowance Act of June 15, 1945, provided an allowance for each child after the first. By 1968 this had been increased from 5 to 18 shillings a week for the second child and 20 shillings for each younger child. The children must be under fifteen for those who leave school at that age, sixteen for certain handicapped children, and nineteen for those who are continuing their education full time or are apprentices with low earnings.

EXTENSION OF SOCIAL SECURITY. The Labour government of 1945 set itself at once to the task of implementing the promises made during the war for a general extension of social services. In 1946 three major bills were passed: the National Insurance Act combined health, old age, and unemployment benefits, the cost of which was met through a single weekly payment by the employer, the employee, and the state; the National Health (Industrial Injuries) Act provided benefits beyond those furnished when the employer was alone liable; the National Health Service Act granted free medical service and supplies, hospital care, and nursing aid to every Briton. These acts were supplemented by the National Assistance Act of 1948, which superseded the old Poor Law and provided for assistance to any person whose needs were not met under the National Insurance provisions. The above four broad measures, which were on the whole extensions of previous practices, went into effect July 5, 1948. The most radical innovation was the extension of free medical aid to every Briton, a measure that in the United States was commonly referred to as the socialization of medicine. Each doctor who adhered to the program received a fixed salary plus an additional fee according to the number of families who selected him as their doctor. He was permitted also to continue his private practice. People were free to choose their own doctors, and provision was made for specialized surgical care.

The Health Insurance was very popular, and over 95 percent of the population soon were registered under the plan. Practically all British dentists and over 90 percent of the doctors participated in the service. To the large group of the underprivileged, the act brought long-needed assistance, as is well attested by the extraordinary demand for eyeglasses, dental plates, artificial limbs, and other such items. Adequate prenatal care, maternity aid, and child care meant much to the poor. A change was made in the 1951–52 budget providing for a nominal charge (increased by 2.5 percent in 1969) for dentures, eyeglasses, and certain other appliances and services. In 1968 abortions were made available on broad social and medical grounds under the National Health Service.

On July 27, 1967, a private member bill was passed providing that homosexual behaviour between consenting adults in private should no longer be a criminal offense. This measure finally implemented the main recommendations made in 1957 by the Wolfenden Committee on Homosexual Offenses and Prostitution. The question had repeatedly been before the Houses of Parliament since that time. Another much debated measure was enacted in December, 1969, abolishing the death penalty.

Economic Developments

NATIONALIZATION. In the election campaign of 1945 foreign policy had not been an issue, and all parties emphasized the need for more housing, social security, improved health measures, and full employment. The Fabian Socialists, who greatly influenced the philosophy of the Labour party, had long stressed municipal ownership. With one municipality merging into another, with local areas losing their importance in practically all things that affect the life of the people, with the increased mobility of the population, the development of large-scale industries, and the increased nationalization of the revenue and taxation system, there was a growing demand for public ownership on a national basis. In Britain, nationalization of certain industries was an old story. The telegraph and telephone systems had long been run by the Post Office Department. With the formation of a National Grid System in 1926 the government began the sale of electricity on a wholesale basis; the British Broadcasting System took over the radio in 1927; the London transport system was nationalized in 1933 and the mineral rights of the coal mines in 1938. Pledged to a policy of furthering public ownership, the Labour government nationalized the Bank of England (1946); the overseas cable and wireless services (1946); civil aviation (1946); the operation of the coal mines (1947); railroads, road haulage, canals, and docks (1947); and electrical supply and gas works (1948). This nationalization was achieved by various procedures, and in all cases the government did not confiscate but gave fair compensation to the previous owners. In most cases government corporations were established to run the new industries. The Labour government intended to round out its nationalization policy by taking over the iron and steel industry. In December, 1949, a bill nationalizing the steel industry was enacted, but it was not implemented until after the general election in 1950. On February 15, 1951, the Iron and Steel Corporation of Great Britain became sole owner of the country's principal iron and steel companies, the shareholders being compensated by special government-guaranteed bonds. The government-owned holding company by the end of its financial year on September 1, 1951, showed a fair net profit after providing for reserves, interest, and taxes. The Conservative party, however, always opposed the nationalization of steel and after winning the election in October, 1951, proceeded to denationalize it again. In 1953 road haulage (trucking) was also turned back to private operators, although three years later long-distance haulage was again returned to a division of the British Transport Commission, which runs railways and related services. The Conservative government did not undertake denationalization in any other fields. The Labour government which took over in October, 1964, announced as part of its program the renationalization of the steel industry, which was accomplished in 1967.

CRISIS IN FOREIGN TRADE. Instead of immediately removing World War II controls, the government was for a time forced to extend them. The rationing of clothing was not lifted until the spring of 1949; and food rationing, which had begun in 1940 and was partially removed in 1948, was not completely ended until July 3, 1954, when meat and bacon, the sole remaining items, were freed. Because of the shortage of coal, domestic consumers still had to register for each allocation. The "austerity" program was made necessary by the excess of imports over exports, which had come about through the need to replace wartime losses and deterioration of machinery. In order to cut down the amount of foreign exchange used for the importation of food, the government in 1947 launched a four-year program. to expand agricultural production even further.

British industries made a rapid recovery, and the shipping fleet was enlarged through an active building program. In this reconstruction, loans from the United States were helpful, especially one of $3.75 billion made in 1946 to be repaid between 1951 and 2001 at 2 percent interest, if trade conditions warranted. Britain participated in the European Recovery Program, and loans were also forthcoming from the dominions. In spite of an increase in exports, the balance of trade remained unfavorable. In the summer of 1949 the problem seemed particularly acute, and conferences were held with the dominion ministers and also with officials of the United States. With the approval of the International Monetary Fund, Britain on September 19, 1949, devalued the pound sterling from $4.03 to $2.80, a step that was immediately followed in a number of other states whose currencies were closely linked to sterling. This drastic step provided at least temporary relief from the shortage in dollars. For a period British industry and prosperity reached new heights, yet the total trade balance remained unfavorable to Britain. Too many manufactured goods went for domestic consumption and not enough into exports.

When the Labour government took over in 1964, the balance of payments deficit was estimated at over $2 billion. The government took drastic steps, levying a temporary surcharge of 15 percent on all imports except food. The gasoline tax was raised seven cents a gallon, and the standard rate of personal and income tax was increased from 38.75 percent to 41.25 percent. A run on the British pound developed the fiercest speculative attack on the pound sterling in three decades. The Bank of England was able to steady affairs by negotiating a $3 billion loan from the central banks of the United States, Canada, Japan, and eight European countries, and by drawing the $1 billion stand-by credit available under Britain's agreement with the International Monetary Fund. Some temporary relief was obtained. Yet in spite of further austerity measures, as well as additional international financial aid, the balance of payments deficit became ever more precarious, leading to a further devaluation of the pound (by 14.3 percent to $2.40 United States) on November 18, 1967. Unfortunately the export of the fashion of long hair for men, popularized by a singing group known as The Beatles, and of the mini-skirt for women did not bring in much hard cash. To ease the strain on the economy Britain drastically reduced its defense outlay. Agreements were negotiated whereby West Germany pays for most of the cost of the British forces stationed within its territory. Britain also cut its military and naval bases abroad and announced its intention to recall all its forces east of Suez, except for those at Hong Kong, by 1971.

These measures began to pay off, and at the end of 1969 for the first time in years the pound sold above par on the exchanges. The trade balance showed a marked surplus in contrast to the deficit of about a million dollars annually the past two years. As a sign of better times the government lifted the restriction (it had been $120) on the amount of British currency that vacationers could spend abroad.

Britain has pushed the use of atomic power for industrial purposes and by 1967 over 10 percent of its electricity was being produced by nuclear reactors. A tremendous boost for the economy was the discovery under the North Sea of large off-shore natural gas fields which were put into production in 1967.

Empire and Commonwealth

In 1929 the British government in the face of the great depression had appropriated £1 million a year for the economic development of outlying regions of the Empire. An economic department was established within the colonial office as a center for economic planning in the colonies. An act of 1940 increased this appropriation five-fold, and the British Colonial Development and Welfare Acts of 1945, 1950, and 1955 provided for £220 million to be spent by 1960 on colonial improvement.

These sums were materially increased by grants from the treasuries of the respective colonies. Such measures were in line with a statement made by Churchill during the war that he had not become His Majesty's Prime Minister in order to preside over the dissolution of the British Empire.

THE NEW COMMONWEALTH OF NATIONS. It was soon clear, however, that the concepts of Empire and Commonwealth were changing. The most devastating blow to old relationships came when Britain officially withdrew from India on August 15, 1947, and the two dominions of Pakistan and the Union of India were established [see below, pp. 814–17]. In June, 1948, King George VI dropped "Emperor of India" from his titles, at the same time that Lord Mountbatten was succeeded as Governor General of India by a native Indian. Prime Minister Jawaharlal Nehru was determined to give the Union of India a republican constitution with an elective head, which required some change in Commonwealth practice, since heretofore the king had always been recognized as sovereign of each dominion. Conferences were held in London in October, 1948, and April, 1949, attended by representatives of the United Kingdom, Canada, Australia, New Zealand, South Africa, India, Pakistan, and Ceylon, the last having achieved dominion status in February, 1948. In these talks it was agreed to drop the word "British" and to refer henceforth to the mutual association of these states as the Commonwealth of Nations. The thorny question of the position of the king was solved when India specifically expressed the "desire to continue her full membership of the Commonwealth of Nations and her acceptance of the king as the symbol of the free association of its independent member nations, and, as such, the head of the Commonwealth." In 1953 Pakistan voted that henceforth it was to be known as the Islamic Republic of Pakistan. The republic retained its ties with the Commonwealth, recognizing Elizabeth II as "Queen of the United Kingdom and her other Realms and Territories," but did not designate her "Queen of Pakistan." In fact the title "Head of the Commonwealth," first used in 1949 to accommodate India, was by 1953 to be the sole designation common to all the dominions.

When the Republic of Ireland broke away from the United Kingdom on April 18, 1949, unlike India and Pakistan, it disassociated itself completely from the Commonwealth and withdrew its memberships [see below, pp. 788–90]. Northern Ireland continued as part of the United Kingdom and thus was in the Commonwealth, but not as a separate member. Since then, as various former colonies or protectorates have obtained their independence most of them have accepted membership in the Commonwealth. Because of the severe criticism of its racial policies by other Commonwealth members, South Africa, however, withdrew its request for continued membership in the Commonwealth when it became a Republic on May 31, 1961. [See Appendix VII for list of Commonwealth members and dates of admission.]

The British Commonwealth as originally constituted in the late 1920s [see above, pp. 289–291] was composed of predominantly white

English-speaking states. This racial character changed with the dropping of the designation "British" and the establishment of the Commonwealth. But the use of English as a common language is still an important tie among these diverse self-governing states. There are many other such bonds—schools patterned on the British model, British practices of government, British legal codes and procedures (at times even a bewigged judiciary), British trade connections with monetary linkups to the pound sterling, and not to be underrated—cricket, rugby, horse racing, and the spit and polish of British military training.

ADMINISTRATIVE REORGANIZATION. The gradual transformation of the British Empire into a Commonwealth of Nations as a governing concept can perhaps be brought home by a brief enumeration of changes in administration and nomenclature. After World War I the affairs of the Empire, apart from the United Kingdom, were dealt with by the Colonial Office. In July, 1925 a Secretaryship of State for Dominion Affairs was established and took care of the relations between the United Kingdom and the dominions. In 1947 this secretaryship and the Dominion Office became the Secretary of State for Commonwealth Relations and the Commonwealth Relations Office. When India and Pakistan became independent the venerable India Office ceased to be, and its staff and responsibilities, so far as they continued to exist, were transferred to the Commonwealth Relations Office. The Colonial Office was likewise merged with the Commonwealth Office on August 1, 1966, and the Secretary of State for Commonwealth Relations became Secretary of State for Commonwealth Affairs. The office of Secretary of State for the Colonies was finally ended the next year. The Secretary of State for Commonwealth Affairs is now responsible for relations with all the independent members of the Commonwealth, with the Associated States, and the remaining United Kingdom colonies and protectorates. A holdover from former times, and indicative of British desires to retain Ireland within the family, is that relations with the Irish Republic continue to be the responsibility of the Secretary for Commonwealth Affairs and not of the Foreign Office.

These changes in names and administrative reorganization reveal the profound shifts which have taken place in the British Empire. The Commonwealth has meanwhile continued its old decentralized development. Officials of the Commonwealth governments hold frequent meetings, including usually an annual conference of premiers, to discuss common problems. These are customarily held in London. At the Commonwealth Prime Ministers Conferences in 1964 and 1965 a Commonwealth Secretariat was established. This is indicative of a desire to establish somewhat closer integration and give emphasis to its cooperative character. Arnold Smith, a Canadian, became the first Secretary-General.

Besides conferences of government leaders there have been meetings of other groups, such as Commonwealth scientists, medical men, and men of the universities. In March, 1966, a Commonwealth Foundation was established to promote interchanges between Commonwealth organizations and professional groups. There is also a Commonwealth Development Corporation and a Commonwealth Development Finance Company, both largely funded by Britain.

There have at times been serious differences at these various conferences and meetings. Britain's Commonwealth Immigration Act of 1968 which restricted the number of immigrants who had no substantial and close connection with Britain aroused concern. The act was specifically designed to reduce the number of Asian immigrants from East Africa, particularly from Kenya where the government was pressuring its Indian residents either to assume Kenyan citizenship or emigrate. In 1965, when Britain refused to take armed measures to coerce Rhodesia on the declaration of independence by a white dominated government, two African members of the Commonwealth—Ghana and Tanzania—cut their diplomatic ties with the United Kingdom. These, however, were soon resumed. The policies to be followed in regard to both Rhodesia and South Africa have aroused great differences of opinion, but not enough to disrupt the Commonwealth [see below, pp. 847–51]. After all, the Commonwealth countries are not bound to follow either a common domestic or a common foreign policy.

The policy of trade preference within the Commonwealth has been continued. Without weakening the association of the Commonwealth, each member participates in other regional groupings. Thus, Canada has a special defense agreement with the United States; the United Kingdom, Australia, New Zealand, and Pakistan have special Far East commitments and joined (1954) with other powers in the Southeast Asia Treaty Organization (SEATO); while only the United Kingdom and Canada are members of the North Atlantic Treaty Organization. Only the African Commonwealth members are members of the Organization of African Unity. Kenya, Uganda, and Tanzania joined hands in order to negotiate jointly with the European Common Market.

The history of each dominion cannot be surveyed. Suffice it to point out that each dominion had its own peculiar problems of postwar reconstruction. After much debate Newfoundland in 1949 became a province of Canada. In December, 1949, the British Parliament passed the North America Bill, which established the independence of Canada from all control by the British Parliament in matters relating to the amendment of the Canadian constitution. At the same time appeals from the Canadian courts to the Privy Council in London were abolished. Not without political strife, Canada adopted its own distinctive (maple leaf design) flag in December, 1964. Australia and New Zealand are undergoing rapid industrialization, a process that was greatly stimulated by the war. Both countries have welcomed a large number of immigrants from Europe, but still restrict Asiatics and Africans. [See Chapter 33 for a discussion of some of the other dominions.]

CONTINUING CHANGES IN THE EMPIRE. There have been other changes and transformations within the post-World War II British Empire besides the development of the Commonwealth. In the Near East, Britain withdrew as the mandatory power from Palestine. British influence in Jordan subsequently declined rapidly, and the last British troops stationed there by agreement were withdrawn in July, 1957. After long and difficult negotiations British troops were withdrawn in 1956 from the Sudan and Egypt as these countries achieved their full independence. After Egypt internationalized the Suez Canal on July 26, 1956, Egyptian-British relations deteriorated rapidly, leading to British-French-Israeli intervention against Egypt in October, 1956 [see below, pp. 831–33]. In 1964 Malta became independent and joined the Commonwealth. Defense agreements provided that British forces could remain on Malta for ten years, and the Maltese do not wish to see them leave for economic reasons. Gibraltar, in spite of much Spanish pressure and harassment, remains the last rock of the British colonial possessions in the Mediterranean. Spurred on by U.N. Assembly resolutions favoring the independence of all colonial areas, Britain cut its commitments in South Arabia. None of the Arab states where England was formerly dominant have become members of the Commonwealth.

In the Caribbean area Guyana (formerly British Guiana) became independent on May 26, 1966, and proclaimed itself a republic on February 23, 1970. The islands of Antigua, St. Kitts-Nevis-Anguilla, Dominica, Grenada, and St. Lucia entered into a new form of association with Britain in 1967. Britain continues to be responsible for external affairs and defense, but each island controls its own internal affairs and has the right to amend its own constitution. This group of islands is part of a larger Caribbean Free Trade Area (CARIFTA) established in 1968 among other Commonwealth countries in the Caribbean area. Some commodities were exempt from the free trade agreement but tariffs on these are to be removed within the next ten years. That the United Kingdom still is prepared at times to use the stick was demonstrated when a leader in the small island of Anguilla attempted in 1969 to proclaim the independence of that island. Two royal frigates, some helicopters and a hundred-man force were dispatched to occupy the island, which they did without opposition. The London papers had a good time ribbing the government on its great military victory.

There are a variety of territories still dependent on the United Kingdom and in this way remotely and rather indirectly a part of the Commonwealth. The following classification is often applied to them. There are, first of all, the dependent territories belonging through settlement, conquest, or annexation to the British Crown, such as Gibraltar, Hong Kong, the Falkland Islands, and numerous other small islands scattered about the world. Then there are the protectorates, territories which have never been formally annexed but over which by treaty or grant the Crown has power and jurisdiction, as for example, the British Solomon Islands. A third classification, the Protected State, is fast disappearing. These are territories under the protection of the Crown where the Crown has control over their foreign affairs but does not exercise jurisdiction in internal affairs —although this distinction is often rather academic. The best examples of these were former Bechuanaland (Botswana), Basutoland (Lesotho), Swaziland, and Rhodesia in southern Africa or the protected Sultanates in the southern part of the Arabian peninsula. British policy, controls, and governmental procedures are by no means uniform in these various territories. They are constantly changing and in great measure being adapted to modern concepts and ideals. Therein lies the strength of British policy, and it keeps the Union Jack fluttering, if not exactly flying at its former height, throughout the world.

CHAPTER

30

The Fourth and Fifth French Republics

The Establishment of the Fourth Republic

WITH the fall of France in 1940 two French "governments" came into being, one under Marshal Pétain at Vichy, the other—the Free French Movement—under General de Gaulle at London. Within France numerous resistance groups sprang up which by the spring of 1943 were effectively formed into a National Council of Resistance.

This organization entered into formal relationship with De Gaulle in London. After the successful Allied invasion of North Africa, the French National Committee in London was merged (June 3, 1943) with the French North African administration to form the French Committee of National Liberation. With the establishment of a Provisional Consultative Assembly in Algiers in November, 1943, to which the Council of Resistance within France appointed forty delegates, there existed one center around which the anti-Vichy forces could unite.

THE PROVISIONAL GOVERNMENT. On the liberation of France in June, 1944, the Provisional Consultative Assembly, dominated by De Gaulle, was transferred to Paris and enlarged by the inclusion of more representatives from the resistance groups. The latter had perfected their organizations and by their armed co-operation as the "French Forces of the Interior" played an important part in the Allied victory. The leading role of the Communists in the resistance movement gave this party great prestige in liberated France. On September 9, 1944, General de Gaulle named a cabinet as the Provisional Government of the French Republic. This cabinet had at its side the Provisional Consultative Assembly, which, even if it did not exercise great power, served the very useful purpose of giving representation to the many groups who thought they should share in determining the future of France. There is thus a clear thread of organizational continuity between De Gaulle's proclamation of the Free French Movement and the establishment of the new French government.

For the next fifteen months De Gaulle and his cabinet governed France largely by executive decree, although important measures were brought before the Consultative Assembly. It was a difficult time. The French economy, particularly the transportation system, lay in ruins. Before the liberation, the resistance groups had issued pronouncements in favor of nationalization of important sectors of the economy. These resistance groups had considerable political power, while on the other hand many of the large industrialists had been guilty of gross collaboration with the Nazis. Under such conditions, with industry completely disorganized, De Gaulle was forced to undertake a policy of nationalization. From December, 1944, to December, 1945, the coal mines of northern France, the Renault works, the *Gnome et Rhône* aircraft company, civil aviation, and banking and credit were nationalized. In 1946, after De Gaulle left office, complete nationalization of the coal mines, gas, and electricity took place.

With Allied help a respectable French army was created by the Provisional Government and it shared in the final victory. Above all it was in a position to take over a zone of occupation, although a specific French zone in Germany and Austria had originally not been planned. De Gaulle constantly strove to assert France's position as a great power with what may be considered remarkable success. On December 10, 1944, he concluded a twenty-year treaty of alliance and mutual assistance with the Soviet Union. It was while France was under the Provisional Government that it again began to share in directing European affairs, although at the Potsdam Conference France was not represented.

With liberation the Provisional Government began a wholesale arrest of collaborators. In 1945 Marshal Pétain was condemned to death, but his sentence was commuted to life imprisonment in view of his great age and his previous distinguished service to France. He was held on an island in the Bay of Biscay, where he died July 23, 1951. Pierre Laval, the arch-collaborator among Vichy officials, was condemned to death and shot. The judicial procedure followed in these early trials aroused much criticism, and, although more trials were held, the many prosecutions that had been expected did not materialize.

The Provisional Government from the beginning worked toward broadening its base of support among the people of France. In October, 1945, elections were held for a National Assembly, and in a special plebiscite held at that time 96.4 percent of the voters favored drawing up a new constitution for France. As a result of this election the Communists had the largest single delegation, and a combination of leftist parties definitely controlled the chamber. Although De Gaulle was again acclaimed head of the Assembly, on January 20, 1946, he resigned over a question of military credits, and France was again on the familiar path leading to a succession of premiers in the following years. With remarkable speed a new constitution was drawn up and submitted to a referendum on May 5. General de Gaulle came out in opposition to the document, his chief criticism being directed at the overwhelming power given to the single-chamber legislative body. It was generally feared that this body might come under the control of the Communists, leaving no check to the communization of France. This constitution was defeated, and in new elections on June 2 the Communists took second place to the *Mouvement Républicain Populaire* (MRP), a right-center party that had the support of the Catholic Church. This time the Socialists and the MRP worked together, and a more traditional constitution was drafted. In spite of the continued opposition of De Gaulle, who believed the executive had not been granted enough powers, the French people approved the constitution on October 13, 1946, by a majority of over a million. In a period of little over a year, elections were held five times without serious disorder; these elections indicated remarkable stability as to relative party strength, the Communists polling between 25 and 30 percent of the vote in each election.

THE CONSTITUTION OF THE FOURTH REPUBLIC. The new constitution, which did not differ greatly from that of the Third Republic, provided for a president with nominal powers elected by parliament for a seven-year term. Since World War II, women had had the vote in France, and under an electoral law of May, 1951, the National Assembly (627 members) was directly elected under a modified form of proportional representation. The Council (320 members), which replaced the old Senate, was indirectly elected by electoral colleges in the departments.

Under the Fourth Republic the old practice of giving various overseas departments and colonies representation in both houses of parliament in Paris was extended.

Local government remained much as it had been under the Third Republic and continued to be supervised closely by the central government in Paris. The judiciary system also remained much the same, and France continued to have, beside the regular and criminal courts, a fine system of administrative courts. The multiple-party system prevailed and at each election, in addition to the Communists, Socialists, and MRP, there were a number of lesser parties.

THE FRENCH UNION. A new organization for the Empire, known as the French Union, was established. This Union was declared to "be composed, on the one hand, of the French Republic which comprises the overseas Departments and Territories, and on the other hand, of the Associated Territories and States." The overseas departments originally consisted of the three old departments of Algeria (twelve since 1956) and four newly established ones: Martinique, Guadeloupe, Réunion, and French Guiana. The rest of the French possessions were classed as overseas territories except Tunisia, Morocco, and the Indochinese Federation, which were called Associated Territories and States. At the head of the French Union was the President of France and a High Council consisting of representatives from the French government and from each associated state. An indirectly elected Assembly completed the picture, half the members of this body representing Metropolitan France and half the overseas departments, territories, and associated states. It was a rather ingenious governmental arrangement and reflected the desire of the French to unify and centralize the empire. This was very different from the British practice, in which decentralization continued to be the order of the day. The French Union was not effective, and decisions in regard to the colonies were still made by the French cabinet and the French parliament. The overseas governments were slow to move, and it was not until 1956 that any considerable extension of suffrage to the natives was made.

Internal and External Affairs

ECONOMIC RECOVERY. On January 7, 1947, France adopted the so-called Monnet Plan. It was not an overall economic blueprint, but it established production goals for a four-year period (1947–50) for six key industries: coal, power, steel, cement, agricultural machinery, and transport. Heavy importation of raw materials and of machinery for the rehabilitation and modernization of French industry formed a vital part of the program. A huge power development in the Rhone valley was undertaken. By 1947–48, production in French industry as a whole equaled or even exceeded prewar levels, and it continued to expand. Prisoners of war made an important contribution to the French labor supply until their return to Germany in 1948.

Inflation and rising living costs were at the root of a whole series of strikes in these years, although some of them no doubt were inspired by the Communists to embarrass the government. The latter is usually held to have been the case in the serious coal-mine strike in the fall of 1948, which brought clashes between miners and troops. As after World War I, a split occurred in the ranks of organized labor. There were two large union confederations—the first allied with the Communist party, the second with the Socialists. In addition there was a smaller group consisting mainly of Catholic unions.

At the end of the war approximately a third of the working population of France was still engaged in agriculture, and their earnings represented about a quarter of the national income. In the first years large importations of wheat were necessary, partly because of several very poor crop years. Since then, considerable mechanization has taken place on French farms. To make the use of modern machinery practicable, many of the small scattered holdings, which were typical of much of France, needed to be consolidated, and the government has appropriated large grants to facilitate this reparceling. This is a democratic answer, on a small scale to be sure, to the challenge of the collective farms of Eastern Europe.

The French economy was plagued by a bad financial situation. The decline in the value of the franc, the need to increase salaries for governmental employees, the financing of reconstruction projects, the rebuilding of the army, the fighting of a costly colonial war in Indochina, and later the necessity of repressing armed rebellion in Algeria made the problem of balancing the budget very difficult. New taxes were imposed, but the long-needed thorough revision of the French tax structure did not take place. The government was able to obtain large loans from the United States and lesser amounts from other states, as a necessary if temporary way out. The Organization for European Economic Co-operation (OEEC), under the Marshall Plan, was worked out by conferences in Paris, and France was one of the leading countries benefiting from this aid. After 1950 under new programs much military and economic aid was extended to France by the United States.

OVERSEAS FRANCE. The internal situation in France was further strained by developments in overseas France. Attempts to re-establish control in all its former mandates and colonies involved France in continual armed conflict until 1958. These wars were on a scale for which the Foreign Legion no longer sufficed, although conscripts could not be sent to some areas, for example, Vietnam. This placed a heavy toll on volunteers, especially in the officers' corps. With reluctance the French government withdrew completely from Lebanon and Syria and recognized the independence of these states. In Indochina efforts to establish a regime of Associated States was never really successful and led to severe conflict in Vietnam. India forced the surrender of century old French enclaves, and belated efforts to reform the colonial administrations in Sub-Saharan Africa only increased demands for more autonomy and self-government. Rising nationalism led eventually to a recognition of Moroccan independence and after a long conflict to the independence of Tunis and Algeria [see below, pp. 824–28]. This withering away of the French Empire, together with differences over colonial policy and the costs inevitably associated with it, added to the political instability of the era. Nor did this continuing round of colonial withdrawals do anything to bolster the French ego and the traditional concept of grandeur. All this helped to undermine the French Fourth Republic and pave the way for De Gaulle's return to power.

ALLIANCES AND REGIONAL GROUPS. France in the early postwar years tried to act as a sort of bridge between Russia, the United States, and Britain. Assured a place in the occupation of Austria and Germany, the French opposed any policy that promised to bring a united Germany into being. French policy favored the internationalization of the Ruhr and the establishment of a weak federal Germany. It was the French who brought about the separation of the Saar Basin from the rest of the French occupation zone. This territory was established as an autonomous state (1947) in economic union with France. Great Britain and the United States recognized the economic union of the Saar with France, while the USSR protested it. The Saar government as established under French guidance outlawed pro-German political parties and worked intimately with the French government. In Germany the issue of the Saar aroused great feeling, and the opposition Social Democratic party took up the cause with gusto.

As differences between Russia and the West increased, France began to co-operate more closely with Great Britain and the United States. On March 4, 1947, France signed at Dunkirk an alliance with Britain, and on March 17, 1948, at Brussels this was expanded into a fifty-year alliance with Britain, the Netherlands, Belgium, and Luxembourg, known as the Western European Union. France is a member of the Council of Europe; indeed, the headquarters are at Strasbourg [see above, pp. 694–95]. Robert Schuman, the long-time French foreign minister, was largely responsible for establishing in 1952 the European Coal and Steel Community (ECSC) with its common market for steel and coal. In 1954 France joined with seven other Eastern and Western nations to establish a collective security system for Southeast Asia (SEATO) [see Appendix VII].

France has been inclined to move cautiously in everything affecting Germany. Having held out for months, France in 1948–49 consented to merge her occupation zone of Germany with the American and British zones (Bizonia) [see above, p. 618]. After the outbreak of the Korean war the United States boldly came out for a policy of rearming Germany in order to strengthen the defenses of Western Europe. France made proposals (the Pleven Plan) for a "European Army," and these eventually were transmuted into a plan for a European Defense Community (EDC) consisting of France, West Germany, Italy, and the Benelux countries (1952). However, EDC aroused widespread criticism in France, and cabinets continually postponed bringing it up for ratification. Finally Premier Mèndes-France in August, 1954, had the courage to do so, although he refused to take a positive stand on the issue. The treaty was defeated by the Assembly, whereupon Great Britain took the initiative and called a conference at London to work out new agreements (September 27 to October 3, 1954). Here the EDC powers were joined by Britain, the United States, and Canada. Agreement was reached on the restoration of German sovereignty, the rearming of Germany, and Germany's membership in the Western European Union and in NATO.

The French government made agreement on the Saar a condition for accepting this Western German settlement. The long series of postwar Saar negotiations was climaxed on October 19, 1954, when Premier Mendès-France and Chancellor Konrad Adenauer signed an agreement providing for the Europeanization of the Saar within the framework of the Western European Union. After the Saar Statute was drawn up, all restrictions on political activities in the Saar were to be removed for a period of three months, at the end of which the people were to vote on the proposed statute.

With the Saar issue temporarily settled, all the London Conference agreements on Germany were signed on October 23, 1954. The French chambers subsequently ratified them without serious opposition. The approval of the treaties led the Soviet Union in May, 1955, to denounce the French-Soviet treaty of alliance of 1944. France, nevertheless, continued to be an advocate of negotiation with the Russians.

The plebiscite on the Saar Statute was held on October 23, 1955, and this plan for Europeanization was decisively rejected. The Saar elections in the following December resulted in a victory of the parties favoring reunification with Germany. French leaders, and public opinion as well, came to realize that the return of the Saar to Germany was inevitable. Further negotiations with Germany led to an agreement under which France received special economic concessions in regard to the Saar, some of them extending even beyond a special three-year transitional period. Germany also agreed to co-operate in canalization of the Moselle. In return the Saar was admitted as the tenth state of the Federal Republic of Germany on January 1, 1957.

The way was now cleared for furthering the collaboration begun in the European Coal and Steel Community. On January 1, 1958, France joined with West Germany, Italy, Belgium, the Netherlands, and Luxembourg in establishing the European Economic Community (Common Market) and the European Atomic Energy Community (Euratom).

Under the influence of the North Africa problem, France adopted an anti-Arab policy. The nationalization of the Suez Canal Company, which was predominantly a French-controlled organization, brought close collaboration with England and Israel against Egypt. The armed attack on Egypt in October, 1956, was one of the most popular military expeditions that France had undertaken in recent years [see below, pp. 833–34]. The sharp opposition expressed by the United States on this occasion as well as the generally critical attitude of Americans to French policy in Indochina and North Africa aroused considerable anti-American sentiment in France. But in spite of all differences of opinion, France remained bound to the United States and Britain. Soviet support of the Arabs, and Communist aid to anticolonial agitators in numerous French overseas possessions, were factors enough to warrant a continued pro-Western policy and French membership in NATO. Although France sent a fleet to the Eastern Mediterranean in July, 1958, when American and British troops were sent into Lebanon and Jordan, French landing operations were discouraged by her allies in view of the hostility of the populace toward France.

POLITICAL DEVELOPMENTS. In 1947 General de Gaulle re-entered the political scene and launched his "Rally of the French People" (*Rassemblement du Peuple Français*; R.P.F.). His program was not well defined and consisted largely of an attack on French disunity, for which he blamed the political parties. He hoped to gain strength by cutting across party lines, and he soon had a following in the French parliament, although the deputies wore other party labels. In general he advocated a rightist national state and in the municipal elections of November, 1947, was able to capture about a third of the vote, mostly at the expense of the MRP. To combat what they considered extremist dangers from the Communists on the one side and the Gaullists on the other, leaders of the Socialists, MRP, and Radical Socialists united in January, 1948, under the banner of the "Third Force."

A new electoral law was passed in May, 1951, which permitted parties to form coalition lists and modified the prevailing system of proportional representation. The law actually was devised to cut Communist influence in the Assembly, and the general elections held in June showed its effect. Although the Communists polled about the same popular vote as before (25.88 percent), they were reduced from 187 to 103 seats. The MRP representation was also cut in half (166 to 85), but their loss was largely due to the shift of both leaders and membership to General de Gaulle's party, which won 118 seats. General de Gaulle, however, did not assume important leadership in the Assembly and, after disastrous losses in the municipal elections of 1953, took his party out of direct participation in party politics. The result was that his followers split into several factions and formed new political groups.

From the time the new constitution came into force (1947) to May, 1958, France had nineteen cabinets. In this series the premiership of Pierre Mendès-France (June 24, 1954 to February 5, 1955) was the most important. He not only adopted a vigorous foreign policy, bringing the long Indochinese conflict to a close, inaugurating needed reforms in Tunisia, and participating in the agreements that restored sovereignty to Western Germany, but he also introduced important domestic reforms. He had the courage to tackle the problem of excessive wine and alcohol production and received much publicity as the milk-drinking Frenchman.

Yet his notable achievements did not spare him the usual fate of French premiers, and a strange coalition of Communists, MRP, and rightist deputies was able to bring about his downfall in a debate on North African policy.

The North African problem continued to plague succeeding cabinets. A proposed change in the electoral law brought even more serious disputes, which resulted in the dissolution of the Assembly before the expiration of its mandate, a rare occurrence in French politics. In elections held in January, 1956, the Communists emerged as the largest party (144 seats), while a rightist group of small shopkeepers, known as the Poujadists, won considerable support (about 49 seats). In view of these gains by the extremist parties, the Socialists—the second largest group—agreed to participate in a Republican Front government. Since 1951 they had refused to join the cabinet because of differences with the center parties over government aid to Roman Catholic schools. On this point they retained their freedom of action, but the expected legislation on this issue was not introduced because of more urgent problems.

The Socialist leadership became deeply involved in trying to suppress the Algerian revolt. They advocated free elections in Algeria but insisted on restoration of peace and order as a prerequisite for these elections. In spite of an even larger commitment of French troops, no end could be brought to the Algerian rebellion. On May 13, 1958, while France was just emerging from one of its ever-recurring cabinet crises, French army leaders seized power in Algeria. They demanded that General de Gaulle should be named premier. Instead, Pierre Pflimlin became head of the government and was granted extraordinary powers by the chambers. The army revolt, however, spread to Corsica, and elements within the French navy joined the dissident generals. Unable to carry out an effective policy, Pflimlin and President Coty undertook negotiations with De Gaulle, who took over the government on June 1, 1958, on his own conditions.

The Assembly granted De Gaulle full powers for six months to act by decree in domestic and international affairs, and also authority to submit constitutional reforms directly to the people for a referendum without first submitting them for approval to the parliament. De Gaulle had long been demanding that the constitution should be changed to give the executive more power.

He made an immediate visit to Algeria and obtained the co-operation of the army leaders there. His policy of federalism and of granting Moslems equal status did not meet with full approval by the European French element, but at least he seemed to offer better prospects for a "correct settlement" than any other French politician.

The Establishment of the Fifth Republic

On assuming power De Gaulle set himself two main tasks. One was to offer France a new form of government, and the other was to end the war in Algeria. Constitutional reform got under way at once with the appointment on June 12 of a group of juridical experts to assist De Gaulle in drawing up a new constitution. The draft was then submitted to an advisory committee made up of seventeen deputies, ten senators, and twelve persons prominent in public affairs. Although he was in no way obligated to do so, De Gaulle did accept some of their suggested changes, as well as those made by the Council of State, France's highest court for constitutional matters, and by President René Coty. On September 4, 1958, the eighty-eighth anniversary of the fall of the Second Empire, Premier de Gaulle in an elaborate ceremony in the *Place de la République* presented a new constitution to the French people.

THE CONSTITUTION. The constitution as proposed did not outline in detail the government of the French Republic. Much was left to be regulated by future organic laws. The constitution simply stated, for example, that parliament was to consist of a directly elected National Assembly and an indirectly elected Senate. The size, method of election, and distribution of seats was left to future determination. Even the exact scope of the parliament's powers was not stated, but clearly it was not to have as much power as under the Third and Fourth Republics. Under the constitution, the government (cabinet) may ask parliament for power for a limited period of time to implement its program by ordinance, such ordinances becoming invalid if a bill for ratification is not submitted to parliament before the date for the expiration of the special powers. After the expiration of this period, parliament has the power to modify these ordinances only in those matters lying within its legislative domain (Article 48). While parliament thus has the opportunity to accept or reject the ordinances, delaying tactics could easily avoid a showdown. The National Assembly (not the Senate) can force the resignation of the premier by a majority vote of its total membership. Motions of censure must be signed by one tenth of the membership and can be voted on only forty-eight hours after the motion is submitted.

The constitution clearly vests dominant power in the president, who was to be elected for a term of seven years, at first by an electoral college comprising the members of parliament and representatives of departments, overseas territories, and communal councils. In 1962 the constitution was amended to provide for the direct election of the president, a change which the Assembly opposed but which was approved by 62.25 percent of the electorate in a referendum. The president has the usual executive functions, is granted wide appointive powers, and specifically is given the duty of naming the premier. He can request a rereading by parliament of any law or parts thereof which are submitted to him for signature and promulgation. After consulting the premier and the presidents of the assemblies, the president can dissolve parliament. Article 16 gives him the right in case of emergency to assume dictatorial powers by his own decision, but he must consult the Constitutional Council on the measures he undertakes. During the period when he exercises exceptional powers, the National Assembly cannot be dissolved.

The constitution further establishes a Constitutional Council of nine members, three appointed by the President of the Republic, three by the President of the Assembly, and three by the President of the Senate. The Council supervises the election of the president and carries out all referendums. Before promulgation, organic (that is, constitutional) laws must, and ordinary laws may, be submitted to the Constitutional Council, which decides whether or not they are in conformity with the constitution. A provision declared unconstitutional cannot be promulgated, and decisions of the Council cannot be appealed. A law once promulgated cannot, however, be declared unconstitutional by the process of judicial review as practiced in the United States.

In respect to overseas territories, with the notable exception of Algeria, the constitution established a new French Community in place of the highly centralized French Union of the Fourth Republic. In internal affairs all member states of the Community were to enjoy autonomy, and they had the right to secede at any time. It is clear that in establishing the Community, France was preparing for a major change in colonial policy. Centralized control was to give way to close cooperation among freely associated states.

In a referendum held on September 28, 1958, the constitution was approved in Metropolitan France by a majority of four to one. It was not so much agreement with the detailed provisions of the constitution as fear of civil conflict and disorder if De Gaulle should resign that led to the approval of the document. Among the parties only the Communists, a section of the Radical Socialists led by Pierre Mendès-France, and the Poujadists were in opposition.

In a whirlwind tour of the African territories at the end of August, De Gaulle had offered all the overseas territories, except Algeria, the alternative of voting for the constitution and becoming a member of the French Community, or voting no and securing independence. In the latter case France would end all economic aid, and the territories would lose their privileged position in the French tariff system. The new constitution was approved in all the territories with the exception of Guinea. Although Algeria had not been offered such a choice, the French settlers feared that a negative vote would lead to a separation from France. Consequently, although the constitution did not meet their demands fully, the referendum also showed a favorable majority there.

New Elections. Thus on October 4, after twelve years of precarious existence, the Fourth Republic came to an end, and the new constitution came into effect with the establishment of the Fifth Republic. De Gaulle immediately set about implementing the main provisions of the constitution. A new electoral law was enacted dividing Metropolitan France into 465 electoral districts, each with about 93,000 inhabitants. If in these single-member districts no candidate received a majority of the votes cast, a run-off election was to be held a week later in which a mere plurality would suffice to elect. Elections were held at the end of November with victory going to the supporters of De Gaulle. As anticipated, the new electoral system worked to the disadvantage of the Communist party, which obtained only ten seats as compared to 144 in the last parliament of the Fourth Republic. On December 21 De Gaulle was elected the first president of the Fifth Republic.

Internal and External Affairs

TRANSFORMATION OF OVERSEAS FRANCE. Settlements had been reached in Indochina, Morocco, and Tunis before the end of the Fourth Republic, but it was left to De Gaulle to work out new arrangements in Algeria, Sub-Saharan Africa, and various scattered French territories.

De Gaulle had been raised to power largely because of the failures of the previous governments in Algeria. By a series of promotions and new appointments to high army commands he was able to break the power of the All-Algerian Committee of Public Safety and bring the government there under the control of Paris authorities. More troops were sent to Algeria but they made little headway against the determination of the Algerian guerrillas. Terrorism and incendiarism, long a part of the Algerian scene, were now unleashed by Algerians in Metropolitan France itself. Repeated attempts by De Gaulle to bring about a cessation of hostilities failed. Finally in mid-1960 De Gaulle indicated rather vaguely that he would be willing to enter into discussions with Algerian leaders under certain conditions. The possibility of coming to a negotiated agreement led some prominent Frenchmen in Algeria to form a "Front for French Algeria." They were determined to halt De Gaulle's plans, which they maintained could only separate Algeria from France. Divisions also increased in France, and De Gaulle assumed emergency powers, carrying on by decree legislation.

In a plebiscite held in January, 1961, De Gaulle won the support of the people of France and Algeria for his Algerian policy, ill-defined as it was, and prospects for negotiations seemed improved. With the prospect of a negotiated settlement, four army generals in Algeria attempted a *coup d'état*, with the support of other dissident officers, about 20,000 Foreign Legion troops, and 25,000 paratroopers. In the name of the Secret Army Organization (OAS) they took over control of Algiers and some other cities on April 21, 1961. Rumors prevailed that they would attempt to seize Paris. De Gaulle took to radio and television and in a forceful speech called on the people to save France from the "partisan, ambitious, and fanatical" officers who threatened a national disaster. Reservists were called up in Paris and security forces brought into the city. The political parties except some extreme right groups assured the government of their support, and throughout France people stopped work for an hour to demonstrate their support of De Gaulle. The army, air force, and navy remained firm, and on the night of April 25–26 loyal forces entered Algiers. The danger of the coup was ended, but the OAS continued to cause serious difficulties.

DE GAULLE French Premier Charles de Gaulle voting in the parliamentary elections of November 30, 1958, which confirmed the popularity of his leadership under the new constitution of the Fifth Republic.

On May 20, 1961, talks between the French government and Algerian leaders began at Évian-les-Bains. The negotiations were soon deadlocked and broken off. Shooting, bombings, assassinations, and burnings raged on in Algerian and French towns. Meanwhile discussions were carried on intermittently, and finally on March 18, 1962, a cease-fire was signed at Évian-les-Bains. After eight years of the worst colonial warfare in modern times, and for the first time since September, 1939, France was at peace.

The Évian accords provided for a referendum on independence for Algeria. Meanwhile Algeria was to be governed by a French High Commissioner and a twelve-man provisional executive. The many emergency measures were to be gradually rescinded. France promised to continue its financial support after the referendum and to negotiate a continuation of the special preferential tariff, marketing, and other commercial arrangements which were of direct benefit to Algeria. The Saharan oil fields were to be developed and exploited to the mutual benefit of France and Algeria, which led subsequently to some differences. There were to be guarantees for French citizens in an independent Algeria and inhabitants were to choose within three years if they wanted to become Algerians or remain French. France was gradually to reduce her troops, but was guaranteed a fifteen-year lease of the Mers-el-Kebir naval base. France actually withdrew from this base January 31, 1968, nine years before the date specified.

The terms were no doubt a victory for the Algerian nationalists. In the next weeks the OAS as a manifestation of its bitter hostility to the agreement continued its policy of terrorism. But the people of both France and Algeria were ready for peace. On April 8, Metropolitan France accepted the Évian accords by 90 percent of the votes cast. On July 1, Algeria showed its approval by voting 5,975,581 to 16,534 for independence and co-operation with France. For some time Europeans had been fleeing Algeria and the numbers now increased. It was estimated that in 1962–63, 900,000 out of the million Europeans living in Algeria fled to France. Housing in France for this influx was inadequate and in some of the larger cities grave economic and social problems arose. The returnees also added a dissident element to the political scene, but De Gaulle retained his mass support and swept the parliamentary elections in November, 1962 [see below, p. 751].

In Sub-Saharan Africa De Gaulle also had to make important concessions to the rising wave of anticolonialism. As has been pointed out already, when he sought the approval of the constitution of the Fifth Republic he promised all colonies, except Algeria, that if they approved the constitution they would remain in the French Community with all the privileges and aid that entailed, or if they disapproved they could have their independence. Guinea was the only colony which voted no and it was immediately granted its independence on October 2, 1958. The colonies which had voted yes were now given the opportunity of choosing within six months their status in the French Community. The institutional framework of this organization was gradually erected in 1959, only to be abandoned the next year when all the French territories in Africa, exclusive of French Somaliland, established their independence [see below, pp. 851–53]. In a stormy referendum in 1967 French Somaliland again chose to continue to be associated with France with increased autonomy rather than to become independent. In the United Nations Trusteeship Council France sponsored the granting of independence of its two trust territories of Togoland and the Cameroons. [For dates of independence, and old and new names of the Republics, see Appendix VIII.]

Independence, achieved in peaceful fashion and with little turbulence, brought into being a "transformed" or "second" Community whose highest organ was a Council of Heads of State and Government. Here supposedly the leaders could gather and on a basis of equality discuss mutual problems. Besides Guinea, six states—Mali, Dahomey, Ivory Coast, Niger, Upper Volta, and Mauritania—did not take their place in the Community, although France continued to offer them her helping hand. The French Community, never a thriving institution, soon lost what little significance it once had, although technically remaining in existence.

None of the former colonies cut themselves off completely from France, and their currencies remained linked with the French franc. Through bilateral arrangements and grants of aid France salvaged a leading position in most of the states. She obtained the right to intervene in stated circumstances and to station troops at various bases. These developed into highly trained mobile units which at times have come to the rescue of existing governments, as for example in Chad in the spring of 1970. France also has a special unit, the *Force d'Intervention* consisting of about 16,500 men, which is stationed near Toulouse and can be airlifted to anyplace in Africa in a matter of hours.

THE FRENCH-SPEAKING WORLD. French-speaking in contrast with English-speaking Africa was a reality. And France was not the only one who sought to maintain old ties. It was the President of Senegal Leopold Sédar Senghor, who writes poetry in French, who first proposed in 1964 the establishment of an agency to further cultural ties between the French-speaking countries of the world. The idea was taken up by others and representatives of thirty countries (France, Belgium, Luxembourg, Switzerland, Canada, Haiti; fourteen former French and three former Belgian nations in Africa; Madagascar and Mauritius in the Indian Ocean; Lebanon, Laos, Cambodia, and South Vietnam) met at Niamey, the capital of Niger, in February, 1969. Here it was tentatively decided to create an agency with headquarters in the Paris area. Its function would be to act as a clearing house for member countries in the field of culture and technology. It would further the exchange of teachers, students, and learning in general, and reduce duplication of effort, as for example by consolidating schools for civil servants in African countries. The agency would not infringe on the sovereignty of member countries or the use of other national languages. France actually stayed in the background in the negotiations, although it has traditionally been active in seeking to win friends and influence people through the spread of the French language. A second conference at Niamey in March, 1970, led to the formal signing by twenty-one countries of a convention establishing the agency at Paris and naming Jean-Marc Léger, a Canadian, as its head [see Appendix VII for membership]. Canada agreed to underwrite 32 percent of the organization's budget, France 40, Belgium 12, while the remainder is to be supplied by the other member states. The Niamey agreement is at least a move in the direction of establishing a cultural commonwealth.

DOMESTIC POLICY. As the Fifth Republic came into being, affairs within France were dominated by De Gaulle. When he assumed the presidency on January 8, 1959, he appointed his long-time disciple Michel Debré as premier. The makeup of the cabinet remained about the same, only the Socialist members withdrawing. The was some reshuffling of cabinet posts in the next months, but Debré carried on until April 14, 1962, when, after the signature of the Évian accords, he resigned. He was replaced by a banker and close friend of De Gaulle, Georges Pompidou. Parliament faded in significance as the president assumed emergency powers. In October, 1962, the Assembly did attempt to assert itself when De Gaulle planned to by-pass it by submitting a constitutional amendment directly to the people providing for popular election of the president. After a fifteen-hour debate the Assembly overthrew the government. De Gaulle promptly dissolved the chamber and won a landslide victory both in the referendum on the constitutional change and in the ensuing parliamentary elections. His party, the Union for the New Republic and Democratic Union of Labor, won 230 seats as compared to 67 for the Socialists, 53 for the Democratic Center (Popular Republicans, Independents, and others), 41 for the Communists, with a scattering going to other parties. No Communist-Socialist left front materialized in the succeeding years. The Communists were hard hit by the death of their long-time leader Maurice Thorez on July 12, 1964.

The first direct election of a president on December 5, 1965, in which De Gaulle had five opponents, gave no one an absolute majority, De Gaulle receiving 44 percent of the vote. The necessity for run-off elections in which only the top two candidates participated was considered a blow to De Gaulle's prestige. It was not so much the strength of his leading opponent, the veteran leftist, François Mitterrand, who was supported by both Socialist and Communist parties, but the desertion of a large portion of the bourgeoisie for a third surprise candidate, Jean Lecanuet, which gave these elections significance. The run-off elections of December 19 gave De Gaulle only a 55 percent majority. This campaign demonstrated that the political parties were in a process of re-formation, and for the first time in seven years the people of France had been offered serious political debate in all information media. The Assembly elections of 1967 showed that the opposition forces were back in stride when the Gaullists obtained a bare majority, 269 to 245 seats. Local elections also indicated growing political opposition.

At the time De Gaulle came to power the French economy had slowed down in comparison with the boom years of 1953–57, and he was confronted with an inflationary situation, a treasury and foreign trade deficit. The war in Algeria proved a steady drain on finances. Yet slowly the situation began to improve. Effective December 29, 1958, the franc was devalued by 17.55 percent: from 420 to 493.7 francs to the dollar. It remained stable, and on January 1, 1960, a new heavy franc at 100 old francs to one (4.937 to a dollar) was introduced. In 1959 for the first time in years the foreign trade balance was reversed and exports exceeded imports. In part this was the result of free trade with the countries of the Common Market. France continued to plan its economy with the Third Modernization and Equipment Plan, 1958–61, the Fourth, 1962–65, and the Fifth, 1966–70. The last called for an annual growth in the economy of slightly less than 5 percent and an increase in foreign trade of more than 55 percent. In trade as in other foreign fields De Gaulle sought to push the position of France. Gold and foreign exchange reserves steadily increased, very much at the cost of the United States gold supply.

Not as dynamic as industrial expansion in Germany or Italy, French industry nevertheless made steady progress. It accounts for about 50 percent of the gross national product. Agriculture, in which about 25 percent of the active population is engaged, remains the backbone of the economy. The farmers were hard hit by De Gaulle's efforts to prevent inflation by holding the price level. Farmers blockaded roads and markets with their trucks and tractors: surplus products which could not be sold profitably were dumped in government buildings and on streets. Their tumultuous demonstrations brought clashes with troops in 1961. The government was forced to take cognizance of their plight and fell back on a farm support program covering cereals, meat, poultry, milk products, wines, fruits, and vegetables. It also furnished funds for research, for the modernization and consolidation of farms, granted tax relief, and extended some social benefits to farmers. Yet little headway was made toward improving the antiquated marketing system with most products distributed via Paris. It has been estimated that the cost of a peach is increased by 1,150 percent between the grower and the consumer.

There have also been many serious strikes among civil servants, miners, transportation workers, and other groups of workers. Reluctantly the government has acceded at least in part to their demands. Wages have increased, but have not kept up with the increase in prices. There is a shortage of workers, and France—like Germany, but not to the same extent—recruits many foreign workers from abroad. Housing still remains inadequate, modernization comes slowly in both household and factory, superhighways are a rarity, but France again is one of the most prosperous and wealthy countries of the world.

By a decree issued in January, 1959, the whole system of public education was reorganized. However, there still is a shortage of schools, the teachers receive comparatively low salaries, and the scholarship grants for secondary and higher education are inadequate. In 1961, 80 thousand teachers in Paris and neighboring departments struck for a modest 5 percent increase. University students in Paris repeatedly demonstrated against the lack of classroom and laboratory space. These demonstrations were particularly turbulent in the spring of 1968 [see below, p. 755]. The insufficiency of government funds for public free education has intensified the opposition in sections of the left against the increased subsidies to church schools which De Gaulle inaugurated in 1959.

FOREIGN AFFAIRS. As in domestic matters, De Gaulle strove to refurbish the glory of France in foreign affairs. France must be a great power, strong and independent, its sovereignty unblemished. Pacts and alliances must be a union, not a merger of independent states; Europe must become not one state but a *Europe des patries*. Decision-making must be the result of negotiation; it must not be vested in a body where France could be outvoted or where France would not have a decisive voice. These basic attitudes have governed French policy toward the Common Market, NATO, the development of atomic power, and toward the UN.

When De Gaulle took over, the European Economic Community (EEC) was well established and on its way toward bringing about greater unity in Western Europe. The market was so advantageous to French farmers and industrialists that De Gaulle had no choice but to continue to co-operate in the organization. But he proved to be a hard bargainer and slowed the progress of integration. He consistently opposed the extension of power of the EEC's Central Commission, with its ever enlarging group of "European Civil Servants." Although the other members of the market approved, De Gaulle in January, 1963, vetoed the admission of Great Britain to the organization. Back of the veto was opposition to the enlargement of the EEC, for British membership would surely have soon brought in the other members of the European Free Trade Association and Ireland as well. Such an enlarged organization would inevitably make it harder for France to play a dominant role in its affairs. Britain was insular and maritime, had special relations with the Commonwealth, and the reservations she asked for in regard to agriculture were not acceptable to France. Agricultural policy was always a crucial consideration in the Common Market negotiations and led to a crisis in the closing months of 1964. It was resolved only when the other EEC members agreed to the French position. But the agricultural differences were far from settled, and in July, 1965, France withdrew its members from some of the important committees and also her permanent representative to the Commission. The dispute ostensibly involved farm subsidy programs and financial arrangements for the joint agricultural market; back of it lay the increased authority which these measures would give to the Common Market Commission and the further political integration of Europe which would result. Since all EEC decisions require the unanimous approval of the members, the French boycott for a time stymied the organization.

Within the Common Market, France has attempted to consolidate its position, most notably by an effort to establish close relations with West Germany. Chancellor Adenauer was a firm believer in French-West German ties, and was only too glad to sign a Treaty of Cooperation with France on January 22, 1963. It provided that there were to be regular meetings of the chiefs and foreign ministers of the two countries in order to co-ordinate their policies within EEC and in international affairs in general. The meetings were held, but without too much success. De Gaulle saw in the agreement a means of strengthening his position against what he considered the Anglo-Saxon domination by Britain and the United States. West Germany, which favored more European unity than De Gaulle desired, did not go along with France's stiff and cool policy toward the United States.

In relation to NATO De Gaulle maintained a hostile attitude, for he considered it too much under American direction, and a restriction on French sovereignty. To show his displeasure he withdrew the French fleet from NATO command in July, 1963, and this policy was extended in various degrees to other services and even to the Command Headquarters itself. By late 1964 only two reduced French divisions in Germany and three air wings remained under NATO's Supreme Headquarters. France exploded its first atomic bomb in February, 1960, and De Gaulle insisted on developing France's own atomic striking force. France did not sign the 1968 treaty on the nonproliferation of nuclear weapons. De Gaulle refused to have any part in developing a NATO multilateral nuclear fleet and never hid his desire to have a general revision of the NATO agreements. On July 1, 1966, he terminated French participation in the NATO command organization and forced the removal of all foreign as well as NATO military installations from French territory by April 1, 1967. Protests from NATO partners were of no avail. On January 1, 1967, he stopped payment of France's 12 percent share of the military expense. Yet in spite of his uncooperative attitude, he did not withdraw entirely from NATO, and the other members of the alliance chose to put a good face on a bad situation. Without withdrawing completely, he discontinued active participation in the Southeast Asia Treaty Organization (SEATO) and denied any obligation under that treaty in respect to Vietnam as the United States became deeply involved in war in that country.

De Gaulle's attitude toward the UN was similar. Such organizations restricted the independence of France, and he considered them ineffective. He opposed the UN Assembly's attempt to bring about a settlement of the Algerian problem. In the Congo crisis he also departed from UN policy and like Russia refused to pay the assessment for the Congo peacekeeping force. He likewise refused to contribute to the UN force in Cyprus; instead he offered his personal services as mediator. Yet France continued to participate in the many UN agencies, made substantial contributions to some of the voluntary funds, and usually voted with the Western powers on crucial issues.

De Gaulle was far from breaking his ties with either the United States or Britain, but he refused to do anything which might be considered "hanging on to their coattails." He cultivated better relations with Russia and with the states of Eastern Europe. Much to the consternation of the United States he recognized Red China on January 27, 1964. He condemned the policy of the United States in Vietnam and called for the neutralization of all Southeast Asia. He made spectacular tours of many countries, including those in Central and Latin America, in an effort to improve the image of France in these areas and, incidentally, to better trade relations. On a visit to Canada to attend the International Exposition at Montreal in 1967 it was generally held that he overstepped the bounds of courtesy when he went out of his way to encourage the French separatists in Quebec by ending his speech with their slogan "*Vive le Québec libre.*" Everywhere and at all times he sought, not without some success, to further his own ideas of France's national honor and special glory.

The End of an Era

Although De Gaulle provided France with a strong personal rule, it was not a dictatorship according to Fascist or Communist patterns. The chambers continued to meet, political parties as well as labor unions were never outlawed, and Frenchmen could still grumble and voice their feelings. Above all they were free to strike, and there were every year many strikes by all kinds of workers, including civil servants. Reluctantly the government acceded to at least part of their demands. Wages increased, but did not keep up with the increase in prices. Housing remained inadequate, and modernization of both household and factory proceeded slowly. Yet on the whole the economy was strengthened and France became one of the most prosperous and high-priced countries of the world. But there were weak spots and in general the business boom declined in 1967. This formed part of the background for the serious disturbances which paralyzed France in the spring of 1968.

GROWING DOMESTIC UNREST. The trouble began with student riots at the Nanterre campus of the University of Paris in March and soon spread to the Sorbonne. Buildings were occupied and the government sent in strong forces of riot troops. Barricades were thrown up, and in the confused street fighting much property was destroyed. In May the student revolt was joined by a rash of illegal trade union strikes. Although there were some extremists, in general the students wanted only long-overdue reforms and reasonable facilities for education and employment. The overcrowding of classrooms and laboratories was a long-tolerated disgrace. The workers demanded a forty hour week, a guaranteed wage of about $200 a month, and retirement at the age of sixty. For some weeks the government seemed inclined to permit the demonstrations to continue. Differences between the workers and students appeared, and the impatience, disgust, and fear of the population increased over the disruption of services and general destruction that was taking place. Garbage piled up in the streets, farmers blocked highways with their tractors, and a black market sprang up. Even some players and the girls at the Folies Bergére went on strike; the situation was indeed serious.

De Gaulle waited. Finally on May 30, having secured the support of the army generals in a secret meeting at Baden-Baden where French troops were still stationed, he addressed the nation. He made a vigorous statement, squashed rumors that he would resign, and promised to see things through. He dissolved parliament, issued a decree granting a 35 percent increase in minimum wages, which did much to appease the workers, and promised educational reforms. There were widespread demonstrations of support for De Gaulle and these were confirmed when in the June Assembly elections the Gaullists tok 358 of the 487 seats. Maurice Couve de Murville, the long-time foreign minister, replaced Georges Pompidou as the new premier. On the surface at least, France was returning gradually to a normal state of affairs.

Profit margins were cut by the wage increases and price restraints. When a severe financial crisis arose in November, De Gaulle was adamant in refusing to devalue the franc. Only international aid helped France to survive. The necessary additional austerity measures including a very unpopular sales tax built up dissatisfaction among the people.

A broad educational reform bill became law on October 11. The power vested in the Ministry of Education was drastically reduced; steps were taken to democratize and rationalize the secondary school system. Universities were henceforth to be run by councils elected by faculty and students. The council would elect the university president, control budgets, determine curriculum, hire faculty, and allocate research funds. Existing rectors appointed by the Minister of Education would continue as chancellors with power to advise and even delay some council decisions. This did not meet all the student demands, but it did break the stranglehold the government bureaucracy traditionally held on education. The necessary expansion of facilities, of course, remained to be carried out.

RESIGNATION OF DE GAULLE. The post-riot election was obviously a strong endorsement of De Gaulle, and he determined to make full use of it. For some time he had contemplated changing the makeup and role of the Senate, for it no longer served as a checking body of the Assembly, that role being passed to the president. The Senate was to be merged with the Economic and Social Council and given only advisory functions. At the same time more power was to be given to regional councils throughout the country. De Gaulle chose to refer this directly to the people rather than to submit it first to the Assembly. This had been the procedure followed when the direct election of the President had been instituted. Many held that this was incorrect practice. There was also the long tradition of the Senate in France and the opposition of most existing senators to overcome. De Gaulle chose to consider the referendum as a vote of confidence and stated he would resign if the people did not approve what he considered an essential political reform. In the election held on April 27, 1969, 10,905,453 (47.69 percent) supported him while 12,004,970 (52.40 percent) voted no. True to his word De Gaulle resigned as president the next day.

POST-DE GAULLE FRANCE. According to the constitution Alain Poher, president of the Senate, became interim president. He chose to be a candidate for the office but was defeated in the election on June 15 by Georges Pompidou. De Gaulle had taken himself and wife on a vacation in Ireland and played no role in the campaign. Yet he no doubt was pleased that a Gaullist carried the day.

The transition of power went smoothly. Pompidou announced no radical changes and the new cabinet, headed by Premier Jacques Chaban-Delmas, could still rely on the Gaullist controlled chamber. The austerity measures introduced by De Gaulle had not solved the currency problem and on August 8 it became necessary to devalue the franc by 12 percent to $.18005 United States. This led to immediate devaluation in fourteen African countries (Mauritania, Senegal, Ivory Coast, Dahomey, Togo, Niger, Mali, Upper Volta, Congo [Brazzaville], Central African Republic, Chad, Gambon, Cameroon, and Madagascar) where the currency is pegged to the French franc. It also had severe repercussions in other former French territories such as Algeria, Tunisia, and Morocco where the currency is less closely related. In France the government was forced to enact various price and wage control measures in an effort to prevent the beneficial effects of devaluation from being dissipated.

While there was no startling change in foreign policy a greater degree of flexibility was soon evident. On December 2, 1969, the French agreed with their Common Market partners that negotiations should be undertaken with the United Kingdom and subsequently with other countries on the question of joining that organization. Statements were made expressing French loyalty to NATO, and relations with the United States were improved. France also undertook to enhance her position in the Arab world, agreeing to sell modern French fighting planes to Libya. Meanwhile she continued her arms embargo to Israel, refusing to recognize the right of that country to annex the territory seized in the Six-Day War of 1967, although supporting the right of Israel to exist as a state. To safeguard her position as a power in the Mediterranean and her access to vital oil supplies, France also sought closer ties with Spain and Greece through the sale of planes of advanced design. France indeed has come a long way since those dark days when De Gaulle, faced by a near revolutionary situation, had the courage and foresight to end the Algerian War.

The sudden death of General de Gaulle on November 9, 1970, plunged the whole country into mourning, for in spite of political differences, it was generally recognized that he had done much for France. The leaders of the world, among them President Nixon, journeyed to Paris to pay their respects to his memory.

CHAPTER

— 31 —

Italy
and the Vatican

Establishment of the Republic: *Post-Fascist Governments; The New Republican Constitution.*

Internal and External Affairs: *The Political Kaleidoscope; Economic Recovery; Foreign Relations.*

The Vatican: *Pius XII in the Postwar Era; John XXIII and the Calling of Vatican Council II; Paul VI and the Changing Church.*

Establishment of the Republic

POST-FASCIST GOVERNMENTS. On July 25, 1943, Mussolini was forced to resign by the Fascist Grand Council, and Marshal Badoglio, the conqueror of Ethiopia, headed the new government. It was the latter who signed the armistice terms with the Western Allies in September, 1943, and they supported his regime in southern Italy. Unlike Germany, where unconditional surrender brought the disappearance of all central authority, Italy always had a recognized Italian government headed by the king and cabinet. Mussolini, who had been held captive, was freed by German paratroopers on September 11 and established a new Fascist Republican regime in northern Italy. For many months, more of Italy was under Mussolini's German-sponsored republic than under the Italian royal government, and this division of Italy sharpened the ever-present differences between north and south. Opposition to its Fascist rulers made the north the great center of the partisan movement which, like the French resistance, felt that it should do the reconstructing.

The Italian forces in the south were loyal to Badoglio, who brought Italy into the war against Germany as a cobelligerent of the Allies on October 13, 1943. The Italian fleet in particular performed valuable transport and convoy services. Badoglio, nevertheless, was too tainted with fascism for the Italians themselves. He was forced to reform his cabinet four times to take in leaders of the anti-Fascist movement. Thus, men of such diverse views as the great philosopher-historian Benedetto Croce, Count Sforza, who returned to Italy from the United States, and the Communist leader Togliatti, who came from the USSR, were members of his last cabinet. On the liberation of Rome (June 4, 1944) Badoglio was succeeded by Bonomi, an old pre-Fascist political leader. Gradually the Allied Military Government (AMG), which was merged with the Allied Control Commission (ACC), extended the jurisdiction of the Italian government. In February, 1945, the Italian government was given the right to deal directly again with foreign states. On January 1, 1946, all northern Italy except the region about Trieste was turned over to the control of the Italian authorities.

The end of the war brought a reorganization of the Italian cabinet, and a Consultative Chamber was formed in September, 1945, consisting of 429 members nominated by the government from lists submitted by the political parties, trade unions, and various professional associations. On December 10, De Gasperi, who was to prove to be the ablest politician of the new Italy, formed his first cabinet. Although in the succeeding years he was forced to change the personnel of his cabinet on eight occasions, he managed to remain head of the government until 1953.

These first Italian governments were faced with all the pressing problems of immediate postwar reconstruction. A widespread famine made necessary large shipments of UNRRA supplies, $450 million worth being sent in 1946 alone. In addition, the state had to be purged of fascism, which meant not only taking action against former leading officials, but also making a thoroughgoing examination of many organizations and the whole legal system. One of the first bits of fascism to go by the board were the Italian racial laws. National elections for a Constituent Assembly were held in June, 1946, and in a referendum held at this time 12,717,932 votes were cast for a republic and 10,719,284 for the monarchy. In a belated attempt to popularize the monarchy, Victor Emmanuel III had abdicated on May 9 in favor of his son, who was proclaimed Humbert II. The new king, true to his promise to abide by the result of the plebiscite, withdrew to Portugal, and on June 18, 1946, Italy officially became a republic.

THE NEW REPUBLICAN CONSTITUTION. The Constituent Assembly did not set itself seriously to drafting the new constitution until after the signature of the peace treaties [see above, pp. 609–10] and the termination

of the Allied Military Government on March 1, 1947. At the beginning
of December, 1947, the last British and American troops were withdrawn
from Italy, and that same month the new constitution was approved by
the Assembly.

The constitution in general represents the views of the Christian Democrats and establishes a rather conventional parliamentary form of government. The president is elected for a term of seven years by parliament,
which for this purpose is augmented by three delegates from each of the
twenty regions into which Italy has been divided. The latter are new
governmental subdivisions, and in turn are subdivided into the traditional
provinces (992) and communes (8,007). The regions are intended to
bring about a lessening of centralism. Until final legislation was passed
in 1970, only five regions had achieved semi-autonomy and their own
regional parliaments. Among them was the controversial union in 1948
of the two provinces of Bolzano and Trentino into the region of Trentino-
Alto Adige (South Tyrol). [See below, pp. 767–68.] Under agreements
reached in 1969 by the Italian government with Austria and the political
parties of the provinces, this region is to be divided again into its two
historic parts. Since a number of the local parliaments would almost
certainly come under Communist party control there was much political
maneuvering involved in establishing the regions. Bitter rivalry was aroused
between cities in some regions as to where the capital was to be located,
for the new regional offices meant additional jobs, public work contracts,
and considerable influence. The regions served as electoral districts for
the Senate, electing a senator for each 200,000 inhabitants by universal
suffrage of voters over twenty-five years of age. The term, originally six
years, was changed to five years in 1962 to make it coincide with that of the
second chamber. In addition the president can appoint five life-senators
from citizens who have shown distinction in scientific, artistic, literary, and
social fields; ex-presidents also become *de jure* senators for life. The Chamber of Deputies is elected for five years by voters over twenty-one years
of age. The two bodies have equal powers, and the ministry, which constitutes the real executive, is responsible to them. In an effort to avoid the
danger of rule by executive decree, careful provision is made as to the conditions under which parliament may delegate legislative power. A Constitutional Court of fifteen judges has powers similar to those of the
Supreme Court of the United States; it decides on the constitutionality of
laws and decrees and judges disputes between the state and regions and
between regions. The constitution contains a bill of rights, and it sanctions the settlement of 1929 with the Vatican. Catholic religious instruction is compulsory in all state elementary and secondary schools. A church
marriage ceremony is sufficient for a legal marriage, a civil ceremony being
optional, and divorce was prohibited, until December 18, 1970, when a
rather restricted divorce law went into effect. While other faiths are
tolerated, only the Catholic Church receives state subsidies.

Internal and External Affairs

THE POLITICAL KALEIDOSCOPE. The Constituent Assembly was dissolved on February 1, 1948, and elections were set for the following April. A bitter election campaign was soon under way. The Vatican came out openly in support of the Christian Democrats and urged the defeat of the Communists. The election was fought as if it would determine the outcome of the Cold War between Western and Eastern Europe. Italians in the United States were urged to write their relatives to vote anti-Communist. The United States government made a gift of twenty-nine ships to Italy as a sign of American friendship and faith in Italian democracy; it was intimated that all American aid to Italy would cease in case of a Communist victory, and Congress hurriedly passed an interim aid bill for Italy. Britain and the United States took this occasion to announce unilaterally that they favored the restoration of the free territory of Trieste to Italy. France and the United States also promised to support Italy's claim to trusteeship over her former colonies. The Christian Democrats won the elections, obtaining 48.7 percent of the vote and 53.5 percent of the seats in the Chamber of Deputies. In spite of all the internal and external pressure, the Communists held their own. The Communist and left-wing Socialists together captured 31 percent of the total vote. In a country where 99 percent of the people are Roman Catholics, this indicates again that many Italians pray and vote while facing in different directions. The extreme poverty that prevails among a large part of the population and the Communist-led labor unions are important factors in maintaining the Communist vote.

The election results were such as to give the coalition cabinet headed by the Christian Democratic leader De Gasperi a good working majority. Luigi Einaudi, a distinguished economist and long a member of the Italian Senate, was elected president of Italy in 1948 and held that office until he was succeeded in 1955 by Giovanni Gronchi, a left-wing Christian Democrat who had been president of the Chamber of Deputies. Municipal elections in 1951–52 showed a gain for parties on the left and also for a neo-Fascist group. To prevent a possible deadlock by a combination of extreme left and right groups, De Gasperi pushed through an electoral reform law in the spring of 1953. It provided that a party or group of parties that obtained 50 percent of the popular vote would be assigned a considerable majority of seats in the Chamber of Deputies. The center parties confidently expected that this arrangement would assure them a resounding victory in the election scheduled for June. However, they won only 49.1 percent of the popular vote and had to be content with the bare majority of seats which they managed to win. The Communists polled 22 percent of the vote and together with the left-wing Socialists accounted for 35.3 percent of the total.

This time De Gasperi was unable to form a government because of divisions in his own Christian Democratic party and the failure of the Democratic Socialists to support him. It was an unstable political situation, and from 1953 to 1958 Italy was ruled by a series of coalition cabinets under various leaders. The elections of May, 1958, brought gains to the center coalition parties, largely at the expense of the Monarchists and neo-Fascists, with the left-wing parties also gaining a few seats. The Communist vote declined slightly but the party still captured 140 seats. The chronic political stalemate continued, for the Christian Democrats, the largest single party, lacked a clear majority and had to seek allies either by an "opening to the right" (Liberals, Monarchists, neo-Fascists) or by an "opening to the left" (Republicans, right-wing Democratic Socialists and especially with Pietro Nenni's Socialists). A series of right-center governments followed. Finally in February, 1962, after Nenni had renounced his policy of "unity of action" with the Communists, Premier Fanfani decided to strengthen his position by shifting to the left. Agreements were negotiated, and although the Socialists did not actually join the revised cabinet they supported it. It was an unsatisfactory arrangement and Premier Fanfani dissolved parliament in February, 1963. The ensuing elections brought a sharp set-back to the Christian Democrats, whose popular vote dropped from 42.3 percent in 1958 to 38.3 percent in 1963, while the Communists rose from 22.7 percent to 25.3 percent. It was the last triumph for the long-time leader of the Communists, Palmiro Togliatti, for he died on a visit to Russia in August, 1964. Luigi Longo now took over the leadership of the party.

The elections were followed by a long period of cabinet negotiations. It was clear, however, that the "opening to the left" had to be pursued. Finally at the end of 1963 a four-party coalition—Christian Democrats, Socialists, Democratic Socialists, and Republicans—was formed under Premier Aldo Moro, a Christian Democrat, with Nenni as vice premier. Angered by Nenni's decision to participate in the government, a left-wing faction broke away (January, 1964) from the Socialists and formed a more radical Socialist party of Proletarian Unity (PSIUP). The Christian Democratic party was also divided into factions, and the right wing undertook to limit the program of extensive social and economic reforms on which the coalition rested. This led to the resignation of the government in June, 1964, but the new cabinet, again headed by Moro, was almost identical with the old one. Only one prominent member, the Socialist budget minister, was missing. He refused to go along with the revised compromise program which was characterized as being "more realistic" because it tempered and stretched out the proposed five-year reform plan. More attention was to be given to immediate anti-inflationary measures and to the co-ordination of the economic program with the needs of a free economy and membership in the Common Market.

When in December, 1964, President Antonio Segni, a Christian Democrat like those before him, was forced to resign because of ill health, a sharp political conflict developed over choosing his successor. On the twenty-first ballot, with the aid of the Communists, Giuseppi Saragat, a right-wing Socialist who had served as deputy premier in several cabinets, was elected president.

In 1966 the two Socialist parties ended their nineteen-year-old split to form the Italian Socialist party. This party continued participation in the left-center coalition led by Premier Moro. The parliamentary elections of 1968 brought a slight decline for the United Socialists, for part of their support went to a left-wing schismatic Proletarian Socialist party and to the Communists who polled 26.9 percent of the total vote. A rash of student demonstrations and industrial strikes with their usual demands added to the turmoil of the campaign. The old left-center combination of Christian Democrats, United Socialists, and Republicans still commanded a majority of the seats after the balloting. The United Socialists, however, in order to strengthen their bargaining power over against their coalition partners withdrew from the government, which led to a short-lived minority cabinet. Their strategy worked, and by the end of 1968 they were back in a government headed by Premier Mariano Rumor.

The old question of church-state relations, never far below the surface in Italy, beset the coalition government. The dominant Christian Democratic party, being church oriented, was reluctant to meet the desires of its leftist coalition partners in this field. The Socialists in general supported the enactment of legislation permitting divorce, although this was a question which cut across party lines. They pointed out that it would bring greater liberty to many Italians and would lead to the legalization of many family relationships. Without divorce many Italians struck up permanent liaisons with more congenial partners. Children born to such unions were regarded by law as illegitimate and were not considered for family allowances. A strong argument for a divorce law was that such parents could free themselves from their former spouses, remarry, and thus legitimize their offspring. The Vatican consistently opposed all divorce legislation and maintained that a divorce law violated the concordat of 1929.

Another disturbing problem is the taxation of the Roman Catholic Church. Taxes have been levied on dividends from investments in Italy held by the church. The issue is whether these taxes should be continued and whether other church property should be added to the tax rolls.

There are other differences among these left-center coalition partners, none more difficult than their relationship to the strong Communist party which, either alone or in cooperation with Socialists, controls many municipalities. There are those who want to carry this cooperation over to the national government, where since 1948 it has been the practice that a government must resign rather than stay in power with the aid of Communist votes. In July, 1969, the recently united Socialists split again on this basic problem which involves all sorts of practical and theoretical issues. A faction of the party led by Francesco de Martino was charged with carrying on a flirtation with the Communists, whereupon Minister

Mario Tanassi led a walkout of thirty-nine deputies to form a secessionist Unitary Socialist party. The split came in spite of the efforts of the veteran Socialist leader Pietro Nenni to preserve the unity of the party. The result was that, as so often before, the cabinet resigned and a prolonged government crisis ensued. The Unitary Socialists wanted a hard and fast pledge against co-operating with the Communist party before they would enter into a new coalition government. Party discipline is notoriously weak in Italy and such a pledge if made by party leaders would have been difficult to keep. In the end Mariano Rumor formed a minority cabinet consisting of only members of his own Christian Democrats, the largest Italian party but still a minority group. The Republicans and Socialists agreed to support it by their votes, but refused to share as coalition partners. The sharp divisions among the political left which have plagued Italian politics for years remained and led to a new government crisis in February, 1970, triggered by the problem of negotiations with the Vatican over the proposed divorce bill. After various attempts to construct a new government had failed, Rumor was successful in forming a four-party cabinet on March 28. The Republicans, Unitary Socialists, and Socialists agreed to cooperate with the Christian Democrats on the promise that an *ad hoc* committee headed by Socialist Pietro Nenni would undertake speedy negotiations with the Vatican on the divorce issue.

Pressing economic problems, widespread demand for the extension of social services, and a rash of serious strikes bedeviled the new government. But it was again the old question of political cooperation with the Communists which brought the downfall in July, 1970, of Italy's thirty-first postwar cabinet. When the Socialists agreed to join with the Communists in establishing the administrations in two of the new regions, the governing coalition fell apart. A new cabinet with a slightly different political complexion was again achieved, but at present there seems little prospect of stopping the ever circling Italian political merry-go-round.

After public demonstrations and protracted political wrangling, a divorce law was finally passed and became effective December 18, 1970. The law is a limited one and permits a divorce only after waiting periods of five to seven years, depending on the nature of the separation and whether the applicant is judged to be at fault. Clearly Rome is in no danger of becoming the Reno of Europe.

ECONOMIC RECOVERY. After World War I it was the fashion for a time to speak of "have" and "have not" powers. Italy was classed among the latter because she possessed few raw materials, and her economy did not suffice to take care of the expanding population. World War II only aggravated this problem. Postwar discovery of rich methane-gas deposits as well as the discovery of some oil, notably in Sicily, has added to Italy's supply of power. Also, the ever-expanding electric power industry was nationalized in 1962. Italy, however, remains a country with too many people for its arable land, material resources, and capital. During the decades around the turn of the century approximately 30 percent of the natural increase in population emigrated. This meant a large influx of gold to Italy, for the emigrants sent generous remittances to their relatives. Today migration is everywhere restricted, and emigrants average around 150,000 a year. Those countries that still desire immigrants are looking for skilled, trained workers, and of these Italy has no excess. In more recent years many Italians have journeyed to Switzerland, Germany, and France as contract laborers. In 1953 a parliamentary committee investigated the poverty in which many Italians live. It reported that the housing of 2,793,000 families, 24.1 percent of the population, was subnormal. In southern Italy, 57 percent of the population maintained a low or subnormal standard of living. Housing projects have been high on the list of the government's modernization program, but housing still remains inadequate. Since 1952 the number of Italians engaged in industry has outstripped those engaged in agriculture. In spite of the constant stream of agricultural workers to the city, there is not enough land to support those who remain behind. All the easily available land has been reclaimed, although the government has begun new reclamation projects. In 1950 a moderate agrarian expropriation program was enacted for certain districts in southern Italy which has since been extended to other regions. Assigned holdings may vary in size from 5 to 123 acres, but the average farm is about 12.5 acres. Breaking up the large estates will perhaps stifle some social unrest, but it also raises economic considerations. Increased mechanization, which is sorely needed, is usually not adapted to an agricultural system based on many tiny holdings. More is to be gained by the greater use of fertilizers, for Italy's yield per acre is still low, and by shifting from wheat to more intensive crops. The government is moving along these lines, and real progress has been made.

The manufacturing plants of the great northern cities were not destroyed in the last days of conflict. But even here much unemployment or partial employment existed for a considerable period. A policy of spreading what work was available was adopted, and industries were forced to keep people on the payroll who might well have been dispensed with. The Italian economy was bolstered by outright grants as well as by loans from the United States. Aid under the Marshall Plan along with subsequent economic and military assistance did much to improve conditions. Great advances were made and the Italians in referring to the expansion of the years 1958–62, speak of the economic miracle. By the time the economy had begun to level off, unemployment which had long hovered around the two million mark had been reduced to around 750 thousand. Foreign trade expanded, but Italian imports regularly exceeded exports. The trade deficit was in large part covered by the increasing influx of tourists. The Italians have done much to lure the auto traveler. Roads have improved and in October, 1964, Italy's modern Sun Highway, the longest superhighway in Europe, was opened from Milan to Naples. This 470 mile stretch is to be extended southward to the very toe of Italy. A 165-mile connecting link to Bari and Brindisi on the Adriatic was opened in December, 1969. In co-operation with France and Switzerland a seven-mile two-lane tunnel was built under Mt. Blanc-Chamonix, France to Courmayeur, Italy. It was opened on July 16, 1965, and cuts the distance from Geneva to Turin by about 35 miles in summer and 322 miles in winter when the passes are closed by snow.

In order to lessen the traditional differences between northern and southern Italy, the government undertook a special fifteen-year development program (1950-65; later extended to 1980) for southern Italy, Sicily, and Sardinia. Billions of lira were poured into both public and private projects. A special five-year plan drawn up in 1964 (revised later to extend to 1970) called for unprecedented state intervention in a continued attempt to liquidate the imbalances between north and south, industry and agriculture, urban and rural areas.

FOREIGN RELATIONS. Italy's application for membership in the United Nations unfortunately became linked with those of Hungary, Rumania, Finland, and Bulgaria, all of which failed to receive the support of the permanent members of the Security Council until December, 1953. Count Sforza, who was minister of foreign affairs in the immediate postwar years, gave Italy a distinctive Western orientation which has been followed ever since. In spite of the noisy opposition of the Communists, Italy joined the Marshall Plan, NATO, the Council of Europe, and the European Coal and Steel Community (ECSC), and was willing to share the burdens of the European Defense Community (EDC). When this plan was defeated by France, Italy participated in the London Conference, which led to agreement on the restoration of sovereignty to Germany and the entrance of Italy and Germany into the Western European Union. In 1957 Italy played host to the final conference preceding the establishment of the European Economic Community (EEC) and the European Atomic Energy Community (Euratom). Italy has since been a staunch member of these organizations. She supported Britain's application to the Common Market, and has favored policies designed to further European integration. This has led her to side more with West Germany than with France on EEC issues. The establishment of the Common Market did much to promote Italian prosperity; West Germany has become Italy's chief trading partner.

As a result of the war Italy lost its African possessions of Libya, Eritrea, and Somaliland [see above, p. 610]. Under the Peace Treaty of February, 1947 [see above, p. 609] a free Territory of Trieste was created. Zone A (86 sq. mi.; population 298,000, mostly Italians), which included the city proper, was to be administered by Britain and the United States, while Zone B (199 sq. mi.; population 73,500, mostly Slovenes and Croats) was to be under the charge of Yugoslavia. As early as 1948, Britain, the United States, and France, without consulting Russia (also a party to the peace treaty), announced that Trieste should be returned to Italy. This statement naturally brought protests from Russia and Yugoslavia. Britain and the United States gradually turned much of the administration of their zones over to Italians. In October, 1953, Marshal Tito was able to block British and United States withdrawal, but in the succeeding months agreement was reached by the four powers directly concerned. On October 26, 1954, American and British troops were withdrawn and Zone A, minus about five square miles in the vicinity of Crevatini, was handed over to Italy. Yugoslavia obtained Zone B plus the small addition from Zone A. The city of Trieste retained its status as a free port and the political, cultural, and economic rights of ethnic minorities in both areas are safeguarded. The city of Rijeka (Fiume) is its Yugoslav counterpart.

Italy has not played a spectacular role in the higher policy of the powers. Her statesmen have made many official visits to other countries and have in turn received many guests. The traditional ties of friendship with Britain have been reknit; relations with the United States have been consistently friendly. In 1967 President Nikolai V. Podgorny of the USSR paid an official visit to Rome, the first Russian head of state to visit Italy since Tsar Nicholas II did so in 1909. He even conferred with the Pope. The visit furthered new Italian-Soviet accords covering cultural, economic, scientific and technical fields. The Italian Fiat Company obtained the right to manufacture automobiles in Russia and Air Alitalia inaugurated service between Italy and Moscow. These strengthened ties to Russia did not, however, keep the Italian government from criticizing Russian Near Eastern policy or its 1968 takeover in Czechoslovakia. The growing Russian naval presence in the Mediterranean was not welcomed by Italy.

Italy has steadfastly co-operated fully in NATO and met her UN obligations. Only with Austria has there been dispute. In establishing the region of Trentino-Alto Adige, Italy united the predominantly German-speaking South Tyrolese province of Bolzano with the predominantly Italian-speaking province of Trento. Austria charged that this action along with other policies deprived the German-speaking Tyrolese of the autonomy envisaged in the 1946 Austro-Italian agreement. Activists among the inhabitants resorted to bombing of electric power lines and other terroristic acts. Austria brought the question to the attention of the UN Assembly in 1960 and 1961. On both occasions the Assembly recommended the resumption of discussions between the two countries. Italy took a long step forward in solving the problem by appointing a nineteen-member Parliamentary Commission to study the Alto-Adige in September, 1961. On April 10, 1964, the Commission recommended a new statute which would broaden the area's autonomy and strengthen the rights of the German-speaking population. Italy and Austria then appointed a committee to prepare an agreement on the basis of the report. In the summer of 1969 a provisional agreement was reached which was narrowly approved by the dominant German party in South Tyrol. With this acceptance accomplished the foreign ministers of Austria and Italy signed a formal accord on November 30. It provides for the dissolution of the merger of Trentino and Bolzano, the name Alto Adige is to be dropped, and the German-speaking province will again be known officially as South Tyrol. As the population now stands it will have a ratio of about 230,000

German-speaking to 130,000 Italian-speaking inhabitants. South Tyrol will have a substantial increase in local autonomy and the chief administrative officials will be locally appointed. There are many safeguards in respect to the use of German in schools and in administrative and judicial procedures. The accord was subsequently approved by the Austrian and Italian parliaments. Its implementation requires an amendment of the Italian constitution and the enactment of numerous other measures. A four-year timetable for carrying out the projected steps has been established.

The Vatican

PIUS XII IN THE POSTWAR ERA. Cordial relations have existed between the Italian government and the Vatican in the postwar years. Whereas the Pope never gave outright support to Sturzo's Populist party after World War I, Pius XII and his successors have given direct aid to the present Christian Democratic party. This is in line with the Vatican's general policy of supporting Catholic parties in those continental countries where there are substantial numbers of Catholic believers.

In Eastern Europe this policy led to direct conflict with the Communist governments which, following their United Front policy, were bent on establishing single-party states. In certain countries the governments closed convents and confiscated church lands in the process of carrying out their policy of land distribution. Another major issue in these countries was the complete secularization of the school systems. In general, religious education in the schools was handicapped although not universally abolished, but private religious schools were closed. Notable conflicts between the Catholic Church and the state centered in the imprisonment and trial of Archbishop Stepinac in Yugoslavia in 1946 and of Cardinal Mindszenty in Hungary in 1949. Under pressure from the Soviet government the Uniate churches of Ruthenia and the former provinces of Poland declared (1946) their allegiance to the Patriarch of Moscow. The Uniate churches of Rumania were later (1948–49) incorporated into the Rumanian Orthodox Church. The Papacy naturally deplored the loss of these Eastern-rite Christians, and thus the conflict between the Vatican and communism grew sharper.

In the summer of 1949, as the governments in Czechoslovakia and Poland began drastically to curb the privileges of the Roman Catholic Church, the Papacy (July 13) took the unusual step of excommunicating all persons who were Communists or in any way aided the cause of communism. In Czechoslovakia the government answered by declaring it would charge any priest with treason who tried to enforce the papal edict. In Italy, France, and most Western countries the priests made no particular effort to enforce the excommunication ban, although it was universal in its application. There was also some question as to exactly who did come under the ban. An authoritative article published in the *Osservatore Romano* stated that there were many people, particularly in

Italy, Belgium, and France, who, "fooled by the promises of the Communists or desirous of social reforms, favor communism even though they do not accept its fundamental doctrine." The latter were not excommunicated, although the Holy See called their attention to "the grave responsibilities they incurred by supporting the arch-enemies of the Christian church."[1] Relations between the Papacy and the churches behind the Iron Curtain, although far from satisfactory have tended to improve, and leading churchmen have even been permitted to visit Rome. On September 15, 1964, the Vatican signed a treaty with Hungary in which the Hungarian government recognized papal appointments to the Hungarian hierarchy. The Hungarian episcopate also resumed administration of the Papal Hungarian Institute in Rome.

In the immediate postwar years the Pope issued many statements asking for reconciliation among the peoples of the world. The Catholic Church, however, refused to co-operate in the World Council of Churches, which was formally constituted on August 23, 1948, at Amsterdam, by delegates representing 147 churches from 44 different countries. At the meeting of the World Council in Evanston, Illinois, in 1954, Roman Catholics were forbidden to take part even as observers. Pius XII took occasion to make numerous statements explaining Catholic teaching on particular subjects and on the duties of Catholics. Many of the Papal pronouncements called for an advanced social solution of the problems of industry. An unusually large number of canonizations have taken place in the postwar years, among them that of Pius X (1954) which was exceptional in that it was proclaimed only forty years after his death. Special recognition was accorded Catholicism in Africa by the canonization of twenty-two young men who were slain in Uganda in 1885–87 because they refused to renounce their Catholic faith. A special shrine to these martyrs was consecrated by Pope Paul VI when he visited Uganda in 1969.

In 1946 the Pope created thirty-two cardinals to bring the College of Cardinals up to its historic full complement of seventy members. For the first time since the fourteenth century, non-Italians held the majority. The church was strengthened through the establishment of new dioceses in many countries, and the first local hierarchies in Africa in fourteen centuries were formed in 1950 in Nigeria, the Cameroons, Togoland, the Gold Coast, and Sierra Leone. Norway, for the first time since the Reformation, received a hierarchy in 1953. The activity of Catholic Action, which represents various lay organizations sponsored by the church, has been greatly expanded. The church has made wide use of radio and television, and several popular and influential speakers have made their appearance not only in America but also on the continent. Italy has granted the Vatican extraterritorial rights over 1,335 acres on the outskirts of Rome for the erection of a powerful radio station. The ever-widening conflict between the Vatican and communism set the keynote for the prayers and observ-

[1] *The New York Times,* July 27, 1949.

ances of the Holy Year of 1950, when special indulgences were proclaimed for the benefit of all pilgrims to Rome. The Pope brought the Holy Year to a close by making use for the first time of the powers granted to the Papacy by the Vatican Council in 1870 to define matters of faith and morals. On November 1, 1950, he proclaimed the dogma of the corporal assumption of the Blessed Virgin Mary. The Pope in 1952 dedicated the people of Russia to the Virgin and placed them under her special protection. The position of the Virgin in the church was further enhanced when the year 1954, the hundredth anniversary of the proclamation of the doctrine of the Immaculate Conception, was proclaimed a special Marian year. Many special observances were held, and the Pope proclaimed a new feast of the Queenship of Mary to be celebrated each May 31.

JOHN XXIII AND THE CALLING OF VATICAN COUNCIL II. The death of Pius XII on October 7, 1958, brought to a close one of the most significant pontificates in recent times. All cardinals except Mindszenty of Hungary, who was not granted permission to leave the country, and Stepinac of Yugoslavia, who was ill, attended the conclave that elected Angelo Giuseppe Cardinal Roncalli, Patriarch of Venice, the 262nd official successor of St. Peter. The new Pope, born in northern Italy the son of humble peasant parents, chose to be called John XXIII and was crowned on November 4, 1958. He immediately took steps to strengthen the administration of the church by filling several posts that had long been vacant. In line with this policy he broke with tradition by increasing the College of Cardinals to seventy-four in a consistory on December 15. It was subsequently enlarged and in March, 1969, totaled 134. Since many of the new cardinals came from African and Eastern churches, the Italians became an even smaller minority.

John XXIII, nearly seventy-seven years old, was widely considered to have been chosen as an interim or compromise pope. In fact he did have the shortest pontificate in the last 130 years, reigning slightly over four and one-half years. Far from establishing a caretaker regime, he proved to be an innovator and man of action. He not only initiated a revision of Canon Law, but issued eight encyclicals, two of them being of major significance. On May 15, 1961, in *Mater et Magistra* he dealt with man's pressing social problems and touched on such practical matters as the depressed state of agriculture in an increasingly technological world. His *Pacem in Terris* (April 11, 1963) addressed to the whole world and not merely to Catholics, was a plea for peace on earth, a clarion call for disarmament and a nuclear test ban, for the rights of minorities and interracial justice, and for more co-operation between all faiths and nations. Most important of all, on January 25, 1959, he announced his intention to convoke an Ecumenical Council of the Church, the first to be held since the Vatican Council of 1870. He issued a call for *aggiornamento*—the updating of theological teachings and discipline; he desired to bring an inner renewal of the church, to open its windows to "the winds of change." He hoped too through the

Council to bring about more unity not only among Christian communities, but also among people of all faiths. Commissions were appointed to prepare the work of the Council and Pope John was able to preside over the first session of Vatican Council II, October 11 to December 8, 1962.

Over 2,500 cardinals, archbishops, bishops, and heads of the major religious orders attended the Council. An innovation was the presence of thirty-four representatives of various Protestant churches and two representatives of the Orthodox Church in Russia as observers; the Union of Greek Orthodox Churches headed by Archbishop Athenagoras at Istanbul did not attend. This session of the Council was given over largely to preparatory work. Pope John pointed the way by decreeing on November 13, 1962, the first change in the canon of the Mass since the early seventh century. Henceforth the name of Saint Joseph, the spouse of the Virgin Mary, was inserted into one of the nine prayers of the canon immediately following that of Mary.

PAUL VI AND THE CHANGING CHURCH. On June 3, 1963, John XXIII died. Few, if any, popes achieved the admiration and love which was accorded him by people of all faiths, ranks, and conditions of life. He was succeeded by Giovanni Battista Cardinal Montini of Milan, who took the name of Paul VI. He was noted as a scholar and intellectual. In his coronation address he announced his intention to resume the Ecumenical Council which had technically been ended by the death of his predecessor. The second session met September 29 to December 4, 1963. The Council endorsed the principle of collegiality, which maintains the collective governing and teaching authority of the bishops; that the bishops as successors of the apostles share with the pope in the government of the church. It also sanctioned the use of the vernacular in the administration of the sacraments and in parts of the Mass. This retreat from Latin received the endorsement of the Pope and began to take effect throughout the world the following year. At this session, as already at the previous one, a definite cleavage between so-called progressive and conservative groups was in evidence.

When Pope Paul VI made the pilgrimage to Jerusalem, January 4–6, 1964, he was the first supreme pontiff to leave Italy since 1814, the first to visit the Holy Land, and the first to travel by air. He received a tremendous reception, and his many well-wishers made it difficult for him to visit the holy places. Orthodox Patriarch Athenagoras of Istanbul made a visit to Jerusalem at the same time, and the meeting between the leaders of the two churches—the first in over 500 years—was a significant landmark in ecumenical co-operation. The Pope continued to travel new paths when he attended the International Eucharistic Congress in Bombay, December 2–5, 1964. He addressed his remarks to Christians and non-Christians, urging members of all faiths to come closer together. He also took the occasion to make a plea to the governments of the world to end the arms race and devote a larger share of their resources to fighting poverty.

On October 4, 1965, he continued his far-flung journeys when he visited New York City to address the United Nations.

At the third session of the Council, September 14 to November 21, 1964, three representatives of the Orthodox Church at Istanbul were also in attendance. For the first time women were present when fifteen feminine auditors, religious and lay, were invited. Again collegiality received a strong affirmative vote. The church fathers also approved the establishment of a permanent order of deacons (diaconate) as a separate order in the hierarchy rather than as a last step prior to priesthood. This order is to help alleviate the shortage of priests in some areas and is to be established by the competent territorial bishops with the approval of the supreme pontiff. Statements about the relation of the church to non-Christians, including Jews, as well as a statement on religious liberty, caused a rather sharp division among the Council Fathers and were held over for the next session.

The actions and decisions of the Council required approval and proclamation by the Pope. In closing the third session the Pope decreed the statement on ecumenism approved by the Council. In proclaiming the formulation of the Constitution of the Church (*De Ecclesia*) the Pope made nineteen amendments to the text as approved by the Council. In this Constitution the principle of collegiality was accepted, although how it is to be implemented was not defined. The decree reaffirms the doctrine of Papal Infallibility and significantly states:

> But the College or body of bishops has no authority unless it is understood together with the Roman Pontiff the successor of Peter as its head. The Pope's power of primacy over all, both pastors and faithful, remains whole and intact. In virtue of his office, that is as Vicar of Christ and pastor of the whole church, the Roman Pontiff has full, supreme and universal power over the church. And he is always free to exercise this power.[2]

The Council in its lengthy statement on the Virgin Mary, which constitutes Chapter VIII of *De Ecclesia*, had carefully avoided granting the title "Mother of the Church" to the Virgin. In rather pointed fashion the Pope overruled the Council in his address at the closing congregation of the third session, November 21, 1964, when he proclaimed Mary the Mother of the Church.

The fourth and final session of the Council met September 14 to December 8, 1965. In his opening address the Pope announced his decision to establish a synod of Catholic bishops "for consultation and collaboration" with him in the government of the church. The elected membership will consist of one delegate from national conferences having fewer than 25 bishops, 2 from those with fewer than 50, 3 from conferences up to

---

[2] Text of Vatican Council's Constitution *De Ecclesia* as proclaimed by Pope Paul VI, Chapter III, *The New York Times*, November 23, 1964.

POPE PAUL VI MEETING WITH PATRIARCH ATHENAGORAS
in Jerusalem, January, 1964.

100, and 4 from those with more than 100 bishops. In addition the Pope will appoint 15 percent of the members, and the heads of offices of the Roman curia will be *ex officio* members. The synod when established will have a membership of between 200 and 300. It is designed purely as a consultative body and what use the Pope will make of it remains to be seen. It is, however, a recognition of the principle of collegiality so strongly endorsed by the fathers in the second session.

At the final session of the Council, two more constitutions (that is, formal, significant doctrinal statements) were added to those already proclaimed (on the Liturgy, December 4, 1963, and on the Church, November 21, 1964); they were on Divine Revelation, November 18, 1965, and on the Church in the Modern World, December 8, 1965. Decrees, dealing with more practical matters of church affairs, were formulated in regard to monastic orders and seminaries, on the apostolate of the laity, and on missions and priestly life. Declarations, which are statements of principle, were adopted on the relationship of the church and non-Christian religions, on Christian education, and on religious liberty. It was these declarations, which renounced the continuing responsibility of Jews for the death of Christ and considered the position of Protestants in predominantly Catholic countries, that particularly attracted worldwide attention.

The Pope in a *moto proprio* (a decision by papal authority alone) dated December 7 ended the right of the four-century-old Sacred Congregation of the Holy Office to serve as prosecutor, defender, and judge in the secret trial of persons charged with heresy. This Office in the past had established and administered the dread Inquisition and supervised the *Index of Forbidden Books*. The Office is henceforth to be known as the Congregation for the Doctrine of the Faith and its tribunals must operate under the norms of canon law rather than by secret procedures. The *Index of Forbidden Books*, which first appeared in 1569 and was last reissued in 1947, no longer has the force of church law. The problem of heresy, however, remains. In 1969 the Pope established a new theological commission to trace the boundary between heresy and legitimate innovation in the church.

On December 7, 1965, the day before the formal closing of the Council, the Pope in Rome and the Orthodox Patriarch Athenagoras in Istanbul, in the presence of official delegations from both church bodies, made identical statements deploring and nullifying the excommunications of 1054 which led to the schism between the two churches. To what extent the Patriarch's action was approved by the other Orthodox Church leaders is uncertain, but the joint statements were significant intimations of past errors and of hope for reconciliation and reunion.

The Orthodox-Roman Catholic dialogue was continued when Pope Paul paid a visit to Istanbul in July, 1967, and Patriarch Athenagoras returned the visit the following October. In line with the growing spirit of ecumenism the Pope was also visited by the Archbishop of Canterbury, the President of the World Council of Churches, and other non-Catholic leaders. There were also Catholic observers at the meeting of the World Council of Churches at Uppsala, Sweden in 1968. In June, 1969, the Pope continued his travels by visiting Geneva, the home of the Calvinist Reformation and today the headquarters of the World Council of Churches, which now has 229 full member and 13 associate member churches, the latter being churches with less than 10,000 members. While the edges of age-old religious controversies were gradually losing some of their sharpness, Christian unity remained a distant goal. As the Pope himself acknowledged in a statement to the Vatican's Secretariat for Christian Unity in 1967, his own position of primacy and authority was "without doubt the most grave obstacle on the road to ecumenism." Paul VI was the first pope ever to visit the Far East when he journeyed to Manila in the fall of 1970, making various stopovers on the way.

The Papacy has continued to update church practices and administration. In 1966, fasting was made obligatory for Latin rite Catholics only on Ash Wednesday and Good Friday. Friday abstinence (no eating of meat) remained, but national conferences of bishops were given the power to abrogate this. This has been done in most countries, although the regulations vary. On January 1, 1967, an apostolic constitution set new norms for obtaining indulgences and the practice of referring to them in terms of years and days was dropped. The calendar of saints has also been revised (1969) and some saints of doubtful authenticity have been dropped. Saint Christopher, the patron of travelers, no longer has an official feast day on the church calendar but can still be venerated. The rules on mixed marriages have been eased but remain basically the same. The non-Catholic partner can now make oral rather than written promises to rear any offspring in the Catholic faith and Catholics no longer are subject to excommunication by contracting a marriage before a non-Catholic minister. In 1970 the practice of permitting the laity to receive both bread and wine at communion was extended, and local conferences of bishops are to decide whether this practice is to be followed in their dioceses. The papal directive stated that when there are large numbers of communicants only the wafer is still to be used and that the wine could be given by the priest either directly from the chalice, through a straw, or with a spoon. The regulations regarding cooperation and worshiping with Protestants on the part of clergy and laity have been liberalized. In France, Germany and some other countries, Protestant and Catholic leaders have agreed on a common text for the Lord's Prayer. Progress is also being made on obtaining a common text of the Bible. The use of Luther's great chorale "A Mighty Fortress is Our God" is general in Catholic churches today.

In keeping with the decision of Vatican Council II the first Synod of Bishops was convened in Rome in 1967. It deliberated for a month on problems facing the church and the world, but no definite decisions were made. On March 1, 1968, a major reorganization of the curia, the first since 1908, went into effect. Henceforth all sacred congregations will enjoy equal jurisdiction. In general the various national conferences of bishops are becoming more active and creating more diversity within the church. The Dutch hierarchy for example sponsored a new catechism (1966) which aroused much attention throughout the world. It was granted an imprimatur in the United States but this was later withdrawn. It was subject to severe criticism by Vatican theologians who charged it contained ten major and forty-eight minor heresies. A commission of six cardinals reviewed the matter and recommended for correction in future editions misleading omissions, obscurities, and interpretations in ten doctrinal areas. Cardinal Alfrink of Utrecht bowed, but did not give way, agreeing only that these changes would henceforth be printed separately as a supplement to the catechism.

On a visit to Uganda in 1969 the Pope gave his blessing to the creation of a loose confederation of the twenty-eight episcopal conferences of Africa The Pope's statement on that occasion is a good summary of the conflict between unity and diversity which confronts the Catholic Church today and also reflects on the wider problem of Christian unity. Bidding the African bishops and all African Catholics to be "missionaries to yourselves" he went on to say:

A burning and much-discussed question arises concerning your evangelizing work, and it is that of the adaption of the gospel and of the church to African culture. Must one church be European, Latin, Oriental, or must she be African? Your church must be first of all Catholic. That is, it must be entirely founded upon the identical, essential, constitutional patrimony of the selfsame teaching of Christ, as professed by the authentic and authoritative tradition of the one true church. This condition is fundamental and indisputable.

The expression, that is, the language and mode of manifesting this one faith, may be manifold; hence it may be original, suited to the tongue, the style, the character, the genius and the culture of the one who professes this one faith. From this point of view, a certain pluralism is not only legitimate but desirable.

The liturgical renewal is a living example of this. And in this sense you may, and you must, have an African Christianity.

There are two big issues confronting the church which have brought some differences among the various national conferences of bishops, the Vatican, and individual clergy. The one is the continuance of the church rule on celibacy for the clergy. This is a practice which applies to the priests of the Roman rite but not to those of the Oriental rites in the Catholic Church. Many would relax this prohibition and feel that to do so would help relieve the growing shortage of priests. The issue has been widely debated, and groups among the clergy have openly advocated it. The Vatican, however, definitely reaffirmed its traditional policy on celibacy in the encyclical *Sacerdotalis Celebatus* (Priestly Celibacy) which was issued on June 23, 1967. Nevertheless there have been an increasing number of withdrawals from both the secular and regular clergy by members who are no longer in accord with this teaching. Here again the Dutch hierarchy is in advance of others in trying to devise methods of keeping the services of priests who marry, permitting them to preach and conduct prayer services, but not to say Mass. In January, 1970, the Dutch bishops formally called upon the church to modify its stand on celibacy, but the Pope steadfastly refused to change his position.

Opposition to celibacy was nothing compared to the upheaval which the Papal stand on birth control engendered. This problem had been up for study by ecclesiastical officials ever since the close of Vatican Council II. There were some indications that the church's teaching on this burning issue—in view of the burgeoning demographic problems facing the world—would be modified. Instead, the Pope in the encyclical *Humanae vitae* on July 29, 1968, again proclaimed the church's prohibition against all forms of artifical birth control. Various national conferences of bishops, notably in Austria, Belgium, Canada, France, Germany, and the Netherlands, issued statements pointing out that the encyclical was not a dogmatic utterance and in their interpretation left considerable latitude to the consciences of individuals in applying the doctrine. Sociological studies would seem to indicate that most Catholic married couples do follow their consciences rather than the Pope in their conduct.

The second Council of Bishops which convened in Rome October 11–28, 1969, led to more critical debate and expression of divergent views than was manifest at the synod two years previously. The Pope had set the agenda of the meeting, and topics such as celibacy and birth control, although raised, were not discussed. The bishops by a series of votes gave clear expression to their desire to have a greater share in the future government of the church. In his final address to the synod the Pope responded to the bishops' proposals by agreeing to summon a synod every two years rather than at irregular intervals; to increase the role of the synod secretariat; to consider having permanent representation of diocesan bishops at the Rome secretariat; and to give "utmost consideration" to the proposal that individual bishops and national conferences be permitted to propose agenda items for future synods. Subsequently the Pope established that fifteen bishops should assist the permanent secretariat in preparing for future synods; twelve of these bishops are to be elected by the Synod Assembly and three nominated by the Pope. In a number of public statements, however, he took occasion to assert that his office and authority was a divine one, and that the church could not be governed democratically, like a secular state. On November 23, 1970 the Pope issued a decree barring cardinals past the age of 80 from participating in the election of a new pope. This affected 25 of the 127 members of the Sacred College as it was then constituted. The cardinals would, however, retain all other rights and prerogatives associated with their offices.

CHAPTER

32

The Small States of Western and Southern Europe

Austria: *Governmental Reorganization; Economic Development; Foreign Affairs.*

Switzerland: *Politics and Economy; Foreign Affairs.*

The Lowlands: *Re-establishment of Governments; Economy; Political Development.*

Ireland: *Severance from Britain; Relations with Ulster.*

The Scandinavian States: *Political Scene; Economic Developments; Social Legislation; Religion; Foreign Affairs.*

Finland: *Political Development; Economy.*

The Iberian States: *Spain; Portugal.*

The Aegean States: *Turkey; Greece; Cyprus.*

———— ◆ ————

THE HISTORY of the small states of Europe in the post-World War II years in many ways reflects the history of the great powers. The colonial empires of Belgium and the Netherlands have been largely liquidated like those of Italy, France, and Great Britain. Only Portugal has so far been able to retain its colonies. All states follow more or less a common foreign policy in that they join the United Nations (Switzerland is the sole exception and even it adheres to some of the UN related organizations), and such regional pacts as the Council of Europe, the Common Market, the European Free Trade Association, or NATO. All countries large or small are subject to much the same current economic, social, religious, and political stresses, but not necessarily to the same degree On the other hand, the histories of the small states are not replicas of those of the great powers. They have their unique problems and make their singular contribution to modern civilization. Space and time force a briefer consideration of their history, but this is no reason why they should be neglected entirely. In many ways the small powers have a style of their own which deserves study and evaluation, particularly if history is considered to be something more than power politics.

Austria

GOVERNMENTAL REORGANIZATION. On April 29, 1945, three weeks after the Russian armies entered Vienna, the formation of a provisional government for Austria under the leadership of Dr. Karl Renner was announced. He was an old, respected Socialist leader, who had taken a leading part in establishing the Austrian Republic after World War I. The Soviet government immediately recognized the Renner government, which was a coalition of Socialist, Communist, and People's (Catholic) party leaders. All laws dating from the Hitlerian period were abolished, and persons who were members of the Nazi party between July, 1933, and April 25, 1945, were called upon to register. From the start the Austrian government assumed responsibility for denazification. The Western powers took over the occupation zones previously agreed upon, but it was not until August 23, 1945, that arrangements could be made with the Russians for them to take over their respective occupation zones in the

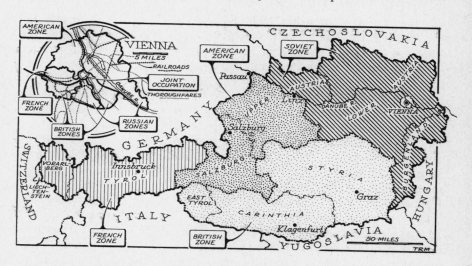

MAP 28   *Austria After World War II*

city of Vienna. A small district in the center of the city was reserved for joint control by the occupying powers. Vienna became the headquarters for the Allied Control Council, and on October 20, 1945, this body officially recognized the Renner government. Thus, unlike Germany, Austria from the first had one central government of its own which operated under the supervision of the Allied powers.

In order to broaden the basis of his government, Renner called a meeting of representatives of the Austrian provinces. They endorsed his government and his program of returning to the Constitution of October 1, 1920, as amended in 1929. This meant that Austria was again to have a president elected by parliament, which consists of an upper chamber chosen by the provincial diets and a lower chamber elected directly by the people. The Occupying Powers licensed only three parties, and in the elections held on November 25, 1945, the People's party won 85 seats, the Socialists 75, and the Communists 4. Renner was elected president, an honor fully deserved, and Figl, a member of the People's party, became chancellor at the head of a three-party coalition cabinet. The occupation authorities lent this government their support and on January 6, 1946, announced their recognition of Austria as a state, with the frontiers of 1937, pending a final delimitation. This meant that Austria could establish a diplomatic corps and begin again to conduct foreign relations. In June, 1946, a new control plan was agreed to, under which Austrian laws (other than constitutional provisions) and international agreements (other than those with the four occupying powers) automatically went into effect thirty-one days after their passage, unless unanimously disapproved by the Allied Control Council. This plan did much to strengthen the Austrian government and prevented many one-power vetoes. It is true that this provision was not always observed. In July, 1946, for example, the Austrian government passed a far-reaching nationalization bill. The Soviet authorities refused to recognize the law in their zone, since it would have included some industries that they were claiming as German assets. As long as the law was not universally applied throughout Austria, the other powers also refused to recognize it for their zones.

The Austrian government was able to extend its administration over all Austria, although it ran into more hindrances in some zones than in others. While there were differences between the occupying powers, they did not approach in seriousness those which developed among the four powers in Germany. The Austrian government was always able to focus attention on Austria as a whole. Its efforts to win back southern Tyrol from Italy failed, but it played a part in rebuffing Yugoslavia's claims for frontier rectifications. It was also preliminary Austrian-Russian discussions that paved the way for the conclusion of the long delayed State Treaty on May 15, 1955 [see above, pp. 618–20]. Under this treaty Austria again became a sovereign, independent, democratic state, but was required to affirm her unceasing neutrality, which the powers promised to respect. To ensure this neutrality Austria undertook never to enter into any military alliances or permit the establishment of military bases on her territory by a foreign power. Austria was permitted to have its own army. Political or economic union between Germany and Austria was specifically forbidden. The ratifications were completed on July 27 and withdrawal of troops proceeded without delay. Austria could celebrate the opening of its rebuilt opera house with Beethoven's "Fidelio" on November 5, with no foreign troops on its soil.

Up to 1970 the postwar parliamentary elections resulted in a slight edge for the People's party over the Socialists, with a few seats going to minor groups. When the Communists withdrew their representative from the cabinet in 1947 as a protest against a currency measure, the succeeding governments until 1966 consisted of a coalition of the two major parties, leaders of both these parties wisely foregoing the possibility of governing through an alliance with a minor group. By agreement, the two parties shared in appointments to public office. The chancellors were regularly members of the People's party: Leopold Figl until 1953, Julius Raab, who represented a different wing of the party, until 1961, then Alfons Gorbach who was followed by Joseph Klaus in 1964. When the 1966 elections gave the People's party a clear majority over the Socialist and the Freedom parties combined, and agreement could not be reached with the Socialists, Chancellor Klaus formed a single-party cabinet. The next election on March 1, 1970, brought a reversal, the Socialists winning the most seats and Bruno Kreisky became the first postwar Socialist chancellor, heading a minority government. The Austrian president is elected for a six-year term by popular vote and in these elections the Socialists have regularly carried the day, as they also have in the city elections in Vienna.

Although the republic is firmly established and universally accepted, the Habsburgs are still a political issue. In 1962 the Supreme Administrative Court confirmed the legality of Archduke Otto's renunciation of membership in the imperial house of Habsburg-Lorraine and his declaration of loyalty to the Austrian republic. These were prerequisites for the end of his exile and return to Austria. While the People's party was inclined to go along with the court's ruling the Socialists raised a clamor. The issue became involved in a cabinet crisis, and by agreement between the two parties the decrees barring Otto from Austria remained in effect.

ECONOMIC DEVELOPMENT. After World War I it was necessary to rush to Vienna large food shipments and to supply international loans to revive the Austrian economy. The same was true after World War II. UNRRA furnished much aid, and the United States provided even more in outright gifts, amounting to about a billion and a half dollars by 1955. While the French and Russian occupying forces, at least in the first years, lived off the land, Britain and the United States supplied more than their own rations. The cost of the occupying armies was a heavy drain on the Austrian budget. On July 1, 1947, the United States government returned most of the payments it had received and agreed that henceforth the United States would pay its own occupation costs. Russia waived occupation costs in 1953, and Britain and France the following year. Since the Austrian economy had been so closely linked with Germany, serious repercussions were felt from events in that country. Inability to obtain replacement parts for broken-down machinery alone constituted a real problem. Rupture of trade relations with Southeastern Europe was also a serious handicap.

Three times since the war Austria has undertaken currency reforms, which went off in orderly fashion and helped to stabilize the economy. Austria participated in the Marshall Plan, and a good part of the funds was spent for the erection of dams and the expansion of heavy industry in the Western Zones. Although there were differences as to controls in the four zones and there was not always free movement between them, Austrian economy in general functioned as a unit. The conclusion of the State Treaty in 1955 restored to Austria control over its oil fields and provided for Austrian repurchase of the Danube Shipping Company. While the terms of the payment [see above, pp. 618–19] and the agreed deliveries of oil and other goods to Russia, over a period of ten years, constituted a heavy burden, they were so much more reasonable than previous demands that they were willingly accepted by Austria. In July, 1958, the USSR agreed to a 50 percent reduction of the seven million tons of oil still to be delivered, and in February, 1964, a formal statement confirmed the fact that Austria's obligations to the Soviet Union under the treaty had been fulfilled. The oil fields are administered by a semi-public corporation under government auspices, and Austria ranks fifth among Europe's oil producers. Hydroelectric power has been greatly expanded, notably by a series of dams on the Danube. An excellent network of superhighways is under construction. In general the economy flourishes. Austria has successfully integrated the refugees who remained there after the war and again after the Hungarian revolt of 1956 and the Czechoslovak crisis of 1968. It has even begun to recruit workers in nearby frontier countries.

FOREIGN AFFAIRS. Austria was one of the sixteen countries which were admitted to the United Nations on December 14, 1955, in the so-called package deal. Since then it has been a firm supporter of that organization and has served a term as one of the elected members of the Security Council. In 1960 and 1961 it brought the dispute with Italy over South Tyrol before the UN Assembly. This is an issue which lies close to the hearts of most Austrians and finally in the fall of 1969 preliminary agreement was reached with Italy on a solution to the problem [see above, pp. 767–68]. As a participant in the Council of Europe, the Organization for Economic Cooperation and Development (OECD), the General Agreement on Tariffs and Trade (GATT), and the European Free Trade Association (EFTA), Austria has undertaken a progressive lowering of tariffs. Over 50 percent of Austria's trade is with the Common Market countries, and it has sought unsuccessfully to join the European Economic Community. Beginning in 1960 Austria undertook a modest foreign aid program, much of it devoted to putting Austria's excellent scientific and educational facilities at the disposal of the underdeveloped countries.

Switzerland

POLITICS AND ECONOMY. During the war the activity and power of the federal government in Switzerland were rapidly expanded. Rationing, price control, and all the other things that go with the supervision of a nation's economy had to be done on a federal rather than on a cantonal level. With the end of hostilities Swiss opinion was divided on the question of whether these state controls should be retained. In 1947 a national referendum was held and a series of amendments to the constitution were approved, giving the federal government wide powers to control the nation's economy under certain conditions and for certain ends. At this time by a large majority the people approved an old-age security and insurance plan to be administered by the federal government. For a time the emergency taxing powers of the federal government were retained, but in 1953 they were returned to the cantons by referendum.

Postwar elections have shown no striking changes in party alignment, although the leftist parties have as everywhere gained a few seats. The Communist party, which had been banned in 1940, was permitted to participate in the 1947 elections and won 7 out of a total of 196 seats. In the next election the Communist seats were reduced to five, and subsequently to three or four. Communism has no great appeal to the Swiss and the party has no members in the second chamber, which represents the cantons. In the parliamentary elections held every four years Democrats, Radical Democrats, and Catholic Conservatives have consistently shown about equal strength, each securing approximately one quarter of the seats, the rest going to various small parties. In 1957–58 the Swiss chambers adopted proposals giving women the right to vote in federal elections, to be elected to the federal parliament, and to be appointed to the Supreme Federal Court. These proposals being a constitutional amendment were subject to a referendum in 1959, which failed to approve them, leaving Switzerland and tiny Liechtenstein the only countries in Europe where women do not vote. Women's suffrage in cantonal affairs is a matter for each canton to decide; so far nine cantons, Vaud, Neuchatel, Basel Stadt, Bern, Ticino, Valais, Lucerne, Zurich, and Geneva have adopted female suffrage. In addition, some cantons have made it optional for communes to permit women to vote in local affairs. In 1970 parliament again approved an amendment to the constitution which would give women the right to vote and run for office in national elections. It was submitted to a referendum in February, 1971, and was approved.

The government has negotiated trade pacts on liberal credit terms with most European countries and trades with countries on both sides of the Iron Curtain. Trade, however, is largely with the countries of the European Economic Community, especially West Germany, and Switzerland has applied for associate membership in that organization. So far negotiations have been unsuccessful. Over half the annual output of the country's chief industrial products—watches, chemicals, textiles, and machinery—are exported. The Swiss watch industry exports approximately 95 percent of its output, which accounts for approximately 16 percent of the total exports. Employment and prosperity have reached new heights, and the government has initiated some rather drastic measures to stop the inflationary trend. One method is to curb the number of foreign workers recruited by Swiss industry; these numbered over 816,000 in 1964. From 1965 to 1969 establishments with foreign workers were forced to cut their number by 17 percent. In March, 1970, a new restriction was imposed limiting the number of workers admitted each year to 40,000. Foreign workers are not allowed to bring their families to Switzerland until they have lived there at least ten years, and their children born in Switzerland are not granted Swiss citizenship. Counting the workers, their dependents, and the ever-present tourists and political exiles there must be about a million foreigners in a total population of slightly over six million. There are those who fear this large foreign element will somehow change the Swiss way of life. Two thirds of the workers come from Italy, many from Spain, both predominantly Catholic countries, and some see in this a danger of upsetting Switzerland's historical racial and religious balance. Yet it is not easy to see how Switzerland's industry could continue to prosper without this additional labor supply.

Foreign Affairs. In the spring of 1946 diplomatic relations, which had been suspended since 1919, were resumed with the USSR. Long and difficult negotiations took place between the Swiss and Allied governments over the return of German assets secreted in Swiss banks. The Swiss for a long time refused to meet the Allied demands, but finally agreed to turn over 50 percent of the Nazi funds to the Inter-Allied Reparation Agency for the rehabilitation of countries devastated by Germany. This agreement was mutually terminated in 1952, when Switzerland agreed to make a lump-sum payment of 121,500,000 Swiss francs in settlement of Allied claims. At the same time the West German government approved the settlement of Swiss claims against the former German Reich. Switzerland has not applied for membership in the United Nations but is a member of the International Court of Justice and most of the specialized agencies. In no way a "joiner," it was not until 1963 that Switzerland became a member of the Council of Europe. The Swiss government accepted the invitation to collaborate in the Marshall Plan with a reservation safeguarding her traditional neutrality, but did not actually receive any Marshall Plan funds. It regularly appropriates a substantial sum for aid to developing countries. In keeping with its strict neutrality, Switzerland has again become a place for important international conferences.

The Lowlands

Re-establishment of Governments. Belgium and Luxembourg were completely liberated in September, 1944, although sections of both were temporarily overrun in the Battle of the Bulge in December of that year. Most of Holland, however, remained in enemy hands until the very last. Luxembourg had been incorporated directly into Germany in 1942, but with liberation the government-in-exile returned and was able to take over direction of affairs without difficulty. In Belgium Prince Charles, the younger brother of the King, was made regent in 1944, as Leopold III was still held captive in Germany, and parliament for a time continued this arrangement after the war. Many Belgians objected to the King's capitulation in 1940, his subsequent marriage to a commoner, and his supposedly authoritarian leanings. Leopold's cause became involved in the Flemish question, since his wife was a Fleming and Flanders is the stronghold of the Catholic party, which supported him. The Flemish movement had gained in strength during the German occupation. The return of the King was an issue in the elections of 1949, at which women voted for the first time. The Catholic party made notable gains, and in a special referendum on March 12, 1950, 57.7 percent of the vote was cast in favor of Leopold's resuming the throne. On his return to Belgium on July 22, after six years of exile, the Socialist opposition became so virulent, threatening revolution, that Leopold agreed to retire at once and to abdicate in 1951 when his son Baudouin would become of age. This solution was accepted, and in August, 1950, Baudouin was invested with the royal power, formally ascending the throne the following year.

The re-establishment of the government in the Netherlands after the war was accomplished without undue political strife. Many collaborators were arrested, and the execution of two of them marks the first break since 1854 in Holland's abstention from capital punishment. After celebrating her fiftieth anniversary on the throne Queen Wilhelmina abdicated, and on September 6, 1948, her daughter Juliana took the oath as Queen of the Netherlands.

ECONOMY. By the time the Netherlands could start rebuilding, the economy of Belgium was functioning again and earning valuable foreign exchange through services to the Allied armies. Belgium was soon classed as the most prosperous of the states of Europe that had been at war. Recovery in Holland was slower, but by the end of 1945 all the flooded areas were drained, and a real beginning had been made on the rehabilitation of agriculture, the most important Dutch occupation. The revival of the German market benefited the Lowland countries, for Germany has always accounted for a large share of their exports and imports. In 1954 a forty-five-mile Amsterdam-Rhine canal under construction since 1931 was opened, cutting shipping time from the German border to Amsterdam to twenty hours. Both Belgium and Holland have pursued an aggressive policy of extension and modernization of their internal waterway system. In 1963 the two countries undertook to build a new canal joining the Scheldt and the Rhine shortening the water route to Antwerp by about twenty-five miles.

Granting independence to former Dutch colonies in the East Indies and to Belgian colonial territories in the Congo [see below, pp. 822, 853] necessitated many economic adjustments which have been successfully made. By a statute of December, 1954, the Netherlands and the two Caribbean territories of Netherlands Antilles (formerly Netherlands West Indies) and Surinam (formerly Netherlands Guiana) were constituted a single realm under the House of Orange. Each of the states have autonomy in domestic affairs, but defense and foreign affairs are decided by a Council of the Realm at The Hague in which the two overseas areas are represented by ministers plenipotentiary. It is a new attempt to solve the problem of colonialism along the lines of self-government.

Not only were the last colonial conflicts costly, but they involved heavy losses from investments. Returning colonials had to be absorbed into the economy at home. In Belgium an austerity program involving reduction in social insurance benefits and increased taxation brought a rash of strikes. To alleviate some of the grievances the government in December, 1963, passed a national insurance law that covered more than two thirds of the population. It set up a rate of standard fees for medical care and provided free treatment for invalids, orphans, and widows. The doctors maintained the fees were too low and that the entire law was the first step toward socialized medicine; they staged a remarkably effective eighteen-day strike. A compromise provided for higher fees without an increase in insurance charges, the deficit to be absorbed by the national budget.

In the Netherlands the discovery in 1961 of natural gas brought an important addition to the limited supply of natural resources. Subsequent drilling explorations indicate the presence of large supplies of gas and oil in coastal waters. The Dutch natural gas reserves are now considered to be second only to those of Texas; the Netherlands promise to become a chief supplier of energy for their European neighbors. In 1967 the Netherlands, Belgium, and West Germany agreed to build a $100 million fast-breeder nuclear reactor capable of generating 300 megawatts of electricity.

In a convention drawn up in London in 1944, the Dutch and Belgian governments agreed to adopt a common customs policy after the war. In 1946 a council was established to integrate the tariff systems, a difficult task since the Belgian and Luxembourg tariffs were relatively high and specific, while the Dutch rates were low and levied on an ad-valorem basis. A compromise was reached which had the effect of substantially increasing Dutch rates. This agreement was the basis of the Benelux Union of Belgium, the Netherlands, and Luxembourg, which went into effect on January 1, 1948. While it provided a common tariff against outside states, it did not bring free internal trade. Varying excise taxes remained which were collected when goods passed from one country to another. Salt, for example, bore an excise in Holland but not in Belgium, and the reverse was true of matches and vinegar. Complete economic union, originally planned for 1950, was not then achieved, due primarily to wage differences and agricultural costs, but economic integration constantly increased in the fifties. On

February 3, 1958, a series of agreements establishing the Benelux Economic Union were signed. The treaties, which went into effect November 1, 1960, and are to run for fifty years, consolidated the arrangements that had gradually been achieved. These freed all trade between the countries from tariffs and liberated about 97 percent of it from restrictions on volume, brought reduction on tax differences and a common trade and payments policy toward other nations, and established a single labor market with free movement of workers. Negotiations for trade agreements with other countries now take place on a joint Benelux basis. The agreements are administered by a committee of ministers, which makes major decisions that are then referred to their respective national parliaments for ratification and by an Inter-Parliamentary Advisory Council (20 representatives each from Belgium and the Netherlands, 9 from Luxembourg) with the aid of a secretariat-general. Benelux economy has been greatly benefited by the establishment of the Common Market.

While the original Benelux Agreement was purely an economic one, the three states have tended to carry their co-operation over into the political field. This was evident in the negotiation of the Brussels Pact (1948) leading to the Western European Union (1955), and by their participation in the Organization for European Economic Cooperation (OEEC, 1948), the Council of Europe (1948), the North Atlantic Treaty Organization (NATO, 1949), the European Coal and Steel Community (ECSC, 1952), the European Economic Community (Common Market, 1958), and the European Atomic Energy Community (Euratom, 1958). When De Gaulle forced the withdrawal of Supreme Headquarters of the Allied Powers Europe (SHAPE) from France in 1967 it was shifted to Castreau, Belgium, and the Headquarters of NATO to Brussels. On questions of foreign policy the Benelux states tend to follow a common line.

POLITICAL DEVELOPMENT. In all three countries the first postwar elections indicated the increase in strength of the Catholic parties. Unable to command a clear majority, they were forced to co-operate with other parties, frequently with the Socialists. In the Netherlands there are numerous minor parties to offset the ideological clash between Clericals and Socialists. The Dutch Catholic Church has been at the forefront of the movement to modernize the Catholic Church [see above, p. 776] and politically as well has been by no means conservative. In Belgium, however, party lines are more sharply drawn. Here three great political issues clouded the scene. One was the question of Leopold III's return, which aroused much strife before it was settled. The second was the old problem of state subsidies for Catholic-controlled schools. These grants were increased when pro-Catholic cabinets were in power; but under a Socialist-Liberal cabinet in 1955, in an effort to strengthen state schools, a substantial reduction in state subsidies to Catholic schools was undertaken. This caused serious unrest and led to mass protest demonstrations. When the three major parties— Christian Socialists, Socialists, and Liberals—finally reached an agreement, parliament passed an education law in May, 1959, which has allayed the controversy. A special fund was created to overcome the shortage of state schools; these would be established if a sufficient number of parents in a district requested one. Church schools would be given the same subsidies as public schools, and parents would be free to choose which type of school their children should attend. Fees for secondary education were also abolished.

Like the second, the third great political issue in Belgium was of long standing. This was the conflict between the Flemings and Walloons, and it has many facets. The coal industry, the mainstay in the economy of the Walloon sections, has become obsolete, and the newer industries have shifted to the Flemish sections. The balance between the two groups has been affected by the higher birthrate among the Flemings, who now outnumber the Walloons by a 5:3 ratio. Politically Flanders constitutes the stronghold of the Christian Socialists, while the Socialists and Liberals are strongest in the less clerically-minded Walloon areas. As so often happens, nationality conflicts come to center on linguistic differences. A law of 1932 required the exclusive use of the predominant language in each community. To determine which language predominated was not easy and traditional practices were continued, which usually gave an advantage to French. Under pressure the government drew a dividing line in 1962 (revised in 1963) which provided for the administrative division of the country into unilingual Flemish and Walloon regions, reserving greater Brussels as a bilingual enclave. This meant doing away with former bilingual administrative and educational systems in many localities. Further laws provided for a completely bilingual state administration, extending even to the diplomatic service. Feeling ran high on all these measures and there were many public demonstrations. The Catholic University of Louvain is located just inside the Flemish linguistic border and beginning in 1965 the Flemings demanded that it become an entirely Flemish teaching institution. There were serious riots and the Bishops divided along nationality lines in an unsuccessful attempt to find a way out. This led ultimately to a government crisis in 1968, and further measures to ensure absolute parity between Flemings and Walloons in all spheres of national life resulted. Henceforth there are to be dual ministers for education, culture, and community relations. The Bishops made a strategic retreat and announced plans for a new French language university at Ottignies in Wallonia and the transfer of the French language medical faculty from Louvain to Brussels. Extremists in both groups called for the establishment of a Federated Belgium made up of Flanders (Flemish speaking), Wallonia (French speaking), and Brussels (bilingual). So far this has not been done and Belgium with all its divisive influences remains a centralized state.

Ireland

SEVERANCE FROM BRITAIN. Ireland was the only dominion of the British Commonwealth which was able to preserve its neutrality during World

War II. This meant she was not classed as one of the peace-loving states and hence was not one of the charter members of the United Nations. It was not until 1955 that she achieved membership under the so-called package deal when sixteen states were admitted at once. Since then Ireland has taken an active part in UN affairs and has furnished contingents to some of the peace-keeping forces.

In November, 1948, the parliament of Eire repealed the "External Relations Act" and broke the last legal ties connecting that country with Britain. In commemoration of the Easter Rebellion of 1916 this act went into effect on Easter Monday, April 18, 1949. With it the name of Eire was officially changed to the Republic of Ireland and Ireland ceased to be a member of the Commonwealth. Every effort was made to persuade Ulster to join with Ireland, but elections since held in the northern counties show unmistakably that the majority of these people prefer to remain a part of the United Kingdom. The government in London recognized Ireland as no longer belonging to the King's Dominions. It however refused to class it as a foreign state and relations with the republic are handled by the Secretary for Commonwealth Affairs, not by the Foreign Minister. The new British nationality act which went into effect on January 1, 1949, created three types of citizens: United Kingdom citizens, Commonwealth citizens, and Irish citizens. In general the act provided that the three categories of citizens will enjoy equal rights and privileges in the United Kingdom, rights not enjoyed by citizens of any other countries. Citizens of the Irish Republic, for example, if they live in a British constituency, are entitled to be included in the registry of electors and can vote. Whatever they will be, it is quite clear that the Irish are not yet considered foreigners in Britain, although there can be no doubt how the Irish of the republic consider themselves. The economies of the two countries remain closely linked, and the English pound circulates freely alongside Irish currency within Ireland. When Britain devalued the pound in 1967, Ireland immediately took similar action. On July 1, 1966, a free trade agreement between Ireland and Britain went into effect under which import duties in both countries will be gradually reduced until such duties are abolished by 1975. Ireland is economically quite dependent on Britain which in 1969 accounted for 65 percent of Ireland's exports and 53 percent of her imports. In addition to trade ties, Ireland and Great Britain concluded (1961) a reciprocal social security agreement. When Britain applied for membership in the Common Market Ireland followed suit, but both suffered a French veto.

RELATIONS WITH ULSTER. In 1959 Eamon de Valera, who held the office of prime minister six times, decided to give up his post and run for the presidency, an office he easily won and an honor he richly deserved. He was re-elected in 1966. Relations with North Ireland gradually improved. The Irish Republican Army, which had sought to force unity through a policy of terrorism, in February, 1962, announced the end of its campaign. It was estimated that in the previous five years it had caused damage of

$14 million and had been responsible for the death of six North Irish policemen. For the first time since partition the prime ministers of Ireland and Ulster held a conference in January, 1965, and similar meetings have taken place in subsequent years. In spite of more contacts between the two countries and more cooperation on the governmental level, antagonism between the Irish of the Republic and the Irish of Ulster continues to flare up. Within Ulster itself the general unrest of the late 1960s has produced violent confrontations between Catholics and Protestants. Serious rioting occurred in Ulster in October, 1968, and with increasing violence through 1971. The Catholics, a minority in Ulster, charge that they are discriminated against by the Protestant dominated government. The riots got out of hand, and British troops were called in to re-establish order. The Republic of Ireland did not hide its sympathy for the Ulster Catholics and called on the UN for intervention. This was vetoed by both the governments of Belfast and London on the ground that the disturbances were clearly an internal affair and therefore not subject to UN consideration. The uneasy situation continues; there is no sign at present that Ulster desires a federation, let alone a merger with the republic.

The Scandinavian States

The effects of the war were not by any means the same in the various Scandinavian states. While Sweden benefited from its neutrality, its great contributions to the relief of distress in Finland and in the rest of Europe should be noted. It granted asylum to many political refugees and helped in many ways to preserve the liberal tradition in time of war. The end of the conflict found many displaced persons in Norway and Denmark. As the Russian armies advanced, over a quarter-million Germans fled to Denmark, and it was not until 1948 that all of these had been returned to Germany. Denmark was the least disturbed of any of the occupied states, although the establishment of Iceland as an independent republic in 1944 was in part the result of wartime events. After the war some Danes raised a claim to South Schleswig, but the government never took this position. Denmark and Norway were original members of the United Nations, and Sweden and Iceland were admitted in 1946. Norway and Denmark sent contingents to serve in the British occupation zone of Germany.

POLITICAL SCENE. Only the Norwegian government was in exile during the war, and it promised from the very beginning to resign immediately on its return to Norway. A new cabinet consisting partly of old officials and partly of resistance leaders was formed without a political crisis. In both Denmark and Norway collaborators were arrested by the thousands, and the leaders, among them the notorious Norwegian Quisling, were executed. Elections in all these states showed a remarkable continuation of the prewar pattern. The Communist party, whose influence was at its height in the immediate postwar elections when it polled about 10 percent of the vote, has since declined. The Social Democrats, except for brief interludes, have consistently headed the governments. In Norway, the

Labor party dominated for thirty years, but in 1965 was defeated by a coalition of four Conservative and Liberal parties. Here as in most other countries the Socialists no longer proclaim their adherence to the Marx-Engels ideology, and have adopted a gradualist-reformist attitude. Agrarian parties are also strong, and most cabinets have represented a Socialist-Agrarian coalition. In all three countries monarchy remains an accepted and popular institution. On April 21, 1947, Frederick IX succeeded his father as king of Denmark. Denmark accepted a new constitution in 1953 which introduced a unicameral legislature (Folketing) and provided for direct representation in that body from Greenland and the Faeroe Islands. The voting age was reduced from twenty-five to twenty-three, and female succession to the throne was recognized. In 1952 Norway passed an important electoral reform bill rectifying the overrepresentation of rural districts. After a reign of fifty-two years Haakon VII died in 1957, and Olav V became the second king of Norway's modern era. Venerable Gustav V of Sweden died at the age of ninety-two in 1950 and was succeeded by his son Gustav VI Adolf. In 1970–71 a major constitutional reform was inaugurated in Sweden when the bicameral system was replaced by a 350-member unicameral parliament elected for a three-year term. Like Germany, Sweden has adopted measures to curb splinter parties which often result from proportional representation. A party henceforth must receive at least 4 percent of the total votes cast, or obtain at least 12 percent in any one of the country's 28 constituencies in order to gain parliamentary representation. In the first election under the new system, held in September, 1970, the Social Democrats lost their clear majority, winning 163 seats to 170 for the right-center parties and 17 for the Communists. Social Democratic Premier Olof Palme, however, continued in power as the head of a minority government with the tacit support of the Communists.

ECONOMIC DEVELOPMENTS. The economy of Denmark was not greatly disrupted by the war. Not more than a third of her merchant fleet was lost, as compared to Norway's loss of nearly one half. Sweden, too, lost much shipping, but her industry and agriculture as a whole prospered during the war years. The collapse of the German market, which before the war took 17 percent of Sweden's exports and furnished 22 percent of her imports, was a serious blow and necessitated a revision of trade channels in the immediate postwar years. The three Scandinavian states, and Iceland as well, joined in the Marshall Plan.

No radical departures have been made in postwar legislation. A mixed economy, with government ownership or control dominating the utility and public service industries, continues to be the rule in all these states. To help pay for imports through shipping services Norway has rebuilt her merchant fleet so that it ranks third in the world as compared to fourth before the war. In 1952 the Norwegian government launched a ten-year economic development plan for northern Norway. The development of water power in this region is keyed to the rich ore deposits in neighboring Sweden. All the states have become more industrialized and agriculture has suffered a relative decline. The number of farms is steadily diminishing as more mechanization takes place. Today only some 20 to 26 percent of the Scandinavian population are fully employed in agriculture. Agricultural exports in the form of dairy products are most important in Denmark.

At meetings of the foreign ministers of Denmark, Iceland, Norway, and Sweden in 1947 and 1948 it was decided to set up a Committee on Economic Cooperation with a permanent secretariat. This committee was to investigate the possibilities of establishing a common tariff schedule, reduction of inter-Scandinavian customs duties, limitation of quantitative trade restrictions, and in general an increase in economic co-operation among the Scandinavian states. In 1952 a consultative Nordic Council was founded made up of representatives from the above four states. Finland was invited to join, but did not participate until December, 1955, when Russia no longer objected to Finnish co-operation in the Council. Attended by cabinet and parliament representatives, the Council has discussed and planned a wide variety of measures envisaging greater co-operation among the northern powers.

In October, 1957, the Committee on Economic Cooperation submitted a detailed report to the governments outlining a draft convention for a customs union. The plan for a Scandinavian tariff union was superseded by the conclusion of the European Free Trade Association (EFTA, Outer Seven) in 1960, in which the three Scandinavian states were joined by Austria, Britain, Portugal, and Switzerland. Finland joined with the group in 1961. Norway and Denmark, following Britain's lead, subsequently sought membership in the European Economic Community (Common Market), but when France vetoed the British request, this also affected applications by other EFTA states. Sweden, always more concerned to preserve its strict neutrality because of its proximity to Russia and Finland, held aloof from direct ties with EEC until July 28, 1967 when it made inquiry about associate membership. The negotiations of all three Scandinavian states with the Common Market proved abortive, and on January 15, 1969, the governments of Denmark, Norway, Sweden, and Finland released plans for the economic integration of the four countries into a Nordic Economic Union. This still remains (1970) in the negotiation stage, as does the renewed application of the three Scandinavian states for membership in the Common Market.

SOCIAL LEGISLATION. Social-insurance legislation has been regularly extended in all the Scandinavian countries. In 1954 agreements were reached between Denmark, Norway, and Sweden, covering the principal fields of social security, which enabled workers to go from country to country without losing their benefits. This, along with the abolition of earlier work permits, did much to establish a common labor market. Iceland and Finland joined in this movement for labor co-operation on a more limited scale. In Denmark government-subsidized health-insurance programs cover about 80 percent of the population on a voluntary basis. The obligatory health-insurance program was expanded in Norway in 1956 to cover all Norwegians. On January 1, 1955, a broad universal health-insurance plan went into effect in Sweden. An extension of older programs, it is financed by premiums paid by the insured (44 percent), contributions from employers (29 percent) and from the state (27 percent). By another law the famous Bratt liquor-rationing system was ended on October 1, 1955. The state retains the monopoly of all sales of spirits, wines, and strong beers. Consumption is discouraged by imposing high taxes; for example, taxes make up 89 percent of the price of a bottle of aquavit. Restaurants can dispense spirits only under a strict licensing system and driving under the influence of liquor is heavily penalized. The government also sponsors an active temperance program. Serious differences arose in Sweden in the fall of 1957 over whether an additional old-age pension plan should be obligatory or voluntary. This dispute led to a cabinet crisis, and in a referendum the compulsory plan advocated by the Socialists won over the voluntary plans advocated by the Agrarians and Liberals. Under the Socialist scheme, enacted into law in 1959, a pensioner's income at the age of 67 equals 65 percent of his average salary during the fifteen best working years prior to retirement. Old-age pensions have also been increased in Norway and Denmark.

The Swedish film industry has prospered and led the way in the production of avant-garde films. In Denmark the laws restricting publishing and sale of all sex literature, including admittedly pornographic material, have been repealed, although there are still some restrictions limiting sale to adults. A lively export trade has developed in these items. On October 3, 1967, Sweden aligned itself with the rest of Europe (only Great Britain and Ireland remain the exception) by instituting right-hand driving on its streets and highways. The innovation was undertaken in an effort to cut down the number of accidents, notably along the Norwegian-Swedish border, resulting from the increase in tourist traffic.

RELIGION. Religious liberty exists in fact as well as in law, although the Lutheran Church continues to be the established church. In 1949 Sweden liberalized its laws so as to place other religious bodies on a standing equal to that of the established church. The Catholic Church is headed by a Vicar Apostolic in Denmark and Sweden and since 1953 by a Bishop in Norway. Religion is a regular subject of instruction in the schools.

FOREIGN AFFAIRS. Attempts to negotiate a Scandinavian defense pact collapsed in the spring of 1949, since the negotiations touched upon the defense plans of the Western powers. Sweden, which has not been at war since the French Revolutionary era, preferred to adhere to her traditional neutrality. To have reversed this policy would almost certainly have brought greater Russian pressure on Finland, which the Swedes wished to avoid. Norway, having been confronted with the delicate task of refusing a Russian pact of mutual assistance, found no alternative but to cast in

her lot with the Western powers in the Atlantic Pact, as did Denmark and
Iceland. Denmark has one of the finest airfields in Europe at Karup, Jutland, but so far, like Norway, has refused to permit the permanent stationing of Allied NATO forces on its soil. On the other hand, by a twenty-
year treaty in 1951 the United States obtained air and naval bases in
Greenland which will be used by other NATO powers as well. Denmark
in 1956 re-established normal trade relations with Russia—the last of the
northern states to do so. Minor disputes have arisen with Russia, and the
various states have always sought to follow a correct, but nevertheless
independent, policy toward their powerful neighbor.

The Nordic Council, an excellent example of a regional group within
the United Nations, although engaged largely in furthering economic and
social co-operation among its members, at times does devote its attention
to broader international affairs. Thus in 1954 a resolution was adopted
advocating the admission of Red China to the United Nations. Norway
as second-largest user of the Suez Canal was greatly affected by the Suez
Crisis of 1956. She co-operated in the peaceful solution of this problem
and furnished substantial contingents for the United Nations forces which
took over this area. After the closing of the Suez Canal resulting from the
Israeli-Arab War of June, 1967, Norwegian ship owners immediately placed
orders for large super-tankers to share in the profitable oil route around
the Cape of Good Hope. The Scandinavian countries have consistently
supported United Nations efforts to further peace, and Sweden has furnished contingents for the peace-keeping operations in the Congo and
in Cyprus. United States policy in Vietnam has come under severe
criticism in all three countries, but particularly so in Sweden. Sweden has
granted asylum to numerous defectors from the United States armed
forces and on January 10, 1968, granted official recognition to North Vietnam.

Finland

Finland fought the war as a bitter enemy of Russia, and after the war
was burdened by heavy reparations and by a vigorous Communist party, yet
it managed to maintain both a neutral policy in foreign affairs and political
democracy at home. The relative freedom of action retained by Finland,
at a time when the Baltic states were reincorporated into Russia and all
the states of Eastern Europe except Yugoslavia came under tight Soviet
control, may be explained by two factors. One of these was the desire of
the Soviet government to retain the neutrality of Sweden. Soviet annexation of Finland would probably have driven Sweden into the arms of
the West, and this Russia wished to avoid. Moreover, the cost to Russia
was not high, as Finland did not represent a route of invasion and it could,
in any case, be occupied in the event of a crisis. The second factor that
accounts for Finnish freedom is the vigor with which the traditional leaders
of the country have resisted attempts at Communist infiltration. Ever
since the civil strife following World War I and the struggles of World

War II, Finland's rulers have had a realistic view of communism, and the Russians, in turn, have had a healthy respect for the determination of the Finns.

Finland's postwar relations with Russia were founded on the armistice terms and the peace treaty, which were severe but not unbearable [see above, pp. 609–10]. The armistice terms provided, among other things, for the trial of war criminals, and early in 1946 eight prominent wartime cabinet ministers were given prison sentences of from two to ten years. They were released well before the end of their sentences, however, and the whole procedure was characteristic of the independent spirit of the Finns. Similarly, when in 1948 the Soviet government invited Finland to negotiate a ten-year treaty of friendship and mutual assistance, the Finns were able to obtain terms confirming their sovereign rights. Unlike Russia's treaties with the other states of Eastern Europe, this treaty explicitly recognizes Finland's neutral position. Military co-operation is provided for only in case of an attack by Germany or a state allied with Germany, and the two states must confer before the treaty goes into operation.

POLITICAL DEVELOPMENT. Finland thus stands outside the Soviet alliance system, and is not a member of the Warsaw Pact [see above, pp. 633–34]. In 1955, during the period of relaxation in Soviet-Western relations in which the Austrian treaty was concluded and the summit conference was held at Geneva, the Soviet government terminated its fifty-year lease of the naval base at Porkkala-Udd, and the treaty of mutual assistance was extended for another twenty years. A year later the Karelo-Finnish SSR, one of the sixteen constituent republics of the USSR, was demoted to the status of an autonomous republic of the RSFSR. This republic, bordering on Finland and including territories annexed from that country in 1940, was inhabited largely by Finns. It was created in 1940 under circumstances that led most observers to conclude that it was designed to serve as a base for annexing the whole of Finland, or at least as an ominous reminder to the Finnish government. Its dissolution consequently seemed to signify a further relaxation of pressure on Finland. Otto Kuusinen, the veteran Finnish Communist leader who had headed the Karelo-Finnish SSR from the start, was now given an honorary position on the Presidium of the Communist party of the Soviet Union which he occupied until his death in 1964. This new relaxation of Soviet-Finnish tension also permitted Finland to join the Nordic Council, created in 1952 to promote closer social and economic relations among the Scandinavian states. At the same time, Finland gained admission to the United Nations, after a ten-year deadlock resulting from East-West difficulties.

In domestic politics, the struggle with communism was, on the whole, more strenuous than in the realm of foreign relations. Since the war the Communists have joined with other left-wing groups to form the Democratic Union, and in the election of March, 1945, this party won a quarter of the seats in the Diet. On the basis of this electoral strength the Communists played a prominent role for three years in a coalition cabinet with

Social Democrats and Agrarians, and worked hard to gain control of the key ministry of interior. In this they failed, due to the astuteness and vigor of the rival parties, and when the electoral strength of the Democratic Union fell to 19 percent in 1948 it was dropped from the cabinet. In the following year widespread Communist led strikes almost succeeded in paralyzing the government, but in the end they also failed. During this period the Soviet government refrained from giving the Finnish Communists overt material support, and the latter did not have sufficient domestic strength to obtain their objectives. For practical purposes, the Social Democrats and the Agrarians shared political power throughout the postwar period, although they represented rival interests within the country. Juho Paasikivi, the veteran nonparty leader, served as President from 1946 to 1956, when he was succeeded by Urho Kekkonen, the leader of the Agrarians. The Communist-led Democratic Union retained close to 20 percent of the vote in the decade after 1948, but when its strength rose to 23 percent in 1958 the delicate balance between the Agrarians and the Social Democrats was upset. Kekkonen was now able to form a predominantly Agrarian government with Communist support in parliament, and the Soviet government was quick to take advantage of its new opportunity. In 1958–59 and again in 1961–62 the USSR brought great pressure to bear on Finland by means of demands and threats, and in effect agreed to favor Kekkonen's government in return for economic concessions as well as his assurance that political leaders unfriendly to the USSR would not receive government positions. This ominous development in Finnish-Soviet relations resulted in part from the adroit use by the USSR of political divisions within the country, and in part from Kekkonen's personal conviction that Finland could not count on West European support and must learn to get along with the USSR at any cost. The elections of 1962 and 1968 renewed Kekkonen's term of office as president and continued the predominance of centrist and leftist parties on which his policy was based. A major split within the Communist party between moderates and neo-Stalinists in the late 1960s, however, tended to weaken the role of the party in the coalition.

ECONOMY. Throughout the postwar years Finland labored under a heavy economic burden. The delivery of materials for war reparations to Russia, reduced by Moscow in 1948, was completed in 1952. These payments approximately equaled in value the budget of the Finnish government for one year. In addition, there was extensive war destruction to be repaired, not the least of which was caused by the retreating German troops. More difficult was the resettlement of some 56,000 families from territories ceded to the USSR. The government took full responsibility for this operation, and found a place for all by subdividing existing land holdings and opening up new lands. During the 1950s, as much as one third of the gross national product of Finland was reinvested each year in permanent agricultural and industrial installations. While this placed a great burden on the Finnish people, and no doubt accounts for some of the social unrest, the rapid investment resulted in a significant growth of the Finnish economy. Many industries, such as shipbuilding, expanded rapidly, and the pace of industrialization was reflected in the growth of the urban population from one third in 1950 to one half in 1970. As a member of the Nordic Council and an associate member of the European Free Trade Association, Finland more than doubled its foreign trade in the 1950s and 1960s, with the USSR accounting for about 15 percent of its imports and exports. The development of Finland in the quarter of a century since the war was admired by other countries as evidence of the independence and moderation of the Finnish people.

The Iberian States

The economy of Spain and Portugal as neutral states was closely linked with that of the Axis during the war years, although they also traded with the Western powers. The rupture of these former Axis connections, the unprecedented drought in the early postwar years, and the reluctance of some states to return to normal trade relations caused a severe economic crisis. Spain, which formerly exported food, was forced to buy high-priced Argentinian wheat under a credit arrangement that helped the Franco regime to survive. In 1948 France opened the frontier to trade with Spain, and Spanish trade, notably with Britain, also increased. Portugal's trade relations were more favorable, but it remains basically a poverty-stricken state. In both Spain and Portugal the population is increasing rapidly, which only complicates the problem of raising the standard of living through more equal distribution of wealth. In Spain about 13 percent and in Portugal about 38 percent of the people are illiterate.

SPAIN. At the first meeting of the United Nations in San Francisco, this body voted to bar the Franco regime in Spain permanently from membership. At the Potsdam Conference a special communiqué denouncing Franco was issued. In 1946 the Assembly of the United Nations passed a resolution requesting all member states to withdraw their diplomatic representatives from Madrid. But in 1948 an active bloc, led by South American states, appeared in the Assembly, urging that Spain be admitted to the United Nations. Thus, as the lines of the anti-Communist conflict became more sharply drawn, the hostility to the dictatorial Spanish regime lessened. Russia, alone of the great powers, consistently maintained her anti-Franco policy, but Spain was able to squeeze into the United Nations under the package admission deal of 1955. Spain was not admitted to the Marshall Plan nor was she asked to join the Atlantic Pact. In September, 1953, the United States, with the somewhat reluctant confirmation of Britain and France, negotiated a mutual-aid agreement with Spain. It was a real feather in Franco's cap. Under this agreement the United States furnished Spain military and economic aid, and in return was granted joint use of military and naval bases in Spain. Five air bases (one naval), radar sites, supply and ammunition depots, and a 485-mile oil pipeline were

built. The treaty was to run for ten years with the possibility of renewal
for two five-year periods. At the last moment it was renewed for five years
in 1963 and again in 1969. At the expiration of the treaty the bases will
revert to Spain. These huge expenditures, along with additional United
States economic aid, have done much to bolster the economy of Franco's
regime.

The United States policy toward Spain also contributed greatly to
Spain's decreasing isolation in international affairs. In 1958 Spain joined
the International Monetary Fund, the International Bank for Reconstruction, and the Organization for European Economic Cooperation. Spain
would like to become a member of NATO but has never been admitted.
Her application for associate membership in the European Economic
Community was turned down, along with all the other states that sought
ties with that organization. Spain negotiated its first direct trade agreement with the Soviet Union in 1966 and has slowly extended its trade and
cultural ties with other East European countries. Spain and Portugal have
drawn closer together, the dictatorial leaders of the two countries finding it
rather easy to collaborate.

Tangier, which Spain had occupied in 1940, was again put under international control in 1945, when Spanish troops were forced to withdraw.
This city, as well as Northern Spanish Morocco, was transferred to the
sovereignty of the Kingdom of Morocco in April, 1956, after that state had
achieved its independence from France. Ceuta and Mellila, both ancient
Spanish coastal enclaves in North Africa governed as parts of Spanish
provinces, were not affected by the transfer. Subsequently clashes occurred
between a self-styled irregular "Liberation Army of the Moroccan Sahara"
and Spanish troops in the Spanish colonies along the West African coast.
In April, 1958, Spanish South Morocco—a desert region of some 10,000
square miles—was transferred to Moroccan jurisdiction. The same year
Spanish West Africa was divided into the province of Ifni, a small enclave
valuable as a port for Spanish fishermen, and the province of Spanish
Sahara (Rio de Oro and Saguiet el Hamra). These regions were also
claimed by Moroccan nationalists. On January 4, 1969, Spain handed
back the 740-square mile enclave of Ifni to Morocco, thus ending its
thirty-four-year occupation of this territory. A special convention guaranteed Spain reciprocal fishing rights in the territorial waters. Spain also
controlled Spanish Guinea which consisted of the two provinces of Rio
Muni and Fernando Po. Known as Equatorial Guinea since 1963, the
colony was granted its independence on October 12, 1968, ending 104
years of Spanish rule [see below, p. 856]. Repeated restrictive measures
levied against Gibraltar in the late 1960s have failed to bring Britain's
surrender of this bastion to Spain.

In spite of early postwar opposition, General Franco has been able
to maintain his rule without any serious changes. A law of 1947 abolished
the republic, and Spain became a monarchy; at the same time Franco
was assured life tenure as Chief of State. This was confirmed in a new

constitution which was approved in a national referendum in December, 1966. Hailed as introducing a more liberal regime, the constitution actually changed little. About one fourth of the members of the Cortes were now to be elected directly, and married women were given the right to vote. However, no political parties were recognized as legal institutions by the constitution, and the people had little more than the liberty of approving the government sponsored lists. In July, 1969, amid great fanfare Franco designated Prince Juan Carlos of Bourbon, the grandson of Alfonso XIII (abdicated 1931), as his successor as chief of state. He was accorded the title of Prince of Spain and Royal Highness and will be known as such until he becomes king on the death or incapacitation of Franco. Prince Juan is married to Princess Sophie of Greece.

Spain remains at present a Fascist state, with all that designation implies in regard to civil liberties. Occasional student riots, increasing in number and virulence since 1966, a large number of labor strikes, and, more recently, even some critical articles in the clerical press, indicate that dissatisfaction exists. A concordat was concluded with the Vatican in 1953 recognizing Roman Catholicism as "the only religion of the Spanish Peoples" and providing for the nomination of bishops by the Spanish government. The state appropriates money for the Catholic Church, and the church exercises a controlling hand over Spanish schools. The Spanish church remains in the hands of a conservative hierarchy, but there is a growing split between liberal and conservative forces in the church. Many priests, as well as some bishops, are siding with the students and workers in their strikes for reform. The provision of the concordat which gives the government a deciding voice in the nomination of bishops is also under attack by the progressive churchmen. In this protest they are supported by the Vatican, which has at various times indicated its desire to update the church in Spain.

Over 99 percent of the population is Roman Catholic; Protestants are usually held to number around 30,000 and Jews 5,000. The minority religions, a minuscule group in a population of about 32 million, suffer under many legal as well as extra-legal discriminations. For years their places of worship could not be marked, they were not allowed to hold public processions or services of any kind, they had no legal status as corporate bodies, marriages celebrated by their clergy were not recognized by the state, they could not have their own schools or publications, and they were discriminated against in all public service appointments. In 1955 a Spanish court did rule that civil marriage between a baptized Catholic and a Protestant (mixed marriage) could be contracted, although the decision was not free from qualifications. A gradual relaxation of restrictions became discernible in the early 1960s. In 1963 the British and Foreign Bible Society was allowed to resume activities. General Franco surprised everyone in January, 1965, by stating in a speech to the nation that he favored "the exercise of freedom of conscience." A law to implement this more liberal policy, drastically revised under the influence of the hierarchy, was

finally passed by the Cortes in June, 1967. It still does not bring equality
or liberty to Spain's religious minorities. Especially objectionable to them
is the provision that they must solicit the approval of the Ministry of
Justice and register with the government as a religious association. This
gives the government the power to demand a list of the members of the
association as well as a statement of its financial accounts. The minorities
remain restricted in their right to establish educational, cultural, charitable, and social associations. Yet on December 16, 1968, the 462-year-old
ban of Jews in Spain was ceremoniously lifted on the occasion of the
opening of the first new synagogue in Spain in 600 years.

In Spain a new political force has come to the fore as the Falange
(which was merged with the National Movement, the only legally constituted political organization) has declined in power and position. This
is the Sacerdotal Society of the Holy Cross and *Opus Dei* (Work of God)
which was founded in Spain by Msgr. José Maria Escrivà de Balaguer y
Albás in 1928. This is an association of Roman Catholic laymen and
priests whose purpose is to bring religious practice into its members' daily
life and particularly into their daily work. The association gained no real
foothold until after the end of the Spanish Civil War and World War II.
On February 23, 1947, the Vatican formally approved it as the first
secular institute to be authorized to operate throughout the world. It
now (1970) claims a membership of around 50,000 in 73 countries with
20,000 in Spain alone. It comprises both celibate and married members,
many of them highly educated and very dedicated men. The members
meet, usually in small groups, for religious retreats, lectures, and discussions. Each member is assigned a lay director in addition to his con-
fessor, who keeps watch on his spiritual life and counsels him on how to
improve it. Although the core membership is not large, they have a
wide circle of adherents in Spain, estimated at between 100,000 to 200,-
000 "cooperators," who make regular financial contributions and participate
in some of the movement's religious activities. In keeping with its aim of
helping Christians to be better persons, *Opus Dei* has established a considerable number of educational, social, sport, and recreational centers.
Its members have infiltrated and gained a leading role in a large part of
Spain's banking, insurance, construction, and communication industries.
In the cabinet shifts at the end of October, 1969, *Opus Dei* members
virtually achieved complete domination of the government. The political
activity of the movement has aroused controversy, for it is obviously another avenue of asserting church influence in Spain.

PORTUGAL. In Portugal after World War II Salazar as premier retained his firm grip on affairs, and his party consistently won all elections.
Opposition to the regime persisted as was evidenced by constantly recurring arrests of persons charged with "activity threatening the security of
the government." In the 1958 presidential elections an opposition candidate, campaigning under great handicaps, received 20 percent of the vote.
This was a rather disturbing expression of opinion, and shortly after the

election, in a televised speech, Salazar announced that the presidential popular elections might not be held in the future, because "it is not convenient to have an opposition party." True to his word the constitution was amended in 1959, providing that henceforth the president should be chosen by an electoral college made up of the National Assembly, the appointive Corporative Chamber, and representatives from the municipalities and overseas legislative councils. While antigovernment demonstrations continually occurred, they were not permitted to get out of hand; Portugal remained a dictatorial state.

In spite of his authoritarian government Salazar was generally accepted by the Western states, and Portugal would have been admitted to the United Nations long before 1955 had it not been for the Russian veto. Portugal participated in the Marshall Plan, is a member of NATO, and belongs to the European Free Trade Association (Outer Seven). During the war the United States and Britain made use of the Portuguese Azores as an air base, and postwar negotiations have extended some of these privileges. There are also two large air bases in Portugal used primarily by British and American forces. The old Portuguese-British alliance still continues and has played its part in establishing Portugal's postwar international position.

Portugal has undertaken a number of six-year plans to expand basic industries. These have been relatively successful, business and manufacturing showing marked increases. Yet Portugal continues to have one of the lowest standards of living in Europe and the highest rate of illiteracy. In 1951 the status of the overseas possessions was changed from "colonies" to "overseas territories," but the territories continued to be administered in much the same old authoritarian fashion. In the African territories over 95 percent of the natives were illiterate, there was practically no secondary or higher education for natives, forced labor was resorted to, and only a few thousand natives were given *assimilado* status. To obtain this status, legally equal to that of Europeans, the natives had to meet certain rather rigorous educational, occupational, and other requirements.

For a time it seemed as if Portugal might escape the rising tide of native nationalism and anticolonialism. In 1955 diplomatic relations with India were severed as a result of a dispute over Portugal's tiny colonial outposts in India which Portugal refused to surrender [see map, p. 815]. India's blocking the right of passage from one Portuguese colony to the other over Indian territory was taken to the International Court of Justice for settlement, where the ruling (1960) was in India's favor. Portugal turned a deaf ear to India's repeated demands for a negotiated surrender. Finally on December 18–19, 1961, the Indian government sent troops into the colonies and incorporated them into the Indian Union. Portugal complained of India's action to the Security Council of the UN, but division among the great powers forestalled any investigation or official censure of India.

It was not until 1961 that serious nationalist uprisings, triggered by

events in the neighboring Congo, broke out in Portuguese Angola. The
Portuguese answer was to move in more troops. Fighting has continued
ever since, with the Portuguese fairly successful in asserting their authority.
In 1963 nationalist guerrilla warfare spread to Portuguese Guinea. Mozambique has been less affected, but here also uprisings occurred in the
northern sections of the territory in 1964. The bitter fighting in Angola
led the UN Assembly in 1962 to adopt a resolution by a vote of 92–2 (Spain
and South Africa dissenting) calling upon Portugal to cease repressive
measures against the people of Angola. Portugal has consistently denied
the competence of the UN to deal with these disturbances since they are
internal affairs, the overseas territories being an integral part of a unitary
state. Portugal claims that there is no question of granting these peoples
independence, since they are already free and have equal status with the
Portuguese homeland in Europe. Needless to say this euphemism is not
accepted by the vast majority of the natives in the African territories, nor
by most of the members of the United Nations.

In September, 1968, Premier Salazar, after forty years in power, was
incapacitated by a cerebral hemorrhage, and President Americao Deus
Thomaz appointed Marcelo Caetono as his successor. A law professor,
the latter had long been closely associated with Salazar and on taking
office announced that he would continue his predecessor's policies. Portugal would fight to retain its territorial possessions in Africa, communism
would be suppressed, and public order maintained. There was some indication that the rigid censorship of the past would be relaxed and more
political activity permitted. This did not materialize and a report of
the Council of Europe in April, 1970, stated that despite a certain laizali-
zation by the new regime Portugal was not yet eligible for membership in
the Council which admits only democratic states. It cited serious limitations on individual rights, the ban on political parties, the continued censorship, and the absence of universal suffrage.

Portugal maintains an army of over 120,000 men in its various African
possessions. The discovery of extensive mineral deposits have made Angola and Mozambique more valuable than ever in Portuguese eyes. In
December, 1968, a subsidiary of the American Gulf Oil Corporation began
production from off-shore wells in the small enclave of Cabinda which is
separated from Angola by a narrow strip of Congolese territory. Production from these and certain other newly discovered wells is expected to
make Portugal soon self-sufficient so far as oil is concerned. Portugal has
attempted to introduce certain reforms and has launched a $1.56 billion
development program in its African lands. It hopes to convince the
natives that they will be better off if Portugal retains possession of these
territories than if they become independent. Meanwhile the guerrilla
warfare continues. The neighboring African states are so taken up with
their own problems that they have not been able to interfere substantially
in the Portuguese-native conflicts. For Portugal it is a heavy drain on
its economy, but so far the casualty lists have been relatively light.

The Aegean States

TURKEY. Turkey's strict neutrality until almost the end of World War II was born of its disastrous experiences in the many European wars in which it had participated in the past. The Turkish government considered that it could best protect the country's interests by remaining neutral. This was particularly true since both Germany and Russia had designs on Turkey's independence. For Germany, Turkey was important both as a means of outflanking Russia and as a route to the Arab countries. In the view of Russia, Turkey occupied an important strategic position that would be controlled by enemies of the Soviet regime if it were not controlled by the Soviet Union itself. While the war was in progress the Turkish government succeeded in preserving a nice balance between these two pressures, and refrained from joining the United Nations coalition until March, 1945. With the defeat of Germany, however, the danger to Turkey inherent in the Soviet aims became more immediate. Early in 1945, when the defeat of Germany was imminent, the Soviet Union denounced the Russian-Turkish nonaggression pact of 1925 on the ground that a reconsideration of its terms was necessary. It soon became clear that Russia not only wanted to participate in the defense of the Turkish Straits, but also desired to annex a small strip of territory in northeastern Turkey. This pressure was vigorously resisted by Turkey, which rejected subsequent Russian proposals regarding the Straits as "not compatible with the inalienable rights of sovereignty of Turkey or with its security."

Despite the foreign threat, Turkey made substantial progress during the first postwar years and began to move from a one-party to a multiparty political system. The long tenure of the official People's party, headed by President Inönü after 1938, had led to favoritism and corruption that attracted a great deal of criticism. Turkey also suffered from the economic effects of the war. The cost of living rose some 400 percent in the course of the war, and this was matched by no comparable rise in salaries and wages. The government made various efforts to relieve the burden of the inflation, but its measures amounted to little more than gathering increasing power into the hands of the cautious bureaucracy. The initiative was therefore taken by Bayar, a follower of Atatürk and a former prime minister, to organize a Democratic party in 1946. This new party favored limiting state ownership to key industries and giving freer rein to private initiative and competition. The Democrats gained only a small number of seats in the National Assembly in the elections of 1946, a defeat which they attributed to illegal practices on the part of the People's party, but in 1950 they came to office after a landslide electoral victory. This was the first time in Turkish history that a government had been changed as a result of free elections, and it was generally regarded as a step in the direction of democratic government as known in the West.

Turkish efforts at modernization in this period were greatly assisted by the American aid program. This started modestly with $100 million in 1947 as part of the Truman Doctrine, but in the course of the next decade some $2 billion was advanced to Turkey. Of this amount about three quarters was for military purposes. The new government elected in 1950, with Bayar as president and Menderes as prime minister, made many important gains during its long tenure of office. Economic growth in particular was greatly stimulated. In the decade after 1948, agricultural production was doubled and industrial production increased by about one half. In such specialized fields as electric power, road-building, and merchant shipping, expansion was much more rapid. Turkey extended her international ties by joining NATO in 1951, the Balkan Alliance in 1953, and in 1954 the Middle East Treaty Organization (known until 1959 as the Baghdad Pact and thereafter as the Central Treaty Organization or CENTO). Turkey also was active in the Council of Europe and in the United Nations. In the latter connection she participated in the Korean war with a brigade of 4,500 troops, which fought bravely in some of the bitterest battles. Despite incessant Soviet pressure, Turkey stood firm in defense of its independence and was respected as a strong and progressive state.

These gains by the Democratic regime were nevertheless bought at a high price. In the economic sphere, Turkish investments in industry and transportation greatly surpassed her ability to pay for them. Unlike Greece, Turkey built up a large indebtedness to West European creditors which she could pay for only with American economic aid. The Democrats felt that Turkey was so vital to NATO that the United States would continue to pay her debts. Yet the United States refused to expand its aid to this extent, and by the late 1950s Turkey found it very difficult to get foreign credit. The import of consumer goods was severely restricted, inflation increased, and popular discontent grew. As its domestic situation became more difficult, the Democratic regime took increasingly harsh measures against its political opponents. Starting in 1953, the government adopted laws restricting the freedom of speech and of the press, and jailed prominent members of the opposition on flimsy charges. Thanks in part to such measures, and in part to its success in winning the support of the peasantry, which the People's party had neglected, the Democrats remained in office. In the elections of 1954 they retained their large parliamentary majority, but in 1957 they received only 48.5 percent of the popular vote as against 41 percent for the People's party. Owing to the peculiarities of the Turkish electoral system the Democrats still retained a large parliamentary majority, but their policies provoked increasing criticism at home and abroad. This growing discontent with the policies of Menderes culminated in a *coup d'état* on May 27, 1960, by a group of army officers under the leadership of General Cemal Gürsel.

The action of the military leaders was in response to a widespread discontent, and the fall of Menderes was generally greeted as the end of a period of tyranny. The new leaders did not, however, have any well-formulated policies to introduce in place of those that they had so boldly overthrown. General Gürsel became president of the republic, and direct military rule continued for eighteen months until the military leaders agreed on the appointment of Ismet Inönü as prime minister in November, 1961, following the adoption of a new constitution. The new prime minister had been Kemal Atatürk's principal assistant and had succeeded him as president from 1938 to 1950. He was also a figure around whom all Turks could rally, and with the aid of the Republican People's party he supervised the restoration of parliamentary government. Nevertheless Inönü was seventy-seven when he returned to office, and he was inclined to continue the policy of a rather rigid bureaucratic control of the economy that his party had initiated when Turkey was still underdeveloped. Disappointments in Cyprus added to the discontent caused by bureaucratic rigidity, and in 1965 Inönü was defeated in parliament and forced to resign.

Under the Justice party, whose principle leader was Suleyman Demirel, Turkey now embarked on a new and more independent policy of economic development. Instead of relying so completely on the United States and NATO, it sought to develop friendly relations with East as well as West and succeeded in negotiating substantial development loans from both the USSR and the Organization for European Cooperation and Development. The Turkish second five-year plan (1968–72) provided for very substantial new investments in support of an annual rate of growth of 7 percent. Within the framework of this program Turkey appeared to be faring better than most countries in its efforts to solve the complex problems of political and economic development.

GREECE. When King George II and the Tsouderos cabinet went into exile in May, 1941, after the Axis invasion of their country, they carried with them the burdensome heritage of the authoritarian regime of Metaxas, who had died a few months earlier. In the course of the war numerous changes were made in the Greek government-in-exile to give it a more representative character, although it long remained under the influence of extreme nationalist elements. In occupied Greece, at the same time, a powerful coalition group, known as the EAM (National Liberation Front), was formed with a view to organizing resistance to the Axis occupation forces. While it contained many democratic leaders in its membership, the EAM gradually came under the domination of the Communists as a result of their well-developed united-front infiltration technique. By the end of the war, the EAM had an armed force under its command sufficiently powerful to seize control of the government if necessary. The moderate democratic leaders, who would normally have had the support of a majority of Greeks in peacetime, were now divided in their loyalties between the government-in-exile and the EAM. Just before the end of the war, however, the moderates managed to form a government of national unity under Papandreou, a Social Democrat, which included representatives of the EAM. It was this government that returned to Greece upon the liberation of that country in October, 1944, accompanied by British troops under General Scobie.

Many issues faced the Papandreou coalition in Greece. The question of the return of King George had led to a long controversy that was still unsolved. Some form of parliamentary government had to be established to replace that destroyed by Metaxas in 1936. The most immediate issue, however, was that of unifying all armed forces in Greece under the command of General Scobie, including those of the powerful EAM guerrillas. This measure had been agreed to by all parties on the eve of the return to Greece, but the EAM now realized that the loss of their armed forces was a sacrifice they could not make. After failing to obtain a compromise that would have permitted them to retain part of the armed forces, the EAM ministers resigned from the cabinet on December 1, 1944, and called a general strike. Within a few days armed conflict broke out, and the fighting lasted for six weeks. A truce in the middle of January was followed by an agreement concluded at Varkiza, on February 12, 1945, which provided that the EAM should surrender its arms. By this time almost all the moderate elements had left the EAM, and it was generally recognized to be an instrument of the Communist party. While surrendering some of their arms, the Communists retained substantial supplies of weapons and ammunition in northern Greece. They also regrouped their best fighting forces and retired beyond the Greek frontier to prepared camps in Albania, Bulgaria, and Yugoslavia. From these positions they ventured forth again in 1946 in an attempt to seize power in Greece.

In the meantime, a return to representative government was under way. The Papandreou cabinet resigned during the civil strife and was succeeded by several nonparty governments which attempted to steer the nation back to civil order and reconstruction. Under the supervision of an Allied Mission composed of British, American, and French observers, elections were held in March, 1946, in which the conservative parties headed by the Populists won a solid majority. The EAM leaders boycotted the election, but the Allied Mission declared it to be free and fair and estimated that no more than 15 percent of the registered voters had abstained in response to the EAM boycott. The conservative trend of Greek opinion at this juncture was generally attributed to a revulsion against the excesses of the EAM and to fear of domination by Russia. A Populist government was now organized under Constantine Tsaldaris, nephew of the Populist leader of the prewar period, and in a plebiscite held in September the return of King George II was voted by a modest majority. When he died in 1947 he was succeeded by his brother Paul, whose son Constantine in turn took his place in 1964.

The tasks faced by the Populist regime were almost overwhelming. The Axis occupation and the civil strife that followed it had caused immense physical damage, had destroyed the financial structure of the country, and had undermined the morale of the civil service. What was needed most of all was sufficient assistance so that Greece's own productive facilities could be set to work again. Substantial aid was in fact received during the immediate postwar period from lend-lease and UNRRA, but this was only short-term assistance. Moreover, the renewed attacks of the guerrillas interfered very greatly with the work of reconstruction.

At the same time Britain, which had taken primary responsibility for the security of the Eastern Mediterranean in the postwar period, announced that the financial burden was now too great. Greece therefore turned to the United States, and in March, 1947, President Truman declared that the security of Greece was vital to American national interest. This policy, which was known as the Truman Doctrine and embraced Turkey as well as Greece, was the starting point of the very substantial American program of financial and military assistance in this region. In 1947 no more than $300 million in American aid was designated for Greece, but by 1956 some two and a half billion dollars had been advanced in economic and military aid. The needs of war-devastated Greece were so great, and its position as a line of defense against possible Soviet expansion was so important, that this aid program was widely hailed as a vital enterprise.

In purely economic terms, Greece made remarkable gains in the period after 1947. In agriculture, production of wheat and rice was greatly expanded, and the profitable tobacco business was restored. By 1950 agricultural production had passed the prewar level, and by 1955 it had increased again by one half. Similar gains were scored in industrial production, which by 1956 had reached almost double the prewar level. These gains were made possible primarily because of the shipment of modern equipment to Greece and the technical advice provided by the American economic mission. Accompanying this growth in production was an extensive road-building, irrigation, and electrification program. Within a few years a revolution was produced in Greek internal communications, and electricity was brought to several hundred villages. Two principal long-term economic benefits resulted from this aid: production now began to expand more rapidly than the population, thus raising the hope of a steady improvement in living standards; and Greece was able for the first time to raise enough food to feed itself without imports.

Accompanying these economic gains was a hard-won victory in attaining the political objectives of the aid program. After a long and bloody campaign, the Communist guerrillas were finally defeated. Until 1949 the guerrillas showed no signs of giving up, and indeed increased in strength in some areas despite the best efforts of the Greek army. The turning point came as a result of two factors: the retraining and re-equipment of the Greek army, and a split in the ranks of the Communists. American aid began to arrive late in 1947, but it was not until the following year that the full danger of the military situation was recognized. With this aid, and the assistance of American military specialists, the Greek army gained rapidly in striking power. The split in Communist ranks was caused primarily by the ousting of Tito from the Soviet orbit. Yugoslavia had provided the bulk of the support for the guerrillas, and when its frontiers were closed in 1949 it greatly limited their freedom of action.

The American aid program brought a period of stability to Greek politics. Strong majority governments under Papagos (1952–55), Karamanlis (1955–1963), and Papandreou (1963–65) provided a continuity of policy that Greece had not known in the twentieth century. For a time American aid officials played an active role in the government through their control of the purse strings, and when American assistance was gradually terminated a new generation of younger Greek officials was prepared to take over. In these years the Greek economy ranked high in rate of growth, and as an associate member of the European Economic Community after 1962 it had prospects of participating in Europe's new affluence. The new political stability of Greece was reflected in many aspects of public life, but it did not result in the disappearance of Communism. The Communist party was outlawed in 1947, but a Communist-sponsored united-front movement known as the Union of the Democratic Left continued to play an active role in parliament and in public life. When Prime Minister Papandreou resigned in the summer of 1965 after coming into conflict with King Constantine over army appointments, the left-wing forces took advantage of the prolonged political crisis and contributed much to the violence that upset the long period of orderly development.

The challenge to King Constantine II and his conservative entourage by the aging Georgios Papandreou and his American-educated son Andreas was accompanied by street riots which soon led to political chaos. The crisis was finally resolved when a group of army colonels led by Georgios Papadopoulos seized power in April, 1967. The king initially cooperated with the new government, but in December he tried unsuccessfully to overthrow it and was obliged to flee to exile in Italy.

The new military government established firm control over the country, despite considerable unpopularity at home and abroad, but it did not inaugurate any bold new policies designed to solve Greece's political and economic problems. Its brutal suppression of rival political groups within the country led to widespread criticism in Europe, and in December, 1969, Greece withdrew from the Council of Europe in anticipation of formal censure. Although the Greek colonels had originally come to power as an anti-Communist government, their isolation from the West now forced them to adopt a milder attitude toward the Communist countries. Despite the difficulties in which they found themselves, Papadopoulos and his colleagues sought to maintain order and to work for the economic development of Greece.

CYPRUS. The extension of American aid to Greece and Turkey brought these countries more closely into the Western orbit, and before long this aid also became an integral part of the larger American assistance program that developed in this period. In 1951 Greece, like Turkey, became a member of NATO, and their military forces now came within the scope of general NATO planning. A NATO headquarters for the Eastern Mediterranean was established at Izmir (Smyrna), in Turkey, and the military personnel of the two countries were brought into close co-operation. In 1953 these two countries concluded a treaty with Yugoslavia, which was not a member of NATO. In the following year this treaty, which provided only for military consultation, was transformed into a military defense agreement for a twenty-year period. A permanent council of the three foreign ministers was established, and frequent consultation was planned.

This Balkan alliance, combined as it was with membership in NATO, brought a marked improvement in the position of Greece and Turkey, which only a few years ago had been isolated and threatened by the USSR and its allies. This unity of purpose and interest was soon fundamentally disturbed, however, by the controversy over Cyprus. This strategic island, under British rule since 1878 and a crown colony since 1925, had played an important role as a British base in World War II. Some 80 percent of its population of 600,000 was Greek, and for a generation there had been an active movement in Cyprus as well as on the Greek mainland favoring the annexation of Cyrus by Greece. The Turks, on the other hand, pointed to the fact that 18 percent of the population of Cyprus was Turkish, and that the island was only 40 miles from Turkey, while it was some 660 miles from the Greek mainland. The fact that Cyprus was a major British military base was also an important consideration. It was not only valuable as a location for airfields, but it was in fact the only remaining location in this area where the British could freely maintain sizable armed forces. In the postwar period, Cyprus thus became a bitter issue not only between Greece and Great Britain, but also between Greece and Turkey.

After the war the Labour government in Britain took steps to give the Greeks a more active role in the government of Cyprus and to improve economic conditions. These efforts met with hostility, however, and were further complicated by the strife in Greece itself. Once the Communists in Greece were defeated, Cyprus became the major issue for Greek nationalists. The Communists also seized on this issue as a means of salvaging some of their popularity. The situation in Cyprus now deteriorated rapidly, with the Greeks resorting to terrorism and the British replying with the harsh rule of martial law. Initial British proposals for a compromise met with failure, as did the efforts of the Greeks to obtain support for their point of view in the United Nations. At the same time Greek-Turkish relations rapidly became embittered. In September, 1955, Turkish mobs destroyed the Greek section of Istanbul, wrecking the stores of many merchants and thus undermining the economic position of the important Greek minority in Turkey's largest city. The Greeks replied by bombing the Turkish consulate in Salonika. In 1960, after several thousand lives had been lost in bitter civil strife, the Greek and Turkish governments negotiated a compromise under which an independent Republic of Cyprus was created. The constitution of this new state, which was under the joint guarantee of Britain, Greece, and Turkey, provided for a Greek president, a Turkish vice-president with co-equal powers in vital matters of policy, and a ratio of 7 to 3 for the two nationalities in the assembly and in the public services.

This arrangement had some of the elements of a genuine compromise of the issues under dispute, but it left both sides discontented. The Greeks were dissatisfied because they had placed great hopes on reunion with Greece. They were also concerned that the Turks, with only 18 percent of the population, should have a 30 percent representation in the government and a veto on major policy matters at the executive level. The Turks, for their part, did not believe that the Greeks sincerely intended to implement the 1960 compromise, and were particularly concerned about the rights of the Turks in the five major cities where the population was mixed. Before long these disagreements and misunderstandings led to the collapse of the compromise and renewed civil strife on a large scale.

Early in 1964 the United Nations established a peace-keeping force in Cyprus to maintain order. Order was preserved until the military government that came to power in Greece in 1967 began to adopt a more aggressive policy, and for a while it seemed again that war might break out between Greece and Turkey over possession of the island. A compromise was nevertheless finally reached under which Greek and Turkish troops were withdrawn from the island, and the UN force was given a predominant role in preserving order. This settlement offered a new opportunity for the independent republic established in 1960 to solve the island's problems with less direct interference by Greece and Turkey.

CHAPTER

33

The Decline of Colonialism

Asia: *Former British Possessions; Former French Possessions; Former Dutch Possessions; Portuguese Possessions.*

The Arab World: *The Western Arabs; The Middle East; The Arabian Peninsula.*

Sub-Saharan Africa: *Former British Possessions; Former French Possessions; Former Belgian Possessions; Spanish and Portuguese Possessions.*

The Movement Toward African Unity.

———◆———

IT WAS NOTED earlier in this volume that in 1914 almost 500 million people in Asia and Africa were ruled by Europeans. By 1970 this number had been reduced to 21 million, of which some 15 million were ruled by Portugal, the last colonial power. Some would add to this category the independent republics of South Africa and Rhodesia, where the white minorities broke with Britain so that they could maintain their rule over the African peoples, but these countries are not colonies in the ordinary sense of the term.

The process of decolonization may be said to have started in 1898 with the Spanish-American war, but it advanced only slowly after the First World War and it was not until after the Second that most of the colonies gained their independence. The pace of decolonization depended initially on the decline of the coercive power of the European states due to the two world wars, but its ultimate success was due to movements initiated within the colonies themselves, by political leaders who believed that the political, economic, and social development of their peoples was being retarded by colonial policies.

The Second World War brought opportunities for national liberation in several forms. It required the colonial states to concentrate their military power to a greater extent than before in Europe, and in some cases led them to enlarge native colonial armed forces so that some could be used in Europe. It also upset peacetime commercial relations and led the colonies to rely to a greater extent on their own resources. The share of the colonies in the world trade of the colonial powers declined steadily throughout the twentieth century, and this decline was accelerated by the war. In the case of the Pacific colonies, independence was further hastened by Japan's occupation policy which encouraged native nationalist leaders to turn against European colonial administrations. Finally, the struggle against German aggression within Europe had the effect of strengthening those trends of world opinion that favored independence for colonies. It was in this spirit that the Atlantic Charter of August, 1941, a joint declaration of Roosevelt and Churchill, asserted "the right of all peoples to choose the form of government under which they will live."

The forms taken by decolonization after 1945 varied according to the traditions and policies of the colonial powers. Britain had been relatively little concerned with the domestic affairs of its colonies, and this policy formed the basis for the gradual transfer of authority to native leaders which was largely completed between 1947 and 1960. The French had sought to a much greater degree to extend their own institutions to their colonies. For them decolonization meant a sharper break, and after independence they maintained a closer relationship than the British with their former colonies. Belgian and Dutch colonial policy had not greatly affected the colonies under their rule, and these had only a most limited administrative basis on which to build an independent statehood. The Portuguese, on the other hand, have refused to relinquish their colonies (with the exception of Goa), and in 1961 granted their colonial peoples Portuguese citizenship in an effort to retain them as overseas territories rather than as colonies.

From the perspective of the 1970s, the older controversies over the exploitation resulting from colonialism and neocolonialism have tended to give way to issues of a somewhat different character. The record of European colonialism tends to show that colonial rule brought certain advantages to the colonies in terms of the development of administrative structures and national resources, but only to the extent that these were needed for the limited economic and security objectives of the colonial powers. Colonial rule had relatively little effect on the great majority of the peoples inhabiting the colonies, and to the extent that European institutions were adopted they were on the whole not particularly suited to local conditions.

Most of the former colonies found that they could continue to benefit from the role in world trade that they had achieved before independence. In most other respects, however, they had to build their own political, economic, and social institutions as best they could to meet the requirements and opportunities offered by the modern world. From the standpoint of the colonial powers, only in the case of Britain had their colonies played a large role in their world trade, and these patterns of trade were not altered as much by independence as the proponents of colonialism had predicted.

An important role in decolonization has been played by the United Nations, and throughout the process it has pressed the view that all peoples have a right to live under a government of their own choice. This view was expressed in the Declaration on the Guaranteeing of Independence to Colonial Countries and Peoples adopted in 1960, and a Special Committee was established by the General Assembly to report on the implementation of this Declaration. By 1970 the principal concern of the United Nations with regard to colonial peoples was in connection with the Trust Territories [see pp. 596–97], but it also continued to interest itself in the territories under Portuguese administration and in Rhodesia and South West Africa.

Asia

FORMER BRITISH POSSESSIONS. After the defeat of Japan, Britain again took over control of Hong Kong, and Singapore once more became Britain's Far Eastern naval base. A good deal of unrest akin to the difficulties in French Indochina and in the Dutch East Indies developed in British Malaya. A new Federation of Malaya was constituted in January, 1948, through pacts signed with the various rulers of the Malayan states, and on August 31, 1957, this federation assumed independent membership in the Commonwealth. The enlargement of the federation in September, 1963, into the Federation of Malaysia, including Sabah (North Borneo), Sarawak, and Singapore aroused protests from the Philippines and the bitter opposition of Indonesia. Armed conflict ensued, several conferences were held, and the dispute came before the UN. No settlement was reached; raids and guerrilla attacks by Indonesia continued. In this conflict Britain and other members of the Commonwealth (Australia, New Zealand, Canada) furnished naval and military aid to the federation.

Suddenly on August 9, 1965, Singapore, on the insistence of Prince Abdul Rahman, the Malay leader who was Prime Minister of Malaysia, withdrew from the federation. Rahman maintained that the withdrawal was necessary in order to prevent the outbreak of communal strife between the Chinese (who constituted 75 percent of the population of Singapore and who, he claimed, were seeking to dominate the federation) and the Malayans. The separation agreement provided for continued close co-operation in matters of commerce and defense between Singapore and the federation and for the continuance of British bases on the 217 square mile island of Singapore. The prime minister of the federation promised to support Singapore's application for separate membership in the United Nations and in the Commonwealth. The withdrawal of Singapore was hailed by Indonesia as the first step in the dissolution of the federation; Indonesia welcomed the prospect of re-establishing close trade relations with the city which for years had served as the great *entrepôt* of East Indian trade. Singapore is now officially a republic.

England's Asiatic island territories were further diminished when Tongo proclaimed its independence on June 4, 1970. Tongo is a Polynesian kingdom of some 150 islands with a total area of 269 square miles and a population of about 80,000. As a member of the Commonwealth Tongo will still have ties with London.

During World War II the Japanese, who posed as liberators, proclaimed Burma independent, and it was clear that a restoration to its former status within the British Empire would be impossible. Negotiations in 1947 between the Burma Executive Council and the British government led to an agreement providing for the independence of Burma as a country "not within His Britannic Majesty's dominions and not entitled to His Britannic Majesty's protection." For ten years the Union of Burma, which formally came into existence on January 4, 1948, functioned under a parliamentary form of government, but since then has been under the control of General Ne Win. He has pushed a left-socialistic program and gone far in his policy of nationalization. He has not been able to achieve internal unification, and local guerrilla conflicts—some under leaders of differing Communist persuasions—continue to plague the country. In foreign affairs Burma has followed a policy of nonalignment in the Cold War, but at the same time has energetically tried to reduce Western influence.

The greatest impact upon Asia came from the British withdrawal from India on August 15, 1947, and the establishment of the two dominions of Pakistan and the Union of India. The division of India had been a bitterly debated question, but was finally accepted by the leaders of the Congress party. The name "Pakistan" is a coined word derived from the names of the provinces which were to make up the new state, and in Persian means "Land of the Pure." Extended discussions led to arrangements whereby both Pakistan and India retained relationship with the United Kingdom through membership in the Commonwealth of Nations [see above, p. 731].

Pakistan, by far the smaller of the two states (365,929 square miles), is divided with two sections on opposite sides of the Indian peninsula and has a population of about 109 million (1968), most of them Mohammedan. Until his death in 1948, Mohammed Ali Jinnah directed the affairs of Pakistan. In the beginning there were some bloody riots, and more than ten million Hindu and Mohammedan refugees flocked from one state to the other. Armed conflict developed over the question of whether the state of Kashmir should belong to Pakistan or the Union of India. Its government requested admission to India, although the population is largely Mohammedan. The dispute was submitted to the United Nations,

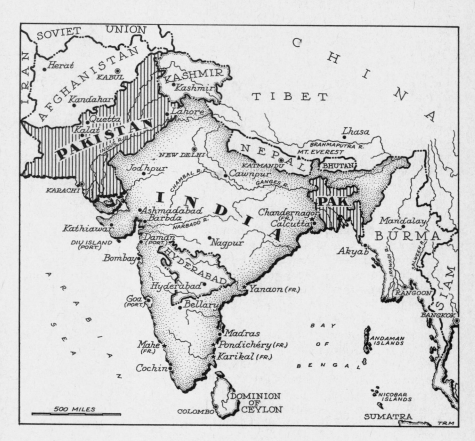

Map 29   *India and Pakistan, 1948*

which was able to bring about a cessation of hostilities. A commission was sent out to study the situation and a plebiscite proposed, but the voting never took place. UN observers keep under surveillance the cease-fire line of January 1, 1949. About half the state, containing approximately one-fourth the population, is occupied by Pakistan, and the rest by India, which, however, claims jurisdiction over the whole area.

In April, 1965, fighting broke out over the frontier line in the Rann of Cutch, a desolate area along the Arabian Sea, which is salt marsh for half the year and desert the other half. Thanks largely to the patient efforts of Britain, which undertook to act as mediator, a cease-fire agreement was reached at the end of June. The troops, which had been massed along the whole border, were now to be withdrawn except along the old Jammu-Kashmir cease-fire line, and the two governments were to attempt to reach a decision on the boundary which involved a territory of about 3,500 square miles. This settlement was lost sight of in the armed conflict which broke out again between Pakistan and India in Kashmir in August, 1965. The border fighting threatened to develop into a general conflict and was complicated by renewed Chinese claims on India along the Sikkim border. As a result of vigorous pressure by the UN Security Council a cease-fire was accepted by Pakistan and India on September 23. The terms called for the cessation of warfare of any type and the withdrawal of armed personnel to the positions held before August 5, 1965. An international arbitration commission on February 19, 1968 awarded Pakistan 317 square miles of the 3,500-square-mile disputed area in the Rann of Cutch. Reluctantly both countries accepted the decision.

In 1958 there were serious disturbances within Pakistan and the president declared martial law, dismissed the central and local governments, abolished all parties, and abrogated the constitution. The Army Commander-in-Chief, General Mohammed Ayub Khan, was appointed chief martial law administrator, and he was given full powers to govern the country. Elected president in 1960, it was not until 1962 that Ayub Khan proclaimed a new constitution. Supported by controlled elections, he ran the government as he saw fit. For some years opposition to his rule mounted both in West and East Pakistan. In the latter there was a marked growth of East Pakistani (Bengali) nationalism and pressure for regional autonomy. A major political crisis began in the fall of 1968 with agitation by students for educational reforms. Old political leaders raised their voices, and in the following January a Democratic Action Committee was formed by leaders of eight opposition parties. There were serious clashes with the police as demonstrations increased, and as a result Ayub Khan announced his final and irrevocable decision not to seek re-election as president in 1970. This led to constitutional talks with opposition leaders, but when these were unsuccessful Ayub Khan resigned from office on March 25, 1969, turning all governmental powers over to General Agha Mohammed Yahya Khan, the Commander-in-Chief of the Army. Martial law was immediately proclaimed, the constitution abrogated, and the national and provincial political assemblies dissolved. Peace was more or less restored, students again returned to their classes, some reforms were made, but the future political course remained uncertain.

In November, 1970, the Ganges Delta of East Pakistan was hit by a devastating cyclone and tidal waves. Hundreds of thousands were killed in one of the world's major natural disasters. It was feared that this might be taken as an excuse to cancel the national elections scheduled to be held on December 7, for a national assembly to draft a new constitution (the third since independence). The elections, however, went off in orderly fashion. In East Pakistan the autonomy party made great gains, partly a result of the tardy and insufficient relief efforts of the West Pakistan officials. The Bengalis of East Pakistan have long been at odds with the Punjabis of the West, for there are few common interests or ties between the two sections of the country, and this hostility led in 1971 to a bloody civil war.

The Union of India (1,262,275 square miles) has a territory about one-third the size of the United States with a population estimated at about 534 million (1968). Most of these are Hindu, although the number includes about 47 million Moslems. Gandhi, the great Indian leader, was assassinated by a Hindu extremist on January 30, 1948. He had lived long enough to see the British leave India, and the shock of his death played no small part in reducing the fraternal strife between Hindu and Moslem. From the beginning the Union of India was under the direction of Nehru. The new government was able very early to negotiate agreements with the more than 550 former Princely States within its borders whereby their rulers transferred to it the powers (defense, foreign affairs, and communications) formerly exercised by Britain. Subsequently many of these territories were consolidated with neighboring provinces or grouped into larger units and subfederations within the union. The large state of Hyderabad at first refused to make an agreement, but in November, 1949, signed the instrument of accession to the Union. Under a Reorganization Act of 1956, India is divided into 16 states and 9 centrally administered territories. In August, 1949, India signed an agreement with the independent kingdom of Bhutan on its northern frontier placing this state under India's protection in return for a generous annual subsidy paid by India. The small state of Sikkim between Bhutan and Nepal, which had long been under British paramountcy, continues under the protectorate of India by an agreement of December 5, 1950. Sikkim hit the American press when the Crown Prince, who since has succeeded to the throne, married an American citizen (Hope Cooke) in March, 1964. India on July 31, 1950, signed a treaty recognizing the complete sovereignty, independence, and territorial integrity of Nepal. Later agreements have increased economic and cultural ties between the two states, but currently Nepal is seeking to lessen Indian influence in its affairs. Tibet was recognized as a part of China in a nonaggression pact concluded with Communist China in 1954. Disputes, however, arose about the Tibet-Indian border and led to clashes between military patrols in 1959. No settlement was reached and in October, 1962, China attacked. After initial success the Chinese announced a cease-fire and their withdrawal to a line which would leave them in control of the disputed territory. Relations between the two countries remained unsatisfactory, and China's settlement of her frontier difficulties with Pakistan did not ease the situation as far as India was concerned.

After much delaying action France turned over the last French enclaves to Indian administration in 1954. Attempts to reach an agreement on the surrender of the Portuguese enclaves failed repeatedly. Three bits of Portuguese territory were incorporated into India in August of 1961, and the following December Indian troops occupied the larger enclaves of Goa, Amao, and Diu. Portugal protested the action as an act of aggression to the Security Council of the UN, but a Soviet veto prevented the adoption of a resolution calling for a cease-fire and withdrawal of troops. Portugal has not recognized the seizure, and manifested its continued hostility by protesting the papal visit to India in December, 1964, as an affront to its own historic loyalty to the church.

Nehru did much to strengthen and modernize India. Untouchability was abolished, and there is no legal discrimination on the ground of race, religion, cast, or sect, although the law has not been able to eradicate age-old customs and tabus in practice. Though much of the foreign aid contributed by the United States, as well as by other countries, has been devoted to building up heavy industry, large amounts of aid have had to be used to provide food since the steady and rapid increase of population overshadows all of India's problems. Nehru did much to assert India's position in international affairs. By calling two conferences on Asian relations in 1947 and 1949, which were attended by nearly all countries in Asia, Nehru gave India a leading voice in the independence and anti-imperialist movements in the East. India has also supported the nationalist awakening in Africa and has been one of the leaders in denouncing the racial policies of South Africa. Nehru tried to follow a policy of non-alignment in the Cold War, but was personally more oriented toward the West than to communism. On his death on May 21, 1964, he was succeeded as prime minister by Lal Bahadur Shastri. Although known for his energy, ability, and political skill, the latter could hardly be expected to equal Nehru's influence in Indian or world affairs. He died suddenly in January, 1966, while on a visit to Tashkent, Russia, where he and the President of Pakistan had met on the invitation of Premier Kosygin to attempt a settlement of Indo-Pakistan conflicts. The "Tashkent Resolution" did bring some amelioration of differences. Shastri was succeeded as prime minister by Mrs. Indira Gandhi, Nehru's daughter. She was not spared political bickering and had to shift cabinet members several times in the next years. In 1969 she forced through the nationalization of the large banks of India.

FORMER FRENCH POSSESSIONS. With the independence of India the position of the five long-established French trading stations there was bound to be challenged. It was agreed that plebiscites should be held in each area, but after one plebiscite (Chandernagor) went overwhelmingly pro-India, the French government kept postponing further balloting. Finally under Indian pressure a settlement was negotiated with France, and on November 1, 1954, Yanaon, Pondicherry, Karikal, and Mahé were joined with India [see map, p. 815].

Immediately after the end of the war the French government attempted to establish a Federation of Indochina. New French-sponsored governments were established in the Republic of Cochin China (1946), the Kingdom of Cambodia (1946–47), and the Kingdom of Laos (1947), and these were proclaimed free states within the Federation of Indochina and the French Union. France also recognized in principle the independence of the Republic of Vietnam (1946), consisting for the time being of Tonkin and northern Annam. Final boundaries were to be determined later, and this played a part in future difficulties. Vietnam—the name means "Southern Land" and was the ancient name for the province of Annam—was under the leadership of a vigorous Republican (Vietminh) group, which was subject to strong Communist influence.

Renewed warfare broke out between the French authorities and the Vietminh under the leadership of Ho Chi Minh in December, 1946, and continued during the following years. The French Foreign Legion, although fortified by many recruits from the demobilized armies of Europe, was not strong enough to cope with the situation, and volunteer troops from Metropolitan France were sent to the area. (Under a special French law no French conscripts could be sent to Indochina.) In 1948 the French government installed a promonarchist Vietnam regime at Saigon under former Emperor Bao Dai of Annam and attempted to support it as the government of the state; in March, 1949, the French authorities signed a broad treaty with Bao Dai according Vietnam considerable independence within the French Union. The boundaries of Vietnam had by this time been extended to include Tonkin, Annam, and Cochin China, thus covering 123,979 of Indochina's 286,000 square miles. Ho Chi Minh's Democratic Republic of Vietnam gradually won control of the northern sections and important areas along the coast.

With the outbreak of the Korean war the Indochinese conflict received attention as another struggle against the spread of communism. The United States supplied military and financial aid not only to France but to regular Vietnam forces, and after 1952 carried the greater share of the financial burden of the war. In the spring of 1954 French efforts to strike a knockout blow were defeated at Dienbienphu, and Ho Chi Minh extended his control. The war had long been subject to bitter criticism in France, and the French government decided to salvage what it could. At a conference in Geneva (April 26 to July 21, 1954) a cease-fire agreement was negotiated. Vietnam was divided roughly along the 17th parallel, the part to the north to be occupied by Vietminh forces, the southern part by French Union forces. An International Supervisory Commission (composed of representatives from India, Canada, and Poland) was established, and elections were scheduled for July, 1956, to form a united government. These elections were never held, and two states, the Republic of Vietnam in the south and the Democratic Republic of Vietnam in the north, continue their independent existence. French influence constantly diminished in South Vietnam. In 1956 the French expeditionary force was withdrawn and the high commissioner replaced by an ambassador.

As the French withdrew, the United States through its policy of financial aid and through its civil and military advisers to the government achieved considerable influence in South Vietnam. But the influence also brought hostility, particularly from the old Vietminh forces, which were soon known as the Vietcong because of their Communist connections. The strife-ridden government of South Vietnam was unequal to coping with the increased number of Vietcong infiltrators from North Vietnam. Gradually the United States was drawn into active participation in the armed conflict, and in the spring of 1964, began to bomb Vietcong bases in both South and North Vietnam. Step by step the United States stumbled reluctantly into a conflict similar to the one waged by France in the early postwar years.

No attempt can be made here to chronicle the events of the war or the long weary steps toward negotiating a peace. Through constantly increasing supplies of material and men (well over 500,000) the United States had soon "Americanized" the war. Much was said in Washington about combating communism and of living up to the obligations of the SEATO alliance. Some of the members of that alliance grouping—but not France, the United Kingdom, or Pakistan—lent token support, as did South Korea. But world opinion in general condemned United States policy. Within the United States itself opposition to the war slowly but relentlessly increased. At first concentrated largely in colleges, universities, and churches, it finally carried over into political circles. Senators Wayne Morse and Ernest Gruening, for a long time the only consistent opponents to the conflict in the Senate, were now joined by others. It suddenly became acceptable politically to be opposed to the conflict. On March 31, 1968, President Johnson ordered a partial halt to the bombing of North Vietnam and announced his intention not to seek re-election. Three days later the United States and North Vietnam agreed to establish diplomatic contacts to discuss the opening of peace negotiations. A month later it was announced that the peace talks would be held in Paris. Much time was spent in wrangling over what delegations should participate and at what kind of table they should be seated—rectangular, square, or round! Meanwhile, the bitter, inconclusive fighting continued. By the time President Nixon assumed office in January, 1969, it was clear that it would be extremely difficult to find support for an acceleration of the conflict, even if he had been inclined to advocate it. In the summer of 1969 token withdrawals of United States troops were made, and by the summer of 1971, the troop level had been reduced from 550,000 to 250,000 men. The ending of the war and the conclusion of peace nevertheless remained the will-o'-the-wisp which no one seemed able to lay hands on.

The kingdoms of Cambodia and Laos, which occupy the western half of the Indochinese peninsula, received new constitutions in 1947, and in

PEOPLE'S REPUBLIC OF **CHINA**

Canton

BURMA

RED R.

MEKONG R.

Dienbienphu

Hanoi

Haiphong

GULF OF TONKIN

Hong Kong (BR)

Luang Prabang

NORTH VIETNAM

HAINAN (COM.CHINA)

LAOS

Vientiane

17TH PARALLEL

THAILAND

Hué

SOUTH

Bangkok

CAMBODIA

MEKONG R.

SOUTH VIETNAM

CHINA

Phompenh

MEKONG

SEA

Saigon

GULF OF THAILAND

FEDERATION OF **MALAYA**

TONKIN

HAINAN (FR)

FRENCH INDOCHINA

Kuala Lumpur

BURMA (BR)

SIAM

LAOS ANNAM

STRAIT OF MALACCA

CAMBODIA

COCHIN CHINA

SUMATRA (INDONESIA)

Singapore (BR)

SUMATRA (NETH.)

MALAY STATES (BR)

250 MILES

SOUTHEAST ASIA

1939

250 MILES

TRM

INDOCHINA, 1954

MAP 30

1949 were recognized as independent states within the French Union. But here too anti-French feeling increased, and after the Geneva Accords of 1954, these states assumed separate status in international affairs, being admitted to the UN in December of 1955.

FORMER DUTCH POSSESSIONS. At the end of World War II the vast Dutch colonial empire in the East presented great problems. Since Dutch forces were in no position to occupy the East Indies on the capitulation of Japan, the British were given the job. Instead of combating the Indonesian Republic, which a group of Indonesians led by Sukarno proclaimed in August, 1945, the British tended to co-operate with it, much to the dissatisfaction of the Dutch, who considered the whole Republican movement the action of rebels. The Dutch government fought the independence movement in every possible way, organizing friendly governments in the outlying islands and increasing its military forces rapidly. Before the British withdrew in November, 1946, they were able to get the Dutch and Republican leaders to initial an agreement to negotiate their differences, but militant groups in both the Netherlands and Indonesia found excuses to abandon this agreement. The Dutch continued to land forces, and in January, 1947, undertook a stringent blockade of the Republic under the guise of enforcing import and export controls. Armed conflicts never actually ceased, and in July the Dutch swept forward on all fronts in a vast "police action." Britain and the United States protested to the Dutch government, while India and Australia brought the affair to the attention of the Security Council of the United Nations. This raised the point of whether the United Nations could interfere in a colonial conflict, which the Netherlands insisted was an internal affair. Nevertheless the Security Council continued its mediatory attempts and the United Nations Committee for Indonesia finally was able to arrange a conference at The Hague, where it was agreed to form the United States of Indonesia as a free and sovereign partner of the Netherlands in a union under the Dutch Crown, similar to the British Commonwealth of Nations. On December 27, 1949, the United States of Indonesia officially came into being with Sukarno as its first president. Grave differences soon developed over Dutch New Guinea, which Indonesia claimed, but which the Dutch insisted on retaining under their direct control. On August 10, 1954, at The Hague a protocol was signed terminating the Netherlands-Indonesian Union, and the last member of the Netherlands Military Mission left Indonesia that month. The protocol was never ratified and, when further negotiations failed, Indonesia on February 14, 1956, unilaterally abrogated the Union Statute and the accompanying financial and economic agreements. President Sukarno in February, 1957, announced a program for "guided democracy" and included a Communist in the coalition cabinet. This aroused opposition of liberal-rightist elements, who revolted in some of the islands. Sukarno, however, remained in control of the central government. At the end of 1957 he seized the multimillion-dollar Dutch plantation properties in Indonesia, which were later nationalized, and many of the Dutch colonists were forced to leave.

Having lost Indonesia the Netherlands seemed determined to hold on to Netherlands New Guinea. The garrisons there were strengthened and agreements were made with Australia for co-ordinating policies on the island. Sukarno, the belligerent head of Indonesia, insisted to the contrary that Dutch New Guinea must be joined to his country. In June, 1960, Indonesia banned all Dutch ships from Indonesian waters and two months later broke off diplomatic relations with The Hague. Indonesia then began to send armed "infiltrators" to New Guinea. Relations became so bad that the Netherlands on September 21, 1961, offered to relinquish sovereignty over New Guinea to United Nations jurisdiction. This offer eventually led to a settlement. After seven months of administration by the UN, authority over West Irian, its new official name, was transferred to Indonesia. As part of the agreement Indonesia was obligated to conduct a plebiscite under UN supervision by the end of 1969 to determine whether the population of West Irian wished to remain a part of Indonesia or preferred independence. It turned out to be a *pro forma* referendum supporting Indonesia.

Relations between Indonesia and the Netherlands improved rapidly. In June, 1964, Indonesia removed the ban on Netherlands shipping and the following year resumed diplomatic relations. This paved the way for the conclusion of a technical co-operation agreement in April, 1964, and the establishment of a commission to consider Dutch claims arising from the transfer of West Irian to Indonesia.

In October, 1965, a leftist coup was attempted under circumstances which are still obscure. A military regime was set up under General Suharto, which began immediately to exterminate all trace of communism, and in the resulting fighting hundreds of thousands (some estimates are in excess of a million) Communists lost their lives. For a time Sukarno, shorn of all power, remained in office, but he was replaced as president of Indonesia by General Suharto in 1968. Relations with the West have steadily improved, especially with the Netherlands, and on a new basis the Dutch are again returning to the East Indies.

PORTUGUESE POSSESSIONS. In the modern era Portugal retained only two scattered possessions in Asia. Under pressure from India [see above, p. 818] she was forced to cede her tiny enclaves along the Indian coast, a cession she has steadfastly refused to recognize. This left her only the colony of Macao on the south coast of China. Riots in 1966–67 forced the Portuguese to agree to Chinese demands, for it was clear, even to the hardheaded statesmen in Lisbon, that Portugal could retain possession of this territory only through the goodwill and sufferance of Red China. Like Hong Kong to the north, Macao gives China important trade and other contacts with the Western world, and for the time being the present status is advantageous to all.

The Arab World

The Arab peoples are united by a common culture and increasingly by a common political outlook, but they have lived under widely diverse conditions and their paths to independence have taken different routes. The peoples living in the Western Arab states of Morocco, Algeria, Tunis, and Libya came under predominantly French, Spanish, and Italian influence in the nineteenth century, and gained their independence after the Second World War. The Arab peoples of the Middle East, in Egypt, Sudan, Syria, Lebanon, Iraq, and Jordan developed along a somewhat different pattern under British and French influence, and gained the substance of their independence in the interwar period [see pp. 411–22]. Since 1945 their principal political concern has been the challenge of the establishment of Israel in the predominantly Arab-inhabited Palestine mandate. In the Arabian peninsula, Kuwait, Saudi Arabia, Yemen, Southern Yemen, Muscat and Oman, and the Persian Gulf States have evolved under predominantly British influence and have been the latest to make the transition from a traditional to a modern way of life.

THE WESTERN ARABS. *Morocco.* The growing influence of European values and institutions led to domestic strife in Morocco in the 1940s and 1950s between tribal and religious leaders who wished to preserve the traditional way of life and the rising nationalist groups in the cities that sought independence from French rule. After a period of acute civil disturbance, France granted independence to Morocco in 1956 under a nationalist government. A reforming sultan who had earlier been exiled was restored as King Mohammed V, and upon his death in 1961 he was succeeded by his son Hassan II. Spain associated itself with the French action by relinquishing its Moroccan territories except for the two tiny enclaves of Ceuta and Melilla. Tangier, under an international administration established in 1923 and renewed in 1945, was likewise transferred to Morocco.

Morocco embarked on independence with only modest resources, and with a population deeply divided between a rapidly growing modern sector and a much larger element still loyal to religious and tribal practices. The role of the king and the government has been to mediate between these groups, and the government has sought to develop the country with American and Soviet aid and through association with the Common Market. When the political tensions of development paralyzed the government in 1965, King Hassan suspended parliament and ruled through the bureaucracy. An attempt by republican officers to overthrow the government failed in the summer of 1971, and the King now sought to reform his administration and to give greater consideration to the needs of the growing urban population.

Algeria. For many years Algeria was regarded as an integral part of France, and its division into departments, at first restricted to coastal regions, was extended to all Algeria in 1947. This was part of the Algerian Statute of 1947, which granted Algerians French citizenship, established

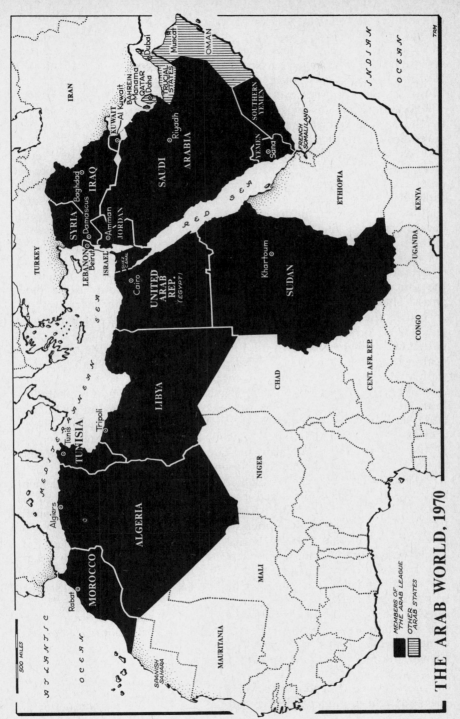

THE ARAB WORLD, 1970

MAP 31

an Algerian legislative assembly, and extended the franchise to include Moslem women; the Moslem male population had obtained the right to vote three years earlier. The electorate, however, was divided into two electoral colleges; one college consisted of approximately 8.5 million Moslems, the other of 1.2 million Europeans in Algeria, mostly French. The local assembly was largely an advisory body, effective power being held by the French resident minister appointed by and responsible to the government in Paris.

Many leading Algerian nationalists had been schooled in French ideas and rejected these political arrangements as well as the unequal economic status of most of the native population as hardly in line with the vaunted French principles of "Liberty, Equality, and Fraternity." Unrest continued and serious insurrections that broke out in November, 1954, developed into a long-drawn-out civil war. A French parliamentary committee presented a critical report on conditions in Algeria in June, 1955, but no agreement could be reached on what changes should be made. Discovery of oil in the hinterland of Algeria and in neighboring regions of the Sahara only heightened French determination to hold fast to those areas. The French army of over 400,000 sought without success to put an end to the guerrilla warfare, and the Arab nationalists inaugurated a policy of terrorism not only against the French in Algeria but also against natives who collaborated with the French. The French authorities in turn dealt with the nationalists as rebels; neither side followed the rules of warfare prescribed by the Geneva conventions. In April, 1956, the Algerian Assembly was suspended. France inaugurated various governmental reform projects, but none of them were acceptable to the nationalists. The latter no doubt received aid from neighboring Morocco and Tunis, as well as from other Arab states, notably Egypt. Several times, over the protest of France, the Algerian question was discussed in the Assembly of the United Nations, without achieving a settlement.

The European (French) colonials in Algeria opposed any settlement that threatened their privileged position. They wanted Algeria to be integrated closely with France and governed as part of Metropolitan France. It was largely this group that prevented the adoption of far-reaching reform plans, although the Arab nationalists proclaimed they would accept nothing short of independence. It was the French *colons* who backed the army leaders in defying the Paris civilian authorities in May, 1958, and thus brought De Gaulle to power and the establishment of the Fifth Republic.

De Gaulle was brought to power by French nationalists who hoped that he would save Algeria for France, but as the situation developed he came to realize that no solution that gave a privileged position to the French and other Europeans would be accepted by the Arabs [see above, pp. 749–50]. It took De Gaulle almost four years to lead France out of this impasse. In this period he won French opinion over to recognizing Algeria's right to independence, and he also broke up an attempt of dissident French officers to seize control of Algeria and possibly of France as well. In the course of prolonged negotiations with a Provisional Government established by the Algerian nationalists, De Gaulle reached agreement at Evian in March, 1962, on a cease-fire. The Evian accords also provided for a transfer of political authority from France to Algeria, on condition of approval by the French people. In a referendum held in April, 90 percent of the votes supported De Gaulle's solution, and the crisis was finally terminated.

When Algeria became independent in July, 1962, the French High Commissioner withdrew, and sovereignty was transferred to the Provisional Executive. Bitter strife for the leadership of Algeria followed. The Évian accords had brought the liberation of Ahmed Ben Bella who had been imprisoned in France since 1956. He was one of the founders of the National Liberation Front (FLN) and had commanded the forces which launched the revolution. Backed by Colonel Boumedienne and his exile army of 30,000 to 40,000 which had been forced to sit out the war because the French prevented them from getting to Algeria, Ben Bella displaced Ben Kheda, seizing the premiership of the provisional government. There were other changes in government personnel, so that Ben Bella and his group were able to dominate the drafting of the constitution. It provided for a strong presidential system, under which the president heads the cabinet and designates the ministers, who are, however, responsible to the unicameral Assembly. Ben Bella was elected president and for a term of five years was given full powers enabling him to by-pass not only the Assembly, but also the FLN which was declared the sole political party. Ben Bella made use of his powers. Men who had played important roles in the rebellion and now differed from him were removed—some exiled, others imprisoned.

It was no easy task to put Algeria on its feet again. The exodus of Europeans had immobilized much of Algeria's economy and deprived the country of much technical skill. Land which had belonged to Europeans was nationalized with partial compensation and placed under the control of peasants' and workers' committees. Fortunately, France continued to provide aid (estimated at $350 million in 1964), the United States supplied surplus wheat to prevent an acute food shortage, and Algeria also obtained large credits from the USSR. Most important was the large cash inflow from oil. In 1964 Algeria was the eighth largest source of crude oil in the world. Mutual exploitation of this resource constitutes a continuing bond between France and Algeria. France also continues to supply Algeria with many teachers and technicians.

Ben Bella established a leftist regime and sought leadership among the developing African states. Unfortunately for the cause of Arab unity in North Africa, armed border conflict broke out in October, 1963, with Morocco. A cease-fire was soon arranged but the dispute has not been settled. There were also border difficulties with Tunisia. These differences did not prevent Algeria from taking part in Arab summit conferences, or from joining with the countries of the Maghreb (Libya, Tunisia, and Morocco) in signing an accord in November, 1964, for the co-ordination of their economies and the ultimate establishment of a trade and customs union.

After thirty-three months of personal rule, Ben Bella was overthrown in June, 1965, in a bloodless *coup d'état* led by his former supporter Colonel Houari Boumedienne, the Minister of Defense. A twenty-six-member Revolutionary Council composed largely of army officers took over authority with a new cabinet headed by Boumedienne exercising executive authority. Inclusion of some leaders in the cabinet from Kabylia, the mountainous coastal region of Algeria, indicated a desire to conciliate the Berbers of this area who had never made their peace with Ben Bella. The new government promised a policy of "non-alignment, to work for the development of an Arab Maghreb [North Africa] and to further a socialistic policy." Peking, unlike Moscow, enthusiastically endorsed the new regime and urged no change in plans for an African-Asian Conference in Algiers, which was, however, postponed.

Boumedienne's government has in general been more moderate than that of Ben Bella, even though it has relied heavily on the USSR for military equipment. After the euphoria produced by their hard-won independence, the Arabs in Algeria have found it difficult to come to grips with the realities of political, economic, and social development. The departure of almost a million Frenchmen deprived Algeria of much of its skilled manpower, and despite the availability of oil resources, its natural wealth is not sufficient to provide substantial revenues. The country has therefore had to follow the slow, hard path of training manpower, establishing industries, and thus gradually increasing the standard of living. This has been a severe blow for the many Arabs who thought that their poverty had been due to French policies and that independence would bring prosperity. One of the principal tasks of the government has been to restore the self-confidence of a people to whom the nationalists had promised more than they could deliver.

Tunisia. The transformation of Tunisia from a French protectorate to an independent state was less turbulent than in Morocco and Algeria. This was due in part to the fact that the Arab leaders had a better working relationship with the French and were able to make the necessary adjustments through negotiation rather than violence. The difference was due also in considerable measure to Habib Bourguiba, who has been one of the most skillful modernizing leaders in the Arab world.

Independence from France in 1956 was followed by the overthrow of the Bey of Tunis, the traditional ruler, and in the following year Bourguiba became president. Although Tunisia is officially a democratic republic, Bourguiba ran the country to a large extent by himself until he suffered the first of a series of heart attacks in 1967. His domestic policies favored state initiative in promoting industry and education, and he did not hesitate to impose heavy burdens on the taxpayers. He also used forceful methods in coercing peasants to enter cooperatives, as a means of raising the technological level of agriculture. These policies, as well as the use of force against trade unions and students, led to civil disturbances when Bourguiba's health began to fail. The political unity that had marked his leadership also faltered when Ladgham, his political heir, came into conflict with and finally ousted Ben Salah, Bourguiba's principal economic administrator. The very considerable success of Bourguiba's policies thus contained elements of political turbulence, which may well emerge more prominently in the 1970s.

Libya. The difference between Libya and the other three Western Arab states is that it has been a much poorer and more sparsely settled land, and under Italian colonial rule it enjoyed far less autonomy. Libya came under British and French military occupation upon the defeat of Italy, and in 1952 it gained independence by vote of the UN General Assembly. The government that came to power was a conservative one under King Idris, and its close reliance on the West was symbolized by the presence of a large American air base used as a transit point for the movement of troops.

Since gaining independence Libya has undergone two revolutions, economic and political. The economic revolution resulted from the discovery of vast oil resources which it began to export in 1961. This new affluence raised Libya's per capita GNP from $50 to $1,000 in a decade and has been accompanied by both the opportunities and the problems of rapid economic growth.

The political revolution occurred in 1969, when King Idris was overthrown by a group of army officers who established a Libyan Arab Republic. The government called for the abandonment of the American air base and other forms of Western influence and proclaimed allegiance to the cause of Arab nationalism and unity along lines favored by Nasser's Egypt. The long-term program of this new regime was not immediately apparent, but the fact that a revolution had taken place served to alert other traditional Arab regimes to what might be in store for them.

THE MIDDLE EAST. *Israel.* Since the Second World War the entire attention of the Arab world has focused on the problem of Palestine, for the war brought a great change in the balance of forces that had led to the adoption of the British White Paper in 1939 [see above, pp. 416–20]. The most important of these changes was the increased pressure on the part of Zionist leaders for Jewish immigration to Palestine, as a result of the decimation of the Jews in Europe.

Of the nine million Jews who came under Axis rule during the war, some six million were deliberately killed by the Germans, while about a million managed to escape. At the end of the war there remained somewhat over one million Jews in Central and Eastern Europe, exclusive of the Soviet Union, many of whom were refugees in camps for displaced persons while others were living in a state of despair and misery. This was the greatest holocaust in the history of the world, and as the full horror of this German policy became known after the war political leaders in many countries felt a moral obligation to support the Zionist leaders. The United Kingdom was prepared to give up its mandate in Palestine, and the United States, the home of a large and influential Jewish community, was prepared to offer its political and economic assistance.

Recognizing that a broad solution of this problem would have to be sought, the British and American governments appointed in 1945 an "Anglo-American Committee of Inquiry Regarding the Problems of European Jewry and Palestine" to conduct an investigation and make recommendations. In its report issued in April, 1946, the Anglo-American Committee proposed that Palestine be transformed from a British mandate into a United Nations trust territory, and that in the meantime 100,000 Jews be permitted to immigrate immediately instead of the 1,500 a month allowed under existing British policy. The British government rejected these recommendations, on the ground that it could not bear the military and financial burdens their implementation would involve. Instead it placed the issue before the UN General Assembly, which in turn established a Special Committee on Palestine in May, 1947, to study the problem. The Special Committee completed its report by the end of the summer, and recommended by a vote of 7 to 3 that Palestine be partitioned with a view to establishing an Arab state, a Jewish state, and an international City of Jerusalem under UN administration. The Arabs objected violently to this proposal, since it meant dividing up an area where they constituted a two-thirds majority of the population. The Jews favored the idea, however, since it at least gave them an independent state. To the majority of UN members, partition appeared to be with all its faults the most feasible solution, and on November 29, 1947, the General Assembly adopted the recommendations of the Special Committee by a vote of 33 to 13, with 10 abstentions.

The implementation of this decision proved to be most difficult in view of the strong passions that had been aroused. Palestine now had a population of some two million, of which over 800,000 Arabs and a few thousand Jews were to be included in an Arab state. The Jewish state, on the other hand, had a mixed population of over 500,000 Jews and almost 400,000 Arabs. The City of Jerusalem had a population of more than 200,000, in which the two rival groups were almost equally divided. The mixed character of the population and the complex nature of the proposed frontiers of the two states made a peaceful implementation of the UN proposals impossible. Violent fighting between the Jews and the armed forces of the Arab League broke out in December, 1947, and continued throughout the winter and spring. The Palestine Commission sent by the UN to supervise partition was entirely ineffectual and was soon disbanded. In its place the Security Council appointed Count Bernadotte of Sweden as UN Mediator for Palestine in May, 1948, but his efforts to negotiate a truce came to an untimely end in September, 1948, when he was assassinated by a Zionist terrorist. Negotiations were continued by Ralph Bunche, the Acting Mediator, and a temporary truce agreed to in November was followed by general armistice terms signed between February and July, 1949, giving Israel more land than originally awarded to it by the UN [see map, p. 832]. In the meantime a UN Conciliation Commission took up the more difficult task of negotiating a permanent settlement in Palestine. The Zionist troops had proved to be more effective than the divided and weak forces of the Arab League and were reluctant to give up the advanced positions they had won. The Arabs, on the other hand, refused to discuss terms until over 900,000 Palestinian Arabs who had sought refuge in neighboring countries were repatriated to Palestine. Still, the complex issues that continued to confront the United Nations in Palestine did not obscure the fact that it had already made an important contribution to a peaceful settlement.

In the meantime, as soon as the British had brought their mandate to an end in May, 1948, the Zionists established an independent state of Israel with Weizmann as president and Ben-Gurion as prime minister. A constitution was adopted which provided for a parliamentary democracy based on universal suffrage, and a single-chamber assembly elected for a four-year term. The first general elections were held in January, 1949. In the following May, Israel achieved its final recognition as a member of the international community by being admitted as the fifty-ninth member of the United Nations. The problems of domestic politics and even of a peaceful settlement with the Arabs were less troublesome, however, than those of settling the continuing influx of Jewish refugees. It was to this task that the Israeli government now turned its attention, and in the decade that followed, very substantial results were achieved. Domestic policy was dominated by two central problems: the desire to permit free immigration of Jews from all over the world, and the need for capital for economic and social development.

By 1965 the population had grown to 2.5 million of which 90 percent was Jewish. To settle and train these immigrants, many of whom came not from Europe but from Africa and Asia, required extensive economic assistance. There was also an arid and largely undeveloped country to be cultivated and industrialized. These tasks could not have been accomplished without the extensive aid received from the United States. Part of this aid took the form of government loans, part came from the sale of Israeli bonds, and part from donations collected by the United Jewish Appeal. Israel also received reparations from the German Federal Republic. At the same time Israel's trade expanded rapidly, and by the mid-1960s it had achieved a promising record of economic growth. The demand for imports to support a rising standard of living nevertheless outpaced the country's export capacity, and the growing trade deficit which reached half a billion dollars in 1964 posed a critical problem of economic self-discipline.

Weizmann, the founder of Zionism, was president of Israel until his death in 1952, and was succeeded first by Ben-Zvi (1952–63) and then

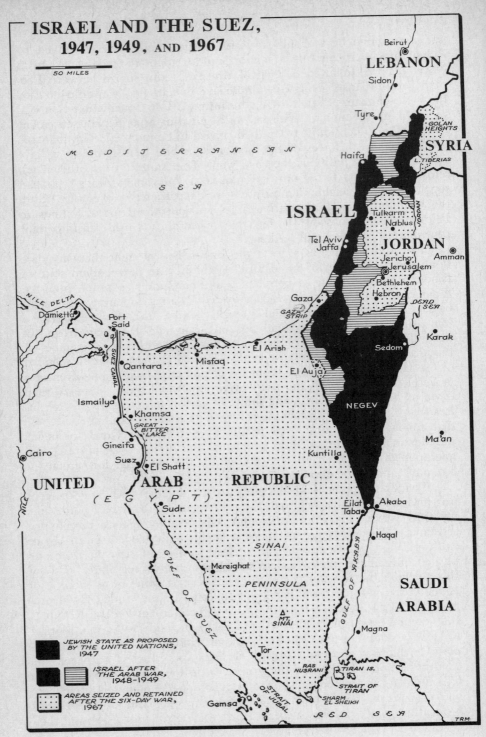

ISRAEL AND THE SUEZ, 1947, 1949, AND 1967

50 MILES

MEDITERRANEAN SEA

LEBANON
Beirut
Sidon
Tyre

Haifa

GOLAN HEIGHTS
SYRIA
L. TIBERIAS

ISRAEL
Tulkarm
Nablus
Tel Aviv
Jaffa
JORDAN
Jericho
Jerusalem
Amman
Bethlehem
Hebron
DEAD SEA
Karak

NILE DELTA
Damietta
Port Said
Gaza
GAZA STRIP
El Arish
Qantara
Misfaq
El Auja
Sedom

Ismailya

SUEZ CANAL

Khamsa
GREAT BITTER LAKE
NEGEV

Gineifa
Cairo
Suez
El Shatt
Kuntila
Ma'an

UNITED ARAB REPUBLIC
(EGYPT)

NILE

Sudr

Eilat
Taba
Akaba
Haqal

SINAI
GULF OF SUEZ
Mereighat
PENINSULA
GULF OF AKABA
SAUDI ARABIA
Magna
△ MT. SINAI

Tor
RAS NUSRANI
TIRAN IS.
STRAIT OF TIRAN
Gemsa
GULF OF JUBAL
SHARM EL SHEIKH
RED SEA

TRM

JEWISH STATE AS PROPOSED BY THE UNITED NATIONS, 1947
ISRAEL AFTER THE ARAB WAR, 1948-1949
AREAS SEIZED AND RETAINED AFTER THE SIX-DAY WAR, 1967

MAP 32

by Shazar. The dominant political figure throughout this period was Ben-Gurion, who headed the government from 1948 to 1953 and again from 1955 to 1963. The later years of his tenure of office were clouded by his stormy controversy with Defense Minister Lavron over a scandal in the Israeli foreign espionage organization, and when he was succeeded as prime minister by Eshkol in 1963 Ben-Gurion's prestige as a public figure was seriously tarnished.

Throughout these years the government's principal concern in foreign policy was to safeguard Israel's security in a situation in which its Arab neighbors continued to regard its very existence as an act of aggression against Arab national rights. This situation was exacerbated by the over 900,000 Arab refugees from Israel who lived in misery in the neighboring states and were cared for by the United Nations Relief and Works Agency. Endless border strife resulted from this situation, and it came to a head after Egypt announced in 1955 its intention to obtain arms from the Soviet orbit and subsequently nationalized the Suez Canal Company in 1956. After a period of mounting tension, Israel launched a preventive war in October, 1956, with the aim of breaking Egypt's military power before it was sufficiently strong to threaten Israel. Israel was shortly joined by Britain and France, who moved in to re-establish international control over the Suez Canal Company and to overthrow Nasser. The United Nations, reflecting world opinion and backed by the policies of the United States and the Soviet Union, nevertheless compelled the aggressors to withdraw. A United Nations Emergency Force was established to supervise a zone between Egypt and Israel, and the slow process of clearing the Suez Canal of war damage was started. Israel succeeded in destroying the Egyptian forces east of the Suez, but it was unable to annex any territory and provoked widespread antagonism in the Arab world and beyond. The new explosion of Arab nationalism in Iraq in 1958 soon demonstrated the inherent difficulty of Israel's position in a hostile Arab world.

In the years immediately after the war of 1956, both Israel and its Arab neighbors returned to the tasks of domestic development. This was a period of armistice rather than of peace, however, and each party to the conflict was on the alert lest the opponent gain an advantage. It was in this atmosphere of increasingly strident raids and counter-raids that Nasser decided to test Israel in May, 1967. He apparently was seeking to challenge Israel in a way that would lead it to initiate a conflict which would provoke the neighboring local states to unite and eventually strike back with full force.

The challenge took the form on May 18 of an Egyptian demand for the withdrawal of the UN Emergency Force that had been policing the Egyptian-Israeli border since 1956, followed by occupation of Sharm el Sheikh on the Strait of Tiran in order to close the Gulf of Akaba to Israeli shipping. These actions were followed by a period of negotiation during which Israel mobilized and the Arab states formed a new coalition providing for military cooperation. Although the Arabs did not plan to attack first, Israel felt that the odds were against her in the long run. At dawn on June 5 she launched a surprise attack on Egypt, Jordan, and Syria, designed to make it impossible for them to retaliate. This was done by destroying the greater part of their air power on the ground, and then crushing the Arab ground forces that were defenseless without air protection. In the process Israel also occupied the Sinai peninsula up to the Suez, the Gaza Strip, the west bank of Jordan (including Jerusalem, internationalized in 1948), and the strategic Golan Heights in Syria.

This Six-Day War (June 5–10, 1967) was in a sense one of the quickest and most decisive military victories in history, but it was only one battle in a much longer war that had started in 1948 and that had no end in sight. The immediate aim of Israel, security from the type of attack that it had just delivered, was bought at a high price. The major foreign states concerned did not support Israel's action. After prolonged debates, the UN Security Council adopted unanimously a resolution on November 22, 1967, calling upon Israel to withdraw its armed forces from territories occupied in the conflict, urging respect for the sovereignty of every state in the area (that is, that the Arab states should recognize Israel), and requesting the UN Secretary-General to designate a special representative in the Middle East to promote a peaceful settlement of the dispute.

This resolution established the framework for a settlement, but it had little effect on the situation. Gunnar V. Jarring, the Swedish diplomat appointed as the Secretary-General's special representative, found that neither side was willing to make the concessions called for by the Security Council. Extended negotiations on the part of Britain, France, the United States, and the USSR likewise failed to produce results.

Israel's stubbornness in resisting compromise was due to the belief that retention of the occupied territories was her only bargaining power in her effort to gain Arab recognition. The adamant attitude of the Arabs, despite their disastrous defeat, was due to significant changes in their position after 1967. The development of guerrilla tactics made possible continuing raids into Israel and bombings of Israeli airliners, to which Israel could respond with retaliatory raids. The possibilty of another Israeli surprise attack was reduced by the deployment of Soviet missiles in Egypt, accompanied by the re-equipment of Arab military forces and the presence of Soviet pilots to protect Egypt's strategic positions. Arab military strength was thus able to recuperate under an umbrella of Soviet protection that severely restricted Israeli retaliatory power.

By 1970 Israel was thus in a more difficult position than in 1967, and the nation rallied resolutely to meet the new dangers. Golda Meir succeeded Levi Eshkol as prime minister following his death in 1969, and she led a government pledged to a tough foreign policy. At the same time, the 1967 war and its consequences led to profound changes within Israeli society. Until then the life of the country had been dominated by the older generation of Zionists who had sought a homeland where they could practice the traditional faith in a predominantly agricultural setting. The rise of a new generation and the development of the technological skills necessary to maintain Israel's industrial and military position in the 1960s brought to the forefront leaders more concerned with the creation of a modern society than with the fulfillment of traditional goals.

International concern that a continuing deadlock and escalating conflict might have grave consequences for the general peace led the American government in the summer of 1970 to negotiate a 90-day cease-fire between Egypt, Jordan, and Israel. The purpose of this truce, which went into effect on August 7, was to enable the two countries to renew their efforts to achieve a peaceful settlement with the mediation of Ambassador Jarring under the auspices of the United Nations. The prospects for negotiations were almost immediately endangered, however, when Israel accused Egypt of violating the cease-fire by moving additional missiles into the Suez truce zone. The validity of these accusations was initially denied, but American reconnaissance flights over the Canal soon confirmed them. Although Egypt and Israel continued to respect the cease-fire, and refrained from military activity, negotiations between the two countries were not resumed until January, 1971. At this time Ambassador Jarring noted that the two sides had reduced their differences on some of the key issues, although basic disagreements remained as to the final terms of a settlement.

Egypt. Egypt emerged in 1945 from the war essentially unchanged, for its leaders continued to be concerned primarily with the game of domestic politics. The Nationalist Wafd party alternated in office with one or another of the more moderate groups, and King Farouk played them off against each other as best he could. Egypt wanted to end British tutelage, which now consisted chiefly of control of the Sudan and the stationing of British forces in the Suez Canal Zone, but it did not have the unity of purpose to assert itself. The frustration of Egypt's position was revealed with particular clarity during the Palestine War in 1948. Although Egypt was an established state with a population of over 20 million and had the assistance of several allies, its military forces made a very poor showing. While the reaction to these events was in many ways emotional, there was an underlying belief that domination by Britain was preventing Egypt from developing a strong state and a modern society.

The intensity of Egyptian feeling was expressed in the extensive anti-Western riots in Cairo in January, 1952, which destroyed many foreign commercial enterprises. These events were followed in July by a revolution carried out by a group of army officers known as the Army Revolutionary Council. This group was initially led by General Naguib, and one of its first acts was to send King Farouk into exile. In 1953 Egypt was proclaimed a republic, and a new constitution was drafted which vested essential authority in the Army Revolutionary Council. In 1954 Naguib was replaced by Colonel Nasser, the actual leader of the Council, who became both prime minister and president of the republic.

The policy of the new regime was based on a desire to transform Egypt into a modern state as rapidly as possible. An agrarian reform was proclaimed, but it could offer assistance to only a fraction of the land-hungry peasants. More promising was the hope offered by the construction of the High Aswan dam, which would greatly increase the area under irrigation, but the project required capital not available to the government. The agrarian poverty that lay at the heart of Egypt's troubles was complicated by a high birthrate. With a population growing more rapidly than production, in spite of the agrarian reforms that Nasser was able to implement, on a per capita basis Egypt seemed doomed to grow steadily poorer. Attempts to solve the problem by industrialization likewise met with fundamental difficulties. Shortage of power and fuel, and particularly the lack of capital, placed narrow limits on the growth of manufacturing. In the social field the new regime soon adopted modern reforms. Hereditary titles were abolished, the legal system was secularized, the interests of the worker were protected, and graft in the civil service was prosecuted. In the balance, despite sincere and vigorous efforts, no revolutionary change in Egypt's economic position took place during the first five years of the new regime.

It was in the foreign rather than the domestic field that Nasser scored his early achievements. The first step was the negotiation in 1954 of Egypt's outstanding controversies with Britain concerning the Suez and the Sudan. The nationalist feeling of the Egyptian leaders made them more determined than ever to obtain a settlement, and the altered strategic situation brought about by modern weapons resulted in a greater British willingness to make concessions. As to the Suez, the British now agreed to withdraw their troops within two years, while retaining the right of re-entry in case of an emergency affecting Egypt's control of the Canal. Egypt, for its part, promised to uphold the 1888 Convention providing for freedom of traffic through the Suez Canal, which was operated by an international company. As to Sudan, the agreement provided that the Sudanese should decide, after a transition period of no more than three years, whether to join Egypt or to form an independent state. At the end of 1955 the Sudan took the latter course and severed its relations with Egypt.

This treaty of 1954, which terminated Egypt's ties with Britain, was accompanied by a more independent policy on the part of Egypt. The United States made a substantial loan to Egypt in 1953 and agreed to support the construction of the High Aswan dam on the upper Nile. Nasser was basically inclined toward the West at this stage and successfully banned propaganda by the Communist party in Egypt. He nevertheless saw the advantage of playing the Soviet Union off against the West and, when the latter refused to sell him arms, he concluded an agreement in

September, 1955, to purchase Soviet military equipment through Czechoslovakia. From this point on, Egypt's relations with the West deteriorated rapidly. American support of the High Aswan dam was withdrawn in July, 1956. In reply, Nasser immediately seized the Suez Canal Company in violation of the 1888 Convention, which he had pledged himself to uphold three years earlier. At the end of October, Israel attacked Egypt with the support of British and French landings in the Suez Canal Zone, and it was only the intervention of the United Nations that saved Nasser. Indeed, although his military forces were severely defeated, Nasser emerged as a hero in an Arab world that was now increasingly hostile to Western domination and interference.

Nasser's domestic policy, which sought to develop a form of Arab socialism, met with some success despite great obstacles. Industrial production expanded rapidly in the 1960s, and it remained Egypt's principal hope for a rising standard of living. It has been estimated that Egypt's real per capita income was no greater in 1954 than in 1900 because of the rapid growth in population, and even when the Aswan Dam is completed in the 1970s, agriculture alone will not be able to contribute a great deal to the race between production and population. In an effort to stimulate industry to the utmost, in 1961 Nasser nationalized all larger banks, industries, and insurance companies in the hope that state initiative would result in more rapid growth. This emphasis on the role of the state is the most characteristic feature of Nasser's version of Arab socialism, and he has sought to convert Arab leaders in neighboring countries to this point of view.

Throughout the 1960s domestic policy in Egypt was closely related to international relations. Indeed, the key to Arab politics is the relationship between the domestic development of each country and the need for unity among the Arab states in an effort to bring under one policy the natural resources (primarily oil) of the less developed countries and the skilled manpower of the more developed. In this process Israel plays a critical role as a challenge to Arab poverty and also as an anvil on which Arab unity can be hammered out. The very existence of Israel is regarded by the Arabs as a challenge, since it has been established on territory inhabited predominantly by Arabs for a thousand years. Specific phases of Arab hostility toward Israel, however, are due more to rivalries for initiative among the leaders of the various Arab states than to the particular security needs of the countries concerned.

The form taken by the Arab-Israeli conflict is also molded to a very considerable extent by the international environment. The withdrawal of Britain and France from the Eastern Mediterranean, despite their final effort in 1956 to reassert their influence, left the United States and the USSR as the principal foreign powers with an active presence, and with China playing a secondary role. In the course of the past century the United States has done much to support education and development in the Arab countries, but as the principal sponsor of Israel since 1948

ARAB SUMMIT CONFERENCE   *Hussein, Nasser, and Faisal at the meeting in Khartoum, Sudan, August, 1967.*

it has become closely linked with the enemy in Arab eyes and has thus lost much of its influence. The main goal of Soviet policy is to strengthen its security in the Middle East by encouraging the withdrawal of all Western influence. It was originally one of the strongest supporters of Israel, since the establishment of that country involved the withdrawal of Britain from Palestine, but since then it has found in Arab nationalism a ready-made vehicle for expanding its influence.

Both the challenge of Nasser to Israel in 1967 and the subsequent enhancement of his role despite his defeat can best be understood in terms of this setting. The defeat served further to radicalize Arab politics, which strengthened Nasser by comparison with the more conservative Arab leaders, and it also gave the USSR an opportunity to increase its influence by virtue of its role as the principal provider of economic and military assistance. By 1970 the Arabs were again able to harass Israel effectively and were safer from retaliation because of stronger Soviet support.

The difficulties faced by Nasser in seeking to mold Arab opinion are reflected in the fact that almost a quarter of a century after the establishment of Israel the Arab countries remain divided. Oil-rich Saudi Arabia, Kuwait, and Libya have been providing Egypt with support in the amount of a quarter of a billion dollars a year since the defeat in 1967, but there has been little agreement on policy. There are prospects since the revolutions in 1969 that Libya and Sudan may join Egypt in a reconstituted United Arab Republic, which would have a population of 50 million and could draw on the vast oil resources of Libya. In practical terms, however, Egypt finds it difficult to cooperate with the more important states of Syria, Lebanon, and Jordan which border on Israel.

The principal vehicle for seeking common political action has been the Arab League, established in 1945 with a formal Council, six committees, and a permanent secretary-general. It has headquarters at Cairo, and generally reflects the view of Egypt and of the Arabs displaced from Palestine by the establishment of Israel. It has had some success in the cultural and economic fields, but has not overcome the basic differences among Arab leaders. More recently Arab guerrilla activities against Israel have come to play an important role in the conflict. In 1970 ten guerrilla organizations were united under a Central Committee headed by Yasir Arafat, leader of Al Fatah, the largest guerrilla group. The basis of Arab unity lay in agreement among the leaders of the Arab states, and in 1971 this was not yet in sight. The death of Nasser of a heart attack in September, 1970, did not affect the balance among the Arab countries, and his successor, Anwar Sadat, continued in his tradition.

Sudan. Since attaining independence in 1956 Sudan has been ruled successively by civilian and military leaders, none of whom have had much success in developing the country. The military coup in 1969 by Gafaar el-Nimeiry established a regime that is dedicated to Arab socialism and prepared to cooperate closely with Egypt. The economic poverty of the country, which depends primarily on the export of cotton, has been aggravated by prolonged civil strife in southern Sudan. The Nilotic and Negro peoples of this region, who constitute a third of the population of the country, have been conducting a guerrilla revolution against the dominant Arab majority virtually throughout the period of independence and have seriously drained the country's resources.

Syria and Lebanon. The development of events in Syria and Lebanon was somewhat similar to that in Egypt. After some armed conflict, Syria became independent from France in 1945. A republic was established by the leaders who had fought long for independence, but their defeat in the Palestine War soon brought an end to their influence. Between May and December, 1949, three *coups d'état* were made by army groups favoring a more modern and dynamic form of government. The third, headed by Colonel Shishakli, established a military regime that lasted for over four years and provided a degree of stability. A more parliamentary regime replaced Shishakli in 1954, but it was rent by internal strife.

As in Egypt, Syrian nationalists were increasingly frustrated by the failure of the West to support their aims, and they turned to the Soviet Union as an alternative. Syria had an active Communist party, and a number of leading army officers were pro-Soviet. When a group of these officers seized control of the army in 1957, the action was widely regarded as the first step toward the establishment of a Soviet satellite. Arab nationalism was stronger than pro-Soviet feeling, however, and when Syria joined with Egypt in 1958 to form the United Arab Republic, the leader of the Syrian Communists was forced to flee the country. Nasser was firmly opposed to communism at home, and now his policy was also enforced in Syria. The formation of the United Arab Republic nevertheless raised almost as many problems as it solved for Syria. The Egyptian economy was much weaker than that of Syria, and any thorough-going integration would only serve to impoverish the latter. At the same time, the thriving commerce of Syria was traditionally free from governmental restrictions, whereas commerce in Egypt was regulated by the state. Many Syrian leaders also objected to Nasser's ban on political parties. This discontent culminated in a revolution in 1961 by national-ist leaders who severed ties with Egypt and sought to develop their coun-try along independent lines. A further revolution in 1963 brought to power the Baath (Renaissance) party, which was also opposed to union with Egypt but which favored a policy of economic development under state initiative, not unlike that of Nasser.

The defeat by Israel in June, 1967, which Syria shared with Egypt and Jordan, led to a further radicalization of Syrian politics. Dissatis-faction with the leadership of the Baath party resulted in an increased role of the military in Syrian politics and a further stiffening of attitudes toward Israel. Syria has become one of the principal sponsors of guerrilla activity against Israel, and the exchange of raids and acts of terrorism be-tween the two countries has continued despite efforts to negotiate a set-tlement. At the same time, the strain of this conflict on Syrian society is reflected in the fact that over one-half the national budget is devoted to military expenditures.

Likewise in Lebanon, the republic established in 1945 after the de-parture of the French did not enjoy great stability. The Israeli victory in 1948 was a major blow to Lebanon's strength and undermined public confidence in the ability of the traditional leaders to further the country's interests. An opposition movement, the Social and Nationalist Front, now came forward with a program of social and economic reform. This movement came to power in 1952 as a result of a bloodless coup, and Chamoun, one of its leaders and a Christian Arab, was elected to the presidency. Despite this initial success, Chamoun's regime did not carry out significant reforms and many of his associates soon broke with him.

Unlike Egypt and Syria, Lebanon adhered to a pro-Western foreign policy. This alienated in particular the Moslem Arabs, who formed about one-half the population of Lebanon. In the spring of 1958 these differences broke out into active civil strife between Chamoun's government and an opposition composed of a variety of nationalist elements. While this strife was nominally over Chamoun's desire for a second term as president, it was in fact an attack on his conservative and pro-Western policy. The rebels received active support from neighboring Syria, at that time part of the United Arab Republic. When the revolt in Iraq in July, 1958, seemed to presage a similar move by the nationalists in Lebanon, the United States, at the request of President Chamoun, sent in Marines and Army paratroopers to help protect the government. In August, as a result of American mediation, the Lebanese assembly elected to the presidency General Chehab, the chief of staff of the army. This compromise resulted in the establishment of a stable regime, and the American forces were able to withdraw within three months. Lebanon under President Chehab pursued a nonaligned policy in international affairs, and has succeeded in co-operating with the other Arab states without sacrificing its domestic independence to the extreme nationalists. In 1964 Chehab was succeeded as president by Charles Helou in an election that reflected continuing political stability.

This stability was nevertheless upset by the war of June, 1967. Even though Lebanon was not directly involved, nationalist elements within the country argued with increasing vehemence against the more moderate leaders in office that the country should not stand aside from the struggle being waged by neighboring Arab countries. Despite the policies of its government, Lebanon was drawn into the conflict when Syrian-based guerrillas used its territory for attacks on Israel. When Israel responded in 1968 with an air raid against the international airport at Beirut, conflict within Lebanon sharpened. The army was not successful in preventing use of Lebanese territory by the guerrillas, and civil strife on this issue assumed menacing proportions.

Iraq and Jordan. In Iraq a traditional form of conservative government survived until 1958, although it had certain distinctive features that set it apart from other governments in his region. The leading statesman of Iraq was Nuri as-Said, who had participated with Colonel Lawrence in the Arab uprisings during World War I and since then had served as prime minister fifteen times. Young King Faisal II, who ascended the throne in 1953 at the age of eighteen, played only a secondary role in the government of the country. Iraq, like its neighbors, participated in the war against Israel in 1948, but despite strong nationalist feeling the government tried to steer a moderate course. In 1955 Iraq signed the Baghdad Pact, a mutual-defense agreement with Turkey. Within a few months Britain joined the Pact, and at the same time agreed to the abrogation of the Anglo-Iraqi Treaty of 1930, under which Britain had enjoyed a privileged position. Britain thus remained as Iraq's chief protector, but as a part of the broader Baghdad Pact that Iran and Pakistan soon joined.

In domestic affairs, the main achievement was the negotiation in 1952 of an agreement with the foreign oil companies guaranteeing to Iraq 50 percent of their profits. Within a short time this new income more than doubled state revenue. Provision was made that 70 percent of oil revenues be assigned to a Development Board, which devoted this new wealth primarily to major capital investments.

Despite significant gains, the government of Nuri as-Said provoked opposition on both domestic and foreign grounds. At home, nationalist leaders were severely repressed. While the pace of economic development was quickened, the initial benefit accrued not to the undernourished peasantry but to the wealthy landowners who were able to develop their estates with modern equipment. The substantial progress that was made was thus carried out within a conservative framework, and the public as a whole did not get a sense of participating in the gains. Even more controversial was the foreign policy of Nuri as-Said, which vigorously opposed Nasser's aims and remained friendly to American and British interests. This policy was in direct conflict with dominant nationalist feeling, which maintained that only through Arab unity and the overthrow of Western influence could progress be made. On July 14, 1958, the Iraqi monarchy was overthrown by a group of Army officers led by General Karim el-Kassem. King Faisal and Nuri as-Said were both assassinated, and a government was established which resembled that of Nasser in Egypt in its main outlines. This revolt was greeted with widespread support both in Iraq and in the Arab world in general, and the landings of American forces in Lebanon and of British forces in Jordan were made in order to prevent the further spread of Nasser's influence. The initial measures taken by the new regime were less radical than had been anticipated, despite the activity of a vigorous Communist party, and it soon received the recognition of the United States and the United Kingdom and participated in the deliberations of the United Nations. The new government now asserted its independence by denouncing the Baghdad Pact, and in 1959 a reorganized Central Treaty Organization (CENTO) linked Turkey, Iran, and Pakistan without the participation of Iraq.

General Kassem initially assumed a strong position of leadership, but his revolution released political forces that before long overwhelmed him. These forces were represented by rival versions of socialism and nationalism, of which the most prominent were the Communist party and the Baath party, which as in Syria favored an Arab variant of socialism. In 1963 the Baath leaders seized power, killing Kassem in the process, and a few months later a military dictatorship was established by Colonel Aref. Aref died in a helicopter accident in 1966, and two years later Major General Ahmed Hassan al-Bakr emerged as head of the government. The various military and civilian leaders who have alternated in power since 1963 have all been associated with the program of the Baath party and have generally been sympathetic to Nasser's goals. Although

Iraq played only a limited role in the Six-Day War, it shared in the general Arab desire to rise to the challenge of defeat. Iraq has also faced in its northern provinces bordering on Iran and Turkey the constant threat of revolt by its Kurdish minority, and in 1970 the government finally agreed to grant the Kurds local autonomy and proportional representation in the central government.

The Emirate of Transjordan was created by the British after World War I and was ruled by Abdullah, son of King Hussein of the Hashimite Dynasty, with the aid of a British subsidy. Despite its shortage of resources and population, the strong Arab legion the British created under General Glubb gave Abdullah the possibility of playing a prominent political role in the Arab world. In 1946 Transjordan was given its independence, but under a treaty agreement Britain retained a privileged position. Abdullah played an active role in the Palestine War in 1948, and as a result annexed central Palestine. The inhabitants of these new territories, together with a large influx of refugees from Palestine, now tripled the population of the country. Abdullah had assumed the title of King in 1946, and in 1949 he changed the name of his country to the Hashimite Kingdom of Jordan. Of the 1.5 million inhabitants of Jordan in the late 1950s, native tribesmen comprised one third and the remainder were divided about equally between the residents of the newly annexed territories and refugees from Israel.

This heritage forced the new kingdom to follow an ambiguous course in international affairs. Abdullah was a proud monarch, eager to pursue a leading policy in the Arab world. He was also under pressure from extreme nationalists, particularly among his new Palestinian subjects, to break with Britain, on whose financial support he was dependent. Abdullah was assassinated in 1951 by a Moslem fanatic; his son Talan, who succeeded him, was mentally incapacitated, and in 1953 his grandson, Hussein, became king at the age of seventeen. Hussein, like his grandfather, recognized the value of British support but also felt the necessity of acknowledging Arab nationalism. It was the latter force which was dominant in the 1950s and which determined many of Jordan's policies. Thus in 1955 nationalist opinion prevented Jordan from joining the Baghdad Pact, and in the following year Hussein dismissed General Glubb in an act of defiance against British influence. Despite this gesture the British decided to continue their substantial subsidy to Jordan, and American technical assistance and economic aid, starting in 1954, helped to sustain the government. Jordan joined with Iraq in February, 1956, to form the Arab Union as a counterpoise to the United Arab Republic of Egypt and Syria, but this union was terminated five months later when the Iraqi government was overthrown. Isolated once more in a sea of nationalist feeling, King Hussein again called on the British to come to his assistance, and a battalion of paratroopers flown in from Cyprus remained until October to help keep order. The weakness of the King's position lay in the opposition to his policies by the two thirds of his inhabitants who as Palestinian Arabs were powerfully attracted by the magnetic influence of Nasser's nationalism. To bolster his position, however, Hussein had the support of a well-disciplined army and the temporary presence of British troops. A continuing flow of American economic aid and a new spirit of mutual tolerance between Jordan and Egypt resulted in a period of unprecedented stability and prosperity in the 1960s. The continuing friction with Israel, accompanied by frequent border incidents, was at the same time further exacerbated by the controversy over the use of the Jordan River.

Jordan was the principal loser in the Six-Day War, since the territories of Jerusalem and the West Bank occupied by Israel comprise over one-half Jordan's population and economic resources. This loss has greatly increased nationalist pressure on King Hussein and has brought the country to a state of acute crisis. It is now supported by grants from the richer and more conservative Arab countries, but at the same time many political leaders are attracted by the radical views favored by Nasser and by the Baath parties in Syria and Iraq.

The principal opposition to Hussein came from the Palestinian guerrillas, who deeply resented his policy of joining with Egypt in 1970 to seek a negotiated peace with Israel. In September, 1970, guerrillas representing the Popular Front for the Liberation of Palestine hijacked three jet airlines by diverting them to Jordan, and held the passengers hostage in return for the release of Arab guerrillas held prisoner by Israel, Great Britain, West Germany, and Switzerland. While negotiations were under way to exchange the prisoners for the hostages, open civil war broke out in Jordan between the guerrillas and the government. Hussein's troops finally regained control over the country after two weeks of fighting, but internal order in Jordan remained precarious.

THE ARABIAN PENINSULA. South of Jordan and Iraq stretches a large and sparsely populated peninsula that is rich in oil and poor in almost every other resource. The greater part of this peninsula lies within the frontiers of Saudi Arabia, but bordering it on the south and east are Yemen, Southern Yemen, Muscat and Oman, the Persian Gulf States, and Kuwait.

Only in recent years has Saudi Arabia emerged from obscurity, and its rise has been tied to the wealth produced by its oil resources. Although neutral in the war, King Ibn Saud received British and American support, and in 1944 he permitted the United States to construct a large air base at Dhahran. More important, however, were the profits from the American oil concessions, which by the late 1950s were bringing into the King's treasury well over a quarter of a billion dollars a year. While very substantial sums were expended on the royal household and on the army, much of this new income went for such basic investments as railroads, harbors, and electric power. These resources also strengthened Ibn Saud's position, and he became a powerful force favoring a moderate pro-Western policy despite the fact that, like most Arabs, he was antagonistic to Israel. The weakness of Ibn Saud's position, however, was that he relied heavily on his personal prestige among his Arab tribesmen and did not have the backing of a fully organized government. When he died in 1953 he was succeeded by Saud, whose younger brother, Faisal, was named crown prince. King Saud did not have his father's personal prestige within his kingdom, and his opposition to Nasser provoked domestic unrest. For all practical purposes Saud was replaced in 1958 by Faisal, who served as prime minister and was not averse to working with Nasser. Four years later Faisal formally seized full government powers, and in 1964 he dethroned Saud and succeeded him as king. Faisal is a reforming ruler who seeks to transform his country from a tribal existence to a modern way of life without revolutionary excesses. Relying for four-fifths of his income on revenue from oil, he has sought to diversify the economy and attract foreign capital.

King Faisal and his associates face a difficult problem in seeking to meet the challenge of left-wing Arab nationalism. On the one hand they have sought to preserve the security of their government by opposing Nasser's effort to support republicanism in Yemen. On the other, they have joined with Kuwait and Libya in making substantial financial contributions to the support of Egypt after its defeat in the Six-Day War. Their principal effort, however, has been to demonstrate through the development of their own countries that moderation can be as successful as radicalism.

In Yemen, nationalist forces succeeded in 1948 in overthrowing the traditional system of government and assassinating the ruler, Imam Yahyah. The revolt was short-lived, however, for within a month the old regime was restored with the Crown Prince Ahmed as the new imam. In 1955 Ahmed suppressed another nationalist uprising and then decided to embark on a program of modernization. He sought both American and Soviet aid, and seemed eager to lead his country away from its traditionally tribal way of life. At the same time, he became involved in a bitter struggle with the Aden Protectorate, a large area that Britain dominated through Aden Colony. This conflict broke out into open warfare in 1957 and led Ahmed to seek Soviet arms and technical assistance. Yemen also aligned itself with the United Arab Republic when the latter was formed in 1958 and thus associated its policies with those of Nasser. A republican revolt in 1962 overthrew Imam Ahmed, but was unable to establish effective control over the country until 1969. The royalists retreated into the rugged mountains and received substantial support from Saudi Arabia. It took 10,000 Egyptian troops to help the republicans turn the tide, and also extensive aid from the USSR and China, before a reasonably secure republican regime could be established.

The radical trend of republicanism in Yemen has been in part a reaction to the process of decolonization in the former British Aden Colony and Aden Protectorate. A long period of civil strife finally culminated in the establishment in 1967 of a People's Republic of Southern

Yemen under a leftist National Liberation Front government. The new government has sought to balance the urban interests in Aden with those of the mountain tribes, and it has maintained a precarious stability that is constantly threatened by popular frustration arising from desperate poverty. The last strongholds of Arab tribal rule, represented by all the countries south of Iraq except Yemen and Southern Yemen, are now threatened by the People's Front for the Liberation of the Occupied Arabian Gulf (PFLOAG). Based in Southern Yemen, and supported by Soviet and Chinese advisers, PFLOAG seeks to capitalize on the discontent aroused by the conservatism of the traditional sheikhdoms which are only now beginning to awaken to the realities of the modern world.

The approach of the scheduled British withdrawal in 1971 from the remaining Arab sheikhdoms was unsettling for the traditional rulers. In July, 1970, the 32-year reign of Sultan Said bin Taimur of Muscat and Oman came to an end when he was ousted by his British-educated son, Qabus bin Said. The new sultan changed the name of his country to Oman, to emphasize its unity, and opened it to foreign support for the sweeping economic and social reforms that he planned. While seeking to lead his country into the modern world, Sultan Qabus also faced active warfare in his western province of Dhofar, which was infiltrated by guerrillas based in Southern Yemen.

The neighboring sheikhdoms of Bahrein, Qatar, and the seven Trucial States, whose defense and foreign relations had been handled by Britain under the terms of treaties concluded in the nineteenth century, sought to bolster their security by establishing a federation after the British departure. The problems of these oil-rich areas under traditional leadership are reflected in Kuwait, which was a British protectorate until 1961. It is able to provide free education and medical services for its population of half a million. It also contributes heavily to the support of the larger Arab countries that bore the brunt of the Six-Day War, thus acknowledging that their great wealth should be made available to Arabs generally. While the Arab crisis lasts the more modern Arab governments are likely to tolerate the oil sheikhdoms because of the support that they offer, but in the long run these oases of affluence will face demands for their incorporation into some form of larger Arab commonwealth.

Sub-Saharan Africa

FORMER BRITISH POSSESSIONS. As Britain's strategic position in the Mediterranean weakened, she placed more emphasis on her position in East Africa. In Kenya colony a violent antiwhite secret society known as the Mau Mau began in 1952 a policy of terrorism which forced Britain to undertake major armed intervention. By 1957 the situation showed such marked improvement that most of the emergency regulations could be relaxed. Under a constitution worked out by a conference in London, Kenya received its independence on December 12, 1963, as a member of the Commonwealth. Exactly a year later it declared itself a republic, and Jomo Kenyatta, who had long led the native nationalist forces, became president.

Kenyatta exercised a firm control of affairs. The remnants of the Mau Mau who refused an amnesty were subdued by military action. There were difficulties with Somalia and Ethiopia over borders and the tribesmen who wander back and forth across them. A settlement was eventually reached by negotiation. China made a definite bid for influence in Kenya, but Kenyatta rejected communism as "somebody else's nationalism" and insisted on a policy of nonalignment. In 1966 he won a political life-or-death struggle with a powerful leftist rival, Oginga Odinga, who, however, is still active in politics. Kenyatta has backed a Kenyanization policy designed to place Kenyan citizens in control of political, industrial, and commercial life. This hit many Indian residents who, under the 1963 agreement granting Kenya independence, had been permitted to keep British passports. They began to flock to England, which led the British government in February, 1968, to restrict Asian immigration from Kenya to an annual quota of 1,500 heads of families and their dependents. This policy of the British government was bitterly criticized both in Kenya and in Britain.

Kenya has been the recipient of much economic aid from the United States and Britain. Under the skillfull leadership of its minister of economics, Tom Mboya, it made great industrial progress. This brought with it labor strife, and Kenya was plagued by strikes and political unrest. In July, 1969, Tom Mboya was assassinated. At that time he was considered one of the most able leaders in Kenya and a possible successor of Kenyatta.

Elsewhere in British Africa, notably in West Africa, there has been steady and on the whole peaceful economic and political development toward self-rule. Ghana (formerly the Gold Coast and the British trust territory of Togoland) became an independent member of the Commonwealth on March 7, 1957, to be followed by Nigeria (1960), Sierra Leone (1961), Tanganyika (1961), Uganda (1962), Zanzibar (1963), and Gambia (1965). On April 26, 1964, Tanganyika and Zanzibar merged and the following October adopted the name Tanzania.

In 1953 the protectorates of Northern Rhodesia, Nyasaland, and the self-governing colony of Southern Rhodesia were joined in a federation. Following the dissolution of this federation in 1963, Nyasaland achieved independence in 1964 as the state of Malawi, as did Northern Rhodesia which became Zambia. In 1966 Botswana (formerly Bechuanaland) and Lesotho (Basutoland) became independent, as did Swaziland and the Island of Mauritius in 1968.

Southern Rhodesia (after October 24, 1964, simply Rhodesia) reverted to its status as an internal self-governing colony. Bitter strife between the dominant 200,000 white settlers, who hold most of the cultivable land, and the 4,000,000 underprivileged native Africans delayed independence. The predominantly white electorate voted overwhelmingly for independence on November 6, 1964, but the British government warned the Rhodesians against declaring independence without its approval, such approval being contingent on a satisfactory agreement being implemented between Africans and whites. Nevertheless, under the leadership of Prime Minister Ian D. Smith, Rhodesia on November 11, 1965, declared its independence. This step was condemned in London as well as at the UN, and the British government undertook economic sanctions, including an oil embargo, against its rebellious territory. The United States cooperated in this policy. The unwillingness of England to use armed force against Rhodesia was condemned by the Organization of African Unity, and nine members of the OAU temporarily severed relations with Britain as a tangible manifestation of their dissatisfaction with what they considered Britain's too patient handling of the Smith regime. Negotiations between the Rhodesian government and London led to no agreement, and in 1969 Rhodesia adopted a new constitution which would perpetuate white rule. In the constitutional referendum the voters overwhelmingly approved the establishment of a republic and severing all governmental links with Britain. This action was not recognized by the London authorities, who insisted that any settlement of the Rhodesian dispute must rest on "unimpeded progress within a reasonable time towards [black] majority rule." Only South Africa and Portugal supported Rhodesia and helped to bolster its economy. On March 2, 1970, Rhodesia officially proclaimed itself a republic.

The independence of various former British colonies was achieved with relatively little bloodshed. But independence did not solve all the problems. In Nigeria bitter strife developed, and this came to the fore in the first nationwide parliamentary elections which were held on December 30, 1964. The basic question was whether Nigeria should be dominated by the large Northern Region or by a combination of the smaller Western, Midwestern, and Eastern regions. This was complicated by tribal and religious differences. New elections in 1965 added only to the political turmoil and led to two bloody army-led *coups d'état* in 1966. In these, leaders from the Northern Region who favored a more centralized united Nigerian government won. Unfortunately in all this strife some units of the army got out of hand and many Ibo tribesmen who had moved into the Northern Region were killed. Others fled back to the Eastern Region, their tribal center. This area is the most important oil-producing region of Nigeria, and control over this huge mineral wealth was a factor (how significant is hard to evaluate) in the civil war which soon broke out. The governor of the Eastern Region, Lt. Col. Odumegiou Ojukwu, was suspicious of the aims of the central authorities and wanted supreme power vested in the regions. On May 30, 1967, he declared the independence of the Eastern Region as the Republic of Biafra. The central government under the direction of Major General Yakubu Gowon immediately dispatched troops to suppress the rebel movement.

This attempt at coercion developed into a long bloody war. The

Nigerian army seized the Biafran coast cities and came to control the Niger River. This meant Biafra was blockaded, and starvation set in among the thousands of Ibo refugees. The Red Cross and various church agencies undertook to supply food, which had to be flown in at night. Collections were held in Europe, America, and other countries as well to help the "starving Biafrans." However, ways were also found to send military supplies to Biafra, most of this coming from nearby Gabon. Efforts by the UN and by the Organization of African Unity to arrange a settlement were unsuccessful. Four African states, Tanzania, Ivory Coast, Zambia, and Gabon granted Biafra recognition in 1968. The policies of the great powers were not clear-cut. Britain on the whole favored the central authorities, while France finally announced in 1968 that it supported the principle of self-determination for Biafra. Although the greater part of its territory was occupied by the Nigerian forces, the Republic of Biafra held on, and the bloodshed and starvation continued. After the seizure of the most important airfield by Nigerian troops, Biafra surrendered on January 12, 1970, thus ending the thirty-one-month civil war. The Nigerian government at once took over the distribution of relief supplies to the many refugees, refusing to take aid from countries and groups which had been supplying the Biafrans.

In the former British Dominion of South Africa the race problem has become acute and has been a subject of repeated discussion and censure in the UN [see above, p. 597]. South Africa steadfastly maintains that the issues raised are her own internal concern and not subject to the purview of the UN. Serious clashes have occurred between natives, Indians who migrated to that country years ago as laborers, and whites. In the general election of 1948 Premier Smuts was defeated, and Daniel F. Malan, at the head of a coalition of Nationalist and Afrikander parties, took over. Malan was the exponent of a policy based on a definite statutory separation of races, which is known as *Apartheid*, a policy which was vigorously continued under Johannes A. Strijdom, who held the premiership from 1954 to 1958, and by Hendrik F. Verwoerd who succeeded him. In 1956 Johannesburg was designated an area for purely white settlement, and as a consequence large numbers of Africans and Indians had to be moved beyond the city limits. In the same year the Nationalist government was able, by reconstituting the Senate, to muster the two-thirds vote necessary to pass an Amendment Act removing the colored voters in Cape Province from the common electoral roll to a separate roll. The legality of the procedure was challenged in the courts, where it was upheld. Another act was passed in 1957, consolidating and extending those statutes under which the state controls and regulates the lives of Africans. Thus the minister of native affairs can "direct that no native shall attend any church or other religious service" if his presence might be considered a "nuisance." To such regulations the churches, with the exception of the Dutch Reformed Church, are in general offering resistance.

Nevertheless the stringency of the government's *Apartheid* policy has increased rather than diminished. The numerous measures needed to implement it have passed in parliament with little opposition. Censorship prevails and a law, commonly called the Sabotage Act, enacted in 1962, provides for a wide range of harsh penalties for deeds committed in order to change "the economic or social order." Under this law a large number of people, including Albert J. Luthuli, winner of the 1960 Nobel Peace Prize, have been placed on a list whose members may not be quoted in writing under penalty of a five-year prison term. While the racial policy is largely carried out by manifold restrictions, the government has also undertaken what is sometimes referred to as positive *Apartheid*. Toward this end it has undertaken to establish eight native governmental areas known as Bantustans where administration and self-government will be turned over to natives. The government has also attempted to provide housing for natives. But all this is far from granting nonwhites equal status, and there never has been the slightest intention of doing so.

The sentiment for a republic has always been strong among the Afrikanders. In 1957 the use of "God Save the Queen" and the Union Jack was prohibited. A plebiscite in 1960 on the establishment of a republic carried 850,458 to 775,878, and the date for its proclamation was set for May 31, 1961. When India, Pakistan, and Ghana became republics they requested continuing membership in the Commonwealth. Verwoerd at first made a similar request at the meeting of the prime ministers of the Commonwealth states in London in March. Such severe criticisms of South Africa's racial policies were made by some of the prime ministers that, seeing the handwriting on the wall, Verwoerd withdrew his request and announced that South Africa would part from the Commonwealth on becoming a republic. Although in no way approving *Apartheid*, Britain and some of the other members of the Commonwealth have sought to follow a friendly policy toward South Africa, while the hostility of other members has sharpened.

On September 6, 1967, Prime Minister Verwoerd died of stab wounds inflicted by a deranged immigrant of Greek extraction from Mozambique. He was succeeded as head of the National party and as premier by Balthazar Johannes Vorster. The new prime minister pledged himself to carry forward his predecessor's policies. *Apartheid* has been tightened by new laws, but at the same time more self-government has come to colored areas through the organization of local assemblies. The *Apartheid* program continues to win votes in South Africa and condemnation at the UN and in most countries of the world. Because of its racial policies South Africa was barred from the 1964 and 1968 Olympic games. In spite of the discriminatory racial practices, realistic economic arrangements have been established with neighboring Malawi, Swaziland, Lesotho, and Botswana, all of which are dependent on transit through South African territory. Repeated attacks in the UN [see below, p. 866] have not kept Vorster from continuing the policy of integrating South West Africa into South Africa. He has also followed a policy of cooperating with Rhodesia and has not supported the UN sponsored economic block-ade of that country. Economically South Africa has prospered, and it is by far the leading industrial country in Africa. It won a first in the medical world when Dr. Christian N. Barnard in December, 1968, per-formed the first successful heart transplant.

Out of the English possessions have emerged the only two states in Africa where the governments are dominated by descendents of the original white settlers. Many of these white families in South Africa and Rhodesia have long been resident in their respective countries and regard themselves as Africans, at least politically, and not as Europeans. They face the task of establishing a satisfactory relationship with their more numerous black neighbors who constitute the great labor force of both countries.

FORMER FRENCH POSSESSIONS. At the close of World War II the French government sought to re-establish its presence not only in Asia and in the Mediterranean area, but also in its Sub-Saharan colonies. Serious difficulties arose first in Madagascar when a revolt in 1947 was suppressed with great loss of life. In line with tradition and practice, France sought to centralize its colonial administration by joining its chief colonies into two federations: French West Africa and French Equatorial Africa. Re-forms inaugurated in 1957 provided for greater decentralization in both federations and for more native participation in government through new territorial institutions. In spite of large-scale development programs in these areas there was much unrest politically, and early in 1958 additional troops had to be sent to the Cameroons to suppress a reputedly "Com-munist-led uprising." In both federations political parties existed which demanded independence.

It was therefore a bold step by De Gaulle when he gave the colonies the alternative choice of approving the constitution of the Fifth Republic in the referendum on September 28, 1958 and staying within the French Community, or rejecting the constitution and becoming independent. Only Guinea opted for independence, which was formally granted on October 2, 1958. The following December, Guinea was admitted to the UN. Agree-ments negotiated with France in January, 1959, provided that Guinea was to remain in the French franc area and receive technical assistance from France. French was to be retained as the official language. Guinea never joined the French Community and under President Sekou Touré sought and received aid from the USSR. A long step toward re-establishing closer relations with France was taken by the signing of a number of agreements in May, 1963. Monetary problems were regulated, and French teachers were to replace most of the foreign teachers in the Guinea schools.

The other French African territories all approved De Gaulle's con-stitution and subsequently voted to become self-governing states within the French Community [see above, pp. 749–50]. But the climate of opinion in Africa was changing rapidly and by 1960 all the French colonies had become independent except for French Somaliland. [For the ways in which the old colonial areas were divided, the names of the new states

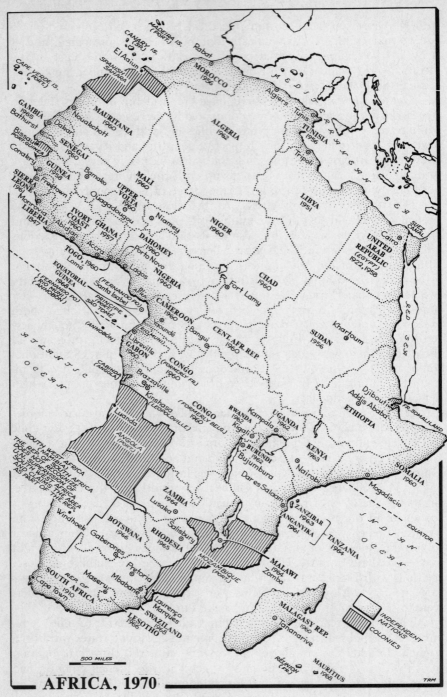

MADEIRA IS. (PORT.)
CANARY IS. (SP.)
El Aaiun
Rabat
MOROCCO 1956
CAPE VERDE IS. (PORT.)
SPANISH SAHARA
Algiers
Tunis
TUNISIA 1956
MEDITERRANEAN SEA
Cairo
SUEZ CANAL
GAMBIA 1965
Bathurst
Nouakchott
MAURITANIA 1960
Dakar
ALGERIA 1962
Tripoli
LIBYA 1951
UNITED ARAB REPUBLIC (EGYPT) 1922, 1958
RED SEA
Bissau PORT. GUINEA
Conakry
SENEGAL 1960
GUINEA 1958
Bamako
MALI 1960
Niamey
NIGER 1960
CHAD 1960
SIERRA LEONE 1961
Freetown
Monrovia
LIBERIA 1847
UPPER VOLTA 1960
Ouagadougou
IVORY COAST 1960
GHANA 1957
Abidjan
Accra
DAHOMEY 1960
Porto Novo
Lagos
NIGERIA 1960
Fort Lamy
Khartoum
SUDAN 1956
TOGO 1960
Lome
EQUATORIAL GUINEA 1968 (FERNANDO PO) (RIO MUNI) (ANNOBON)
(FERNANDO PO) Santa Isabel
PRINCIPE
SAO TOME
(ANNOBON)
CAMEROON 1960
Yaounde
(RIO MUNI)
Bangui
CENT. AFR. REP. 1960
ATLANTIC OCEAN
Libreville
GABON 1960
CONGO (FORMERLY FR.) 1960
Brazzaville
CABINDA (ANGOLA)
Kinshasa
CONGO (FORMERLY BELG.) 1960 (LEOPOLDVILLE)
Luanda
RWANDA 1962
Kigali
BURUNDI 1962
Bujumbura
Kampala
UGANDA 1962
Djibouti
Addis Ababa
FR. SOMALILAND
ETHIOPIA
KENYA 1963
Nairobi
SOMALIA 1960
Mogadiscio
ANGOLA (PORT.)
SOUTH WEST AFRICA THE REP. OF SOUTH AFRICA DOES NOT RECOGNIZE THE U.N. SUPERVISION OF THIS AREA. SOUTH WEST AFRICA CLAIMS IT AS PART OF THE REP.
Windhoek
ZAMBIA 1964
Lusaka
Dar es Salaam
ZANZIBAR 1963
TANGANYIKA 1961
TANZANIA 1964
INDIAN OCEAN
EQUATOR
BOTSWANA 1966
Gaberones
RHODESIA 1965
Salisbury
MOZAMBIQUE (PORT.)
MALAWI 1964
Zomba
REP. OF SOUTH AFRICA 1910
Cape Town
Maseru
Mbabane
Pretoria
Lourenço Marques
SWAZILAND 1968
LESOTHO 1966
MALAGASY REP. 1960
Tananarive
RÉUNION (FR.)
MAURITIUS 1968
INDEPENDENT NATIONS
COLONIES
500 MILES

AFRICA, 1970

MAP 33

TRM

with the dates of independence, and their membership in the United Nations, see the map on p. 852 and Appendices IV and VIII.]

FORMER BELGIAN POSSESSIONS. After World War II the rich Belgian Congo continued to supply the Belgian government with much-needed revenue and scarce foreign exchange. In 1957 the first steps toward elective government were taken in the Congo when partially-elected town councils were established. Self-government never went very far, and the Congo was usually considered a showpiece of European paternalism in Africa. But developments in the French colonies were not without influence in the Congo, where nationalist riots broke out in Leopoldville in January, 1959, and continued spasmodically here and in other cities during the year. Troops had to be called in to maintain order. Belgium, in an effort to meet the demands of the natives, announced a program for the gradual attainment of self-rule in the Belgian Congo. This was rejected by such leaders as Joseph Kasavubu and Patrice Lumumba. The Africans demanded immediate independence. A visit by King Baudouin and his premier to the Congo in December convinced the Belgians that the demand for independence was not to be ignored. The government decided forthwith to call a round-table conference to meet January 20, 1960, in Brussels. Forty-four Congolese delegates, drawn from various parties, attended. Although holding diverse views on many issues, they presented a united front in insisting on immediate independence. At the conference it was agreed that the Congo should become independent on June 30 of that year, and a timetable was worked out for drawing up the constitution, holding elections, and establishing a government.

Elections were held at the end of May; the Belgian parliament approved a provisional constitution which embraced the decisions of the round-table conference on June 19; the first Congolese cabinet headed by Patrice Lumumba took office on June 24, and that same day Joseph Kasavubu was elected president of the new state by the two chambers of parliament; on June 29 a treaty of friendship and co-operation was signed at Leopoldville by Belgian and Congolese representatives, and according to schedule at midnight on June 30 by royal proclamation of King Baudouin the Belgian Congo became the independent Republic of the Congo.

From this enumeration of key steps it is obvious that the shift from a paternalistic colonial administration to independence had gone very fast, too fast as it soon appeared. The native leaders were untrained and inexperienced. They were not united as to policy, nor did they have the loyal backing of disciplined parties. It had been assumed that the transition period would go smoothly, since Belgian advisers and Belgian officers had been retained on a temporary basis. But early in July native troops mutinied against their Belgian officers, and there were numerous incidents of violence against Belgian civilians. Belgium reacted quickly and flew in troops, whereupon on July 12 the Congolese government appealed to the United Nations for military assistance. With unprecedented speed, in accordance with a resolution of the Security Council, the first detachment of a UN force arrived at Leopoldville airport on July 15. The troops of the UN Operation in the Congo (ONUC, derived from the French title) were drawn mostly from Africa, but also had contingents from Sweden, Ireland, and other non-African states. ONUC was to serve as a politically neutral stabilizing power resorting to fighting only in self-defense. The Security Council called upon Belgium to withdraw its military personnel.

Meanwhile civil war had in fact broken out in the Congo. On July 11, Moise Tshombe, the pro-Belgian premier of mineral-rich Katanga province, had proclaimed the secession of Katanga from the central government. Other provinces threatened to break away. The authorities in Leopoldville, divided among themselves, were unable to assert control. In mid-July Premier Lumumba, who wanted the UN forces to throw Tshombe out of Katanga, in desperation appealed to the Soviet Union for aid. The Security Council had specifically passed a resolution against unilateral aid by any power, but by late August some Soviet aircraft, other materials, and Soviet personnel had arrived. The Secretary-General had in the meantime arranged by negotiation with Tshombe for the entrance of UN troops into Katanga on August 12, and Belgian forces were withdrawn.

The Congolese central government, however, was in turmoil as a result of conflicting policies. President Kasavubu dismissed Premier Lumumba, who refused to step down and in turn dismissed the President. The premier was subsequently arrested and held by an army contingent. What unanimity there had been among the great powers in the Security Council was also dissolving. Things came to a head over the question of approval of the policies undertaken by Secretary-General Dag Hammarskjöld in implementing UN policy. The USSR submitted a resolution calling for the end of UN interference in the internal affairs of the Congo. This was defeated, whereupon the Soviets vetoed a draft resolution proposed by Ceylon and Tunisia calling upon the Secretary-General to give vigorous implementation to previous UN resolutions. The whole future UN policy in the Congo was at stake. To circumvent the Soviet veto the United States was able to have a resolution approved in the Security Council (8–2 with one abstention) referring the Congo problem to a special session of the General Assembly under the "Uniting for Peace" resolution of 1950. The Soviets have always rejected action under this resolution. They opposed the Assembly's draft resolution sponsored by the African states which asked for continued UN aid to the Congo, appealed for financial contributions, and called upon all states to refrain from giving military assistance outside the United Nations. Although the Security Council repeatedly discussed the Congo, it was Assembly action which henceforth was responsible for the continuation of ONUC. Russia, France, and other states maintained that the Security Council and not the Assembly is responsible for peace-keeping actions and refused to pay the assessments which were eventually necessary to support the Congo peace-keeping force [see below, p. 865].

Premier Lumumba, having escaped detention, attempted to regain authority, but was killed on February 13, 1961, probably by mercenaries employed by Katanga authorities. The situation deteriorated so badly that the Security Council on February 21, 1961, with France and the USSR abstaining, authorized the UN forces to use force to prevent the recurrence of civil war in the Congo. After further negotiations failed to restore Congo unity the UN forces in September, 1961, began to assert control over Katanga. It was, at this time, not a question of fighting their way into the province, but rather of resisting expulsion by the mercenary-led local gendarmerie. On a visit in connection with this action Secretary-General Hammarskjöld was killed in an airplane crash. The UN forces not only established effective control of Katanga, but of other provinces as well. In June, 1963, Tshombe announced his withdrawal from politics and flew to Paris for medical treatment. The Republic of the Congo entered upon a period of relative stability under the administration of Premier Adoula. By the end of 1963 the UN contingent which had at one time numbered close to 20,000 men and officers was cut back to 5,350.

The Congo assembly elected in 1960 which was to draw up a definitive constitution to replace the basic law drafted by Belgium never got around to it. This assembly was dissolved in September, 1963, and a commission of 127 members began drafting a new constitution. The latter was approved by popular vote in June–July, 1964. On June 30 the last UN forces were withdrawn; the Congo was starting out afresh. A new government was established with Kasavubu as president, and Tshombe, who returned from Spain where he had been living in exile, as premier. The return of Tshombe had the approval of both Belgium and the United States.

Civil strife, in part inspired by foreign-supported influences, again developed, and the rebel movement made considerable headway. The rebels soon came to hold many Belgian and other white civilians and officials, as well as many missionaries as hostages. On November 24, 1964, United States planes with the authorization of the Tshombe government dropped Belgian paratroopers at Stanleyville for the sole purpose of rescuing hostages. About 2,000 people were evacuated in a limited four-day operation, but it was too late to save many of them. The action was labeled by some as unbridled imperialistic intervention. A group of African nations pressed for condemnation of the United States and Belgium by the Security Council to which the Council responded with a harmless resolution asking for the end of foreign intervention, a cease-fire, the withdrawal of mercenaries, and a government of reconciliation.

Elections were held in the Congo March 18 to April 30, 1965, and Tshombe's newly formed National Congolese Convention (CONACO) won an overall majority of 86 seats in the chamber. However, the Appeal Court in Leopoldville invalidated the election, because of irregularities in three key central provinces, and elections were repeated there in August. These went against Tshombe, and dissension also arose within his loosely organized CONACO grouping. On October 8 President Kasavubu dismissed the Tshombe government. The new cabinet headed by Evariste Kimba failed to receive parliamentary approval. At the President's request he continued as premier, and new elections were announced for the spring of 1966. In a move to end the political feuding between Kasavubu and Tshombe, Major General Joseph D. Mobutu, the army commander, on November 25, 1965, seized power. He ousted Kasavubu, organized a new cabinet without including Tshombe, canceled the coming elections and announced that he would rule as president for five years.

The situation remains far from stable, but during the past years the central government has gained in strength. Belgian-Congo relations have had their ups and downs; nevertheless, Belgian technicians and teachers have returned to the Congo; Belgian advisers are training the new Congolese army. Although Belgium has lost the colony, she actually has regained considerable influence and status in the Congo.

SPANISH AND PORTUGUESE POSSESSIONS. In the postwar years, Spain yielded certain of its territories in the western bulge of Africa to Morocco, retaining for the time being Spanish Sahara and a couple of enclaves along the Mediterranean Coast [see above, pp. 797–98]. In Sub-Saharan Africa she possessed the ancient colony of Spanish Guinea, consisting of the territory of Rio Muni, wedged in between Cameroon and Gabon, on the mainland, the larger islands of Fernando Po and Annobón and three tiny nearby islands. The colony known as Equatorial Guinea since 1963 had an area of slightly over 10,000 square miles and a population of about 200,000. Early in 1968 the Spanish government, in line with recommendations by the UN Special Commission on Colonialism, began negotiations with native leaders for a transfer of sovereignty. On October 12, 1968, Equatorial Guinea became the thirty-eighth African country to gain its independence since the end of World War II.

Like other African countries, Equatorial Guinea is beset with tribal differences. There is discord between the Bubis of Fernando Po and the more numerous Fangs of Rio Muni. The Bubis have a literacy rate of around 90 percent and are far more prosperous than the people on the mainland. Disputes also arose with Spain about withdrawal of garrisons which had remained to protect Spanish citizens. In the spring of 1969, the president of Equatorial Guinea appealed to the UN for aid. Secretary-General U Thant sent a special envoy to lend his good offices in bringing about a settlement. Here as elsewhere, the transfer from colonial status to independence brought serious problems. Old trade and cultural ties will no doubt assure Spain a continuing role in the republic's development.

Unlike Spain and the other great powers who have granted independence to their Sub-Saharan colonies, Portugal is determined to retain her possessions of Portuguese Guinea, Angola, and Mozambique [see above, pp. 800–2]. Her efforts to hold back the mounting waves of anticolonial feeling in the world has already cost her years of warfare which promise to continue in the future.

The Movement Toward African Unity.

The establishment of a growing number of independent African states led to the formation of regional groupings for various purposes. A conference of Independent African States met at Accra in Ghana, in 1958, and eventually three major groups came into being, known by the cities in which the founding conference had met. These were the Brazzaville, Casablanca, and Monrovia groups, all having an indefinite geographical or ideological basis for union [see Appendix VII]. These unions met with little success, and finally representatives of all three groups agreed to participate in a meeting of African states to be held at Addis Ababa, Ethiopia, in May, 1963. Emperor Haile Selassie I was host to the meeting and contributed much to its success. Thirty states were represented and agreed to establish an Organization of African Unity (OAU). The Charter which outlines the aims and establishes the administrative bodies, resembles in many ways the UN Charter. The principles of the United Nations and the Universal Declaration of Human Rights are affirmed, and the OAU functions as one of the regional groupings foreseen by the UN Charter. Morocco and Tunis, which were not represented at Addis Ababa, signed the Charter shortly thereafter. Since then as African states have become independent, they have immediately sought and obtained admission [see Appendix VII].

The Charter establishes a permanent secretariat and various commissions to further economic, social, and cultural activities.[1] Twice yearly the foreign (or other designated) ministers meet as a Council of Ministers, and the Heads of States assemble once a year, or if needed, in extraordinary session. Procedural matters require only a majority, but decisions require a two-thirds vote. There is no arrangement to impose sanctions if a member does not agree with decisions reached; the aim is to provide a forum for discussion and action by reaching a consensus. It is recognized that African unity does not exist today, and there are basic differences and problems confronting the Mediterranean states and those below the Sahara. Yet there are many things the states have in common, for example, an antagonism to colonialism and a need for modernization of their societies with all that this entails. The OAU has been effective in settling some controversies among member states, even if it has not been able to prevent all resort to arms. It also has created something of a united front and serves to present the African point of view at the United Nations.

The existence of the OAU does not preclude the formation of other regional groupings. There are approximately some fifty such regional associations in Africa today. Two of the more important economic groupings are the Central African Economic and Customs Union and the East African Community [see Appendix VII]. The latter grouping, consisting of Kenya, Tanzania, and Uganda, was formed for the definite purpose of negotiating an agreement with the Common Market. Whereas eighteen former

---

[1] See the succinct pamphlet issued by the Department of State: *The Organization of African Unity* (Department of State Publication 8444, Washington, D.C., 1969).

French, Belgian, and Italian African colonies had previously been accorded associate membership in the Common Market, these were the first former British colonies to seek such membership [see above, pp. 648–49]. On September 1, 1969, associate agreements between Morocco, Tunisia, and the Common Market went into effect. To describe the activity of all the regional associations would be to write the recent history of the whole continent; it must suffice here merely to note the trends to African unity.

CHAPTER

34

Europe and the World

The United Nations in Action: *Disputes Before the Council; Disputes Before the Assembly; Vanishing Trusteeships; The Economic and Social Council and the Specialized Agencies; Growth of Regionalism; Disarmament; Use of Armed Forces; Financial Crisis; Disputes Before the International Court of Justice.*
Twentieth-Century Trends: *Freedom and Security; Evolution of European Society.*

IT IS EASY to tear down but hard to build up, it is easy to divide but difficult to unite again, it is easy to start a quarrel or war but it is a long, laborious process to establish friendships or make peace. These aphorisms are amply illustrated by the history of Europe and the world in all periods, but in none more so than in the years since the close of World War II. And during this time it has been the United Nations that has offered a constructive hope, an organization which has attempted to build anew, which has sought to unite rather than divide, which has steadfastly fostered friendship and peace, and done much to alleviate the sufferings of mankind. The cleavages and antagonisms existing among the nations have indeed been manifested in the UN and have circumscribed its effectiveness. Yet a rapid survey of its activities will show, except to those who are unwilling to see, that it has achieved much and holds the hope of achieving more.

The United Nations in Action

The post of Secretary-General proved to be a most exacting one. Trygve Lie, its first incumbent, was re-elected to a second term and on his resignation in 1953 was succeeded by Dag Hammarskjöld, Swedish Minister of State. Hammarskjöld was a most effective administrator and vigorously extended the activities of the organization. This was notably true in the peace-keeping operations in the Near East and in the Congo. His policies in the Congo particularly aroused the ire of Khrushchev, who in an address to the General Assembly on September 19, 1960, advocated the removal of Hammarskjöld and the replacement of the Secretary-General's office by a three-man body representing Eastern, Western, and neutral states. Nothing came of this so-called *troika* (three horse) proposal. Having won the endorsement of the Assembly, Hammarskjöld continued his attempts to bring peace to the Congo and while on a mission to that country was killed in an airplane crash on September 18, 1961. A deadlock occurred over the choice of his successor, but after some deft negotiation the Security Council made a unanimous recommendation to the Assembly that U Thant of Burma be named Acting Secretary-General. This was done on November 3 and the following November he was appointed Secretary-General for a term expiring on November 3, 1966, five years after his original appointment. Although personally reluctant to do so, because of the diverse and uncooperative policies of the great powers, he was, however, prevailed upon to accept election to a second term.

DISPUTES BEFORE THE COUNCIL. Although the activities of the United Nations and its many agencies are manifold, it is its actions in relation to disputes, wars, or threats of war on which the attention of the world focuses. A large number of "disputes" or "situations" [see above, p. 592, for the technical distinction between the two] have been brought before the Security Council. Many of them have already been discussed and so need only be brought to mind here.

The first was a complaint by Iran in January, 1946, charging Russian interference in Iranian affairs. The Council heard both parties and recommended direct settlement. Eventually the USSR withdrew its troops, and so the crisis passed. Since then the Council has been called upon to deal with such diverse problems as the existence of fascism in Spain; the sinking of British destroyers in the Corfu Channel by Albanian mines; the Palestine question; the problem of India and Pakistan and their relation to Kashmir; the Soviet blockade of Berlin in 1948; the administration of Trieste; frontier difficulties between Greece and its neighbors; the Anglo-Iranian oil question; restrictions by Egypt on the passage of shipping through the Suez Canal; the invasion of South Korea by North Korea; armed hostilities off the coast of China in 1955; the Hungarian Revolution; the Suez Crisis; the Iraq-Lebanon-Jordan Crisis of 1958; various incidents involving Loas, Cambodia, and Vietnam (1959–65); violation of Russian airspace by United States reconnaissance planes (RB–47 and U-2 incidents, 1960); violation of Argentine sovereignty by Israel in kidnapping Adolf Eichmann (1960); several complaints by Cuba of United States harassments (1960–62) as well as the United States-Russia crisis over the existence of Russian missile bases in Cuba in 1962; incidents involving strife in the Congo (1960–64); the Portuguese African colonies (1963); Cyprus (1963); Dominican Republic (1965); armed conflict between Pakistan and India over Kashmir (1965); the unilateral declaration of independence by the white minority government in Rhodesia (1965) when the UN went so far as to impose economic sanctions (1966, 1968) against that country; the war in Vietnam (1966); the civil war in South Arabia (1966); the Israeli-Arab War (1967 f.); and the Warsaw Pact invasion of Czechoslovakia (1968). Many of these problems have been before the Council repeatedly. At times incidents were never really dealt with because discussion was killed in the early steps by a veto. Many other thorny problems such as the independence movements in Morocco, Tunisia, and Algeria in the 1950s were called to the attention of the Council but were not placed on the agenda for official action.

One of the most important problems to come before the Security Council was the Korean question. After World War II Korea north of the 38th parallel was placed under Russian occupation, the territory to the south under that of the United States. Negotiations for establishing an independent united democratic Korea broke down and the issue was referred to the United Nations General Assembly in 1947. The Assembly recommended holding elections and appointed a commission to supervise them. The Soviet authorities, however, refused to admit the commission to North Korea and supervised elections were held only in South Korea. The General Assembly thereupon recognized the government of President Syngman Rhee as the legitimate government of South Korea, and the United States withdrew its occupation forces. Russia, however, sponsored a government of North Korea and on June 25, 1950, North Korean troops invaded South Korea.

The United States immediately requested the Security Council to consider the issue. Russia had boycotted the Council since January 13 because of the continued representation of Nationalist China on that body, and with Russia absent the Council by a unanimous vote declared the North Korean action a breach of the peace. North Korea was asked to withdraw its troops. The Commission on Korea which was in South Korea at the time was asked to submit a factual report. On June 26 the United States resolved to aid the forces of South Korea in repelling the invasion and the next day the Security Council recommended that "members of the United Nations aid the Republic of Korea in repelling the armed attack so as to restore international peace and security in the area." Subsequently the Security Council requested the President of the United States to appoint a Supreme Commander of all United Nations forces in Korea. General Douglas MacArthur received the command.

The presidency of the Security Council rotates monthly among the members states; in August it was Russia's turn to assume the office, which it did, thus ending its six and one-half month boycott of the Council. Russia, through its power of veto, soon stalled effective action by the Council on Korean matters, and the Assembly inherited the problem. It was primarily this body that dealt with Korea subsequently and supervised the cease-fire and truce agreement of July 27, 1953, made at Panmunjom [see map, p. 863]. The task of establishing a free democratic unified Korea was left to future negotiations.

A conference was held at Geneva from April 26 to June 15, 1954, but no agreement could be reached on how a united Korea was to be established. Meanwhile two UN bodies that had been established in 1950, the United Nations Commission for the Unification and Rehabilitation of Korea (UNCURK), and the United Nations Korean Reconstruction Agency (UNKRA), continued to function although their activity was limited to South Korea. A Neutral Nations Supervisory Commission to oversee the implementation of the armistice terms was found to be ineffective and was deactivated in June, 1956. A year later the Assembly voted to dissolve UNKRA. Most of the funds for this agency had been supplied by the United States. When the American government ceased to channel large funds through the UN, preferring to bolster South Korea by its own program of military and economic aid, the life blood of UNKRA was sapped. The UN Military Command still functions (1970) with two divisions of United States troops and a few small units from other countries who fought in the war remaining in South Korea. Also, the UN Assembly regularly hears reports on Korea and passes resolutions calling for the reunification of the country. The Korean settlement remains an uneasy one; neither Korea has been able to coerce the other, and each goes its own way—the one under Communist auspices, the other nurtured by the United States and the free world.

The Security Council has not been particularly successful in solving the issues placed before it; yet it has served the very useful purpose of providing a forum for discussion and argument when problems threatened to become critical. The Council has in many cases made it possible to keep negotiations alive and to postpone decisions when too great haste might have led to armed conflict. The commissions which have been sent out, such as those to study the problems of Greece and India, have contributed much to the clarification of issues and the correct orientation of public opinion.

DISPUTES BEFORE THE ASSEMBLY. The maintenance of peace is primarily the work of the Security Council, but according to Article 10 the Assembly can discuss any question that may arise under the Charter. It cannot, however, make recommendations when the Security Council is considering a "dispute or situation," except on the request of the Council. In practice the Security Council by a majority vote has removed certain matters from its agenda, thus enabling the General Assembly to discuss them and make recommendations. This was done, for example, in

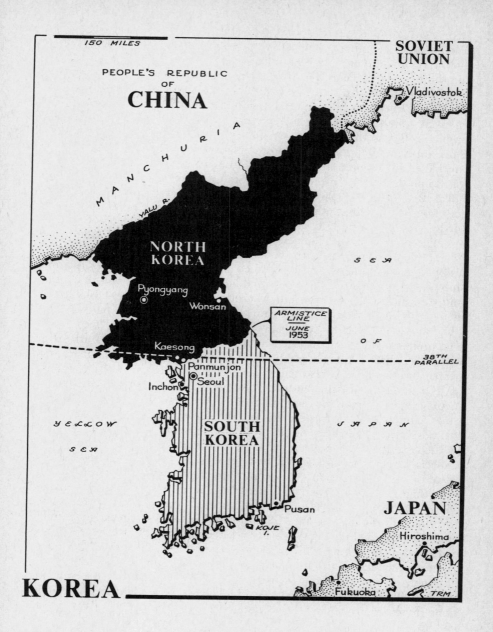

KOREA

MAP 34

regard to the Polish appeal on the question of fascism in Spain and to the Greek appeal charging Albania, Bulgaria, and Yugoslavia with supporting guerrillas in Greece. The Assembly and Council have both dealt with the thorny issue of Palestine. This matter first came before the Assembly, which in turn referred it to the Council. The Council later requested the Secretary-General to call a special meeting of the Assembly to take up the Palestine question. Both bodies have since repeatedly discussed the problem. It was the General Assembly that sent a Commission to study the question and appointed a "United Nations Mediator," but both bodies considered his reports. It was largely through the efforts of Acting Mediator Ralph J. Bunche of the United States, who took over after Count Folke Bernadotte of Sweden had been assassinated, that a temporary cessation of hostilities was arranged between Israel and the Arab states (1949) [see above, pp. 830–31].

The failure of the Council to do anything about Spain led to consideration of this matter by the Assembly. In December, 1946, a resolution was passed recommending that Franco Spain be debarred from membership in the specialized agencies, that all member states withdraw their ministers and ambassadors from Madrid, and that if no suitable government were established soon in Spain the Security Council should consider what measures were to be taken. This resolution was not lived up to. The problem of the mistreatment of Indians in the Union of South Africa was placed before the Assembly by the Indian Government. It aroused heated discussions and resulted in a resolution stating that the treatment of Indians should be in line with international obligations. Both governments were to report on action taken. The topic was broached several times later but never passed beyond the discussion stage. Greece's difficulties with its northern neighbors illustrate another procedure followed by the Assembly. When the case came before it, the Assembly established a special committee and sent it to Greece in 1947 for the purpose of observation and conciliation. This committee reported to the Assembly, and from then until May 28, 1954, United Nations military observers remained on the frontiers of Greece. On that date, at the request of the Greek government, the mission was discontinued, and the Greek government officially expressed its thanks to the United Nations for the success of its endeavors in the interest of international peace. The Assembly also played an important part in the Korean dispute, particularly after Russia resumed its attendance at the Council meetings and the action of that body was stalemated. At various times the Assembly has discussed and passed resolutions in regard to the strife in Indonesia, Morocco, Tunis, Algeria, and Cyprus.

In 1956 when the USSR vetoed the Council's resolution calling for the cessation of Russian intervention in the Hungarian Revolution and when France and Britain vetoed the Council's resolution on a cease-fire in the Suez Invasion, both these issues came before the Assembly in accordance with the "Uniting for Peace Resolution" of 1950 [see above, p. 591].

The Assembly and its agencies worked out a solution of the Suez affair and supervised the clearing of the blocked Canal. The Hungarian government refused a committee of the Assembly permission to visit Hungary, but the Commission nevertheless was able to draw up a lengthy, well-substantiated report on the Hungarian Revolution. This was endorsed by the Assembly, which passed a resolution calling upon Hungary and the USSR "to desist from repressive measures against the Hungarian people." Similarly when the Council was unable to come to any agreement on the Iraq-Lebanon-Jordan Crisis this problem passed to the Assembly.

The Assembly has repeatedly debated and passed resolutions concerning problems arising out of the establishment of new independent states in Africa and Asia. In 1960 Nikita Khrushchev of the USSR in an address to the General Assembly proposed that in keeping with the principles of the Charter, the United Nations must declare itself in favor of the "immediate and complete elimination of the colonial system in all its forms and manifestations." Two draft declarations—one proposed by the USSR, the other by the forty-three African and Asian members of the UN—were debated and the latter one was adopted. In order to implement this "Declaration on the Granting of Independence to Colonial Countries and Peoples" the Assembly in 1961 appointed a committee of seventeen members (enlarged to twenty-four in 1962), which has developed into one of the most active UN committees. It has gathered much information on various colonial territories and has prodded the Assembly into taking an ever-increasing activity in this field. The Assembly played a very active role in the prolonged crisis and civil war which ensued when the Congo achieved independence from Belgium in 1960. It was the Assembly that was largely instrumental in establishing the UN Temporary Executive Authority (UNTEA) which supervised the transfer of West New Guinea (West Irian) from the control of the Netherlands to Indonesia (1962–63). It has regularly passed resolutions condemning the *Apartheid* policies in South Africa and has waged a continuing skirmish with that country over the administration of South West Africa [see above, p. 849]. The Assembly in 1961 established a Special Committee on Territories under Portuguese Administration and has passed resolutions at various times condemning Portugal's colonial policies as well as the action of the white dominated government in Rhodesia.

VANISHING TRUSTEESHIPS. On March 6, 1957, British Togoland, as part of the new state of Ghana, was the first trust territory to attain the goal set by the system of trusteeship. It achieved its independence as a result of careful negotiations between the Trusteeship Council and the administering power, as well as through a supervised plebiscite. Since then all other trust territories in Africa and also Western Samoa (January 1, 1962) and Nauru (January 1, 1968) have become independent. Only two trust territories remain: New Guinea with neighboring islands (Australia) and the Trust Territory of the Pacific Islands administered by the United States.

The Trusteeship Council over the years has conducted many investigations and has stimulated the adoption of important reforms in the trust territories and in other colonial lands as well. Altogether the trustee system has been one of the most successful projects undertaken by the United Nations.

The Trusteeship Council, as well as the Council or the Assembly, have, however, been unable to arrange a satisfactory settlement in respect to South West Africa. The Union of South Africa, which held a mandate over this former Germany colony as a result of the World War I settlement, always refused to negotiate a trusteeship agreement. In April, 1949, the South African legislature admitted representatives of South West Africa to the Union parliament, thus removing it to their satisfaction from mandate status. Up to that time, although denying its obligation to do so, South Africa submitted a report on South West Africa to the Assembly for its information. This practice was now discontinued, and the General Assembly requested an advisory opinion from the International Court of Justice. The court delivered its opinion on July 11, 1950, holding that South West Africa remained under the mandate system and that South Africa was not competent to modify its status without the consent of the United Nations. South Africa had the obligation to submit reports to the United Nations and to transmit petitions of the inhabitants of South West Africa. South Africa, however, was not legally obligated to place the territory under the trusteeship system. Asked again by the Assembly for a further advisory opinion, the Court in 1956 held that South Africa continued to have international obligations under the League of Nations Covenant and Mandate, and the UN Committee on South West Africa as the successor body to the League Mandates Commission had a right to grant oral hearings to petitioners from South West Africa. The General Assembly has repeatedly considered the status of South West Africa and has appointed special committees to investigate the situation. The extreme racial policy of *Apartheid* in South Africa [see above, pp. 849–51] and the extension of this policy to a territory that had been for a time under international supervision is involved.

In November, 1960, Ethiopia and Liberia instituted proceedings before the International Court of Justice charging that South Africa was not living up to its obligations as a mandatory power for South West Africa, that it was practicing *Apartheid* in that territory, and was not promoting to its utmost the material and moral well-being and social progress of the inhabitants of that territory. The judiciary wheel ground slowly, and it was not until 1966 that the Court gave its final decision. By an 8–7 vote it held that Ethiopia and Liberia had not established any legal right or interest in their claims and therefore they were rejected. This adverse decision led the Assembly that same year to declare that South Africa had not fulfilled its obligations in regard to South West Africa and that the mandate was therefore terminated. South West Africa was made the "direct responsibility" of the UN. An *ad hoc* committee was created to recommend to a special session of the Assembly in April 1967 a practical means by which the territory should be administered. A special UN Council for South West Africa and a UN Commissioner to administer the territory were established. However, South Africa did not withdraw its forces or its administration as requested, and none of the great powers were willing to sanction coercive measures. Nevertheless in 1968 the Assembly went bravely forward and proclaimed that South West Africa was henceforth to be known as Namibia and called upon the Security Council to take effective measures to secure the removal of South African presence in the territory and secure its independence. So far these resolutions, like so many others which have been passed censuring South Africa, have produced no tangible results.

THE ECONOMIC AND SOCIAL COUNCIL AND THE SPECIALIZED AGENCIES. No attempt can be made here to summarize all the multifarious activities of these bodies or of the many commissions and committees they have established. Their work is often technical in nature and their achievements must be reserved for the appreciation of specialists, as for example the history and significance of the World Bank. Yet a few things of more general nature may be noted.

The UN commissions and committees have one and all served as fact-finding and study agencies. The information they have assembled is often worldwide in scope and studies of this magnitude have never been available before. More regionally centered projects are not neglected and the reports of the Economic Commission for Europe form, for example, an expert analysis of the conditions and needs of Europe. The program carried on by the United Nations Educational, Scientific and Cultural Organization is varied, extensive, and truly to be admired. The Commission on Human Rights, on which Mrs. Franklin D. Roosevelt represented the United States for many years, drafted a Universal Declaration on Human Rights, which was approved by the General Assembly in December, 1948. An *ad hoc* committee also prepared a Convention on Genocide which has the purpose of preventing the extermination of racial, religious, or national groups. Basic human rights were furthered by a Convention on the Political Rights of Women (1954), the Declaration of the Rights of the Child (1959), and a Convention on Consent to Marriage, Minimum Age for Marriage, and Registration of Marriage (1964). A Declaration on the Elimination of Racial Discrimination was adopted in 1965.

Realizing that the need to care for children would continue after the dissolution of UNRRA, the General Assembly in 1946 established the United Nations Children's Fund (UNICEF). At first considered largely as a means of helping children in war-devastated countries, its activities have been expanded, and in 1953 the Assembly voted to continue the fund indefinitely. It is financed by voluntary contributions from governments and by private gifts from individuals and organizations. Its activity has been centered on combating such diseases as tuberculosis, malaria, yaws, trachoma, and leprosy, and in establishing maternal and child welfare services. Family-planning programs are conducted when requested by governments in the over one-hundred countries and territories where the agency operates. UNICEF's great humanitarian work was recognized when it was awarded the Nobel Peace Prize for 1965.

When the International Refugee Organization, which had functioned as a specialized agency, was discontinued, it was replaced by the Office of the United Nations High Commissioner for Refugees which began functioning in January, 1951. The Commissioner and his staff were charged with searching out permanent solutions for the refugees. This office has worked closely with other organizations established to deal with special refugee problems, notably the United Nations Relief and Works Agency (UNRWA), which was charged specifically with the care of the Arab refugee camps in the states bordering Israel. The work of this agency was greatly increased by the added number of refugees resulting from the Israeli-Arab War of 1967. The Hungarian revolution in 1956, the persistent flight of refugees from behind the Iron Curtain, the influx of Chinese to Hong Kong, have continually brought new problems for the High Commissioner. Originally established for three years, the term of the office has repeatedly been renewed.

The Interim Commission administering the General Agreement on Tariffs and Trade (GATT) has brought about extraordinary results in lowering and stabilizing tariffs. On May 4, 1964, the sixth general round (the Kennedy Round) of GATT tariff negotiations opened in Geneva. They were named in honor of the late President because of his program for freer trade embodied in the United States Trade Expansion Act of 1962. These negotiations, more comprehensive than those of previous sessions, were not concluded until June 30, 1967. Substantial tariff reductions were agreed upon in both agricultural and industrial products; these were to be implemented by stages between January 1, 1968, and January 1, 1972.

In 1964 the United Nations Conference on Trade and Development (UNCTAD) was established as a permanent organ of the General Assembly with headquarters in Geneva and a liaison office in New York. It is composed of all members of the UN and its related agencies and seeks to deal with particular problems relating to international trade. It carries on year-round activity through its numerous subsidiary committees and holds large international conferences at intervals of not more than three years.

The great humanitarian services performed by some of the specialized agencies were recognized by the Nobel prize authorities when they awarded the Nobel Peace Prize to the United Nations High Commission for Refugees in 1954, to the United Nations Children's Fund in 1965, and to the International Labor Organization in 1969. The latter award came on the fiftieth anniversary of the founding of the ILO, which was then, as it still is, deeply engaged in helping find productive labor opportunities for the people of the poorer countries, along with dealing with the rapidly increasing world population problem.

GROWTH OF REGIONALISM. The Charter of the United Nations not only recognized the existence of certain regional groupings but expressly permitted the formation of others. Most of these have been explained earlier and need only be brought into context here, for they have affected the day-to-day operations of the UN. The Inter-American System is among the oldest existing regional groups. It rests on numerous agreements and statements going back to the Monroe Doctrine of 1823; these agreements were consolidated into the "Charter of the Organization of American States" at the Bogota Conference of 1948. The Commonwealth of Nations is the product of evolutionary growth and has little regional unity beyond being united by the seven seas. The Arab League resulting from a pact signed in March, 1945, not only has a general regional unity but is united by common racial, religious, and cultural ties. The Soviet Union, by a series of bilateral treaties, a common defense pact (Warsaw), a Council for Mutual Economic Assistance (COMECON or CEMA), and through adherence to common political ideologies, has created a regional grouping in Eastern Europe. France, Britain, Belgium, the Netherlands, and Luxembourg in negotiating their fifty-year treaty of collaboration and self-defense (known as the Brussels Pact or Western European Union) in March, 1948, were careful to bring it in line with the Charter as a regional pact. The group in April, 1949, joined with Denmark, Norway, Iceland, Portugal, Canada, the United States, and even Italy, to form a North Atlantic Pact [see above, pp. 634–38]. Later the group was joined by states as remote from the North Atlantic as Turkey and Greece and also by West Germany. It is clear that the Atlantic Pact (North Atlantic Treaty Organization, NATO) was designed to create an alliance system to counterbalance Communist Eastern Europe. It aroused sharp protests from Russia on the score that it was an offensive rather than a defensive regional grouping. There have been attempts to form certain African blocs but thier membership has not been stable, which is also true of the combination of African-Asian states which has held conferences and at times co-operated at the UN. [For membership in some of the more important regional groups see Appendix VII.]

DISARMAMENT. Whereas the League of Nations Covenant envisaged a program of disarmament, the United Nations Charter stresses, if anything, the regulation of armaments rather than their limitation or reduction. In 1946 the General Assembly established an Atomic Energy Commission charged with the task of making specific proposals for the international control of atomic energy. But since the United States and the USSR could not agree, this Commission accomplished nothing. The United States insisted on a system of international control and inspection which would be a protection from willful violation of the agreement. This the USSR rejected, objecting to inspection or supervision of its internal affairs. The doubts of the British and American officials as to the good faith of Russia, under a system of voluntary controls, bore a striking resemblance to the fears of Metternich when Alexander I of Russia proposed disarmament after the Napoleonic Wars. In 1816 Metternich wrote to the British foreign minister: "The disadvantage of affording in the outset information of this nature, and the difficulty always of obtaining any true data from Russia, no one could better appreciate than your Lordship. To take the initiative here, uncertain of a reciprocity of confidence, would be impossible."

In 1947, on the recommendation of the Assembly, the Council established a Commission for Conventional Armaments to consider the reduction of armaments and armed forces, along with an effective system of guarantees. This commission was no more effective than the one on atomic energy, and in 1950 the Soviet Union withdrew from both over the question of the representation of China. Both commissions were subsequently dissolved in 1952, when on January 11 of that year the Assembly created a single Disarmament Commission to carry on the tasks previously assigned to its two predecessors.

In April, 1954, acting on a suggestion from the General Assembly, the Disarmament Commission established a subcommittee of five— Canada, France, the United Kingdom, the United States, and the USSR— to "seek in private an acceptable solution to the disarmament problem." This committee held many sessions but accomplished little more than summarizing proposals made by the various states. The United States insisted that improved political conditions, notably the reunification of Germany, were a prerequisite to any material reduction in the size of the army, while the Soviet Union demanded the suspension of nuclear weapons tests as a prerequisite for considering other disarmament measures. Other lesser points were also at issue, notably freedom for inspection by air, and although there was much discussion in the Disarmament Commission, in the Assembly, and in the press, no concrete steps toward disarmament were achieved. On the theory, perhaps, that many heads were better than few, in November, 1957, the Disarmament Commission was expanded to twenty-five by adding representatives of fourteen nations to the eleven members of the Security Council who were already on the commission. A year later it was enlarged to include all UN members. The commission has been moribund; for instance, it did not meet from August, 1960, until April, 1965. Actual disarmament discussions have been passed on to another smaller group. On September 7, 1959, the United States, the USSR, Great Britain, and France in identically-worded statements announced the establishment of a new ten-power Disarmament Committee—five representatives from the Western powers and five from the Warsaw Pact countries. This was a concession to the Soviet demand for parity in international disarmament discussions. The new committee was not an organ of the UN but used its facilities, and some of its proposals were printed as UN documents. Its ambivalent nature was resolved when, following a

Russian proposal, the Assembly adopted a resolution establishing an eighteen-member Disarmament Committee by adding eight "uncommitted" countries to the previous ten-member committee. In March, 1962, France refused to participate any longer, largely on the ground that the committee was ineffective and that negotiations on nuclear disarmament should be limited to the four nuclear powers (at that time the United States, Russia, Britain, and France). The refusal of France to participate accounts for the fact that the committee is often referred to as the seventeen- rather than eighteen-member Committee on Disarmament. In 1969 the membership was expanded to twenty-six. Discussions in the committee paved the way for initialing the United States-Russian-British Nuclear Test Ban Treaty on July 25, 1963. This treaty has subsequently been adhered to by most nations of the world, the two notable exceptions being France and Red China. The committee also drafted the Treaty on Nonproliferation of Nuclear Weapons, which was reported to the General Assembly on March 14, 1968. The treaty was subsequently signed by the United States, the Soviet Union, and the United Kingdom in London on July 1 and by over eighty non-nuclear-weapons states. The treaty obligates the nuclear-weapons states not to transfer nuclear weapons or explosive devices to any other state. Non-nuclear-weapons states undertake to carry on their civilian nuclear activities—such as research and power reactors—under safeguard agreements negotiated with the International Atomic Energy Committee.

Somewhat more fruitful than many of the exchanges on disarmament have been the deliberations of the UN Scientific Committee on the Effects of Radiation which was established in 1955. It has studied among other things the genetic effects of radiation and the measurement of radioactive fallout. This committee has provided for an exchange of information on a purely scientific level.

USE OF ARMED FORCES. While no United Nations International Police Force has ever been established, the Korean war did result in a so-called army of the United Nations, composed largely of United States forces with some assistance from other powers. The Suez Crisis of 1956 ended with a UN occupation force taking over as French, British, and Israeli troops were withdrawn. The United Nations Emergency Force (UNEF), from which were barred contingents from the permanent members of the Security Council and from neighboring Near Eastern countries, patrolled the frontier separating the Gaza Strip from Israel and the Sinai border between Egypt and Israel. All troops wore their national uniforms, except for a UN armband and UN designation on their headgear. The force numbered about 5,000 men and was under a commander appointed by the General Assembly and responsible to it. The force was withdrawn on the eve of the six-day Israeli-Arab War in 1967. The United Nations Truce Supervisory Organization (UNTSO), which dates back to 1949, still has military observers on duty seeking to maintain the cease-fire line of 1967.

The UNEF served as a model for the United Nations Operation in the Congo (ONUC, from the French title *Operation des Nations Unies au Congo*) which served in the Congo from July 15, 1960, to June 30, 1964. This was a much larger force, reaching for a period a strength of 19,000 to 20,000 men, and at times was called upon to take part in active combat [see above, pp. 853–55]. In March, 1964, a United Nations peace-keeping force in Cyprus (UNFICYP) was organized. To be financed by voluntary contributions, it was to supervise the cease-fire agreement between the Greek and Turkish Cypriote communities. Originally created for a three-month period, its term has been periodically extended, and it is still functioning effectively (1970).

The United Nations has at various times sent small contingents as observers, as well as maintaining important truce observation contingents. Among the more important of these are: United Nations Truce Supervision Organization in Palestine (UNTSO); the United Nations Military Observer Group for India and Pakistan (Kashmir Problem), and the United Nations Yemen Observation Mission (June, 1963–September 4, 1964). They have performed most useful functions and are one way of establishing what has been termed "United Nations presence" in troubled areas.

FINANCIAL CRISIS. The high costs of the peace-keeping forces in the Near East and in the Congo led to financial difficulties which for a time paralyzed the UN. The Charter provides that the expenses of the organization shall be apportioned among the members by the Assembly. This is regularly done and the percentages vary slightly from year to year, ranging from approximately 30 percent for the United States, 15 percent for Russia, 7.5 percent for the United Kingdom, to 0.04 percent for such countries as Albania, El Salvador, Gabon, and Yemen. At times the UN has assumed large-scale operations which have not been financed through the regular budget but from a special budget or fund raised by voluntary contributions. The United Nations Children's Fund (UNICEF) was the first such subagency, and collections gathered under "trick or treat" by children in the United States on Halloween add their mite to this special budget. The Expanded Program for Technical Assistance (EPTA) and the United Nations Relief and Works Agency for Palestine Refugees (UNRWA) are other examples of agencies financed by special budgets. The number of states contributing to these special budgets have been relatively few, and their work has often had to be curtailed.

When the United Nations Emergency Force (UNEF) was established in connection with the Suez Crisis of 1956 it was decided to finance it through a special fund. The force had to be gathered immediately and the Assembly approved (November 26, 1956) an original grant of $10 million, the method for raising the funds to be decided later. The Assembly by resolution on December 21, 1956, decided that the ten million should be raised by regular assessment of its members. The USSR and other members opposed this method saying the cost should be paid by the aggressor states: France, the United Kingdom, and Israel. They also maintained that the Assembly had no right to institute military operations, such matters being within the purview of the Security Council. More funds were necessary, and under a compromise proposed by the United States the costs were to be met partly by assessment and partly by voluntary contributions. Aside from the countries which supplied troops, twenty-two states during 1957–62 made contributions totaling $26 million, about 21 percent of the UNEF's entire cost.[1] Russia steadfastly refused either to make voluntary contributions or to pay its special assessments.

The financial difficulties were enhanced by the establishment of the peace-keeping force in the Congo (ONUC) in 1960. This too was to be financed by a special account, but this time in an Assembly resolution it was stated that the 1960 costs for the Congo force constituted expenses of the UN within the meaning of Article 17 of the Charter, and the assessments for the *ad hoc* account were "binding legal obligations." Subsequent financial resolutions aroused much debate and disagreement; specific references to Article 17 were omitted. Arrears in assessment payments mounted, and in December 1961 the Assembly decided to ask the International Court of Justice for an advisory opinion whether the expenditures authorized by the Assembly for the financing of the UNEF and ONUC constituted expenses of the UN that could be assessed upon its members. Meanwhile to cover the deficit it authorized a $200 million bond issue bearing a 2 percent interest rate and redeemable over twenty-five years, the bonds to be repaid by adding some $10 million annually to the regular budget.

Twenty-one governments submitted briefs and nine made oral presentations to the Court. By a 9-5 decision the Court on July 21, 1962, advised that the obligations incurred for the peace-keeping operations were legal obligations which the General Assembly could apportion among its members under Article 17. The Court held that while the Security Council's responsibility for peace and security affairs was primary, it was not exclusive, and the Assembly could initiate peace-keeping operations.

Since the opinion was only advisory, it was not technically binding. France joined Russia and others in refusing to pay the assessments for ONUC, or that part of the regular budget which was designated for the repayment of the bonds. These states maintained that only the Security Council could levy peace-keeping assessments. Repeated efforts to find a way out of the impasse failed as the arrears increased.

Article 19 of the Charter provides that any member owing more than equivalent "contributions due from it for the preceding two full years" shall have no vote in the General Assembly. By the time the Assembly met on December 1, 1964, eight states (seven Communist mem-

[1] See Chap. VII in Gabriella Rosner, *The United Nations Emergency Force* (New York, 1963).

bers from Eastern Europe and Yemen) were in arrears. Russia was the largest debtor, owing $52.6 million. The situation was further complicated by the fact that France would also be in arrears on January 1, 1965. The United States, weary of making more than its share of voluntary contributions and desiring to clarify the UN financial situation, served notice that it would challenge Russia's right to vote at the Assembly unless she paid up. Frantic negotiations did not produce a settlement but did achieve a temporary solution; the Assembly would operate by consensus without formal voting. The Assembly met, debated, and even elected a new president, admitted three new members, chose the nonpermanent members of the Security Council and approved the budget of 1965 without taking a vote. As the Assembly was about to adjourn, the delegate from Albania demanded that the Assembly resume regular roll calls. According to the rules there was no way of avoiding a vote, unless the demand was withdrawn. The Albanian delegate refused to do this. Finally the United States, on the ground that this was a procedural not a substantive matter, announced that it would raise no objection to a procedural vote. This upheld 97 to 2 (Albania and Mauretania) the Assembly President's ruling that the Albanian demand was out of order. One of the last acts of the Assembly at the session was to appoint a Special Committee on Peace-Keeping Operations which was instructed to make a comprehensive review of "peace-keeping operations in all their aspects, including ways of overcoming financial difficulties of the organization."

On August 16, 1965, Arthur J. Goldberg, who had become the United States representative at the United Nations after the death of Adlai Stevenson, announced to the Special Committee that ". . . without prejudice to the position that Article 19 is applicable, the United States recognizes, as it simply must, that the General Assembly is not prepared to apply Article 19 in the present situation and that the consensus of the membership is that the Assembly should proceed normally. We will not seek to frustrate that consensus, since it is not in the world interest to have the work of the General Assembly immobilized in these troubled days." At the same time he made it clear that if any member can insist on making an exception to the principle of collective financial responsibility the United States reserved the same option if in its view strong and compelling reasons exist for doing so. Russia had already conceded a bit in offering to make a voluntary contribution to the peace-keeping efforts once the point had been recognized that it was not obligated to make the payment.[2] This reversal of policy on the part of the United States enabled the UN to proceed normally when it met at the next regular

[2] The nations liable under Article 19 in August, 1965 were as follows: USSR, $62,236,882; France, $17,752,565 (paid for Middle East but not the Congo); Albania, $95,952; Belgium, $3,271,651; Byelorussia, $2,107,165; Cuba, $690,633; Czechoslovakia, $4,069, 638; Hungary, $2,257,c74; Poland, $4,322,387; Rumania, $926,994; South Africa, $1,117,647; the Ukraine, $8,049,135; Yemen, $127,129.

session. The peace-keeping operations continued to be supported by voluntary contributions.

DISPUTES BEFORE THE INTERNATIONAL COURT OF JUSTICE. The Court was organized in 1946 and the first case to come before it was the Corfu Channel dispute between Britain and Albania. On October 22, 1946, two British ships were damaged by mines in the Corfu Channel causing the death of forty-four officers and sailors and the wounding of forty-two others. The British government charged Albania with illegally laying these mines. The Albanians denied doing so, but charged that the British ships were trespassing in Albanian territorial waters. The dispute was first brought before the Security Council, which, being unable to effect an agreement, recommended that the two parties submit the question to judicial settlement. Albania, although not a member of the Court, consented to come before it. Arguments were held in 1948 and the Court handed down its decision in April, 1949. Albania was held responsible, since it had failed to notify shipping in general of the minefield in Albanian waters, nor had it warned the British warships of their imminent danger. On the other hand, the Court unanimously held that British action in sweeping mines several weeks after the accident without Albania's consent was a violation of Albania's sovereignty. The Court invited the parties to indicate their views as to the amount of damages. Albania failed to comply within the prescribed time and the amount of compensation was fixed by the Court in December, 1950. Albania has refused so far to make this payment.

The Court has actually been used very little. About a third of the cases have involved advisory opinions on such questions as the admission of states to membership in the United Nations, interpretation of the peace treaties with Bulgaria, Hungary, and Rumania, and the international status of South West Africa. Some of the other contentious cases typical of the issues coming before the Court involved a fishery dispute between Norway and Britain; a question of asylum between Colombia and Peru; a dispute between France and the United States over trade in Morocco; a question involving the Anglo-Iranian Oil Company; a territorial problem of whether the small Channel islands of Minquiess and Ecrehos belonged to Britian or France; a dispute between Guatemala and Liechtenstein involving the nationality and assets of wealthy German-born Friedrich Nottebohn; a case concerning the guardianship of an infant between the Netherlands and Sweden; a boundary dispute between Honduras and Nicaragua going back to the arbitral award made by the King of Spain in 1906; a case involving the question whether the Temple of Preah Vihear, a sacred place of pilgrimage, was in Cambodia or Thailand; a dispute between the Republic of Cameroons and the United Kingdom; a suit by Ethiopia and Liberia against South Africa in regard to the administration of South West Africa; a difference between Belgium and Spain involving the Barcelona Traction, Light, and Power Company; and a question over the jurisdiction of the North Sea Continental Shelf involving Denmark, the Federal Republic of Germany, and the Netherlands. No doubt the Court would be used more if the political cleavages among the nations of today were not so sharp. Many of the important issues which arise are by nature political questions which do not lend themselves to judicial settlement. Whether an independent state of Israel, Indonesia, or North Korea should be established is, for example, not a question for a court to decide. The Court, of course, constitutes only one of the procedures for pacific settlement provided by the United Nations, and its greater use depends on stable world conditions.

Twentieth-Century Trends

FREEDOM AND SECURITY. The conditions that were to lead to two world wars and a world depression during the first half of the twentieth century were all present at its start, although the nature and direction of these forces were still only incompletely understood. Some observers agreed with the American historian Brooks Adams, who predicted in his *Law of Civilization and Decay* (1895) that economic competition would lead to a loss of energy on the part of society and eventually to complete disintegration. More popular was the Marxian theory that the continued development of capitalism would lead to increasingly violent conflicts between owners and workers, until the latter would finally assume control. The liberal point of view, expressed with less vigor and tenacity than its more arrogant rivals, was that with the extension of parliamentary democracy the various peoples of Europe would find a satisfactory solution to their problems by means of discussion and compromise.

All these views, and many variants of them expressed before the turn of the century, nevertheless failed to take cognizance of the central problem of the emerging European crisis. For the individual it was a question of reconciling the ideal of personal freedom, which the tradition of Western civilization had taught him to value, with the desire for a degree of economic welfare which seemed possible only if many important decisions were left to a powerful and largely impersonal government. For the sovereign states of Europe it was a question of reconciling the increasing responsibility they found it necessary to assume for the welfare of their citizens with the economic interdependence brought on by the requirements of industrialism, which rapidly reduced the ability of any individual state to control the forces affecting its economy.

There can be little doubt that the chief concern of any political doctrine must be that of raising the material and spiritual level of the average individual. The weakness of the liberal approach after World War I was not that it failed to concern itself with the security of the individual as well as with his freedom, but that it placed too great a reliance for the guarantee of that security on the free working of the economic system within the traditional framework of national states. The Communists, at the other extreme of political thought, claimed that the individual possessed no freedom except insofar as his security was guaranteed, and they attempted to guarantee it through the mechanism of a totalitarian system that in theory recognized no national frontiers. To the nationalistic and still relatively individualistic peoples of Central Europe, the international-ism of the Communists was as distasteful as the economic free enterprise of the liberals was unattainable. It was therefore not surprising that they should have been attracted after the disasters of the depression by the pro-grams of facism or Nazism, which attempted to achieve the security of limited national groups by extending the sovereignty of a few states over the whole of Europe.

Whatever popularity fascism may have enjoyed in Europe was derived from the fact that it offered a rough-and-ready solution to the economic and emotional insecurity so widely prevalent in the 1930s. Much of the support that fascism might have attracted by its recognition of this cru-cial European problem was nevertheless lost as the methods it intended to employ became more evident. The ruthlessness with which it ignored the national sovereignty of its victims was alone enough to alienate many groups who might otherwise have been willing to join its ranks. More re-volting to the great majority of Europeans, however, was the measureless brutality of fascism towards all individuals not belonging to the favored group that claimed it as their destiny to rule Europe. The perceptive British publicist H. G. Wells had already remarked, in the widely-read tract for world government which he entitled *The Outline of History* (1920), that as a result of World War I there had been "a slipping off of ancient restraints; a real decivilization of men's minds." While the in-creased brutalization of human conduct was evident throughout Europe, nowhere did it reach the calculated extremes practiced by the followers of Hitler. The enemies of Hitlerism thus in the end accumulated more rapidly than its friends, and the war its doctrines inevitably provoked led finally to its complete defeat.

The defeat of fascism weakened one of the leading ideologies that claimed to offer a solution to the problems facing the individual in an age of industrialism, but it did not thereby bring agreement among the peoples of Europe as to how the relations of the individual and the state should be adjusted within the larger framework of economic activity. The gen-eral trend towards the welfare state was indeed evident throughout the European world, from the extreme Stalinist form of communism at the Eastern pole to the mild socialism of the West European states. There is much to be said for the view that the differences between East and West in this regard lie less in the degree of government participation in the social and economic life of the country than in the political systems within which the various governments operate. It may thus be held that the differences between countries such as Norway and Yugoslavia, if not those between the Soviet Union and the United States, are merely a reflection of relative differences in the opportunities for and tradition of self-govern-ment over the past several generations.

Yet it is clear that the matter is not this simple, for the peoples of Europe live less on a continent or in a world than in a very rigid structure of sovereign national states. An important result of the rise of the welfare state has in fact been to strengthen greatly the national exclusiveness of the European countries. If the emotional nationalism of the type exhibited by the Nazis and the Fascists is no longer so apparent, the welfare states of the 1970s, with their vast concentration of economic responsibility, find it more difficult to reach compromises than did their predecessors in 1910 or 1930. At the same time the independent economic forces that in the past tended to break down national barriers, such as commerce, banking, and business, have lost most of their influence. Similarly such internationally organized ideologies as Catholicism and socialism, which during World War I could deal with the problems confronting Europe with considerable objectivity, no longer enjoy European-wide influence. While Catholicism exerts an important influence in the key states of Germany and Italy, as well as in such peripheral countries as Spain, Portugal, and Ireland, it is restricted in Eastern Europe. Likewise, socialism has ceased to be a force for unity in Europe. After splitting into the warring factions of moderate socialism and communism at the end of World War I, each of the two factions was weakened by national frictions. Even the well-disciplined doctrine of communism was not entirely successful after World War II in imposing its authority on the states within its sphere of influence. It was, therefore, more than ever the case that in the middle of the twentieth century the freedom and security of the individual in Europe depended less on the degree of responsibility the various governments took for his welfare than on the European system of states and its relation to world society.

EVOLUTION OF EUROPEAN SOCIETY. By the middle of the twentieth century there was reason enough for Europeans to question whether the organization of their society into sovereign national states did not lie at the heart of their difficulty. A general feeling of pessimism had been voiced ever since World War I, and the gloomy predictions of Oswald Spengler's *Decline of the West* (1918–22) that the great urbanization and materialism of European society would soon lead to its decay were read by many with approval. Others followed the efforts of Arnold J. Toynbee, who in his *Study of History* (1933–54) sought the key to the ills of the West in a comparative study of the rise and fall of earlier civilizations. While Toynbee offered some hope that man might learn from past experience, the sociologist Pitirim Sorokin presented in his *Social and Cultural Dynamics* (1937–41) a view of history that saw only a series of fluctuations between spiritual and secular ages which organized society could not hope to alter. The Communists alone welcomed the decline of the Europe the nineteenth century had known, for they believed that its collapse was a necessary prerequisite to the establishment of the proletarian society that it was their task to organize.

If one judges European society by its success in coping with the problems of modernization in the course of the twentieth century, one emerges with mixed conclusions. At the start of the century Europe was unquestionably at the forefront of human progress, although its standard of living was already falling behind that of the United States. In no field was Europe's predominant position more apparent than in the political. Not only did Europeans rule directly over some half-billion inhabitants in other parts of the world, but they guided the destinies of the world in innumerable other ways. It is precisely in the political field that Europe's failure in the twentieth century has been most striking. The overseas territories have now become independent states that no longer look to Europe for guidance. The nationalism that in the nineteenth century liberated the peoples of Europe from dynastic rule and gave wings to their aspirations for a more modern way of life had by the twentieth become a heavy burden, causing endless political disturbance and placing confining bonds on material growth. In the new era it seemed that only nations with territories continental in scope, such as the United States and the USSR, could enjoy economic growth within the confines of national frontiers. Even for these giants, it was questionable how long their relative self-sufficiency would last in a rapidly expanding age. The apostles of political and economic integration maintain that for Europe political disunity is a temporary handicap that can be overcome by further progress along the path pioneered by the Europe of the Six. In the 1970s union is nevertheless a hope rather than an accomplishment. One can envisage a future united Europe that could rival the United States and the USSR in some respects and would surpass them in many. Western Europe surpasses both the United States and the USSR in population, in trade, and in coal production, and is well ahead of the latter in the production of steel, electricity, and many other commodities. If resources of this order were assembled under a single political leadership, Western Europe would at least be restored to a permanent place in world affairs on a footing similar to that of the United States and the USSR.

In the economic and social spheres Europe has had less difficulty maintaining its position, although here again it has lost the leading role that it occupied before World War I. A ranking on the basis of per capita economic and social levels would find the United States, Canada, Australia, and New Zealand ahead of the European states, and the USSR would rank about twentieth with Japan, Uruguay, Argentina, and Italy not far below. Czechoslovakia, Poland, and Hungary would also be within this range of development, but the other states of Eastern Europe as well as Spain and Portugal would be well below it. What has occurred of course is not a European decline, for in fact Europe is enjoying unprecedented prosperity. It is rather that the modern technology developed initially in Western Europe has been adopted by other states that have the resources and skills required to rival or surpass the production and living standards achieved by Europe. This is not a process that can be greatly expanded in the foreseeable future, for few states enjoy the conditions necessary for such an achievement. The countries of Europe are thus in no danger of losing their position among the top twenty or twenty-five in the world that have achieved high economic and social levels.

In the cultural sphere it is more difficult to judge in national, let alone quantitative, terms. In those aspects of scientific research that require large-scale economic and technological support, Europe has lagged behind the United States and the USSR. In the field of nuclear research only Britain and France have kept up in some measure with the two super-powers, and they share with China the role of minor nuclear powers. In those aspects of culture in which the individual alone can excel, provided he is free from limiting controls, it cannot be said that Europe has lost its predominant position. No doubt more literature, music, art, and philosophy are created outside the European world today than at the turn of the century, but in its concern with fundamental human problems European culture retains its distinctive position.

In evaluating the course of European development over seven decades it is again therefore to the realm of politics that one must turn in seeking the explanation for the crises that have wracked European society. It is not the substance but the organization of the European heritage that must be held to account for its relative, and perhaps temporary, eclipse. The achievements of the countries of the New World, and of Russia, Japan, and the other more advanced countries, are based in very considerable measure on their acceptance and application of the body of modern knowledge that is largely West European in origin. Europe's institutions cannot be transferred to foreign soil as readily as its technology, but its original and continuing contributions to modern knowledge lie at the basis of the hopes of mankind for peace and prosperity.

Appendices

Bibliography

Index

Appendix I

Area and Population of the States of Europe and the Near East c. 1900, c. 1925, c. 1970[1]

COUNTRY	c. 1900			c. 1925			c. 1970		
	AREA SQ. MI.	DATE OF CENSUS	POPULATION	AREA SQ. MI.	DATE OF CENSUS	POPULATION	AREA SQ. MI.	DATE OF CENSUS	POPULATION
Albania	4,516[2]	1900e	322,000	10,629	1927	833,618	10,629	1968e	2,019,000
Austria-Hungary[3]	264,204	1900	46,810,981						
Austria	115,903[2]	1900	26,150,597	32,369	1923	6,535,759	32,369	1968	7,350,000
Hungary	125,039[2]	1900	19,092,292	35,875	1920	7,980,143	35,902	1969e	10,256,000
Belgium	11,373	1900	6,693,810	11,752	1920	7,465,782	11,755	1968e	9,619,000
Bulgaria	24,380[2]	1900	3,733,189	39,814	1920	4,861,439	42,796	1968e	8,370,000
Czechoslovakia				54,207	1921	13,613,172	49,381	1969e	14,418,000
Denmark	15,360	1901	2,464,770	16,604	1921	3,267,831	16,576	1968e	4,870,000
Estonia				18,353	1922	1,110,538	17,610[2]	1968e	1,300,000
Finland	144,255[2]	1897	2,592,778	132,550	1920	3,366,507	117,975	1969e	4,703,000
France	204,092	1901	38,595,580	212,659	1926	39,402,491	212,659	1969e	50,330,000
Germany	208,830	1900	56,367,178	180,985	1925	62,410,619	138,000	1968e	77,249,000[4]
Greece	25,014	1896	2,433,806	49,912	1928	6,204,684	51,182	1968e	8,803,000
Iceland	39,756[2]	1901	78,470	39,709	1920	94,690	39,709	1968e	201,000
Ireland	32,583[2]	1901	2,197,739	27,345	1926	2,971,992	27,345	1969e	2,921,000
N. Ireland				5,462[2]	1926	1,256,561	5,462[2]	1966	1,484,775
Italy	110,646	1901	32,449,754	119,710	1928	41,168,000	116,235	1968e	52,750,000
Latvia				25,409	1920	1,503,193	25,200[2]	1968e	2,300,000
Liechtenstein	65	1912	10,716	65	1912	10,716	62	1968e	21,000
Lithuania				21,553	1923	2,168,971	25,500[2]	1968e	3,100,000
Luxembourg	998	1900	236,543	999	1922	260,767	999	1968e	336,000
Monaco	.6	1900	15,180	.6	1928	24,927	.6	1968e	23,000
Netherlands	12,648	1899	5,104,137	12,587	1920	6,865,314	12,868	1969e	12,873,000
Norway	124,130[2]	1900	2,240,032	124,964	1920	2,649,775	124,556	1969e	3,851,000
Poland	49,159[2]	1897	9,455,943	149,958	1921	27,176,717	121,131	1969e	32,555,000
Portugal	34,528	1900	5,016,267	34,254	1920	5,621,977	34,207	1968e	9,465,000
Rumania	50,700	1899	5,912,520	122,282	1925e	17,393,149	91,671	1968e	19,721,000
Russia	8,660,395	1897	129,004,514	8,241,921	1926	120,716,341	8,708,070	1968e	237,798,000

Country	Area	Date	Population	Area	Date	Population	Area	Date	Population
San Marino	23	1896	9,500	38	1928	13,013	38	1968e	18,000
Montenegro	3,630	1900e	228,000				5,333[2]	1961	471,894
Serbia	18,630	1900	2,492,882				34,116[2]	1961	7,642,227
Yugoslavia				96,134	1921	12,017,323	98,826	1969e	20,351,000
Spain	194,783	1900	18,618,086	194,800	1923	21,763,147	195,504	1969e	32,949,000
Sweden	172,876	1900	5,136,441	173,156	1920	5,904,489	173,426	1969e	7,969,000
Switzerland	15,976	1900	3,315,443	15,940	1920	3,880,320	15,944	1968e	6,147,000
United Kingdom	120,979	1901	41,605,323	94,279[4]	1921	43,174,814	94,279[5]	1969e	55,534,000[5]
Vatican City							.17	1969e	1,000
Turkey	1,115,046[6]	1900e	24,931,600	294,416	1927	13,648,270	294,194	1969e	34,375,000
Egypt	400,000[2]	1900e	9,821,045	383,800	1927	14,177,864	386,198	1969e	32,501,000
Hejaz	96,500[2]	1900e	300,000	150,000	1925e	3,500,000	150,000[2]	1969e	2,000,000
Nejd				425,000	1925e	3,000,000	425,000[2]	1968e	4,000,000
Saudi Arabia							927,000e	1968e	6,000,000
Jordan				30,000	1920e	200,000	37,500	1968e	2,103,000
Iran (Persia)	628,000	1900e	9,000,000	628,000	1925e	10,000,000	629,343	1968e	26,985,000
Iraq				143,250	1920e	2,849,282	117,599	1968e	8,634,000
Israel (Palestine)				10,000	1922	757,182	7,992	1969e	2,822,000
Kuwait							6,178	1968e	540,000
Lebanon				3,400[2]	1920e	628,863	4,015	1968e	2,580,000
Libya							679,358	1969e	1,869,000
Morocco	219,000[2]	1900e	5,000,000	231,500	1925e	6,000,000	158,612	1969e	15,050,000
Southern Yemen							111,075	1968e	1,195,000
Sudan	950,000[2]	1900e	10,000,000	1,014,000	1924e	5,825,247	967,500	1969e	15,186,000
Syria	109,509[2]	1900e	3,317,600	60,000[2]	1920e	2,000,000	72,234	1969e	5,866,000
Tunisia	51,000[2]	1900e	1,900,000	48,300	1921	2,095,090	60,166	1968e	4,666,000
Yemen	77,200[2]	1900e	750,000	75,000	1930e	3,000,000	75,000	1969e	5,000,000

[1] Table compiled from various editions of the *Statesman's Year-Book*, *United Nations Monthly Bulletin of Statistics*, and other standard reference works. Official areas of states vary from time to time as more accurate surveys are made, although no boundary changes took place; "e" is used as an abbreviation for estimate; Hungary is listed next to Austria; Montenegro and Yugoslavia next to Serbia, in order to show their relation to these states; the Near Eastern states are grouped at the end.

[2] Provinces, vilayets, or component parts of other sovereign states.

[3] Includes Bosnia-Herzegovina.

[4] East Germany 16,002,000; West Germany 58,015,000; East Berlin 1,082,000; West Berlin 2,150,000.

[5] Includes Northern Ireland.

[6] Territorial areas of old Turkey and of the Turkish succession states are largely estimates which vary greatly in different sources.

Appendix II

Statements of Peace Aims by President Wilson

1. THE FOURTEEN POINTS OF JANUARY 8, 1918[1]

. . . We entered this war because violations of right had occurred which touched us to the quick and made the life of our own people impossible unless they were corrected and the world secured once for all against their recurrence. What we demand in this war, therefore, is nothing peculiar to ourselves. It is that the world be made fit and safe to live in; and particularly that it be made safe for every peace-loving nation which, like our own, wishes to live its own life, determine its own institutions, be assured of justice and fair dealing by the other peoples of the world as against force and selfish aggression. All the peoples of the world are in effect partners in this interest, and for our own part we see very clearly that unless justice be done to others it will not be done to us. The programme of the world's peace, therefore, is our programme; and that programme, the only possible programme, as we see it, is this:

I. Open covenants of peace, openly arrived at, after which there shall be no private international understandings of any kind, but diplomacy shall proceed always frankly and in the public view.

II. Absolute freedom of navigation upon the seas, outside territorial waters, alike in peace and in war, except as the seas may be closed in whole or in part by international action for the enforcement of international covenants.

III. The removal, so far as possible, of all economic barriers and the establishment of an equality of trade conditions among all the nations consenting to the peace and associating themselves for its maintenance.

IV. Adequate guarantees given and taken that national armaments will be reduced to the lowest point consistent with domestic safety.

V. A free, open-minded, and absolutely impartial adjustment of all colonial claims, based upon a strict observance of the principle that in determining all such questions of sovereignty the interests of the populations concerned must have equal weight with the equitable claims of the government whose title is to be determined.

VI. The evacuation of all Russian territory and such a settlement of all questions affecting Russia as will secure the best and freest co-operation of the other nations of the world in obtaining for her an unhampered and unembarrassed opportunity for the independent determination of her own political development and national policy and assure her of a sincere welcome into the society of free nations under institutions of her own choosing; and, more than a welcome, assistance also of every kind that she may need and may herself desire. The treatment accorded Russia by her sister nations in the months to come will be the acid test of their goodwill, of their comprehension of her needs as distinguished from their own interests, and of their intelligent and unselfish sympathy.

VII. Belgium, the whole world will agree, must be evacuated and restored, without any attempt to limit the sovereignty which she enjoys in common with all other free nations. No other single act will serve as this will serve to restore confidence among the nations in the laws which they have themselves set and determined for the government of their relations with one another. Without this healing act the whole structure and validity of international law is forever impaired.

VIII. All French territory should be freed and the invaded portions restored, and the wrong done to France by Prussia in 1871 in the matter of Alsace-Lorraine, which has unsettled the peace of the world for nearly fifty years, should be righted, in order that peace may once more be made secure in the interest of all.

IX. A readjustment of the frontiers of Italy should be effected along clearly recognizable lines of nationality.

X. The peoples of Austria-Hungary, whose place among the nations we wish to see safeguarded and assured, should be accorded the freest opportunity of autonomous development.

[1] *Congressional Record*, Vol. 56, pp. 680–1 (65 Cong., 2d. Sess., Jan. 8, 1918).

XI. Rumania, Serbia, and Montenegro should be evacuated; occupied territories restored; Serbia accorded free and secure access to the sea; and the relations of the several Balkan states to one another determined by friendly counsel along historically established lines of allegiance and nationality; and international guarantees of the political and economic independence and territorial integrity of the several Balkan states should be entered into.

XII. The Turkish portions of the present Ottoman Empire should be assured a secure sovereignty, but the other nationalities which are now under Turkish rule should be assured an undoubted security of life and an absolutely unmolested opportunity of autonomous development, and the Dardanelles should be permanently opened as a free passage to the ships and commerce of all nations under international guarantees.

XIII. An independent Polish state should be erected which should include the territories inhabited by indisputably Polish populations, which should be assured a free and secure access to the sea, and whose political and economic independence and territorial integrity should be guaranteed by international covenant.

XIV. A general association of nations must be formed under specific covenants for the purpose of affording mutual guarantees of political independence and territorial integrity to great and small states alike.

2. THE "FOUR PRINCIPLES" OF FEBRUARY 11, 1918[2]

. . . The principles to be applied are these:

First, that each part of the final settlement must be based upon the essential justice of that particular case and upon such adjustments as are most likely to bring a peace that will be permanent;

Second, that peoples and provinces are not to be bartered about from sovereignty to sovereignty as if they were mere chattels and pawns in a game, even the great game, now forever discredited, of the balance of powers; but that

Third, every territorial settlement involved in this war must be made in the interest and for the benefit of the populations concerned, and not as a part of any mere adjustment or compromise of claims amongst rival states; and

Fourth, that all well-defined national aspirations shall be accorded the utmost satisfaction that can be accorded them without introducing new or perpetuating old elements of discord and antagonism that would be likely in time to break the peace of Europe and consequently of the world.

3. THE "FOUR ENDS" OF JULY 4, 1918[3]

There can be but one issue. The settlement must be final. There can be no compromise. No halfway decision would be tolerable. No halfway decision is conceivable. These are the ends for which the associated peoples of the world are fighting and which must be conceded them before there can be peace:

I. The destruction of every arbitrary power anywhere that can separately, secretly, and of its single choice disturb the peace of the world; or, if it cannot be presently destroyed, at the least its reduction to virtual impotence.

II. The settlement of every question, whether of territory, of sovereignty, or economic arrangement, or of political relationship, upon the basis of the free acceptance of that settlement by the people immediately concerned, and not upon the basis of the material interest or advantage of any other nation or people which may desire a different settlement for the sake of its own exterior influence or mastery.

III. The consent of all nations to be governed in their conduct towards each other by the same principles of honour and of respect for the common law of civilized society that govern the individual citizens of all modern states in their relations with one an-

[2] *Congressional Record*, Vol. 56, p. 1937 (65 Cong. 2d. Sess., Feb. 11, 1918).
[3] *Congressional Record*, Vol. 56, p. 8671 (65 Cong. 2d. Sess., July 5, 1918).

other, to the end that all promises and covenants may be sacredly observed; no private plots or conspiracies hatched, no selfish injuries wrought with impunity, and a mutual trust established upon the handsome foundation of a mutual respect for right.

IV. The establishment of an organization of peace which shall make it certain that the combined power of free nations will check every invasion of right and serve to make peace and justice the more secure by affording a definite tribunal of opinion to which all must submit and by which every international readjustment that cannot be amicably agreed upon by the peoples directly concerned shall be sanctioned.

4. THE "FIVE PARTICULARS" OF SEPTEMBER 27, 1918[4]

. . . But these general terms do not disclose the whole matter. Some details are needed to make them sound less like a thesis and more like a practical program. These, then, are some of the particulars, and I state them with the greater confidence because I can state them authoritatively as representing this Government's interpretation of its own duty with regard to peace:

First. The impartial justice meted out must involve no discrimination between those to whom we wish to be just and those to whom we do not wish to be just. It must be a justice that plays no favorites and knows no standard but the equal rights of the several peoples concerned.

Second. No special or separate interest of any single nation or any group of nations can be made the basis of any part of the settlement which is not consistent with the common interest of all.

Third. There can be no leagues or alliances or special covenants and understandings within the general and common family of the league of nations.

Fourth. And more specifically, there can be no special, selfish, economic combinations within the league and no employment of any form of economic boycott or exclusion except as the power of economic penalty by exclusion from the markets of the world may be vested in the league of nations itself as a means of discipline and control.

Fifth. All international agreements and treaties of every kind must be made known in their entirety to the rest of the world.

Appendix III

Statements of the United Nations Peace Aims

1. THE ATLANTIC CHARTER OF AUGUST 14, 1941[1]

Joint declaration of the President of the United States of America and the Prime Minister, Mr. Churchill, representing His Majesty's Government in the United Kingdom, being met together, deem it right to make known certain common principles in the national policies of their respective countries on which they base their hopes for a better future for the world.

FIRST. Their countries seek no aggrandizement, territorial or other;

SECOND. They desire to see no territorial changes that do not accord with the freely expressed wishes of the peoples concerned;

THIRD. They respect the right of all peoples to choose the form of government under which they will live; and they wish to see sovereign rights and self-government restored to those who have been forcibly deprived of them;

FOURTH. They will endeavor, with due respect for their existing obligations, to further the enjoyment by all states, great or small, victor or vanquished, of access, on equal terms, to the trade and to the raw materials of the world which are needed for their economic prosperity;

[4] *Congressional Record*, Vol. 56, p. 10887 (65 Cong., 2d. Sess., Sept. 28, 1918).
[1] *Congressional Record*, Vol. 87, p. 7217 (77 Cong., 1st Sess., Aug. 21, 1941).

FIFTH. They desire to bring about the fullest collaboration between all nations in the economic field with the object of securing, for all, improved labor standards, economic advancement, and social security;

SIXTH. After the final destruction of the Nazi tyranny, they hope to see established a peace which will afford to all nations the means of dwelling in safety within their own boundaries, and which will afford assurance that all the men in all the lands may live out their lives in freedom from fear and want;

SEVENTH. Such a peace should enable all men to traverse the high seas and oceans without hindrance;

EIGHTH. They believe that all of the nations of the world, for realistic as well as spiritual reasons, must come to the abandonment of the use of force. Since no future peace can be maintained if land, sea, or air armaments continue to be employed by nations which threaten, or may threaten, aggression outside of their frontiers, they believe, pending the establishment of a wider and permanent system of general security, that the disarmament of such nations is essential. They will likewise aid and encourage all other practicable measures which will lighten for peace-loving peoples the crushing burden of armaments.

Franklin D. Roosevelt
Winston S. Churchill

2. THE "FOUR FREEDOMS" FROM PRESIDENT ROOSEVELT'S ADDRESS TO CONGRESS OF JANUARY 6, 1941, REAFFIRMED IN HIS ADDRESS OF JANUARY 6, 1942[2]

. . . In the future days, which we seek to make secure, we look forward to a world founded upon four essential human freedoms.

The first is freedom of speech and expression everywhere in the world.

The second is freedom of every person to worship God in his own way everywhere in the world.

The third is freedom from want, which, translated into world terms, means economic understandings which will secure to every nation a healthy peacetime life for its inhabitants everywhere in the world.

The fourth is freedom from fear—which, translated into world terms, means a world-wide reduction of armaments to such a point and in such a thorough fashion that no nation will be in a position to commit an act of physical aggression against any neighbor—anywhere in the world.

Appendix IV

Membership of the United Nations

1. THE DECLARATION BY UNITED NATIONS, JANUARY 1, 1942

The Governments signatory hereto,

Having subscribed to a common program of purposes and principles embodied in the Joint Declaration of the President of the United States of America and the Prime Minister of the United Kingdom of Great Britain and Northern Ireland dated August 14, 1941, known as the Atlantic Charter;

Being convinced that complete victory over their enemies is essential to defend life, liberty, independence and religious freedom, and to preserve human rights and justice in their own lands as well as in other lands, and that they are now engaged in a common struggle against savage and brutal forces seeking to subjugate the world,

[2] *Congressional Record*, Vol. 87, p. 46 (77 Cong., 1st Sess., Jan. 6, 1941); see also Vol. 88, p. 33 (77 Cong., 2d. Sess., Jan. 6, 1942).

DECLARE:

(1) Each Government pledges itself to employ its full resources, military or economic, against those members of the Tripartite Pact and its adherents with which such government is at war.

(2) Each Government pledges itself to co-operate with the Governments signatory hereto and not to make a separate armistice or peace with the enemies.

The foregoing declaration may be adhered to by other nations which are, or which may be, rendering material assistance and contributions in the struggle for victory over Hitlerism.

DONE at Washington, January First, 1942.

2. ORIGINAL SIGNATORIES OF THE DECLARATION BY UNITED NATIONS OF JANUARY 1, 1942, WITH OFFICIAL DATE OF ADMISSION TO THE UN ORGANIZATION

America, United States of: October 24, 1945
Australia: November 1, 1945
Belgium: December 27, 1945
Canada: November 9, 1945
China: October 24, 1945
Costa Rica: November 2, 1945
Cuba: October 24, 1945
Czechoslovakia: October 24, 1945
Dominican Republic: October 24, 1945
El Salvador: October 24, 1945
Greece: October 25, 1945
Guatemala: November 21, 1945
Haiti: October 24, 1945
Honduras: December 17, 1945

India: October 30, 1945
Luxembourg: October 24, 1945
Netherlands: December 10, 1945
New Zealand: October 24, 1945
Nicaragua: October 24, 1945
Norway: November 27, 1945
Panama: November 13, 1945
Poland[1]: October 24, 1945
Union of South Africa: November 7, 1945
Union of Soviet Socialist Republics: October 24, 1945
United Kingdom: October 24, 1945
Yugoslavia: October 24, 1945

3. STATES WHICH SUBSEQUENTLY ADHERED TO THE DECLARATION BY UNITED NATIONS, WITH OFFICIAL DATE OF ADMISSION TO THE UN ORGANIZATION IN PARENTHESES

Mexico: June 5, 1942 (November 7, 1945)
Philippines: June 10, 1942 (October 24, 1945)
Ethiopia: July 28, 1942 (November 13, 1945)
Iraq: January 16, 1943 (December 21, 1945)
Brazil: February 8, 1943 (October 24, 1945)
Bolivia: April 27, 1943 (November 14, 1945)
Iran: September 10, 1943 (October 24, 1945)
Colombia: December 22, 1943 (November 5, 1945)

Liberia: February 26, 1944 (November 2, 1945)
France: December 26, 1944 (October 24, 1945)
Ecuador: February 7, 1945 (December 21, 1945)
Peru: February 11, 1945 (October 31, 1945)
Chile: February 12, 1945 (October 24, 1945)
Paraguay: February 12, 1945 (October 24, 1945)
Venezuela: February 16, 1945 (November 15, 1945)
Uruguay: February 23, 1945 (December 18, 1945)

[1] Poland, not having a government recognized by all the sponsoring powers, was the only signatory of the Declaration by United Nations which did not participate in the San Francisco Conference. A Polish government, recognized by the four powers, signed the Charter on October 15, 1945.

Turkey: February 24, 1945 (October 24, 1945)

Egypt: February 27, 1945 (October 24, 1945)

Saudi Arabia: March 1, 1945 (October 24, 1945)[2]

Syria: March 1, 1945 (October 24, 1945)[2]

Lebanon: March 1, 1945 (October 24, 1945)

4. ADDITIONAL STATES WHICH PARTICIPATED IN THE SAN FRANCISCO CONFERENCE APRIL—JUNE, 1945, WITH OFFICIAL DATE OF ADMISSION TO THE UN ORGANIZATION

Argentina: October 24, 1945

Byelorussian Soviet Socialist Republic, October 24, 1945

Denmark: October 24, 1945

Ukrainian Soviet Socialist Republic: October 24, 1945

5. STATES SUBSEQUENTLY ADMITTED TO MEMBERSHIP IN THE UNITED NATIONS WITH OFFICIAL DATE OF ADMISSION TO UN ORGANIZATION

Afghanistan: November 19, 1946
Iceland: November 19, 1946
Sweden: November 19, 1946
Thailand: December 16, 1946
Pakistan: September 30, 1947
Yemen: September 30, 1947
Burma: April 19, 1948
Israel: May 11, 1949
Indonesia: September 28, 1950[3]
Albania: December 14, 1955
Austria: December 14, 1955
Bulgaria: December 14, 1955
Cambodia: December 14, 1955
Ceylon: December 14, 1955
Finland: December 14, 1955
Hungary: December 14, 1955
Ireland: December 14, 1955
Italy: December 14, 1955
Jordan: December 14, 1955
Laos: December 14, 1955
Libya: December 14, 1955
Nepal: December 14, 1955
Portugal: December 14, 1955
Rumania: December 14, 1955

Spain: December 14, 1955
Morocco: November 12, 1956
Sudan: November 12, 1956
Tunisia: November 12, 1956
Japan: December 18, 1957
Ghana: March 8, 1957
Malaya: September 17, 1957[4]
Guinea: December 12, 1958
Cameroon: September 20, 1960
Central African Republic: September 20, 1960
Chad: September 20, 1960
Congo (Brazzaville): September 20, 1960
Congo (Leopoldville): September 20, 1960
Cyprus: September 20, 1960
Dahomey: September 20, 1960
Gabon: September 20, 1960
Ivory Coast: September 20, 1960
Madagascar (now Malagasy Republic): September 20, 1960
Niger: September 20, 1960
Somalia: September 20, 1960
Togo: September 20, 1960
Upper Volta: September 20, 1960

[2] Following a plebiscite held on February 21, 1958, Egypt and Syria united to form the United Arab Republic which continued as a single member of the UN. Syria, having resumed its independent status on September 28, 1961, resumed its separate membership in the UN on October 13, 1961. The United Arab Republic continued as a member of the UN.

[3] Withdrew from membership January 21, 1965; effective March 1, 1965; resumed membership September 19, 1966, and the General Assembly approved this action September 28, 1966.

[4] On September 16, 1963, Singapore, Sabah (North Borneo), and Sarawak joined with Malaya to form the Federation of Malaysia and succeeded to Malaya's membership in the UN September 17, 1963. On August 9, 1965, Singapore withdrew from Malaysia and was admitted to the UN on September 23, 1965.

Mali: September 28, 1960
Senegal: September 28, 1960
Nigeria: October 7, 1960
Sierra Leone: September 27, 1961
Mauritania: October 27, 1961
Mongolia: October 27, 1961
Tanganyika: December 14, 1961[5]
Burundi: September 18, 1962
Rwanda: September 18, 1962
Jamaica: September 18, 1962
Trinidad and Tobago: September 18, 1962
Algeria: October 8, 1962
Uganda: October 25, 1962
Kuwait: May 14, 1963
Kenya: December 16, 1963
Zanzibar: December 16, 1963[5]

Malawi: December 1, 1964
Malta: December 1, 1964
Zambia: December 1, 1964
Gambia: September 23, 1965
Maldive Islands: September 23, 1965
Singapore: September 23, 1965
Guyana: September 20, 1966
Botswana: October 17, 1966
Lesotho: October 17, 1966
Barbados: December 9, 1966
Southern Yemen: December 14, 1967
Mauritius: April 24, 1968
Swaziland: September 24, 1968
Equatorial Guinea: November 12, 1968
Fiji: October 13, 1970[6]

Appendix V

Declarations of War in World War I in Chronological Order[1]

1. THE CENTRAL POWERS

Austria-Hungary: July 28, 1914
Germany: August 1, 1914

Turkey: November 3, 1914
Bulgaria: October 11, 1915

2. THE ALLIED AND ASSOCIATED POWERS

Serbia: July 28, 1914
Russia: August 1, 1914
Luxembourg: August 2, 1914
France: August 3, 1914
Belgium: August 4, 1914
British Empire: August 4, 1914
Montenegro: August 9, 1914
Japan: August 23, 1914
Italy: May 25, 1915
San Marino: June 1, 1915
Portugal: March 9, 1916
Rumania: August 27, 1916
Greece: November 24, 1916[2]

United States: April 6, 1917
Cuba: April 7, 1917
Siam: July 22, 1917
Liberia: August 4, 1917
China: August 14, 1917
Brazil: October 26, 1917
Panama: November 10, 1917
Guatemala: April 22, 1918
Nicaragua: May 6, 1918
Costa Rica: May 24, 1918
Haiti: July 15, 1918
Honduras: July 19, 1918

[5] Tanganyika and Zanzibar having united on April 26, 1964, to form a United Republic of Tanganyika and Zanzibar, Zanzibar on May 13, 1964, ended its separate membership in the UN. The new state assumed the name of the United Republic of Tanzania on October 29, 1964.

[6] Total membership as of January 1, 1971, stands at 127.

[1] Not all Allied and Associated Powers were at war with all of the Central Powers, and declarations of war by one member of a coalition against different members of the other coalition did not occur at the same time. For example, Italy declared war against Austria-Hungary on May 24, 1915, Turkey August 21, 1915, Bulgaria October 19, 1915, and Germany August 28, 1916. Reference is made only to the first declaration of war in this table which is adapted by permission from Quincy Wright: A *Study of War* (2 vols.; Chicago, 1942), vol. I, p. 646, Table 42.

[2] Declaration by Provisional Government at Salonika under Venizelos; declaration by Royal Government June 27, 1917, after abdication of Constantine.

3. NEW STATES RECOGNIZED BY THE ALLIES WHICH BECAME INVOLVED IN THE WAR AND SIGNED SOME OF THE PEACE TREATIES

Hijaz: March 19, 1917   Poland: November 2, 1918
Czechoslovakia: June 30, 1918

4. STATES WHICH BROKE RELATIONS WITH SOME OF THE CENTRAL POWERS AND SIGNED SOME OF THE PEACE TREATIES

Bolivia: April 14, 1917   Uruguay: October 17, 1917
Peru: October 6, 1917   Ecuador: December 17, 1917

Appendix VI

Entrance of States into World War II in Chronological Order[1]

1. THE AXIS AND SATELLITE STATES

Germany: September 1, 1939
Italy: June 11, 1940
Hungary: April 10, 1941
Bulgaria: April 24, 1941
Rumania: June 22, 1941
Finland: June 25, 1941 (Previously at war with the USSR Nov. 30, 1939 to March 12, 1940)

Japan: December 7, 1941
Manchukuo: December 8, 1941
Slovakia: December 12, 1941
Croatia: December 14, 1941
Albania: December 17, 1941
Thailand: January 25, 1942
Nanking government of China: January 9, 1943

2. THE COALITION AGAINST THE AXIS (AFTER JAN. 1, 1942 KNOWN AS THE UNITED NATIONS)

Poland: September 1, 1939
United Kingdom: September 3, 1939
France: September 3, 1939
India: September 3, 1939 (Action taken by government in London)
Australia: September 3, 1939
New Zealand: September 3, 1939
Union of South Africa: September 6, 1939
Canada: September 10, 1939
Norway: April 8–9, 1940
Belgium: May 10, 1940
Luxembourg: May 10, 1940
Netherlands: May 10, 1940
Greece: October 28, 1940
Yugoslavia: April 6, 1941
Union of Soviet Socialist Republics: June 22, 1941 (Previously invaded Poland Sept. 17, 1939; at war with

Finland Nov. 30, 1939 to March 12, 1940; declared war on Japan August 8, 1945)
United States: December 7, 1941
Philippine Commonwealth: December 7, 1941
Panama: December 7, 1941
Costa Rica: December 8, 1941
Dominican Republic: December 8, 1941
Nicaragua: December 8, 1941
El Salvador: December 8, 1941
Haiti: December 8, 1941
Honduras: December 8, 1941
Guatemala: December 9, 1941
Cuba: December 9, 1941
China: December 9, 1941 (Chinese-Japanese incident had begun July 7, 1937)

[1] Table compiled from Katherine E. Crane: "Status of Countries in Relation to the War, August 12, 1945." *Department of State Bulletin.* (1945) 13:230–241; Royal Institute of International Affairs: *Chronology of the Second World War.* (London: 1947).

Czechoslovakia: December 9, 1941 (Government-in-Exile)
Brazil: May 2, 1942
Mexico: May 22, 1942
Ethiopia: December 1, 1942
Iraq: January 16, 1943
Bolivia: April 7, 1943
Iran: September 9, 1943
Colombia: November 26, 1943 (State of Belligerency with Germany)
Liberia: January 27, 1944
Ecuador: February 2, 1945
Paraguay: February 8, 1945
Peru: February 11, 1945 (State of Belligerency with Germany and Japan)
Chile: February 12, 1945 (State of Belligerency with Japan)

Venezuela: February 14, 1945 (State of Belligerency with Germany and Japan)
Uruguay: February 22, 1945
Turkey: February 23, 1945
Egypt: February 26, 1945
Syria: February 26, 1945
Lebanon: February 27, 1945
Saudi Arabia: March 1, 1945
Argentina: March 27, 1945 (Declared war against Germany and Japan, but not a signatory to Declaration by United Nations)
Mongolian People's Republic: August 9, 1945 (Declared war against Japan, but not a signatory to Declaration by United Nations)

3. AXIS SATELLITES WHICH SUBSEQUENTLY DECLARED WAR AGAINST THE AXIS

Italy: October 13, 1943
Rumania: August 24, 1944
Bulgaria: September 8, 1944

Finland: September 15, 1944
San Marino: September 21, 1944
Hungary: January 20, 1945

Appendix VII
Regional Groups and Organizations After World War II
(ARRANGED CHRONOLOGICALLY BY AREA)

Europe and the Near East

COMMONWEALTH OF NATIONS
(BRITISH COMMONWEALTH OF NATIONS BEFORE APRIL 27, 1949)

Original members (Dominions), December 11, 1931 (Statute of Westminster)
Australia and dependencies
Canada
[Ireland—ceased membership April 18, 1949]
[Newfoundland—ceased membership (became Canadian province) March 31, 1949]
New Zealand and dependencies
[Union of South Africa and dependencies—ceased membership May 31, 1961]
United Kingdom and dependencies

Later additions
India, August 15, 1947 (became republic January 26, 1950)
Pakistan, August 15, 1947 (became republic November 2, 1953)
Ceylon, February 4, 1948
Ghana, March 6, 1957 (became republic July 1, 1960)
Federation of Malaya, August 31, 1957 (renamed Federation of Malaysia September 16, 1963, including Sabah [North Borneo], Sarawak, and Singapore; Singa-

pore withdrew from the Federation August 9, 1965, and as an independent state
was admitted to the Commonwealth on October 16, 1965)

Nigeria, October 1, 1960 (became republic October 1, 1963)

Cyprus, March 13, 1961 (became republic August 16, 1960)

Sierra Leone, April 27, 1961

Tanganyika, December 9, 1961 (became republic December 9, 1962; merged with
Zanzibar April 26, 1964; adopted name of Tanzania October 29, 1964)

Jamaica, August 5, 1962

Trinidad and Tobago, August 31, 1962

Uganda, October 9, 1962 (became republic October 9, 1963)

Zanzibar, December 10, 1963 (merged with Tanganyika April 26, 1964; adopted
name of Tanzania October 29, 1964)

Kenya, December 12, 1963 (became republic December 12, 1964)

Malawi, July 6, 1964 (formerly Nyasaland; became republic July 6, 1966)

Malta, September 21, 1964

Zambia, October 10, 1964 (formerly Northern Rhodesia)

Gambia, February 18, 1965 (became republic April 23, 1970)

Singapore, October 16, 1965 (became republic August 9, 1965)

Guyana, May 26, 1966 (formerly British Guiana; became republic February 23,
1970)

Botswana, September 30, 1966 (formerly Bechuanaland; a republic)

Lesotho, October 4, 1966 (formerly Basutoland; a kingdom)

Barbados, November 30, 1966

Mauritius, March 12, 1968

Swaziland, September, 1968 (a kingdom)

Nauru, November 29, 1968 (special limited membership)

Tonga, June 4, 1970 (a kingdom)

Fiji, October 13, 1970 (a republic)

BENELUX ECONOMIC UNION (BENELUX)

Original members, September 5, 1944 (agreement revised March 14, 1947, and
February 3, 1958)

Belgium
Luxembourg
The Netherlands

THE ARAB LEAGUE

Original members, March 22, 1945

Egypt	Lebanon
Iraq	Jordan
Saudi Arabia	Yemen
Syria	

Later additions

Libya, March 28, 1953

Sudan, January 19, 1956

United Arab Republic, February 1, 1958 (Egypt, Syria; Syria withdrew September
8, 1961)

Morocco, October 1, 1958

Tunisia, October 1, 1958

Kuwait, July 20, 1961

Algeria, August 16, 1962

Southern Yemen, 1968

THE COMMUNIST INFORMATION BUREAU (COMINFORM; DISSOLVED
APRIL 17, 1956)

Original members, October 5, 1947 (Communist parties of these countries)

Bulgaria
Czechoslovakia
France
Hungary
Italy

Poland
Rumania
Union of Soviet Socialist Republics
Yugoslavia (expelled June 28, 1948)

BRUSSELS TREATY ORGANIZATION (BRUTO OR WESTERN UNION) AND AFTER
MAY 6, 1955, WESTERN EUROPEAN UNION (WEU)

Original members, March 17, 1948

Belgium
France
Luxembourg

The Netherlands
United Kingdom

Later additions resulting from agreements signed October 23, 1954

German Federal Republic, May 6, 1955
Italy, May 6, 1955

ORGANIZATION FOR EUROPEAN ECONOMIC CO-OPERATION (OEEC); REORGANIZED
AS ORGANIZATION FOR ECONOMIC CO-OPERATION AND DEVELOPMENT (OECD)
SEPTEMBER 30, 1961

Original members, April 16, 1948

Austria
Belgium
Denmark
France
Greece
Iceland
Ireland
Italy
Luxembourg

The Netherlands
Norway
Portugal
Sweden
Switzerland
Turkey
United Kingdom
Germany (Bizonia and French zone; until
   October 31, 1949)

Later additions

Free territory of Trieste, July, 1948, to October, 1954
German Federal Republic, October 31, 1949
United States and Canada associated with OEEC June 2, 1950; full membership
   in OECD September 30, 1961
Spain, July 20, 1959
Finland, Japan, and Yugoslavia participate in some OECD activities

COUNCIL FOR MUTUAL ECONOMIC AID (COMECON) REORGANIZED
DECEMBER, 1959; JUNE, 1962

Original members, January 25, 1949

[Albania, resigned December, 1962]
Bulgaria
Czechoslovakia
Hungary

Poland
Rumania
Union of Soviet Socialist Republics

Later additions

German Democratic Republic, September 29, 1950
Mongolia, June 7, 1962

NORTH ATLANTIC TREATY ORGANIZATION (NATO)

Original members, April 4, 1949

Belgium	Luxembourg
Canada	The Netherlands
Denmark	Norway
France	Portugal
Iceland	United Kingdom
Italy	United States

Later additions

Greece, February 20, 1952
Turkey, February 20, 1952
German Federal Republic, May 5, 1955

COUNCIL OF EUROPE

Original members, May 5, 1949

Belgium	Luxembourg
Denmark	The Netherlands
France	Norway
Iceland	Sweden
Italy	United Kingdom

Later additions

Greece, August 9, 1949 (withdrew under pressure December 12, 1969)
Turkey, August 9, 1949
Iceland, March 7, 1950
The Saar (Associate Member), May 13, 1950 to December 31, 1956
German Federal Republic (Associate Member) July 13, 1950
                            (Full Member) May 2, 1951
Austria, April 16, 1956
Cyprus, May 24, 1961
Switzerland, May 6, 1963
Malta, April 29, 1965

EUROPEAN PAYMENTS UNION (EPU); REPLACED BY EUROPEAN MONETARY AGREEMENT (EMA) DECEMBER 27, 1958; EMA IS ADMINISTERED BY OECD

Original members, July 1, 1950

Austria	The Netherlands
Belgium-Luxembourg	Norway
Denmark	Portugal
France	Sweden
German Federal Republic	Switzerland
Greece	Turkey
Iceland	United Kingdom (and Ireland)
Italy	

Later addition

Spain, July 20, 1959

EUROPEAN COAL AND STEEL COMMUNITY (ECSC; SCHUMAN PLAN)

Original members, April 18, 1951
  Belgium   Italy
  France   Luxembourg
  German Federal Republic   The Netherlands

Later additions
  United Kingdom (Associate Agreement), December 21, 1954
  Switzerland (Consultation Agreement), May 7, 1956

EUROPEAN DEFENSE COMMUNITY (EDC; PROPOSED BUT NEVER
IMPLEMENTED)

Proposed members, April 18, 1951
  Belgium   Italy
  France   Luxembourg
  German Federal Republic   The Netherlands

NORDIC COUNCIL

Original members, March 1952
  Denmark   Norway
  Iceland   Sweden

Later addition
  Finland, December 30, 1955

BALKAN ALLIANCE

Original members, February 28, 1953 (Military Agreement August 9, 1954)
  Greece
  Turkey
  Yugoslavia

EASTERN SECURITY TREATY (WARSAW PACT)

Original members, May 14, 1955
  Albania   Hungary
  Bulgaria   Poland
  Czechoslovakia   Rumania
  Democratic Republic of Germany   Union of Soviet Socialist Republics

MIDDLE EAST TREATY ORGANIZATION (METO; BAGHDAD PACT); RENAMED
CENTRAL TREATY ORGANIZATION (CENTO) AUGUST 21, 1959

Original members, February 24, 1955
  Turkey
  [Iraq—ceased membership March 24, 1959]

Later additions

United Kingdom, April 4, 1955
Pakistan, September 23, 1955
Iran, November 3, 1955
United States assumes close partnership, July 28, 1958

EUROPEAN ATOMIC ENERGY COMMUNITY (EURATOM)

Original members, January 1, 1958

Belgium
France
German Federal Republic

Italy
Luxembourg
The Netherlands

EUROPEAN ECONOMIC COMMUNITY (EEC; COMMON MARKET)

Original members, January 1, 1958

Belgium
France
German Federal Republic

Italy
Luxembourg
The Netherlands

Associate members

Greece, November 1, 1962
Burundi, June 1, 1964
Cameroon, June 1, 1964
Central African Republic, June 1, 1964
Chad, June 1, 1964
Congo (Brazzaville), June 1, 1964
Congo (Kinshasa), June 1, 1964
Dahomey, June 1, 1964
Gabon, June 1, 1964
Ivory Coast, June 1, 1964
Malagasy, June 1, 1964
Mali, June 1, 1964
Mauritania, June 1, 1964
Morocco, September 1, 1969
Niger, June 1, 1964
Rwanda, June 1, 1964
Senegal, June 1, 1964
Somalia, June 1, 1964
Togo, June 1, 1964
Tunisia, September 1, 1969
Upper Volta, June 1, 1964
French Overseas Territories and Departments, June 1, 1964
Netherland Antilles, October 1, 1964
Turkey, December 1, 1964

EUROPEAN FREE TRADE ASSOCIATION (EFTA: OUTER SEVEN)

Original members, May 3, 1960

Austria
Denmark
Norway
Portugal

Sweden
Switzerland
United Kingdom

Later addition
  Iceland, March 1, 1970

Associate member
  Finland, March 27, 1961

Far East

FAR EASTERN COMMISSION (FEC); DISSOLVED, 1951

Original members, February 26, 1946

Australia   New Zealand
Canada   Philippines
China   Union of Soviet Socialist Republics
France   United Kingdom
India   United States
The Netherlands

SOUTH PACIFIC COMMISSION

Original members, February 6, 1947

Australia   New Zealand
France   United Kingdom
The Netherlands   United States

COLOMBO PLAN FOR CO-OPERATIVE ECONOMIC DEVELOPMENT IN SOUTH AND SOUTHEAST ASIA (COLOMBO PLAN)

Original members, July 1, 1951

Australia   New Zealand
Canada   Pakistan
Ceylon   United Kingdom with Malaya, British
India   Borneo, and Singapore

Later additions

Cambodia, 1951   Thailand, 1954
Laos, 1951   Malaysia, full membership, 1957
South Vietnam, 1951   Singapore, full membership, 1959
United States, 1951   Bhutan, 1962
Burma, 1952   South Korea, 1962
Nepal, 1952   Afghanistan, 1963
Indonesia, 1953   Maldive Islands, 1963
Japan, 1954   Iran, 1967
Philippines, 1954

PACIFIC OR ANZUS COUNCIL (ANZUS)

Original members, September 1, 1951

Australia
New Zealand
United States

SOUTHEAST ASIA COLLECTIVE DEFENSE TREATY (SEATO; SOUTHEAST ASIA
TREATY ORGANIZATION; PACIFIC CHARTER)

Original members, September 8, 1954

Australia
France
New Zealand
Pakistan

Philippines
Thailand
United Kingdom
United States

Africa

UNION AFRICAINE ET MALGACHE (UAM; BRAZZAVILLE GROUP; REORGANIZED
AS UNION AFRICAINE ET MALGACHE DE COOPERATON ÉCONOMIQUE
[UAMCE], MARCH 7–10, 1964); REORGANIZED AS THE ORGANISATION COMMUNE
AFRICAINE ET MALGACHE [OCAM], FEBRUARY 10–12, 1965

Original members, December, 1960

Cameroon
Central African Republic
Chad
Republic of Congo (Brazzaville)
Dahomey
Gabon

Ivory Coast
Malagasy Republic
Mauritania
Niger
Senegal
Upper Volta

Later additions
Togo, 1963
Rwanda, 1963
Congo (Kinshasa), 1965

THE AFRICAN STATES OF THE CASABLANCA CHAPTER (CASABLANCA GROUP)

Original members, January 3–7, 1961

Ghana
Guinea
Mali

Morocco
United Arab Republic

Later addition
Algeria, 1962

INTER-AFRICAN AND MALAGASY STATES ORGANIZATION (IAMSO;
MONROVIA GROUP)

Original members, May 8–12, 1961; January 25–30, 1962; Charter, December 20,
1962

Cameroon
Central African Republic
Chad
Congo (Brazzaville)
Congo (Kinshasa)
Dahomey
Ethiopia
Gabon
Ivory Coast
Liberia

Malagasy
Mauritania
Niger
Nigeria
Senegal
Sierra Leone
Somalia
Togo
Upper Volta

ORGANIZATION OF AFRICAN UNITY (OAU)

Original members, May 22–25, 1963

Algeria	Malagasy
Burundi	Mali
Cameroon	Mauritania
Central African Republic	Niger
Chad	Nigeria
Congo (Brazzaville)	Rwanda
Congo (Kinshasa)	Senegal
Dahomey	Sierra Leone
Ethiopia	Somalia
Gabon	Sudan
Ghana	Tanganyika (Tanzania)
Guinea	Tunisia
Ivory Coast	Uganda
Liberia	Upper Volta
Libya	United Arab Republic

Later additions

Morocco, 1963	Botswana, 1966
Togo, 1963	Lesotho, 1966
Kenya, 1964	Mauritius, 1968
Malawi, 1964	Swaziland, 1968
Zambia, 1964	Equatorial Guinea, 1968
Gambia, 1965	

UNION DOUANIERE ET ÉCONOMIQUE DE L'AFRIQUE CENTRALE (UDEAC); CENTRAL AFRICAN ECONOMIC AND CUSTOMS UNION

Original members, January 1, 1966

Cameroon	Congo (Brazzaville)
Central African Republic	Gabon
Chad	

EAST AFRICAN COMMUNITY

Original members, December 1, 1967

Kenya
Tanzania
Uganda

The Americas

ORGANIZATION OF AMERICAN STATES[1]

Original members, April 30, 1948

Argentina	Chile
Bolivia	Colombia
Brazil	Costa Rica

[1] These American states have also agreed to an Inter-American Treaty of Reciprocal Assistance (Rio Treaty), which was signed at Rio de Janeiro on September 2, 1947, and entered into force on December 3, 1948.

Cuba   Nicaragua
Dominican Republic   Panama
Ecuador   Paraguay
El Salvador   Peru
Guatemala   United States
Haiti   Uruguay
Honduras   Venezuela
Mexico

Later additions
    Trinidad and Tobago, February 23, 1967
    Barbados, November 15, 1967

CARIBBEAN FREE TRADE AREA (CARIFTA)

Original members, December 15, 1965
    Antigua
    Barbados
    Guyana

Later additions
    Trinidad and Tobago, May 1, 1968   St. Lucia, July 1, 1968
    Dominica, July 1, 1968   St. Vincent, July 1, 1968
    Grenada, July 1, 1968   Jamaica, August 1, 1968
    St. Kitts-Nevis-Anguilla, July 1, 1968   Montserrat, August 1, 1968

AGENCY FOR CULTURAL AND TECHNICAL COOPERATION AMONG FRENCH-SPEAKING
NATIONS (PAYS FRANCOPHONES)

Original members, March 20, 1970
    Belgium   Madagascar
    Burundi   Mali
    Cameroon   Mauritius
    Canada   Monaco
    Chad   Niger
    Ivory Coast   Rwanda
    Dahomey   Senegal
    France   Togo
    Gabon   Tunisia
    Upper Volta   South Vietnam
    Luxembourg

Appendix VIII

African States and Territories

INDEPENDENT STATES

	Former status or name	Capital	Date of Independence
Algeria	French departments	Algiers	July 3, 1962
Botswana	Br. Bechuanaland	Gaborone	Sept. 30, 1966
Burundi	Part of Belg. trust territory of Ruanda-Urundi	Bujumbura	July 1, 1962
Cameroon	Br. and Fr. trust territories of Cameroons	Yaounde	Jan. 1, 1960 (Fr.) Oct. 1, 1961 (Br.)

	Former status or name	Capital	Date of Independence
Central African Republic	Part of Fr. Eq. Africa	Bangui	Aug. 13, 1960
Chad	Part of Fr. Eq. Africa	Fort Lamy	Aug. 11, 1960
Congo (Brazzaville)	Part of Fr. Eq. Africa	Brazzaville	Aug. 15, 1960
Congo[1] (Kinshasa)	Belgian Congo	Kinshasa	June 30, 1960
Dahomey	Part of Fr. W. Africa	Porto Novo	Aug. 1, 1960
Equatorial Guinea	Sp. col. of Fernando Po, Rio Muni	Santa Isabel	Oct. 12, 1968
Ethiopia	Known also as Abyssinia	Addis Ababa	Ancient
Gabon	Part of Fr. Eq. Africa	Libreville	Aug. 17, 1960
Gambia	British colony	Bathurst	Feb. 18, 1965
Ghana	Br. Gold Coast and Br. trust territory of Togoland	Accra	March 6, 1957
Guinea	Part of Fr. W. Africa	Conakry	Oct. 2, 1958
Ivory Coast	Part of Fr. W. Africa	Abidjan	Aug. 7, 1960
Kenya	British colony	Nairobi	Dec. 12, 1963
Lesotho	Br. Basutoland	Maseru	Oct. 4, 1966
Liberia	Ex-U.S. slave settlement	Monrovia	July 26, 1847
Libya	Italian colony	Tripoli	Dec. 24, 1951
Malagasy	Madagascar; Fr. colony	Tananarive	June 26, 1960
Malawi	Nyasaland; Br. colony	Zomba	July 6, 1964
Mali	French Sudan	Bamako	Sept. 22, 1960
Mauritania	Part of Fr. W. Africa	Nouakchott	Nov. 28, 1960
Mauritius	British colony	Port Louis	March 12, 1968
Morocco	French protectorate	Rabat	March 2, 1956
Niger	Part of Fr. W. Africa	Niamey	Aug. 3, 1960
Nigeria	British colony	Lagos	Oct. 1, 1960
Rhodesia[2]	Internal self-governing colony	Salisbury	Nov. 11, 1965
Rwanda	Part of Belg. trust territory of Ruanda-Urundi	Kigali	July 1, 1962
Senegal	Part of Fr. W. Africa	Dakar	Aug. 20, 1960
Sierra Leone	British colony	Freetown	April 27, 1961
Somalia	Br. and Ital. Somaliland	Mogadiscio	July 1, 1960
South Africa[3]	Dutch and Br. colonies British Dominion	Capetown	May 31, 1910 (Dom.) May 31, 1961 (Rep.)
Sudan	Anglo-Egyptian Sudan	Khartoum	Jan. 1, 1956
Swaziland	Br. protectorate	Mbabane	Sept. 6, 1968
Tanzania	Tanganyika and Zanzibar Br. trust terr.; colony	Dar es Salaam	Dec. 9, 1961 (Tan.) Dec. 10, 1963 (Zan.) April 26, 1964 (Union)

[1] Officially named Democratic Republic of the Congo in 1964. Kinshasa, formerly Leopoldville, is the capital and the country is referred to as Congo (Kinshasa), although Congo (Leopoldville) is still sometimes used.

[2] Rhodesian independence has not been recognized by Britain, and its international status is not clear; it is not a member of the United Nations. Rhodesia became a republic March 2, 1970.

[3] South Africa considers its former mandatory state of South West Africa as part of South Africa. The Assembly of the United Nations, however, has made South West Africa a "direct responsibility" of the UN and renamed it Namibia.

	Former status or name	Capital	Date of Independence
Togo	Fr. trust terr. of Togo-land	Lomé	April 27, 1960
Tunisia	French protectorate	Tunis	March 20, 1956
Uganda	British colony	Kampala	Oct. 9, 1962
United Arab Republic	Egypt; Br. protectorate	Cairo	Feb. 28, 1922 Feb. 21, 1958 (UAR)
Upper Volta	Part of Fr. W. Africa	Ouagadougou	Aug. 5, 1960
Zambia	N. Rhodesia; Br. colony	Lusaka	Oct. 24, 1964

FRENCH OVERSEAS TERRITORIES

French Somaliland		Djibouti

PORTUGUESE OVERSEAS TERRITORIES

Angola	Province; includes Cabina at the estuary of the Congo	Luanda
Mozambique	Province	Lourenco Marques
Portuguese Guinea	Province	Bissau

SPANISH OVERSEAS TERRITORIES

Spanish Sahara	Province	El Aaiún
Spanish North Africa	Ports of Alhucemas, Ceuta, Chafarinas, Melilla, and Peñón de Vélez along the Med. coast of Morocco; included in different Spanish provinces	

Appendix IX

Vanishing Royalty, 1900–70

EUROPE

1900	1925	1950–70
Albania (Established 1912–13) Prince William of Wied, 1914	(Regency and Republic 1918–28) King Zog, 1928–39	
Austria-Hungary Francis Joseph, 1848–1916 Charles I, 1916–18	(Regency under Admiral Horthy in Hungary 1920–1944)	

	1900	1925	1950–70

Belgium
Leopold II, 1865–1909
Albert, 1909–34

Albert, 1909–34
Leopold III, 1934–

(Regency under Prince
  Charles 1944–50)
Leopold III, 1950–51
Baudouin, 1951–

Bulgaria
Ferdinand I, Prince 1887–
  1908; King 1908–18
Boris III, 1918–43

Boris III, 1918–43
Simeon II, 1943–46

Denmark
Christian IX, 1863–1906
Frederick VIII, 1906–12
Christian X, 1912–47

Christian X, 1912–47
Frederick IX, 1947–

Frederick IX, 1947–

Germany
William II, 1888–1918

Greece
George I, 1863–1913
Constantine I, 1913–17
Alexander I, 1917–20
Constantine I, 1920–22
George II, 1922–23

(Republic, 1924–35)
George II, 1935–44
Regency, 1944–46
George II, 1946–47
Paul I, 1947–64

Paul I, 1947–1964
Constantine II, 1964–

Italy
Victor Emmanuel III,
  1900–44

Victor Emmanuel III, 1900–
  1944
Umberto II, regent 1944–6
Umberto II, May-June,
  1946

Ireland
Victoria, 1837–1901
Edward VII, 1901–10
George V, 1910–36

George V, 1910–36
Edward VIII, 1936
George VI, 1936–49

Liechtenstein
John II, 1858–1929

John II, 1858–1929
Francis I, 1928–38
Francis Joseph II, 1938–

Francis Joseph II,
  1938–

Luxembourg
Adolf, 1890–1905
Wilhelm, 1905–12
Adelaide, 1912–19
Charlotte, 1919–64

Charlotte, 1919–64

Charlotte, 1919–1964
Jean, 1964–

1900	1925	1950–70
Monaco Albert I, 1899–1922 Louis II, 1922–49	Louis II, 1922–49 Rainier III, 1949–	Rainier III, 1949–
Montenegro Nicholas I, Prince 1860– 1910; King 1910–18		
The Netherlands Wilhelmina, 1890–1948	Wilhelmina, 1890–1948 Juliana, 1948–	Juliana, 1948–
Norway Haakon VII, 1905–57	Haakon VII, 1905–57	Haakon VII, 1905–57 Olav V, 1957–
Portugal Carlos I, 1889–1908 Manuel II, 1908–10		
Rumania Carol I, Prince 1866–81; King 1881–1914 Ferdinand I, 1914–27	Ferdinand I, 1914–27 Michael I, 1927–30 Carol II, 1930–40 Michael I, 1940–47	
Russia Nicholas II, 1894–1917		
Serbia (Yugoslavia) Alexander I (Obrenovich), 1889–1903 Peter I (Karageorgevich), 1903–21 Alexander I, 1921–34	Alexander I, 1921–34 Peter II, 1934–45	
Spain Alfonso XIII, 1886–1931	Alfonso XIII, 1886–1931	
Sweden Oscar II, 1872–1907 Gustav V, 1907–50	Gustav V, 1907–50	Gustav V, 1907–50 Gustav VI (Gustav Adolf), 1950–
United Kingdom Victoria, 1837–1901 Edward VII, 1901–10 George V, 1910–36	George V, 1910–36 Edward VIII, 1936 George VI, 1936–52	George VI, 1936–52 Elizabeth II, 1952–

NEAR EAST AND NORTH AFRICA

1900	1925	1950–70
Turkey Abdul Hamid, 1876– 1909 Mohammed V, 1909–18 Mohammed VI, 1918–1922		
Egypt Abbas Hilmi, 1892–1914 Hussein Kamil, 1914–17 Fuad I, 1917–36	Fuad I, 1917–36 Farouk, 1936–52	Farouk, 1936–52 Ahmed Fuad, 1952–53
Ethiopa Menelek II, 1889–1913 Lij Yasu, 1913–16 Empress Zauditu, 1916– 1930	Empress Zauditu, 1916–30 Haile Selassie, 1930– (King 1928–)	Haile Selassie, 1930–
Iran (Persia) Muzaffar-ed-din, 1896– 1907 Mohammed Ali, 1907–09 Sultan Ahmad, 1909–25	Riza Khan Pahlavi, 1925– 1941 Mohammed Reza Pahlavi, 1941	Mohammed Reza Pahlavi, 1941–
Iraq	Faisal I, 1921–33 Ghazi, 1933–39 Faisal II, 1939–58	Faisal II, 1939–58
Jordan (Transjordan)	Abdullah ibn-Husein, 1921– 1951	Abdullah ibn-Husein, 1921–51 Talal, 1951–52 Hussein, 1952–
Kuwait Sheikh Mubarrak, 1896–1915 Sheikh Jabir, 1915–17 Sheikh Salem, 1917–21	Ahmad Ibn Jabir al-Subah, 1921–50	Abdullah al-Salim al-Subah, 1950–65 Sabah al-Salim al-Subah, 1965–
Libya (Established 1951)		Mohammed Idris et Senussi, 1951–69

1900	1925	1950–70

Morocco
  Moulay-Abd-el-Aziz,
    1894–1908
  Moulay-Abd-el-Hafid,
    1908–12
  Moulay Youssef,
    1912–27
	Moulay Youssef, 1912–27
	
	Sidi Mohammed ben
	  Youssef,1927–53
		Sidi Mohammed ben
		  Youssef, 1927–53
		Sidi Mohammed ben
		  Moulay Arafa,
		  1953–55
		Sidi Mohammed ben
		  Youssef, 1955–61
		  (King Mohammed
		  V since Aug. 18,
		  1957)
		Hassan II, 1961–

Saudi Arabia
  (Established 1932;
    formerly Hejaz, Nejd,
    etc.)
	Ibn Saud, 1926–53	Ibn Saud, 1926–53
		Saud ibn Abdul-Aziz,
		  1953–64
		Faisal ibn Abd-al-Aziz,
		  1964–

Tunisia
  Sidi Ali, 1882–1902
  Sidi Mohammed el Hadi,
    1902–06
  Sidi Mohammed en Nasr,
    1906–22
  Sidi Mohammed el
    Habib, 1922–29
	Sidi Mohammed el Habib,
	  1922–29
	Sidi Ahmed, 1929–42
	Sidi Mohammed al Mousif,
	  1942–43
	Sidi Mohammed al Amin,
	  1943–57
		Sidi Mohammed al
		  Amin, 1943–57

Yemen
  Imman Yahya, 1904–48
	Imman Yahya, 1904–48
	Imman Ahmad, 1948–62
		Imman Ahmad, 1948–
		  1962

Appendix X

Roman Popes, 1900–70

1878–1903 Leo XIII (Gioacchino Pecci)
1903–14   Pius X (Giuseppe Sarto)
1914–22   Benedict XV (Giacomo della Chiesa)
1922–39   Pius XI (Achille Ratti)
1939–58   Pius XII (Eugenio Pacelli)
1958–63   John XXIII (Angelo Roncalli)
1963–   Paul VI (Giovanni Battista Montini)

Appendix XI

Chronology

NINETEENTH-CENTURY ORIGINS OF WORLD WAR I ALLIANCE SYSTEMS

1873

JUNE 6: Three Emperors' League (Germany, Austria-Hungary, Russia); informal arrangement followed by an alliance in 1881.

1879

OCT. 7: Dual Alliance (Germany, Austria-Hungary); in force until 1918.

1881

JUNE 18: Alliance of Three Emperors (Germany, Austria-Hungary, Russia); in force until 1887.

1881

JUNE 28: Austro-Hungarian-Serbian treaty; in force until 1895.

1882

MAY 20: Triple Alliance (Germany, Austria-Hungary, Italy); in force until World War I.

1883

OCT. 30: Rumania adheres to Triple Alliance; remains a member until World War I.

1887

JUNE 18: German-Russian Treaty ("Reinsurance Treaty"); in force until 1890.

1891

AUG. 21–JAN. 4, 1894: Conclusion of French-Russian Military Convention; in force until 1917.

SELECT LIST OF DATES, 1900–70

1900

JUNE 12: Second German naval law provides for great expansion of fleet.
JUNE 13–AUG. 14: Boxer Uprising in China.
DEC. 14: French-Italian agreement on Morocco and Tripoli.

1901

JULY 1: Associations law in France; Separation of church and state 1901–05.

1902

JAN. 30: Signature of Anglo-Japanese Alliance.
MAY 31: End of Boer War (begun Oct. 9, 1899).

1903

JUNE 10: Assassination of King Alexander and Queen Draga of Serbia; Peter Karageorgevich becomes king.
OCT. 2: Mürzsteg Program of Reform in Macedonia.

1904

FEB. 4: Start of the Russian-Japanese War.
APR. 8: Anglo-French Entente.

1904 *(continued)*

APR. 12: Secret Treaty of Alliance and a public Treaty of Friendship between Serbia and Bulgaria.
OCT. 3: French-Spanish Treaty in regard to Morocco.
OCT. 21: The Dogger Bank Incident.

1905

JAN. 22: Bloody Sunday; Revolutionary Agitation in Russia.
MAR. 31: William II of Germany visits Tangier; leads to First Morocco Crisis.
JULY 24: Treaty of Björkö between Russia and Germany.
AUG. 12: Renewal of Anglo-Japanese Treaty of Alliance.
SEPT. 5: Treaty of Portsmouth ends Russo-Japanese War.
OCT. 30: October Manifesto; Emperor grants a constitution to Russia with a representative Duma.

1906

JAN. 10: Beginning of military and naval conversations between England and France.
JAN. 16–APRIL 7: Algeciras Conference; settles First Morocco Crisis.
DEC. 13: Tripartite Accord between Great Britain, France, and Italy on Ethiopia.

1907

JUNE 10: Franco-Japanese agreement for equality of treatment in China.
JUNE 15–OCT. 18: Second Hague Peace Conference. (First Conference May 18–July 29, 1899.)
JULY 30: Russo-Japanese Agreement for equality of treatment in China.
AUG. 31: Anglo-Russian Entente.

1908

JULY 6–24: Young Turk Revolution.
SEPT. 16: Buchlau Conference (Austrian and Russian Foreign Ministers).
SEPT. 25: Casablanca Affair; arrest of German deserters from French Foreign Legion.
OCT. 5: Bulgarian independence proclaimed.
OCT. 6: Austria-Hungary annexes Bosnia-Herzegovina; beginning of the Annexation Crisis.
OCT. 28: Daily Telegraph Affair; tension between Germany and Britain.

1909

FEB. 9: French-German Morocco settlement; end of Casablanca Affair.
MAR. 31: Serbia recognizes annexation of Bosnia-Herzegovina; end of crisis.
APR. 27: Deposition of Sultan Abdul Hamid by Young Turks.
OCT. 24: Racconigi Agreement between Russia and Italy over the Near East.

1910

MAY 7: Death of Edward VII; accession of George V.
JULY 4: Russo-Japanese agreement on Manchuria.
AUG. 22: Japan annexes Korea.
AUG. 29: Montenegro proclaimed a kingdom.
OCT. 5: Portugal proclaimed a republic.
NOV. 4–5: Potsdam Agreement between Germany and Russia on the Near East.

1911

JULY 1: Germany sends gunboat *Panther* to Agadir; Second Morocco Crisis.
JULY 13: Anglo-Japanese Treaty renewed.
AUG. 10: British Parliament Act finally accepted by House of Lords.
AUG. 19: German-Russian agreement over Persia and the Baghdad Railway.
SEPT. 29: Start of Tripolitan War.
NOV. 4: German-French agreement over Morocco and the Congo; end of Second Morocco Crisis.

1912

FEB. 8–11: Haldane mission to Berlin; failure of Anglo-German naval negotiations.
FEB. 12: China proclaimed a republic.
MAR. 13: Alliance between Bulgaria and Serbia; beginning of agreements which led to Balkan League (Bulgaria, Serbia, Greece, Montenegro).
JULY 8: Secret treaty between Russia and Japan in regard to northeastern Asia.
JULY 16: Naval Convention between France and Russia.
OCT. 8: Montenegro declares war on Turkey; joined by Bulgaria, Serbia, and Greece on Oct. 18; First Balkan War.
OCT. 15: Secret Treaty of Ouchy ends Tripolitan War; confirmed in public Treaty of Lausanne Oct. 18.
NOV. 21–22: Grey-Cambon letters.
DEC. 17: Beginning of Conference of Ambassadors in London to deal with matters relating to Balkan War.

1913

MAY 7: Ambassadorial Conference at St. Petersburg forces Bulgaria to cede Southern Dobruja to Rumania.
MAY 30: Treaty of London ends First Balkan War; Balkan states left to divide former Turkish lands in Europe beyond Enos-Media line.
JUNE 1: Alliance between Serbia and Greece against Bulgaria.
JUNE 29–30: Start of Second Balkan War.
AUG. 10: Treaty of Bucharest ends Second Balkan War.
OCT. 18: Austro-Hungarian ultimatum to Serbia demanding evacuation of Albanian territory.
NOV. 5: Russian-Chinese agreement over Mongolia.
NOV.–DEC.: Liman von Sanders Crisis; question of German influence in Turkey.

1914

JUNE 28: Assassination of Archduke Francis Ferdinand.
JULY 20–23: Poincaré visits St. Petersburg.
JULY 23: Austro-Hungarian ultimatum to Serbia.
JULY 28: Austria-Hungary declares war on Serbia.
JULY 30: General mobilization ordered in Russia.
AUG. 1: Germany declares war on Russia.
AUG. 2: Turkish-German Treaty of Alliance.
AUG. 2: German ultimatum to Belgium.
AUG. 3: Germany declares war on France.
AUG. 4: England declares war on Germany.
OCT. 29: Turkish cruisers bombard Russian Black Sea ports.
NOV. 2: Russia declares war on Turkey, followed by England and France on Nov. 5.
NOV. 5: England annexes Cyprus (British protectorate since 1878).

1915

MAR. 18: Russia receives promise of acquisition of Constantinople from France and Britain.
APR. 25: British start landings in Gallipoli campaign.
APR. 26: Secret Treaty of London between Allies and Italy.
MAY 23: Italy enters the war against Austria-Hungary.
JULY 22: Turkey grants Bulgaria part of Thrace; treaty not signed until Sept. 22.
SEPT. 6: Bulgaria concludes alliance with Germany and Austria-Hungary.
OCT. 3–5: British and French land at Salonika.
OCT. 14: Bulgaria and Serbia declare war on each other.

1916

JAN. 6: Compulsory military service bill adopted in Great Britain.
APR. 24: Easter Rebellion in Ireland.
APR. 26: British-French-Russian agreement on partition of Asiatic Turkey.

1916 (*continued*)

MAY 9–16: Sykes-Picot Agreement between Britain and France.
AUG. 27: Rumania declares war on Austria-Hungary.
NOV. 21: Death of Francis Joseph of Austria-Hungary; Charles I succeeds to the throne.
DEC. 18: President Wilson transmits peace proposals to belligerents.
DEC. 4: Lloyd George becomes Prime Minister.
DEC. 30: Rasputin assassinated.

1917

FEB. 1: Unrestricted submarine war by Germany.
FEB. 16: British-Japanese agreement on disposition of German Asiatic possessions.
FEB–JUNE: Emperor Charles of Austria attempts secret peace negotiations.
MAR. 12 (Feb. 27 Old Style): Provisional Government established in Russia.
MAR. 15: Emperor Nicholas II abdicates.
APR. 6: United States declares war on Germany; declares war on Austria-Hungary Dec. 7, 1917.
APR. 16: Lenin returns to Russia.
APR. 19–21: Agreement of St. Jean de Maurienne partitioning Asia Minor.
JUNE 27: Greece officially enters war on side of Allies.
JULY 20: Pact of Corfu; agreement between Serbs, Croats, and Slovenes.
JULY 20: Kerensky becomes head of the Russian government.
NOV. 2: Balfour declaration on Palestine.
NOV. 7 (Oct. 25 Old Style): Bolsheviks seize power in Russia.
DEC. 5: Russia and Central Powers conclude armistice.
DEC. 23: French and British understanding on spheres of influence in Southern Russia.

1918

JAN. 8: President Wilson announces his Peace Program of Fourteen Points.
MAR. 3: Treaty of Brest-Litovsk between Russia and the Central Powers.
MAY 7: Treaty of Bucharest between Rumania and the Central Powers.
JULY 16: Emperor Nicholas II and his family executed at Ekaterinburg.
SEPT. 29: Bulgaria concludes armistice at Salonika.
OCT. 4: King Ferdinand of Bulgaria abdicates.
OCT. 30: Turkey concludes armistice at Mudros.
NOV. 3: Austria-Hungary concludes armistice.
NOV. 3: Mutiny in German high seas fleet.
NOV. 9: Abdication of William II.
NOV. 9: Rumania re-enters the war.
NOV. 11: Germany concludes armistice.
NOV. 13: Hungary signs special armistice ("Military Convention") at Belgrade.
DEC. 14: British hold "Khaki Election."
——— Civil War in Russia; ends 1920.

1919

JAN. 18: Peace Conference assembles at Paris.
MAR. 2: Formation of Third International.
MAR. 22.: Bela Kun overthrows Karolyi government in Hungary.
MAY 7: Peace Treaty submitted to German delegation.
MAY 14: Greeks land at Smyrna with consent of Allies.
JUNE 28: Treaty of Versailles with Germany signed.
AUG. 4: Rumanians capture Budapest.
AUG. 11: Weimar Constitution goes into effect in Germany.
SEPT. 10: Treaty of St. Germain with Austria signed.
NOV. 27: Treaty of Neuilly with Bulgaria signed.
DEC. 10: Allies force Rumanians to withdraw from Hungary.

1920

JAN. 10: League begins official existence.
FEB. 10: Plebiscite in Northern zone of Schleswig (March 14 in Southern zone).

1920 (*continued*)

MAR. 13–17: Kapp Putsch; German government flees Berlin.
APR. 25–OCT. 12: War between Russia and Poland.
JUNE 4: Treaty of Trianon with Hungary signed.
JUNE 22: Beginning of Greek offensive in Anatolia (Greek–Turkish war ends 1923).
AUG. 10: Treaty of Sèvres with Turkey.
AUG. 14: Czech-Yugoslav Treaty of Alliance; beginning of the Little Entente treaties.

1921

FEB. 19: French-Polish military alliance.
MAR. 3: Polish-Rumanian Treaty of Alliance.
MAR. 8: French occupation of Ruhrort, Duisburg, Düsseldorf (withdrew Aug. 25, 1925).
MAR. 16: Turkish-Russian treaty (territorial).
MAR. 18: Treaty of Riga between Russia and Poland.
MAR. 20: Plebiscite in Upper Silesia.
APR. 23: Rumanian-Czech Treaty of Alliance.
APR. 27: Reparation commission sets total of 132 billion gold marks.
JUNE 27: Yugoslav-Rumanian alliance; completion of Little Entente.
AUG. 24–25: United States concludes peace with Austria and Germany.
OCT. 21: Second attempt of King Charles to obtain throne of Hungary.
———— New Economic Policy in Russia.

1922

FEB. 2: Conclusion of Washington Conference.
FEB. 15: Opening of Permanent Court of International Justice at The Hague.
APR. 16: Russo–German treaty of Rapallo.
OCT. 30: Mussolini becomes Italian Premier.
DEC. 26: Reparation Commission votes Germany in default on timber deliveries.

1923

JAN. 11: France and Belgium occupy the Ruhr.
FEB. 16: Lithuania's seizure of Memel recognized by Council of Ambassadors.
FEB. 16: Japan returns Kiaochow to China; Shantung treaty.
MAR. 14: Vilna given to Poland by Council of Ambassadors.
JULY 24: Treaty of Lausanne with Turkey.
AUG. 29: Italy seizes Corfu (evacuates Sept. 27).
SEPT. 13: Primo de Rivera seizes power in Spain.
SEPT. 26: End of passive resistance in Ruhr.
NOV. 8–11: Beer Hall Putsch in Munich.

1924

JAN. 14: Dawes Committee begins work.
JAN. 21: Death of Lenin.
JAN. 25: French-Czechoslovak Treaty of Alliance.
JAN. 27: Italian-Yugoslav treaty; Fiume annexed to Italy.
MAR. 3: Abolition of the Caliphate.
APR. 9: Dawes Plan presented.
JUNE 10: Matteotti assassinated in Rome.
OCT. 2: Geneva Protocol (compulsory arbitration, definition of aggressor).
NOV. 18: Evacuation of Ruhr completed.
———— Great Britain (Feb. 1), Italy (Feb. 7), and France (Oct. 28) recognize Russia.

1925

JAN. 21: Albanian National Assembly proclaims a republic.
APR. 26: Hindenburg elected German President.
MAY 5: England restores Gold Standard.
OCT. 5–16: Locarno Conference, treaties signed Dec. 1.

1926

MAY 3: British general strike.
MAY 12–14: Pilsudski coup in Poland.
SEPT. 8: Germany admitted to the League of Nations.
NOV. 18: Close of Imperial Conference; autonomy of the Dominions foreseen.

1927

JAN. 31: End of Inter-Allied commission of military control in Germany.
MAY 26: Britain breaks relations with Soviet Russia (resumed Oct. 1, 1929).
JUNE 20–AUG. 4: Naval disarmament conference at Geneva.
DEC. 27: Banishment of Trotsky.
———— Chiang Kai-shek breaks with the Communists.

1928

JUNE 20: Radić shot in Yugoslav parliament.
AUG. 27: Briand-Kellogg Pact (Pact of Paris).
OCT. 1: First Five-year Plan in USSR.

1929

FEB. 9: Litvinov protocol; Russia, Poland, Rumania, Estonia, Latvia renounce war.
FEB. 11: Lateran pact; agreement between Italy and the Vatican.
JUNE 7: Young Plan announced.
OCT. 23: Stock Exchange crash in United States.
NOV. 30: French evacuate Coblenz Zone.
DEC. 22: Young Plan acceptance upheld in referendum in Germany.

1930

JAN. 21–APR. 2: London Naval Conference.
JAN. 28: Primo de Rivera forced to resign in Spain.
JUNE 30: Evacuation of Rhineland.
SEPT. 14: Nazis make great gains in German elections.
OCT. 1: Wei-hai-wei restored to China by Britain.
OCT. 5–12: First Balkan Conference at Athens.

1931

MAR. 21: Proposed German-Austrian customs union announced.
APR. 14: Alfonso XIII flees Spain; Spanish Republic established.
MAY 11: Failure of the Austrian *Kreditanstalt*.
JUNE 20: Hoover Moratorium.
SEPT. 18: Mukden Incident; start of Japanese occupation of Manchuria.
DEC. 10: Lytton Commission appointed to investigate Manchurian situation.
DEC. 11: Statute of Westminster; regulates status of Dominions in the British Commonwealth of Nations.

1932

JAN. 7: Stimson notifies Nine-Power Treaty signatories that United States will recognize no territorial gains obtained through armed force.
FEB.–JULY: First meeting of Disarmament Conference at Geneva.
FEB. 18: Independence of Manchukuo proclaimed.
APR. 10: Hindenburg defeats Hitler in presidential election.
MAY 20: Brüning resigns as Chancellor; Von Papen his successor.
JULY 21–AUG. 21: Ottawa Imperial Conference; Ottawa Agreements establish preferential tariffs.
OCT. 4: Lytton Report submitted to League.
DEC. 2: Von Schleicher Chancellor of Germany.

1933

JAN. 30: Hitler becomes Chancellor of Germany.
FEB. 2–OCT. 14: Meeting of Disarmament Conference.

1933 (continued)

FEB.: Reorganization of Little Entente; Permanent Council established.
MAR. 4: Franklin D. Roosevelt inaugurated as President of the United States.
MAR. 23: Enabling Act passed by Reichstag giving Hitler full power.
MAY. 27: Japan announces her withdrawal from League.
JUNE 12–JULY 27: World Economic Conference at London.
JULY 15: Conclusion of Mussolini-sponsored Four Power Pact.
SEPT. 30: German-Vatican Concordat ratified.
OCT. 14: Germany withdraws from Disarmament Conference and from League.
NOV. 17: United States recognizes Russia.

1934

JAN. 11: Franco-Russian Trade Pact.
JAN. 26: German-Polish Nonaggression Treaty.
FEB. 9: Conclusion of Balkan Pact.
MAR. 18: Rome Protocols signed (Italy, Austria, Hungary).
JUNE 30: Nazi Blood Purge.
JULY 25: Attempted Nazi Putsch in Austria; murder of Dollfuss.
AUG. 2: Death of Hindenburg.
SEPT. 13: Poland repudiates its obligations under the minorities treaty.
SEPT. 14: Treaties of Baltic Entente signed.
SEPT. 19: Russia enters League.
OCT. 9: King Alexander and Barthou murdered at Marseilles.

1935

JAN. 7: Franco-Italian agreement concerning Africa.
JAN. 13: Saar Plebiscite.
MAR. 16: Reintroduction of military service in Germany.
MAR. 23: Russia sells her interest in Chinese Eastern Railway in Manchukuo.
APR. 11–14: Stresa Conference.
MAY 2: Franco-Russian Pact signed.
MAY 12: Death of Marshal Pilsudski.
MAY 16: Russian-Czech Pact signed.
JUNE 18: Anglo-German Naval Agreement.
OCT. 3: Italian invasion of Ethiopia.
OCT. 11: League imposes sanctions on Italy; effective Nov. 18.
NOV.–DEC.: Hoare-Laval plan for settling Ethiopian crisis at Ethiopia's expense.

1936

MAR. 7: Reoccupation of Rhineland by German army; denunciation of Locarno Treaties by Germany.
MAR. 25: Conclusion of London Naval Conference (England, France, United States).
MAY 3: Popular Front victories in French elections.
MAY 5: End of Italian Campaign in Ethiopia.
JULY 18: Spanish Civil War begins.
JULY 20: International conference at Montreux approves Turkish request to refortify the Straits.
OCT. 25–27: German-Italian pact concerning Austria, beginning of Rome-Berlin Axis.
NOV. 27: German-Japanese Anti-Comintern Pact.
DEC. 5: New Constitution in Russia.
DEC. 12–25: Chiang Kai-shek reaches an agreement with Chinese Communists.

1937

JAN. 2: Anglo-Italian "Gentlemen's Agreement" in regard to Mediterranean interests.
JULY 7: Lukouchiao (Marco Polo Bridge) Incident; Sino-Japanese Incident.
AUG. 29: Nonaggression pact between China and Russia.
SEPT. 9: Nyon Conference in connection with Spanish Civil War.
NOV. 6: Italy joins German-Japanese Anti-Comintern Pact.

1937 (*continued*)

NOV. 15: Brussels Conference (Far Eastern Conflict).
DEC. 11: Italy withdraws from League.
DEC. 12: *Panay* Incident.

1938

MAR. 12–13: Germany occupies Austria.
MAR. 16–19: Polish ultimatum to Lithuania; settlement of Vilna controversy.
APR. 16: Anglo-Italian Pact (Ethiopia, Spain).
AUG. 21–23: Little Entente recognizes Hungary's right to rearm.
SEPT. 29: Munich Agreement on Czech-German Crisis.
OCT. 2: Polish forces occupy Teschen.
OCT. 8: Ruthenia granted full autonomy.
NOV. 2: Hungary awarded strip of southern Slovakia.
NOV. 30: Anti-French demonstrations in Italian Chamber.
DEC. 6. French-German agreement guaranteeing common frontiers.

1939

FEB. 24: Hungary and Manchukuo join Anti-Comintern Pact.
MAR. 15: Germany seizes Prague; Slovakia nominally independent.
MAR. 15: Hungary occupies Ruthenia.
MAR. 21: Germany annexes Memel.
MAR. 28: End of Civil War in Spain with surrender of Madrid.
MAR. 31–APR. 6: Anglo-French guarantee to Poland.
APR. 7: Spain joins Anti-Comintern Pact.
APR. 7: Italy seizes Albania.
APR. 11: Hungary withdraws from League.
APR. 13: Great Britain and France guarantee independence of Rumania and Greece.
APR. 27: Great Britain introduces military conscription.
APR. 28: Hitler denounces German-Polish agreement of 1934 and Anglo-German naval agreement of 1935.
MAY 3: Molotov replaces Litvinov who had been commissar for foreign affairs since 1930.
MAY 9: Spain withdraws from League.
MAY 12: Anglo-Turkish mutual assistance pact.
MAY 22: Italian-German Political and Military Alliance (Pact of Steel).
JUNE 23: French-Turkish agreement; Turkey receives Hatay.
AUG. 23: German-Russian Pact; revised Sept. 29.
SEPT. 1: Germany attacks Poland.
SEPT. 3: England and France declare war on Germany.
SEPT. 29: Estonia signs mutual assistance pact with Soviet Union.
OCT. 5: Latvia signs mutual assistance pact with Soviet Union.
OCT. 10: Lithuania signs mutual assistance pact with Soviet Union.
OCT. 15, 30: Germany signs protocols with Estonia and Latvia for return of Baltic Germans to the Reich.
OCT. 19: Turkey signs mutual assistance pacts with Great Britain and France.
NOV. 4: United States amends neutrality laws (Cash and Carry).
NOV. 30: Russia attacks Finland.
DEC. 14: Russia expelled from League of Nations.

1940

MAR. 5: Allied Supreme War Council decides to help Finns.
MAR. 12: Russo-Finnish peace signed.
APR. 8: Allies announce laying of mine fields in Norwegian waters.
APR. 9: German invasion of Denmark and Norway.
APR. 28–JUNE 8: British occupy Narvik.
MAY 2–3: Last Allied troops leave southern Norway.
MAY 9: British troops occupy Iceland.

1940 (*continued*)

MAY 10: German invasion of Holland, Belgium, and Luxembourg.
MAY 10: Churchill becomes Prime Minister.
MAY 17: French line broken at Sedan.
MAY 28: King Leopold capitulates.
JUNE 4: Germans occupy Dunkirk.
JUNE 10: Italy declares war on France and Great Britain.
JUNE 15–16: Russian troops occupy Lithuania, Latvia, and Estonia.
JUNE 22: Armistice signed between France, Germany, and Italy.
JUNE 27: Rumania cedes Bessarabia and Northern Bukovina to Russia.
JULY 1: Rumania renounces Anglo-French guarantee.
JULY 5: British attack French fleet at Oran; leads to rupture of French-British relations.
JULY 18: Burma Road closed.
AUG. 8: Beginning of large-scale air raids on Britain.
AUG. 30: Northern Transylvania awarded to Hungary at Vienna Conference.
SEPT. 3: United States–Great Britain destroyer-base exchange.
SEPT. 6: King Carol II of Rumania abdicates; Michael becomes king, General Antonescu dictator.
SEPT. 7: Rumania cedes Southern Dobruja to Bulgaria.
SEPT. 16: Selective service act passed in the United States.
SEPT. 27: German-Italian-Japanese Tripartite Pact (Pact of Berlin).
OCT. 18: Great Britain reopens Burma Road.
OCT. 28: Italian invasion of Greece.
NOV. 12: Molotov in Berlin for three-day conference.
NOV. 20–25: Hungary, Rumania, Slovakia adhere to Tripartite Pact.

1941

JAN. 10: New trade pact between Germany and Russia.
MAR. 1: Bulgaria adheres to Tripartite Pact.
MAR. 11: United States Congress passes Lend-Lease Act.
MAR. 25: Yugoslavia adheres to Tripartite Pact.
MAR. 26: Political coup in Belgrade; Peter II king.
APR. 6: German invasion of Yugoslavia and Greece.
APR. 10: Proclamation of independent Croatia.
APR. 13: Russo-Japanese Neutrality Treaty.
MAY 2–31: Revolution in Iraq; suppressed by Great Britain.
MAY 6: Stalin takes office as Premier of the Soviet Union.
MAY 20: German invasion of Crete.
MAY 27: Roosevelt proclaims unlimited state of national emergency.
JUNE 14: President Roosevelt freezes Axis funds in the United States.
JUNE 16–21: United States closes German and Italian consulates; United States consulates closed in Germany and Italy.
JUNE 18: Treaty of Friendship between Germany and Turkey.
JUNE 22: German invasion of Soviet Union.
JUNE 23: Japan seizes control of French Indochina.
JULY 12: British-Soviet mutual aid pact.
JULY 25: United States and Great Britain freeze Japanese funds.
AUG. 14: Churchill and Roosevelt issue Atlantic Charter.
OCT. 11: General Hideki Tojo becomes premier of Japan.
OCT. 27: President Roosevelt's speech asserting that "shooting has started."
NOV. 6: U.S. grants one-billion dollars lend-lease credit to USSR.
NOV. 12: Finland rejects American request to make peace with Russia.
NOV. 26: Strong American note to Japan.
DEC. 7: Pearl Harbor.
DEC. 8: United States declares war on Japan.
DEC. 11: Germany and Italy declare war on the United States.
DEC. 13: Hungary and Bulgaria declare war on the United States.
DEC. 22: Churchill in Washington for conference.

1942

JAN. 1: Declaration by United Nations signed by twenty-six states at Washington.
FEB. 15: Japanese capture Singapore.
APR. 9: United States forces on Bataan Peninsula surrender to Japan.
MAY 6: United States forces on Corregidor surrender.
MAY 7: Battle of the Coral Sea.
MAY 11–27: Second Washington Conference between Churchill and Roosevelt.
MAY 26: Twenty-year alliance between England and the USSR.
JUNE 4: Battle of Midway Island.
JULY 1: General Rommel halted at El Alamein, 70 miles west of Alexandria.
AUG. 7: United States lands troops on Japanese-held island of Guadalcanal; beginning of the road back.
AUG. 12–16: Visit of Churchill to Moscow.
OCT. 23–NOV. 10: British African offensive drives Germans from Egypt.
NOV. 8: United States and Britain land forces in French North Africa.
NOV. 11: German forces take over Unoccupied France.
DEC. 24: Assassination of Admiral Darlan, French Chief of State in North Africa.

1943

JAN. 14–26: Conference at Casablanca (Roosevelt, Churchill).
FEB. 2: Germans surrender at Stalingrad.
MAY 8–12: End of conflict in North Africa.
MAY 11: Third Washington Conference between Churchill and Roosevelt.
MAY 18: United Nations Food Conference at Hot Springs, Virginia.
MAY 22: Official Dissolution of The Third International (Comintern) announced.
JULY 10: Invasion of Sicily.
JULY 25: Marshal Badoglio replaces Mussolini as head of the Italian government.
AUG. 24: First Quebec Conference; Churchill and Roosevelt meet.
AUG. 29: Death of Boris III of Bulgaria; Simeon II (6 years old) king.
SEPT. 3: Invasion of southern Italy.
SEPT. 8: Announcement of Italian armistice signed at Algiers on Sept. 3.
SEPT. 10: German troops occupy Rome.
SEPT. 15: Mussolini rescued by German paratroopers; re-establishes Fascist regime in northern Italy.
OCT. 19–30: Moscow Conference of foreign secretaries (Hull, Eden, Molotov).
NOV. 9: Establishment of United Nations Relief and Rehabilitation Administration (UNRRA).
NOV. 22–26: Cairo Conference (Roosevelt, Churchill, Chiang Kai-shek).
NOV. 28–DEC. 1: Tehran Conference (Roosevelt, Churchill, Stalin).
DEC. 4–6: Roosevelt, Churchill, and President Inönü of Turkey in conference at Cairo.
DEC. 12: Czech-Soviet Pact.

1944

JAN. 22: Allied landings on Anzio Beach.
MAR. 8–21: Unsuccessful Finnish-Russian armistice negotiations.
MAR. 22: Germans take over government of Hungary; end of Admiral Horthy's regime.
JUNE 4: Rome captured by Anglo-American troops.
JUNE 6: Allied invasion of Normandy; D-Day.
JULY 1–15: International Monetary Conference at Bretton Woods.
AUG. 11: U.S. forces recapture Guam.
AUG. 15: Allied landing in the south of France.
AUG. 21–SEPT. 29: Dumbarton Oaks Conference, Washington, D.C.
AUG. 23: King Michael dismisses General Antonescu; Rumania accepts Allied armistice terms.
AUG. 25: Liberation of Paris.
SEPT. 4: Finnish-Russian fighting stops; armistice signed Sept. 10.
SEPT. 5: USSR declares war on Bulgaria.
SEPT. 9: Bulgarian armistice; terms signed at Moscow Oct. 28, 1944.

1944 (*continued*)

SEPT. 10: Second Quebec Conference between Churchill and Roosevelt.
OCT. 9: Churchill and Eden in Moscow for a conference on the Polish problem.
OCT. 14: Athens occupied by Allied forces.
OCT. 20: Belgrade occupied by Russian and Yugoslavian forces.
OCT. 21–22: Battle of Leyte Gulf follows landing by United States forces on island of Leyte, Oct. 19.
NOV. 1: International Civil Aviation Conference opens at Chicago.
DEC. 16: The German army launches its last great offensive in the Ardennes; Battle of the Bulge.
DEC. 25: Churchill visits Greece and arranges settlement of Greek Civil War.

1945

JAN. 9: United States forces land on Luzon in Philippines.
JAN. 11: Russians capture Warsaw.
JAN. 20: Hungarian government at Debreczen signs armistice.
FEB. 4–12: Yalta Conference (Roosevelt, Churchill, Stalin).
FEB. 19–MAR. 17: Battle for Iwo Jima.
MAR. 4: Finland declares war on Germany as of Sept. 15, 1944.
MAR. 12: Stalin turns over Northern Transylvania to Rumania.
APR. 1: Invasion of Okinawa.
APR. 5: USSR denounces five-year nonaggression pact with Japan.
APR. 12: Death of President Franklin D. Roosevelt; Harry S Truman becomes President.
APR. 13: Vienna taken by Russian troops.
APR. 21: USSR and Polish Provisional Government sign twenty-year Treaty of Mutual Assistance.
APR. 25–JUNE 26: San Francisco Conference draws up United Nations Charter.
APR. 29: Mussolini executed by partisans.
APR. 30: Suicide of Hitler in bunker of Reich Chancellery in Berlin.
MAY 7: Unconditional surrender of Germany by Provisional Government under Admiral Doenitz.
MAY 8: V-E Day.
JUNE 29: Czechoslovakia cedes Ruthenia to USSR.
JULY 17–AUG. 2: Potsdam Conference (Truman, Stalin, Churchill and later Attlee).
JULY 26: Announcement of victory of Labour party in British general elections held July 5.
AUG. 6: First atomic bomb dropped on Hiroshima.
AUG. 8: Russia declares war on Japan.
AUG. 9: Second atomic bomb dropped on Nagasaki.
AUG. 14: Japanese unconditional surrender.
AUG. 15: V-J Day.
SEPT. 2: Formal signature by Japanese of surrender terms on U.S.S. *Missouri* in Tokyo Bay.
OCT. 20: Austrian Provisional Government established April 25 recognized by Allied Council for Austria.
NOV. 20: Opening of Nuremberg Trial of twenty top Nazi leaders.
DEC. 16–27: First session of Council of Foreign Ministers meets at Moscow.

1946

MAR. 5: Churchill delivers "Iron Curtain" speech at Westminster College, Fulton, Missouri.
APR. 18: League of Nations Assembly holds final session at Geneva.
APR. 25–JULY 12: Second session of Conference of Foreign Ministers meets at Paris.
JUNE 3: Italians reject monarchy in plebiscite.
JULY 1: Italian-Yugoslavian boundary delimited by foreign ministers at Paris.
JULY 29–OCT. 15: Peace Conference at Paris. Delegates from twenty-one nations

1946 *(continued)*

consider draft of peace treaties with Italy, Rumania, Bulgaria, Hungary, and Finland.

SEPT. 8: Bulgaria rejects monarchy in a plebiscite; proclaimed a People's Republic Sept. 15.

SEPT. 28: George II returns to Athens as King of Greece.

OCT. 13: French approve new constitution.

OCT. 16: Execution of ten leading Nazis as a result of conviction in Nuremberg Trial; Goering commits suicide.

NOV. 4–DEC. 12: Third Session of Council of Foreign Ministers meets at New York.

DEC. 2: Anglo-United States agreement for economic merger of their occupation zones in Germany (Bizonia).

1947

FEB. 10: Signature of Peace Treaties with Italy, Finland, Rumania, Bulgaria, and Hungary, at Paris.

MAR. 4: France and Britain sign fifty-year treaty of alliance.

MAR. 10–APR. 24: Fourth session of Council of Foreign Ministers meets at Moscow.

MAR. 12: Announcement of "Truman Doctrine" to halt spread of communism; Congress asked to aid Greece and Turkey.

JUNE 5: Secretary Marshall in an address at Harvard suggests a plan for aiding Europe; leads to so-called Marshall Plan (European Recovery Program).

JUNE 30: Official end of UNRRA.

JULY 12: Representatives of sixteen European states meet in conference at Paris to lay the basis for the "Marshall Plan"; Russia refuses to co-operate.

AUG. 15: End of British rule in India; Dominions of India and Pakistan come into being.

OCT. 5: Announcement of the formation of a Communist Information Bureau (Cominform) with headquarters at Belgrade; agreement made by Communist parties of the USSR, France, Italy, Poland, Czechoslovakia, Hungary, Rumania, Bulgaria, and Yugoslavia.

NOV. 25–DEC. 15: Fifth session of Council of Foreign Ministers at London.

DEC. 30: King Michael of Rumania abdicates.

1948

JAN. 1: Benelux Customs Union inaugurated.

JAN. 4: Burma becomes an independent republic.

JAN. 30: Mohandas K. Gandhi assassinated.

FEB. 4: Ceylon becomes a self-governing dominion.

FEB. 25: Communists seize control of the government of Czechoslovakia.

MAR. 17: France, Britain, the Netherlands, Belgium, and Luxembourg sign fifty-year Brussels pact; Western Union.

MAY 15: British mandate in Palestine expires; state of Israel proclaimed.

JUNE 18: Currency reform in three Western zones of Germany.

JUNE 19: Soviet authorities start blockade of Berlin; develops into general blockade between Eastern and Western zones.

JULY 5: Labour government's broad health and security program goes into effect in the United Kingdom.

DEC. 27: Hungarian government arrests Joseph Cardinal Mindszenty; sentenced to life imprisonment Feb. 8, 1949.

1949

JAN. 20: Nineteen Middle and Far Eastern countries meet in New Delhi to discuss Asian affairs.

APR. 1: Newfoundland becomes the tenth province of Canada.

APR. 4: North Atlantic Treaty Organization (NATO) agreements signed in Washington, D.C.

APR. 18: Eire officially becomes completely independent as the Republic of Ireland.

1949 *(continued)*

APR. 21–7: Conference of British Commonwealth prime ministers in London; India agrees to remain in what in the future is to be known as "The Commonwealth of Nations" with the king at its head as the symbol of the free association of its members.

MAY 5: Agreement by the United States, Britain, France, and USSR to end blockade between Western and Eastern zones (including Berlin) on May 12th.

MAY 5: Statute of the Council of Europe signed by ten European states in London; Strasbourg chosen as seat of the Council.

MAY 8: Parliamentary Council at Bonn adopts final draft of a constitution for Western Germany; German Federal Republic.

MAY 23–JUNE 20: Sixth session of the Council of Foreign Ministers at Paris.

JULY 13: Publication of the Papal ban of excommunication of all Communists.

SEPT. 19: United Kingdom devalues currency; similar action follows in many other states.

OCT. 7: German Democratic Republic (Russian zone) proclaimed.

NOV. 22: UN Assembly reaches a decision on Italian colonies of Libya and Somaliland.

DEC. 16: Revision of Parliament Act of 1911 further restricting power of the House of Lords.

DEC. 27: Independence of United States of Indonesia under Dutch crown officially proclaimed.

1950

JAN. 6: Great Britain recognizes Communist government of China.

JAN. 26: Formal proclamation of the Republic of India.

JAN. 26: United States and South Korea sign pact for United States arms aid.

MAR. 12: Referendum in Belgium favors return of King Leopold.

APR. 1: Italy takes over trusteeship of Somaliland.

JUNE 25: South Korea invaded by North Korean forces; leads to United Nations intervention spearheaded by the United States.

JULY 8: General Douglas MacArthur appointed commander of combined UN forces in Korea.

OCT. 4, 5: Turkey and Greece accept invitation to join NATO; membership effective 1952.

NOV. 28: Poland and East Germany ratify Oder-Neisse Line as their common frontier.

DEC. 19: General Dwight D. Eisenhower appointed supreme commander of NATO forces in Europe.

1951

FEB. 1: UN General Assembly declares Communist China guilty of aggression in Korea.

FEB. 2: France and India sign agreement ceding Chandernagor to India.

APR. 11: General MacArthur dismissed as commander of UN forces in South Korea; succeeded by Lieut. Gen. Matthew Ridgway.

APR. 30: Iranian Senate approves oil nationalization bill; leads to controversy with Great Britain.

JULY 1: Colombo Plan for co-operative economic development in South and Southeast Asia goes into effect.

SEPT. 1: United States, Australia, and New Zealand sign Pacific Security Agreement.

SEPT. 8: Signature of Japanese Peace Treaty by 49 countries in San Francisco.

OCT. 24: United States proclaims end of state of war with Germany.

DEC. 24: Independence of Libya proclaimed.

1952

MAR. 1: Heligoland restored to German Republic.

APR. 28: Japanese Peace Treaty and United States-Japanese security pact take effect; end of Allied occupation.

MAY 27: European Defense Treaty and related protocols are signed by France, Germany, Italy, and Benelux countries; agreements are never ratified by all powers.

1952 *(continued)*

JULY 23: General Mohammed Naguib seizes power in Egypt; King Farouk abdicates three days later.

JULY 25: European Coal and Steel Community treaty enters into force.

NOV. 4: Election of Dwight D. Eisenhower as President of the United States.

1953

FEB. 12: Britain and Egypt sign agreement recognizing self-government for the Anglo-Egyptian Sudan.

FEB. 28: Treaty of friendship and collaboration between Greece, Turkey, and Yugoslavia signed at Ankara.

MAR. 5: Death of Stalin at the age of 73; Georgi M. Malenkov succeeds as premier.

JUNE 2: Coronation of Elizabeth II in London.

JUNE 17: Demonstrations in East Berlin.

JUNE 18: Egypt proclaimed a republic.

JULY 27: Korean armistice signed at Panmunjom.

AUG. 20: French depose Sultan Sidi Mohammed ben Youssef of Morocco; Moroccan nationalists oppose new Sultan Sidi Mohammed ben Moulay Arafa.

DEC. 4–8: Meeting of President Eisenhower, Prime Minister Churchill, and Premier Laniel of France in Bermuda.

1954

JAN. 25–FEB. 18: Berlin Conference of Big Four Powers.

APR. 2: Turkey and Pakistan sign mutual defense agreement.

APR. 26–JULY 21: Geneva Conference on Korea and Indochina.

APR. 29: India and Communist China sign eight-year nonaggression pact in Peking; Tibet recognized as part of China.

JULY 21: Indochina cease-fire agreements signed in Geneva.

AUG. 5: Iran initials agreement with oil companies settling oil dispute.

AUG. 9: Yugoslavia, Greece, and Turkey sign twenty-year military alliance at Bled, Yugoslavia.

AUG. 10: Agreement ending Netherlands-Indonesian Union signed at The Hague.

AUG. 30: French National Assembly rejects European Defense Community (EDC) treaty.

SEPT. 6–8: Southeast Asia Defense Conference at Manila; United States, Britain, France, Australia, New Zealand, Pakistan, Thailand, and the Philippines sign Southeast Asia Collective Defense Treaty and Pacific Charter (SEATO).

SEPT. 28–OCT. 3: Nine-power conference in London on West German sovereignty and rearmament.

OCT. 5: Italy, Yugoslavia, United States, and Britain initial agreement dividing Trieste territory between Italy and Yugoslavia.

OCT. 11: Russian-Chinese agreement on Russian evacuation of Port Arthur and on various other matters announced.

OCT. 19: British-Egyptian agreement on transfer of Suez Canal Zone to Egypt signed; full evacuation of British garrison by June, 1956.

OCT. 21: France agrees to turn her remaining Indian stations (Yanaon, Pondicherry, Karikal, Mahé) over to India.

OCT. 23: French-West German agreement on the Europeanization of the Saar; protocols on sovereignty and rearmament of Germany signed.

DEC. 2: United States and National China sign mutual defense treaty.

1955

FEB. 8: Resignation of Malenkov as premier of Russia; succeeded by Nikolai M. Bulganin.

APR. 5: Resignation of Sir Winston Churchill as prime minister of the United Kingdom; succeeded by Anthony Eden.

APR. 18–24: Asian-African Conference at Bandung in Indonesia.

MAY 5: West German Federal Republic becomes a sovereign state, as 1954 Paris Agreements go into effect.

1955 *(continued)*

MAY 7: USSR cancels friendship treaties with France and England.

MAY 11–14: Warsaw Conference of 8 East European states; Eastern Security Pact concluded.

MAY 15: Signature of Austrian State Treaty by Britain, France, the Soviet Union, the United States, and Austria; effective July 27.

JULY 18–23; Meeting of the heads of state of Britain, France, the Soviet Union, and the United States at Geneva (Summit Conference).

OCT. 28: Big Four foreign ministers' conference at Geneva.

NOV. 3: Sidi Mohammed ben Youssef (Mohammed V) restored as Sultan of Morocco.

DEC. 14: Package deal results in admission of sixteen new members to UN.

DEC. 18: Saar elections won by pro-German parties.

1956

JAN. 1: Sudan becomes independent republic; end of Anglo-Egyptian condominium.

JAN. 26: USSR returns Porkkala naval base to Finland.

FEB. 14: Nikita S. Khrushchev attacks Stalin and "cult of the individual" at 20th Communist party Congress in Moscow.

APR. 16: Announcement of the dissolution of the Cominform.

JUNE 13: Last British troops leave Suez Canal; end of 74-year British occupation.

JUNE 23: Premier Nasser elected president of Egypt.

JUNE 28–30: Riots in Poznan, Poland.

JULY 19: United States withdraws offer to aid Egypt in construction of Aswan dam.

JULY 26: Egypt nationalizes Suez Canal.

OCT. 19: Japan and USSR end state of war; renew diplomatic relations.

OCT. 21: Polish Communist Central Committee elects new Politburo with Wladyslaw Gomulka as first secretary; "Spring in October" revolution.

OCT. 24: Start of Hungarian Revolution; suppressed by USSR.

OCT. 29: Israel invades Sinai Peninsula of Egypt.

OCT. 30: France and Britain issue ultimatum to Egypt; attack next day by air.

NOV. 7: Cease-fire in Egypt results from UN actions.

DEC. 22: French and British forces complete their withdrawal from Egyptian territory.

1957

JAN. 1: Saar becomes tenth state of Federal Republic of Germany.

JAN. 10: Harold Macmillan succeeds Anthony Eden as prime minister of Great Britain.

MAR. 4: Israel orders withdrawal of troops from Gaza strip and Gulf of Akaba area.

MAR. 6: Ghana (former British Gold Coast) achieves independence and becomes a member of the Commonwealth of Nations.

MAR. 9: Eisenhower Doctrine; United States to aid Middle Eastern countries requesting help in combatting Communist aggression.

MAR. 29: Suez Canal reopened after being blocked since Nov. 1, 1956.

MAY 7: Reorganization of Soviet production; 92 economic regions established.

JUNE 20: UN report indicts USSR for crushing Hungarian Revolution and replacing legal Nagy government.

JULY 1: Beginning of International Geophysical Year.

JULY 3: Molotov, Malenkov, Kaganovich, and Shepilov ousted from Central Committee of Communist party of Russia.

JULY 25: Tunisia becomes a republic.

AUG. 31: Federation of Malaya becomes an independent nation and member of the Commonwealth of Nations.

OCT. 4: USSR launches first earth satellite, Sputnik I; Sputnik II on Nov. 3.

1958

JAN. 1: European Atomic Energy Community and European Economic Community established (France, German Federal Republic, Italy; the Netherlands, Belgium, Luxembourg).

1958 *(continued)*

JAN. 31: First United States earth satellite orbited by the army, Explorer I.

FEB. 1: Egypt and Syria form United Arab Republic; later approved by plebiscites.

MAR. 2: Yemen affiliates with United Arab Republic.

MAR. 27: Khrushchev becomes Premier of USSR; remains First Secretary of the Central Committee of Communist party of the USSR.

MAY 13: General Raoul Salan and Brig. Gen. Jacques Massu lead army coup in Algeria; call for return of General Charles de Gaulle to power.

JUNE 1: De Gaulle becomes premier of France; granted wide powers.

JULY 13: Agreement reached on compensation to be paid Universal Suez Canal Company by United Arab Republic.

JULY 14: Overthrow of monarchy in Iraq; assassination of king and prime minister.

JULY 15: The United States sends marines to Lebanon in response to request for aid by the President of Lebanon.

JULY 17: British paratroopers land in Jordan at request of King Hussein.

JULY 24: USSR grants 50 percent reduction in Austrian oil deliveries.

AUG. 21: UN General Assembly in special session unanimously adopts resolution facilitating early withdrawal of United States forces from Lebanon and British forces from Jordan.

SEPT. 19: Algerian government-in-exile established at Cairo.

SEPT. 28: Constitution of Fifth Republic worked out by De Gaulle is approved in French election; goes into effect Oct. 5.

OCT. 2: Republic of Guinea proclaimed at Conakry.

OCT. 9: Death of Pope Pius XIII; Angelo Giuseppe Cardinal Roncalli, Patriarch of Venice, elected his successor (Oct. 28); becomes John XXIII.

DEC. 27: France revalues currency; joins with the United Kingdom (and sterling area), West Germany, the Benelux countries, Italy, Norway, Sweden, and Denmark in widening currency convertibility.

1959

JAN. 4–5: Serious riots in the Belgian Congo.

FEB. 19: Agreement signed establishing Cyprus as an independent republic; effective Aug. 16, 1960.

MAR. 24: Iraq withdraws from Baghdad Pact.

MAY 11–JUNE 20; JULY 13–AUG. 5: Big Four foreign ministers' conference at Geneva on German problem; agree to form a ten-nation Disarmament Committee.

AUG. 15–27: Khrushchev visits the United States.

OCT. 8: Conservative Party sweeps British elections.

NOV. 20: Convention initialed establishing European Free Trade Association (EFTA; Outer Seven); Austria, Denmark, Norway, Sweden, Portugal, Switzerland, and United Kingdom.

1960

JAN. 1: French Cameroon becomes independent republic.

FEB. 13: France explodes its first atomic bomb.

APRIL 27: Togo becomes independent republic.

MAY 1: U.S. reconnaissance plane U-2 shot down near Sverdlovsk, USSR.

MAY 16: Summit Conference in Paris attended by Eisenhower, Macmillan, De Gaulle and Khrushchev; Khrushchev torpedoes conference with speech against U.S. on U-2 incident.

JUNE 30: Belgian Congo becomes independent Republic of the Congo; riots and civil war follow.

JULY 14: Security Council authorizes sending UN forces to the Republic of the Congo.

AUG. 12: UN forces enter Katanga province in the Congo.

DEC. 14: Agreements signed changing Organization for European Economic Cooperation (OEEC) to Organization for Economic Cooperation and Development (OECD); effective Sept. 30, 1961.

1961

JAN. 3: U.S. severs diplomatic relations with Cuba.

MARCH 1: U.S. establishes Peace Corps.

APRIL 12: Soviet Major Yuri A. Gagarin the first man to orbit earth in space.

APRIL 17: U.S. involved in attempt of Cuban rebels to invade Cuba; Bay of Pigs incident.

MAY 31: South Africa severs ties with Commonwealth and becomes a republic.

JUNE 3–4: President Kennedy and Premier Khrushchev confer in Vienna; mounting crisis over status of Berlin.

JUNE 19: Kuwait achieves independence.

AUG. 13: German Democratic Republic erects wall between East and West Berlin.

SEPT. 18: Dag Hammarskjöld, Secretary-General of the UN, killed in airplane crash in Northern Rhodesia.

SEPT. 28: Syria withdraws from United Arab Republic; Egypt to continue to be known as United Arab Republic.

DEC. 10: USSR and Albania sever diplomatic relations.

DEC. 18–19: India forcibly takes over Portuguese Dao, Damao, and Din.

DEC. 26: Yemen's federation with United Arab Republic ended.

1962

FEB. 20: John H. Glenn first U.S. astronaut to orbit earth.

MARCH 18: Cease-fire agreement signed at Évian-les-Bains, ending seven years of war in Algeria; effective March 19.

APRIL 8: French voters in referendum approve Algerian peace settlement.

JULY 1: Algerians vote overwhelmingly for independence.

JULY 20: Advisory Opinion of International Court of Justice on financial obligation of UN members for peace-keeping operations.

AUG. 15: Dutch-Indonesian agreement on West New Guinea.

OCT. 11–DEC. 6: First Session of Vatican Council II.

OCT. 20: Serious Chinese-Indian border conflict breaks out.

OCT. 22: USSR involved in U.S.–Cuban crisis over missile bases.

1963

JAN. 14: President de Gaulle of France pronounces against Britain's application for membership in the European Economic Community (Common Market); officially vetoed at meeting of EEC in Brussels Jan. 29.

JAN. 22: French-German treaty of friendship and reconciliation signed.

APRIL 10: John XXIII issues encyclical *Pacem in Terris* calling for a world community to insure peace.

MAY 23–26: Summit Conference of African powers in Addis Ababa; Charter of African Unity.

JUNE 3: Pope John XXIII dies; succeeded by Paul VI.

JUNE 20: Agreement between U.S. and USSR for establishment of direct Washington-Moscow telephone line to reduce chance of a nuclear war.

JULY 25: Initialing of nuclear test ban treaty by U.S., USSR and the United Kingdom; signed Aug. 5.

SEPT. 16: Federation of Malaysia, comprising Malaya, Singapore, Sarawak and Saban (North Borneo) formally established; Indonesia and Philippines oppose establishment.

SEPT. 29–DEC. 4: Second session Vatican Council II.

NOV. 22: Assassination of President Kennedy in Dallas, Texas.

DEC. 21–24: Clashes between Turkish and Greek Cypriotes; lead to prolonged crisis in Cyprus.

DEC. 31: Termination of ten-year Federation of Rhodesia and Nyasaland.

1964

JAN. 4–6: Pope Paul VI visits Holy Land; meets with Patriarch Athenagoras of Eastern Orthodox Church.

1964 (*continued*)

JAN. 13–17: Summit meeting of Arab League in Cairo on Israel's projected diversion of waters from Jordan River.

JAN. 27: France recognizes Communist China.

MARCH 6: Death of King Paul I of Greece; succeeded by Constantine II.

MAY 27: India Prime Minister Jawaharlal Nehru dies.

JUNE 30: Last UN troops leave Congo.

SEPT. 14–NOV. 21: Third Session of Vatican Council II; Pope proclaims the Virgin Mary Mother of the church.

OCT. 14–15: Khrushchev deposed; Leonid I. Brezhnev succeeds him as First Secretary of the Party and Aleksei N. Kosygin as Chairman of the Council of Ministers (Premier).

OCT. 15: Labour wins British election; Harold Wilson becomes prime minister.

OCT. 16: Red China explodes its first atomic bomb; world's fifth nuclear power.

OCT. 20: Death of Herbert Hoover.

NOV. 24–28: U.S.–Belgian military rescue mission in Congo.

DEC. 1: UN session hamstrung by U.S.–USSR dispute over payment of assessments for peace-keeping operations.

DEC. 2–5: Pope Paul VI attends International Eucharistic Council in Bombay.

1965

JAN. 21: Indonesia withdraws from UN; effective March 1.

JAN. 24: Sir Winston Churchill dies; born Nov. 30, 1874.

FEB. 7: U.S. commences bombing raids in Vietnam.

FEB. 24–MARCH 2: Walter Ulbricht, head of East Germany, pays visit to United Arab Republic; leads to crisis between West Germany and Arab states and exchange of ambassadors between West Germany and Israel (Aug.).

APRIL 28: U.S. lands marines in Dominican Republic during governmental crisis.

JULY 26: Britain grants independence to Maldive Islands.

AUG. 9: Singapore withdraws from Federation of Malaysia.

SEPT. 4: Death of Dr. Albert Schweitzer in Lambarene, Gabon.

SEPT. 14–DEC. 8: Fourth and final session of Vatican Council II.

OCT. 4: Pope Paul VI at UN in New York.

NOV. 11: Rhodesia proclaims its independence; not recognized by Great Britain.

DEC. 9: Nikolai V. Podgorny succeeds Anastas I. Mikoyan as Chairman of the Presidium of the Supreme Soviet.

1966

FEB. 24–26: President Kwame Nkrumah of Ghana ousted by military coup.

MARCH 12–13: President Sukarno yields power to military leaders in Indonesia; Communist party banned.

APRIL 1: Labour party under Prime Minister Wilson obtains ninety-seven-seat majority in parliamentary elections in Britain.

MAY 26: British Guiana becomes independent and assumes name of Guyana.

AUG. 11: Malaysia and Indonesia sign agreement ending hostilities begun in 1963.

SEPT. 30: Bechuanaland becomes independent as Republic of Botswana.

OCT. 4: Basutoland becomes independent as Kingdom of Lesotho.

NOV. 30: Barbados becomes independent after 341 years of British control.

DEC. 3: U Thant re-elected as Secretary General of the United Nations for another five-year term.

1967

MARCH 19: French Somaliland in a referendum decides to continue association with France rather than become independent.

MARCH 21: Svetlana Alliluyeva, daughter of Joseph Stalin, defects to the West.

APRIL 19: Konrad Adenauer, former Chancellor of West Germany, dies at age of ninety-one.

APRIL 21: Military coup in Greece.

1967 (continued)

APRIL 28–OCT. 29: Expo 67, international exposition at Montreal.

MAY 15: General Agreement on Tariffs and Trade (GATT) delegations reach agreement on reduction of import duties in Kennedy Round of negotiations.

MAY 30: Republic of Biafra declares itself independent from Nigeria; bitter fighting develops.

JUNE 5–10: Israel defeats Arab states in Six-Day War; UN Security Council adopts cease-fire resolutions.

JUNE 17: Communist China explodes its first hydrogen bomb.

JUNE 23–25: Soviet Premier Kosygin and President Johnson confer at Glassboro, New Jersey.

JULY 24–26: President de Gaulle of France pays official visit to Canada; calls for a "Free Quebec" in speech at Montreal.

AUG. 4: West Germany and Czechoslovakia establish diplomatic relations on consular level.

SEPT. 3: Nguyen Van Thieu elected president of South Vietnam.

NOV. 18: British devalue pound 14.3 percent; equivalent to U.S. $2.40.

NOV. 30: Aden and South Arabia become independent as the People's Republic of Southern Yemen.

DEC. 3: Dr. Christian Barnard of South Africa performs the first human heart transplant.

DEC. 13–14: King Constantine goes into exile in Rome after an unsuccessful attempt to remove military junta.

1968

JAN. 5: Alexander Dubček elected head of Communist party in Czechoslovakia; replaces Antonin Novotny who remains as president.

JAN. 23: United States intelligence ship *Pueblo* seized by North Korean patrol boats; crew held captive.

JAN. 30: Vietcong Tet offensive in South Vietnam.

FEB. 19: Arbitration Commission awards 300 square miles of Rann of Cutch to Pakistan, 3,000 square miles to India.

MARCH 1: Great Britain curtails immigration of British subjects of Asian ancestry into Britain.

MARCH 30: General Ludvik Svoboda replaces Antonin Novotny as President of Czechoslovakia.

MARCH 31: President Johnson announces he will not seek re-election and orders partial halt of bombing of North Vietnam.

APRIL 3: United States and North Vietnam agree to discuss peace talks.

APRIL 4: Martin Luther King, Jr., assassinated in Memphis, Tennessee; James Earl Ray later apprehended and convicted.

MAY: Serious student riots and industrial strikes in France.

MAY 3: North Vietnam and United States agree on Paris as site of peace talks.

JUNE 5: Robert F. Kennedy, candidate for Democratic nomination for President of the United States, shot by Sirhan Bishara Sirhan at Los Angeles; Kennedy dies June 6.

JUNE 10: Gen. Creighton W. Abrams replaces Gen. William C. Westmoreland as United States commander in Vietnam.

JUNE 30: Gaullists win large majority in National Assembly elections in France.

JULY 1: The United States, Great Britain, the USSR, and fifty-eight non-nuclear states sign nuclear nonproliferation treaty.

JULY 29: Pope Paul VI issues encyclical condemning artificial methods of birth control; widespread opposition to encyclical in Catholic circles.

AUG. 21: After a series of negotiations, troops of the USSR, Poland, Hungary, Bulgaria, and East Germany invade Czechoslovakia to halt Czech liberalization program.

AUG. 22: Pope Paul VI attends 39th International Eucharistic Congress in Bogotá, Colombia.

1968 *(continued)*

SEPT. 6: Swaziland becomes independent.

SEPT. 27: Marcelo Caetano replaces critically ill Antonio de Oliveira Salazar as premier of Portugal.

OCT. 4: Czechoslovak leaders accede to Soviet demands on ending liberalization program and agree to stationing of Soviet troops on Czech soil.

OCT. 30: Law enacted in Czechoslovakia establishing a Czech and Slovak federal state effective January 1, 1969.

OCT. 31: President Johnson ends bombing of North Vietnam.

NOV. 5: Richard Nixon elected President of the United States.

DEC. 23: North Korea releases crew of U.S.S. *Pueblo*.

1969

JAN. 4: Spain cedes Ifni to Morocco.

FEB. 17–20: At a conference at Namey, Niger, some thirty French-speaking countries agree to establish an agency in Paris to facilitate cultural and technological cooperation and exchange.

MARCH 5: Despite East German harassments, West Germany holds election for its president in West Berlin; Gustave Heinemann, a Socialist, elected.

MARCH 25: Mohammed Ayub Khan resigns as President of Pakistan; succeeded by Agha Mohammed Yahya Khan.

MARCH 28: Former President Dwight D. Eisenhower dies.

APRIL 17: Gustav Husak replaces Alexander Dubček as First Secretary of the Communist party in Czechoslovakia.

APRIL 28: De Gaulle resigns presidency of France following rejection of constitutional reforms in a referendum.

JUNE 10: Pope Paul VI addresses International Labor Organization in Geneva and visits headquarters of the World Council of Churches.

JUNE 16: Georges Pompidou defeats Alain Poher in French presidential election.

JULY 20: Neil A. Armstrong, Col. Edwin E. Aldrin, Jr., and Lt. Col. Michael Collins carry out first landing of man on the moon.

JULY 29: Membership of Geneva Disarmament Conference raised to twenty-six; had been raised from eighteen to twenty in May.

JULY 30–AUG. 2: Pope Paul VI visits Uganda; dedicates shrine to African saints martyred in 1885 and 1887.

AUG. 8: France devalues franc by 12.5 percent; 1 franc equals 18.004 cents U.S.

SEPT. 2: Military junta overthrows monarchy in Libya and establishes Libyan Arab Republic.

SEPT. 3: President Ho Chi Minh of North Vietnam dies.

OCT. 15: Vietnam Moratorium Day in the United States; nationwide antiwar protest.

OCT. 24: Germany revalues mark by 9.29 percent; 1 mark equals 27.3224 cents U.S.

NOV. 14–24: Astronauts Charles Conrad, Alan L. Bean, and Richard F. Gordon, Jr. carry out second landing on the moon.

DEC. 2: European Economic Community agrees to open negotiations in 1970 on British membership.

DEC. 21–23: Conference of Arab leaders at Rabat, Morocco.

1970

JAN. 12: Biafran surrender ends thirty-one-month civil war in Nigeria.

MARCH 2: Rhodesia becomes a republic.

MARCH 5: Nuclear nonproliferation treaty goes into effect.

MARCH 19: Chancellor Willy Brandt of the German Federal Republic and Premier Willi Stoph of the German Democratic Republic meet at Erfurt; first meeting of chiefs of government of West and East Germany.

MARCH 26: United States, Britain, France, and USSR hold first four-power talks since 1959 on Berlin; subsequent meetings held.

APRIL 30: President Nixon sends United States troops into Cambodia; this action arouses great protest at home and throughout the world.

1970 (*continued*)

JUNE 4: Tonga, former British protectorate, proclaims its independence.

JUNE 11: United States formally yields, after sixteen years of operation, Wheelus Air Force Base to the Libyan government.

JUNE 18: Conservative party under leadership of Edward Heath sweeps the British elections.

JUNE 22: Law lowering voting age to eighteen enacted in the United States.

JULY 1: United States troops leave Cambodia.

AUG. 7: United States proposal for ninety-day cease-fire and resumption of Arab-Israeli peace talks agreed to by United Arab Republic, Jordan, and Israel goes into effect.

AUG. 12: The Federal Republic of Germany and the USSR sign the "Moscow Treaty" —a treaty of reconciliation and peaceful cooperation.

SEPT. 28: President Gamal Abdel Nasser of the United Arab Republic dies; succeeded by Anwar Sadat.

OCT. 9: Cambodia formally proclaimed a republic.

OCT. 10: Fiji becomes independent after ninety-six years of British rule.

NOV. 9: General Charles de Gaulle of France dies.

NOV. 18: West German-Polish Treaty of Reconciliation initialed; signed December 7.

NOV. 26–DEC. 5: Pope Paul VI journey to the Far East.

DEC. 15–19: Serious uprisings in Gdansk and other Polish cities; triggered by increase in food prices.

DEC. 20: Edward Gierek replaces Wladyslaw Gomulka as First Secretary of the Polish Communist party; other Polish leaders replaced.

1971

FEB. 15: Britain adopts decimal currency.

MARCH 25: Independence declaration in East Pakistan leads to civil war.

MARCH 30–APRIL 9: Soviet Communist party holds 24th Congress.

JUNE 17: United States agrees to return Okinawa to Japan by 1972.

JUNE 23: Agreement reached on terms of British entry into Common Market.

JULY 10: Attempted republican coup fails in Pakistan.

JULY 15: President Nixon announces that he will visit Peking before May 1972.

AUG. 23: France, USSR, Britain, and United States accept draft agreement on status of West Berlin.

BIBLIOGRAPHY

THE FOLLOWING REFERENCES are offered as a guide for those desiring to pursue further the topics discussed in this volume. Only a fraction of the vast literature already published on the twentieth century is included, but an effort has been made to select those items that are of particular interest to the student and the general reader. As a rule only works in the English language are cited, but in exceptional cases reference is also made to works in foreign languages. The following is an outline of the classifications under which these volumes are listed:

1. Reference Works

Bibliographies:
    General Bibliographies; Serial Bibliographies.   931

General References:
    Facts and Figures; Interpretations of Contemporary History; International Relations.   932

2. General Works by Country and Region

United Kingdom, Empire and Commonwealth:
    General; Biographies and Memoirs; Foreign Relations; Economy; Government and Parties; Special Topics; General Books on the Commonwealth and Empire; Australia and New Zealand; Canada and Newfoundland; Ceylon and Malaysia; India and Pakistan; Ireland and Ulster; South Africa.   933

France:
    General Books on the Third Republic; Biographies and Memoirs; Economic Questions; Government; Special Topics; France and World War II; France Under the Fourth and Fifth Republics; Overseas France.   940

Italy and the Vatican:
    General; Economy; Foreign Affairs; Italy Since 1945; The Vatican and the Catholic Church.   944

3. International Problems

1. Reference Works

BIBLIOGRAPHIES

General Bibliographies

Besterman, T.: *A World Bibliography of Bibliographies* (4 ed., 5 vols., 1965–66).
Foreign Affairs Bibliography (1919 ff.). A most valuable research aid in serial volumes
    edited by W. L. Langer and H. F. Armstrong for 1919–32 (1933), R. G.
    Woolbert for 1932–42 (1945), and H. L. Roberts for 1942–52 (1955), and
    1952–62 (1965); with current bibliographies appearing in the quarterly
    journal *Foreign Affairs*.
Franz, G. (ed.): *Bücherkunde zur Weltgeschichte* (1956). A general bibliography
    with references in several languages.
Howe, G. F., et al. (eds.): *Guide to Historical Literature* (1961). The standard
    guide for general history.
Launay, J. de: *The Two World Wars: A Selected Bibliography* (1965).
Paklons, L. L.: *European Bibliography* (1964). A reference work centering on the
    European movement.
Pehrsson, H., and H. Wulf: *The European Bibliography* (1965).
Roach, John (ed.).: *A Bibliography of Modern History* (1969). One of three sections
    covers the period 1793–1945.

Serial Bibliographies

Bibliographic Index (annual, 1937 ff.). Lists current bibliographic material.
Cumulative Book Index (semiannual, 1928 ff.).
Essay and General Literature Index (annual, 1934 ff.).
Historical Abstracts (quarterly, 1955 ff.). Abstracts in English of periodical articles
    published throughout the world on the period 1775–1945.
International Bibliography of Historical Sciences (annual, 1930 ff.).
International Index to Periodicals (annual, 1920 ff.).
Public Affairs Information Service, *Bulletin* (annual, 1915 ff.). Includes pamphlets,
    articles, and government documents, as well as books, in the field of economics
    and public affairs.
Readers' Guide to Periodical Literature (annual, 1900 ff.).
U.S. Library of Congress: *Catalogue—Books: Subjects* (quarterly, annual, cumulative,
    1950 ff.). Books, pamphlets, periodicals, and other serials currently received
    and catalogued by the Library of Congress and other large American libraries.
    An outstanding bibliographical aid.

GENERAL REFERENCES

Facts and Figures

Annual Register of World Events (1954 ff.); formerly The Annual Register (1825–1953).

Banks, A. S., and R. B. Textor: A Cross-Polity Survey (1963). A comparative study of the political characteristics of the countries of the world, using computer techniques.

Current Biography Yearbook (1955 ff.); formerly Current Biography: Who's News and Why (1940–1954).

Europa Year Book (1926 ff.).

European Yearbook (1955 ff.). Published under the auspices of the Council of Europe.

Facts on File Yearbook (1941 ff.).

Ginsburg, N.: Atlas of Economic Development (1961).

Helmreich, E. C.: History at a Glance: Chronological Chart of European Civilization (1965).

Keesing's Contemporary Archives (1931 ff.).

Langer, W. L. (ed.): Encyclopedia of World History (4th ed., 1968).

New York Times Index (1913 ff.).

Political Handbook and Atlas of the World (1927 ff.).

Russett, B. M., et al. (eds.): World Handbook of Political and Social Indicators (1964).

Statesman's Year-Book (1864 ff.).

United Nations: Statistical Yearbook (1948 ff.).

United Nations Yearbook (1946 ff.).

Woytinsky, W. S., and E. S. Woytinsky: World Commerce and Governments (1955).

———: World Population and Production (1955).

Interpretations of Contemporary History

Albrecht-Carrié, R.: The Unity of Europe: An Historical Survey (1965).

Barraclough, G.: An Introduction to Contemporary History (1964).

Beloff, M.: Europe and the Europeans (1957).

Dorpalen, A.: Europe in the 20th Century: A History (1968).

Fourastié, J.: La grande metamorphose du XXᵉ siècle (1961).

Freymond, J.: Western Europe Since the War: A Short Political History (1964).

Graubard, S. R. (ed.): A New Europe? (1964).

Halecki, O.: The Limits and Divisions of European History (1950).

Holborn, H.: The Political Collapse of Europe (1951).

Lukacs, J. A.: The Decline and Rise of Europe (1965).

Ware, C. F., F. M. Panikler, and J. M. Romein: The Twentieth Century (1967).

International Relations

Carr, E. H.: International Relations Between the Two Wars, 1919–1939 (1948).

Craig, G. A., and F. Gilbert (eds.): The Diplomats, 1919–1939 (1955).

Donnelly, D.: Struggle for the World: The Cold War 1917–1965 (1965).

Duroselle, J. B.: Histoire diplomatique de 1919 à nos jours (3rd ed., 1962).

Gathorne-Hardy, G. M.: A Short History of International Affairs, 1920–1939 (4th ed., 1960).

Hayter, W.: The Diplomacy of the Great Powers (1961).

Langer, W. L. (ed. C. E. and E. Schorske): Explorations in Crisis: Papers on International History (1969).

Lerche, C. O., Jr., and A. A. Said: Concepts of International Politics (2nd ed., 1970).

Potemkin, V. P. (ed.): *Histoire de la diplomatie* (3 vols., 1946–47). The official Soviet
    interpretation, of which the third volume covers the period 1919–39. A revised
    edition is being prepared under the editorship of V. A. Zorin (1959 ff.).
Renouvin, P.: *Les crises du XXᵉ siècle*: Vol. I, *De 1914 à 1929* (1957); Vol. II, *De
    1929 à 1945* (1958). Outstanding surveys, published as volumes seven and
    eight in the *Histoire des relations internationales* edited by Renouvin.
Taylor, A. J. P.: *From Sarajevo to Potsdam* (1965).
Wiskemann, E.: *Europe of the Dictators, 1919–1945* (1966).

2. General Works by Country and Region

UNITED KINGDOM, EMPIRE AND COMMONWEALTH

General

Calleo, D. P.: *Britain's Future* (1969).
Cole, G. D. H.: *The Post-War Condition of England* (1956).
Dangerfield, G.: *Strange Death of Liberal England* (1961).
Derry, T. K.: *The United Kingdom: A Survey of British Institutions To-Day* (1963).
Havighurst, A. F.: *Twentieth-Century Britain* (1966).
Martin, K.: *The Magic of Monarchy* (1937).
Maurois, A.: *The Edwardian Era* (1933).
Medlicott, W. N.: *Contemporary England, 1914–1964* (1967).
Middleton, D.: *These Are the British* (1957).
Nowell-Smith, S. (ed.): *Edwardian England, 1901–1914* (1964).
Reynolds, E. E.: *Britain in the Twentieth Century* (1966).
Smellie, K. D.: *The British Way of Life* (1955).
Taylor, A. J. P.: *English History, 1914–1945* (1965).

Biographies and Memoirs

Asquith, Lady C. M. E.: *Diaries 1915–1918* (1968).
Attlee, C. R.: *As It Happened* (1954). Autobiography of the leader of the Labor
    party.
Birkenhead, F. W. F. S.: *Halifax: The Life of Lord Halifax* (1965).
Blake, R.: *Unrepentant Tory: The Life and Times of Andrew Bonar Law, 1858–1923*
    (1956).
Bowle, J.: *Viscount Samuel: A Biography* (1957).
Brome, V.: *Aneurin Bevan* (1953).
Bullock, A.: *The Life and Times of Ernest Bevin* (2 vols., 1960–67).
Cooke, C.: *The Life of Richard Stafford Cripps* (1957).
Cooper, D.: *Old Men Forget: The Autobiography of Duff Cooper (Viscount Norwich)*
    (1954).
Dalton, H.: *Memoirs* (3 vols., 1953–57).
De Mendelssohn, P.: *The Age of Churchill* (1961).
Dugdale, B. E. C.: *Arthur James Balfour* (2 vols., 1936).
Eden, A.: *Days for Decision* (1950).
———: *Facing the Dictators: The Memoirs of Anthony Eden* (1962).
———: *Full Circle: The Memoirs of Anthony Eden* (1960).
———: *The Reckoning: The Memoirs of Anthony Eden* (1965).
Feiling, K.: *The Life of Neville Chamberlain* (1947).
Garvin, J. L.: *The Life of Joseph Chamberlain* (4 vols., 1932–51); Vol. IV by J.
    Amery.
Jones, T.: *A Diary with Letters, 1931–1950* (1954). A record of service under four
    prime ministers.

————: *Lloyd George* (1951).

Koss, S. E.: *Lord Haldane: Scapegoat for Liberalism* (1969).

Lee, S.: *King Edward VII: A Biography* (2 vols., 1925–27). The standard account.

Macmillan, H.: *Winds of Change, 1939–1941* (1966).

————: *The Blast of War, 1939–1945* (1967).

————: *Tides of Fortune, 1945–1955* (1969).

————: *Riding the Storm, 1956–1959* (1971).

Nicolson, H.: *Curzon: The Last Phase, 1919–25* (1935). Primarily an account of his work at the foreign office.

————: *Diaries and Letters,* ed. by Nigel Nicolson (3 vols., 1966–68).

————: *King George The Fifth: His Life and Reign* (1952).

Owen, F.: *Tempestuous Journey: Lloyd George, His Life and Times* (1954). The most comprehensive biography yet published.

Petrie, C.: *Life of Sir Austen Chamberlain* (2 vols., 1940).

Postgate, R. W.: *The Life of George Lansbury* (1951).

Raymond, J.: *The Baldwin Age* (1962).

Spender, J. A.: *The Life of The Right Hon. Sir Henry Campbell-Bannerman* (2 vols., 1923).

Strauss, W. L.: *Joseph Chamberlain and the Theory of Imperialism* (1942).

Templewood, Viscount: *Nine Troubled Years* (1954). The memoirs of Sir Samuel Hoare, British foreign secretary.

Trevelyan, G. M.: *Grey of Fallodon* (1937).

Wheeler-Bennett, J. W.: *King George VI: His Life and Reign* (1958).

Wilson, H.: *The Labour Government, 1964–1970* (1971).

Young, G. M.: *Stanley Baldwin* (1952).

Zetland, L. J. L. D.: *The Life of Lord Curzon* (1928).

(See also sections on biography under the First and Second World Crises.)

Foreign Relations

Busch, B. C.: *Britain and the Persian Gulf, 1894–1914* (1967).

Churchill, W.: *The Aftermath* (1929).

————: *Arms and the Covenant* (1938).

————: *Blood, Sweat and Tears* (1941).

————: *The Second World War* (6 vols., 1948–53).

————: *Step by Step, 1936–1939* (1939).

————: *While England Slept* (1938).

————: *The World Crisis* (4 vols., 1923–29). About World War I.

Colvin, I.: *Vansittart in Office* (1965).

Eade, C. (ed.): *The War: Speeches of the Rt. Hon. Winston Churchill* (3 vols., 1952).

Epstein, L. D.: *British Politics in the Suez Crisis* (1964).

Fitzsimmons, M. A.: *Empire by Treaty: Britain and the Middle East in the Twentieth Century* (1964).

————: *The Foreign Policy of the British Labour Government, 1945–1951* (1953).

Fowler, W. B.: *British-American Relations, 1917–1918: The Role of Sir William Wiseman* (1969).

George, M.: *The Warped Vision; British Foreign Policy, 1933–1939* (1965).

Gilbert, M.: *Britain and Germany Between the Wars* (1964).

————: *The Roots of Appeasement* (1966).

Gordon, M. R.: *Conflict and Consensus in Labour's Foreign Policy 1914–1965* (1969).

Grenville, J. A. S.: *Lord Salisbury and Foreign Policy at the Close of the Nineteenth Century* (1964).

Kennedy, J. F.: *Why England Slept* (1940). A discussion of policy in the thirties.

Marwick, A.: *Britain in the Century of Total War: War, Peace and Social Change, 1900–1967* (1968).

Monger, G. W.: *End of Isolation: British Foreign Policy, 1900–1907* (1963).

Northedge, F. S.: *The Troubled Giant: Britain Among the Great Powers, 1916–1939* (1966).

Reynolds, P. A.: *British Foreign Policy in the Inter-War Years* (1954).

Strang, W.: *The Foreign Office* (1955).

Tucker, W. R.: *The Attitude of the British Labour Party Towards European and Collective Security Problems, 1920–1939* (1950).

Ullman, R. H.: *Anglo-Soviet Relations, 1917–21* (2 vols., 1961–68).

Ward, A. W., and G. P. Gooch (eds.): *The Cambridge History of British Foreign Policy, 1783–1919* (3 vols., 1923).

Watt, D. C.: *Britain Looks to Germany: A Study of British Opinion and Policy Towards Germany* (1965).

Williams, A.: *Britain and France in the Middle East and North Africa* (1968).

Wolfers, A.: *Britain and France Between Two Wars: Conflicting Strategies of Peace Since Versailles* (1940). Excellent.

Economy

Allen, V. L.: *Power in Trade Unions* (1954). Analysis of British trade unions.

Benham, F. C.: *Great Britain Under Protection* (1941). Excellent nontechnical account.

Clapham, J. H.: *The Bank of England* (2 vols., 1944).

Collins, H., and C. Abramsky: *Karl Marx and the British Labor Movement* (1964).

Conan, A. R.: *The Sterling Area* (1952).

Court, W. H. B.: *A Concise Economic History of Britain 1750 to Recent Times* (1954).

De Neuman, A. M.: *The Economic Aspects of Nationalization in Great Britain* (1952).

Dietz, F. C.: *An Economic History of England* (1942). Includes some excellent chapters on the twentieth century.

Gregg, P.: *A Social and Economic History of Britain, 1760–1950* (1950).

Kindleberger, C. P.: *Economic Growth in France and Britain: 1851–1950* (1964).

McGrone, G.: *Scotland's Economic Progress 1951–1960* (1965).

O'Brien, T. H.: *British Experiments in Public Ownership and Control* (1938).

Patterson, S.: *Immigrants in Industry* (1968).

Reid, W. S.: *Economic History of Great Britain* (1954).

Rogow, A. A.: *The Labour Government and British Industry, 1945–1951* (1955).

Government and Parties

Allen, C. K.: *Law and Orders: An Inquiry into the Nature and Scope of Delegated Legislation and Executive Powers in England* (1947).

Attlee, C. R.: *The Labour Party in Perspective—And Twelve Years Later* (1949). History of the Labour party and how its aims have been carried out.

Beaverbrook, W.: *Politicians and the War, 1914–1916* (1928).

Brand, C. F.: *British Labour's Rise to Power* (1941). Historical account of the growth of the Labour party.

Butler, D. E.: *The British General Election of 1951* (1952).

———: *The British General Election of 1955* (1955).

———: *The Electoral System in Britain, 1918–1951* (1953).

———: *Electoral System in Britain Since 1918* (1963).

———, and A. King: *The British General Election of 1964* (1965).

Carter, B. E.: *The Office of Prime Minister* (1956).

Cole, G. D. H.: *A History of the Labour Party from 1914* (1948).

Cross, C.: *The Fascists in Britain* (1961).

Ehrman, J.: *Cabinet Government and War, 1890–1940* (1958).

Finer, H.: *English Local Government* (1934).

Hewart, Lord: *The New Despotism* (1929). An important study of legislation by Orders in Council.

Jackson, R. M.: *The Machinery of Justice in England* (1953).

Jennings, W. I.: *The British Constitution* (3rd ed., 1950).

———: *Cabinet Government* (2nd ed., 1950).

———: *Parliament* (2nd ed., 1957).

————: *Party Politics* (2 vols., 1960–61).
Keith, A. B.: *The British Cabinet System, 1830–1938* (1939).
————: *The Constitution of England from Queen Victoria to George VI* (2 vols., 1940).
————: *Introduction to British Constitutional Law* (1931).
Laski, H. J.: *Parliamentary Government in England* (1938). A penetrating and critical study.
Le May, G. H. L.: *British Government, 1914–1953* (1955).
Lowell, A. L.: *The Government of England* (2 vols., 1912). A classic account.
Lyman, R. W.: *The First Labour Government, 1924* (1957).
May, T. E.: *Treatise on the Law, Privileges, Proceedings and Usage of Parliament* (16th ed., 3 vols., 1957).
McBriar, A. M.: *Fabian Socialism and English Politics, 1884–1918* (1962).
McCarran, M. P.: *Fabianism in the Political Life of Britain, 1919–1931* (1952).
McKenzie, R. T.: *British Political Parties: The Distribution of Power Within the Conservative and Labour Parties* (1955). Organization of the parties.
Milibrand, R.: *Parliamentary Socialism* (1964).
Pelling, H.: *The British Communist Party* (1958).
————: *The Origins of the Labour Party, 1880–1900* (1954).
————: *Short History of the Labour Party, 1900–60* (3rd ed., 1968).
Reid, J. H. S.: *The Origins of the British Labour Party* (1955).
Wheare, K. C.: *Government by Committee* (1955).

Special Topics

Abel-Smith, B.: *Cost of National Health Service in England and Wales* (1956).
Beck, G. A.: *The English Catholics, 1850–1950* (1950).
Davies, H. (ed.): *The English Free Churches* (1952).
Eckstein, H.: *The English Health Service: The Origins, Structure, and Achievement* (1958).
Lewis, H.: *The Navy of Britain* (1948).
Lloyd, R.: *The Church of England in the Twentieth Century* (2 vols., 1948–50).
Luvaas, J.: *The Education of an Army: British Military Thought, 1815–1940* (1964).
Mack, E. C.: *Public Schools and British Opinion Since 1860* (1941).
Macmillan, N.: *The Royal Air Force* (4 vols., 1942–50).
Marwick, A.: *The Deluge: British Society and the First World War* (1964).
Mayfield, G.: *The Church of England: Its Members and Its Business* (1958).
Newman, T. S.: *Digest of British Social Insurance* (1947, and later supplements).
Patterson, S.: *Immigration and Race Relations in Britain 1960–64* (1969).
Rait, Sir R., and G. S. Prvde: *Scotland* (2nd ed., 1954).
Ross, Sir J. S.: *National Health Service in Great Britain* (1952).
Schweinitz, K. de: *England's Road to Social Security* (1943). A historical survey, 1349–1942.
Sheppard, E. W.: *Short History of the British Army* (4th ed., 1950).
Spinks, G. S.: *Religion in Britain Since 1900* (1952).
Williams, A.: *A History of Modern Wales* (1950).
Wood, M.: *Communism and British Intellectuals* (1959).
Woodward, L.: *Great Britain and the War of Nineteen Fourteen to Eighteen* (1967).

General Books on the Commonwealth and Empire

Arnold, G.: *Economic Co-operation in the Commonwealth* (1967).
Crick, W. F.: *Commonwealth Banking Systems* (1965).
Cross, C.: *The Fall of the British Empire, 1918–1968* (1968).
Currey, C. H.: *The British Commonwealth Since 1815* (2 vols., 1950–51).
Eayrs, J. C.: *The Commonwealth and Suez; a Documentary Survey* (1964).
Eckles, R. B.: *Britain, Her Peoples and the Commonwealth* (1954).
————: *The Empire and Commonwealth Yearbook* (1952 ff.).

Fitzsimmons, M. A.: *Empire by Treaty: Britain and the Middle East in the Twentieth Century* (1964).

Hamilton, W. B. (ed.): *A Decade of the Commonwealth, 1955–1964* (1966).

Hancock, W. K.: *Survey of British Commonwealth Affairs* (2 vols., 1964).

Jennings, W. I.: *Constitutional Laws of the Commonwealth* (2nd ed., 1952).

———: *Problems of the New Commonwealth* (1958).

Keith, A. B.: *Constitutional Law of the British Dominions* (1933).

———: *The Dominions as Sovereign States: Their Constitutions and Governments* (1938).

———: *The Governments of the British Empire* (1935).

Mansergh, N.: *The Commonwealth Experience* (1969).

McCleary, S. F.: *Peopling the British Commonwealth* (1955).

Miller, J. D. B.: *Britain and the Old Dominions* (1966).

Parry, C.: *Nationality and Citizenship Laws of the Commonwealth and of Ireland* (1957).

Perkins, J. O. N.: *The Sterling Area, the Commonwealth and World Economic Growth* (1967).

Roberts-Wray, K. O.: *Commonwealth and Colonial Law* (1966).

Rose, J. H., A. P. Newton, and E. A. Benians (eds.): *The Cambridge History of the British Empire* (8 vols., 1929–36).

The Round Table. A quarterly review published since 1911 which is devoted to Commonwealth problems.

Simon, J. A. S.: *Crown and Commonwealth* (1953).

Taylor, D.: *The Years of Challenge: The Commonwealth and the British Empire, 1945–1958* (1960).

Watts, R. L.: *New Federations: Experiments in the Commonwealth* (1966).

Wheare, K. C.: *The Constitutional Structure of the Commonwealth* (1960).

Winks, R. W. (ed.): *The Historiography of the British Empire-Commonwealth: Trends, Interpretations and Resources* (1966).

(See also The Eastern Mediterranean Region, Africa, The Far East.)

Australia and New Zealand

Best, E.: *The Maori* (2 vols., 1924).

Caiger, G. (ed.): *The Australian Way of Life* (1953).

Cameron, W. J.: *New Zealand* (1965).

Clark, C. M. H.: *A History of Australia* (2 vols., 1962–68).

Condliffe, J. B., and W. T. G. Airey: *A Short History of New Zealand* (8th ed., 1957).

Cumberland, K. B.: *Southwest Pacific: A Geography of Australia, New Zealand and Their Pacific Neighbourhoods* (1954).

Elkin, A. P.: *The Australian Aborigines* (3rd ed., 1954).

Greenwood, G.: *Australia: A Social and Political History* (1955).

———: *Australia in World Affairs, 1950–55* (1957).

Hall, D. O. W.: *Portrait of New Zealand* (3rd ed., 1961).

Holmes, J. M.: *Australia's Open North* (1963).

Horsfall, J. C.: *Australia* (1955).

Miller, J. D. B.: *Australian Government and Politics* (1954).

The Modern Encyclopedia of Australia and New Zealand (1964).

Preston, R. (ed.): *Contemporary Australia: Studies in History, Politics, and Economics* (1969).

Robson, J. L. (ed.): *New Zealand: The Development of Its Laws and Constitution* (1954).

Shaw, A. G. L.: *Australia in the Twentieth Century: An Introduction to Modern Society* (1967).

Wilkes, J. (ed.): *New Guinea and Australia* (1959).

Yarwood, A. T.: *Asian Migration to Australia; the Background to Exclusion* (1964).

Canada and Newfoundland

Allen, R.: *Ordeal by Fire: Canada, 1910–1945* (1961).
Chadwick, St. J.: *Newfoundland: Island into Province* (1967).
Creighton, D.: *Dominion of the North: A History of Canada* (rev. ed., 1958).
Dawson, R. M.: *The Conscription Crisis of 1944* (1962).
————: *William Lyon Mackenzie King, 1925–1932* (1963).
Deener, D. R. (ed.): *Canada–United States Treaty Relations* (1963).
Easterbrook, W. T., and H. G. J. Aitken: *Canadian Economic History* (1956).
Hutchison, B.: *Canada: Tomorrow's Giant* (1957).
————: *The Incredible Canadian: A Candid Portrait of Mackenzie King* (1952).
Keenleyside, H. L..: *Canada and the United States* (rev. ed., 1952).
Lower, A. R. M.: *Colony to Nation: A History of Canada* (1946).
————, et al.: *Evolving Canadian Federalism* (1958).
McInnis, E.: *Canada: A Political and Social History* (1952).
Parker, J.: *Newfoundland, 10th Province of Canada* (1950).
Phillips, C. E.: *The Development of Education in Canada* (1957).
Smallwood, J. R. (ed.): *The Book of Newfoundland* (2 vols., 1936).
Wade, M.: *The French Canadians, 1760–1945* (1955). Five-hundred pages on the period since World War I.

Ceylon and Malaysia

Arasaratnom, S.: *Ceylon* (1964).
Brackman, A. C.: *Southeast Asia's Second Front; the Power Struggle in the Malay Archipelago* (1966).
Djojomadikwsumo, S., and J. Pandel: *Trade and Aid in South East Asia* (4 vols., 1968–). So far, 2 volumes dealing with Malaysia and Singapore, East Malaysia and Brunei have been published.
Freeman, R. A.: *Socialism and Private Enterprise in Equatorial Asia, the Case of Malaysia and Indonesia* (1968).
Ginsburg, N.: *Malaya* (1958).
Gullick, J.: *Malaya* (rev. ed., 1964).
Jones, S. W.: *Public Administration in Malaya* (1953).
Kennedy, J.: *A History of Malaya* (1962).
King, F. H. H.: *The New Malayan Nation: A Study of Communalism and Nationalism* (1957).
Ludowyk, E. F. C.: *The Modern History of Ceylon* (1966).
Miller, H.: *A Short History of Malaysia* (1967).
Mills, L. A.: *British Rule in Eastern Asia: A Study of Contemporary Government and Economic Development in British Malaya and Hong Kong* (1942).
————: *Ceylon* (1950).
————: *Malaya: A Political and Economic Appraisal* (1958).
Oliver, H. M., Jr.: *Economic Opinion and Policy in Ceylon* (1957).
Purcell, V.: *The Chinese in Malaya* (1948).
Pye, L. W.: *Guerrilla Communism in Malaya: Its Social and Political Meaning* (1956).
Roff, W. R.: *The Origins of Malay Nationalism* (1967).
Ryan, N.: *The Making of Modern Malaya: A History from Earliest Times to the Present* (1963).
Wriggins, W. H.: *Ceylon: Dilemma of a New Nation* (1960).

India and Pakistan

Ali, Chaudhri Muhammad: *The Emergence of Pakistan* (1967).
Aziz, K. K.: *The Making of Pakistan: A Study of Nationalism* (1967).
Birdwood, Lord: *India and Pakistan* (1954). Internal and foreign affairs including the Kashmir dispute.

Brecher, M.: *The Struggle for Kashmir* (1953).
Callard, K.: *Pakistan: A Political Study* (1957). Government and politics.
Campbell, R. D.: *Pakistan: Emerging Democracy* (1963).
Feldman, H.: *Revolution in Pakistan: A Study of the Martial Law Administration* (1967).
Fischer, L.: *The Life of Mahatma Gandhi* (1951).
Gadgil, D. R.: *Planning and Economic Policy in India* (2nd ed., 1962).
Gandhi, M. K.: *Gandhi's Autobiography: The Story of My Experiments with Truth* (1948).
————: *Untouchability* (1944).
————: *Women and Social Injustice* (1945).
Gokale, B. G.: *Indian Thought Through the Ages; A Study of Some Dominant Concepts* (1961).
Griffiths, P.: *Modern India* (1957).
Ilbert, C. P.: *The Government of India* (1922). Best account of Government Act of 1919.
Indian Statutory Commission: *Report of the Indian Statutory Commission* (2 vols., 1930). The first volume, which surveys Indian conditions, is particularly valuable.
Isaac, H. E.: *India's Ex-Untouchables* (1965).
Jennings, I.: *Constitutional Problems in Pakistan* (1957).
Joshi, G. N.: *The New Constitution of India* (1937). A criticism of the 1935 constitution.
Kabir, H.: *Education in New India* (1956).
Kahin, G. M. (ed.): *Major Governments of Asia* (1958). Includes India and Pakistan.
Karan, P. P., and W. M. Jenkins: *The Himalayan Kingdoms: Bhutan, Sikkim and Nepal* (1963).
Keith, A. B.: *A Constitutional History of India, 1600–1935* (1969).
Lacy, C.: *The Conscience of India: Moral Traditions in the Modern World* (1965).
Mahar, J. M.: *India: A Critical Bibliography* (1964).
Mehrotra, S. R.: *India and the Commonwealth 1885–1929* (1964).
Moracs, F.: *Jawaharlal Nehru: A Biography* (1956).
Mosley, L.: *The Last Days of the British Raj* (1962).
Nehru, J.: *The Discovery of India* (2nd ed., 1947). History and conditions in India.
————: *Toward Freedom: The Autobiography of Jawaharlal Nehru* (1941).
Papanek, G. F.: *Pakistan's Development, Social Goals, and Private Incentives* (1967).
Singh, V.: *Economic History of India, 1857–1956* (1965).
Sitaramagya, P.: *History of the Indian National Congress* (2 vols., 1946–47).
Smith, D. E.: *India as a Secular State* (1963).
Spear, T. G. P.: *India, a Modern History* (1961). A volume in the University of Michigan series.
Srinivas, M. N.: *Caste in Modern India and Other Essays* (1962).
Tayyeb, Ali: *Pakistan; a Political Geography* (1966).
Tennyson, H.: *India's Walking Saint: The Story of Vinoba Bhave* (1955). The great leader of land reform in India.
Vakil, C. (ed.): *Economic Consequences of Divided India* (1950). Chapters on aspects of Indian economy by various scholars.
Varma, V. P.: *Modern Indian Political Thought* (1964).
Vorys, K. von: *Political Development in Pakistan* (1965).
Weiner, M.: *The Politics of Scarcity: Public Pressure and Political Response in India* (1962).
Wilcox, W. A.: *Pakistan; the Consolidation of a Nation* (1963).
Wolpert, S.: *India* (1965).

Ireland and Ulster

Ayearst, M.: *The Republic of Ireland; its Government and Politics* (1969).
Barry, T. B.: *Guerrilla Days in Ireland: A Firsthand Account of the Black and Tan War, 1919–1941* (1956).

Blanshard, P.: *The Irish and Catholic Power* (1953).   Critical.
Coffey, T. M.: *Agony at Easter. The 1916 Irish Uprising* (1969).
Coogan, T. P.: *Ireland Since the Rising* (1966).
Evans, E. E.: *Irish Heritage: The Landscape, the People and Their Work* (1945).
Hayden, M., and G. Moonan: *A Short History of the Irish People* (2 vols., 1960).
Holt, E.: *Protest in Arms: The Irish Troubles 1916–1923* (1961).
MacColl, R.: *Roger Casement: A New Judgment* (1957).
MacManus, M. J.: *Eamon de Valera* (1946).
Mansergh, N.: *The Government of Northern Ireland: A Study in Devolution* (1936).
————: *The Irish Free State: Its Government and Politics* (1934).
————: *The Irish Question, 1840–1921: A Commentary on Anglo-Irish Relations and on Social and Political Forces in Ireland in the Age of Reform and Revolution* (1965).
Martin, F. X., et al.(eds.): *The Irish Struggle, 1916–1926* (1966).
McDowell, R. B.: *The Irish Administration 1801–1914* (1964).
O'Hegarty, P. S.: *A History of Ireland Under the Union, 1801–1922* (1952).
Ryan, D.: *The Fenian Chief: A Biography of James Stephens* (1969).
Stewart, A. T. Q.: *The Ulster Crisis* (1967).
Williams, D. (ed.): *The Irish Struggle 1916–1926* (1966).
Wilson, T. (ed.): *Ulster Under Home Rule* (1955).

South Africa

Carter, G. M.: *The Politics of Inequality: South Africa Since 1948* (1958).
Cope, J.: *South Africa* (1967).
Feit, E.: *African Opposition in South Africa* (1967).
Gibbs, H.: *Background to Bitterness: The Story of South Africa, 1652–1954* (1954).
Hancock, W. K.: *Smuts* (2 vols., 1962–68).
————, and J. van der Poel (eds.): *Selections from the Smuts Papers* (4 vols., 1966–   ).
Horwitz, R.: *The Political Economy of South Africa* (1967).
Lovell, R. I.: *The Struggle for South Africa, 1875–1899: A Study in Economic Imperialism* (1934).
Mansergh, N.: *South Africa 1906–1961: The Price of Magnanimity* (1962).
Marquard, L.: *The Peoples and Policies of South Africa* (3rd ed., 1962).
Munger, E. S.: *Afrikaner and African Nationalism* (1967).
Neame, L. E.: *The History of Apartheid: The Story of the Colour War in South Africa* (1962).
Rhoodie, N., and H. J. Venter: *Apartheid, a Socio-Historical Exposition of the Origin and Development of the Apartheid Idea* (1960).
Robertson, H. M.: *South Africa: Economic and Political Aspects* (1957).
Thompson, L. M.: *Politics in the Republic of South Africa* (1966).
Wellington, J. H.: *South Africa* (2 vols., 1955).
Zacklin, R.: *Challenge of Rhodesia. Toward an International Public Policy* (1969). No. 575 of *International Conciliation.*

FRANCE

General Books on the Third Republic

Albrecht-Carrié, R.: *France, Europe, and the Two World Wars* (1960).
Brogan, D. W.: *France Under the Republic: The Development of Modern France, 1870–1939* (1940).
Earle, E. M. (ed.): *Modern France: Problems of the Third and Fourth Republics*

(1951). Twenty-eight chapters on different aspects of French life and government.

Evans, E. E.: *France: A Geographical Introduction* (1946). Brief but thorough.

Guérard, A.: *France: A Modern History* (1959). A volume in the University of Michigan series.

Harvey, D. J.: *France Since the Revolution* (1968).

Joll, J. (ed.): *The Decline of the Third Republic* (1959).

Knapton, E. J.: *France Since Versailles* (1952).

Ralston, D. B.: *The Army of the Republic. The Place of the Military in the Political Evolution of France, 1871–1914* (1967).

Roe, F. C.: *Modern France: An Introduction to French Civilization* (1956).

Scott, J. A.: *Republican Ideas and the Liberal Tradition in France, 1870–1914* (1951).

Shirer, W. H.: *The Collapse of the Third Republic. An Inquiry into the Fall of France in 1940* (1969).

Thomson, D.: *Democracy in France Since 1870* (5th ed., 1969). Covers events to end of 1968.

Wright, G.: *France in Modern Times, 1760 to the Present* (1962).

Biographies and Memoirs

Aron, R.: *An Explanation of De Gaulle* (1966).

Bankwitz, P. C. F.: *Maxime Weygand and Civil-Military Relations in Modern France* (1967).

Brogan, D. W.: *French Personalities and Problems* (1947).

Clemenceau, G.: *Grandeur and Misery of Victory* (1930).

Colton, J.: *Léon Blum, Humanist in Politics* (1966).

Daladier, E.: *In Defense of France* (1939). A collection of speeches.

De Gaulle, C.: *War Memoirs* (5 vols., 1955–1960).

Duclos, J.: *Mémoires: 1896–1924* (1968).

François-Poncet, A.: *The Fateful Years: Memoirs of a French Ambassador in Berlin, 1931–1938* (1949).

Herriot, E.: *Episodes, 1940–1944* (1950).

———: *In Those Days: Memoirs* (1952). Before World War I.

Huddleston, S.: *Pétain: Patriot or Traitor?* (1951).

Jackson, J. H.: *Clemenceau and the Third Republic* (1948).

Laval, P.: *Notes et mémoires* (1947).

Paul-Boncour, J.: *Recollections of the Third Republic* (vol. I, 1958).

Reynaud, P.: *In the Thick of the Fight, 1930–1945* (1955).

Ryan, S.: *Pétain the Soldier* (1968).

Schoenbrun, L.: *The Three Lives of Charles De Gaulle* (1968).

Stokes, R. L.: *Léon Blum: Poet and Premier* (1937).

Warner, G.: *Pierre Laval and the Eclipse of France* (1969).

Weinstein, H. R.: *Jean Jaurès: A Study of Patriotism in the French Socialist Movement* (1936).

Werth, A.: *Lost Statesman: The Strange Story of Pierre Mendès-France* (1958).

———: *De Gaulle, A Political Biography* (1966).

(See also sections on the First and Second World Crises.)

Economic Questions

Clough, S. B.: *France: A History of National Economics* (1939).

Ehrmann, H. W.: *French Labor from Popular Front to Liberation* (1947).

Einaudi, M., M. Bye, and E. Rossi: *Nationalization in France and Italy* (1955).

Haight, F. A.: *A History of French Commercial Policies* (1941). Excellent.

Lorwin, W. R.: *The French Labor Movement* (1955).

Wright, G.: *Rural Revolution in France: The Peasantry in the Twentieth Century* (1964).

Government

Brower, D. R.: *The New Jacobins: The French Communist Party and the Popular Front* (1968).
Cafelle, R. B.: *The M. R. P. and French Foreign Policy* (1963).
Campbell, P.: *French Electoral Systems and Elections, 1789–1957* (1958).
Cantril, H., and D. Rodnick: *On Understanding the French Left* (1956).
Furniss, E. S.: *The Office of the Premier in French Policy-making* (1954).
Greene, N.: *Crisis and Decline. The French Socialist Party in the Popular Front Era* (1969).
King, J. C.: *Generals and Politicians: Conflict between France's High Command, Parliament, and Government, 1914–1918* (1951).
Larmour, P. J.: *The French Radical Party in the 1930's* (1964).
Marcus, J. T.: *French Socialism in the Crisis Years, 1933–36* (1958).
Micaud, C. A.: *Communism and the French Left* (1963).
———: *The French Right and Nazi Germany, 1933–9* (1943). A penetrating study.
Noland, A.: *The Founding of the French Socialist Party* (1956).
Osgood, S. M.: *French Royalism under the Third and Fourth Republics* (1960).
Plumyene, J., and R. Lasierre: *Les fascismes français* (1963).
Rieber, A. J.: *Stalin and the French Communist Party 1941–1947* (1962).
Rossi, A.: *The Communist Party in Action: An Account of Its Organization and Operations in France* (1949).
Sharp, W. R.: *The French Civil Service: Bureaucracy in Transition* (1931).
———: *The Government of the French Republic* (1938).
Soltau, R. H.: *French Parties and Politics, 1871–1930* (1931).
Tannenbaum, E. R.: *The Action Française: Die-hard Reactionaries in Twentieth Century France* (1962).
Weber, E.: *Action Française: Royalism and Reaction in Twentieth Century France* (1969).
Wohl, R.: *French Communism in the Making, 1914–1924* (1966).
Wright, G.: *Raymond Poincaré and the French Presidency* (1942).

Special Topics

Bosworth, W.: *Catholicism and Crisis in Modern France: French Catholic Groups at the Threshold of the Fifth Republic* (1962).
Caute, D.: *Communism and the French Intellectuals 1914–1960* (1964).
Challener, R. D.: *The French Theory of the Nation in Arms, 1866–1939* (1955).
Dansette, A.: *Religious History of Modern France* (2 vols., 1961). An excellent account.
Gwynn, D.: *The Catholic Reaction in France* (1924).
Laurens, F. D.: *France and the Italo-Ethiopian Crisis, 1935–1936* (1967).
Paul, W.: *The Second Ralliement: The Rapprochement between Church and State in France* (1967).
Phillips, C. S.: *The Church in France, 1848–1907* (1936).
Ralston, D. B.: *The Army of the Republic: The Place of the Military in the Political Evolution of France, 1871–1914* (1967).
Saurat, S.: *Modern French Literature, 1870–1940* (1946).
Siegfried, A.: *France: A Study in Nationality* (1930). A brilliant brief analysis.
Talbott, J. E.: *The Politics of Educational Reform in France, 1918–1940* (1969).

France and World War II

Arnoult, P.: *Les finances de la France et l'occupation allemande, 1940–44* (1951).
Aron, R., and G. Elgey: *The Vichy Regime, 1940–44* (1958).
Beaufre, André: *1940: The Fall of France* (1968).

Deporte, A. W.: *De Gaulle's Foreign Policy, 1944–1946* (1968).
Farmer, P.: *Vichy: Political Dilemma* (1955). Views the Vichy regime as a conserva-
    tive, not Fascist, movement.
Giraud, A. (Pertinax): *The Gravediggers of France* (1944).
Horne, A.: *To Lose a Battle: France, 1940* (1969).
Huddleston, S.: *France: The Tragic Years, 1939–47* (1955).
Hytier, A. D.: *Two Years of French Foreign Policy: Vichy 1940–1942* (1958).
Lazareff, P.: *Deadline: The Behind the Scenes Story of the Last Decade in France*
    (1942).
Marchal, L.: *Vichy: Two Years of Deception* (1943).
Maurois, A.: *Tragedy of France* (1940).
Pickles, D. M.: *France Between the Republics, 1940–1945* (1945).
Tissier, P.: *The Government of Vichy* (1942).
Viorst, M.: *Hostile Allies: FDR and Charles De Gaulle* (1965).
Weygand, J.: *The Role of General Weygand: Conversations With His Son* (1948).
White, D. S.: *Seeds of Discord: De Gaulle, Free France, and the Allies* (1964).

France Under the Fourth and Fifth Republics

Aron, R.: *France, Steadfast and Changing: The Fourth to the Fifth Republic* (1960).
DePorte, A. W.: *De Gaulle's Foreign Policy: 1944–1946* (1968).
Ehrmann, H. W.: *Politics in France* (1968).
Einaudi, M., and F. Goguel: *Christian Democracy in Italy and France* (1952). A
    discussion of Catholic political parties.
Furniss, E. S.: *De Gaulle and the French Army: A Crisis in Civil-Military Relations*
    (1964).
Gavin, C. I.: *Liberated France* (1955).
Godfrey, E. D.: *The Government of France* (2nd ed., 1963).
Kulski, W. W.: *De Gaulle and the World; the Foreign Policy of the Fifth French
    Republic* (1966).
Lafonce, J. A.: *The Government of the Fifth Republic* (1960).
Lüthy, H.: *France Against Herself* (1955).
Menard, O. D.: *The Army and the Fifth Republic* (1967).
Mendès-France, P.: *The Pursuit of Freedom* (1956).
Novick, P.: *The Resistance versus Vichy: The Purge of Collaborators in Liberated
    France* (1968).
Pierce, R.: *French Politics and Political Institutions* (1968).
Serfaty, S.: *France, De Gaulle, and Europe: The Policy of the Fourth and Fifth
    Republics toward the Continent* (1968).
Tannenbaum, E. R.: *The New France* (1961). Social and cultural history.
Touraine, A.: *Le mouvement de mai, ou le communisme utopique* (1968).
Wallace-Hadrill, M. M.: *France: Government and Society* (1957).
Werth, A.: *France, 1940–1955* (1956).
Williams, P. M.: *The French Parliament, 1958–1967* (1968).

Overseas France

Alleg, H.: *The Question* (1958). About the war in Algeria.
Brace, R. M.: *Morocco, Algeria, Tunisia* (1965).
Bret, H.: *Histoire de la colonisation française* (3 vols., 1946–50).
Cady, J. F.: *The Roots of French Imperialism in Eastern Asia* (1954).
Catroux, G.: *The French Union* (1953).
Cole, A. B. (ed.): *Conflict in Indochina and International Repercussions: A Documen-
    tary History, 1945–1955* (1956).
Gordon, D. C.: *The Passing of French Algeria* (1966).
Hammer, E. J.: *The Struggle for Indo-China* (1954).

Hanotaux, G. (ed.): *Histoire des colonies françaises et l'expansion de la France dans le monde* (6 vols., 1934).

Knight, M. M.: *Morocco as a French Economic Venture: A Study of Open Door Imperialism* (1937).

Lacouture, J.: *Vietnam: Between Two Truces* (1966).

McAlister, J. T.: *Viet Nam: The Origins of Revolution* (1969).

Mus, P.: *Viet Nam: Sociologie d'une Guerre* (1952).

Pickles, D.: *Algeria and France: From Colonialism to Cooperation* (1963).

Priestly, H. I.: *France Overseas: A Study in Modern Imperialism* (1938).

Robequain, C.: *The Economic Development of French Indo-China* (1944).

Roberts, S. H.: *History of French Colonial Policy, 1870–1925* (2 vols., 1929).

Roberts, W. A.: *The French in the West Indies* (1942).

Thompson, V.: *French West Africa* (1958).

Tillion, G.: *Algeria* (1958).

Zartman, I. W.: *Morocco: Problems of New Power* (1964).

Ziadeh, N. A.: *Origins of Nationalism in Tunisia* (1962).

(See also under the Eastern Mediterranean Region, Africa, and Southeast Asia.)

ITALY AND THE VATICAN

General

Albrecht-Carrić, R.: *Italy from Napoleon to Mussolini* (1950).

Battaglia, R.: *The Story of the Italian Resistance* (1957).

Borgese, G. A.: *Goliath: The March of Fascism* (1937). An excellent account.

Cassels, A.: *Fascist Italy* (1968).

Detzell, C. F.: *Mussolini's Enemies: The Italian Anti-Fascist Resistance* (1961).

Fermi, L.: *Mussolini* (1961).

Germino, D. L.: *The Italian Fascist Party in Power: A Study of Totalitarian Rule* (1959).

Halperin, S. W.: *Mussolini and Italian Fascism* (1964).

Kogan, N.: *A Political History of Postwar Italy* (1966).

Mack Smith, D.: *Italy: A Modern History* (1959). A volume in the University of Michigan series.

Minio-Paluello, L.: *Education in Fascist Italy* (1946).

Monelli, P.: *Mussolini: An Intimate Life* (1953).

Mussolini, B.: *My Autobiography* (1928).

Nitti, F. F.: *Escape* (1930). Gripping account of an escape from an Italian penal colony:

Rossi, A.: *The Rise of Italian Fascism, 1918–22* (1938).

Rusinow, D. I.: *Italy's Austrian Heritage 1919–1946* (1969).

Salomone, A. W.: *Italy in the Giolittian Era: Italian Democracy in the Making* (1960).

Salvadori, M.: *Italy* (1965).

Salvemini, G.: *The Fascist Dictatorship in Italy* (1927).

———: *Under the Axe of Fascism* (1936). Outstanding.

Schneider, H. W.: *The Fascist Government of Italy* (1936).

———: *Making the Fascist State* (1928). One of the best books on the rise of fascism.

———, and S. B. Clough: *Making Fascists* (1929).

Seton-Watson, C.: *Italy from Liberalism to Fascism, 1870–1925* (1967).

Sondern, F., Jr.,: *Brotherhood of Evil: The Mafia* (1959).

Steiner, H. A.: *Government in Fascist Italy* (1938).

Thayer, J. A.: *Italy and the Great War: Politics and Culture, 1870–1915* (1964).

Trevelyan, J. P.: *A Short History of the Italian People* (1956).

Wiskemann, E.: *Fascism in Italy: Its Development and Influence* (1969).

(For the theory of fascism see the section on Political Thought.)

Economy

Clough, S. S.: *The Economic History of Modern Italy* (1964).
Dickinson, R. C.: *The Population Problem of Southern Italy: An Essay in Social Geography* (1955).
Horowitz, D. L.: *The Italian Labor Movement* (1963).
Longobardi, C.: *Land Reclamation in Italy: Rural Revival in the Building of a Nation* (1936).
Lutz, V.: *Italy; a Study in Economic Development* (1962).
Martellaro, J. A.: *Economic Development in Southern Italy, 1950–1960* (1965).
Meenan, J.: *The Italian Corporative System* (1945). One of the best studies.
Neufeld, M. F.: *Italy: School for Awakening Countries. The Italian Labor Movement in Its Political, Social, and Economic Setting from 1800 to 1960* (1961).
Royal Institute of International Affairs: *The Economic and Financial Position of Italy* (2nd ed., 1935).
Schmidt, C. T.: *The Corporate State in Action: Italy Under Fascism* (1939).
————: *The Plough and the Sword: Labor, Land, and Property in Fascist Italy* (1938).
Welk, W. G.: *Fascist Economic Policy: An Analysis of Italy's Economic Experiment* (1938).

Foreign Affairs

Askew, W. C.: *Europe and Italy's Acquisition of Libya, 1911–1912* (1942). A fine study.
Badoglio, P.: *The War in Abyssinia* (1937). By the Italian conqueror of Ethiopia.
Baer, G. W.: *The Coming of the Italian-Ethiopian War* (1967).
Barker, A. J.: *The Civilizing Mission: A History of the Italo-Ethiopian War* (1968).
Barros, J.: *The Corfu Incident of 1923: Mussolini and the League of Nations* (1965).
Croce, B.: *Croce, the King and the Allies: Extracts from a Diary by B. Croce, July 1943–June 1944* (1950).
Currey, M. I.: *Italian Foreign Policy, 1918–1932* (1935). Sympathetic.
Deakin, F. W.: *The Brutal Friendship: Mussolini, Hitler and the Fall of Italian Fascism* (1962).
Del Boca, A.: *The Ethiopian War 1935–1941* (1968).
Duroselle, J. B.: *Le conflit de Trieste 1943–1954* (1966).
Gibson, H. (ed.): *The Ciano Diaries, 1939–1943: The Complete Unabridged Diaries of Count Galeazzo Ciano, Italian Minister for Foreign Affairs, 1936–1943* (1946).
Harris, B.: *The United States and the Italo-Ethiopian Crisis* (1964).
Hess, R. L.: *Italian Colonialism in Somalia* (1966).
Kogan, N.: *The Politics of Italian Foreign Policy* (1963).
Laurens, F. D.: *France and the Italo-Ethiopian Crisis 1935–1936* (1967).
Macartney, M. H. H., and P. Cremona: *Italy's Foreign and Colonial Policy, 1914–1937* (1938).
Muggeridge, M.: *Ciano's Diplomatic Papers: Being a Record of Nearly 200 Conversations Held During the Years 1936–42 with Hitler, Mussolini, Franco, and Others* (1948).
Potter, P. B.: *The Wal Wal Arbitration* (1938). A detailed account.
Salvadori, M.: *Brief History of the Patriot Movement in Italy, 1943–1945* (1954).
Villari, L.: *Italian Foreign Policy under Mussolini* (1956). Friendly to Fascist policy.
(See also books on First and Second World Crises.)

Italy Since 1945

Carrillo, E. A.: *Alcide de Gasperi: The Long Apprenticeship* (1965).
Einaudi, M., and F. Goguel: *Christian Democracy in Italy and France* (1952).

Grindrod, M.: *The Rebuilding of Italy: Economics and Politics, 1945–1955* (1955).
Hughes, H. S.: *The United States and Italy* (1953).
La Palombara, J.: *The Italian Labor Movement: Problems and Prospects* (1957).
Mammarella, G.: *Italy After Fascism: A Political History, 1945–1965* (1966).

The Vatican and the Catholic Church

Abbott, W. M. (ed.): *The Documents of Vatican II, in a New and Definitive Translation, with Commentaries and Notes by Catholic, Protestant and Orthodox Authorities* (1966).
Albrecht, D. (ed.): *Der Notenwechsel zwischen dem Heiligen Stuhl und der Deutschen Reichsregierung* (2 vols., 1965–69).
Alix, C.: *Le Saint Siège et les Nationalismes en Europe, 1870–1960* (1962).
Attwater, D.: *The Christian Churches of the East* (1948). On the Uniates.
————: *Eastern Catholic Worship* (1945).
Bea, Augustin (Cardinal): *The Church and the Jewish People; a Commentary on the Relation of the Church to non-Christian Religions* (1966).
Bernhart, J.: *The Vatican as a World Power* (1939). A sympathetic treatment, translated from the German.
Binchy, D. A.: *Church and State in Fascist Italy* (1942).
Bucci, P. V.: *Chiesa e Stato: Church-State Relations in Italy within the Contemporary Constitutional Framework* (1969). On the post-World War II period.
Bull, G. A.: *Vatican Politics at the Second Vatican Council, 1962–5* (1966).
Burn-Murdoch, H.: *The Development of the Papacy* (1954). Largely historical, with a useful chapter on definition of important doctrines.
Camp, R. L.: *The Papal Ideology of Social Reform: A Study in Historical Development 1878–1967* (1969).
Carlen, M. C.: *A Guide to the Encyclicals of the Roman Pontiffs from Leo XIII to the Present Day, 1878–1937* (1939).
Cianfarra, C. M.: *The Vatican and the War* (1944). Favorably inclined.
Dushnyck, W.: *The Ukrainian-rite Catholic Church at the Ecumenical Council, 1962–1965* (1967).
Eckhardt, C. C.: *The Papacy and World Affairs* (1937). Historical; two chapters deal with the twentieth century.
Goerner, E. A.: *Peter and Caesar; the Catholic Church and Political Authority* (1965).
Graham, R. A., Jr.: *Vatican Diplomacy* (1959).
Hales, E. E.: *The Catholic Church in the Modern World* (1958).
Halperin, S. W.: *The Separation of Church and State in Italian Thought from Cavour to Mussolini* (1937).
Jemolo, A. C.: *Church and State in Italy 1850–1950* (1960).
Kerwin, J. G.: *The Catholic Viewpoint on Church and State* (1960).
Manhattan, A.: *The Catholic Church Against the Twentieth Century* (1947). A critical account of Vatican policy in relation to various European countries.
Moody, J. N. (ed.): *Church and Society: Catholic Social and Political Thought and Movements, 1789–1950* (1953). Arranged primarily by countries.
Nichols, P.: *The Politics of the Vatican* (1968).
O'Dea, T. F.: *The Catholic Crisis* (1968).
Powers, F. J. (ed.): *Papal Pronouncements on the Political Order* (1952). A selection covering the years 1878 to 1951.
Regan, R. J.: *Conflict and Consensus; Religious Freedom and the Second Vatican Council* (1967).
Rynne, X.: *Vatican Council II* (1968).
Schneider, B., P. Blet, and A. Martin (eds.): *Die Briefe Pius XII au die Deutschen Bischöfe 1939–1944* (1966).
Schöppe, L.: *Konkordate seit 1800. Originaltext und deutsche Übersetzung der geltenden Konkordate* (1964). Well-edited.
Secretairerie d'état de Sa Sainteté: *Actes et documents du Saint Siège relatifs à la Seconde Guerre Mondial* (vol. I; 1965 ff.).

Smith, G. D. (ed.): *The Teaching of the Catholic Church: A Summary of Catholic Doctrine* (2 vols., 1949). Authoritative statement by a group of Catholic scholars.

Teeling, W.: *Pope Pius XI and World Affairs* (1937).

Webb, L. C.: *Church and State in Italy 1947–1957* (1958).

Webster, R. A.: *The Cross and the Fasces: Christian Democracy and Fascism in Italy* (1960).

(See also bibliographies on various states for church-state relations.)

THE SMALLER COUNTRIES OF WESTERN EUROPE

Belgium, Luxembourg, and the Netherlands

Anstey, R.: *King Leopold's Legacy, the Congo under Belgian Rule, 1908–1960* (1966).

Arango, E. R.: *Leopold III and the Belgian Royal Question* (1963).

Barnouw, A. J.: *The Dutch; a Portrait Study of the People of Holland* (1940). One of the best books on the Netherlands.

Belgian Ministry of Foreign Affairs: *Belgium: The Official Account of What Happened, 1939–1940* (1941).

Boolen, J. J., and J. C. van der Daes: *Five Years of Occupation: The Resistance of the Dutch Against Hitler-Terrorism and Nazi-Robbery* (1945).

Cammaerts, E.: *Albert of Belgium* (1935).

Campen, S. I. P. van: *The Quest for Security: Some Aspects of Netherlands Foreign Policy 1945–1950* (1958).

Clough, S. B.: *A History of the Flemish Movement in Belgium* (1930).

De Meeus, A.: *History of the Belgians* (1962).

Eyck, F. G.: *The Benelux Countries* (1959).

Goris, J. (ed.): *Belgium* (1945).

————: *Belgium Under Occupation* (1947). Good chapters on various aspects of Belgian life and economy.

Herchen, C. J. P. A.: *History of the Grand Duchy of Luxemburg.* (5th ed., 1950).

Hoover, H.: *An American Epic.* Vol. I, *The Relief of Belgium and Northern France* (1959).

Kalken, F. van: *Histoire de la Belgique et de son expansion coloniale* (rev. ed., 1954).

Kleffens, E. N. van: *Juggernaut over Holland: The Dutch Foreign Minister's Personal Story of the Invasion of the Netherlands* (1941).

Landheer, B. (ed.): *The Netherlands* (1943).

Mallison, V.: *Power and Politics in Belgian Education, 1815 to 1961* (1963).

Miller, J. K.: *Belgian Foreign Policy Between Two Wars, 1919–1940* (1951).

Overstraeten, R. van (ed.): *The War Diaries of Albert I, King of the Belgians* (1954).

Pausw, G. A. de: *The Educational Rights of the Church and Elementary Schools in Belgium* (1953). Written from a Catholic viewpoint.

Rousseau, A.: *Belgium and Luxembourg* (1950).

Simon, C. A.: *Le parti Catholique Belge, 1830–1945* (1958).

Slade, R.: *King Leopold's Congo: Aspects of the Development of Race Relations in the Congo Independent State* (1962).

Stengers, J.: *Belgique et Congo: L'Elaboration de la Charte Coloniale* (1963).

Vandenbosch, A.: *Dutch Foreign Policy Since 1815* (1958).

Warmbrunn, W.: *The Dutch Under German Occupation 1940–1945* (1963).

Weber, P.: *Geschichte Luxemburgs im zweiten Weltkrieg* (1947).

Zuylen, P. van: *Les Mains libres: politique extérieure de la Belgique, 1914–1940* (1950).

Scandinavian States: General Surveys

Anderson, S. V.: *The Nordic Council: A Study of Scandinavian Regionalism* (1968).

Arneson, B. A.: *The Democratic Monarchies of Scandinavia* (2nd ed., 1949).

Childs, M.: *This Is Democracy: Collective Bargaining in Scandinavia* (1938).
Friis, H. (ed.): *Scandinavia Between East and West* (1950).
Kenney, R.: *The Northern Tangle* (1946). Scandinavia during World War II.
Lindgren, R. E.: *Norway-Sweden: Union, Disunion, and Scandinavian Integration* (1959).
Scott, F. D.: *The United States and Scandinavia* (1950). Informative and interesting.
Wuorinen, J. H.: *Scandinavia* (1965).

Denmark and Iceland

Danstrup, J.: *A History of Denmark* (1948).
Jensen, A. E.: *Iceland: Old-New Republic* (1954). Popular survey.
Koch, H.: *Grundtvig* (1952). Biography of the founder of folk high schools in Denmark.
Lampe, D.: *The Savage Canary: The Story of Resistance in Denmark* (1957).
Lauring, P.: *A History of Denmark* (1960).
Mannicke, P.: *Denmark: A Social Laboratory* (1939). Co-operatives, folk high schools, social legislation.
Nuechterlein, D. E.: *Iceland: Reluctant Ally* (1961).
Rothery, A.: *Denmark: Kingdom of Reason* (1937).
Stefanson, V.: *Iceland: The First American Republic* (1939). Descriptive.
Thordarson, B.: *Iceland: Past and Present* (2nd ed., 1945).
Westergaard, H.: *Economic Development in Denmark Before and During the World War* (1922).

Norway

Bourneuf, A.: *Norway: The Planned Revival* (1958).
Collinder, B.: *The Lapps* (1949).
Curtis, M. (ed.): *Norway and the War: September 1939–December 1940* (1941).
Galenson, W.: *Labor in Norway* (1949).
Gjessing, G.: *Changing Lapps* (1954).
Hardy, G.: *Norway* (1925).
Johnson, A.: *Norway: Her Invasion and Occupation* (1948).
Koht, H.: *Norway: Neutral and Invaded* (1941). By an eminent historian who was also minister of foreign affairs.
Larsen, K.: *A History of Norway* (1948).
Riste, O.: *The Neutral Ally: Norway's Relations with Belligerent Powers in the First World War* (1965).
Vorren, O. (ed.): *Norway North of 65* (1960).

Sweden

Abrahamson, S.: *Sweden's Foreign Policy* (1957).
Ander, O. F.: *The Building of Modern Sweden: The Reign of Gustav V, 1907–1950* (1958).
Andersson, I.: *A History of Sweden* (1955).
Childs, M.: *Sweden: The Middle Way* (1947). A thought-provoking presentation.
Cole, M., and S. Smith: *Democratic Sweden* (1939).
Heckscher, E. F.: *An Economic History of Sweden* (1954).
Oakley, S.: *A Short History of Sweden* (1966).
Rosenthal, A. H.: *The Social Programs of Sweden* (1967).
Rustow, D. A.: *The Politics of Compromise: A Study of Parties and Cabinet Government in Sweden* (1955).
Tomasson, R. F.: *Sweden: Prototype of Modern Society* (1971).
Verney, D. V.: *Parliamentary Reform in Sweden, 1866–1921* (1957).

Switzerland

Bonjour, E., et al.: *A Short History of Switzerland* (1952).
Bozeman, A. B.: *Regional Conflicts Around Geneva* (1949).
Huber, H.: *How Switzerland Is Governed* (1947).
Hughes, C.: *The Federal Constitution of Switzerland: Translation and Commentary* (1954).
Hunold, A.: *The Industrial Development of Switzerland* (1954).
Kohn, H.: *Nationalism and Liberty: The Swiss Example* (1956).
Mayer, K. B.: *The Population of Switzerland* (1952).
Meier, H. K.: *Friendship under Stress: U.S.-Swiss Relations 1900–1950* (1969).
Rappard, W. E.: *The Government of Switzerland* (1936).
Siegfried, A.: *Switzerland, a Democratic Way of Life* (1950).
Soloveytchik, G.: *Switzerland in Perspective* (1954).

Spain and Portugal

Blanshard, P.: *Freedom and Catholic Power in Spain and Portugal* (1962).
Bolloten, B.: *The Grand Camouflage: The Spanish Civil War and Revolution, 1936–1939* (1968).
Bowers, C. G.: *My Mission to Spain: Watching the Rehearsal for World War II* (1954). Memoirs of a United States ambassador to Spain.
Brenan, G.: *The Spanish Labyrinth* (1943).
Carr, R.: *Spain 1808–1939* (1966).
Cattell, D. T.: *Communism and the Spanish Civil War* (1955).
———: *Soviet Diplomacy and the Spanish Civil War* (1957).
Delpech, J.: *The Oppression of Protestants in Spain* (1955).
Descola, J.: *A History of Spain* (1963).
Duffy, J.: *Portugal in Africa* (1962).
Feis, H.: *The Spanish Story: Franco and the Nations at War* (1948). Contains much on United States policy toward Spain.
Hammond, R. J.: *Portugal and Africa, 1815–1910, a Study in Uneconomic Imperialism* (1966).
Hayes, C. J. H.: *Wartime Mission in Spain, 1942–1945* (1945). By the United States ambassador to Madrid.
Hughey, J. D., Jr.: *Religious Freedom in Spain* (1956).
Jackson, G.: *The Spanish Republic and the Civil War* (1965).
Johnston, V. B.: *Legions of Babel: The International Brigades in the Spanish Civil War* (1967).
Kleine-Ahlbrandt, W. L.: *The Policy of Simmering: A Study of British Policy During the Spanish Civil War, 1936–1939* (1962).
Livermore, H. V.: *A History of Spain* (1958).
———: *A New History of Portugal* (1966).
Madariaga, S. de: *Spain: A Modern History* (1958).
Merkes, M.: *Die deutsche Politik gegenuber dem Spanischen Bürgerkrieg, 1936–1939* (1961).
Nowell, C. E.: *A History of Portugal* (1952).
Padelford, N. J.: *International Law and Diplomacy in the Spanish Civil War* (1939).
Payne, S. G.: *Franco's Spain* (1967).
Peers, E. A.: *The Church in Spain 1737–1937* (1948). A good discussion.
———: *The Spanish Tragedy, 1930–36: Dictatorship, Republic, Chaos* (1936).
Puzzo, D. A.: *Spain and the Great Powers, 1936–1941* (1962).
Ramos, O. A.: *Politics, Economics and Men of Modern Spain, 1808–1946* (1946).
Sanchez, J. M.: *Reform and Reaction; the Politico-Religious Background of the Spanish Civil War* (1964).
Sufrin, S. C.: *The Economy of Spain* (1952).
Thomas, H.: *The Spanish Civil War* (1961).

Traina, R. P.: *American Diplomacy and the Spanish Civil War* (1968).
Trend, J. B.: *Portugal* (1958).
Ullman, J. C.: *The Tragic Week: A Study of Anticlericalism in Spain, 1875–1912* (1968).
Whitaker, A. P.: *Spain and Defense of the West: Ally and Liability* (1961).

GERMANY

General

Bruck, W. F.: *Social and Economic History of Germany, 1888–1938* (1938).
Chalmers, D. A.: *The Social Democratic Party of Germany: From Working Class Movement to Modern Political Party* (1964).
Craig, G. A.: *The Politics of the Prussian Army, 1640–1945* (1955).
Epstein, K.: *The Genesis of German Conservatism* (1966).
Eyck, E.: *Das persönliche Regiment Wilhelms II: Politische Geschichte des Deutschen Kaiserreiches von 1890 bis 1914* (1948).
Gerschenkron, A.: *Bread and Democracy in Germany* (new ed. 1966).
Goerlitz, O. W.: *History of the German General Staff* (1953). About half the volume is devoted to World War II.
Gooch, G. P.: *Germany* (1925). A fine interpretive study.
Holborn, H.: *A History of Modern Germany* (3 vols., 1959–69). Vol. III covers the period 1840–1945.
Jacob, H.: *German Administration Since Bismarck* (1963).
Kochan, L.: *The Struggle for Germany 1914–1945* (1963).
Kohn, H.: *The Mind of Germany* (1960).
Manchester, W.: *The Arms of Krupp 1587–1968* (1968).
Mann, G.: *The History of Germany Since 1789* (1968).
Meinecke, F.: *The German Catastrophe: Reflections and Recollections* (1950).
Rohr, D. G.: *The Origins of Social Liberalism in Germany* (1963).
Rosenberg, A.: *The Birth of the German Republic, 1871–1918* (1931).
Schorske, C. E.: *German Social Democracy, 1905–1917: The Development of the Great Schism* (1955).
Snyder, L. L.: *German Nationalism: The Tragedy of a People* (1952).
Stolper, G.: *German Economy, 1870–1914* (1940). Clear, nontechnical account.
Taylor, A. J. P.: *The Course of German History* (1946).
Valentin, V.: *The German People: Their History and Culture from the Holy Roman Empire to the Third Reich* (1946).

Biographies and Memoirs

Adenauer, K.: *Erinnerungen* (4 vols., 1966–   ).
Beck, E. R.: *Verdict on Schacht: A Study of the Problem of Political Guilt* (1956).
Booth, M. (trans.): *Prisoner of Peace* (1954). Memoirs of Rudolf Hess.
Bullock, A.: *Hitler: A Study in Tyranny* (1953).
Cecil, L.: *Albert Ballin: Business and Politics in Imperial Germany, 1888–1918* (1967).
Epstein, K.: *Matthias Erzberger and the Dilemma of German Democracy* (1959).
Frischauer, W.: *The Rise and Fall of Hermann Goering* (1951).
Frölich, P.: *Rosa Luxemburg: Her Life and Work* (1940).
Hanfstaengl, E.: *Unheard Witness* (1957).
Hassell, U. von: *The von Hassell Diaries, 1938–1944: The Story of the Forces Against Hitler Inside Germany as Recorded by Ambassador Ulrich von Hassell, a Leader of the Movement* (1947).
Heiber, H. (ed.): *The Early Goebbels Diaries, 1925–1926* (1962).
Heiden, K.: *Der Fuehrer: Hitler's Rise to Power* (1944).

————: *Hitler: A Biography* (1936).
Kersten, F.: *The Kersten Memoirs, 1940–1945* (1957).
Kessler, H.: *Walter Rathenau: His Life and Work* (1930).
Lockner, L. (ed.): *The Goebbels Diaries* (1948).
Manvell, R., and H. Fraenkel: *Doctor Goebbels; His Life and Death* (1960).
Martiensen, A. K.: *Hitler and His Admirals* (1949).
Olden, R.: *Hitler* (1936).
————: *Stresemann* (1930).
Peterson, E. N.: *Hjalmar Schacht: For and Against Hitler* (1954).
Raeder, E.: *My Life* (1960).
Rauschning, H.: *The Voice of Destruction* (1940). Talks between Hitler and the
    former president of the Danzig Senate.
Ribbentrop, J. von: *The Ribbentrop Memoirs* (1954).
Schacht, H.: *My First Seventy-six Years* (1955).
Scheidemann, P.: *The Making of New Germany: The Memoirs of Philipp Scheidemann*
    (2 vols., 1929). By one of the leaders of the Social Democratic party.
Schellenberg, W.: *The Labyrinth: Memoirs of Hitler's Secret Service Chief* (1956).
Schmidt, P.: *Hitler's Interpreter* (1951).
Severing, C.: *Mein Lebensweg* (2 vols., 1950). Memoirs of one of the leading states-
    men of the Weimar Republic.
Smith, B. F.: *Adolf Hitler: His Family, Childhood and Youth* (1967).
Speer, A.: *Inside the Third Reich: Memoirs* (1970). One of the most important
    memoirs of a Nazi leader.
Stein, G. (ed.): *Hitler* (1968).
Steinberg, J.: *Yesterday's Deterrent, Tirpitz and the Birth of the German Battle Fleet*
    (1965).
Strasser, O.: *Hitler and I* (1940).
Sutton, E. (ed.): *G. Stresemann: Diaries, Letters, Papers* (3 vols., 1935–40).
Weizsäcker, E. H.: *Memoirs* (1951).
Weymar, P.: *Adenauer: His Authorized Biography* (1957).
Wheeler-Bennett, J. W.: *Hindenburg the Wooden Titan* (1936).
(See also books listed under First and Second World Crises.)

Weimar Republic

Angress, W. T.: *Stillborn Revolution; the Communist Bid for Power in Germany,
    1921–1923* (1963).
Anschütz, G.: *Die Verfassung des Deutschen Reichs vom 11. August, 1919* (3rd ed.,
    1930). The best commentary on the Weimar Constitution.
Badia, G.: *Histoire de l'Allemagne Contemporaine, 1917–1962* (2 vols., 1962–64).
Bracher, K. D.: *Die Auflösung der Weimarer Republik* (1960). Has an extensive
    bibliography.
Bretton, H. L.: *Stresemann and the Revision of Versailles: A Fight for Reason* (1935).
Carsten, F. L.: *The Reichswehr and Politics 1918 to 1933* (1966).
Castellan, G.: *Le réarmement clandestine du Reich, 1930–1935* (1954). Author relies
    on archives of the French General Staff.
Deak, I.: *Weimar Germany's Left-Wing Intellectuals: A Political History of the
    Weltbühne and its Circle* (1968).
Dorpalen, A.: *Hindenburg and the Weimar Republic* (1964).
Edwards, M. L.: *Stresemann and the Greater Germany, 1914–1918* (1963).
Eyck, E.: *A History of the Weimar Republic* (2 vols., 1962–63). A translation.
Fischer, R.: *Stalin and German Communism: A Study in the Origins of the State
    Party* (1948). A history of the German Communist party by a former member.
Flechtheim, O. K.: *Die KPD in der Weimarer Republik* (1969).
Gatzke, H.: *Stresemann and the Rearmament of Germany* (1954).
Gay, P.: *Weimar Culture: The Outsider as Insider* (1968).
Gordon, H. J.: *The Reichswehr and the German Republic, 1919–1926* (1957).

Hertzman, L.: DNVP: *Right-Wing Opposition in the Weimar Republic 1918–1923* (1963).

Hunt, R. N.: *German Social Democracy, 1918–1933* (1964).

Kaufmann, W. H.: *Monarchism in the Weimar Republic* (1953).

Lebovics, H.: *Social Conservatism and the Middle Class in Germany, 1914–1933* (1969).

Mitchell, A.: *Revolution in Bavaria, 1918–1919: The Eisner Regime and the Soviet Republic* (1965).

Nicholls, A. J.: *Weimar and the Rise of Hitler* (1968).

Ringer, F. K.: *The Decline of the German Mandarins: The German Academic Community, 1890–1933* (1969).

————: *The German Inflation of 1923* (1969).

Rosenbaum, K.: *Community of Fate: German-Soviet Diplomatic Relations 1922–1928* (1965).

Rosenberg, A.: *A History of the German Republic, 1918–1930* (1936).

Ryder, A. J.: *The German Revolution of 1918; A Study of German Socialism in War and Revolt* (1967).

Scheele, G.: *The Weimar Republic: Overture to the Third Reich* (1946). A sober appraisal.

Turner, H. A.: *Stresemann and the Politics of the Weimar Republic* (1963).

Ullmann, R. K., and S. King-Hall: *German Parliaments: A Study of the Development of Representative Institutions in Germany* (1954).

Vermeil, E.: *Germany in the Twentieth Century: A Political and Cultural History of the Weimar Republic and the Third Reich* (1956).

Waite, R. G. L.: *Vanguard of Nazism: The Free Corps Movement in Postwar Germany, 1918–1923* (1952).

Watkins, F. M.: *The Failure of Constitutional Powers under the German Republic* (1939).

Watt, R. M.: *The Kings Depart: Versailles and the German Revolution* (1969).

Wheeler-Bennett, J. W.: *The Nemesis of Power: The German Army in Politics, 1918–1945* (1954).

Wunderlich, F: *Labor Under German Democracy, 1918–1933* (1940).

Ziegler, D. J.: *Prelude to Democracy: A Study of Proportional Representation and the Heritage of Weimar Germany 1871–1920* (1958).

The Third Reich

Allen, W. S.: *The Nazi Seizure of Power: The Experience of a Single German Town, 1930–1945* (1965).

Almond, G. A. (ed.): *The Struggle for Democracy in Germany* (1949). A discussion of the German resistance movement during the war and of postwar reconstruction.

Baumont, M., J. H. E. Fried, and E. Vermeil (eds.): *The Third Reich* (1955). Essays by twenty-eight scholars of different nationalities.

Beck, E. R.: *The Death of the Prussian Republic: A Study of Reich-Prussian Relations 1932–1934* (1959).

Bengston, J. R.: *Nazi War Aims; the Plan for the Thousand Year Reich* (1962).

Bernstein, V. H.: *Final Judgment: The Story of Nuremberg* (1947). A summary of the trials.

Blond, G.: *The Death of Hitler's Germany* (1954). A translation of a French account of the last nine months of the Third Reich.

Bracher, K. D.: *Die deutsche Diktatur. Enstehung, Struktur und Folgen des Nationalsozialismus* (1969).

————, W. Sauer, and G. Schulz: *Die National-sozialistische Machtergreifung. Studien zur Errichtung des totalitären Herrschaftssystems in Deutschland 1933/1934* (1960). A thorough study.

Brandt, K.: *Germany's Agricultural and Food Policies in World War II* (1953).

Bramsted, E. K.: *Goebbels and National Socialist Propaganda, 1925–1945* (1965).

Broszat, M.: *German National Socialism, 1919–1945.* (1966).

Burckhardt, C. J.: *Meine Danziger Mission, 1937–1939* (2nd ed., 1960).

Burden, H. T.: *The Nuremberg Party Rallies* (1967).

Davidson, E.: *The Trial of the Germans: An Account of the Twenty-two Defendants before the International Military Tribunal at Nuremberg* (1966).

Delarue, J.: *The Gestapo: A History of Horror* (1964).

Deutsch, H. C.: *The Conspiracy Against Hitler in the Twilight War* (1968).

Donohoe, J.: *Hitler's Conservative Opponents in Bavaria, 1930–1945: A Study of Catholic, Monarchist, and Separatist Anti-Nazi Activities* (1961).

Feder, G.: *Hitler's Official Programme* (1934). Commentary by the man who formulated the twenty-five-point program.

Fitz-Gibbon, C.: *Denazification* (1969).

———: *20 July* (1956).

Foertsch, H.: *Schuld und Verhaengnis: Die Fritsch-Krise im Frühjahr 1938 als Wendepunkt* (1951).

Fried, J. H. E.: *The Exploitation of Foreign Labor by Germany* (1945). A study sponsored by the International Labor Office.

Frye, A.: *Nazi Germany and the American Hemisphere, 1933–1941* (1967).

Gallin, M. A.: *German Resistance to Hitler: Ethical and Religious Factors* (1962).

Hale, O. J.: *The Captive Press in the Third Reich* (1964).

Harris, W. R.: *Tyranny on Trial* (1954). Analysis of the Nuremberg trials.

Heiber, H. (ed.): *Reichsführer! Briefe an und von Himmler* (1968).

Heiden, K.: *A History of National Socialism* (1934). One of the best books on the subject.

Hilberg, R.: *The Destruction of the European Jews* (1961).

Hoffmann, P.: *Widerstand, Staatsstreich, Attentat* (1969). About half the 960 pages are on assassination attempts before the one of July 20, 1944.

Höhne, H.: *The Order of the Death's Head: The Story of Hitler's S.S.* (1970).

Homze, E. L.: *Foreign Labor in Nazi Germany* (1967).

Jenks, W. A.: *Vienna and the Young Hitler* (1960).

Klein, B. H.: *Germany's Economic Preparations for War* (1959).

Koehl, R. L.: *RKFDV: German Resettlement and Population Policy, 1939–45* (1958).

Loewenstein, K.: *Hitler's Germany: The Nazi Background of the War* (1939).

Lüdde-Neurath, W.: *Regierung Dönitz: Die letzten Tage des Dritten Reiches* (1953).

Milward, A. S.: *The German Economy at War* (1965).

Mosse, G. L.: *The Crisis of German Ideology: Intellectual Origins of the Third Reich* (1964).

Neumann, F. L.: *Behemoth: The Structure and Practice of National Socialism* (1942).

Orlow, D.: *The History of the Nazi Party: 1919–1933* (1969).

Peterson, E. N.: *The Limits of Hitler's Power* (1969).

Poliakov, L., and J. Wulf (eds.): *Das Dritte Reich und die Juden: Dokumente und Aufsaetze* (1955).

Pollock, J. K.: *The Government of Greater Germany* (1938). With a well-selected bibliography.

Prittie, T.: *Germans Against Hitler* (1964).

Pulzer, P. G. J.: *The Rise of Political Anti-Semitism in Germany and Austria* (1964).

Reitlinger, G. R.: *The Final Solution: The Attempt to Exterminate the Jews of Europe, 1939–1945* (1953).

———: *The S.S.: Alibi of a Nation, 1922–1945* (1956).

Ritter, G.: *Carl Goerdeler und die deutsche Widerstandsbewegung* (1954).

Rothfels, H.: *The German Opposition to Hitler. An Assessment* (1961).

Schlabrendorff, F. von (trans. by H. Simon): *The Secret War Against Hitler* (1965).

Schweitzer, A.: *Big Business in the Third Reich* (1964).

Shirer, W. L.: *Berlin Diary: The Journal of a Foreign Correspondent, 1934–1941* (1941).

———: *The Rise and Fall of the Third Reich* (1960).

Stern, F.: *The Politics of Cultural Despair: A Study in the Rise of German Ideology* (1961).
Taylor, T.: *Sword and Swastika: Generals and Nazis in the Third Reich* (1952).
Trevor-Roper, H. R.: *The Last Days of Hitler* (1947). Best account of Hitler's death.
Woetzel, R. K.: *The Nuremberg Trials in International Law* (1960).
Zeller, E. (trans. by R. P. Hellre and D. R. Masters): *The Flame of Freedom: The German Struggle against Hitler* (1969).
Zeman, Z. A. B.: *Nazi Propaganda* (1964).
Zimmermann, E. (ed.): *Germans Against Hitler, July 20, 1944* (3rd ed., 1960).
(For National Socialist philosophy see books listed under Political Thought.)

Foreign Policy

Balfour, M. L. G.: *The Kaiser and His Times* (1964).
Bathurst, M. E.: *Germany and the North Atlantic Community* (1956).
Carr, E. H.: *German-Soviet Relations between the Two World Wars, 1919–1939* (1951).
Cowan, L. G.: *France and the Saar, 1680–1948* (1950).
Craig, G. A.: *From Bismarck to Adenauer: Aspects of German Statecraft* (1958).
Dirksen, H. von: *Moscow, Tokyo, London: Twenty Years of German Foreign Policy* (1952).
Dyck, H. L.: *Weimar Germany and Soviet Russia, a Study in Diplomatic Instability* (1966).
Fischer, F.: *Germany's Aims in the First World War* (1967).
Hilger, G., and A. G. Meyer: *The Incompatible Allies: A Memoir-History of German-Soviet Relations, 1918–1941* (1953).
Hirszowicz, L.: *The Third Reich and the Arab East* (1966).
Iklé, F. W.: *German-Japanese Relations, 1936–1940* (1956).
Kalijarvi, T. V.: *The Memel Statute: Its Origin, Legal Nature, and Observation to the Present Day* (1937). A careful study.
Kimmich, C. M.: *The Free City: Danzig and German Foreign Policy, 1919–1934* (1968).
Kochan, T.: *Russia and the Weimar Republic* (1954).
Leonhardt, H. L.: *Nazi Conquest of Danzig* (1942).
Marrow, I. F. D.: *The Peace Settlement in the German Polish Border Lands* (1936).
Mason, J. B.: *The Danzig Dilemma* (1946). A thorough discussion.
Offner, A. A.: *American Appeasement: United States Foreign Policy and Germany* (1969).
Orlow, D.: *The Nazis in the Balkans: A Case Study of Totalitarian Politics* (1968).
Rosenbaum, K.: *Community of Fate: German-Soviet Diplomatic Relations, 1922–1928* (1965).
Russell, F. M.: *The Saar: Battleground and Pawn* (1951).
Schmokel, W. W.: *Dream of Empire: German Colonialism, 1919–1945* (1964).
Seabury, P.: *The Wilhelmstrasse: A Study of German Diplomats under the Nazi Regime* (1955).
Speier, H. (ed.): *West German Leadership and Foreign Policy* (1957).
Trumpener, U.: *Germany and the Ottoman Empire, 1914–1918* (1968).
Weinberg, G. L.: *German-Soviet Relations, 1939–1941* (1954).
Wiskemann, E.: *Germany's Eastern Neighbors* (1956).
(See also books listed under First and Second World Crises.)

Education and Religion

Albrecht, D.: *Der Notenwechsel zwischen dem Heiligen Stuhl und der Deutschen Reichsregierung* (vol. 1, 1965).
Butler, E. M.: *Saint Simonian Religion in Germany: A Study of the Young German Movement* (1968).

Cochrane, A. C.: *The Church's Confession Under Hitler* (1962). Concentrates on the Synod of Barmen.

Conway, J. S.: *Nazi Persecution of the Churches* (1968).

Deuerlein, E.: *Das Reichskonkordat* (1956).

Dibelius, O.: *In the Service of the Lord: The Autobiography of Bishop Otto Dibelius* (1964).

Frey, A.: *Cross and Swastika: The Ordeal of the German Church* (1938). A good statement of the issues.

Friedlander, S.: *Pius XII and the Third Reich. A Documentation* (1966).

Heer, F.: *Der Glaube des Adolf Hitlers* (1968).

Helmreich, E. C.: *Religious Education in German Schools: An Historical Approach* (1959).

Hermelink, H.: *Kirche im Kampf: Dokumente des Widerstands und des Aufbaus in der Evangelischen Kirche Deutschlands von 1933 bis 1945* (1950). A very important collection of material.

Hylla, E. J., and F. O. Kegel: *Education in Germany: An Introduction for Foreigners* (1954).

Klügel, E.: *Die lutherische Landeskirche Hannovers und Ihr Bischof 1933–1945* (1964). One of the more important books on the church struggle under Hitler; well footnoted.

Kneller, G. F.: *The Educational Philosophy of National Socialism* (1941).

Lewy, G.: *The Catholic Church and Nazi Germany* (1964).

Liddell, H.: *Education in Occupied Germany* (1949).

Littell, F. H.: *The German Phoenix* (1960). The German Evangelical Church.

Luckey, H.: *Free Churches in Germany* (1956).

Meier, K.: *Die Deutschen Christen* (1964). A volume in the series *Arbeiten Zur Geschichte Des Kirchenkampfes* sponsored by the "Kommission der Evangelischen Kirche in Deutschland für die geschichte des Kirchenkampfes"; all these important volumes cannot be listed here.

Mosse, G. L. (trans. by S. Attanasio): *Nazi Culture; Intellectual, Cultural and Social Life in the Third Reich* (1966).

Neuhäusler, J.: *Kreuz und Hakenkreuz: Der Kampf des Nationalsozialismus gegen die katholische Kirche und der kirchliche Widerstand* (1946). Various aspects of the Catholic Church's conflict with Hitler.

Niemöller, W.: *Kampf und Zeugnis der Bekennenden Kirche* (1947). Probably the most important of Niemöller's many books on the *Kirchenkampf*.

Pilgert, H. P.: *The West German Educational System* (1953).

Riede, D. C.: *The Official Attitude of the Roman Catholic Hierarchy in Germany toward National Socialism 1933–1945* (Ann Arbor: University of Michigan, University Microfilms, 1957).

Samuel, R. H., and R. H. Thomas: *Education and Society in Modern Germany* (1949).

Solberg, R. W.: *God and Caesar in East Germany: The Conflicts of Church and State in East Germany Since 1945* (1961).

Stammler, E.: *Churchless Protestants* (1964). About the Evangelical Church in Germany.

Volk, L.: *Der bayerische Episkopat und der Nationalsozialismus* (1966).

Wenke, H.: *Education in Western Germany: A Postwar Survey* (1953).

Wurm, T.: *Erinnerungen aus Meinem Leben* (1953). Memoirs of the Protestant bishop of Württemberg during the Third Reich.

Zahn, G. C.: *German Catholics and Hitler's Wars; a Study in Social Control* (1962).

Germany Since 1945

Balfour, M., and J. Mair: *Four Power Control in Germany and Austria* (1956).

Childs, D.: *East Germany* (1969).

Davison, W. P.: *The Berlin Blockade; a Study in Cold War Politics* (1958).

Dornberg, J.: *The Other Germany* (1968). East Germany.

Edinger, L. J.: *Kurt Schumacher; a study in Personality and Political Behavior* (1965).
Friedrich, C. J., et al.: *American Experiences in Military Government in World War II* (1948).
Gillen, J. F. J.: *State and Local Government in West Germany, 1945–1953* (1953).
Gimbel, J.: *The American Occupation of Germany: Politics and the Military, 1945–1949* (1968).
Golay, J. F.: *The Founding of the Federal Republic of Germany* (1958).
Gottlieb, M.: *The German Peace Settlement and the Berlin Crisis* (1960).
Hanhardt, A. M., Jr.: *The German Democratic Republic* (1969).
Hanrieder, W. F.: *West Germany Foreign Policy, 1949–1963; International Pressure and Domestic Response* (1967).
Hiscocks, R.: *The Adenauer Era* (1966). Published in England under the title *Germany Revived.*
Legien, R.: *The Four Power Agreements on Berlin* (1960). Brief.
Litchfield, E. H., et al.: *Governing Postwar Germany* (1953). Chapters on all important aspects of German government.
Lowenberg G.: *Parliament in the German Political System* (1967).
Mander, J.: *Berlin: Hostage for the West* (1962).
Nettle, J. P.: *The Eastern Zone and Soviet Policy in Germany, 1945–50* (1951). A scholarly work well supplied with tables and charts.
Oppen, B. R. von: *Documents on Germany Under Occupation, 1945–1954* (1955).
Plischke, E.: *Contemporary Governments of Germany* (1969).
———: *History of the Allied High Commission for Germany: Its Establishment, Structure and Procedures* (1953).
Pollock, J. K.: *German Democracy and Work* (1955).
———, et al.: *Germany Under Occupation* (2nd ed., 1949). A valuable collection of documents.
Schmidt, H. G.: *Economic Assistance to West Berlin, 1949–1951* (1952).
Schwarz, L. W.: *Refugees in Germany Today* (1957).
Slusser, R. M.: *Soviet Economic Policy in Postwar Germany* (1953).
Smith, J. E.: *The Defense of Berlin* (1963).
Snell, J. L.: *Wartime Origins of the East-West Dilemma over Germany* (1959).
Stahl, W. (ed.): *The Politics of Postwar Germany* (1963).
Stolper, W. F.: *The Structure of the East German Economy* (1960).
Tauber, K. P.: *Beyond Eagle and Swastika: German Nationalism Since 1945* (1967).
Vali, F. A.: *The Quest for a United Germany* (1967).
Wallich, H. C.: *Mainsprings of the German Revival* (1955).
Warburg, J. P.: *Germany: Key to Peace* (1953). Critical analysis of United States postwar policy.
Wettig, G.: *Entmilitärisierung und Wiederbewaffnung in Deutschland, 1943–1955* (1967).
Willis, F. R.: *France, Germany, and the New Europe, 1945–1963* (1965).
Windsor, P.: *City on Leave: A History of Berlin 1945–1962* (1963).
Zentner, H.: *Aufstieg aus dem Nichts: Deutschland von 1945 bis 1953. Eine Soziographie in zwei Bänden* (2 vols., 1954). A gripping photographic account.
Zink, H.: *American Military Government in Germany* (1947).
———: *The United States in Germany, 1944–1955* (1957).

THE DANUBIAN REGION

Austro-Hungarian Monarchy

Austrian History Yearbook (1965 ff.).
Burian, S.: *Austria in Dissolution* (1925).
Crankshaw, E.: *The Fall of the House of Habsburg* (1963).
Engel-Janosi, F.: *Österreich und der Vatikan, 1846–1918.* Vol. 1, *Die Pontifikate Pius' IX und Leos XIII, 1846–1903* (1958).

Glaise-Horstenau, E. von: *The Collapse of the Austro-Hungarian Empire* (1930).
    Valuable on the Dual Monarchy during World War I.
Janetschek, O.: *The Emperor Franz Joseph* (1953).
Jaszi, O.: *The Dissolution of the Habsburg Monarchy* (1929). A mine of information
    on Austria-Hungary.
Jelavich, B.: *The Habsburg Empire in European Affairs 1814–1918* (1969). Has a
    selected bibliography.
Kann, R. A.: *The Multinational Empire: Nationalism and National Reform in the
    Habsburg Monarchy, 1848–1918* (2 vols., 1950). Excellent sections on each
    nationality.
Kienast, E. M., and R. Rie (trans. and eds.): *The Incredible Friendship, the Letters
    of Emperor Franz Joseph to Frau Katharina Schratt* (1966).
Kiszling, R.: *Erzherzog Franz Ferdinand von Österreich-Este* (1953).
Macartney, C. A.: *The Habsburg Empire 1790–1918* (1969).
McGuigan, D. G.: *The Hapsburgs* (1966).
May, A. J.: *The Hapsburg Monarchy, 1867–1914* (1951). The best volume on this
    period.
————: *The Passing of the Hapsburg Monarchy, 1914–1918* (2 vols., 1966).
Miskolczy, J.: *Ungarn in der Habsburger-Monarchie* (1959).
Redlich, J.: *Austrian War Government* (1929). The opening chapter is a good
    discussion of the government of the Dual Monarchy.
————: *Emperor Francis Joseph of Austria: A Biography* (1929). Authoritative and
    understanding.
Shepherd, G. B.: *The Last Habsburg* (1968).
Sugar, P. F.: *Industrialization of Bosnia-Hercegovina 1878–1918* (1963).
Taylor, A. J. P.: *The Habsburg Monarchy, 1809–1918* (1948).
Walter, F.: *Die Nationalilätenfrage in Alten Ungarn und die Sudostpolitik Wiens*
    (1959).
Wandruszka, A. (trans. by C. and H. Epstein): *The House of Habsburg: Six Hundred
    Years of European Dynasty* (1964).
Zeman, A.: *The Break-up of the Habsburg Empire, 1914–1918* (1961).

The Succession States

Czernin, F.: *Versailles, 1919: The Forces, Events, and Personalities That Shaped the
    Treaty* (1964).
Dallin, A., et al.: *Russian Diplomacy in Eastern Europe, 1914–1917* (1963).
Deak, F.: *Hungarian-Rumanian Land Dispute* (1928).
Hertz, F.: *The Economic Problem of the Danubian States: A Study in Economic Nation-
    alism* (1947). Many valuable tables.
Lukacz, J. A.: *The Great Powers and Eastern Europe* (1953). Much on World War II.
Macartney, C. A., and W. W. Palmer: *Independent Eastern Europe: A History* (1962).
Mitrany, D.: *The Effect of the War in Southeastern Europe* (1936).
Pasvolsky, L.: *Economic Nationalism of the Danubian States* (1928). A study spon-
    sored by the Brookings Institution.
Roucek, J. S., et al.: *Central-Eastern Europe: Crucible of World Wars* (1946).
    Countries to the east of Germany, including Russia.
Royal Institute of International Affairs: *The Balkan States: A Review of the Economic
    and Financial Development of Albania, Bulgaria, Greece, Romania, and
    Yugoslavia Since 1919* (1936).
————: *South-Eastern Europe: A Political and Economic Survey* (1939). Hungary,
    Yugoslavia, Albania, Bulgaria, Greece, and Turkey.
Schlesinger, R.: *Federalism in Central and Eastern Europe* (1945). An excellent study
    with a historical approach.
Seton-Watson, H.: *Eastern Europe Between the Wars, 1918–1941* (3rd ed., 1962).
    An outstanding volume concentrating on Poland, Czechoslovakia, Hungary,
    Rumania, Yugoslavia, and Bulgaria.
Wanklyn, H. G.: *The Eastern Marchlands of Europe* (1941). A fine study by a

geographer, on the Baltic states, Poland, Czechoslovakia, Hungary, Yugoslavia.

Zagoroff, S. D., et al.: *The Agricultural Economy of the Danubian Countries, 1935–1945* (1955).

Danubian States Since 1945

Bain, L. B.: *The Reluctant Satellites: An Eyewitness Report of East Europe and the Hungarian Revolution* (1960).

Betts, R.: *Central and South East Europe, 1945–1948* (1950).

Birke, E., and R. Neumann (ed.): *Die Sowjetisierung Ost Mitteleuropas. Untersuchungen zu ihrem Ablauf in den einzelnen Ländern* (1963).

Black, C. E. (ed.): *Challenge in Eastern Europe* (1954).

Borsody, S.: *The Triumphs of Tyranny: The Nazi and Soviet Conquest of Central Europe* (1960).

Brown, J. F.: *The New Eastern Europe: The Khrushchev Era and After* (1966).

Burks, R. V.: *The Dynamics of Communism in Eastern Europe* (1961).

Gsovski, V. (ed.): *Church and State Behind the Iron Curtain: Czechoslovakia, Hungary, Poland, Romania, with an Introduction on the Soviet Union* (1955). A survey with extensive quotations from laws and decrees.

Gyorgy, A.: *Governments of Danubian Europe* (1949). Post-World War II governments.

————, et al.: *Soviet Satellites: Studies in Politics in Eastern Europe* (1949).

Ionescu, G.: *Breakup of the Soviet Empire* (1965).

————: *The Politics of the European Communist States* (1967).

Kertesz, S. D. (ed.): *East Central Europe and the World: Developments in the Post-Stalin Era* (1962).

————: *The Fate of East-Central Europe* (1956).

Meyer, P., et al.: *The Jews in the Soviet Satellites* (1953).

Osborne, R. H.: *East-Central Europe: An Introductory Geography* (1967).

Pounds, N. J. G.: *Eastern Europe* (1969).

Ripka, H.: *Eastern Europe in the Post-War World* (1961).

Rothschild, J.: *Communist Eastern Europe* (1964).

Roucek, J. S., and K. V. Lottich: *Behind the Iron Curtain; the Soviet Satellite States: East European Nationalisms and Education* (1964).

Sanders, I. T. (ed.): *Collectivization of Agriculture in Eastern Europe* (1958).

Seton-Watson, H.: *The East European Revolution* (3rd ed., 1956). One of the best reviews of the Iron Curtain countries.

Skilling, H. G.: *Communism National and International: Eastern Europe after Stalin* (1964).

Spulber, N.: *The Economies of Communist Eastern Europe* (1957).

Starr, R. F.: *The Communist Regimes of Eastern Europe* (1969).

Sztachova, J. (ed.): *Mid-Europe: A Selective Bibliography* (1953).

Tobias, R.: *Communist-Christian Encounter in Eastern Europe* (1956).

Wellisz, S.: *The Economies of the Soviet Bloc: A Study of Decision Making* (1964).

Zauberman, A.: *Industrial Development in Czechoslovakia, East Germany and Poland, 1937–56* (1958).

The Balkan States

Anderson, M. S.: *The Eastern Question, 1774–1923: A Study in International Relations* (1966).

Barker, E.: *Macedonia: Its Place in Balkan Power Politics* (1950). An objective study on a controversial area.

Geshkoff, T. I.: *Balkan Union: A Road to Peace in Southeastern Europe* (1940). A study of attempts at federation.

Hoffmann, G. W.: *The Balkans in Transition* (1963).

Iatrides, J. O.: *Balkan Triangle Birth and Decline of an Alliance Across Ideological Boundaries* (1968).
Jelavich, C., and B. Jelavich (eds.): *The Balkans in Transition: Essays in the Development of Balkan Life and Politics Since the Eighteenth Century* (1963).
Kerner, R. J., and H. N. Howard: *The Balkan Conferences and the Balkan Entente, 1930–1935* (1936).
Pribichevich, S.: *World Without End: The Saga of Southeastern Europe* (1940).
Schevill, F., and W. M. Gewehr: *A History of the Balkan Peninsula* (1933).
Stadtmüller, G.: *Geschichte Südosteuropas* (1950).
Stavrianos, L. S.: *Balkan Federation: A History of the Movement Toward Balkan Unity in Modern Times* (1944). Best study on this subject.
————: *The Balkans Since 1453* (1958). Has an extensive bibliography.
Wilkinson, H. R.: *Maps and Politics: A Review of the Ethnographical Cartography of Macedonia* (1952).
Wolff, R. L.: *The Balkans in Our Times* (1956).

Albania

Amery, J.: *The Sons of the Eagle: A Study in Guerrilla War* (1948).
Durham, M. E.: *High Albania* (1909).
————: *Some Tribal Origins, Laws and Customs of the Balkans* (1928).
————: *The Struggle for Scutari* (1914).
————: *Twenty Years of Balkan Tangle* (1920).
Frasheri, K.: *The History of Albania: A Brief Survey* (1964).
Griffith, W. E.: *Albania and the Sino-Soviet Rift* (1963).
Hamm, H.: *Albania—China's Beachhead in Europe* (1963).
Hasluck, M.: *The Unwritten Law in Albania* (1954). Describes the pre-Communist social structure.
Pano, N. C.: *The People's Republic of Albania* (1969).
Robinson, V.: *Albania's Road to Freedom* (1942). Largely descriptive.
Skendi, S. (ed.): *Albania* (1956). A handbook with bibliography.
————: *The Albanian National Awakening, 1878–1912* (1966).
Stickney, E. P.: *Southern Albania or Northern Epirus in European International Affairs, 1912–1913* (1926).
Swire, J.: *Albania* (1929).
————: *King Zog's Albania* (1937).
Thomas, J. I.: *Education for Communism. School and State in the People's Republic of Albania* (1969).

Austria

Allard, S.: *Russia and The Austrian State Treaty* (1968).
Bader, W. B.: *Austria Between East and West, 1945–1955* (1966).
Ball, M. M.: *Post-War German-Austrian Relations: The Anschluss Movement, 1918–1936* (1937). Impartial, with a good bibliography.
Braunthal, J.: *The Tragedy of Austria* (1948). Failure of Social Democracy, with an appendix on Dollfuss' role.
Burghardt, A. F.: *Borderland: A Historical and Geographical Study of Burgenland, Austria* (1962).
Buttinger, J.: *In the Twilight of Socialism: A History of the Revolutionary Socialists of Austria* (1953). A history of the Socialist underground from Dollfuss to Hitler.
Diamant, A.: *Austrian Catholics and the First Republic: Democracy, Capitalism, and the Social Order, 1918–1934* (1960).
Eichstadt, U.: *Von Dollfuss zu Hitler: Geschichte des Anschlusses Österreichs, 1933–1938* (1955).
Fraenkel, J. (ed.): *The Jews of Austria: Essays on their Life, History and Destruction* (1967).

Gehl, J.: *Austria, Germany, and the Anschluss, 1931–1938* (1963).

Gruber, K.: *Between Liberation and Liberty: Austria in the Post-War World* (1955).

Gulick, C. A.: *Austria from Habsburg to Hitler* (2 vols., 1948). Strong on the economic side, and written from a Socialist point of view.

Hiscocks, C. R.: *The Rebirth of Austria* (1953). A sympathetic account.

Kann, R. A.: *A Study in Austrian Intellectual History* (1960).

Latour, C. F.: *Südtirol und die Achse Berlin-Rome, 1938–1945* (1962).

Ludwig, E.: *Österreichs Sendung im Donauraum* (1954). Austrian domestic and foreign policy, 1918–1953.

Macdonald, M.: *The Republic of Austria, 1918–1934: A Study in the Failure of Democratic Government* (1946). Entirely political.

Rothschild, K. W.: *Austrian Economy Since 1945* (1951).

————: *Austria's Economic Development Between the Two Wars* (1947).

Rüdiger, E.: *Between Hitler and Mussolini: Memoirs of Ernst Rüdiger Prince Starhemberg* (1942). By the leader of the Heimwehr.

Schuschnigg, K.: *Austrian Requiem* (1947).

————: *My Austria* (1938).

Shell, K. L.: *The Transformation of Austrian Socialism* (1962).

Shepherd, G.: *The Anschluss* (1963).

————: *The Austrian Odyssey* (1957).

Siegler, H.: *Austrian Problems and Achievements* (1964).

Stadler, K. R.: *The Birth of the Austrian Republic, 1918–1921* (1966).

————: *Österreich 1938–1945 im Spiegel der NS-Akten* (1966).

Stearman, W. L.: *The Soviet Union and the Occupation of Austria: An Analysis of Soviet Policy in Austria, 1945–1955* (1961).

Strong, D. F.: *Austria, October 1918–March 1919* (1939). Scholarly account of the founding of the Republic.

Bulgaria

Black, C. E.: *The Establishment of Constitutional Government in Bulgaria* (1944).

Black, F. H.: *The American College of Sofia: A Chapter in American-Bulgarian Relations* (1958).

Brown, J. F.: *Bulgaria under Communist Rule* (1970).

Danailov, G. T.: *Les effets de la guerre an Bulgarie* (1932).

Dellin, L. A. D. (ed.): *Bulgaria* (1957). A handbook with bibliography.

Evans, S. G.: *A Short History of Bulgaria* (1960).

Genov, G. P.: *Bulgaria and the Treaty of Neuilly* (1935). Nationalistic but nevertheless informative.

Khristov, K., et al.: *A Short History of Bulgaria* (1963).

Logio, G. C.: *Bulgaria, Past and Present* (1936).

Manning, C.: *A History of Modern Bulgarian Literature* (1960).

Markham, R. H.: *Meet Bulgaria* (1931).

Muir, N.: *Dimitri Stancioff: Patriot and Cosmopolitan* (1957).

Pasvolsky, L.: *Bulgaria's Economic Position* (1930). A thorough study.

Pundeff, M. V.: *Bulgaria: A Bibliographic Guide* (1965). A valuable reference work, published by the Library of Congress.

Rothschild, J.: *The Communist Party of Bulgaria: Origins and Development 1883–1936* (1959).

Sipkov, I.: *Legal Sources and Bibliography of Bulgaria* (1956).

Swire, J.: *Bulgarian Conspiracy* (1940). An account of the IMRO.

Todorov, K.: *Balkan Firebrand: The Autobiography of a Rebel Soldier and Statesman* (1943). An account of Bulgarian politics by a leader of the Agrarian party.

Czechoslovakia

Beneš, E.: *Eduard Beneš in His Own Words: Three-score Years of a Statesman, Builder and Philosopher* (1945).

————: *Memoirs of Dr. Eduard Beneš: From Munich to New War and New Victory* (1954).

Busek, V., and N. Spulber (eds.): *Czechoslovakia* (1957). A handbook with bibliography.

Czechoslovak Academy of Sciences (Robert Littel, ed.): *The Czech Black Book* (1969). A day-by-day account of Russian intervention in 1968.

Jesina, C. (ed.): *The Birth of Czechoslovakia* (1968). A collection of documents and pictures.

Kerner, R. J. (ed.): *Czechoslovakia* (1940).

Kirschbaum, J. M.: *Slovakia: Nation at the Crossroads of Central Europe* (1960).

Korbel, J.: *The Communist Subversion of Czechoslovakia 1938–1948* (1959).

Lettrich, J.: *History of Modern Slovakia* (1955).

Löbl, E.: *Stalinism in Prague: The Löbl Story* (1967).

Luza, R.: *The Transfer of the Sudeten Germans: A Study of Czech-German Relations, 1933–1962* (1964).

Markus, V.: *L'Incorporation de L'Ukraine Subcarpathique à L'Ukraine Soviétique, 1944–1945* (1956).

Masaryk, T. G.: *The Making of a State: Memoirs and Observations, 1914–1918* (1927). The best book on the founding of Czechoslovakia.

Mikus, J. A.: *Slovakia: A Political History, 1918–1950* (1963).

Nemec, F.: *The Soviet Seizure of Subcarpathian Ruthenia* (1955).

Perman, D.: *The Shaping of the Czechoslovak State: Diplomatic History of the Boundaries of Czechoslovakia, 1914–20* (1962).

Raschhofer, H.: *Die Sudetenfrage: Ihre Voelkerrechtliche Entwicklung vom ersten Weltkrieg bis zur Gegenwart* (1953).

Remington, R. A. (ed.): *Winter in Prague: Documents on Czechoslovak Communism in Crisis* (1969).

Ripka, H.: *Czechoslovakia Enslaved: The Story of the Communist Coup d'Etat* (1950).

Schwartz, H.: *Prague's 200 Days: The Struggle for Democracy in Czechoslovakia* (1969).

Seton-Watson, R. W.: *A History of Czechs and Slovaks* (1943). A sympathetic account by a British expert.

Sturm, R.: *Czechoslovakia: A Bibliographic Guide* (1967).

Suda, Z.: *The Czechoslovak Socialist Republic* (1969).

Taborsky, E.: *Communism in Czechoslovakia, 1948–1960* (1961).

Textor, L. E.: *Land Reform in Czechoslovakia* (1923). An excellent objective study.

Thomson, S. H.: *Czechoslovakia in European History* (2nd ed., 1953).

Wanklyn, H.: *Czechoslovakia: A Geographical and Historical Study* (1954). An important study well supplied with maps.

Windsor, P.: *Czechoslovakia, 1968: Reform, Repression, and Resistance* (1969).

Wiskemann, E.: *Czechs and Germans* (1938).

Zeman, Z. A. B.: *Prague Spring* (1969).

Zinner, P. E.: *Communist Strategy and Tactics in Czechoslovakia, 1918–48* (1963).

Hungary

Aczél, T.: *The Revolt of the Mind: A Case History of Intellectual Resistance Behind the Iron Curtain* (1959).

———— (ed.): *Ten Years After; the Hungarian Revolution* (1966).

Bethlen, A.: *The Treaty of Trianon and European Peace* (1934).

Braham, R. L.: *The Hungarian Jewish Catastrophe; a Selected and Annotated Bibliography* (1962).

———— (ed.): *The Destruction of Hungarian Jewry; a Documentary Account* (2 vols., 1963).

Bucsay, M.: *Geschichte des Protestantismus in Ungarn* (1959).

Dreisziger, N. A. F.: *Hungary's Way to World War II* (1968).

Halász, Z. (ed.): *Hungary* (2nd ed., 1963). An official informative handbook.

Helmreich, E. C. (ed.): *Hungary* (1957). A handbook with bibliography.

Horthy, M.: *The Confidential Papers of Admiral Horthy* (1965).
———: *Memoirs* (1956).
Jászi, O.: *Revolution and Counter-Revolution in Hungary* (1924).
Kallay, N.: *Hungarian Premier: A Personal Account of a Nation's Struggle in the Second World War* (1954). Very informative.
Karolyi, M.: *Memoirs: Faith without Illusion* (1956).
Keeskemeti, P.: *The Unexpected Revolution: Social Forces in the Hungarian Uprising* (1961).
Kertesz, S. D.: *Diplomacy in a Whirlpool: Hungary between Nazi Germany and Soviet Russia* (1953). Foreign policy of Hungary in the interwar period.
Kovács, I. (ed.): *Facts about Hungary: The Fight for Freedom* (rev. ed., 1966).
Macartney, C. S.: *Hungary* (1934).
———: *Hungary and Her Successors: The Treaty of Trianon and Its Consequences, 1919–1937* (1937).
———: *Hungary: A Short History* (1962).
Nagy, I.: *Imre Nagy on Communism: In Defense of the New Course* (1957).
Nagy-Talavera, N. M.: *The Green Shirts and the Others: A History of Fascism in Hungary and Rumania* (1969).
Nyers, R.: *The Cooperative Movement in Hungary* (1963).
Seton-Watson, R. W.: *Treaty Revision and the Hungarian Frontiers* (1934). Opposed to revision.
Sinos, D.: *History of Hungary* (1959).
Tokes, R. L.: *Bela Kun and the Hungarian Soviet Republic; the Origins and Role of the Communist Party* (1967).
UN Special Committee on the Problem of Hungary: *Report* (1957).
Váli, F. A.: *Rift and Revolt in Hungary: Nationalism versus Communism* (1961).
Vambery, R.: *Hungary to Be or Not to Be* (1946). Critical.
Völgyes, I.: *The Hungarian Soviet Republic: 1919. An Evaluation and a Bibliography* (1969).
Zinner, P. E.: *Revolution in Hungary* (1962).

Rumania

Cretzianu, A. (ed.): *Captive Rumania: A Decade of Soviet Rule, 1945–1955* (1956).
———: *The Lost Opportunity* (1957). Much on Rumanian affairs during World War II.
Fischer-Galati, S. A.: *The New Rumania: From People's Democracy to Socialist Republic* (1967).
———: *Rumania. A Bibliographic Guide* (1963).
———: *The Socialist Republic of Rumania* (1969).
Floyd, D.: *Rumania, Russia's Dissident Ally* (1965).
Gafencu, G.: *Last Days of Europe: A Diplomatic Journey in 1939* (1948).
———: *Prelude to the Russian Campaign: From the Moscow Pact (August 21, 1939) to the Opening of Hostilities in Russia (June 22, 1941)* (1945).
Hillgruber, A.: *Hitler, König Carol and Marschall Antonescu: Die Deutsch-Rumänischen Beziehungen, 1938–1944* (1954). A good study, but written mostly from German sources.
Ionescu, G.: *Communism in Rumania, 1944–1962* (1964).
Iorga, N.: *A History of Roumania* (1926). By Rumania's great historian.
Marie, Queen of Rumania: *The Story of My Life* (1934).
Mitrany, D.: *The Land and the Peasant in Rumania* (1930). A good analysis.
Oprea, I. M.: *Nicholae Titulescu's Diplomatic Activity* (1968).
Pop, N.: *Kiriche unter Hammer und Sichel: Die Kirchenverfolgung in Rumänien, 1945–1951* (1953). Largely an account of the fate of the Uniate churches.
Roberts, H. L.: *Rumania: Political Problems of an Agrarian State* (1951). Chiefly on the interwar period.
Seton-Watson, R. W.: *A History of Roumania from Trajan to Trianon* (1934).

Spector, S. D.: *Rumania at the Paris Peace Conference; a Study of the Diplomacy of Ioan I. C. Bratianu* (1962).

Yugoslavia

Armstrong, H. F.: *Tito and Goliath* (1951). Tito and his relations with Russia.
Avakumovic, I.: *History of the Communist Party of Yugoslavia* (1964).
Baerlein, H.: *The Birth of Yugoslavia* (2 vols., 1922).
Bonifacić, A. (ed.): *The Croatian Nation in Its Struggle for Freedom and Independence* (1955).
Byrnes, R. F. (ed.): *Yugoslavia* (1957). A handbook with bibliography.
Campbell, J. C.: *Tito's Separate Road: America and Yugoslavia in World Politics* (1967).
Clissold, S.: *A Short History of Yugoslavia* (1967).
Darby, H. C., et al.: *A Short History of Yugoslavia from Early Times to 1966* (1966).
Djilas, M.: *Anatomy of a Moral* (1959).
——: *Conversations with Stalin* (1962).
——: *Land Without Justice* (1958).
——: *The New Class: An Analysis of the Communist System* (1957).
Dragnich, A. N.: *Tito's Promised Land: Yugoslavia* (1954). Critical of the new order.
Eterovich, F. H. (ed.): *Croatia: Land, People, Culture* (1964).
Fotitch, C.: *The War We Lost* (1948). By a former Yugoslav ambassador to the United States.
Halpern, J. M.: *A Serbian Village* (1958).
Hoffman, G. W., and F. W. Neal: *Yugoslavia and the New Communism* (1962).
Hoptner, J. B.: *Yugoslavia in Crisis, 1934–1941* (1962).
Kerner, R. J. (ed.): *Yugoslavia* (1949).
Korbel, J.: *Tito's Communism* (1951).
Kostelski, Z.: *The Yugoslavs: The History of the Yugoslavs and Their States to the Creation of Yugoslavia* (1952). Good on the history of the different provinces.
Maček, V.: *In the Struggle for Freedom* (1957). Memoirs.
Maclean, F.: *The Life and Times of Josip Broz-Tito* (1957).
McVicker, C. P.: *Titoism: Pattern for International Communism* (1957).
Neal, F. W.: *Titoism in Action* (1958).
Peter II, King of Yugoslavia: *A King's Heritage: Memoirs* (1955).
Ristić, D. N.: *Yugoslavia's Revolution in 1941* (1966).
Roberts, A.: *The Lottery that Killed a King: The Assassination of Louis Barthou and King Alexander I of Yugoslavia* (1970).
Tomasevich, J.: *Peasants, Politics and Economic Changes in Yugoslavia* (1955).
Trouton, R.: *Peasant Renaissance in Yugoslavia, 1900–50* (1950).
Ulam, A. B.: *Titoism and the Cominform* (1952).
Vucinich, W. S. (ed.): *Contemporary Yugoslavia: Twenty Years of Socialist Experiment* (1969).
West, R.: *Black Lamb and Grey Falcon: A Journey Through Yugoslavia* (2 vols., 1941). A classic travel account.
Yugoslavia's Way: The Program of the League of the Communists (1958). An official publication.
Zaninovich, M. G.: *The Development of Socialist Yugoslavia* (1969).

THE BALTIC REGION

General

Jackson, J. H.: *The Baltic* (1940).
Kirchner, W.: *The Rise of the Baltic Question* (1954).
Reddaway, W. F.: *Problems of the Baltic* (1940).
Tarulis, A. N.: *American-Baltic Relations, 1918–1920: The Struggle Over Recognition* (1965).

Warner, O.: *The Sea and the Sword: The Baltic, 1630–1945* (1965).
Wittram, R.: *Baltische Geschichte: Die Ostseelände: Livland, Estland, Kurland, 1180–1918* (1954).
Woods, E. G.: *The Baltic Region* (1932). Geographical background.

Finland

Gripenberg, G. A.: *Finland and the Great Powers, Memoirs of a Diplomat* (1965).
Jackson, J. H.: *Finland* (1938).
Jakobson, M.: *The Diplomacy of the Winter War: An Account of the Russo-Finnish Conflict, 1939–40* (1961).
————: *Finnish Neutrality: A Study of Finnish Foreign Policy Since the Second World War* (1969).
Jutikkala, E., and K. Pirinen: *A History of Finland* (1962).
Lundin, C. L.: *Finland in the Second World War* (1957).
Mazour, A. G.: *Finland Between East and West* (1956).
Mead, W. R.: *Finland* (1968).
Memoirs of Marshal Mannerheim (1954).
Rintala, M.: *Four Finns: Political Profiles* (1969). Political portraits of Mannerheim, Tannes, Stahlberg, and Paasikivi.
————: *Three Generations: The Extreme Right Wing in Finnish Politics* (1962).
Schwartz, A. J.: *America and the Russo-Finnish War* (1960).
Smith, C. J.: *Finland and the Russian Revolution, 1917–1922* (1958).
Tanner, V.: *The Winter War: Finland Against Russia, 1939–1940* (1957).
Upton, A. F.: *Finland in Crisis 1940–1945: A Study in Small Politics* (1964).
Wright, J. H.: *Finland: An Economic Survey* (1953).
Wuorinen, J. H. (ed.): *Finland and World War II, 1939–1944* (1948).
————: *A History of Finland* (1965).
————: *Nationalism in Modern Finland* (1931). A fundamental study of historical background.

The Baltic States

Berzins, A.: *The Unpunished Crime* (1963). An indictment of Soviet policy in Latvia.
Bilmanis, A.: *A History of Latvia* (1951). By a leading Latvian diplomat who represented his country in Moscow and Washington before World War II.
Kalijarvi, T. V.: *The Memel Statute: Its Origins, Legal Nature, and Observation to the Present Day* (1937).
Nodel, E.: *Estonia: Nation on the Anvil* (1963).
Page, S. W.: *The Formation of the Baltic States: A Study of the Effects of Great Power Politics upon the Emergence of Lithuania, Latvia, and Estonia* (1959).
Pick, F. W.: *The Baltic Nations: Estonia, Latvia, and Lithuania* (1945).
Royal Institute of International Affairs: *The Baltic States* (1938). An excellent study.
Senn, A. E.: *The Emergence of Modern Lithuania* (1959).
————: *The Great Powers, Lithuania and The Vilna Question, 1920–1928* (1968).
Spekke, A.: *History of Latvia: An Outline* (1951).
Swettenham, J. A.: *The Tragedy of the Baltic States* (1952). Mostly on World War II and after.
Tarulis, A. N.: *Soviet Policy Toward the Baltic States, 1918–1940* (1959).
Urch, R. O. G.: *Latvia: Country and People* (1938).
Uristalu, E.: *The History of the Estonian People* (1952).
Vardys, V. S. (ed.): *Lithuania Under the Soviets: Portrait of a Nation, 1940–65* (1965).
Watson, H. A.: *The Latvian Republic: The Struggle for Freedom* (1965).

Poland

Bor-Komorowski, T.: *The Secret Army* (1951).
Budurowycz, B. B.: *Polish-Soviet Relations, 1932–1939* (1963).

Ciechanowski, J.: *Defeat in Victory* (1947). Memoirs of the Polish wartime ambassador in Washington.

Cienciala, A. M.: *Poland and the Western Powers, 1938–1939: A Study in the Interdependence of Eastern and Western Europe* (1968).

Cyprian, T.: *Nazi Rule in Poland, 1939–1945* (1961).

Debicki, R. (ed.): *Foreign Policy of Poland, 1919–59: From the Rebirth of the Polish Republic to World War II* (1962).

Dziewanowski, M. K.: *The Communist Party of Poland* (1959).

———: *Joseph Pilsudski: European Federalist* (1969).

Gross, F.: *The Polish Worker: A Study of a Social Stratum* (1945).

Halecki, O.: *A History of Poland* (1956). By a leading Polish historian.

——— (ed.): *Poland* (1957). A handbook with bibliography.

Heymann, F. G.: *Poland and Czechoslovakia* (1966).

Hiscocks, R.: *Poland: Bridge for the Abyss? An Interpretation of Developments in Post-War Poland* (1963).

Horak, S.: *Poland's International Affairs, 1919–1960* (1964).

Jordan, Z.: *The Oder-Neisse Line* (1952). A study of the Polish-German frontier.

Korbel, J.: *Poland Between East and West: Soviet and German Diplomacy Toward Poland, 1919–1933* (1963).

Korbonski, A.: *Politics of Socialist Agriculture in Poland: 1945–1960* (1965).

Korbonski, S.: *The Story of the Polish Underground State, 1939–1945* (1956).

Lane, A. B.: *I Saw Poland Betrayed: An American Ambassador Reports to the American People* (1948).

Mikolajczyk, S.: *The Rape of Poland: Pattern of Soviet Aggression* (1948). By the exiled leader of the Polish Peasant party.

Morrison, J. F.: *The Polish People's Republic* (1969).

Pilsudska, A.: *Pilsudski: A Biography by His Wife* (1941).

Reddaway, W. F., et al. (eds.): *The Cambridge History of Poland* (2 vols., 1941–50).

Roos, H. (trans. by J. R. Foster): *A History of Modern Poland from the Foundation of the State in the First World War to the Present Day* (1966).

Rothschild, J.: *Pilsudski's Coup d'Etat* (1966).

Rozek, E. J.: *Allied Wartime Diplomacy: A Pattern in Poland* (1958).

Sharp, S. L.: *Poland: White Eagle on a Red Field* (1953). Critical of interwar Poland.

Staar, R. F.: *Poland, 1944–1962: The Sovietization of a Captive People* (1962).

Stankiewicz, W. J., and J. M. Montias: *Institutional Changes in the Postwar Economy of Poland* (1955).

Stypulkowski, Z.: *Invitation to Moscow* (1951). By a Polish leader who attempted to work with the Russians.

Syrok, K.: *Spring in October: The Story of the Polish Revolution, 1956* (1957).

Taylor, J.: *The Economic Development of Poland, 1919–1950* (1952).

Umiastowski, R.: *Poland, Russia, and Great Britain, 1941–1945: A Study of Evidence* (1946).

Wandycz, P. S.: *Soviet-Polish Relations, 1917–1921* (1969).

Zawodny, P. E.: *Death in the Forest: The Story of the Katyn Forest Massacre* (1962).

Zielinski, H.: *Population Changes in Poland, 1939–1950* (1954).

Ziffer, B.: *Poland: History and Historians* (1952).

Zoltowski, A.: *A Border of Europe: A Study of the Polish Eastern Provinces* (1950).

THE SOVIET UNION

General

Black, C. E. (ed.): *Rewriting Russian History: Soviet Interpretations of Russia's Past* (rev. ed., 1962).

——— (ed.): *The Transformation of Russian Society: Aspects of Social Change Since 1861* (1960).

Curtiss, J. S. (ed.): *Essays in Russian and Soviet History* (1963).

Daniels, R. V.: *Russia* (1964).

Fisher, H. H. (ed.): *American Research on Russia* (1959).

Florinsky, M. T.: *Russia: An Interpretation* (2 vols., 1953). The best general history in English of the period to 1917.

————: *Russia: A Short History* (1964).

Masaryk, T. G.: *The Spirit of Russia* (2 vols., 2nd ed., 1955).

Morley, C.: *Guide to Research in Russian History* (1951). A valuable handbook.

Outline History of the U.S.S.R. (1960). Translation of a Soviet textbook.

Riasanovsky, N. V.: *A History of Russia* (1963).

Seton-Watson, H. *The Russian Empire, 1801–1917* (1967).

Shapiro, D.: *A Select Bibliography of Works in English on Russian History, 1801–1917* (1962).

Simmons, E. J. (ed.): *Continuity and Change in Russian and Soviet Thought* (1955).

Smirnov, I. I. (ed.): *A Short History of the U.S.S.R.* (2 vols., 1965). A Soviet interpretation.

Sumner, B. H.: *A Short History of Russia* (1944).

Treadgold, D. W.: *Twentieth Century Russia* (1964).

Last Years of the Empire

Baron, S. H.: *Plekhanov: The Father of Russian Marxism* (1963).

Byrnes, R. F.: *Pobedonostsev: His Life and Thought* (1968).

Curtiss, J. S.: *Church and State in Russia: The Last Years of the Empire, 1900–1917* (1940).

Fischer, G.: *Russian Liberalism: From Gentry to Intelligentsia* (1958).

Florinsky, M. T.: *The End of the Russian Empire* (1951).

Gurko, V. I.: *Features and Figures of the Past: Government and Opinion in the Reign of Nicholas II* (1939).

Haimson, L. H.: *The Russian Marxists and the Origins of Bolshevism* (1955). With special reference to the period before 1905.

Harcave, S. S.: *First Blood: The Russian Revolution of 1905* (1964).

Kokovtsov, V. M.: *Out of My Past* (1935). By the Russian minister of finance, 1904–14.

Leroy-Beaulieu, A.: *The Empire of the Tsars and the Russians* (3 vols., 1893–1902).

Levin, A.: *The Second Duma: A Study of the Social-Democratic Party and the Russian Constitutional Experiment* (1940).

Lyashchenko, P. I.: *History of the National Economy of Russia to the 1917 Revolution* (1949). A standard account by a Soviet scholar.

Mendel, A. P.: *Dilemmas of Progress in Tsarist Russia: Legal Marxism and Legal Populism* (1961).

Miliukov, P.: *Russia and Its Crisis* (1905). On the revolution of 1905.

————: *Political Memoirs, 1905–1917* (1967).

Owen, L. A.: *The Russian Peasant Movement, 1900–1917* (1937).

Pares, B.: *The Fall of the Russian Monarchy* (1939).

Pavlovsky, G.: *Agricultural Russia on the Eve of the Revolution* (1930).

Pobyedonosteff, K. P.: *Reflections of a Russian Statesman* (1898). Memoirs of one of the leading Russian conservatives in the last years of the empire.

Robinson, G. T.: *Rural Russia Under the Old Regime* (new ed., 1949).

Schwarz, H.: *The Russian Revolution of 1905* (1966).

Seton-Watson, R. W.: *The Decline of Imperial Russia, 1855–1914* (1952).

Stavrou, Theofanis (ed.): *Russia Under the Last Tsar* (1969). Topical essays.

Tcharykov, N. V.: *Glimpses of High Politics: Through War and Peace, 1855–1929* (1931).

Treadgold, D. W.: *Lenin and His Rivals: The Struggle for Russia's Future, 1898–1906* (1956).

Von Laue, T. H.: *Sergei Witte and the Industrialization of Russia* (1963).

Wallace, D. M.: *Russia* (rev. ed., 1912).

Witte, S.: *Memoirs* (1921). The leading Russian statesman at the turn of the century.

Russian Revolution

Abramovich, R. R.: *The Soviet Revolution, 1917–1939* (1962).

Browder, R. P., and A. F. Kerensky (eds.): *The Russian Provisional Government, 1917: Documents* (3 vols., 1961). A valuable collection of sources, many translated for the first time.

Bullitt, W. C.: *The Bullitt Mission to Russia* (1919). A first-hand account of the beginnings of Soviet-American relations.

Carr, E. H.: *The Bolshevik Revolution, 1917–1923* (3 vols., 1951–53). Volumes I–III in his *History of Soviet Russia.*

Carroll, E. M.: *Soviet Communism and Western Opinion, 1919–1921* (1965).

Chamberlin, W. H.: *The Russian Revolution, 1917–21* (2 vols., 1935). An able account by an American journalist.

Chernov, V.: *The Great Russian Revolution* (1936). By a leader of the Socialist Revolutionary party.

Curtiss, J. S.: *The Russian Revolution of 1917* (1957). A brief interpretation.

Daniels, Robert V.: *Red October: The Bolshevik Revolution of 1917* (1967).

Deutscher, I.: *The Prophet Armed: Trotsky, 1879–1921* (1954).

———: *The Prophet Unarmed: Trotsky, 1921–1929* (1959).

———: *The Prophet Outcast: Trotsky, 1929–1940* (1963).

Farnsworth, B.: *William C. Bullitt and the Soviet Union* (1967).

Ferro, M.: *La revolution de 1917* (1967).

Fleming, P.: *The Fate of Admiral Kolchak* (1963).

Footman, D.: *Civil War in Russia* (1961).

Francis, D. R.: *Russia From the American Embassy* (1921). An account by the American ambassador, 1916–18.

Katkov, G.: *Russia 1917: The February Revolution* (1967).

Kazemzadeh, F.: *The Struggle for Transcaucasia, 1917–1921* (1951).

Kennan, G. F.: *The Decision to Intervene* (1958). This and the following volume are part of a multivolume history of Soviet-American relations, 1917–1920.

———: *Russia Leaves the War* (1956).

Kerensky, A. F.: *Russia and History's Turning Point* (1965).

Pipes, R.: *The Formation of the Soviet Union: Communism and Nationalism, 1917–1923* (rev. ed., 1964).

——— (ed.): *Revolutionary Russia* (1968).

Rabinowitch, A.: *Prelude to Revolution: The Petrograd Bolsheviks and the July 1917 Uprising* (1968).

Radkey, O. H.: *The Agrarian Foes of Bolshevism: Promise and Default of the Russian Socialist Revolutionaries, February to October, 1917* (1958).

———: *The Election to the Russian Constituent Assembly of 1917* (1950).

Reed, J.: *Ten Days That Shook the World* (1926). A sympathetic account by an American journalist.

Reshetar, J. S., Jr.: *The Ukrainian Revolution, 1917–1920* (1952).

Rodzianko, M. V.: *The Reign of Rasputin* (1927). Memoirs of the leader of the Octobrist party.

Serge, V.: *Memoirs of a Revolutionary, 1901–1941* (1963).

Sobolev, P. M. (ed.): *History of the October Revolution* (1966). The Soviet interpretation.

Stewart, G.: *The White Armies of Russia: A Chronicle of Counter-Revolution and Allied Intervention* (1933).

Sukhanov, M. N.: *The Russian Revolution, 1917: A Personal Record* (1955).

Trotsky, L.: *History of the Russian Revolution* (3 vols., 1934). By the organizer of the Red Army.

Ullman, R. H.: *Intervention and the War: Anglo-Soviet Relations, 1917–1921* (3 vols., 1961–72).

Unterberger, B. M.: *America's Siberian Adventure, 1918–1920: A Study of National Policy* (1956).

Von Laue, T. H.: *Why Lenin? Why Stalin? A Reappraisal of the Russian Revolution,
     1900–1930* (1964).
Warth, R. D.: *The Allies and the Russian Revolution* (1954).
White, J. A.: *The Siberian Intervention* (1950).
Woytinsky, W. S.: *Stormy Passage: A Personal History through Two Russian Revolu-
     tions to Democracy and Freedom, 1905–1960* (1961).

Ideology and Politics

Armstrong, J. A.: *The Politics of Totalitarianism: The Communist Party of the
     Soviet Union from 1934 to the Present* (1961).
————: *Ukrainian Nationalism, 1939–1945* (1955).
Barghoorn, F. C.: *Soviet Russian Nationalism* (1956).
Berdyaev, N.: *Origin of Russian Communism* (1937).
Brzezinski, Z.: *Ideology and Power in Soviet Politics* (1962).
————: *The Permanent Purge: Politics in Soviet Totalitarianism* (1956).
————, and S. P. Huntington: *Political Power: USA/USSR* (1964). An original and
     stimulating comparative study.
Carr, E. H.: *The Interregnum, 1923–24* (1954). Volume IV in his *History of Soviet
     Russia.*
————: *Socialism in One Country, 1924–26* (2 vols., 1958–59). Volumes V and VI
     in his *History of Soviet Russia.*
Carroll, E. M.: *Soviet Communism and Western Opinion 1919–1921* (1965).
Conquest, R.: *Power and Policy in the U.S.S.R.: The Struggle for Stalin's Succession,
     1945–1960* (1967).
————: *The Great Terror: Stalin's Purge of the Thirties* (1968).
Daniels, R. V.: *The Conscience of the Revolution: Communist Opposition in Soviet
     Russia* (1960).
Denisov, A., and M. Kirichenko: *Soviet State Law* (1960). A Soviet text in political
     science.
Deutscher, I.: *Stalin: A Political Biography* (1949).
Fainsod, M.: *How Russia Is Ruled* (rev. ed., 1963). The standard account of the
     Soviet political system.
————: *Smolensk Under Soviet Rule* (1958).
Fischer, G.: *Soviet Opposition to Stalin: A Case Study in World War II* (1952).
Fischer, L.: *The Life of Lenin* (1964).
————: *Men and Politics* (1941). By one of the best-informed American journalists
     in the USSR in the 1930s.
Frankland, M.: *Khrushchev* (1967).
Fundamentals of Marxism-Leninism (rev. ed., 1963). Official version of the Soviet
     ideology.
Gehlen, M. P.: *The Communist Party of the Soviet Union* (1969).
Hazard, J. N.: *The Soviet System of Government* (rev. ed., 1964).
History of the Communist Party of the Soviet Union (1960). The Soviet account.
Howe, I. (ed.): *The Basic Writings of Trotsky* (1963).
Hunt, R. N. C.: *The Theory and Practice of Communism* (1950).
Leites, N.: *A Study of Bolshevism* (1953).
Lenin, V. I.: *Selected Works* (12 vols., 1935–36).
Linden, C. A.: *Khrushchev and the Soviet Leadership 1957–1964* (1966).
Marcuse, H.: *Soviet Marxism: A Critical Analysis* (1958).
Meyer, A. G.: *Leninism* (1957).
Moore, B., Jr.: *Soviet Politics: The Dilemma of Power* (1950).
————: *Terror and Progress U.S.S.R.: Some Sources of Change and Stability in the
     Soviet Dictatorship* (1954).
Payne, R.: *The Life and Death of Lenin* (1964).
Pethybridge, R.: *A Key to Soviet Politics: The Crisis of the Anti-Party Group* (1962).
Ploss, S. I.: *Conflict and Decision-Making in Soviet Russia: A Case Study of Agricul-
     tural Policy, 1953–1963* (1965).

Possony, S. T.: *Lenin: The Compulsive Revolutionary* (1964).
Rigby, T. H.: *Communist Party Membership in the U.S.S.R., 1917–1967* (1968).
————: *Stalin* (1968).
Rush, M.: *Political Succession in the U.S.S.R.* (1965).
Schapiro, L. B.: *The Communist Party of the Soviet Union* (1960).
————: *The Origin of Communist Autocracy: Political Opposition in the Soviet State, First Phase, 1917–1922* (1965).
———— (ed.): *The U.S.S.R. and the Future: An Analysis of the New Program of the CPSU* (1962).
Schlesinger, R.: *Soviet Legal Theory* (1946).
Scott, D. J. R.: *Russian Political Institutions* (1958).
Selznik, P.: *The Organizational Weapon: A Study of Bolshevik Strategy and Tactics* (1952).
Shub, D.: *Lenin: A Biography* (1948).
Smith, E. E.: *The Young Stalin: The Early Years of an Elusive Revolutionary* (1967).
Stalin, J. V.: *Works* (13 vols., 1952–55). Official edition of Stalin's writings to 1934.
Swearer, H. R.: *The Politics of Succession in the U.S.S.R.* (1964).
Tatu, M.: *Power in the Kremlin: From Khrushchev to Kosygin* (1969).
Triska, J. F. (ed.): *Soviet Communism: Programs and Rules* (1962).
Tucker, R. C., and S. F. Cohen: *The Great Purge Trial* (1965).
Ulam, A. B.: *The Bolsheviks: The Intellectual and Political History of the Triumph of Communism in Russia* (1965).
Vakar, N. P.: *Belorussia: The Making of a Nation* (1956).
Vyshinsky, A. Y.: *The Law of the Soviet State* (1948). An official statement of the Soviet view in the Stalin era.
Wolfe, B. D.: *Three Who Made a Revolution* (1948). The lives of Lenin, Trotsky, and Stalin in the prerevolutionary period.
Wolin, S., and R. W. Slusser (eds.): *The Soviet Secret Police* (1957).

Society and Economics

Bacon, E.: *Central Asians Under Russian Rule: Study in Culture Change* (1966).
Bauer, R. A.: *The New Man in Soviet Psychology* (1952).
————, A. Inkeles, and C. Kluckhohn: *How the Soviet System Works* (1956).
Beck, F., and W. Godin: *Russian Purge and the Extraction of Confession* (1951).
Bergson, A. (ed.): *Soviet Economic Growth: Conditions and Perspectives* (1953).
————, and S. Kuznets (eds.): *Economic Trends in the Soviet Union* (1963).
Berliner, J. S.: *Factory and Management in the U.S.S.R.* (1957).
Bunyan, J.: *The Origin of Forced Labor in the Soviet Union, 1917–1921* (1967).
Cang, J.: *The Silent Millions: A History of the Jews in the Soviet Union* (1968).
Curtiss, J. S.: *The Russian Church and the Soviet State* (1953).
Erlich, V.: *The Soviet Industrialization Debate, 1924–1928* (1960).
Field, M. G.: *Soviet Socialized Medicine* (1967).
Fisher, R. T.: *Pattern for Soviet Youth* (1959).
Fletcher, W. C., and A. J. Strover (eds.): *Religion and the Search for New Ideals in the U.S.S.R.* (1967).
Granick, D.: *Management of the Industrial Firm in the U.S.S.R.* (1954).
Gregory, J. S.: *Russian Land, Soviet People* (1968). A geography.
Hazard, J. N.: *Law and Social Change in the U.S.S.R.* (1953).
Hodgman, D. R.: *Soviet Industrial Production, 1928–1951* (1954).
Inkeles, A.: *Public Opinion in Soviet Russia* (1950).
————, and R. A. Bauer: *The Soviet Citizen: Daily Life in a Totalitarian Society* (1959).
Karcz, J. F. (ed.): *Soviet and East European Agriculture* (1967).
Kolarz, W.: *Religion in the Soviet Union* (1961).
Lewin, M.: *Russian Peasants and Soviet Power* (1968).
Liberman, S. I.: *Building Lenin's Russia* (1945).
Lorimer, F.: *The Population of the Soviet Union: History and Prospects* (1946).

Maynard, J.: *Russia in Flux* (1946).
Nutter, G. W.: *Growth of Industrial Production in the Soviet Union* (1962).
Pipes, R. (ed.): *The Russian Intelligentsia* (1961).
Reshetar, J. S., Jr.: *Problems of Analyzing and Predicting Soviet Behavior* (1955).
Sakharov, A. D. (annotated by H. E. Salisbury): *Progress, Coexistence, and Intellectual Freedom* (1970). Unorthodox views of a Soviet scientist.
Schlesinger, R.: *The Family in the U.S.S.R.* (1949).
———— (ed.): *The Nationalities Problem and Soviet Administration* (1956).
Schwartz, H.: *The Soviet Economy Since Stalin* (1965).
Simmons, E. J. (ed.): *Through the Glass of Soviet Literature: Views of Russian Society* (1953).
Sorlin, P.: *The Soviet People and Their Society from 1917 to the Present* (1968).
Spulber, M.: *The Soviet Economy: Structure, Principles, Problems* (1962).
Strauss, E.: *Soviet Agriculture in Perspective: A Study of Its Successes and Failures* (1969).
Stroyen, W. B.: *Communist Russia and the Russian Orthodox Church 1943–1962* (1967).
Sutton, A. C.: *Western Technology and Soviet Economic Development, 1917 to 1930* (1968).
Timasheff, N. S.: *The Great Retreat: The Growth and Decline of Communism in Russia* (1946).
————: *Religion in Soviet Russia, 1917–1942* (1942).
Volin, L.: *A Century of Russian Agriculture: From Alexander Second to Khrushchev* (1970).
Yarmolinsky, A.: *Literature under Communism* (1960).
Zaleski, E.: *Planning Reforms in the Soviet Union, 1962–1966* (1967).

Foreign Policy and International Communism

Allard, S.: *Russia and the Austrian State Treaty* (1970).
Aspaturian, V. V.: *The Union Republics in Soviet Diplomacy: A Study of Soviet Federalism in the Service of Soviet Foreign Policy* (1960).
Barghoorn, F. C.: *The Soviet Cultural Offensive* (1960).
————: *The Soviet Image of the United States* (1950).
————: *Soviet Foreign Propaganda* (1964).
Beloff, M.: *The Foreign Policy of Soviet Russia, 1929–41* (2 vols., 1947–49).
Bishop, D. G.: *The Roosevelt-Litvinov Agreements. The American View* (1965).
Black, C. E., and T. P. Thornton (eds.): *Communism and Revolution: The Strategic Uses of Political Violence* (1964).
Borkenau, F.: *European Communism* (1953).
Browder, R. P.: *The Origins of Soviet-American Diplomacy* (1953).
Brzezinski, Z.: *The Soviet Bloc: Unity and Conflict* (1960).
Cattell, D. T.: *Soviet Diplomacy and the Spanish Civil War* (1957).
Dallin, A.: *German Rule in Russia, 1941–1945* (1957).
Deane, J. R.: *The Strange Alliance: The Story of Our Efforts at Wartime Cooperation With Russia* (1947).
Degras, J.: *The Communist International, 1919–1943: Documents* (2 vols., 1956–60).
———— (ed.): *Soviet Documents on Foreign Policy* (3 vols., 1951–53). A fundamental collection.
Dennett, R., and J. E. Johnson (eds.): *Negotiating with the Russians* (1951).
Fischer, L.: *Russia's Road from Peace to War: Soviet Foreign Relations, 1917–1941* (1969).
————: *The Soviets in World Affairs: A History of the Relations Between the Soviet Union and the Rest of the World, 1917–1929* (2 vols., 2nd ed., 1951).
Gankin, O. H., and H. H. Fisher: *The Bolsheviks and the World War: The Origins of the Third International* (1940).
Garthoff, R. L.: *Soviet Military Doctrine* (1953).
————: *Soviet Strategy in the Nuclear Age* (1958).

Graubard, S. R.: *British Labour and the Russian Revolution, 1917–1924* (1956).
Hammond, T. T. (ed.): *Soviet Foreign Relations and World Communism* (1965). A selected, annotated bibliography of 7,000 books in thirty languages. An outstanding reference work.
Hilger, G., and A. G. Meyer: *The Incompatible Allies: A Memoir-History of German-Soviet Relations, 1918–1941* (1953).
Kapur, H.: *Soviet Russia and Asia 1917–1927: A Study of Soviet Policy Towards Turkey, Iran, Afghanistan* (1967).
Kennan, G. F.: *Russia and the West under Lenin and Stalin* (1961).
———: *Soviet Foreign Policy, 1917–1941* (1960).
Kulski, W. W.: *Peaceful Co-existence: An Analysis of Soviet Foreign Policy* (1959).
Lederer, I. J. (ed.): *Russian Foreign Policy: Essays in Historical Perspective* (1962).
Mackintosh, J. M.: *Strategy and Tactics of Soviet Foreign Policy* (1962).
McLane, C. B.: *Soviet Policy and the Chinese Communists, 1931–1946* (1958).
Mosely, P. E.: *The Kremlin in World Politics* (1960).
North, R. C.: *Moscow and the Chinese Communists* (2nd ed., 1963).
Pethybridge, R. (ed.): *The Development of the Communist Bloc* (1965).
Possony, S. T.: *A Century of Conflict: Communist Techniques of World Revolution* (1953).
Rubinstein, A. Z.: *The Soviets in International Organizations* (1964).
Salisbury, H. E.: *War Between Russia and China* (1969).
Seton-Watson, H.: *From Lenin to Malenkov: The History of World Communism* (1953).
Shulman, M. D.: *Stalin's Foreign Policy Reappraised* (1963).
Smith, W. B.: *My Three Years in Moscow* (1950). Memoirs of the American ambassador, 1946–49.
Stettinius, E. R.: *Roosevelt and the Russians: The Yalta Conference* (1949). By the American Secretary of State, 1944–45.
Thompson, J. M.: *The Russian Problem at the Paris Peace Conference, 1919* (1966).
Thornton, T. P. (ed.): *The Third World in Soviet Perspective* (1964).
Treadgold, D. W. (ed.): *Soviet and Chinese Communism: Similarities and Differences* (1967).
Triska, J. F., and R. M. Slusser: *The Theory, Law and Policy of Soviet Treaties* (1962).
Werth, A.: *Russia at War, 1941–1945* (1964).
White, J. A.: *The Diplomacy of the Russo-Japanese War* (1964).
Wolfe, T. W.: *Soviet Power and Europe, 1945–1970* (1970).
Zagoria, D. S.: *The Sino-Soviet Conflict, 1956–1961* (1962).

THE EASTERN MEDITERRANEAN REGION

General

Belot, R.: *The Struggle for the Mediterranean, 1939–1945* (1952).
Davison, R. H.: *The Near and Middle East: An Introduction to History and Bibliography* (1959).
De Novo, J. A.: *American Interests and Policies in the Middle East, 1900–1939* (1963).
Fisher, S. N.: *The Military in the Middle East: Problems in Society and Government* (1963).
——— (ed.): *Social Forces in the Middle East* (1955).
Fisher, W. B.: *The Middle East: A Physical, Social, and Regional Geography* (4th ed., 1961).
Halpern, M.: *The Politics of Social Change in the Middle East and North Africa* (1963).
Hudson, G. F.: *Turkey, Greece and the Eastern Mediterranean* (1939).
Hurewitz, J. C.: *Diplomacy in the Near and Middle East: A Documentary Record* (2 vols., 1956). The second volume covers the period 1914–56.

————: *Middle East Politics* (1968).
Karpat, K. H. (ed.): *Political and Social Thought in the Contemporary Middle East* (1968).
Kirk, G. E.: *A Short History of the Middle East* (1964).
Lenczowski, G.: *The Middle East in World Affairs* (3rd ed., 1962).
Lerner, D., et al.: *The Passing of Traditional Society: Modernizing the Middle East* (1958).
Lewis, B.: *The Middle East and the West* (1964).
Love, K.: *Suez: The Twice-Fought War. A History* (1969).
Marlowe, J.: *World Ditch; the Making of the Suez Canal* (1964).
Marriott, J. A. R.: *The Eastern Question* (4th ed., 1940).
Merlin, S.: *The Big Powers and the Present Crisis in the Middle East* (1968).
Miller, H. C. M.: *Constitutions, Electoral Laws, Treaties of States in the Near and Middle East* (1947).
Miller, W.: *The Ottoman Empire and Its Successors, 1801–1927, with an Appendix, 1927–36* (4th ed., 1936).
Nevakivi, J.: *Britain, France, and the Arab Middle East, 1914–1920* (1969).
Playfair, T. S. O.: *The Mediterranean and the Middle East* (1954).
Polk, W. R.: *The United States and the Arab World* (1969).
Reitzel, W.: *The Mediterranean: Its Role in American Foreign Policy* (1948).
Royal Institute of International Affairs: *The Middle East: A Political and Economic Survey* (2nd ed., 1954).
Sachar, H. M.: *The Emergence of the Middle East 1914–1924* (1969).
Speiser, E. A.: *The United States and the Near East* (1947).
Spencer, W.: *Political Evolution in the Middle East* (1962).
Stavrianos, L. S.: *The Balkans Since 1453* (1958). A valuable survey, with a good account of Greece.
Walker, D. S.: *The Mediterranean Lands* (2nd ed., 1962).
Warriner, D.: *Land and Poverty in the Middle East* (1948).

The Arabs and Islam

Abu-Lughod, I. (ed.): *The Arab-Israeli Confrontation of 1967* (1970).
Antonius, G.: *The Arab Awakening: The Story of the Arab National Movement* (1939).
Atiyah, E. S.: *The Arabs* (1955).
Berger, M.: *The Arab World Today* (1962). A comprehensive survey.
Brace, R. M.: *Morocco, Algeria, Tunisia* (1964).
Brockelman, C.: *History of the Islamic Peoples* (1947).
Faris, N. A., and M. T. Husayn: *The Crescent in Crisis: An Interpretive Study of the Modern Arab World* (1955).
Flory, M.: *Les Régimes politiques des pays arabes* (1968).
Frye, R. N. (ed.): *Islam and the West* (1957).
Gallagher, C. F.: *The United States and North Africa: Morocco, Algeria and Tunisia* (1963).
Gibb, H. A. R.: *Modern Trends in Islam* (2nd ed., 1950).
Hazard, H. W.: *Atlas of Islamic History* (1951).
Hitti, P. K.: *The Arabs: A Short History* (rev. ed., 1949).
————: *History of the Arabs* (8th ed., 1963). The standard work.
Hollingworth, C.: *The Arabs and the West* (1952).
Hourani, A. H.: *Minorities in the Arab World* (1947).
Kerr, M. H.: *The Arab Cold War, 1958–1967* (1967).
Khadduri, M.: *Modern Libya: A Study in Political Development* (1963).
Lawrence, T. E.: *Seven Pillars of Wisdom* (1935). Dramatic memoirs of one of the organizers of the Arab uprising in World War I.
Lewis, B.: *The Arabs in History* (1962).
MacDonald, R. W.: *The League of Arab States: A Study in the Dynamics of Regional Organization* (1965).

Musrey, A. G.: *An Arab Common Market: A Study in Inter-Arab Trade Relations, 1920–1967* (1969).
Nuseibeh, H. Z.: *The Ideas of Arab Nationalism* (1956).
Smith, W. C.: *Islam in Modern History* (1957). The best general introduction.

Greece

Allborough, L. G.: *Crete: A Case Study of an Underdeveloped Area* (1953).
Andréadès, A.: *Les effets économiques et sociaux de la guerre en Grèce* (1928).
Campbell, J., and P. Sherrard: *Modern Greece* (1968).
Carey, J. P. C.: *The Web of Modern Greek Politics* (1968).
Chandler, G.: *A Divided Land: An Anglo-Greek Tragedy* (1959).
Forster, E. S.: *A Short History of Modern Greece, 1821–1940* (1941).
Kaltchas, N.: *Introduction to the Constitutional History of Modern Greece* (1940).
Kousoulas, D. G.: *The Price of Freedom: Greece in World Affairs, 1939–1953* (1953).
———: *Revolution and Defeat: The Story of the Greek Communist Party* (1965).
Legg, K. R.: *Politics in Modern Greece* (1969).
Mavrogordato, J.: *Modern Greece, 1800–1931* (1931).
McNeill, W. H.: *Greece: American Aid in Action, 1947–1956* (1957).
———: *The Greek Dilemma: War and Aftermath* (1947).
O'Ballance, E.: *The Greek Civil War, 1944–1949* (1966).
Psomiades, H. J.: *The Eastern Question: The Last Phase. A Study in Greek-Turkish Diplomacy* (1968).
Sophocles, S. M.: *A History of Greece* (1961).
Stavrianos, L. S.: *Greece: American Dilemma and Opportunity* (1952).
Sweet-Escott, B.: *Greece: A Political and Economic Survey, 1939–1953* (1954).
Woodhouse, C. M.: *Apple of Discord: A Survey of Recent Greek Politics in Their International Setting* (1948).
Xydis, S. G.: *Greece and the Great Powers, 1944–1947* (1963).

Cyprus

Alastos, D.: *Cyprus in History* (1955).
Arnold, P.: *Cyprus Challenge: A Colonial Island and Its Aspirations* (1956).
Grivas, G.: *General Grivas on Guerrilla Warfare* (1964).
Hill, S. F.: *A History of Cyprus* (4 vols., 1940–52).
Lee, D. E.: *Great Britain and the Cyprus Convention Policy of 1878* (1934). A fundamental study.
Mayes, S.: *Cyprus and Makarios* (1960).
Newman, P.: *A Short History of Cyprus* (1940).
Purcell, H. D.: *Cyprus* (1969).
Royal Institute of International Affairs: *Cyprus: Background to Enosis* (1957). A brief but informative statement of the British viewpoint.
Turkey and Cyprus: A Survey of the Cyprus Question with Official Statements of the Turkish Viewpoint (1956).

Turkey

Ahmad, F.: *The Young Turks, the Committee of Union and Progress in Turkish Politics* (1969).
Berkes, N.: *The Development of Secularism in Turkey* (1964).
Davison, R. H.: *Turkey* (1968). Brief and excellent.
Edib, H.: *Conflict of East and West in Turkey* (2nd ed., 1935).
———: *Turkey Faces West* (1930).
Eren, N.: *Turkey Today and Tomorrow: An Experiment in Westernization* (1963).
Frey, F. W.: *The Turkish Political Elite* (1965).
Harris, G. S.: *The Origins of Communism in Turkey* (1967).
Heyd, U.: *The Foundation of Turkish Nationalism* (1950).

Hovannisian, R. G.: *Armenia on the Road to Independence, 1918* (1967).
Howard, H. N.: *The Partition of Turkey, 1913–1923* (1931).
Karpat, K. H.: *Turkey's Politics: The Transition to a Multi-Party System* (1959).
Kinross, Baron (Patrick Balfour): *Ataturk: A Biography of Mustafa Kemal* (1964).
Luke, H.: *The Old Turkey and the New: From Byzantium to Ankara* (1955).
Makal, M.: *A Village in Anatolia* (1954). A unique account by a village teacher.
Mikusch, D. von: *Mustapha Kemal* (1931).
Price, M. P.: *A History of Turkey* (1956).
Ramsaur, E. E., Jr.: *The Young Turks and the Revolution of 1908* (1957).
Robinson, R. D.: *The First Turkish Republic* (1963).
Shotwell, J. T., and F. Deak: *Turkey at the Straits* (1940).
Ward, R. E., and D. A. Rustow (eds.): *Political Modernization in Japan and Turkey* (1964). A valuable comparative study.
Webster, D. E.: *The Turkey of Ataturk* (1939).
Weiker, W. F.: *The Turkish Revolution, 1960–1961: Aspects of Military Politics* (1963).
Yalman, A. E.: *Turkey in My Time* (1956).
———: *Turkey in the World War* (1930).

Egypt and Sudan

Abbas, M.: *The Sudan Question: The Dispute over the Anglo-Egyptian Condominium, 1884–1951* (1952).
Berger, M.: *Bureaucracy and Society in Moslem Egypt: A Study of the Higher Civil Service* (1957).
Beshir, M. O.: *Educational Development in the Sudan 1898–1956* (1969).
Corbyn, E. M.: *Survey of the Anglo-Egyptian Sudan, 1898–1944* (1946).
Duncan, J. S. R.: *The Sudan: A Record of Achievement* (1952).
Fabunmi, L. A.: *The Sudan in Anglo-Egyptian Relations, 1800–1956* (1960).
Gaitskell, A.: *Gezira: A Story of Development in the Sudan* (1959).
Hallberg, C. W.: *The Suez Canal: Its History and Diplomatic Importance* (1931).
Harris, C. P.: *Nationalism and Revolution in Egypt: The Role of the Muslim Brotherhood* (1964).
Heyworth-Dunne, J.: *Religious and Political Trends in Modern Egypt* (1950).
Holt, P. M.: *A Modern History of the Sudan from the Firey Sultanate to the Present Day* (1961).
Issawi, C.: *Egypt: An Economic and Social Analysis* (1947).
Jackson, H. C.: *Behind the Modern Sudan* (1955).
Johnson, P.: *The Suez War* (1957).
Lloyd, S. A.: *Egypt Since Cromer* (2 vols., 1933–34).
Longgood, W. F.: *Suez Story: Key to the Middle East* (1957).
MacMichael, H.: *The Sudan* (1954).
Marlowe, J.: *World Ditch: The Making of the Suez Canal* (1964).
Naguib, M.: *Egypt's Destiny: A Personal Statement* (1955).
Nasser, G. A.: *Egypt's Liberation: The Philosophy of the Revolution* (1955).
Nutting, A.: *No End of a Lesson: The Story of Suez* (1967).
Royal Institute of International Affairs: *Great Britain and Egypt, 1914–1951* (1952).
Schonfield, H. J.: *The Suez Canal in Peace and War, 1869–1969* (1969).
Tignor, R. L.: *Modernization and British Colonial Rule in Egypt, 1882–1914* (1966).
Trimingham, J. S.: *Islam in the Sudan* (1949).
Vatikiotis, P. J. (ed.): *Egypt Since the Revolution* (1968).
Wheelock, K.: *Nasser's New Egypt: A Critical Analysis* (1960).
Zayid, M. Y.: *Egypt's Struggle for Independence* (1965).

Israel

Anglo-American Committee on Jewish Problems in Palestine and Europe: *Report* (1946).

Ben-Gurion, D.: *Israel: Years of Challenge* (1963).
Bernstein, M. H.: *The Politics of Israel: The First Decade of Statehood* (1957).
Eban, A. S.: *Voice of Israel* (1957).
Ellis, H. B.: *Israel and the Middle East* (1957).
Eytan, W.: *The First Ten Years: A Diplomatic History of Israel* (1958).
Feis, Herbert: *The Birth of Israel* (1969).
Frank, W.: *Bridgehead: The Drama of Israel* (1957).
Halevi, N., and R. Klinov-Malul: *The Economic Development of Israel* (1968).
Kraines, O.: *Government and Politics in Israel* (1961).
Patai, R.: *Israel Between East and West: A Study in Human Relations* (1953).
Rodinson, M.: *Israel and the Arabs* (1969).
Royal Institute of International Affairs: *Great Britain and Palestine, 1915–1945* (1946).
Safran, N.: *From War to War: The Arab-Israeli Confrontation, 1948–1967* (1969).
Sharabi, H.: *Palestine and Israel: The Lethal Dilemma* (1969).
Weizmann, C.: *Trial and Error* (1949). Memoirs of the Zionist leader.

Syria and Lebanon

Grant, C. P.: *The Syrian Desert* (1937).
Gulick, J.: *Social Structure and Culture Change in a Lebanese Village* (1955).
Haddad, G. M.: *Fifty Years of Modern Syria and Lebanon* (1950).
Hitti, P. K.: *History of Syria* (1951).
———: *Lebanon in History* (1957).
Hourani, A. H.: *Syria and Lebanon: A Political Essay* (1946).
Hudson, M. C.: *The Precarious Republic: Political Modernization in Lebanon* (1968).
Longrigg, S. H.: *Syria and Lebanon under French Mandate* (1958).
Salibi, K. S.: *The Modern History of Lebanon* (1965).
Ziadeh, N. A.: *Syria and Lebanon* (1957).

Iraq and Jordan

Doherty, K. B.: *The Jordan Waters Conflict* (1965).
Gallman, W. J.: *Iraq under General Nuri* (1964).
Glubb, J. B.: *The Story of the Arab Legion* (1948).
Hussein, King: *Uneasy Lies the Head: The Autobiography of His Majesty King Hussein I of the Hashemite Kingdom of Jordan* (1962).
Ireland, P. W.: *Iraq: A Study in Political Development* (1938).
Khadduri, M.: *Independent Iraq: A Study in Iraqi Politics Since 1932* (1951).
Langley, K. M.: *The Industrialization of Iraq* (1961).
Longrigg, S. H.: *Iraq, 1900 to 1950: A Political, Social, and Economic History* (1953).
Patai, R.: *The Kingdom of Jordan* (1958).
Salter, J. A.: *The Development of Iraq: A Plan of Action* (1955).
Sparrow, G.: *Modern Jordan* (1961).
Stevens, G. G.: *Jordan River Partition* (1965).
Vatikiotis, P. J.: *Politics and the Military in Jordan: A Study of the Arab Legion, 1921–1957* (1967).

The Arabian Peninsula

Allpree, P. S.: *Warlords of Oman* (1967).
Dickson, H. R. P.: *The Arab of the Desert: A Glimpse into Bedouin Life in Kuwait and Saudi Arabia* (1949).
———: *Kuwait and Her Neighbours* (1956).
Doughty, C. M.: *Travels in Arabia Deserta* (2 vols., new ed., 1923). A classic travel book.
Fénelon, K. G.: *The Trucial States: A Brief Economic Survey* (1967).

Hazard, H. W.: *Saudi Arabia* (1956).
Heyworth-Dunne, J.: *Al-Yemen: A General Social, Political and Economic Survey* (1952).
Howarth, D. A.: *The Desert King: A Life of Ibn Saud* (1964).
Ingrams, W. H.: *The Yemen: Imams, Rulers, and Revolution* (1963).
Kelly, J. B.: *Eastern Arabian Frontiers* (1964).
King, G.: *Imperial Outpost: Aden, Its Place in British Strategic Policy* (1964).
Landen, R. G.: *Oman Since 1856: Disruptive Modernization in a Traditional Arab Society* (1967).
Lebkicher, R., et al.: *The Arabia of Ibn Saud* (1952).
Lipsky, G. A.: *Saudi Arabia: Its People, Its Society, Its Culture* (1959).
Miles, S. B.: *The Countries and Tribes of the Persian Gulf* (1966).
Morris, J.: *Sultan in Oman* (1957).
Moyse-Bartlett, H.: *The Pirates of Trucial Oman* (1966).
O'Shea, R.: *The Sand Kings of Oman* (1957).
Philby, H. S.: *Saudi Arabia* (1955).
Phillips, W.: *Oman: A History* (1967).
Sanger, R. H.: *The Arabian Peninsula* (1954).
Tritton, A. S.: *The Rise of the Imams of Sanaa* (1925).
Twitchell, K. S.: *Saudi Arabia: With an Account of the Development of Its Natural Resources* (1947).
Winder, R. B.: *Saudi Arabia in the Nineteenth Century* (1965).

AFRICA

General

Aboyade, O.: *Foundations of an African Economy* (1966).
Anene, J. C. (joint editor): *Africa in the Nineteenth and Twentieth Centuries: A Handbook for Teachers and Students* (1967).
Beetham, T. A.: *Christianity and the New Africa* (1967).
Bohannan, P.: *Africa and Africans* (1964).
Brzezinski, Z. K. (ed.): *Africa and the Communist World* (1963).
Busia, K. A.: *Africa in Search of Democracy* (1967).
Carter, G. M. (ed.): *African One-Party States* (1962).
————: *Independence for Africa* (1960).
Doob, L. W.: *Communication in Africa; a Search for Boundaries* (1961).
Easton, S. C.: *The Twilight of European Colonialism: A Political Analysis* (1960). A fine historical survey.
Emerson, R.: *Africa and United States Policy* (1967).
Fortes, M. (ed.): *African Political Systems* (1963).
Hance, W. A.: *African Economic Development* (1967).
————: *The Geography of Modern Africa* (1964).
Hapgood, D.: *Africa: From Independence to Tomorrow* (1965).
Hatch, J.: *A History of Postwar Africa* (1965).
Miner, H.: *The City in Modern Africa* (1967).
Oliver, R., and J. D. Fage: *A Short History of Africa* (1962).
Ottenberg, S., and P. Ottenberg (eds.): *Cultures and Societies of Africa* (1960).
Prothero, R. Mansell (ed.): *Geography of Africa* (1969).
Rotberg, R. T.: *A Political History of Tropical Africa* (1965). An excellent introductory history.
Wallerstein, I.: *Africa: The Politics of Independence* (1961).
Wattenberg, B., and R. L. Smith: *The New Nations of Africa* (1963).
Woolf, Leonard S.: *Empire and Commerce in Africa: A Study in Economic Imperialism* (1968).

Federation and Union

African Conference on Progress through Cooperation: *Africa: Progress through Coopera-tion* (1966).

Currie, D. P. (ed.): *Federalism and the New Nations of Africa* (1964).

Hazlewood, A. (ed.): *African Integration and Disintegration: Case Studies in Economic and Political Union* (1967).

Le Vine, V. T.: *Political Leadership in Africa* (1967).

Mazrui, Ali A.: *The Anglo-African Commonwealth; Political Friction and Cultural Fusion* (1967).

Newbury, C. W.: *The West African Commonwealth* (1964). Ghana and Nigeria.

Nkrumah, K.: *Africa Must Unite* (1963).

Okigbo, P. N. C.: *Africa and the Common Market* (1967).

Areas and Countries

Adamson, J.: *The People of Kenya* (1967).

Anene, J. C.: *Southern Nigeria in Transition* (1966).

Apter, D. E.: *The Political Kingdom in Uganda* (1967).

Basden, G. T.: *Among the Ibos of Nigeria* (1966).

Bennett, G.: *Kenya: A Political History: The Colonial Period* (1963).

Birmingham, W.: *A Study of Contemporary Ghana* (1966).

Carter, G. M. (ed.): *Five African States: Responses to Diversity: The Congo, Dahomey, the Cameroun Federal Republic, the Rhodesias and Nyasaland [and] South Africa* (1963).

Deschamps, H.: *Histoire de Madagascar* (1960).

Diamond, S.: *The Transformation of East Africa* (1966).

———: *Nigeria: Model of a Colonial Failure* (1967).

Fage, J. D.: *Ghana: A Historical Interpretation* (1959).

Gann, L. H., and P. Duignan: *Burden of Empire. An Appraisal of Western Colonialism in Africa South of the Sahara* (1969).

Gerteiny, A. G.: *Mauritania* (1967).

Ghai, D. P.: *Portrait of a Minority: Asians in East Africa* (1965).

Gower, L. C. B.: *Independent Africa* (1967).

Haight, M. V. J.: *European Powers and South-East Africa* (1967).

Herskovits, M. J.: *The Human Factor in Changing Africa* (1962). Sub-Saharan Africa.

Ingham, K.: *A History of East Africa* (1965).

Kimble, D.: *A Political History of Ghana; the Rise of Gold Coast Nationalism, 1850–1928* (1963).

Kimble, G. H. T.: *Tropical Africa* (2 vols., 1960).

Kingsnorth, G. W.: *Africa South of the Sahara* (1962).

Lemarchand, R.: *Political Awakening in the Belgian Congo* (1964).

Lofchie, M. F.: *Zanzibar: Background to Revolution* (1968).

Louis, W. R.: *Ruandi-Urundi, 1884–1919* (1963).

Mboya, T.: *Freedom and After* (1963). On Kenya.

Mveng, E.: *Histoire du Cameroun* (1963).

Neres, P.: *French-Speaking Africa: From Colonial Status to Independence* (1962).

Nkrumah, K.: *Ghana: The Autobiography of Kwame Nkrumah* (1957).

Nsarkoh, J. K.: *Local Government in Ghana* (1964).

Oliver, R. A. (ed.): *History of East Africa* (1963).

Rhoodie, E.: *South West; The Last Frontier in Africa* (1967).

Rotberg, R. I.: *The Rise of Nationalism in Central Africa: The Making of Malawi and Zambia, 1873–1964* (1965).

Rutman, G. L.: *The Economy of Tanganyika* (1968).

Spiro, H. J.: *Politics in Africa: Prospects South of the Sahara* (1962).

Stevens, R. P.: *Lesotho, Botswana, and Swaziland* (1967).

Stratton, A.: *The Great Red Island* (1964). Madagascar.
Thompson, V.: *The Malagasy Republic* (1965).
Tindall, P. E. N.: *A History of Central Africa* (1968).
Touval, S.: *Somali Nationalism* (1964).
Ward, W. E. F.: *A History of the Gold Coast* (1949).
Wills, A. J.: *An Introduction to the History of Central Africa* (1964).

EAST ASIA

General

Beckmann, G.: *The Modernization of China and Japan* (1962).
Bloch, K.: *German Interests and Policies in the Far East* (1940).
Buss, C. A.: *Asia in the Modern World* (1964).
Friedman, I. S.: *British Relations with China, 1931–1939* (1940).
Griswold, A. W.: *The Far Eastern Policy of the United States* (1938).
Hubbard, G. E.: *British Far Eastern Policy* (1943).
Lach, D. F.: *Asia in the Making of Europe* (2 vols., 1965–70).
Lensen, G. A.: *Russia's Eastward Expansion* (1964).
Levy, R., G. Lacam, and A. Roth: *French Interests and Policies in the Far East* (1941).
Lower, A. R. M.: *Canada and the Far East* (1940).
Michael, F. H., and G. E. Taylor: *The Far East in the Modern World* (rev. ed., 1964).
Milner, I. F. G.: *New Zealand's Interests and Policies in the Far East* (1940).
Mitchell, K. L.: *Industrialization of the Western Pacific* (1942).
Reischauer, E. O.: *Beyond Vietnam: The United States and Asia* (1967).
———, J. K. Fairbank, and A. M. Craig: *A History of East Asian Civilization* (2 vols., 1960–65).
Romein, J.: *The Asian Century: A History of Modern Nationalism in Asia* (1962).
Tamagna, F. M.: *Italy's Interests and Policies in the Far East* (1941).

China

Asia Research Center (ed.): *The Great Cultural Revolution in China* (1968).
Barnett, A. D.: *Communist China: The Early Years* (1964).
———, and E. O. Reischauer (eds.): *The United States and China: The Next Decade* (1970).
Biggerstaff, K.: *The Earliest Modern Government Schools in China* (1961).
Bloodworth, D.: *The Chinese Looking Glass* (1967).
Blum, R.: *The United States and China in World Affairs* (1966).
Brandt, C.: *Stalin's Failure in China, 1924–27* (1958).
——— et al.: *A Documentary History of Chinese Communism* (1952).
Buchan, A. (ed.): *China and the Pearl of Asia* (1966).
Chassin, L. M.: *The Communist Conquest of China: A History of the Civil War, 1945–1949* (1965).
Ch'en, Hsi-en: *The Chinese Communist Regime; Documents and Commentary* (1967).
Cheng, Tien-fong: *History of Sino-Russian Relations* (1957).
Chiang Kai-shek: *Soviet Russia in China: A Summing-up at Seventy* (1957).
Chubb, O. E.: *Twentieth Century China* (1964).
Doolin, J.: *The Chinese People's Republic* (1966).
Eckstein, A.: *Communist China's Economic Growth and Foreign Trade; Implications for U.S. Policy* (1966).
———, W. Galenson, and Ta-chung Liu (eds.): *Economic Trends in Communist China* (1968).
Fairbank, J. K. (ed.): *Chinese Thought and Institutions* (1957).
———: *The United States and China* (rev. ed., 1958).

Goodrich, L. C.: *A Short History of the Chinese People* (1944).
Harrison, J. A.: *China Since 1800* (1967).
Hinton, H. C.: *Communist China in World Politics* (1966).
Hsu, I. C. Y.: *The Rise of Modern China* (1970).
Isaacs, H. R.: *The Tragedy of the Chinese Revolution* (2nd ed., 1961).
Karol, K. S.: *China: The Other Communism* (1967).
Latourette, K. S.: *The Chinese: Their History and Culture* (4th ed., 1964).
Levenson, J. R.: *Confucian China and Its Modern Fate* (1968).
Lewis, J. W. (ed.): *Party Leadership and Revolutionary Power in China* (1970).
Linebarger, P. M. A.: *The China of Chiang Kai-shek: A Political Study* (1941).
Liu, C.: *A Military History of Modern China, 1924–1949* (1956).
MacNair, H. F. (ed.): *China* (1946).
Mao Tse-tung: *Selected Works* (4 vols., 1954–56).
Melby, J. F.: *The Mandate of Heaven: A Record of a Civil War; China 1945–49* (1968).
North, R. C.: *The Foreign Relations of China* (1969).
———: *Moscow and the Chinese Communists* (1953).
Pollard, R.: *China's Foreign Relations, 1917–31* (1933).
Powell, R. L.: *The Rise of Chinese Military Power, 1895–1912* (1955).
Purcell, V. W.: *The Boxer Uprising, A Background Study* (1963).
Schiffrin, H. Z.: *Sun Yat-sen and the Origins of the Chinese Revolution* (1968).
Schurmann, F.: *Ideology and Organization in Communist China* (2nd ed., 1968).
———, and O. Schell (eds.): *The China Reader* (3 vols., 1966–67).
Schwartz, B.: *Chinese Communism and the Rise of Mao* (1951).
Steele, A. T.: *The American People and China* (1966).
Stuart, J. L.: *Fifty Years in China: The Memoirs of John Leighton Stuart, Missionary and Ambassador* (1954).
Sun, I.: *Chinese Railways and British Interests, 1898–1911* (1954).
Sun Yat-sen: *Memoirs of a Chinese Revolutionary* (1918).
Tan, C. C.: *The Boxer Catastrophe* (1955).
Teng, Ssu-yu, and J. K. Fairbank: *China's Response to the West: A Documentary Survey, 1839–1923* (1954).
Thomson, J. C.: *While China Faced West: American Reformers in Nationalist China, 1928–1937* (1969).
Tung, W. L.: *The Political Institution of Modern China* (1964).
United States Department of State: *United States Relations with China, with Special Reference to the Period 1944–1949* (1949).
Van Slyke, L. P.: *Enemies and Friends; the United Front in Chinese Communist History* (1967).
Walker, R. L.: *China Under Communism: The First Five Years* (1955).
Wang Shih, et al.: *Brief History of the Communist Party* (1958). An official party history.
Wang, Y. C.: *Chinese Intellectuals and the West, 1872–1949* (1966).
Young, A. N.: *China and the Helping Hand, 1937–1945* (1963).

Manchuria and Mongolia

Bawden, C. R.: *The Modern History of Mongolia* (1968).
Friters, G.: *Outer Mongolia and Its International Position* (1950).
Jones, F. C.: *Manchuria Since 1931* (1949). An account of Japanese economic policy.
Lattimore, O.: *Inner Asian Frontiers of China* (1951).
———: *Manchuria: Cradle of Conflict* (1935).
———: *Nationalism and Revolution in Mongolia* (1955).
———: *Nomads and Commissars: Mongolia Revisited* (1962).
Rupen, R. A.: *Mongols of the Twentieth Century* (2 vols., 1964).
Schumpeter, E. B. (ed.): *The Industrialization of Japan and Manchukuo, 1930–1940* (1940).
Smith, S. R.: *The Manchurian Crisis, 1931–32: A Tragedy in International Relations* (1948).

Stimson, H. L.: *The Far Eastern Crisis: Recollections and Observations* (1936).
Tang. S.: *Russian and Soviet Policy in Manchuria and Outer Mongolia 1911–1931* (1959).
Willoughby, W. W.: *The Sino-Japanese Controversy and the League of Nations* (1935).

Japan

Beasley, W. G.: *The Modern History of Japan* (1963).
Borg, D.: *The United States and the Far Eastern Crisis of 1933–1938* (1964).
Borton, H.: *Japan's Modern Century* (1955). The best general account.
Butow, R. J. C.: *Japan's Decision to Surrender* (1954).
————: *Tojo and the Coming of the War* (1961).
Clinard, O. J.: *Japan's Influence on American Naval Power, 1897–1917* (1947).
Cohen, B. C.: *The Political Process and Foreign Policy: The Making of the Japanese Peace Settlement* (1957).
Cohen, J. B.: *Japan's Post-War Economy* (1958).
Cole, A. B.: *Japanese Society and Politics: The Impact of Social Stratification and Mobility on Politics* (1957).
Dunn, F. S.: *Peace Making and the Settlement in Japan* (1963).
Feis, H.: *Contest over Japan* (1967).
Grew, J. C.: *Ten Years in Japan* (1944).
Ike, N.: *Japanese Politics: An Introductory Survey* (1957).
Ito, M.: *The End of the Imperial Japanese Navy: From Pearl Harbor to Leyte* (1962).
James, P. H.: *The Rise and Fall of the Japanese Empire* (1952).
Jansen, M. B.: *The Japanese and Sun Yat-sen* (1954).
Jones, F. C.: *Japan's New Order in East Asia: Its Rise and Fall, 1937–1945* (1954).
Kawai, K.: *Japan's American Interlude* (1960).
Latourette, K. S.: *The History of Japan* (rev. ed., 1957).
Lockwood, W. W.: *The Economic Development of Japan: Growth and Structural Change, 1868–1938* (1954).
Maxon, Y. C.: *Control of Japanese Foreign Policy: A Study of Civil-Military Rivalry, 1930–1945* (1957).
Moore, F.: *With Japan's Leaders: An Intimate Record of Fourteen Years as Counsellor to the Japanese Government Ending December 7, 1941* (1942).
Ogata, S. N.: *Defiance in Manchuria: The Making of Japanese Foreign Policy 1931–1932* (1964).
Potter, J. D.: *Yamamoto; the Man Who Menaced America* (1965).
Reischauer, E. O.: *The United States and Japan* (rev. ed., 1964).
————: *Japan: The Story of a Nation* (1970).
Samson, G. B.: *A History of Japan* (3 vols., 1958–63).
Starry, R.: *The Double Patriots: A Study of Japanese Nationalism* (1957).
————: *A History of Modern Japan* (1960).
Swearingen, R., and P. Langer: *Red Flag in Japan* (1952). Communism 1918–51.
Yoshihashi, T.: *Conspiracy in Mukden: The Rise of the Japanese Military* (1963).

Formosa and Korea

Ballantine, J. W.: *Formosa: A Problem for United States Foreign Policy* (1952).
Barclay, G. W.: *Colonial Development and Population in Taiwan* (1954).
Conroy, F. H.: *The Japanese Seizure of Korea, 1868–1910* (1960).
Goodrich, L. M.: *Korea: A Study of U.S. Policy in the United Nations* (1956).
Grajdanzev, A. J.: *Modern Korea* (1944).
Hulbert, H. B.: *History of Korea* (2 vols., 1962).
Kim, C. I. E., and Han-kyo Kim: *Korea and the Politics of Imperialism 1876–1910* (1967).

Mancall, M. (ed.): *Formosa Today* (1964).
Meade, E. G.: *American Military Government in Korea* (1951).
Oliver, R. T.: *Syngman Rhee: The Man Behind the Myth* (1954).
Rees, D.: *Korea: The Limited War* (1964).
Reeve, W. P.: *The Republic of Korea: A Political and Economic Study* (1963).
Scalapino, R. A. (ed.): *North Korea Today* (1963).

Southeast Asia and the Pacific Islands

Allen, S. C.: *Western Enterprise in Indonesia and Malaya* (1957).
Aziz, M. A.: *Japan's Colonialism and Indonesia* (1955).
Brackman, A. C.: *Indonesian Communism* (1963).
Brookings Institution: *Vietnam After the War* (1968).
Cady, J. F.: *A History of Modern Burma* (1958).
————: *Southeast Asia: Its Historical Development* (1964).
Corson, W. R.: *The Betrayal* (1968). Vietnam conflict.
Crawford, A. (Caddell): *Customs and Culture of Vietnam* (1968).
Du Bois, C.: *Social Forces in Southeast Asia* (1949). Essays on nationalism in this
    region.
Duncanson, D. J.: *Government and Revolution in Vietnam* (1968). A British study.
Elsbree, W. H.: *Japan's Role in Southeast Asian Nationalist Movements, 1940–1945*
    (1953).
Falk, R. A. (ed.): *The Vietnam War and International Law* (1968).
Fall, B. B.: *Last Reflections on a War* (1967). Vietnam.
————: *Street Without Joy: Indochina at War, 1946–1954* (1961).
————: *Viet-Nam Witness, 1953–66* (1966).
Fifield, R. H.: *The Diplomacy of Southeast Asia* (1958).
Grant, B.: *Indonesia* (1964).
Halberstam, D.: *The Making of a Quagmire* (1964).
Hall, G. D. E.: *A History of South-East Asia* (2nd ed., 1964).
Harvey, H. E.: *British Rule in Burma (1824–1942)* (1946).
Hoang-van-Chi: *From Colonialism to Communism; A Case History of North Vietnam*
    (1964).
Hyma, A.: *The Dutch in the Far East* (1942).
Jacoby, E. H.: *Agrarian Unrest in Southeast Asia* (1961).
Kahin, G. M., and J. W. Lewis: *The United States in Vietnam* (new ed., 1969).
Legge, J. D.: *Indonesia* (1964).
Leur, J. C. van: *Indonesian Trade and Society* (1955).
MacDonald, M.: *Borneo People* (1958). By the former Governor General of Malaya
    and British Borneo.
McAlister, J. T., Jr.: *Viet Nam: The Origin of Revolution* (1969).
————, and P. Mus: *The Vietnamese and Their Revolution* (1970).
McVey, R. T.: *Indonesia* (1965).
Mende, T.: *South-East Asia Between Two Worlds* (1955).
Pike, D.: *Viet Cong: The Organization and Techniques of the National Liberation
    Front* (1966).
————: *War, Peace, and the Viet Cong* (1969).
Purcell, V. W.: *The Chinese in Southeast Asia* (1951).
Pye, L. W.: *Guerrilla Communism in Malaya* (1956).
Rose, S.: *Britain and Southeast Asia* (1962).
Rupen, R. A., and R. Farrell (eds.): *Vietnam and the Sino-Soviet Dispute* (1967).
Salisbury, H. E.: *Behind the Lines—Hanoi, December 23, 1966–January 7, 1967*
    (1967).
Schiller, A.: *The Formation of Federal Indonesia, 1945–1949* (1955).
Skinner, G. W.: *Leadership and Power in the Chinese Community of Thailand*
    (1958).
Starner, F. L.: *Magsaysay and the Philippine Peasantry* (1961).

Tanham, G.: *Communist Revolutionary Warfare: Viet Minh in Indochina* (1961).
Thompson, V. M.: *Left Wing in Southeast Asia* (1950).
The Pentagon Papers (1971).
Trager, F. N. (ed.): *Marxism in Southeast Asia* (1959).
Vandenbosch, A.: *The Dutch East Indies: Its Government, Problems, and Politics* (1942).
Vlekke, B. H. M.: *The Story of the Dutch East Indies* (1945).
Vo Nguyen Giap: *People's War, People's Army* (1962).
———: *"Big Victory, Great Task"; North Viet-Nam's Minister of Defense Assesses the Course of the War* (1968).
Woodman, D.: *The Republic of Indonesia* (1955).
(See also France: Overseas, and United Kingdom: Ceylon and Malaya).

3. International Problems

FIRST WORLD CRISIS

Diplomatic Background

Albertini, L.: *The Origins of the War of 1914* (3 vols., 1952–57).
Albrecht-Carrié, R.: *A Diplomatic History of Europe Since the Congress of Vienna* (1958).
Brandenburg, E.: *From Bismarck to the World War* (1927). By a leading German historian.
Fay, S. B.: *The Origins of the World War* (2 vols., rev. ed., 1930). A pioneering study that remains the standard general work.
Fellner, F.: *Der Dreibund: Europaische Diplomatie vor dem Ersten Weltkrieg* (1960).
Gooch, G. P.: *Before the War: Studies in Diplomacy* (2 vols., 1936–38).
———: *Studies in Diplomacy and Statecraft* (1942).
Lafore, L.: *The Long Fuse: An Interpretation of the Origins of World War I* (1965).
Langer, W. L.: *The Diplomacy of Imperialism, 1890–1902* (2 vols., 1935).
———: *European Alliances and Alignments, 1871–1890* (1931).
———: *The Franco-Russian Alliance, 1890–1894* (1929).
Laqueur, W. (ed.): *1914: The Coming of the First World War* (1966).
Mansergh, N.: *The Coming of the First World War: A Study in the European Balance, 1878–1914* (1949).
Mish, I. H.: *The Anglo-Japanese Alliance: The Diplomacy of Two Island Empires, 1894–1907* (1966).
Potemkin, V. P. (ed.): *Histoire de la diplomatice* (3 vols., 1946–47). French translation of an official Soviet account. The second volume covers the period 1870–1919. A revised version is being prepared by V. A. Zorin (5 vols., 1959–).
Renouvin, P.: *The Immediate Origins of the War* (1928). A French interpretation.
———: *Le XIXe siècle: Vol. II, De 1871 à 1914: l'apogée de l'Europe* (1955). This is volume six of the *Histoire des relations internationales* edited by Renouvin.
Ritter, G.: *The European Powers and the Wilhelminian Empire, 1890–1914* (1969). Translation of the second volume of Ritter's *The Sword and the Scepter: The Problem of Militarism in Germany*.
Schmitt, B. E.: *The Coming of the War: 1914* (2 vols., 1930). The most detailed study of the problem in English.
Taylor, A. J. P.: *The Struggle for Mastery in Europe 1848–1918* (1954).
Tuchman, B. W.: *The Proud Tower: A Portrait of the World before the War, 1890–1914* (1966).

Wegerer, A. von: *Des Ausbruch des Weltkrieges* (2 vols., 1939). A full statement of the German case.
———: *A Refutation of the Versailles War Guilt Thesis* (1930).

Biographies and Memoirs

Asquith, H. H.: *The Genesis of the War* (1923).
Bernstoff, J. H. von: *Memoirs* (1936). By the German ambassador in Washington during the War.
Bethmann-Hollweg, T. von: *Reflections on the World War* (1920).
Buchanan, G.: *My Mission to Russia* (2 vols., 1923). By the British ambassador in St. Petersburg, 1910–17.
Giolitti, G.: *Memoirs of My Life* (1923).
Grey, Viscount, of Fallodon: *Twenty-Five Years, 1892–1916* (2 vols., 1925).
Hammann, O.: *The World Policy of Germany, 1890–1912* (1927). By an official in charge of German press relations.
Hantsch, H.: *Leopold Graf Berchtold, Grandseigneur und Staatsmann* (2 vols., 1963).
Herriot, E.: *In Those Days: Vol. I, Before the First World War* (1952). Memoirs of the French statesman.
Hymans, P.: *Mémoires* (2 vols., 1958).
Isvolsky, A.: *Recollections of a Foreign Minister* (1921).
Jagow, G. von: *Ursachen und Ausbruch des Weltkrieges* (1919). By the German state secretary for foreign affairs, 1913–16.
Jonescu, T.: *Some Personal Impressions* (1920). Memoirs of a Rumanian statesman.
Kürenberg, J. von: *The Kaiser: A Life of William II, Last Emperor of Germany* (1954).
Lichnowsky, K. M.: *Heading for the Abyss: Reminiscences* (1928). By the German ambassador at London.
Nicolson, H.: *Portrait of a Diplomatist* (1930). Life of Sir Authur Nicolson.
Paléologue, G. M.: *An Ambassador's Memoirs* (3 vols., 1923–25). By the French ambassador at St. Petersburg, 1914–17.
Porter, C. A.: *The Career of Théophile Delcassé* (1936).
Radoslawoff, V.: *Bulgarien und die Weltkrise* (1923). By the Bulgarian premier during the war.
Rich, N., and M. H. Fisher (eds.): *The Holstein Papers* (4 vols., 1955–63).
Salandra, A.: *Italy and the Great War* (1932).
Sazonov, S.: *Fateful Years, 1906–1916: Reminiscences* (1928).
William, H.: *My Memoirs, 1878–1918* (1922).

Special Studies in Prewar Diplomacy

Anderson, E. M.: *The First Moroccan Crisis, 1904–1906* (1930).
Andrew, C.: *Théophile Delcassé and the Making of the Entente Cordiale: A reappraisal of French Foreign Policy, 1898–1905* (1968).
Askew, W. C.: *Europe and Italy's Acquisition of Libya, 1911–1912* (1942).
Barlow, J. C.: *The Agadir Crisis* (1940).
Carroll, E. M.: *French Public Opinion and Foreign Affairs, 1870–1914* (1931).
Churchill, R. P.: *The Anglo-Russian Convention of 1907* (1939).
David, W. D.: *European Diplomacy in the Near Eastern Question, 1906–1909* (1940).
Dedijer, V.: *The Road to Sarajevo* (1966).
Gifford, P., and W. R. Louis (eds.): *Britain and Germany in Africa: Imperial Rivalry and Colonial Rule* (1967).
Gollwitzer, H.: *Europe in the Age of Imperialism 1880–1914* (1969).
Gottlieb, W. W.: *Studies in Secret Diplomacy During the First World War* (1957).
Hale, O. J.: *Germany and the Diplomatic Revolution: A Study in the Diplomacy of the Press, 1904–1906* (1931).
Helmreich, E. C.: *The Diplomacy of the Balkan Wars, 1912–1913* (1938, reprinted 1969).

Hoffman, J. W.: *The Austro-Russian Rivalry in the Balkans, 1909–1912* (1940).
Kazemzadeh, F.: *Russia and Britain in Persia 1864–1914* (1968).
Martin, B. G.: *German-Persian Diplomatic Relations 1873–1912* (1959).
Mathews, J. J.: *Egypt and the Formation of the Anglo-French Entente of 1904* (1939).
Pribram, A. F.: *Austrian Foreign Policy, 1908–1918* (1923).
Remak, J.: *Sarajevo: The Story of a Political Murder* (1959).
Schmitt, B. E.: *The Annexation of Bosnia, 1908–1909* (1937).
Seton-Watson, R. W.: *Germany and the Great Powers, 1866–1914* (1938).
————: *The Role of Bosnia in International Politics, 1875–1914* (1932).
————: *Sarajevo: A Study in the Origins of the Great War* (1928).
Thaden, E. C.: *Russia and the Balkan Alliance of 1912* (1965).
Thompson, G. M.: *The Twelve Days: 24 July to 4 August 1914* (1964).
Uebersberger, H: *Osterreich zwischen Russland und Serbien: zur sudslawischen Frage und der Entstehung des Ersten Weltkrieges* (1958).
Vucinich, W. S.: *Serbia Between East and West: The Events of 1903–1908* (1954). A carefully documented study.
Walton, C. C.: *Kiderlen-Wächter and the Anglo German Problem* (1949).
Wedel, O. H.: *Austro-German Diplomatic Relations, 1908–1914* (1932).
White, J. A.: *The Diplomacy of the Russo-Japanese War* (1964).
Williamson, S. R., Jr.: *The Politics of Grand Strategy: Britain and France Prepare For War, 1904–1914* (1969).
Wolf, J. B.: *The Diplomatic History of the Bagdad Railroad* (1936).
Woodward, E. L.: *Great Britain and the German Navy* (1935).

General Histories of the War

Baldwin, H.: *World War I, an Outline History* (1962). Brief.
Chambers, F. P.: *The War Behind the War, 1914–1918: A History of the Political and Civilian Fronts* (1939).
Cruttwell, C. R. M. F.: *A History of the Great War, 1914–1918:* (1934). The most useful general history.
Dickson, M.: *The Food Front in World War I* (1944).
Frothingham, T. G.: *The Naval History of the World War* (3 vols., 1924–26).
Lasswell, H. D.: *Propaganda Technique in the World War* (1938).
Liddell Hart, B. H.: *A History of the World War, 1914–1918* (1934).
————: *The War in Outline, 1914–1918* (1936).
McEntee, G. L.: *Military History of the World War* (1937).
Shotwell, J. T. (ed.): *Social and Economic History of the War* (150 vols., 1921–37). Indispensable volumes on the nonmilitary aspects of the war, covering all the major participants.
Stallings, L. (ed.): *The First World War: A Photographic History* (1933). A vivid picture of the period.
Thommin, R. L.: *The First World War* (Am. ed., 1964). Translated from the French by M. Keiffer.
Van der Slice, A.: *International Labor: Diplomacy and Peace, 1914–1919* (1941).

Special Studies on the War

Adams, J. C.: *Flight in Winter: Serbia's Struggle Against the Central Powers, 1914–1916* (1942). A vivid account of the Balkan front.
Asprey, R. B.: *The First Battle of the Marne* (1962).
Barnett, C.: *The Swordbearers: Studies in Supreme Command in the First World War* (1963).
Birnbaum, K. F.: *Peace Moves and U-boat Warfare: A Study of Imperial Germany's Policy towards the United States April 18, 1916–January 9, 1917* (1958).

Bonham-Carter, V.: *The Strategy of Victory, 1914–1918: The Life and Times of the Master Strategist of World War I: Field-Marshall Sir William Robertson* (1964).

Ellis, C. H.: *The British "Intervention" in Transcaspia, 1918–1919* (1963).

Falls, C. B.: *Armageddon: 1918* (1964). Near Eastern campaigns.

Fischer, F.: *Germany's Crimes in the First World War* (1967).

Fuller, J. F. C.: *Tanks in the Great War, 1914–1918* (1920).

Gatzke, H.: *Germany's Drive to the West* (1950).

Gibson, L., and J. E. T. Harper: *The Riddle of Jutland* (1934). On the controversial naval engagement.

Golovin, N. N.: *The Russian Army in the Great War* (1931).

Hanak, H.: *Great Britain and Austria-Hungary During the First World War. A Study in the Formation of Public Opinion* (1962).

Hankey, M. P. A. H.: *The Supreme Command, 1914–1918* (2 vols., 1961).

Harne, A.: *The Price of Glory: Verdun, 1916* (1962).

Higgins, T.: *Winston Churchill and the Dardanelles; a Dialogue in Ends and Means* (1963).

Horn, Daniel: *The German Naval Mutinies of World War I* (1969).

Hubatsch, W.: *Die Ära Tirpitz: Studien zur deutschen Marinepolitik 1890–1918* (1955).

James, R. R.: *Gallipoli* (1965).

Kennan, G. F.: *The Decision to Intervene* (1958).

————: *Russia Leaves the War, 1917–1920* (1956).

Kluck, A. von: *The March on Paris and the Battle of the Marne, 1914* (1920).

Langer, W. L.: *Gas and Flame in World War I* (1965).

Lasswell, H. D.: *Propaganda Technique in the World War* (1938).

Lettow-Vorbeck, P. von: *East African Campaigns* (1957).

Linde, G.: *Die deutsche Politik in Litauen im Ersten Weltkrieg* (1965).

Moberly, F. J.: *The Campaign in Mesopotamia* (4 vols., 1923–27).

Moorehead, A.: *Gallipoli* (1956).

Morley, J. W.: *The Japanese Thrust into Siberia, 1918* (1957).

Raleigh, W., and H. A. Jones: *The War in the Air* (6 vols., 1922–37). The official British history.

Ritter, G.: *The Schlieffen Plan: Critique of a Myth* (1958).

Siney, M. G.: *The Allied Blockade of Germany, 1914–1916* (1957).

Sokol, E. D.: *The Revolt of 1916 in Russian Central Asia* (1954).

Terraine, J.: *The Western Front, 1914–1918* (1965).

Trumpener, U.: *Germany and the Ottoman Empire, 1914–1918* (1968).

Tuchman, B. W.: *The Guns of August* (1962).

Tyng, S.: *The Campaign of the Marne, 1914* (1935).

Warth, R. D.: *The Allies and the Russian Revolution* (1954).

Wavell, A. P.: *Allenby: A Study in Greatness* (1941).

Zeman, Z. A. B. (ed.): *Germany and the Revolution in Russia, 1915–1918, Documents from the Archives of the German Foreign Ministry* (1958).

War Memoirs

Beneš, E.: *My War Memoirs* (1928).

Brusilov, A. A.: *A Soldier's Notebook* (1930).

Churchill, W.: *The World Crisis, 1911–1918* (4 vols., 1923–27).

Clemenceau, G.: *The Grandeur and Misery of Victory* (1930).

Coffman, E. M.: *The War to End All Wars: American Experience in World War I* (1968).

Conrad von Hotzendorf, F.: *Aus Meiner Dienstzeit, 1906–1918* (5 vols., 1921–25). By the Austrian chief of staff.

Czernin, O.: *In the World War* (1920). By the minister of foreign affairs of Austro-Hungary, 1916–17.

Foch, F.: *Memoirs* (1931).
Hamilton, I.: *Gallipoli Diary* (2 vols., 1920).
Hindenburg, P. von: *Out of My Life* (2 vols., 1921).
Hoffmann, M.: *War Diaries and Other Papers* (2 vols., 1929).
Jellicoe, J. R. J.: *The Crisis of the Naval War* (1920).
Joffre, J. J. C.: *Personal Memoirs* (2 vols., 1932).
Lawrence, T. E.: *Revolt in the Desert* (1926).
————: *Seven Pillars of Wisdom* (1935).
Liman von Sanders, O.: *The Dardanelles Campaign* (1931).
————: *Five Years in Turkey* (1927).
Lloyd George, D.: *War Memoirs* (6 vols., 1933–37).
Ludendorff, E.: *Ludendorff's Own Story, August 1914–November 1918* (2 vols., 1920).
Maximilian of Baden, Prince: *Memoirs* (2 vols., 1928).
Pétain, H. P.: *Verdun* (1930).
Poincaré, R.: *Au service de la France* (9 vols., 1926–32).
Sarrail, M. P. E.: *Mon commandement en Orient, 1916–1918* (1920).
Scheer, R.: *Germany's High Sea Fleet in the World War* (1920).
Suchomlinow, N. A.: *Erinnerungen* (1924). Memoirs of the Russian minister of war, 1909–15.
Tirpitz, A von: *My Memoirs* (2 vols., 1919).

American Participation

Bailey, T. A.: *The Policy of the United States Towards Neutrals, 1917–1918* (1942).
Baker, R. S. (ed.): *Woodrow Wilson: Life and Letters* (8 vols., 1927–39).
Buehrig, E. H.: *Wilson's Foreign Policy in Perspective* (1957).
Cohen, W. I.: *The American Revisionists: The Lessons of Intervention in World War I* (1967).
Daniels, J.: *The Wilson Era: Years of War and After 1917–1923* (1946).
Freidel, F. B.: *Over There: The Story of America's First Great Overseas Crusade* (1964).
Gelfand, L. E.: *The Inquiry; American Preparations for Peace, 1917–1919* (1963).
Hendrick, B. J.: *Life and Letters of Walter H. Page* (3 vols., 1922). A biography of the United States ambassador at London.
Hoover, H. C.: *The Ordeal of Woodrow Wilson* (1958).
Lansing, R.: *War Memoirs* (1935).
Link, A. S.: *Wilson* (5 vols., 1947–65).
Mamatey, V. S.: *The United States and East Central Europe, 1914–1918: A Study in Wilsonian Diplomacy and Propaganda* (1957).
March, P. C.: *The Nation at War* (1932). By the United States chief of staff.
Martin, L. W.: *Peace Without Victory: Woodrow Wilson and the British Liberals* (1958).
May, E. R.: *The World War and American Isolation 1914–1917* (1959).
Millis, W.: *The Road to War: America, 1914–1917* (1935).
Mock, J. R.: *Censorship, 1917* (1941).
Paxson, F. L.: *American Democracy and the World War* (2 vols., 1939).
Pershing, J. J.: *My Experiences in the World War* (2 vols., 1931).
Peterson, H. C.: *Propaganda for War: The Campaign Against American Neutrality, 1914–1917* (1939).
Read, J. M.: *Atrocity Propaganda, 1914–1919* (1941).
Seymour, C.: *American Diplomacy During the World War* (1934).
————: *American Neutrality, 1914–1917* (1936).
———— (ed.): *The Intimate Papers of Colonel House* (4 vols., 1926–28).
Smith, G.: *When the Cheering Stopped: The Last Years of Woodrow Wilson* (1964).
Spencer, S. R.: *Decision for War, 1917; The Laconia Sinking and the Zimmermann Telegram as Key Factors in the Public Reaction Against Germany* (1953).
Tansill, C. C.: *America Goes to War* (1938).

Tuchman, B. W.: *The Zimmermann Telegram* (1958).
Unterberger, B. M.: *America's Siberian Expedition 1918–1920: A Study of National Policy* (1956).

PEACE SETTLEMENT

Termination of Hostilities

Forster, K.: *The Failures of Peace: The Search for a Negotiated Peace during the First World War* (1941).
Kann, R. A.: *Die Sixtusaffäre und die geheimen Friedensverhandlungen* (1966).
Lutz, R. H.: *The Causes of the German Collapse in 1918* (1934). A collection of documents.
Maurice, F.: *The Armistice of 1918* (1943).
Nowak, K. F.: *The Collapse of the Central Powers* (1924).
Rudin, H. M.: *Armistice, 1918* (1944).

The Peace Conference

Bailey, T. A.: *Woodrow Wilson and the Great Betrayal* (1945).
————: *Woodrow Wilson and the Lost Peace* (1944).
Bonsal, S.: *Suitors and Suppliants: The Little Nations at Versailles* (1946).
————: *Unfinished Business* (1944).
Hankey, M. P. A. H.: *The Supreme Council at the Paris Peace Conference 1919; a Commentary* (1963).
House, F. M., and C. Seymour (eds.): *What Really Happened at Paris: The Story of the Peace Conference, 1918–1919, by American Delegates* (1921).
Howard, H. N.: *The King-Crane Commission: An American Inquiry in the Middle East* (1963).
Lansing, R.: *The Big Four and Others of the Peace Conference* (1921).
————: *The Peace Negotiations: A Personal Narrative* (1921).
Lloyd George, D.: *Memoirs of the Peace Conference* (2 vols., 1939).
Low, A. D.: *The Soviet Hungarian Republic and the Paris Peace Conference* (1963).
Mantoux, P.: *Les délibérations du conseil des quatre (24 Mars–28 Juin): Notes de l'officier interprète* (2 vols., 1955).
Marston, E. S.: *The Peace Conferences, 1919; Organization and Procedure* (1945).
Miller, D. H.: *My Diary at the Conference of Paris, with Documents* (21 vols., 1928).
Nicolson, H.: *Peacemaking, 1919* (1933).
Palmer, F.: *Bliss, Peacemaker: The Life and Letters of General Tasker Howard Bliss* (1934).
Riddell, G.: *Lord Riddell's Intimate Diary of the Peace Conference and After, 1918–1923* (1933).
Seymour, C. (ed. by Harold B. Whiteman, Jr.): *Letters from the Paris Peace Conference* (1965).
Shotwell, J. T.: *At the Paris Peace Conference* (1937).
Temperley, H. (ed.): *History of the Peace Conference* (6 vols., 1920–24). The standard work.
Thompson, J. M.: *Russia, Bolshevism, and the Versailles Peace* (1966).
Tillman, S. P.: *Anglo-American Relations at the Paris Peace Conference of 1919* (1961).
Wade, R. A.: *The Russian Search for Peace, February–October 1917* (1969).
(For further bibliographical references see R. C. Binkley: "Ten Years of Peace Conference History," *Journal of Modern History* (1929), 1:607–29, and P. Birdsall: "The Second Decade of Peace Conference History," *Journal of Modern History* (1939), 11:362–78.

The Peace Treaties and Special Aspects of the Settlement

Albrecht-Carrié, R.: *Italy at the Paris Peace Conference* (1942).

————: *The Meaning of the First World War* (1965).

Almond, N., and R. H. Lutz: *The Treaty of St. Germain* (1934).

Birdsall, P.: *Versailles Twenty Years After* (1914).

Bretton, H. L.: *Stresemann and the Revision of Versailles: A Fight for Reason* (1953).

Burnett, P. M. (ed.): *Reparation at the Paris Peace Conference from the Standpoint of the American Delegation* (2 vols., 1940).

Carnegie Endowment for International Peace: *The Treaties of Peace, 1919–1923* (2 vols., 1924).

Dallin, A., et al.: *Russian Diplomacy and Eastern Europe 1914–1917* (1963).

Dawes, C. G.: *A Journal of Reparations* (1939).

Deák, F.: *Hungary at the Paris Peace Conference: A Diplomatic History of the Treaty of Trianon* (1942).

Donald, D.: *The Tragedy of Trianon* (1928).

Fifield, R. H.: *Woodrow Wilson and the Far East: The Diplomacy of the Shantung Question* (1952).

Fraenkel, F.: *Military Occupation and the Rule of Law: Occupation Government in the Rhineland, 1919–1923* (1944).

Gerson, L. L.: *Woodrow Wilson and the Rebirth of Poland, 1914–1920: A Study in the Influence on American Policy of Minority Groups of Foreign Origin* (1953).

Hubatsch, W.: *Germany and the Central Powers in the World War, 1914–1918* (1963).

Keynes, J. M.: *The Economic Consequences of the Peace* (1920).

King, J. C.: *Foch versus Clemenceau: France and German Dismemberment, 1918–1919* (1960).

Laroche, J. A.: *Au Quai d'Orsay avec Briand et Poincaré, 1913–1926* (1957).

Lederer, I. J.: *Yugoslavia at the Paris Peace Conference: A Study in Frontiermaking* (1963).

Louis, W. R.: *Great Britain and Germany's Lost Colonies 1914–1919* (1967).

Luckau, A. M.: *The German Delegation at the Peace Conference* (1941).

Mantoux, E.: *The Carthaginian Peace: Or the Economic Consequences of Mr. Keynes* (1952).

Mayer, A. J.: *Political Origins of the New Diplomacy, 1917–1918* (1959).

————: *Politics and Diplomacy of Peacemaking: Containment and Counter-Revolution at Versailles, 1918–1919* (1968).

Myers, D. P. (ed.): *The Treaty of Versailles and After: Annotations of the Treaty* (1947).

Nelson, H. I.: *Land and Power; British and Allied Policy on Germany's Frontiers, 1916–19* (1963).

Pink, T. P.: *The Conference of Ambassadors: Paris, 1920–1931* (1942).

Roth, J. J. (ed.): *World War I: A Turning Point in Modern History* (1967). Four essays by leading scholars on the significance of the war.

Saucerman, S.: *International Transfers of Territory in Europe with names of the affected subdivisions as of 1910–1914* (1937).

Scherer, A., and J. Grunewald: *L'Allemagne et les problèmes de la paix pendant la première guerre mondiale; documents extraits des archives de l'Office allemand des affaires étrangères* (1962).

Spector, S. D.: *Rumania at the Paris Peace Conference. A Study of the Diplomacy of Ion I. C. Bratianu* (1962).

Stein, B. E.: *Die Russische Frage auf der Pariser Friedenskonferenz, 1919–1920* (1953). A translation from the original Russian published in 1949.

Thompson, J. M.: *Russia, Bolshevism, and the Versailles Peace* (1966).

United States Department of State: *Papers Relating to the Foreign Relations of the United States: The Paris Peace Conference 1919* (13 vols., 1942–47). Vol. XIII is a carefully annotated edition of the Treaty of Versailles.

Wambaugh, S.: *Plebiscites Since the World War* (2 vols., 1933).

LEAGUE OF NATIONS

General

Aufricht, H.: *Guide to League of Nations Publications: A Bibliographical Survey of the Work of the League, 1920–1947* (1951). A guide to the documents published by the League and its agencies.
Barros, J.: *Betrayal from Within: Joseph Avenol, Secretary-General of the League of Nations, 1933–1940* (1969).
Burton, M. E.: *The Assembly of the League of Nations* (1941).
Carroll, M. J.: *Key to League of Nations Documents, 1920–29* (1930). This and later supplements are an excellent guide to the many League publications.
Dexter, B. V.: *The Years of Opportunity; the League of Nations, 1920–1926* (1967).
Hemleben, S .J.: *Plans for World Peace Through Six Centuries* (1943). A useful study with a good bibliography.
Hill, M.: *The Economic and Financial Organization of the League of Nations: A Survey of Twenty-five Years' Experience* (1945).
Institute on World Organization: *World Organization: A Balance Sheet of the First Great Experiment* (1942).
Kolasa, J.: *International Intellectual Cooperation: The League Experience and the Beginnings of UNESCO* (1962).
Latané, J. H. (ed.): *Development of the League of Nations Idea: Documents and Correspondence of Theodore Marburg* (2 vols., 1932).
Lodge, H. C.: *The Senate and the League of Nations* (1925).
Miller, D. H.: *The Drafting of the Covenant* (2 vols., 1928).
Myers, D. P.: *Handbook of the League of Nations* (1935).
Ranshoffen-Wertheimer, F. F.: *The International Secretariat: A Great Experiment in International Administration* (1945).
Renborg, B. A.: *International Drug Control: A Study of International Administration By and Through the League of Nations* (1947).
Shotwell, J. T., and M. Slavin: *Lessons on Security and Disarmament: From the History of the League of Nations* (1949). A critical appraisal of the League.
Walters, F. P.: *A History of the League of Nations* (2 vols., 1952). The most comprehensive history of the League.
Wilson, W.: *The Case for the League of Nations* (1923). A collection of the President's speeches on the League.
Winkler, H. R.: *The League of Nations Movement in Great Britain, 1914–1919* (1952).
Zimmern, A. E.: *The League of Nations and the Role of Law* (1936). By a British authority.
(Attention is also called to the League of Nations' *Statistical Year Book, Armaments Year Book, Review of World Trade,* and *World Economic Survey.*)

The International Labor Organization

Calhoun, L. J.: *The International Labor Organization and United States Domestic Law* (1953).
Follows, J. W.: *Antecedents of the International Labor Organization* (1951).
Haas, Ernst B.: *Beyond the Nation-State: Functionalism and International Organization* (1964).
International Labour Office: *Automation and Other Technological Developments: Labour and Social Implications* (1957).
————: *International Survey of Social Security, Comparative Analysis and Summary of National Laws* (1950).
————: *Trente ans de combat pour la justice sociale, 1919–1949* (1950).
Jenks, C. W.: *The International Protection of Trade Union Freedom* (1957).
Lowe, B. E.: *The International Protection of Labor: International Organization, History and Law* (rev. ed., 1935).

Shotwell, J. T. (ed.):*The Origins of the International Labor Organization* (2 vols., 1934).

The Permanent Court of International Justice and the International Court of Justice

Bowett, D.: *The Law of International Institutions* (1963).

Carlston, K. S.: *Law and Organization in World Society* (1962).

Davis, C. D.: *The United States and the First Hague Peace Conference* (1962).

Fleming, D. F.: *The United States and the World Court* (1945).

Hambro, E.: *The Case Law of the International Court: A Repertoire of the Judgments, and Advisory Opinions and Orders of the Permanent Court of International Justice and of the International Court of Justice* (1952).

Hudson, M. O.: *The Permanent Court of International Justice, 1920–1942: A Treatise* (rev. ed., 1943).   The best book on the subject.

International Court of Justice: *Reports of Judgments, Advisory Opinions and Orders* (1947 ff.).

————: *Selected Documents Relating to the Drafting of the Statute* (1946).

————: *Yearbook.*

Jenks, C. W.: *The Proper Law of International Organizations* (1962).

————: *The Prospects of International Adjudication* (1964).

Lissitzyn, O. J.: *The International Court of Justice: Its Role in the Maintenance of International Peace and Security* (1951).

McDougal, M. S., et al.: *Studies in World Public Order* (1964).

————, and F. P. Felicano: *Law and Minimum World Public Order* (1964).

Peaslee, A. J.: *International Governmental Organizations: Constitutional Documents* (1961).

Rosenne, S.: *The International Court of Justice* (1957).

The Mandate System

Andrews, F. F.: *The Holy Land Under Mandate* (1931).

Beer, G. L.: *African Questions at the Paris Conference, with Papers on Egypt, Mesopotamia, and the Colonial Settlement* (1923).   By the chief of the colonial division of the American delegation to negotiate peace.

Goldblatt, I.: *The Mandated Territory of South West Africa in Relation to the United Nations* (1961).

Hall, H. D.: *Mandates, Dependencies and Trusteeship* (1948).   A comparative study.

Hanna, P. L.: *British Policy in Palestine* (1942).

Hocking, W. E.: *The Spirit of World Politics: With Special Studies of the Near East* (1932).   Good chapters on mandates.

Logan, R. W.: *The African Mandates in World Politics* (1948).

Margolith, A. M.: *The International Mandates* (1930).   A general survey.

Royal Institute of International Affairs: *Great Britain and Palestine, 1915–1945* (3rd ed., 1946).   The best single account.

Secretariat of the League of Nations: *The Mandates System: Origins, Principles, Application* (1945).

Upthegrove, C. L.: *Empire by Mandate: A History of the Relations of Great Britain with Permanent Mandate Commission of the United Nations* (1959).

Wright, Q.: *Mandates Under the League of Nations* (1930).   An excellent volume with maps, tables, and an extensive bibliography.

Protection of Minorities

Azcarate, P. E.: *League of Nations and National Minorities: An Experiment* (1945).   By the former director of the Minorities Questions Section of the League of Nations.

Barros, J.: *The Aland Islands Question: Its Settlement by the League of Nations* (1968).
Claude, I. L.: *National Minorities: An International Problem* (1955).
Glower, R.: *The Hungarian Minorities in the Succession States* (1937).
Hourani, A. H.: *Minorities in the Arab World* (1947). Deals mostly with pre-World War II conditions.
Janowsky, O. I.: *Nationalities and National Minorities (With Special Reference to East-Central Europe)* (1945).
Kaeckenbeeck, G.: *International Experiment of Upper Silesia, 1922–37* (1942).
Kulischer, E. M.: *The Displacement of Population in Europe* (1943).
———: *Europe on the Move* (1948).
Ladas, S. P.: *The Exchange of Minorities, Greece and Turkey* (1935).
Laponce, J. A.: *The Protection of Minorities* (1960).
Macartney, C. A.: *National States and Minority Rights* (1934).
Mair, L. D.: *The Protection of Minorities* (1928).
Malony, W. O.: *Nationality and the Peace Treaties* (1934).
Meillet, A.: *Les langues dans L'Europe nouvelle* (1928). Contains an extended statistical summary of all the languages of Europe.
Les minorités ethniques en Europe Centrale et Balkanique (1946). One of the most accurate studies with maps, prepared by the French Government.
Robinson, J. (ed.): *Were the Minorities Treaties a Failure?* (1943).
Schechtman, J. B.: *European Population Transfers, 1939–1945* (1946).
Simpson, G. E.: *Racial and Cultural Minorities: An Analysis of Prejudice and Discrimination* (3rd ed., 1965).
Stone, J.: *International Guarantees of Minority Rights* (1932).
———: *Regional Guarantees of Minority Rights: A Study of Minorities Procedure in Upper Silesia* (1933).
Viefhaus, E.: *Die Minderheitenfrage und die Enstehung der Minderheitenschutzvertrag auf der Pariser Friedenskonferenz 1919* (1960).
Wyman, D. S.: *Paper Walls: America and the Refugee Crisis 1938–1941* (1968).

War, Security, and Disarmament

Barnet, R. J., and R. A. Falk (eds.): *Security in Disarmament* (1965).
Bechhoefer, B. C.: *Postwar Negotiations for Arms Control* (1961).
Bull, H.: *The Control of the Arms Race* (1965).
Coles, H. (ed.): *Total War and Cold War: Problems in Civilian Control of the Military* (1962).
Edwards, D. V.: *Arms Control in International Politics* (1969).
Etzioni, A.: *The Hard Way to Peace: A New Strategy* (1962).
Ferrell, R. H.: *Peace in Their Time: The Origins of the Kellogg-Briand Pact* (1952).
Hoag, C. L.: *Preface to Preparedness: The Washington Disarmament Conference and Public Opinion* (1941).
Lefever, F. W. (ed.): *Arms and Arms Control: A Symposium* (1962).
Lieberman, J. T.: *The Struggle to Control Atomic Weapons, 1945–1949* (1970).
Melman, S. (ed.): *Disarmament, Its Politics and Economics* (1962).
Miller, D. H.: *The Geneva Protocol* (1925).
———: *The Peace Pact of Paris* (1928).
Myers, D. P.: *Origin and Conclusion of the Paris Pact* (1929).
Noel-Baker, P. J.: *The Geneva Protocol for the Pacific Settlement of International Disputes* (1925).
O'Connor, R. G.: *Perilous Equilibrium: The United States and the London Naval Conference of 1930* (1962).
Rappard, W. E.: *The Quest for Peace Since the World War* (1940).
Shotwell, J. T.: *On the Rim of the Abyss* (1936).
———: *War as an Instrument of National Policy and Its Renunciation in the Pact of Paris* (1929).
Stockholm International Peace Research Institute: *Yearbook of World Armaments and Disarmament, 1968–69* (1969).

Tate, M.: *The Disarmament Illusion: The Movement for a Limitation of Armaments to 1907* (1942).
Vagts, A.: *A History of Militarism: Romance and Realities of a Profession* (1937).
Wright, Q.: *A Study of War* (2 vols., 1942). A monumental study of war and its causes.

ECONOMIC PROBLEMS

General

Ashworth, W.: *A Short History of the International Economy, 1850–1950* (1952).
Bell, J. F.: *A History of Economic Thought* (1953).
Clark, C.: *The Conditions of Economic Progress* (2nd ed., 1951).
Clough, S. B., and C. Cole: *Economic History of Europe* (3rd ed., 1953).
Drucker, P. F.: *The Age of Discontinuity: Guideline to Our Changing Society* (1969).
Ellsworth, P. T.: *The International Economy* (1950).
Friedlaender, H. E., and J. Oser: *Economic History of Modern Europe* (1953).
Giedion, S.: *Mechanization Takes Command* (1948).
Hayek, F. A. (ed.): *Capitalism and the Historians* (1954).
Hutchison, T. W.: *A Review of Economic Doctrines, 1870–1929* (1953).
James, E.: *Histoire de la pensée économique au XXe siècle* (2 vols., 1955).
Lewis, W. A.: *Economic Survey, 1919–1939* (1949).
Postan, M. M.: *An Economic History of Western Europe, 1945–1964* (1967).
Rostow, W. W.: *The Stages of Economic Growth: A Non-Communist Manifesto* (1960).
Seligman, B. B.: *Main Currents in Western Economics: Economic Thought since 1870* (1962).
Svennilson, I.: *Growth and Stagnation in the European Economy* (1954). An outstanding interpretation.
United Nations: *The Growth of World Industry, 1953–1965* (1967).
Viner, J.: *The Long View and the Short: Studies in Economic Theory and Policy* (1958).

World Depression

Dulles, E. L.: *Depression and Reconstruction* (1936).
Einzig, P.: *The World Economic Crisis, 1929–1932* (1932).
Galbraith, J. K.: *The Great Crash, 1929* (1955).
Haberler, G.: *Prosperity and Depression: A Theoretical Analysis of Cyclical Movements* (3rd ed., 1941).
Mitchell, W. C.: *Business Cycles and Their Causes* (1941).
Moulton, H. G.: *Controlling Factors in Economic Development* (1949).
Ropke, W.: *International Economic Disintegration* (1942).
Rothbard, M. N.: *America's Great Depression* (1963).
Schumpeter, J. A.: *Business Cycles* (2 vols., 1939).
Shannon, D. A. (ed.): *The Great Depression* (1960).

Special Topics

Aitken, H. S. J. (ed.): *The State and Economic Growth* (1959).
Brandt, K., et al.: *Management of Agriculture and Food in the German-Occupied and other Areas of Fortress Europe* (1953).
Brown, W. A., Jr.: *The International Gold Standard Reinterpreted, 1914–1934* (1941).
Burn, D. L.: *Economic History of Steelmaking, 1867–1934* (1940).

Feis, H.: *Europe the World's Banker, 1870–1914* (1930).
Keynes, J. M.: *The General Theory of Employment, Interest and Money* (1936).
Kulischer, E. M.: *Europe on the Move: War and Population Changes, 1917–47* (1948).
League of Nations: *The Agricultural Crisis* (1931).
Lewis, W. A.: *The Theory of Economic Growth* (1955).
Morgan, O. S. (ed.): *Agricultural Systems of Middle Europe* (1933).
Ridgeway, G. L.: *Merchants of Peace: The History of the International Chamber of Commerce* (1959).
Ropke, W.: *The International Order and Economic Integration* (1959).
Stettinius, E. R., Jr.: *Lend-Lease: Weapon for Victory* (1944).
Sturmthal, A.: *The Tragedy of European Labor, 1918–1939* (1943).
United States Bureau of the Budget: *The United States at War: Development and Administration of the War Program of the Federal Government* (1946).
Von Neumann, J., and O. Morgenstern: *Theory of Games and Economic Behavior* (3rd ed., 1953).

POLITICAL THOUGHT

Political Theory of Various States

Bochenski, J. M.: *Soviet Russian Dialectical Materialism* (1963).
Bowen, R. H.: *German Theories of the Corporative State, with Special Reference to the Period 1870–1919* (1947).
Chabod, F.: *A History of Italian Fascism* (1963).
Cohen, H. E.: *Recent Theories of Sovereignty* (1937). Contains chapters on the British Empire and pluralism.
Cross, C.: *The Fascists in Britain* (1961).
Emerson, E.: *State and Sovereignty in Modern Germany* (1928). German political theory and federalism.
Fraenkel, E.: *The Dual State: A Contribution to the Theory of Dictatorship* (1941). Special reference to Germany.
Hallowell, J. H.: *The Decline of Liberalism as an Ideology with Particular Reference to German Politico-Legal Thought* (1943).
Joll, J.: *The Anarchists* (1966).
Jordan, Z. A.: *Philosophy and Ideology: The Development of Philosophy and Marxism-Leninism in Poland Since the Second World War* (1963).
Klemperer, K. von: *Germany's New Conservatism: Its History and Dilemma in the Twentieth Century* (1957).
Krieger, L.: *The German Idea of Freedom: History of a Political Tradition* (1957).
Magid, H. M.: *English Political Pluralism: The Problem of Freedom and Organization* (1941).
Marcuse, H.: *Soviet Marxism: A Critical Analysis* (1958).
Mayer, J. P.: *Political Thought in France from the Revolution to the Fourth Republic* (rev. ed., 1949). A brief, useful account with a good bibliography.
Muret, C. T.: *French Royalist Doctrines Since the Revolution* (1933).
Payne, S. G.: *Falange: A History of Spanish Fascism* (1961).
Soltau, R.: *French Political Thought in the Nineteenth Century* (1931).
Webster, R. A.: *Christian Democracy in Italy, 1860–1960* (1961).
Wetter, G. A.: *Dialectical Materialism: A Historical and Systematic Survey of Philosophy in the Soviet Union* (1958).

Nationalism and Imperialism

Barghoorn, F. C.: *Soviet Russian Nationalism* (1956).
Baron, S. W.: *Modern Nationalism and Religion* (1947).

Cobban, A.: *National Self-Determination* (1944). A consideration of how this problem affects different areas of the world.

Deutsch, K. W.: *Nationalism and Social Communications: An Inquiry into the Foundations of Nationality* (1953).

——, and Richard W. Merritt (eds.): *Nationalism and National Development: An Interdisciplinary Bibliography* (1970).

Emerson, R.: *From Empire to Nation: The Rise to Self-assertion of Asian and African Peoples* (1960).

Hayes, C. J. H.: *Essays on Nationalism* (1926).

——: *Historical Evolution of Modern Nationalism* (new ed., 1949).

Hertz, F.: *Nationality in History and Politics: A Study of the Psychology and Sociology of National Sentiment and Character* (1944).

Joseph, B.: *Nationality: Its Nature and Problems* (1929).

Kedourie, E.: *Nationalism* (1960).

Kemilainen, A.: *Nationalism: Problems Concerning the World, the Concept and Classification* (1964).

Kohn, H.: *The Age of Nationalism: The First Era of Global History* (1962).

——: *The Idea of Nationalism* (1944).

——: *Nationalism: The Meaning and History* (1955).

——: *Pan-Slavism: Its History and Ideology* (1953). The best volume on this important subject.

Parkes, J.: *The Emergence of the Jewish Problem, 1878–1939* (1946). An objective survey of different European countries, sponsored by the Royal Institute of International Affairs.

Royal Institute of International Affairs: *Nationalism* (1940). A report by a study group, thorough and broad in scope.

Schumpeter, J. A.: *Imperialism and Social Classes* (1951). Stresses sociological causes of imperialism.

Shafer, B. C.: *Nationalism: Interpreters and Interpretations* (1959).

——: *Nationalism: Myth and Reality* (1955). Excellent, with a good selected bibliography.

Snyder, L. L.: *The Dynamics of Nationalism: Readings in Its Meaning and Development* (1964).

——: *The New Nationalism* (1968).

Strausz-Hupé, R., and H. W. Hazard (eds.): *The Idea of Colonialism* (1958).

Sturzo, D. L.: *Nationalism and Internationalism* (1946).

Valentin, H.: *Antisemitism Historically and Critically Examined* (1936).

Whitaker, V. G. (ed.): *Nationalism and International Progress* (rev. ed., 1961).

Winslow, E. M.: *The Pattern of Imperialism: A Study in the Theories of Power* (1948). (See also the bibliography on minorities in the section on the League of Nations.)

Totalitarianism

Adorno, T. W., et al.: *The Authoritarian Personality* (1956).

Arendt, H.: *The Origins of Totalitarianism* (rev. ed., 1966).

Buchheim, H.: *Totalitarian Rule: Its Nature and Characteristics* (1968).

Cobban, A.: *Dictatorship: The History and Theory* (1939).

Drucker, P. F.: *The End of Economic Man: A Study of the New Totalitarianism* (1939).

Friedrich, C. J. (ed.): *Totalitarianism* (1954). A series of papers presented at a conference.

——, M. Curtis, and B. R. Barber: *Totalitarianism in Perspective* (1969).

Gregor, A. J.: *Contemporary Radical Ideologies: Totalitarian Thought in the Twentieth Century* (1968).

Kornhauser, W.: *The Politics of Mass Society* (1959).

Talmon, J. L.: *The Rise of Totalitarian Democracy* (1952).

Wittfogel, R. A.: *Oriental Despotism: A Comparative Study of Total Power* (1957).

Modernization

Almond, G. A., and J. S. Coleman (eds.): *The Politics of the Developing Areas* (1960).

Apter, D. E.: *The Politics of Modernization* (1965).

Black, C. E.: *The Dynamics of Modernization: A Study in Comparative History* (1966).

——, and R. A. Falk (eds.): *The Future of the International Legal Order* (5 vols., 1969–).

Brode, J. (ed.): *The Process of Modernization: An Annotated Bibliography of the Sociocultural Aspects of Development* (1969).

Coleman, J. S. (ed.): *Education and Political Development* (1965).

Deutsch, K. W.: *The Nerves of Government: Models of Political Communication and Control* (1963).

Eisenstadt, S. N.: *Modernization: Growth and Diversity* (1963).

Ellmann, R., and C. Feidelson (eds.): *The Modern Tradition: Background of Modern Literature* (1965).

Ellul, J.: *The Technological Society* (1964).

Frey, F. W., P. Stephenson, and K. A. Smith (eds.): *Survey Research in Comparative Social Change: A Bibliography* (1969).

Hagen, E.: *On the Theory of Social Change: How Economic Growth Begins* (1962).

Haskins, C. P.: *The Scientific Revolution and World Politics* (1964).

Hunter, G.: *Modernizing Peasant Societies: A Comparative Study in Asia and Africa* (1969).

Huntington, S. P.: *Political Order in Changing Societies* (1968).

La Palombara, J. (ed.): *Bureaucracy and Political Development* (1963).

Levy, M. J.: *Modernization and the Structure of Societies* (2 vols., 1966).

Moore, B., Jr.: *Social Origins of Dictatorship and Democracy: Lord and Peasant in the Making of the Modern World* (1966).

Morse, C., et al.: *Modernization by Design: Social Change in the Twentieth Century* (1969).

Nash, M.: *The Golden Road to Modernity: Village Life in Contemporary Burma* (1965).

Parsons, T.: *Structure and Process in Modern Societies* (1960).

Pye, L. W. (ed.): *Communications and Political Development* (1963).

——, and S. Verba (eds.): *Political Culture and Political Development* (1965).

Richtar, R. (ed.): *Civilization at the Crossroads: Social and Human Implications of the Scientific and Technological Revolution* (3rd ed., 1969).

Riggs, F. W.: *Administration in Developing Countries: The Theory of Prismatic Society* (1964).

Rustow, D. A.: *A World of Nations: The Dynamics of Modern Politics* (1966).

Shils, E. A.: *Political Development in the New States* (1962).

Sinai, I. R.: *The Challenge of Modernization* (1965).

——: *In Search of the Modern World* (1967).

Spengler, J. J., and R. Braibanti (eds.): *Tradition, Values, and Socio-Economic Development* (1961).

Spitz, A. A.: *Developmental Change: An Annotated Bibliography* (1969).

Vallier, I.: *Catholicism, Social Control, and Modernization in Latin America* (1970).

Wallas, G.: *The Great Society: A Psychological Analysis* (1914).

Ward, R. E., and D. A. Rustow (eds.): *Political Modernization in Turkey and Japan* (1964).

Weiner, M. (ed.): *Modernization: The Dynamics of Growth* (1966).

Liberalism

Ascoli, M., and F. Lehmann (eds.): *Political and Economic Democracy* (1937).

Bryn-Jones, D.: *Toward a Democratic Order* (1945).

Bullock, A., and W. Shick (eds.): *The Liberal Tradition: From Fox to Keynes* (1957).

Bunke, H. C.: *The Liberal Dilemma* (1964).
Burnham, J.: *Suicide of the West: An Essay on the Meaning and Destiny of Liberalism* (1964).
Cole, C. D. H.: *Some Relations Between Political and Economic Theory* (1934).
Croce, B.: *Politics and Morals* (1945). Pertinent essays by the leading Italian historian and philosopher.
Fogarty, M. P.: *Christian Democracy in Western Europe, 1820–1953* (1957).
Friedrich, C. J.: *Constitutional Government and Democracy: Theory and Practice in Europe and America* (rev. ed., 1950).
Greene, T. M.: *Liberalism: Its Theory and Practice* (1957).
Grimond, J.: *The Liberal Challenge* (1963).
Laski, H. J.: *Reflections on the Revolution of Our Time* (1943).
———: *The Rise of Liberalism* (1937).
Lippmann, W.: *The Good Society* (1937). An analysis of collectivism and liberalism.
Lodge, G. C.: *Spearheads of Democracy: Labor in the Developing Countries* (1962).
Lowi, T. J.: *The End of Liberalism: Ideology Policy, and the Crisis of Public Authority* (1969).
Mises, L. von: *The Free and Prosperous Commonwealth: An Exposition of the Ideas of Classical Liberalism* (1963).
Pemrock, J. R.: *Liberal Democracy: The Merits and Prospects* (1950).
Rossiter, C. L.: *Constitutional Dictatorship: Crisis Government in the Modern Democracies* (1948).
Salvadori, M.: *Liberal Democracy* (1957).
Schlesinger, A. M., Jr.: *The Vital Center* (1949).
Taylor, O. H.: *The Classical Liberalism, Marxism, and the Twentieth Century* (1960).
Watkins, F.: *The Political Tradition of the West: A Study of the Development of Modern Liberalism* (1948).

Fascism and National Socialism

Ascoli, M., and A. Feiler: *Fascism for Whom?* (1938). Theory and practice in Italy and Germany.
Baynes, N. (ed.): *Hitler's Speeches* (2 vols., 1942). Well-edited and useful volumes.
Borgese, G. A.: *Goliath: The March of Fascism* (1937).
Carsten, F. L.: *The Rise of Racism* (1967).
Chamberlain, H. S.: *Foundations of the Nineteenth Century* (1912).
Chandler, A. R.: *Rosenberg's Nazi Myth* (1945).
Cole, G. D. H.: *Socialism and Fascism, 1931–1939* (1960). The fifth volume in his *History of Socialist Thought*.
Florinsky, M. T.: *Fascism and National Socialism* (1936).
Ford, G. S. (ed.): *Dictatorship in the Modern World* (2nd ed., 1939). Chapters on various dictatorial regimes.
Gobineau, A. de: *The Inequality of Human Races* (1915).
Gooch, G. P.: *Dictatorship in Theory and Practice* (1935). A stimulating lecture by one of England's leading historians.
Hitler, A.: *Mein Kampf* (1925–27); published in abridged form in America as *My Battle* (1933) and in England as *My Struggle* (1933); a complete and unabridged English translation appeared as *Mein Kampf* (1939) in both America and England.
Hitler's Secret Conversations, 1941–1944 (1953).
Hoffman, R.: *The Organic State: An Historical View of Contemporary Politics* (1939). Fascism and national socialism.
Mosca, G.: *The Ruling Class* (1939).
Mussolini, B.: *The Political and Social Doctrine of Fascism* (1933). A translation of his article in the *Enciclopedia Italiana*.
Neumann, F.: *Behemoth* (1942).
Palmieri, M.: *The Philosophy of Fascism* (1936).
Rauschning, H.: *The Revolution of Nihilism* (1939).

Rocco, A.: *The Political Doctrine of Fascism* (1926).
Rosenberg, A.: *Der Mythus des 20. Jahrhunderts* (1930).

Socialism and Communism

Beckwith, B. P.: *The Economic Theory of a Socialist Economy* (1948). An analyt-
    ical treatment by topic.
Berlin, I.: *Karl Marx* (2nd ed., 1948). A good brief biography.
Bernstein, E.: *Evolutionary Socialism* (1909).
Bochenski, J. M., and G. Niemeyer (eds.): *Handbook on Communism* (1962).
Borkenau, F.: *European Communism* (1953). The best general survey.
Burns, E.: *A Handbook of Marxism* (1935). The convenient collection of Marxist
    sources.
Chambre, H.: *From Karl Marx to Mao Tse-tung* (1963).
Cole, G. D. H.: *A History of Socialist Thought* (5 vols., 1953–60).
Daniels, R. V. (ed.): *A Documentary History of Communism* (1960).
————: *The Nature of Communism* (1962).
Djilas, M.: *The New Class: An Analysis of the Communist System* (1957).
Einaudi, M., et al.: *Communism in Western Europe* (1951).
Fundamentals of Marxism-Leninism (rev. ed., 1962). An official Soviet treatise.
Gay, P.: *The Dilemma of Democratic Socialism: Eduard Bernstein's Challenge to
    Marx* (1952).
Gyorgy, A.: *Issues of World Communism* (1966).
Hunt, R. N. C.: *A Guide to Communist Jargon* (1957).
————: *Marxism: Past and Present* (1955).
————: *The Theory and Practice of Communism* (rev. ed., 1957).
Joll, J.: *The Second International, 1889–1914* (1955).
Kautsky, K.: *Communism and Socialism* (1932).
Leites, N.: *A Study of Bolshevism* (1953). Studded with quotations arranged under
    various topics.
Lichtheim, G.: *Marxism: An Historical and Critical Study* (1961).
Mehring, F.: *Karl Marx: The Story of His Life* (1935).
Meyer, A. G.: *Communism* (1957).
————: *Leninism* (1957).
————: *Marxism: The Unity of Theory and Practice* (1955).
Plamenatz, J.: *German Marxism and Russian Communism* (1954).
Rosenberg, A.: *A History of Bolshevism* (1934).
Rossiter, C. L.: *Marxism: The View from America* (1960).
Rumyantsev, A. M.: *Categories and Laws of the Political Economy of Communism*
    (1969).
Salvadori, M.: *Rise of Modern Communism* (1952).
Seton-Watson, H.: *Nationalism and Communism: Essays 1946–1963* (1964).
Ulam, A. B.: *The Unfinished Revolution: An Essay on the Sources of Influence of
    Marxism and Communism* (1960).
Wilson, E.: *To the Finland Station* (1940). On the Western background of Com-
    munist thought.
Wolfe, B. D.: *Marxism: One Hundred Years in the Life of a Doctrine* (1965).
Yearbook on International Communist Affairs (1967 ff.). Follows summary volume
    World Communism: A Handbook 1918–1965 (1966). Domestic and inter-
    national activities of individual Communist parties throughout the world.
(See also books on the Soviet Union.)

Revolution in Theory and Practice

Arendt, H.: *On Revolution* (1963).
Bienen, H.: *Violence and Social Change* (1968).

Black, C. E., and T. P. Thornton (eds.): *Communism and Revolution: The Strategic Uses of Political Violence* (1962).

Brinton, C.: *The Anatomy of Revolution* (rev. ed., 1965).

Coser, L. A.: *Continuities in the Study of Social Conflict* (1968).

Crozier, B.: *The Rebels: A Study of Post-War Insurrections* (1960).

Dahrendorf, R.: *Class and Class Conflict in Industrial Society* (1959).

Drachkovitch, M. M. (ed.): *The Revolutionary Internationals, 1864–1943* (1966).

Eckstein, Harry (ed.): *Internal War* (1964).

Friedrich, C. J. (ed.): *Revolution* (1966).

Gurr, T. R.: *Why Men Rebel* (1970).

Hobsbawm, E. J.: *Social Bandits and Primitive Rebels: Studies of Archaic Forms of Social Movements in the 19th and 20th Centuries* (1959).

Johnson, C.: *Revolutionary Change* (1966).

Leiden, C., and K. M. Schmitt (eds.): *The Politics of Violence in the Modern World* (1968).

Luttwak, E.: *Coup d'état: A Practical Handbook* (1968).

Malaparte, C.: *Coup d'état: The Technique of Revolution* (1932).

Mazlish, B., et al. (eds.): *Revolution: A Reader* (1971).

Paret, P., and J. W. Shy: *Guerrillas in the 1960's* (1964).

Pettee, G. A.: *The Process of Revolution* (1938).

Ponomarev, B. W.: *World Revolutionary Movement of the Working Class* (1967).

Tucker, R. C.: *The Marxian Revolutionary Idea* (1969).

Wolf, E.: *Peasant Wars of the Twentieth Century* (1969).

Historical Interpretations of the Twentieth Century

Berdyaev, N.: *The Meaning of History* (1936). A general religious approach by a Russian scholar, originally presented as lectures in 1919–20.

Clough, S.: *The Rise and Fall of Civilizations: An Inquiry into the Relationship between Economic Development and Civilization* (1951).

Geyl, P.: *Debates with Historians* (1958).

———: *Use and Abuse of History* (1955).

Halecki, O.: *The Limits and Divisions of European History* (1950).

Halperin, S. W. (ed.): *Some 20th Century Historians; Essays on Eminent Europeans* (1961).

Hay, D.: *Europe: The Emergence of an Idea* (1968).

Mayer, A. J.: *Dynamics of Counterrevolution in Europe, 1870–1956: An Analytic Framework* (1971).

McNeill, W. H.: *Past and Future* (1954).

———: *The Rise of the West* (1963). A reply to Spengler.

Sontag, R. J.: *A Broken World, 1918–1939* (1971).

Sorokin, P. A.: *The Crisis of Our Age: The Social and Cultural Outlook* (1941).

Spengler, O.: *The Decline of the West* (2 vols., 1926–28).

Toynbee, A. J.: *A Study of History* (11 vols., 1934–59).

———: *A Study of History* (2 vols., 1947–57). An abridged version.

SECOND WORLD CRISIS

Diplomatic Background

Bishop, D. G.: *The Roosevelt-Litvinov Agreements: The American View* (1965).

Carr, E. H.: *German-Soviet Relations Between the Two World Wars, 1919–1939* (1951).

Compton, J. V.: *The Swastika and the Eagle: Hitler, the United States and the Origins of World War II.* (1967).

Craig, G. A., and F. Gilbert (eds.): *The Diplomats, 1919–1939* (1953). A series of valuable essays on various diplomats.

Documents and Materials Relating to the Eve of the Second World War (2 vols., 1948). A collection of German documents published by the Soviet government.

Documents on German Foreign Policy, 1918–1945 (1949 ff.). Published under the editorship of a committee of American, British, and French scholars.

Duroselle, J.-B.: *Histoire diplomatique de 1919 à nos jours* (rev. ed., 1962).

Eubank, K.: *Munich* (1963).

——:*The Origins of World War II* (1969). A short account.

Gantenbein, J. W. (ed.): *Documentary Background of World War II, 1931–1941* (1948).

Hilger, G., and A. G. Meyer: *The Incompatible Allies: A Memoir-History of German-Soviet Relations, 1918–1941* (1953).

Jarausch, K. H.: *The Four Power Pact, 1933* (1965).

Kennan, G. F.: *From Prague after Munich: Diplomatic Papers 1938–1940* (1968).

Lafore, L.: *The End of Glory. An Interpretation of the Origin of World War II* (1970).

Litvinov, M.: *Against Aggression* (1939). A collection of public statements.

Meskill, J. M.: *Hitler and Japan: The Hollow Alliance* (1966).

Molotov, V.: *Soviet Peace Policy* (1941). A collection of public statements.

Mosley, L.: *On Borrowed Time. How World War II Began* (1969).

Namier, L. B.: *Diplomatic Prelude, 1938–1939* (1948).

——: *Europe in Decay: A Study in Disintegration* (1950).

Nazi Conspiracy and Aggression (8 vols., 1946). The official records of the International Military Tribunal that tried the German war criminals at Nuremberg.

Nixon, E. B. (ed.): *Franklin D. Roosevelt and Foreign Affairs* (3 vols., 1968).

Offner, A. A.: *American Appeasement: U.S. Foreign Policy and Germany 1933–1938* (1969).

Potemkin, V. P. (ed.): *Histoire de la diplomatie* (3 vols., 1946–47). French translation of an official Soviet account. The third volume covers the period 1919–39. A revised version is being prepared by V. A. Zorin (5 vols., 1959–   ).

Renouvin, P.: *Les crises du XXᵉ siècle: Vol. I, De 1914 à 1929* (1957); *Vol. II, De 1929 à 1945* (1958). These are Volumes VII. and VIII. of the *Histoire des relations internationales* edited by Renouvin.

Rossi, A.: *The Russo-German Alliance August 1939 to June 1941* (1950).

Schroeder, P. W.: *The Axis Alliance and Japanese-American Relations, 1941* (1958).

Taylor, A. J. P.: *The Origins of the Second World War* (1963).

Thorne, C.: *The Approach of War, 1938–1939* (1967).

Toscano, M.: *The Origins of the Pact of Steel* (1967).

Weinberg, G. L.: *Germany and the Soviet Union, 1939–1941* (1954).

Wiskemann, E.: *The Rome-Berlin Axis: A History of the Relations Between Hitler and Mussolini* (1949).

Woodward, E. L., and R. Butler (eds.): *Documents on British Foreign Policy, 1919–1939* (1946 ff.).

Political Memoirs and Accounts

Alfieri, D.: *Dictators Face to Face* (1955). Memoirs of the Italian ambassador to Hitler's Germany.

Anfuso, F.: *Rom-Berlin im diplomatischen Spiegel* (1951).

Armstrong, A.: *Unconditional Surrender: The Impact of the Casablanca Policy upon World War II* (1961).

Beck, J.: *Dernier rapport: Politique polonaise, 1926–1939* (1951). Memoirs of Poland's minister of foreign affairs.

Bluecher, W. von: *Gesandter zwischen Diktatur und Demokratie* (1951). Memoirs of the German minister to Finland.

Blum, L.: *L'oeuvre de Léon Blum: Mémoires, 1940–1945* (1955).

Bonnet, G.: *Défense de la paix* (2 vols., 1946–48).

Butow, R. J. C.: *Tojo and the Coming of the War*.

Byrnes, J. F.: *Speaking Frankly* (1947). By the secretary of state, 1945–47.

Chadwin, M. L.: *The Hawks of World War II* (1968).

Churchill, W.: *History of the Second World War* (6 vols., 1948–53).

Correspondence Between the Chairman of the Council of Ministers of the U.S.S.R. and the Presidents of the U.S.A. and the Prime Minister of Great Britain During the Great Patriotic War of 1941–1945 (2 vols., 1957). An official Soviet edition of Stalin's wartime correspondence.

Coulondre R.: *De Staline à Hitler: Souvenirs de deux ambassades, 1936–1939* (1950). Memoirs of a French ambassador at Moscow and Berlin.

Davies, J. E.: *Mission to Moscow* (1941).

Deane, J. R.: *The Strange Alliance: The Story of Our Efforts at Wartime Collaboration with Russia* (1947).

Dirksen, H. von.: *Moscow, Tokyo, London: Twenty Years of German Foreign Policy* (1952). By a German ambassador.

Divine, R. A.: *Roosevelt and World War II* (1969).

Feis, H.: *Churchill, Roosevelt, Stalin: The War They Waged and the Peace They Sought* (1957).

Fischer, A. (ed.): *Teheran, Jalta, Potsdam. Die sowjetischen Protokolle von den Kriegskonferenzen der "Grossen Drei"* (1968).

François-Poncet, A.: *The Fateful Years: Memoirs of a French Ambassador in Berlin, 1931–1938* (1949).

Friedlander, S.: *Prelude to Downfall: Hitler and the United States* (1967).

Gafencu, G.: *Last Days of Europe: A Diplomatic Journey in 1939* (1948).

———: *Prelude to the Russian Campaign* (1945).

Gamelin, M. G.: *Servir* (2 vols., 1946).

Gibson, H. A. (ed.): *The Ciano Diaries, 1939–1943* (1946).

Grew, J. C.: *Turbulent Era* (2 vols., 1952). Memoirs of the United States ambassador to Japan.

Henderson, N.: *Failure of a Mission* (1940).

———: *Water Under the Bridge* (1945).

Hugessen, H.: *Diplomat in Peace and War* (1949). Diary of the British minister to the Baltic states and to Turkey 1939–44.

Hull, C.: *Memoirs* (2 vols., 1948).

Ickes, H. L.: *The Secret Diary of Harold L. Ickes* (3 vols., 1953–54). Inside view on the making of U.S. policy 1933–39.

Ike, N. (trans. and ed.): *Japan's Decision for War. Records of the 1941 Policy Conferences* (1967).

Kennan, G. F.: *American Diplomacy, 1900–1950* (1951). Includes two articles on containment of Russia.

———: *Realities of American Policy* (1954).

Kordt, E.: *Wahn und Wirklichkeit: Die Aussenpolitik des Dritten Reiches* (1948).

Krosby, H. P.: *Finland, Germany, and the Soviet Union, 1940–1941: The Petsamo Dispute* (1968).

Langer, W. L., and E. S. Gleason: *The Challenge to Isolation, 1937–1940* (1952).

———: *Undeclared War, 1940–41* (1953). Authoritative accounts of American policy.

McNeill, W. H.: *America, Britain and Russia: Their Co-operation and Conflict, 1941–1946* (1953).

Medlicott, W. N.: *The Economic Blockade* (2 vols., 1952–59).

Meissner, O.: *Staatssekretar unter Ebert-Hindenburg-Hitler* (1950).

Muggeridge, M. (ed.): *Ciano's Diplomatic Papers* (1948).

Papen, F. von: *Memoirs* (1952). An apology, but nevertheless informative.

Reynaud, P.: *Au coeur de la melée, 1930–1945* (1951).

———: *La France a sauvé l'Europe* (2 vols., 1947).

Ribbentrop, J. von: *Zwischen London und Moskau: Erinnerungen und letzte Aufzeichnungen* (1953). Apology of Hitler's minister of foreign affairs.

Rintelen, E. von: *Mussolini als Bundesgenosse: Erinnerungen des Deutschen Militärattachés in Rom, 1936–1943* (1951).

Schmidt, P.: *Hitler's Interpreter* (1951).

Sherwood, R. E.: *Roosevelt and Hopkins: An Intimate History* (1948).

Stettinius, E. R., Jr.: *Roosevelt and the Russians: The Yalta Conference* (1949).
Stimson, H. L.: *On Active Service in Peace and War* (1948).
Toynbee, A. J. (ed.): *Survey of International Affairs, 1939–1946* (11 vols., 1952–58).
Weizsäcker, E. von: *Memoirs* (1951). By the head of the German foreign office.
Welles, S.: *Seven Decisions That Shaped History* (1951). By the United States under-secretary of state.
Weygand, M.: *Recalled to Service: The Memoirs of General Maxime Weygand* (1952).

Military Memoirs and Accounts

Alexander, H. R.: *The Alexander Memoirs, 1940–1945* (1962).
Allen, W. E. D., and P. Muratoff: *The Russian Campaigns of 1941–1943* (1944).
Anders, W.: *An Army in Exile: The Story of the Second Polish Corps* (1949).
———: *Hitler's Defeat in Russia* (1953).
Armstrong, J. A. (ed.): *Soviet Partisans in World War II* (1968).
Arnold, H. H.: *Global Mission* (1949). By the chief of the United States air forces.
Bateson, C.: *The War With Japan: A Concise History* (1969).
Bekker, C. D.: *Defeat at Sea: The Struggle and Eventual Destruction of the German Navy, 1939–1945* (1955).
Belot, R. de: *The Struggle for the Mediterranean* (1951).
Bor-Komorowski, T.: *The Secret Army* (1951). An account of the Polish under-ground forces.
Burdick, C. B.: *Germany's Military Strategy and Spain in World War II* (1968).
Butcher, H. C.: *My Three Years with Eisenhower, 1942–1945* (1946).
Clark, M. W.: *From the Danube to the Yalu* (1954).
Colvin, I. G.: *Master Spy: The Incredible Story of Admiral Wilhelm Canaris* (1952). An account of the German secret service.
Craven, W. F., and J. L. Cate (eds.): *The Army Air Force in World War II* (6 vols., 1948–55).
Davis, K. S.: *Experience of War, The United States in World War II* (1965).
De Gaulle, Charles: *War Memoirs* (5 vols., 1955–60).
Detwiler, Donald S.: *Hitler, Franco, und Gibraltar. Die Frage des spanischen Eintritts in den zweiten Weltkrieg* (1962).
Eisenhower, D. D.: *Crusade in Europe* (1949).
Erickson, J.: *The Secret High Command: A Military-Political History, 1918–1941* (1962).
Feis, H.: *Between War and Peace: The Potsdam Conference* (1960).
Fuller, J. F. C.: *The Second World War, 1939–45: A Strategical and Tactical History* (1949).
Gallagher, M. P.: *The Soviet History of World War II: Myths, Memories, and Realities* (1963).
Galland, A.: *The First and the Last: The Rise and Fall of the German Fighter Forces, 1938–1945* (1954).
Garfield, B.: *The Thousand Mile War: World War II in Alaska and the Aleutians* (1969).
Gilbert, F. (ed.): *Hitler Directs The War: The Secret Records of His Daily Military Conferences* (1950).
Goddard, D. C.: *The War in the Far East, 1941–1945* (1969).
Greenfield, K. R.: *American Strategy in World War II: A Reconsideration* (1963).
Guderian, H.: *Panzer Leader* (1952).
Harris, A. T.: *Bomber Offensive* (1947).
Higgins, T.: *Hitler and Russia, the Third Reich in a Two-Front War, 1937–1943* (1966).
Hinsley, F. H.: *Hitler's Strategy* (1951). Brief military history of the war.
Hubatch, W.: *"Weserübung": die deutsche Bezetzung von Danemark und Norwegen 1940* (1960).
Ismay, H. L.: *Memoirs* (1960).

Jackson, W. G. F.: *The Battle for Italy* (1967).

Jones, R. H.: *The Roads to Russia: United States Lend-Lease to the Soviet Union* (1969).

Keitel, W.: *The Memoirs of Field-Marshal Keitel* (trans. by D. Irving, 1966).

Kesselring, A.: *Memoirs* (2nd ed., 1954). By the German commander in Italy.

Killen, J.: *A History of the Luftwaffe* (1968).

Kimball, W. F.: *The Most Unsordid Act: Lend-Lease, 1939–1941* (1969).

Kimmel, H. E.: *Admiral Kimmel's Story* (1955). By the commander in chief of the Pacific Fleet at the time of Pearl Harbor.

King, E. J.: *U.S. Navy at War, 1941–1945* (1946). By the wartime chief of naval operations.

Kingston-McCoughry, E. J.: *Defense: Policy and Strategy* (1960).

Kleist, P.: *Zwischen Hitler und Stalin, 1939–45* (1950). German policy in Russia during the war.

Leverkuehn, P.: *German Military Intelligence* (1954).

Lewin, R.: *Rommel as Military Commander* (1968).

Liddell Hart, B. H.: *The Rommel Papers* (1953).

————: *Strategy: The Indirect Approach* (1954). A discussion of military strategy from the Greeks on down, with two thirds of the book on the years after 1914.

Lindbaek, L.: *Norway's New Saga of the Sea: The Story of Her Merchant Marine in World War II* (1969).

Long, G.: *Greece, Crete and Syria* (1953). An account of World War II campaigns in these areas from the Australian point of view.

Manstein, E. von: *Lost Victories* (1958).

Matloff, M., and E. M. Snell: *Strategic Planning for Coalition Warfare* (2 vols., 1953–59).

Montgomery, B. L.: *El Alamein to the River Sangro* (1949).

————: *Normandy to the Baltic* (1948).

Morison, S. E.: *History of United States Naval Operations in World War II* (11 vols., 1947–57).

————: *Strategy and Compromise* (1958).

Moulton, J. L.: *The Norwegian Campaign of 1940: A Study of Warfare in Three Dimensions* (1966).

Nobécourt, J.: *Hitler's Last Gamble: The Battle of the Bulge* (1967).

O'Ballance, E.: *The Red Army: A Short History* (1964).

Pavlov, D. V. (trans. J. C. Adams): *Leningrad, 1941: The Blockade* (1965).

Puleston, W. D.: *The Influence of Sea Power in World War II* (1947).

Roginski, W. V., et al. (eds.): *SSSR v Velikoi Otechestvennoi Voine, 1941–1945 gg.* (1964). An official Soviet account.

Salisbury, H. E.: *The 900 Days: The Siege of Leningrad* (1969).

Shtemenko, S. M.: *The Soviet General Staff at War, 1941–1945* (1970).

Smith, J. E.: *The Defense of Berlin* (1963).

Snell, J. L.: *Illusion and Necessity: The Diplomacy of Global War 1939–1945* (1963).

Snyder, L. L.: *The War: A Concise History, 1939–1945* (1960).

Speidel, H.: *Invasion 1944* (1949). By a German general.

Stacey, C. P.: *The Canadian Army, 1939–1944* (1948).

Stein, G. H.: *The Waffen SS: Hitler's Elite Guard at War 1939–1945* (1966).

Theobald, R. A.: *The Final Secret of Pearl Harbor* (1954). A criticism of Roosevelt's policy by a United States admiral.

Trevor-Roper, H. R. (ed.): *Blitzkrieg to Defeat: Hitler's War Directives 1939–1945* (1965).

Tsatsos, J.: *The Sword's Fierce Edge: A Journal of the Occupation of Greece, 1941–1944* (1969).

United States Army in World War II (1947 ff.). Some ninety-nine volumes planned in this official series.

Warlimont, W.: *Inside Hitler's Headquarters, 1939–45* (1964).

Webster, C. K.: *The Strategic Air Offensive Against Germany, 1939–1945* (4 vols., 1961).

Werner, H.: *Iron Coffins: A Personal Account of the German U-Boat Battles in World War II* (1969).
Wilmot, C.: *The Struggle for Europe* (1952). A military history of World War II.
Wright, Gordon: *The Ordeal of Total War 1939–1945* (1968).
Zhukov, G. K.: *Marshal Zhukov's Greatest Battles* (1969). Partial translation of Zhukov's memoirs (Moscow, 1969).

THE UNITED NATIONS

Documents

Documents of the United Nations Conference on International Organization, San Francisco, 1945 (16 vols., 1945–46). The official record.
Peaslee, A. J.: *International Governmental Organizations: Constitutional Documents* (2 vols., 2nd ed., 1961). Constitutions of all specialized agencies and also of the organizations.
Sohn, L. B. (ed.): *Basic Documents of the United Nations* (1956). A convenient collection of the most important documents.
United Nations: *Official Records* (1946 ff.).
United States Congress, Senate Committee on Foreign Relations: *Review of the United Nations Charter: A Collection of Documents* (1954). A very useful commentary.
United States Department of State: *The United Nations Conference on International Organization, San Francisco, April 25 to June 26, 1945: Selected Documents* (1946).
World Peace Foundation: *The United Nations in the Making: Basic Documents* (1945).

Organization, Procedures, Commentaries

Asamoah, Obed Y.: *The Legal Significance of the Declarations of the General Assembly of the United Nations* (1966).
Asher, R. E., et al.: *The United Nations and Promotion of the General Welfare* (1957). Human rights, education, underdeveloped countries, and so forth.
Bailey, S. D.: *The General Assembly of the United Nations: A Study of Procedure and Practice* (1960).
———: *The Secretariat of the United Nations* (1962).
———: *Voting in the Security Council* (1969).
Cheever, D. S., and H. F. Haviland, Jr.: *International Organization in World Affairs* (1954). Structure, condition, and functions of existing international organizations and agencies.
Clark, G., and L. B. Sohn: *World Peace Through World Law* (1958). Proposed revision of UN Charter.
Claude, I. L., Jr.: *The Changing United Nations* (1967).
Cohen, B.: *The United Nations: Constitutional Developments, Growth and Possibilities* (1961).
Goodrich, L. M.: *The United Nations* (1959).
———, E. Hambro, and A. P. Simons: *Charter of the United Nations: Commentary and Documents* (3rd. ed., 1969).
———, and A. P. Simons: *The United Nations and the Maintenance of International Peace and Security* (1955). First of a series of volumes on the United Nations sponsored by the Brookings Institution.
Goodspeed, S. S.: *The Nature and Function of International Organization* (2nd ed., 1968).

Griffin, G. E.: *The Fearful Master: A Second Look at the United Nations* (1964).

Gross, E. A.: *The United Nations: Structure for Peace* (1962).

Hadwen, J. G.: *How United Nations Decisions Are Made* (1960).

Hammarskjöld, D.: *The International Civil Servant in Law and in Fact* (1961).

Higgins, R.: *The Development of International Law through the Political Organs of the United Nations* (1963).

Jiménez de Aréchaga, E.: *Voting and the Handling of Disputes in the Security Council* (1950).

Lawson, R. C.: *International Regional Organization: Constitutional Foundations* (1962).

Lie, T.: *In the Cause of Peace* (1954). Memoirs by the first secretary general of the UN.

Moore, R. A.: *The United Nations Reconsidered* (1963).

Nicholas, H. G.: *The United Nations as a Political Institution* (1959).

Schwebel, S. M.: *The Secretary-General of the United Nations: His Political Powers and Practice* (1952).

Sharp, W.: *The United Nations Economic and Social Council* (1969).

Singh, N.: *Termination of Membership of International Organizations* (1958).

Stevenson, A. E.: *Looking Outward: Years of Crisis at the United Nations* (1963). Speeches and papers.

Stoessinger, J. G.: *Financing the United Nations System* (1964).

Werners, S. E.: *The Presiding Officers in the United Nations* (1967).

Wilcox, F. O., and C. M. Marcy: *Proposals for Changes in the United Nations* (1955).

Specialized Activities

Ahluwalia, K.: *The Legal Status, Privileges and Immunities of the Specialized Agencies of the United Nations and Certain Other International Organizations* (1964).

Green, J. F.: *The United Nations and Human Rights* (1956).

Holborn, L. W.: *The International Refugee Organization of the United Nations: Its History and Work, 1946–1952* (1956).

Keenleyside, H. W.: *International Aid: A Summary with Special Reference to the Programmes of the United Nations* (1966).

Mangone, G. J. (ed.): *UN Administration of Economic and Social Programs* (1966).

McDonald, A. H.: *Trusteeship in the Pacific* (1949).

Menon, M. A. K.: *Universal Postal Union* (1965).

Murray, J. N.: *The United Nations Trusteeship System* (1957).

Pillsbury, K.: *UNESCO Education in Action: A Field Study of the UNESCO Department of Education* (1963).

Sady, E. J.: *The United Nations and Dependent Peoples* (1956).

Schwartz, L. E.: *International Organizations and Space Cooperation* (1962).

Toussaint, C. E.: *The Trusteeship System of the United Nations* (1956).

Wrightman, D.: *Toward Economic Cooperation in Asia: The United Nations Economic Commission for Asia and the Far East* (1963).

(See also books on the International Labor Office and the International Court of Justice in section above on League of Nations.)

National Policies and Peace-Keeping Forces

Bloomfield, L. P.: *The United Nations and U.S. Foreign Policy; a New Look at the National Interest* (rev. ed., 1967).

Borvett, D.: *United Nations Forces: A Legal Study* (1964).

Brooke, D.: *Preface to Peace; the United Nations and the Arab-Israel Armistice System* (1964).

Burns, A. L., and N. Heathcote: *Peace-keeping by U.N. Forces from Suez to the Congo* (1963).

Burns, E. L. M.: *Between Arab and Israeli* (1962). Truce supervision in Palestine.

Calvocoressi, P.: *World Order and New States: Problems of Keeping the Peace* (1962).

Dallin, A.: *The Soviet Union at the United Nations; an Inquiry into Soviet Motives and Objectives* (1962).

Epstein, L. D.: *British Politics in the Suez Crisis* (1964).

Finer, H.: *Dulles over Suez: The Theory and Practice of His Diplomacy* (1964).

Gardner, R. N.: *In Pursuit of World Order: U.S. Foreign Policy and International Organization* (1964).

Goodrich, L. M.: *Korea: A Study of U.S. Policy in the United Nations* (1956).

Goodwin, G. L.: *Britain and the United Nations* (1957).

Gordenker, L. *The UN Secretary-General and the Maintenance of Peace* (1967).

Gordon, K.: *The United Nations in the Congo: A Quest for Peace* (1962).

Gross, F. B. (ed.): *The United States and the United Nations* (1964).

Haas, E. B.: *The Web of Interdependence: The United States and International Organizations* (1969).

Halderman, J. W.: *The United Nations and the Rule of Law: Charter Development through the Handling of International Disputes and Situations* (1966).

Higgins, R.: *United Nations Peacekeeping, 1946–1967: Documents and Commentary,* Vol. I: The Middle East (1969).

Hovet, T., Jr.: *Africa in the United Nations* (1963).

Kay, D. A.: *The New Nations in the United Nations, 1960–1967* (1970).

Lefever, E. W.: *Crisis in the Congo: A UN Force in Action* (1965).

Miller, L.: *World Order and Local Disorder: The United Nations and Internal Conflicts* (1967).

Miller, R. I.: *Dag Hammarskjold and Crisis Diplomacy* (1961).

O'Brien, C. C.: *To Katanga and Back: A UN Case History* (1963).

Riggs, R. E.: *Politics in the United Nations: A Study of United States Influence in the General Assembly* (1958).

Robertson, T.: *Crisis: The Inside Story of the Suez Conspiracy* (1964).

Rosner, G.: *The United Nations Emergency Force* (1963).

Rubinstein, A. Z.: *The Soviets in International Organizations: Changing Policy toward Developing Countries, 1953–1963* (1964).

Russell, R. B.: *The United Nations and United State Security Policy* (1968).

Stegenga, J. A.: *The United Nations Force in Cyprus* (1968).

Towney, R.: *The United Nations: A View from Within* (1968).

Uhl, A.: *The US and the UN: Partners for Peace* (1962).

Wohlgemuth, P.: *The Portuguese Territories, and the United Nations* (1963).

(See also Africa, Formosa and Korea, Southeast Asia.)

Periodicals, Handbooks, Yearbooks

Annuaire des organisations internationales (Yearbook of International Organizations) (12th ed., 1968–69).

Annual Review of United Nations Affairs (1949 ff.). Edited by C. Eagleton et al.

Chamberlin, W. (ed.): *A Chronology of the United Nations, 1941–1964* (1964).

Everyman's United Nations: A Ready Reference to the Structure, Functions and Work of the United Nations and Its Related Agencies (1968 ff.).

International Organization (1947 ff.). A quarterly that covers the work of the UN and other international organizations.

UN Monthly Chronicle (monthly, May 1964 ff.), preceded by *United Nations Weekly Bulletin, 1946–1947, United Nations Bulletin, 1948–1954,* and *United Nations Review, 1954–1964.*

United Nations Documents Index: United Nations and Specialized Agencies, Documents and Publications (1950 ff.).

U.S. Participation in the UN (1946 ff.). Annual report by the President to Congress.

Yearbook of the United Nations (1947 ff.). Indispensable.

Yearbook on Human Rights (1946 ff.).

RECONSTRUCTION OF EUROPE

Peace Settlement

Cohen, B. C.: *The Political Process and Foreign Policy: The Making of the Japanese Peace Settlement* (1957).

Dunn, F. S.: *Peace-making and the Settlement with Japan* (1963).

Harris, W. R.: *Tyranny on Trial: The Evidence at Nuremberg* (1954). A full discussion of the international trial of war criminals.

Kecskemeti, P.: *Strategic Surrender: The Policy of Victory and Defeat* (1958).

Knapp, W.: *A History of War and Peace 1939–1965* (1967).

Leiss, A. C., and R. Dennett (eds.): *European Peace Treaties after World War II* (1954). Negotiations and texts of the treaties with Italy, Bulgaria, Hungary, Rumania, and Finland.

Molotov, V. M.: *U.S.S.R. at the Paris Peace Conference* (1946). Speeches.

Murin, M.: *Les tentatives de paix dans la seconde guerre mondiale, 1935–45* (1949).

Neumann, W. L.: *Making the Peace, 1941–5: The Diplomacy of the Wartime Conferences* (1950).

Opie, R., et al.: *The Search for Peace Settlements* (1951).

Pick, F. W.: *Peacemaking in Perspective: From Potsdam to Paris* (1950).

United States Department of State: *Making the Peace Treaties, 1941–1947* (1947).

————: *Paris Peace Conference 1946: Selected Documents* (1947).

————: *Treaties of Peace with Italy, Bulgaria, Hungary, Roumania and Finland* (1947). A convenient collection of the English texts of the treaties.

Economic and Social Reconstruction

Asher, R. E., et al.: *The United Nations and Economic and Social Co-operation* (1957).

Brown, W. A., Jr., and R. Opie: *American Foreign Assistance* (1953).

Claude, I. L., Jr.: *National Minorities: An International Problem* (1955). A study of minorities during and after World War II.

Diebold, W.: *Trade and Payments in Western Europe: A Study in Economic Co-operation, 1947–51* (1952).

Frings, P.: *Das Internationale Fluchtingsproblem, 1919–1950* (1951). A discussion of various agencies that have dealt with refugees.

Frumkin, G.: *Population Changes in Europe Since 1939* (1951).

Myrdal, G.: *An International Economy: Problems and Prospects* (1956).

Organization for European Economic Cooperation: *Annual Reports* (1949 ff.).

Price, H. B.: *The Marshall Plan and Its Meaning* (1955).

Schechtman, J. B.: *Postwar Population Transfers in Europe, 1945–1955* (1962).

Svennilson, I.: *Prospects of Development in Western Europe, 1955–1975* (1959).

Tinbergen, J.: *Shaping the World Economy: Suggestions for an International Economic Policy* (1962).

Weil, G. E.: *The European Convention on Human Rights: Background, Development and Prospects* (1963). Deals with European integration.

European Integration

Axline, W. A.: *European Community Law and Organizational Development* (1968).

Beloff, M.: *Europe and the Europeans: An International Discussion* (1957).

Collier, D. S. (ed.): *Western Integration and the Future of Eastern Europe* (1962).

————, and K. Glaser (eds.): *Western Integration and the Future of Eastern Europe* (1966).

Council of Europe: *Concise Handbook of the Council of Europe* (rev. ed., 1956).

————: *European Culture and the Council of Europe* (rev. ed., 1956).

Diebold, W.: *The Schuman Plan* (1959).
Feld, W.: *The European Common Market and the World* (1967).
Haviland, H. F.: *The United States and the Western Community* (1957).
Isenberg, I.: *An Outlook for Western Europe* (1970).
Jensen, F. B., and T. Walter: *The Common Market: Economic Integration in Europe* (1965).
Kitzinger, U. W.: *The European Common Market and Community* (1967).
Lindberg, L. U.: *The Political Dynamics of European Economic Integration* (1963).
Lister, L.: *Europe's Coal and Steel Community: An Experiment in Economic Union* (1960).
Mason, H. L.: *The European Coal and Steel Community: Experiment in Supranationalism* (1955).
Palmer, M., et al.: *European Unity: A Survey of the European Organization* (rev. ed., 1968).
Robertson, A. A.: *The Council of Europe: Its Structure, Functions and Achievements* (1956).
Rogger, H., and E. Weber (eds.): *The European Right: A Historical Profile* (1965).
Royal Institute of International Affairs: *Britain in Western Europe: WEU and the Atlantic Alliance* (1956).
Savage, K.: *The History of the Common Market* (1969).
Schmitt, H. A.: *The Path to European Union: From the Marshall Plan to the Common Market* (1963).
Spinelli, A.: *The Eurocrats: Conflict and Crisis in the European Community* (1966).
Valentin, D. G.: *The Court of Justice of the European Coal and Steel Community* (1955).
Weil, G. L.: *A Handbook on the European Economic Community* (1965).

Europe in World Politics

Acheson, D.: *Present at the Creation: My Years at the State Department* (1969).
Betts, R. F.: *Europe Overseas: Phases of Imperialism* (1968).
Black, C. E., R. A. Falk, K. Knorr, and O. R. Young: *Neutralization and World Politics* (1968).
Blackett, P. M. S.: *Atomic Weapons and East-West Relations* (1956).
Bohlen, C. E.: *The Transformation of American Foreign Policy* (1969).
Buchan, A. (ed.): *Europe's Futures, Europe's Choices: Models of Western Europe in the 1970's* (1969).
Council of Europe: *Focus on East-West Relations: A Policy for Europe* (1956).
Dahl, R. A. (ed.): *Political Oppositions in Western Democracies* (1966).
Dennett, R., and J. F. Johnson (eds.): *Negotiating with the Russians* (1951). A series of essays by different experts.
Fleming, D. F.: *The Cold War and its Origins, 1917–1960* (2 vols., 1961).
Gehlen, M. P.: *The Politics of Coexistence: Soviet Methods and Motives* (1967).
Gaitskell, H. T.: *The Challenge of Coexistence* (1957).
Grimal, H.: *Le décolonisation, 1919–1963* (1965).
Halle, L. J.: *The Cold War as History* (1967).
Hammond, P. Y.: *The Cold War Years: American Foreign Policy Since 1945* (1969).
Herz, M. F.: *Beginnings of the Cold War* (1966).
Inozemtsev, N. N. (ed.): *Mezhdunarodnye otnosheniya posle vtoroi mirovoi voiny* (3 vols., 1962–65). A Soviet survey of international relations since World War II.
Israilian, V. L.: *Soviet Foreign Policy: A Brief Review, 1955–65* (1967).
Kennan, G. F.: *Russia, the Atom and the West* (1958).
Laqueur, W.: *The Rebirth of Europe* (1970).
Lindberg, L. U., and S. A. Scheingold: *Europe's Would-be Polity: Patterns of Change in the European Community* (1969).
Lukacs, J.: *Decline and Rise of Europe: A Study in Recent History, with Particular Emphasis on the Development of a European Consciousness* (1965).

————: A History of the Cold War (1961).

Mayne, R.: The Recovery of Europe from Devastation to Unity (1970).

Miller, J. D. B.: The Politics of the Third World (1967). The uncommitted nations.

Moore, B. T.: NATO and the Future of Europe (1958).

Padelford, N. J.: The Dynamics of International Politics (1962).

Rees, D.: The Age of Containment: The Cold War 1945–1965 (1968).

Sampson, A.: Anatomy of Europe: A Guide to the Workings, Institutions, and Character of Contemporary Europe (1968).

Shulman, M. D.: Beyond the Cold War (1966).

Snell, J. L. (ed.): The Meaning of Yalta: Big Three Diplomacy and the New Balance of Power (1956).

Wainhouse, D. W.: International Peace Observation: A History and Forecast (1966).

Willis, F. R.: France, Germany, and the New Europe, 1945–1967 (rev. ed., 1968).

INDEX

A NOTE ON THE TYPE

This book is set in Linotype ELECTRA, *designed by W. A. Dwiggins. This face cannot be classified as either "modern" or "old-style." It is not based on any historical model, nor does it echo any particular period or style. It avoids the extreme contrast between "thick" and "thin" elements that marks most "modern" faces, and attempts to give a feeling of fluidity, power, and speed.*

The book was composed, printed, and bound by The Haddon Craftsmen, Inc., Scranton, Pennsylvania.

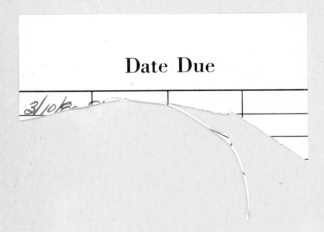

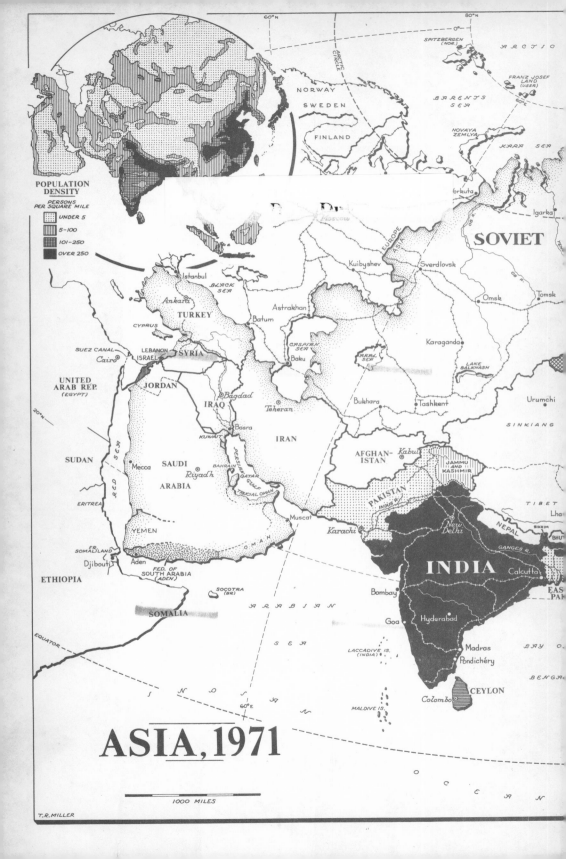

ASIA, 1971

POPULATION
DENSITY

PERSONS
PER SQUARE MILE

UNDER 5
5-100
101-250
OVER 250

SOVIET

NORWAY
SWEDEN
FINLAND

SPITZBERGEN
(NOR.)

FRANZ JOSEF
LAND
(USSR)

BARENTS
SEA

NOVAYA
ZEMLYA

KARA
SEA

Vorkuta

Igarka

Moscow

EUROPE
ASIA

Kuibyshev
Sverdlovsk

Omsk
Tomsk

Istanbul

BLACK SEA

Ankara
TURKEY

Batum

Astrakhan

CASPIAN
SEA

Baku

Karaganda

ARAL
SEA

LAKE
BALKHASH

CYPRUS

SUEZ CANAL
Cairo
LEBANON
ISRAEL
SYRIA

Bukhara
Tashkent

Urumchi

SINKIANG

UNITED
ARAB REP.
(EGYPT)

JORDAN

Bagdad
IRAQ

Teheran

IRAN

AFGHAN-
ISTAN

Kabul

JAMMU
AND
KASHMIR

TIBET

Lha

SUDAN

Mecca

KUWAIT

Basra

SAUDI
Riyadh
ARABIA

BAHRAIN
QATAR
TRUCIAL OMAN

PERSIAN GULF

Muscat

PAKISTAN

INDUS R.

Karachi

New
Delhi

NEPAL

SIKKIM

BHU

GANGES R.

INDIA

Calcutta

EAS
PA

ERITREA

RED SEA

YEMEN

OMAN

Bombay

FR.
SOMALILAND
Djibouti

Aden

FED. OF
SOUTH ARABIA
(ADEN)

SOCOTRA
(BR)

ARABIAN

SEA

Goa

Hyderabad

Madras
Pondichéry

TIBET

BAY O

BENGA

ETHIOPIA

SOMALIA

LACCADIVE IS.
(INDIA)

Colombo

CEYLON

EQUATOR

20°N

60°E

MALDIVE IS.

O
C
A
N

1000 MILES

T.R.MILLER